BLACK LITERATURE
CRITICISM

BLACK LITERATURE
C R I T I C I S M

Excerpts from Criticism of the Most Significant Works
of Black Authors over the Past 200 Years

VOLUME 1: Achebe-Ellison

James P. Draper, Editor

 **Gale Research Inc.** · *DETROIT* · *LONDON*

STAFF

James P. Draper, *Editor*

Andrea M. Gacki, Kyung-Sun Lim, *Assistant Editors, Black Literature Criticism*

Robyn Young, *Contributing Editor*

Cathy Falk, Marie Lazzari, Sean R. Pollock, David Segal, Bridget Travers,
Contributing Associate Editors

Jennifer Brostrom, John P. Daniel, Judy Galens, Tina Grant, Alan Hedblad, Elizabeth P. Henry,
Andrew M. Kalasky, Christopher K. King, Susan M. Peters, James Poniewozik, Mark Swartz, Janet M.
Witalec, *Contributing Assistant Editors*

Jeanne A. Gough, *Permissions & Production Manager*

Linda M. Pugliese, *Production Supervisor*
Maureen Puhl, Jennifer VanSickle, *Editorial Associates*
Donna Craft, Paul Lewon, Lorna Mabunda, Camille Robinson, Sheila Walencewicz, *Editorial Assistants*

Maureen Richards, *Research Supervisor*
Paula Cutcher-Jackson, Judy L. Gale, Robin Lupa, Mary Beth McElmeel, *Editorial Associates*
Tamara C. Nott, *Editorial Assistant*

Sandra C. Davis, *Permissions Supervisor (Text)*
Josephine M. Keene, Denise M. Singleton, Kimberly F. Smilay, *Permissions Associates*
Maria L. Franklin, Michele Lonoconus, Shelly Rakoczy (Co-op), Shalice Shah, Nancy K. Sheridan,
Rebecca A. Stanko, *Permissions Assistants*

Margaret A. Chamberlain, *Permissions Supervisor (Pictures)*
Pamela A. Hayes, *Permissions Associate*
Nancy M. Rattenbury, Keith Reed, *Permissions Assistants*

Mary Beth Trimper, *Production Manager*
Mary Winterhalter, *Production Assistant*

Arthur Chartow, *Art Director*
C. J. Jonik, *Keyliner*
Kathleen A. Mouzakis, *Graphic Designer*

The paper used in this publication meets the minimum requirements
of American National Standard for Information Sciences—Permanence Paper for Printed Library Materials, ANSI Z39.48-1984. ∞™

Copyright © 1992
Gale Research Inc.
835 Penobscot Building
Detroit, MI 48226-4094

ISBN 0-8103-7929-5 (3-volume set)
ISBN 0-8103-7930-9 (Volume 1)
A CIP catalogue record for this book is available from the British Library

Printed in the United States of America

Published simultaneously in the United Kingdom
by Gale Research International Limited
(An affiliated company of Gale Research Inc.)

Contents of Volume 1

Introduction

A Comprehensive Information Source on Black Literature

*B*lack Literature Criticism (*BLC*) presents a broad selection of the best criticism of works by major black writers of the past two hundred years. Among the authors included in *BLC* are eighteenth-century memoirist Olaudah Equiano, poet Jupiter Hammon, and poet Phillis Wheatley; nine-teenth-century autobiographer Frederick Douglass, poet Paul Laurence Dunbar, diarist Charlotte Forten, and essayist Booker T. Washington; such twentieth-century masters as novelist Chinua Achebe, novelist James Baldwin, poet Gwendolyn Brooks, poet Countee Cullen, novelist Ralph Ellison, dramatist Lorraine Hansberry, poet Langston Hughes, fiction writer Zora Neale Hurston, novelist Toni Morrison, novelist Ngugi wa Thiong'o, dramatist Wole Soyinka, and novelist Richard Wright; and emerging writers Andrea Lee, Charles Johnson, Lewis Nkosi, and August Wilson. The scope of *BLC* is wide: one hundred twenty-five writers representing the United States, Nigeria, South Africa, Jamaica, and over a dozen other nations are covered in comprehensive author entries.

Coverage

This three-volume set is designed for high school, college, and university students, as well as for the general reader who wants to learn more about black literature. *BLC* was developed in response to strong demand by students, librarians, and other readers for a one-stop, authoritative guide to the whole spectrum of black literature. No other compendium like it exists in the marketplace. About half of the entries in *BLC* were selected from Gale's acclaimed Literary Criticism Series and completely updated for publication here. Typically, the revisions are extensive, ranging from completely rewritten author introductions to wide changes in the selection of criticism. Other entries were prepared especially for *BLC* in order to furnish the most comprehensive coverage possible. Authors were selected for inclusion based on the range and amount of critical material available as well as on the advice of leading experts on black literature. A special effort was made to identify important new writers and to give the greatest coverage to the most studied authors.

Each author entry in *BLC* attempts to present a historical survey of critical response to the author's works. Typically, early criticism is offered to indicate initial responses, later selections document any rise or decline in literary reputations, and retrospective analyses provide modern views. Every endeavor has been made to include the seminal essays on each author's work along with recent commentary providing current perspectives. Interviews and author statements are also included in many entries. Thus, *BLC* is both timely and comprehensive.

Organization of Author Entries

Information about authors and their works is presented through eight key access points:

■ The **Author Heading** cites the name under which the author most commonly wrote, followed by birth and death dates. Uncertain birth or death dates are indicated by question marks. Name variations, including full birth names when available, are given in parentheses on the first line of the **Biographical and Critical Introduction**.

■ The **Biographical and Critical Introduction** contains background information about the life and works of the author. Emphasis is given to four main areas: 1) biographical details that help reveal the life, character, and personality of the author; 2) overviews of the major literary interests of the author—for example, novel writing, autobiography, social reform, documentary, etc.; 3) descriptions and summaries of the author's best-known works; and 4) critical commentary about the author's achievement, stature, and importance. The concluding paragraph of the **Biographical and Critical Introduction** directs readers to other Gale series containing information about the author.

■ Most *BLC* entries include an **Author Portrait**. Most also contain **Illustrations** documenting the author's career, including holographs, title pages of works, letters, or pictures of important people, places, and events in the author's life.

■ The **List of Principal Works** is chronological by date of first book publication and identifies the genre of each work. For non-English-language authors whose works have been translated into English, the title and date of the first English-language edition are given in brackets beneath the foreign-language listing. Unless otherwise indicated, dramas are dated by first performance rather than first publication.

■ **Criticism** is arranged chronologically in each author entry to provide a useful perspective on changes in critical evaluation over the years. Most entries contain a detailed, comprehensive study of the author's career as well as book reviews, studies of individual works, and comparative examinations. To ensure timeliness, current views are most often presented, but never to the exclusion of important early pieces. For the purpose of easy identification, the critic's name and the date of the critical work are given at the beginning of each piece of criticism. Unsigned criticism is preceded by the title of the source in which it appeared. Within the criticism, titles of works by the author are printed in boldface type. Publication information (such as publisher names and book prices) and certain numerical references (such as footnotes or page and line references to specific editions of works) have been deleted at the editor's discretion to provide smoother reading of the text.

■ Critical essays are prefaced by **Explanatory Notes** as an additional aid to readers of *BLC*. These notes may provide several types of valuable information, including: 1) the reputation of the critic; 2) the perceived importance of the work of criticism; 3) the commentator's approach to the author's work; 4) the apparent purpose of the criticism; and 5) changes in critical trends regarding the author. In some cases, **Explanatory Notes** cross-reference the work of critics within the entry who agree or disagree with each other.

■ A complete **Bibliographical Citation** of the original essay or book follows each piece of criticism.

■ An annotated **Further Reading List** appears at the end of each entry and suggests resources for additional study.

Other Features

BLC contains three distinct indexes to help readers find information quickly and easily:

■ The **Author Index** lists all the authors appearing in *BLC*. To ensure easy access, name variations and name changes are fully cross-indexed.

■ The **Nationality Index** lists all authors featured in *BLC* by nationality. For expatriate authors and authors identified with more than one nation, multiple listings are offered.

■ The **Title Index** lists in alphabetical order all individual works by the authors appearing in *BLC*. English-language translations of original foreign-language titles are cross-referenced to the foreign titles so that all references to a work are combined in one listing.

Citing *Black Literature Criticism*

When writing papers, students who quote directly from *BLC* may use the following general forms to footnote reprinted criticism. The first example is for material drawn from periodicals, the second for material reprinted from books.

Robert B. Stepto, "Storytelling in Early Afro-American Fiction: Frederick Douglass' 'The Heroic Slave'," *The Georgia Review*, XXXVI (Summer 1982), 355-68; excerpted and reprinted in *Black Literature Criticism*, ed. James P. Draper (Detroit: Gale Research, 1992), pp. 585-88.

Edward Margolies, *Native Sons: A Critical Study of Twentieth-Century Negro American Authors* (J. B. Lippincott, 1968); excerpted and reprinted in *Black Literature Criticism*, ed. James P. Draper (Detroit: Gale Research, 1992), pp. 59-64.

Acknowledgments

The editor wishes to acknowledge the valuable contributions of the many librarians, authors, and scholars who assisted in the compilation of *BLC* with their responses to telephone and mail inquiries. Special thanks are offered to *BLC*'s two chief advisors: Clarence Chisholm, Chairman of the Afro-American Studies Section of the Association of College and Research Libraries, and Arnold Rampersad, Woodrow Wilson Professor of English and Director of American Studies at Princeton University.

Comments Are Welcome

The editor hopes that readers will find *BLC* to be a useful reference tool and welcomes comments about the work. Send comments and suggestions to: Editor, *Black Literature Criticism*, Gale Research Inc., Penobscot Building, Detroit, MI 48226-4094.

Authors Included
in *Black Literature Criticism*

Chinua Achebe 1930-

Jamil Abdullah Al-Amin (H. Rap Brown) 1943-

Maya Angelou 1928-

Ayi Kwei Armah 1939-

William Attaway 1911?-1986

James Baldwin 1924-1987

Toni Cade Bambara 1939-

Amiri Baraka (LeRoi Jones) 1934-

Barry Beckham 1944-

James Madison Bell 1826-1902

Louise Bennett 1919-

Mongo Beti (Alexandre Biyidi) 1932-

Arna Bontemps 1902-1973

David Bradley 1950-

William Stanley Braithwaite 1878-1962

Gwendolyn Brooks 1917-

Claude Brown 1937-

Sterling Brown 1901-1989

William Wells Brown 1816?-1884

Dennis Brutus 1924-

Ed Bullins 1935-

J. E. Casely-Hayford 1866-1930

Aimé Césaire 1913-

Charles W. Chesnutt 1858-1932

Alice Childress 1920-

John Pepper Clark 1935-

Austin Clarke 1934-

Eldridge Cleaver 1935-

Lucille Clifton 1936-

Joseph Seamon Cotter, Sr. 1861-1949

Countee Cullen 1903-1946

Frank Marshall Davis 1905-1987

Samuel R. Delany 1942-

William Demby 1922-

Owen Dodson 1914-1983

Frederick Douglass 1817?-1895

W. E. B. Du Bois 1868-1963

Paul Laurence Dunbar 1872-1906

Cyprian Ekwensi 1921-

Lonne Elder III 1931-

Ralph Ellison 1914-

Buchi Emecheta 1944-

Olaudah Equiano 1745?-1797

Frantz Fanon 1925-1961

Nuruddin Farah 1945-

Jessie Redmon Fauset 1882-1961

Rudolph Fisher   1897-1934

Charlotte L. Forten   1837?-1914

Charles Fuller   1939-

Ernest Gaines   1933-

Marcus Garvey   1887-1940

Nikki Giovanni   1943-

Donald Goines   1937?-1974

Nicolás Guillén   1902-1989

Alex Haley   1921-

Jupiter Hammon   1711?-1800?

Lorraine Hansberry   1930-1965

Frances Ellen Watkins
   Harper   1825-1911

Robert Hayden   1913-1980

Bessie Head   1937-1986

Chester Himes   1909-1984

Pauline Elizabeth Hopkins   1859-
   1930

Langston Hughes   1902-1967

Zora Neale Hurston   1901?-1960

Charles Johnson   1948-

Fenton Johnson   1888-1958

James Weldon Johnson   1871-
   1938

Gayl Jones   1949-

Adrienne Kennedy   1931-

Jamaica Kincaid   1949-

Martin Luther King, Jr.   1929-
   1968

Etheridge Knight   1931-1991

George Lamming   1927-

Nella Larsen   1891-1964

Camara Laye   1928-1980

Andrea Lee   1953-

George Washington Lee   1894-
   1976

Audre Lorde   1934-

Joaquim Maria Machado de
   Assis   1839-1908

Haki R. Madhubuti (Don L.
   Lee)   1942-

Clarence Major   1936-

Malcolm X (Malcolm Little; El-
   Hajj Malik El-Shabazz)
   1925-1965

Paule Marshall   1929-

Claude McKay   1889-1948

Ron Milner   1938-

Thomas Mofolo   1876-1948

Toni Morrison   1931-

Ezekiel Mphahlele   1919-

S. E. K. Mqhayi   1875-1945

Walter Dean Myers   1937-

Gloria Naylor   1950-

Ngugi wa Thiong'o   1938-

Lewis Nkosi   1936-

Christopher Okigbo   1932-1967

Sembène Ousmane   1923-

Gordon Parks   1912-

Okot p'Bitek   1931-1982

Adam Clayton Powell, Jr.   1908-
   1972

Dudley Randall   1914-

Ishmael Reed   1938-

Jacques Roumain   1907-1944

Sonia Sanchez   1934-

Léopold Sédar Senghor   1906-

Ntozake Shange   1948-

Wole Soyinka   1934-

Wallace Thurman   1902-1934

Melvin B. Tolson   1898?-1966

Jean Toomer   1894-1967

Desmond Tutu   1931-

Amos Tutuola   1920-

Derek Walcott   1930-

Alice Walker   1944-

Margaret Walker   1915-

Booker T. Washington   1856-1915

Phillis Wheatley   1753?-1784

Walter White   1893-1955

John Edgar Wideman   1941-

John A. Williams   1925-

Sherley Anne Williams   1944-

August Wilson   1945-

Harriet Wilson   1827?-?

Charles Wright   1932-

Richard Wright   1908-1960

Frank Yerby   1916-

Al Young   1939-

ACKNOWLEDGMENTS

The editor wishes to thank the copyright holders of the excerpted criticism included in this volume, the permissions managers of many book and magazine publishing companies for assisting in securing reprint rights, and Anthony Bogucki for assistance with copyright research. The editor is also grateful the staffs of the Detroit Public Library, Wayne State University Purdy/Kresge Library Complex, and the University of Michigan Libraries for making their resources available. Following is a list of the copyright holders who have granted permission to reprint material in this volume of *BLC*. Every effort has been made to trace copyright, but if omissions have been made, please let the editor know.

COPYRIGHTED EXCERPTS IN *BLC*, VOLUME 1, WERE REPRINTED FROM THE FOLLOWING PERIODICALS:

African Literature Today, n. 4, 1969; n. 11, 1980; n. 14, 1984. Copyright (c) 1969, 1980, 1984 by Heinemann Educational Books Ltd. All rights reserved. All reprinted by permission of Africana Publishing Company, New York, NY.—*America,* v. 144, May 30, 1981. (c) 1981. All rights reserved. Reprinted with permission of America Press, Inc., 106 West 56th Street, New York, NY 10019.—*American Literature,* v. 43, November, 1971. Copyright (c) 1971 Duke University Press, Durham, NC. Reprinted with permission of the publisher.—*The American Poetry Review,* v. 13, January-February, 1984 for "The French Connection" by Marjorie Perloff. Copyright (c) 1984 by World Poetry, Inc. Reprinted by permission of the author.—*The American Scholar,* v. 32, Summer, 1963. Copyright (c) 1963 by the United Chapters of Phi Beta Kappa Society. Reprinted by permission of the publishers./ v. 18, Winter, 1948-49. Copyright 1948, renewed 1976 by the United Chapters of Phi Beta Kappa Society. Reprinted by permission of the publishers.—*American Studies,* v. 29, Fall, 1988 for "Down from Slavery" by Robert Butler. Copyright (c) Mid-America Studies Association, 1988. Reprinted by permission of the publisher and the author.—*Ariel: A Review of International English Literature,* v. 17, January, 1986 for "The Troubadour: The Poet's Persona in the Poetry of Dennis Brutus" by Tanure Ojaide. Copyright (c) 1986 The Board of Governors, the University of Calgary. Reprinted by permission of the publisher and the author.—*The Atlantic Monthly,* v. 221, June, 1968 for "Black Anger" by Robert Coles. Copyright 1968 by The Atlantic Monthly Company, Boston, MA. Reprinted by permission of the author.—*Black American Literature Forum,* v. 19, Fall, 1985 for an interview with Frank Marshall Davis by John Edgar Tidwell. Copyright (c) 1985 Indiana State University. Reprinted by permission of Indiana State University, the Literary Estate of Frank Marshall Davis and John Edgar Tidwell./ v. 13, Fall, 1979 for "Ed Bullins Was Steve Benson (But Who Is He Now?)" by Richard G. Scharine; v. 13, Fall, 1979 for "Who Is He Now: Ed Bullins Replies" by Ed Bullins; v. 18, Spring, 1984 for "All Our Farewells Cry to Thee: A Memory of an Evening with Owen Dodson" by James V. Hatch; v. 18, Summer, 1984 for "The Insistent Presence of Black Folk in the Novels of Samuel R. Delany" by Sandra Y. Govan; v. 21, Spring- Summer, 1987 for "Work and Culture: The Evolution of Consciousness in Urban Industrial Society in the Fiction of William Attaway and Peter Abrahams" by Cynthia Hamilton. Copyright (c) 1979, 1984, 1987 Indiana State University. All reprinted by permission of Indiana State University and the respective authors.—*Black Creation,* v. 4, Winter, 1973 for a review of "Runner Mack" by Jim Walker. Copyright 1973 by the Institute of Afro-American Affairs. Reprinted by permission of the author.—*Black Images,* v. 3, Autumn, 1974 for an interview with Barry Beckham by Sanford Pinsker. Reprinted by permission of Barry Beckham and Sanford Pinsker.—*Black Orpheus,* n. 16, October, 1964 for "Like Goats to Slaughter: Three Plays, by John Pepper Clark" by Anthony Astrachan. Copyright (c) 1964 by the author. Reprinted by permission of Georges Borchardt, Inc. for the author./ n. 20, August, 1966 for "Voices Out of the Skull" by Paul Theroux. (c) Mbari Ibadan. Reprinted by permission of the author.—*Book World—The Washington Post,* May, 11, 1969 for "Who Has the Truth?" by Charles V. Hamilton. (c) 1969 Postrib Corp. Reprinted with permission of *The Washington Post* and the author./ September 23, 1979; March 30, 1980. (c) 1979, 1980, *The Washington Post.* Both reprinted with permission of the publisher.—*Books Abroad,* v. 37, Spring, 1963. Copyright 1963 by the University of Oklahoma Press. Reprinted by permission of the publisher.—*Books in Canada,* v. 9, June-July, 1980 for "Little England Made Him" by Dan Hilts; v. 15, October, 1986 for "Hollow Laughter" by Paul Wilson. Both reprinted by permission of the respective authors.—*Callaloo,* v. 6, February, 1983 for an interview with Aimé Césaire by Philippe Decraene. Copyright (c) 1983 by Charles H. Rowell. All rights reserved. Reprinted by permission of Philippe Decraene./ v. 7, Spring-Summer, 1984 for an interview with David Bradley by Susan L. Blake and James A. Miller. Copyright (c) 1984 by Charles H. Rowell. All rights reserved. Reprinted by permission of David Bradley, Susan L. Blake and James A. Miller./ v. 7, Fall, 1984 for an interview with Samuel Delany by Charles Johnson. Copyright (c) 1984 by Charles H. Rowell. All rights reserved. Reprinted by permission of the author.—*The Canadian Forum,* v. XLVIII, April, 1968 for a review of "The Meeting Point" by James Dale. Reprinted by permission of the author.—*The Christian Science Monitor,* May 20, 1981 for "Well-Made Novel Sifts

COPYRIGHTED EXCERPTS IN *BLC*, VOLUME 1, WERE REPRINTED FROM THE FOLLOWING BOOKS:

Abramson, Doris E. From *Negro Playwrights in the American Theatre: 1925-1959.* Columbia University Press, 1969. Copyright (c) 1967, 1969 Columbia University Press. Used by permission of the publisher.—Achebe, Chinua. From *Morning Yet on Creation Day: Essays.* Anchor Press/Doubleday, 1975. Copyright (c) 1975 by Chinua Achebe. All rights reserved. Used by permission of Doubleday, a division of Bantam Doubleday Dell Publishing Group, Inc. In Canada by the author.—Andrews, William L. From *The Literary Career of Charles W. Chesnutt.* Louisiana State University Press, 1980. Copyright (c) 1980 by Louisiana State University Press. All rights reserved. Reprinted by permission of the publisher.—Baker, Houston A. From *The Journey Back: Issues in Black Literature and Criticism.* University of Chicago Press, 1980. (c) 1980 by The University of Chicago. All rights reserved. Reprinted by permission of the publisher and the author.—Baker, Houston A., Jr. From *A Many-Colored Coat of Dreams: The Poetry of Countee Cullen.* Broadside Press, 1974. Copyright (c) 1974 by Houston A. Baker, Jr. Reprinted by permission of the publisher.—Bambara, Toni Cade, and Claudia Tate. From an interview in *Black Women Writers at Work.* Edited by Claudia Tate. Continuum, 1983. Copyright (c) 1983 by Claudia Tate. All rights reserved. Reprinted by permission of the publisher.—Barthold, Bonnie J. From *Black Time: Fiction of Africa, the Caribbean, and the United States.* Yale University Press, 1981. Copyright (c) 1981 by Yale University Press. All rights reserved. Reprinted by permission of the publisher.—Bell, Bernard W. From *The Afro-American Novel and Its Tradition.* The University of Massachusetts Press, 1987. Copyright (c) 1987 by The University of Massachusetts Press. All rights reserved. Reprinted by permission of the publisher.—Bigsby, C. W. E. From *The Second Black Renaissance: Essays in Black Literature.* Greenwood Press, 1980. Copyright (c) 1980 by C. W. E. Bigsby. All rights reserved. Reprinted by permission of Greenwood Publishing Group, Inc., Westport, CT.—Bone, Robert. From *Down Home: Origins of the Afro-American Short Story.* Columbia University Press, 1988. Copyright (c) 1975 Robert Bone. Used by permission of the publisher.—Bone, Robert. From *The Negro Novel in America.* Revised edition. Yale University Press, 1965. Copyright (c) 1965 by Yale University.— Bontemps, Arna. From "The Negro Contribution to American Letters," in *The American Negro Reference Book.* Edited by John P. Davis. Prentice-Hall, 1966. (c) 1966 by Prentice-Hall, Inc. Used by permission of Prentice Hall/A division of Simon & Schuster, Englewood Cliffs, NJ.—Bontemps, Arna. From an introduction to *Black Thunder.* Beacon Press, 1968. Introduction (c) 1968 by Arna Bontemps. All rights reserved. Used by permission of Beacon Press.—Bontemps, Arna and John O'Brien. From an interview in *Interviews with Black Writers.* Edited by John O'Brien. Liveright, 1973. Copyright (c) 1973 by Liveright. All rights reserved. Reprinted by permission of Liveright Publishing Corporation.— Brawley, Benjamin. From *The Negro Genius: A New Appraisal of the Achievement of the American Negro in Literature and the Fine Arts.* Dodd, Mead, 1937. Copyright, 1937 by Dodd, Mead & Company, Inc. Renewed 1965 by Thaddeus Gaillard. All rights reserved. Reprinted by the Literary Estate of Benjamin Brawley.—Bronz, Stephen H. From *Roots of Negro Racial Consciousness, the 1920's: Three Harlem Renaissance Authors.* Libra Publishers, Inc., 1964. (c) 1964 by Stephen H. Bronz. All rights reserved. Reprinted by permission of the publisher.—Brown, Lloyd W. From *Amiri Baraka.* Twayne, 1980. Copyright 1980 by Twayne Publishers. All rights reserved. Reprinted with the permission of Twayne Publishers, a division of G. K. Hall & Co., Boston.—Childress, Alice. From an interview in *Interviews with Contemporary Women Playwrights.* Edited by Kathleen Betsko and Rachel Koenig. Beech Tree Books, 1987. Copyright (c) 1987 by Kathleen Betsko and Rachel Koenig. All rights reserved. Reprinted by permission of Beech Tree Books, a division of William Morrow and Company, Inc.—Clark, Norris B. From "Gwendolyn Brooks and a Black Aesthetic," in *A Life Distilled: Gwendolyn Brooks, Her Poetry and Fiction.* Edited by Maria K. Mootry and Gary Smith. University of Illinois Press, 1987. (c) 1987 by the Board of Trustees of the University of Illinois. Reprinted by permission of the publisher and the author.—Clifton, Lucille. From "A Simple Language," in *Black Women Writers (1950-1980): A Critical Evaluation.* Edited by Mari Evans. Anchor Press/Doubleday, 1984. Copyright (c) 1983 by Mari Evans. All rights reserved. Used by permission of Doubleday, a division of Bantam Doubleday Dell Publishing Group, Inc.— Cudjoe, Selwyn R. From "Maya Angelou and the Autobiographical Statement," in *Black Women Writers (1950-1980): A Critical Evaluation.* Edited by Mari Evans. Anchor Press/Doubleday, 1984. Copyright (c) 1983 by Mari Evans. All rights reserved. Used by permission of Doubleday, a division of Bantam Doubleday Dell Publishing Group, Inc.— Dathorne, O. R. From *The Black Mind: A History of African Literature.* University of Minnesota Press, 1974. (c) Copyright 1974 by the University of Minnesota. All rights reserved. Reprinted by permission of the publisher.—Davis, Arthur P. From *From the Dark Tower: Afro-American Writers, 1900-1960.* Howard University Press, 1974. Copyright (c) 1974 by Arthur P. Davis. All rights reserved. Reprinted by permission of the publisher.—Dodson, Owen, and John O'Brien. From an interview in *Interviews with Black Writers.* Edited by John O'Brien. Liveright, 1973. Copyright (c) 1973 by Liveright. Reprinted by permission of the publisher.—Ekwensi, Cyprian. From a letter in *Cyprian Ekwensi.* By Ernest Emenyonu. Evans Brothers Limited, 1974. (c) Ernest Emenyonu 1974. All rights reserved.—Farrison, William Edward. From *William Wells Brown: Author and Reformer.* The University of Chicago Press, 1969. (c) 1969 by The University of Chicago. All rights reserved. Reprinted by permission of the publisher.—Gates, Henry Louis, Jr. From *Figures in Black: Words, Signs, and 'Racial' Self.* Oxford University Press, 1987. Copyright (c) 1987 by Henry Louis Gates, Jr. All rights reserved. Reprinted by permission of Oxford University Press, Inc.—Gayle, Addison, Jr. From *The*

PHOTOGRAPHS AND ILLUSTRATIONS APPEARING IN *BLC*, VOLUME 1, WERE RECEIVED FROM THE FOLLOWING SOURCES:

BLACK LITERATURE

CRITICISM

Chinua Achebe

1930-

Nigerian novelist, short story writer, poet, essayist, editor, and author of children's books.

Achebe is considered one of the most important figures in contemporary African literature. His novels, which chronicle the colonization and independence of Nigeria, are among the first works in English to present an intimate and authentic rendering of African culture. His major concerns, according to Abiola Irele, involve "the social and psychological conflicts created by the incursion of the white man and his culture into the hitherto self-contained world of African society, and the disarray in the African consciousness that has followed." Critics praise Achebe's innovative and successful fusion of folklore, proverbs, and idioms from his native Ibo tribe with Western political ideologies and Christian doctrines. Margaret Laurence noted: "Chinua Achebe's careful and confident craftsmanship, his firm grasp of his material and his ability to create memorable and living characters place him among the best novelists now writing in any country in the English language."

The son of Ibo missionary teachers, Achebe was born in Nigeria in 1930. He attended Church Mission Society in Ogidi and Government College in Umuahia before obtaining his Bachelor of Arts degree from Ibadan University in 1953. He began working for the Nigerian Broadcasting Company a year later. Dissatisfied with the political situation in Lagos, he resigned in 1966 and moved to Eastern Nigeria, now devoting all his time to writing poetry, short stories, and juvenilia. Poems written during this period were collected in *Beware, Soul Brother and Other Poems* (1971) and in *Christmas in Biafra and Other Poems* (1973). In the early 1970s Achebe accepted a visiting professorship at the University of Massachusetts and later at the University of Connecticut. While in the United States, he taught literature, founded and edited the literary magazine *Okike: A Nigerian Journal of New Writing,* and continued his writing of novels. In 1976 he returned to Nigeria and began teaching at the University of Nigeria-Nsukka.

Achebe's first novel, *Things Fall Apart* (1958), is considered a classic of contemporary African fiction for its realistic and anthropologically informative portrait of Ibo tribal society before colonization. Set in the village of Umuofia in the late 1880s, when English missionaries and bureaucrats first appeared in the region, this book traces the conflict between tribal and Western customs through Okonkwo, a proud village leader, whose refusal to adapt to European influence leads him to murder and suicide. Arthur Ravenscroft noted: *"Things Fall Apart* is impressive for the wide range of what it so pithily covers, for the African flavour of scene and language, but above all for the way in which Achebe makes that language the instrument for analyzing tragic experience

and profound human issues of very much more than local Nigerian significance." *No Longer at Ease* (1960), set in the Nigerian city of Lagos during the late 1950s, details the failure of Obi Okonkwo, the grandson of Okonkwo from *Things Fall Apart,* to successfully combine his traditional Ibo upbringing with his English education and affluent lifestyle. While *No Longer at Ease* was less universally praised than *Things Fall Apart,* some critics defended its stylistic weaknesses as a deliberate attempt to demonstrate the consequences of one culture's dilution by another.

In his third novel, *Arrow of God* (1964), Achebe returned to Umuofia to describe life in the village during the 1920s. This book centers on Ezeulu, the spiritual leader of the region, who sends his son Oduche to a missionary school to discover Western secrets. Upon his return, Oduche attempts to destroy a sacred python, setting in motion a chain of events in which Ezeulu is stripped of his position as high priest and imprisoned by the English. Critics noted a change of thematic direction in

Achebe's next novel, *A Man of the People* (1966). Here, focusing on the tribulations of a teacher who joins a political organization endeavoring to remove a corrupt bureaucrat from office, Achebe condemned the widespread graft and abuse of power among Nigeria's leadership following its independence from Great Britain. Adrian A. Roscoe commented: "Achebe's first three novels showed the author as teacher . . . . From instructing his society to lashing it with satire; from portraying with a touching nostalgia the beauty of a vanishing world to savagely pillorying what is succeeding it—*A Man of the People* indeed marks a new departure."

Anthills of the Savannah (1988), Achebe's first novel in two decades, garnered widespread acclaim as his most accomplished work of fiction. In this book, according to Nadine Gordimer, "22 years of harsh experience, intellectual growth, self-criticism, deepening understanding and mustered discipline of skill open wide a subject to which Mr. Achebe is now magnificently equal." Set in Kangan, an imaginary West African nation, *Anthills of the Savannah* is about three childhood friends who become leaders in their country's government. Ikem is the editor-in-chief of the state-owned newspaper; Sam is a military leader who becomes President of Kangan; and Chris serves as Sam's Minister of Information. Their friendship ends tragically when Sam fails in his attempt to be elected President-for-Life and begins to suppress his opposition. Ikem is murdered by Sam's secret police for publishing several articles denouncing the government; Sam's corpse is later discovered in a shallow grave on the palace grounds following a military coup; and Chris is killed in a street riot. In *Anthills of the Savannah*, Achebe examined the ways in which individual responsibility and power are often exploited to the detriment of an entire society. He also emphasized the roles of women and the urban working class while retaining the use of Ibo proverbs and legends to enhance his themes. Ben Okri stated: "All those who have inundated Achebe with critical analysis, and who spoke of him as the grandfather of African literature before he was 36, have [*Anthills of the Savannah*] to wrestle with for some time to come. Chinua Achebe has found new creative fire."

Achebe's most recent work, *Hopes and Impediments: Selected Essays* (1988), a collection of fourteen political essays and speeches, has been praised as "brilliant." In addition to a controversial essay attacking Joseph Conrad's *Heart of Darkness* as "racist," it also contains a tribute to James Baldwin as well as biting commentaries about Africa and the social forces that have shaped it. Critic Joe Wood noted: "Though Mr. Achebe sometimes fails to pursue his ideas with rigor [in *Hopes and Impediments*], . . . his thoughts always pack a provocative wallop."

Recognized as perhaps the finest living Nigerian novelist, Achebe is credited with helping launch the field of modern African literature. His novels are praised for their balanced examination of contemporary Africa and are often the standards by which other African works

are judged. Critics note, however, that Achebe's writing reverberates beyond the borders of Nigeria and beyond the arenas of anthropology, sociology, and political science. As literature, it deals with universal qualities. And, as Douglas Killam observed: "Achebe's novels offer a vision of life which is essentially tragic, compounded of success and failure, informed by knowledge and understanding, relieved by humour and tempered by sympathy, embued with an awareness of human suffering and the human capacity to endure. . . . Sometimes his characters meet with success, more often with defeat and despair. Through it all the spirit of man and the belief in the possibility of triumph endures."

(For further information about Achebe's life and works, see *Black Writers; Contemporary Authors,* Vols. 1-4; *Contemporary Authors New Revision Series,* Vols. 6, 26; *Contemporary Literary Criticism,* Vols. 1, 3, 5, 7, 11, 26, 51; *Children's Literature Review,* Vol. 20; and *Something about the Author,* Vols. 38, 40. For related criticism, see the entry on Nigerian Literature in *Twentieth-Century Literary Criticism,* Vol. 30.)

PRINCIPAL WORKS

Things Fall Apart (novel) 1958
"The Sacrificial Egg" (short story) 1959; published in periodical *Atlantic Monthly*
No Longer at Ease (novel) 1960
The Sacrificial Egg and Other Stories (short stories) 1962
"Where Angels Fear to Tread" (essay) 1962; published in periodical *Nigeria Magazine*
Arrow of God (novel) 1964
Chike and the River (juvenilia) 1966
A Man of the People (novel) 1966
Beware, Soul Brother and Other Poems (poetry) 1971
How the Leopard Got His Claws [with John Iroaganachi] (juvenilia) 1972
Christmas in Biafra and Other Poems (poetry) 1973
Girls at War and Other Stories (short stories) 1973
Morning Yet on Creation Day (essays) 1975
Don't Let Him Die: An Anthology of Memorial Poems for Christopher Okigbo [coeditor with Dubem Okafor] (anthology) 1978
The Drum (juvenilia) 1978
The Flute (juvenilia) 1978
The Trouble with Nigeria (essays) 1983
African Short Stories [coeditor with C. L. Innes] (anthology) 1984
Anthills of the Savannah (novel) 1988
Hopes and Impediments: Selected Essays (essays) 1988

Kate Turkington (essay date 1971)

[*In the following essay, Turkington discusses the theme of "compromise or die" in Achebe's novels.*]

Achebe's first three novels, *Things Fall Apart, No Longer at Ease* and *Arrow of God* have been published as a trilogy. His last novel to date (and surely, now, there must come a book about the recent Nigerian/Biafran conflict) is *Man of the People.* Superficially, however, the novels fall into two camps. *Things Fall Apart* and *Arrow of God* are "traditional" novels in that they are situated firmly in the past, in the traditional Ibo culture and way of life. *No Longer at Ease* and *Man of the People* are present-day situation novels, dealing as they do with educated young men versus corrupt politicians. The differences are superficial, however, because the main theme as it seems to me, the tragedy of the man who can't or won't adapt, is implicit in all the novels. And it is in the deeper meanings of the novels that I would suggest that Achebe is not dealing with parochial trivia. "This no be them country" may be geographically and ethnically true for non-West Africans, but the problems and issues that Chinua Achebe raises are relevant to most peoples and cultures.

Things Fall Apart, Achebe's first novel, has probably been paid the most critical attention of the four, not only because of its position in the brief history of the Nigerian novel, but also, because it gave for the first time in English, in a strong, confident, subtle prose, a picture of an alien society that most people outside West Africa had never heard about or been interested in. The British may have 'occupied' Nigeria for 100 years, but they knew little or nothing of the indigenous culture they imposed their own civilization upon. At first glance then, *Things Fall Apart* is an historical novel. It gives us a vivid picture of an Ibo society that was dying when Achebe wrote about it, and that recent events have done little to improve. Okonkwo, "one of the greatest men of his time" in the village of Umuofia destroys himself finally because he cannot unbend himself and his traditional ways in the face of change, represented by the white man and his new religion. He kills the white man's messenger. (pp. 205-06)

Okonkwo is Everyman facing the unknown. The situation is universal, the reaction particular. Because he is the simple, inexperienced product of an ancient and ordered way of life he becomes inarticulate in the face of things he cannot understand. This inability to comprehend becomes translated into violent action which in turn will result in his own violent death. But he dies pure, because he lives up to the ideals that his background and culture have given him. But this is more than simple narrative. Achebe is delineating a problem not only concerned with Africans tragically under pressure in a changing world. The key sentence in [one of the passages] is, "He heard voices asking: 'Why did he do it?'"

These are the voices of universal 'survivors' for whom compromise is easy. The question Achebe poses here is a subtle one. To survive you must adapt and therefore adopt some kind of compromise. But does this entail a loss of personal honour which can only be satisfied by holding on to what you believe in? Which is better,

expediency equalling survival, or a failure or refusal to adapt, thus maintaining personal integrity? Okonkwo is a fine man and the hardness of his character must be judged by the standards of his day and traditional society, not ours. But there is something elemental about him which almost symbolizes man against lesser men. Achebe understandably is less sympathetic in his treatment of the white man in this book. He presents a savage satire on the bumbling District Officer and his refusal to attempt a compromise....[The official's intention to write a book entitled *The Pacification of the Primitive Tribes of the Lower Niger*] is not pretty irony; there are echoes here of Robinson Crusoe's view of the black man. "I taught him to say Master, and then let him know, that was to be my name." However, Achebe does show more compassion towards Mr. Brown, the missionary, who was "respected even by the clan because he trod softly on their faith".

Achebe deals with the same problem of compromise in *No Longer at Ease.* And the very titles of these first two novels underline the issue. Here the setting is the present, but the dilemma facing Obi Okonkwo, the dead Okonkwo's grandson, although more sophisticated, is basically the same. Obi returns from four years' studying in England to try to find his position in life, literally and metaphorically. But his 'been-to' experience forces him into a situation where he must mould and adapt this 'European' experience to the African and Ibo tradition. Ironically it only limits his powers of adaptation and compromise. He had been sent to England with the high hopes of Umuofia behind him. (pp. 206-07)

Achebe carefully relates back Obi's character to that of his proud grandfather, 'his self-will was not new'. The conflict is yet embryonic. When Obi returns to Nigeria he is unable to compromise both his own personal integrity and his new 'European' habits and ideals to what his people expect from him....The irony is that Obi knows full well what is expected of him, but cannot or will not bring himself to do it. But like his grandfather in *Things Fall Apart* this is not simply a failure in humility. It is also a failure of compromise and perhaps of imagination.

In the world of Achebe's novels it does not seem possible to exist successfully in any arbitrary scheme of ideals. To do so is to invite disaster and retribution.... Hopelessly in debt, Obi is forced to shelve his integrity and to accept bribes in return for government scholarships, although he still tries to pretend to himself that he has not lost all his honour by only considering candidates who have satisfied the minimal educational and other requirements. Old Okonkwo refused to attempt any kind of compromise. Obi attempts a half-hearted one and fails. And just like the 'survivors' in his grandfather's time who had asked 'Why did he do it?' everyone now asks the same question of Obi. (pp. 208-09)

The theme is explored again in *Arrow of God.* This novel brings into conflict again, not only the old and the new,

African experience confronting European experience, but also expediency versus honour. Ezeulu, the old priest, brings personal tragedy upon himself because he refuses to compromise his pride and his traditional beliefs.

In the final novel, **Man of the People,** Odili, the idealistic and honest young schoolmaster is drawn pell-mell into the whirling, robust, boisterous world of present-day African politics which is not only extremely funny but extremely sad too. Odili's motives are pure. He wants to fight corruption and right wrongs and his innocence leads him to believe that he can triumph in a political society that makes the eighteenth-century Hustings look like one of Mrs. Gaskell's tea parties. He joins the new political party, C.P.C., the Common People's Convention, that has been formed by Max, his friend from University days. Odili's scruples are easily overcome. (p. 210)

These novels are not only about Nigeria. They represent too some of the issues that face us all in a world where ideals become more and more slippery in such a rapidly changing period of moral transition. But if, as I suggest, Achebe is presenting us with the recurrent theme of compromise or die, what is he then offering as a positive solution? Okonkwo failed to adapt and died. Max tried to compromise but also died. Odili and Obi die spiritual deaths when their ideals are shattered by reality. Achebe, I think, makes no arbitrary stand. He puts a relevant world problem into a West African setting and observes, reports and then leaves us to our own judgement. And although there is so much humour in his books he means them to be sad books. (pp. 211-12)

The language of Achebe's novels presents a highly skillful hand. He has a wonderful, true ear for Nigerian and English speech rhythms and a simple-seeming but very sophisticated use of metaphor. He has understood and mastered, and made it a dominant feature of his writing, the English philosophy of understatement and its concomitant bare narrative style. And much of his narrative style has its roots in a very wide literary tradition. The writings of many nations have been concerned with the effects of dramatic change on traditional ways of life. This conflict is often sharpened by glorifying or semi-deifying the 'traditional' hero. (p. 212)

Themes in literature are rarely original. It is in their individual treatment that they take on their own particular coloration. Achebe's novels define not only situations common to the Old Icelandic Sagas but ones which recur in much of modern literature. Because he places them in his own environment, which although, specifically Nigeria, is still a microcosm of a much larger world, he gives to them a fresh colour and insight. "This no be them country" may be metaphorically true of Okonkwo and Odili in that they cannot exist successfully in a period of social and moral transition, but it is not true for us, Achebe's readers, because his "country" can be for and of all of us. It is not so much a narrow canvas

as one that rather affords us a sharply angled view of a familiar human condition. (p. 214)

Kate Turkington, "'This No Be Them Country'—Chinua Achebe's Novels," in English Studies of Africa, *Vol. 14, No. 2, September, 1971, pp. 205-14.*

G. D. Killam (essay date 1971)

[*In the following review essay, Killam discusses theme, setting, and characterization in Achebe's novels.*]

Chinua Achebe is Nigeria's best-known novelist, and possibly the best-known writer of fiction in black Africa. He has written four novels which are widely read in Africa and are now achieving an audience in Europe and North America. Achebe attracted considerable attention when the publication of his fourth book, **A Man of the People** —the closing scenes of which describe a military take-over from a corrupt civil regime in a West African country—coincided with the first military coup in Nigeria, in January 1966. Yet his reputation rests principally on his first novel, **Things Fall Apart,** published in 1958, the first novel by a Nigerian writer to have serious claim to consideration as literature.

Things Fall Apart is about Iboland, in the eastern region of present-day Nigeria, in the period between 1850-1900; that is, the period just prior to and after the arrival of white men in this part of West Africa. The setting is Umuofia and Mbanta, the two principal villages in a union called the "nine villages". Okonkwo, the hero of the novel, a great wrestler in his youth, is, when we meet him, a renowned warrior, celebrated in songs at religious festivals, and one of the most wealthy, powerful, and influential people in Umuofia. The language of Okonkwo and the other villagers is expressed in the idiom of the Ibo villages as Achebe transmutes it into modern English. The conflict in the novel, vested in Okonkwo, derives from the series of crushing blows which are levelled at traditional values by an alien and more powerful culture, causing, in the end, the traditional society to fall apart. Thus the significance of the title of the book taken from Yeats's *The Second Coming:*

> Turning and turning in the widening gyre
> The falcon cannot hear the falconer;
> Things fall apart; the centre cannot hold;
> Mere anarchy is loosed upon the world.

Things Fall Apart is a vision of what life was like in Iboland between 1850 and 1900. Achebe makes a serious attempt to capture realistically the strains and tensions of the experiences of Ibo people under the impact of colonialism. It is not wholly true, however, to say that the novel is written consistently from their point of view. Achebe is a twentieth-century Ibo man, and recognizes the gulf which exists between his present-day society and that of Ibo villagers sixty years ago, sixty years which have seen remarkable changes in the texture and structure of Ibo society. Achebe is able to view objectively the forces which irresistibly and inevitably destroyed traditional Ibo social ties and with them the quality of Ibo life. His success proceeds not from his interest in the history of his people and their folklore and legend in an academic sense, but from his ability to create a sense of real life and real issues in the book and to see his subject from a point of view which is neither idealistic nor dishonest.

Things Fall Apart is written in three parts: the first and most important is set in Umuofia before the coming of the white man—before his existence is even known. The second part dramatizes Okonkwo's banishment from Mbanta, the village of his mother's people, for sins committed against the Earth Goddess, and describes, mostly through reports, the coming of the white man to the nine villages, the establishment of an alien church, government, and trading system, and the gradual encroachment of these on the traditional patterns of tribal life. The third section and the shortest brings the novel swiftly to a close, dramatizing the death of the old ways and the death of Okonkwo.

Okonkwo is a character of intense individuality, yet one in whom the values most admired by Ibo peoples are consolidated. He is both an individual and a type. The first paragraphs of the book indicate the deftness and certainty with which Achebe establishes not only the character but the ethical and moral basis of his life and, by extension, the ethical and moral basis of the life of the clan. (pp. 514-16)

In the second and third parts of the novel the critical social conflict takes place. These sections present the social and psychological effects and the tragic consequences which result from the clash between traditional Ibo society and British Christian imperialism. In the second section, as well, the relationship between Okonkwo and his refractory son Nwoye is delineated in such a way as to transmute the broader cultural conflict to the personal level. (p. 521)

The third part of the novel begins by describing Okonkwo's return to Umuofia after his seven years of exile, a return less auspicious than he hoped it would be. Again Achebe emphasizes the heroic stature of Okonkwo: he has withstood reversals of fortune and personal calamities which would have crushed a less resilient spirit. "It seemed to him as if his *chi* might be making amends for past disasters!" (p. 526)

The novel is in fact a structure of ironies—irony of the tragic kind which shows an exceptional man who sees his best hopes and achievements destroyed through an inexorable flow of events which he is powerless to restrain, tragic irony suggested and supported by a carefully integrated pattern of minor ironies throughout the work: the accidental shooting which brings about his exile; the irony of the appeal of Christianity to Nwoye, Okonkwo's first-born, in whom he had placed his hopes; the irony contained in the persistent comment by Okonkwo that his daughter Ezinma ought to have been born a male child. And there is the more general irony

made explicit in the closing paragraph of the book, but implicit in the encounter between the Africans and Europeans throughout the second and third parts: that Christianity, seen as a "civilizing agent", acts as a catalyst in destroying a civilization which heretofore had strength and cohesion.

Achebe's second novel, *No Longer at Ease,* is set in the present (1960) and has as its hero Obi Okonkwo, the grandson of Okonkwo in *Things Fall Apart.* The novel opens with Obi on trial for accepting bribes when a Civil Servant, and the book takes the form of a long flashback which leads up to the trial. The novel tells of Obi's return from England where he has recently completed his B.A. degree. Filled with idealism, Obi is determined to assist in ridding his country of corruption and to help create a better nation. A second and parallel plot concerns Obi's affair with Clara, a nurse with whom he falls in love on the boat returning them to Nigeria. Clara is *"osu"* among the Ibo, a descendant of cult slaves, and according to tradition she must live apart from the free-born.

The novel records Obi's professional, social and moral decline. He begins well enough on his return; he is appointed Scholarship Secretary at the Federal Ministry of Education. He resists attempts at bribing him. The relationship with Clara is at first a happy one. But a series of conflicting and simultaneous demands are made on him which undermine his security and eventually his integrity. (pp. 530-31)

The novel reveals the pressures placed upon a young man like Obi, the wide gulf between his idealism which is based on his western education, and the actuality of his status as an individual within a complex and contradictory society in which the old values maintain sway and influence. Thus the significance of the title, taken from a line of T. S. Eliot's "Journey of the Magi":

> We returned to our places, these Kingdoms,
> But no longer at ease here, in the old dispensa-
> tion,
> With an alien people clutching their gods.
> I should be glad of another death.

The novel closes with Obi's conviction, and Achebe writes:

> Everybody wondered why. The learned judge, as we
> have seen, could not comprehend how an educated
> young man and so on and so forth. The British
> Council man, even the men of Umuofia, did not
> know. And we must presume that, in spite of his
> certitude, Mr. Green did not know either.

The questions posed in the closing paragraph of the novel are rhetorical. The novel has offered implicitly, and in dramatic form, the answers to them.

The book is an attempt by Achebe at writing modern tragedy and it is in this regard that the novel's most serious limitation is revealed. There is an element of the *roman à thèse* in the novel which proceeds not from Achebe's attempt to create a modern tragedy but from the need he seems to have felt to define what he is going to do and then deliberately to illustrate this. At the interview for appointment to the Civil Service post a discussion takes place between Obi and the chairman on the nature of tragedy, and concludes with this speech by Obi:

> 'Real tragedy is never resolved. It goes on hopelessly for ever. Conventional tragedy is too easy. The hero dies and we feel a purging of the emotions. A real tragedy takes place in a corner, in an untidy spot, to quote W. H. Auden. The rest of the world is unaware of it. Like that man in *A Handful of Dust* who reads Dickens to Mr. Todd. There is no release for him. When the story ends he is still reading. There is no purging of the emotions for us because we are not there.'

Here Achebe momentarily loses his objectivity and breaks the dramatic pattern of the novel by obtruding himself between his book and his readers.

Achebe's third book, *Arrow of God,* is set in the period between that of *Things Fall Apart* and *No Longer at Ease.* The locale is Umuaro and the other villages which form a union of six villages. Achebe presents this area as the center of the values and experience of the people of the novel. As in *Things Fall Apart* the presence of white men suggests a world and peoples outside Umuaro, but the significance is in the power and influence of white men as they shape the day-to-day destinies of the Umuaro villagers.

The principal character in the novel is Ezeulu, chief priest of Ulu—a god created to supersede the older village deities at the time when the six villages banded together for protection against the slave raids. When we meet him Ezeulu's power is supreme. A powerful, forceful, and noble character, Ezeulu resembles Okonkwo in the first novel but experiences none of the inner doubts and uncertainties of the latter. Yet though his power and influence are secure, they need to be protected from outside pressures which threaten to undermine them. Against a carefully developed plot which describes Umuaro's history through a series of births, deaths, marriages, ceremonies, Achebe displays the pressures brought to bear on Ezeulu which lead to tragic consequences at both the individual and social levels. (pp. 533-35)

A Man of the People marks a change in Achebe's approach to novel-writing. In his first three books he explored in various ways the results of the confrontation between Africa and Europe and centered his novels in the stories of heroes whose lives end tragically, partly because of flaws in their natures which cause them to make miscalculations at critical moments, and partly because they are caught up in historical circumstances which they are powerless to control and which overwhelm them. Achebe's approach in these books is insistently ironic but it is irony of a tragic kind. In *A Man of the People,* which presents situations and events exactly contemporary with its writing, Achebe employs the irony of the satirist in order to ridicule and condemn the moral political situations which the book describes and which determine its pattern.

The novel tells, in the first person, the story of Odili, a university graduate and teacher, and of his involvement with Chief the Honourable M. A. Nanga, M.P., and with the political life of the country. Scornful of Nanga's fraudulent political behavior, Odili is nearly overwhelmed by Nanga's charm and seduced to Nanga's opportunistic way of thinking and acting. But when Nanga steals his mistress from him, Odili, mostly from motives of revenge but partly because of a political idealism which reasserts itself, joins a rival political party which contests the election, receives a brutal beating from Nanga's hired thugs, and sees the leader of his party—a close personal friend—murdered. The novel closes with a military take-over of the country, with Odili, now happily married, determined to found a school to honor the martyred leader of the party he has served.

Achebe achieves balance and proportion in his theme of political corruption by showing both the absurdity of much of the behavior of the principal characters and the destructive consequences of that behavior to the commonwealth. Of the chief characters, Odili, Nanga, and Odili's father are the most successful, and for different reasons. Odili's motives are never entirely disinterested: capable of idealism and a desire to rid the country of political corruption, he nevertheless acts often out of self-interest and spite in his dealings with his protagonist, Nanga. He is not a stereotyped character of a kind familiar in novels treating this theme.

Nanga is a compelling character. In Achebe's words,

> Chief Nanga was a born politician; he could get away with almost anything he said or did. And as long as men are swayed by their hearts and stomachs and not their heads the Chief Nangas of this world will continue to get away with anything. He had that rare gift of making people feel—even while he was saying harsh things to them—that there was not a drop of ill will in his entire frame. I remember the day he was telling his ministerial colleague over the telephone in my presence that he distrusted our young university people and that he would rather work with a European. I knew I was hearing terrible things but somehow I couldn't bring myself to take the man seriously. He had been so open and kind to me and not in the least distrustful. The greatest criticism a man like him seemed capable of evoking in our country was an indulgent: 'Make you no min'am.'
>
> This is of course a formidable weapon which is always guaranteed to save its wielder from the normal consequences of misconduct as well as from the humiliation and embarrassment of ignorance. For how else could you account for the fact that a Minister of Culture announced in public that he had never heard of his country's most famous novel and received applause—as indeed he received again later when he prophesied that before long our great country would produce great writers like Shakespeare, Dickens, Jane Austen, Bernard Shaw and—raising his eyes off the script—Michael West and Dudley Stamp.

The character of Odili's father is presented as both a type and an individual, one who embodies attitudes typical of the generality of Nigerians of his generation, yet capable of independent and at times noble action.

The appropriateness of the language Achebe uses is as evident here as in the earlier books. Here, too, he makes use of "pidgin", the *lingua franca* of West Africa. Used generally as the language of extravagant and sometimes grotesque comic presentation, "pidgin" has, as Achebe shows, a close correlation to the sentiments of the common man and can be used to reflect serious as well as comic considerations.

A Man of the People attracted considerable attention when it was published because the closing actions it describes coincided with the military coup which took place in Nigeria in January, 1966. The novel had, and perhaps still has, topicality. There is no necessary correlation between topicality and art: a novel achieves the status of art when it transcends the local and particular circumstances which inspire it. Achebe is aware of this and has stated that "the writer's duty is not to beat the morning's headlines in topicality, it is to explore the depth of the human condition." (pp. 539-41)

> G. D. Killam, "Chinua Achebe's Novels," in The Sewanee Review, *Vol. LXXIX, No. 4, Autumn, 1971, pp. 514-41.*

Charles R. Larson (essay date 1972)

[*In the following excerpt, Larson reviews* Things Fall Apart, *describing it as the "archetypal African novel."*]

Things Fall Apart has come to be regarded as more than simply a classic; it is now seen as the archetypal African novel. The situation which the novel itself describes— the coming of the white man and the initial disintegration of traditional African society as a consequence of that—is typical of the breakdown all African societies have experienced at one time or another as a result of their exposure to the West. And, moreover, individual Africans all over the continent may identify with the situation Achebe has portrayed. (p. 28)

Although *Arrow of God* is in some ways probably artistically superior to *Things Fall Apart,* it is fated to run a second place in popularity to Achebe's first work. [*Things Fall Apart*] may also be regarded as archetypal because of Achebe's reshaping of a traditional Western literary genre into something distinctly African in form and pattern. (p. 29)

Achebe's dialogue in *Things Fall Apart* is extremely sparse. Okonkwo [the protagonist] says very little at all; not of any one place in the novel may it be said that he has an extended speech or even a very lengthy conversation with another character. And as for authorial presentations of his thoughts, they are limited to two or three very brief passages. Indeed, Achebe relies for the development of his story usually on exposition rather than the dramatic rendering of scene, much as if he were telling an extended oral tale or epic in conventional narrative fashion—almost always making use of the preterit. Again and again the reader is told something about Okonkwo, but he rarely sees these events in action. (pp. 40-1)

I have . . . . noted the strong aversion that many Western critics have toward the anthropological overtones present in African fiction, except for the anthropologist, of course, who is looking for this kind of thing. This aversion of the literary critics, however, is no doubt due to their equation of the anthropological with the local colorists at the end of the last century and the beginning of this one. However, in a work such as *Things Fall Apart,* where we are not presented with a novel of character, the anthropological is indeed important. Without it there would be no story. The only way in which Achebe can depict a society's falling apart is first by creating an anthropological overview of that culture, and it should be clear that it is not going to Okonkwo's story that Achebe is chronicling as much as the tragedy of a clan. It is the village of Umuofia, which has been sketched in so carefully, which he will now show as falling apart, crumbling from its exposure to Western civilization. (pp. 43-4)

The piling up of ethnological background, I suggest, is often the equivalent of atmospheric conditioning in Western fiction. Achebe's anthropological passages are what Hardy's descriptive passages are for him—equivalent to Hardy's evocation of atmosphere and mood. Indeed, it is extremely difficult to find a passage of pure description of a natural setting anywhere in Anglophone African writing of the first generation. There is very little that can be related to "landscape painting" in English fiction except for the anthropological passages. (p. 44)

The concluding chapter of *Things Fall Apart* is one of the highlights of contemporary African fiction. In less than three pages, Achebe weaves together the various themes and patterns he has been working with throughout much of his novel. Technically, the most significant aspect of this final chapter is Achebe's sudden shifts in point of view. (p. 57)

The shifting point of view back and forth between an African and a Western viewpoint symbolizes the final breakup of the clan, for *Things Fall Apart,* in spite of the subtitle on the first American edition, *The Story of a Strong Man,* is only in part Okonkwo's story, and, as we have noted, as the book progresses, the story becomes increasingly that of a village, a clan. Achebe clearly indicates this in the final paragraph of his novel where he reduces Okonkwo's story to nothing more than a paragraph in a history book, for history is facts and not individuals, and the history of the coming of the white man to Africa is not the story of the pacification of individuals but of entire tribes of people and even beyond that . . . . Achebe has moved throughout his book away from the individual (Okonkwo) to the communal

(Umuofia) and beyond that to the clan. And in the last paragraph, the extension is even further beyond the Ibo of Southeast Nigeria to that of the *Primitive Tribes of the Lower Niger,* ergo, the entire African continent.

The conclusion to *Things Fall Apart* has often been considered over-written, anti-climactic, unnecessarily didactic.... Certainly it can be argued that Achebe takes pains to make his message clear, but I feel that the shift to the District Commissioner's point of view strengthens rather than weakens the conclusion. It seems impossible for any one to read Achebe's last chapter without being noticeably moved, and if it is didactic in the sense of tying things up a little too nicely, then I would have to insist that this was Achebe's intention from the beginning and not merely an accident because of his background of oral tradition.... Achebe has written ... [that] the novelist in an emergent nation cannot afford to pass up a chance to educate his fellow countrymen.... [Furthermore], contemporary African literature and other forms of African art have inherited a cultural inclination toward the didactic which in regard to African tradition may be called functionalism.

The ending of *Things Fall Apart* also illustrates the dichotomy of interpretations which cultural backgrounds impose upon a reader. Most Western readers of Achebe's novel seem to interpret the story of Okonkwo's fall as tragic if not close to pure tragedy in classical terms. They cite Okonkwo's pride, his going against the will of the gods (for instance, breaking the Week of Peace, and killing Ikemefuna), and interpret the ending as tragic and inevitable, citing, usually, a parallel to Oedipus. Achebe's own feelings about Okonkwo and the conclusion to the novel, however, would tend to indicate a rather different interpretation. The most obvious clue is Achebe's title, *Things Fall Apart,* taken from William Butler Yeats's poem, "The Second Coming." Although Yeats's title may be applied ironically to Achebe's story, the indications are that Achebe views the new dispensation as something inevitable, perhaps even desirable. His criticism is clearly of the old way of life which is unsatisfactory now that the West has arrived. This interpretation is supported by several comments Achebe has made about his novel.... Lack of adaptability ... is what Achebe implies led to the collapse of traditional Ibo society. (pp. 59-61)

Of the three major divisions of the book, only the trajectory of Parts II and III resembles the traditional Western well-made novel with conflict—obstacles to be overcome by the protagonist. Part I is especially loose, incorporating as it does section after section of anthropological background. The effect is, of course, to re-create the entire world of day-to-day existence in traditional Ibo society, and Achebe takes pains to make certain that the major stages of life are included: birth, marriage, and death. In the symbiosis which results, Umuofia, rather than Okonkwo, becomes the main character of *Things Fall Apart,* and the transformation it undergoes is archetypal of the entire breakdown of traditional African cultures under exposure to the West.

The novel itself, as I stated at the beginning, must also be regarded as archetypical for the form and patterns Achebe has given it. If we compare the novel very briefly with Joyce Cary's *Mister Johnson* it is readily evident that *Things Fall Apart* is not a story about a character as is Cary's novel and as I feel we tend to regard Western novels as being. For example, Achebe could never have called his novel *Okonkwo,* though it could have been given the name of Okonkwo's village if Achebe had thought that the situation did not extend beyond that one locale within Nigeria. Okonkwo himself does not alter at all throughout the novel. He is the same at the ending as he is at the beginning of the story. Thus, *Things Fall Apart,* because of its emphasis on community rather than individuality, is a novel of situation rather than of character, and this is undoubtedly its major difference from the traditional Western genre, which in the twentieth century, at least, has emphasized the psychological depiction of character. (pp. 62-3)

Let it simply be noted here that the situational plot is indeed the most typical narrative form one encounters in contemporary African fiction. The reason for this is that by and large the major theme of African writing to date has been the conflict of Africa with the West, whether this is shown in its initial stages, as in Achebe's *Things Fall Apart,* or at any one of several different later stages. All four of Achebe's novels are examples of the situational plot, for what happens is ultimately more significant for the group than for the individual whom Achebe uses to focus the situation. The significance, then, is felt by the village, the clan, the tribe, or the nation. (pp. 63-4)

Things Fall Apart does not necessarily give the impression that the story is "plotless" in spite of the fragmentary nature of many of the substories or tales.... Achebe's use of the proverb can act as a serious counterpart for the more continuous surface progression of the story.... The other unities which he relies on to give form and pattern to the story are the traditional oral tale or tale within a tale—a device no longer in favor with contemporary Western novelists, yet a convention at least as old as the "Man in the Hill" episode in Fielding's *Tom Jones.* The use of the leitmotif and its associations with stagnancy in Umuofia, masculinity, land, and yam also act as connective links throughout the narrative. It is because of these unities and others, which are vestiges of his own traditional culture, that Achebe's *Things Fall Apart* deserves its position in the forefront of contemporary African writing. Achebe has widened our perspective of the novel and illustrated how a typically Western genre may be given a healthy injection of new blood once it is reshaped and formed by the artist whose vision of life and art is different from our own. (pp. 64-5)

Achebe has increased the importance of dialogue in [*Arrow of God*]—especially dialogue which makes use of materials drawn from traditional oral literature such as the proverb. Hardly a page of his story passes without the presence of a proverb or two; sometimes there will be as many as half-a-dozen, piled one upon another.... The use of these oral examples is a primary means of characterization, and it is the adults in Achebe's novel who make the greatest use of these materials—giving the impression of great wisdom. The majority of the proverbs in *Arrow of God* are spoken as dialogue rather than as part of authorial commentary. The unique aspect of Achebe's characterization, then, is his use of oral literary material—far more frequently than almost all other African writers. (pp. 150-52)

Achebe's European characters in *Arrow of God* are generally a little less convincing than they could be, for, in truth, they are examined only from the outside, are stereotyped and one-dimensional, efficient little machines meant to do a job in the British Foreign Service, and, necessarily, I suppose, are in too many ways typical of the men who were in the colonial service. (p. 153)

Almost all—if not all—of Achebe's characters in *A Man of the People* are stereotypes, because with this novel Achebe moved into a new area: satire. In many ways the novel is his weakest so far, and I am convinced that its popularity with the African reading audience bears little correlation to its literary merits; however, the novel accomplishes exactly what it set out to do—satirize life in Nigeria in the mid-1960's. Many of the situations satirized can only be appreciated by someone who lived in Nigeria during those years: political corruption, the increasing bureaucracy, the postal strike, the census, the means of communication, the daily news media.

It probably is not fair to criticize Achebe's cardboard characters in *A Man of the People*, since satire rarely is built on believable characters. Even the fact that the story is told in the first person results in no great insight into Achebe's narrator, Odili Samalu, or any of the other characters. The thin story thread is more reminiscent of the novels of Cyprian Ekwensi than of Achebe's earlier works.... When the story line gets out of control, Achebe conveniently draws his political morality to an end by having the nation succumb to a military coup. In spite of the de-emphasis on character development, there is certainly more dialogue than Achebe has ever used before, especially in dialects such as Pidgin English, as a means of characterization. The conversation at times is witty, but the whole affair—Odili's entering politics because he has lost his girl—is unconvincing and rather overdrawn. Everybody gets satirized, however, educated and uneducated Africans, the British and the Americans, even the Peace Corps.... *A Man of the People* should be acknowledged for exactly what is is: an entertainment, written for Africans. Achebe no longer tries to explain the way it is, to apologize for the way things are, because this is exactly the point: this is the way things are. The characters are ineffectual, and Achebe's satire itself will be short-lived. The story and

the characters have none of the magnitude or the nobility of those in *Things Fall Apart* or *Arrow of God.* (pp. 153-55)

> *Charles R. Larson, "Chinua Achebe's 'Things Fall Apart': The Archetypal African Novel" and "Characters and Modes of Characterization: Chinua Achebe, James Ngugi, and Peter Abrahams," in his* The Emergence of African Fiction, *revised edition, Indiana University Press, 1972, pp. 27-65, 147-66.*

Eustace Palmer (essay date 1972)

[*In the following excerpt, Palmer presents a critical overview of* Things Fall Apart, A Man of the People, *and* No Longer at Ease, *noting that Achebe's novel* Things Fall Apart *is "unquestionably his best."*]

Chinua Achebe's first novel, *Things Fall Apart* is unquestionably his best. Never again was he to demonstrate such mastery of plot construction, such keen psychological insight, and such an ability to hold his themes steadily before his mind and pursue them convincingly to a logical conclusion. *Things Fall Apart* derives its strength from the quality of the author's perception of the social forces at work in an ancient and proud society, and from his admirable knowledge of human psychology shown in the development of Okonkwo's character. There are distinct affinities between the work of Achebe and that of Hardy. Both show a keen awareness of the movement of social forces and their effect on the destiny of ordinary people. (p. 48)

The theme of the novel is stated clearly on page 160: 'He has put a knife on the things that held us together and we have fallen apart.' With the arrival of the white man and his new religion and administration, traditional society's cracks and weaknesses, hitherto concealed by the common fear of the ancestors and the gods, break open and the once-stable community collapses. In order to impress on the reader the tragedy of its collapse, Achebe devotes great skill in evoking his society as it used to be; and this is one of the reasons for the novel's enduring appeal. Those who open this novel hoping to find a description of noble savagery where the tensions of modern Western society do not exist, are likely to be disappointed. Umuofia society is proud, dignified, and stable, because it is governed by a complicated system of customs and traditions extending from birth, through marriage to death. It has its own legal, educational, religious, and hierarchical systems, and the conventions governing relations between the various generations are as elaborate as any to be found in a Jane Austen novel. (pp. 48-9)

There is a school of social anthropologists who rhapsodize over traditional African society seeing it as a welcome antidote to the materialism and commercial technology of Western society, with its morbid preoccupation with worldly possessions, status symbols, rapid promotion, and all the trappings of the rat-race. Such anthropologists are likely to have second thoughts on reading *Things Fall Apart,* for this society is just as competitive, just as materialistic, and just as concerned with status as any to be found in the Western world. (pp. 51-2)

The apparent prosperity of this society is overshadowed by the everbrooding presence of danger, fear, and death. There was the fear of evil and capricious gods and magic, the fear of the forest, and 'of the forces of nature, malevolent, red in tooth and claw'. It is fear, especially the fear of the gods and of evil, that motivates the many acts of apparent brutality in this community. (p. 52)

It is a mark of Achebe's intelligent objectivity, that conscious though he is of the strength and stability of traditional Umuofia society, he is not blind to its brutality. He does not merely record these instances of savagery without implying any judgement, for he carefully leaves clues and hints, structural as well as textual, as comments on the nature of the society he describes. (pp. 52-3)

The need for sociological detail to create a sense of society dictates the novel's construction. The first part may appear sluggish, with a number of apparently irrelevant digressions, while the second moves with astonishing rapidity and is much more unified. This is necessary, for Achebe is not concentrating on action in the first part, but on the evocation of Ibo society which requires the description of episodes some of which, like Ezinma's illness, or the trial scene, could even be transposed elsewhere, without materially damaging the story. (p. 61)

In a sense, Achebe could not avoid using proverbs since they are highly prized in the society he has set himself the task of portraying. He tells himself that the art of conversation is highly regarded among the Ibos and 'proverbs are the palm-oil with which words are eaten'.... Proverbs do not merely convey a quaint charm, nor are they only part of the elaborate conventions of Ibo society, they have a very important role to play in conversation and are an indispensable aspect of Achebe's style. (pp. 61-2)

As in *Things Fall Apart,* Achebe's insight into the working of social forces shapes [*No Longer at Ease*]. The novel derives its interest largely from this social analysis. But *No Longer at Ease* has flaws. Firstly, the hero is weak and insufficiently realized.... The failure to take us close enough to Obi's consciousness is the basic cause of our ignorance of the mainspring of the hero's actions and this, in its turn, results in a number of psychological implausibilities in the novel. (pp. 68-9)

Another major flaw is the imperfect blending of the two main themes. Achebe wishes to show that Obi's love affair with Clara is destroyed by his society's conservatism. However, Achebe does *not* demonstrate that social forces are to blame.... The affair is destroyed, not by the clash between the old and the new, but by Clara's unreasonable behaviour.

The third major weakness of the novel is structural. *No Longer at Ease* is too episodic to form a coherent whole. We saw in our study of *Things Fall Apart* that although some of the scenes were not causally related and could be transposed without materially affecting the novel's meaning, yet each was absolutely necessary in the presentation of Okonkwo and his society. With *No Longer at Ease,* some of the scenes are not only transposable, but are also irrelevant. (pp. 69-70)

Finally, Achebe does not seem to have been able to resist melodramatics, for example, Obi's outburst at the meeting of the Umuofia Progressive Society, or the scene in which Clara returns Obi's ring.

What gives this novel its interest is Achebe's social concern and his terse, ironic, lucid, unpretentious style. His scintillating wit, which is itself the index of his objectivity and maturity of outlook, is everywhere apparent. (p. 71)

Thematically *A Man of the People* belongs to the same tradition as *Things Fall Apart* and *No Longer at Ease*.... Stylistically, however, *A Man of the People* is very different from the earlier novels. Firstly, it is a first person narrative; secondly, it is that rare bird in the corpus of African literature—a comic novel. After the tragic grandeur of *Things Fall Apart* and the pessimism of *No Longer at Ease,* it is refreshing to turn to a novel which occasionally stirs a belly laugh. One of the puzzles of African literature is that our verbal humour never seems to carry through to our writing. Perhaps we take ourselves and our leaders far too seriously to expose them publicly in a comic novel, although we are quite prepared to caricature them in private. However, African intellectuals are becoming more ready to laugh at aspects of their society—witness the publication of four satirical novels: *A Man of the People*, *Mission to Kala,* *The Interpreters,* and *The Beautyful Ones Are Not Yet Born.* (pp. 72-3)

[Despite its humour], *A Man of the People* looks like a tract for the times in which Achebe's dominant preoccupation is the exposure of the evils of his country's political system. But he is so full of his didactic mission that he fails to create situations, characters, and a plot which can convincingly carry the message. Consequently, the political intention is always obtrusive, especially in the last sections of the novel, where Achebe becomes more of a journalist than a novelist. One is disappointed not to see more of the process whereby law and order broke down. The conclusion of the novel is also unsatisfactory, for if Chief Nanga deserved to end on the rubbish heap, Odili did not deserve much better.

The weaknesses of *A Man of the People* should not blind us to its merits, although it is a flawed work, it is a necessary and an important one. (p. 84)

Eustace Palmer, "Chinua Achebe," in his An Introduction to the African Novel, *Africana, 1972, pp. 48-84.*

Chinua Achebe with Victoria K. Evalds (interview date 1976)

[*In the following 1976 interview, Evalds and Achebe discuss "the social change in Achebe's novels" and "Achebe's current goals and future plans."*]

[Evalds]: *Considering your novels in sequence, the flow of social history is interrupted by the missing volume of the Okonkwo trilogy which would have been centered on Nwoye/Issac. Could you explain why you chose to skip this generation?*

[Achebe]: Well, I did plan to deal with that generation. As a matter of fact, **Things Fall Apart** as originally conceived, covered all three generations. But in writing, I realized that it would be spreading the story over too wide an area, so I decided on three books. The idea of that middle generation was something that was in my mind originally, and I did plan to go back to it after I finished **No Longer at Ease.**

Why did I decide to skip it in the first place? I have been trying to explain that to myself. I really don't know, except that I have said that I found it difficult to cope with that generation. That is my father's generation, and there is a kind of difficulty that I have in being able to explain their psychology. There is a certain "generation gap" problem. And, although I came to understand my father and to admire him, there are still some things about that generation I cannot clearly understand. I hope I will go back some day with more understanding.

Then you do plan to complete the trilogy?

I certainly have that "on the cards". I am not sure when.

Concerning **No Longer at Ease,** *why are nationalist groups and activities not more in evidence in the novel? Would not a young man of Obi's background and sentiments be drawn into some type of nationalist activity?*

Well, some men of Obi's generation obviously were, but Obi, by nature was not attracted.

Would it have made Obi too strong a character to have had him involved with nationalist politics?

That is an interesting point, but I do not accept the idea that Obi was a weak character. I think he is very strong; it is just that his strength is not the kind that is particularly appreciated in the West. He was more of an artist than an activist. He meditated rather than acted, but he was not weak. It is also a matter of my preference in what I wanted to deal with in the novel; when you are writing you must be selective to a certain extent.

I realize you have stated your distaste for using tribalism as my generalization to explain the Nigerian political situation. However, the factor of ethnicity was certainly in evidence in Nigeria when you wrote **Man of the People;** *why then is ethnicity not given more attention in the novel?*

Again, I will say that I do not think that everything that is going on in the world must get into a novel simply because it is written at that point; the novelist must be selective. Now there is a certain amount of ethnicity in **Man of the People,** but it is very indirect. For example, one character claims he lost a job because someone from another group got it. But it seemed to me that there were other more important things for me to be dealing with than ethnic differences. If I had wanted to write on the dangers of ethnicity, I would have done it; but I was concerned with something else, and it seemed to me that ethnic considerations were not central to that. Also, I think the ethnic question is quite often exaggerated to the point where every problem in Africa is dismissed as a "tribal" one; and I just did not want to get into that.

In re-reading your novels, I was struck by the fact that the role of women is more fully portrayed in the novels dealing with the traditional society. Does your treatment of modern women represent your own, perhaps unconscious, male orientation? Or does it reflect a certain ambivalence in modern male-female relationships due to the changing role of women in African society?

That is a tough question. I think you are right about my portrayal of traditional women. The reason must be that their roles were defined and clear, and basically accepted. There is always some kind of war between the sexes you know, but in the traditional society it was good humored. One understood that the man was boss, but the name given to children was "Mother is supreme". In other words, there was an arrangement in which one formally accepted male dominance, but in practice one made obeisance to the female role and influence. And generally, I think these roles were understood, and there was not too much friction or confusion. This is one way of dealing with problems in the world.

In the modern society I think the roles are still in a state of flux. Many people are confused about the role of women, and I myself am not very clear on just how to handle this subject.

I cannot help but notice a certain attitude toward women in the modern novels—of their being objects rather than persons. In line with your idea of teaching people about their own society, I wonder perhaps if you have slighted women by not giving them models which they could look up to or follow?

Well, you must distinguish between my ideas and the ideas of my characters. As a matter of fact, although I am not giving central roles to women, you can gauge the development of the male personalities by their attitude toward women. Take Odili in **Man of the People;** he starts off treating women as objects, but he ends up changing his ideas completely. In my view this is a measure of his growth. What I am saying is that I am not totally identifiable with the actions of my male characters, and that you can sense my sympathy or attitude (toward women) by the attitude of my characters toward them. (pp. 16-17)

I would like to conclude with some questions about your goals as a writer and your future plans. As a writer who has been concerned with examining the African past, what do you think of recent criticism which contends that African writers are using the past as a form of escapism and are not dealing with current problems and their solutions?

Well those critics who make that comment do not know what they are talking about. What they are really concerned with is the criticism of the role of the Europeans (by African authors). As they see it, if a writer talks about the past and how that past was destroyed, he is somewhat putting the blame on the Europeans. And they are tired of hearing this.

So you feel it is still necessary to examine the past?

It is necessary to do both. Every people has a past, a present, and a future. But to say, well, we talked about our past yesterday, today let us talk about our present is ridiculous. I think one flows into the other—there is no cut-off point.

Any writer who feels that there is something that he can pull out of the past, either in the way of story, of analogy, or whatever, should do so. Now if an African writer does not want to deal with the past that is fine; but if he is not able to deal with the past that is another matter.

These people who criticize do not know anything about the past, and what is worse, they do not care. So they propound the theory that we are now "modern", that we are no longer a tribal people, and therefore all our concerns should be about today. Sometimes it has even gone beyond Africa to being concerned about the Third World, with all oppressed peoples. Now I do not have any time for that kind of thing because that is a real escape, a real evasion.

Concerning the recent past, has enough time elapsed for you and other writers to consider the War? As part of your role of teacher and social critic, do you feel a responsibility to write about this period of your people's history?

I will be writing. And I am not even sure that the novel I am working on now won't reflect some aspects of the War, although it is not about the War specifically. There is no way you can go through such an experience and not write about it even though you are not writing a specific story. Its influence on your thinking about yourself and the rest of the world is bound to come through. And I notice, when I stop to look at what I have written, that this is already happening. Of course a certain amount of distance is necessary, a certain amount of time to recover—how long depends on who is writing.

I am sure you are aware that your novels are often quoted by social scientists writing on non-literary themes. Do you feel an artist should be aware of this type of potential influence when he is writing?

I believe that the writer is a teacher; there is no way he can get away from this role unless he is not read. If he is read, then his work will have certain effects on others. So long as the writer does not let the idea of the possible effects cramp his style, so long as he does not stop on every page to consider what the social scientist will say, then the writer will be all right.

Would you advise younger writers to maintain a stream of committed writing aimed at the general public rather than exploring some symbolic and interpretative modes of writing?

I do not lay down the law for any writer. I am not that wise to be able to say to the young people, this is what you should be doing. Anyway, a writer who is doing what other people are doing, or what somebody tells him to do, has not yet become a writer. He still has not found his voice. When you find your voice you follow it whether it takes you into that area that is supposed to be symbolic, or not. What is important will suggest itself to a good writer. And good writers will emerge without all this aid from me, the critics, or anyone else.

But you still feel a necessity for commitment to the society whatever the mode of writing?

If it is commitment you are talking about rather than modes of writing, that is a different question. I do not think one can ever be a serious writer and do away with commitment. I just do not accept that as a possibility.

Since you feel commitment is necessary for writers, do you feel that it is possible for Nigerian authors to freely criticize their society at this time? Is any form of censorship currently being exercised by the military government on Nigerian writers?

Criticizing the society is a must (for writers). There is no direct censorship in Nigeria; the government has not forbidden anything as far as I know. However, many people assume that a military government calls for caution, so there is a form of self-imposed censorship. The writer has to find out how far he can go and to decide what is sensible without being counterproductive. And we have had some fairly outspoken people, not only in literature but in journalism.

Do you feel that the commitment of African writers to their society necessitates them working to change the society through channels other than literature?

For some people, yes, it might. One can very easily be led away from literature to other forms of activity, including direct action. And sometimes one can be led to doubting the value of literature. At that point I think one ought to stop and think it all through again. I think it would be a pity if all the literary people stopped writing and went on to something else, but at the same time I do not accept the idea that a writer is such a special person that even if the world is burning, all he can do is sit and write about it. I believe it is a question of the right balance.

What of current Nigerian writing? Do you find that the bitterness, cynicism and introspection of the first post-War writings is giving way to a more positive outlook?

Yes, I think so. There is a certain amount of bitterness, but I think the best artists are able to surmount that and to go on to something else. Just bitterness itself is self-destructive and does not leave you with very much.

You have expressed an interest in children's literature, indigenous publishing and the creation of an African aesthetic. Are these still concerns of yours? Do you view your efforts in these areas as fostering a framework of cultural independence from the West?

The short answer to that question is yes.

And in the future, are you going to work in all these areas?

As many of them as I can find time for. I find that the area of children's literature is particularly important.

And you wish to use literature to help reinforce the African heritage for this generation of African children?

Yes, exactly.

The creation of an African aesthetic seems to be a particularly volatile issue. How do you view the role of your journal, Okike, *in this regard?*

Well, to consider *Okike* is to start from the end of the story. It is an attempt to enter the case, one of the contending cases you see. *Okike* is an attempt to make sure our case is heard, to make plain that this is a culture with something to offer the world. There are other offerings, other attitudes, other ways of looking at the world; but this is the one we have, and we have an obligation to present it for what it is worth. The world is made up of different peoples and cultures; and all people, however modest their circumstances, have been working and creating. The world is poorer for not understanding this, for not looking for the specific strengths of various cultures.

As more and more Africans have input into literary criticism and the creation of aesthetic criteria, do you feel some of the bitterness in literary discussion can be overcome?

Yes, at the moment it is probably somewhat shrill. I do not know if this is peculiar to our case, but I suspect that it probably happens at this point in the life of other cultures. People take what they do seriously, which is a good thing, and they challenge the judgements of other people. Perhaps the time will come when it will not be necessary to shout.

Can you tell me about your plans for the future? You have said you are working on another novel, and you are publishing the journal. Are you going to continue to teach?

I am going back to Nsukka in the summer, I hope to teach at the University of Nigeria. My original position there did not involve much actual classroom teaching. I hope it will be that way again, at least for the first few years, so I can work on various projects. And I will be working on this novel; I had hoped to finish it here but that has not been possible.

Thank you so much; you have been most kind to answer these rather diverse questions. I am sure we all wish you a safe journey home and success in whatever activities you undertake. (pp. 18-20)

> Chinua Achebe with Victoria K. Evalds, in an interview in Studies in Black Literature, *Vol. 8, No. 1, Spring, 1977, pp. 16-20.*

Eileen Battersby (essay date 1987)

[*In the following excerpt, Battersby offers a generally positive review of* Anthills of the Savannah, *concluding: "It is not a great novel . . . [but] worth reading."*]

[*Anthills of the Savannah* is an] extremely political novel, . . . its value lying more in what Achebe is saying than in how he says it. Yet it is hard to accept the didactic message when it is conveyed through such unconvincing stereotypes telling their own stories. Sam is a parody of every scared megalomaniac history has ever produced, while Ikem and Chris are largely interchangeable—both are clever, brash, opinionated and very exasperated. Chris's lover Beatrice, beautiful and brilliant (whom Achebe unnecessarily hampers with a First in English from London University), provides a central consciousness, but inspires some of the weakest writing: 'Chris saw the quiet, demure damsel whose still waters nonetheless could conceal deep overpowering eddies of passion.'

It's a novel of rhetoric: 'What must a people do to appease an embittered history?' It's also a novel of inspired moments—a traffic jam, confrontations with stupid policemen, a memorable scene in which an old man takes the stage and tells Kangan's story from the peasant viewpoint. Achebe is at his best when his characters are speaking Pidgin, or are quoting proverbs: 'A man who answers every summons by the town crier will not plant yams in his field.' The richness of traditional African folklore and native speech are contrasted with the sterile politicking inherited from outsiders who ruled, influenced, then left.

Anthills of the Savannah does not approach the brilliance of *Things Fall Apart* or the comic artlessness of *A Man of the People.* It is not a great novel. Its awkward phrasing, often jagged dialogue, stylistic unevenness and unexceptional multiperspective narrative are too glaring for that. But its truth and realism make it an important statement about the nature of power. During an address to the local student union, Ikem declares: 'Story-tellers are a threat . . . they threaten all champions of control'. Later, he adds: 'Writers don't give prescriptions . . .

writers give headaches.' Chinua Achebe is expressing his own political sentiments, his fears and anger—these are the elements which make this, his first novel after an 18-year silence, worth reading.

Eileen Battersby, "'Story-tellers Are a Threat'," in The Listener, Vol. 118, No. 3033, October 15, 1987, p. 29.

Cherry Clayton (essay date 1988)

[In the following review, Clayton declares Hopes and Impediments to be a work of a "new and superior order." In an unexcerpted portion of the essay, he also reviews J. M. Coetzee's White Writing: On the Culture of Letters in South Africa.]

The critical work represented in the selected essays of the South African novelist J. M. Coetzee and the Nigerian author Chinua Achebe is of a new and superior order, mobilizing the best creative and critical energies of two writers as committed to their craft as they are to exposing what Achebe calls the "monster of racist habit". In both cases the critique of a "white" culture (whether European, American, or South African)—its assumptions, blind spots, abuses of language, logic or humanity—is based on a scrupulous examination of evidence, as it emerges within early travel writing, anecdotes, or the work of individual authors who appear to be transmitting the "truth" of a continent and its indigenous peoples, but are often perpetuating Western conceptual grids. The result, as they see it, is the entrenching of dehumanizing myths. The pervasiveness and harm of such myths are driven home with a new force by two highly intelligent writers with insight, humour and moral passion . . . .

Like Coetzee, Achebe is both rooted in his own culture and critical of it, though he has a richer and more dynamic culture to draw on, which may partly account for his less cerebral, but vigorous, humane and humorous voice. The "essays" in **Hopes and Impediments** are often the texts of occasional talks, and thus they gain the fuller dimension of personality, and the cutting edge of a spoken denunciation, counter-argument, and reiteration of principle and belief which the genre offers. The collection begins with a convincing demonstration of Joseph Conrad's racism, and the ways in which Heart of Darkness has been appropriated by teachers and critics. Anyone who has not yet quietly removed Heart of Darkness from their undergraduate syllabus and substituted Things Fall Apart will do so after reading this essay. But perhaps the best idea would be to go on teaching Heart of Darkness with Achebe's essay as accompaniment.

Though Achebe's revelation of certain offensive tones and assumptions is unanswerable, his real concern, shown throughout these essays, is to address racism as such, as a habit of mind which cannot conceive of the African as an equal, and uses Africa as a giant projection screen for its own Western fantasies and flaws. Like Coetzee, he sees the imaginative annexation of a territory, without an eye for the "recognizable humanity" within it, as deeply culpable and artistically distorting. In reply to this skewed perspective, he enlists many of the values he defines in Igbo art: an "outward, social and kinetic quality", together with a space for the private and contemplative. His own inclusive and life-enhancing definitions of art clearly draw on traditions within Nigerian cultural life: "Even if harmony is not achievable in the heterogeneity of human experience, the dangers of an open rupture are greatly lessened by giving to everyone his due in the same forum of social and cultural surveillance."

Achebe's emphasis on human beings as creatures who find their fulfilment not in individualism, consumerism, or an ideal of free, uncluttered space, but in "a presence—a powerful, demanding presence limiting the space in which the self can roam uninhibited . . . an aspiration by the self to achieve spiritual congruence with the other", is healthy and corrective. This belief is the core of his critique of some Western writers and of his appraisal of undervalued or misunderstood African writers, such as Amos Tutuola, of whose novel The Palm-Wine Drinkard he offers a vigorous and illuminating reading.

The collection begins with his analysis of Conrad and ends with a tribute to James Baldwin. Along the way there are speeches on broad topics, such as **"The Truth of Fiction"** and **"Thoughts on the African Novel"**, a personal tribute to Christopher Okigbo, and passing reflections on the present needs of his own society. Despite the more glaring practical deficiencies operating within his own modernizing society, he still values a literary culture and sees its role as crucial:

> Literature . . . gives us a second handle on reality; enabling us to encounter in the safe, manageable dimensions of make-believe the very same threats to integrity that may assail the psyche in real life; and at the same time providing through the self-discovery which it imparts a veritable weapon for coping with these threats whether they are found within problematic and incoherent selves or in the world around us.

It is in this valuing of "benevolent" fictions, which know themselves as fictions, and the discrediting of the "malignant fiction" of racism, which is fiction masquerading as truth, that Achebe and Coetzee are united directing their considerable eloquence.

Cherry Clayton, "Uprooting the Malignant Fictions," in The Times Literary Supplement, No. 4460, September 23-29, 1988, p. 1043.

Joe Wood (essay date 1989)

[In the following essay, Wood reviews Hopes and Impediments, describing it as a "brilliant collection."]

Throughout this brilliant collection, the Nigerian novel-ist Chinua Achebe seems, in a quiet way, to fancy himself continental Africa's answer to the American cultural critic James Baldwin. ***Hopes and Impediments*** opens with a clearly worded examination of Joseph Conrad's "Heart of Darkness" that hammers the author for perpetuating "comforting"—and racist—myths about Africa. Conrad's story, Mr. Achebe writes, "projects the image of Africa as 'the other world,' the antithesis of Europe and therefore of civilization, a place where man's vaunted intelligence and refinement are finally mocked by triumphant bestiality." Most Westerners— and, in fact, most people touched by the West—on some level share Conrad's bigoted perspec-tive, according to Mr. Achebe. By means of these 14 essays and speeches, written over 23 years, Mr. Achebe rather convincingly reminds us of this, along the way spicing keen cultural analysis with pungent personal anecdotes. And he does not let matters end there. How can we, the writer energetically asks, change the old prejudices and simultaneously create a new Africa? Among his answers: new myths and socially "beneficent fiction," both of which he believes provide a base upon which Africans, and the rest of us, can re-create the continent's societies and peoples. Thought Mr. Achebe sometimes fails to pursue his ideas with rigor (the essays are mostly lectures and addresses, not scholarly writ-ings), his thoughts always pack a provocative wallop. In the end, Mr. Achebe aims to nudge readers to think past their stubborn preconceptions, and he succeeds marve-lously.

> *Joe Wood, in a review of "Hopes and Impedi-ments: Selected Essays," in* The New York Times, *November 12, 1989, p. 55.*

FURTHER READING

Busby, Margaret. "Bitter Fruit." *New Statesman* 114, No. 2948 (25 September 1987): 34.
> Appraises *Anthills of the Savannah,* noting: "Reading *Anthills of the Savannah* is like watching a master carver skillfully chiselling away from every angle at a solid block of wood. . . . True, there are occasional slips, lines one might wish less awkward, but the overall effect is undeniably powerful."

Evalds, Victoria K. "Chinua Achebe: Bio-Bibliography and Recent Criticism, 1970-75." *A Current Bibliography on African Affairs* 10, No. 1 (1977-78): 67-87.
> Comprehensive bio-bibliography of Achebe. Contains brief summary of criticism on his works.

Linfors, Bernth. "The Palm Oil with Which Achebe's Words Are Eaten." *African Literature Today* 1 (1968): 3-18.
> Examines Achebe's use of proverbs in *Things Fall Apart, Arrow of God, No Longer at Ease,* and *A Man of the People.*

Okafor, Clement A. "Chinua Achebe: His Novels and the Environment." *CLA Journal* XXXII, No. 4 (June 1989): 433-42.
> Considers the African environment in Achebe's nov-els. The critic writes: "[Achebe] is a highly talented craftsman who has skillfully used his environment in creating seminal works that have blazed a new path along which modern African writers have travelled for the better part of the last three decades."

Ponnuthurai, Charles Sarvan. "The Pessimism of Chinua Achebe." *Critique: Studies in Modern Fiction* XV, No. 3 (1974): 95-109.
> Examines Achebe's protagonists and their flaws, con-cluding that Achebe is "essentially a pessimistic writ-er."

Rogers, Philip. "Chinua Achebe's Poems of Regeneration." *Journal of Commonwealth Literature* 10, No. 3 (1976): 1-9.
> Discusses major themes in Achebe's poetry.

Jamil Abdullah Al-Amin

1943-

(Born Hubert Gerold Brown; became known as H. Rap Brown; assumed present name during 1970s) American autobiographer.

Al-Amin is best known as the author of *Die Nigger Die!* (1969), a highly charged autobiography that focuses on what it means to be black in America. He came to prominence in the late 1960s, when he was widely known as H. Rap Brown, and won fame as an outspoken young black leader. *Die Nigger Die!,* his political and social testament, documents his emergence, from boyhood onwards, as a public figure and recounts his experiences in the civil rights movement. In the aftermath of the struggle by Martin Luther King, Jr., to win black civil rights through nonviolent protest, some in Brown's generation believed that a more direct confrontation with white racism was necessary. Brown became known for his belief that blacks should be prepared to use guns to assert their rights, and many opponents charged that he was an advocate of violence. Brown countered that his views were necessitated by the virulence of racism. "I preach a response to violence," he wrote in *Die Nigger Die!*—"Meet violence with violence." If someone deprives you of your human rights, Brown contended, he is being violent. "It's your responsibility to jump back" at your oppressor, he claimed, because "if you don't, he knows that you're scared and that he can control you." Reactions to Brown and *Die Nigger Die!* varied widely. *Newsweek* magazine accused him of "hate-mongering," for example, while Kiarri Cheatwood, writing in *Black World* in 1975, called him "a young man of deep sensibilities."

Brown was born in Baton Rouge, Louisiana, in 1943, the son of Eddie C. Brown, an oil company worker, and Thelma Warren Brown. He enrolled at Southern University in 1960 and spent the summers of 1962 and 1963 in Washington, D.C., where he participated in demonstrations organized by the Nonviolent Action Group (NAG), an affiliate of the Student Nonviolent Coordinating Committee (SNCC). In 1964 he quit school and moved to Washington, becoming chairman of NAG in the fall. He worked in local antipoverty programs during 1965 and as an SNCC organizer in Greene County, Alabama, in 1966. He was named Alabama state project director of SNCC later in the year. In May 1967 he succeeded Stokely Carmichael, a leading spokesman for the Black Power Movement, as chairman of SNCC. Brown quickly captured public attention by claiming in a televised statement that "Violence is as American as cherry pie." He claimed in full: "This country was born of violence. Violence is as American as cherry pie. Black people have always been violent, but our violence has always been directed toward each other. If nonviolence is to be practiced,

then it should be practiced in our community and end there." He added: "If Washington, D.C., doesn't come around, Washington, D.C., should be burned down." He also accused white America of conspiring "to commit genocide against black people," advised blacks to "get yourself some guns," and called President Lyndon Johnson a "wild, mad dog, an outlaw from Texas" who dispatched "honky, cracker federal troops into Negro communities to kill black people."

In August 1967, at Senate Judiciary Committee hearings, police cited an inflammatory speech by Brown as "sole reason" for a riot in Cambridge, Maryland. According to police testimony, Brown told his audience to get their guns and that they "should've burned...down long ago" an all-black school in the city. Moments after Brown finished his address, a fire broke out in the school and spread rapidly, destroying nearly 20 buildings in a predominantly black business district. Brown was indicted by a Maryland grand jury and later arrested on charges of carrying a concealed weapon across state lines while under indictment. In a statement issued on August 20, he claimed that he was being held as a political prisoner. He was released on bond on August 22. During Columbia University disorders in April 1968, Brown and Carmichael met with demonstrators at Hamilton Hall. The next month Brown was convicted of violating the Federal Firearms Act and sentenced to five years in prison—the maximum sentence. After serving jail time near New Orleans, he was released on bond in July 1969 when the Louisiana Court of Appeals vacated the conviction. His trial for the 1967 Cambridge incident was set for May 1970, but Brown went underground. As a result, he was immediately placed on the FBI's ten-most-wanted list. The riot and arson charges were dropped in 1973 in a plea-bargain arrangement. (Earlier, in January 1971, a Maryland prosecutor admitted fabricating evidence relating to the arson charge.) In October 1971 Brown was shot by police officers in New York while trying to make a getaway from an armed robbery he committed at the Red Carpet Lounge on Manhattan's West 85th Street. Brown was defended at his trial by William Kunstler; Imamu Baraka appeared as a character witness. Convicted of taking part in the holdup, Brown was sentenced to 5 to 15 years and was held at Attica State Prison in New York state. During his incarceration he converted to Islam and adopted his current name, Jamil Abdullah Al-Amin. Paroled in 1976, he moved to Atlanta, Georgia, where he operates a small grocery.

Brown wrote *Die Nigger Die!* in 1969 at the height of his fame. The book garnered mixed reactions, as had its author. Some commentators expressed shock at the work's strong, forthright language and puzzled over its message. Others viewed *Die Nigger Die!* as a timely testament of the social, cultural, and political injuries suffered by blacks in contemporary America. John Leonard of the *New York Times* found the work unsatisfactory both as autobiography and as political commentary, charging that Brown was "so busy proving his *machismo* that his material never comes into focus." But in the *New York Times Book Review,* Shane Stevens asserted that *Die Nigger Die!* expresses the author's "essential humanism . . . , cloaked though it may be in fear and hate." Citing Brown's ability to combine his outrage with an irreverent sense of humor, Stevens wrote that "the cutting edge of deep pain is there. But so is the raucous, sometimes slightly hysterical, laughter of life." Critic Kiarri Cheatwood stressed Brown's political analyses, lauding his "depth," "historically-shaped consciousness," and "mature thought." As an example, Cheatwood observed that "perhaps better than anyone before him," the author outlined "the responsibilities of Black students to their people."

Although Brown himself is no longer in the national headlines, *Die Nigger Die!* remains a seminal document of the civil rights movement in America. Since his parole, Brown has given occasional interviews to journalists. In 1985 he met with *Washington Post* columnist George F. Will, who found him "enveloped in a strange serenity." Brown's life, Will suggested, was now cen-

tered on his Muslim faith, and the onetime political activist was working with neighbors on plans for a religious school. "Many people reckon time from the '60s," Brown observed, because "time stopped for them then." He added, "I don't miss the '60s."

(For further information about Al-Amin's life and works, see *Black Writers* and *Contemporary Authors,* Vols. 112, 125.)

PRINCIPAL WORK

Die Nigger Die! [as H. Rap Brown] (autobiography) 1969

H. Rap Brown (essay date 1969)

[*The following essay first appeared as the introduction to* Die Nigger Die! *in 1969. The author prefaced his remarks with this quotation from John O'Neal's* Black Theater *article "Motion in the Ocean": "Racism systematically verifies itself when the slave can only break free by imitating the master: by contradicting his own reality." Here, Brown examines distinctions and variations in the use of the word "nigger" in contemporary America. The introduction ends with a poem by Don L. Lee, an American poet, essayist, and critic now known by his Swahili name Haki R. Madhubuti. Madhubuti is widely admired for his contributions to black literature and the Black Arts Movement, including:* Black Pride *(1967),* Dynamite Voices I: Black Poets of the 1960s *(1971),* Directionscore: Selected and New Poems *(1971),* Enemies: The Clash of Races *(1978),* Killing Memory, Seeking Ancestors *(1987), and* Say That the River Turns: The Impact of Gwendolyn Brooks *(1987).*]

When a Black man looks at Black people with a Black mind and Black soul, it is immediately apparent that Black people possess certain unique characteristics which not only distinguish them from whites and negroes, but which have greatly contributed to the survival of Blacks. Whites recognize this and have always attempted to eradicate these characteristics or discredit them. In instances where they have succeeded, negroes have been created.

Negroes have always been close allies of whites in trying to eliminate Black resistance to undesirable acculturation. Negroes see poor and uninstitutionalized Blacks as niggers. They find it necessary to prove to whites that they are not niggers, failing to realize that whites see all Black people as niggers, no matter how rich or how poor.

Some Blacks prefer to be called negroes because they like to distinguish themselves from other Blacks. They fear that if they called themselves Blacks, they might antagonize whites. And if they antagonized whites, they would lose their position as negroes—the white-appointed overseers of Blacks. Thus, negroes have always tried to aid and impress whites by eliminating Blackness. Negroes know that whites prefer institutionalized Blacks, i.e., Blacks who give their allegiance to white cultural, political, social and economic institutions. Non-institutionalized Blacks are difficult to control, because their allegiance is to Blacks and not to white institutions. It is negroes who strain to send their children to white schools so that the nigger in them may be killed and they may thereby become better institutionalized.

Any action or behavior which is not endorsed by whites, negroes consider "acting a nigger." What was "acting a nigger" two years ago is now accepted as "soul." Naturally, this was endorsed by whites before being accepted by negroes. The conversation in negro america has always been, "What are we going to do about them niggers?" never, "What are we going to do about them white folks?" Negroes always said, "Niggers holding us back!" "Niggers ain't shit!" "Don't go around acting a nigger!"

Negroes say:

> Nobody but niggers curse and use "poor English."
> Nobody but niggers steal.
> Nobody but niggers are always loud.
> Nobody but niggers listen to the blues.
> Nobody but niggers burn and loot.
> Nobody but niggers eat watermelon.
> I don't call you nigger 'cause you're mine,
> I call you nigger 'cause you shine.

While negroes are saying this about poor and uninstitutionalized Blacks, whites say this about all Blacks. The negro, being unable to recognize who is the true enemy, becomes an enemy of Blacks. Negroes prefer "living" to being free.

To be Black in the country is to be a nigger. To be a nigger is to resist both white and negro death. It is to be free in spirit, if not body. It is the spirit of resistance which has prepared Blacks for the ultimate struggle. This word, "nigger," which is taboo in negro and white america, becomes meaningful in the Black community. Among Blacks it is not uncommon to hear the words, "my nigger," (addressed to a brother as an expression of kinship and brotherhood and respect for having resisted), or "He's a bad nigger!," meaning, He'll stand up for himself. He won't let you down. He'll go down with you. When Blacks call *negroes* "niggers," however, it takes on the negativeness of white and negro usage.

Negroes and whites have wished death to all Blacks, to all niggers. Their sentiment is "Die Nigger Die!"— either by becoming a negro or by institutionalized or active genocide.

Blacks know, however, that no matter how much or how hard negroes and whites may try, ultimately it will be the negro and his allies who will "Dye, die, die!"

> America calling.
> negroes.
> can you dance?
> play foot/baseball?
> nanny?
> cook?
> needed now.negroes
> who can entertain
> ONLY.
> others not
> wanted.
> (& are considered extremely dangerous.)

                    Don L. Lee

                                        (pp. v-vii)

H. Rap Brown, in an introduction to his Die Nigger Die!, *The Dial Press, Inc., 1969, pp. v-vii.*

Charles V. Hamilton (essay date 1969)

[*Hamilton is an American authority on black politics. In the following essay, he praises* Die Nigger Die! *for its pointedness but faults Brown himself for portraying other black spokesmen as if he had "some sort of monopoly on truth."*]

This short book [*Die Nigger Die!*] reflects many of the emotions, strengths, weaknesses and ambivalences of a large segment of the Black protest movement today in this country. For that reason, it is an important book. It tells where a lot of people (particularly younger ones) are in their thinking and acting. H. Rap Brown admits that he is more a spokesman than a leader:

> When I was head of SNCC, that's all I was. I was not a leader of Black people. I had a public platform because I was Chairman of SNCC and therefore what I said got heard by a lot of people. But I don't think I can articulate the sentiments of Black folks any better than the brothers and sisters did in Detroit. I'm just in a position where maybe I can explain what the brother is talking about, because there're a lot of negroes who don't understand.

Brown traces his career from early childhood in Louisiana to his current battles with the courts, and the reader is given a good glance at the kind of experiences that go into the making of an intense, alienated Black activist. Many will read this book looking for his "position on violence." The author is to the point:

> Societies and countries based on the profit motive will never insure a new humanism or eliminate poverty and racism...The power necessary to end racism, colonialism, capitalism and 'imperialism' will only come through long, protracted, bloody, brutal and violent wars with our oppressors.

The book discusses most of the issues one hears discussed in activist circles these days, and on one subject especially it is characteristically ambivalent. At one point, Brown talks about "tribalism." "This tribalism has extended into what is called the 'Movement.' 'Militant' tribes compete against other 'Militant' tribes and 'Moderate' tribes, to promote tribal interests and not the interests of the Race or the Masses. We treat Revolution as if it is an historic process rather than an evolutionary movement. In other words we all got a monopoly on truth." But then at the end of the book, he succumbs to a favorite self-hate pastime of blasting other Black spokesmen, and in a manner that would tend to make the reader think that he, in fact, had some sort of monopoly on truth.

> Inside the united states this [lack of common political motion] is a paramount problem where groups of Blacks are struggling in various ways for liberation. This struggle is being checked through the lack of a common political objective. The concept of Black Power, for instance, has been diluted and prostituted to the point where even the most conservative negroes, are now for the Black Power. 'Whitey' Young [and this is always sure to get a laugh of approval from the young Black revolutionaries in the audience], dictator of the urban league, preaches for Black pride and acclaims that Black Power is attainable through Black capitalism. A lot of cats said the blood is coming home, but look again, he's still following his master, Floyd McKissick, former director of CORE, who once argued for Black Power maintains that Black people need Black capitalism.... All Black folks considering revolutionary work must be aware of these pitfalls. We must study how revolutions are aborted, how independence movements are stifled, how people are cheated of the fruits of their efforts, how the foot soldier or the Mau Mau gets betrayed by the bourgeois nationalist—these are things that all revolutionaries must understand.

This is nonsense. And it represents an enlightenment and arrogance not justified by the author's revealed insights or demonstrated talents. But the Movement is prolific with it today. While on the one hand there is the warning against trying to out-militant or out-revolutionary each other, there is, on the other, this tendency to disparage others working just as diligently in their own way. The fact is that Brown is right when he indicates that no one (including himself) has a monopoly on truth.

A most important thing is that the major Black spokesmen are beginning to write their own stories, to speak for themselves. It will be more difficult to misrepresent what they believe, and this alone is a valuable contribution to understanding these turbulent times, especially when they are as clear and as forceful as Brown. The book should be read carefully. There is a lot in it to understand.

> *Charles V. Hamilton, "Who Has the Truth?"*
> in Book World—The Washington Post, *May 11, 1969, p. 8.*

Shane Stevens (essay date 1969)

[*Stevens is an American novelist and critic. He is best known as the author of* Go Down Dead *(1967), a novel about black life in Harlem. Commentators have noted that Stevens, who is white, showed a remarkable understanding of black issues in this work. According*

to James R. Frakes, the book depicts a Harlem "you've never seen before.... What this novel shouts is that 'you'd better believe it!'" In the following 1969 review, Stevens examines the method and intent of Die Nigger Die!]

America, this manifest white middle-class utopia founded on the principles of equality and justice for all, is at a crossroads. And I don't mean just the obvious breaking point of generational life styles. I refer to a crisis of identity, almost a mental breakdown, as it were, in the body politic.

In a calmer time, all of five or six years ago, integration was believed by most to be the answer to racial antagonism. Today that belief is viewed as a product of some distant Golden Age. Now the cry is for separation of the races, but a separation of *choice* by the black population with, of course, the blessing of many whites. Separate but equal has come to signify a cleavage that goes bone deep into our national identity. It is, in some ways, a giving up of the American dream.

How did America come to this? Much of the answer is found in the black man's belief—constantly reinforced by events—that the white majority really does not want him here. That white America literally wants the black man to die. Action and reaction ensure, and the paranoia grows on each side. As the dialogue ceases, the shouting increases. We are today seeing the results of the collapse of this national dialogue.

Evidence of this paralysis can be seen in the present volume by H. Rap Brown. In a rather horrific way, the title tells the story. **Die Nigger Die!** is a hymn of hate for white America. Hate yes, but sorrowful disappointment as well. Mr. Brown—who succeeded Stokely Carmichael as chairman of the Student Nonviolent-Coordinating Committee for 1967-68, before that organization joined with the Black Panthers—believes white America is out to destroy the American black man. In the strongest of language, he argues that this country is waging genocide on its largest minority group. He sees America, in fact as the oppressor of black people around the world.

The book purports to be a personal history, an "autobiography in action," but, of course, it is more than that. It is also a moving and rather eloquent plea—for all its cool rap—for a revolutionary struggle of oppressed peoples everywhere; not so much a handbook of revolution as an earthy and somehow very appealing look at the making of one revolutionist. Exaggerated, even distorted, yet the essential humanism of the man is here, cloaked though it may be in fear and hate. The author sees and feels and tells us much, yet there is a sense of style and grace of wit about him that perhaps tells us even more.

His recounting of his early years as a Cub Scout marching in endless parades behind apparently diarrheic horses is pure gold. So too is the story of his meeting with former President Johnson. After informing Johnson that most of the blacks who had voted for him wish they had gone fishing instead, Brown rose to go and "to show . . . what I thought about the whole meeting, I stole some stuff out of the White House. I liberated everything I could! Sure did. Show you what I think . . . . I was trying to figure how to get a painting off the wall and put it under my coat. I figured it belonged to me anyhow."

Again, in discussing his education, Brown brings out the comedy as well as the tragedy of what goes on in our schools. For example, in high school,

> I saw no sense in reading Shakespeare. After I read Othello, it was obvious that Shakespeare was a racist. From reading his poetry, I gathered that he was a faggot. But we never discussed the racist attitude expressed in his works. This was when I really began to raise questions. I was in constant conflict with my teachers . . . . I would interpret the thing one way and they would say it's wrong. Well, how could they tell me what Shakespeare was thinking. I knew then that something was wrong, unless the teachers had a monopoly on truth or were communicating with the dead.

And for those wishing to liberate themselves from Army service, as well as those wishing to see a master con man at work, Brown's tale of his encounter with the draft is required reading. In all of the above examples, the cutting edge of deep pain is there. But so is the raucous, sometimes slightly hysterical, laughter of life.

Equally appealing is Brown's disclaimer of any personal heroics. Indeed, the man's sense of proportion about himself—though not about the world around him—is refreshing. And I must add quickly, almost unique among so-called black militant "leaders." In writing of his year as chairman of S.N.C.C., for example, Brown candidly evaluates his position:

> When I was head of S.N.C.C., that's all I was. I was not a leader of Black people. I had a public platform . . . and therefore what I said got heard by a lot of people. But I don't think I can articulate the sentiments of Black folks any better than the brothers and sisters did in Detroit.

As for black "militants," Brown sees clearly the problem of self-serving identity hangups. Most of them, he believes are "further away from being revolutionaries than the poor people who are not militantly political. But the coffeehouse intellectual, the Black militant, thinks he's political because he reads Fanon." Spending "all their time trying to program white people into giving them money," the black militants "are willing to be anything, as long as they can be Black first. Black capitalists, Black imperialists, Black oppressors—anything, so long as it's Black first."

Sound familiar?

For Brown, the country's structure is divided into three categories: "white America," "negro America" and "Black America." The difference between "negro America" and "Black America"? "If you're Black, then you do everything you can to fight white folks. If you're

negro, you do everything you can to appease them." The threat to the existing establishment comes, of course, from black America. It is, therefore, black America which will be the vanguard of the inevitable revolution.

On the subject of violence, Brown's "cherry pie" speech is well-known. He sees violence as a necessary part of any revolutionary struggle. He considers himself not so much violent as willing to react to violence. His penchant for carrying a gun is public knowledge. Forgetting the obvious psychoanalytic interpretations, this makes Brown himself as American as cherry pie.

Is there in fact a conspiracy in America to destroy the black man? I'm not sure the question is relevant any longer to many blood brothers. There is, of course, no aboveground conspiracy mapped out by common consensus. But white America does seem to nourish the almost undisguised wish that the black man would disappear. For those, like Brown, who have borne the brunt of poverty, pain and neglect, this is tantamount to a national policy of race destruction.

That Brown has suffered ignominiously at the hands of white America is tragic. That it has left him despairing is wholly understandable. His paranoia—fed by the jailings and abuse—is little different in kind from that disease which causes the Ku Klux Klan and their ilk to view all blacks as inferior beings. Brown is no more "sick" than the society that produced him, no more paranoid than that society which sees him as a "dangerous nigger."

No man is all good or all evil. To believe that is to make a mere caricature of man. What is needed, desperately, is a dialogue of similarities among us. Brown obviously feels that the dialogue between black and white is no longer operative. In this sense I, sadly, agree with him. And in the absence of any meaningful dialogue, I see the fires of paranoia burning blood red. And that may well be the final irony. That our blood—the river of life for all of us—is all the same color. (pp. 6, 38)

> *Shane Stevens, in a review of "Die Nigger Die!" in* The New York Times Book Review, *June 15, 1969, pp. 6, 38.*

Angus Calder (essay date 1970)

[Calder is an English-born historian, editor, and literary critic. In the following 1970 New Statesman *review essay, he places* Die Nigger Die! *among other recent works written by those "to whom violence has been done [and who] are at last talking about doing violence in return."]*

'American violence is public life, it's a public way of life, it becomes a form, a detective story form.' This is from the great Chester Himes, creator of the black Harlem cops, Coffin Ed and Gravedigger. Himes responds to interview with all the cold intelligence one would have hoped for, in a new paperback-periodical called *Amistad* which results either from some publisher's understanding that there's money to be made from the boom in Black Studies, or from a guilty conscience. Alas, the two aren't incompatible.

One can't, in fact, see Himes's macabre stories as straight documentary, 'just plain and simple violence in narrative form'. But does anyone doubt now that the crime thriller is close to American reality? Or that the Western, that other pre-eminent gift of White America to world culture, reflects a national ethos which persists in cities where blacks get shot like injuns? And what Black America gives the world is jazz; a music of love, yes, but also a shout of pain turning towards anger. The distance from Jonny Dodds keening into a clarinet to Archie Shep pouring rage into a sax is one which Himes himself travelled decades ago, in company with Richard Wright (whose classic *Native Son* and *Black Boy* now return in a handsome reprint). Those to whom violence has been done are at last talking about doing violence in return.

America looks from some angles much like the Russia of the 1860s. There are the same mindless stampings of state power; the same ineffectual disposition to introduce essential reforms half a century late; the same proliferation of unlikely panaceas and petty messiahs amongst relatively small dissident groups; the same absence of any one feasible left-wing strategy that could give dissidence any hope of real success. So far, the world of Dostoevsky; the only one in which the Manson 'family' would make sense. But in the absence of censorship and in the presence of the mass media, everything becomes invested in the helpless clarity of art. To adapt a good joke by Chester Himes, one trouble with the Negro Problem is that it provides mass entertainment for millions of liberals, and makes a fair number of people a great deal of money. The starving in India aren't such good business.

For instance, Piri Thomas's *Down These Mean Streets* arrives in Britain after three years with a note on the dust jacket: 'To be filmed by Warner Bros-Seven Arts as a major motion picture.' Suppose the money to be spent on that film went directly to alleviate conditions in Spanish Harlem, where Piri Thomas comes from? His autobiography turns out to be as good as Claude Brown's well-known *Manchild in the Promised Land,* and to tell a very similar story of childhood and adolescence; gang fights, petty crime, drugs, big crime, wounded attempting a robbery, jail. It lacks Brown's pleasing dryness, but is better structured, and even more vivid; it contains the extra factor that Thomas, a Puerto Rican, had a black father and a white mother. He chose to regard himself as black while his father saw the Spanish language as the key to establishing the family's whiteness, and the resulting domestic rows are described at length. He went to the South as a sailor to establish his own blackness: a fact thoroughly confirmed by his later voyages:

> Wherever I went—France, Italy, South America, England—it was the same. It was like Brew said: any language you talk, if you're black, you're black. My

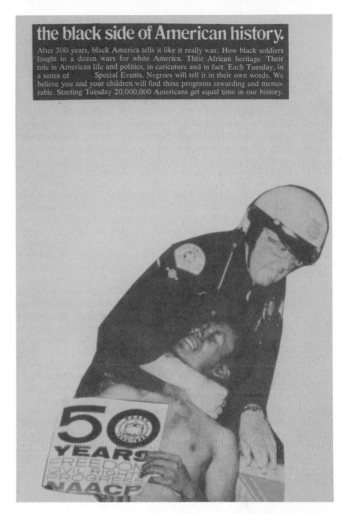

An illustration from Die Nigger Die! *depicting "the black side of American life."*

> hate grew within me. *Dear God, dear God,* I thought, *I'm going to kill, I'm going to kill somebody.*

But one wouldn't describe Thomas as 'bitter', though no doubt some paperback publisher will. There is too much implicit invocation of that Christian myth of human brotherhood which we had all better stop believing in. As Julius Lester puts it in *Look Out Whitey!,* 'nothing kills a nigger like too much love.' What emerges as fully from Thomas's book as from Claude Brown's, or from Rap Brown's perfunctory autobiographical excursions in **Die Nigger Die!,** is that the most all-American aspect of ghetto life is the way in which respect can only be achieved by violence. 'Whether you're right or you're wrong, as long as you're strong, you're right' was the lesson Thomas drew from a fight over a girl in a dance hall, and Brown, past chairman of SNCC, derives a virtually identical one from a successful confrontation between blacks and a white sheriff in the South. 'They had met "the man" and found out that when you stop being controlled by fear, then the people you were once afraid of are afraid of you.' Himes carries the logic to a bleak conclusion:

I think the only way a Negro will ever get accepted as an equal is if he kills whites; to launch a violent uprising to the point where the people will become absolutely sickened, disgusted; to the place where they will realise that they have to do something...

But there is still an implicit appeal to 'the people' lodged in the phrasing, just as in Brown's now notorious statement that 'violence is as american as cherry pie'. 'The people'; the ruinous American Dream. Rap Brown may deprive America of its capital letter. But he argues that Black Americans

hold the key to liberation round the world ... because this country is the chief oppressor around the world. If we view this country as an octopus, then we see that her tentacles stretch around the globe. Like in Vietnam, Africa, Latin America... If these countries cut off a tentacle, it can be replaced. But we got his eye; we live in the belly of the monster. So it's up to us to destroy its brain.

The logic is very much like that which argues that America is in South East Asia to save the world for democracy, and is no more likely to be appreciated in Black Africa. Brown's colleague in SNCC, Julius Lester, demonstrates very ably that the North fought the South not to free the slaves but to keep its pockets full, but he still (why, *why*?) quotes Lincoln for his epigraph. The fact that Abe said that the institutions belong to the people, so they can overthrow them by violence when they want to, does not help anyone to overthrow the American government now; but, like so many of Abe's sayings, it cheers people up and helps to keep their faces away from the facts.

Lester's book is very good most of the time, written with grace, wit and scholarship, and providing, though too briefly, a socialist analysis of WPP (White People's Power). His reaction to the pledge by the Establishment of new investments in the ghetto is well worth remembering—'it's the old investments that are causing the problem now.' But he peters out at the end in sentimental millenarianism. 'Everything must be secured clean... The new order is coming, child. The old is passing away.' The strategies which will permit the scouring to begin have not been revealed, and Rap Brown's book doesn't help to locate them. Vague Fanonisms about the Third World and incessant reiterations of the case for violence, except on the part of the police, will develop on a useful scale, and with coherent aims.

That Brown is an honest revolutionary we have no right to doubt. The risk he has accepted, in trying to translate words into reality, is that of near-certain death by violence. He remarks, of a 43-day fast he made in prison: 'I figured there wasn't no better place to die than in a united states jail.' But his lively, confused and repetitious book illustrates the trouble with the Negro problem. The best passage is perhaps his description of 'the Dozens'. His skill at this game in childhood earned him his nickname, "Rap." The aim is to 'totally destroy somebody else with words'. *Die Nigger Die!* is most

charitably regarded as a game of the Dozens with 'white america'. The people who are going to like it will mostly be whites in love with their guilt complex. It will make money presumably (the shrieking dust jacket of the English edition is not designed to hinder this process), but it will bring a socialist America no nearer.

Himes is well aware of the dangers involved in this kind of thing:

That's one of the saddest parts about the black man in America—that he is being used to titillate the emotions of the white community in various aspects... I want these people just to take me seriously. I don't care if they think I'm a barbarian, a savage, or what they think; just think I'm a serious savage.

And he suggests that the immense publicity for such black leaders as Malcolm X and Stokely Carmichael was designed to weaken their position with the black community, to identify them in effect with WPP. He must have something there; even in Malcolm X's doggedly dedicated autobiography, there are signs that the treatment he got from the media mellowed him. Rap Brown knows the danger too:

Black militants grow naturals to appear on TV as cops shooting blacks for this country. There is not one negro on TV that has a politically meaningful role... All of these shows play against black people; they might help individuals but never the masses. They are designed to keep blacks militantly happy. Black militants talk about revolution while seriously programming white people for money.

These books, together and singly, make depressing reading. There is so much American charm, so much American vitality, so much American dream, so little sign that anything will really change. Where are the Wobblies now, and what happened to all the idealism which made people believe in a New Deal? Wafted away on their own hot air. (pp. 242-43)

Angus Calder, "Playing the Dozens," in New Statesman, *Vol. LXXX, No. 2058, August 28, 1970, pp. 242-43.*

The Times Literary Supplement (essay date 1971)

[*In the following excerpt from an unsigned 1971* Times Literary Supplement *review essay titled "White against Black and Black against White," the critic contends that* Die Nigger Die! *"is not to be taken seriously."*]

It is now almost seventy years since the distinguished Negro social scientist W. E. B. DuBois produced the prophecy which has since adorned so many title-pages: that the problem of the twentieth century would be the problem of the colour line. Events since then make it difficult (to put it mildly) to demonstrate that his judgment was mistaken; yet intense perplexity persists about the root causes of problems associated with race. Indeed, dispute still rages about problems as basic as the terminology employed in the debate. The use of the word "race" itself—to take the most basic example—has provoked bitter and prolonged dispute in which the bona fides of the participants is frequently and bitterly impugned by their opponents.

Another particularly striking indication of the extent to which disagreement on basic premises persists is the stubborn refusal of at least two identifiable groups among those who have concerned themselves with this issue to accept that such an entity as race relations even exists. The critiques of these groups proceed from diametrically opposed assumptions, but both are in essence conspiracy theories. Each rests on the belief that concern with race as such is artificially induced, through the exploitation of emotional anxieties without rational foundation. The left-wing protest industry (it is alleged in one version) and the animators of the industrial-military complex (in its polar opposite) exploit the issue in this way in order to achieve their political goals. Yet while it is quite impossible not to agree with such critics that there is a good deal of shoddy rhetoric being passed off for analysis in this field, it is equally impossible to swallow the conclusion they draw, that race and colour have no reality at all. And if the field of study is ill-defined and much campaigned over, it is also a remarkably vital one. Judged only by the crudest of yard-sticks—the amount of recent work in print—race must rank very high among social problem topics. (p. 169)

It is, of course, nothing new for those involved in a field of study engaging human emotions as intensely as this one to find the "scientific" objectivity they have been taught to bring to their work difficult to formulate and apply. Past attempts to approach the subject from the angle of those on whom events bear particularly hard have encountered heavy criticism on the grounds that proper academic standards risk being jettisoned in the process. Professor R. A. Schermerhorn has labelled this trend "victimology"; it involves, he suggests, a Burkean pity for the plumage of individual suffering rather than the proper concern for the dying bird of a society organized around exploitation, with which social scientists can, at this stage, more profitably concern themselves. The latest generation of young academics accept this challenge and conceive of themselves as enlisting, literally as well as figuratively, in a war of liberation designed to end inequality and repression once and for all, by overturning the whole structure of that society.

Even this kind of involvement has not proved sufficient to close the breach between investigators and participants. The basic reason for the persistence of this division is the new ethnic exclusiveness that has come to characterize the Black liberation movement in the United States after its abrupt change of direction away from the attempt to achieve civil rights by non-violent protest towards direct action. Despite the willingness—eagerness; indeed—of White radical academics to enlist and turn their talents to equipping the revolution with the intellectual rationalizations required to transmit its objectives to the White audience, the trend has been toward the exclusion of all White participation, whatever the intention of the participant. In the new Black studies programmes that have been established in universities all over the United States, the emphasis has lain heavily on the rediscovery and further analysis of the Black experience by Black academics and students working together without intrusion by outsiders, however well-intentioned or well-informed.

The Black studies programmes are, of course, only one facet of this new departure which has begun to succeed; where earlier initiatives have failed; in conferring a new sense of identity on Black Americans. The practical implications of this new development are that many Black Americans now feel that they belong to a distinctive culture with a validity of its own—though there are sharp variations in the conclusions they have drawn from this discovery. An account of these beliefs and the actions which have been based upon them have been diffused in a distorted form to a far wider audience through the intense and detailed coverage that events in the United States have received in the press and television services of the world. The descriptions that the participants in this process have provided of these developments, and especially those that have taken place since 1966—the year of Black Power—are in many ways influenced by this consciousness of speaking to an audience wider than has ever before been achieved by spokesmen for Black America. Moreover, they are for the first time their own interpreters. In addressing this new audience, the temptation to heighten the drama by painting in primary colours, is often irresistible.

The books under review [H. Rap Brown, **Die Nigger Die!**; Julius Lester, *Look Out Whitey! Black Power's Gon' Get Your Mama*; Bobby Seale, *Seize the Time*; Robert L. Allen, *A Guide to Black Power in America*; James Boggs, *Racism and the Class Struggle*; Earl Ofari, *The Myth of Black Capitalism*; Ed Bullins, *The Electronic Nigger*; Joseph S. Roucek and Thomas Kiernan, editors, *The Negro Impact on Western Civilization*; Tom Stacey, *Immigration and Enoch Powell*; John Rex, *Race Relations in Sociological Theory*; Sami Zubaida, editor, *Race and Racialism*] divide sharply into two categories—accounts by participants, and academic analyses—and the contrasts between them are so marked that to read them consecutively is sometimes to wonder whether the events they describe took place on the same planet, let alone in the same society. Not only do the two groups differ drastically both in content and in the style in which they are presented; perhaps most important of all, they are conceived as serving entirely different purposes.

The books of the Black militants are intended not as explanations but as weapons. In guerrilla warfare they may rank below Molotov cocktails in effectiveness, but they are part of the same armoury. Half a dozen of the works under review fall into this category; and Ed Bullins's plays—particulary *Electronic Nigger*—provide marginal content. Through all of them run a number of common themes: the uniqueness both of the contemporary situation of Blacks in America and of the quality of the experience through which they have passed: the value of this experience in helping to create a culture which has enabled Black Americans to sustain the destructive experience of slavery; the persistence and intensification of exploitation. (p. 170)

The most straightforward of the six, in this and in other ways, is H. Rap Brown's *Die Nigger Die!* Brown has had the distinction of being high on the F.B.I.'s list of wanted men (the new radical prestige symbol); he has also specialized in the shock statement designed to appall a White audience. Brown's most famous essay in this direction was his pronouncement that "violence is as American as cherry pie"; his book is an extension of this role and is not to be taken seriously. As a virtuoso exercise in the art of invective it rates quite high: there are some enjoyable cracks worked off, even if one has the irresistible impression that they have been rehearsed in too many lecture halls and television studios. There are also the customary bitter side-swipes at other claimants to the role of Black spokesman. But setting these elements on one side, little more remains than a polished platform performer talking into a tape recorder. Occasionally, his account takes on unconsciously pathetic overtones, as in the descriptions of his childhood. Wholly incredible boasts about the sexual exploits of the seven-year-old Rap alternate with banal descriptions of events such as form the common stuff of urban childhood. It gradually dawns on the reader that Brown himself may be unaware of what is uncommon in his experience and what is universal; in this way he achieves an involuntary pathos through underlining the degree of social separation that still exists between Black and White America. (pp. 170-171)

"White against Black and Black against White," in The Times Literary Supplement, *No. 3598, February 12, 1971, pp. 169-72.*

FURTHER READING

Cheatwood, Kiarri. *"Die Nigger Die! (On a Requiem from a Bold Young Oppression-Fighter)."* *Black World* XXIV, No. 12 (October 1975): 51-2, 82-7.
   Surveys the critical reception given to *Die Nigger Die!* and briefly identifies some of the major issues raised in the work. Cheatwood concludes: "In summation, despite his acidious poignancy and burning humor, H. Rap Brown shows himself in his book to be a young man of deep sensibilities."

Harrington, Stephanie. "The Guardian Celebrates: John Brown's Roll to Rap Brown's Rock." *The Village Voice* 8, No. 3 (2 November 1967): 1, 25, 31.
   Summarizes Brown's political views as he himself presented them in a speech at the 19th anniversary celebration of the National Guardians.

Weinstein, James. "Since Malcolm's Death." *The Nation* 209, No. 4 (11 August 1969): 118-19.
   Reviews recent works about black militancy, noting: "*Die Nigger Die!*, in contrast to [Robert Scheer's] *Eldridge Cleaver,* is not a good book even though the politics of Cleaver and H. Rap Brown are similar. The book is most valuable as a partial biography of Brown, and as an example of his agitational style. Too much of it, however, is Brown honking his own horn, or else pure jive."

Maya Angelou

1928-

(Born Marguerite Johnson) American autobiographer, poet, scriptwriter, dramatist, nonfiction writer, composer, and editor.

Hailed as one of the great voices of contemporary African-American literature, Angelou is best known for *I Know Why the Caged Bird Sings* (1970), the first of her series of five autobiographical novels. Her autobiography and poetry have generated great interest because they reflect her tenacity in overcoming social obstacles and her struggle for self-acceptance. Critics particularly praise her dynamic prose styles, poignant satire, and her universal messages relevant to the human condition. Angelou herself explained: "I speak to the black experience but I am always talking about the human condition—about what we can endure, dream, fail at and still survive."

Angelou wrote the first volume of her autobiography after friends, among them such notable writers as James Baldwin and Jules Feiffer, suggested she write about her childhood spent between rural, segregated Stamps, Arkansas, where her pious grandmother ran a general store, and St. Louis, Missouri, where her worldly, glamorous mother lived. *I Know Why the Caged Bird Sings* chronicles Angelou's life up to age sixteen, providing a child's perspective of the perplexing world of adults. Angelou described herself as "a too big Negro girl, with nappy black hair, broad feet and a space between her teeth that would hold a number-two pencil." Although her grandmother instilled pride and confidence in her, her self-image was shattered when she was raped at the age of eight by her mother's boyfriend. Angelou was so devastated by the attack that she refused to speak for approximately five years. *I Know Why the Caged Bird Sings* concludes with the sixteen-year-old Angelou having regained self-esteem and caring for her newborn son, Guy. In addition to being a trenchant account of a black girl's coming-of-age, this work affords insights into the social and political tensions of the 1930s. Sidonie Ann Smith echoed many critics when she wrote: "Angelou's genius as a writer is her ability to recapture the texture of the way of life in the texture of its idioms, its idiosyncratic vocabulary and especially in its process of image-making."

The next four volumes of Angelou's autobiography—*Gather Together in My Name* (1974), *Singin' and Swingin' and Gettin' Merry Like Christmas* (1976), *The Heart of a Woman* (1981), and *All God's Children Need Traveling Shoes* (1986)—continue to trace the author's psychological, spiritual, and political odyssey. As she emerges from a disturbing and oppressive childhood to become a prominent figure in contemporary American literature, Angelou's quest for self-identity and emotional fulfillment results in extraordinary experiences, such

as encounters with Malcolm X and Dr. Martin Luther King, Jr. Angelou's personal involvement with the civil rights and feminist movements both in the United States and in Africa, her developing relationship with her son, and her knowledge of the hardships associated with the lower class of American society are recurrent themes throughout the series. The four subsequent works are generally considered inferior to *I Know Why the Caged Bird Sings;* critics cite lack of moral complexity and failure to generate empathy or universal appeal. Lynn Z. Bloom believes that perhaps the decreasing popularity of subsequent volumes resulted because Angelou appeared a "less admirable" character as her autobiography progressed. In *Gather Together in My Name,* for example, Angelou barely escapes a life of prostitution and drug addiction; in the process, Bloom maintains, Angelou "abandons or jeopardizes the maturity, honesty, and intuitive good judgment toward which she had been moving in *Caged Bird*." Nevertheless, critics continue to praise Angelou's narrative skills and her impassioned responses to the challenges in her life.

All God's Children Need Traveling Shoes, Angelou's latest autobiographical installment, is distinctive in its examination of black America's intellectual and emotional connections with post-colonial Africa. In this work, Angelou describes her four-year stay in Ghana where she worked as a free-lance writer and editor. The overriding theme in this volume is the search for "home." Angelou finds much to praise in Africa, but gradually realizes that although she has cultural ties to the land of her ancestors, she is nevertheless distinctly American and in many ways isolated from traditional African society. Angelou observed: "If home was not what we had expected, nevermind, our need for belonging allowed us to ignore the obvious." Wanda Coleman summed up general critical opinion of *All God's Children Need Traveling Shoes* when she noted that Angelou's work is "an important document drawing much needed attention to the hidden history of a people both African and American."

Angelou's poetry, which is collected in such volumes as *Just Give Me a Cool Drink of Water 'fore I Diiie* (1971) and *And Still I Rise* (1976) is fashioned almost entirely of short lyrics and jazzy rhythms and addresses social issues pertaining to African-Americans. Although her poetry has contributed to her reputation and is especially popular among young people, most commentators reserve their highest praise for her prose. Angelou's dependence on alliteration, her heavy use of short lines, and her conventional vocabulary has led several critics to declare her poetry superficial and devoid of her celebrated humor. Some reviewers praise her poetic style as refreshing and graceful, however.

Angelou's autobiographical volumes have an important place in the African-American tradition of personal narrative, and they continue to garner praise for their honesty and moving sense of dignity. Although an accomplished poet and dramatist, Angelou is dedicated to the art of autobiography. Angelou explained that she is "not afraid of the ties [between past and present]. I cherish them, rather. It's the vulnerability . . . it's allowing oneself to be hypnotized. That's frightening because we have no defenses, nothing. We've slipped down the well and every side is slippery. And how on earth are you going to come out? That's scary. But I've chosen it, and I've chosen this mode as my mode."

(For further information about Angelou's life and works, see *Black Writers; Contemporary Authors,* Vols. 65-68; *Contemporary Authors New Revision Series,* Vol. 19; *Contemporary Literary Criticism,* Vols. 12, 35, 64; *Dictionary of Literary Biography,* Vol. 38: *Afro-American Writers After 1955: Dramatists and Prose Writers; Something About the Author,* Vol. 49.)

PRINCIPAL WORKS

Cabaret for Freedom [with Godfrey Cambridge] (drama) 1960
The Least of These (drama) 1966
I Know Why the Caged Bird Sings (autobiography) 1970

Just Give Me a Cool Drink of Water 'fore I Diiie (poetry) 1971
Ajax [adaptor; from the drama *Ajax* by Sophocles] (drama) 1974
Gather Together in My Name (autobiography) 1974
Oh Pray My Wings Are Gonna Fit Me Well (poetry) 1975
And Still I Rise (drama) 1976
Singin' and Swingin' and Gettin' Merry Like Christmas (autobiography) 1976
And Still I Rise (poetry) 1978
The Heart of a Woman (autobiography) 1981
Shaker, Why Don't You Sing? (poetry) 1983
All God's Children Need Traveling Shoes (autobiography) 1986
Now Sheba Sings the Song (poetry) 1987
I Shall Not Be Moved (poetry) 1990

Selwyn R. Cudjoe (essay date 1984)

[*In the following excerpt, Cudjoe evaluates several volumes of Angelou's autobiography as part of an African-American literary tradition of autobiographical statement.*]

The Afro-American autobiographical statement is the most Afro-American of all Afro-American literary pursuits. During the eighteenth and nineteenth centuries, thousands of autobiographies of Afro-American slaves appeared expressing their sentiments about slavery, the most cruel of American institutions. The practice of the autobiographical statement, up until the contemporary era, remains the quintessential literary genre for capturing the cadences of the Afro-American being, revealing its deepest aspirations and tracing the evolution of the Afro-American psyche under the impact of slavery and modern U.S. imperialism. (p. 6)

There is nothing in the autobiographical statement that makes it essentially different from fiction except, of course, that which has been erected by convention. Michael Ryan, picking up on the observations of Jacques Derrida, has argued that inherent in the structure of the autobiographical statement is the necessary death of the author as a condition for the existence of the referential machinery. "The writing," he states, "must be capable, from the outset, of functioning independently of the subject, of being repeated in the absence of the subject. Strictly speaking, then, its referent is always 'ideal' of fictional—produced and sustained by convention."

To the degree, however, that the referent is present in the autobiography (it being absent or "ideal" in fiction), there is really nothing in the autobiography that guarantees that it will not be read as fiction or vice versa. In fact, any discussion on the Afro-American autobiography is always likely to raise this question: "Is it really true?" and almost always the author must present strong evidence that the work is unquestionably autobiographical. . . . (p. 7)

Autobiography and fiction, then, are simply different means of arriving at, or (re)cognizing the same truth: the reality of American life and the position of the Afro-American subject in that life. Neither genre should be given a privileged position in our literary history and each should be judged on its ability to speak honestly and perceptively about Black experience in this land. (p. 8)

[Maya Angelou's] *I Know Why the Caged Bird Sings* . . . explores growing up Black and female in the American South during the second quarter of this century. . . . The world to which Angelou introduces us is embroidered with *humiliation, violation, displacement,* and *loss.* From the outset Angelou sounds the pervading themes when she declares: "If growing up is painful for the Southern Black girl, being aware of her displacement is the rust on the razor that threatens the throat. It is an unnecessary insult." From this introduction she wends her way to the end of her work, where she concludes: "The Black female is assaulted in her tender years by all those common forces of nature at the same time that she is caught in the tripartite crossfire of *masculine prejudice, white illogical hate* and *Black lack of power.*"

This is the burden of the work: to demonstrate the manner in which the Black female is violated, by all of the forces above, in her tender years and to demonstrate the "unnecessary insult" of Southern girlhood in her movement to adolescence.

Southern life, as Angelou demonstrates, is one of harshness and brutality. It is exemplified by the conditions under which the workers of Stamps lived, the fear engendered by the Ku Klux Klan, the wanton murder of Black folks (which led Mother Henderson to send Maya and her brother Bailey to their mother in California), the racial separation of the town, and the innumerable incidents of denigration which made life in the South an abomination against God and man. Not that moments of happiness were entirely absent from her childhood life, but such moments came, as Thomas Hardy characterized them in *The Mayor of Casterbridge,* as but "the occasional episode[s] in a general drama of pain."

Such cruelty led to a well-defined pattern of behavior on the part of the South's citizens and the adoption of certain necessary codes if one was to exist in that part of the country. As Angelou points out: "The less you say to white folks (or even powhitetrash) the better." The insults of the powhitetrash had to be accepted and the spiritual and emotional manner in which the whites tried to debase the Blacks had to be fended off at each moment of existence.

As the text charts Angelou's movement from *innocence* to *awareness,* from childhood to an ever quickening sense of adolescence, there were certain ideological apparatuses, inserted into the social fabric, which Angel-

ou had to overcome in order to maintain a sense of relative liberation and autonomy. It is the virtue of Angelou and the strength of the statement that, as she develops, she is able to detect the presence of these apparatuses, to challenge them and to withstand their pervasive and naturalizing tendencies.

In this country, as in any other capitalist country, religion, education, and sports are supposed to function in certain ideological ways so that the subject accepts certain well-defined practices. Thus, while religion is designed to keep the Afro-American in an oppressed condition, here Black people subverted that institution and used it to assist them to withstand the cruelty of the American experience. (pp. 11-13)

One of the most poignant moments of the ideological unveiling comes when Angelou describes her graduation exercises of 1940 at Lafayette County Training School. As she listens to the condescending and racist manner in which Mr. Edward Donleavy, the featured speaker, insulted the intelligence of her class, hearing the approving "amens" of her elders as he made his invidious comparisons with Central, the white school of the area, Angelou, a young sensitive Black female, could only think: "It was awful to be Negro and have no control over my life. It was brutal to be young and already trained to sit quietly and listen to charges brought against my color with no chance of defense. We should all be dead. I thought I should like to see us all dead, one on top of the other."

And here the sense of collective responsibility, a sensibility charged by the disparagement of the group, is reflected. In the impotence of childhood there is nothing she can do, but the charges which have been leveled against her people will not be soon forgotten.

Indeed, the act colors the texture of her world; she realizes the emptiness of the sentiments which were expressed in the valedictory address: "I am master of my fate, I am captain of my soul." Observing the inherent falsehood of the statement "To be or not to be," she could only observe in ironic tones: "Hadn't he heard the whitefolks? We couldn't *be,* so the question was a waste of time." It is out of this web of reality that she takes her first, fumbling steps toward her social development in Stamps, Arkansas.

According to the text, then, the major crime of the society is that it attempts to reduce all Negroes to a sense of impotence and nothingness. This is the internal "rust" which threatens the "personhood" of Black people (young and old) in all of America. It is the inherent homicidal tendency of an oppressive and racist society which pushes these young people to the brink of spiritual waste and physical destruction. For Maya, such a milieu becomes the point of departure from which she struggles to salvage a sense of dignity and personhood, the necessary prerequisite before any sense of femaleness can be expressed.

Maya Angelou understands that to be Black and female is to be faced with a special quality of violence and violation. This peculiarity is brought into sharp focus when Maya goes to live with her mother and is subsequently raped by her mother's boyfriend. When she is faced with this catastrophe, her first reaction is to withdraw into herself. Yet because of the strength of her individual will, she is able to work herself back to a point where she can function in a seemingly productive manner in her social world. Nevertheless, the rape of this eight-year-old by an almost impotent adult Black male—who, it would seem, was unable to enjoy a relatively mature and respectful relationship with an adult Black woman—can be seen as symbolic of only one aspect of this internal dimension of Black life. (pp. 14-15)

Angelou wants to suggest that the power, the energy, and the honesty which characterized our examination of our relationship with our oppressor (i.e., at the external level) must now be turned inward in an examination of some of the problems which seem to have inhibited our own level of social development and our quest for liberation. In other words, the problem of Afro-American liberation is to be seen as both an *internal* and an *external* reality, the former of which must be our exclusive concern. It is this internal probing which characterizes [*I Know Why the Caged Bird Sings*] and marks the writings of the Black female writer.

One cannot, however, simply read the shortcoming of Black life back into the text and forget the complicity of white society, which is the major causative agent of Black denigration. On the larger canvas from which this life is drawn, the villain is to be recognized as a society which reduces men to impotence, women to lives of whoredom, and children to victimization by their fathers' lust and impotence. Indeed, it is the perception of what constitutes femininity and beauty which leads Maya into a sexual liaison that eventually produces an unplanned pregnancy. Certainly at the age of sixteen she was not prepared financially or emotionally to take care of a child.

But to argue for the cruelty and brutality of the society does not deny the episodes of beauty which relieve the monotony of life in Stamps or the violence of California. Nor can one deny the progressive tendency of the religious life of Stamps's Black community. It is to argue, however, that the cruelty so overwhelms the sensibility of the Black person in the South that it makes it very difficult for him/her to exist in the society. For a Black woman it further demonstrates the pain which growth and awareness demand. As Angelou says: "Without willing it, I had gone from being ignorant of being ignorant to being aware of being aware. And the worst part of my awareness was that I didn't know what I was aware of." This realization of her status is bought at a price: her subjection to the tripartite force of which she speaks (masculine prejudice, white illogical hate, and Black powerlessness).

One of the shortcomings of the text revolves around the manner in which the story is told from the point of view of an adult, who imposes the imagination, logic, and language of an adult upon the work and thus prevents the reader from participating in the unfolding of childhood consciousness as it grows into maturity. The tone of the work is even and constant, which causes the text to be almost predictable in its development. The rationalization of later years tends almost to destroy the flow of the text. Indeed many times one is forced to question the authenticity of her response to incidents in her life. (pp. 15-16)

The task of autobiography, then, does not consist in the mere reproduction of naturalistic detail but, because it involves the creative organization of ideas and situations and makes an ethical and moral statement about the society, must generate that which is purposeful and significant for our liberation. . . .

The intense solidity and moral center which we observed in *Caged Bird* is not to be found in *Gather Together in My Name*. . . . The richly textured ethical life of the Black people of the rural South and the dignity with which they live their lives are all but broken as we enter the *alienated* and *fragmented* lives which the urban world of America engenders. It is these conditions of *alienation* and *fragmentation* which characterize the life of Maya Angelou as she seeks to situate herself in urban California during her sixteenth to nineteenth years. (pp. 16-17)

Gather Together reveals a more selective vision of Afro-American life. In this work, the author writes about one particular kind of Afro-American whom she meets through the kind of work she does. When one considers that Angelou has been a short-order cook, a waitress at a nightclub, a madam in charge of her own house of prostitution, a nightclub dancer, a prostitute, and the lover of a drug addict who stole dresses for a living, it becomes apparent that the range of characters whom she encountered during this period of emotional and social upheaval were indeed limited to the declassed elements of the society. And this is what differentiates *Gather Together* from both *Caged Bird* and *Singin' and Swingin' and Gettin' Merry Like Christmas*.

The violation which began in *Caged Bird* takes on a much sharper focus in *Gather Together*. To be sure, the author is still concerned with the question of what it means to be Black and female in America, but her development is reflective of a particular type of Black woman at a specific moment of history and subjected to certain social forces which assault the Black woman with unusual intensity.

Thus when she arrives in Los Angeles she is aware that even her mother "hadn't the slightest idea that not only was I not a woman, but what passed for my mind was animal instinct. Like a tree or a river, I merely responded to the wind and the tides." In responding to the indifference of her mother's family to her immaturity, she complains most bitterly, "they were not equipped to understand that an eighteen-year-old mother is also an eighteen-year-old girl." Yet is is from this angle of vision—that of "a tree in the wind" possessing mostly "animal instinct" to an "unequipped" eighteen-year-old young woman—that we must prepare to respond to Angelou's story.

Neither politically nor linguistically innocent, *Gather Together* reflects the imposition of values of a later period in the author's life. Undoubtedly, in organizing the incidents of text in a coherent manner (i.e., having recourse to memorization, selection of incidents, etc.), the fictive principle of which we spoke in our introduction comes fully into play. The fact is that with time the perception of the subject changes, which demonstrates that the autobiographical statement indicates one's *attitudes* toward the fact, rather than the presentation of the facts (i.e., the incidents) as given and unalterable. It is that *attitude toward the facts* to which critics should respond.

For example, it is difficult for the reader to believe that the young Angelou set out to organize the prostitution of Johnnie Mae and Beatrice because she wanted to take revenge on those "inconsiderate, stupid bitches." Nor can we, for that matter, accept the fact that she turned tricks for L.D. because she believed that "there was nothing wrong with sex. I had no need for shame. Society dictated that sex was only licensed by marriage documents. Well, I didn't agree with that. Society is a conglomerate of human beings, and that's just what I was. A human being."

As a justification, it rings too hollow. Society is not a conglomeration merely of human beings. Society is a conglomeration of *social beings* whose acts make them *human* or *nonhuman*. To the degree that those acts *negate* our humanity, they can be considered wrong. To the degree that they *affirm* our humanity they can be considered correct. Such reasoning, though, is only to keep the argument within the context in which Maya Angelou has raised the question.

For me, the importance of the text—its social significance—lies in its capacity to signify to, and from, the larger social context from which it originates. Clearly, *Caged Bird* and *Gather Together* assume their largest meaning or meanings within the context of the larger society. As a consequence, one cannot reduce important attitudes of social behavior by mere strident comments of dissent. Such attitudes and values are derived from the larger *social* context of Afro-American life. Correspondingly, one questions Angelou's attitude toward Johnnie Mae when she cries out that she has been wounded: "And, ladies, you decided in the beginning that you were going to screw me one way or the other. Look at us now. Who did the screwing?" It is imperious, but is it correct?

In spite of this imperious attitude, and a certain degree of life-saving pride, Maya is an extremely lonely young woman; a young woman more isolated in bustling California than she was in the quietude of Stamps; a young woman who had to use both that imperious attitude and her life-saving pride to exist. . . . Yet precisely because she is drifting through this phase of her life, none of this advice is particularly fruitful to her nor does she seem particularly proud of her activity during those "few tense years" of sixteen through eighteen. Of course, it is not so much that these incidents took place; what is more important is what she made of these incidents in terms of her own social development. While this question cannot be answered here, we hesitate to accept in an unquestioning manner her interpretation of what these events meant to her life.

Finally, two horrendous and dramatic incidents make her realize how much on the brink of catastrophe she had been. The kidnapping of her child (i.e., the near-loss of her child, her most important and significant achievement thus far) and her being saved from a life of drugs by the generosity of Troubadour Martin really gave her that rebirth into innocence; a rebirth at a higher level of dialectical understanding.

Yet in a curious way the book seems not to succeed. Its lack of moral weight and ethical center deny it an organizing principle and rigor capable of keeping the work together. If I may be permitted, the incidents of the book appear merely gathered together in the name of Maya Angelou. They are not so organized that they may achieve a complex level of signification. In fact, it is the absence of these qualities which make the work conspicuously weak.

The language has begun to loosen up and this becomes the work's saving grace. Where there were mere patches of beautiful writing in *Caged Bird,* there is a much more consistent and sustained flow of eloquent and almost honey-dipped writing. The simplicity of the speech patterns remains, yet there is a much more controlled use of language. The writing flows and shimmers with beauty; only the rigorous, coherent and meaningful organization of experience is missing.

At the end of the work, the author attempts to recover some of the powerful ideological unfoldment of the society which we encountered in *Caged Bird.* Whereas, however, she presented herself as an integral part of the society in *Caged Bird,* in *Gather Together* she separates herself from the daily life and sufferings of her people and projects a strikingly individual ethos. . . . (pp. 17-20)

This kind of distance and assumption weakens the work because it begins to rely almost exclusively on individual exploits rather than to reflect the traditional collective wisdom and/or sufferings of the group. Because of this absence, the work reduces itself at times to a titillating account of a personal life bereft of the context of the larger society. The narrowly private existence of the subject is substituted for the *personal universalized* (which gives such great power to the Afro-American autobiographical statement), and the importance of *Gather Together* is diminished. (p. 20)

Thus, where she announces at the end of *Caged Bird* that she "had gone from being ignorant of being ignorant to being aware," at the end of *Gather Together* she declares for a certain type of innocence which cannot be really regarded in the same light as that which we found at the beginning of *Caged Bird.* It must be regarded as the (re)discovery of that primal innocence, at a higher level of consciousness, which was lost in her original encounter with the American dream. The sinking into the slime of the American abyss represents the necessary condition of regeneration and (re)birth into a new and, hopefully, more consciously liberated person. Thus, if *Caged Bird* sets the context for the subject, *Gather Together* presents itself as the necessary purgation through which the initiate must pass in order to (re)capture and to (re)define the social self to function in a relatively healthy manner in white America.

Singin' and Swingin' explores the adulthood of Maya Angelou, again major protagonist, as she moves back into and defines herself more centrally within the mainstream of the Black experience. In this work, she encounters the white world in a much fuller, more sensuous manner, seeking to answer, as she does, the major problem of her works: what it means to be Black and female in America. We would see that this quest, in the final analysis, reduces itself to what it means to be Black and person in America; the urgency of being Black and female collapses into what it means to be Black and person. In order to achieve this, the book is divided into two parts: part one, in which the writer works out her relationship with the white American world, and in part two, in which she makes a statement about her own development through her participation in the opera *Porgy and Bess,* and her encounter with Europe and with Africa.

Singin' and Swingin' opens with a scene of displacement in which Angelou feels a sense of being "unanchored" as the family bonds of her youth are torn asunder under the impact of urban life in California. Under these new circumstances the author examines her feeling and her relationship with the larger white society as she encounters white people on an intimate personal level for the first time. As the reader will recall, Blacks and whites lived separately in Stamps and the occasion for shared and mutual relations did not exist. Before Angelou can enter into any relationship, though, she must dispense with all the stereotypical notions she has about white people. Indeed it is no longer possible to argue: "It wasn't nice to reveal one's feelings to strangers. And nothing on earth was stranger to me than a friendly white woman."

As the autobiography gradually unfolds, she observes that most of the stereotypical pictures which she has of whites are designed to protect her feelings from the cruelty of white hate and indifference. Yet as she grows into adulthood, these notions are punctured and eventually discarded, the biggest test coming when she is forced to make a decision about marrying Tosh, a white man, who is courting her through her son. Part of the

difficulty arises from Angelou's awareness that whites had violated her people for centuries and that "Anger and guilt decided before my birth that *Black was Black and white was white* and although the two might share sex, they must never exchange love."

Angelou confronts the problem with a sort of evasion when she tells herself that Tosh "was Greek, not white American; therefore I needn't feel that I had betrayed my race by marrying one of the enemy, nor could white Americans believe that I had so forgiven them the past that I was ready to love a member of their tribe." She is not entirely satisfied by the truce she makes with her Blackness and for the rest of her marriage has to contend with the guilt created by her liaison with a white male.

With the end of her marriage, the tears came and the fright that she would be cast into "a maelstrom of rootlessness" momentarily embroidered her mind. Soon, however, it gave way to the knowledge that she would be ridiculed by her people in their belief that she was another victim of a "white man [who] had taken a Black woman's body and left her hopeless, helpless and alone." At the end of this encounter, however, she would be better prepared to deal with her own life, having gained a certain entrance to the white world and possessing, already, the stubborn realities of Black life.

One of the significant facets of the author's relationship to Tosh revolves around the manner in which she effaces her own identity within the framework of the marriage. But the compromises which she makes to secure a stronger marriage cannot be seen only in the context of the *subjection* of wife to husband or Black female to white male. It can also be read as the subjection of the central values of the Black world (and, as a consequence, of the Black woman) to the dominant totality of white values.

In this context, it is to be noted that in spite of the fact that Angelou finds many aspects of white culture objectionable, most of the dominant images of perfection and beauty remain fashioned by the ethos of white society. Yet the tensions which keep the first section of the work together center around the general tendency of her wanting to be absorbed into the larger ambit of American culture (i.e., white culture) and her struggle to maintain a sense of her Black identity. (pp. 21-3)

As Angelou begins the second phase of her development (i.e., her evolution towards adulthood) her Southern origins became the necessary basis on which she begins to evaluate the major transformations which have taken place in her life thus far. . . . The identification of her people's sufferings in the minds of the ordinary European, their immediate identification of her with Joe Louis, the enthusiastic manner in which the Europeans welcomed the *Porgy* cast and the spirituals of her people, led to some of the most revealing moments of her development. The recognition that "Europeans often made as clear a distinction between Black and white Americans as did the most confirmed Southern bigot . . .

[in that] Blacks were liked, whereas white Americans were not," did much to raise her self-esteem and a recognition of her emergent place in the world. (pp. 23-4)

It is, however, the success of *Porgy* which seemed paradigmatic of her evolution as an autonomous and fully liberated person. The pride which she takes in her company's professionalism, their discipline onstage, and the wellspring of spirituality that the opera emoted, all seem to conduce toward an organic harmony of her personal history as it intertwined with the social history of her people. The triumph of *Porgy,* therefore, speaks not only to the dramatic success of a Black company, it speaks, also, to the personal triumph of a remarkable Black woman. *Singin' and Swingin'* is a celebration of that triumph.

In 1970 Maya Angelou produced her first work, a volume concerned with what it meant to be Black and female in America. By 1976 she had enlarged her concerns to address what it meant to be Black and person in America, given the social, political, and economic constraints which militate against any achievement in contemporary America. (p. 24)

> Selwyn R. Cudjoe, "Maya Angelou and the Autobiographical Statement," in Black Women Writers (1950-1980): A Critical Evaluation, *edited by Mari Evans, Anchor Press/Doubleday, 1984, pp. 3-37.*

Priscilla R. Ramsey (essay date 1984-85)

[*In the following excerpt, Ramsey argues that in her poetry Angelou acknowledges and then transcends despair and unhappiness.*]

Maya Angelou's physical shifts from Stamps, Arkansas' Lafayette County Public School to the Village Gate's stage in Manhattan and from New York to a teaching podium at Cairo University in Egypt represent an intellectual and psychological voyage of considerable complexity—one of unpredictably erratic cyclic movement. She has chronicled some of this voyage in her three autobiographies. . . . Additionally she has written three collections of poetry: *Oh Pray My Wings are Gonna Fit Me Well* (1975), *And Still I Rise* (1971), and *Just Give Me a Cool Drink of Water 'fore I Die* (1971). (p. 139)

The public achievements have been many and yet the private motivation out of which her writing generates extends beyond the mere search for words as metaphors for purely private experience. Her poetry becomes both political and confessional. Significantly, one sees in her autobiographies a role-modeling process—one paradigmatic for other women—while not allowing the didactic to become paramount in either the poetry or the autobiographies.

Her autobiographies and poetry reveal a vital need to transform the elements of a stultifying and destructive personal, social, political and historical milieu into a sensual and physical refuge. Loneliness and human distantiation pervade both her love and political poetry, but are counterposed by a glorification of life and sensuality which produces a transcendence over all which could otherwise destroy and create her despair. This world of sensuality becomes a fortress against potentially alienating forces, i.e., men, war, oppression of any kind, in the real world. This essay examines the outlines of this transcendence in selected examples from her love and political poetry. . . . (p. 140)

Drawing upon her scholarly and gifted understanding of poetic technique and rhetorical structure in modern Black poetry, Ruth Sheffey explains:

> Genuine rhetoric, indeed all verbal art, coexists with reason, truth, justice. All of the traditions of rational and moral speech are allied to the primitive idea of goodness, to the force of utterance. Because the past is functional in our lives when we neither forget it nor try to return to it, the new Black voices must reach the masses in increasingly communal ways, must penetrate those hidden crevices of our beings only recognizable and reachable by poetry.

Professor Sheffey speaks here to the fundamental meaning and significance Black poetry holds for its private community. Sheffey's remarks could not more appropriately describe Maya Angelou's poetic voice in terms of motive, content and audience. By way of example consider:

>   No No No No
> No
> the two legg'd beasts
> that walk like men
> play stink finger in their crusty asses
> while crackling babies
> in napalm coats
> stretch mouths to receive
> burning tears
> on splitting tongues
> JUST GIVE ME A COOL DRINK OF
>   WATER 'FORE I DIE . . .
>
>   (pp. 140-41)

Her metynomic body imagery functions as poetic referent further chronicling and transporting her prophetic message: stop the assault on Black people and recognize their humanness. As prophecy, her succinct assertions for change beginning with napalmed babies, epitomized in hopeful dreams as the poem progresses—disintegrate ironically into the decayed emptiness of an old man's "gaping mouth." (pp. 142-43)

The audience, a Black one, cannot help but understand the universal message this poem imports. It is a collectively oriented statement (the persona's "I" operating synedochically for the group), and one of hope, although a hope which ironically collapses at poem's end.

A similar transcendence becomes the ironically complicated prophetic message in ["**The Calling of Names**"]:

He went to being called a Colored man
after answering to "hey nigger,"
Now that's a big jump,
anyway you figger,
    Hey, Baby, Watch my smoke.
From colored man to Negro.

With the "N" in caps
was like saying Japanese
instead of saying Japs.

    I mean, during the war.

The next big step
was change for true
From Negro in caps
to being a Jew.

    Now, Sing Yiddish Mama.

Light, Yello, Brown
and Dark brown skin,
were o.k. colors to
describe him then,

    He was a bouquet of Roses.

He changed his seasons
like an almanac,
Now you'll get hurt
if you don't call him "Black"

    Nigguh, I ain't playin' this time.

As significant referents, words are used to recreate a personal reality, but as verbal discourse they remain very close to the writer's understanding of truth. Maya Angelou brings to the audience her own perceptions of historical change and their relationship to a new reality. With the exception of a long ago Phyllis Wheatley, whose poems speak almost exclusively of God, nature and man, few Black artists have focused their poetic gifts outside history, politics and their changing effects upon Black life. Here Maya Angelou engages in this lifelong tradition of speaking to the concerns of a historical and political Black presence in World War II, Voter and Civil Rights legislation of the fifties; finally the Black Power Movement of the sixties—these events name only a few of the historical and political meanings the synedochic imagery of naming has signalled for Blacks in America.

From the ancient African rituals which gave a child a name harmonious with his or her chi to the derogatory epithets coming out of slavery's master-servant relationships—naming has always held a reality redefining importance for black people. It has reached the level contemporarily with the recreation of one's destiny, an incantation signalling control over one's life. Hence the proliferation of African names with significant meanings.

But as the incantation and the structure of the poem's ideas have evolved out of historical and political event, one hears the old degrading epithets merging into new and more positive meanings.

Her title with its article "the" and preposition "of" signal, perhaps, the only formalizing or distancing

aesthetic techniques in the poem. Her emphasis is primarily upon the concrete, the substantive movement back to a derogatory black history and a clearly assertive statement about a more positive future. Like many of the poems in this collection this one also work toward the notion of a positive identity, a positive assertion of what and who Black people have decided they will be. Her formal rhyme scheme here is one in which the initial stanzas rhyme the second and fourth lines, a rhyming pattern more constricted than in much of her other political poetry. Less metaphorical transformation and less abstraction appear in this poem, however, and while that makes it aesthetically less pleasing, its meaning speaks more directly to the concrete issues of evolving importance to Afro-American history and politics. The abstractions of metaphor perhaps then do not apply here. (pp. 143-44)

While Maya Angelou's political poetry suggests the irony of emotional distantiation by using bodily imagery as her objective correlative, her love poetry almost equally as often employs this series of patterns to capture an image, an instant, an emotional attitude. Moreover, fantasy often rounds out the missing parts of the human whole when reality fails to explain fully what she sees. Here in the following poem, "**To a Man**" she explores this mystery, this distantiation from the understanding of a man:

My man is
Black Golden Amber
Changing.
Warm mouths of Brandy Fine
Cautious sunlight on a patterned rug
Coughing laughter, rocked on a whirl of French
tobacco
Graceful turns on woolen stilts
Secretive?
A cat's eye.
Southern, Plump and tender with navy bean sul-
lenness
And did I say "Tender?"
The gentleness
A big cat stalks through stubborn bush
And did I mention "Amber"?
The heatless fire consuming itself.
Again. Anew. Into ever neverlessness.
My man is Amber
Changing
Always into itself
New. Now New
Still itself.
Still

If indeed this poem talks about a man and not some more hidden and abstract object we cannot define, then "**To a Man**" explores the mysteries of a baffling and emotionally distant human being through a persona's fantasy, her worshipping recreation of an artifice rather than of any more luminous understanding of his many selves. And while she does not name him in the poem and he could be reminiscent of any of the men she knew, her description of him evokes a picture of Make, a South African freedom fighter and the man who became her second husband. She recounts this marriage and its end in her final autobiography, *The Heart of a Woman.*

Whether a husband or not, his mystery constitutes her poem's ostensible statement, through her persona's particular visual gestalt, i.e., approach. The persona's failure to (penetrate) her subject's overpreoccupation with his own personal style as a wall against intimacy becomes a source of the poem's interesting aesthetic and emotional tension. Her subject cannot be captured, i.e., "understood" and he is cut off from the persona's concentrated engagement by this barrier that she creates—his personal style. The word choices she selects to describe or rather, guess as what she comprehends about him are words suggesting the altering and varying nature of his physical and psychic characteristics. She looks at him seeing only the qualities of an ambiance he creates around himself through the deliberateness of his studied poses. He moves "Cat like." She images his moving dynamism concretely in "woolen stilts" which both regalize and thrust him backward spatially and temporally to a time when he could have been a royal African chieftain dancing on tall stilts.

She magnificently combines the auditory, tactile and visual into the imagery of his ". . . coughing laughter rocked on a whirl of French tobacco" graphically capturing what we take to be—given all she has said before—still, his moving and elegant dynamism. His sight, sound, smell—even his smoke concretized in French rather than in some ordinary domestic. (pp. 146-47)

Like a musical recitative, she repeats in . . . "To a Man," descriptions framed in rhetorical questions drawing attention all the more to his stolid mystery. In using the repeated rhetorical questions, she counterposes her technique against the traditional way in which modern Black poets use repetition. Modern Black poets use repetitious phrasing for emphasis, clarity and to signal an end to complexity. In Angelou's work the rhetorical questions, increase tension and complexity and build upon his opaque mystery. Why?

Some of the explanation might lie in the fact that writers often repeat the issues and conflicts of their own lives throughout much of the art until either concrete conditions or the art brings insight and resolution. Witness Richard Wright's unending preoccupation with the Communist Party's orthodoxy and demanding control over his work, or Gwendolyn Brooks' mid-career, philosophical redirection after attending the Fisk University Black Writer's Conference. The seeds for a similar obsession lie in her autobiographies and project into Angelou's poetry. She berates herself for her overly romantic ability to place men on pedestals, to create a rose-colored fantasy around them at a distance only to later discover her cognitive error. Her relationships with men in *Caged Bird* and *Gather Together* have this fantasy quality where she overelaborates their personalities in her own mind confusing their concrete behaviors and her day-dream. She does this, sometimes out of her own unconscious desire for their unconditional love—wanting almost a symbiotic object-subject attachment to them. In the final analysis, each of these men exploits

Drawing by Tom Feelings from Angelou's 1987 work Now Sheba Sings the Song, *a poem celebrating black women.*

her because all are morally and characterologically flawed in ways her own emotional neediness causes her to miss as her fantasy life recreates their personalities. One lover, temporarily stationed close to her home in San Diego, uses her companionship while his naval assignment lasts then leaves her. He returns to his wife. A fast living "sugar daddy" cons her into prostitution to "help" him with a non-existent gambling debt. Again concrete conditions force her into looking beneath the surface he presents. She finds that her "giving" provided pretty dresses for his wife. Nothing more! Finally, when at last she marries, and her fantasies tell her she has found nirvana in the white picket fenced-cottage she has dreamed of she learns its hidden price: she will become prisoner rather than mistress of the house and husband. (pp. 147-48)

The narcissistic male is always the one most attractive to [Angelou] and the one most mysterious—ultimately he will always turn out to be the man most destructive to her and her capacity to invest too much of her dependency and need in him too quickly. The wonder which underlies her perceptions in **"To a Man"** are not surprising provided one has read her autobiographies and identified this common psychic pattern she recurringly illustrates. What she identifies as mystery and wonder are part of the guardedness and distance he sustains—keeping her always at a safe length away from himself. One would expect anger from her rather than wonder.

Anger would have been more appropriate toward his self-protection and yet she does not express anger. Perhaps also the absence of anger affirms the passivity Lillian Arensberg has seen in Angelou's writing. We must, however, not overlook another important factor which accounts for what may be occurring here from an aesthetic and artistic rather than a purely psychic point of view. Her persona's opportunity to draw attention to it—rather than to her male subject. Thus, in doing this, she can draw upon her female audience's alleged universal bafflement with the mysterious male psyche. The poem would be better called "To a Woman" in that case, if one accepts this less direct reading of the poem. (pp. 149-50)

While Maya Angelou's poetry may not have taken us into every nook and cranny of her long and complex life starting with the Lafayette County Training School—its various movements and insights have nonetheless helped us understand the themes, the issues even some of the conflicts which have pervaded her inner life. Thus, while we could not share the objective events in all their entirety . . . , her various poetic stances have given us some lead into parts of that subjective voyage. (p. 151)

Her love poetry . . . suggests her relationship to a world which can be stultifying, mystifying and oppressive, but one she will not allow to become these things and overwhelm her. The voyage through her life has not been filled with soft and pliable steps each opening into another opportunity for self acceptance. Her voyage has instead been anything but that and yet she has filled those voids with fantasy, song, hope and the redefinition of her world's view through art. (pp. 152)

> *Priscilla R. Ramsey, "Transcendence: The Poetry of Maya Angelou," in* A Current Bibliography on African Affairs, *Vol. 17, No. 2, 1984-85, pp. 139-53.*

Lucinda H. MacKethan (essay date 1985)

[*In the following excerpt, MacKethan explores Angelou's use of humor in* I Know Why the Caged Bird Sings.]

The expression "Mother Wit" has three associations: according to Alan Dundes, it is, first, "a popular term in black speech referring to common sense"; secondly, it is "the kind of good sense not necessarily learned from books or in school"; and thirdly, "with its connotation of collective wisdom acquired by the experience of living and from generations past," it is "often expressed in folklore." In his collection of essays related to Afro-American folklore, Dundes consistently pairs mother wit with laughter and humor, for, as he says, "it is what makes a people laugh that reveals the soul of that people." When we look, however, at the word *mother,* in relation to mother wit, we might wonder how the term applies to the traditional experience of the Afro-American mother from slavery times forward; the question we could ask is, Why are these women laughing? . . . [The experiences of the black woman in the autobiographical works of] Maya Angelou [reveal] little cause for laughter. (p. 51)

Angelou's story of her girlhood is in many places a lyrical testament to language as providing her one saving image of self; from a childhood in which she tried to live wordlessly as a means of protecting herself against knowledge that was certain pain, Angelou emerged armed, she says, with a "secret word which called forth the djinn who was to serve me all my life: books."

The woman's brand of mother wit that we see in the works of . . . Angelou is tied to [her] special sense of the capacities of language as an enabling power. That power first reveals itself in the humor of caricature, in broad slaps of ridicule applied to the backsides of oppressors who include white men, white women, and black men too. Secondly, the power of language appears in the humor of exaggeration, a device which comes into play particularly when [Angelou portrays] the gulf that existed between what [she] had the right to expect and what the world was willing to allow. And finally, the power of mother wit resides perhaps most plentifully in . . . representations of [her] own mothers' words of wisdom; in [Angelou's] works mother figures offer the practical, loving, yet also tough and disciplining advice for life that they know their black daughters must acquire if they are to have any hope of being more than the mules of the world. . . . (pp. 52-3)

The development of verbal humor as a survival strategy . . . is a unifying device for the events of her life that Maya Angelou selected for *I Know Why the Caged Bird Sings.* Angelou the autobiographer takes her childhood self, who goes by many names, on a kind of quest for a name and for words. . . . The progress of this girl's life is made possible by a series of word-bringers—her brother, her teachers, her mother's con men friends, her mother herself—who gradually open to her the potential of language; words alone can free her from her fear of and dependency on others' conceptions. Thus, with no ability to raise the words she needs, Margeurite in the first scene is betrayed by the white world's view of beauty: "Because I was really white," she tries to think, "and because a cruel fairy stepmother, who was understandably jealous of my beauty, had turned me into a too-big Negro girl, with nappy black hair, broad feet, and a space between her teeth that would hold a number-two pencil." By the end of the book, Maya is not only talking but she has an edge on her white school mates; she and her friends "were alert to the gap separating the written word from the colloquial. We learned to slide out of one language and into another without being conscious of the effort."

The most important of the word-bringers in Maya's life is her mother—a savvy, sassy, street-wise Mama who makes Black beautiful and language a gift of the body as well as an art of the mind. Vivian Baxter Johnson can dance, can shoot a crooked business partner, can make her living in the tough blues joints of St. Louis and San Francisco. Yet most of all she can talk, and unlike Maya's conservative southern grandmother's, her talk is full of hope, irreverence for tradition, and scorn for anyone who thinks they can keep her down. When she repeats the old report, "They tell me the whitefolks still in the lead," she says it, Angelou tells us, "as if that was not quite the whole truth." Vivian's words are a compendium of mother wit: "She had a store of aphorisms," Angelou remarks, "which she dished out as the occasion demanded": "The Man upstairs, He don't make mistakes;" "It ain't no trouble when you pack double;" "Nothing beats a trial but a failure;" and perhaps most to our point, "Sympathy is next to shit in the dictionary, and I can't even read."

While we are given no explicit statement at the end of her story that Margeurite Johnson has fully absorbed what she needs of her mother's verbal capacities, Maya's own nascent motherhood, and her attitude toward becoming a mother, indicate that a survivor is coming into being. She tells us her feelings as a young, unwed mother who managed to hide her pregnancy from her family for almost eight months, and her words have a kind of triumph in them. . . . Gone is the girl who could see her Blackness only as some cruel fairy godmother's revenge. With a real mother, and mother wit, Maya has the preparation she needs to become the writer, the word-bringer, who created **I Know Why the Caged Bird Sings.**

One joke that the Black American community has shared for a long time shows a young black girl gazing into the fabled mirror to ask, "Who's the fairest of all?," whereupon the mirror, of course, answers back: "It's Snow White, you Black bitch, and don't you forget it." The joke, we can bet, is a trick on that tired white trope, locked as it is in the blind and self-reflexive looking glass of impotent white hate. The [autobiography of Maya Angelou reveals] . . . that, beginning in slavery times, women found the means, in the company of other nurturing women, to change the joke and slip the yoke. So indeed, they don't call it Mother Wit for nothing. (pp. 59-60)

Lucinda H. MacKethan, "Mother Wit: Humor in Afro-American Women's Autobiography" in Studies in American Humor, *n.s. Vol. 4, Nos. 1 & 2, Spring & Summer, 1985, pp. 51-61.*

Deborah E. McDowell (essay date 1986)

[*In the following excerpt, McDowell offers a mixed review of* All God's Children Need Traveling Shoes.]

No genre has captured the Afro-American literary imagination as has autobiography. Beginning with the slave narratives—Frederick Douglass' *Narrative of the Life of Frederick Douglass* (1845) and Linda Brent's *Incidents in the Life of a Slave Girl* (1861) among the best examples—Afro-American writers have returned compellingly to the genre that selects and records the incidents of a life and shapes them into an image of self. . . .

To this collection, Maya Angelou has added five volumes, a number unequalled, to my knowledge, by any other Afro-American writer. **All God's Children Need Traveling Shoes** is the latest of the chronicle which began with the very popular and justly acclaimed **I Know Why the Caged Bird Sings** (1970). These volumes cover miles of geographical territory and milestones of personal history. . . .

This latest installment departs from the singular constant of Afro-American autobiography: the confrontation of a Black self with a racist American society that ever threatens to destroy it. Angelou's first four volumes record that confrontation, illuminating an aspect unique to the Black woman. In her life, the oppression of race joins with the oppression of gender to create "the rust on the razor that threatens [her] throat." Taken together, Angelou's autobiographies show a self that defies the rusted razor, a self that—true to the demands of the genre—survives and triumphs.

The personal survival and triumph recorded in **All God's Children Need Traveling Shoes** are not the consequence of a confrontation with a racist American social structure. This is, rather, a confrontation with an African heritage, a heritage she has viewed primarily in abstract and sentimental terms: Africa was an "ancient trial soul," "an all sepia paradise," a mother into whose arms she could "snuggle down" much as "a baby snuggles in a mother's arms." The book records the sometimes painful process of exchanging that faulty and naive understanding of Africa for one more realistic and complex. Its unifying, if sometimes overdrawn theme and metaphor, is *home.*

Like so many Afro-Americans in the sixties, Angelou regarded Africa as a haven from racist America. They formed an "unceasing parade of naive travelers who thought that an airline ticket to Africa would erase the past and open wide the gates to a perfect future." In Africa they would be received in "the welcoming arms of the family . . . bathed, clothed with fine raiment and seated at the welcoming table." In other words, Africa would be the home that America never was and could never be. But this fantasy is shattered soon after Angelou's arrival in Ghana. . . .

[Angelou] arrives in a Ghana basking in its five-year-old independence and lauding the achievement and promise of its president, Kwame Nkrumah. W. E. B. DuBois is already living there as an expatriate; Malcolm X visits, enlisting support for his newly-formed Organization of Afro-American Unity, designed to link the civil rights struggles of Black Americans with newly-independent African nations.

Against this backdrop of progressive politics, Angelou's most startling and disappointing experiences stand out and take on added significance. When she looks for employment at the Ghana Broadcasting Office, she is first patronized then scornfully treated by a receptionist who volunteers that "American Negroes are always crude." . . . The receptionist's scorn seems mild, however, compared to the treatment of Black Americans when they are suspected of involvement in an attempt on Nkrumah's life.

Not all of Angelou's experiences deal with the sober hardships of rejection and displacement, however. She is warmly welcomed, befriended and supported by some Africans, including the writer Efua Sutherland. Her accounts of these relationships are leavening, at times even funny. In one episode she hires an African beautician to braid her hair "Ghanaian fashion"; instead, the woman gives her a style like that worn by pickaninnies "to teach [her] a lesson on the foolishness of trying to 'go native'."

For a little over one-third of the book, Angelou manages to capture convincingly these and other complexities of Black Americans living in Africa. She portrays with telling candor the Africa of shattered fantasies, the Africa that did not greet her homecoming with open arms. But finally, perhaps because of some vestigial longing for "home," Angelou is seduced by those same fantasies, creating, at the end of the book, an "illusory place, befitting [her] imagination." The latter part of the book seems to wash over all the earlier convincingly rendered details of rejection, unrecognition and displacement as it rushes to an unearned and unconvincing conclusion—an embrace, if you will, with the African mother who had earlier closed her arms. Blending clichés and stereotypes (however much their basis is in historical fact), Angelou fashions a reconciliation that seems schematic and false, the stuff of textbooks, robbed of feeling.

For example, on a weekend trip into the bush, she stops for gas in Cape Coast, the inglorious site of a former holding fort for captured slaves. Having avoided the place for a year, she hurries out of the town back onto the highway, but she cannot escape; "history had invaded [her] little car." . . .

But these passages seems prefabricated, dead to the feeling that the reader has come to expect of Angelou's record of her African sojourn. It is their cumulative effect that creates a sense of inauthenticity and contributes to the reader's detachment from her story.

Shortly before returning to America, Angelou visits Eastern Ghana and is given a tour of Keta, a town whose population was nearly decimated by the slave trade. There she is accosted by an Ewe woman who "had the wide face and slanted eyes of my grandmother." The woman appears hostile, but because of the language barrier she and Angelou are unable to communicate. The guides comes to the rescue, explaining that the woman has mistaken Angelou for the daughter of a friend, for a descendant "from those stolen mothers and fathers" from the village of Keta. Angelou sums up this experience in terms that have a disappointingly generic ring:

> I had not consciously come to Ghana to find the roots of my beginnings, but I had continually and accidentally tripped over them or fallen upon them in my everyday life . . . And here in my last days in Africa, descendants of a pillaged past saw their history in my face and heard their ancestors speak through my voice. . . . The women wept and I wept. I too cried for the lost people, their ancestors and mine. But I was also weeping with a curious joy. Despite the murders, rapes and suicides, we had survived. The middle passage and the auction block had not erased us. . . . There was much to cry for, much to mourn, but in my heart I felt exalted knowing there was much to celebrate. Although separated from our languages, our families and customs, we had dared to continue to live. We had crossed the unknowable ocean in chains and had written its mystery into "Deep River, my home is over Jordan."

It could be argued that what I'm calling a generic summary is simply evidence that the slave experience is so embedded in the collective unconscious of all Black Americans that images evoking that experience are inevitable and to be expected. That notwithstanding, I had hoped to find a sharper, more quickened personal idiom amid this collective story of slave-trading, the Middle Passage and the auction block. But then, perhaps it is impossible to mine and inscribe a personal idiom, given that story's weight and complexity.

In this sense, *All God's Children Need Traveling Shoes* fits squarely in the tradition of Afro-American autobiography. As one student of the genre has observed, the "self" of Afro-American autobiography is not an "individual with a private career, but a soldier in a long, historic march toward Canaan."

> *Deborah E. McDowell, "Traveling Hopefully," in* The Women's Review of Books, *Vol. IV, No. 17, October, 1986, p. 17.*

Maya Angelou with Carol E. Neubauer (interview date 1987)

[In the following excerpt of an interview conducted by Neubauer in 1987, Angelou discusses the art of autobiography and the process of remembering.]

[Neubauer]: I see autobiography in general as a way for a writer to go back to her past and try to present what is left

in memory but also to recover what has been lost through imagination and invention.

[Angelou]: Autobiography is for me a beloved which, like all beloveds, one is not given by family. One happens upon. You know, you turn the corner to the left instead of to the right. Stop in the parking lot and meet a beloved, or someone who becomes a beloved. And by the time I was half finished with **Caged Bird** I knew I loved the form—that I wanted to try to see what I could do with the form. Strangely enough, not as a cathartic force, not really; at any rate I never thought that really I was interested or am interested in autobiography for its recuperative power. I liked the form—the literary form—and by the time I started **Gather Together** I had gone back and reread Frederick Douglass' slave narrative. Anyway, I love the idea of the slave narrative, using the first person singular, really meaning always the third person plural. I love that. And I see it all the time in the black literature, in the blues and spirituals and the poetry, in essays James Baldwin uses it. But I've tried in each book to let the new voice come through and that's what makes it very difficult for me not to impose the voice of 1980 onto the voice I'm writing from 1950, possibly.

And so when you say you look for a new voice you don't mean the voice of the present or the time of writing the autobiographical account, but rather of that period of your past. That must be difficult.

Very. Very difficult, but I think that in writing autobiography that that's what is necessary to really move it from almost an "as told to" to an "as remembered" state. And really for it to be a creative and artistic literary art form. I believe I came close to recreating the voice in **Gather Together** of that young girl—erratic, sporadic, fractured. I think in each case I've come close. Rather a sassy person in **Singin' and Swingin'**

*It seemed that in **The Heart of a Woman,** either the voice was more complex or else there was more than one voice at work. There seemed to be the voice of that time in your life and yet another voice commenting on that time.*

It seems so, but I looked at that quite carefully and at the period I think it is the voice because I was really coming into a security about who I was and what I was about, but the security lasted sometimes for three or four days or maybe through a love affair or into a love affair or into a job. I think it would be like smoke in a room. It would just dissipate and I would suddenly be edgewalking again. I would be one of those children in the rye, playing very perilously close to the precipice and aware of it. I tried very hard for the voice. I remember the woman very well.

*What I saw in **Heart of a Woman** was not so much that there were two voices talking against one another, but rather that a voice from a more recent time commented ironically on the predominant voice of that time in the past. The irony of you as the writer and the autobiographical presence coming through.*

It is really one of the most difficult. First, well, I don't know what comes first in that case. Whether it is the insistence to write well while trying to speak in a voice thirty years ago. I'm now writing a new book and trying to speak in that voice—the voice of 1963 and what I know about writing in 1984. It really is difficult.

Does it become more difficult the closer you get to the present?

Yes, absolutely. Because by '63 my command of English was *almost* what it is today and I had been very much influenced by Vus Make. He had really influenced my thinking, and his English was exquisite. My reading in other languages also by that time had very much influenced my speaking and I was concerned about eloquence by 1960. So this book is really the most difficult and I've been ducking and dodging it too. I know this morning I should call my editor and tell him I have not forgotten him. He's very much on my mind and the work is very much on my mind. I don't know what I'm going to do when I finish this book. I *may* try to go back and pick up some of the incidents that I left out of maybe **Caged Bird** or **Gather Together** or any of the books. I don't know how to do that.

Are you thinking of autobiography?

Yes.

*That's fascinating. One of the things I'm interested in particularly is how the present influences the autobiographical past. I think what you're engaged in doing now and have been since **Caged Bird** is something that's never been done before in this scope. Each volume of yours is a whole and has a unity that works for that volume alone. If you were to go back to the period of **Caged Bird** that would add another wrinkle in this question of time and different voices.*

I don't know how I will do it, and I don't know if I'll be able to do it. But I think there are facets. When I look at a stained glass window, it's very much like this book. I have an idea that the books are very much like the Everyman stories so that there is greed and kindness and generosity and cruelty, oppression, and sloth. And I think of the period I'm going to write about and I try to see which of the incidents in which greed, say it's green, which of these that happened to me during that period will most demonstrate that particular condition. Now some are more rich, but I refuse them. I do not select them because it's very hard to write drama without falling into melodrama. So the incidents I reject, I find myself unable to write about without becoming melodramatic. I just can't see how to write it. In **Gather Together** there is an incident in which a man almost killed me—tried to, in fact—and kept me for three days and he was a mad man, literally. My escape was so incredible, literally incredible, that there was no way to write it, absolutely, to make it credible and not melodramatic.

Have you ever chosen to take another incident in that case, perhaps one that might not have even happened, and use that as a substitute?

No, because there were others which worked, which did happen, and which showed either cruelty or the irony of escape. So I was able to write that rather than the other.

I see. So you didn't have to sacrifice the core of the experience.

No, I never sacrificed. It's just choosing which of those greens or which of those reds to make that kind of feeling.

It's a beautiful metaphor, the greens, the reds and the light coming through the window. Because in a sense, memory works that way; it filters out past work. And yet an autobiographer has a double task—at least double, probably triple or quadruple—in some ways the filtering has been done beyond your control on an unconscious level. But as a writer working in the present you, too, are making selections or choices, which complicate the experience.

There is so much to talk to you about on this subject. I have, I think, due to all those years of not talking, which again, I chose to minimize in *Caged Bird* because it's hard to write that without, again, the melodramas leaking in. But because of those years of muteness, I think my memory was developed in queer ways, because I remember—I have total recall—or I have none at all. None. And there is no pattern to the memory, so that I would forget all the good and the bad of a certain time, or I will remember *only* the bad of a certain time, or I will remember *only* the good. But when I remember it, I will remember *everything* about it. *Everything.* The outside noises, the odors in the room, the way my clothes were feeling—everything. I just have it, or I remember nothing. I am sure that is a part of the sort of psychological problems I was having and how the memory went about its business knitting itself.

Almost as a treasure chest or a defense.

Yes, both, I guess. But in a sense, not really a defense, because some of the marvelous things I've not remembered. For instance, one of the promises I've exacted from every lover or husband who promised to be a permanent fixture was that *if* I die in the house, if something happened, get me outside. Please don't let me die in the room, or open the window and let me see some rolling hills. Let me see, please. Now, my memory of Stamps, Arkansas, is flat, dirt, the trees around the pond. But everything just flat and mean. When I agreed to go to join Bill Moyers for his creativity program, I flew to Dallas and decided to drive to Stamps because I wanted to sneak up on Stamps. It's, I guess, 200 miles or more. When I drove out of Texas into Arkansas, Stamps is 30 miles from Texas. I began to see the undulating hills. I couldn't believe it! I couldn't believe it! It's beautiful! It's what I love. But the memory had completely gone.

When you're working, for example, on your present book, are there things that help you remember that period or any period in the past better?

Well, a curious thing has happened to me with every book. When I start to work—start to plan it—I encounter people whom I have known in that time, which is really queer. I've wondered if I would encounter them anyway, or if it's a case of "when the student is ready the teacher appears." If I simply wouldn't see their value if I would encounter them and wouldn't see their value for what I'm working on, because I wouldn't be working on that. That is one of the very interesting things. I'm working on Ghana now and this summer I went to London to write a play. I saw a sister friend there from Ghana and suddenly about fifteen Ghanaians; soon I was speaking Fanti again and they were reminding me, "Do you remember that time when?" and suddenly it all came right up my nostrils. But what I do is just pull myself away from everything and everybody and then begin the most frightening of the work. And that is going back. I'm always afraid I'll never come out. Every morning I wake up, usually about 5:30 and try to get to my work room. I keep a little room in a hotel. Nothing on the walls, nothing belonging to me, nothing. I go in and I try to be in by 6:30 and try to get back, get back. Always, for the first half hour is spent wondering if anybody cares for me enough to come and pull me out. Suppose I can't get out?

That's a difficult road to retrace—to find.

Like an enchanted . . . I know that sounds romantic, but you know how I mean. But I do get back and I remember one thing and I think, "Yes, and what are the other things like that that happened?" And maybe a second one will come. It's all there. *All of it* is there.

Even down to the finest details and the dialogues, what you said to the people you were with.

The sound of the voices. And I write wurrrrrrrrrrrrrrr.

How long do you write if you go in at 6:30?

Well, I'm out by 12:30, unless it's really happening. If it's really happening I'll stay till 2:00, but no longer. No longer. And then get out and go home and shower and make a lovely lunch and drink a lot of wine and try to come down. Get back. Stop in a shop, "Hi, how are you? Fine. . . ." So I can ascertain that I do live and people remember me.

Do you leave it in the middle of an incident so that you have a way back, or do you write to the end of each one?

No, I can't write to the end of the incident. I will write to a place that's safe. Nothing will leak away now; I've got it. Then at night I'll read it and try to edit it.

The same night?

The same night. Try to edit it for writing, a little of it. And then begin again the next day. Lordy.

Is it a frightening journey because of the deep roots from that time to the present? Do you feel a kind of vulnerability?

I am not afraid of the ties. I cherish them, rather. It's the vulnerability. It's like using drugs or something. It's allowing oneself to by hypnotized. That's frightening, because then we have no defenses, nothing. We've slipped down the well and every side is slippery. And how on earth are you going to come out? That's scary. But I've chosen it, and I've chosen this mode as my mode.

How far will the fifth volume go?

Actually, it's a new kind. It's really quite a new voice. I'm looking at the black American resident, me and the other black American residents in Ghana, and trying to see all the magic of the external quest of human beings to go home again. That is maybe what life is anyway. To return to the Creator. All of that naiveté, the innocence of trying to. That awful rowing towards God, whatever it is. Whether it's to return to your village or the lover you lost or the youth that some people want to return to or the beauty that some want to return to.

Writing autobiography frequently involves this quest to return to the past, to the home. Sometimes, if the home can't be found, if it can't be located again, then that home or that love or that family, whatever has been lost, is recreated or invented.

Yes, of course. That's it! That's what I'm seeing in this trek back to Africa. That in so many cases that idealized home of course is non-existent. In so many cases some black Americans created it on the spot. On the spot. And I did too. Created something, looked, seemed like what we have idealized very far from reality. It's going to be a painful, hard book to write, in that not only all the stuff

that it cost me to write it, but there will be a number of people who will be disappointed. So I have to deal with that once the book is out. The main thing is getting it out. (pp. 286-91)

Maya Angelou and Carol E. Neubauer in an interview in The Massachusetts Review, *Vol. XXVIII, No. 2, Summer, 1987, pp. 286-92.*

FURTHER READING

Lupton, Mary Jane. "Singing the Black Mother: Maya Angelou and Autobiographical Continuity." *Black American Literature Forum* 24, No. 2 (Summer 1990): 257-76.
   Academic examination of Angelou's autobiographical method.

Neubauer, Carol E. "Displacement and Autobiographical Style in Maya Angelou's 'The Heart of a Woman'." *Black American Literature Forum* 17, No. 3 (Fall 1983): 123-29.
   Analysis of *The Heart of a Woman.* Neubauer argues that in this work Angelou introduces a new element in her autobiography: the "displacement" of her own life as well as that of her son.

Tate, Claudia. "Maya Angelou." In her *Black Women Writers at Work,* pp. 1-11. New York: Continuum Publishing Co., 1983.
   Interview with Angelou in which she discusses the nature of both her poetry and prose works.

Washington, Carla. "Maya Angelou's Angelic Aura." *The Christian Century* 105, No. 3 (23 November 1988): 1031-32.
   Explores Angelou's spirituality as evidenced in her poetry and autobiographies.

Ayi Kwei Armah

1939-

Ghanaian novelist, short story writer, nonfiction writer, poet, and scriptwriter.

Considered one of Africa's leading prose stylists, Armah has garnered substantial critical acclaim as a novelist. In 1968, with the lauded *The Beautyful Ones Are Not Yet Born,* he began a ten-year period during which he would publish five novels. *Fragments* and *Why Are We So Blest?* followed in 1970 and 1972. In these works, Armah criticized corruption and neocolonialism in contemporary Africa. Later, in the historical novels *Two Thousand Seasons* (1973) and *The Healers* (1978), Armah radically shifted his frame of reference to Africa's past, calling for a return to traditional African culture and values.

Born in the Ghanaian coastal city of Takoradi, Armah studied at Achimota College in his native country. After completing his secondary education, he worked as a Radio Ghana scriptwriter, reporter, and announcer and later won a scholarship to study in the United States. There he studied for one year at Groton, a preparatory school in Massachusetts, before entering Harvard University in 1960. Countering a common misconception that he was only an infant when he left Ghana, Armah stated in his 1985 essay "One Writer's Education": "I was already nineteen years old, and had experienced life as an independent working adult in Accra, when I left for America." Armah left Harvard in 1963 before completing his courses and examinations. As he noted of himself: "By my final undergrad year such matters as academic kudos, social status, and professional careers had already come to seem profoundly irrelevant to me." Influenced by African revolutionary movements and by the "persons and groups that had worked to create new, better social realities in place of those they had found at birth," Armah set out on a 7,000-mile trip over four continents to pursue a truly "creative existence." The experience left him hospitalized, drained and spent. He wrote, "It's an understatement to say I had a nervous breakdown: it was my entire being, body and soul, that had broken down."

With that life of creativity "closed" to him, Armah turned to writing, receiving his B.A. degree at Harvard and later an M.F.A. at Columbia. In 1968 he published *The Beautyful Ones Are Not Yet Born,* a novel often described as existentialist. The protagonist, simply known as "the man," is a railway clerk in Ghana during the regime of Kwame Nkrumah, the African leader who took power when Ghana gained independence from Britain. In this Ghana, filth and excrement are everywhere, serving in the novel as metaphors for the corruption that permeates society. The man, however, resists this corruption. He fights the "gleam" that causes almost all Ghanaians to pursue material wealth and

power through bribery and other foul deeds. Like "the man," the protagonists of Armah's next two novels are alienated in their respective societies, and like Armah, they have studied in the United States. In *Fragments,* a returning student, Baako, is expected to flaunt his education and status as a "been-to," an African who has been abroad, but instead he wants only to write. In their inability to understand that Baako does not share their own desires of wealth and prestige, his family has him committed to an insane asylum. *Why Are We So Blest?,* Armah's third novel, is the story of Modin, an African student studying at Harvard. He leaves school and returns to Africa with his white girlfriend Aimée to participate in a revolutionary struggle. Modin is ultimately destroyed in Armah's complex tale, which explores, among other things, sexual relationships and the hierarchy of race as Modin is subjugated and sped to destruction by Aimée. Critics generally praised these three works, especially *The Beautyful Ones Are Not Yet Born;* many compared Armah's writing ability with that of such celebrated Western writers as James Joyce and

Joseph Conrad. But other critics—notably Nigerian writer Chinua Achebe—accused Armah of portraying Africa in a European manner. This accusation may have struck Armah, for in subsequent novels he changed his subject matter and style dramatically. As American poet Gwendolyn Brooks recorded in her 1972 autobiography *Report from Part One,* Armah "now deplores" *The Beautyful Ones Are Not Yet Born* because "the *address* is 'not right.' Future books, he assures us, will have an African focus, an absolutely African focus."

In his first three novels, Armah wrote about the struggles, alienation, and failures of individuals in contemporary African society. In *Two Thousand Seasons,* however, Armah began to portray entire African communities in a historical context—and in their struggles, these communities would succeed. Writing in 1980, Bernth Lindfors claimed of *Two Thousand Seasons:* "Instead of witnessing the anguish of a doomed, fragmented individual, we are shown the joy of a mini-tribe united in the struggle against evil. Instead of existential despair, there is revolutionary hope." *Two Thousand Seasons* marked a striking change from Armah's earlier novels. The novel covers one thousand years of African history and approaches epic proportions in its descriptions of battles, use of folk mythology, and compressed meanings. In the work Armah condemned the Arab "predators" and European "destroyers," calling for the reclamation of Africa's traditional values. With *The Healers,* he took this hope a step further, developing the idea of spiritual inspiration as a reparative force. The young protagonist, Densu, studies to become a healer at a time when Africa is being ravaged by a virulent plague of non-African origin. Densu condemns violence and disunity among his people, embracing instead a communal philosophy. As with *Two Thousand Seasons,* Armah emphasized in *The Healers* the need to return to traditional African culture as a model for the future.

Since the publication of his last novel in 1978, Armah has chiefly written essays on such topics as the role of Marxism in Africa, the need for a native publishing industry, and the benefits to be gained from establishing a dominant African language in Africa instead of continuing to use European ones. Nevertheless, it is not known why Armah has not published another novel. Commenting on this issue, Derek Wright, in his 1989 study *Ayi Kwei Armah's Africa: The Sources of His Fiction,* noted: "Two recent essays [by Armah], which stress the little creative time available to the writer earning his living as a freelance translator and lament the lack of an independent African publishing industry, suggest some possible explanations. Even then, a decade-long silence following the publication of five novels in the previous decade is a puzzling affair. . . ." Wright added: "[Whether there is] any real possibility that the two fictional worlds of the early and late novels might yet be brought into a more organic relationship by the evolution of another new narrative mode" in Armah's writing must remain a matter of speculation "until the

appearance of some more major fiction by this most unpredictable and enigmatic of African writers."

(For further information about Armah's life and works, see *Black Writers; Contemporary Authors,* Vols. 61-64; *Contemporary Authors New Revision Series,* Vol. 21; and *Contemporary Literary Criticism,* Vols. 5, 33.)

PRINCIPAL WORKS

"La mort passe sous les blancs" (essay) 1960; published in periodical *L'Afrique littéraire et artistique*
"Contact" (short story) 1965; published in periodical *The New African*
"Asemka" (short story) 1966; published in periodical *Okyeame*
"African Socialism: Utopian or Scientific" (essay) 1967; published in periodical *Présence africaine*
"Pour les ibos, le régime de la haine silencieuse" (essay) 1967; published in periodical *Jeune Afrique*
"An African Fable" (short story) 1968; published in periodical *Présence africaine*
The Beautyful Ones Are Not Yet Born (novel) 1968
"Yaw Manu's Charm" (short story) 1968; published in periodical *Atlantic*
"Fanon: The Awakener" (essay) 1969; published in periodical *Negro Digest*
"A Mystification: African Independence Revalued" (essay) 1969; published in periodical *Pan-African Journal*
"The Offal Kind" (short story) 1969; published in periodical *Harper's Magazine*
"Aftermath" (poem) 1970; published in *Messages: Poems from Ghana*
Fragments (novel) 1970
Why Are We So Blest? (novel) 1972
Two Thousand Seasons (novel) 1973
"Sundiata, An Epic of Old Mali" (essay) 1974; published in periodical *Black World*
"Chaka" (essay) 1975; published in periodical *Black World*
"Larsony, or Fiction as Criticism of Fiction" (essay) 1976; published in periodical *Asemka*
The Healers (novel) 1978
"Halfway to Nirvana" (short story) 1984; published in periodical *West Africa*
"Islam and 'Ceddo'" (essay) 1984; published in periodical *West Africa*
"Masks and Marx: The Marxist Ethos vis-à-vis African Revolutionary Theory and Praxis" (essay) 1984; published in periodical *Présence africaine*
"The View from PEN International" (essay) 1984; published in periodical *West Africa*
"The Caliban Complex" (essay) 1985; published in periodical *West Africa*
"Flood and Famine, Drought and Glut" (essay) 1985; published in periodical *West Africa*
"The Lazy School of Literary Criticism" (essay) 1985; published in periodical *West Africa*
"One Writer's Education" (essay) 1985; published in periodical *West Africa*

"Our Language Problem" (essay) 1985; published in periodical *West Africa*

"The Oxygen of Translation" (essay) 1985; published in periodical *West Africa*

"The Teaching of Creative Writing" (essay) 1985; published in periodical *West Africa*

"Africa and the Francophone Dream" (essay) 1986; published in periodical *West Africa*

"Dakar Hieroglyphs" (essay) 1986; published in periodical *West Africa*

"The Third World Hoax" (essay) 1986; published in periodical *West Africa*

"Writers as Professionals" (essay) 1986; published in periodical *West Africa*

"Seed Time" (poem) 1988; published in periodical *West Africa*

"Doctor Kamikaze" (short story) 1989; published in periodical *Mother Jones*

Charles Miller (essay date 1968)

[*In the following excerpt from an essay originally published in the* Saturday Review *in 1968, Miller applauds Armah's handling of difficult subject matter in* The Beautyful Ones Are Not Yet Born.]

Ghana under Kwame Nkrumah is the scene of this outstanding novel [*The Beautyful Ones Are Not Yet Born*] by Ayi Kwei Armah, a Ghanaian television writer. But the story could take place in almost any new nation of Africa, since it deals with that handmaiden of fledgling African sovereignty: corruption in "people's" governments....

The Beautyful Ones Are Not Yet Born turns on the purgatory of a railway clerk (we never learn his name) who will end his days as a railway clerk because he carries the terrible burden of principle in a climate of ethics that permits advancement only under the table. In and out of his job fast-buck offers abound but he spurns them all, to the bewilderment of the high-living mediocrities and incompetents who are eager to make him a man of means for a price. Although, being human, he's not entirely immune to temptation, the degrading payola atmosphere stiffens his resistance. . . .

Nor can he find inner reward in his virtue, tortured as he is by the memory of just a few years earlier, when a dynamic young leader brought the fruits of freedom within the Ghanaian people's reach—and then handed them over to a rookery of corner-cutting political hacks. The bitterness of hope betrayed has become poison in his mind; everyday life is a lockstep march through a prison yard. On February 24, 1966, the long-awaited day of reckoning, a shout of joy echoes across the nation as Nkrumah and his gang get the heave-ho—and the wheeling-dealing goes on under new management. Or at least so it seems to the clerk. He continues to walk his treadmill of hopelessness.

Armah's handling of the clerk's ordeal is, to put it mildly, unusual. In fact, quite a few readers are going to find it revolting. For his message almost seems to be that power corrupts while absolute power defecates. The extent to which Armah relies on human waste to symbolize the decay of personal integrity is all but breathtaking—and this can, if you wish, refer to holding the nose. In brief, it really hits the fan.

This is literary talent? You bet it is. And I say that as one who finds most scatological prose not only disgusting but badly written. It calls for no small gift to expound on excreta and neither offend nor bore, even greater ability if this unlovely topic is to be made valid within the context of a novel. Armah brings it off, his objective being, of course, to convey a moral lesson—by highlighting his protagonist's uncompromising ethical rectitude through personal fastidiousness. To the clerk, going to the toilet is a nightmare, not only because the public lavatories which he uses happen to violate every rule of hygiene but because they also represent, in a very physical sense, the moral contamination which surrounds him—sometimes even tempts him in its foul way—and against which he must always be on guard. Armah has treated a most indelicate function with remarkable skill—and force. (p. 24)

I register two small objections. Now and then, Armah's lampoonery may go below the belt. His portrayal of the old United Gold Coast Convention Party (although it's not identified by name) as an assemblage of Uncle Toms strikes me as unfair to a group that did much to spearhead Ghanaian independence. (It's also an injustice to the party's leader, Dr. J. B. Danquah, regarded by some, myself included, as Ghana's real founding father.) And I can't buy the impression he creates that despite Nkrumah's overthrow, nothing in Ghana has changed for the good. All right, the country has yet to become a model of freedom, but it would be very wrong to overlook certain impressive strides made by Ghana's National Liberation Council toward restoration of the constitutional democracy that Nkrumah so callously dismantled.

It would also be a mistake to let these two shortcomings prejudice the reader against a valid and uncommonly arresting view of the abuse of power in that part of the world which may be least able to afford so outrageous an indulgence. (pp. 24-5)

> *Charles Miller, "The Arts of Venality," in* Saturday Review, *Vol. LI, No. 35, August 31, 1968, p. 24-5.*

Charles R. Larson (essay date 1972)

[*In the following review of* Why Are We So Blest?, *Larson praises the "unsettling" nature of the novel.*]

When Ayi Kwei Armah published his first two novels, *The Beautyful Ones Are Not Yet Born* and *Fragments,* many of his countrymen were offended at the picture he presented of life in post-Independence Day Ghana. Armah depicted an African wasteland, where corruption in the government was rampant and where the African intellectual, educated abroad, felt totally out of place, frustrated to the point of rage or despair by his inability to make any change in the system. Although Armah's criticism was specifically aimed at the sterility of contemporary Ghanaian life, indirectly it was pointed away from Africa—especially at Western commercialism and neo-colonialism. Thus it seemed inevitable that it would only be a matter of time before this most talented of the younger African novelists would more directly vent his spleen at the source: The West, and especially the United States, where Armah received much of his higher education. This expectation is confirmed in *Why Are We So Blest?,* in many ways his most unsettling, novel.

In *Why Are We So Blest?* Armah has presented the quintessential learning experience for the African student—education in the United States. Although the main action takes place in North Africa, lengthy sections of the narrative flash back to record the main character's higher education in Cambridge, Massachusetts. When the novel opens, Modin Dofu, who has been a student at Harvard, has come to North Africa in hopes of joining a revolutionary group plotting the liberation of Portugal's African colonies. With him is Aimée Reitsch, a white American student whose sexual fantasies, rooted in her stereotyped dreams of deepest, darkest Africa, underlie the master-slave relationship she has established over Modin.

Solo Nkonam is another Ghanaian who has been educated overseas—in Lisbon. His function within *Why Are We So Blest?* is much like Marlow's in Conrad's *The Heart of Darkness:* to act as the recording consciousness for the protagonist's moral disintegration. Solo realizes that previously he himself has played a variant of the slave role Modin is now enacting with Aimée, but Solo has temporarily found release by working as a translator in North Africa—far from his own people. As he muses early in the novel, "What is ordained for us I have not escaped—the fate of the *évolué,* the turning of the assimilated African, not into something creating its own life, but into an eater of crumbs in the house of slavery." Solo sees himself as a ghostly wanderer, a man diminished by his Western education. "What a farce, scholarships! That blood money never went to any of us for our intelligence. It was payment for obedience. . . . The end of a Western education is not work but self-indulgence."

The heart of the novel, however, is Modin's plight in America. His education, he realizes, has been designed to make him a cog in the neo-colonial machine. Frigid white women throw themselves at him, expecting that he will liberate them from their sexual fetters. As Modin reflects, "These women I have known have had deep needs to wound their men. I have been an instrument in

their hands." The novelist writes of the effect upon Modin: "Imprisoned in whiteness, now trained to desire all flesh that is white, he has come to think of his imprisonment as the essence of his freedom."

Armah's new novel may offend some readers. The ending, for example, is the most graphic and sickening portrayal of physical torture I can recall having encountered. At the same time, this violent denouement is by no means arbitrary: the author has carefully prepared his reader for it. Masterfully constructed, *Why Are We So Blest?* is disturbing in many ways: in the sharpness of its focus on the psychological by-products of racial prejudice—among others, emasculation and self-contempt—and in the implications it makes about race relations. Yet it is these very elements which, I predict, will make people talk about this book for a long time to come. (pp. 73-4)

Charles R. Larson, in a review of "Why Are We So Blest?" in Saturday Review, *Vol. LV, No. 10, March 18, 1972, pp. 73-4.*

Chinua Achebe (essay date 1973)

[*Nigerian novelist Achebe is widely regarded as one of the greatest African writers of the twentieth century. In his works, which chronicle the colonization and independence of Nigeria, he has rendered an intimate and authentic representation of African culture. Achebe's major concerns, according to Abiola Irele, involve "the social and psychological conflicts created by the incursion of the white man and his culture into the hitherto self-contained world of African society, and the disarray in the African consciousness that has followed." In the following excerpt from his celebrated 1973 article "Africa and Her Writers," Achebe accuses Armah of not understanding Ghana in* The Beautyful Ones Are Not Yet Born.]

There is a brilliant Ghanaian novelist, Ayi Kwei Armah, who seems to me to be in grave danger of squandering his enormous talents and energy in pursuit of the *human condition.* In an impressive first novel, *The Beautyful Ones Are Not Yet Born,* he gives us a striking parable of corruption in Ghana society and of one man who refuses to be contaminated by this filth.

It is a well-written book. Armah's command of language and imagery is of a very high order indeed. But it is a sick book. Sick, not with the sickness of Ghana, but with the sickness of the *human condition.* The hero, pale and passive and nameless—a creation in the best manner of existentialist writing—wanders through the story in an anguished half-sleep, neck-deep in despair and human excrement of which we see rather a lot in the book. Did I say he *refused* to be corrupted? He did not do anything as positive as refusing. He reminded me very strongly of that man and woman in a Jean-Paul Sartre novel who sit in anguished gloom in a restaurant and then in a sudden access of nihilistic energy seize table knives and stab their hands right through to the wood—to prove some very obscure point to each other. Except that Armah's hero would be quite incapable of suffering any seizure.

Ultimately the novel failed to convince me. And this was because Armah insists that this story is happening in Ghana and not in some modern, existentialist no man's land. He throws in quite a few realistic ingredients like Kwame Nkrumah to prove it. And that is a mistake. Just as the hero is nameless, so should everything else be; and Armah might have gotten away with a modern, "universal" story. Why did he not opt simply for that easy choice? I don't know. But I am going to be superstitious and say that Africa probably seized hold of his subconscious and insinuated there this deadly obligation—deadly, that is, to universalistic pretensions—to use his considerable talents in the service of a particular people and a particular place. Could it be that under this pressure Armah attempts to tell what Europe would call a modern story and Africa a moral fable, at the same time; to relate the fashions of European literature to the men and women of Ghana? He tried very hard. But his Ghana is unrecognizable. This aura of cosmic sorrow and despair is as foreign and unusable as those monstrous machines Nkrumah was said to have imported from Eastern European countries. Said, that is, by critics like Armah.

True, Ghana was sick. And what country is not? But everybody has his own brand of ailment. Ayi Kwei Armah imposes so much foreign metaphor on the sickness of Ghana that it ceases to be true. And finally, the suggestion (albeit existentially tentative) of the hero's personal justification without faith nor works is grossly inadequate in a society where even a lunatic walking stark naked through the highways of Accra has an extended family somewhere suffering vicarious shame.

Armah is clearly an alienated writer, a modern writer complete with all the symptoms. Unfortunately Ghana is not a modern existentialist country. It is just a Western African state struggling to become a nation. So there is enormous distance between Armah and Ghana. There is something scornful, cold and remote about Armah's obsession with the filth of Ghana. . . . (pp. 38-40)

Armah is quoted somewhere as saying that he is not an African writer but just a writer. Some other writers (and friends of mine, all) have said the same thing. It is a sentiment guaranteed to win applause in Western circles. But it is a statement of defeat. A man is never more defeated than when he is running away from himself. (pp. 41-2)

> *Chinua Achebe, "Africa and Her Writers," in his* Morning Yet on Creation Day: Essays, *Anchor Press/Doubleday, 1975, pp. 29-45.*

Bernth Lindfors (essay date 1980)

[*In the following excerpt, Lindfors analyzes Armah's portrayal of Africa in* Two Thousand Seasons *and* The Healers.]

[Both *Two Thousand Seasons* and *The Healers*] present Africa as a victim of outside forces that it resists but cannot contain. These depredations of the past are responsible for the chaos one sees in Africa at present, and only by properly understanding that past and present will Africans collectively be able to tackle the problems of the future: how to get the victim back on its feet, how to raise the materially oppressed and downtrodden, how to heal the spiritually sick. Instead of merely cursing various symptoms of the colonial disease, as he had done in his first three books, Armah now wants to work towards effecting a cure. (p. 87)

[*Two Thousand Seasons*] is an interesting scenario and a fascinating contrast to Armah's earlier fiction. Instead of watching one man struggle fruitlessly to maintain his purity or sanity in an atmosphere of rank corruption, we see a communal group, activated by the highest ideals, actually *succeed* in their military manoeuvres against extraordinarily powerful antagonists. Instead of witnessing the anguish of a doomed, fragmented individual, we are shown the joy of a mini-tribe united in the struggle against evil. Instead of existential despair, there is revolutionary hope. Instead of defeat, victory.

But the optimism in Armah's new view of man and society in Africa is predicated on certain assumptions which it is difficult to credit as reasonable. Foremost among these is the belief that Africa, before being polluted by contact with the outside world, was a Garden of Eden, at least in terms of social organization. People lived in harmonious communities, sharing the fruits of their labour and never striving to compete against their neighbours for the acquisition of superior status or material goods. Rulers did not exist; the communities were acephalous, completely democratic and devoted to the principle of reciprocity. This principle was the very essence of what Armah calls 'our way, the way'. . . . Africans were a creative, productive, hospitable, non-oppressive, healthy and sharing people—until the invaders came. Africans should now strive to return to 'our way, the way' by destroying the destroyers of their former paradise.

The villains in this stark melodrama are portrayed as the obverse of the heroes. This may be a dramatic necessity, in as much as one needs very potent Manichean forces to overwhelm such a superabundance of virtue as is said to have existed in prehistoric Africa. But it also assumes that entire races of people can be reduced to the level of primal forces, that one be characterized as inherently predisposed towards good, another addicted to evil. This kind of xenophobic oversimplification used to be found in B-grade films manufactured in Hollywood during the Second World War, in which fanatical kamikaze pilots and fat, stupid, goose-stepping German generals represented all that was reprehensible in the world. (pp. 89-90)

The trouble with Armah's cartoon history of Africa is that it ultimately is not a positive vision, even though it promises future happiness. All it really offers is negation of negation. The most creative act imaginable is destruction of the destroyers. . . . This is a philosophy of paranoia, an anti-racist racism—in short, negritude reborn. In place of a usable historical myth, *Two Thousand Seasons* overschematizes the past, creating the dangerous kind of lie that Frantz Fanon used to call a 'mystification'. (p. 90)

In his latest novel *The Healers* Armah moves a step closer to fleshing out his nightmare vision of the past by substituting concrete substance for abstract symbol. If *Two Thousand Seasons* was his theory of history, *The Healers* is an adumbration of the theory using actual recorded events as proof of the hypotheses advanced. Armah takes the fall of the Ashanti Empire as emblematic of Africa's destruction, and he attributes the calamity not only to the rapacity of the West but also to the disunity within Africa itself. It is towards the reunification of Africa tomorrow that Africans must work today if they wish to repair the damage done yesterday. History is again seen as a guide to a better future.

The novel itself is unified by the imagery of disease. Africa has been prostrated by a foreign plague against which it had no natural immunity, and some of its members, infected beyond all possibility of recovery, have turned against the parent body itself, spreading the disabling disorder still further. Any manifestation of division in society is regarded as a symptom of the malady, a crippling indisposition requiring a cure. (p. 91)

It is clear that Armah himself wants to assist in the healing process. The role of the writer, he seems to be saying, is to inspire Africa to be true to its own spirit so it can be reunited as the harmonious community it once was before the predators and destroyers came. This is a noble goal, even if the 'paradise lost' theme is rather naïve as an interpretation of human history. Armah evidently is trying to do something constructive in his fiction, something far more positive than he had done in his first three novels. Giving Africa a new, clean image of itself is a much more wholesome occupation than rubbing its nose in dung.

And, indeed, *The Healers* is a better-balanced book, a saner piece of fiction, than *Two Thousand Seasons*. Gone, but not totally forgotten, are the Arab and European demons who were objects of such intense hatred in Armah's earlier venture into history. Gone, too, are the scenes of sexual perversion and the almost Homeric descriptions of bloodshed, gore and corporeal mutilation, descriptions which told in gleeful, gloating detail exactly where a bullet or blade entered an enemy's body and where it exited. Gone as well is the over-idealized band of forest guerrillas, those glamorous

outlaws descended from a romantic blend of Mao, Mau Mau and Robin Hood, who, instead of offering the reader some semblance of fidelity to African life, gave imaginary life to African fidelity. Gone, in short, are the delirious fantasies that pushed *Two Thousand Seasons* beyond the dimensions of viable myth into the wilder liberties of nightmare.

The Healers, it must be admitted, also has its good guys and bad guys, its heavy-handed moralizing and its propensity to force history to fit a predetermined ideological paradigm, but it is not a harmful book to put into the hands of young people. For one thing, it does not encourage xenophobia. For another, it emphasizes creativity ('inspiration') rather than destruction. And by concentrating on real events and weaving fiction into the fabric of fact, it could help young Africans to reshape their perspective on the past and come to a better understanding of the world in which they currently live. In other words, it offers an interpretation of human experience that seems valid because it is rooted in an imaginable reality.

Yet it is still a cartoon, still comic-strip history. It will not persuade many adults because it falsifies far more than it authenticates and in the process fails to avoid the pitfalls of oversimplification. Nevertheless, some grown-ups will be able to enjoy it at the level of popular fiction, for it is good cops-and-robbers, cowboys-and-indians stuff. It even includes a murder mystery to bait the reader's interest. But basically it is juvenile adventure fiction of the *Treasure Island* or *King Solomon's Mines* sort, the only major difference being that it is thoroughly *African* juvenile adventure fiction. (pp. 94-5)

I am not saying this to belittle the novel's importance. Obviously, *The Healers* is a major attempt by a major African writer to reinterpret a major event in African history. But I think it will have its major impact on young people, and this is as it should be in any remythologizing of Africa. One must aim at winning the hearts and minds of the young, imbuing them with the highest ideals and making them proud and happy to be Africans. This *The Healers* does better than any other novel Armah has written. And this is why it is potentially his most important book and certainly his healthiest. One can no longer complain that his vision is warped or his art sick. (p. 95)

Bernth Lindfors, "Armah's Histories," in African Literature Today, *No. 11, 1980, pp. 85-96.*

Bonnie J. Barthold (essay date 1981)

[*In the following excerpt from her 1981 study* Black Time: Fiction of Africa, the Caribbean, and the United States, *Barthold examines symbolism and characterization in* Why Are We So Blest?]

Armah's third novel moves from the isolated vision of the man in *The Beautyful Ones Are Not Yet Born* or the portrayal of fragmentation and loss in *Fragments* to the relationship of three individuals to a revolution in progress in an unspecified Portuguese colony in Africa, identified as "Congheria," in its description very much like Guinea-Bissau on the northern Guinea Coast of West Africa. But in *Why are We So Blest?* the attempt at action proves as impotent as vision does in Armah's other novels. None of the three figures succeeds in actually taking part in the revolution and each is shown as unable to overcome the destructive isolation of his own psyche.

Solo Nkonam, a translator for an Algerian magazine, looks back on his past participation in revolution with disillusionment. Modin Dofu, a Ghanaian student, and Aimée Reitsch, a neurotic American girl, fail in their attempt to join the revolutionaries. The story is a narrative of political failure, and political failure manifests a larger, spiritual failure, their distance from the revolution reflecting their spiritual isolation and their imprisonment in self. In the world of *Why Are We So Blest?*, as in the traditional ideal community, this isolation in self is equivalent to spiritual death. Both Solo's names signal this isolation; his surname, loosely translated from Akan, means "lonely stranger." There is irony too in the names Modin Dofu (in Akan, "I am called a person who loves") and Aimée ("one who is loved"); in the symbolic interplay of isolation and sexuality that structures the novel, love breeds only destruction.

Solo narrates the story, largely on the basis of the notebooks kept by Aimée and Modin, which have come into his hands. A passage from the first entry in Modin's notebook fuses the narrative interplay of sexuality and isolation. The passage deals with Earl Lynch, who "in 25 years might be the first black professor at Harvard." Lynch uses sex as a means of racial retaliation, and makes a point of having affairs with as many of his white colleagues' wives as he can. His use of sex is also an attempt to break out of his own imprisonment in self, an imprisonment that is imaged in Modin's description of Lynch's "secret library." Lynch shares his secret with Modin, who learns that the library is comprised of "standard reading" on Marxism, available "at any book shop." But above the bookshelves, dominating the room, hangs an African mask, which according to Lynch "doesn't have any meaning":

> The design was a mask: a pained, human face, a huge head, huge bulbous, all-seeing eyes, pained, distorted ears open to all possible sounds, superimposed on a shriveled mouth and nostrils cramped with hard control. The limbs—emaciated, reduced to spindly lines—were attached indirectly to the human spider-head. The design gave the creature no chest, no stomach, no groin. From its existence of pain the faculties lodged in those organs had been subtracted by the carver. There were just eight crawly, elongated little limbs about the spider face.

As described by Modin, the mask has "a powerful meaning," part of which comes from the character of the folklore figure it portrays—Ananse, the cunning

spider of countless West African stories. The "wisdom of Ananse" is a misguided, self-centered wisdom that often loses touch with reality. In one story, for example, Ananse decides that he will gather up all the wisdom in the world and store it in a calabash at the top of a tall coconut palm. When he thinks he has it all, he ties the calabash around his neck, allowing it to hang down in front—thus making it impossible for him to climb the coconut palm. Ananse's son, Ntikumah, begins to laugh as he watches his father's struggles, and tells him that he would do better to put his load on his back. Realizing the wisdom of Ntikumah's words, Ananse also realizes that he has failed in his attempt to gather up *all* wisdom. In frustration and anger, he drops the calabash, which shatters, allowing wisdom to spread once again throughout the world.

In *Why Are We So Blest?*, Earl Lynch has his own calabash in his secret library. But in Modin's words, it contains only the wisdom of "the white desert." "Caught in the white net of minds," Lynch ironically seeks a "break for his spirit" in "the whitest of philosophies, Marxism." The web of Ananse becomes a circle of imprisonment rather than reciprocity, and Lynch's attempt to escape has only enmeshed him further.

For Modin, the web itself is a symbol of the choices available to the black intellectual.

> Those who stay in the peripheral areas intellectually, emotionally, psychologically, totally, are not lonely. They are in touch with home, not cut off. The price they pay for not being lonely, however, is that they suffer the crudest forms of manipulation, mystification, planned ignorance.
>
> Those who shift from the periphery to the center can hope to escape some of these cruder forms of manipulation. But the price they pay is loneliness, separation from home, the constant necessity to adjust to what is alien, eccentric to the self.

At the center of the web is an insensitive Lynch, who sees no meaning in the mask of Ananse. At the center, too, is Solo. Fully aware of his alienation, he opens his narrative by remarking, "Even before my death I have become a ghost." Modin, whom we see as a younger double of Solo, remarks, "The directions made available to me within this arrangement are all suicidal. I am supposed to get myself destroyed but of my own free-seeming choice. Earl [Lynch] is a suicide." At the center of the web is the spiritual death of Lynch and Solo. Aware of this, Modin seeks to reconnect with the periphery, though from the beginning he sees his choice only as a more meaningful choice of death:

> The real question is not whether to commit suicide but how best to invest my inevitable destruction. . . . Outside of investing my death in an ongoing effort to change things as they are, it wouldn't matter much what kind of death I chose. . . . All existent methods are absurd and deadly outside of a revolutionary commitment to Africa.

To his credit, Modin is repelled by Lynch's use of sex as a racial weapon. Though he has a series of relationships with white women, initially at least his purpose is pleasure, and the relationships are portrayed with tenderness. When he becomes aware of sex as an idea, as a weapon, he is revolted. This and his own sense of survival combine after he is nearly stabbed to death by a woman's husband, and he swears off even a tacit involvement in such a battle. Given this, he begins his relationship with Aimée—also white, but unmarried—only reluctantly; and when he realizes that she is fantasizing about him as a black violator of white purity, he nearly breaks it off. Instead of severing the relationship, however, he converts her—as he sees it—to his own genuine tenderness.

But the relationship between Modin and Aimée is only peripherally grounded in psychology. More centrally, it is a symbolic relationship between a destroyer, a Circe of sorts, insensitive to the pain she causes, and a victim who seems to realize from the beginning that he is fated for destruction. They meet when Modin, having rejected his white-funded scholarship stipend, takes a job as a paid volunteer in a psychological study of pain. Aimée has volunteered for the study as well, not for the money but for the "experience." The experiment in pain is an obvious foreshadowing of the conclusion of the novel: Aimée's threshold of pain is extraordinarily high, and the experimenters leave off increasing the voltage of the shocks they are using for fear of physiological damage. Modin, by contrast, experiences pain almost immediately. Aimée's insensitivity here—her desire in fact to know what the experience of pain is—prophesies the conclusion when she joins in the sexual torture of Modin that leads to his death.

Disillusioned with intellectual passivity, Aimée and Modin both decide to "discontinue their studies"—he at Harvard, she at Radcliffe—and go to Algeria, where they hope to join forces with the anti-Portuguese revolutionaries who have their headquarters there. From there, they plan to move on to Congheria and the revolution itself. The Congherians in Algeria reject the couple, Aimée because she is white, Modin because he is "too intellectual." But they do this tacitly, stringing the couple along with a perpetual "Come back in two weeks." Modin and Aimée's money runs out. Solo invites them to share his apartment. Months pass. Tired of waiting, the two strike out on their own for Congheria.

A French motorist who has offered them a ride returns later with three friends. They beat Modin and rape Aimée, and after an extended sexual torture in which Aimée—not unwillingly—participates, they cut off Modin's penis with a piece of thin wire and leave him to bleed to death as they take Aimée back to a nearby village. The novel concludes with Aimée's description of the event:

> They used me to get Modin hard. The wounded man gave a yell of pain and pulled hard on the wire. First his friend was surprised, then he too pulled. The

snapping off of the tip of Modin's prick was slow. I thought it would fall just like that, but the wire cut into his flesh and then in spite of all that tension nothing seemed to happen. Modin did not scream. I was thinking the wire had broken when the tip of his penis snapped off and hung by just a bit of skin from the bottom. I gathered all my strength and shook myself free of the two men holding me. They let me go. They were laughing, all of them.

> Modin started bleeding. The blood curved out in a little stream that jerked outward about every second. I reached him and without thinking of what I was doing I kissed him. His blood filled my mouth. I wanted him to speak to me. He had groaned a little when I took him and kissed him, but he said nothing.

> I asked him, "Do you love me?"

> He didn't answer me.

Modin leaves the center of the web to find a recapitulation of Ananse's pain, in a movement of fatal circularity. He has written earlier that when he travels, "it is the past that fills my mind. . . . It always happens when I travel. . . . As my body is taken forward, my mind becomes hungry for places and things behind me. . . . Everything comes together rapidly. Every journey in this way becomes a return, another visit into myself." The reader is left to imagine Modin's awareness that the end of his journey was embodied in its beginning, in Ananse's web and in his meeting with Aimée. (pp. 169-73)

> *Bonnie J. Barthold, "Ayi Kwei Armah: 'Why Are We So Blest?'" in her* Black Time: Fiction of Africa, the Caribbean, and the United States, *Yale University Press, 1981, pp. 169-73.*

Ayi Kwei Armah (essay date 1985)

[*In the following excerpt from his 1985 essay "One Writer's Education," Armah describes the effect of the 1961 murder of Patrice Lumumba, the first Premier of Congo (now Zaire) and first Pan-African nationalist, on his education and goals.*]

When I entered Harvard in 1960, it was my intention to specialise in Literature. In my first year, however, my centre of interest shifted from the contemplation of arrangements of symbols, images and words, to a scrutiny of the arrangements of the social realities buried under those words, images and symbols. This shift of intellectual focus had, not altogether incidentally, been accelerated by the events of the Congo crisis, culminating in the murder of Patrice Lumumba.

The assassination of Lumumba created in me the kind of deep-running sadness usually provoked by some irreplaceable personal loss. The reason is not really hard to find. I had long had a sense of myself not simply as an Akan, an Ewe, a Ghanaian and a West African, but most strongly and significantly as an African. It was as an African, then, that I contemplated, then understood, Lumumba's murder.

I used, then as now, to read both carefully and widely. I therefore knew Lumumba had worked to create a unified national movement in a fragmented land, had come to power through democratic elections, and, to judge by all he said, aspired to move together with all Africans from a servile to an independent, self-reliant status. When he was murdered even the most obtuse African student knew it was because the West, America in the lead, did not want to see potentially creative Africans in power.

In my general reading I had come to be suitably impressed by the consistency with which America and the West promoted parasitic, dictatorial regimes outside their own home grounds, supporting Chiang against Mao in China for instance, Diem against Ho in Vietnam, Somoza against Sandino in Nicaragua, Batista against Castro in Cuba. I kept relating this pattern of Western political preferences to developments at home in Africa, and, against the background of abundant historical evidence, the conclusion that presented itself to my mind was inexorable: if we Africans were to rise from the abyss of exploitation and contempt, we would be obliged to do so against murderous opposition from the West, America in the lead, the same way the Chinese, the Vietnamese, the Cubans had.

And yet my personal truth was that the Americans were my hosts, excellent ones at that. From my first minute in America I'd been treated courteously and kindly, and persons who were by any reckoning part of that country's power elite had made me a welcome friend in their homes. If anyone is qualified to speak of having lived through an idyllic spell of youth, I am.

Still, in my attempt to attain knowledge of the world in which I was to become a fully conscious adult, and perhaps to reach a clear understanding of my own probable function within that world; I was trying to balance the kindness, the respect and the abundant love bestowed on my individual person against the enormity of the crime committed against Lumumba, the Congo, Africa. In this attempt I felt initially hampered by the fact that I had not systematically studied the economic, social, political and, ultimately, philosophical and cultural issues at stake not only in the Congo but also in Angola, Azania, Zimbabwe, Namibia, in Africa as a whole and in the world at large. I wanted to end this state of relative ignorance. I decided to switch from Literature to the Social Sciences.

I had precise ideas about what I needed to study. But at first I could find no single department at the university offering the full range of interdisciplinary courses I was determined to take. Persistent investigation revealed there was indeed a likely programme, but it was a pilot programme not yet advertised in the academic catalogue. Admissions was restricted to Social Science students meeting specific academic standards. I registered for the requisite courses, met the stipulated standards and got into the experimental Social Studies programme.

It was just what I'd been searching for. It opened up the various Social Science disciplines in such a way that the interconnections between the economics of continents, the politics of nations and the sociology and culture of peoples were made systematically clear.

The consummation of this new love did not mean an abandonment of Literature. But there too my interest shifted significantly, from appreciation to production, from literary theology to create and expository writing as craft and art.

Something else happened. My old respect and affection for authors whose work had moved me was now transferred, not indeed to eminent sociologists, but to persons and groups that had worked to create new, better social realities in place of those they had found at birth. These, after all, were practically involved in creativity of a more difficult and necessary type, and it mattered not at all that their work was essentially anonymous. It was to that kind of creativity that I wanted to engage my life.

It took a 7,000-mile trip over four continents plus a certain amount of hardship for me to discover that the way to a really creative existence was in fact closed to me. Nine months after I'd left Harvard, I found myself with only one exit. It led back to the world I'd sought not simply to abandon but to work actively against. Less importantly but more pressingly, my health, till then always excellent, had been destroyed by months of malnourishment, poor accommodation and sheer uncertainty. For the first time in my life I was ill enough to be hospitalised, first in Algiers, then in Boston. It's an understatement to say I had a nervous breakdown: it was my entire being, body and soul, that had broken down.

The physical damage alone took months in hospital to repair. After that a worse problem remained: how to work up some semblance of motivation for living in a world dying for change, but which I couldn't help to change. I knew I could write, but the question that immobilised me then remains to this day: of what creative use are skillfully arranged words when the really creative work—changing Africa's social realities for the better—remains inaccessible?

For I saw and still see the neo-colonial order we're all living with as profoundly destructive, its ruling arrangements incurably parasitic. That knowledge had long killed in me any desire to commit my life to any career in this old world masquerading as new. In all kindness I was offered the healing virtues of psychoanalysis. In all politeness I declined. I needed no disciple of Freud, Adler or Horney to tell me why my soul felt repelled by the world as it happens to be.

In the end, I waited till I felt marginally strong enough, then made the inescapable decision: I would revert to writing, not indeed as the most desired creative option, but as the least parasitic option open to me. When I returned to Ghana in 1964, there was nothing at home so unexpected as to shock me. Rather, I was in the position of a spore which, having finally accepted its destiny as a fungus, still wonders if it might produce penicillin. (pp. 1752-53)

Ayi Kwei Armah, "One Writer's Education,"
in West Africa, No. 3548, August 26, 1985,
pp. 1752-53.

Neil Lazarus (essay date 1987)

[*In the following excerpt, Lazarus discusses alternatives to worshipping the "gleam" (Armah's symbol for materialism) in* The Beautyful Ones Are Not Yet Born.]

[*The Beautyful Ones Are Not Yet Born*] is transparently a moral work, whose prevailing tenor is subjectivistic. This sense of moral earnestness ought not, however, to be interpreted as idealistic, for it stems not from any abstract consideration as to how the "good" or the "just" life might be led, but rather from an appraisal of what was actually possible in Ghana after decolonization—of what seemed, indeed, to be prefigured in the style of the decolonizing movement itself. Armah's vision may be subjectivistic, but it derives from a material observation of the Procrustean tendencies of real human history, not from a contemplation of ideal, transhistorical forms. In this respect it is reminiscent of much of [Frantz] Fanon's work. Above all it seems to me, *The Beautyful Ones* needs to be read in the light of Fanon's classic essay "The Pitfalls of National Consciousness." In this essay Fanon mounts a stinging critique of bourgeois nationalist ideology in Africa. "National consciousness," he argues, was parasitic, unimaginative, and wholly lacking in energy or initiative:

> The national bourgeoisie of under-developed countries is not engaged in production, not in invention, nor building, nor labour; it is completely canalized into activities of the intermediary type. Its innermost vocation seems to be to keep in the running and to be part of the racket. The psychology of the national bourgeoisie is that of the businessman, not that of a captain of industry. . . .
> [The historic mission of the national bourgeoisie] has nothing to do with transforming the nation; it consists prosaically, of being the transmission line between the nation and a capitalism, rampant though camouflaged, which today puts on the masque of neo-colonialism. The national bourgeoisie will be quite content with the role of the Western bourgeoisie's business agent, and it will play its part without any complexes in a most dignified manner. But this same lucrative role, this cheap-jack's function, this meanness of outlook and this absence of all ambition symbolize the incapability of the national middle class to fulfil its historic role of bourgeoisie. Here, the dynamic pioneer aspect, the characteristics of the inventor and the discoverer of new worlds which are found in all national bourgeoisies are lamentably absent. . . .
> Because it is bereft of ideas, because it lives to itself and cuts itself off from the people, undermined by its hereditary incapacity to think in terms of all the problems of the nation as seen from the point of view of the whole of the nation, the national middle class will have nothing better to do than to take on the role of manager for Western enterprise, and it will in practice set up its country as the brothel of Europe. (*Wretched of the Earth*)

Fanon's essay was written at the time of independence and was intended to serve as an admonition. The end of colonialism was in sight, but Fanon wanted to show that if the places of the departing colonial officers were filled by members of the national bourgeoisies, independence would not have been won. Armah's presentation in *The Beautyful Ones* proceeds directly from this analysis. However, there is one crucial difference: *The Beautyful Ones* was first published in 1968, ten years *after* Ghana's acquisition of political independence. What Fanon had posed as a potential threat is taken by Armah unambiguously to have come true. And even more than this is involved for Armah: for what Fanon had spoken of as "national consciousness," the ideology of a small, if powerful elite within the wider society, seems to Armah in the years since independence to have imprinted itself upon the society at large.

In *The Beautyful Ones,* Armah offers us a picture of this dominant ideology at work. His chief device in this presentation is the literary construct of the gleam. The reader is introduced to the gleam near the beginning of the novel. As [the protagonist] "the man" walks to work in the early morning, the dark shape of Yensua Hill is beginning to be visible against the background of the dawn sky:

> On top of the hill, commanding it just as it commanded the scene below, its sheer, flat, multistoried side an insulting white in the concentrated gleam of the hotel's spotlights, towered the useless structure of the Atlantic-Caprice. Sometimes it seemed as if the huge building had been put there for a purpose, like that of attracting to itself all the massive anger of people in pain. But then, if there were any angry ones at all these days, they were most certainly feeling the loneliness of mourners at a festival of crazy joy. Perhaps then the purpose of this white thing was to draw onto itself the love of a people hungry for just something such as this. The gleam, in moments of honesty, had a power to produce a disturbing ambiguity within. It would be good to say that the gleam never did attract. It would be good, but it would be far from the truth. And something terrible was happening as time went on. It was getting harder and harder to tell whether the gleam repelled more than it attracted, attracted more than it repelled, or just did both at once in one disgustingly confused feeling all the time these heavy days.

The Atlantic-Caprice is a tourist hotel and the venue of elaborate social functions attended by all of the local "big men." The hotel's gleaming spotlights speak of success, and thoughts of success consume the waking minds and haunt the sleeping thoughts of almost everybody in *The Beautyful Ones.* People are attracted to the gleam because of its brilliance. Its sparkle seems to promise splendor, power, prestige, and luxury. Within the massively deprived universe of the novel, such a promise is not lightly to be ignored. The fact that certain individuals have managed to "arrive" at the gleam serves to strengthen the belief of the thousands aspiring toward it, the belief that their desires are capable of fulfillment. The power of the gleam is such that every human action is judged less in terms of its social utility or even its legality than in terms of its efficiency. The sole criterion of judgment is whether or not the action in question has propelled its instigator closer to riches or ease. The society has become fetishistic in its obsession with ostentation and gratuitous consumption and in its eschewal of all principles except those related to materialism and accumulation.

What is at issue here is not simply "false" consciousness. Armah's account is sharpened by his stress upon the scarcity of commodities. In the universe of the novel, the passion with which commodities such as television sets or long-grained rice are sought is inversely proportional to their availability. The entire society has internalized the imperatives of the gleam, and yet a life of luxury is well out of reach of all but an infinitesimal fraction of the whole population.

It follows naturally from the social obsession with the gleam and the near impossibility of its ever being reached that "alternative" methods of approaching it are everywhere attempted. One discovers very early in the novel that corruption is so rampant as to be positively *conventional*. Fraud is so prevalent that it is not only resignedly accepted as a "fact of life" but actively endorsed as a way to "get ahead." The all-consuming but invariably fruitless and self-torturing quest after the luxuries that only the gleam can bring is such as to transform the end of reaching it into a matter of far greater significance within the public consciousness than the mere means of doing so. The gleam is regarded as a stage or condition to be sought and gained at any cost. Qualitative distinctions between means and ends are first blurred, then eroded, and finally come to be envisaged only as hindrances to success, rationalizations of failure, the trademarks of cowards and fools. (pp. 147-50)

Strictly speaking, there are only two ways of living against the gleam. The first of these is to concede the central province of reality to it and to retreat into marginality. In the novel this is the strategy that Teacher, Maanan, and Rama Krishna all adopt, each in his or her own particular way. The second way of living against the gleam is to refuse to accept its domination of social reality, to campaign against it on its own purloined ground, to set oneself to conquer it by living affirmatively in the face of its negatory imperatives. This is the strategy that is adopted by "the man" and that is ultimately endorsed in *The Beautyful Ones.*

The idea of fleeing from the degraded world is demonstrated, in the novel, to be both futile and self-destructive. This is the case irrespective of where the soul in flight is attempting to flee toward: whether it be toward asociality (as with Teacher), madness (Maanan), or spirituality (Rama Krishna). (p. 162)

The most important advocate of flight from the gleam in the novel is unquestionably Teacher. Accordingly, it is in the implicit comparison between his existential strategy and "the man"'s that the novel's debate about different ways of opposing the gleam is most rigorously posed. At first sight it might appear that of the two blueprints Teacher's is by far the more satisfactory and effective. After all, he is possessed of a degree of intellectual certainty about the validity of his own position and stance, whereas "the man" is constantly racked by doubt and insecurity about the morality of his. Furthermore, however inauthentic his freedom might be, Teacher is free whereas "the man," wage slave and family member, is not. And third, although both he and "the man" suffer the depredations of acute loneliness, at least Teacher has chosen his life-style of aloofness and asociality; "the man" is more acted upon than actor in this regard, being ostracized by a society at large that regards his integrity as antisocial and even, possibly, subversive.

Some commentators have, indeed, suggested that Teacher serves as a foil for Armah's own opinions in the novel. Kofi Yankson, for instance, has argued that the novel's central inference is that escape, not combat, is the only practical means of living against the gleam. But a careful examination of *The Beautyful Ones* is enough to dispel this impression that it is Teacher's policy of self-imposed internal exile rather than "the man"'s strategy of resolute struggle with the here and now that is ultimately vindicated in the novel. (pp. 163-64)

Teacher's flight from the world is the indirect consequence of his commitment to Nkrumahism. The extent of his present anomie is inversely proportional to the intensity of his past allegiance. [Too] much of Teacher had been caught up in Nkrumahism to enable him to recover from the disillusion which attended its collapse. Nkrumah's "betrayal" of the African revolution became in Teacher's eyes much more than a contingent failure or act of treachery. The bitterness of the experience now makes it impossible for him to see in Nkrumah's career anything less than an eternal African sequence of hope, betrayal, and despair.

Teacher's alienation is comprehensive. All meaning and purpose have been drained from his existence, and the universe seems to him bound by the irresistible natural cycles of birth and decay, life and decomposition. Even the social process is now cast in his eyes as entropic. Hope gives way inevitably to disillusion, and disillusion is made all the harder to bear by the lingering memory of the hope in whose ashes it has arisen. For teacher there is no lasting hope to be found anywhere. He adopts this conviction as though it were an incontrovertible metaphysical principle: "It is not a choice between life and death, but what kind of death we can bear, in the end. Have you not seen there is no salvation anywhere?"

Applying this dissipative philosophy to social reality, Teacher concludes that although situations inspiring hope might arise in the world, the hope thus aroused would best not be trusted, being transient in its very nature and containing its endings and the threat of its decay in its beginnings and its first, embryonic promises of things to come:

> The man remembered times when Teacher had talked with eagerness about hopeful things, but then always there was the ending, when he would deliberately ask whether the rot and weakness were not after all the eternal curse of Africa itself, against which people could do nothing that would last. Sometimes this death of hope would spread all over the world. When Teacher had talked of people standing up and deciding then and there to do what ages and millions had called impossible, had talked of the Chinese Mao and the Cuban Castro struggling in the face of all reasonable hope, even then Teacher's mind would look beyond the clear awakening and see after the dawn the bright morning and the noonday, the afternoon, dusk, and then another night of darkness and fatigue. Once he had asked whether it was true that we were merely asleep, and not just dead, never to aspire anymore. So even after the big movements he hopes for, the question always remains with Teacher; is it all worthwhile, then? And he sighs from long habit, reproaching himself for wishing after impossible dreams.

In Teacher's eyes, there is nothing in social reality upon which to ground a public morality. Time passes; whisperings swell into movements, into mass activity, and then subside, decay, and dissolve: "So much time has gone by, and still there is no sweetness here." Such changes as do occur appear to be synchronized by an inexorable logic forever beyond the control of human action, a logic which stamps its processes of life and death upon natural and social realms alike. Teacher is often moved to talk

> of the cycle of life and death, youth and age, newness and decay, of the good food we eat and the smelly shit it turns into with time. . . . this was the way with all of life. . . . there was nothing anywhere that could keep the promise and the fragrance of its youth forever. . . . everything grows old. . . . the teeth that once were white would certainly grow to be encrusted with green and yellow muck, and then drop off leaving a mouth wholly impotent, strong only with rot, decay, putrescence, with the smell of approaching death. Yet out of the decay and the dung there is always a new flowering. Perhaps it helps to know that. Perhaps it clears the suffering brain, though down in the heart and within the guts below, the ache and the sinking fear are never soothed.

Teacher's metaphysical outlook on events is not to be confused with cowardice, as [Kolawole] Ogungbesan seems to have imagined ("Symbol and Meaning") [see Further Reading]. Nor is his inactivity to be regarded as the outcome of an overintellectualization of the problems of commitment. His is a post- and not a pre-commitment mentality. His inactivity derives from his conviction (which in turn derives from his own experience) that political action is futile and that all hope is doomed to betrayal. Logically speaking, as he well appreciates, despair entails hope, and hope constantly speaks of renewal. But he is resolved never again to heed the inspirational voice of hope: "I will not be entranced by the voice, even if it should swell as it did in the days of hope. I will not be entranced, since I have seen the destruction of the promises it made. But I shall not resist it either. I will be like a cork."

Teacher understands that this resolution condemns him endlessly to a life of emptiness. Perpetually on the run from the gleam, he is incapable of raising his hand to assist those combating it and dreaming of the construction of a new order, however far in the future this might be. He knows that in one sense he is as dead as the loved ones trying to welcome him into a different type of death. He has chosen one type of death, they another. In a world in limbo he expends all of his energy fleeing the touch of other dead beings. He has no beliefs, and if he is still left with desires, they are useless, since he will not allow them conscious expression. He has his freedom, but it is a freedom whose exercise is indistinguishable from its nonexercise:

> It makes no difference. If we can't consume ourselves for something we believe in, freedom makes no difference at all. You see, I am free to do what I want, but there is nothing happening now that I want to join. There used to be something, and you know what I mean. . . . I don't feel any hope in me any more. I can see things, but I don't feel much. When you can see the end of things even in their beginnings, there's no more hope, unless you want to pretend, or forget, or get drunk or something. No. I also am one of the dead people, the walking dead. A ghost. I died long ago, so long ago that not even the old libations of living blood will make me live again.

By contrast with Teacher, "the man" is unfree. But, also by contrast with Teacher, he chooses life rather than a form of living death as his personal stance. The quality of this "life," as one might have expected from Armah's description of the debased environment within which it is conducted, is impoverished in the extreme. "The man"'s domestic and material circumstances are squalid and miserable. Furthermore, they appear highly unlikely to improve significantly during his own lifetime. Yet within the context of these demeaning circumstances, "the man" manages to invest his struggle for bare existence with great dignity and to wrench from this struggle a note of hope for the future. (pp. 164-67)

Besides his moral perspicacity and social integrity, "the man"'s cardinal virtue consists in his self-discipline. His is not an easy existence. It is one that, if it is to be borne long and in sanity, requires a levelheaded abandonment of false optimism. The world must be taken and grappled with as it is found. It will not help to pretend that its transformation is imminent if it is not, for such a pretence can only lead to subsequent disillusion. Individuals are obliged to live their lives from day to day, not from revolutionary conjuncture to revolutionary conjuncture. "The man" realizes this. He moves toward the realization, too, that with social revolution seemingly not a viable proposition for the time being, progress has to be assessed negatively, in terms of resistance to the hegemonic order, rather than positively, in terms of the construction of a new one. It is only at the end of the novel that he learns to rest content with his existential stance in the face of the appalling near-certainty that his generation will not live to celebrate the birth of the "beautiful ones." Up until this point in the novel, "the man" can find no means of defending his own convictions against the charge that it is ultimately absurd or, worse, perverse to uphold a principle or set of principles whose immediate social relevance is nil and whose direct usefulness to posterity is at best massively problematical.

"The man" has to learn to accept that none of the victories that he might be capable of forging from everyday life can possibly be world historical ones. Many of these victories, indeed, will not even seem to be victories at all. To the mind anxious for results and for clear indications that its judgments have been sound, this knowledge, that all that can be expected from the present is that it will not foreclose every single one of the future's progressive options, is difficult to bear. For in such a context success is unheralded and carries with it no banners of glory. "The man" struggles toward an awareness that his strategy for living is justified, even though it might never be hailed as such. The understanding that he might well die without ever seeing so much as a single brick laid toward the concretization of his dreams calls upon "the man" to exercise tremendous self-control in sustaining himself upon his course of action. Sometimes it seems to him that his tenacity in refusing to contemplate fraud in a world in which success is only ever achieved through corruption, is stubborn and selfish. His resistance of corruption exhausts him. The utmost vigilance is needed merely to keep the gleam at bay, and so much strength is sapped in each encounter with it that nothing remains with which to begin the task of reconstruction. (pp. 167-68)

All of "the man"'s victories, hence, are small (imperceptible, in fact, from any macrosociological viewpoint) and desperately hard in the earning. They are nevertheless indisputably victories, and in a novel in which every other strategy for resistance is shown to result in a form of living death, "the man"'s small triumphs against the forces of degradation stacked against him are sufficient to occasion the reader's great admiration. In his unquenchable determination to make his life yield a positive meaning and purpose, "the man" approaches heroic stature. His denial of the gleam is creative, for it leaves the way open for the "beautiful ones" of the novel's title. Theirs will be the future, and theirs also must be the task of revolution, for the hands of the present generation are tied by the constraining ropes of social and personal possibility. "The man"'s life may well continue to be harsh and excruciatingly painful, but it will possess none of the inauthenticity that characterizes Teacher's. As such, it would seem to be vindicated where Teacher's is not, for while Teacher's strategy of escape leaves him feeling forever marginalized, "the man" discovers that his policy of dogged refusal offers

him moments—no matter how qualified—of happiness. (p. 169)

Neil Lazarus, "Pessimism of the Intellect, Optimism of the Will: A Reading of Ayi Kwei Armah's The Beautiful Ones Are Not Yet Born," in Research in African Literatures, *Vol. 18, No. 2, Summer, 1987, pp. 137-75.*

Derek Wright (essay date 1989)

[*In the following excerpt from his 1989 study* Ayi Kwei Armah's Africa: The Sources of His Fiction, *Wright, an expert on Armah's life and works, surveys the author's writing since the publication of* The Healers.]

The essays that have trickled in a steady stream from Armah's pen since the publication of *The Healers* have pushed deeper into the polemics of the histories but in pursuit, principally, of their practical dimensions and potential for creative action. The mechanics of mental decolonization and the subsequent possibilities for the reindigenization of African cultural and political life are investigated in the specific areas of historical scholarship, language, publishing, translation, nomenclature, and political ideology, each of which has to be rescued from a disfiguring dependency upon Western concepts and controls.

"Dakar Hieroglyphs" applauds the "rehabilitation of African humanity in the context of world history" represented by the late Cheikh Anta Diop's development of palaeographic studies at the University of Dakar. Long frustrated by the neocolonial sycophancy of the pro-French Senghor regime, this endeavour has at last succeeded in providing for African scholars direct access to Egyptian hieroglyphic texts, without mediation by or interference from Western interpretation, and is pushing the academic study of the African past far beyond a few grudging Western concessions to oral history and the achievements of medieval Sudanic kingdoms. Armah's group of essays devoted to the problem of language calls for the linguistic reunification of the African continent through the *lingua franca* of Kiswahili—a concern shared by other African writers such as Soyinka—and itemizes the possible immediate gains. Firstly, according to **"Our Language Problem"**, African writers working in their native microlanguages would also have a common African language in which to make their work available to other Africans (as Soviet ethnic groups have Russian), which need is not fulfilled by the continuing hegemony of the colonial language: "The vitality of individual ethnic and national languages depends on their organised connection to a central language that serves as an international universe. Unless organised around such a linguistic centre of their own, they invariably face an unpleasant choice: to be sucked into the orbit of some potent alien language, or to die." Secondly, argues **"The Oxygen of Translation"**, a common language would serve as the medium through which the world's entire intellectual and scientific knowledge might be transmitted to Africa's educational institutions and communications media and, conversely, from which the intellectual products of Africa's scientists, philosophers and artists might be translated into the world's major languages. Thirdly, runs the argument of **"Africa and the Francophone Dream"**, an African *lingua franca* would at least be a positive alternative to propping up declining colonial languages such as French, which now depends largely upon Africa for the maintenance of its international status and which, now that its hegemony is threatened, ironically looks to francophone African elites to help it resist the precise fate—a subordination tantamount to suppression—which the French themselves have imposed on all African languages in their own colonial *espace*. Taking up a point made in passing by **"The Oxygen of Translation"**, the essay **"Writers as Professionals"** calls upon African authors, businessmen, publishers and distributors to form a continental cooperative for the establishment of an entirely independent African publishing industry, devoted to the marketing of books, regular journals and literary translations produced by Africans (Armah, who must himself command at least four languages and who is currently adding Russian and Ancient Egyptian to his store, has strong feelings about the importance of translation and traces the traditional hostility towards it in university English departments to ethnocentric prejudices which prevent a properly broadminded approach to world literature). Only a strong independent organization of this kind would be able to break the stranglehold of those multinational European and American publishing outfits which profit from the absence or fragility of indigenous publishing enterprises whilst refusing "to make the sort of investment necessary to left African writing to professional plateaux of viability and performance" since the process of indigenization that normally follows from professionalization would drive them out of business. In **"The Third World Hoax"** the derogatory appellation "Third World", interiorized by Africans who still lazily depend upon European definitions of their own realities, is seen as another fraudulent and obsolete Western export which its originators have long ceased to have any use for: in this case, a variant on the term "Third Estate", revived from the junkyard of European history. The African intellectual is exhorted to commence his own healing cure by breaking his addiction to "obsolete machinery, mildewed theories, unworkable development plans, structural adjustment programmes . . . shoddy goods and rotten ideas" dumped upon Africa by Europe. **"The View from PEN International"** and **"The Lazy School of Literary Criticism"** fire off shafts at two latterday and diehard practitioners of "Larsony" [in reference to Armah's disagreements with critic Charles Larson], Per Wästberg of the PEN presidency and an English research student chasing occult Faulknerian connections with Armah's work; both of whom persist in bygone colonial assumptions about African history and literature which reduce Africa to an historical and cultural zero, and neither of whom, ludicrously unaware as they are of the present state of research in these subjects,

deserve the intelligent refutation with which Armah compliments them. **"One Writer's Education"** corrects some mistaken impressions concerning the writer's educational career, provides some valuable insights into both this and the breakdown that led to his American hospitalization, and insists upon the irrelevance to the African writer of concepts of creativity which do not incorporate the changing of Africa's social and political realities.

The most substantial of this batch of writings is, however, the long article, **"Masks and Marx: The Marxist Ethos vis-á-vis African Revolutionary Theory and Praxis."** Armah is concerned here to rescue the universal occurrences of revolution and communism, and of systematic thinking about them, from those Marxist monopolies which have recently become a significant variant on Western intellectual proprietorship in African ideological circles. His argument is that Marxism is, demonstrably, as colonial-imperialist, assimilationist-Eurocentric, and racist-evolutionist as its capitalist counterpart, and is equally unhistorical in its thinking about non-Western peoples and its unexamined assumption that the world and civilization are coterminous with the West. One by one, Marxist myths are stripped of their mystifying jargon and universalist pretensions by their subjection to the scrutiny of "Third World" revolutionary theory and practice. (pp. 265-68)

These essays, like the conclusions to the two historical novels, issue calls to action, make positive probes towards an alternative vision of Africa's future, and are written in a dauntless, determinedly optimistic mood. The polemic is resolutely forward looking and when the past is called to the aid of the argument, as in the restatement of the ancient professional pedigrees of oral literature and translation in Africa, its use is constructive, not consolatory: 'for our purpose, knowledge of our past is a springboard, not a mattress to doze on". To a hopeful long-term view is added the recommendation of immediate action. Linguistic unity, though frustrated by events in the present, "is both immediately sensible and ultimately achievable" and writers, though unable to accomplish the task alone, may begin by making "a concerted effort to bring the principle down to earth" and setting themselves to "examine the most promising attempts now being made to find exits from the language trap". Once a possible other case of the future has been established and a radical alternative to the present imaginatively entertained, the possibilities are boundless:

> If at some point in the near or distant future Africans became sufficiently conscious of our own interests to intelligently organise the immense cultural and linguistic resources we do have . . . that one African *lingua franca* would become a potent instrument of cultural advancement, a trunk language ensuring simultaneous, permanent contact with roots and a confident flowering into the great wide universe.

This buoyancy is, however, earthed by a hard-headed realism as regards the probabilities of short-term success. All of this "presupposes a new generation of

African decision-makers . . . no longer willing to have the continent's people, languages and culture serve as cannon fodder in wars between rival imperialists", and always, compared to the alternative of drifting along with a neocolonical tide of ready-made, second-hand ideas, "the liberatory option is unattractively hard." Armah's appeal is to the Africans themselves and his target, as always, is the Westernized elite:

> Marx has become a functional, philosophical, ancestral mentor-surrogate for intellectuals either ignorant of, or simply deprived of, their own philosophical lineages—they are intellectual orphans. The non-Western world in these neo-colonial times is a breeding ground of young intellectuals who never had their own ideational family trees revealed to them . . . The majority of non-Western intellectuals educated in colonial or neo-colonial institutions are trained to be ignorant of their own philosophical antecedents while struggling to assimilate data, theories and father-figures from the Western arsenal . . . As for those who do, in fact, have their own lineages but have been trained not to recognize them, some will cling with combative desperation to the *ersatz* fathers they have found, thinking them even better than the real ones they might have had. But the most intelligent will keep searching for the truth until they find their lost ancestors and selves.

Thus it seems that Armah's faith in Africa's future, restated with uncompromising integrity and a wry humour that has mellowed over the years, is still placed principally in a few superior specimens of the intelligentsia and their kindred spirits and potential followers among the masses: "One lucky fact remains: most Africans do not refer to themselves as Third World people. Only certain African intellectuals do". It is up to the enlightened few to rally together—"If we are to be the antenna probing the way to the future unity, we ourselves will have to bring our minds together first"— and to persuade and convince the rest of their class. Armah does not waste time blaming Europeans for dumping third-rate goods, ideas and definitions upon Africa, for the real question to be answered is why Africans themselves are so receptive, indeed addicted, to these things and therefore deserving of the contempt implied by the intellectual lassitude of the West in its recourse to Third World identity tags. Similarly, the good or ill will of foreign publishers towards Africa is irrelevant since the kind of commitment that can short-circuit them can come only from within the culture itself: "As long as major African writers are happy to depend on Western publishers or their local placemen, we shall remain blocked at pre-professional levels", and it makes no sense for such writers to "attach African politicians for their chronic dependence on foreign patrons" whilst remaining "heroically mute about our own dependence on publishers in those same imperial centres". Armah's appeal to African intellectual elites— writers, scholars, businessmen and politicians—is consistently coupled with the sceptical fear that this hand-picked group has so deeply internalized Western habits of thought that it will not be able to respond to the call: "Meanwhile it is clear that the French authorities have picked the right elite to promote *la francophonie* . . .

African leaders eager to sacrifice the development of a viable African language to the development of *anglophonie, francophonie* or any other *phonie* . . ." The emancipation of African publishing houses "will have to wait until our rulers and businessmen are hit by a near-fatal attack of intelligence". On the broader issue of mental and moral decolonization Armah entertains no illusions about the difficulties of the task ahead:

> Against the minority of the African elite with enough intelligence and initiative to seek re-Africanization, the barriers are formidable. Among the strongest intellectual barriers is the Manichaean stigmatization of African values. It is impossible for anyone, African or foreigner, to co-operate harmoniously with Africans if that person has been trained to think of Africans as primitive, savage, barbarous or what have you—in other words, if culturally the person is a Westerner.

This, as Cabral argues, is the fundamental problem and source of all others, and must be returned to and resolved before the others can be confronted.

Armah's recent essays have explored the practical implications of the polemics contained in the last two novels but have suggested no new areas of artistic development and, since **The Healers,** he has published only one minor piece of fiction. This is the short story **"Halfway to Nirvana"**, a poignant satire on the lives of United Nations conferees who spend their lives wining and dining on Africa's catastrophic drought and hunger. Its ironic hero, Christian Mohamed Tumbo (the ecumenical symmetry of his name suggests the degree of foreign incursion), graduates from the life of a starving schoolteacher, via a Swedish foundation and "Anti-Drought Organization", to the earthly "Nirvana" of the UN system: "European salaries diplomatic status tax exemption duty free goodies travel galore clean paperwork cool hotels, per diems in dollars." Tumbo fatalistically accepts that "drought and floods have been part of Africa's history for thousands of years" and announces with cynical frankness that "it will be a sad day for some of us when this catastrophic drought is over. Fortunately . . . it will go on. And on." Finally, at one of the conferences which he regularly sleeps through, Tumbo's cynicism catches both himself and his colleagues out. At the point where delegates are theorizing about "the implementational modalities for achieving the objective of the total eradication of poverty and injustice in Africa by, at the latest, the year plus 4000", he embarrasses the whole conference with what is most likely an expression of its own unstated feeling by crying out in his drunken sleep "Vive la Sécheresse!", thus carrying to its logical conclusion what he has earlier referred to as "the technique of the griot"—the adoption of "a bantering attitude to truths others prefer to bury under taciturn official masks". Western aid-systems, the tale alleges, suck into their orbit mainly opportunists and frustrated careerists who have nowhere to go except deeper into mindless hedonism or cynical self-loathing. **"Halfway to Nirvana"** is biting, and sometimes bitter, satire, reverting to the tone of the early novels and demonstrating that Armah has lost none of his sureness of touch. (pp. 272-76)

> *Derek Wright, "Current Work and Conclusion," in his* Ayi Kwei Armah's Africa: The Sources of His Fiction, *Hans Zell Publishers, 1989, pp. 265-84.*

FURTHER READING

Aidoo, Christina Ama Ata. Introduction to *The Beautyful Ones Are Not Yet Born,* by Ayi Kwei Armah, pp. vii-xii. New York: Collier Books, 1969.
   Historical interpretation of Armah's portrayal of Ghana.

Bishop, Rand. "The Beautiful Ones Are Born: Armah's First Five Novels." *World Literature Written in English* 21, No. 3 (Autumn 1982): 531-37.
   Reviews Robert Fraser's book on Armah's oeuvre (see below).

Fraser, Robert. *The Novels of Ayi Kwei Armah: A Study in Polemical Fiction.* London: Heinemann, 1980, 113 p.
   First extensive study of Armah's five novels.

Gakwandi, Shatto Arthur. "Freedom As Nightmare: Armah's *The Beautyful Ones Are Not Yet Born* and Duodu's *The Gab Boys.*" In his *The Novel and Contemporary Experience in Africa,* pp. 87-109. London: Heinemann, 1977.
   Analyzes *The Beautyful Ones Are Not Yet Born* as a portrayal of the horrors of independence in Africa.

Lazarus, Neil. *Resistance in Postcolonial African Fiction.* New Haven: Yale University Press, 1990, 262 p.
   Examines trends in African fiction since the colonial era, viewing Armah's work as a prototype.

Nama, Charles. "Ayi Kwei Armah's Utopian World." *World Literature Written in English* 28, No. 1 (Spring 1988): 25-35.
   Describes *The Healers* as a traditional Ashanti epic, proposing that Armah uses African traditions of the historical novel and epic to portray the "classical age of African greatness."

Ogbang, P. Mego. "Reflections on 'Language, Vision and the Black Writer'." *Black World* XXII, No. 2 (December 1972): 40-7.
   Praises a passage from *Fragments* for its commentary on African society and values.

Ogungbesan, Kolawole. "Symbol and Meaning in *The Beautyful Ones Are Not Yet Born.*" *African Literature Today* 7 (1975): 93-110.
   Examines symbolism in *The Beautyful Ones Are Not Yet Born.*

Palmer, Eustace. "Ayi Kwei Armah: *The Beautyful Ones Are Not Yet Born.*" In his *An Introduction to the African Novel,* pp. 129-42. London: Heinemann, 1972.
   Analyzes *The Beautyful Ones Are Not Yet Born* as an example of the "decolonization" of African literature.

Priebe, Richard. "Demonic Imagery and the Apocalyptic Vision in the Novels of Ayi Kwei Armah." *Yale French Studies,* No. 53 (1976): 102-36.
   Examines Armah's first three novels in light of a definition of myth in which a hero ventures to an area of supernatural wonder and returns home victorious.

Sale, J. Kirk. "The Man in the Middle." *The New York Times Book Review* (22 September 1968): 34.
   Early laudatory review of *The Beautyful Ones Are Not Yet Born,* attesting to the universality of the novel despite its distinctly Ghanaian traits.

Review of *The Beautyful Ones Are Not Yet Born,* by Ayi Kwei Armah. *The Times Literary Supplement,* No. 3500 (27 March 1969): 333.
   Profiles the preponderance of olfactory imagery in Armah's first novel, noting, "It would be impossible for someone who had never possessed the sense of smell to understand *The Beautyful Ones Are Not Yet Born.*"

Tucker, Martin. "Tragedy of a Been-to." *The New Republic* 162, No. 5 (31 January 1970): 24, 26.
   Reluctantly praises *Fragments,* concluding, "I think the novel fails of its promise—for the first novel promised more than fragments. It still succeeds as a tone poem of powerful allegorical force."

Wright, Derek. "Saviours and Survivors: The Disappearing Community in the Novels of Ayi Kwei Armah." *Ufahamu* XIV, No. 2 (1985): 134-56.
   Examines the nature of "community" in Armah's first three novels.

———. "Requiems for Revolutions: Race-Sex Archetypes in Two African Novels." *Modern Fiction Studies* 35, No. 1 (Spring 1989): 55-68.
   Compares race-sex stereotypes and relations in Armah's *Why Are We So Blest?* and Nuruddin Farah's *A Naked Needle.*

William Attaway

1911?-1986

(Full name William Alexander Attaway) American novelist, essayist, short story writer, playwright, screenwriter, and songwriter.

Attaway is remembered chiefly for two novels, *Let Me Breathe Thunder* (1939) and *Blood on the Forge* (1941). Although he continued to write in other genres after the publication of the latter work, he never again achieved much critical success. Most commentators agree that *Blood on the Forge,* which chronicles the experiences of three brothers at a steel mill in Pennsylvania, is the classic portrayal of the Great Migration—the migration of blacks from the agrarian South to the industrialized North in the United States in the period after World War I.

Born in Greenville, Mississippi, Attaway was himself a part of the migration northward. His parents, physician William S. Attaway and schoolteacher Florence Parry Attaway, moved their family to Chicago when their son was young. As Attaway told *Current Biography* in 1941, his father "did not want his children to grow up under the Southern caste system, so he packed up his family and followed the great migration North." In Chicago, Attaway attended a vocational school, initially planning to become an auto mechanic. Around this time, however, having been introduced to the poetry of Langston Hughes by one of his teachers, he decided to become a writer. Under pressure from his parents, he enrolled at the University of Illinois. He dropped out, however, after his father's death and lived as a hobo for two years. A string of occupations followed—seaman, salesman, and labor organizer—as Attaway pursued a variety of experiences in preparation for the writing career he anticipated for himself. In 1935 Attaway helped write the Federal Writers' Project guide to Illinois and befriended another Mississippi-born black author, Richard Wright, who was also with the project. The same year saw the production of Attaway's drama *Carnival* at the University of Illinois, where he had returned to study.

In 1936 Attaway published his first story, "Tale of the Blackamoor." He also received his B.A. degree and, later in the year, moved to New York City. There he worked at odd jobs and even tried acting with the help of his sister Ruth, an actress. Attaway was performing with the traveling production of Moss Hart and George S. Kaufman's *You Can't Take It With You* when he learned that his first novel, *Let Me Breathe Thunder,* had been accepted for publication. This work, the story of two white hoboes, Ed and Step, and their attachment to a nine-year-old Mexican boy, Hi-Boy, was favorably received by critics. While some early reviewers found it significant that the main characters in the work are white, not black, other commentators noted that Ed and

Step are basically outcasts, possessing a social status generally analogous to that of blacks. Aided by a two-year grant from the Julius Rosenwald Fund, Attaway immediately began work on his next novel, *Blood on the Forge.* This work is about three brothers—Big Mat, Chinatown, and Melody Moss—who leave their lives as Southern sharecroppers to work in a Northern steel mill. But even in the North, which held for them the promise of greater racial equality and better job opportunities, the Moss brothers encounter only pain and tragedy. Although most of the early reviews of *Blood on the Forge* were laudatory, the book was not a commercial success.

It is not known why Attaway stopped writing novels. After *Blood on the Forge,* he wrote songs, books about music, and screenplays. Two works are especially notable: *Calypso Song Book* (1957), a collection of songs, and *Hear America Singing* (1967), a children's history of popular music in America. He also wrote songs for his friend Harry Belafonte, at whose home he was married in 1962. Later, Attaway, his wife, and their two children lived in Barbados for eleven years. According to Samuel B. Garren, in Barbados Attaway fulfilled "a lifelong desire of his to live in a country with a black government, black law enforcement, and black professional people." Attaway's last years were spent in California writing screenplays. He died in June 1986.

While Attaway's two novels were initially well received by critics, author Richard Wright seized the public spotlight with his novel *Native Son* (1940) just before Attaway's second novel was published. Critics have suggested that Wright's work somehow made *Blood on the Forge* less impressive to the reading public, thereby drawing attention away from Attaway at a critical time in his literary development. In an introduction to a 1970 edition of *Blood on the Forge*, Edward Margolies speculated that "Attaway's book may have looked tame to an America preparing for another war and whose reading public had already found its Negro 'spokesman' in the virile Wright." More recently, scholars have reclaimed an important position for Attaway among black American writers. *Blood on the Forge* is studied today as a consummate proletarian novel, as a leading fictional account of the Great Migration, and for its elements of black history and folklore. It remains Attaway's greatest work and, some critics believe, the greatest inter-war depiction of the plight of black American workers.

(For further information about Attaway's life and works, see *Dictionary of Literary Biography*, Vol. 76: *Afro-American Writers, 1940-1955*.)

PRINCIPAL WORKS

Carnival (drama) 1935
"Tale of the Blackamoor" (short story) 1936; published in periodical *Challenge*
Let Me Breathe Thunder (novel) 1939
Blood on the Forge (novel) 1941
"Death of a Rag Doll" (short story) 1947; published in periodical *Tiger's Eye*
Calypso Song Book (songs) 1957
Hear America Singing (nonfiction) 1967

Stanley Young (essay date 1939)

[*In the following review, Young, a playwright and publisher, eagerly commends theme and language in* Let Me Breathe Thunder.]

This first novel [*Let Me Breathe Thunder*] by a 25-year-old Negro quite definitely proves two things: That it is possible for a Negro to write about whites, and that William Attaway has a legitimate reason to face a typewriter in the years to come. His tough and tender story of two young box-car wanderers and their love for a little Mexican waif who rides the reefers with them has

some of the emotional quality and force of the familiar relationship of George and Lennie in *Of Mice And Men*. We see two rootless men faced by hard reality yet still susceptible to dreams and affection.

Ed and Step, the major characters, represent in these times the vast army of drifting young Americans who grab their scenery from the top of a freight and take their emotions from an empty stomach. They are apparently living from day to day and waiting for nothing. They are not professional hoboes given to talk about the "romance of the road." Their single thought is to keep alive, to push on over the next mountain, to pick hops in California, berries in Washington, back-doors in Ohio, until by some miracle they land and take root.

In New Mexico Ed and Step meet Hi-Boy, an inarticulate Mexican kid with dreams in his eyes and a wistful, trusting way that breaks through their casual, tough veneer until the men appoint themselves as road guardians to the boy. It is in no way the average jocker-lamb relationship of the hobo jungle. The kid becomes a kind of domestic symbol to the wanderers and a kind of outlet for their affection and all the tenderness which is missing in their abnormal lives.

No matter what brothel or bar or circumstance Step's primitive urges lead him into, Hi-Boy's reactions to the scene take precedence over everything else. They delight in him when they find he is a crack shot with a rifle; they are paternally concerned when he is ill. He is their cub and they want to keep him happy and rolling in the sun they have not seen. When the rancher at Yakima Valley wants to keep Hi-Boy, the men are torn between their desire for the boy's future and their own need of him, and William Attaway makes their decision seem urgent and humanly important.

All the emotions of the book are direct and primitive, and the bareness of the speech cuts the action to lean and powerful lines. The scenes in Mag's roadhouse, Step's relations with the emotionally starved rancher's daughter, Hi-Boy's moment when he jabs a fork into his hand to prove his courage to Step—these and a dozen other incidents are as jabbing to the nerves as a power-drill. Less ably written the book would only be melodrama and sentimentality, but the characterizations are sure and the dialogue distilled to the point that a poet writing a cablegram could not better.

It is surely true, however, that the understated writing and the hard-boiled characters cloaking their semi-conscious good intentions are ingredients of novels that have become rather familiar of late. Before James Cain or Edward Newhouse or Benjamin Appel or even the early Hemingway, this book would have caused great excitement. It is no particular discredit to William Attaway to say that in his first work he has paralleled the style of his more eminent contemporaries. He has, in many moments of this book, equaled them, and, in the poetic overtones of the writing, occasionally surpassed them. He is an authentic young artist not to be watched tomorrow but now.

Stanley Young, "Tough and Tender," in The New York Times Book Review, *Part 6, June 25, 1939, p. 7.*

Milton Rugoff (essay date 1941)

[*In the following review, Rugoff praises Attaway for the "rich vein of human experience" he brought to the writing of* Blood on the Forge.]

It is inevitable that **Blood on the Forge** should recall the work of Richard Wright—not simply because the author is Negro, but because he writes of the frustration and suffering of his people and does so with crude power and naked intensity. **Blood on the Forge** is a short novel packed with the same sense of the animal terrors of the hunted and the dream of the long oppressed that marked *Uncle Tom's Children*. Mr. Attaway is willing to portray Negro life at its lowest in order to make stunningly clear to what a pass life in a white land has brought his people. But this is implicit and it may well be that some readers will be content to think his book merely violent and sensational.

At the opening the Moss brothers are sharecropping a piece of worked-out Kentucky earth, starving, clinging desperately, with childish faith, to the soil. The three men act as foils for each other: Big Mat, a giant of a man, twisted by a strangled desire to preach; Melody, who turns his troubles into guitar music, and China-town, he of the slant eyes and the lazy joking. In each the thwarted craving for recognition of personality has its strange outlet: Big Mat occasionally flies into insane rages, Melody indulges in wistful-dream games, and Chinatown treasures a gold tooth in his mouth as though it were the window of his soul. Their farm is a Negro *Tobacco Road*—which means that it belongs even lower on the social scale than the demesne of the Lesters, descending, in fact, into a region where the only relief is an iron stoicism or crazy yearnings.

When Big Mat finally rises against the boss and the trio are forced to flee they are lured by strikebreaking agencies to Northern steel mills. If the picture of Negroes-against-the-soil seemed raw and shocking, that in the post-war Pennsylvania steel towns is like something out of a revivalist's damnation-sermon conception of hell—a vision of writhing souls seen through smoke and flame, heightened by glimpses of the debauchery of Sodom and Gomorrah and the smouldering dump heaps of Gehenna.

On the soil the brothers had at least been able to breathe untainted air, grapple with an element, earth, that was capable of giving life; here there are only the monstrous machines disembowelling and consuming the earth, with puny creatures chained to them in a slavery that drained them utterly, that shriveled them until even the green-corn whiskey, the city whores and strike-breakers' extra pay could not slake the thirsts of body and soul.

The Moss brothers sense what is happening to them but cannot understand it. Frantically groping for life, haunted, moreover, by a steel mill superstition that the earth resents their work and in the end will take its toll in flaming flesh and pulverized bone, they lead incredibly hectic lives—brawling, drinking, gambling from bleak dawn to dawn. The climax comes when a catastrophe resulting from neglect by the management precipitates a strike. It is by no means an unusual climax, but the reactions of the three brothers certainly are—particularly that of Big Mat, who gets his big chance to assert his personality, to strike back at white men, when he is made a strikebreaker deputy. He realizes dimly that he is fighting his fellow workers, but greater than his sympathies or even his fear of death is his soul's need to cast off the feeling of his own impotence and nothingness. All other outlets having been cut off, he turns, like Bigger Thomas, to the anti-social, killing blindly.

There are in **Blood on the Forge** flashes of the humour, the lazy good nature, the music, the exuberance of the traditional Negro of fiction, but here these are obviously the mechanisms of defeated, aimless spirits. The keynotes in these lives are spiritual strangulation, social maladjustment, cravings that break out in myth-making dreams or desperate orgies of the senses. Mr. Attaway has a rich vein of human experience to explore, and he has, I think, the equipment to do so. **Blood on the Forge** is only a beginning.

Milton Rugoff, in a review of "Blood on the Forge," in New York Herald Tribune Books, *August 24, 1941, p. 8.*

Drake de Kay (essay date 1941)

[*In the following review of* Blood on the Forge, *de Kay praises Attaway for his skillful and unsentimental portrayal of the Great Migration.*]

During and for several months after the close of the first World War a shortage of man power existed in the Pennsylvania and West Virginia steel industry. Attracted by wages of $4 a day, Southern farm Negroes moved North to enter the steel mills. From the point of view of tenant farmers living in a state of virtual peonage the low wages of the mill workers seemed riches, while there was an additional inducement to desert the land in the expectation of enjoying greater social freedom. The mass migration which drained large sections of the South of its farm labor, causing a new problem for agriculturists, also created a series of problems for Northern employers and labor leaders. At the time the unions were conducting their initial efforts to organize the steel industry on a closed-shop basis and the employers were relying increasingly on Negroes as strike-breakers. Consequently the unions watched this influx with mounting anxiety. Also to be reckoned with was the fear of the white workers that they might eventually be displaced by Negroes willing to accept lower wages and working conditions. These and other aspects of the Southern Negro migration are touched upon in this story of the three Moss brothers—Melody, Chinatown and Big Mat—who abandon their worn-out tenant farm in the red clay hills of Kentucky to work in a West Virginia steel mill. Through the narration of their experience as industrial workers we perceive social and economic issues that are part of the history of an epoch.

Written by a Negro author with notable objectivity, [*Blood on the Forge*] is a starkly realistic story involving social criticism as searching as any to be found in contemporary literature; but Mr. Attaway, though his protagonists are of his own race, has not singled out the Negro as the sole victim of unjust conditions. He shows native white Americans and immigrant Slavs working under the same system of low pay, cruelly long hours and unnecessary hazards to life and limb. Many of these injustices have since been rectified, but that fact does not detract from the story value of a tale which holds one's attention primarily by its realistic characterizations, the vividness and intensity of dramatic moments and its pathos. There is a double theme: the Negro competing with the white man in an abnormal condition of the labor market, and the man of the soil forced to make an adjustment with urban industrial life.

Big Mat, a physical giant with the mentality of a child who has never learned to play, tries to remain faithful to his wife, Hattie, who waits in Kentucky until he shall have earned enough money to send for her. He reads his Bible regularly and saves his pay. His brothers persuade him to attend a dog fight, where he meets Anna, a Mexican girl of the red light district, and yields to the urgings of his physical nature. Like other unmarried steel workers, Melody and Chinatown spend their pay on corn whiskey, dice and women. The greater social freedom for Negroes turns out to be largely delusive, for their chief competitors, the Slavs, hate them, while white Americans and Irish preserve a guarded attitude. When the union organizers appear the black workers are easily brought into the employers' camp, being persuaded that, as the least efficient racial group, their only chance of continuing on the job consists in making the best of present conditions.

Working in the terrific heat of blast furnaces and open hearths while under a complex of moral and emotional tensions, the brothers fall under the spell that ensnares all steel men. But one sees in the attitude of these black men something more—a transference of their mystical worship of earth to that other primal element, fire, yet not without a struggle and a haunting sense of apostasy. Earth will be avenged for man's presumption in converting it into steel.

This novel portraying life in the raw is not for those who shun the unlovely aspects of human nature, who have a distaste for bloodshed and the cruder manifestations of sex. Indeed one of its chief claims to literary distinction consists in the author's refusal to sentimentalize his earthy men and women. The artistic integrity Mr. Attaway evinced in his first book, *Let Me Breathe*

Thunder, is equally evident in the faithful depiction of the primitive approach to life of a social group on whose laborious efforts the whole scheme of modern industrial life is based.

> *Drake de Kay, "The Color Line," in* The New York Times Book Review, *Part 6, August 24, 1941, pp. 18, 20.*

Edward Margolies (essay date 1968)

[*In the following excerpt from his* Native Sons: A Critical Study of Twentieth-Century Negro American Authors, *Margolies, a leading authority on Attaway's life and works, examines the author's novel* Blood on the Forge *and evaluates Attaway's standing among black writers.*]

There persists to this day a widely held belief that the deep South, with its brutal caste system and its savage history of racial atrocities, represents for Negroes an image of steaming hell. Such a view is constantly reinforced by spokesmen for civil rights organizations and activists of various liberal persuasions. It serves their political convenience and humanitarian goals, which is all to the good, but unfortunately it muddles their thinking. For it is grounded on the assumption that people are political and economic entities whose motivations and behavior may be simplistically understood. Since Negroes have been systematically exploited and oppressed in the South, it follows they must hate the South that has persecuted them. There are partial truths here—how else explain the vast northward migrations that have been taking place over the past fifty or so years? But what of the large numbers who have stayed behind? Partial truths are not satisfactory to the artist, for he understands that people often leave the place of their origins not simply out of hatred, but because they want to continue to love their homes. And they carry their love with them to the dismal ghettos of the North and cherish it all the more for their adversity. Jean Toomer, for all his woozy romanticism, persuades because his South represents a heartfelt need, and even racial militants like Richard Wright, may, on occasion, speak lyrically of "down-home" times. They miss especially the soil, the seasons, the sense of community they once knew; they regale one another with stories and fables and legends of family, friends, and relatives they left behind; and they attempt to adapt their older ways to the anarchy of city life. Frequently they return South for visits in order to renew themselves.

Calvin Hernton, in a recent book of essays, describes the mixed feelings of some of these visitors:

> The fact that Negroes are alienated from the broader life of the South and its deeper mysteries does not frequently pull them away, but binds them ever more closely to the bosom of Down-Home. The South is the mother-matrix out of which and in which the Negro's mind has been fashioned; it is at the same time the festering ache in the republic of his heart. This, more than anything else, is why they go back.

Such ambivalence has seldom been expressed with more skill or emotional impact than in William Attaway's *Blood on the Forge* (1941), a narrative describing the first stage of the Negro's journey North from his ancestral home. It recounts the experiences of the three brothers Moss in a steel-mill town in western Pennsylvania after leaving their Kentucky hill-country tenant farm during World War I. In the course of the novel one of the brothers is killed, and as the book closes the two remaining brothers move on to the city, where they hope to acquire new roots.

The novel not only records a critical moment in the Negro's history but expands its significance by reference to some of the larger events of the American experience. It takes into account the looming strife between incipient labor unions and the steel companies, the psychology and culture of east European immigrants as they work alongside Southern Negroes, and the specific work conditions under which they all struggle. But it would be a mistake to regard *Blood on the Forge* as a tract, for Attaway rendered the usual subject matter of the proletarian novel into a work of art. He transcended his materials to describe a strange odyssey of the human spirit—without losing several familiar sociological truths. Indeed, what may puzzle the reader is a certain cold realism combined with what can only be described as fervored romantic pessimism.

The failure of the novel to attain popularity may perhaps be ascribed to this paradoxical achievement. On the face of it, *Blood on the Forge*—even its title—suggests simply another of the interminable working-class novels dealing with the downtrodden and their efforts to succeed to a dignified life. Or perhaps the novel was read as naturalistic fiction, but because it did not quite fit the "uplift" formula of its day, it was ignored and relegated to the dustbin of the ideologically confused. Whatever the reasons, it is clear that neither the "aesthetes" who wanted their art to eschew all sociological comment, nor the "socially committed" who wanted their art to point the way, would have looked favorably on *Blood on the Forge,* since in form and subject matter it seems to lie somewhere in a no man's land. Attaway has ideological axes to grind, but they are honed in peculiarly traditional American accents. He urges the primacy of the life of the soil over the life-denying machine, and projects the American image of men of different nationalities and colors working and living together. For all that, his books may have appeared a little foreign to American readers. Possibly the publication of Richard Wright's more sensational *Native Son* the preceding year had something to do with it. Wright's novel was less polished, but it contained rather startling revelations for white readers unused to racial complexities. The American reading public apparently could take only one Negro at a time. Wright became a "spokesman"; Attaway never published another novel.

Attaway prepared the way for *Blood on the Forge* with *Let Me Breathe Thunder,* a novel he published two years

earlier in 1939. In one sense Attaway is less inhibited in his first book because he is writing primarily about white characters whose point of view would not be readily understood as racial. Yet his protagonists, hobo migrant farm workers, are Negroes under the skin—pariahs, consumed at the same time with wanderlust and the desire to stay put. Their agony is a Negro agony, and their allusions to race problems are more "inside" than Attaway might have cared to admit. They speak on more than one occasion of interracial sex and its conspiratorial acceptance in middle-class communities, of the various kinds of racial prejudice they meet throughout the country—and the fact that only hoboes do not appear to discriminate; of the private humiliations "outsiders" experience in a bourgeois milieu, and above all of their uneasiness in accommodating themselves to the patterns of American life, and their desire not to do so. They are the alienated, the uncommitted, whose discontents may one day be marshaled toward revolution—but not necessarily of the doctrinaire, ideological variety. They do not yet know what they want, but they know what they dislike. Once they are aware of what they seek, they are perhaps capable of changing their world.

Attaway here does not understand his people. His solution, like Toomer's, is a return to the soil. A character named Sampson, who owns orchards and farm lands, has suffered considerably during his life; his wife and sons have died and he lives alone with an adolescent daughter. But his strong sense of identification with the land serves to renew him and give him perspective and emotional balance. Sampson is portrayed most sympathetically, but Attaway cannot make him ring altogether true. And the hoboes whom he asks to stay with him on the land cannot believe in him either; as the novel closes, they leave to try their luck elsewhere. Attaway's inability to make Sampson believable stems as much from anachronism as from failure of craftmanship. The American dream of the independent farmer was outmoded by the Depression years, and Attaway was simply unable to cope with his nostalgia.

The plot of *Let Me Breathe Thunder* is unsophisticated and sometimes Hollywoodishly sentimental. (pp. 47-51)

The novel celebrates the loyalty and decency of men on the move, and the essential virtues of the life of the soil. Attaway's Negro themes, as we have seen, are muted and disguised, which allows him to speak the language of protest without using its rhetoric. In shying away from making his main characters Negroes, Attaway was perhaps fearful of having his novel labeled protest fiction. The two Negro characters who do appear in the novel have no especial "Negro" traits, and although one of them is nearly lynched for the supposed attempted rape of a white girl, scarcely any allusion is made to his race. It appears as if Attaway were bending over backwards to assure his readers that he is not writing "sociology." Such a position is absurd, since any reader would naturally associate lynchings and imaginary sex crimes with race. The novel falters on other counts: the characters rarely spring to life, and their situations vaguely suggest those Steinbeck described two years earlier in *Of Mice and Men.* Yet for all that, the narrative does possess a certain verve, and the prose is economical and clean in the Hemingway manner—objective but replete with undertones of irony and sadness.

In **Blood on the Forge,** the Hemingway style is transformed by Negro tones and rhythms. As the novel traces the deterioration of the Negro peasant under the crush of industrial life, Attaway rings changing images of the natural Southern landscape against the hearths, blast furnaces, and smoking chimneys of the steel-mill town. Implicit in the language is a kind of hell-death-decay imagery. His "green men" glance about them upon their arrival in Allegheny County and remember their former homes, the red clay hills, where "there was growing things everywhere and crab-apple trees bunched—stunted but beautiful." What they see now is an "ugly, smoking hell out of a backwoods preacher's sermon." Later they ask, "Where are the trees? They so far away on the tops of the low mountains that they look like the fringe on a black wear-me-to-a-wake dress held upside down against the sky." Attaway foreshadows the disintegration of black men under these conditions when the brothers, on their first day in the Pennsylvania community, spy a Negro whore approaching them on the street. At first they are attracted, but as she passes alongside, they are nearly overcome by a sickening odor. They are told afterward that one of her breasts is rotting away.

The reduction of the brothers begins almost immediately. Surrounded by rusty iron towers, brick stacks, magnets, traveling cranes, and steam shovels, they appear even to themselves physically diminished in size:

> They had always thought of [Mat, the elder] as big and powerful as a swamp tree. Now, in their eyes, he was getting smaller and smaller. Like spiral worms, all their egos had curled under pressure from the giants around them. Sooner or later it came to all the green men.

Attaway does not, however, confine this effect entirely to Negroes. The other workers in the mills—Irish, Italians, Slovaks, and Ukrainians—in one sense make better adjustments to industrial life. They raise families—for them their children are "growing things"—while the Negroes make no attempt to send home for their wives and children. Yet the white workers fare scarcely better: their children fornicate and commit incest in the weeds outside their homes, and their grown daughters become whores.

Steel, the indestructible symbol of industry, assumes a powerful impersonal force, brutalizing and degrading to the human spirit.

> The fire and flow of metal seemed an eternal act which had grown beyond men's control. It was not to be compared with crops that one man nursed to growth and ate at his own table. The nearness of a farmer to his farm was easily understood. But no man was close to steel. It was shipped across endless

tracks to all the world. On the consignment slips were Chicago, Los Angeles, New York, rails for South America, tin for Africa, tool steel for Europe. This hard metal held up the new world. Some were shortsighted and thought they understood. Steel is born in the flames and sent out to live and grow old. It comes back to the flames and has a new birth. But no man could calculate its beginning or end. It was old as the earth. It would end when the earth ended. It seemed deathless.

But if Attaway deplores the evils of the industrial North, he does not conversely romanticize the virtues of the pastoral South. Unlike Toomer, he savagely portrays the South as being too oppressive for Negroes. In the first part of the novel the three brothers live together (with Hattie, Mat's wife) as tenant farmers in the Kentucky red-clay hills. They are on the verge of starvation and enslaved in debt. Even farming is largely useless because most of the topsoil has been washed away over the course of years. What remains for the brothers is the memory, the idea, the "dream" of the land as it must have been before they and the land were exploited by racist owners. The erosion of the land suggests the erosion of their morale which, in a sense, washes them off the land. The immediate cause of their hasty departure, however, is a beating administered by Mat to a white overseer. In order to escape the inevitable lynch mob, the brothers go North to the steel mills. Circumstances keep Mat from taking Hattie along, and Mat's separation from his wife signals the beginning of the dissolution of their family life.

The Kentucky sequence serves to introduce the major characters, who together suggest a composite Negro folk personality. Melody, who will manage best in the ordeal ahead, is sensitive and poetic. He is so named because of his skill with the guitar and because he is capable of articulating in song the folk life of the peasant. Chinatown is simple, lazy, sensual, and hedonistic. He lives by outward symbols; his greatest source of pride is his gold tooth, because, as he puts it later, it shines and smiles at him. Mat, the dominant figure of the group, is huge, brooding, and sullen. All his life he has suffered insults and humiliation at the hands of whites, but he has managed for the most part to suppress his rage and adopt a glazed expression when he is most hurt. An intensely religious man, Mat reads the Bible constantly to discover the causes of his agony. He believes he is cursed because he was conceived in sin, and that the curse has manifested itself in Hattie's inability to give birth to a child. Six times pregnant, Hattie has "dropped" her baby each time before it was born—and this is the central metaphor that supports Attaway's main theme, for Hattie's infertility corresponds to the infertility of the Southern soil that can no longer give sustenance to Negro life. Hence the brothers seek to sink roots in soil elsewhere. Insofar as they cannot do so, they will diminish and wither.

The second part of the novel relates the journey of the brothers to Pennsylvania—crouched and huddled in a dark boxcar with numerous other Negroes who are being brought North to work in mills.

> Squatted on the straw-spread floor of a boxcar, bunched up like hogs headed for market, riding in the dark for what might have been years, knowing time only as dippers of warm water gulped whenever they were awake, helpless and dropping because they were headed into the unknown and there was no sun, they forgot even that they had eyes in their heads and crawled around in the boxcar, as though it were a solid thing of blackness.

The screech, the rattle, the roar of the train, the fetid air, the smell of urine demoralized the men. "The misery that stemmed from them was a mass experience." Not even Mat could "defend his identity against the pack." Chinatown whimpers, terrified that someone in the dark may try to steal his gold tooth. He tells Melody that "without it I ain't nobody." Nor can Melody play his guitar and sing in the deafening noise. It is as if the train journey has suddenly and shockingly severed them from all connection with the past—a feeling not unlike what their African ancestors must have experienced in the holds of the slave ships. Yet in another sense the boxcar is a kind of womb preparing to disgorge them into a new life.

But the life of the steel mills is even more dehumanizing than the one they have fled. Once the green men overcome their initial bewilderment at the sterile, ugly grayness of the community, they attempt to acclimate themselves. They learn from bunkhouse talk how to survive in their dangerous work. They feel the hostility of the white workers, who fear—with justification—that the Negroes have been transported North in order to weaken the union. They learn above all the drudgery of the mill, the tedium, the immense physical stamina required of steel workers on twelve-hour shifts. Their off hours at first are spent sleeping, but soon they begin to enjoy dice games in the bunkhouses, drinking corn whiskey, "whoring" in Mex Town, and attending dog fights. Even Mat allows himself to be drawn into these frivolities after he learns by letter that Hattie has lost her seventh baby. Melody has meanwhile fallen in love with a fifteen-year-old Mexican-American prostitute, Anna, whose earthy nature is adulterated somewhat by her pathetic longings for dance-hall dresses and high-heeled shoes. When Melody fails to satisfy her at their first encounter, she throws herself at Mat, whose brute strength and courage in a melee at the dog fights had rescued her from physical harm.

In certain respects Mat appears to adjust more easily to the life of a steel worker than his brothers. His physical strength is put to the test, and he proves himself more than equal to it. He wins a grudging respect among his fellow workers, and his self-abasement under the glare of the white man seems to disappear. Yet after breaking with his puritanical, Bible-oriented moorings, Mat will need something more than the knowledge that he can stand up to any white man in order to sustain his emotional balance.

Chinatown, on the other hand, makes the worst adjustment. His gold tooth does not count for much in the gray steel community. Nor can he, in his casual South-ern way, easily withstand the pressures and tensions of the world he has entered. He misses the out-of-doors, the feel of the earth beneath his bare feet, the sun and the warmth. Melody tries to keep the brothers together but is troubled by a sense of loss. He cannot play his guitar and sing as he once did. He is aware of a need for other melodies, other rhythms in his new environment, yet he cannot quite catch them. His impotence with Anna suggests the signal impotence of all three brothers in their new life.

There is a remarkable soliloquy in this section of the novel, delivered by a crippled Negro named Smothers. Smothers has lost the use of his legs in an accident in the mills some years before, but he is retained on the job by the steel company as a watchman. He is regarded tolerantly by his fellow workers despite his obsessive tirades against steel. Smothers is prophetic—a crippled Tiresias announcing the apocalypse if men persist in their materialist pursuits. His harangues restate the view implicit at the start of the novel that the earth gives moral and spiritual sustenance to men, and that its destruction transgresses nature and denies men their potentialities. On one occasion he rises in the bunkhouse to utter the following words:

> It's wrong to tear up the ground and melt it up in the furnace. Ground don't like it. It's the hell-and-devil kind of work. Guy ain't satisfied with usin' the stuff that was put here for him to use—stuff on top of the earth. Now he got to git busy and melt up the ground itself. Ground don't like it, I tells you. Now they'll be folks laugh when I say the ground got feelin'. But I knows what it is I'm talkin' about. All the time I listen real hard and git scared when the iron blast holler to git loose, an' them big redhead blooms screamin' like the very heart o' the earth caught between them rollers. It jest ain't right . . . .

> Can't blame the ground none. It give warnin'. Yessir, they was warnin' give a long time ago. Folks say one night there's somethin' fall right outen the sky, blazin' down, lightin' up this ol' river in the black o' night . . . . A solid hunk o' iron it be, big around as a house, fused together like it been worked by a puddler with a arm size of a hundred-foot crane. Where it come from? Where this furnace in the sky? You don't know. I don't know. But it were a warning to quit meltin' up the ground.

Later in the same section, Attaway describes a dog fight which the brothers attend along with other workers. The event is particularly savage but evidently serves to relieve the spectators of their built-up murderous frustrations. Its effect on Mat, however, is quite the opposite, as he begins to strike out wildly and indiscriminately at the other workers like a starved dog loosed from its leash.

The passage of time brings the further decline of the brothers. Mat has rented a shack and is now living with Anna. He has given up all thoughts of sending for Hattie and has left his Bible behind in the bunkhouse. Melody broods over the loss of Anna and schemes to get her back. He calls on her while Mat is working at the mill. Anna suspects his motives, and her suspicions are confirmed when he announces that he wants to give Mat a letter from Hattie. Anna wrestles with him to take the letter away from him. Exhausted and unsuccessful, she gives up the fight and she and Melody make love. It soon becomes clear that Anna is not happy living with Mat, who does not allow her to go out and show off the sequined dress and high-heeled shoes he bought her with money he had been saving for Hattie. The next day Anna disappears, and when she returns two days later Mat assumes she has been "lying" with someone and beats her savagely. Actually she has been lying on the hills near the big homes of wealthy townspeople, fantasying that she is the mistress of a rich man.

Events move swiftly now. Melody has an accident at the mill which severely damages his guitar-playing hand. Then Mat is arrested in Pittsburgh for attempting to kill a man. Melody drives to Pittsburgh to bail him out, and on the return trip Mat, crushed and defeated, tells him that Anna no longer truly gives herself to him.

The portents of disaster build. Again steel serves as the underlying metaphor to suggest the hellish antilife man has created, and it is again the raving Smothers who calls up the image of a monster that demands human sacrifice. Smothers senses impending death. "Ever'body better be on the lookout. Steel liable to git somebody today. I got a deep feelin' in my bones," he says. The men laugh and Bo, the foreman, promises Smothers, "If it's you...we make you up into watch fobs. The boys round the bunkhouse'll wear you across their vests for luck." Smothers tells the hair-raising story of how he lost his legs in the mill and how afterward, "All the time in the hospital I kin hear that steel talkin'... I kin hear that steel laughin' an' talkin' till it fit to bust my head clean open... I kin hear when cold steel whisper all the time and hot roll steel scream like hell. *It's a sin to melt up the ground....*"

Melody, too, has come to sense steel as a death god. "Suddenly Melody was aware of the warning. He started up. There was great danger. Something screamed it inside him.... Perhaps the monster had gotten tired of an occasional victim. Perhaps he was about to break his chains. He would destroy masses of men, flesh, bones and blood, leaving only names to bury."

And then there is a blinding flash, followed by "a mushroom cloud, streaked with whirling red fire...." Several workers, Smothers included, are killed. Chinatown is blinded.

In a sense each of the brothers has now been rendered impotent: Chinatown, who lives by outward symbols, can no longer see; Melody, who lives through his music, can no longer play the guitar; and Mat has become a hulking shell of a man because Anna no longer loves him. All three brothers go to live with Anna. She no longer sleeps with Mat, but takes care of Chinatown, whose eyes are like "old eggs rotting in their ragged half shells, purple and revolting."

Racial tensions are rising in the town. The union is moving toward a strike and the steel interests are countering by bringing more Negroes in from the South. Negro leaders have been bought off and are directing Negro workers not to join the union. Meanwhile the depleted Mat has taken to walking alone among the hills on the edge of town. On one occasion he is approached by the law and sworn in as a deputy, ostensibly to maintain order but really to help break the forthcoming strike. He views this as an opportunity to redeem his faltering manhood with Anna—and at the same time, unconsciously, to wreak his vengeance on whites.

On the day of the strike, Melody, in order to bolster Chinatown's dashed ego, takes him to a brothel. Inadvertently he discovers Anna has been secretly working there nights, and rushes back to the shack to accuse her—and to beg her to run away with him. Suddenly Mat returns. Overhearing their conversation, he savagely beats Anna into a heap, then shambles back to town and brutally provokes some of the strikers on orders of the sheriff. In the ensuing melee, Mat kills and injures a number of them before he is himself hacked down.

The novel closes on Melody and Chinatown headed for Pittsburgh, where they will begin life anew.

Part of the strength of this final section of the novel lies in Attaway's generally successful fusion of naturalistic and metaphysical elements. The social and economic forces that drive the brothers from the Kentucky hills and divide the steel community in bloody conflict are in themselves crimes against nature. The same pride and greed that destroy the soil manifest themselves again as racial tension and industrial strife. Attaway focuses these perceptions on Mat just prior to his death. Having been rejected by Anna, Mat tries to redeem his ego by identifying himself with steel.

> Big Mat looked at the mills, and the big feelings were lifting him high in the air. He was big as God Almighty....He could have spit and quenched a blast furnace....Smothers had been a liar. Steel couldn't curse a man. Steel couldn't hurt him. He was the riding boss. How could those dead mills touch him? With his strength he could relight their fires or he could let them lie cold.

But like some epic Greek hero, Mat recognizes his *hubris* at the moment of his death, and intuits that his brutality in attacking the workers is just like the brutality to which he himself had been subjected in the South. And he recognizes too that the young Slav who is striking at him with a pickaxe handle is not unlike the Mat who struck out violently at a white man in Kentucky. Like Oedipus, Mat is his own persecutor and victim.

Unfortunately, for Mat (and the Negro by implication) vision comes too late. Attaway contrasts Mat's vision at death to Chinatown's continuing blindness in life. On the train that carries Melody and Chinatown to Pittsburgh, the brothers meet a blind Negro soldier who used to be a steel worker. When Chinatown asks why he left the mills, the soldier explains that he responded to a deep feeling inside him—a sound of guns. He tells Chinatown that he too can hear the guns if he listens carefully. Chinatown strains, and "their noise came over the rumble of the train."

> "Sound like somethin' big an' important that a fella's missin', don't it?" asked the soldier.
>
> Chinatown nodded.
>
> Melody watched the nod. He looked at the two blind men closely. Their heads cocked to one side, listening for sounds that didn't exist. They were twins.

And so the blind lead the blind. Just as the soldier was lured away from home by the nonexistent glory of war, so Melody and his brothers have been seduced from their homes by promises of freedom and security in the North. And thus it would always be for men like Chinatown and the soldier. (pp. 52-61)

Attaway ends his novel on a note of defeat. Yet even in defeat, his protagonists persist—though not very hopefully—in their struggle for survival and identity. The brothers' renewed search for the good life seems doomed from the start. One knows that the entire cycle of hope, passion, and defeat will begin again with such persons as the blind "twins," Chinatown and the soldier—blind because they will continue to be deluded by unattainable dreams and promises.

One wonders, naturally, whether their author was himself as overcome with the hopelessness of his prognosis. Born in Mississippi . . . , the son of a physician, Attaway was himself part of the great migration North. He attended public schools in Chicago and, after an interim as a hobo, he worked at a variety of jobs before returning to the University of Illinois to complete his education. It was in high school, Attaway writes, that he developed an interest in becoming an author. He had always assumed that Negro success was to be won in genteel professions like medicine, but upon first reading Langston Hughes, his outlook was transformed. Prior to the appearance of his two novels, he published little. His first novel, as we have seen, was promising; his second, a classic of its kind. Why then did Attaway stop writing fiction? He was only twenty-nine when **Blood on the Forge** appeared. It is, of course, always hazardous to guess at the motives of a writer, but possibly some clues may be found in the works themselves.

It is first of all clear that Attaway had no intention of writing "race" fiction. He did not want his novels to stop short at "protest," but rather hoped to make some grand metaphysical statement about the conditions of life and human experience, in which, possibly, Negro characters figured. But such a wholly laudable ambition was not, as has already been suggested, something the American reading public was prepared to accept from a Negro author—especially at the outset of World War II, when the great tasks ahead appeared to lie more in action and less in reflection. Attaway may simply have been discouraged at the response to his book—and quit.

Another alternative, however, suggests itself. It is perhaps in the realm of ideas that we may look for the source of Attaway's arrested artistic development. Basically Attaway is a romantic. **Let Me Breathe Thunder,** for all its praise of stable family life and the virtues of farming, ultimately celebrates the free-wheeling bohemianism of hoboes—and Attaway, by manipulating his plot this way and that, manages to free his protagonists from any social and moral obligations. In another romantic vein, **Blood on the Forge** projects the myth of the "good" soil corrupted by man's greed, whose logical absurdity manifests itself in the manufacture of steel. While no one would deny that the excesses of American capitalism have produced cruel and dehumanizing injustices, it is hard, after Darwin, to ascribe moral virtues to nature. And since it is scarcely possible any longer to look to nature as something apart and holy, Attaway may well have written himself out of subject matter.

And yet if one grants Attaway his premises, it is undeniable that he has written a beautiful and moving novel. Nor can one deny that his vision of earth as sanctified remains persistently embedded in the American *mythos*. It is, after all, out of such nostalgia that art is created. (pp. 62-4)

> *Edward Margolies, "Migration: William Attaway and 'Blood on the Forge'," in his* Native Sons: A Critical Study of Twentieth-Century Negro American Authors, *J. B. Lippincott Company, 1968, pp. 47-64.*

Phyllis R. Klotman (essay date 1972)

[*In the following essay, Klotman assesses Attaway's use of "whiteness" in* Blood on the Forge.]

William Attaway's **Blood on the Forge** was reissued in 1969, the same year that saw the renascence of Jean Toomer's *Cane,* as well as the publication of several significant novels by contemporary Afro-American writers, such as Paule Marshall's *The Chosen Place, The Timeless People* and Ishmael Reed's *Yellow Back Radio Broke—Down.* Attaway's important but ignored book about the three Moss brothers, who leave the depleted farmland of Kentucky for the steel mills of Pennsylvania, poignantly but realistically tells the story of one facet of the Great Black Migration during the first World War.

Blood on the Forge was originally published in 1941, only one year after *Native Son,* but Attaway does not deal with whiteness in character and symbol in the same terms that Richard Wright used. Attaway eschews the stereotypical; his white characters, with the exception of the sheriff and "Boss" Johnston, are essentially complex and well-rounded figures. Nor is whiteness his central symbol. The steel mill is. Big Mat, Melody and Chinatown are seduced North by the promise of jobs and decent wages, but are gradually beaten down and stripped of their manhood by the uncompromising and brutal, man-eating monster, the steel mill. Behind the faceless monster is the white power structure, manipulating the lives of white immigrants and black unskilled workers—who are shipped in by cattle car, a disgusting and dehumanizing experience—for the sake of feeding the mill and filling their coffers. The bosses are never seen; their power is felt mainly through their underlings who set white worker against black, deputize strikebreakers, and generally control through fear or famine.

Racism as an omnipotent factor does not exist in the lives of the three brothers after they leave Kentucky. At least for a time. They are accepted by the Slavs, the Irish and the Italians with whom they work in the mill; they drink, gamble and whore together. As a friend, old Zanski warns that they'll never be happy until they send for their families—a man needs children in his home and a wife to put up curtains—he admonishes. In a word, stability. But few black workers move out of the bunkhouse. Their separation from their past—rootedness in the soil, the folk, religion, family—is almost as complete as that of their ancestors who traveled to a new and ugly life in the dark bellies of slave ships instead of airless boxcars. When Mat does finally set up "housekeeping," it is with Anna, the Mexican prostitute, who wants an "Americano" because she is tired of "peons." (Anna suffers from the delusion that all "Americanos" are rich, regardless of color.) The three brothers are systematically unmanned by the dehumanizing process of forging steel. Chinatown is blinded in an accident which eats up the lives of fourteen men; Melody's hand is smashed so that he is no longer able to play his guitar; Big Mat is killed during the strike in which he has become an unwitting tool the bosses wield against the white workers. Earlier his skill and strength earned him the approbation of his fellow workers and the title "Black Irish"; later he comes to be "hated by his fellow workers. He was a threat over their heads. The women covered their faces at the sight of him, the men spat; the children threw rocks. Always within him was that instinctive knowledge that he was being turned to white men's uses. So always with him was a basic distrust of a white. But now he was a boss. He was the law. After all, what did right or wrong matter in the case? Those thrilling new words were too much to resist. He was a boss, a boss over whites."

There is very little about the unionizing process that the black workers, including the Moss brothers, understand or identify with. The backbreaking hazardous work in the mill has been a kind of salvation for them. Having sharecropped all of their lives, always on the verge of starvation, they are neither shocked nor dismayed by the twelve-hour day in the mill. At least they get paid. They have not begun to think about the possibility of better working conditions—an eight-hour day, better wages, unions—a fact that the Northern industrialists well knew and used to their advantage in controlling the "socialist" oriented, organizing aspirations of the white immigrants: "Big Mat was not thinking about the labor trouble. Yet he knew he would not join the union. For a man who had so lately worked from dawn to dark in the fields twelve hours and the long shift were not killing.

For a man who had known no personal liberties even the iron hand of the mills was an advancement."

One of the things that drives the Moss brothers North is the impossibility of paying off a $40 debt to Mr. Johnston, the landowner to whom they are perpetually in debt. Fear of the control the white boss has over their very ability to stay alive is a given with the black sharecropper. It inspires Mat's hate: "Deep inside him was the familiar hatred of the white boss." There are only a few stereotypical characters in *Blood on the Forge.* Mr. Johnston, the Kentucky landowner, is a classic bigot, indigenous to the South, but interestingly enough, he uses the black sharecroppers against the white just as the bosses in the northern mill use the black workers against the immigrants. Johnston explains to Mat why he doesn't have white sharecroppers work his land: "well, they's three reasons: niggers ain't bothered with the itch; they knows how to make it the best way they kin and they don't kick none." They don't "kick" because they have no recourse. If their anger gets out of control, the resultant violence always turns against them. When Mat explodes in anger and fury, killing the mule that killed their mother in the fields, he puts them all in Johnston's debt to the point of starvation. They don't run because they have no place to go, and Johnston thinks he can keep them from getting the "itch" by manipulation and innuendo, an "old Master" tactic, in the plantation tradition: "My ridin' boss tells me there some jacklegs around, lyin' to the niggers about how much work they is up North. Jest you remember how I treat you and don't be took in by no lies."

They don't get taken in by northern lies; they leave because they know southern truths. One of these truths is never to look at or touch a white woman. Melody knows that Mat has "more sense than to talk to a white lady"; Chinatown agrees: "It's dangerous . . . . 'member young Charley from over in the next county got lynched jest cause he stumble into one in the broad daylight." Another of those old-fashioned southern truths is never strike a white man a semi-lethal blow. When the riding boss refuses to give Big Mat the mule Johnston has promised him ("If Mr. Johnston got good sense you won't never git another mule . . . . You'd be run off the land if I had my say. Killin' a animal worth forty dollars, 'cause a nigger woman got dragged over the rocks—"), Mat in a blind rage stikes him down. Realizing that the man will live "to lead the lynch mob against him," Mat and his brothers reluctantly leave the land they have worked so lovingly yet for so little reward.

The white line drawn about their lives in the South is straight, clear, immovable. The Moss brothers are powerless to effect change, to shift that boundary in any direction, but they understand their role in the schema and derive some satisfaction from a sense of belonging to the land. Big Mat is a powerful man who seems to draw strength from the soil's blackness which is like his own. When he goes North he becomes unmoored, confused by the change in the pattern, but he adapts to the work better than his brothers, better even than the whites. What he doesn't understand is that hate can be generated to meet the needs of new situations. When the white workers become politicized enough to strike, more blacks are shipped in, in boxcars, and the brothers remember, identify with those men—"bewildered and afraid in the dark, coming from hate into a new kind of hate." Bo, the only black foreman, knows the pattern—they only send for black men when there's trouble.

Big Mat is a tragic figure, reminiscent of the one slave on every plantation who refused to be whipped by the soul driver, a man of tremendous physical power and courage who could never be submissive. As developed by the early black fictionists, he becomes the black hero or the "bad nigger," feared by everyone. Big Mat has some of these characteristics, but in *Blood on the Forge* he is also an Othello-like figure, proud, jealous, and formidable. And his blackness is played off against a white Iago, a sneaky little boss-sheriff who manipulates him by appealing to his new-found sense of manhood. "Deputize this man," the sheriff says, "assign him his hours. He won't need a club. Just give him a couple of boulders. He'll earn his four dollars Monday." Actually the bosses save the four dollars. Mat destroys and is destroyed, as so many are in the struggle for steel. Most of Attaway's characters—black, white, all shades of ethnic groupings—are handled well. Many have real nuances of complexity, including the two brothers, Chinatown and Melody, who are left derelict at the end; Anna, the grasping but pathetic Mexican girl; Zanski's granddaughter Rosie, a union sympathizer who turns prostitute for the scabs in order to support the starving strikers in her family; and Smothers, the black prophet of doom, who understands that all men will have to pay for ravaging the earth: "*It's a sin to melt up the ground,* is what steel say. *It's a sin.* Steel bound to git ever'body 'cause o' that sin. They say I crazy, but mills gone crazy 'cause men bringin' trainloads of ground in here and meltin' it up."

One of the tragic outcomes in the novel is the loss of continuity in the lives of the men who are almost human sacrifices to the industrial Moloch created by an unseen hand grasping for profits. And that hand is white. If we used to think that free enterprise meant freedom to exploit all the resources of our country—both human and natural—to destroy the land and leave it in waste, we have since been forced to change our minds. There is something very timely in Attaway's implicit warning, as Edward Margolies suggests in his introduction to the 1969 edition of *Blood on the Forge:* "Possibly he [Attaway] saw his worst fears realized in the rapid spread of industrial wastelands and the consequent plight of urban Negroes. From one point of view his feelings about the sanctity of nature now seem almost quaint in an age of cybernetics. Yet given what we are told is the dangerous pollution of our environment, who can tell but that Attaway may not have been right?"

What is most interesting about the "rediscovery" of such novels as *Blood on the Forge* is their contemporaneity. We have now, some twenty-eight years later,

reached the point of no return in our violation of the environment and of each other. Yet we are as unseeing as Chinatown and the soldier at the end of the novel—"blind men facing one another, not knowing." (pp. 459-64)

Phyllis R. Klotman, "An Examination of Whiteness in 'Blood on the Forge'," in CLA Journal, *Vol. XV, No. 4, June, 1972, pp. 459-64.*

James O. Young (essay date 1973)

[*In the following excerpt from his 1973 study* Black Writers of the Thirties; *Young classes and examines* Blood on the Forge *as proletarian fiction.*]

In his eloquent novel, *Blood on the Forge* (1941), William Attaway delved into the history of the black man in America. But, like Richard Wright in his folk history of the migration, instead of dramatizing the exploits of a historic race hero, Attaway looked with the scrutiny of a sociologist at the brutal experience of the mass of blacks who migrated from the agrarian South into the industrial North at the time of the First World War. Like [Arna Bontemps'] *Black Thunder*, Attaway's novel should be classed as proletarian fiction. In fact, the general structure of the novel conformed more closely to the typical proletarian novel than did Bontemps' because the setting was more contemporary and the exploitation of the workers was placed in an industrial environment. But Attaway's book was not the run-of-the-mill, artless formula-novel which was characteristic of so much proletarian fiction. For in addition to portraying the persecution and exploitation of the workers, black and white, Attaway also intelligently dramatized the erosion of the old southern folkways by the immense and impersonal force of the machine.

Blood on the Forge was Attaway's second novel. In 1939, he had published *Let Me Breathe Thunder,* a picaresque novel about two depression era hoboes. Perhaps the most interesting note about this novel is that its principal characters are white. Though in many ways Attaway's first novel is very effective, it relies too heavily on melodrama; his protagonists are just a bit too naïve and sentimental to be believable. Such is not the case with *Blood on the Forge* which ranks as one of the finest novels of the depression era.

Attaway's main characters are three brothers. Chinatown is lazy, hedonistic, and lives by outer symbols—his proudest possession is his golden tooth about which he explains "can't 'ford to lose this tooth." Melody is introspective, intelligent, and sensitive—the music he makes on his guitar is expressive of his personality. And, finally, Big Mat, the oldest brother, is a physical giant who, in hopes of some day receiving a call to preach, reads his Bible every day. Wrote Attaway, "To almost everybody but his close kin he was a stupid, unfeeling giant, a good man to butcher hogs .... Melody alone knew him completely. Melody, from his dream world, could read the wounds in Big Mat's eyes." The essential characteristic of each of the three men will be destroyed by the new machine environment.

All three brothers are tenant farmers in the green hills of Kentucky. They are forced to flee from those hills when Big Mat, pouring out the bitterness of years of humiliation and persecution, thrashes the white riding boss: "The riding boss fell to the ground, blood streaming from his smashed face. He struggled to get to his feet. A heavy foot caught him in the side of the neck. His head hung over his shoulder at an odd angle." Aside from the immediate necessity of escaping white retaliation, their flight has another level of meaning for Attaway. They are leaving the land because it has become infertile. It is worn out, incapable of sustaining the black folk any longer. "The land has jest give up, and I guess it's good for things to come out like this," observes Big Mat as they prepare to leave.

They meet an agent from a northern steel mill who gives them passage to the mill on board a freight car. The blackness of the boxcar is symbolic of a womb out of which they will be reborn into the industrial environment. But it is also a coffin, symbolic of the impending death of the folk consciousness: "Squatted on the straw-spread floor of a boxcar, bunched up like hogs headed for market, riding in the dark for what might have been years, knowing time only as dippers of warm water gulped whenever they were awake, helpless and drooping because they were headed into the unknown and there was no sun, they forgot even that they had eyes in their heads and crawled around in the boxcar, as though it were a solid thing of blackness."

When the new men arrive at the mills, Attaway contrasts them to the men who have already been conditioned to the sterile monotony of the industrial existence: "Everything was too strange for the green men to comprehend. In a daze, they were herded to the mill gates and checked in. The night shift was getting off. They mingled for a few minutes at the mill gates. All of them were gray in the dirty river mist." The idea that the green men will become gray men is skillfully developed by Attaway. He never deviates from the attitude that as bad as the feudalistic southern environment was, it was still alive; it was still characterized by very personal relationships between human beings, not the impersonal, mechanized quality of the northern environment. Social scientists like E. Franklin Frazier, looking toward long-range goals, had optimistically observed the destruction of the old folk culture as a positive development accelerating integration into the mainstream of American society. Attaway had carefully dramatized this process, but without the optimism of the sociologists. His artistic consciousness was much more sensitive to immediate suffering, and it told him that possibly something valuable was being destroyed.

It does not take long for the three brothers to become gray men, stripped of their folk identities by the mills. Melody finds that "the old music was going," and after

an accident to his hand in the mills he ceases to play his guitar altogether. Chinatown is blinded by an explosion in the mills and he is no longer capable of seeing those outward symbols through which he had lived: "Now those symbols were gone, and he was lost." Big Mat, because of his enormous strength, fares best in the competition with the monster machines. But even he succumbs eventually, losing his religion and becoming shamefully impotent—a mere hulk of the virile man he once was.

The last sections of the novel revolve around Mat and his efforts to regain his manhood. There is rising dissatisfaction among the workers at the mills and they decide to strike. Big Mat has no intention of joining the union. And through his attitude the author attempts to explain why black men were successfully employed as strike-breakers for so many years. "Big Mat was not thinking about the labor trouble. Yet he knew that he would not join the union. For a man who had so lately worked from dawn to dark in the fields twelve hours and the long shift were not killing. For a man who had ended each year in debt any wage at all was a wonderful thing. For a man who had known no personal liberties even the iron hand of the mills was an advancement. In his own way he thought these things. As yet he could not see beyond them. Mat is signed up as a company deputy and he regains his manhood through violence. "He had handled people, and they feared him. Their fear had made him whole." But this feeling of manhood is only temporary, it has no strength against feelings or ideas such as those behind the expression "nigger." He can maintain his manhood only through repeated violence.

Attaway reintroduces the proletarian theme within the context of Mat's anti-union violence. He understands Mat's position, but clearly disagrees with it. Mat achieves proletarian consciousness only as he is being beaten to death by one of the union men. He suddenly suspects that he has taken over the role of the riding boss. "Maybe somewhere in these mills a new Mr. Johnson was creating riding bosses," realizes Mat, "making a difference where none existed." Big Mat's sudden, intuitive realization rings perhaps the one false note in Attaway's novel. The attempt to submerge race conflict within the context of class conflict was no more convincing when portrayed dramatically than when it was proclaimed by radical politicians and scholars. (pp. 225-29)

James O. Young, "Black Reality and Beyond," in his Black Writers of the Thirties, *Louisiana State University Press, 1973, pp. 203-35.*

L. Moody Simms, Jr. (essay date 1975)

[In the following excerpt, historian Simms favorably appraises Attaway's portrayal of the black experience in his two novels.]

Undoubtedly, Mississippi's best known native-born black writer is Richard Wright. Wright's reputation, which has grown steadily since the publication of his *Native Son* in 1940, is justly deserved. Yet over the years, Wright's achievement has tended to overshadow and obscure the work of other Mississippi-born black writers. One of them whose work deserves to be better known is William Attaway. His *Blood on the Forge* (1941) is an excellent novel which stands up well when compared with any other fiction dealing with blacks written during the past three decades. (p. 13)

Attaway's first novel, *Let Me Breathe Thunder,* appeared in 1939. It is the tough and tender story of two young box car wanderers and their love for a little Mexican waif. The major characters, Ed and Step, are rootless white men faced by hard, precarious reality, yet still capable of dreaming and caring. They represent the large numbers of young people who drifted about America during the difficult depression years of the 1930's. They live from day to day, waiting for nothing in particular. Ed and Step are not professional hoboes given to pointing out the "romance of the road;" their single object is to stay alive and keep moving. They support themselves through brief stretches of farm work.

During a stop in New Mexico, Ed and Step meet an inarticulate Mexican boy named Hi-boy. His wistful and trusting way soon breaks through their casual, seemingly tough veneer. Ed and Step appoint themselves the boy's guardian and take him on the road as they continue their roaming. Hi-Boy becomes an outlet for their affection and for the tenderness missing from their rootless lives. For Ed and Step, Hi-Boy's welfare comes to take precedence over all else. Quite naturally, when a Yakima Valley rancher wants to take Hi-Boy permanently into his family, Ed and Step are torn between their own need for the boy and their concern for his future.

Attaway's *Let Me Breathe Thunder* has some of the emotional force and quality of the relationship between George and Lennie in John Steinbeck's *Of Mice and Men* (1937). Less ably written, the book would be melodramatic and overly sentimental. But the characterizations are sure, the dialogue is crisp and natural, and careful attention is given to physical detail. All told, *Let Me Breathe Thunder* is a solid first novel and makes the point that a black writer can deal successfully with a work made up primarily of white characters.

Published in 1941, Attaway's second and best novel, *Blood on the Forge,* is set for the most part in an Allegheny Valley steel-mill community during World War One. During and for several months after the end of the war, a manpower shortage existed in the West Virginia and Pennsylvania steel industry. Attracted by wages of four dollars a day, many Southern farm blacks moved north to work in the mills. To these black tenant farmers living in a state of near peonage, the low wages of steel workers seemed like true riches. The prospect of enjoying greater social freedom provided an additional inducement for deserting the land.

This northward migration of blacks looking for a better life in the mill towns created problems for northern employers and labor leaders. At the time, unions were engaged in initial efforts to organize the steel industry on a closed shop basis. When strikes resulted, the employers relied increasingly on black strike breakers. The unions consequently watched the black influx with growing anxiety. Many white workers came to fear that they might be permanently displaced by blacks who were willing to accept lower wages and poorer working conditions.

Set against this background, *Blood on the Forge* is the story of three black brothers—Mat, Chinatown and Melody Moss—who abandon their worn-out tenant farm in Kentucky's red clay hills to work in an Allegheny Valley steel mill. The novel thus has a double theme: blacks competing with whites in an abnormal condition of the labor market and men of the soil attempting to adjust to modern industrial life.

Mat, the eldest brother, at first appears to be making an adjustment to his new environment better than his brothers. Heretofore, he had stoically coped with life through his own understanding of the Bible. In the mill, his tremendous physical strength gains him a respect he had never gotten in the South. But Mat's new-found self-confidence proves to be an illusion. Discarding his Bible, he finds that his virility is not enough to sustain him. It counts for little with Anna, his Mexican mistress, who dreams of becoming the mistress of a wealthy mill-owner. Playing on Mat's false sense of himself, the owners easily turn him against his fellow workers as they attempt to organize.

Chinatown, the hedonist, fares worse than Mat. Delighting in the senses, he spends his pay on corn whiskey, dice, and women. He is utterly dependent on his brothers. Of the three, he is hit the hardest physically by the harsh life of the mill worker. Eventually, he is left blind by an explosion in the mill.

The third brother, Melody, survives best. A musician in the South, he is still something of a poet after his move northward. But his new environment renders him impotent. His old songs don't seem to have any meaning any more; he is unable to play his guitar. Yet even though he appears at best indifferent to the manipulation of his fellow blacks by both the owners and white workers, he does manage to come through his Northern experience, unlike his two brothers, in one piece, physically and mentally.

Throughout the novel, Attaway reveals that the blacks' dream of greater social freedom in the mill towns is largely delusive. Many of their fellow white workers—especially the Slav and Irish immigrants—hate them and see them as a threat. When the union organizers appear, the employers easily manipulate the black workers into their camp. The blacks, being convinced that they are the lowest group in the racial pecking order, see their only chance of continuing on the job as bending to the desire of the owners.

Yet Attaway does not simply single out the blacks as the sole victim of the unjust conditions which he vividly portrays. He shows the European immigrants and native whites working under and being exploited by the same system of low pay, long hours, and unnecessary hazards to life and limb. He compassionately shows the blighted dream of the immigrants for a new life in America.

In **Blood on the Forge,** Attaway has mined a rich vein of human experience. His outlook is not very optimistic in this work, but he writes about his people knowingly and with warm appreciation. At once, his main characters are likable, humorous, bewildered, and stout-hearted. The dialogue sounds completely authentic.

Unfortunately, Attaway has published only the two novels considered above. The best of these, **Blood on the Forge,** has only recently begun to receive the critical recognition it merits. Edward Margolies has noted [in the introduction to the Collier Books' edition of **Blood on the Forge**], one of the reasons why Attaway's novel was largely ignored when it was first published: "Appearing one year after Richard Wright's sensational *Native Son,* Attaway's book may have looked tame to an America preparing for another war and whose reading public had already found its Negro 'spokesman' in the virile Wright." In any event, a careful reading of **Blood on the Forge** leads one to believe that, excepting Wright's *Native Son,* it is the strongest of black novels dealing with the plight of blacks and racial violence written during the inter-war period. (pp. 13-17)

> *L. Moody Simms, Jr., "In the Shadow of Richard Wright: William Attaway," in* Notes on Mississippi Writers, *Vol. VIII, No. 1, Spring, 1975, pp. 13-18.*

Cynthia Hamilton (essay date 1987)

[*In the following excerpt, Hamilton compares Attaway's portrayal of work and culture in* Blood on the Forge *with that of Peter Abrahams in his 1963 novel* Mine Boy.]

What is the meaning of "everyday life," of the ordinary actions of ordinary men and women? How can a writer take the ordinary, everyday work experience of characters and give us a glimpse of human transformation, even social transformation? William Attaway and Peter Abrahams have done just that in their novels **Blood on the Forge** and *Mine Boy.* Theirs is not a picture of everyday life as the sum total of mundane necessities in the city, e.g., consuming and producing. Rather, they show us characters who come to understand that "everyday" is the whole of modern life, actions as well as intentions. When ordinary working people reach out to reappropriate from their oppressions the whole of everyday life, societal transformation may occur. The

fragmentation of everyday life, the isolation of actions, and the disjointedness of behaviors help to perpetuate domination of workers by others. Attaway's and Abrahams' novels are about the transformation of individuals from a state of dependency and domination into men who glimpse purpose and intent, men who grasp "meaning" in ordinary, day-to-day actions. They do so at great cost, experiencing pain, even the loss of things familiar. But in their personal transformations they alter the institutions of work, family, and community, and social values in general.

Attaway's novel **Blood on the Forge** is a masterpiece of social analysis. He alone, among all black writers, makes work the center of his sociological imagination. Without charts and statistics, without the language of detached objectivity, Attaway presents to the sensitive reader the dynamics of the process of migration and the transition from the Kentucky sharecropper South to the industrial North of Pennsylvania (specifically, Allegheny County). In the first section of his book, Attaway destroys myths which social scientists are responsible for creating: myths which served to motivate black migration northward, like the idea that the North was a "promised land," and myths regarding the behavior of Blacks while in the South, particularly those centering on acquiescence to oppression. In Attaway's novel the trip north by the main characters—Mat, Melody, and Chinatown Moss—, though facilitated by a labor recruiter who tells them about the midnight freight train (after leaving ten dollars as a sign of his legitimacy), is truly an act of necessity. Mat, the oldest of the three brothers, had that very day struck an overseer whom he thought died from the blow, so the trio has to leave town. Such unilateral decisions were common among black men of the South, a necessity not frequently emphasized in historical treatments of migration.

Mat's wife Hattie, who stands "barefoot... in the doorway" as the brothers leave, is likewise a part of the history which is not well articulated. What happened to those left behind to fend for themselves? How did these women "endure"? Would they too travel "up north," alone, to a hostile environment? The patterns of migration show that men and women often had to travel alone because industrial cities rarely had work for women, while cities that developed around service work were more accessible to women. In particular, domestic and other service work opportunities for women existed in cities in which upper-class whites had not yet departed in their effort to escape immigrants and industry. However, some European immigrants, including the Irish, were not adverse to domestic service, and black women might find themselves without even that option. If women could not find work in the same cities as their men, families would be broken apart, and without families it was impossible to recreate strong communities. The family has always posed an economic threat to employers: Members of stable communities are inclined to challenge low wages and bad working conditions. If we are in doubt about how social policy regarding the family is used as a mechanism of social control, South

Africa provides a haunting example. There, individual isolation on the job and in the urban environment, coupled with the systematic dismantling of the family, has been an aid to political repression, the centerpiece of apartheid.

The distorting ideology of patriarchy added another dimension to industrial policies. As Bell Hooks has observed, when black and white men were put in a work situation in which neither had permanent female and family attachments, there was the illusion of "equality," whereas when women, black or white, entered the picture, the behavioral codes of the color bar became more overt. Attaway demonstrates this irony in exchanges between the men in his novel. The labor recruiter is the first to introduce the policy of segregation by gender: He quickly explains to the Moss brothers that the freight trains north don't transport women, but they could "surely" come later. The illusion of male equality in industrial cities with the absence of "attached women" provided a major service to employers. The role of women can therefore be seen as critical for the discussion of the survival of culture and community in new, hostile, urban industrial environments. By degrading women's status and excluding women's roles from the labor process, capital thwarted the process of self-expression and discovery, as well as patterns of continuity, within immigrant communities. (pp. 147-49)

We might imagine that three brothers traveling to a new environment would be able to keep their families intact, especially since family would lend cultural and moral support. Mat, the oldest brother, even promises to send for his wife Hattie as soon as his first check comes. However, after six months, Mat not only has given up the idea of bringing Hattie north, but he also stops reading the Bible, one of his daily activities in the South. The family unit as a central cultural variable is missing in the steel towns. Here, work is devastating, life fragmented by shifts. At the mill, men are cramped together in bunkhouses, one fire in the middle of each for cooking and warmth. Everything centers around the mill. There are no diversions except those usually practiced by groups of men in such situations, serving to lull the pain of the hours before the furnace. As many labor historians have noted, industrialists manipulated the production and provision of alcohol, drugs, and sex; religious education; and dancing and sports to induce patterns of obedience, servility, and acceptance of the debilitating conditions of work. In mill and mining towns, men paid women for a bit of pleasure and attention; the rest of the salary went for liquor and gambling. The emphasis was placed on those "things" which money could buy. Attaway has his character Mat assume that he can buy a home and a woman to attend to it. He cannot understand that "Hatties" like those he had known in the past do not fit into this environment, for the women who find themselves in the mill town are no longer guided by the old norms of marriage and family. They too have been swept up in the tide of materialism which causes them to set their standards according to the life-styles of the bourgeoisie: The mill owners' neighborhoods and mansions which lie over the hill become the standard to which they aspire.

Even in situations in which families have been reconstituted, Attaway shows their decimation, as daughters turn to prostitution and wives to waitressing, bartending, and running boarding houses in an effort to augment the family income. Women worked factory jobs during the day and still found it necessary to earn more, so some worked the brothels at night, as this conversation between two of the novel's characters indicates:

> "Well, it is kinda funny. Most all the other girls here work in the box factory in the daytime—come here at night."
>
> "Yeah," he said.
>
> It would not have been polite for him to voice his curiosity, but she knew of it through his face.
>
> "You can't take home just eight dollars every week," she explained. "Not if everybody is gonna eat."
>
> "What about the men in your family?"
>
> "Ah-h-h . . . " She made a gesture. "They are all with the union. My brothers—they have not been on job since a month ago. They go crazy. But they got to stick by the union . . . .
>
> "I'm for the union too," she went on, "but all of the trade here comes from scabs and strike breakers. Nobody else got any money."

In preventing the newcomers from retaining part of their past through the institution of the family, industrialists were able to manipulate social relations and, thus, control behavior. The old Slav Zanski says, " 'Feller from long way off die like plant on rock. Plant grow if it get ground like place it come from.' "

Paradoxically, steel and railroad industries in the nineteenth and early twentieth centuries encouraged irregular and undisciplined behavior *off* the job; their workers, all men, lived in company boarding arrangements, and they had to look outside for food, amusement, and any small comforts of home. These men were completely rootless, the factory their only common frame of reference. Without community, wife, or family, they were easy sources of scab and low-wage labor. Social historian Herbert Gutman explains that " '. . . these men rarely protested in collective ways, and for good reason. They did not plan to stay in the steel mills long. Most had come to the United States as single men (or married men who had left their families behind) to work briefly in the mills, save some money, return home, and purchase farmland." Meanwhile, on the inside, industrialists found undisciplined behavior disruptive and resorted to fines for drinking; tardiness; talking, eating, and reading on the job; and so forth. (pp. 149-51)

[Isolation, detachment, and anomie, coupled] with high turnover rates of employment, served American and South African industry well by creating an environment in which men work like machines and their jobs provide the only outlet for their energies and anxieties. Living with memories of their rural past and the hope of rejoining their families, the men might find almost any conditions tolerable precisely because of the air of impermanence. Moreover, were conflict and strikes to occur, the employer could replace these human machines with new ones recruited in similar fashion. Workers could be pitted against each other not simply because of ethnic and racial prejudices, which they were assumed to (and did indeed) harbor, but precisely because the environment mitigated against the creation and maintenance of strong social bonds. (p. 151)

In spite of the conditions of anomie, workers made constant efforts to reconstruct their old familial patterns. Some men moved out of the barracks into boarding houses where at least there could be meals in common and casual talk. Attaway's character Mat moves into a little shack where he attempts to recreate family. Unaccustomed to the instability of urban social relations . . . , he assumes that a family can be created by placing a woman in a house where she will hang clean curtains. Women, too, like Attaway's character Anna, long for family despite their obsession with fancy dresses and dance shoes. The bourgeoisie, it seems, serves as the only real model for new relations. As both authors emphasize, money—and the material possessions it can buy—replaces social bonds in the city. In this sense, the past of the displaced rural migrants has failed them, for they can draw from it no models for defense in the urban setting where old values and behavior are dysfunctional. Therefore, we watch them struggle to create new models. (pp. 152-53)

Not only can the urban environment disrupt social bonds and values created by the migrants' rural past, it distorts their vision as well, disrupts their relationship to the surrounding physical space. The urban industrial environment is immediately antagonistic, threatening, intimidating, and alienating. There is nothing which welcomes or beckons one's participation. This environment belittles people, pushes them to the periphery rather than placing them at the center of activity. When the Moss brothers get off the freight train in **Blood on the Forge** after hours of darkness, they "see the things that they would see for a long time to come": "The mills were as big as creation when the new men had ridden by on the freight. From the bunkhouse they were just so much scrap iron, scattered carelessly, smoking lazily. In back of them ran a dirty-as-a-catfish-hole river with a beautiful name: the Monogahela. Its banks were lined with mountains of red ore, yellow limestone and black coke. None of this was good to the eyes of men accustomed to the patterns of fields." (p. 154)

I have thus far concentrated on the externalities of work presented in **Blood on the Forge** and *Mine Boy*. But Attaway's and Abrahams' novels also present work's internalities: the image which men create of themselves as a consequence of their productive activity. Unlike the rural work place, in which laborers could see the concrete results of their efforts, the urban industrial setting separated workers from the products of their labor. Every day the work was the same, with little evidence of what had been produced. The result was alienation.

For Attaway's character Mat, the mill becomes an adversary, a challenge to overcome. His strength and size are pitted against steel, and it is to prove his manhood that he returns daily. But his brother Melody finds no meaning in the work, and his fingers can no longer find their way on his guitar strings: "Here at the mill it felt right to find quick chords with the fingers—a strange kind of playing for him, but it was right for that new place." For the third brother, Chinatown, the fear of the first encounter with steel remains, as he joins the others, reluctantly, on his shift. Ironically, it is Chinatown whom "steel" identifies as defenseless when it lashes out and blinds him in a furnace explosion which kills twelve men. Known as the joy of the crowd, Chinatown seemed to smile constantly; his habit of narrowing his eyes like those of a Chinaman earned him his nickname. The steel mill takes from him the one thing from the past which assured his identity, his eyes: "He had been a man who lived through outward symbols. Now those symbols were gone, and he was lost." Maybe Melody had been right; maybe "'the Judgment [was] jest a steel mill.'"

Attaway's portrayal of the brothers presents symbolically what may have been the three primary consequences of urban acculturation. Mat destroys himself while trying to adjust to the new environment, using the only tools he has, those of the past. Chinatown, in fear and rejection, really never attempts to participate in the new environment; he goes to his shift at the mill, rarely works, but still cannot escape its oppression. With Melody we sense that Attaway is presenting the painful process of transformation. Though the urban industrial setting is just as alienating for Melody as it is for his brothers, he tries to adapt some of the old values and effect transformation. For example, his rural Southern music becomes the blues in the urban North, and while others are taking sides on a strike, Melody decides to stay home with his blind brother, familial obligation taking precedence over political conflict. In the end we feel that Melody will adjust to the city, but on his own terms, taking his brother and his music with him wherever he goes. (pp. 155-56)

Xuma [in Abrahams' *Mine Boy*] and Mat are problematic characters. While work is their new source of identity and each professes to feel his manhood at work alone, we see that work is destroying them, physically and psychologically. Moreover, there is a tendency to see these two as simple personalities—big, trusting, vulnerable, and tragic—, but we must also see Xuma and Mat as "process," the evolving "new" men of urban industrialization. These were the men that came to dominate the labor force of heavy industry in the U.S. at the turn of the century, as well as the migrants who have labored in South African industry, workers from rural areas for the most part. These were the men who were subjected to the early experiments in industrial organization by those determined to ensure management's control of the work process.

The industrialization campaign in the U.S. had its counterpart on the African continent, particularly in South Africa. The mining corporations in South Africa took their lead from Ford and International Harvester in the U.S., where language training for migrants was mandatory. In South Africa, "a special language was constructed from Zulu and Afrikaans, called Fanacalo, in order to instruct raw recruits from diverse ethnic backgrounds, inhibiting communication between workers except in the quasimilitary language invented by the bosses."

These rural migrants were the men industry feared precisely because of their strength and work knowledge; their sense of loyalty and commitment was threatening because it was a possible source of workers' independence. Therefore the new organization of industry replaced all other compensation for work with material compensation. Workers were encouraged not to be concerned with the end product of their labor but to become specialists at some minute task, like attaching a nut to a bolt ten to twelve hours a day. For efficiency and high productivity, money was to be the reward for workers. Men and women were encouraged to think solely of their own well-being, not that of fellow workers, relatives, or friends.

But these new men, like Xuma and Mat, were not driven by money, as their employers assumed. Nor were they receptive to carrot-and-stick methods of positive and negative material incentives. These men were driven by forces within: their old standards of self-reliance and self-sufficiency, their unyielding nature in the face of force, and their traditional conceptions of manhood, which centered around a silent tolerance and endurance of pain and the constant desire for respect. Ironically, the combination drove them, helplessly, into the arms of capital, which transformed all of these motives into profits for the owners and bosses.

These men looked to work for meaning and self-affirmation, but they found only alienation and exploitation. Attaway and Abrahams identify this important element for the process of changing behavior and the resulting social consciousness. Their characters must come to a new self-consciousness before they can identify group interest or action. They must learn to see again, to define new meanings in the decay of a past which cannot service the present. This process of unlearning appears in the arena of social relations in *Blood on the Forge:* "Someday," thinks Melody,

> the mills would be his and Big Mat's home. Mat had faced a mick who said the word that passed only between black men. Back in Kentucky everybody had called them "nigger." It was something for Mat to have so soon unlearned that. He himself had unlearned a lot of things. The old music was going. Now when he took down his guitar he felt the awe of a

night—white with leaping flames. Sure the mills would be their home. But the mills couldn't look at China's gold tooth and smile. In the South he had worn that tooth like a badge.

The hardest lesson of the new urban environment involves the irony of the disparity between the individual and the group. While urban society emphasizes individualism, the older tradition of rural migrants was one of group identification. Ironically, in this new, hostile environment that group identity was also necessary for survival but discouraged by the "bosses." Therefore, group formations, whether family, church, union, or community, would be critical political tools, and it is precisely this fact which determined industrialists to try to thwart the development of such formations.

Ultimately, Attaway's and Abrahams' protagonists, who had always derived a sense of self and meaning in life through their relations with others, must face the future alone. Only one of the Moss brothers survives Allegheny County in one piece and ends up traveling to Pittsburgh to yet another industrial experience. (pp. 157-59)

Many first-generation urban immigrants were destroyed by the attempt to develop a new consciousness out of the collision between old cultural values and habits and new industrial/urban necessities. The clearest example of the effect of this process of urbanization and the development of a new group consciousness is, of course, the labor movement itself and the fight for unionization, particularly among the unskilled. Whether in the West or the Third World, the real test of "consciousness" is workers' ability to organize for their own interests and against the control of capital. Though much has been written on labor movements, we are rarely provided with insights that allow us to understand the process which propels some workers into organized opposition against their bosses, while others resist organization, sometimes in sympathy with fellow workers and sometimes not. This subject becomes sensitive indeed when the variable of race is added, but Attaway and Abrahams brave the controversy with startling insight.

When strike talk emerges in Attaway's *Blood on the Forge,* it is hard for the Eastern Europeans to arrive at a conclusion. They talk in secret, for the most part, relying on the past; shared language and standards of behavior allow them to communicate with each other. In the church, a special service is held, and the men publicly express their loyalty through sacred symbols: In kissing the Cross, they make a vow not only among men but between men and something more remote and commanding. Most of the Blacks get word of the strike just in time to decide whether or not they will stay out of the line of fire, for violence is assured. Some, like Melody, stay home—not, in his case, out of conscious political conviction but in order to care for his recently blinded brother. He knows the mill is an evil to be confronted, but he needs more time to decide how he might confront it. Mat, on the other hand, is torn: Because he still longs to be steel's equal, to prove and exhibit his strength and courage to the men, the mill security forces are able to recruit him to "crack heads" in the Poles' strike quarters. The real reasons for his acceptance and the reasons attributed to him by the mill owners (and, implicitly, some labor historians) are different.

Labor historians have been wont to see Blacks as scabs; organizers have looked at the job insecurity of Blacks; and both have assumed a vulnerability which would necessarily thrust Blacks into the arms of management. The truth is that, although vulnerable, Blacks, as a group, have rarely identified with management or the paternalism of industrial welfare, even when they—like Mat in Attaway's novel—became management's unwitting henchmen. The Black race has produced its share of traitors and informers, as have other immigrant groups, but they are a small minority of the Black community.

Attaway depicts Bo, a gang boss, as an informer, something the Moss brothers don't realize initially. But they find out:

> "Maybe them guys was fired 'cause I said I seen 'em goin' in the union place. But hell! I got to keep my job. I got to do what they say. Don't forget I'm the only nigger in the mill got micks under him."

> This was true. Bo was a big man in the mill. Melody did not want Bo against him. If Bo was able to get white men put off the job he could even more easily do the same to black men. Melody became afraid. He pulled Big Mat away, for fear of what might be said.

> "How come you pull me? . . . I don't like no stool pigeons," grunted Big Mat [to Melody].

> "But we on their side, looks like."

> "I ain't on no stool pigeon's side."

> "But you ain't with the union."

> "Naw, I guess I ain't."

There is a clear distinction here between Mat, whom management uses to beat up strikers, and Bo, who is a silent informer for management. Though their actions serve the same ends for the owners of the mill, their own conceptions and justifications for what they do are very different. Mat's personal reasons for accepting the nightstick and breaking into the Slav's meeting hall are clear only to him (and to the reader) moments before his death. Attaway's description is one of the most moving passages in the book:

> The blow on the back of his head took him without warning. His eyes had been the measure of the whole river front. His big eyes could not have seen the young Slav and the pickax handle . . . .

> Like a reflection in disturbed water, the face of the young Slav came into his vision. He looked at that face from a great distance. It would only be a moment before he must crash to the ground. His eyes were objective. He had all the objectivity of a man who is closer to death than life. From that dark place he looked back at the world . . . .

> It seemed to him that he had been through all of this once before. Only at that far time he had been the

arm strong with hate. Yes, once he had beaten down a riding boss. A long time ago in the red hills he had done this thing and run away. Had that riding boss been as he was now? Big Mat went further away and no longer could distinguish himself from these other figures. They were all one and all the same. In that confusion he sensed something true. Maybe somewhere in these mills a new Mr. Johnston was creating riding bosses, making a difference where none existed. (pp. 159-61)

Political consciousness is not the product of ideology or mere oppression. It is self-appraisal, the affirmative result of the integrative process by which many experiences which derive from the conditions created by work—on and off the job—are brought meaningfully together. Only when the individual forges a synthesis of so many experiences fragmented by capitalist society can he or she act definitively, for only then can the person truly see. Attaway explains this in reference to his characters: "Big Mat and Melody were vastly different men. But both of them approached the world alike. Ideas of union and nonunion could only confuse them until that time when their own personal experience would give them the feeling necessary for understanding."

Attaway and Abrahams allow us to see and feel the process of consciousness evolving in their characters Mat, Xuma, and Melody. For Blacks throughout the diaspora, it was the artist who first expressed the pains of "modernization." The new man of the cities confronted by technology was portrayed in music and dance, in painting and literature. It should not be surprising to the social analyst that this would be so, for it is the artist who feels and is moved by the pulse of cultural transformation.

According to Toni Morrison, the black artist's literary view of the city is more telling than that of mainstream American writers because " . . . the positive and negative aspects of urbanism can best be articulated by those who know it, but who have no vested political, cultural or philosophical interests in supporting or rejecting it as it presently exists and who seldom see themselves as disengaged from society." Individualism and the urge to autonomy, seen as virtues in white society, are not consciously pursued Black ideals. For Blacks, including the Black writer, the city or the village takes on significance within the context of a collective—the neighborhood, the significant grouping within. An individual seeks identity within a group, not outside it. Therefore, the problems of consciousness which affect Attaway's and Abrahams' characters, and which I have suggested are symbolic of real-life crises, occur because the characters have no clearly established group to provide identification and direction. There are no established people or points of reference which connect to the past, yet these focal points are imperative if social development is to occur. Individuals must be able to identify themselves in the present with relation to a past before they can move on to defy the system, provide alternate wisdom, and establish, maintain, and sustain generations.

Social analysts have suggested a methodological framework which recognizes the connection between culture and work; indeed, such an approach is necessary to complete the analysis of urbanization, for only when we appreciate the dialectic of culture and work can we produce analyses which project the conflicts and contradictions inherent in all patterns of behavior. Attaway and Abrahams recognize these strains and transformations in human character and have provided us a basis for a new understanding of both history and culture as seen through the prism of everyday life. According to Henri Lefebvre, "the revolutionary process begins by shaping the everyday and finishes by reestablishing it." Only when work is understood as Attaway and Abrahams present it—as the center of the urban experience, that which shapes all other social as well as productive relations—can we interpret history with the objective of providing a richer future. (pp. 161-62)

Cynthia Hamilton, "Work and Culture: The Evolution of Consciousness in Urban Industrial Society in the Fiction of William Attaway and Peter Abrahams," in Black American Literature Forum *Vol. 21, Nos. 1-2, Spring-Summer, 1987, pp 147-163.*

FURTHER READING

Barthold, Bonnie J. "William Attaway, *Blood on the Forge*." In her *Black Time: Fiction of Africa, the Caribbean, and the United States,* pp. 164-68. New Haven: Yale University Press, 1981.

Examines the black experience of time as presented in seven representative novels, including Attaway's *Blood on the Forge*.

Campbell, Jane. "Visions of Transcendence in W.E.B. DuBois's *The Quest of the Silver Fleece* and William Attaway's *Blood on the Forge*." In her *Mythic Black Fiction: The Transformation of History,* pp. 64-86. Knoxville: University of Tennessee Press, 1986.

Compares Attaway's depiction of impoverished black workers in *Blood on the Forge* with that of W.E.B. DuBois in *The Quest of the Silver Fleece*.

Felgar, Robert. "William Attaway's Unaccommodated Protagonists." *Studies in Black Literature* 4, No. 1 (Spring 1973): 1-3.

Attempts to gain recognition for Attaway by synopsizing and briefly analyzing his two novels.

Garren, Samuel B. "Playing the Wishing Game: Folkloric Elements in William Attaway's *Blood on the Forge*." *CLA Journal* XXXII, No. 1 (September 1988): 10-22.

Examines the "wishing game" and other examples of black folklore in *Blood on the Forge*.

Review of *Let Me Breathe Thunder,* by William Attaway. *Saturday Review of Literature* 20 (1 July 1939): 20.

Assesses the merits and faults of *Let Me Breathe Thunder*. According to the critic: "Attaway writes easily, the way a man walks or tells a tale, with natural vigor and his objective clear every foot of the way . . . . On the debit, we must note that Mr. Attaway has projected much of his dramatic experience . . . into his writing. Too many of his scenes are plainly stagy, seen as tableaus in terms of groups and gestures, or heard as dramatic speeches, with an eye towards effective curtains and black-outs."

James Baldwin

1924-1987

(Full name James Arthur Baldwin) American novelist, essayist, dramatist, nonfiction and short story writer, poet, scriptwriter, and author of children's books.

Baldwin is recognized as one of the most important writers in twentieth-century American literature. In his works he exposed racial and sexual polarization in American society and challenged readers to confront and resolve these differences. Baldwin's influence and popularity reached their peak during the 1960s, when he was regarded by many as the leading literary spokesperson of the civil rights movement. His novels, essays, and other writings attest to his premise that the black American, as an object of suffering and abuse, represents a universal symbol of human conflict.

Much of Baldwin's work is loosely based on his childhood and adolescence. Baldwin was born and raised in Harlem under very trying circumstances. His stepfather, an evangelical preacher, struggled to support a large family and demanded the most rigorous religious behavior from his nine children. According to John W. Roberts, "Baldwin's ambivalent relationship with his stepfather served as a constant source of tension during his formative years and informs some of his best mature writings.... The demands of caring for younger siblings and his stepfather's religious convictions in large part shielded the boy from the harsh realities of Harlem street life during the 1930s." As a youth Baldwin read constantly and even tried writing; he was an excellent student and sought escape from his environment through literature, movies, and theatre. During the summer of his fourteenth birthday he underwent a dramatic religious conversion, partly in response to his nascent sexuality and partly as a further buffer against the ever-present temptations of drugs and crime. He served as a junior minister for three years at the Fireside Pentecostal Assembly, but gradually he lost his desire to preach as he began to question blacks' acceptance of Christian tenets that had, in essence, been used to enslave them.

Shortly after he graduated from high school in 1942, Baldwin was compelled to find work in order to help support his brothers and sisters. He took a job in the defense industry in Belle Meade, New Jersey, and there, not for the first time, he was confronted with racism, discrimination, and the debilitating regulations of segregation. The experiences in New Jersey were closely followed by his stepfather's death, after which Baldwin determined to make writing his sole profession. He moved to Greenwich Village in New York City and began to write a novel, supporting himself by performing a variety of odd jobs. In 1944 he met author Richard Wright, who helped him obtain the 1945 Eugene F. Saxton fellowship. Despite the financial freedom the

fellowship provided, Baldwin was unable to complete his novel that year. Moreover, he found the social and cultural tenor of the United States increasingly stifling. Eventually, in 1948, he moved to Paris, using funds from a Rosenwald Foundation fellowship to pay his passage. Most critics believe that this journey abroad was fundamental to Baldwin's development as an author.

"Once I found myself on the other side of the ocean," Baldwin told the *New York Times*, "I could see where I came from very clearly, and I could see that I carried myself, which is my home, with me. You can never escape that. I am the grandson of a slave, and I am a writer. I must deal with both." Through some difficult financial and emotional periods, Baldwin undertook a process of self-realization that included both an acceptance of his heritage and an admittance of his fundamental homosexuality. Critic Robert A. Bone noted that Europe gave the young author many things: "It gave him a world perspective from which to approach the question of his own identity. It gave him a tender love affair which would dominate the pages of his later fiction. But above all, Europe gave him back himself. The immediate fruit of self-recovery was a great creative outburst. First came two [works] of reconciliation with his racial heritage. *Go Tell It on the Mountain* (1953) and *The Amen Corner* (1955) represent a search for roots, a surrender to tradition, an acceptance of the Negro past. Then came a series of essays which probe, deeper than anyone has dared, the psychic history of this nation. They are a moving record of a man's struggle to define the forces that have shaped him, in order that he may accept himself."

Following the publication of *Go Tell It on the Mountain,* Baldwin was hailed by critics as a major novelist and a worthy successor to Ralph Ellison and Richard Wright. The book dramatizes the events leading to the religious confirmation of John Grimes, a sensitive Harlem youth struggling to come to terms with his confusion about his sexuality and his religious upbringing. At the core of the novel is a family's legacy of brutality and hate, augmented by the destructive relationship between John and his stepfather, a fundamentalist preacher whose insecurities over his own religious commitment result in his abusive treatment of John and his emotional neglect of his family. Baldwin earned unanimous praise for his skillful evocation of his characters' squalid lives and for his powerful language, which some critics likened to a fire-and-brimstone oratory.

While most critics regarded *Go Tell It on the Mountain* as a cathartic novel in which Baldwin attempted to resolve the emotional anguish of his adolescence, others viewed his next work, *Giovanni's Room* (1956), as the one in which he truly confronted his homosexuality for the first time. The novel was controversial, apparently because Baldwin was one of the first black writers to openly discuss homosexuality in his fiction. *Giovanni's Room,* which is set in Paris, is the story of an ill-fated love affair between a white American student and an Italian bartender. Many critics were outraged by Baldwin's blunt language and his controversial topic, though some reviewers echoed David Littlejohn's assessment that the work is "certainly one of the most subtle novels of the homosexual world." Baldwin continued his investigation of racial and sexual politics in the novel *Another Country* (1962), which provoked even more debate. Although it received largely negative reviews due to Baldwin's candid depiction of sexual relations, some commentators considered *Another Country* superior to *Giovanni's Room* in terms of thematic scope and descriptive quality.

Baldwin's fiction of the late 1960s and 1970s was primarily influenced by his involvement in the civil rights movement. *Tell Me How Long the Train's Been Gone* (1968) centers on two brothers and their different approaches to escaping the ghetto; one finds success in the entertainment industry, while the other is nearly destroyed by racism and violence. *If Beale Street Could Talk* (1974) further examines blacks living in a hostile

environment. In *Just above My Head* (1979), Baldwin returned to his earlier themes of religion and sexuality in a complex story of a homosexual gospel singer. Although these works were best-sellers, they signaled for most critics a decline in Baldwin's creative talents due to his reliance on didacticism.

Because Baldwin sought to inform and confront whites, and because his fiction contains interracial love affairs, he early came under attack from writers of the Black Arts Movement, who called for a literature exclusively by and for blacks. Baldwin refused to align himself with the movement; he continued to call himself an "American writer" as opposed to a "black writer" and continued to confront the issues facing a multi-racial society. Eldridge Cleaver, in his book *Soul on Ice,* accused Baldwin of a hatred of blacks and "a shameful, fanatical fawning" love of whites. What Cleaver saw as complicity with whites, Baldwin saw rather as an attempt to alter the real daily environment with which American blacks have been faced all their lives.

Although Baldwin is best known as a novelist, his nonfiction works have received substantial critical acclaim. The essay "Everybody's Protest Novel," published in 1949, introduced him to the New York intelligentsia and generated controversy for its attack on authors of protest fiction, including Richard Wright, who, Baldwin maintained, perpetuated rather than condemned negative racial stereotypes. While Baldwin viewed this piece as an exploration of the thematic options that black writers could follow, Wright considered it a personal affront and subsequently terminated his professional alliance with Baldwin. Nevertheless, critics praised Baldwin for his perceptive analysis of protest literature and for his lucid prose. Baldwin earned additional critical praise for the essays collected in *Notes of a Native Son* (1955) and *Nobody Knows My Name: More Notes of a Native Son* (1961). In these volumes, Baldwin optimistically examined the state of race relations in the United States and abroad in essays that range from poignant autobiographical remembrances to scholarly literary and social criticism. He also used personal experience to address the problems artists face when drawn to political activism. Critics viewed Baldwin's next nonfiction work, *The Fire Next Time* (1963), as both a passionate plea for reconciliation between the races and as a manifesto for black liberation.

As racial tensions escalated in the mid-1960s, Baldwin's vision of America turned increasingly bitter and his prose more inflammatory. After the publication of *No Name in the Street* (1972), Baldwin was faulted for abandoning his deft powers of persuasion in favor of rhetoric and was accused by some of racism. Keneth Kinnamon summed up the change in Baldwin's attitude and literature during this period: "[The] redemptive possibilities of love seemed exhausted in that terrible decade of assassination, riot, and repression.... Violence, [Baldwin] now believes, is the arbiter of history, and in its matrix the white world is dying and the third world is struggling to be born.... Though love may still be a sustaining personal force, its social utility is dubious." One of Baldwin's last nonfiction works, *The Evidence of Things Not Seen* (1985), is about the Atlanta child murders, which claimed the lives of more than twenty black children and young adults between 1979 and 1981. In this treatise, Baldwin combined straight reportage with an examination of the tragedy, perceiving the murders as a prelude to an apocalyptic confrontation between blacks and whites.

In addition to his numerous books, Baldwin was one of the few black authors to have had more than one of his plays produced on Broadway. Both *The Amen Corner,* another treatment of storefront pentecostal religion, and *Blues for Mister Charlie,* a drama based on the racially-motivated murder of Emmett Till in 1955, had successful Broadway runs and numerous revivals. Fred L. Standley commented that in both plays, "as in his other literary works, Baldwin explores a variety of thematic concerns: the historical significance and the potential explosiveness in black-white relations; the necessity for developing a sexual and psychological consciousness and identity; the intertwining of love and power in the universal scheme of existence as well as in the structures of society; the misplaced priorities in the value systems in America; and the responsibility of the artist to promote the evolution of the individual and the society." In *The Black American Writer: Poetry and Drama* (1969), Walter Meserve offered remarks on Baldwin's abilities as a playwright. "Baldwin tries to use the theatre as a pulpit for his ideas," Meserve stated. "Mainly his plays are thesis plays—talky, over-written, and cliche dialogue and some stereotypes, preachy, and argumentative. Essentially, Baldwin is not particularly dramatic, but he can be extremely eloquent, compelling, and sometimes irritating as a playwright committed to his approach to life." Meserve added, however, that although the author was criticized for creating stereotypes, "his major characters are the most successful and memorable aspects of his plays. People are important to Baldwin, and their problems, generally embedded in their agonizing souls, stimulate him to write.... A humanitarian, sensitive to the needs and struggles of man, he writes of inner turmoil, spiritual disruption, the consequence upon people of the burdens of the world, both White and Black."

At the time of his death from cancer late in 1987, Baldwin was still working on two projects—a play, *The Welcome Table,* and a biography of Martin Luther King, Jr. Although he lived primarily in France, he had never relinquished his United States citizenship and preferred to think of himself as a "commuter" rather than as an expatriate. The publication of his collected essays, *The Price of the Ticket: Collected Nonfiction, 1948-1985* (1985), and his subsequent death sparked reassessments of his career and comments on the quality of his lasting legacy. "Mr. Baldwin has become a kind of prophet, a man who has been able to give a public issue all its deeper moral, historical, and personal significance," remarked Robert F. Sayre in *Contemporary American*

Novelists. "Certainly one mark of his achievement...is that whatever deeper comprehension of the race issue Americans now possess has been in some way shaped by him. And this is to have shaped their comprehension of themselves as well." Perhaps the most telling demonstration of the results of Baldwin's achievement came from other black writers. Orde Coombs, for instance, concluded: "Because he existed we felt that the racial miasma that swirled around us would not consume us, and it is not too much to say that this man saved our lives, or at least, gave us the necessary ammunition to face what we knew would continue to be a hostile and condescending world." Playwright Amiri Baraka offered a similar assessment in his funeral eulogy to Baldwin. "This man traveled the earth like its history and its biographer," Baraka said. "He reported, criticized, made beautiful, analyzed, cajoled, lyricized, attacked, sang, made us think, made us better, made us consciously human.... He made us feel...that we could defend ourselves or define ourselves, that we were in the world not merely as animate slaves, but as terrifyingly sensitive measurers of what is good or evil, beautiful or ugly. This is the power of his spirit. This is the bond which created our love for him." In a posthumous profile for the *Washington Post,* Juan Williams wrote: "The success of Baldwin's effort as the witness is evidenced time and again by the people, black and white, gay and straight, famous and anonymous, whose humanity he unveiled in his writings. America and the literary world are far richer for his witness. The proof of a shared humanity across the divides of race, class and more is the testament that the preacher's son, James Arthur Baldwin, has left us."

(For further information about Baldwin's life and works, see *Black Writers; Concise Dictionary of American Literary Biography, 1941-1968; Contemporary Authors,* Vols. 1-4, 124; *Contemporary Authors Bibliographical Series,* Vol. 1; *Contemporary Authors New Revision Series,* Vol. 3; *Contemporary Literary Criticism,* Vols. 1, 2, 3, 4, 5, 8, 13, 15, 17, 42, 50; *Dictionary of Literary Biography,* Vols. 2, 7, 33; *Dictionary of Literary Biography Yearbook: 1987;* and *Something about the Author,* Vol. 9.)

PRINCIPAL WORKS

Go Tell It on the Mountain (novel) 1953
The Amen Corner (drama) 1955
Notes of a Native Son (essays) 1955
Giovanni's Room (novel) 1956
Nobody Knows My Name: More Notes of a Native Son (essays) 1961
Another Country (novel) 1962
The Fire Next Time (essays) 1963
Blues for Mister Charlie (drama) 1964
Going to Meet the Man (short stories) 1965
Tell Me How Long the Train's Been Gone (novel) 1968
No Name in the Street (essay) 1972
One Day, When I Was Lost (screenplay) 1972
If Beale Street Could Talk (novel) 1974
The Devil Finds Work (criticism) 1976

Little Man, Little Man: A Story of Childhood (juvenile
    fiction) 1976
Just above My Head (novel) 1979
The Evidence of Things Not Seen (nonfiction) 1985
Jimmy's Blues: Selected Poems (poetry) 1985
The Price of the Ticket: Collected Nonfiction, 1948-1985
    (essays) 1985

Anthony West (essay date 1953)

[*In the following review, originally published in the*
New Yorker *in 1953, West offers a generally favorable
assessment of Baldwin's first novel,* Go Tell It on the
Mountain.]

James Baldwin's **Go Tell It on the Mountain** is a first
novel of quite exceptional promise, centering on a
church in Harlem. The church is one of those enthusiastic and declamatory Bible-thumping tabernacles characteristic of religiosity in decay, and the noble idea of man
speaking directly to his God has betrayed a preacher
into being a medium through whom the inner voices of
fear, vanity, and hunger for love and power speak
violently and repulsively. The Temple of the Fire
Baptized is the scene of a conflict between a growing boy
with a real vocation and his preacher stepfather, a
compulsive lecher whose sense of guilt, rather than a
true call, has brought him to the pulpit. The soured and
corrupt man does his best to try to beat a sense of shame
and misery into his stepson, but the boy, withdrawing
from the squalor and tensions of his home into a private
world of dream and ecstasy, at last arrives at the state of
grace and peace the stepfather has always desired and
never achieved. Mr. Baldwin, who heard the call and
preached in just such a chapel when he was fourteen,
gives an extraordinarily vivid picture of the intellectual
seediness and poverty of this kind of religious life and of
the secular life that produces it, since all the characters,
particularly the women in the tormented stepfather's
life, have histories that inevitably bring them into the
Temple of the Fire Baptized.

But for all its abundant virtues there is something
lacking in the book; its perfections are wooden and it is
without vitality in spite of its realism. When one
compares it with Ralph Ellison's *Invisible Man,* the
deficiency immediately declares itself. Ellison's novel
was emotionally disturbing and extremely serious, but it
was also rich in comic invention. It made its points with
the same sort of broad farce effects that Dostoevski used
time and again, and that any novelist who aspires to be
serious must use to give a rounded picture of the
business of being a man. A Harlem without laughter is
as incredible as *The Brothers Karamazov* without Kras-
sotkin, Mme. Hohlakov, and the doctor who stands in
Captain Snegiryov's poverty-stricken rooms advising
him to send his wife to Paris and Ilusha to Italy for their
health. Ellison's white man pretending he is better than

the colored one and the man with gas pains pretending
that his belchings are God's voice speaking through him
are comic figures by any honest system of values, and
comedy not only tells the truth about them but is also
the essential truth. Mr. Baldwin's God-intoxicated lecher, with his roving eye and his inflamed conscience,
which always arrives on the scene too late, carries farce
with him wherever he goes, and if one treats him with
Kafkaesque solemnity, the life goes out of him and the
spiritual tragedy of his congregation loses a dimension.
Ellison gives the whole picture in the two and a half
pages in which the Invisible Man visits the Holy Way
Station of the Reverend B. P. Rinehart, the Spiritual
Technologist, whose slogan is "No Problem Too Hard
for God." The whole thing is grotesque. And the
situation in which the Invisible Man is mistaken for the
Spiritual Technologist by the innocent Sister Harris and
Sister Judkin is low comedy, with a background of
sacred boogie-woogie beaten out on a piano and an
electric guitar, but the farce goes right to the heart of the
innocence of the two women and the hero's despair. Mr.
Baldwin's novel is humorless, and the result is that it
seems not more dignified or more understanding but
less penetrating.

> *Anthony West, "Sorry Lives," in* The New
> Yorker, *Vol. XXIX, No. 18, June 20, 1953, p.*
> *93.*

Langston Hughes (essay date 1956)

[*A major literary figure of the Harlem Renaissance,
Hughes devoted his versatile and prolific career to
portraying the urban experience of working-class
blacks. In the following 1956* New York Times Book
Review *essay, he praises the theme, content, and prose
style of* Notes of a Native Son.]

James Baldwin writes down to nobody, and he is trying
very hard to write up to himself. As an essayist he is
thought-provoking, tantalizing, irritating, abusing and
amusing. And he uses words as the sea uses waves, to
flow and beat, advance and retreat, rise and take a bow
in disappearing.

In *Notes of a Native Son,* James Baldwin surveys in
pungent commentary certain phases of the contemporary scene as they relate to the citizenry of the United
States, particularly Negroes. Harlem, the protest novel,
bigoted religion, the Negro press and the student milieu
of Paris are all examined in black and white, with
alternate shutters clicking, for hours of reading interest.
When the young man who wrote this book comes to a
point where he can look at life purely as himself, and for
himself, the color of his skin mattering not at all, when,
as in his own words, he finds "his birthright as a man no
less than his birthright as a black man," America and
the world might well have a major contemporary
commentator.

Few American writers handle words more effectively in
the essay form than James Baldwin. To my way of

thinking, he is much better at provoking thought in the essay than he is in arousing emotion in fiction.... In his essays, words and material suit each other. The thought becomes poetry, and the poetry illuminates the thought.

> Langston Hughes, "From Harlem to Paris," in The New York Times Book Review, February 26, 1956, p. 26.

Stephen Spender (essay date 1963)

[*Spender is an English poet and essayist. In the following excerpt, he analyzes Baldwin's views about love and race, concluding: "The great contribution of Mr. Baldwin is that he finds words to express what one knows to be true: how it feels to be an American Negro."*]

Baldwin's power is his ability to express situations—the situation of being a Negro, and of being white, and of being human. Beyond this, he is perhaps too impatient to be a good novelist, and although he is a powerful essayist [as shown in *The Fire Next Time*] his experiences are so colored with feelings that he seems unable to relate the thoughts which arise from his feelings to parallel situations that have given rise to other men's thoughts. (p. 256)

Mr. Baldwin would admit, I think, that when (and this is quite often) he is guided by his emotions he finds himself in a position not far from that of the Black Muslims. He quite rightly resents the claims of whites that they are superior to colored people. But in fact he thinks that the colored are superior. (p. 257)

Mr. Baldwin asserts that the white American does not recognize death because he does not recognize life. He does not recognize the "constants" of life in himself, and therefore he does not recognize them in the Negro. If he recognized the Negro as a being like himself, then he would recognize in himself those constants which he acknowledges in the Negro. Thus the black can "save" the white by making the white conscious of his humanity....

Although Mr. Baldwin considers love is the only answer to the American race problem, it is not at all evident from his book that he loves white Americans, and at times it is even doubtful whether he loves his own people. Not that I blame him for this. What I do criticize him for is postulating a quite impossible demand as the only way of dealing with a problem that has to be solved. (p. 258)

The great contribution of Mr. Baldwin is that he finds words to express what one knows to be true: how it feels to be an American Negro. Within his own works he has solved the problem of integration: not by love, but by imagination using words which know no class nor color bars. (p. 260)

> Stephen Spender, "James Baldwin: Voice of a Revolution," in Partisan Review, Vol. XXX, No. 2, Summer, 1963, pp. 256-60.

Philip Roth (essay date 1964)

[*Roth is an American novelist, essayist, and literary critic. Among his best-known works are* Goodbye, Columbus, and Five Short Stories *(1959).* Portnoy's Complaint *(1969). and a series of presumed semiautobiographical volumes featuring novelist Nathan Zuckerman. In the following excerpt, he discusses theme and characterization in Baldwin's* Blues for Mr. Charlie.]

[The direction **Blues for Mr. Charlie**] takes is an expression of the will of one of the characters, Richard's father, who searches for the meaning of [his son's] murder for himself, for his son, and for the man who committed it....

[Richard] is rich with anger, and yet in the very first scene with his father, he surrenders to him the pistol he has brought back with him from the North, an act for which he will in the end have to pay with his life.

Why does he surrender the pistol? Meridian himself does not demand it, although his values may seem to. Instead, at his son's provocation, Meridian admits that the mother was in fact pushed, and did not slip as apparently he had once tried to make his son believe. Richard now gives him the gun supposedly because Meridian has given up the truth, and given it up to him. But this truth his father speaks only verifies what Richard had already known. Surrendering the gun at this point, then, is either psychological perversity on Richard's part (a clue to a motive of which he himself is unaware), or sentimentality on the part of the writer, who may so want a scene of loving and forgiveness between a father and a son on the stage that he will have one even if it means destroying the most authentic facts about his own characters. Or else it is just so much piety about that word *truth*. Whatever the cause, at the most important dramatic moment of the act (and maybe of the play) the sense of the drama is hopelessly distorted: Meridian Henry, rather than disputing his son's judgment of him, accepts it, asks to be forgiven; and Richard, instead of finding his strength of purpose hardened by his father's truthfulness, surrenders his purpose by surrendering the gun....

[This distortion of character] may tell us that beneath the play presented, there is a hidden play about a Negro father and a Negro son.... How to the point of what the play at first appears to be about, if Meridian had said, "You cannot live in my house with a gun"; if Richard had replied, "That's how you killed my mother"—and if Meridian had answered, "You are wrong. I want the gun." Then that struggle which also seems to remain confused in the heart of the writer, the struggle between love and hate, would have been untangled in the drama, even if it could not, and cannot, be resolved for either the playwright or the audience. But this required the dramatist to permit one of his characters to become a hero, and his play, perhaps, to aspire to tragedy. For a while, I thought Baldwin had chosen Meridian to fill the role of tragic hero in what is really a tragic story. If he had, then real blues might have been sung in the end for the Negro rather than those spurious blues for Mr. Charlie, who is the white man, and who can hardly be said to be the play's hero either. (p. 10)

But in the remaining two acts of the play all the purposes of the first act collapse; indeed, everything collapses, sense, craft, and feeling. The duty to understand is replaced with a duty to do what is practically its opposite, to propagandize.... When the curtain goes up on Act Two the circumstances and the people of Act One are pretty much swept aside. Now we are over in Whitetown, in the home of Lyle Britten, who is the murderer, but not the villain—as, in a way, Richard is the victim without being the hero. Both are dummies who only move their mouths while the real hero and villain air their views. For the real hero of these last two acts is blackness, as the real villain is whiteness....

[*Blues for Mister Charlie*] is soap opera designed to illustrate the superiority of blacks over whites. The blues Baldwin may think he is singing for Mr. Charlie's sinning seem to me really to be sung for his inferiority....

His making a hero of blackness, combined with his sentimentalizing of masculinity, blinds Baldwin to the fact that Richard's condition is no less hideously comic than Lyle Britten's. There is no glory or hope, not a shred of it, to be found in the life of either the black man or the white. What these characters give evidence to, what the play seems to be about really, is the small-mindedness of the male sex. It is about the narcissistic, pompous, and finally ridiculous demands made by the male ego when confronted by moral catastrophe. (p. 11)

> *Philip Roth, "Channel X: Two Plays on the Race Conflict," in* The New York Review of Books, *Vol. II, No. 8, May 28, 1964, pp. 10-13.*

Robert A. Bone (essay date 1965)

[*Bone is a distinguished American literary critic and an authority on African-American literature. In the following excerpt from an essay first published in* Tri-Quarterly *in 1965, he surveys theme and plot in* Go Tell It on the Mountain, Giovanni's Room, *and* Another Country.]

Go Tell It on the Mountain (1953) is the best of Baldwin's novels, and the best is very good indeed. It ranks with Jean Toomer's *Cane,* Richard Wright's *Native Son,* and Ralph Ellison's *Invisible Man* as a major contribution to American fiction. For this novel cuts through the walls of the storefront church to the essence of Negro experience in America. This is Bal-

dwin's earliest world, his bright and morning star, and it glows with metaphorical intensity. Its emotions are his emotions; its language, his native tongue. The result is a prose of unusual power and authority. One senses in Baldwin's first novel a confidence, control, and mastery of style which he has not attained again in the novel form. (p. 5)

Baldwin sees the Negro quite literally as the bastard child of American civilization. In Gabriel's double involvement with bastardy, we have a re-enactment of the white man's historic crime. In Johnny, the innocent victim of Gabriel's hatred, we have an archetypal image of the Negro child. Obliquely, by means of an extended metaphor, Baldwin approaches the very essence of Negro experience. That essence is rejection, and its most destructive consequence is shame. But God, the Heavenly Father, does not reject the Negro utterly. He casts down only to raise up. This is the psychic drama which occurs beneath the surface of John's conversion....

The quality of Negro life, unending struggle with one's own blackness, is symbolized by Baldwin in the family name, *Grimes.* One can readily understand how such a sense of personal shame might have been inflamed by contact with the Christian tradition and transformed into an obsession with original sin. (p. 8)

Given this attack on the core of the self, how can the Negro respond? ... There is ... the path of self-hatred and the path of self-acceptance. Both are available to Johnny within the framework of the church, but he is deterred from one by the negative example of his father.

Consider Gabriel. The substance of his life is moral evasion. A preacher of the gospel, and secretly the father of an illegitimate child, he cannot face the evil in himself. In order to preserve his image as the Lord's anointed, he has sacrificed the lives of those around him. His principal victim is Johnny, who is not his natural child. In disowning the bastard, he disowns the "blackness" in himself. Gabriel's psychological mechanisms are, so to say, white. Throughout his work Baldwin has described the scapegoat mechanism which is fundamental to the white man's sense of self. To the question, Who am I?, the white man answers: I am *white,* that is, immaculate, without stain. I am the purified, the saved, the saintly, the elect. It is the *black* who is the embodiment of evil. Let him, the son of the bondwoman, pay the price of my sins.

From self-hatred flows not only self-righteousness but self-glorification as well.... When the Negro preacher compares the lot of his people to that of the children of Israel, he provides his flock with a series of metaphors which correspond to their deepest experience. The church thus offers to the Negro masses a ritual enactment of their daily pain. It is with this poetry of suffering, which Baldwin calls the power of the Word, that the final section of the novel is concerned.

The first fifteen pages of Part III contain some of Baldwin's most effective writing. As John Grimes lies before the altar, a series of visionary states passes through his soul. Dream fragments and Freudian sequences, lively fantasies and Aesopian allegories, combine to produce a generally surrealistic effect. Images of darkness and chaos, silence and emptiness, mist and cold—cumulative patterns developed early in the novel—function now at maximum intensity. These images of damnation express the state of the soul when thrust into outer darkness by a rejecting, punishing, castrating father-figure who is the surrogate of a hostile society. The dominant emotions are shame, despair, guilt, and fear. (pp. 8-9)

On these harsh terms, Baldwin's protagonist discovers his identity.... To the question, Who am I?, he can now reply: I am he who suffers, and yet whose suffering on occasion is "from time set free." And thereby he discovers his humanity, for only man can ritualize his pain. We are now very close to that plane of human experience where art and religion intersect. What Baldwin wants us to feel is the emotional pressure exerted on the Negro's cultural forms by his exposure to white oppression. And finally to comprehend that these forms alone, through their power of transforming suffering, have enabled him to survive his terrible ordeal.

Giovanni's Room (1956) is by far the weakest of Baldwin's novels. There is a tentative, unfinished quality about the book, as if in merely broaching the subject of homosexuality Baldwin had exhausted his creative energy. Viewed in retrospect, it seems less a novel in its own right than a first draft of *Another Country*. The surface of the novel is deliberately opaque, for Baldwin is struggling to articulate the most intimate, the most painful, the most elusive of emotions. The characters are vague and disembodied, the themes half-digested, the colors rather bleached than vivified. We recognize in this sterile psychic landscape the unprocessed raw material of art.

And yet this novel occupies a key position in Baldwin's spiritual development. Links run backward to *Go Tell It on the Mountain* as well as forward to *Another Country*. The very furniture of Baldwin's mind derives from the storefront church of his boyhood and adolescence. When he attempts a novel of homosexual love, with an all-white cast of characters and a European setting, he simply transposes the moral topography of Harlem to the streets of Paris. When he strives toward sexual self-acceptance, he automatically casts the homosexual in a priestly role. (p. 10)

At the emotional center of the novel is the relationship between David and Giovanni. It is highly symbolic, and to understand what is at stake, we must turn to Baldwin's essay on André Gide. Published toward the end of 1954, about a year before the appearance of *Giovanni's Room,* this essay is concerned with the two sides of Gide's personality and the precarious balance which was struck between them. On the one side was his sensuality, his lust for the boys on the Piazza d'Espagne, threatening him always with utter degradation. On the

other was his Protestantism, his purity, his otherworldliness—that part of him which was not carnal, and which found expression in his Platonic marriage to Madeleine. As Baldwin puts it, "She was his Heaven who would forgive him for his Hell and help him to endure it." It is a drama of salvation, in which the celibate wife, through selfless dedication to the suffering artist, becomes in effect a priest.

In the present novel, Giovanni plays the role of Gide; David, of Madeleine.

Possessing the power to save, David rejects the priestly office. Seen in this light, his love affair with Giovanni is a kind of novitiate. The dramatic conflict of the novel can be stated as follows: does David have a true vocation? Is he prepared to renounce the heterosexual world? When David leaves Giovanni for Hella, he betrays his calling, but ironically he has been ruined both for the priesthood and the world.

It is Giovanni, Baldwin's doomed hero, who is the true priest. For a priest is nothing but a journeyman in suffering.... It is a crucial distinction for all of Baldwin's work: there are the relatively innocent—the *laity* who are mere apprentices in human suffering—and the fully initiated, the *clergy* who are intimate with pain. Among the laity may be numbered Americans, white folks, heterosexuals, and squares: among the clergy, Europeans, Negroes, homosexuals, hipsters, and jazzmen. (p. 11)

The patterns first explored in *Giovanni's Room* are given full expression in *Another Country*. Rufus is a Negro Giovanni—a journeyman in suffering and a martyr to racial oppression. Vivaldo and the other whites are mere apprentices, who cannot grasp the beauty and the terror of Negro life. Eric is a David who completes his novitiate, and whose priestly or redemptive role is central to the novel. There has been, however, a crucial change of tone. In *Giovanni's Room,* one part of Baldwin wants David to escape from the male prison, even as another part remains committed to the ideal of homosexual love. In the later novel, this conflict has been resolved. Baldwin seems convinced that homosexuality is a liberating force, and he now brings to the subject a certain proselytizing zeal.

Another Country (1962) is a failure on the grand scale. It is an ambitious novel, rich in thematic possibilities, for Baldwin has at his disposal a body of ideas brilliantly developed in his essays. When he tries to endow these ideas with imaginative life, however, his powers of invention are not equal to the task. The plot consists of little more than a series of occasions for talk and fornication. Since the latter is a limited vehicle for the expression of complex ideas, talk takes over, and the novel drowns in a torrent of rhetoric.

The ideas themselves are impressive enough. At the heart of what Baldwin calls the white problem is a moral cowardice, a refusal to confront the "dark" side of human experience. The white American, at once over-protected and repressed, exhibits an infuriating tendency to deny the reality of pain and suffering, violence and evil, sex and death. He preserves in the teeth of human circumstance what must strike the less protected as a kind of willful innocence. (p. 12)

By projecting the "blackness," of his own being upon the dark skin of his Negro victim, the white man hopes to exercise the chaotic forces which threaten to destroy him from within.

The psychic cost is of course enormous. The white man loses the experience of "blackness," sacrificing both its beauty and its terror to the illusion of security. In the end, he loses his identity. For a man who cannot acknowledge the dark impulses of his own soul cannot have the vaguest notion of who he is. (pp. 12-13)

There are psychic casualties on the Negro side as well. No human personality can escape the effects of prolonged emotional rejection. The victim of this cruelty will defend himself with hatred and with dreams of vengeance, and will lose, perhaps forever, his normal capacity for love. Strictly speaking, this set of defenses, and the threat of self-destruction which they pose, constitutes the Negro problem.

It is up to the whites to break this vicious circle of rejection and hatred. They can do so only by facing the void, by confronting chaos, by making the necessary journey to "another country." What the white folks need is a closer acquaintance with the blues....

What dramatic materials are employed to invest these themes with life? A Greenwich Village setting and a hipster idiom.... A square thrown in for laughs. A side trip to Harlem (can we be *slumming*?). A good deal of boozing, and an occasional stick of tea.... Five orgasms (two interracial and two homosexual) or approximately one per eighty pages, a significant increase over the Mailer rate. Distracted by this nonsense, how can one attend to the serious business of the novel?

In one respect only does the setting of *Another Country* succeed. Baldwin's descriptions of New York contain striking images of malaise, scenes and gestures which expose the moral chaos of contemporary urban life. The surface of his prose reflects the aching loneliness of the city with the poignancy of a Hopper painting. (p. 13)

At the core of Baldwin's fiction is an existentialist psychology.... Sexual identity—all identity—emerges from the void. Man, the sole creator of himself, moves alone upon the face of the waters....

[Eric holds a] pivotal position in the novel. Through his commitment to Yves, he introduces an element of order into the chaos of his personal life. This precarious victory, wrested in anguish from the heart of darkness, is the real subject of *Another Country*. Images of chaos proliferate throughout the novel. (p. 15)

Eric is the first of Rufus' friends to face his demons and achieve a sense of self. He in turn emancipates the rest.

From this vantage point, one can envision the novel that Baldwin was trying to write. With the breakdown of traditional standards—even of sexual normality—homosexuality becomes a metaphor of the modern condition.... The homosexual becomes emblematic of existential man.

What actually happens, however, is that Baldwin's literary aims are deflected by his sexual mystique. Eric returns to America as the high priest of ineffable phallic mysteries. His friends, male and female, dance around the Maypole and, *mirabile dictu,* their sense of reality is restored....

For most readers of *Another Country,* the difficulty will lie in accepting Eric as a touchstone of reality.... [Few] will concede a sense of reality, at least in the sexual realm, to one who regards heterosexual love as "a kind of superior calisthenics."... To most, homosexuality will seem rather an invasion than an affirmation of human truth. Ostensibly the novel summons us to reality. Actually it substitutes for the illusions of white supremacy those of homosexual love. (p. 16)

The drama of reconciliation is enacted by Ida and Vivaldo. Through their symbolic marriage, Ida is reconciled to whites; Vivaldo, to women. This gesture, however, is a mere concession to majority opinion. What Baldwin really feels is dramatized through Rufus and Eric. Rufus can neither be fully reconciled to, nor fully defiant of, white society. No Bigger Thomas, he is incapable of total hate. Pushed to the limits of endurance, he commits suicide. Similarly, Eric can neither be fully reconciled to women, nor can he surrender to the male demi-monde. So he camps on the outskirts of Hell. In the case of Rufus, the suicidal implications are overt. With Eric,... Baldwin tries to persuade us that Hell is really Heaven. (pp. 16-17)

Coupled with these racial sentiments are manifestations of sexual Garveyism. Throughout the novel, the superiority of homosexual love is affirmed. Here alone can one experience total surrender and full orgastic pleasure: here alone the metaphysical terror of the void. Heterosexual love, by comparison, is a pale—one is tempted to say, white—imitation. In many passages hostility to women reaches savage proportions.... (p. 17)

In *Another Country,* the sharp outlines of character are dissolved by waves of uncontrolled emotion. The novel lacks a proper distancing. One has the impression of Baldwin's recent work that the author does not know where his own psychic life leaves off and that of his characters begins. What is more, he scarcely cares to know, for he is sealed in a narcissism so engrossing that he fails to make emotional contact with his characters. If his people have no otherness, if he repeatedly violates their integrity, how can they achieve the individuality which alone will make them memorable? (p. 18)

Properly regarded, *Another Country* will be seen as the celebration of a Black Mass. The jazzman is Baldwin's priest; the homosexual, his acolyte. The bandstand is his altar; Bessie Smith his choir. God is carnal mystery, and through orgasm, the Word is made flesh. Baldwin's ministry is as vigorous as ever. He summons to the mourners' bench all who remain, so to say, hardened in their innocence. Lose that, he proclaims, and you will be saved. To the truly unregenerate, those stubborn hetero-sexuals, he offers the prospect of salvation through sodomy. With this novel doctrine, the process of inver-sion is complete. (p. 19)

[Baldwin] has already devoted two novels to his sexual rebellion. If he persists, he will surely be remembered as the greatest American novelist since Jack Kerouac. The future now depends on his ability to transcend the emotional reflexes of his adolescence. So extraordinary a talent requires of him no less an effort. (p. 20)

> Robert A. Bone, "The Novels of James Baldwin," in Tri-Quarterly, *No. 5, Winter, 1965, pp. 3-20.*

David Littlejohn (essay date 1966)

[*In the following excerpt from his* Black on White: A Critical Survey of Writing by American Negroes, *Littlejohn examines* Go Tell It on the Mountain, Giovanni's Room, *and* Another Country, *proposing that each work is "a staving off of death, a matter of survival" for Baldwin.*]

Each of James Baldwin's three novels [*Go Tell It on the Mountain, Giovanni's Room,* and *Another Country*] has been written out of some personal necessity of the author's, a necessity which it describes, conveys, and, hopefully, enables the author to transcend. Everything he writes—when he writes well—bears this sense of an inner necessity, of the whole of himself told and overcome. From no other contemporary author does one get such a sensation of writing as life; it is all so open and desperate and acute, minute by minute and word by word. The captivation of the reader, the feeling of rightness comes from Baldwin's absolute honesty, from his yielding, however unwillingly, to necessity. A reader *feels* the desperation—if the man had not written this book, and written it so, he could not have survived. Each book is a renewed effort to stay alive and upright through the finding and placing of perfect words. Each book is a staving off of death, a matter of survival.

If this is the case, it can scarcely be considered illegiti-mate or extra-literary prying to regard the novels as essentially about him, the man, James Baldwin. Autobi-ographical exactness, after all, is the very source of their sting, their astringent modern taste. It is not anti-literary, therefore, or anti-poetic, to talk of *James Baldwin's* family, or experience, or pain, in these novels, rather than John's or David's. It is no more nasty to write of his inversion than of Proust's. When a writer makes it so clear that he is not lying, one should do him the honor of believing him.

There is more than one kind of honesty in writing, of course. A self-dissolving symbolist may tell truth as well as a self-displaying realist, and Baldwin's honesty is only his, the latest variety: the need to tell "all" the truth, with no pretenses, no fictions, no metaphors—the quality one associates with his best essays. Such a need (cf. Mailer, Genet) may ultimately render unusable all the standard props of fiction. In this new, needful, stripped-bare kind of nervous truth, one tells far more than is customarily told, in order to stay this side of insanity. Baldwin allows himself, for example, none of Ellison's objectivity, very little of his distance from his fictions. Like Richard Wright, ultimately, he is probably more a symbolic Negro than a typical one; but, again, like Richard Wright, he is no less useful, or even less necessary, for that.

Each novel, for Baldwin, has been a stage; a stage to be lived through, transformed into words, then exorcised and transcended. The next novel begins a new stage, and the process goes on. This does not, of course, mean that he will ever reach the shores of fulfillment and rest. It seems, in fact, highly unlikely, unless he should begin to lie.

Go Tell It on the Mountain (1952) was the first stage, Baldwin's baptism of fire. It is the testament of his coming to terms with, his defining and transcending, the experience of his boyhood—his family, his religion, his Harlem youth. (The story is told again in **"Notes of a Native Son"**; it is told a third time, far less honestly, in **The Fire Next Time.**) The telling was necessary for Baldwin, in the same way that telling *Look Homeward, Angel* was necessary for Thomas Wolfe. *Go Tell It on the Mountain* has, in fact, much the same kind of effect as Wolfe's great novel, the effect of autobiography-as-exor-cism, of a lyrical, painful, ritual exercise whose necessity and intensity the reader feels. The impact on a reader, in books of this sort, appears to be in direct relation to the amount of truth the author is able to tell himself. At the end of *Go Tell It on the Mountain,* the hero, John, has "come through"; one presumes that Baldwin had as well. (pp. 119-21)

Baldwin is as unafraid of glorious prose as he is of honest prose, and the book is woven out of both. But the strength, at last, is that of his own personal necessity, a necessity that the reader can vicariously share. It is the strength of a harrowing prayer, simple and felt, of a small tragic truth that enlarges the heart. The book is carven with love. Because of its peculiar kind of necessary, very personal truth, it remains one of the few, the very few, essential Negro works.

Giovanni's Room (1956) served its purpose too, I sus-pect. Baldwin's personal uncertainties are not limited to the racial, religious, and familial. (pp. 123-24)

It is certainly one of the most subtle novels of the homosexual world, not as poetic and outspoken as Genet's, not as trashy as John Rechy's; but the emotions are more to be observed than to be shared. It has something of the lyrical allusiveness of *Go Tell It on the*

Mountain, of its squeezing, sonnetlike smallness—Giovanni's room is the perfect symbolic setting, as cluttered and oppressively closed as one of Pinter's settings. But the effect, on the whole, is slight. (p. 124)

Another Country, and the sick truths it tells Americans about themselves, had to wait for the emergence of a new style: a style one may designate as New York-1960's.... It is used, at its shrillest, most wide-open, by Baldwin, Edward Albee, LeRoi Jones, Norman Mailer, Lenny Bruce, *The Realist,* the new Grove Press novelists, some of the Jewish Establishment journalists and critics (*The New York Review, The New Leader, Partisan Review*), and probably by hundreds of New Yorkers whose names we will never know. It has correspondences with softer manifestations like pop art, Jules Feiffer, Nichols and May, *A Hard Day's Night.* Jane, Vivaldo's "beat chick" in *Another Country,* is a splendid specimen: she is brittle, bitchy, fresh from the shrink, with sex like broken glass; a frenzied neurotic with every nerve bare and bleeding loud; first cousin to Lula in *The Dutchman.*

This style almost entirely carries the book, a style of screaming, no-holds-barred verbal violence. The revolving sequence of events, the inter-ringing figures of the sex dance (everyone mixing with everyone else), even, ultimately, the characters in the dance themselves, white and black, homo-, hetero-, and bi-sexual, exist primarily to provide voices and vehicles for the screamy exchanges, the ear-piercing insults, the excruciating displays of mutual torment. (pp. 125-26)

The race war, as depicted in this novel, is a difficult thing to understand. First of all, Baldwin has almost entirely excluded "average" people, the simple white American bourgeoisie or lower orders, whose prejudice is so obvious and so stupid it bores even more than it disgusts him. The few representatives of *that* world, the upstairs world, who foolishly drop into the plot are usually dissolved into steam with single drops of acid. (A pair of white heterosexual liberals, the Silenskis, so square they are married and have children and make money, degenerate into the crudest samples of sick America before the book is through, despite Baldwin's obvious efforts to be fair. Their racial liberality, it develops, is as fragile as their sexual assurance. So much for "normal" people.)

So all we have left to fight the race war are a few outlaw blacks and highly emancipated whites. In such a context the war loses its social relevance (except perhaps symbolically), and takes on the dimensions of a private duel. But the issues are no less clear. "Somewhere in his heart the black boy hated the white boy because he was white. Somewhere in his heart Vivaldo had hated and feared Rufus because he was black." Baldwin tries, or at least the top of his mind tries, to keep the sides equal, and the fighting fair. The white combatants, Leona, Vivaldo, especially Eric, are created with affection and care: these are no evil, ill-understood Wrighteous puppets. But the Negroes have all the trumps. It is *they,* always, who

carry the whip, and no white lover, friend, or reader dares to deny them the right. (pp. 126-27)

At their most intense, these race-war combats always transmute into sex combats—which illustrates Baldwin's theory of the fundamentally sexual character of racism. This aspect of the novel, however, is even more unsettled and unsettling, because of the case Baldwin is trying to make for inversion. (p. 128)

The over-lyrical poeticizing of homosexual love is one of the real flaws of the book. Surely Genet's pictures, or even Baldwin's in *Giovanni's Room,* of the foul *and* fair of inversion, are more just. (pp. 129-30)

Another Country has, in its frantic new writer's world called New York, much of the same necessity, the same quality of desperate exorcism as Baldwin's earlier works. But things here are less under control. Almost all of the thinking, the non-imaginative thinking of Baldwin's essays is sandwiched into the fiction, bearing a suggestion that the man is now writing more from his ideas than his imagination. The piercing one-note tone of repetitiousness of so much of this long book supports this dissatisfying notion. Another dangerous sign is the confusion of narrative authority, very like the confusions of self-identity which mar so many of Baldwin's latest and weakest essays. His own opinions mingle with those of his characters, subjectivity jars with objectivity in such a way as to indicate that the author is unaware of the difference: i.e., that James Baldwin, through the 1950's the sole master of *control* in American prose, in the 1960's has begun to lose control.

What is there to salvage and prize? A number of things. More often than not, between the explosions, *Another Country* reminds the reader that James Baldwin is still one of the genuine stylists of the English language. (p. 130)

He is the most powerful and important American essayist of the postwar period, perhaps of the century. *Notes of a Native Son* and *Nobody Knows My Name* will maintain their place among the small collection of genuine American classics. They have already been adopted as standard texts and models of style in American college courses; and this is not just a "vogue," an offshoot of the Civil Rights movement. Two such books would sustain any reputation, as long as men can tell the true from the false. (pp. 135-36)

Baldwin has shown more concern for the painful exactness of prose style than any other modern American writer. He picks up words with heavy care, then sets them, one by one, with a cool and loving precision that one can feel in the reading. There are no bright words in his best essays, no flashes, allusions, delusions, no Tynanesque "brilliance." His style is like stripped conversation, saying the most that words can *honestly* say. If it hurts, if it ties one down and hammers its words on one's mind, it is simply the effect of his won't-let-go rigor. There is good and bad prose, there is moral and immoral.

This does not of course imply that the style is flat, because it is not like champagne. Baldwin is fully aware of the ambiguities and ironies implicit in his subjects (primary among them the sick paradox that calls itself America), and he weaves these same ambiguities and ironies into his prose. He is also drivingly and constantly self-critical, which is why his writing is so strong and clear, his thinking so often unassailable. His paragraphs work like a witty colloquy of two sharp minds. Baldwin's and his critic's, one within the other: the devastating qualifiers, the cool understatements, the parentheses, the litotes, the suggestions and quiet parallels display the double mind of the self-critic at work.

Writing like this can be more harrowing, more intense than *any* of the works we are considering [elsewhere in the book]. As Baldwin himself admits, Negro literature "is more likely to be a symptom of our tension than an examination of it," and this includes his own three novels, his plays, and his stories. The exhilarating exhaustion of reading his best essays—which in itself may be a proof of their honesty and value—demands that the reader measure up, and forces him to learn. (pp. 136-37)

> *David Littlejohn, in his* Black on White: A Critical Survey of Writing by American Negroes, *Grossman Publishers, 1966, pp. 119-37.*

Alfred Kazin (essay date 1973)

[*In the following excerpt, Kazin explores Baldwin's treatment of sexual and emotional issues in his major works.*]

As a writer Baldwin is as obsessed by sex and family as Strindberg was, but instead of using situations for their dramatic value, Baldwin likes to pile up all possible emotional conflicts as assertions. But for the same reason that in *Giovanni's Room* Baldwin made everybody white just to show that he could, and in *Tell Me How Long the Train's Been Gone* transferred the son-father quarrel to a quarrel with a brother, so one feels about *Another Country* that Baldwin writes fiction in order to use up his private difficulties; even his fiction piles up the atmosphere of raw emotions that is his literary standby. Why does so powerful a writer as Baldwin make himself look simpleminded by merely asserting an inconsequential succession of emotions? (p. 222)

[In] *Notes of a Native Son, Nobody Knows My Name, The Fire Next Time,* Baldwin dropped the complicated code for love difficulties he uses in his novels and simplified himself into an "angry Black" very powerfully indeed—and this just before Black nationalists were to turn on writers like him. The character who calls himself "James Baldwin" in *his* nonfiction novel is more professionally enraged, more doubtfully an evangelist for his people, than the actual James Baldwin, a very literary mind indeed. But there is in *Notes of a Native Son* a genius for

bringing many symbols together, an instinctive association with the 1943 Harlem riot, the streets of smashed plate glass, that stems from the all too understandable fascination of the Negro with the public sources of his fate. The emphasis is on heat, fire, anger, the sense of being hemmed in and suffocated; the words are tensed into images that lacerate and burn. Reading Baldwin's essays, we are suddenly past the discordancy that has plagued his fiction—a literal problem of conflict, for Baldwin's fiction shows him trying to transpose facts into fiction without sacrificing the emotional capital that has been his life. (pp. 223-24)

> *Alfred Kazin, "The Imagination of Fact: Capote to Mailer," in his* Bright Book of Life: American Novelists & Storytellers from Hemingway to Mailer, *Atlantic-Little, Brown, 1973, pp. 207-41.*

John W. Aldridge (essay date 1974)

[*In the excerpt below, Aldridge briefly surveys Baldwin's development as a writer, lamenting what he perceives to be the author's deteriorating skills as a novelist.*]

Over the past twenty years Baldwin has become the most influential prophet and polemicist and perhaps the most distinguished writer of his race, and he has earned a position in the moral community of our time comparable only to that of Norman Mailer as a monitor of conscience and a remaker of consciousness. His fame now secure, we have accorded him the highest honor we can bestow upon a public intellectual: We have disarmed him with celebrity, fallen in love with his eccentricities, and institutionalized his outrage (along with Mailer's obscenity and Capote's bitchiness) into prime-time entertainment.

Yet his role as America's favorite token black is not without its advantages for Baldwin the writer, however responsible it may have been for converting the realities of his cause into the clichés of rhetoric. His strategy has always been to keep constantly before us the reminder that he is a *black* writer and that black is his subject. The absolute rightness of his cause coupled with his self-righteousness in proselytizing for it have very effectively kept at bay many commentators who might otherwise have approached him with the critical skepticism they habitually bring to the work of his white contemporaries. Baldwin has, to be sure, been the object of negative criticism, but all too often its force has been blunted or misdirected to peripheral issues seemingly in deference to the idea that the act of critical discrimination just might possibly be considered discriminatory. Where other writers may be judged on the strength of their artistry, Baldwin's artistry has frequently been placed beyond judgment because of the sacredness of his subject. One can only wonder whether his other and, in some respects, more central subject, interracial sexuality and homosexuality, would be quite so effective as a silencer of opposition . . . .

Baldwin's blackness has caused him to perceive and conceive experience almost exclusively within the charged polarities of black and white, and in spite of his intelligence and remarkable powers of narration—qualities displayed more impressively in his essays than in his novels—he has repeatedly produced fictional characterizations that represent the most simplistic vision of the racial conflict. There is considerable irony in this because Baldwin, very early in his career [in the essay *"Everybody's Protest Novel"*], brilliantly stated the case against the very kind of fiction he later came to write.... However sensitive Baldwin may be to the unique quality of the individual human being, he has been generally unsuccessful in creating characters who exist independently of their categorization....

[Baldwin's failure] would appear to be the result of an inability to extricate his powerful feelings for individuals from his far more powerful feelings for them as victims of racial oppression.

Perhaps in an effort to break out of the confines and to generalize the implications of his own form of the protest novel, Baldwin has repeatedly tried to convince his readers that there is finally no difference between the dilemma of his black characters and that of just about everybody else in our corrupt society....

Baldwin's preoccupation with sexual love between blacks and whites may be yet another symptom of his effort to extend the thematic range of his fiction beyond the boundaries of race. Sexual love emerges in his novels as a kind of universal anodyne for the disease of racial separatism, as a means not only of achieving personal identity but also of transcending false categories of color and gender.... As the forces of discrimination grow stronger in the outside world, the characters grow more undiscriminating in their sexuality, achieving through countless combinations and recombinations of relationships some brief sense that they are still alive.... The remarkable thing about these people, apart from their indefatigability, is that they are really not interested in one another at all. In fact, they are no more real to one another than they are as characters.... One might have assumed on the evidence of his essays and early fiction that Baldwin would be consumed in the fires of hate and that his future as a novelist could well depend on his achievement of compassion and objectivity. But it seemed probable after the appearance of *Another Country* and the later novel, *Tell Me How Long the Train's Been Gone,* that he might instead be destined to drown in the throbbing seas of sentimental love, and, regrettably, his new novel. *If Beale Street Could Talk,* only makes that probability seem a certainty....

It is extremely sad to see a writer of Baldwin's large gifts producing, in all seriousness, such junk. Yet it has been evident for some time that he is deteriorating as a novelist and becoming increasingly a victim of the vice of sentimentality. This seems a particular pity because Baldwin may have one great novel left within him which it would take the most radical courage to write, the story

of a talented black writer who achieves worldwide success on the strength of his anger and, in succeeding, gradually loses his anger and comes to be loved by everybody. Clearly, such acceptance can be considered a triumph for a black man in America, but it can be death for a black writer in whom anger and talent are indivisible.

John W. Aldridge, "The Fire Next Time?" in Saturday Review/World, *June 15, 1974, pp. 20, 24-5.*

Edmund White (essay date 1979)

[*White is an American novelist, dramatist, and literary critic who has written widely on homosexuality in contemporary America. He is especially known for two works:* A Boy's Own Story *(1982), a bildungsroman about a homosexual boy's coming to terms with his sexual identity, and* States of Desire *(1980), a sociological study of homosexual lifestyles in the United States. In the following excerpt, he reviews* Just above My Head, *focusing on Baldwin's portrayal of homosexuality in the novel.*]

Of all the well-known novelists of the day, James Baldwin is among the warmest, the most companionable, the least ironic. So many contemporary writers seem incapable of presenting loyalty, innocence or happiness, especially family happiness, but Baldwin inhabits these feelings with great naturalness and intensity. He can show, as he does more than once in *Just Above My Head,* parents and children exchanging gifts at Christmas or during a reunion. The family members have tears in their eyes, not of regret but of anticipation, not of loneliness but of love. Looked at merely as a literary fashion (and it is, of course, much, much more), the direct depiction of such ardor is unique today; one has to go back to Dickens to find a similar impulse in a major writer, though in Dickens the happy moments are all too often bathetic, whereas in Baldwin they glow with the steadiness and clarity of a flame within a glass globe....

[The book's most remarkable character is Julia]. Julia is a hypocrite, an eerily controlled monster of vanity and manipulation bent on destroying her mother and seducing her father. Of such stuff melodramas are made, and Baldwin drains every bit of juice from this juiciest of material. True melodrama, however, with its demand for villains and heroes, is a failure of compassion, and Baldwin is above all a wise and compassionate writer. Accordingly, once Julia achieves her monstrous goals..., she turns in terror from her victory, loses her faith, renounces her ministry—and, after years of self-degradation, grows into a woman of formidable dignity and understanding.

The central figure, Arthur, is another test for Baldwin's delicacy of sentiment, for his powers as a diplomat of the emotions, because Arthur is both black and homosexual. To present a homosexual character in the round and with sympathy is still, I suppose, a challenge even to a white writer, but granting acceptance to male homosexuality in the black community is a still greater problem, historically and politically. (p. 5)

In *Just Above My Head* Baldwin has successfully placed the black male homosexual back into the context of black society. Baldwin is not, it seems, arguing for gay liberation.... [The] attitude embodied in this novel is one of tolerance and acceptance of all forms of sexuality so that the crusaders for black rights can march forward, united.... The scenes in which [Arthur and Crunch] discover their love for each other are the best written in the book—hushed, concentrated, immaculately detailed.... Again and again homosexual alliances are paralleled by those that are heterosexual until the reader begins to respond to the emotions and experiences of individuals, regardless of their affectional preferences. As a young man Baldwin wrote *Giovanni's Room,* a homosexual love story in which the characters are white. He has before and since written many books about blacks who happen to be heterosexual.... His decision to bring homosexuality and blackness together is courageous, given the tense political situation; that he has done so with such tact is a sign of his decency and artistry.

But this novel is not merely about a character's exploration of his homosexuality. Arthur—and Julia and Hall and all the other characters—must also come to terms with their blackness. (pp. 5, 9)

[The] integration struggles of the 1960s in the South are swiftly and dramatically related at the heart of the novel. For young people to whom those days are nothing but a dry chapter in history, this book will serve to put human flesh on schematic bones. Never has the story of the heroic civil rights movement been more powerfully rendered.

Just Above My Head is not a perfect novel: fiction that is politically engaged is always less elegant than reactionary fiction, which lavishes on form the attention a progressive literature must also devote to content. Arthur—and especially Arthur's death—are disappointingly shadowy. Too much of "Book One" is carelessly written. Too many scenes occur in bars and restaurants as anecdotes exchanged over dinner and drinks, as though Baldwin is so eager to tell stories that he forgets to show actions. No matter. In whole long sections the style is imbued with Baldwin's peculiarly indirect vision, his idiosyncratic way of catching the imprecision, the blurriness, of experience. And, despite the clinking of forks and cocktail glasses, the tale does move forward on coiled muscles—this is the work of a born storyteller

Dust jacket of Baldwin's Tell Me How Long the Train's Been Gone, *the author's last novel of the 1960s.*

at the height of his powers, a man who, now that he is older and more mature, has truly come into his own. As the most celebrated black American novelist, Baldwin has given his readers a comprehensive and comprehending examination of race and sexuality and suggested some of the ways in which the politics of color can shape the transactions of love. (p. 9)

> *Edmund White, "James Baldwin Overcomes," in* Book World—The Washington Post, *September 23, 1979, pp. 5, 9.*

Emmanuel S. Nelson (essay date 1985)

[*In the following essay, Nelson explores Baldwin's portrayal of sexuality, chiefly homosexuality, in his novels and essays.*]

The international reputation of James Baldwin has rested largely on his insightful analyses of American race relations (e.g., *The Fire Next Time*) and on his poignant interpretations of the nightmarish Black experience (e.g., *Go Tell It On the Mountain*). Such a reputation has served to deemphasize the fact that he is one of the most important and influential homosexual writers of the twentieth century. Therefore, to grasp the full literary and cultural significance of Baldwin's works, one has to bear in mind that central to Baldwin's life and art is his confrontation with and acceptance of his sexuality. A black homosexual in a racist and homophobic culture, he struggles toward a healing and liberating sense of self-acceptance. Each of his six novels is a record of his struggle; collectively, they are a testament to the growing maturity of his vision.

Baldwin's growth as an individual and novelist can be divided into three major stages. In his first two novels, *Go Tell It on the Mountain* (1953) and *Giovanni's Room* (1956), we see a young Baldwin attempting to come to terms with his sexual self. In his first work his rebellion is hesitant and his liberation tentative; in the second novel his defiance is more open and courageous. Artistically he is most effective at this stage. In the second phase of his development—*Another Country* (1961) and *Tell Me How Long the Train's Been Gone* (1967)—he becomes defensive and polemical in his treatment of the homosexual theme. But his art, largely because of his confrontational posture, suffers. *If Beale Street Could Talk* (1974) and *Just Above My Head* (1979), his two most recent novels, signal the third stage of his struggle. Free from sexual polemics, these works suggest that he has at last reached a new plateau of awareness: a healing acceptance of his sexuality. The maturity of his vision and freedom from defensiveness enhance the quality of his art, although he rarely attains the creative heights of his early work. Thus Baldwin moves from tentative sexual rebellion to polemical confrontation to mature sexual self-acceptance; artistically, however, his first two novels remain his strongest, the next two show some weakening in novelistic energy, and the last two evince renewed vigor.

One of the central thematic concerns of *Go Tell* is the developing sexuality of John Grimes, the fourteen-year-old autobiographical protagonist. For a proper understanding of Baldwin's handling of the homosexual theme, we should consider his attitude toward homosexuality at the time of the publication of his first novel. In *"Male Prison,"* an essay he wrote in 1954, he vehemently attacks Andre Gide for his somewhat explicit handling of the homosexual theme in *Madeleine* and vehemently declares:

> And his homosexuality, I felt, was his own affair which he ought to have hidden from us, or, if he needed to be so explicit, he ought at least to have managed to be a little more scientific—whatever, in the domain of morals, that word may mean—less logical, less romantic.

This curious and somewhat ambiguous assertion reveals Baldwin's personal confusion over his own homosexuality and his indecision regarding the relationship between his sexuality and his art. The young Baldwin who made this statement is clearly hiding in the closet.

Baldwin's reluctance to deal openly with his homosexuality partly accounts for the subdued nature of his treatment of that topic in *Go Tell.* But there is also a crucial artistic reason. John, the protagonist, is only fourteen, and the narration is limited to his internal point of view. Since he is too young and too confused about his sexuality to articulate and define his homosexual longings, such desires can only be suggested, not explained, to the reader. The result, however, is one of the most effective portrayals of the developing adolescent homosexual sensibility in American fiction, comparable to Truman Capote's expert handling of an almost identical situation in *Other Voices, Other Rooms.*

The reader gets the first hint of John's homosexual proclivity when the young protagonist keeps staring at Elisha, as the seventeen-year-old Sunday-school teacher explains the lesson. John finds himself "admiring the timbre of Elisha's voice, much deeper and manlier than his own, admiring the leanness and grace, the strength, the darkness of Elisha in his Sunday suit." When the teacher asks him a question, John becomes "ashamed and confused, feeling the palms of his hands become wet and his heart pound like a hammer." When Elisha dances in a state of religious frenzy, the adolescent protagonist is fascinated by "the muscles leaping and swelling in his long, dark neck," and his thighs that move "terribly against the cloth of his suit." John feels guilty about his recently learned habit of masturbation, but what terrifies him most is that his masturbatory fantasies largely center around the boys he sees in the school restroom, boys who are "older, bigger, braver, who made bets with each other as to whose urine could arch higher." Such fantasies produce in him "a transformation of which he would never dare speak."

John and Elisha's playful wrestling on the church floor has obvious sexual overtones. Wrestling, as James Giles points out, has often been used by writers as "a significant device for underscoring covert homosexual attraction (e.g., Lawrence's *Women in Love*)." After the wrestling, the protagonist stares "in a dull paralysis of terror at the body of Elisha" and looks at the older boy's face with "questions he would never ask." Toward the end of the novel, after John's experience of spiritual conversion, he touches Elisha's arm and finds "himself trembling." He looks at his Sunday-school teacher and struggles "to tell him something . . . all that could never be said." When Elisha places a "holy kiss" on John's forehead, the new convert views it as "a seal ineffaceable forever," thus suggesting a new awareness of his part. Thus Baldwin reveals his doubts, fears, anxieties and moments of dim excitement that accompany the awakening and gradual growth of homosexual awareness in John's adolescent psyche.

Equally subtle and effective is Baldwin's use of his protagonist's homosexuality as a means of symbolic revolt against sexually repressive religion. John grows up in the stifling atmosphere of Protestant fundamentalism. He is taught to view the desires of the flesh as satanic in origin. Such an attitude is reinforced in him when he sees Elisha and his girl friend, Ella Mae, being reprimanded by the preacher for possibly considering premarital sex. He is further confused by the vast hiatus between his father's profession and actual practice of Christianity. Therefore he rebels; his rebellion takes a specifically sexual form. He experiences his earliest homosexual stirrings in the church, in the holy temple of God. His homosexual wrestling with Elisha takes place in the church, under the providential eyes. Elisha, whose biblical name is obviously chosen intentionally, "redeems" John by nurturing the adolescent's spiritual as well as sexual growth. Baldwin's blending of the erotic and the spiritual indicates his rebellious stance. By presenting homosexual attraction in a specifically religious context, he "consecrates" homosexuality and defiantly mocks at the religion of his childhood.

Homosexuality emerges as a vehicle of rebellion also against a hostile and authoritarian father. John, rejected by his stepfather, searches for a father-figure. The very fact of his illegitimacy serves as a powerful metaphor for his condition of alienation from the elder Grimes. Frequently subjected to his father's violent rage, John begins to hate him and wishes to see him tormented in hell. His hatred propels him toward Elisha, who shows him the protective love and affection that he desperately longs for. This movement away from the father toward a father-figure culminates in the final scene, in which the protagonist walks away from his father toward Elisha and touches his arm, while uncomfortably feeling the presence of the old man. John, thus, clearly rejects his father in favor of his handsome Sunday-school teacher.

But Baldwin is yet to reach any substantial level of liberation. He is hesitant to make his sexual rebellion overt. And an aspect of his treatment of the homosexual theme betrays his internationalization of society's negative attitude toward the homosexual: his introduction of the Oedipal motif suggests his subscription to the popular misconception that male homosexuals are disturbed products of defective families with hostile or absent fathers and overprotective mothers. His incorporation of such a heterosexist belief regarding the etiology of male homosexuality into his protagonist's quest for sexual identity clearly indicates that Baldwin is far from achieving a healthy acceptance of his own sexuality.

Go Tell, then, is Baldwin's record of his initial attempt to reconcile himself to his sexual self. He has taken the first step toward liberation. His rebellion is hesitant, but his tentativeness proves to be a major artistic strength. He portrays in a sensitive and thoroughly convincing manner the emerging adolescent homosexual consciousness and gently rebels against religion that menaces honest forging of sexual identity. It is this theme of sexual identity that dominates his next novel.

Prior to the publication of *Giovanni's Room,* Baldwin had already established his reputation as an eloquent essayist *(Notes of a Native Son),* a successful playwright *(The Amen Corner),* and a gifted novelist *(Go Tell).* Readers and critics had come to recognize him as a brilliant writer whose analyses of race relations had bruised the American conscience and as an authentic interpreter of the Black experience. Therefore, *Giovanni's Room,* with its explicit and sympathetic handling of homosexuality, shocked and disappointed many. Moreover, it was published in the mid-fifties, when the sociopolitical climate in America was hardly conducive to a novel that handled with dignity and romantic intensity the sexual love between men. Baldwin's decision to write and publish such a work was a single act of personal and literary rebellion, because by doing so he risked his professional reputation and the very real possibilities of alienating a substantial segment of his growing white audience and antagonizing a large number of blacks. But he has survived numerous critical attacks. Now, after more than twenty-five years after its publication, it remains a classic piece of American homosexual fiction.

Giovanni's Room deals with the romantic involvement of David, a young white American, and Giovanni, a handsome Italian. Their relationship fails because David, unable to accept his homosexual self, refuses to commit himself to his lover. He abandons Giovanni to degrading circumstances which eventually lead to the young Italian's death at the guillotine. Though an element of sensationalism is inherent in the plot, Baldwin forcefully reveals one of the central dilemmas of the American homosexual: on the one hand, he is faced with rigid social definitions of masculinity and cultural expectations of heterosexual behavior; on the other hand, he has to deal with his sexual feelings for other men, feelings that conflict with all belief systems. The crisis resulting from such a conflict provides the central drama of Baldwin's second novel.

Giovanni's Room signals a crucial point in Baldwin's quest for sexual self-acceptance; it marks a new stage in his growth as an artist and as an individual. In *Go Tell* he gave us the impression of one still largely hiding in the closet but cautiously trying to get out. In *Giovanni's Room,* however, we see him out of the closet and defiantly confronting the American sexual Establishment. His decision to deal with homosexuality openly and compassionately shows that he is willing to face honestly his own sexual dilemma.

Although *Giovanni's Room* indicates that Baldwin is well on his way toward achieving the liberating sense of sexual self-acceptance, it also suggests that he has yet to go a long way. For instance, in spite of his overt sexual rebellion, he has not freed himself from the internalization of homophobic beliefs regarding the origin of male homosexual impulses. Once again he creates for his protagonist a weak father and domineering mother and thus implies that David's homosexuality is a result of unresolved Oedipal conflicts. He continues to collaborate unwittingly with those who view homosexuality as a form of pathological condition. But in his next novel, for the first time, he rejects such "vulgarly Freudian" explanations and moves closer to a mature acceptance of himself.

The publication of *Another Country*—Baldwin's third and most controversial novel—indicates his entry into the second major phase of his personal and artistic development. In his search for sexual self-acceptance he shows enhanced maturity. But he becomes defensive in his treatment of homosexuality, and his elaborate polemics undermine the quality of his art.

Baldwin's maturity becomes evident in his refusal to rely on Freudian theories to explain his characters' homosexuality. Refreshingly absent from the novel are ineffectual fathers, overprotective mothers and homosexually rebellious children. In effect, he rejects the psychiatric explanations for homosexual behavior. He now recognizes the naturalness of homosexual feelings; therefore he realizes that homosexuality, like heterosexuality, needs no explanation or justification.

Baldwin's heightened maturity is also evident in his refusal to categorize men into the conventional and rigidly distinct camps of homosexuals and heterosexuals. He views human sexuality in terms of a homosexual-heterosexual continuum: while some may be exclusively homosexual and some others exclusively heterosexual, many possess varying degrees of bisexual potential. This concept of sexuality is not new; it is merely a recognition of scientific facts. Kinsey's findings, which have been more than amply confirmed by recent research, show that while only about four percent of American males are exclusively homosexual, a whopping thirty-seven percent have at least one post-adolescent homosexual orgasm. Many of Kinsey's countrymen, however, hastily ignore such disquieting statistics that menace their fanciful personal and national definitions.

Baldwin is among the first American writers to treat such a scientifically sound view of human sexuality in an open, elaborate and artistically serious manner. Such an approach enables him to illustrate the sheer naturalness of homosexual desire. And by making basically heterosexual and thoroughly masculine characters like Vivaldo and Rufus engage in homosexual activities, he also challenges the stereotype of male homosexuals as effeminate and limp-wristed. Many heterosexual readers are likely to be shocked by the spectacle of perfectly "normal" men going to be with one another, but Baldwin compels us to an honest reevaluation of our view on human sexuality.

In spite of such mature and enlightened approach to human sexuality, however, Baldwin has not yet resolved his struggle with his own sexuality. Largely because of his growing eminence as a public figure and as a racial spokesman, he feels pressured to defend homosexuality. His polemical stance in *Another Country* is so obvious and unrelenting that Robert Bone accuses Baldwin of presenting homosexuality with "proselytizing zeal" [see essay dated 1965]. Whenever he describes homosexual acts, he becomes eloquently sentimental. For example, he presents Eric's first homosexual experience primarily in a passionately liturgical language. But he frequently betrays a general distaste and contempt for heterosexuality. He often shows sex between a man and woman as "a brutal, indecent spectacle."

Baldwin's polemical posture is also responsible for the flaws in the plot. In his zealous defense of homosexuality, he makes Eric a "redeemer." But it is precisely his redemptive role that weakens the plot and credibility of the action. Stephen Adams argues [in *The Homosexual as Hero in Contemporary Fiction* (1980)] that it is not Eric's homosexuality that makes him redemptive, but the self-knowledge that he has gained through suffering and existential confrontation with life. While it is true that Eric has a stronger sense of self than any other character in the novel, that attribute alone does not convince us that he can mend marriages and relationships by having sex with one of the partners.

Another Country not only created a critical furor, but also elicited angry responses from black militants. Eldridge Cleaver and LeRoi Jones were outraged by Baldwin's celebration of homosexuality and handling of the theme of interracial homosexuality. Their anger was further exacerbated by his growing popularity among whites and increasing prominence in the Civil Rights Movement. Since they considered homosexuality as a disease peculiar to white males, they certainly did not want a "faggot" to be a racial spokesman for blacks. Criticism from black militants put Baldwin on the defensive; therefore, he continues his polemical stance in his next novel, *Tell Me.*

In *Tell Me,* as in *Another Country,* Baldwin continues to cast the homosexual in redemptive role. Christopher, a politically active black homosexual, not only emerges as someone with a potential to save the world, but becomes an "actual agent of . . . transformation." Christopher's name itself suggests his redemptive role; his commitment to political militancy shows that he is a vital part of a transforming process that is changing the sociopolitical complexion of America. Thus the black homosexual becomes an instrument in changing the world into a more humane and livable place.

Although Baldwin is not entirely convincing in his defensive glorification of the positive potential of homosexuality, one should try to understand the author's views in terms of his larger posture of rebellion. He has chosen the black homosexual—the perennial outcast who is an embodiment of much that is despised in America—and has made him a suffering but redeeming figure. He has chosen the lonely, rejected outsider, and, while recognizing his pain, crowned him with dignity and magnificently reaffirmed his humanity. One should not hastily brush aside Baldwin's views regarding the potential of the black homosexual to save the world as an untenable part of a highly subjective vision, although one may challenge the novelist's ability to convey such ideas convincingly in his work. After all, Baldwin's life itself proves that these views are not utterly invalid. He has channeled his racial outrage and homosexual anguish into his eloquent essays, speeches, debates, novels and plays; by doing so, he has made an indelible mark on the American conscience and has made a substantial contribution to interracial understanding in general and to the Civil Rights Movement in particular. In other words, he has surely helped transform America. Therefore, has he not proved that a gifted black homosexual can indeed change the world?

Tell Me not only reveals Baldwin's general sexual defensiveness, but also indicates that he is in part responding to negative criticism from black militants. By combining racial radicalism and homosexuality in Christopher, he implies that there is no fundamental conflict between the two traits. Also, by making the militant Christopher go to bed with Leo Proudhammer, the novel's autobiographical protagonist, Baldwin is determined to have the last laugh.

But Baldwin does seem to make some minor concessions to Cleaver and other angry militants. He makes homosexuality in *Tell Me* primarily intraracial. All white homosexuals, who make only brief appearances, are masochistic in their sexual attraction to black men. Such a presentation may be designed to pacify black militants like LeRoi Jones (who makes his white homosexual character in *The Baptism and the Toilet* a pathetic wretch who is brutally abused by a gang of black youths) and Cleaver (one of whose major objections to *Another Country* is Baldwin's positive portrayal of Eric, a Southern white homosexual). But it perhaps also reflects Baldwin's own desire for racial and sexual revenge on white males.

Tell Me indicates that Baldwin has not yet succeeded entirely in his quest for liberation through self-acceptance. Although he has made significant strides, he is still polemical in his treatment of the homosexual theme. His defensiveness itself is a clear indication of his lingering discomfort with his sexuality.

If Beale Street Could Talk, published seven years after *Tell Me,* marks the crucial final stage in Baldwin's struggle toward healing sexual self-acceptance. A poignant love story, it is his first and only exclusively heterosexual novel. It has none of the tiresome sexual polemics of *Tell Me* and *Another Country,* but has the emotional immediacy of *Go Tell* and the lyrical grace of *Giovanni's Room.* Clearly one of his finest accomplishments, it is an expression of personal and artistic triumph.

The conspicuous absence of homosexuality in *Beale Street* is a significant feature of the novel. Except for some passing references to Fonny's adolescent experimentation and to reports of rape in the all-male environment of prisons, Baldwin avoids the topic. There are three possible explanations for his decision to eschew the homosexual theme. Perhaps he wants to demonstrate to his readers and critics that he is indeed capable of writing an entirely heterosexual novel. (One must note that homosexual writers like Oscar Wilde, E.M. Forster, Truman Capote, Tennessee Williams and many others have produced highly successful and entirely heterosexual works—a fact that testifies to their imaginative strength.) Critics like James Giles argue that Baldwin has "dramatically played down the homosexual content of his fiction" in order to appease angry black critics ["Religious Alienation and Homosexual Consciousness in *City of Night* and *Go Tell It on the Mountain*" (*College English,* November, 1974)]. Giles' observation sounds plausible, but underestimates Baldwin's courage and defiance. While Baldwin has earlier shown some willingness to make minor concession to critics whose indignation might concern him, he is too strong an individual to be dictated to by others. If he is that afraid of and vulnerable to negative criticism, he would not have said or written much of what he has since the publication of *Go Tell* nearly thirty years ago. Therefore, his decision to avoid the homosexual theme should be found in his changed attitude toward that subject.

In the first novel we saw him reluctantly coming out of the closet. In the three subsequent works of fiction, we saw him openly and defiantly but, most of the time, polemically confronting the heterosexual Establishment. But his defensiveness itself was a sign that he was not yet entirely comfortable with his sexuality. *Beale Street,* then, indicates that he has moved into a new phase: calm and complete acceptance of his sexuality. He no longer feels the need to polemicize; he has made peace with his sexual self and, therefore, disengages himself from a defensive preoccupation with the subject of homosexuality.

That Baldwin has reached a new plateau of sexual awareness is also evident in his descriptions of heterosexual acts in *Beale Street.* His first four novels reveal that he is rather "helpless before the mysteries of heterosexual love," but poignantly eloquent while describing sexual feelings between men. He has always had a tendency to show heterosexual acts as unpleasant and lacking in the inner satisfaction and sense of liberation which he believes homosexual acts proffer. In *Beale Street,* however, he views heterosexual acts as intensely satisfying and spiritually invigorating. In other words, he is now willing to concede that heterosexuality, after all, is just as good as homosexuality.

Such a broad and enlightened view of human sexuality suggests Baldwin's personal maturity. His avoidance of defensive sexual parochialism reveals internal liberation. Since he no longer feels the psychological need to maintain his confrontational posture and to engage in elaborate polemics, he is able to devote more of his creative energy to the artistic aspects of his work. Therefore, it is reasonable to assert that the artistic superiority of *Beale Street* over his two earlier novels, amply evident in the multitude of exuberant reviews it has received, is at least partly a result of his achievement of personal freedom through calm sexual self-acceptance.

Baldwin's latest novel, *Just Above My Head,* confirms our perception that he has indeed gained liberation through acceptance and awareness. Homosexuality reappears in this story about a spectacularly successful black homosexual gospel singer, but it is "less accentuated" and "more thoroughly integrated into the overall structure" of the novel. He does not rely on Freudian beliefs to explain or justify his character's homosexuality; he refrains from conceiving of homosexuality merely as an instrument of rebellion against an abusive father or an arbitrary God; he is no longer defensive or polemical; and he is not any more intent on establishing the "superiority" of homosexuality over heterosexuality. He has now come to terms with his sexual self; therefore, he is able to view calmly the joys and agonies of homosexual life. Nearly three decades ago, in *Go Tell,* he voiced his hesitant sexual rebellion, while largely hiding in the closet. Since then he has defiantly kicked open the closet door to march out and polemically confront the American sexual Establishment. More recently he has achieved complete liberation through healing sexual self-acceptance. The development of his art testifies to his growing personal maturity.

From *Go Tell* to *Just Above My Head* Baldwin has indeed "come full circle." Each of his novels bears witness to his successful struggle with his sexuality in his quest for freedom through awareness and acceptance. By creating art out of his personal struggle and by rendering his private dilemma a matter of public drama, he has effectively challenged a nation and its most cherished values and illusions. His collective protagonist—from John, the adolescent character of *Go Tell,* to the phenomenally successful, middle-aged musician of *Just Above My Head*—symbolizes profound changes in the author and in his country. Though he chided Gide in 1954 for being too openly homosexual, he himself has since then moved from sexual secrecy to angry revolt to mature self-acceptance. But America too has changed dramatically during those years. Sexual fascism has given way to a climate of relative tolerance. Baldwin's

passionate eloquence certainly has played a role in pleading for—and sometimes demanding—understanding of and tolerance for sexual diversity. His works signal the growing maturity of his vision, and his extraordinary critical and commercial success suggests that America, too, is gradually coming of age.

Emmanuel S. Nelson, "The Novels of James Baldwin: Struggles of Self-Acceptance," in Journal of American Culture, *Vol. 8, No. 4, Winter, 1985, pp. 11-16.*

Terry Teachout (essay date 1985)

[*In the following excerpt from an essay first published in* Commentary *in 1985, Teachout discusses what he terms the "undermining" of Baldwin's artistic career.*]

"The failure of the protest novel," James Baldwin wrote in 1949, "lies in its rejection of life, the human being, the denial of his beauty, dread, power, in its insistence that it is his categorization alone which is real and which cannot be transcended." It was around this time that American critics first began to speak of Baldwin as a writer with the sensibility and detachment of a potentially first-rate artist; with the 1953 publication of *Go Tell It on the Mountain,* a beautifully written first novel about Harlem life, he proved them correct.

That book, together with the best of his early essays for *Commentary* and *Partisan Review,* quickly gave James Baldwin a well-deserved reputation as an outstandingly gifted writer—and the only black writer in America capable of staying out of what Lionel Trilling called in another connection "the bloody crossroads" between literary art and politics. Soon his name began to appear regularly in middlebrow magazines like *Harper*'s and the *New Yorker*.

But Baldwin's qualifications for playing the "Great Black Hope," as he later characterized his role, began to look a little more problematic with each passing year. He had, after all, abandoned Harlem for Paris with what looked suspiciously like enthusiasm. His ornate prose style reminded readers more of Henry James than of Richard Wright. And he was, though he did not advertise it at first, a homosexual. None of this seemed to have much to do with the kinds of things people like Martin Luther King, on the one hand, or Malcolm X, on the other hand, were saying in public. Younger and more militant blacks took elaborate pains to distance themselves from Baldwin; Eldridge Cleaver, in *Soul on Ice,* went so far as to accuse Baldwin of harboring a "shameful, fanatical, fawning, sycophantic love of the whites."

Eventually, perhaps in response to such criticism, the tone of Baldwin's work began to take on a raw, politicized stridency which had not previously been a part of his literary equipment. This stridency fatally compromised his standing as a writer of fiction; *Another Country* was the last of his novels to be taken at all seriously by the critics (and by no means all of them). But Baldwin's essays, early and late, have somehow remained impervious to revaluation—which makes it all the more useful to have this new volume of his "collected nonfiction."

The Price of the Ticket contains, complete and unabridged, *Notes of a Native Son; Nobody Knows My Name; The Fire Next Time; Nothing Personal; The Devil Finds Work; No Name in the Street;* and a couple of dozen previously uncollected articles of largely exiguous interest. The only important omissions are the autobiographical preface to *Notes of a Native Son* and Baldwin's latest book, an essay on the Atlanta child murders called *The Evidence of Things Not Seen.* [*The Price of the Ticket*] is a fat omnibus, clearly a gesture to posterity, and an attempt to consolidate Baldwin's shaky literary reputation. Times and tastes have changed profoundly since Baldwin published his first important essay... forty-odd years ago, and so one inevitably wonders: does he still *sound* like a major writer? Is the literary value of his work compromised by his consuming obsession with race? Is his message as compelling as ever—or simply irrelevant?

Baldwin's first collection of essays, *Notes of a Native Son* (1955), was received with more or less uncritical admiration.... But *Notes of a Native Son* is likely to strike today's reader as uneven in a way that Baldwin's first novel, for all its flaws, is not. Baldwin spends the whole first part of the book searching for the right things to write about and the right tone in which to write about them. Though he is reasonably competent at it, straight reportage obviously does not become him; as for his initial attempts at literary criticism, these come out sounding hopelessly stilted.

What finally pulled Baldwin's nonfiction writing up to the level of the best parts of *Go Tell It on the Mountain* was his discovery, in a 1953 essay (also collected in *Notes of a Native Son*), *"Stranger in the Village,"* of the great good pronoun of his literary destiny: the concrete, liberating "I" which, as with Proust's "Marcel," would bring his idiosyncratic style into the sharpest focus. In this piece Baldwin finally learned to do in his writing what, as a budding young preacher in Harlem, he must have heard about in the cradle: to begin with anecdote and end in generalization:

> From all available evidence no black man had ever set foot in this tiny Swiss village before I came. I was told before arriving that I would probably be a "sight" for the village; I took this to mean that people of my complexion were rarely seen in Switzerland, and also that city people are always something of a "sight" outside the city. It did not occur to me—possibly because I am an American—that there could be people anywhere who had never seen a Negro.

With the simple but pregnant discovery of autobiography as a vehicle for social criticism, Baldwin had at last struck a workable balance between the two most characteristic aspects of his artistic personality, the fiery Harlem preacher and the urbane Parisian memoirist. In

the 1955 essays *"Equal in Paris"* and *"Notes of a Native Son,"* both written in the first person, it is the latter aspect which dominates; these two pieces, like *Go Tell It on the Mountain,* are devoid of an overtly political content, and the author's angry message emerges through stylish dramatized narrative rather than vague sermonizing.... (pp. 76-8)

"Equal in Paris" and *"Notes of a Native Son"* come close to justifying every word of praise ever uttered about *Notes of a Native Son.* On the other hand, Baldwin's second collection, *Nobody Knows My Name,* which also received high praise, contains nothing that comes anywhere near matching the remarkable quality of those two essays. Baldwin largely restricts himself here to reportage about the desperate condition of Southern blacks; while these articles are, as reportage, far more professional than their earlier counterparts in *Notes of a Native Son,* their literary value is strictly that of good celebrity journalism. And when Baldwin does use explicitly autobiographical material, the results, particularly in *"The Black Boy Looks at the White Boy,"* are diminished by a distressing new quality: an extreme, even mannered, self-consciousness.

Yet whatever may have been wrong with *Nobody Knows My Name,* readers of the November 17, 1962 *New Yorker* who opened their copies in order to read a report by James Baldwin on the Black Muslims called *"Letter from a Region in My Mind"* suddenly found in their hands the literary equivalent of a pinless grenade. The opening paragraph of this extraordinary essay, which quickly found its way between hard covers as *The Fire Next Time,* was riveting....

Baldwin, describing the religion of his youth with incomparable vividness, concludes in *The Fire Next Time* that it is no longer sufficient. In light of the long history of racism, "whoever wishes to become a truly moral human being... must first divorce himself from all the prohibitions, crimes, and hypocrisies of the Christian church." He interprets the rise of the Black Muslims, who preach that Allah is black and the white man the devil, as the predictable outcome of the moral decadence of Christianity; though he rejects the simple-minded demonology and racial separatism of Elijah Muhammad and Malcolm X, he finds in it rough justice for the sins of the white man. (p. 78)

The Fire Next Time is not without its stylistic miscalculations, the worst of which is *"My Dungeon Shook,"* a four-page preface bearing the subtitle "Letter to My Nephew on the One Hundredth Anniversary of the Emancipation" and through whose resolute platitudes one slogs with dismay. But Baldwin's writing in the rest of *The Fire Next Time* is generally quite marvelous. It is, in fact, so good that something like an act of will is needed to ask the key question: what is being said here? What is being recommended?

"I was always exasperated by his notions of society, politics, and history," James Baldwin once said of Richard Wright, "for they seemed to me to be utterly

Dust jacket of Baldwin's 1961 collection of essays on "the question of color."

fanciful." These harsh words are even more readily applicable to Baldwin himself, who is in a very real sense a man with neither politics nor philosophy. The political impact of his best work was previously achieved through implication alone; *The Fire Next Time* reveals that his specific responses to the condition of blacks in America are wholly emotional. (p. 79)

Despite its still formidable reputation as a central document in the struggle for equality, *The Fire Next Time* turns out to have little of interest to say about the question of racial politics. Its impact comes solely from the fact that it is so exquisitely written. And Baldwin's timing was immaculate. His passionate prophecies of impending doom scorched the collective consciousness of middle-class Americans in a way that no amount of sober analysis could have rivaled.

But *The Fire Next Time* was the last point at which the curve of James Baldwin's career intersected with the *Zeitgeist* of the Great Society. Public black rhetoric came to be dominated, just as Baldwin had predicted it would, by loveless images of violence. And Baldwin's response to this change was, to say the least, disheartening.

Though *The Fire Next Time* was full of the language of extremism, its message was not yet one of racial hate. That was still to come. In *No Name in the Street,* his 1972 sequel to *The Fire Next Time,* Baldwin's striking

prose style, that arresting amalgam of Henry James and the Old Testament, remained largely intact. But the ends to which he now directed this style were another matter altogether. For even the most casual reading of *No Name in the Street* revealed that the literary control manifested in *The Fire Next Time* had now been coarsened by aimless, free-floating political hysteria. . . .

After a career spent dancing in and out of "the bloody crossroads," Baldwin had at last faltered. The lapse was to be permanent. Aside from *The Devil Finds Work,* an erratic and frequently embarrassing volume of autobiography masquerading as film criticism, he published only a handful of political essays after *No Name in the Street.* They are shocking in their abandonment of all pretense to literary detachment; in them Baldwin luxuriates in the foul rhetoric of zealotry that for more than a decade poisoned this country's political discourse. . . .

It is impossible to read the second half of *The Price of the Ticket* without feeling an intense sadness at the literary tragedy it embodies. And it is equally difficult to read the rest of the book without coming to feel that of its seven hundred pages one would willingly, even gratefully, part with all but *The Fire Next Time* and a handful of shorter essays. To revisit James Baldwin's nonfiction is to understand the full extent to which the trivializing claims of radical politics undermined the artistic career of the man about whom Edmund Wilson once said: "He is not only one of the best Negro writers that we have ever had in this country, he is one of the best writers that we have." (p. 80)

> *Terry Teachout, "Tragic Decline," in* Commentary *Vol. 80, No. 6, December, 1985, pp. 76-80.*

Nathan Glazer (essay date 1985)

[*In the following excerpt, Glazer reviews* The Evidence of Things Not Seen *and* The Price of the Ticket, *focusing on Baldwin's treatment of social issues in both works.*]

James Baldwin's collected nonfiction, *The Price of the Ticket,* appears simultaneously with his latest work of nonfiction, *The Evidence of Things Not Seen,* a small book on the trial of Wayne Williams, who was suspected of killing many black children and youths in Atlanta but put on trial only for two of these murders, as Baldwin reminds us again and again. It is a strange book. Little in it deals with either Atlanta, or the child killings, or the trial. (p. 40)

It is a very hard book to read. What we recall as the icy clarity of Baldwin's prose, the precision of his writing (he loves the word "precisely"), here melts and becomes somewhat muddy. The words are still there, the wonderful quotations from spirituals and blues and the Bible. But all one gets is the rush of anger and despair over the black situation, and what whites have done to make it so.

It was not always like this. Not that the tone of *The Evidence of Things Not Seen* is completely new—one finds the same in much of the writing collected in *The Price of the Ticket*. But that is just the problem. The black situation has changed. America has changed. Baldwin has not. Or, insofar as he has, it has been to get angrier and less precise about the targets of his anger, and to give up all hope, it seems, for black existence and the black future in America.

Which is strange indeed. His first pieces of writing date from 1948. A good deal has happened since then. Among other things, Baldwin tells us in *The Evidence of Things Not Seen,* we have had the only two presidents since perhaps Jefferson for whom "Blacks have had any human reality at all." But they are, "exquisitely, the exceptions that prove the rule." We leave out comment on the word "exquisitely," another Baldwin favorite. Why do they *prove* this rule? They are, after all, two of our last five presidents. (pp. 40-1)

The very first essay in [*The Price of the Ticket*], and Baldwin's first substantial piece of writing, is *"The Harlem Ghetto,"* from *Commentary* in 1948. I was on the editorial staff then; how he came to us I don't recall, but I do recall our pleasure that a remarkable young black writer—how remarkable we didn't yet know—had come to us. At that time, *Commentary* was a much more exclusively Jewish magazine than it would later become, and all we could think of suggesting to Baldwin was that he write about blacks and Jews. *"The Harlem Ghetto"* is much more than that. It exhibits a fully developed style as well as almost every theme that was to recur in Baldwin's nonfiction, and indeed many that were to be part of his fiction.

There is an immediate sense of the congestion and claustrophobia of Negro life in America, affecting every social class and every occupation. There are perceptive comments on the Negro press, in all its variants; on black leadership—political, lay, and clerical; observations on the difficulties of black intellectuals in relating to the black community, which were not so different from the difficulties Jewish intellectuals writing in *Commentary* then had in relating to the official Jewish community. (pp. 41-2)

And he describes the complex relationship between Negroes and Jews with remarkable sensitivity, by way of analysis of an archetypal sermon. It begins with the traditional accusation that the Jews killed Christ, "which is neither questioned nor doubted," but

> the term Jew actually operates to include all infidels of white skin.... The preacher begins by accusing the Jews of having refused the light and proceeds from there to a catalog of their subsequent sins and the sufferings visited upon them by a wrathful God.

But he is also describing "the trials of the Negro, while the sins recounted are those of the American republic." (p. 42)

There is much else in these few pages, which are worth rereading today—one will of course notice wryly that the disappearance of the few Jews from Harlem has done nothing to improve matters. But my point is that this is a complex and subtle analysis of the relationship of Jew and Negro, of symbols and reality, in the ghetto. An incredibly distinctive voice came from a 24-year-old whose last formal education had been in a New York City high school. Where had he acquired that voice, so stinging and so elegant? It was a mystery, but a circle of editors, almost all Jewish, were ready to listen to, and publish, whatever he had to say.

It was not until the late 1950s that Baldwin broke away from the *New Leader-Commentary-Partisan Review-Encounter* connection, and began to publish in magazines and journals of wider circulation. The road to *Playboy,* which sent him to Atlanta to cover the story of the murdered children, was reached through the friendly and accepting channels of the New York intellectuals. And the notes of hope—particularly when Baldwin wrote from Paris, where he covered a Congress of Negro and African writers for *Encounter* in 1951, and compared French justice less than favorably with American in *Commentary* in 1950—were not completely absent even in his own writing. Consider the guarded optimism in his report from the Paris Congress:

> For what ... distinguished the Americans from the Negroes who surrounded us, men from Nigeria, Senegal, Barbados, Martinique ... was the banal and abruptly quite overwhelming fact that we had been born in a society, which, in a way quite inconceivable for Africans, and no longer real for Europeans, was open, and, in a sense which has nothing to do with justice or injustice, was free.

One will find nothing like this in Baldwin's writing since the civil rights revolution. Indeed, one would think, in the light of his blazing rhetoric since the early 1970s, that the movement had failed rather than succeeded. To Baldwin it *has* failed, as he writes in *The Evidence of Things Not Seen:* "Others may see American progress in economic, racial, and social affairs—I do not. I pray to be wrong, but I see the opposite, with murderous implications, and not only in North America."

One hesitates to resort to mere facts in dealing with such unqualified pessimism, and yet his very excess will lead many readers to involuntarily contrast what they think is happening in America with what Baldwin insists is the case. Consider the following (before the 1980 election): "[In] a couple of days, blacks may be using the vote to outwit the Final Solution." Or: "The educational system of this country is, in short, designed to destroy the black child. It does not matter whether it destroys him by stoning him in the ghetto or by driving him mad in the isolation of *Harvard*." And if one were to respond in amazement, "Black students are being destroyed *at Harvard?*" Baldwin would undoubtedly answer, "White students are being destroyed there, too." Little distinction is made among blacks–or among whites. Blacks are slaves, and have remained slaves. (But whites are slaves, too).

There is the same lack of specificity when Baldwin recurs (as he does on occasion) to the black-Jewish theme of his first essay. Between *"The Harlem Ghetto"* and *"Negroes are anti-Semitic because they are anti-White"* . . . , the voice becomes harder and harsher. The Jews are subsumed completely in the denunciation of white America ("the Negro is really condemning the Jew for having become an American white man"). One wants to protest, there are differences among Jews, and among whites. But it is all swept away in rhetoric. All this disables Baldwin from offering any precise or differentiated account of what goes on in America—and particularly of the panic over the murdered black children and the subsequent trial in Atlanta. For Baldwin, nothing has changed in America; it is as if he is frozen in a time capsule. The passage of time has only had the effect of dulling his perception of the distinctions and subtleties that were evident to him 30 years ago.

Writing of the Atlanta child killings and the trial of Wayne Williams, Baldwin draw parallels and makes references to scarcely relevant and distant events. It seems the 13th victim was a boy from the North, and it is this that "precipitated the [official] hue and cry." This reminds Baldwin of Emmett Till, another black boy visiting in the South from the North, who whistled at a white woman and was killed for it. But what indeed is the connection? That Atlanta's black establishment only takes account of Northern blacks, not its own native citizens? That Southern whites now as then kill black boys for uppityness? In Baldwin's mind there is a connection; in the reader's there can only be mystification. (pp. 42, 44)

Baldwin has become an accusing voice, but the accusation is so broad, so general, so all-embracing, that the rhetoric disappears into the wind. No one escapes, nothing is to be done, and we can only await "The Fire Next Time." There is enough that is badly amiss with blacks to justify gloom and foreboding, and yes, expectations of disaster. But just what is amiss? It is not, it cannot be, that blacks serve on juries, or become mayors or police chiefs or judges, or become middle class. Yet all this makes no difference to Baldwin at all, or makes things worse: he refuses to consider why, if such progress hasn't made a difference, it hasn't.

"I agree with the Black Panther position concerning black prisoners," he wrote in *No Name in the Street* in 1972. "Not one of them has ever had a fair trial . . . , white middle-class America is always the jury . . . and this fact is not altered, it is rendered even more implacable, by the presence of one or two black faces in the jury box." Is one wrong to detect here that kind of recent French philosophical logic that reverses traditional French clarity—the logic by which one demon-

strates a point not *despite* the existence of opposite facts, but *because* of them? How could the situation be "rendered even more implacable" by the presence of black jurors? One grasps for an explanation. Because the blacks are forced to accept white logic? Because they are intimidated by whites? What? His friend is the mayor of Atlanta, the police chief is black, the judge is black—but all this to Baldwin is simply proof that the power still lies in white hands and whites are exclusively responsible for black distress.

Baldwin is still worth reading, for many things: for the early essays in particular; for the rhetorical power of *The Fire Next Time;* for the snatches of autobiography, as in *The Devil Finds Work,* where he does make distinction (and in which whites appear as individuals, not wrapped in an all-embracing thunder); for the wonderful analyses of the movies of the white world that a very sensitive and gifted young black boy saw (in the company sometimes of a white teacher or another white friend) 50 years ago, and for much else. But his vision of America seems increasingly to be shaped by projections made up of inner nightmares and crude leftist pictures of America. We have nightmares enough of our own. God knows, and the Atlanta child murders—which have been repeated again and again in recent years, with whites in all roles—are one of them. But I find little illumination now in a rhetoric that once struck me as sharp and precise, yet now wraps everything in darkness and disaster. (p. 44)

Nathan Glazer, "The Fire This Time," in The New Republic, *Vol. 193, No. 27, December 30, 1985, pp. 40-2, 44.*

James Baldwin with David C. Estes (interview date 1986)

[*In the following interview, Estes and Baldwin discuss the making of* The Evidence of Things Not Seen *and survey Baldwin's development as an autobiographical essayist and novelist.*]

[Estes]: *Why did you take on the project to write about Wayne Williams and the Atlanta child murders? What did you expect to find when you began the research for* **The Evidence of Things Not Seen?**

[Baldwin]: It was thrown into my lap. I had not thought about doing it at all. My friend Walter Lowe of *Playboy* wrote me in the south of France to think about doing an essay concerning this case, about which I knew very little. There had not been very much in the French press. So I didn't quite know what was there, although it bugged me. I was a little afraid to do it, to go to Atlanta. Not because of Atlanta—I'd been there before—but because I was afraid to get involved in it and I wasn't sure I wanted to look any further.

It was an ongoing case. The boy was in jail and there were other developments in the city and among the parents and details which I've blotted out completely which drove me back to Atlanta several times to make sure I got the details right. The book is not a novel nor really an essay. It involves living, actual human beings. And there you get very frightened. You don't want to make inaccuracies. It was the first time I had ever used a tape recorder. I got hours of tape. At one moment I thought I was going crazy. I went to six, or seven, or eight places where the bodies had been found. After the seventh or the eighth, I realized I couldn't do that any more.

There is a sense in the book that you were trying to keep your distance, especially from the parents of both the victims and the murderer. In fact, you state at one point in it that you "never felt more of an interloper, a stranger" in all of your journeys than you did in Atlanta while researching this case.

It wasn't so much that I was trying to keep my distance, although that is certainly true. It was an eerie moment when you realize that you always ask "How are the kids?" I stopped asking. When I realized that, I realized I'm nuts. What are you going to say to the parents of a murdered child? You feel like an interloper when you walk in because no matter how gently you do it you are invading something. Grief, privacy, I don't know how to put that. I don't mean that they treated me that way. They were beautiful. But I felt that there was something sacred about it. One had to bury that feeling in order to do the project. It was deeper than an emotional reaction; I don't have any word for it.

It wasn't that I was keeping my distance from the parents. I was keeping a distance from my own pain. The murder of children is the most indefensible form of murder that there is. It was certainly for me the most unimaginable. I can imagine myself murdering you in a rage, or my lover, or my wife. I can understand that, but I don't understand how anyone can murder a child.

The carefully controlled structure of your earlier essays is absent from **Evidence.**

I had to risk that. What form or shape could I give it? It was not something that I was carrying in my imagination. It was something quite beyond my imagination. All I could really hope to do was write a fairly coherent report in which I raise important questions. But the reader is not going to believe a word I say, so I had to suggest far more than I could state. I had to raise some questions without seeming to raise them. Some questions are unavoidably forbidden.

Because you are an accomplished novelist, why didn't you use the approach of the New Journalism and tell the story of Wayne Williams by relying on the techniques of fiction?

It doesn't interest me, and I've read very little of it. Truman Capote's *In Cold Blood* is a very pretty performance, but in my mind it illustrates the ultimate pitfall of that particular approach. To put it another way, when I write a play or a novel, I write the ending and am

responsible for it. Tolstoy has every right to throw Anna Karenina under the train. She begins in his imagination, and he has to take responsibility for her until the reader does. But the life of a living human being, no one writes it. You cannot deal with another human being as though he were a fictional creation.

I couldn't fictionalize the story of the Atlanta murders. It's beyond my province and would be very close to blasphemy. I might be able to fictionalize it years from now when something has happened to me and I can boil down the residue of the eyes of some of the parents and some of the children. I'm sure that will turn up finally in fiction because it left such a profound mark on me. But in dealing with it directly as an event that was occurring from day to day, it did not even occur to me to turn it into fiction, which would have been beyond my power. It was an event which had been written by a much greater author than I.

Reflecting on the writing of the New Journalists, I think the great difficulty or danger is not to make the event an occasion for the exhibition of your virtuosity. You must look to the event. (pp. 59-60)

Now that your collected non-fiction has appeared in **The Price of the Ticket,** *what reflections about your career as an essayist do you have as you look back over these pieces?*

It actually was not my idea to do that book, but there was no point in refusing it either. But there was also something frightening about it. It's almost forty years, after all. On one level it marks a definitive end to my youth and the beginning of something else. No writer can judge his work. I don't think I've ever tried to judge mine. You just have to trust it. I've not been able to read the book, but I remember some of the moments when I wrote this or that. So in some ways it's a kind of melancholy inventory, not so much about myself as a writer (I'm not melancholy about that), but I think that what I found hard to decipher is to what extent or in what way my ostensible subject has changed. Nothing in the book could be written that way today.

My career began when I was twenty-one or twenty-two in *The New Leader.* That was a very important time in my life. I had never intended to become an essayist. But it came about because of Saul Levitas who assigned me all these books to review. I will never know quite why he did that. I had to write a book review a week, and it was very good for me. You can always find turning points looking back, but there was one very long review of *Raintree County,* a novel about an America I had never seen. Between the time that I turned in the review and its publication, the author Ross Lockridge committed suicide. It was very shocking because it was such a sun-lit, optimistic book that had won every prize in sight. But he had blown his brains out. That marked me in a way. I didn't feel guilty about it since he hadn't read my review, but it struck me with great force. It was from that point, in hindsight, that I began to be considered an essayist by other people. (p. 61)

What major artistic problems have you had to confront in your non-fiction?

I was a black kid and was expected to write from that perspective. Yet I had to realize the black perspective was dictated by the white imagination. Since I wouldn't write from the perspective, essentially, of the victim, I had to find what my own perspective was and then use it. I couldn't talk about "them" and "us." So I had to use "we" and let the reader figure out who "we" is. That was the only possible choice of pronoun. It had to be "we." And we had to figure out who "we" was, or who "we" is. That was very liberating for me.

I was going through a whole lot of shit in New York because I was black, because I was always in the wrong neighborhood, because I was small. It was dangerous, and I was in a difficult position because I couldn't find a place to live. I was always being thrown out, fighting landlords. My best friend committed suicide when I was twenty-two, and I could see that I was with him on that road. I knew exactly what happened to him—everything that happened to me. The great battle was not to interiorize the world's condemnation, not to see yourself as the world saw you, and also not to depend on your skill. I was very skillful—much more skillful than my friend, much more ruthless, too. In my own mind I had my family to save. I could not go under; I could not afford to. Yet I knew that I was going under. And at the very same moment I was writing myself up to a wall. I knew I couldn't continue. It was too confining. I wrote my first two short stories, and then I split.

You said earlier that you never intended to become an essayist. Did you ever consider one or the other of the genres in which you worked as being more important than another?

No, as a matter of face I didn't. I thought of myself as a writer. I didn't want to get trapped in any particular form. I wanted to try them all. That's why I say I remember having written myself into a wall. Significantly enough, the first thing I wrote when I got to Paris and got myself more or less together was the essay "**Everybody's Protest Novel**"—a summation of all the years I was reviewing those "be kind to niggers" and "be kind to Jews" books. There was a mountain of them, and every one came across my desk. I had to get out of that, and "**Everybody's Protest Novel**" was my declaration of independence. Then I began to finish my first novel and did *Giovanni's Room,* which was another declaration of independence. And then I was in some sense, if not free, clear.

A striking feature of your work is the great amount of autobiographical material that finds its way into essays which are not primarily autobiographical.

Well, I had to use myself as an example.

When did you realize that you should use yourself in this way?

It was not so much that I realized that I should. It was that I realized I couldn't avoid it. I was the only witness I had. I had the idea that most people found me a hostile black boy; I was not that. I had to find a way to make them know it, and the only way was to use myself.

Does it take some measure of audacity to write autobiography, to expect readers to find your personal life of interest to them?

It didn't occur to me to be audacious. It occurred to me, first of all, to be very frightening. Rather than audacity, it involved a great deal of humility to use myself as a witness, which is different from an example, to the condition of others who are in your condition but cannot speak—or cannot be heard. Jimmie Baldwin himself as a subject is not very interesting. There's nothing special about my life in that way at all. Everybody suffers. Everybody has to make choices. It was only in my social situation that I had to use my personal dilemma to illuminate something. I repeat, I am not speaking from the point of view of the victim. I am speaking as a person who has a right to be here. That's where the humility comes in, for you're setting yourself up to be corrected.

Which works have given you more insight into yourself, your fiction or your autobiographical accounts?

The essay called "**Notes of a Native Son**" was risky trying to deal with the relationship between me and my father and to extrapolate that into a social question. That's risky. On the other hand, *Giovanni's Room* was risky, too, in a very different way. I wouldn't say in a more personal way, but I knew very well what I was setting myself for when I wrote that book. I knew that, too, when I wrote "**Notes,**" but it was much more direct. It involved not only me and my father, but also my family. There was always that delicacy because you are revealing not only your own secrets but those of other people. You simply have to realize that is what you are doing and you don't quite know what the consequences will be. (pp. 61-2)

*On numerous occasions you have written about your teenage years. Yet the focus always changes. For example, the most recent account in "**Here Be Dragons**" touches on homosexual experiences, a subject not mentioned in "**Notes of a Native Son.**"*

You begin to see more than you did before in the same event. It reveals itself—more. There's more to it. It's not a conscious decision to refashion the anecdote. In time one of the things that happens is that you become less frightened because there's less to be frightened of— quite unconsciously. This is not something which is cerebral. I don't know whether you can hunt more and more of your own life or if more and more of your own life will hunt you, but it comes back to you during points in your life in another light. One's relationship to the past changes. Yet that boy, the boy I was, still controls the man I am. If I didn't know as much as I think I do know about that boy, I would still be his prisoner. This happens to many people who are effectively stopped between the ages of seventeen and twenty and when they are fifty or sixty are still imprisoned by the boy or girl they have been. Perhaps what I'm saying is that all the action is to understand enough to be liberated from first of all one's terror and then one's self-image, to keep moving into a larger space. (p. 63)

What is your vision of the America to which you must respond as a writer?

This is a curiously and dangerously fragmented society while, perhaps unlike any society in the past, it has all the stirrings of well-being. It has at its back the resonance of the American Dream and the history of conquest. But it is also based on a lie, the lie of Manifest Destiny. So it's a country immobilized, with a past it cannot explain away. That's why everyone's so cheerful, and the Americans who are crying have to be cheerful. Everyone is friendly, and nobody is friends. Everybody has something to hide, and when you have to hide, you have to cry for despair. Despair is the American crime. So one is trapped in a kind of Sunday purgatory, and the only way out of that is to confront what you are afraid of. The American image of the black face contains everything that terrifies it. It also contains the castrations, the lynchings, the burnings, the continual daily and hourly debasements of life, and you cannot do those things without doing something to yourself.

Do you feel that artists in such a nation as ours can find an audience willing to listen to them?

The artist cannot attempt to answer that question because if he does he'll go mad. The public is going to assume you are a success or a failure, the book was a hit or not. The publisher looks at the market. But if you depend on the market, you might as well become a traveling salesman. The artist has to assume that he creates his audience and that the audience won't be there until he starts to work. The artist is responsible for his audience, which may exist in his lifetime or may never exist until long after he is dead. The artist has to realize that commerce is only a detail. If you try to beat your last success, you stop writing. It's a high risk endeavor. (p. 64)

> *James Baldwin and David C. Estes, in an interview in* New Orleans Review, *Vol. 13, No. 3, Fall, 1986, pp. 59-64.*

William Styron (essay date 1987)

[*Styron, an American novelist, critic, and nonfiction and short story writer, has won acclaim as a Southern writer in the tradition of William Faulkner and Thomas Wolfe. Among his writings are the novels* Lie Down in Darkness *(1951),* Set This House on Fire *(1960),* The Confessions of Nat Turner *(1967), and* Sophie's Choice *(1979). His nonfiction works include* As He Lay Dead, a Bitter Grief *(1981), a critical study of Faulkner and* The Quiet Dust and Other Writings *(1982). Styron and Baldwin became friends in the*

early 1960s. In the following excerpt, Styron recalls the early years of his relationship with Baldwin, noting the paradox inherent in the camaraderie between a white Southerner and a black civil rights activist.]

James Baldwin was the grandson of a slave. I was the grandson of a slave owner. We were virtually the same age and we were both bemused by our close links to slavery, since most Americans of our vintage—if connected at all to the Old South—have had to trace that connection back several generations.

But Jimmy had fresh and vivid images of slave times, passed down from his grandfather directly to his father, a Harlem preacher of a fanatical bent, who left a terrifying imprint on his son's life. Jimmy told me that he often thought that the degradation of his grandfather's life was the animating force behind his father's apocalyptic, often incoherent rage.

By contrast, my impression of slavery was quaint and rather benign; in the late 1930s, at the bedside of my grandmother who was then close to 90, I heard tales of the two little slave girls she had owned. Not much older than the girls themselves, at the outset of the Civil War she knitted socks for them, tried to take care of them during the privations of the conflict and, at the war's end, was as wrenched with sorrow as they were by the enforced leave-taking.

When I told this story to Jimmy he didn't flinch. We were both writing about the tangled relations of blacks and whites in America and, because he was wise, Jimmy understood the necessity of dealing with the preposterous paradoxes that had dwelt at the heart of the racial tragedy—the unrequited loves as well as the murderous furies.

The dichotomy amounted to an obsession in much of his work; it was certainly a part of my own, and I think our common preoccupation helped make us good friends. Jimmy moved into my guest cottage in Connecticut in the late autumn of 1960 and stayed there more or less continuously until the beginning of the following summer. A mutual friend had asked my wife and me to give Jimmy a place to stay, and since he was having financial problems it seemed a splendid idea.

Baldwin was not very well known then—except perhaps in literary circles where he was much admired for his first novel *Go Tell It on the Mountain*—but his fame was gradually gaining momentum and he divided his time between writing in the cottage and trips out on the nearby lecture circuit, where he made some money for himself and where, with his ferocious oratory, he began to scare his predominantly radical chic audiences out of their pants.

His charisma, which had no doubt attended him since his days as a boy preacher in Harlem, was quite apparent; he was often trailed to the cottage by Volkswagen-driving, dirndl-clad, guitar-toting girls who, unaware of his sexual orientation, wanted to bed down with him. Somehow he would elude them. I would see him hurrying towards my house. He had a frail, elfin body that moved with the grace of a ballet dancer. Hopping through the snow drifts, his black face frozen in a smile of maniacal glee, he would burst through the door and howl, 'Baby, save me from these Northern liberals!'

There was more seriousness in that plea than its jollity revealed, Without being in the slightest comforted as a Southerner, or let off the hook, I understood through him that black people regarded *all* white Americans as irredeemably racist, the most simple of them being not the Georgia rednecks (who were in part the victims of their heritage) but any citizen whatever whose *de jure* equality was a façade for *de facto* enmity and injustice.

Also romantic nitwits like those girls. In the cottage Jimmy was writing his novel *Another Country* and was making notes for the essay **"The Fire Next Time."** I was consolidating material, gathered over more than a decade, for a novel I was planning to write—but for which I had no title as yet—on the slave revolutionary Nat Turner. It was a frightfully cold winter, and a good time to learn something about each other.

I was by far the greater beneficiary. Born and reared in a Virginia community where blacks and whites were firmly walled off from each other as in Pretoria, struggling still to loosen myself from the prejudices that such an upbringing engenders, I possessed a residual scepticism: could a Negro really possess a mind as subtle, as richly informed, as broadly inquiring and embracing as that of a white man? My God, what appalling arrogance and vanity. Night after night Jimmy and I talked and talked, drinking whisky through the hours until the chill dawn, and I understood that I was in the company of as marvellous an intelligence as I am ever likely to encounter.

His voice was lilting and silky, but became husky as he chainsmoked. Disconcertingly homely, with an almost misshaped face dominated by popping eyes and a huge mobile mouth in which when laughing (and he laughed often and explosively) the tongue wagged like a bell-clapper, he was spellbinding, and he told me more about the frustrations and anguish of being a black man in America than I had known until then, or perhaps wanted to know. He told me exactly what it was like to be refused service, to be spat at, to be called 'nigger' and 'boy.'

It was as if he were disgorging in private all the pent-up rage and gorgeous passion that a few years later, in **"The Fire Next Time,"** would shake the conscience of the nation.

Sometimes other people, friends of mine, would come in and join our talk. The conversation might then turn more abstract and political. Certain of these people—well-intentioned, tolerant, and 'liberal': all the things Jimmy so intuitively mistrusted—would listen patiently while he spoke, visibly fretting then growing indignant at some pronouncement of his, some scathing *aperçu*.

'You can't mean that!' 'You mean—*burn*... ?'. And, in the troubled silence, Jimmy's face would become a mask of imperturbable certitude. 'Baby,' he would say softly, and glare back with vast glowering eyes. 'Yes baby, I mean *burn*. We will *burn your cities down*.'

Lest I give the impression that the winter was one of unalleviated solemnity, let me say that this was not so. Jimmy was a social animal of manic gusto and we had loud and festive evenings. He was a master chef of soul food—pork chops and collard greens, corn bread and blackeye peas—and I recollect a house often full of after-dinner dancing, the Twist being in vogue then and Jimmy's wiry and nimble little body gyrating at the focus of the centrifuge.

His waif-like form would have invited pathos had it not been so incredibly stuffed with energy. When summer came and he departed for good, heading for his apotheosis—the flamboyant celebrity that the 1960s brought him—he left a silence that to this day somehow resonates through my house.

After that I never saw him as often as I would have liked but our paths crossed from time to time and we always fell on each other with an uncomplicated sense of joyous reunion. Much has been written about Baldwin's effect on the consciousness of the world. It has been enormous.

I shall speak for myself. Even if I had not valued much of his work—which was flawed, like all writing, but which at its best had a burnished eloquence and devastating impact—I would have deemed his friendship inestimable. At his peak he had the fervour of Camus or Kafka. Like them he revealed to me, both in his art and his life, the core of his soul's savage distress and thus helped me to shape and define my own work, and its moral contours. This would be the most appropriate gift imaginable to the grandson of a slave owner from a slave's grandson.

> William Styron, "Social Animal of Manic Gusto," in The Observer, December 6, 1987, p. 10.

Toni Morrison (eulogy date 1987)

[*Morrison, an American novelist, nonfiction writer, editor and educator, has earned acclaim for poetic novels that combine elements of realism and fantasy in their exposition of black American life. These include* The Bluest Eye (1970), Song of Solomon (1973), Sula (1974), Tar Baby (1981), *and* Beloved (1987), *which won the 1988 Pulitzer Prize in Fiction. In the following excerpt from a eulogy she delivered at Baldwin's funeral on December 8, 1987 at the Cathedral of St. John the Divine in New York, she thanks Baldwin for his three gifts to black American writers: new language to express their thoughts, bravery, and love.*]

Jimmy, there is too much to think about you, and too much to feel. The difficulty is your life refuses summation—it always did—and invites contemplation instead. Like many of us left here I thought I knew you. Now I discover that in your company it is myself I know. That is the astonishing gift of your art and your friendship: You gave us ourselves to think about, to cherish. We are like Hall Montana watching "with new wonder" his brother saints, knowing the song he sang is us, "He is us."

I never heard a single command from you, yet the demands you made on me, the challenges you issued to me, were nevertheless unmistakable, even if unenforced: that I work and think at the top of my form, that I stand on moral ground but know that ground must be shored up by mercy, that "the world is before (me) and (I) need not take it or leave it as it was when (I) came in."

Well, the season was always Christmas with you there and, like one aspect of that scenario, you did not neglect to bring at least three gifts. You gave me a language to dwell in, a gift so perfect it seems my own invention. I have been thinking your spoken and written thoughts for so long I believed they were mine. I have been seeing the world through your eyes for so long, I believed that clear clear view was my own. Even now, even here, I need you to tell me what I am feeling and how to articulate it. So I have pored again through the 6,895 pages of your published work to acknowledge the debt and thank you for the credit. No one possessed or inhabited language for me the way you did. You made American English honest—genuinely international. You exposed its secrets and reshaped it until it was truly modern dialogic, representative, humane. You stripped it of ease and false comfort and fake innocence and evasion and hypocrisy. And in place of deviousness was clarity. In place of soft plump lies was a lean, targeted power. In place of intellectual disingenuousness and what you called "exasperating egocentricity," you gave us undecorated truth. You replaced lumbering platitudes with an upright elegance. You went into that forbidden territory, and decolonized it, "robbed it of the jewel of its naïveté," and un-gated it for black people so that in your wake we could enter it, occupy it, restructure it in order to accommodate our complicated passion—not our vanities but our intricate, difficult, demanding beauty, or tragic, insistent knowledge, our lived reality, our sleek classical imagination—all the while refusing "to be defined by a language that has never been able to recognize (us)." In your hands language was handsome again. In your hands we saw how it was meant to be: neither bloodless nor bloody, and yet alive.

It infuriated some people. Those who saw the paucity of their own imagination in the two-way mirror you held up to them attacked the mirror, tried to reduce it to fragments which they could then rank and grade, tried to dismiss the shards where your image and theirs remained—locked but ready to soar. You are an artist after all and an artist is forbidden a career in this place; an artist is permitted only a commercial hit. But for thousands and thousands of those who embraced your text and who gave themselves permission to hear your language, by that very gesture they ennobled themselves, became unshrouded, civilized.

The second gift was your courage, which you let us share: the courage of one who could go as a stranger in the village and transform the distances between people into intimacy with the whole world; courage to understand that experience in ways that made it a personal revelation for each of us. It was you who gave us the courage to appropriate an alien, hostile, all-white geography because you had discovered that "this world (meaning history) is white no longer and it will never be white again." Yours was the courage to live life in and from its belly as well as beyond its edges, to see and say what it was, to recognize and identify evil but never fear or stand in awe of it. It is a courage that came from a ruthless intelligence married to a pity so profound it could convince anyone who cared to know that those who despised us "need the moral authority of their former slaves, who are the only people in the world who know anything about them and who may be, indeed, the only people in the world who really care anything about them." When that unassailable combination of mind and heart, of intellect and passion was on display it guided us through treacherous landscape as it did when you wrote these words—words every rebel, every dissident, revolutionary, every practicing artist from Capetown to Poland from Waycross to Dublin memorized: "A person does not lightly elect to oppose his society. One would much rather be at home among one's compatriots than be mocked and detested by them. And there is a level on which the mockery of the people, even their hatred, is moving, because it is so blind: It is terrible to watch people cling to their captivity and insist on their own destruction."

The third gift was hard to fathom and even harder to accept. It was your tenderness—a tenderness so delicate I thought it could not last, but last it did and envelop me it did. In the midst of anger it tapped me lightly like the child in Tish's womb: "Something almost as hard to catch as a whisper in a crowded place, as light and as definite as a spider's web, strikes below my ribs, stunning and astonishing my heart . . . the baby, turning for the first time in its incredible veil of water, announces its presence and claims me; tells me, in that instant, that what can get worse can get better . . . in the meantime—forever—it is entirely up to me." Yours was a tenderness, of vulnerability, that asked everything, expected everything and, like the world's own Merlin, provided us with the ways and means to deliver. I suppose that is why I was always a bit better behaved around you, smarter, more capable, wanting to be worth the love you lavished, and wanting to be steady enough to witness the pain you had witnessed and were tough enough to bear while it broke your heart, wanting to be generous enough to join your smile with one of my own, and reckless enough to jump on in that laugh you laughed. Because our joy and our laughter were not only all right, they were necessary.

You knew, didn't you, how I needed your language and the mind that formed it? How I relied on your fierce courage to tame wilderness for me? How strengthened I was by the certainty that came from knowing you would never hurt me? You knew, didn't you, how I loved your love? You knew. This then is no calamity. No. This is jubilee. "Our crown," you said, "has already been bought and paid for. All we have to do," you said, "is wear it."

And we do, Jimmy. You crowned us.

> *Toni Morrison, "Life in His Language," in* The New York Times Book Review, *December 20, 1987, p. 27.*

Amiri Baraka (eulogy date 1987)

[*Baraka, an American dramatist, poet, essayist, novelist, and critic, rose to prominence as a controversial and influential voice in the black power movement of the 1960s and 1970s. His works include the poetry collections* Preface to a Twenty Volume Suicide Note *(1961),* Afrikan Revolution *(1973), and* Reggae or Not! *(1982), such dramas as* The Toilet *(1962),* Slave Ship: A Historical Pageant *(1967), and* Weimar 2 *(1981); and a memoir,* The Autobiography of LeRoi Jones *(1984). In the following excerpt from a eulogy he delivered at Baldwin's funeral on December 8, 1987 at the Cathedral of St. John the Divine in New York, he praises the author as a gifted man of letters and an inspiring leader.*]

First of all, Jimmy Baldwin was not only a writer, an international literary figure, he was a man, spirit, voice—old and black and terrible as that first ancestor.

As man, he came to us from the family, the human lives, names we can call David, Gloria, Lover, George, Samuel, Barbara, Ruth, Elizabeth, Paula... and this extension is one intimate identification as he could so casually, in that way of his, eyes and self smiling, not much larger than that first ancestor, fragile as truth always is, big eyes popped out like righteous monitors of the soulful. The Africans say that big ol' eyes like that means someone can make things happen! And didn't he?

Between Jimmy's smile and grace, his insistent elegance even as he damned you, even as he smote what evil was unfortunate, breathing or otherwise, to stumble his way. He was all the way live, all the way conscious, turned all the way up, receiving and broadcasting, sometime so hard, what needed to, would back up from those two television tubes poking out of his head!

As man, he was my friend, my older brother he would joke, not really joking. As man, he was Our friend, Our older or younger brother, we listened to him like we would somebody in our family—whatever you might think of what he might say. We could hear it. He was close, as man, as human relative, we could make it some cold seasons merely warmed by his handshake, smile or eyes. Warmed by his voice, jocular yet instantly cutting. Kind yet perfectly clear. We could make it sometimes, just remembering his arm waved in confirmation or indignation, the rapid-fire speech, pushing out at the world like urgent messages for those who would be real.

This man traveled the earth like its history and its biographer. He reported, criticized, made beautiful, analyzed, cajoled, lyricized, attacked, sang, made us think, made us better, made us consciously human or perhaps more acidly pre-human.

He was spirit because he was living. And even past this tragic hour when we weep he has gone away, and why, and why we keep asking. There's mountains of evil creatures who we would willingly bid farewell to— Jimmy could have given you some of their names on demand—we curse our luck, our oppressors—our age, our weakness. Why and Why again? And why can drive you mad, or said enough times might even make you wise!

Yet this why in us is him as well. Jimmy was wise from asking whys giving us his wise and his whys to go with our own, to make them into a larger why and a deeper Wise.

Jimmy's spirit, which will be with us as long as we remember ourselves, is the only truth which keeps us sane and changes our whys to wiseness. It is his spirit, spirit of the little black first ancestor, which we feel those of us who really felt it, we know this spirit will be with us for "as long as the sun shines and the water flows." For his is the spirit of life thrilling to its own consciousness.

When we saw and heard him, he made us feel good. He made us feel, for one thing, that we could defend ourselves or define ourselves, that we were in the world not merely as animate slaves, but as terrifyingly sensitive measurers of what is good or evil, beautiful or ugly. This is the power of his spirit. This is the bond which created our love for him. This is the fire that terrifies our pitiful enemies. That not only are we alive but shatteringly precise in our songs and our scorn. You could not possibly think yourself righteous, murderers, when you saw or were wrenched by our Jimmy's spirit! He was carrying it as us, as we carry him as us.

Jimmy will be remembered, even as James, for his *word*. Only the completely ignorant can doubt his mastery of it. Jimmy Baldwin was the creator of contemporary American speech even before Americans could dig that He created it so we could speak to each other at unimaginable intensities of feeling, so we could make sense to each other at yet higher and higher tempos.

But that word, arranged as art, sparkling and gesturing from the page, was also man and spirit. Nothing was more inspiring than hearing that voice, seeing that face, and that whip of a tongue, that signification that was his fingers, reveal and expose, raise and bring down, condemn or extol!

It was evident he loved beauty—art, but when the civil rights movement pitched to its height, no matter his early estheticism and seeming hauteur, he was our truest definer, our educated conscience made irresistible by his high consciousness.

Jimmy was a "civil rights leader" too, *at the same time!*, thinkers of outmoded social outrage. He was in the truest tradition of the great artists of all times. Those who understand it is beauty *and truth* we seek, and that indeed one cannot exist without and as an extension of the other.

At the hot peak of the movement Jimmy was one of its truest voices. His stance, that it is *our* judgement of the world, the majority of us who still struggle to survive the beastiality of so-called civilization (the slaves), that is true and not that of our torturers, was a dangerous profundity and as such fuel for our getaway and liberation!

He was our consummate complete man of letters, not as an unliving artifact, but as a black man we could touch and relate to even there in that space filled with black fire at the base and circumference of our souls. And what was supremely ironic is that for all his estheticism and ultra-sophistication, there he was now demanding that we get in the world completely, that we comprehend the ultimate intelligence of our enforced commitment to finally bring humanity to the world!

Jimmy's voice, as much as Dr. King's or Malcolm X's, helped shepherd and guide us toward black liberation.

Let us hold him in our hearts and minds. Let us make him part of our invincible black souls, the intelligence of our transcendence. Let our black hearts grow big world-absorbing eyes like his, never closed. Let us one day be able to celebrate him like he must be celebrated if we are ever to be truly self-determining. For Jimmy was God's black revolutionary mouth. If there is a God, and revolution His righteous natural expression. And elegant song the deepest and most fundamental commonplace of being alive. (pp. 27, 29)

> *Amiri Baraka, "We Carry Him as Us," in* The New York Times Book Review, *December 20, 1987, pp. 27, 29.*

Stanley Crouch (essay date 1988)

[*Crouch, an American critic, musician, and educator, is a music critic for the* Village Voice. *In the following excerpt, he attacks Baldwin's views on racial issues, finding them extremist. For a response to Crouch's argument, see the excerpt below by Bobby Cooley.*]

By 1963, when he published *The Fire Next Time,* James Baldwin's writing had become almost exclusively po-lemical, foreshadowing the narrowing of black commentary into strident prosecution or spiteful apology. Considered the intellectual component of the Civil Rights movement, Baldwin was a seminal influence on the subsequent era of regression in which Stokely Carmichael, Rap Brown, Leroi Jones, and Eldridge Cleaver transformed white America into Big Daddy and the Negro movement into an obnoxious, pouting adolescent demanding the car keys.

The increasing bile and cynicism of Baldwin's generalized charges and his willingness to remove free will from the black lower-class through what he called the "doom" of color, helped foster a disposition that put the Negro movement into the hands of those who had failed at taking it over before: the trickle-down Marxist revolutionaries and cultural nationalists whose flops and follies of imagination Harold Cruse documented so well in *Crisis of the Negro Intellectual.* Those people led many up paths that resulted in imprisonment, spiritual collapse, and death for goals far less logical than acquiring political power through inclusion into the social contract. The alienation of abstract facelessness that Martin Luther King and the civil rights workers had won so many battles against was given greater strength when black political talk became progressively anti-white, anticapitalist, and made threats of overthrowing the system itself.

Before he was swept into the position of a media spokesman, Baldwin had been much more ambitious and much more willing to address the subtleties of being a serious writer. His first book of essays, *Notes of a Native Son,* contains **"Everybody's Protest Novel,"** which was written in 1949 and observes that " . . . the avowed aim of the American protest novel is to bring greater freedom to the oppressed. They are forgiven, on the strength of these good intentions, whatever violence they do to language, whatever excessive demands they make of credibility. It is, indeed, considered the sign of frivolity so intense as to approach decadence to suggest that these books are both badly written and wildly improbable. One is told to put first things first, the good of society coming before the niceties of style or characterization. Even if this were incontestable . . . it argues an insuperable confusion, since literature and sociology are not one and the same; it is impossible to discuss them as if they were."

The turmoil that would so twist Baldwin's intelligence and abuse the possibilities of his talent is also evident in that first book of essays, much of the trouble circulating around his sense of himself as "an interloper," "a bastard of the West." **"Stranger in the Village"** finds him reeling toward the emblematic as he writes of some Swiss hicks in an Alpine town, "These people cannot be, from the point of view of power, strangers anywhere in the world; they have made the modern world, in effect, even if they do not know it. The most illiterate among them is related, in a way that I am not, to Dante, Shakespeare, Michelangelo, Aeschylus, Da Vinci, Rembrandt, and Racine; the cathedral at Chartres says something to them which it cannot say to me, as indeed would New York's Empire State Building, should anyone here ever see it. Out of their hymns and dances come Beethoven and Bach. Go back a few centuries and they are in their full glory—but I am in Africa, watching the conquerors arrive."

Such thinking led to the problem we still face in which too many so-called nonwhite people look upon "the West" as some catchall in which every European or person of European descent is somehow part of a structure bent solely on excluding or intimidating the Baldwins of the world. Were Roland Hayes, Marian Anderson, Leontyne Price, Jessye Norman, or Kiri Te Kanawa to have taken such a position, they would have locked themselves out of a world of music that originated neither among Afro-Americans nor Maoris. Further, his ahistorical ignorance is remarkable, and perhaps willful.

But breaking through the mask of collective whiteness—and collective *guilt*—that Baldwin imposes would demand recognition of the fact that, as history and national chauvinism prove, Europe is not a one-called organism. Such simplifications are akin to the kind of reasoning that manipulated illiterate rednecks into violent attempts at keeping "their" universities clean of Negro interlopers. Or convinced black nationalist automatons that they were the descendants of "kings and queens" brought to America in slave ships and should, therefore, uncritically identify with Africa. Rather than address the possibilities that come both of ethnic cultural identity and of accepting the international wonder of human heritage per se, people are expected to relate to the world only through race and the most stifling conceptions of group history. The root of that vision is perhaps what Shaw spoke of in *Major Barbara,* hatred as the coward's revenge for ever having been intimidated. Baldwin would call it rage, and write, "Rage can only with difficulty, and never entirely, be brought under the domination of the intelligence and is therefore not susceptible to any arguments whatever."

Though his second book of essays, *Nobody Knows My Name,* is the work of a gritty and subtle intelligence, there are more than a few indications of the talent that would soon be lost to polemics. Perhaps the most illuminating is **"Princes and Powers,"** where he takes a remarkably sober look at the Conference of Negro-African Writers and Artists, held in Paris in 1956. Baldwin was faced with an international gathering of black people who were rejecting the justifications used to maintain the colonial structures they groaned under. Here Baldwin introduced themes he would later adapt to the American context: the denial by Europeans of non-Western cultural complexity—or parity; the social function of the inferiority complex colonialism threw over the native like a net; the alignment of Christianity and cruelty under colonialism, and the idea that world views were at odds, European versus the "spirit of Bandung," or the West in the ring with the Third World.

At the time, Baldwin understood quite well the difference between colonized and Afro-American people, whom he rightfully referred to as "the most real and certainly the most shocking contributions to Western cultural life." Though Afro-Americans also suffered under institutionalized prejudice, the nature of their experience was the manifestation of a very specific context. "This results in a psychology very different—at its best and at its worst—from the psychology that is produced by a sense of having been invaded and overrun, the sense of having no recourse whatever against oppression other than overthrowing the machinery of the oppressor. We had been dealing with, had been made and mangled by, another machinery altogether. It had never been in our interest to overthrow it. It had been necessary to make the machinery work for our benefit and the possibility of doing so had been, so to speak, built in."

In assessing the performance of Richard Wright, Baldwin understood the danger of apologizing for brutal, Third World politics that the older writer was condoning. Baldwin didn't miss the implications of Wright's address: " . . . that the West, having created an African and Asian elite, should now 'give them their heads' and 'refuse to be shocked' at the 'methods they will be compelled to use' in unifying their countries. . . . Presumably, this left us in no position to throw stones at Nehru, Nasser, Sukarno, etc., should they decide as they almost surely would, to use dictatorial methods in order to hasten the 'social evolution.' In any case, Wright said, these men, the leaders of their countries, once the new social order was established, would voluntarily surrender the 'personal power.' He did not say what would happen then, but I supposed it would be the second coming."

Listening then to Aimee Cesaire, Baldwin wrote, "I felt stirred in a very strange and disagreeable way. For Cesaire's case against Europe, which was watertight, was also a very easy case to make. . . . Cesaire's speech left out of account one of the great effects of the colonial experience: its creation, precisely, of men like himself." Baldwin could see that Cesaire was a modern man, a writer whose bearing and confidence were proof that, "He had penetrated into the heart of the great wilderness which was Europe and stolen the sacred fire. And this, which was the promise of their freedom, was also the assurance of his power."

Such good sense wouldn't last long in Baldwin's writing. Once he settled into astonishingly lyrical rants such as *The Fire Next Time,* Negro neighborhoods were described as relentlessly grim and so inevitably deforming that only the most naïve could accept Baldwin's having come from such a "ghetto." Ignoring the epic intricacy of Afro-American life, Baldwin began to espouse the kinds of simplistic conceptions Malcom X became famous for: "It is a fact that every American Negro bears a name that originally belonged to the white man whose chattel he was. I am called Baldwin because I was either sold by my African tribe or kidnapped out of it into the hands of a white Christian named Baldwin, who forced me to kneel at the foot of the cross."

Actually, a good number of Negroes named *themselves* after freedom came and the issue of converting slaves to Christianity was a subject of major debate because it broached the idea of slaves having souls. But such facts were of no interest to Baldwin. Rather, he chose to combine the Nation of Islam's venom toward Christianity and toward whites with an overview so committed to determinism that it paralleled the explanatory recipes of the left. When mature thinking was most desperately needed, Baldwin was losing the ability to look at things the way they actually were.

In effect, Baldwin sold out to rage, despair, self-righteousness, and a will to scandalize. The mood he submitted to was one he had pinned down in **"Princes and Powers."** Alioune Diop, editor of *Presence Africaine,* had delivered a talk and Baldwin perceptively noticed this: "His speech won a great deal of applause. Yet, I felt that among the dark people in the hall there was, perhaps, some disappointment that he had not been more specific, more bitter, in a word, more demagogical." In America, there was a very similar attitude among those fat-mouthing Negroes who chose to sneer at the heroic optimism of the Civil Rights Movement; they developed their own radical chic and spoke of Malcolm X as being beyond compromise, of his unwillingness to cooperate with the white man, and of his ideas being too radical for assimilation. Baldwin was sucked into this world of intellectual airlessness. By *The Fire Next Time,* Baldwin is so happy to see white policemen made uncomfortable by Muslim rallies, and so willing to embrace almost, anything that disturbs whites in general, that he starts competing with the apocalyptic tone of the Nation of Islam.

Perhaps it is understandable that Baldwin could not resist the contemptuous pose of militance that gave focus to all of his anger for being the homely duckling who never became a swan, the writer who would perhaps never have been read by so many black people otherwise, and the homosexual who lived abroad most of his adult life in order to enjoy his preferences. Baldwin's increasing virulence had perhaps more than a bit to do with his homosexuality. As a small, even frail, man who wrote of being physically abused by his father, the police, and racists in the Greenwich Village, Baldwin was prone to admire and despise those who handled the world in a two-fisted manner (which comes out clearly in his essay on Norman Mailer, **"The Black Boy Looks at the White Boy"**). He was also given to the outsider's joy when intimidation was possible: "black has *become* a beautiful color—not because it is loved but because it is feared." This same attraction to fear permeated his ambivalent attitude toward Christianity. Condemned to hell as an erotic pariah by Christian doctrine, he was understandably relentless in his counterattacks; at the same time, his alienation did not prevent him from being awed by the particular power and majesty Negroes had brought to the religion. Boldly,

though unconvincingly, in *Another Country* and *Tell Me How Long the Train's Been Gone,* he presented an alternative order in which homosexuals served as priests in a religion based on love.

Baldwin's prose was sometimes coated with the effete sheen of the homosexual straining to present himself as part of an elite, or it could be pickled with the self-defensive snits and bitchiness Lionel Mitchell called "our macho." Beware ye who would condescend: Baldwin's attitude wasn't substantially different from the aggressive defensiveness of any outsiders, be they black nationalists who celebrate Africa at Europe's expense, those feminists who elevate women over men, or any other group at odds with or at a loss for social and political power.

It is also true that Baldwin was the first of his kind, and perhaps the last we shall see for some time: the Negro writer made a celebrity and thrust into the national political dialogue. He had no models to learn from and settled for sassing the white folks when ideas of substance would have been much more valuable. His considerable gift for making something of his own from the language of Henry James and the rhetoric of the black church was largely squandered on surface charges and protest fiction. The talent for writing fiction that Baldwin showed in his first novel, **Go Tell It on the Mountain,** never achieved maturity. Though the rest of the novels are uniformly bad, almost every one contains brilliant passages in which Baldwin's long, long sentences were indicative of his intricate sense of consciousness, boasting finely orchestrated details declarations, and nuances of feeling. But they are, with the exception of the all-white homosexual melodrama *Giovanni's Room,* ruined by the writer's contrived and sentimental conception of race. The purple trumpet in his soul played the same tune over and over, one which depicted Negro life as insufferable, saintly, and infinitely superior to that of whites.

Though homosexuality loomed ever larger in his fiction as the years passed, by the last long essay, *The Evidence of Things Not Seen,* Baldwin streaks away from the issues surrounding the Atlanta child murders, ignoring particularly the exploitation of so many impoverished Negro boys by the homosexual subculture of that city. His eloquence gone, Baldwin reads as though his mind had so eroded that he no longer knew how to build an argument. Very little connects and any subject is an occasion for a forced harangue against the West, the profit motive, Christianity, and so on. It is a disturbingly dishonest book.

One cannot deny James Baldwin his powers, but it is tragic that he was never strong enough to defend and nurture his substantial talent and become the writer even such imposing gifts do not make inevitable. Finally, Baldwin's description of his success as a boy preacher in **The Fire Next Time** says much about the decay of a writer who once seemed poised on greatness: "That was the most frightening time of my life, and quite the most dishonest, and the resulting hysteria lent great passion to my sermons—for a while. I relished the attention and the relative immunity from punishment that my new status gave me...." (pp. 35, 38-9)

Stanley Crouch, "The Rage of Race," in The Village Voice, *Vol. XXXIII, No. 2, January 12, 1988, pp. 35, 38-9.*

Bobby Cooley (essay date 1988)

[*In the following excerpt, Cooley, who is acting director of the African-American Center at Tufts University, responds to Stanley Crouch's negative comments on Baldwin (see excerpt above).*]

Stanley Crouch's article on James Baldwin [see excerpt above] was remarkable for the depth and breadth of its truculence. While reading it, I kept thinking that it was the work of an angry man who was settling an old score. How else to explain the host of crimes of which Baldwin is accused: writings of "bile and cynicism"; a "willingness to remove free will from the black lowerclass through what he called the 'doom' of color"; of helping to "foster a disposition that put the Negro movement into the hands of... trickle-down Marxist revolutionaries and cultural nationalists." This is simply amazing.

It is meaningless and dishonest to suggest that Baldwin's writings led to any such "disposition." After all, some of these same Marxists and cultural nationalists attacked Baldwin (sometimes rather savagely, as in the case of Eldridge Cleaver) for being too white and too willing to be "included in the social contract." Crouch does not mention this, and so descends, in his diatribe, into the very ahistoricism and disregard for fact for which he takes Baldwin to task.

Crouch's anger seems to be based on what he construes as Baldwin's anti-Americanism and his distaste for Baldwin's homosexuality. The article fairly drips with America-the-beautiful sentiment, and Crouch even trots out Leontyne Price and Jessye Norman as proof positive that American society is not racist. That these ladies have succeeded in their field in no way disproves the larger case that James Baldwin made against America. And it is very easy to sneer at Baldwin's homosexuality; after all, it proves pages of psychohistory: tormented homosexual as angry radical writer. This is all rather a lot of nonsense and goes little way toward helping us to usefully assess the life of James Baldwin the man, writer, the intellectual engagé. It merely expresses one man's dislikes and tribal instincts. The writer from Harlem deserves better.

Bobby Cooley, in a letter to the editor in The Village Voice, *Vol. XXXIII, No. 4, January 19, 1988, p. 4.*

FURTHER READING

Bell, Pearl K. "Roth & Baldwin: Coming Home." *Commentary* 68, No. 6 (December 1979): 72-5.
   Examines *Just above My Head* as Baldwin's "most ambitious effort... to portray the black communal life and culture whose absence from the protest novel he lamented long ago...."

Bieganowski, Ronald. "James Baldwin's Vision of Otherness in 'Sonny's Blues' and *Giovanni's Room*." *CLA Journal* XXXII, No. 1 (September 1988): 69-80.
   Explores Baldwin's belief that "To encounter oneself is to encounter the other."

Bloom, Harold, ed. *James Baldwin.* New York: Chelsea House, 1986, 164 p.
   Reprints significant criticism of Baldwin's literary works. Essays include: Marion Berghahn, "Images of Africa in the Writings of James Baldwin"; C. W. E. Bigsby, "The Divided Mind of James Baldwin"; and Stephen Adams, "*Giovanni's Room*: The Homosexual as Hero."

Campbell, James. *Talking at the Gates: A Life of James Baldwin.* New York: Viking, 1991, 288 p.
   Critical biography of Baldwin by one of Baldwin's longtime friends. Campbell provides fresh insight into the writer's inner turmoil and his relationships with Richard Wright, Langston Hughes, Norman Mailer, and the Black Panthers.

Daniels, Lee A. "James Baldwin, Eloquent Essayist in Behalf of Civil Rights, Is Dead." *The New York Times* (2 December 1987): 1, 21.
   Memorial tribute, arguing that Baldwin's essays, not his novels, constitute his most substantial contribution to literature.

Davis, Clive. "Notes of Native Sons." *New Statesman* 110, No. 2853 (29 November 1985): 29-30.
   Mixed evaluation of *The Price of the Ticket.*

Finn, James. "The Identity of James Baldwin." *Commonweal* LXXVII, No. 5 (26 October 1962): 113-16.
   Review of *Another Country.* According to the critic, "*Another Country* is a novel whose parts are more successful than the whole, and the achievement in these parts is of such a high order and of such particularity that we will not, I think, find their counterpart in American writing."

Gilman, Richard. Review of *Just above My Head,* by James Baldwin, *The New Republic* 181, No. 20 (24 November 1979): 30-1.
   Review of *Just above My Head,* noting of the work: "[It is] a melancholy piece of creation. Swollen..., meandering, awkwardly colloquial, and pretentiously elevated by turns, the book agitatedly contains four or five major themes that never are brought into coherence with one another."

Levin, David. "Baldwin's Autobiographical Essays: The Problem of Negro Identity." *The Massachusetts Review* 5, No. 2 (Winter 1964): 239-47.

Generally favorable assessment of *Notes of a Native Son,* labeling the title essay "one of the best autobiographical narratives in our literature."

McCluskey, John. Review of *If Beale Street Could Talk,* by James Baldwin. *Black World* XXIV, No. 2 (December 1974): 51-2, 88-91.
Views *If Beale Street Could Talk* as a synthesis of Baldwin's principal literary concerns: family life, love, religion, and human relationships.

Miller, Karl. "America." *New Statesman* LXVIII, No. 1760 (4 December 1964): 891.
Gauges the impact of Baldwin's involvement with civil rights interests on his development as a writer.

Murray, Donald C. "James Baldwin's 'Sonny's Blues': Complicated and Simple." *Studies in Short Fiction* 14, No. 4 (Fall 1977): 353-57.
Explores imagery of light and dark in "Sonny's Blues."

Porter, Horace A. *Stealing the Fire: The Art and Protest of James Baldwin.* Middletown, Conn.: Wesleyan University Press, 1989, 220 p.
Studies Baldwin's genesis as a writer, focusing on his earliest essays and novels, especially *Notes of a Native Son, Go Tell It on the Mountain,* and *Giovanni's Room.*

Puzo, Mario. "His Cardboard Lovers." *The New York Times Book Review* (23 June 1968): 5, 34.
Review of *Tell Me How Long the Train's Been Gone,* describing the work as "a simple-minded, one-dimensional novel with mostly cardboard characters, a polemical rather than narrative tone, weak invention, and poor selection of incident. Individual scenes have people talking too much for what the author has to say and crucial events are 'told' by one character to another rather than created. The construction of the novel is theatrical, tidily nailed into a predictable form."

Roberts, David H. "James Baldwin (2 August 1924–1 December 1987)." In *American Playwrights Since 1945: A Guide to Scholarship, Criticism, and Performance,* edited by Philip C. Kolin, pp. 42-50. New York: Greenwood Press, 1989.
Examines the production history of Baldwin's two major dramas, *The Amen Corner* and *Blues for Mister Charlie.*

Romano, John. "James Baldwin Writing and Talking." *The New York Times Book Review* (23 September 1979): 3, 33.
Retrospective review essay, focusing on *Just above My Head.*

Sheed, Wilfrid. "The Twin Urges of James Baldwin." *Commonweal* CIV, No. 13 (24 June 1977): 404-7.
Review of *The Devil Finds Work.* Sheed writes: "When James Baldwin goes wrong (as he has taken to doing lately), it usually seems less a failure of talent than of policy. Of all our writers he is one of the most calculating."

Standley, Fred L., and Burt, Nancy V., eds. *Critical Essays on James Baldwin.* Boston: G. K. Hall, 1988, 312 p.
Reprints selected criticism of Baldwin's works. Essays include: Richard K. Barksdale, "Temple of the Fire Baptized"; Leslie A. Fiedler, "A Homosexual Dilemma"; Joyce Carol Oates, "A Quite Moving and Very Traditional Celebration of Love"; Keith E. Byerman, "Words and Music: Narrative Ambiguity in 'Sonny's Blues'"; and Julius Lester, "Some Tickets Are Better: The Mixed Achievement of James Baldwin."

Standley, Fred L., and Pratt, Louis H., eds. *Conversations with James Baldwin.* Jackson: University Press of Mississippi, 1989, 297 p.
Collection of 27 interviews with Baldwin conducted between the years 1961 and 1987. Interviewers include Studs Terkel, David Frost, and Henry Louis Gates, Jr.

Stern, Daniel. "A Special Corner on Truth." *Saturday Review* XLVIII, No. 45 (6 November 1965): 32.
Highly favorable review of Baldwin's short story collection *Going to Meet Me,* noting of the stories: "They are, for the most part, free from the intellectual sin of confusing the Negro's (and/or the white man's) tragedy with the homosexual's psychic deformity. They sing with truth dug out from pain...."

Sweetman, David. "Relations of a Different Order." *The Times Educational Supplement,* No. 3626 (27 December 1985): 17.
Traces Baldwin's development as a writer as evidenced by the essays in *The Price of the Ticket.*

Thompson, John. "Baldwin: The Prophet as Artist." *Commentary* 45, No. 6 (June 1968): 67-9.
Assesses *Tell Me How Long the Train's Been Gone* as "a masterpiece by one of the best living writers in America."

Weatherby, W. J. *James Baldwin: Artist on Fire.* New York: Donald I. Fine, 1989, 412 p.
Full-length biography by one of Baldwin's longtime friends.

Wills, Garry, "What Color Is God?" *National Review* XIV, No. 20 (21 May 1963): 408-14, 416-17.
Review of *The Fire Next Time.* Wills claims: "In some as yet unconfessed way, Baldwin seems to be launched on the self-lacerating task that Ida set herself—to see if, in the amorphous tolerance surrounding the 'accepted' Negro, some fire of human dignity and spontaneity can still be kindled...."

Toni Cade Bambara

1939-

(Born Toni Cade; later acquired surname Bambara) American short story writer, novelist, scriptwriter, editor, and author of children's books.

A writer and social activist, Bambara is "one of the best representatives of the group of Afro-American writers who, during the 1960s, became directly involved in the cultural and sociopolitical activities in urban communities across the country," according to Alice A. Deck. Bambara, who initially gained recognition as a short story writer, has branched out into other genres and media in the course of her career, yet she continues to focus on issues of racial awareness and feminism in her work.

Born Toni Cade in New York City, she later acquired the name "Bambara" after discovering it as part of a signature on a sketchbook in her great-grandmother's trunk. Bambara is generally silent about her childhood, but she has revealed a few details from her youth. In an interview with Beverly Guy-Sheftall in *Sturdy Black Bridges: Visions of Black Women in Literature,* Bambara discussed some women who influenced her work: "For example, in every neighborhood I lived in there were always two types of women that somehow pulled me and sort of got their wagons in a circle around me. I call them Miss Naomi and Miss Gladys, although I'm sure they came under various names. The Miss Naomi types ... would give me advice like, 'When you meet a man, have a birthday, demand a present that's hockable, and be careful.' ... The Miss Gladyses were usually the type that hung out the window in Apartment 1-A leaning on the pillow giving single-action advice on numbers or giving you advice about how to get your homework done or telling you to stay away from those cruising cars that moved through the neighborhood patrolling little girls." After attending Queens College in New York City and several European institutions, Bambara worked as a free-lance writer and lecturer, social investigator for the New York State Department of Welfare, and director of recreation in the psychiatry department at Metropolitan Hospital in New York City. As she told Guy-Sheftall, writing at that time seemed to her "rather frivolous ... something you did because you didn't feel like doing any work. But ... I've come to appreciate that it is a perfectly legitimate way to participate in a struggle."

Bambara's interest in black liberation and women's movements led her to edit and publish an anthology entitled *The Black Woman* in 1970. The work is a collection of poetry, short stories, and essays by such celebrated writers as Nikki Giovanni, Audre Lorde, Alice Walker, and Paule Marshall. *The Black Woman* also contains short stories by Bambara, who was at that time still writing under the name of Cade. According to

Deck, Bambara saw the work as "a response to all the male 'experts' both black and white who had been publishing articles and conducting sociological studies on black women." Another anthology, *Tales and Stories for Black Folks,* followed in 1971. Bambara explained in the introduction to this short story collection that the work's aim is to instruct young blacks about "Our Great Kitchen Tradition," Bambara's term for the black tradition of story-telling. In the first part of *Tales and Stories,* Bambara included works by writers like Langston Hughes, Alice Walker, and Ernest Gaines—stories she wished she had read while growing up. The second part of the collection contains stories by students in a first year composition class Bambara was teaching at Livingston College, Rutgers University. Deck wrote that Bambara's inclusion of professional writers and students in a single work "shows her desire to give young writers a chance to make their talents known to a large audience." Additionally, such a mixture "would have helped her inspire young adults to read, to think critically, and to write."

Most of Bambara's early writings—short stories written between 1959 and 1970 under the name Toni Cade— were collected in her next work, *Gorilla, My Love* (1972). Bambara told Claudia Tate in an interview published in *Black Women Writers at Work* that when her agent suggested she assemble some old stories for a book, she thought, "Aha, I'll get the old kid stuff out and see if I can't clear some space to get into something else." Nevertheless, *Gorilla, My Love* remains her most widely read collection. Deck noted that after the publication of her first collection, "major events took place in Toni Cade Bambara's life which were to have an effect on her writing." Bambara traveled to Cuba in 1973 and Vietnam in 1975, meeting with both the Federation of Cuban Women and the Women's Union in Vietnam. She was impressed with both groups, particularly with the ability of the Cuban women to surpass class and color conflicts and with the Vietnamese women's resistance of their traditional place in society. Furthermore, upon returning to the United States, Bambara moved to the South, where she became a founding member of the Southern Collective of African-American Writers. Her travels and her involvement with community groups like the collective influenced the themes and settings of *The Sea Birds Are Still Alive* (1977), her second collection of short stories. These stories take place in diverse geographical areas, and they center chiefly around communities instead of individuals. With both collections, critics noted Bambara's skill in the genre, and many praised the musical nature of language and dialogue in her stories, which she herself likens to "riffs" and "be-bop."

Although Bambara admittedly favored the short story genre, her next work, *The Salt Eaters* (1980), is a novel. She explained in *Black Women Writers:* "Of all the writing forms, I've always been partial to the short story.... But the major publishing industry, the academic establishment, reviewers, and critics favor the novel.... Murder for the gene-deep loyalist who readily admits in interviews that the move to the novel was not occasioned by a recognition of having reached the limits of the genre or the practitioner's disillusion with it, but rather Career. Economics. Critical Attention. A major motive behind the production of *Salt.*" The novel, which focuses on the recovery of community organizer Velma Henry from an attempted suicide, consists of a "fugue-like interweaving of voices," Bambara's speciality. *The Salt Eaters* succeeded in gaining more critical attention for Bambara, but many reviewers found the work to be confusing, particularly because of breaks in the story line and the use of various alternating narrators. Others appreciated her "complex vision," however, and further praised her ability to write dialogue.

Since the publication of *The Salt Eaters* in 1980, Bambara has devoted herself to another medium, film. She told Tate in *Black Women Writers at Work:* "Quite frankly, I've always considered myself a film person.... There's not too much more I want to experiment with in terms of writing. It gives me pleasure, insight, keeps me centered, sane. But, oh, to get my hands on some movie equipment." Bambara has nevertheless remained committed to working within black communities, and she continues to address issues of black awareness and feminism in her art.

(For further information about Bambara's life and works, see *Black Writers; Contemporary Authors,* Vols. 29-32; *Contemporary Authors New Revision Series,* Vol. 24; *Contemporary Literary Criticism,* Vol. 19; and *Dictionary of Literary Biography,* Vol. 38: *Afro-American Authors After 1955: Dramatists and Prose Writers.*)

PRINCIPAL WORKS

The Black Woman: An Anthology [editor and contributor, as Toni Cade] (poetry, short stories, and essays) 1970
Tales and Stories for Black Folks [editor and contributor] (short stories) 1971
Gorilla, My Love: Short Stories (short stories) 1972
The Sea Birds Are Still Alive: Collected Stories (short stories) 1977
The Salt Eaters (novel) 1980
If Blessing Comes (novel) 1987

Toni Morrison (essay date 1971)

[*Winner of the 1988 Pulitzer Prize for fiction for her novel* Beloved, *Morrison is one of Bambara's friends and editors. Here, in an excerpt originally published in* The New York Times Book Review *in 1971, she gives a glowing review of* Tales and Stories for Black Folks.]

Gretchen and Hazel were eyeing each other. The race is over and Hazel won. "We stand there with the big smile of respect between us. It's about as real a smile as girls can do for each other, considering we don't practice real smiling every day you know, 'cause maybe we too busy being flowers or fairies or strawberries instead of something honest and worthy of respect . . . you know . . . like being people."

Toni Cade Bambara wrote that in **"Raymond's Run,"** the lead story of *Tales and Stories for Black Folks.* It is a most remarkable collection. Joy aches and pain chuckles in these pages, and the entire book leaves you with the impression of silk—which is so nice because it was made by a living thing that had something on its mind, its survival no doubt. Delight. That is the real word for almost every story in this anthology, and I wish there were reams more of them. That all the books George Woods saw fit to send me in those paper bags were like that: books that treated black children like "something honest and worthy of respect . . . you know . . . like . . . people."

What makes this collection so spry, so healing, so genuinely good is what makes any book for children precious: (1) an assumption that the readers are alive and have something to bring to the reading experience. With almost no exception the contributors start with what the kids already know—in their fingers, in their veins—and move on up into their eyes, ears and brains, setting, at last, deep in the muscles of the heart, where everything of consequence ends anyway. (2) That cultural lines of demarcation (in this case black) are worth hanging on to (not instead of something else, not in spite of something else) because the culture is worthy in and of itself. (3) That books are written in language and that *nothing*—not pictures, not binding, no covers—can give them permanent life except language. Take, for example, Albert Murray's opening passage in "Train Whistle Guitar," "Li'l Buddy's Color was that sky blue in which hens cackled; it was that smoke blue in which dogs barked and mosquito hawks lit on barbed-wire fences. It was the color above meadows. It was my color too because it was a boy's color. It was whistling blue and hunting blue, and it went with baseball. . . .Steel blue was a man's color. That was the clean, oil-smelling color of rifle barrels and railroad iron. That was the color that went with Luzana Cholly. . . ."

Some of the tales in Miss Bambara's book are re-tellings of fairy tales with the original violence left intact but translated into contemporary terms. From "The True Story of Chicken Licken" by Lind Homes: "One day Chicken Licken was waiting to cross at the corner when out of the clear blue sky—a policeman walked up and hit her on her head. . . ." Or Bernice Pearson's "The Three Little Brothers": "There once were three little brothers who lived in Newark. Their mother took sick and before she could instruct them on how to make their way in the world she died on the way to Martland Medical Center. The brothers felt they had to move, for the apartment only made them sad about their mother. One brother insisted on buying a straw house. The other wanted a wooden house. The third tried to convince them that a brick house was best. They couldn't agree so they went their separate ways."

Now this book is clearly not meant for the fastidious guardians of the pure, wholesome, good and light—there is a son of a bitch, a few goddam's and somebody says, "I ain't havin no teef pulled"; but it is for children—all children. And though the title implies a limit to its audience, don't count on it. Like so much that is meant for black folks, like so much that black people do for themselves, it ends up in the marrow of the culture at large. So when somebody gives you x-hundred children's books to review you don't really have to scramble around for definitions of and justifications for unless you want to; you just make distinctions between good, bad and neutral. The same way you would read a pile of Russian books for children and not get distracted by questions like "What's so Russian about it?" and "Yes, it's Russian, but is it also human?" Unless there is still some confusion about being both black and human, the hubbub about black literature is cretinous. (p. 3)

So much of the black children's book thing is gap-filling, educational redress and just plain carrot-sticking, that it is hard to find the true and splendid children's book. But there is no question about one. And the lady who produced it is Toni Cade. "I was once a strawberry in a Hansel and Gretel pageant when I was in nursery school and I didn't have no better sense than to dance on tiptoe with my arms in a circle over my head doing umbrella steps and being a perfect fool just so my mother and father could come dressed up and clap. You'd think they'd know better than to encourage that kind of nonsense. I am not a strawberry. I do not dance on my toes. I run. That is what I am all about." Believe it! (p. 43)

Toni Morrison, "Good, Bad, Neutral Black," in The New York Times Book Review, *May 2, 1971, pp. 3, 43.*

Margo Jefferson (essay date 1977)

[*In the following review, originally published in* Newsweek *in 1977, Jefferson praises Bambara for her style and characterization in* The Sea Birds Are Still Alive.]

Short-story writers who are endlessly told that their work doesn't offer the imaginative fullness of a good novel are apt to create a world so precise in geography and tone that each tale seems a chapter rather than a separate story. Grace Paley comes to mind, with her New Yorkers—harassed single mothers, social workers and young toughs whose tangled lives and needs overlap like neighborhood boundaries. Toni Cade Bambara works similarly in this second fine collection of stories, [*The Sea Birds Are Still Alive*].

As in her previous volume, *Gorilla, My Love,* Bambara directs her vigorous sense and sensibility to black neighborhoods in big cities, with occasional trips to small Southern towns. Her people are edgy adolescents, fast-talking the adult world into manageable proportions; grandparents determined to wield the power and shun the pathos of old age; young women and men who formed their political convictions in the fury of the '60s and find themselves grasping for air in the torpor of the '70s; manicurists, singers and students struggling to trim the rhetoric of their wishes to the smaller, tighter fit of reality. "I long," as one character says, "for a long beat between blues notes."

The stories start and stop like rapid-fire conversations conducted in a rhythmic, black-inflected, sweet-and-sour language. Rather than linear plots, Bambara presents situations that build like improvisations on a melody. Honey, the fat singer-actress of **"Witchbird,"** tries to create a persona based on Bessie Smith, Billie Holiday and Lena Horne; she is caught, instead, in a thankless role of big, easygoing landlady for her dashing manager's castoff girlfriends. ("Folks be sneaky with their scenarios and secret casting," she mutters resentfully). A teen-age girl (in **"Christmas Eve at Johnson's Drugs N Goods"**) tries to ward off the blow of not seeing her father, who has left town for a second marriage and a new family, by reasoning with perilous bravado: "I got my life to lead and'll probably leave here myself one day and become an actress or a director. . .It ain't like he'd made any promises about making a home for me with him. So it ain't like he's gone back on his word."

Bambara's people live on their nerve endings—from the manicurist who eases her way out of a husband's life when he ceases calling her "Dahlin'" and begins calling her Mama ("I'm my daughter's mama," she says coldly) to the wary shipboard refugees from a war-ravaged Asian country in the title story, Bambara's single, affecting venture into foreign territory. As drawn with spirit and subtlety, they are—even in their defeats—a pleasure to watch.

> *Margo Jefferson, in a review of "The Sea Birds Are Still Alive," in* Newsweek, *Vol. LXXXIX, No. 18, May 2, 1977, p. 76.*

Anne Tyler (essay date 1980)

[*Tyler is a noted American novelist, short story writer, and critic who won the 1989 Pulitzer Prize for fiction for her novel* Breathing Lessons. *In the following excerpt from a review originally published in* Book World—The Washington Post *in 1980, she describes* The Salt Eaters *as difficult but rewarding reading.*]

[In ***The Salt Eaters***] a black woman is sitting on a stool in a hospital, watching numbly as a fabled healer named Minnie Ransom attempts to bring her out of her depression, or her mental collapse, or perhaps it's simply overwhelming tiredness—whatever led her to slit her own wrists and try to gas herself. As Minnie Ransom hums and flounces her dress and drapes her shawl, as Velma Henry sits frozen in her white gown, scenes from the past and present swim by in no particular order. One scene fades into another, observed by characters who seem chosen almost at random: a lonely bus driver, an ex-pimp, a raging feminist, an intellectual waiter who has no difficulty linking thermodynamics with voodoo and billiards. The shifts are so smooth, sometimes it takes us a moment to realize they occurred. There are flashes of political meetings, cozy conversations in sidewalk cafés, grueling protest marches and animated bouts of "Disposal" (a very funny, surrealistic board game in which players vie to get rid of contaminated nuclear waste).

In short, this book is a long, rich dream pivoting on a hospital stool, widening from the center. . . . (p. 1)

Dreams are not easy to follow, and ***The Salt Eaters*** is not an easy book to read. Too many people swarm by too quickly. Too much is described elliptically, as if cutting through to the heart of the matter might be considered crude, lacking in gracefulness, not sufficiently artistic. There were times (particularly late at night) when the swaying, to-and-froing, roundaboutness of the plot actively irritated me. . . .

But you can't keep a grudge against a writer who talks about an "out-of-town-who's-his-people-anyway husband," and who gives us people so brave and sweet and battle-weary as Velma. . . . Above all, you have to love that down-to-earth mother hen of a healer who knows enough to ask, "Are you sure you want to be well? . . . Wholeness is no trifling matter. A lot of weight when you're well." As in ***Gorilla, My Love*** and ***The Seabirds Are Still Alive***. . . , what pulls us along is the language of its characters, which is startlingly beautiful without once striking a false note. Everything these people say, you feel, ordinary, real-life people are saying right now on any street corner. It's only that the rest of us didn't realize it was sheer poetry they were speaking.

It may seem an outlandish association, but when I closed this book I thought of Isaac Bashevis Singer. Singer's Polish Jews have nothing in common with Toni Cade Bambara's small-town black Americans except their vitality on the page—but it's such a teeming, brimming vitality, made poignant by our foreknowledge of doom, that it comes to be the keynote for both authors. In ***The Salt Eaters*** the sense of foreboding is almost oppressive. Velma may have chosen wholeness, finally, but that's no guarantee of ease or happiness, and Minnie Ransom knows there's worse to come for everybody. Finishing on this note, the novel becomes unexpectedly moving. The small world it illuminates seems more alive than the world around the reader's armchair and the tiny, distant voices of its inhabitants—singing, crying, laughing, cursing—linger in the air. This is a powerful piece of writing. The effort spent in deciphering it is rewarded many times over. (p. 2)

> *Anne Tyler, "At the Still Center of a Dream," in* Book World—The Washington Post, *March 30, 1980, pp. 1-2.*

Toni Cade Bambara with Claudia Tate (interview date 1983?)

[*In the following excerpt from an interview with Claudia Tate, Bambara discusses gender and racial issues in writing.*]

[Tate]: *How does being black and female constitute a particular perspective in your work?*

[Bambara]: As black and woman in a society systematically orchestrated to oppress each and both, we have a very particular vantage point and, therefore, have a special contribution to make to the collective intelligence, to the literatures of this historical moment. I'm clumsy and incoherent when it comes to defining that perspective in specific and concrete terms, worse at assessing the value of my own particular pitch and voice in the overall chorus. I leave that to our critics, to our teachers and students of literature. I'm a nationalist; I'm a feminist, at least that. That's clear, I'm sure, in the work. My story **"Medley"** could not have been written by a brother, nor could **"A Tender Man"** have been written by a white woman. Those two stories are very much cut on the bias, so to speak, by a seamstress on the inside of the cloth. I am about the empowerment and development of our sisters and of our community. That sense of caring and celebration is certainly reflected in the body of my work and has been consistently picked up by other writers, reviewers, critics, teachers, students. But as I said, I leave that hard task of analysis to the analysts. I do my work and I try not to blunder. (pp. 14-5)

Do you see any differences in the ways black male and female writers handle theme, character, situation?

I'm sure there are, but I'd be hard pressed to discuss it cogently and trot out examples. It's not something I think about except in the heat of reading a book when I feel an urge to "translate" a brother's depiction of some phenomena or say "amen" to a sister's. There are, I suppose, some general things I can say. Women are less likely to skirt the feeling place, to finesse with language, to camouflage emotions. But then a lot of male writers knock that argument out—James Baldwin trusts emotions as a reliable way to make an experience available; a lot of young brothers like Peter Harris, Melvin Brown, Calvin Kenley, Kambon Obayani have the courage to be "soft" and unsilent about those usual male silences. One could say that brothers generally set things out of doors, on open terrain, that is, male turf. But then Toni Morrison's *Song of Solomon,* angled from the point of view of a man, is an exception to that. I've heard it said that women tend to aim for the particular experience, men for the general or "universal." I don't know about all that. (p. 19)

Of course, one of the crucial differences that strikes me immediately among poets, dramatists, novelists, storytellers is in the handling of children. I can't nail it down, but the attachment to children and to two-plus-two reality is simply stronger in women's writings; but there are exceptions. And finally, there isn't nearly as large a bulk of gynocentric writing as there is phallic-obsessive writings. I'll tell you—there was a period, back in 1967 or '68, when I thought I would run amok if I heard one more poem with the unzipped pants or the triggered gun or the cathedral spire or the space-missile thrust or the good f—, I'd love to read/hear a really good discussion of just cups, bowls and other motifs in women's writings. We've only just begun, I think, to fashion a woman's vocabulary to deal with the "silences" of our lives. (p. 20)

Do you attempt to order human experience? Or, do you simply record experience?

All writers, musicians, artists, choreographers/dancers, etc., work with the stuff of their experiences. It's the translation of it, the conversion of it, the shaping of it that makes for the drama. I've never been convinced that experience is linear, circular, or even random. It just is. I try to put it in some kind of order to extract meaning from it, to bring meaning to it.

Toni Cade Bambara, circa 1977.

It would never occur to me to simply record, for several reasons. First, it is boring. If I learn in math class that the whole is the sum of its parts, I'm not interested in recording that or repeating that. I'm more interested in finding out whether it is axiomatic in organizing people, or if, in fact, the collective is more than or different from the mere addition of individuals. If I learn in physics that nature abhors a vacuum, right away I want to test it as a law. If it is law, then my cleaned out pocketbook ought to attract some money. Secondly, mere recording is not only boring, it is impolite and may be even immoral. If I wrote autobiographically, for example, I'd wind up getting into folks' business, plundering the lives of people around me, pulling the covers off of friends. I'd be an emotional gangster, a psychic thug, pimp and vampire. I don't have my mother's permission to turn her into a still life. I wouldn't ask a friend to let me impale her/him with my pen or arrest them in print. I wouldn't even know how to ask permission; it seems so rude. Frequently, when I hear a good story, I will ask, "Hey, mind if I use that?" By the time, though, that I convert it my way, it's unrecognizable. Not only because I do not think it's cool to lock people into my head, my words, the type, but also because a usable truth can frequently be made more accessible to the reader if I ignore the actual facts, the actual setting, the actual people, and simply reset the whole thing. I think I hear myself saying that the third reason is that lessons come in sprawled-out ways, and craft is the business of offering them up in form and voice, a way of presenting an emotional/psychic land-scape that does justice to the lesson as quickly and efficiently as possible.

I used to assign my students a writing/thinking exercise: remember how you used to get all hot in the face, slide down in your seat, suddenly have to tie your shoe even though you were wearing loafers back then in the fourth grade whenever Africa was mentioned or slavery was mentioned? Remember the first time the mention of Africa, of Black, made your neck long and your spine straight, made the muscles of your face go just so? Well, make a list of all the crucial, relevant things that happened to you that moved you from hot face to tall spine; then compose a short story, script, letter, essay, poem that make that experience of change available to the young brothers and sisters on your block.

Oh, the agony, the phone calls I got in the middle of the night, the mutterings for days and days, the disrupted whist games, the threats to my life and limb. It was hard. The notes, the outlines, the rough drafts, the cut-downs, the editing, the search for form, for metaphor. Ah, but what wonderfully lean and brilliant pieces they pro-duced. And what they taught themselves and each other in that process of sifting and sorting, dumping, stream-lining, tracing their own process of becoming. Fantastic. And I'm not talking about seasoned writers or well-honed analysts. I'm talking about first-year students from non-writing background at the City College of New York, at Livingston/Rutgers, folks who were not college-bound since kindergarten, folks who had been taught not to value their own process, who had not been encouraged, much less trained, to keep track of their own becoming. Ordering is the craft, the work, the wonder. It's the lifting up, the shaping, the pin-point presentation that matters. I used to listen to those folks teaching younger kids at the campus or at neighborhood centers, giving those kids compact, streamlined "from point A (hot face) to point B (proud)" lessons. Fantastic.

I'm often asked while on the road, "How autobiographi-cal is your work?"—the assumption being that it has to be. Sometimes the question springs from the racist assumption that creative writing and art are the domain of white writers. Sometimes the question surfaces from a class base, that only the leisured and comfortable can afford the luxury of imagination. Sometimes it stems from the fact that the asker is just some dull, normal type who cannot conceive of the possibility that some people have imagination, though they themselves do not, poor things. I always like to dive into that one. It was once argued, still argued, that great art is the blah-blah of the white, wealthy classes. Uh huh. And what works have survived the nineteenth century? The land-

ed-gentry tomes or Frederick Douglass's autobiography? The gentle-lady romances or the slave narratives? After I climb all over that question and try to do justice to those scared little creative writers asking out of sincere concern and confusion, I usually read my **"Sort of Preface"** from *Gorilla, My Love,* which states my case on autobiographical writing; namely, I don't do it . . . except, of course, that I do; we all do. That is, whomsoever we may conjure up or remember or imag-ine to get a story down, we're telling our own tale just as surely as a client on the analyst's couch, just as surely as a pilgrim on the way to Canterbury, just as surely as the preacher who selects a particular text for the sermon, then departs from it, pulling Miz Mary right out of the pew and clear out of her shouting shoes. Can I get a witness? Indeed. But again, the tales of Ernest J. Gaines, of Baldwin, of Gwen Brooks, whomever—the particu-lars of the overall tale is one of the tasks of the critics, and I am compelled to say once again that our critics are a fairly lackluster bunch. (pp. 20-3)

What I strive to do in writing, and in general—to get back to the point I was making in direct response to your question—is to examine philosophical, historical, political, metaphysical truths, or rather assumptions. I try to trace them through various contexts to see if they work. They may be traps. They may inhibit growth. Take the Golden Rule, for example. I try to live that, and I certainly expect it of some particular others. But I'll be damned if I want most folks out there to do unto me what they do unto themselves. There are a whole lot of unevolved, self-destructive wretches out there walk-ing around on the loose. It would seem that one out of every ten people has come to earth for the "pacific" purpose, as grandma would say, of giving the other nine a natural fit. So, hopefully, we will not legislate the Golden Rule into law.

The trick, I suspect, at this point in time in human history as we approach the period of absolute devasta-tion and total renewal, is to maintain a loose grip, a flexible grasp on those assumptions we hold to be true, valid, real. They may not be. The world Einstein conjured or that the Fundamentalists conjure or your friendly neighborhood mystic or poet conjures may be a barrier to a genuine understanding of the real world. I once wrote a story about just that—a piece of it is in the novel, *The Salt Eaters.* A sister with a problem to solve is dawdling in the woods, keeping herself company with a small holding stone, fingering it like worry beads. It falls into a pool; she tries to retrieve it—clutching at water, clutching at water. Better to have pitched it in and stood back to reach the ripples—the effects of her act. The universe is elegantly simple in times of lucidity, but we clutter up our lives with such senseless structures in an effort to make scientific thought work, to make logic seem logical and valuable. We blind ourselves and bind ourselves with a lot of nonsense in our scramble away from simple realities like the fact that everything is one in this place, on this planet. We and everything here are extensions of the same consciousness, and we are co-creators of that mind, will, thought. (pp. 23-4)

Toni Cade Bambara, in an interview with Claudia Tate, in Black Women Writers at Work, *edited by Claudia Tate, 1983. Reprint by Continuum, 1986, pp. 12-38.*

Eleanor W. Traylor (essay date 1984)

[*Traylor is a professor of English and a highly esteemed literary critic; Bambara respects her greatly. In an interview with Claudia Tate in* Black Women Writers at Work *(see interview dated 1983?), Bambara called most other critics a "fairly lackluster bunch." "I'm always struck by that," she continued, "when I compare articles and speeches done by this one or that one to what comes tumbling easily and brilliantly out of the mouth of Eleanor Traylor." In the following essay, originally published in* Black Women Writers (1950-1980): A Critical Evaluation, *Traylor examines Bambara's craft and likens it to "reading jazz."*]

Ultimately the genuinely modern writer "assumes a culture and supports the weight of a civilization." That assumption connects the present moment both to an immediate and to a remote past. From such a writer, we learn that whoever is able to live completely in the present, sustained by the lesson of the past, commands the future. The vitality of the jazz musician, by analogy, is precisely this ability to compose, in vigorous images of the most recent musical language, the contingencies of time in an examined present moment. The jam session, the ultimate formal expression of the jazz musician, is, on the one hand, a presentation of all the various ways, past and present, that a tune may be heard; on the other, it is a revision of the past history of a tune, or of its presentation by other masters, ensuring what is lasting and valuable and useful in the tune's present moment and discarding what is not. Constructing rapid contrasts of curiously mingled disparities, the jam session is both a summing up and a part-by-part examination by various instruments of an integrity called melody. Now a melody is nothing more or less than the musical rendition of what a poet or a historian calls theme. And a theme is no other thing than a noticeable pattern occurring through time as time assumes its rhythmic cycle: past, present, and future. *The Salt Eaters* of Toni Cade Bambara is a modern myth of creation told in the jazz mode.

A narrative which opens with a direct question—"Are you, sure, sweetheart, that you want to be well?"—evokes from us an immediate response. In a time of ubiquitous pollution, unless we are head-buried geese, we answer: Yeah! By leave of our spontaneous response to an irresistible call (the mode of the jazz composer), we enter the improvising, stylizing, re-creative, fecund, and not-so-make-believe world of *The Salt Eaters.* That world, called Claybourne, Georgia, is in a state of definition and transition: "Claybourne hadn't settled on its identity yet. . . . Its history put it neither on this nor that side of the Mason Dixon. And its present seemed to be a cross between a little Atlanta, a big Mount Bayou

and Trenton, New Jersey, in winter." But we enter Claybourne during its preparation for spring festival, and there we discover what resembles a splendid community marketplace: "Tables, tents, awnings, rides, fortunetellers, candy booths, gymnasts with mats, nets, trampolines, oil drums from the islands, congos from who knew where, flat trucks, platforms, pushcarts and stalls of leather crafts, carved cooking spoons, jewelry . . . flower carts, incense peddlers . . . kids racing by with streamers and balloons. . . .Folks readying up for the festival" scheduled to begin when "Hoo Doo Man broke out of the projects with a horned helmet . . . and led the procession through the district to the Mother Earth floats by the old railroad yard." We discover that during festival, "People were supposed to write down all the things they wanted our of their lives—bad habits, bad debts, bad dreams—and throw them on the fire." Claybourne is in preparation for the rites of spring renewal. Yet in the midst of "the fugue-like interweaving of voices" resonant in the streets, we hear the voice of a street-corner preacher admonishing:

> "History is calling us to rule again and you lost dead souls are standing around doing the freakie dickie" . . . "never recognizing the teachers come among you to prepare you for the transformation, never recognizing the synthesizers come to forge the new alliances, or the guides who throw open the new footpaths, or the messengers come to end all excuses. Dreamer? The dream is real, my friends. The failure to make it work is the unreality."

The ominous cry of the street preacher, urging the community to recall its history, manifest its destiny, and heed its loas, intones the themes of its spring celebration: transformation, synthesis, and renewal.

As the community must engage its history in order to decipher the meaning of its own rituals—the rhythmic movement toward its destiny—so the individual self must engage its history in order to be well (whole); for if it does not, it hazards the loss of all that makes it whole. That loss is unaffordable and dread; it abates the power of regeneration.

The voice of the street preacher merges with the voice which has opened the narrative. That voice, its music "running its own course up under the words" is the Ebonic, mythopoeic voice of Minnie Ransom, "fabulous healer" of Claybourne, directly addressing Velma Henry, her patient, the celebrant, who enacts the meaning of the ritual that the entire community prepares to celebrate. It is through Velma's consciousness that we hear and observe everything that we know of Claybourne; it is Velma's personal transformation that we experience and that figures in the possibility of the community's renewal; it is through Velma's negation and acceptance of the actual and her pursuit of the possible that we learn the identity and enormous re-creative powers of those who have eaten salt together and who have learned to reconcile both the brine and the savor of life.

We enter Claybourne at the moment of an emergency—a near-disaster. The neighborhood has just received the news that Velma Henry, one of its most indefatigable workers, has attempted suicide, and is now in treatment at the Southwest Community Infirmary. The Infirmary, standing "at the base of Gaylord Hill facing the Mason's Lodge, later the Fellowship Hall where the elders of the district arbitrated affairs and now the Academy" of the Seven Arts, is as remarkable an institution as is the Academy. The site encompassing both is one of the distinguishing features of Claybourne. Shading the site is a 107-year-old baobab tree planted in the same year in which the Infirmary was built: "The elders . . . [had] planted the young sapling as a gift to the generations to come, as a marker, in case the Infirmary could not be defended. Its roots [are] fed by the mulch and compost and hope . . . gathered from the district's farms, nurtured further by the loa called up in exacting ceremonies. . . ." Minnie Ransom daily placed pots of food and jugs of water for the loa that resided there." "The branches, reaching away from the winter of destruction toward the spring of renewal . . . up over [the buildings] as the collective mind grew . . . promising the . . . fruit of communal actions," enshrine the Infirmary. The reputation of Southwest Community woos the interest of medicine people, "guidance counselors, social workers, analysts, therapists," from surrounding areas who visit to observe its rumored "radical" practices. Built in 1871 by "the courage and resourcefulness of the old bonesetters, the old medicine show people, the grannies and midwives, the root men, the conjure women, the obeah folks, and the medicine people of the Yamassee and Yamacrow," the Infirmary fuses the methods of modern medicine with the traditional healing methods of the old folks. Inscribed in "bas-relief over the Infirmary archway" constructed 107 years ago by "carpenters, smiths and other artisans celebrated throughout the district in song, story and recipe," the compelling words "Health is my right" admit patients and visitors to the place of healing. The east wall of the Academy of the Seven Arts, facing the Infirmary, bears "eight-foot-high figures" of the celebrated builders. The Infirmary is presently administered by Doc Serge—a man of many parts (former pimp, numbers banker, preacher)—a resolved Rinehart whose sane balance of the atoms of his sensibility signifies a Salt Eater. In addition to its medical staff, the Infirmary includes a staff of twelve healers called "The Master's Mind." These twelve, under the supervision of Minnie Ransom, now encircle Velma Henry, whose wrists have been mended, lungs purged of toxic gas, but whose traumatized spirit can hardly "hold a thought" as she sits on a stool, barely hearing Minnie's gentle hum: "Are you sure you want to be whole?"

But the insistent music of Min's voice and the cadence of the voices of the twelve tones of the Master's Mind, "humming in long meter," filter through the twilight zone of Velma's fractured consciousness and urge the chordal riffs of her memory:

> Like babies and doctors and tears in the night.

> Like being rolled to the edge of the bed, to extremes, clutching a stingy share of the corners and about to drop over the side,
> Like getting up and walking, bare feet on cold floor, round to the other side and climbing in and too mad to struggle for warmth, freeze.
> Like going to jail and being forgotten, forgotten, or at least deprioritized cause bail was not as pressing as the printer's bill.
> Like raising funds and selling some fool to the community with his heart set on running for public office.
> Like being called in on five-minute notice after all the interesting decisions had been made, called in out of personal loyalty and expected to break her hump pulling off what the men had decided was crucial for community good . . . being snatched at by childish, unmannish hands . . .
> Like taking on entirely too much: drugs, prisons, alcohol, the schools, rape, battered women, abused children . . . the nuclear power issue . . .
> And the Brotherhood ain't doing shit about organizing [or about] the small-change-half-men, boymen who live off of mothers and children on welfare . . . enclaves unconnected . . .

> Everybody off into the Maharaji this and the right reverend that. If it isn't some far off religious muttery, it's some otherworldly stuff. . .

Plunging down a well of years, Velma's "soul goes gathering." Details of her personal life with Obie, her husband, founder of the Academy of the Seven Arts, swim into focus. They had committed the Academy to the study of seven components of culture: history, mythology, creative motif, ethos, social organization, political organization, and economic organization. They had seen the Academy flower and grow like their young son James Lee (Obie), Jr. But then the factions began, and the splitting apart had seemed to trap Obie in the chasm. And the chasm had engulfed them both; their marriage had seemed to lose its center. Memory spinning, Velma thinks of Palma, her sister, a painter. That memory summons reflections of her own association as pianist for Palma's group, the Seven Sisters of the Grain—an artistic association. Their songs, skits, paintings, dances, and stories articulating themes of unity, self-determination, collective work and responsibility, cooperative economics, purpose, creativity, and faith were the artistic embodiment, Velma had thought, of the teachings of the Academy. Velma remembers, as a dream, her involvement over the past twenty-two years with Claybourne's intense undulating movements toward civil rights, community power, the abolition of war, the affirmation of abundant life for women, the negation of forces which deteriorate the quality and integrity of life in communities, and the absolute restraint of "industrial arrogance and heedless technology" that threatens even the possibility of life itself. But the factions, the incessant babel, the "id ego illogical debates" of the "insulated and inbred" Academy's east wing, the cacophony, the faithlessness, the mutations of the no-longer-faithful, had thrown Velma off balance. No longer able to synthesize, to find the center, she has succumbed, become detritus and "an accomplice in self-ambush."

"Choose," hums Minnie. "Can you afford to be whole?" Velma's sprung consciousness is engaged by the music around her. "Minnie was singsonging . . . the words, the notes ricocheting around the room. Mr. Daniels picked out one note and matched it, then dug under it, then climbed over it. His brother from the opposite side of the circle glided into harmony with him while the rest of the group continued working to pry Velma Henry loose from the gripping power of the disease and free her totally into Minnie Ransom's hand, certain of total cure there." Velma is engulfed by the music; her tortured, fractured sensibility staggers toward it, enters it as through the bell of a glorious horn—down, down, down. Descending thus, she seems to meet and merge with the anguish of other tortured sensibilities: that of a middle aged man, Fred Holt, trapped by his past—unable to decode its symbols, aborting his present, he is a bus driver, dreaming of driving his bus over an embankment; that of a young genius, Campbell, absorbed in plans for his future, neglecting to observe some urgent distinctions, some primary details of his present, he is teetering off balance; that of two women, friends of Velma, Ruby and Jan—one impatient, oversimplifying the crises of her present, aware though she is of the connection between her personal conundrums and those of the community—the other, understanding the complex convulsions of her present, of its relations to her past, yet dumbfounded, unable to summon the energizing force that triggers action—both searching for synthesis, desperate to achieve a center from which to flower; that of the brilliant Dr. Meadows who has masterminded Velma's therapeutic surgery but who regards the healing ritual of the Master's Mind with contempt, skeptical of all experience unverified by the code of a closed system which has become his logic, scorning the circle who seem to surround Velma like twelve planets, he mutters half aloud, "I swear by Apollo the physician . . . by Aesculapius, Hygeia and Panacea . . . to keep according to my ability and my judgment the following oath . . ."

Suspended between sub- and midconsciousness, Velma half hears Meadows' invocation interrupted by Minnie's persistent hum and a "snort" from one of the circle of twelve. Minnie (who had "learned to read the auras of trees and stones and plants and neighbors . . . [had] studied the sun's corona, the jagged petals of magnetic colors and then the threads that shimmered between wooden tables and flowers and children and candles and birds . . . knew each way of being in the world and could welcome them home again, open to wholeness . . ." "Minnie could dance their dance and match their beat and echo their pitch and know their frequency as if her own") croons half to Velma and half to "Spirit Guide," her mentor: "You know as well as I, Old Wife, that we have not been scuffling in this waste-howling wilderness for the right to be stupid." Velma's memory dances away in the music of Min's words. The invocation of Meadows and that of Minnie Ransom provoke a be-bop slide down the corridors of Velma's awakened memory. Barriers fall away between the recent and the past, between the real and the imagined, between adulthood

and childhood, between the known and the half-understood. Images appear, dissolve, and transform in Velma's scatting consciousness. Meadow's invocation has evoked, in her memory, a procession of lore: "Eurydice," "Lot's Wife," "Noah," "Medusa"—the woman with snakes for hair. Looking Medusa straight in the eye, Velma thinks piteously that "she would not have cut her head off . . . she would simply have told the sister to go and comb her hair." But the snakes have engaged the memory of an incident from Velma's childhood when M'Dear Sophie and Daddy Dolphy had taught her the proper uses of salt. Those two could dance on the beach together one minute and fix a salt poultice the next—teaching Velma the difference between "eating salt as an antidote to snakebite and turning into salt, succumbing to the serpent." Memories of M'Dear Sophie and Daddy Dolphy lead to memories of Momma Mae tucking her in bed invoking "Spirits of Blessing," so that Velma could outrun "disaster . . . jinns, shetnoi, soubaka, succubi, innocuii, incubi, nefarii, the demons." Memories of family give way to memories of teachers:

> Giant teachers teaching through tone and courage and inventiveness but scorned, rebuked, beleaguered, trivialized, commercialized, copied, plundered, goofed on by half-upright pianos and droopy-drawers drums and horns too long in hock and spittin up rust and blood, tormented by sleazy books and takers, tone-deaf amateurs and saboteurs, underpaid and overworked and sideswiped by sidesaddle-riding groupies till they didn't know, didn't trust, wouldn't move on the wonderful gift given and were mute, crazy and beat-up. But standing up in their genius anyhow ready to speak the unpronounceable. On the stand with no luggage and no maps and ready to go anywhere in the universe together on just sheer holy boldness.

Memory circling, plunging down as though toward the roots of the baobab tree, Velma enters a region where time melds the dead, the living, and the unborn, where the bold act of imagination weds the actual and the mythical, and where the historical is redeemed by the possible: where "Isis lifted the veil"; where Shango presides over the rites of transformation; where Ogun challenges chaos and forges transition; where Obatala shapes creation; where Damballah ensures continuity and renewal; where Anancy mediates the shapes of Brer Rabbit, Brer Bear, Brer Fox, Brer Terrapin, the Signifyin' Monkey; where the griot memory of mankind mediates its reincarnation as the conjure woman, High John, John Henry, the Flying African, Shine, Stagolee, the Preacher, the blues singer, the jazz makers; where the word sorcerers of African-American literary lineage from the eighteenth century to the present—the immediate present—assemble as Master Minds mediating global experience and metaphorizing possibilities yet unmined. Velma has entered a realm where Minnie Ransom's question resonates like a mighty chorus among "the spirits summoned to regenerate the life of the world." Velma's consciousness has entered a region which gives birth to wholeness. And at the exact moment of that entry, Hoo Doo Man breaks out of the projects to officially begin the spring festival. But, just then, something happens in Claybourne which stuns the population still.

> Is it the drum-trumpet
> sounding the thunderous promise
> of the new rain of spring?
>
> Is it the drum-voice
> medicating the whirlwind?
> or
> Is it the blast eroding forever
> the warpland?

The Salt Eaters, like one complex jazz symphony, orchestrates the chordal riffs introduced in the short stories of Toni Cade Bambara collected, so far, in two volumes: *Gorilla, My Love* (1972) and *The Sea Birds Are Still Alive* (1977). The improvising, stylizing, vamping, re-creative method of the jazz composer is the formal method by which the narrative genius of Toni Cade Bambara evokes a usable past testing its values within an examined present moment while simultaneously exploring the re-creative and transformative possibilities of experience. The method of the jazz composition informs the central themes and large revelation of the world of Bambara's fiction. In that world, time is not linear like clock time; rather, it is convergent. All time converges everywhere in that world in the immediate present; the contemporary, remote, or prehistorical past, and the incipient future are in constant fluid motion. Thus, a play of oppositions and the points of juncture between the past and present form a pattern of summons and response shaping the design of *Gorilla, My Love, The Sea Birds Are Still Alive* and *The Salt Eaters.*

The meaning of ancestry and, consequently, the meaning of modernity is the primary focus of the Bambara narrator. The central vision of both the short and long fiction fixes a view of ancestry as the single most important inquiry of personhood and of community life. But ancestry, in the communities revealed in *Gorilla, My Love,* in *The Sea Birds Are Still Alive,* and in *The Salt Eaters,* is no mere equivalent of the past. Rather, ancestry is the sum of the accumulated wisdom of the race, through time, as it manifests itself in the living, in the *e'gungun,* and in the yet unborn. Often, in the narrative world of Toni Cade Bambara, the search for ancestry is the unconscious quest of the central character as it is for Velma of *The Salt Eaters,* or it is the conscious quest as for Jewel in **"The Survivor"** of *Gorilla, My Love.* And, in the title story of *The Sea Birds Are Still Alive,* the ancestral theme and one of its sharpest images is sounded in the musings of a boat pilot: ". . . it's not the water in front that pulls the river along. It's the rear guard that is the driving force." The pilot, from his cabin, is watching passengers settle themselves on his boat-of-refugees: "they waited, complied, were rerouted, resettled at this camp or that island, the old songs gone, the dances forgotten, the elders and the ancient wisdoms put aside, the memory of home scattered in the wind." On this boat is a "widow woman"; she, like Miss Hazel and Bovanne of

"My Man Bovanne" or Granddaddy Vale of the title story of *Gorilla, My Love* or the bluesman, Mr. Rider, of **"Mississippi Ham Rider"** or even Punjab of **"Playin with Punjab"** or Miss Moore of **"The Lesson"** or Miss Candy of the **"The Survivor"** or 'Dear Mother' of **"Sweet Town"** or Granny and Granddaddy of **"Blues Ain't No Mockin Bird"** or the Mother of the lil' girl-woman "I/Me" voice who is really lil' Hazel Elizabeth Deborah Parker, narrator and celebrant of four stories of the *Gorilla* collection or Maggie of **"Maggie of the Green Bottles"**—all of *Gorilla, My Love* is "the vessel of old stratagems, a walking manual . . ."

The widow woman of the title story of *Sea Birds,* a driving force in her besieged and embattled community, is the voice of experience, the griot voice and the warrior voice, the representative of the finest, most reliable, most nurturing traditions of her tribe. But she is no relic; she is

> the woman who hid the cadres in her storage sheds
> and under her hut, who cooked for the young men of
> the district, proud in her hatred for the enemy, proud
> in her love for the country and the nation coming
> soon. She was doing her part filling up the quivers
> with new arrows, rosining the twine for the crossbow,
> stirring in the pot where the poison brewed.

For reasons, the people of her district are directed by her "as she related, stirring in the pots, how the people of old planted stakes in the water to ensnare and wreck the enemy ships." The widow woman of *Sea Birds* and her like in the stories comprising *Gorilla, My Love* are the chords in the short fiction given full-out symphony performance in the *personae* of Minnie Ransom, Old Wife, and Daddy Dolphy of *The Salt Eaters.* Indeed, the salience and significance of the ancestral theme, pervasive throughout Bambara's fiction, is sounded and dramatized through such *personae* as these. For they represent "the rear guard that is the driving force" of the ancestral best commenting on the worst values and traditions and *ethos* of the race as it evolves and meets the challenges of time, present and future.

Yet the theme of modernity, the parallel of the ancestral theme, is the urgency of the fiction. For modernity, in the world of the stories and novel, not only signifies the immediate present but is "a vision of a society substantially better than the existing one"; it "combines a sense of history and a sense of immediate relevance." It is impulse to "reappraise the past, re-evaluate where we've been, clarify where we are, and predict or anticipate where we are headed." Modernity, for Toni Cade Bambara, is "the crucial assembling of historical jigsaw"; it stresses "[a] sense of continuity, [a will to] keep the hook-up of past and present fluid . . . breaking through any fixed time." Finally, modernity in the fiction is a moment of reassessment and revision. For the widow woman is not the only passenger on the boat-of-refugees whom the captain watches long and hard. He gazes equally searchingly at "young man with a hard brown face" standing at the rail of the ship. The young man, looking out over the waters, is thinking of *home:*

Home for him had been a memory of yellow melons and the elders with their tea sitting right outside his window under the awning. Home after that, a wicket basket and his father's lunch pallet in muddy tent cities, flooded wooden barracks, compounds with loudspeakers but no vegetation and no work to keep one's dignity upright. Meager rations in one country, hostility in the next . . . Then finding home among islanders who remembered home, a color, a sound, the shells, the leaping fish, the cool grottoes. And home among other people foreign but not foreign, people certain that humanity was their kin, the world their home. Home with people like that who shared their next-to-nothing things and their more-than-hoped-for wealth of spirit. Home with people who watched other needles on other gauges that recorded the rising winds.

The vision of *home* as both ancestral past and future possibility modified by informed present perceptions is the vision that restores Velma's balance, pilots her to wholeness, in **The Salt Eaters.** It is this vision that characterizes all of the young healers and shapers and builders and waymakers within the neighborhood-community-world of the stories and novel.

Home—the progenitive energy, the residence of value, the provident of judgment, the measure of propriety, the shaper of *ethos,* rigorous examiner, inflamer of rage, source of passion, architect of love, safe harbor, possibility of wholeness and respite, determinant of *isness*—is the ancestral place available to all who dwell in the fact-o-fictive communities of **Gorilla, Sea Birds** and **The Salt Eaters.** Those who inhabit that finally large yard of space live within the field of its persistent force. They must, because of its atmospheric ether, find the essence of home or be refugee in the constantly shifting sands of uncreated or unre-created order. The young man standing at the rail of the boat of refugees, like Graham and Virginia of **"The Organizer's Wife"** or like Naomi and the narrator of **"The Apprentice"** or like Lacey and Jason of **"Broken Field Running"** or like the shivering she of **"The Long Night"** or Sweet Pea and Larry and Moody and Hector of **"Medley"** or Aisha and Cliff of **"A Tender Man"** or Dada Bibi of **"A Girl's Story"** or Honey, Bertha, and Mary of **"Witchbird"** or Piper/Obatale of **"Christmas Eve at Johnson's Drugs N Goods"**—all of **The Sea Birds Are Still Alive**—locates *home* and, thereby, discovers the principle of fruitful action in his world. He like them is the protagonist of modernity confronting adversity and adversaries like the landlord on the boat of refugees whose ritual act of wanton gluttony and whose unregenerate self-absorption and, consequently, self-delusion violates and obscures any vision, value, or reality other than its own imperious autistic purpose.

Modernity, a jam session constructing rapid contrasts of curiously mingled disparities, is at once an extension of the past and a conduit of some future balancing of the best and worst of human possibilities. Thus, the child, also a passenger on the boat of refugees, snuggling close beside her mother as they grope their way topside to the deck searching a seat, is directed: "the passengers along the way grabbing the small hand and leading the child to the next hand outstretched." This child, like lil' Hazel and baby Jason and Raymond and Ollie and Manny and Patsy and Sylvia and Rae Anne and Horace and all the little girls becoming women and boys becoming men and the communities of the stories in **Gorilla, My Love** and **The Sea Birds Are Still Alive,** lives amid the scheme of oppositions played out in the great conjugation of past and present time mediating future possibilities.

It is this conjugation of time along with its referent—the salient features of a journey into experience conducted by a people who wrenched from a coherent past cast refugee upon a sea of circumstance confront incoherence and give it form—the Afro-American paradigm of creation—which **The Salt Eaters** evokes. Its cast of characters so far consummate the Bambara canon. Velma and Obie of the cast of **The Salt Eaters** are the energy of our possibilities while Campbell, Ruby, Jan, and company are the resources of our strength. Fred Holt, the bus driver of **The Salt Eaters,** is our worst choices able to be redeemed, while Dr. Meadows represents our ability to choose. The entire community of all of them is sufficient to defy the agents of destruction aligned around the malign power plant which seems to tower in their world. The valiant and gorgeous people of **The Salt Eaters** portray the strength of our past, available in the present, able to move our future.

As story, **The Salt Eaters** is less moving tale than brilliant total recall of tale. It is no blues narrative plucking the deep chords of the harp of our soul; no tale of anguish, struggle, lust, and love inspiring and conducting us toward mastery of the spirit and therefore mastery of the demon blues (and whites). It is not a declaration; rather it is an interrogation. It is not indicative in mood; rather it is subjunctive in mood. The novel, which is less novel than rite, begins with a question. It moves around a central word, *if. If* we wish to live, *if* we wish to be healthy, then we must *will* it so. *If* we *will* it so, then we must be willing to endure the act of transformation. **The Salt Eaters** is a rite of transformation quite like a jam session. The familiar tune is played, reviewed, and then restated in a new form.

In the tradition of fiction from which she works, Toni Cade Bambara's first novel faces fabulous first novels. Some among that rich opulence are William Wells Brown's *Clotel,* Du Bois's *Quest of the Silver Fleece,* James Weldon Johnson's *Autobiography of an Ex-Colored Man,* Jean Toomer's *Cane,* Langston Hughes' *Not Without Laughter,* Zora Neale Hurston's *Jonah's Gourd Vine,* Richard Wright's *Native Son,* Ann Petry's *The Street,* James Baldwin's *Go Tell It on the Mountain,* Ralph Ellison's *Invisible Man,* Gwendolyn Brooks' *Maud Martha,* Paule Marshall's *Brown Girl, Brownstone,* Ishmael Reed's *The Free-Lance Pallbearers,* Toni Morrison's *The Bluest Eye,* and Charles S. Johnson's *Faith and the Good Thing.* All of these she knows and knows well. **The Salt Eaters** gestures to these and more. Many of these books belong to the company of the best ever written; all are global in their implications. More in the style of the zany brilliance of a Reed and the cultural ecology of a Johnson, *The Salt Eaters* does not pretend toward the simple splendor of the high elegant blues tradition. Though the work matches the encyclical inclusiveness of single works within that tradition, it dares a wrench. It subdues story, eschews fiction, not for fact but for act. It challenges us to renew and reform our sensibilities so that the high mode—the conquering healing power of main-line Afro-American fiction can reemerge and become again our equipment for living—for life. (pp. 58-69)

> Eleanor W. Traylor, "Music as Theme: The Jazz Mode in the Works of Toni Cade Bambara," in Black Women Writers (1950-1980): A Critical Evaluation, *edited by Mari Evans, Anchor Press/Doubleday, 1984, pp. 58-70.*

Nancy Murray (essay date 1985)

[*In the following review, Murray compares* The Salt Eaters *and* Gorilla, My Love *in terms of scope and style.*]

The writing of Toni Cade Bambara first became available to readers in Britain in 1982, when the Women's Press published her novel, **The Salt Eaters.** It is about the politicisation of black America in the 1960s and 1970s, from the civil rights movement, through Black Power, to the stalled incoherence of the Carter era. It is about fragmentation, and the loss of unit and direction, with the shattered psyche of the central character, Velma, symbolising the centrifugal energy unleashed by the fission of political groups—a destructive, frenzied energy, nourished on disillusion, with a locally-made apocalypse right around the corner.

Shortly before she wrote **The Salt Eaters,** Bambara had visited Cuba and Vietnam, and shed what she called her 'miseducation'. She had immersed herself in community organising and we sense that, like Velma, she 'thought she knew how to build immunity to the sting of the serpent that turned would-be cells, would-be cadres into cargo cults. Thought she knew how to build resistance, make the journey to the centre of the circle, stay poised and centred in the work and not fly off, stay centred in the best of her people's traditions and not be available to madness.' But the centre does not hold, and Velma goes mad. **The Salt Eaters** chronicles her plumbing of the depths and precarious ascent towards health in the Claybourne, Georgia, infirmary, built and maintained for a century by black people. Outside its walls, adrift in the great American emporium, activists get bought off and otherwise maimed, organisations get smashed, and those that remain must find ways to stave off despair.

After Claybourne, Georgia, the New York City of her earlier work, **Gorilla, My Love,** seems like a calm backwater. Although these short stories were written between 1959 and 1972, during the time of Martin Luther King and Malcolm X which she looks back to in

the **The Salt Eaters,** there are only a few echoes here of black political struggles, and grass-root activism. These never appear as more than an aside, from which the narrator keeps an ironic distance. In the most memorable of these stories, we see the world of the urban black neighbourhood through the eyes of a street-wise girl of 10 or 12 years, who is too high-spirited and determined ever to become a bystander or a passive victim: 'ain't nobody gonna beat me at nuthin.' We see her flinging herself at life in that fragile moment when she senses her own worth, and has not yet learned that it is futile to dream. As she grows older, we see her shedding her tough solitariness and getting on the wavelength of another person—inevitably a sister, because men betray women sooner or later. Jewel, the adult actress in **'The Survivor',** finally leaves behind the protective moorings of neighbourhood and, like **The Salt Eaters'** Velma, ends almost in pieces, a reflection of America's destructive fragmentation.

By contrast, the street world of the child, though violent and often lonely, is also home. Its horizons end at the barriers of white America. Only in **'The Lesson'** are the limitations of that world demonstrated to ghetto children. They are taken beyond the barriers to another planet, a downtown toyshop, to learn that they are part of a society 'in which some people can spend on a toy what it would cost to feed a family of six or seven'—a lesson which overwhelms the child narrator who thought she had comprehended the dimensions of the possible. In a few other stories whites intrude into the black world, as bearers of the American ethic, selling either a brand of 'democracy', a new food stamp programme, or buying an old blues singer's songs. In **'The Hammer Man',** they materialise as the jailers, the police who patrol the borders between black and white worlds, and who shoot down anyone who threatens their notion of how an underclass should behave. When the solitary Manny, playing his imaginary basketball game, goes 'into his gliding thing clear up to the blackboard, damn near like he was some kind of very beautiful bird', they watch with a transfixed fascination—and then haul him off to a mental hospital, where, presumably, he will learn to know his place.

The stories of **Gorilla, My Love** are vividly written and never dull. Bambara's style is more tightly controlled here than in **The Salt Eaters,** partly because she seems happier with the short story form, and partly because she is attempting much less. In these stories, one can see the early stirrings of the author's political consciousness; its later target—the America lying beyond the child's horizons. (pp. 108-10)

> Nancy Murray, in a review of "The Salt Eaters" and "Gorilla, My Love," in Race & Class, *Vol. XXVI, No. 4, Spring, 1985, pp. 108-10.*

FURTHER READING

Burks, Ruth Elizabeth. "From Baptism to Resurrection: Toni Cade Bambara and the Incongruity of Language." In *Black Women Writers (1950-1980): A Critical Evaluation,* edited by Mari Evans, pp. 48-57. Garden City: Anchor Books, 1984.

    Analyzes Bambara's use of language and dialogue in her works.

Guy-Sheftall, Beverly. "Commitment: Toni Cade Bambara Speaks." In *Sturdy Black Bridges: Visions of Black Women in Literature,* edited by Roseann P. Bell, Bettye J. Parker, and Beverly Guy-Sheftall, pp. 230-49. Garden City: Anchor Books, 1979.

    Interview with Bambara about her childhood, her own writing, and writing by other black women.

Marcus, Laura. "Feminism into Fiction: The Women's Press." *The Times Literary Supplement,* No. 4303 (27 September 1985): 1070.

    Overview of feminist writings recently published in Great Britain; offers mixed reviews of Bambara's *Gorilla, My Love* and *The Sea Birds Are Still Alive,* diagnosing, "Too much Bambara taken at once can cause indigestion. . . ."

Rosenberg, Ruth. " 'You Took a Name That Made You Amiable to the Music': Toni Cade Bambara's *The Salt Eaters.*" *Literary Onomastics Studies* XII (1985): 165-94.

    Analyzes the origins of the names of the characters in *The Salt Eaters.*

Shipley, W. Maurice. Review of *The Salt Eaters,* by Toni Cade Bambara. *CLA Journal* XXVI, No. 1 (September 1982): 125-27.

    Concludes that Bambara, with her considerable skill in the short story genre, has created a very successful novel with *The Salt Eaters.*

Vertreace, Martha M. "Toni Cade Bambara: The Dance of Character and Community." In *American Women Writing Fiction: Memory, Identity, Family, Space,* edited by Mickey Pearlman, pp. 155-71. Lexington: University Press of Kentucky, 1989.

    Examination of the theme of community in Bambara's literary characterizations. Includes a bibliography of works by and about Bambara.

Amiri Baraka

1934-

(Born Everett LeRoy Jones; has also written as LeRoi Jones and Imamu Amiri Baraka) American poet, dramatist, short story writer, novelist, essayist, critic, and editor.

A controversial writer of the late 1950s and early 1960s, Baraka is considered a seminal figure in the development of contemporary black literature. According to some scholars, he succeeds W. E. B. Du Bois and Richard Wright as one of the most prolific and persistent critics of twentieth-century America. His works, which cover a variety of literary genres, concern the oppression of blacks in white society. He received worldwide acclaim for his first professional production, *Dutchman* (1964), and his subsequent work for the theater has provoked both praise and controversy. Having rejected white values and white society, Baraka strives to create art with a firm didactic purpose: to forge an African-American art that reflects the values of the black community.

Born Everett LeRoy Jones in New Jersey in 1934, Baraka spent his early childhood creating comic strips and writing science fiction stories. He was a descendant of preachers, and he dreamed of becoming a minister because, as he recalled, at that time ministers were the most respected leaders in the black community. "But wow," he told interviewer Isabel Eberstadt in 1964, "there were just too many homosexuals in the church for me." At school Baraka excelled in his studies, graduating from high school at the age of fifteen. About his school experience, he recalled: "When I was in high school, I used to drink a lot of wine, throw bottles around, walk down the street in women's clothes just because I couldn't find anything to do to satisfy myself. Neither sex, nor whiskey, nor drugs would do it." Perhaps hoping to satisfy himself in college, he enrolled at Howard University in 1952. Shortly before his first year at the university, he began spelling his name *LeRoi;* scholar William J. Harris suggests that Baraka may have been trying to create a new identity for himself by altering his name. At Howard he studied with such famous black scholars as E. Franklin Frazier, Nathan A. Scott, Jr., and Sterling A. Brown. Despite these exceptional teachers, Baraka found Howard stifling and flunked out of school in 1954. Shortly thereafter, he joined the United States Air Force. Of his experience in the service, he told interviewer Judy Stone that "the Howard thing let me understand the Negro sickness. They teach you how to pretend to be white. But the Air Force made me understand the white sickness. It shocked me into realizing what was happening to me and others." In 1957, after being dishonorably discharged, he moved to New York's Greenwich Village. There he became a part of the Beat movement and

associated with members Allen Ginsberg, Frank O'Hara, and Charles Olson. During the next few years he established a reputation as a music critic, writing jazz criticism for magazines *Downbeat, Metronome,* and the *Jazz Review.* Along with Hettie Roberta Cohen—a white Jewish woman whom he later married in 1958—he also founded *Yugen,* a magazine forum for the poetry of Beat writers. By the late 1950s, his own poetry began attracting critical attention; his first volume of poetry, *Preface to a Twenty Volume Suicide Note....* (1961), met with general approval for its unconventional style and language. Critics would later observe that this is the only work of Baraka's that is "free from ethnic torment."

In 1960, after reading Baraka's poem "January 1, 1959: Fidel Castro," the New York chapter of the Fair Play for Cuba Committee offered Baraka an invitation to visit Cuba. In *The Autobiography of LeRoi Jones* (1984), he referred to this visit as "a turning point in my life," noting, "Cuba split me open." While there he met Third

World political artists and intellectuals who forced him to reconsider his art and his apolitical stance. They attacked him for being an American and labeled him a "cowardly bourgeois individualist." He tried to defend himself in *Cuba Libre* (1961), an essay reprinted in *Home: Social Essays* (1966), by writing: "Look, why jump on me?...I'm in complete agreement with you. I'm a poet...what can I do? I write, that's all, I'm not even interested in politics." Mexican poet Jaime Shelley answered him: "You want to cultivate your soul? In that ugliness you live in, you want to cultivate your soul? Well, we've got millions of starving people to feed, and that moves me enough to make poems out of." Finally, Baraka came to realize the futility of his unanchored rebellion and began forsaking his life as a literary bohemian to embrace black nationalism. During this transitional period he produced some of his best-known works, including an analysis of contemporary black music, *Blues People: Negro Music in White America* (1963), and a second volume of poetry, *The Dead Lecturer: Poems* (1964).

Although Baraka wrote a number of plays during this period, *Dutchman* is widely considered his masterpiece; Norman Mailer, for example, acknowledged it as "the best play in America." The play received an Obie Award for best Off-Broadway play and rocketed Baraka into the public eye. *Dutchman* centers around an interracial encounter involving Lula, an attractive, flirtatious white woman, and Clay, a young, quiet, well-dressed black intellectual. While on a New York subway, Lula mocks and taunts Clay mercilessly for trying to act white: "You middle-class black bastard"; "You liver-lipped white man"; "You ain't no nigger, you're just a dirty white man." Clay, in a fit of rage, explodes: "I sit here in this buttoned-up suit to keep myself from cutting all your throats. If I'm a middle-class fake white man—let me be. The only thing that would cure my neurosis would be your murder." Feeling justified, Lula stabs Clay to death, and as the play ends, she calmly turns to another black man who has just entered the subway. While some critics praised *Dutchman* for its "power," "freshness," and "deadly wit," others were outraged by its language, its perpetuation of interracial hostility, and its portrayal of whites. Baraka countered: "Lula...is not meant to represent white people—as some critics have thought—but America itself...the spirit of America.... The play is about the difficulty of becoming and remaining a man in America.... Manhood—black or white—is not wanted here."

Baraka's next plays, *The Slave* (1964) and *The Toilet* (1964), also met with mixed reviews. The latter play, about a white homosexual boy who gets beaten up by a gang of black boys, was described by one reviewer as an "obscene, scatological, bloody confrontation of the races in a school lavatory." Critic C. W. E. Bigsby called it "a barely stageable homosexual fantasy in which the setting is a urinal and the theme the sexual nature of violence and the degradation of the white world." Like *The Toilet*, *The Slave* concerns the theme of racial conflict. This time it revolves around a black revolutionary

leader and his discourse with his ex-wife and her husband, both of whom are white. Critics suggest that the protagonist in this play represents Baraka himself as he tried to move away from his role as a mediator between blacks and whites and towards an anti-white, pro-black stance. *"The Slave,"* Baraka reminisced, "was really the last play where I tried to balance and talk to blacks and whites.... [I] began to focus on my own identity about that time and came to the conclusion that it was the black community I must direct myself to—we've tried talking to the white society and it's useless." In 1965 Baraka divorced his white wife, deserted the white literary colony of Greenwich Village, and moved to Harlem. Completely dissociating himself from the white race, Baraka dedicated himself to creating works that were inspired by and spoke to the black community. With increasingly violent overtones, his writings called for blacks to unite and establish their own nation. Experimenting with ritual forms in his drama, he wrote *Slave Ship: A Historical Pageant* (1967), a recreation of the passage of slaves into America. Other works written during his black nationalist period are *The System of Dante's Hell* (1965), his only novel, and *Tales* (1967), a collection of short stories. Around this time Baraka also became more vocal about his hatred of whites; when a white woman came up to him one day and asked what whites could to to help blacks, he retorted, "You can help by dying. You are a cancer." Although some people, especially his white friends, were shocked and upset over his violent outbursts, he continued to denounce all things "white." Hoping to withdraw even further, he approved of his name change in 1968 to Imamu Amiri Baraka, meaning "blessed spiritual leader." According to critic Floyd Gaffney, Baraka's marriage to black woman Sylvia Robinson in 1966 also signaled his "complete commitment to the black cause." Baraka's complex, symbolic plays *Great Goodness of Life (A Coon Show)* (1967), *Madheart: A Morality Play* (1967), and *Police* (1968), Gaffney continued, are further examples of Baraka's new "sociopolitical consciousness."

By 1974 Baraka dropped the spiritual title Imamu, and in a dramatic reversal of his earlier nationalist stance, declared himself an adherent of Marxist-Leninist thought. Categorically rejecting black nationalism, he now advocated socialism, stating: "It is a narrow nationalism that says the white man is the enemy.... The black liberation movement in essence is a struggle for socialism." Explaining his changed philosophy, he told an interviewer in 1980: "...I came to my Marxist view as a result of having struggled as a Nationalist and found certain dead ends theoretically and ideologically, as far as Nationalism was concerned, and had to reach out for a communist ideology." During his socialist period he wrote *Hard Facts: Excerpts* (1975), a volume of poetry, and produced the plays *S-1* (1978), *The Motion of History* (1978), and *The Sidnee Poet Heroical: In 29 Scenes* (1979). In the fall of 1979, he joined the Africana Studies Department at State University of New York at Stony Brook as a teacher of creative writing. In the same year, as cited by Harris,

"[Baraka] was arrested after two policemen allegedly attempted to intercede in a dispute between him and his wife over the price of children's shoes." While serving his sentence at a Harlem halfway house, he wrote *The Autobiography of LeRoi Jones* (1984). Since then he has written "Why's/Wise" (1985), an epic poem; *The Music: Reflection on Jazz and Blues* (1987) with his wife Amina Baraka; and "Reflections" (1988), a poem published in the periodical *Black Scholar.*

In his 1985 retrospective study of Baraka and his work, Harris observed that assessment of Baraka has fallen into two general camps: "The white response...has been either silence or anger—and, in a few cases, sadness.... One general complaint is that Baraka has forsaken art for politics.... Another common accusation holds that Baraka used to be a good poet before he became a virulent racist. The reaction to Baraka in most of the black world has been very different from that in the white. In the black world Baraka is a famous artist. He is regarded as a father by the younger generation of poets; he is quoted in the streets—a fame almost never claimed by an American poet...." Whatever the reaction to Baraka, no one is left unaffected by his works. People bristle at his depictions of "white America," critics assert, because he mirrors the ugly and hideous facets of American society.

Called by one critic as the "Malcolm X of Literature," Baraka's most important contributions may be his influence on other black writers and his "championing" of black people. In a 1975 speech delivered to the Congress of Afrikan People in Detroit, he declared: "Speed the Coming of the Vanguard Party! Build revolutionary united fronts! Expose the illusion of bourgeois democracy and rip the covers off their lackeys! Let the people find out armed struggle is inevitable! Victory to Black people! Victory to the strugglers! Victory to all oppressed people!"

(For further information about Baraka's life and works, see *Black Writers; Concise Dictionary of American Literary Biography, 1941-1968; Contemporary Authors New Revision Series*, Vol. 27; *Contemporary Literary Criticism*, Vols. 1, 2, 3, 5, 10, 14, 33; *Dictionary of Literary Biography*, Vols. 5, 7, 16, 38; and *Dictionary of Literary Biography Documentary Series*, Vol. 8: *The Black Aesthetic Movement.*)

*PRINCIPAL WORKS

A Good Girl Is Hard to Find (drama) 1958
Cuba Libre (essay) 1961
Dante (drama) 1961; also produced as *The Eighth Ditch*, 1964
Preface to a Twenty Volume Suicide Note.... (poetry) 1961
Blues People: Negro Music in White America (essay) 1963
The Moderns: An Anthology of New Writing in America [editor] (anthology) 1963
The Baptism (drama) 1964

The Dead Lecturer: Poems (poetry) 1964
Dutchman (drama) 1964
The Slave (drama) 1964
The Toilet (drama) 1964
Experimental Death Unit #1 (drama) 1965
J-E-L-L-O (drama) 1965
"The Revolutionary Theatre" (essay) 1965; published in periodical *Liberator*
The System of Dante's Hell (novel) 1965
A Black Mass (drama) 1966
Home: Social Essays (essays) 1966
Arm Yourself or Harm Yourself; A One-Act Play: A Message of Self-Defense to Black Men (drama) 1967
Black Art (poetry) 1967
Black Music (essay) 1967
Great Goodness of Life (A Coon Show) (drama) 1967
Madheart: A Morality Play (drama) 1967
Slave Ship: A Historical Pageant (drama) 1967
Tales (short stories) 1967
Black Fire: An Anthology of Afro-American Writings [coeditor with Larry Neal] (anthology) 1968
Black Spring (screenplay) 1968
Home on the Range (drama) 1968
Police (drama) 1968
Black Magic: Sabotage, Target Study, Black Art; Collected Poetry, 1961-1967 (poetry) 1969
Four Black Revolutionary Plays: All Praises to the Black Man (dramas) 1969
Resurrection in Life (drama) 1969
Bloodrites (drama) 1970
In Our Terribleness (Some Elements and Meaning in Black Style) [with Billy Abernathy] (poetry) 1970
It's Nation Time (poetry) 1970
Junkies Are Full of SHHH... (drama) 1970
A Fable (screenplay) 1971
Raise, Race, Rays, Raze: Essays since 1965 (essays) 1971
Strategy and Tactics of a Pan-African Nationalist Party (essay) 1971
Supercoon (screenplay) 1971
Kawaida Studies: The New Nationalism (essay) 1972
Spirit Reach (poetry) 1972
Afrikan Revolution (poetry) 1973
Columbia the Gem of the Ocean (drama) 1973
A Recent Killing (drama) 1973
Crisis in Boston! (essay) 1974
The New Ark's A-Moverin (drama) 1974
Hard Facts: Excerpts (poetry) 1975
Sidnee Poet Heroical or If in Danger of Suit, The Kid Poet Heroical (drama) 1975
Three Books by Imamu Amiri Baraka (LeRoi Jones): The System of Dante's Hell, Tales, The Dead Lecturer (novel, short stories, and poetry) 1975
S-1 (drama) 1976
The Motion of History (drama) 1977
The Motion of History and Other Plays (dramas) 1978
AM/TRAK (poetry) 1979
Selected Plays and Prose of Amiri Baraka/LeRoi Jones (dramas and prose) 1979

Selected Poetry of Amiri Baraka/LeRoi Jones (poetry)
1979
The Sidnee Poet Heroical: In 29 Scenes (drama) 1979
Spring Song (poetry) 1979
*What Was the Relationship of the Lone Ranger to the
     Means of Production?: A Play in One Act* (drama)
     1979
"Afro-American Literature and Class Struggle" (essay)
     1980; published in periodical *Black American
     Literature Forum*
"Confessions of a Former Anti-Semite" (essay) 1980;
     published in periodical *Village Voice*
Dim'Cracker Party Convention (drama) 1980
In the Tradition: For Black Arthur Blythe (poetry) 1980
Boy and Tarzan Appear in a Clearing! (drama) 1981
Reggae or Not! Poems (poetry) 1981
In the Tradition (poetry) 1982
Money: A Jazz Opera (drama) 1982
"Sounding" (poetry) 1982; published in periodical
     Black American Literature Forum
*Confirmation: An Anthology of African American Wom-
     en* [coeditor with Amini Baraka] (anthology) 1983
"The Descent of Charlie Fuller into Pulitzerland and
     the Need for Afro-American Institutions" (essay)
     1983
The Autobiography of LeRoi Jones (autobiography) 1984
Daggers and Javelins: Essays, 1974-1979 (essays) 1984
"Wailers" (poetry) 1985; published in periodical *Calla-
     loo*
"Why's/Wise" (poetry) 1985; published in periodical
     Southern Review
The Music: Reflections on Jazz and Blues [with Amina
     Baraka] (essay) 1987
"Reflections" (poetry) 1988; published in periodical
     Black Scholar

*Works before 1967 were published under the name LeRoi
Jones.

Bernard Bergonzi (essay date 1966)

[*Bergonzi is an English novelist, scholar, and essayist.
In the following excerpt, he appraises* The System of
Dante's Hell.]

LeRoi Jones uses the descending circles of the *Inferno* as
the structure of [*The System of Dante's Hell*], an autobiographical novel about a Negro childhood and adolescence in Newark, N.J. This scaffolding gives the book an
ambitious appearance, but it doesn't seem to me to
serve much organic function, except, possibly, providing
guide-lines to the author's memory and imagination.
Certainly, the reader can do without it: the Hell that Mr.
Jones writes about is terrible enough without bringing in
factitious echoes of Dante. Early on Mr. Jones gives a
brutally uncompromising warning: "This thing, if you
read it, will jam your face in my shit. Now say
something intelligent!" Faced with a challenge like that,

the reviewer needs all the help he can get; fortunately,
Mr. Jones makes his intentions clear in a short epilogue
to the novel called "Sound and Image":

> What is hell? Your definitions.
>
> I am and was and will be a social animal. Hell is
> definable only in those terms. I can get no place else;
> it won't exist. Hell in this book which moves from
> sound and image ("association complexes") into fast
> narrative is what vision I had of it around 1960-61
> and that fix on my life, and my interpretation of my
> earlier life . . . .

"Hell," he concludes, "was the inferno of my frustration. But the world is clearer to me now, and many of its
features more easily definable."

Mr. Jones's conclusion is almost serene, but the preceding narrative is anything but that. The first part of his
book is a rapid, disjunctive series of impressions of the
vitality, squalor, violence, and promiscuity of urban
slum life, in which any kind of coherence or organization is sacrificed to the demands of immediacy and
intensity . . . .

[This prose style] is probably satisfying to write but soon
gets monotonous to read. In spite of the endeavors of
some recent writers, language remains a frail instrument
that can rarely perform all that is asked of it. And
nothing is harder than to convey the sensation of direct,
unmediated physical experience; verbalism soon starts
intruding. Perhaps Mr. Jones wants to break down what
he may regard as "white man's syntax": but the larger
problem involved in using white man's language at all is
still with him.

The "fast narrative" in the second part of the book is
much better; here Mr. Jones's authentic literary powers
are brought into play, notably in the final section about
the experiences of a young northern Negro drafted into
the Air Force and sent to a base in the South. This is a
brutal but superbly written piece of narrative, which
reaches its climax when the airman is beaten up by three
local Negroes . . . .

This novel sticks in the mind, vividly if not very
pleasantly. But it doesn't seem to me a success, not, at
least, by any of the standards I am used to employing. At
the risk of sounding square, one can only reaffirm the
weary truism that it is not the business of art to use
chaos to express chaos (whether physical or moral), and
this, in spite of the achievement of the later sections, is
what Mr. Jones's book, taken as a whole, seems to do. If,
as he says, he wants to jam the reader's face in his shit,
then this is ultimately a political act rather than an
imaginative or creative one. And not, I think, all that
effective. Despite everything, Mr. Jones is a powerful
writer; but many works of popular sociology or journalism would contain more immediate directives in the
cause of Negro emancipation. (p. 22)

Bernard Bergonzi, "Out Our Way," in The
New York Review of Books, *Vol. V, No. 12,
January 20, 1966, pp. 22-3.*

David Littlejohn (essay date 1966)

[*In the following excerpt from a 1966 review essay, Littlejohn evaluates Baraka's works, focusing on the poems in* Preface to a Twenty Volume Suicide Note . . . . *and* The Dead Lecturer.]

The Slave . . . is a blatant, unmodulated scream of racial abuse; its primary purpose, one assumes, was authorial self-gratification. . . . It is so devoid of conflict, of dramatic content—the whites are such pappy, wish-fulfilling projections ("Professor No-Dick"), the gunman such a sick, simple noise, that the only reasonable response, white or black, is one of embarrassed and annoyed detachment. Which, perhaps, is what Jones wanted.

The Dutchman . . . is quite another matter. It may be the most important imaginative literary document of the American race war since *Native Son*. And it works. Jones has here channeled his hate equally into *two* antagonists, a young Negro boy and the violent white female (a stunning part for an actress) who accosts him on a New York subway, and has managed to create in their encounter one of the more genuine and irresistible conflicts of the modern stage.

The dialogue between the two is almost perfect. It conveys the shrill, sharp, absolutely open insult-trading of cool modern neurotics, hiding nothing except everything, all very uptight New Yorky 1964. And just beneath it, one can *feel* the peeled-grape hypersensitivity, the heading-for-a-crackup comic tension. (pp. 74-6)

LeRoi Jones has published (in addition to his plays) [his] volumes of poetry, *Preface to a Twenty-Volume Suicide Note* (1961) and *The Dead Lecturer* (1964), and an expressionistic, semi-autobiographical, semi-pornographic prose thing called *The System of Dante's Hell* (1965). He is the most difficult of all the Negro poets, and it is hard to say whether any reader can be guaranteed a just repayment for his efforts. It is hard, in fact, to say anything sensible or useful about a poet who is himself not simply irrational but anti-rational; whose whole approach to poetic language reaches far beyond mere coherence or what we would call sense; who is highly suspicious of the whole nature of verbal communication. This may be one of those many occasions when the wise critic would simply shut up.

A compromise
would be silence. To shut up, even such risk
as the proper placement
of verbs and nouns. To freeze the spit
in mid-air, as it aims itself
at some valiant intellectual's face.

But to give an idea, not to judge, not to interpret: There is, first, a small group of poems that work very nearly in the manner of ordinary sense (at least for a poet). The title poem and **"The Turncoat"** from the first volume, **"Duncan Spoke of a Process," "If Into Love The Image Burdens," "I Substitute For The Dead Lecturer," "Snake Eyes,"** perhaps **"Footnote To A Pretentious Book,"** and

especially **"The Liar"** from the second volume: these are all quiet, poignantly quiet pieces of introspection, honest and painful, suggestive, intimate, coolly sad: Jones on Jones. They reveal, even in their own moody illogic, a man who wants very much to know who he is, and wants the reader to know and love him too. These are inside poems, straight from the pain. (pp. 96-7)

One familiar with Jones' plays, too, will catch, here and there, the violent racist anger, particularly in the two strong anti-syntactic "speeches," in **"Black Dada Nihilismus,"** a Kill-All-the-Whites manifesto in dada, and in the surrealist abuse of **"Rhythm and Blues"** and **"Green Lantern's Solo,"** two of his strongest poems. The violence here is a kind of nightmare violence, something one puts together out of frightening fragments. The two latter poems (from *The Dead Lecturer*) may be as close to a testament as Jones will ever offer, if one knew where to find it; the most honest possible expression of a man who simply cannot trust words to stay still.

> I am deaf and blind and lost and will not again
> sing your quiet verse. I have lost
> even the act of poetry, and writhe now for
> cool horizonless dawn . . .

More frequently, the communication is nowhere so definable. It is a nonverbal communication that uses words and phrases only as little pressures on the reader's consciousness, a communication that has very little to do with normal syntax or denotative structure. One reads, at best, a tone. The *Suicide Note* poems ("early LeRoi Jones"?) like **"Hymn for Lanie Poo"** have a brash, jazzy, young man's sound—a lot of pop-art black humor, jerky collages à la Rauschenberg of radio serial heroes or comic-strip characters taken seriously. As he admits,

> These words
> are not music. They make no motions
> for a dance.

One is denied even the surface attractions of rhythm, except for a jarring sort of skittery jerkiness, or occasional cool riffs on a theme; the "From an Almanac" poems come nearest to modern jazz. Otherwise, the reader must be content to rest passive, to float along with the unresolved surrealistic progress, as Jones plays about with his parentheses and camp gags and insets of sense in search of a style.

The Dead Lecturer poems are even sparer of sense, less attractive, more steely chill, devoid of even the comic gamey glibness of the earlier Jones. But they are even harder to reject absolutely. We have more odd noodling about with word noises, pages in which no single word group between periods coheres into sense. "Obscure" is too concrete a word: lists, insults, four-letter words, parentheses that don't close, lost commas, cold cuts of sound, allusions, dim suggestions of sex or of characters (there are two hazy "character" sequences, on Crow Jane and Willie Best) blend about in the half light, the murky background of dissonance, not nonsense but not sense. For lines and lines the words may lie positively dead, say nothing at all. Then out of it all leap sudden glints and rills of image or statement or pain, three words, a paragraph, a page. This happens especially in the abstract-expressionist protest poems like **"Rhythm and Blues"**; the evocative and *crafted* poems full of keen dreams and emergent pain: **"A Contract," "The Politics of Rich Painters,"** all lethal and queerly vivid things. Here, in his non-sense, he attacks with surrealist vigor all the common muck that passes for sense.

It is all, ultimately, anti-rational poetry, an attempt at a new stimulation of consciousness through words made malleable. Jones of course is not the only one practicing it, and his identification with Beat poets like Duncan, Olson, and Snyder is appropriate. Rational criticism is unequipped, in the last analysis, to deal with such an effort, and finally irrelevant. It is poetry for the leisured, the patient, the energetic, for those who do not insist on an immediate show of gain for energies expended. (pp. 98-100)

> *David Littlejohn, "Negro Writers Today: The Playwrights," and "Negro Writers Today: The Poets," in his* Black on White: A Critical Survey of Writing By American Negroes, *Grossman Publishers, 1966, pp. 66-78, 79-100.*

Donald P. Costello (essay date 1968)

[*In the following review essay, Costello examines the black man in* Dutchman, The Toilet, *and* The Slave *as victims of "white America."*]

LeRoi Jones, in a 1962 address to the American Society for African Culture, insisted that the job of the Negro writer was to portray "the emotional history of the black man in this country: as its victim and its chronicler." Jones the dramatist has taken his own advice. The black man is the victim in Jones' plays, and Jones himself, with an increasingly strident voice, is the black man's chronicler, and, perhaps, America's chronicler.

The plays have been few. In 1961, 16 performances of Jones' *Dante* were presented at the Off-Bowery Theatre. This was a short dramatization, a modern parallel of the False Comforters theme, from *The Systems of Dante's Hell,* Jones' book of fiction. But 1964 was the big year for LeRoi Jones drama, with productions in New York of *The Baptism, The Toilet, Dutchman,* and *The Slave.*

The Baptism, presented at Writers' Stage Theatre off-Broadway in 1964, is not a racial play. It tries hard to be a comedy-of-cruelty, but it tries harder to be blasphemous. Most of the action takes place on the altar of a Baptist church, with characters including a homosexual in red leotards who does ballet steps, who sprinkles the assembly with confetti, and jokingly asserts that he is "the Son of Man." A 15-year-old girlishly handsome boy comes to be baptized, to be forgiven for 1,095 masturbations, one of which is described in detail, and for which

Jones delights in finding synonyms. The minister claims at the altar that his usherettes are "brides of the Lord's son, our own Jesus Christ"; and they claim that the masturbating boy is actually the Lord's son because "it was he who popped us." After the boy admits that he *is* the Son of God, he kills the usherettes, for "they had no charity." A motorcycle messenger from "The Man" comes to recall this Son of God who, although he was sent to save the earth, has been an absolute failure. God is tired of the world's mess, we are told, and plans to grenade the whole works. But the boy-Christ won't leave, for his job is unfinished; so the messenger hits him with a tire iron and carries him off, home to God, on the back of the motorcycle. In a few hours before the grenade will destroy the world, the homosexual decides to cruise the bars, wondering what happened "to that cute little religious fanatic." Jones strains to be shocking; and the play ends up incoherent and adolescent, with scatter-shot fury. In his racial plays, his fury finds his target.

The Toilet is an ugly but affecting racial play. It was presented at St. Mark's Playhouse in a double bill with **The Slave.** Jones tells us, in an "Introduction by the Playwright," that **"The Toilet** is about the lives of black people. White people tell me it is not. They have no way of knowing, but they insist they do."

In **The Toilet,** the victim—Jones again uses that word in his "Introduction"—is a black boy named Ray Foots who cannot express his love for a white boy named Karolis because of what Jones calls the "brutality" of the "social order." And one of the major achievements of the play is the stunning force with which that social order is shown to *be* brutal. The specific social order created by the play is that of high school boys, most of them black. And the setting is a stinking "latrine of some institution." Throughout the play, comment is made on the social order by boys who turn their backs to the audience to urinate into one of the urinals which make up the visual line of the set, and by a boy who goes behind a toilet partition and is found "pulling his watchamacallit," and by verbal obscenities, some trite and some imaginative.

When Karolis is dragged into the latrine by a group of black boys, he has been beat up, is "crying softly, with blood on his shirt and face." Karolis has been dragged to the toilet to fight Foots, the leader of the Negro gang, because of a homosexual love letter which Karolis has sent Foots, a letter in which Karolis said that Ray Foots was beautiful. Foots feels pity—and a kind of returned love—for Karolis, but because of social pressure from the gang, and because of Karolis' own insistence, Foots does fight the already-beaten Karolis. Eventually Karolis is jumped by all the gang and is left bleeding on the toilet floor, draped with wet toilet paper. Karolis, the white boy, is more obviously—but to Jones less profoundly—a victim than is Foots, the black boy. It is the white boy who is beaten. But the meaning of the play comes from Karolis' revelation that the black boy he really loves is a hidden beautiful boy named Ray, not the Foots of this stinking toilet who is visible to his gang members. "Did I call you Ray in that letter—or Foots?...That's who I want to kill. Foots.... His name is Ray, not Foots. You stupid bastards. I love somebody you don't even know."

After Karolis is left bleeding on the toilet floor, Foots sneaks back in, kneels by Karolis' form and, weeping, cradles his head in his arms as he wipes the blood from Karolis' face. For all of its ugliness, *The Toilet* is, as Jones has written, "a play about love." It is a play about a love between a white boy and a black boy, a love which, because of the social order in which the black people live, cannot be expressed on any level. Brutality results, says Jones, in any social order, "if it is not an order which can admit of any man's beauty." The beauty of Foots remains hidden. Both the black and the white are therefore victims; and the chronicler, Jones, in this play talks—for the last time—about love.

The victim in *Dutchman* is Clay, and this is a play about hatred. *Dutchman* was produced off-Broadway at the Cherry Lane Theatre, and it won the *Village Voice*'s Obie Award for the Best American Play of the 1963-64 season. Subsequently it was presented at the Festival of Two Worlds, at Spoleto. It is the most widely known of Jones' works, primarily through the 1967 movie version, directed by Anthony Harvey.

In *Dutchman,* Jones again, as he had in *The Toilet,* speaks through controlled dramatic art. He controls his form. He embodies his hatred in two characters; he is still a dramatist. In an interview, Jones said, *"Dutchman* is about the difficulty of become a man in America." The boy who is "desperately trying to become a man" is Clay, twenty-year-old Negro. Lula, beautiful young white woman on the make, sits next to Clay on the subway. In brilliant dialogue (by far the best art Jones has shown in any of his plays) Clay's lack of *place* is revealed to the audience. He doesn't belong, for he doesn't acknowledge his blackness. Lula has him pegged: "You're a well-known type," and "I know you like the palm of my hand." He's a suburbanite, living in New Jersey with his parents; in college he thought of himself as Baudelaire. Never did he think of himself as a black nigger. He's a poser, not a man; he doesn't acknowledge what he *is*. Lula takes hold of his jacket and shouts: "Boy, those narrow-shoulder clothes come from a tradition you ought to feel oppressed by. A three-button suit. What right do you have to be wearing a three-button suit and striped tie? Your grandfather was a slave, he didn't go to Harvard."

Scene I ends with Lula's insistence that she knows the truth about Clay. Ivy league clothes won't hide his blackness. And his submission is only a pretense. He cannot be free from his history, the heritage of slavery; and she cannot be free from her history, the heritage of oppression. And simmering under the pretense of Clay's submission to the white order is the necessity of the slave to murder his oppressor: "You're a murderer, Clay, and you know it."

By the end of Scene I the mood of the play is taut. The victim will not stay victimized peacefully. And by this time the observer hears obviously the voice of the chronicler, the tortured autobiographical gropings of LeRoi Jones himself, faced with "the difficulty of becoming a man in America." In a preface to a 1966 collection of essays, ironically called *Home,* Jones tells something about that constant struggle of his own which, in *Dutchman,* is mirrored in the character of Clay: "One truth anyone reading these pieces ought to get is the sense of movement—the struggle, in myself, to understand where and who I am, and to move with that understanding." All these movements, Jones writes, "seem to me to have been always toward the thing that I had coming into the world, with no sweat: my blackness." And, he concludes, "by the time this book appears, I will be even blacker."

In Scene II, Clay becomes blacker. Lula goads him to it. She mocks him, wildly, dancing in the aisle: "You middle-class black bastard." "You liver-lipped white man." "You ain't no nigger, you're just a dirty white man." She commands Clay to do what Jones himself, in his dramatic career, has been doing: "Get up and scream at these people. Like scream meaningless shit in these hopeless faces." Clay finally answers back. He slaps her across the mouth as hard as he can, and announces: "Now shut up and let me talk." And then Clay launches into a long and obscene rage against Lula and against all whites who profess to understand the Negro. Lula cannot understand: "You great liberated whore! You fuck some black man, and right away you're an expert on black people." And neither can any whitey understand or help a black man come to an image of himself. So, Clay insists, through his teeth: "Let me be who I feel like being. Uncle Tom. Thomas. Whoever. It's none of your business." It's as simple as that. Whitey can tell the black man nothing because whitey can understand nothing. As early as 1961, Jones had written: "Liberals think that they are peculiarly qualified to tell American Negroes and the other oppressed peoples of the world how to wage their struggles." In *Dutchman,* the Jones reply to whitey is "It's none of your business."

Clay knows that it is insane to conceal his blackness, but Jones gives him only two alternatives. He can continue the insanity of living half-hidden in whitey's world; or he can relieve his insanity by asserting his blackness through murder: "Murder. Just murder! Would make us all sane." He warns Lula not teach the black man the way of the white man, not to talk too much about the advantages of Western rationalism or the great intellectual legacy of the white man, because if the black man does learn the lesson of the white man, he will adopt his weapon: "All of those ex-coons will be stand-up Western men, with eyes for clean hard useful lives, sober, pious and sane, and they'll murder you." Clay chooses to avoid the easy, luxurious way of murder ("It takes no great effort. To kill you soft idiots."). He chooses, instead, to stay in his insanity, to deny his blackness, to deny the murder that would liberate him: "Ahh, shit,

A scene from The Toilet.

who needs it? I'd rather be a fool. Insane. Safe with my words, and no deaths, and clean, hard thoughts."

But in the Jones world murder is inevitable once white and black confront each other. So, although Clay decides to remain insane by not murdering, Lula turns him into the complete victim by plunging a knife into his chest. In a ritual act, with the collaboration of the rest of the congregation in the subway, whitey kills the black man as indeed whitey has been doing all along. The black man who refuses to murder is himself murdered.

If Clay is the black man, if Clay is Jones (Jones has written often that everything he writes is necessarily written specifically *as* a black man), who is Lula? She is of course America, especially white liberal America who interferes with the black man, who professes friendship as it murders. Jones insists that Clay and Lula are not symbols; but then he goes on to talk of them as if they are. Lula, he insists, "does not represent anything—she is one. And perhaps that thing is America, or at least its spirit." When the critics complained that Lula is too crazy, extreme, neurotic, Jones replied, "You remember America, don't you, where they have unsolved murders

happening before your eyes on television. How crazy, extreme, neurotic, does that sound? Lula, for all her alleged insanity, just barely reflects the insanity of this hideous place."

Harold Clurman has pointed out that if **Dutchman** is angry, **The Slave** is rabid. Anger, he says, has a definite form; rage only smolders and explodes. The form of **The Slave** is supposedly a fable in which a debate takes place. But rather it is a tirade delivered by Walker, a Negro who is leading a violent murderous black rebellion which is in the midst of blowing up "this city . . . this country . . . or world." Walker talks of Easley, the white liberal intellectual who is now married to Walker's white ex-wife. But it is not a debate. It is merely pages of invective in which Walker speaks Jones' doctrine of race violence. "This hideous place" is no longer encompassed into a dramatic space small enough for Jones to control. Here he does not reflect America through a few boys in a toilet or through a white-black couple on a subway; he tries to reflect America in huge, amorphous, prophetic rhetoric. He ignores his own artistic principle that art must reflect man within a "defined world." The chronicler takes over from the artist. The chronicler takes up the role of self-conscious Prophet and shouts hatred.

The Slave holds dramatic interest only in the fact that Jones, as in his other plays, makes the black man a victim, this time—and Jones fully knows this—a victim of his own philosophy. Walker delivers a prologue during which he is dressed as an old field slave; and at the end of the play, as the city explodes, he is again a slave—enslaved by mutual hatred, hatred received and returned. All has been made rotten, we are told again, as we were in *Dutchman,* by the hatred in the heritage of slavery. The Negro writer is, Jones has written, "a chronicler of the Negro's movement from African slave to American slave." The central doctrine of the prologue is "We are liars, and we are murderers."

The slave, who is Walker, who is the black man, who is Jones, is destroyed as well as destroying. The wife knows that the black man has been robbed (like Clay in *Dutchman*) of his image of himself: "I don't even think you know who you are any more. No, I don't think you ever knew.... It must be a sick task keeping so many lying separate uglinesses together...and pretending they're something you've made and understand."

However certain this black man is of his hatred, he is also certain what it has cost him. Hatred has cost the black man everything else that he has desired from life, and it has cost him all his art. The black man has chosen to promote "a bloody situation where white and black people are killing each other...despite the fact that I would rather argue politics, or literature, or boxing, or anything, with you, dear Easley, with you." And the black artist has chosen bloody rebellion knowing "I have killed for all times any creative impulses I will ever have by the depravity of my murderous philosophies."

The leader of the black rebellion knows that another tyranny will result after the rebellion; he is not the Marxist visionary preparing for the happy day after the revolution. The harvest of slavery, with so much hatred, must be bitter; the revolution is only a case of "you had your chance, darling, now these other folks have theirs." He knows it's ugly; but in "this hideous place" there is no alternative to murder and violence. Jones no longer admits Clay's alternative, no longer sees a possible alternative in choosing to remain insane by denying violence. The black man instead seeks the sanity that comes from murder. "God, what an ugly idea," says the white liberal; head in hands, the black man replies, "I know. I know."

Throughout the text of *The Slave,* Jones has the characters talk about "ritual drama." But the play never ascends to the level of ritual drama, to any cleansing emotion. It rants. It establishes no bond between author and audience. It speaks with only one human dimension, racial hatred; its people are partial. The play doesn't even have verisimilitude: Why do the white man and his wife leave their children in the midst of a bombardment? Why does Walker sit around and talk while he should be leading his troops? Why does Walker tell his wife that their children are dead although we hear them scream at the end of the play? Real ritual drama affects one as a transcendent filling up, it exists throughout or even outside of time; this play freezes.

I don't think that *The Slave,* or the bigger question of LeRoi Jones the dramatist, can be understood without examination of Jones' dramatic credo, called "The Revolutionary Theatre," published in *Liberator,* the journal of the Afro-American Research Institute. In 1965, the year after his four off-Broadway productions, Jones reasserts that "Clay in *Dutchman,* Ray in *The Toilet,* Walker in *The Slave* are all victims." And because the black man is victimized by society, the role of black theater is clear: "The Revolutionary Theatre must Accuse and Attack anything that can be accused and attacked. It must Accuse and Attack because it is a theatre of Victims." And that is the difference between *The Slave* on the one hand and *Dutchman* and *The Toilet* on the other. In *The Slave,* Jones is writing "Revolutionary Theatre." Tension is gone because he has made up his mind to Attack and Accuse. *Dutchman* and *The Toilet* are controlled by containing form; Jones is still probing, and the result is the tension that allows art. But in the Attacking and Accusing of *The Slave,* tension is relaxed, form is gone; and propaganda, the Revolutionary Theatre, takes over.

Jones' *Liberator* essay is itself incoherent, frantic, filled with sentences in upper case, with quintuple question marks and double exclamation points. Much of it is inexplicable: "The Revolutionary Theatre must function like an incendiary pencil planted in Curtis Lemay's cap. So that when the final curtain goes down brains are splattered over the seats and the floor, and bleeding nuns must wire SOS's to Belgians with gold teeth." But its central doctrine of hatred is clear enough: "White men will cower before this theatre because it hates them.... The Revolutionary Theatre must hate them for hating.... The Revolutionary Theatre must teach them their deaths." And clear, too, is its call for destruction: "It is a political theatre, a weapon to help in the slaughter of those dim-witted fatbellied white guys who somehow believe that the rest of the world is here for them to slobber on.... It must crack their faces open to the mad cries of the poor.... Americans will hate the Revolutionary Theatre because it will be out to destroy them and whatever they believe is real.... The play that will split the heavens for us will be called THE DESTRUCTION OF AMERICA."

If we are to believe our courts, Jones' life has followed both his art and his theatrical credo. For all of the certitude in *The Slave* that armed rebellion would ruin the artist, the hero-victim of that play took to the streets with guns. And, the courts tell us, so did Jones take to the streets with guns in Newark during last summer's black rebellion. In *The Slave,* the black man has made up his mind to pay the price; in the streets of Newark, Jones apparently made up his mind to pay a similar price. *The Slave* is fearful in its foretelling: in it Jones announces— before Watts and Newark—what will happen and what he will do. Before the riots, *Newsweek* concluded that LeRoi Jones "writes and harangues himself out of the company of civilized men." And, the magazine went on to say, he therefore "forfeits all claim to serious attention." It is, rather, because Jones has decided to leave the company of civilized men that he demands our attention, if not for our interest in art, then for our interest in humanity.

How can the white liberal critic—interested in art and humanity—react to the drama of LeRoi Jones? Jones certainly does not expect acceptance: "My ideas revolve around the rotting and destruction of America, so I can't really expect anyone who is part of that to accept my ideas." Jones intimidates. He predicts that the white liberal critic will attack him on aesthetic grounds. And he's right. That's just what any critic who refuses to abdicate his critical judgment must do in the face of Revolutionary Theatre like *The Slave.*

Jones further intimidates the white liberal critic by insisting—as do black revolutionists both literary and non-literary—that whitey can never understand the black man. Again I suppose that Jones is right. When Jones says, "You cannot understand me," I will not deny it. I am afraid to be patronizing by saying, "I understand." I don't expect to come to understand the foul indignities heaped for centuries on the black man, nor to understand their result—for my skin is white. So how do we react, all boxed in, cowering like a Calvinist sinner before a God who has already decided he is damned? Can the critic do nothing but stand here and plead, "What do you want of me? You, LeRoi Jones, carry your heritage of slavery; I carry my heritage of guilt. Do we just stand here and stare at each other until the murder starts?"

The suffering involved in standing mute while Jones proposes mutual murder seems to be peculiarly the kind of suffering which many white liberals enjoy. When Jones singles out the white liberal as the black man's particular enemy, little response is heard from the self-flagellating liberal who thinks such suffering is good for us. We white liberals might indeed *need* the expiation which Jones offers for our guilt. But if we accept the inevitability of his prophecies, we will be as destructive as Jones.

I think that the white liberal who refuses to give up his rationality must see that Jones' art and philosophy are suicidal as well as murderous. His philosophy is ultimately a betrayal of all of humanity, and particularly of the black man. In fury and despair, Jones says that the black man must accept the white man's way of suppression and murder. This a betrayal not only because it proceeds on the incredible assumption of *The Slave* that the black man would *win* an armed rebellion. (The white ghetto will not stand still, enjoying its punishment, as do we white liberals.) But the Jones philosophy is also a betrayal because it denies the black man the moral superiority over the white man, the moral superiority of non-violence. The conclusion of *The Slave* is that the

answer for the black man is to find himself, and at the same time destroy himself, through killing the white man. But there is no finding there. There is only loss, and a madness. The victim would remain a victim.

So, in spite of the fact that Jones has the power to intimidate into paralysis, the only sane response is to break out, to challenge the rules as Jones has laid them down. I will attack his art on aesthetic grounds, for when form is shattered in art, no shared experience results. And although admitting that full understanding between white and black may be impossible, movement toward understanding must be continued, for we all know that it has been started. We *can* all still remember the "We Shall Overcome" days.

I don't think that Jones, deep down, believes himself when he insists that no understanding is possible. For he writes. He lets white men produce his plays for white audiences. If he truly felt that we could never come to know each other, he might as well talk to a tape recorder. He wears African robes; he insists on calling himself an Afro-American: but he has come to us in his writing. We must assume that he has something to say to us.

We hear obviously enough the hatred for which he has willingly sacrificed his art. Our human reaction is that his vision is so hate-ridden that it is insane, and that we must reject it, must not stand mute before it and watch racial hatred become a self-fulfilling prophecy. But after I reject him, I still am left with fear. *That* cannot be escaped or rejected. And maybe fear finally is the one shared experience that Jones communicates. Perhaps, at this point, poised for the horror which is promised for the summer, the shared experience of fear is what he has to say to us. Perhaps *it* can shake us into the doing—which could bring effective change within the political order.

Is there time for such change? Jones says that political change is only the liberal's game, "palliatives and symbols to remind him of his own good faith." So the fear remains. Is there time? And the prospect of mutual madness. (pp. 436-40)

> *Donald P. Costello, "Black Man as Victim,"*
> *in* Commonweal, *Vol. LXXXVIII, No. 15,*
> *June 28, 1968, pp. 436-40.*

Amiri Baraka with Ossie Onuora Enekwe (interview date 1978)

[*In the following 1978 interview, Enekwe and Baraka discuss Baraka's plays* Dutchman *and* The Motion of History. *They also analyze the "communist phase" of black writers Langston Hughes, Richard Wright, and Ralph Ellison.*]

[Enekwe]: *What are the most crucial periods of your life as a writer?*

[Baraka]: The first period would be right after I got out of the Air Force in the 50's. It gave me the decision to write. Another period would be in the 60's, breaking away from the various influences that I had come under in the village and on the eastside. I decided to cultivate my own sound and my own voice. In the middle of the 60's, I became a cultural nationalist, and by doing so, I left the village, marriage, a lot of things. Next would be the 70's...the whole change from Nationalism to Marxism. These changes in my life have corresponded to the critical periods in my writing career. I had to readjust my views and therefore what I was to say about things. I think the present period is a critical point. I have to try and develop my own work so I can become more clearly and firmly a Marxist writer.

What was it in the Air Force that made you decide to write?

I took some writing courses in High School. When I was in college I read a lot of Elizabethan poetry. When I went into the Air Force, I was isolated, with a few diversions. I had the tendency to write. I also did a lot of reading. I had a chance to bring out the essence of what I really wanted to do. I just wanted to express myself.

How do you consider your present work in relation to your previous work such as **Dutchman?**

I think **Dutchman** has some good things to say. Ideologically there has been a big change since **Dutchman.** I would not disown the play. It's just a totally different thing. What I have to do is try to develop what I'm doing now and work on it, so it will be as powerful as **Dutchman.** A lot of people said they liked **Dutchman.** Now that I write about Socialist Revolution, people refuse to publish my work like before. It's very difficult. I have some manuscripts that have been on my hands for about six years.

Has this problem anything to do with your style?

I would say the content.

How do you think you will improve the situation?

Do some of my own publishing. I don't see any help for that.

If you do your own publishing, when will you find time to write?

It's not hard, just a matter of doing some advertising. That's relatively easy.

I would like you to talk about **The Motion of History.** *I enjoyed it very much. Apart from being instructive, it is entertaining. What's your objective in this play? What kind of problem would you have in trying to structure it for the stage?*

Basically, I need a sophisticated audio-visual equipment and a sophisticated lighting director. I would like the play staged in an even more spare form than it is now.

Basically that's it. I have to relearn my whole method of writing, so I can then put together the whole ideological content that I want. It's possible to have something that's artistically powerful and at the same time politically reactionary. You can go to American movies everyday and see that. This is one of the principal things an anti-imperialist artist has to do: not only write and reflect the struggle in his writing, but take up the struggle itself. It's all interrelated.

What kind of audience do you have in mind, when you write a play such as **The Motion of History?**

Working class people, the advanced workers, people who know something is wrong with the system, and are already organising themselves to fight against it. **The Motion of History** depends on film work, slides. You would have to develop a staging technique for it. We had to settle for a lot in production. If we had the money, like Joe Papp or one of those big time dudes on Broadway, we wouldn't have to grapple with it.

Are you talking in terms of a form similar to Brecht's?

Although I admire Brecht very much, I haven't styled any of my plays like his.

What kind of problem did you have in organizing your ideas?

Trying to develop the form and combine it with the correct content.

Did you have problems articulating the scenes?

The problem is getting from scene to scene. The question is how to make the transition. I began to rely on cinematic techniques. I was trying to make that whole flow of images and information more like a movie reality rather than a play reality. So when you have to actually put it on stage (it's okay to have it on paper like that), you have to think about all this stuff, how you are going to organize it...

Did you ever think that the audience might get bored with the duration of the play? For example, is it supposed to be four hours long? Did you do anything in the play to eliminate boredom?

No, just tried to play it. It could have moved faster. It might be too long. If it's too long, that means I still haven't discovered the appropriate form in which to put this whole chronicle into progression.

You treat the history of the black struggle in this country from the beginning. You bring some new perspectives on the indentured servants. Are they taken from history?

The whole struggle against the ruling class of this society begins with indentured servants, slaves and Indians, the first opposition is composed of those three groups. One book called the *Invention of Racial Slavery* laid out very clearly all the various rebellions and how they became multi-nationalist rebellions of Blacks, Whites and Indians. The ruling class, taking this into consideration, created a new kind of status for white workers. The question of keeping the audience attention in the play depends on how well you stage it. How can you keep that series of energies . . . which is hard to achieve on the stage.

I must say that the play has a lot of suspense. Because you vary the action, one never really knows what to expect. Did you think of it that way?

What I was trying to do is go back to the origin and then come forward and talk about everything I can. When people say it is too long, that is a just criticism, because I try to cover too much. I know a lot of the episodes could have been plays themselves. I like to do that epic kind of thing.

What is the problem with historical plays? How do you deal with the problem of compromising your desire to deal with history with the need to entertain your audience?

The problem is that Broadway plays and Off-Broadway plays are commerce. They belittle the audience's intelligence. What we want to do is develop a theatre where people can be educated and entertained, and at the same time obtain serious theatre.

How do you deal with the problem of performance?

The costumes were all designed and kept clean by us. We didn't have a large budget.

How do you intend to work in the epic theatre?

Intellectually very close. I have to do more studying of Brecht. Reading his writing and poetry convinces me that he can serve as a model. We have put together something called "Images of Struggle Revolution" which is a poetry reading comprising revolutionary poems from around the world, and in that we do a lot of Brecht's poetry.

How does Black Literature develop a sense of identity, especially going beyond the earliest black Africans in this country, to the African roots? In **Blues People** *you mention some of the elements, some cultural traits and values that Africans brought to America. How do you as a writer articulate these ideas so that the Blacks can relate positively to Africa?*

I think that the consciousness is fairly high. It's not at a peak as it was in the late 60's and early 70's. In 1972, 75,000 people marched on African Liberation Day. The question of African liberation has become indelibly placed in Black consciousness. African Liberation Day is a definite part of politically conscious Afro-America. For example, every year there are demonstrations in Washington, San Francisco, New York. You go to the schools, colleges, Afro-American students are at the core of making the colleges divest themselves of their stocks in South Africa.

Political consciousness about Africa is fairly widespread especially among the politically conscious, progressive, advanced forces in this country. To a certain extent it is a mass question. The very fact that they put *Roots* on that T.V. is significant. It was largely an attempt to tap what consciousness they knew existed. They certainly were not creating consciousness of Africa among black people.

Is there anything about Roots *that you considered to be valuable or useful in this sense?*

In that sense it was useful. But, I feel there were a number of contradictions. For instance, *Roots* seems to suggest that there was no class struggle in Africa. It showed the paradise the white man sold us out of, not showing how people were actually *sold* into slavery by an African feudal ruling class. The whole focus in *Roots* was basically on house servants who worked in the kitchen, who drove the coaches, who trained chickens, whereas the majority of the black people worked in the fields picking cotton. The whole question of rebellion was played down, except for one dead dude that was supposed to be with Nat Turner. The impression from *Roots* was that the slaves who talked about freedom, tried to buy their way from it, rather than running and rebelling. Also, the question of the Civil War. In *Roots,* the Civil War was introduced to Blacks via the newspaper, but actually the black people were running away from the plantations, setting fires to the plantations, generally undermining the southern economy and fighting the South; they actually turned the war around. The South was winning the war.

What do you think of Ceddo, *especially its portrayal of Islam?*

I think the movie should have been shown a few years ago.

Did the movie change your views?

Well, my romance with the Muslims was very short lived; that was back in 1968. I knew most things *Ceddo* was talking about, but seeing it on film dramatized like that, made me want to show it to a lot of Afro-Americans, to show the way Islam was imposed on the Africans just like Christianity was. A little truth needed to be learned. A lot of people are still walking around with the idea that Islam is something different.

How would you go about teaching Afro-American Literature? Suppose you were to come to Africa, how would you teach Native Son *and the* Invisible Man?

I would have to give a historical over-view of what was happening in the American society, and to the black people in general. Then I would show with specific sources how it is interrelated to the overall over-view. Just teaching students in a vaccuum without telling them where the books come from, what they are really all about, would not do. You see art flows from life, and if you don't know what the life is about, the art becomes a little abstract. I feel you would have to teach something about American life and history and Afro-American life and history and show how the Blacks fit into that.

At this stage in Afro-American literature, what has been gained, or what do you see as a positive factor or element in the whole movement, the whole history?

There is a revolutionary tradition in Black Literature.

What has happened at the present moment?

At the present moment the bourgeoisie has sensed the strong thrust of Nationalism in the 60's. Now in the 70's a lot of people have sort of disassociated themselves from Black Nationalism—like myself, I have criticized Nationalism. So the bourgeoisie are now pushing a whole movement into a 1950 type of Black Literature, a comprador, non or anti-black "black" literature.

The younger group of Black writers coming out of college don't seem to have many opportunities in getting their work published. Does anything in their writing make you happy?

There are some good young writers coming up. The question is that there has to be some publications organized. We formed an organization called the *Anti-imperialist* Cultural Universe. The first publication was on May 1st. It's called *Main Trend* (magazine). It focuses on popular culture, poetry and essays. We have hopes of attracting the anti-imperialist, more militant literature. There are some publications out like that now and there has to be more. People have to discover they have to publish themselves, they've got to organize.

You don't insist that writers be Marxist before they join the organization?

No, what you have to do is unite with people who are opposed to the imperialist society and the way it is run. They may not be clear as to how it will come. You have to begin by uniting a broad sector of people and the broader the sector the more will eventually become marxists.

Correct me if I'm wrong. It seems to me that Black writers are so concerned with the idea of discipline, or social control, some kind of organizing. They seem too worried about confusion and disunity among black people.

It's no secret that no real change can come without the people organizing. This society will not change of its

Baraka with his wife Amina during auditions for The Motion of History.

own accord. It has to be changed; and it can only be changed if the people are united.

I see you left out the story of the Communist movement in the 1920's-1940's (in **The Motion of History***).*

I just talked about it briefly. I didn't go into the movement. I showed actually the declining Communist party. I tried to lay out in the speech how the views changed. I would love to do a play about the Communist party in the thirties. I think it could be a very interesting piece of work but it would take quite a bit of research on my part. I fully intend to do something like that. As it was, I was trying to show that the party fell apart, thereby making the whole struggle of the working class and the different nationalities impossible. There is a whole spread of people in the United States, not only Black and White, but Asians, Puerto Ricans, Chicanos, Indians, etc., and their struggle cannot be organized without a communist party. I tried to show how the rise of Black nationalism has to be connected with the whole liquidation of the Communist party. Black nationalism becomes intensive in the late 50's and 60's because of the absence of the Communist party. The Communist party ceased to exist in 1957. In the 60's you get intense Black nationalism simply because there is no Communist party, or the "Communist" party that did exist was so backward that the things it said helped to formulate the nationalism. C.P.U.S.A. were so backward that they used to go around putting down Malcolm X. In fact, I think the C.P.U.S.A. did a better job than the bourgeoisie of running Black people away from Communism. It is similar to the "Communist" party in South Africa.

Do you identify two traditions of Black Literature, one beginning with William Wells Brown, and another beginning with Langston Hughes?

I see a revolutionary tradition in Afro-American Literature beginning with slave narratives, pre-civil war revolutionary black nationalistic people like Henry Highland Garnet, David Walker and C. H. Langston. (Also people like Dubois, who is the transitional figure, the connection, between the pre-civil war nationalist and slave narratives and the 20th century. The Harlem Renaissance and Hughes and McKay the most impressive and influential writers of the period. In the 30's, Wright, Theodore Ward, Margaret Walker, in the 40's and on, and then the 60's Black Arts movement, to name a few from that tradition!) I would imagine William Wells Brown would be related to them. I don't put all the Back to Africa people in revolutionary categories. Most of the people who talked about back to Africa really took the same position as the colonization society. After a generation or so the mass of black people didn't want to go to Africa, they wanted to be "free" where they were.

What do you think about Martin Delaney?

He had a strong presence in the Back to Africa movement. He also became an officer in the U.S. army!

Would you reject James Weldon Johnson's The Autobiography of an Ex-Colored Man?

I wouldn't reject it, but I would say it is not part of revolutionary tradition. It is still trying to decide whether to be black or not—but it is a well written book.

Invisible Man *has attracted ambivalent reactions. Some people feel that it is acceptable as long as it shows the oppression of black people.*

Basically, I feel that *Invisible Man* rejects Nationalism and Marxism. It seems to be in favour of individualism, and individualism can't mean anything for the oppressed people, except for the few people who have been hand-picked by the master. There is no such thing as individualism among the oppressed. It is the negative political content that makes the establishment celebrate it! It is well written but reactionary!

What do you think of the Song of Solomon?

I didn't read that book. You will have to ask my wife. I haven't read it. I think Toni Morrison is a skillful writer.

Is there anything you would like to say about your relationship to Africa?

Basically, the question of African liberation is one of the most important questions in the world today. People here, conscious people, revolutionaries, anti-imperialists, are working everyday to help speed up the total liberation of the continent of Africa. We see it as a world struggle and Africa is the beginning of that key in the struggle. I've been in Africa several times and I haven't seen enough of it.

Some of the impulse in the black African struggle came from the U.S. Nationalism of the 1960's. Is there something in the black power movement which you might consider quite positive. Something that might be a stepping stone to the kind of idealizing you are dealing with now?

Basically an anti-imperialism movement is against imperialism. Once you struggle against imperialism you'll find afterwards that a nationalist solution will not work, as Cabral said. Ultimately once the national liberation struggle is won, it has to proceed upward to the socialist revolution. I think people like PAC in South Africa are saying things very clearly not like a few years ago when things were more or less obscure. This is a democratic struggle and once this struggle is won we will proceed to socialist revolution. In that sense the Black Power movement is the democratic national liberation struggle. It sets the stage for the socialist struggle that has to come after that.

Does your relationship with the Communist Party disturb your membership of the Muslim religion?

I was never a Muslim. I was influenced by them. The man who buried Malcolm X gave me the name Ameer Baraka. Later on I met Ron Karenga who was a cultural nationalist in 1967 and he gave me the name Imamu and changed Ameer to Amiri Baraka. I have never been a Muslim, although I have ascribed to their views at one point. Although, I may have suffered from metaphysics and idealism, it definitely wasn't Islam that was the problem.

Why did you drop Imamu from your name?

It was a title that was given to me in the U.S. organization (a cultural nationalist organization of Ron Karenga). I felt that was a way of severing connections with the organization.

So it had nothing to do with the meaning of the name, which is spiritual leader?

In that sense, when I went to Africa in 1974, for instance, I discovered that Imamu is like Reverend here in the U.S. People actually thought you were a preacher and I couldn't take that. I just didn't see that it was appropriate to have it. So I tried to cut it loose.

If someone said to you that other writers have gone through this Communist phase—for example Richard Wright, Langston Hughes, Ralph Ellison—what would be your answer?

Richard Wright and Langston Hughes are the best known of the Black ones. Ellison never went through too much! I taught a course in that at Yale. The course was entitled "Richard Wright and Langston Hughes." My purpose in teaching the course was to have an opportunity to explore their works and their lives. Both fundamentally. Langston Hughes came from a petty bourgeois background. He could never reconcile his wanting to make a living as a writer and having to be ostracized and put down if he was going to be a Marxist writer. (Look at his 30's writings in the book *Good Morning Revolution.*) So, for instance, when the McCarthy period came, he decamped. He was basically afraid that they were going to cut off his livelihood.

Richard Wright came from a Southern urban poor background. His father was a sharecropper who came to the city. His mother did domestic work and he "educated" himself into this pretty bourgeois idealism. If you look at his books very carefully and analyzed them, you'll see his problem—for instance, *American Hunger* which was the second part of *Black Boy,* which I have read twice and analyzed very closely for this course, reveals a great deal about him. First of all, he said that by the time he had gotten to Chicago *he had never had an intimate or sustaining relationship in his life.* He said all of his life came out of books; all of his relationships came out of books!! He had this intellectual approach to life. The closest and the warmest he had ever been toward any group of people was when he joined the John Reed Club which was a mass organization of writers that the Communist party tried to direct. He said that he felt close to these people for the first time. And who were these people? They were middle-class white intellectuals, and he felt closer to them than he did

any other group of people. They selected him president of the John Reed Club. When he went to speak at the South Chicago Cell of the Communist party who were Black, they laughed at him. They said, "You talk like a book." They laughed at the way he dressed in a suit and tie, the complete opposite of the working people in the Communist party. Richard Wright developed a real petty bourgeois consciousness. He also had a problem relating to Black people.

I thought so too. In Native Son, *you find an obsessive repetition of "black". I was beginning to think that perhaps he was disturbed by the color of his skin.*

I think he did develop this problem. His descriptions even in *Black Boy,* if you look at them very closely are quite startling. For instance he said that he wondered why Black people never developed any warmth and love in their relationships. He also said in *American Hunger* that he thought may be what white people said about Black people being childish was true. Those things are quite revealing, he had this sort of schizophrenia, this kind of real petty-bourgeois vacillation. He was opposed to national oppression. He suffered from it, he couldn't escape it, because he was black, but at the same time he felt isolated, he felt he was one of a kind, he thought black people were at a level lower than himself.

Does that explain why he married two white women?

I think so. It explains also why he was that kind of petty bourgeois individual. The demands of the Communists on him were quite modest. What they wanted him to do was help organise the cost of living struggle and write a pamphlet on it. I do that kind of work every week. It's simply a use of your energies. If you say, "This is what I want," and you're a writer, how long does it take to write a pamphlet on the cost of living? I wrote a pamphlet on the Afro-American national question; about the relationship between African and Afro-American Black liberation movement. I mean it's nothing that would tie you up forever to prevent you from writing a novel. He had this overbearing individual sense that "I have to write this novel and nothing can interfere with it." He said once that he wanted to be a Communist, but "my kind of Communist"—such a completely subjective view.

You just mentioned African-Afro-American relationships. It is very clear to any person who is familiar with your work, that you really have Africa on your mind all of the time. Compared to many other Black American writers you seem to have a greater sense of your African roots. I would like to know how you developed this healthy attitude toward Africa?

I think it begins with Malcolm X and his history in Africa. I was greatly influenced by Malcolm. I did a lot of studying about Africa. I was a cultural nationalist. My wife also did a lot of studying about African culture. We studied Swahili for a while and really tried to develop a basic fundamental understanding of Africa. For two reasons—on the negative side—it was because we wanted to impose a sort of pre-capitalist African culture on the black people here in the United States. The positive part of that was that we felt we had to know African history and African culture if we were to fully understand our origin as a people. And now as a Marxist, it's critically important because people in the third world—Africa, Asia and Latin America are really the main force struggling against the imperialists. Right now for instance, the chief struggle is going on in Africa, Rhodesia, South Africa, South West Africa. Those are the most intense struggles going on. Great Britain is involved in Africa. When Great Britain loses its foothold in Africa, I think socialist revolution will happen there. South African investment is still mostly British, although the United States has more political control. South African investment is still economically tied to a great extent to Great Britain. But Imperialism is losing its opportunity to expand itself. Without expansion it dies. So it must expand, must have new raw materials, new markets, new places to invest. Once Britain loses Africa it will collapse. (pp. 97-108)

Amiri Baraka and Ossie Onuora Enekwe, in an interview in Okike: An African Journal of New Writing, *No. 17, February, 1980, pp. 97-108.*

Lloyd W. Brown (essay date 1980)

[*A Jamaican-born writer, Brown is the author of* The Black Writers in Africa and the Americas *(1973) and* Amiri Baraka *(1980). In the following excerpt from the latter work, he evaluates Baraka's skill as a writer.*]

[Amiri Baraka] has been a controversial figure in American politics and literature for the last sixteen years. . . . [While] his poetry, drama, and political activism continue to make him a significant figure in black America, his work as art critic represents an important contribution to the debates of the 1960s and early 1970s. Consequently he has become one of the leading representatives of what is now known as the black aesthetic, or black arts movement, which still seeks to define the alleged peculiarities of the black American's art and art criticism.

But, curiously, for some time serious study of Baraka's work lagged far behind his undoubted achievements and his undeniable reputation. This neglect can be traced, in part, to the fact that Baraka's work has frequently attracted political reaction, or more precisely, political invective, rather than informed and informative analysis. In one sense this kind of reaction is understandable, even inevitable, though not really excusable for all that. Baraka's visibility as black political activist and his frank insistence on the political significance of his literary art have usually aroused unease about his racial militancy, and have encouraged the assumption that his work is political propaganda rather than "serious" art.

However, this kind of assumption has not been very helpful. Although Baraka has been adamant about his political role and vision he has never ceased to produce works that are recognizably distinct from the pamphlets, essays, and speeches that comprise direct political statement. Although he attacks the usual academic insistence on art for its own sake, Baraka clearly makes a distinction between art, even politically committed art, and the tracts, speeches, and other tools of his political activism. Otherwise it would be difficult to account for the fact that during his most politically committed periods he has continued to write as poet and dramatist. In the process he has obviously continued to invite study as a writer whose political activism is integrated with his art (at least on his own terms). And his continuing interest in the creation of literary art forms—albeit fervently committed art forms—implies more than political commitment as such. It also represents a continuing and deep-rooted interest in all of those definable constructs and indeterminate traits which are peculiar to art, whether art is viewed as a self-contained, self-justifying mode or seen as an integral part of a political process. (pp. 7-8)

Each of Baraka's genres—essay, novel, short story, poetry, and drama—reflects certain aspects of his development as politically committed writer, and it simultaneously helps to define the very nature of the experience which it contains. Thus the essays are the direct statements of the political activist and critic. That directness clarifies the relationship between Baraka's personal development and his political ideas. Moreover the special role of the expository essays underlines Baraka's clear distinction between his interest in the written word as committed art and his use of unadorned political statement.

The prose fiction is distinct in Baraka's work, not only as a genre, but also as a form which he abandons relatively early in his career. This abandonment is significant, particularly in view of Baraka's personal view of prose fiction as an inherently white, Western mode. Precisely because of its "alien" cultural sources, Baraka's prose fiction is peculiarly suited to the central themes of his novel (*The System of Dante's Hell*) and his short stories (*Tales*)—the conflict between an "alien" white value system and black identity. This cultural conflict is perversely appropriate for a fictive form since Baraka is always able to dramatize the struggle by continuously striking out at the form itself. Narrative patterns in these works arise, paradoxically, from a violent assault on preconceived notions of fictive form and on the (white, Western) culture that is the source of those notions.

Baraka's dual perception of form and language—both as form of communication and target of attack—runs throughout the poetry. Here, in a genre which spans most of Baraka's career as writer, form and structure have evolved to cohere with his themes in a direct way, rather than by virtue of the paradoxical ironies of the prose fiction. Poetry allows Baraka an unparalleled latitude, accommodating his need to destroy forms, create new structures, and to exploit language itself while demonstrating its limitations. And part of this accomplishment rests in the fact that Baraka's use of black folk forms (music and language, for example) invests his poetry with an "ethnic" legitimacy that the "alien" forms of prose fiction seem to lack in his view.

But in spite of the relatively consistent successes of the poetry it is the drama that most seems to attract Baraka. This fascination lies in his perception of art as commitment and in the peculiar identity of drama itself. As both word and action the form has a special appeal to the political activist who requires, even demands, an artistic mode that is distinct from but complementary to straightforward political activism. This probably explains why, as Baraka's personal activism has intensified and broadened, he has turned more and more to the stage. For example, his most significant work as a convert to socialism has been drama—*The Motion of History* (1976) and *S-1* (1976).

As a result the drama reflects much of Baraka's recent growth as a writer. But for a similar reason his plays comprise his most uneven achievements, ranging from the penetrating insights of *Dutchman* and *The Slave* to the unimaginative baldness of later pieces where committed art seems to have degenerated into a mere preachiness. (pp. 9-10)

[The] unevenness of Baraka's drama is fairly representative of his general achievements as a writer. For even at its least distinguished his writing reflects a continuing tension between the decidedly unsubtle ideologue and the committed artist, between a passion for literal political statement and an interest in art as an imaginatively conceived, expressive, and committed design. And this tension remains in the background even when the interest in imaginative art is merely theoretical. Moreover, as the genre that spans his writing career his drama appropriately reflects a major constant in his writings. That is, despite his ideological shifts, his themes and their underlying social attitudes have remained fairly consistent.

Consequently, his perception of American society is invariably bleak. He always envisions a society of moral corruption and human decay whenever he contemplates America. This moral revulsion at America as a wasteland has a twofold effect. On the one hand it inspires those images of violence and death which characterize much of Baraka's work, ranging from the early radicalism and the black protests and moving to the later revolutionism of the black nationalist and socialist periods. And, on the other hand, this revulsion also triggers a passionate commitment to life, that is, to the moral and social rebirth which he envisages in his successive alternatives (ethnic, socialist, and so forth) to the American wasteland.

Moreover, the moral overview of America is always integrated with his racial themes. The black American's plight as racial victim is both a primary concern in its

own right and an important symptom of America's pervasive ills. And this remains true even in the deliberate emphasis on nonracial criteria in the socialist drama where the issue of racial violence and divisiveness is emphasized as the sign of an exploitive and oppressive ruling elite. Racial anger and moral outrage have always been inextricably interwoven in Baraka's work. Consequently, the thematic complexity of his more substantial work has easily eluded critics, both hostile and sympathetic, who respond only to his ethnic militancy. Finally, it is necessary to recognize the degree to which the shock tactics of moral outrage really arise from the fact that Baraka is a familiar kind of moral idealist, one whose idealism motivates the wasteland images of the "Beat" poetry, the black revolutionism of the middle years, and the more recent themes of socialist revolution.

The underlying thematic continuities of Baraka's work are complemented by certain consistencies in his approach to certain forms or techniques. The images of sight and sound which he emphasizes as a narrative technique in his only novel and in his short stories go back to his earliest poetry. And at the same time these images are adapted to the requirements of the black nationalist poems where the sounds of political statement are indistinguishable from the forms of politically committed art. In the drama the morality play tradition and the interest in ritual forms continue from the earliest plays to the later revolutionary works.

The continuity of certain forms attests to a strong degree of artistic self-awareness in Baraka the writer. This is the kind of self-awareness that springs from his lifelong commitment to the integration of theme with artistic form, and even when that integration is more a matter of promise than practice it makes for a complex context in which to examine Baraka, one in which the reader must be constantly alert to the actual or possible relationship between form and content, rather than neglecting one in favor of the other. This is the major reason for the enormous demands that Baraka's work, even at its worst, places on the reader. At its worst the work suffers from a narrowness of vision and a shrillness of tone that frequently distort the effects of whatever structural achievements might exist. But his best writing is challenging in the other sense: the closely knit relationship between theme and form requires a painstaking attention to the manner as well as the substance of statement—a requirement that has often proven too difficult for those who are overly hostile toward or enthusiastic about the substance.

Finally, Baraka's achievement as a writer should also be weighed on the representative nature of his political activism and art. In fact his career as a whole can be seen as a political weather vane of sorts. The early period reflects that combination of concerns which influences much of American literature and politics in the late 1950s and early 1960s: there is a growing uneasiness about America's world role and the country's relationship with the Third World; and there is increasing recognition that the black civil rights movement raised questions about American society in general as well as about racial relationships. The middle period, the years of Baraka's black nationalism, coincides with the militancy of black America's black power movement and the racial riots in the cities. Finally even the more recent conversion to socialism is not a popular movement in America at this time. His current ideology and writings are representative in that they reflect a general turning away from cultural nationalism and racial confrontation in black American politics since the early 1970s. Although Baraka denounces the "black petite bourgeoisie" who simply exploited black nationalism in order to feather their nests in the mainstream culture, Baraka's own switch to scientific socialism is as much an admission of the failure of black nationalism as is the opportunism that he condemns in the black middle class.

The decline of ethnic politics in black America reflects a marked decrease in political energies, a decrease that can be attributed to the opening of some doors to the mainstream and to the death, imprisonment, or discrediting of the political leaders of the 1960s. Baraka himself is a good example of this decline of political energies. As a scientific socialist he is in the least imaginative phase of his life as a political writer. This relative lack of creativity is not really the fault of the ideology itself. It seems, more likely, to be the reflection of a certain intellectual flabbiness on Baraka's part. Not only in the forgettable poems of *Hard Facts* but also in the plays and essays of the later years, Baraka seems to find it increasingly difficult to go beyond the accepted clichés of political dogma. It has appeared progressively easier for him to offer hackneyed and literal statements in lieu of artistic forms that are both imaginative and sociopolitically significant. Of course the current flabbiness is not necessarily terminal. In light of his career as a whole Baraka is unlikely to remain pedestrian as a political activist or mediocre as an artist. And whatever further developments occur in that career they will, in all likelihood, be closely linked with the literary and political atmosphere of his time. His significance as a mirror of his society has been one of his most enduring characteristics. (pp. 166-68)

> *Lloyd W. Brown, in his* Amiri Baraka, *Twayne Publishers, 1980, 180 p.*

C. W. E. Bigsby (essay date 1980)

[*In the following excerpt, Bigsby offers an overview of Baraka's dramas, focusing on* Dutchman *as "one of the best plays ever written."*]

In terms of the 1960s, black theatre became less a question of establishing specific repertory groups . . . than of creating a drama responsive to the needs and interests of black people and performed in the black communities which it serves. And at the heart of this enterprise, creating the institutions which could facilitate it and elaborating the images, the myths, and the forms of this new theatre, was, most crucially, a single man—LeRoi Jones. It was as a modernist poet, drawing on European and American models, that LeRoi Jones first came to prominence; it was as the colleague of white writers that he first established a reputation, founding *Yugen* Magazine and Totem Press in 1958 and coediting *The Floating Bear* magazine with Diane DiPrima in 1961.

But a changing social world, nationally and internationally, exerted the same moral pressure on Jones that it did on James Baldwin who had been living in Paris while the first events of the civil rights movement were being enacted in America. The change which eventually came over LeRoi Jones was a profound one, one which affected his private, public, and artistic life and made him the most important black writer of the 1960s—a shift, moreover, symbolized by a change of name. He abandoned his "slave name" for an appellation which indicated his new stance—Imamu (leader) Amiri (warrior) Baraka (blessing). In fact, from the beginning, his work had grown out of his own sense of cultural identity but where that had been simply the circumstance of his art, in the late 1960s it became the basis of an artistic and political philosophy. In many ways Baraka has contained within himself the conflict within the black community: avant-garde artist and committed spokesman, putative Black Muslim and secular politician, black nationalist and Marxist ideologue. And the gap between these opposing compulsions—like the space between American promise and fulfillment, revolutionary rhetoric and reality—is always liable to be filled with violence sublimated in artistic form. And it was partly as a writer whose powerful plays were luminous with violent images and articulate anger that he became the leading black playwright of the last decade and a half.

Baraka's arguments with himself have, in essence, been the arguments which split the black community. The irony is that now, as a Marxist-Leninist, he has spent the last few years struggling to escape from a myth of his own construction, that of black political and cultural separation, as in the late 1960s he had had to exorcise his earlier career as experimental writer and proponent of a modernist aesthetic. The alliance which he now seeks between black and white members of the "advanced" working class constitutes a synthesis of the terms of the dialectic which he had identified in the 1960s as constituting mutually exclusive symbolic systems and socially unassimilable propositions. If he was never the true poet of violence which he was taken to be, he was a writer for whom social action and imaginative fiat were symbiotically related. And though he retains that conviction, the components which form his imaginative universe today differ fundamentally from the Manichean elements which constituted his moral battleground a few years ago.

Although his early poetry lays claim to the modernist tradition, there was from the beginning a social compulsion in his work, a drive through the word to the fact.

And his admiration for the Beats was, in part at least, an admiration for people who located a specific environment which became not merely the reason for the literal and stylistic quest, but also, in some ways, its subject. (pp. 235-36)

But the public situation was changing. Africa now stood as a model of revolution rather than as a romantic image of primal innocence as it had in the 1920s.... [Jones's] work, too, was changing. In 1963, he published *Blue People: Negro Music in White America,* and, in 1964, his powerful one-act play, *Dutchman,* was produced at the Cherry Lane Theatre with the assistance of Edward Albee's Playwrights Unit. It was not his first play. *A Good Girl Is Hard to Find* had been produced in Montclair, New Jersey, in 1958, and early in 1964 *The 8th Ditch* (an excerpt from his forthcoming novel, *The System of Dante's Hell*) and *The Baptism* made brief appearances. But it was *Dutchman,* a powerful fable of American race relations, which established his reputation as a dramatist and which turned his career in a new direction. (pp. 236-37)

Dutchman remains one of the best plays ever written by a black author and one of the most impressive works of recent American theatre. Like [Edward Albee's] *The Zoo Story,* it is a potent parable of alienation. If Jones's control of language is reminiscent of Albee's, as is his sense of musical structure, in the person of Clay he has created a far more complex character than Albee's Peter, whose stereotypical role is the one serious flaw in what is otherwise the most impressive first play ever written by an American dramatist. *Dutchman* is a reflexive work. At its heart is a consideration of the artistic process, a debate over the legitimacy of sublimating social anguish into aesthetic form. It addresses itself to a central problem of the black artist who is alive to the evasion which may be implied in the act of writing. It is a debate which Jones has continued throughout his career without ever finding a wholly satisfactory answer.

In part, of course, the play can be read as Jones's confession or critique of his own safe refuge in words, of his own attempts to sublimate racial tensions in art. If this is so it was even more true of a subsequent play, *The Slave,* which is intensely autobiographical and in which he accuses himself and others of remaining slaves to a liberalism which can no longer be validated by reality. (p. 239)

Later the same year, two of his plays were performed at St. Marks Playhouse, *The Toilet* and *The Slave.* The former is a one-act play in which racial violence breaks out in a school lavatory. Yet, beneath the apocalyptic clash is a curiously contradictory belief in the efficacy of love—a Baldwin-like sentimentality expressed in a sexual grace which transcends social realities. The ending, which he explains to have been "tacked on," is strangely out of key with the main thrust of the play. But it does appear to validate his own continuing commitment to the interracial ethos of his Greenwich Village existence. So, black and white come together in the

Robert Hooks and Jennifer West as Clay and Lula in the 1964 Cherry Lane Theatre production of Dutchman.

concluding moment of the play in an epiphany, suggesting thereby that dispossession and exclusion are not exclusively racial experiences.

The Slave, however, pursues racial tensions to their logical conclusion. It takes place at the moment of a black revolt in America. The revolutionary leader, Walker Vessels, formerly married to a middle-class white woman, now visits her and her husband, a white liberal professor, as his troops move in on the city. Himself a writer, he had abandoned the word for the act. But his own presence in his ex-wife's apartment shows that he has not escaped his past, he is still a slave to old ideas and associations. His denunciation of the white liberal is thus largely an exorcism of his own former self. But it is also an assertion that it is precisely liberal equivocation that has transformed the slave into the rebel. Despite his own reservations, however, the logic of his position and of the history in which they are all trapped leads to his shooting the white professor. The play ends as shells hit the building, his former wife is crushed underneath a fallen beam, and the screams of his two children are heard.

For all the violence of the action, the most striking aspect of the play lies in the reservations which it expresses about the act of revolt. He is aware of, and in part still feels, liberal ambiguities about violence and about a social transformation which depends on simple inversion. Lacking any ideological structure for his work, he is left with presenting revolt as generating its own values. In some ways, therefore, it is a work, like Lowell's *The Old Glory,* dedicated to presenting the paradox of revolution. Change is necessary, but the violence of revolt closes the moral gap between oppressed and oppressor. (pp. 239-40)

On the verge of a profound change in his personal life and in the racial situation in America, Jones is all too aware that ideas need judging, that revolutionary symbols fail to deal adequately with the complexity of private or public action. But the play deploys a level of subtlety and ambiguity which he rapidly dispensed with as his own analysis of American society and the racial situation led him to a more stringent and unambiguous stance.

The ironies of the play are magnified when one realizes that shortly afterwards Jones left his white Jewish wife and his two daughters and moved his activities to Harlem where he became the focus for the Black Arts movement of the late 1960s. *The Slave,* therefore, stands as a personal act of exorcism, and the works which followed advocated a clear cultural and political nationalism of a kind which left no space for self-doubt. (p. 242)

Asked, in 1977, what his view of the whole Black Arts movement of the 1960s was, he replied, "There are still progressive black artists who relate what they are doing to the Black Liberation Movement, and to revolution, which is the positive aspect of that. I think the negative aspect has actually been co-opted by the bourgeoisie—I mean the part of black art that just rested with skin identification, so that the very people who first opposed us are given the grants and the money to open the Black Arts Theatres, all around the country, the Negro Ensemble Company, the New Lafayette Company. And now you have exploitation flicks talking about black arts, and there are several people on television who were in plays of mine in the 1960s, who considered themselves revolutionary black artists but who became involved simply with the skin aspect of it. What is black art? It's about black people, they thought. But the point is, it's supposed to be about revolution." It is a view, of course, which necessarily makes him blind to the accomplishments of a work like Ntozake Shange's "Choreo-poem" *For Coloured Girls Who Have Considered Suicide When the Rainbow Is Enuf....* But, then, he has replaced the rigors of one ideological stance by those of another which leaves little space for lyricism.

In his own eyes, of course, the development from *Dutchman* [which espouses Black Nationalism] to *S-1* [which emphasizes the need for blacks and whites to come together and form a Marxist-Leninist Communist Party] represents "a leap from partial truth to a more wholesided reality," from "the feeling and rage against oppression to the beginnings of actual scientific analysis

of this oppression and its true sources." To others, it might appear that he had simply moved from one ideology to another, pressing experience to its extreme edges, to the point at which meaning seems to render itself up only in moral absolutes of chilling determinism. There is indeed a clear line of development visible in his work. Whether or not it is a move in the direction of truth, however, is more debatable. Dramatically, he has abandoned rituals as "bourgeois nationalism" and forsworn the subtleties of his own early work as simply inadequate to confront what he takes to be the unsubtle conflicts of capital and labor. His plays are, he admits, "vehicles for a simple message," and their weakness is perhaps apparent in that description.

His work is now, I suspect, overarticulate. It operates wholly on the surface. All hidden powers are exposed, and the result is both an oversimplified view of political process and a dissipation of dramatic power. No longer interested in the energy generated by the collision of conscious and subconscious or in the potent rhythms of submerged passions, he resolves all tensions into the battle for economic hegemony; all violence becomes literal and political. Character is crushed as effectively by the playwright as it is by the reactionary forces against which he pitches his work. And the risk, clearly, is that in identifying those historical forces which account for the drive towards Marxist-Leninism, he fails to dramatize those human forces which much finally validate it. (pp. 245-46)

But Baraka is not unaware of the problems involved in creating ideological drama. His artistic credo is taken from Mao Tse-tung's *Yenan Forum on Art and Literature:* "What we demand is the unity of politics and art, the unity of content and form, the unity of revolutionary political content and the highest possible perfection of artistic form; ... we oppose both works of art with a wrong political viewpoint and the tendency towards the 'poster and slogan style' which is correct in political viewpoint but lacking in artistic power." As he has indicated in a recent interview, this still eludes him. But he obviously believes that what he has lost—the imaginative brilliance of *Dutchman,* the subtle analysis of *The Slave,* the controlled rhythms and potent rituals of *Slaveship*—is adequately compensated for by the historical significance of his new career. At the moment it is difficult to endorse that view. The question is whether he can yet find a form and a language adequate to his self-imposed task or whether the logic of his present position may not drive him beyond theatre altogether.

Clearly, the pressure for ideological commitment in Baraka is strong, whether it be the shaping myths of black nationalism or those of Marxist-Leninism. But he is a writer of genuine integrity for whom art must always be seen as a public act. His struggle to find a structure capable of expressing the needs of the individual and those of society, his search for a form of transcendence which lies neither in aestheticism nor in a convenient surrender of historical truth, has in essence been that of all black writers in the last two decades. (pp. 246-47)

C. W. E. Bigsby, "Black Drama: The Public Voice," in his The Second Black Renaissance: Essays in Black Literature, *Greenwood Press, 1980, pp. 207-56.*

Maryemma Graham (essay date 1984)

[*In the following essay, Graham offers a generally favorable review of* The Autobiography of LeRoi Jones.]

Autobiographies are written for many different purposes: to explain, to proselytize, to vindicate, to profit. Their popularity as a genre is due, in part, to the fact that they give the writer a chance to present the truth as he/she perceives it, and they give the reader "real" knowledge that no one else will have to verify. Often autobiographies have been kept from the public, as in the case of Richard Wright's *American Hunger,* written in 1944 but not published until 1977, 17 years after the writer's death.

In those cases where a tension exists between the autobiographer's allegiance to the collective and his/her more personal, subjective urges, the reader is often forced to take sides, usually anticipating a celebration of self. In Afro-American autobiography, where this sort of tension is a constant, the writer is likely to bring the two poles together by fusing the singular voice with the collective voice out of the need to demonstrate the effects of a social and economic system on the lives and personalities of the whole people. Thus, in the works of Olaudah Equiana (Gustavus Vassa), Frederick Douglass, W.E.B. Du Bois, Richard Wright, or Ida B. Wells Barnett, our collective history becomes immediately objectified through a single voice.

The Autobiography of LeRoi Jones is the most recent entry in this tradition of political histories. It provides an interesting, although not altogether satisfying or complete, picture of social activism's confluence with the creative spirit as experienced by the most prolific, most written about and most anthologized of contemporary Afro-American writers.

The author has correctly titled this book *The Autobiography of LeRoi Jones,* and not LeRoi Jones/Amiri Baraka, because its major focus is on his early life and rise to distinction as the poet, editor, playwright, and essayist, LeRoi Jones. The child of middle-class parents, Baraka gives us a clear image of his background in "blue-black" Newark during the mid-to-late Depression, of his insistent and doting grandmother, of growing up on bebop music. After graduating from one of Newark's top integrated (meaning mostly white) high schools, Baraka attended Rutgers, then Howard, the "Capstone," where he was repelled by the "middle-class hypocrisy." Opting for the Air Force, he was engulfed by a "white, alienated and racist" world, from which he gradually withdrew to feed his developing intellectual hunger, passion for black music, and latent creativity.

Rendered in highly stylized language, this section of the book creates a hypnotic effect with its rhythms, syntax, and vocabulary alternating between urban folk and fragmented bebop styles. Here are to be found some of the finest examples of Baraka's aesthetic/ideological-prose/poetry blend, as in the interlude, "Black Brown Yellow White":

> The Black was fundamental black life, the life of blues people, the real and the solid and the strong and the beautiful.... The brown was my family and me, half real and half lodged in dream and shadow.... The yellow, the artificial, the well-to-do, the middle class real. Describing by a term like petty bourgeoisie with steel precision, but something else of caste was why my definition came to mean even without me understanding or saying that.

His Air Force apprenticeship having made him a perfect candidate for Bohemia, Baraka fled to New York's Greenwich Village, there to retreat deeper into self-deception. The "Beat" movement's social rebelliousness and aesthetic tastes, in search of "intellectual seriousness" and the "freedom to create," were more than suited to his paradoxical nature. Plunging in, he found the new black music, white women, surrealist art and poetry, and a myriad of hedonistic self-indulgences just fine. But Baraka was not merely a beneficiary, a widely published artist/member, of the beat generation. One of its principal theoreticians and promoters as an editor and publisher (*Zazen, Floating Bear, The Drifting Dear,* Totem Books, Totem/Corinth Books), he earned the title, "King of the Lower East Side."

Eventually, Baraka's apoliticism and alienation were called into question when he encountered some young revolutionaries during a trip to Cuba. By this time, however, he was already set to become a near cult figure, the critic's choice. A long and productive career with William Morrow Publishers was in progress, and offers to write for both the *New York Times* and mainstream left media, as well as offers of creative writing posts at major universities were pouring in.

The death of Malcolm X shocked Baraka and the downtown "core" out of their Bohemian revel. He recalls vividly: "I was stunned. I felt stupid, ugly, useless. Downtown in my mix-matched family and my maximum leader/teacher shot dead while we bullshitted and pretended.... The black core of us huddled there, my wife and family outside the circle." So ended the first phase of his professional and personal life.

The intensity of the social, political and emotional break with his past is reflected in the works of this period: *The System of Dante's Hell, Dutchman, The Slave, The Dead Lecturer, Home.* The next stop, politically, was what Baraka calls the "petty bourgeois fanaticism" of cultural nationalism, highlighted by the founding of two black artists' organizations in the Village and, later, the Black Arts Repertory Theatre/School in Harlem, with a sequel in Newark. He admits that he lacked a formal definition of cultural nationalism, the powerful magnet that attracted many others like him. The politics were confused and the activities were erratic and explosive, a mixture of extreme anti-white sentiments and various cultural practices associated with the Yoruba religion and the Kawaida theory, as well as other sources thought to be associated with "blackness."

Having chosen to omit some experiences, Baraka does not clear up a number of confusions surrounding his background and early history of activism. Yet the "cultural nationalism" portion of the autobiography is most valuable for its concise, lively and analytical discussion of the main aspects of that social and literary movement as reflected in Baraka's own increasing politicalization. The various cultural nationalist tendencies are described, as are the development and contradictions of community-based arts institutions in New York and Newark, which paralleled the emergence of similar institutions throughout the U.S. He recounts the experiences of the Committee for a Unified Newark (CFUN) and analyzes the "opportunism" of Kenneth Gibson, who, after being elected mayor as a result of CFUN's extraordinary work, repudiated it. The discussions of the founding of the Congress of African People (CAP) and the Black Power Conferences are also useful, but it is the critique of the Kawaida doctrine and his break with Ron Karenga's "feudalism," "metaphysics," and "chauvinism," that provide new information about the period. (The force and attraction of Karenga, a key figure, are seldom understood.)

The careful reader will recognize that the Black Arts Repertory Theatre/School and Spirit House are synonymous with the Black Arts Movement of which Baraka was a chief architect. Yet the phenomenon which explains the reality of that period is more implied than stated. Baraka acknowledges the dynamism of that class of artists and intellectuals who were obsessed with what was perceived as "blackness"—indeed this is the book's underlying theme. But his real message is that the Black Arts Movement was not so much the creation of enlightened artists. Rather, it was the overtly political struggle being waged by Blacks on the civil rights battlefront, and by Africans against imperialism and colonialism abroad, that was the breeding ground for new, highly accessible forms of cultural and artistic expression. The Black Arts Movement, therefore, articulated the (somewhat precarious) unity between a young, middle-class leadership and the masses of Black people. Unfortunately, as time passed, the exploding products and forms reflected more and more the deleterious influence of the mass media.

In his failure to interpret the life and death of the Black Arts Movement more critically, Baraka reveals that the movement was meaningful to him primarily as a platform for his own poetry, plays and essays. Highly profiled throughout the movement network and exposed, as well, to a wider audience through *Ebony,* William Morrow and mainstream literary circles, he had exchanged his Greenwich Village notoriety for midtown and uptown celebrity. Indeed, as the Black Arts Movement waned, **Black Fire, Tales, Raise Race Rays Raze,**

Four Black Revolutionary Plays and other works, along with their author's fame, lived on.

Unable to claim, as many Afro-American artists can, that he has not received the critical attention he deserves, Baraka concentrates, instead, on criticizing his critics, those who dwell on his "white life and white wife," and refuse to acknowledge his second marriage to an Afro-American woman. The painstaking details of this second union to Amina and the birth of their five children are clearly important to Baraka, and are intended to suggest how a stable relationship with a woman from a working-class background served as a check on his "petty bourgeois tendencies" and deeply rooted male supremacist attitudes. According to Baraka, it was Amina who first encouraged his Marxism and forced his growth beyond the narrow confines of cultural nationalism.

Baraka might have ended the autobiography with his critique of nationalism and the degree of its complicity with opportunist individuals in the movement, but he goes on, at great cost to clarity and accuracy. As a number of reviewers have commented, his discussion of why and how he came to Marxism leaves much to be desired. The description of events that transpired up to and following October 7, 1974, when he declared himself and CAP Marxist-Leninist, is eclectic, fuzzy and abbreviated—only four-and-a-half pages. One might infer that the struggle to develop into a Marxist-Leninist was neither as intense nor as complex as the break with Bohemia had been some ten years earlier.

The fact is that there is much, much more to the history of the last ten years, during which the debate over Marxism and nationalism has been sharp and ongoing. The truncated description given here obscures what actually happened in CAP, in the years of the African Liberation Support Committee, the National Black Agenda, Malcolm X Liberation University (in North Carolina), when intense struggles split these organizations apart. No attention is given to the role and development of Black Studies, which continues to give many artists and activists, including Baraka, an institutional base. There is no discussion of the impact of left forces on the black liberation movement, whose organizations have been around for many years. He is surely aware of these aspects of his history; we must assume, therefore, that the measly four-and-a-half pages are an advertisement for volume II of the **Autobiography of LeRoi Jones.**

The lingering questions regarding this autobiography are why Baraka chose not to tell it all, whether or not we should accept all of his assumptions, and whether we should subject the information he presents to further analysis. Mainstream readers of this lengthy narrative will undoubtedly come away from it understanding why LeRoi Jones is an extraordinary Afro-American poet/playwright/essayist. For those in "the movement," he will remain enigmatic and vacillating.

But for all readers, this history-according-to-Baraka should be a treasured possession. (pp. 144-48)

Maryemma Graham, "Baraka Tells, but Not All," in Freedomways, *Vol. 24, No. 2, 2nd Quarter, 1984, pp. 144-48.*

Darryl Pinckney (essay date 1984)

[*In the following essay, Pinckney reviews* The Autobiography of LeRoi Jones, *describing it as a "strange mixture."*]

The works of Leroi Jones reveal a mind groping toward orthodoxy. Certainly he Mau-Maued the flak catchers, which was not hard to do in the Sixties. But the swell of black consciousness did not carry him to any liberating heresies. Hating Whitey was not the new frontier it seemed to be at the time. He rowed through the tumult of black nationalism, reinvented himself as Imamu (spiritual leader) Amiri Baraka (blessed prince), and landed on the shores of Marxist-Leninism, as if unaware of the footprints already visible in the sand.

Baraka's odyssey from Beat poet and avant-garde Village playwright, to political activist, mullah of the black masses back in his birthplace, Newark, was an inner migration, its lessons inflamed and splattered on to the cultural scene. Aggressive public acts roared incessantly from the shadows of his private life—his denunciation of white liberals at a Town Hall meeting in 1964, his renunciation of bohemianism and his move to Harlem, where he founded the Black Arts Repertory Theater in 1965. The later vehement poems were themselves incidents, performances by a man who did not like to be upstaged by large events. Now the Angry Young Man, the author of several volumes of poetry, plays, essays, a novel, and a collection of stories, is entering his fiftieth year. His autobiography is "partial evidence" of the swift passage from sullen nonconformist to anointed militant.

Baraka is no lumpen turned avenging angel. He was born in 1934. His father was a postal worker, his mother a social worker. The family held to aspirations of the "lower middle class," a "forward forward upward upward view"—church, piano lessons, the Cotillion, integrated but changing, declining neighborhoods: "It was like a sociologist's joke." Baraka was educated at Howard University. He did a stint in the air force. After his discharge he drifted into New York's hip enclaves, married a nice Jewish girl. It was this background Baraka had to burn before he could turn his back on the Village and take his bags uptown. He was not, like Malcolm X, Eldridge Cleaver, or George Jackson, an autodidact of the jailhouse library, though he remembers the air force ("Error Farce") as a kind of incarceration during which he read avidly and began to think of himself as a writer.

He moved to Harlem at a time when much of one's day was taken up with proving just how black one's

blackness was. A recurring theme in his work is the psychic turmoil that led to and was exacerbated by his determination to extricate himself from his past. The guilt was tinder. Many are the afflictions of the righteous.

His autobiography is a strange mixture, cast in the double-edged amiability of a slangy, funky tone. It is wreathed in nostalgia for his hot youth, for the anarchic parties of "insane hope," the ruthless summers of dudes who were either wrapped too tight or not tight enough, the mad weather of volatile lovers who suspected that a woman was only as good as the man she lay under. There are ragged ends of remorse in Baraka's long book but they are dispensed with like cigarette butts flicked over the Williamsburg Bridge.

It is a story of hanging out until the real thing came along, and hanging out, here, means listening to a great deal of music. Baraka's youth was saturated in rhythm and blues, in bebop. The "emotional anthems" spark a host of associations—grandparents, running buddies, streets, the canteen where he styled in a green Tyrolean hat with a feather band. Dinah Washington coming from a jukebox once inspired him to stand up to a bully. When he remembers the time the streets were heating up, he also recalls that "Heat Wave" by Martha and the Vandellas was the hit record.

In Baraka's downtown days he was a frequent contributor to *Metronome, Downbeat,* and *Jazz,* and he has written on the evolution of jazz as a social art in a fascinating study, **Blues People** (1963), and on religious and secular modes as "racial memory" in the polemical **Black Music** (1967). In his autobiography Archie Shepp, Cecil Taylor, Sun Ra, John Coltrane, Theolonius Monk, Ornette Coleman, Charles Mingus, and Pharoah Sanders make cameo appearances.

Jazz and blues artists populate the landscape of Baraka's poetry as well. He sometimes puns on the musician's language (most noticeably in an early poem, **"The Bridge"**). Spontaneity of line, syntactical idiosyncrasies, dissonant effects—they suggest the feel of jazz, of improvisation. When Baraka began to publish in small magazines, opening up poetry by any means necessary was a concern very much in the air. He counts the Beats, the New York School, Charles Olson, and William Carlos Williams among his influences.

It was not only the verve of the new music that Baraka absorbed for his poetry. Denise Levertov, in a review of Baraka's first collection, **Preface to A Twenty Volume Suicide Note** (1961), observed that Baraka had the "kind of childhood in which the old comic strips...gave to the imagination, for which no other place was provided, a space in which to grow." The book is filled with references to "The Shadow," "Red Lantern," "Charlie Brown," "Lamont Cranston," "Dr. Fu Manchu." His notion of heroism was forged in the movie house. Frank O'Hara once advised the mothers of America to send their kids to the movies so they could learn where candy bars and gratuitous bags of popcorn came from. Baraka's access to popular culture, the natural, campy deployment of its artifacts in his early verse, dramatize his distance from the preceding generation of black poets.

Baraka is an exclusively urban writer. As with most black writing that emerged in the Sixties, there are no echoes of the pastoral South in Baraka's work, no legacy of the hopeful trek up North, no newcomer's terror of failure or disgrace, no waiting for naturalization papers in the cold city. The hash, Baraka notes, had already been settled. His vocabulary is thoroughly of the street corner—nabs, whore, fag, laundromat, horse, cat, your mama, knock me a kiss, Brooks Brothers, mean honking blues. It was a landscape of jobs and cement yards that Baraka invoked in a statement made in 1959 describing his aesthetic. Williams's "irregular foot," Olson's "projective verse" helped him to redefine what was "useful" and could be "saved from the garbage of our lives." The city as quarry, lode, experience.

> Lately I've become accustomed to the way
> The ground opens up and envelops me
> Each time I go out to walk the dog.
> Or the broad edged silly music the wind
> Makes when I run for a bus...
>
> Things have come to that.

Sometimes the stanzas in Baraka's first volume come close to the "I-do-this-I-do-that" poems of O'Hara—("Personism," O'Hara said in his comic manifesto, was invented after lunch with Leroi)—except that Baraka never disallowed big answers to the questions in life. His ambivalence about poetry as a passive activity doubtless had its origins in the cultural conflicts of race. Whereas O'Hara's catalogues of the daily are acquisitive, Baraka's are bitter:

> Monday, I spent most of the day
>   hunting.
> Knocked off about six, gulped down
>   a cou-
> ple of monkey foreskins, then took
>   in a
> flick. Got to bed early.
>
> Tuesday, same thing all day....
>
> Sometimes I think I oughta chuck
>   the whole business.

The early poems show a drifting discontent—"I can't understand what Superman is saying!"—and he is not above letting himself have it in the tender, lyrical love poems. He seems impatient, also, with the things and people around him. Oppositions are generic throughout his poetry, regardless of what phase he happens to be in—correct (engaged) versus cool (detached), black versus white, revolutionary versus bourgeois. The world is perceived as a struggle between *us* and *them*. **"Hymn for Lanie Poo,"** which appeared in his first volume, takes up the opposition between the hip and the square, an issue that became an enduring preoccupation in Baraka's work.

> About my sister.
>   (O, generation revered
>   above all others.
>   O, generation of fictitious
>   Ofays
>   I revere you...
>   You are so beautiful)
> my sister drives a green jaguar
> my sister has her hair done twice a
>   month...
> my sister took ballet lessons...
> my sister doesn't like to teach in
>   Newark
>   because there are too many
>   colored
>   in her classes.
> my sister hates loud shades
> my sister's boy friend is a faggot
>   music teacher
>   who digs Tschaikovsky
> my sister digs Tschaikovsky also

As Baraka remembers his downtown days in the autobiography one gets the feeling of someone on simmer. The clubs and bars, the writers and painters, the black intellectuals and their white lovers, the odd jobs, the gasless flats, the smack—dissatisfaction with living as variously as possible grew along with his literary reputation. Baraka mocks what he calls his "pompous isolation." The civil rights movement sniped at his consciousness. He needed only an occasion. It found him—Cuba. One of Baraka's most famous essays, **"Cuba Libre,"** reprinted in **Home** (1966), is a stirring account of his trip there in 1960 for the anniversary of the revolution. "I carried so much back with me that I was never the same again," Baraka says in the autobiography. Match to the fuse.

The books that followed, **Sabotage** (1963), **The Dead Lecturer** (1964), **Target Study** (1965), and **Black Art** (1966) came in such rapid order that Baraka seemed like a motorcyclist shooting up a ramp and soaring over barrels. They are a radical departure from his previous work. "Will the machinegunners please step forward?" Though the poems share no common form—long line, taut line, print it sideways, let it run off the page—what they say becomes more and more a single-issue campaign and the voice rises to a fierce pitch. "I am inside someone who hates me." The cure for this self-loathing was to "spoil" himself for "casual life," and offer himself up as a vessel of rage. The ironic tone is replaced by a caustic, punitive one. "The white man / at best / is / corny." Or: "Strong beliefs, Hairless, / Very, very white." Baraka sneers at "screaming materialists" "whistling popular Bach."

The poems of this period are characterized by a disgust with Western art and its "guileful treatises." Many of them appear to be addressed to his old friends downtown. **"I don't love you"** is the title of one poem. He taunts: "Death is Not as Natural as You Fags Seem to Think." In **"The Politics of Rich Painters"** he fumes against "So much *taste* / so little understanding, except some up and coming queer explain / cinema and politics while drowning a cigarette." Baraka is searching for a "black poem." "Choice, and / style, / avail / and are beautiful / categories / if you go / for that." He calls them "dagger poems." He envisions a poetry that is not only a reflection of change but its catalyst. Hence, the crusade of wrath, of repudiation. "I am no longer a credit to my race."

Black Power was heavy machinery, as Baraka drove it, a bulldozer mowing down everything in its path. "Banks must be robbed, / The guards bound and gagged." The steel ball of demolition had a wide arc. "I want / to see God. If you know / him. Biblically, have / fucked him. And left him wanting." In **"Black Dada Nihilismus"** he asks an ancient force to "Rape the white girls. Rape / their fathers."

The tempo of revolution is that of publicity and scandal, Kosintsev said—in 1922. Baraka's call for black unity, black pride, produced the side effect of self-love. His ambition, in these collections, is to be emblematic, the epitome of the current mood. His duty is to enumerate the cruelties and failures of American society. Baraka wastes no more time brooding over his own imperfections. He is ready to tell everyone else where to get off.

The drug of anger led to some hyped-up lines which removed from the "multiplicity of definitions," the "powerful motley of experience," the "pushed" English that at one time he felt poetry should honor. Form and technique were curses, deflections, considerations to be kicked out of the historical moment like a body from a speeding car. The moral superiority resulted in bizarre reductions: "Thought is more important than art." In *Home* Baraka slapped black writers around quite a bit, particularly Baldwin and Ellison. The "mediocre" tradition, hatched by Charles Chesnutt, was a consequence of black writers being assimilationist, middle-class, self-serving, pathological, haunted by a need to prove they were not inferior, to show how intelligent, serious, and cultured they were. The odd thing is that Baraka did not seem to realize how quickly the poetry of outrage was absorbed as yet another convention with its own tired premises and rhetorical devices. Showing how bad you are involves the same dangers as showing how refined you are. The matter Baraka never fully addressed was that every black writer wakes up to face the defiled freedom of the blank page.

Baraka has little to say about the works themselves in his autobiography except to note when a play was produced, to place certain ambiguous passages of his surrealistic novel, *The System of Dante's Hell* (1963), in context, or to revisit the background of the autobiographical stories in *Tales* (1968). This is particularly disappointing with the plays. Baraka has produced some of the most arresting black drama since the Federal Theater of the Thirties. *The Toilet* (1964) was not reprinted in *Selected Plays and Prose of Amiri Baraka/Leroi Jones* (1979)—perhaps because its homoerotic elements do not conform to Baraka's current revolutionary morality, which has features similar to that of right-wing fundamentalism. Set in an ugly school toilet, it is about a black gang whose wishes for affection are repressed by the tyranny of manhood. Its action climaxes in an assault on a white boy, a homosexual depicted sympathetically, the individual outside the mainstream.

Henry C. Lacey, in his close reading of Baraka's work, *To Raise, Destroy and Create,* (1981), has pointed out that *The Toilet* is Baraka's "earliest presentation of the skinny, intelligent, bug-eyed, middle-class boy" who is uneasy about being smarter than the others, who gives up much to belong. The self-portrait is also present in the stories based on his experiences at Howard University (which Baraka once dismissed in an interview as a place where "they teach you to be white"), and he returns in the autobiography to what he calls "the runt" but, since he has grown up to be politically "advanced," the self-deprecation seems disingenuous.

Baraka's plays touch on the deep sado-masochism in American race relations and, consequently, sexual metaphors, sexual situations, obscenities, and violent acts are plentiful. They are, as many critics have noted, exorcistic and blasphemous. *Dutchman* (1964) presents a young black intellectual who wants to remain safe with his words but is stabbed to death by an older, contemptuous white woman whom he tries to pick up on a subway. If two people talking around each other puts one in mind of Albee's *The Zoo Story,* then *The Slave* (1964), which juxtaposes the deterioration of an interracial marriage with race war, sounds, in parts, like George and Martha going at it. The economical structures, the symbolism, the reversals of meaning, the fragmented language, the parable mood owe much to absurdist theater and expressionist technique.

As Baraka's commitment to black revolution grew his work in the theater took on the quality of morality plays. He strip-mines stereotypes (Rochester as closet revolutionary in *J-E-L-L-O,* 1965), satirizes institutions (the church in *The Baptism,* 1964, and *Slave Ship,* 1965; the law in *Great Goodness of Life,* 1966), gives black consciousness mythic properties (*A Black Mass,* 1965, *Experimental Death Unit #1,* 1965, *Madheart,* 1966). Sometimes the urge to subvert images, the assertion of black culture, results in stilted language, as if formal, collective theater entailed dispensing with street idioms. The invective of Baraka's essay **"The Revolutionary Theatre"** (included in *Home*) is close in tone to Artaud's idea of theater as a "revenging scourge." Baraka insists that "Americans will hate the Revolutionary Theatre because it will be out to destroy them and whatever they believe is real. American cops will try to close the theaters where such nakedness of the spirit is paraded." Baraka has never suffered from a dearth of incendiary fantasies.

Part of Baraka's gift as a playwright was to find a dramatic equivalent or embodiment for social collisions. The plays are projections, dramas of confrontation and retribution. Even the dialogue seems to have been taken from experience and reordered in a nightmare. But, as with his poetry, ideological self-congratulation took Baraka from the naturalism of *The Toilet* to the comfy didacticism, the home-grown proletarian utilitarianism of *What Was the Relationship of the Lone Ranger to the Means of Production?* (1978). The only interesting thing about the latter play is its title. Heroic workers in an automobile factory triumph over their oppressors. Baraka, in a Brechtian manner, hoped to create a theater that would inspire militancy in its audience, but it could be argued that language not truly of the people is not revolutionary.

Front cover of Baraka's one-act play about self-defense.

Even earlier, as *der schwartze Bohemien,* he was writing against tokenism, against nonviolence because it was a continuation of the status quo. King was an "agent of the middle-class power structure." Baraka's political activism began on behalf of an advocate of armed self-defense in 1961. He was involved with downtown organizations such as The Organization of Young Men and On Guard for Freedom Committee. Harold Cruse remembers, in *The Crisis of the Negro Intellectual* (1967), that in 1961 Baraka was defending white participation and asking why Harlem Negroes should hate whites. The answer: slavery as original sin. Pro-black,

Cruse points out, meant being anti-white. Cruse maintains that Baraka went to Harlem politically "empty-handed." Protest demonstrations and appeals to federally funded anti-poverty programs were naive. The hangup of "black Bakuninism" ensured the mishandling of "yet another promising black organization."

Baraka has written elsewhere on the general history of Harlem but there is little sense of stored communal memory in the autobiography. It is hard to recall the days when the most urgent item on the agenda was the reclamation of black manhood, as if the past were a chronicle of shameful Toms alleviated here and there by incantatory names such as Nat Turner or Denmark Vesey. "Some of us had guns." The ghetto's history was ready to be written by those bloods capable of the brave deed. It was a "great adventure," those "nights of uncertainty," in which they, "informality's children," tried to snatch love out of "some dying white shit." "We felt like pioneers of the new order." People were "dancing in the streets" in Harlem, Detroit, Watts.

Baraka writes in detail about the internal struggles of the Black Arts Repertory Theater. In addition to trying to sustain a cultural program on a shoestring budget, they disrupted rallies staged by black Democrats and Republicans—"cults" he calls them—and refused to receive Sargent Shriver. Most of the organization's problems seemed to stem from the fact that too many lunatics signed up for the voyage and then mutinied. Black pride gave to several lost souls an occupation, just as neoconservatism does today. The warring factions proved too much for Baraka, the helmsman, and he moved abruptly to Newark, his "apprenticeship" to his "real spirit" complete.

Adjusting to this homecoming was a slow process. By 1967 he had founded another theater, Spirit House, and contended every day with the "white power structure." "One thing about the FBI, they're always trying to make you famous." He met members of the Black Panther Party on an extended trip to the West Coast, and if he was not quite taken with their leaders he was immediately drawn to the black nationalism of Ron Karenga. Karenga emphasized African roots, Muslim practices, the "unchanging black values." Morsels of Fanon, Cabral, and Nkrumah were filtered into the stew. Much of Baraka's work in this period is a restatement of a Pan-African catechism. Karenga's doctrine was, for Baraka, the "perfect vehicle for working out the guilt of the overintegrated." Thomas Blair, in *Retreat to the Ghetto* (1977), criticizes Baraka for elevating "reactionary African forms" to a "mystique." Baraka has shed at least one aspect of black nationalism and in the autobiography he takes himself to task for "male chauvinism." Plays from this period in which black women are dealt with harshly have not been reprinted; and one assumes he has changed his mind about the pamphlet *The New Nationalism* (1972), in which he maintains that "We cannot understand what devils and the devilishly influenced mean when they say equality for women. We could never be equals.... Nature has not provided thus."

Baraka devotes several pages to the "rebellion" in Newark in 1967 and the troubles throughout the nation during that hot summer. "In rebellions life goes 156 rpm and the song is a police siren accompanying people's breathless shouts and laughter.... The window breakers would come first. Whash! Glass all over everywhere. Then the getters would get through and get to gettin'." He was beaten, arrested, beaten again, thrown in solitary on charges of possession of weapons, and finally acquitted after a disgraceful trial. It is here that one remembers the trials and assassinations and that the state was armed and trigger-happy. Afterward Baraka believed that he had "changed into a blacker being." He became involved in local and national groups, particularly the Committee for a Unified Newark, which was instrumental in defeating the Imperiale machine and electing Kenneth Gibson. Baraka has written on Newark's corrupt politics in *Raise Race Rays Raze* (1969)—and it is worth reading if one can get through the metaphysical free association with an Islamic accent.

Baraka hasn't a good word to say about any black politician—be it Jesse Jackson, Gibson, or Shirley Chisholm. (Perhaps Baraka has changed his mind since he completed the autobiography. A new poem, "1984," read recently at City College, is a tribute to Jackson's candidacy.) It was their brand of "neo-colonialism" that ended his nationalist phase. He also fell out with Karenga. That helped. And so, in the autobiography, Karenga is exposed as a paranoid, Kawaida, his doctrine, as backward. Karenga ended up doing time in the early 1970s—and Baraka was saved by the thoughts of Mao. He reveals this conversion in the political essays collected in the recent *Daggers and Javelins,* written between 1974 and 1979. In a late poem: "Karenga mouthing social democrat cultural opportunism / in the same slick mohair / buba suits." Poor Angela Davis is a "movie star" "fronting" for the lies of CPUSA. It appears that the only revolutionaries whose motives Baraka trusts are dead ones.

Baraka used to write about Malcolm X in an elegiac vein: "For Malcolm's eyes, when they broke / the face of some dumb white man, For / Malcolm's hands raised to bless us." Then "Malcolm" became the occasion for agit-prop, as in the play **"The Death of Malcolm X,"** a multi-media event about mayhem. Lately, Baraka uses the direct-dialing system and talks to Malcolm as the last remaining disciple. "But Malcolm, brother, comrade / some of us / turned / communist too / there's yr fire / lighting flashes / out our eyeballs / And we're still / in the street / with you / Yeh, big Red," he assures him in *Poetry for the Advanced* (1979).

Baraka's latest polemics are hardly the cutting edge. He has the limits and the force of the *personality.* It is hard to tell to whom Baraka's recent instruction manuals on capitalism are addressed—perhaps to the knowing youths who trashed Tavern on the Green after the Diana Ross concert was rained out. Violence has become so universal a solution that the call to revolution is scarcely audible. No matter. Baraka is "home," in the professional revolutionary business, he who once belittled the martyrdom of the white Freedom Riders, who once told a Columbia University audience that any black reading Marx had fallen for another European trick. He is home, and it must be said for him that home, this USA, will never be quite the same. He is a pure American product. (pp. 19-20, 22, 24)

Darryl Pinckney, in a review of "The Autobiography of LeRoi Jones," in The New York Review of Books, *Vol. XXXI, No. 10, June 14, 1984, pp. 19-20, 22, 24.*

Jay R. Berry, Jr. (essay date 1988)

[*In the following essay, Berry explores the poetic style of* Black Art.]

The Black Artist's role in America is to aid in the destruction of America as he knows it .... The Black Artist must draw out of his soul the correct image of the world. He must use this image to band his brothers and sisters together in common understanding of the nature of the world (and the nature of America) and the nature of the human soul. The Black Artist must demonstrate sweet life, how it differs from the deathly grip of the White Eyes. The Black Artist must teach the White Eyes their deaths, and teach the black man how to bring these deaths about.

This statement, taken from Amiri Baraka's *Home,* coincides with the writing of the poems that comprise *Black Art* (1965-1966) and reflects the book's thematic concerns. As other studies of Baraka's poetry have shown, *Black Art* marks a sharp departure from the more personal and introspective "beat" poetry of *Preface to a Twenty Volume Suicide Note* and *The Dead Lecturer.* Baraka also discusses this departure in the preface to *Black Magic: Collected Poetry, 1961-1967,* a work that contains three books: *Sabotage, Target Study,* and *Black Art:*

You notice the preoccupation with death, suicide, in the early works. Always my own, caught up in the deathurge of this twisted society. The work a cloud of abstraction and disjointedness, that was just whiteness. European influence, etc., just as the concept of hopelessness and despair, from the dead minds the dying morality of Europe. There is a spirituality always trying to get through, to triumph.

Black Magic strategically moves from *Sabotage* ("I had come to see the superstructure of filth Americans call their way of life, and wanted to see it fall") to *Target Study* ("[The poetry is] trying to really study, like bomber crews do the soon to be destroyed cities[,] [l]ess passive now, less uselessly 'literary'") to *Black Art* ("*Black Art* was the crucial seeing, the decisions, the actual move. The strengthening to destroy, and the developing of willpower to build, even in the face of destruction and despair. ...*Black Art* was a beginning, a rebeginning, a coming in contact with the most beautiful part of myself, with our selves. The whole race connected in its darkness, in its sweetness"). *Black Art* is concerned with Black nationalism, nation-building, and the raising of black consciousness; it attempts to glorify all aspects of Afro-American culture. That it is "less passive, less uselessly 'literary'" than his earlier poetry is clearly demonstrated by the book's final poem.

"Black People!" demands that blacks take control of their lives through direct and, if necessary, violent action. The exclamation point in the title calls readers to attention, and the poem itself advocates the development of a black consciousness and nation: "Take their lives if need be, but / get what you want what you need. / ... We must make our own / World, man, our own world, and we can not do this unless the white man / is dead."

Baraka concludes *Black Art* with a compelling poem that reinforces his desire to develop a new black poetry as well as a new black consciousness and nation. This aspect of his poetry has been examined by others. What has not been examined as thoroughly is his keen sense of poetic form and style. This essay will briefly explore some of the stylistic intricacies in *Black Art,* including Baraka's revisions of traditional poetic forms and his use of rhythm and language.

The philosophical underpinnings of *Black Art* are found in the book's title poem. While **"Black Art"** maintains some connections with the Euro-American poetic tradition, it also reformulates the tradition. It is clear, for example, that Baraka's poem is a response to the issues raised in Archibald MacLeish's "Ars Poetica." MacLeish's lofty aesthetic claim that "A poem should be palpable and mute / As a globed fruit ... A poem should be wordless / As the flight of birds .... A poem should not mean / But be" is revised by Baraka: "Poems are bullshit unless they are / teeth or tree or lemons piled / on a step." His **"Black Ars Poetica"** is functional, pragmatic, and, at times, violent as it addresses the everyday reality of Blacks in America:

> We want live
> words of the hip world live flesh and
> coursing blood. Hearts Brains
> Souls splintering fire.
> ....
> We want "poems that kill."
> Assassin poems, Poems that shoot
> guns. Poems that wrestle cops into alleys and take
> their weapons leaving them dead with tongues
> pulled out and sent to Ireland.
> ....
> We want a black poem. And a
> Black World.

Occasionally, Baraka will revise a traditional Euro-American poetic form, such as the sonnet, to express his ideas about the condition of Afro-American life. An example of this tendency is the poem **"leroy."** It does not have lines of rhymed iambic pentameter, and it also has a fifteenth line consisting of one word. Yet the language, while not as formal as one generally finds in

sonnets, is certainly less strident and less colloquial than that of the other poems in *Black Art.* It seems that Baraka consciously revises the traditional sonnet form. He takes a widely used and respected form and, by making certain changes, transforms it into a different and more personal form, one that better reflects his own experiences.

Baraka conveys to the reader a sense of admiration for his mother, who embodied a rich cultural heritage: "I wanted to know my mother when she sat / looking sad across the campus in the later 20's / into the future of the soul ... carrying life from our ancestors, / and knowledge, and the strong nigger feeling." He also conveys the cultural duality in his own personality and his desire to rid himself of the influence of white culture: "May they pick me apart and take the / useful parts, the sweet meat of my feelings. And leave / the bitter bullshit rotten white parts / alone." The fifteenth line could have been added to the end of the previous one. Because of its placement, however, the word is more forceful as it emphasizes Baraka's sense of alienation. Moreover, the stately, ordered, and precise rhythm of the traditional sonnet has given way to a more irregular and intense rhythm that characterizes the cultural and personal situations which he is describing.

Baraka pays careful attention to rhythm, even in poems that do not employ or experiment with traditional forms. **"SOS,"** the opening poem in *Black Art,* contains short, terse, telegraphic phrases that are reminiscent of a radio transmission:

> Calling black people
> Calling all black people, man woman child
> Wherever you are, calling you, urgent, come in
> Black People, come in, wherever you are, urgent,
>   calling you, calling all black people
> calling all black people, come in, black people, come
> on in.

Content and form blend effectively in this poem. The radio transmission asks blacks to "come in" until the final lines, when it asks them to "come / on in." The final line break calls attention to the word change, thereby emphasizing the message. This word change has at least two connotations. On one level, the phrase invites readers into the book of poetry. In this sense it is a fitting opening poem. On another level, it cajoles blacks into claiming their share of the American political, social, and cultural systems on their own terms.

Another poem that effectively employs the line break is **"They have outposts."** The first thirteen lines metaphorically describe the predicament of all the "lost brothers" who are living in the "snowy den" of white society. Images of snow and the blonde actress Virginia Mayo describe the cold, stultifying nature of white culture. In addition, Baraka alludes to Plato's "Allegory of the Cave" to reinforce the awareness of the black condition. The illusionary world created by television and film replaced Plato's shadows, and in this world blacks are lost. Like the inhabitants of Plato's cave, blacks are not able to perceive reality because they are trapped in the illusionary world of the snowy den. Baraka finally asks, "Must I call your names lost brothers?"

At this point he shrewdly utilizes a line break to indicate a shift in thought and emphasis. Whereas earlier he was describing the condition of blacks in white America, now he prescribes a remedy for that condition: "Leave the beast / in its snowy den. Sneak out in the night and run till youre warm. Till your body sweats / and the world makes sense again. Run out from in there, brother. Save yourself." The metaphorical stars refer, of course, to dreams as well as to celestial bodies, and they are carefully distinguished from truth and reality. At present, there is no room for dreams in the lives of black people. The truth and reality for blacks, as Baraka sees it, are the "fat bulging lunatic / eyes, of the white man, which are not stars...." The white man indulges in narcissism and greed at everyone else's expense.

It is at this point that Baraka shifts the focus of his ideas. The last three lines prescribe a violent remedy to correct the injustices described earlier in the poem. By carefully gauging the rhythm of the lines, he is able to change the pace and intensity of the poem as the focus of his ideas shifts. It is not surprising to note, for example, that he employs a line break to emphasize the climactic question: "Why dont / somebody kill the motherfucker?" Nor is it surprising to discover that the number of syllables per line decreases after the question is posed. The verbal violence releases most of the tension that has been built up in the poem, and the rhythm changes accordingly.

Language is also important to the poetry in *Black Art*. Baraka is equally comfortable repeating words and phrases to emphasize a point and using words very sparingly to heighten dramatic effect. **"Incident"** and **"Biography"** are excellent examples of these two uses of language.

"Incident" is a poetic description of the murder of an unknown man. The clauses in the first half of the poem are short and terse. Their staccato sounds and rhythms lend the verse a frenetic, breathless, almost chaotic quality. They seem to capture the act of murder in progress: "He came back and shot. He shot him. When he came / back, he shot, and he fell, stumbling, past the / shadow wood, down, shot, dying, dead, to full halt." The repetition of words such as *shot* underscores the violent theme of the poem. Many of the words Baraka chooses to repeat are verbs—strong action words like *shot, fell,* and *died/dying*. These words possess more force and suggestion of action than adjectives and adverbs, and Baraka's use of them is deliberate. He is attempting to create a dynamic poem.

This is not to say that adjectives, adverbs, and nouns are unimportant. Baraka effectively orchestrates, for example, images of light (life) and darkness (death) within the chaotic action of the poem: "... blood sprayed fine over the killer and the grey light. / Pictures of the dead man, are everywhere. And his spirit / sucks up the light. But

he died in darkness darker than / his soul and everything tumbled blindly with him dying / down the stairs." After the death of the anonymous man is related to the reader, the rhythm and language change. The rhythm of the second half of the poem is slower, more straightforward and matter-of-fact, something like a formal (police?) report: "We have no word / on the killer, except he came back, from somewhere / to do what he did. And he shot only once into the victim's / stare, and left him quickly when the blood ran out. We know / the killer was skillful, quick, and silent...." The language has also become more formal and passive. The verbs are no longer stressed and repeated; adjectives and adverbs control the rhythm and tone.

The action and the report of the action blend together well. Baraka uses a line break to signal the change in rhythm and language. This structural device makes the transition smooth and credible. Two short lines, spatially separated both from each other and from the preceding and following stanzas, indicate the shift. They visually separate the action of the first half from the report of the action in the second half. **"Incident"** thus represents Baraka at his most skillful as he manipulates rhythm, language, tone, and formal structure. These qualities are also manifested in **"Biography"** although in different ways.

"Biography" is an imagistic poem that does not rely on the repetition of words for its power, but on action-oriented language, sparingly used, and the effective use of line breaks. **"Biography"** contains no nonessential words. Each word contributes to the overall sensation of horror that the poem evokes:

> Hangs.
> whipped
> blood
> striped
> meat pulled
> clothes ripped
> slobber
> feet dangled
> pointing....

Many of the words are verbs, and most of them are violent: *hangs, whipped, pulled, ripped, churns, bleeds, sucks, tore.* They describe the painfully ironic and all too frequent "biography" of the Afro-American in a racist American Society. The lynched man's face is reflected against the black sky; his blood falls to the ground, wetting the sticky mud, and the earth "sucks" the man's life blood:

> face
> black sky
> and moon
> leather night
> red
> bleeds
> drips
> ground
> sucks
> blood
> hangs

149

life wetting
sticky
mud.

Perhaps the most startling aspect of the poem is that there are at least two black witnesses to the lynching: "Granddaddy / granddaddy, they tore / his / neck." They must carry this memory with them for the rest of their lives.

The isolation and the intensification of the various images by their placement in one- and two-word lines heighten the dramatic effect of the poem. The structure of the lines forces the reader to dwell on each word, absorbing its full impact. **"Biography"** is the sparest poem in the book and, in some ways, the most compelling.

Occasionally, Amiri Baraka will work with more or less traditional stanzas in **Black Art.** The political content of the poem is, perhaps, uppermost in his mind, but he pays careful attention to poetic style and structure. In **"Ka 'Ba,"** for example, he uses stanzas rather than individual lines to develop ideas. Images and sounds in one stanza lead into similar features in subsequent stanzas. While it is possible to understand the theme apart from the poem's structure, the work becomes more impressive when its formal subtleties are understood.

Aural imagery and physical laws connect the first three stanzas of **"Ka 'Ba."** References to sounds—calls, screams, and chants—and physical movement (or restraint of movement)—walking, failing to walk the air, dancing, sprawling in chains—link ideas presented in the opening stanzas, giving the poem a sense of balance and structural cohesiveness. Baraka is reinforcing the point that blacks are a beautiful people whose world and heritage are filled with sound, vitality, imagination, and possibility, as well as suffering and slavery.

The references to "african imaginations" in the third stanza tie in with ideas and images in the final two stanzas, as Baraka urges blacks to escape from the "grey chains" with which they are bound. He also advocates a return to "the ancient image," to a new awareness of the connection with the black past and black culture:

> We have been captured,
> brothers. And we labor
> to make our getaway, into
> the ancient image, into a new
>
> correspondence with ourselves
> and our black family. We need magic
> now we need the spells, to raise up
> return, destroy, and create. What will be
>
> the sacred words?

The ancient image, black family, magic, spells, and sacred words stem from the "african imaginations" mentioned in the third stanza. Baraka creates a link in form, content, and style between a usable African heritage and culture and the Afro-American situation.

The structural devices employed in **"Ka 'Ba"** strengthen the poem's powerful argument; they also have a resonance that extends beyond this individual poem. The poems in **Black Art,** indeed in all three books collected in **Black Magic: Collected Poetry, 1961-1967,** are the "sacred words," the "magic" needed to "raise up / return, destroy, and create."

Black Art occupies a pivotal position in Amiri Baraka's poetic development. The primary focus of his poetry during this period is its revolutionary ideological content, but he is also deeply concerned with poetic style and structure. As I have tried to show, Baraka's technical excellence and his political concerns fuse in **Black Art** as he attempts to create a new black poetry—vernacular, pragmatic, ideological, formally intricate—to address the everyday reality of black Americans. (pp. 225-34)

> *Jay R. Berry, Jr., "Poetic Style in Amiri Baraka's 'Black Art'," in CLA Journal Vol. XXXII, No. 2, December, 1988, pp. 225-34.*

FURTHER READING

Baraka, Amiri. "Why I Changed My Ideology: Black Nationalism and Socialist Revolution." *Black World* XXIV, No. 9 (July 1975): 30-42.
    Explains his conversion from nationalist to socialist.

Benston, Kimberly W. *Baraka: The Renegade and the Mask.* London: Yale University Press, 1976, 290 p.
    Evaluation of Baraka's literary works, focusing on his plays.

————. "Amiri Baraka: An Interview." *Boundary 2* VI, No. 2 (Winter 1978): 303-16.
    Interview with Baraka. Baraka offers a self-criticism of *The System of Dante's Hell.*

Clark, Norris B. "Aesthetic Theory: Imamu Amiri Baraka." In *Amiri Baraka: The Kaleidoscopic Torch,* edited by James B. Gwynne, pp. 41-60. New York: Steppingstones Press, 1985.
    Examines the relationship between art and aesthetic values in Baraka's poetry.

Dace, Letitia. "Amiri Baraka (LeRoi Jones)." In *Black American Writers: Bibliographical Essays; Richard Wright, Ralph Ellison, James Baldwin, and Amiri Baraka,* edited by M. Thomas Inge, Maurice Duke, and Jackson R. Bryer, Vol. 2, pp. 121-78. New York: St. Martin's Press, 1978.
    Survey of criticism on Baraka's literary work, concluding that "unfortunately not a single critic has thus far informed his or her study with a complete knowledge of Baraka's work."

Dennison, George. "The Demagogy of LeRoi Jones." *Commentary* 39, No. 2 (February 1965): 67-70.

Recalls his reactions to viewing *The Toilet* and *The Slave.* The critic contrasts Baraka's "racial rhetoric" with Jean Genet's *The Blacks,* calling the latter a "true work of art.'

Duberman, Martin. "Visionaries with Blind Spots." *The New York Herald Tribune* CXXVI, No. 43,483 (24 April 1966): 3, 8.
Negative assessment of *Home: Social Essays.* According to Duberman: "Most of these essays are full of private hangups and wild distortions.... My main reaction to these ravings is not anger or fright, but boredom. They are so obviously the effluvium of a disturbed man that they cannot even be taken with the seriousness we accord polemics. Jones is pursuing private catharsis, not communication; there is no room at all for exchange—and apparently Jones couldn't care less."

Gates, Henry Louis, Jr. "Several Lives, Several Voices." *The New York Times Book Review* LXXXIX, No. 11 (11 March 1984): 11-12.
Reviews *The Autobiography of LeRoi Jones,* stating that "Mr. Baraka still has a lot of accounting to do, despite the length, density and lyricism of his narrative."

Harris, William J. *The Poetry and Poetics of Amiri Baraka: The Jazz Aesthetic.* Columbia: University of Missouri Press, 1985, 174 p.
Examines Baraka's literary career as a series of transformations, "of avant garde poetics into ethnic poetics, of white liberal politics into black nationalist and Marxist politics, of jazz forms into literary forms."

Hicks, Granville. "The Poets in Prose." *Saturday Review* XLVIII, No. 50 (11 December 1965): 31-2.
Review of *The System of Dante's Hell,* noting: "Jones writes mostly in violent staccato.... This kind of writing can grow tiresome, but there is a strong cumulative effect."

Hudson, Theodore R. *From LeRoi Jones to Amiri Baraka: The Literary Works.* Durham, N. C.: Duke University Press, 1973, 222 p.
Critical study of Baraka and his works. Analyzing Baraka's prose and dramas, the critic proposes that Baraka is a "romantic."

Kessler, Jascha. "Keys to Ourselves." *Saturday Review* LIII, No. 18 (2 May 1970): 34-6.
Briefly reviews *Black Magic.* The critic writes: "I am troubled by Jones's work and always have been, because I read him as a poet who is both blessed and cursed. He is blessed with the demon of language, and cursed in the way he uses it."

Pinckney, Darryl. "The Changes of Amiri Baraka." *The New York Times Book Review* LXXXIV, No. 5 (16 December 1979): 9, 29.
Presents a review of *Selected Plays and Prose of Amiri Baraka/LeRoi Jones* and *Selected Poetry of Amiri Baraka/LeRoi Jones,* noting of the works: "Selected by Baraka, the work gathered in these two volumes is offered as a summation of his creative life. Baraka's writing is defined by vehement repudiations, littered with discarded identities."

Sollars, Werner. *Amiri Baraka/LeRoi Jones: The Quest for a "Populist Modernism."* New York: Columbia University Press, 1978, 338 p.
Examines Baraka's collected and uncollected works, focusing on *The Dead Lecturer: Poems, The Baptism, The Toilet, Dutchman, The Slave, The System of Dante's Hell,* and *Tales.*

Thielemans, Johan. "From LeRoi Jones to Baraka and Back." In *New Essays on American Drama,* edited by Gilbert Debusscher and Henry I. Schvey, pp. 127-41. Amsterdam: Rodopi, 1989.
Brief biography of Baraka, emphasizing his career as a dramatist.

Barry Beckham

1944-

American novelist, essayist, dramatist, and prose writer.

Beckham is a contemporary black American novelist acclaimed for two works: *My Main Mother* (1969) and, most notably, *Runner Mack* (1972). Both works concern black male protagonists whose search for identity is shaped by a relationship with a fellow black struggler. Being black in America, and its subsequent consequences, is a chief concern in Beckham's works. When *My Main Mother* first appeared in 1969, critic Peter Rowley proclaimed: "If Barry Beckham's second book is as brilliant as the second half of [*My Main Mother*], he may well become one of the best American novelists of the decade." Upon publication of Beckham's second novel, *Runner Mack,* in 1972, critics again offered glowing praise; Joe Weixlmann, for example, called it "a masterpiece." Today, Beckham is recognized as a leading writer of African-American fiction.

Beckham was born in West Philadelphia in 1944. At age nine, he moved with his mother to a black section of Atlantic City, New Jersey. There he attended interracial schools and enjoyed popularity among his peers. He enrolled at Brown University in 1962 as one of only eight black members of the freshman class. In his senior year he began writing his first book, *My Main Mother,* a story about a young black man who kills his adulterous, alcoholic, self-centered mother. "I wrote a great deal of the novel," Beckham later recounted, "in a three-and-one-half room apartment in the Bronx after work while my wife tried to keep our two babies quiet." Completing this book in 1969, he returned to his alma mater a year later as visiting lecturer in Afro-American Studies and English. He was promoted to assistant professor in 1972. During this fruitful year he published *Runner Mack,* produced the play *Garvey Lives!,* and began his third book, *Double Dunk,,* a fictional biography of basketball player Earl "The Goat" Manigault. In 1987 Beckham joined the English department at Hampton University. He retired two years later and founded Beckham House Publishers, specializing in black and educational guidance literature. Since the publication of *Double Dunk* in 1980, Beckham has not written any more novels because, in his words, he's "trying to get the business going."

Although each of Beckham's works has enjoyed popular and critical success, none has garnered more attention and acclaim than *Runner Mack. Runner Mack* is the story of Henry Adams, a naive black man who, tormented by his growing awareness of racial injustice in America, becomes a revolutionary. The plot chronicles Henry's awakening from innocent idealist to militant black activist. Structurally and thematically, *Runner Mack* is divided into two sections. The first describes Henry's urban experiences—living in a run-down apart-

ment with his wife, getting hit by a Mack truck on the way to work, and trying out for a bigoted baseball team. The second section describes Henry's military experience in Alaska. There he meets Runner Mack, a charismatic black revolutionary who radicalizes Henry and persuades him to blow up the White House. But when the mass rally that is to precede the bombing fizzles out due to poor attendance, Runner Mack hangs himself, and Henry rushes into the path of an oncoming Mack truck.

While the plot of *Runner Mack* is fairly simple, the work employs flashbacks and contains a number of intricately-woven satirical episodes. Equally, the complex texture of the work is reflected in its unwillingness to accept facile solutions to ethical problems. According to Weixlmann: Beckham wishes us to realize that the revolutionary dreams of modern-day black militants are no more likely to be realized than were the more modest dreams of those blacks who came north during the Great Migration. Moreover, the book's ending projects the reader into the vacuum created by Henry's death, whether via an onrushing truck or as a character in a novel which has no more printed pages. Rather than proposing some simpleminded solution to the ethical dilemma caused by this country's racial prejudices and its socioeconomic plight, Beckham causes the reader of *Runner Mack* to contemplate what he or she might do to ameliorate the deplorable condition of current-day America.

Beckham stated in a 1974 interview that *Runner Mack* is "about the black man's—in this case the protagonist, Henry Adams'—awareness of himself. The character of Runner Mack makes him understand what has happened to black people, symbolically, over the years." Critics have confirmed Beckham's intentions, interpreting *Runner Mack* as a powerful allegory of Afro-American experience—from the early days of slavery to present-day black militancy.

In general, critical reviews of *Runner Mack* have been positive, with commentators praising the work as an innovative novel of one black man's awareness of himself and his people. Critics have noted, however, that instead of treating this theme in the traditional realistic mode, Beckham crafted *Runner Mack* with what Weixlmann called "evocative dream-reality." Unfortunately, according to critic Jim Walker, this artistry falters in the second half of the book. Beckham's tendency to write "strongly in parts of his novels but falling off in other parts" prompted Walker to dub him "novelist of 'halves'." Other commentators have noted similarities between *Runner Mack* and Ralph Ellison's 1952 novel *Invisible Man.* While not denying the influence of this work on *Runner Mack,* Beckham explained, "If only stylistically there is a much stronger sense of fantasy in my book, as well as the macabre, the gothic, the just plain weird."

After the publication of his first novel in 1969, Beckham commented: "The best fiction for me is the kind that exalts the ordinary man (Malamud), is uproariously funny (Roth), is distressingly violent and tragic (Hawkes), makes full use of the possibilities of the English language (Nabokov), and spurns the impatient reader (Beckett)." By nearly all accounts, *Runner Mack* is such a book. Commentators therefore recognize it as an important work of African-American fiction.

(For further information about Beckham's life and works, see *Contemporary Authors,* Vols. 29-32; *Comtemporary Authors New Revision Series,* Vol. 26; and *Dictionary of Literary Biography,* Vol. 33: *Afro-American Fiction Writers after 1955.*)

PRINCIPAL WORKS

"Listen to the Black Graduate, You Might Learn Something" (essay) 1969; published in periodical *Esquire*
My Main Mother (novel) 1969

"Ladies and Gentlemen, No Salt-Water Taffy Today" (essay) 1970; published in periodical *Brown Alumni Monthly*
Garvey Lives! (drama) 1972
Runner Mack (novel) 1972
"Why It Is Right to Write" (essay) 1978; published in periodical *Brown Alumni Monthly*
Double Dunk (fictional biography) 1980

Barry Beckham (essay date 1969)

[*In the following essay, Beckham briefly discusses theme and technique in* My Main Mother.]

"In *My Main Mother,* a young black cat kills his mother. Without giving the critics too much information, I shall say that thematically I am concerned here with insecurity of the self—the saddening, schizophrenic insecurity that we're all faced with at times—and the limits to which this insecurity will force one before he can feel safe. I wrote a great deal of the novel in a three-and-one-half room apartment in the Bronx after work while my wife tried to keep our two babies quiet. There are few better circumstances under which a man can prove to himself that he wants to be a writer.

"The best writers know they're the best and they feel they can do anything. In my next novel, which I'm very anxious to begin, I have merely images and ideas to guide me. I'm thinking of Kafka, slavery, Harlem, the moon landing, *Gulliver's Travels* and the Vietnam war. If a writer can pull a good story out of that, he can do anything.

"The best fiction for me is the kind that exalts the ordinary man (Malamud), is uproariously funny (Roth), is distressingly violent and tragic (Hawkes), makes full use of the possibilities of the English language (Nabokov), and spurns the impatient reader (Beckett). These are my primary concerns in fiction writing.

"Born in Philadelphia, raised and schooled in Atlantic City, educated at Brown, I live now in Brooklyn and I don't think I'll leave New York City for awhile. I have more ideas than I do time, and I only hope I'll live at least 20 more years to get some of those ideas on paper."

> Barry Beckham, in a review of "My Main Mother," in Library Journal, *Vol. 94, No. 17, October 1, 1969, p. 3473.*

Peter Rowley (essay date 1969)

[*In the following 1969 review, English critic and essayist Rowley offers a generally favorable appraisal of Beckham's first novel,* My Main Mother.]

If Barry Beckham's second book is as brilliant as the second half of [*My Main Mother*], he may well become one of the best American novelists of the decade. Unfortunately, the first 100 or so pages, though seriously written and containing some excellent scenes, are only slightly better than mediocre.

Mitchell Mibbs, Mr. Beckham's protagonist, is also his narrator. As the story opens, we learn that he has murdered his mother. The plot then flashes back to Mitchell age 7. The black family consists of the lonely youth, his beautiful mother who hopes to be a singing star, and his kindly uncle. The boy's father fled before he knew him. Basically, the book is a psychological study of the ruinous effect on a child who is either ignored or tormented by a parent. Thus the title is a triple allusion—to his main "mother," who was his uncle, their living in "Maine," and an indictment of selfish Pearl, who out of her own insecurity dreamed of fame, drank and married an equally spineless ne'er-do-well.

Despite being shunned by mother and step-father, Mitchell, encouraged by the uncle who is his constant companion, becomes the best Negro student in the town public school and receives a full scholarship to Brown. (The author graduated from there in 1966.) There is a brilliant section in which uncle and nephew visit New York in search of Pearl and her husband, now making a final and futile attempt to break into the big time. Of course the couple return to Maine and continue living off the uncle's generosity. The old man's death and the horror of a sordid squabble over his money spur Mitchell into matricide.

The trouble with the childhood part of the novel—as distinct from the adolescent and college sections—is that the hero-narrator is not particularly likable. Though understandably hurt, he is conceited, bitter and belligerent. Mitchell is as cold as Maine in the winter, the treatment of him too acid to be entirely accurate. Writing about children is difficult, and Beckham's compassion for the boy seems lacking. Nevertheless there are a number of redeeming scenes—the ridiculous marriage of his mother and Julius, young Mitchell showing how clever he is in a barber shop, and the boy and his mother on the sailboat of a white man. The pathos and futility and camaraderie of Negro file is sharply etched.

It is in the second half that *My Main Mother* comes to life. Mitchell is now an adolescent. The scenes of Harlem, of how it feels to be an aged black from Maine getting a flat tire on Times Square, of encountering a homosexual in the village, of street gangs and boarding houses, of the ironies of racism by the oh-so-reasonable Maine High School principal and the disdainful behavior of a rich white coed at Brown, and finally the poisoning of Pearl are fantastically vivid and compelling. The climax reminded me of the adolescent violence at the conclusion of the English movie, *If . . ,* when the boarding school boys start a shooting revolution.

The anti-parent novel has been with us since *The Way of All Flesh,* and it is interesting to compare the mental cruelty toward children today with the physical cruelty at the time of Dickens. Not quite as impressive as Frank Conroy's autobiography *Stop-Time,* where the reader can identify fully with the boy-hero, it is to be hoped that *My Main Mother* is a forerunner of remarkable things to come. (pp. 64-5)

> *Peter Rowley, "The Rise and Fall of Mitchell Mibbs," in* The New York Times Book Review, *November 30, 1969, pp. 64-5.*

Mel Watkins (essay date 1972)

[*In the following review essay, Watkins offers an allegorical reading of* Runner Mack.]

On its simplest level *Runner Mack* is the story of Henry Adams, a naive, aspiring professional baseball player who leaves his small, Southern home town and, with his wife Beatrice, comes North to find fame and riches. He gets his chance to try out with the Stars, a big-league team, but before he is told whether he has made it he is drafted and sent to Alaska where his outfit is fighting a capricious war with an unseen enemy. There he meets Runnington Mack, a would-be black revolutionary, who leads Henry to an awareness of himself as a black man and involves him in a plot to bomb the White House and take over the country.

But a recitation of the plot line of his novel reveals almost nothing of what it is about. Unlike Beckham's first novel, *My Main Mother,* which was a subtly rendered, naturalistic account of a black youth driven to matricide by his mother's avarice and promiscuity, *Runner Mack* is an evocative allegory that eschews cinematic and psychological realism. Instead, Beckham employs a satirical narrative voice that, with tightly reined understatement, heightens the macabre effect of the surreal events he relates.

In the opening scene, Henry Adams awakes to find that a putrid liquid is dripping on his forehead from a leak in the ceiling. He confronts Alvarez, the superintendent, who does not speak English. Angered because of the futility of his pantomime attempts and his discovery that the super has stolen a pair of his pajamas, Henry attacks him, only to be driven back to his unheated, leaking apartment and Beatrice's arms by Alvarez's menacing German shepherd. The next morning Henry goes to a job interview. He is jostled by crowds, knocked down, sworn at and hit by a Mack truck. He arrives at the "Home" offices bloodied and limping and goes through a humiliating interview—"Let's see your teeth, Henry . . . open up"—but does get a job in a department where everyone sits at their desks with studied concentration even though no one knows what they are supposed to be doing. Boye, his supervisor, shows him lewd photographs of black women to demonstrate his understanding of blacks, and Henry returns home.

The novel begins, then, with satirical and burlesque episodes and is held together by a matter-of-fact prose that belies their nightmarish qualities. The tone is reminiscent of Kafka's in *The Trial.* Though we discover later, through flashbacks, that Henry's phlegmatic temperament might warrant his passive reaction to the insanity about him, it is clear at the outset that *Runner Mack* has mythic dimensions. Thereafter, in loosely connected episodes, the symbols proliferate.

Throughout, as in Robert Coover's *The Universal Baseball Association* or Bernard Malamud's *The Natural,* baseball is the central metaphor. For Beckham "baseball is *the* America," and only through making the baseball team can Henry be accepted as an American. This thought permeates his consciousness and his every action is affected by it: He is irritable and unable to concentrate at work because he is unsure of the results of his tryout; making love to Beatrice he imagines himself at bat—"an exhilarating contact, sending vibrations to his toes as the bat's fat part caught the ball, and it was already spiraling out and high like bait at the end of a cast line, and the feeling was all over him, a smile forming on his lips"; when he and *Runner Mack* are plotting the bombing of the White House he thinks of himself as a relief pitcher or pinch hitter coming in to save the game. Baseball idioms are an integral part of the narrative. The baseball metaphor, however, fits into a larger allegorical structure.

Runner Mack can be seen as an allegorical chronicle of the Afro-American's historical experience, for Henry Adams's fictional experience parallels black history from slave ship to the present emergence of militant revolutionaries. The opening episodes with Alvarez and the job interview are representative of blacks' plight on slave ships and the auction block. Beatrice is later molested by two uniformed intruders while Henry, a shotgun at his head, watches helplessly (slavery). Henry takes a bizarre subway ride—during which he is protected from a white passenger by a black conductor—to his futile tryout with the Stars (the underground railroad and the attempt to win acceptance as an American).

Within this allegorical structure there are numerous other themes that enhance the symbolic nature of the book. Among these are Beckham's treatment of the strained relationship between black men and women as seen through Henry's relationship with Beatrice. Throughout Beatrice complains, "'We never get to talk. . . . I don't even know about you.'" But each time they are prepared to confront one another honestly there is an intrusion—the two uniformed molesters, the draft notice that is delivered mysteriously in the middle of the night. And when Henry flees the Army and returns, resolved to fight for *his* manhood and to communicate with Beatrice, the incessant clamor of their tenement and the ghetto streets have left her deaf.

Then there is the matter of the Mack (Maccabees?) truck and Runner Mack, the character from whom the title is derived. The truck is seen "looming toward him [Henry] with a grille (smiling) of steel meshwork and headlights (winking) like two glass basketballs. It . . . seemed to be

pouncing, falling from above, about to land on him and swallow him." And when Mack is first encountered: "His eyes were dancing, focused directly on Henry's, and his mouth had a quizzical smile. . . . Something about this moment—the staring eyes, the question—galvanized Henry. It was dreamlike, hypnotic . . . as if he had gone through it before somewhere." Henry is hit by the truck when, angered by someone who swears at him, he turns around to reply—a moment of revolt. But bruised and bloodied, he finds himself at the interview (auction block). Later, he is led into a revolutionary plot by Mack; and, finally, after discovering that Mack has committed suicide, he runs headlong into another Mack truck. The recurring failure of revolt against the system?

But *Runner Mack* need not be read only on a symbolic level. Even though as fable, it is didactic—and occasionally (when symbols are not embedded deeply enough into the texture of the narrative) overly so—each of its episodes, at face value, makes for compelling reading. Beckham's satire and burlesque are effective; this is an enthralling tale. The baseball tryout and Alaskan war episodes, with their caricatures of "Stumpy," the midget manager of the Stars, and Captain Nevins, a demented Army C.O., are hilarious and memorable scenes.

With this latest book, Barry Beckham has moved far beyond the boundaries of his first novel. By creating an ironic verbal world, he has produced an allegory that both illuminates the despair and recurring frustration that has characterized blacks' struggle for freedom and brilliantly satirizes the social conditions that perpetuate that frustration. Its humor and burlesque notwithstanding, it is an unsettling book. As Runner Mack says before he commits suicide: "'I just figured it out. There are no answers. We just keep trying and planning and it doesn't mean anything. History keeps going and we keep trying and nothing happens. . . . We just keep going on and on, hoping it will make sense, but it never does, does it?'" *Runner Mack* reminds us that there is frequently more truth in "fabulation" than in those novels that aspire to a realistic representation. It is a skillfully written and richly imaginative work. It should confirm Barry Beckham's place among the best of contemporary American novelists. (pp. 3, 50)

> *Mel Watkins, in review of "Runner Mack,"
> in* The New York Times Book Review,
> *September 17, 1972, pp. 3, 50.*

Jim Walker (essay date 1973)

[*In the following review essay, Walker presents an overview of* Runner Mack, *focusing on plot, characterization, and literary technique.*]

What do baseball, a satiric rendering of the Vietnam War, images of the decadent North juxtaposed with nostalgia for the South, and a young Black in search for himself have in common? One would have to read Barry Beckham's new (and second), novel, *Runner Mack* to find out, for these are the elements which form the artistic and thematic basis of a most interesting, but not totally successful novel. The title is **Runner Mack,** but the main character of the novel is Henry Adams, who is the young brother in search for himself: who he is and how he got where he is. The novel poses the age-old question "Who am I?" and Beckham's answer is by no means the standard one, basically because he is a gifted writer who uses words to their fullest advantage, even when what he is saying is not worth saying or has been said before.

Beckham divides his novel into 11 chapters, which we can view as being divided roughly in half, each half having its own artistic purpose and design. The first 6 chapters can be seen as Henry Adams' search for meaning and significance in his life; he finds no totally satisfactory answer in anything he does or in anyone he meets and knows, including his wife, Beatrice (whom he loves dearly), or his family still in the South. The remaining 5 chapters introduce us to the second main character of the novel, Runnington Mack, (known also as Runner Mack, Runner and The Run), whose revolutionary beliefs help bring Henry, at least temporarily, to knowledge of himself and thus to manhood. The dustjacket of the novel, quoting from *The New York Times* book review of Beckham's first novel [see excerpt by Peter Rowley dated 1969], said that if Beckham's "second book is as brilliant as the *second part* (italics mine) of his first, he may well become one of the best American novelists of the decade." In my way of thinking, he is only half on that road to literary glory, for the first half of **Runner Mack** is far better in its artistry, in its introduction of themes, in its use of language and in its presentation of characterization than the second half, which is almost an anticlimax to the strengths of the first half. Thus, it would appear that Beckham is a novelist of "halves," writing strongly in parts of his novels but falling off in other parts. But there is little doubt that he can overcome this problem and emerge with a totally satisfying novel.

> In the Twilight, by himself and away from the other workers, Henry Adams stopped to look up at the sky. It was dove-gray. How could he like that sky with its ripples of fading light? But standing in the entrance of a closed-up restaurant, he felt a kinship with it. There was nothing bright about it, nothing cheerful or communicative. It was distant, alone, somber; he was also. He wanted to be by himself, wanted to think things out and enjoy the odd pleasantness of his mood.

These words open Chapter 6 and can as easily serve as the thematic inscription for the Henry of the first half of the novel as they can serve as an introduction to the hauntingly beautiful writing of Beckham. Who and what is Henry Adams? He is characterized at first as a rather lonely, confused brother, who comes North from the South with a host of rather standard advice on living from his family. He aspires to be a major league baseball player but never makes it to the big time, and he probably would not have been happy or fulfilled had he been successful in his quest for baseball fame. Henry needs more than the ephemeral glory of recognition on the baseball diamond for hitting a home run or fielding a ball.

In the first half of the novel Beckham presents a series of episodes that can be viewed as symbolic of actual historical events in the history of the Black man in America, the first of these being Henry's interview for a job at Home Manufacturing. One is puzzled at first by the strange references, images and allusions that are juxtaposed next to the real events of the interview. Then, slowly, Beckham's artistic method begins to become clear. As Henry is being "interviewed" by Mister Peters, head of personnel, at Home Manufacturing, he is introduced to three other department heads, named A. L. Klein, B. J. Kind and M. O. Baby, who advance toward Henry, "pipes in their hands," exhaling smoke, and hiding their faces from him as they stand above him. "Let's see your teeth Henry—voice from behind a screen of smoke—open up." They squeeze his biceps, question him about his belief in God and about his health. In short, they are the slave owners at a slave auction examining and testing a piece of merchandise they will "buy," in this case Henry (for Home Manufacturing). And they literally do "buy" Henry into one of the most impersonal, cold and dehumanizing factories you are ever likely to see in fiction. The entire imagery of the factory section is reminiscent of the best of imagery of Orwell's *1984* or E. M. Forster's "The Machine Stops." In touching upon the effects of contemporary life on the spirit of modern man, Beckham is touching upon one of the great and pervasive themes of all 20th century, dehumanization, Beckham constantly juxtaposes the South with the North, the South being pictured as the place to leave, the North the place to go. The dichotomy is a usual one. Yet, this dichotomy is confused, as Henry finds the supposed "golden North" (His family "expected him to leave. He had a talent that could bring him a better life, fulfillment, freedom, a chance to live, exist; breathe cleanly, comfortably. There was nothing for him down there," in the South) cold, dirty, crowded, smelly, lonely, impersonal, and remembers the South in more nostalgic terms (usually thinking of his family). Perhaps one needs to go away from home to find the beauty of home, while still recognizing, along with Thomas Wolfe, that "You can't go home again." Thus, the essence of the novel is a never-ending search by Henry. He searches for meaning in his relationship with his wife, Beatrice; he questions himself constantly and he specifically questions his pimpled supervisor at Home Manufacturing, Boye (the name "Boye" for a white man is certainly symbolic and ironic!), about why he (Henry) assembles bits and pieces of metallic objects for an end product he never sees. Thus, Henry's question of Boye is the larger philosophical question that all thinking men, and particularly Black men, must ask in a dehumanized 20th century. Boye's initial answer is at best unsettling, for he only reaffirms the individual's unimportance in the world, except as a minute particle of a larger and impersonal whole. "Each part fits into the whole," says Boye, and his answer is reminiscent of the machine imagery of Ellison's novel, *Invisible Man,* itself a novel about a search for identity by a Black man like Beckham's. Black people are only cogs in the well-oiled machinery of the white man. Then Boye expands and enlarges his answer: "As to your questions when you first came in, I don't know the answers, Henry. I don't really know *what* we're doing. Or what it means. Or what I'm doing and if that means anything. I'm supervising. And I get paid for it."

The entire insanity of the factory is underscored beautifully by the appearance of the President of the company on his annual Christmas tour: a hollow, pale man on crutches who can only move with the support of his assistants and whose voice is so soft that his main assistant, Peters, must repeat parrotlike everything he says so the President's words can be heard. Certainly Henry finds no answer in his job with Home Manufacturing, as his own words tell us: He was trying to deal with the disconcerting jumble of his life and so, as he always found it best to do, consciously willed his mind to superimpose another vision. He wasn't asleep, no; he wasn't unconscious either of what was going on before him. But somehow it didn't have much to do with him; had *nothing* to do with him. These men standing in front of all these people who themselves were just as enigmatic as the men—what could they give him, what could they offer? There were other things to consider, things which were swelling up inside him, boiling now, and he needed this respite, this retreat from the demand of focusing on them, to think.

Another event in American history, the underground railway, is rendered in one of the scenes of the novel. The writing in this scene is memorable. Listen to the sound of Beckham's language. It is not only beautiful, but it echoes and underscores the meaning of the words. It is language any artist can be proud of:

> He stepped to the edge of the platform, looked down the canyon of darkness—no subway coming. . .
> Soon the walls were shaking, a rush of air came through the tunnel and the other passengers moved toward the platform edge and Henry had to turn his head away from the blast. He took his hands from his ears. The doors opened. . .
> The clanging, rolling rhythm of the train; a circle of colored saliva on the floor to his right; cracked windows; empty candy boxes on the floor, airborne for a few seconds and skittering down the aisle; folded newspapers left on some seats; profane words crayoned on a sign opposite Henry. He was being taken in by the rhythm, the rolling, the hypnotic commonness of the subway car and its decor, and soon he was in a trance, eyelids heavy, chin dropping against his chest, back to his hometown, back to his mother's living room.

At the end of Chapter 6 Henry is drafted, and is sent to Alaska (to fight in the so-called Alaskan War). This is the turning point in his life, and in the novel. Up to now, Henry has been pictured by Beckham as a man searching for meaning in his life, in his relationship with his wife, in his job, in the city in which he lives, in his futile attempt to be a baseball player. None of these give him full satisfaction. Then he meets Runner Mack in Alaska; he is "ripe for picking," and Runner Mack is the

man to do it. After seeing Mack fly a copter for the first time without panicking or without losing his cool, Henry declares "Runner Mack . . . You . . . are fantastic." And it will be that this fantastic Runner Mack who initiates Henry into the maturity of his years in the remaining pages of the novel. Henry sees Mack from the jump as "vibrant, forceful, hard to ignore." All his life Henry has been searching for someone, anyone, he could talk to and be comfortable with, and he finds that person in Mack: "And Mack. The Run. Runnington. There he was flying this chopper as if he had been doing it for years. Henry wanted to check out carefully this strange, fascinating Black man with his thundering, intense voice and eyes that were deep and flashing. The Run had been a lot of places and seen a lot of things, Henry could tell, and he was certain of himself, sure, positive, unhesitant—the way he walked." Mack tests Henry's belief in God ("What we need, Henry, is our own God. Somebody who looks like us and thinks like us and loves us more than any other people. Do Chinese have a white God? Hell, no. Do Mexicans? No way. Indians? Wake up, Henry, that's what I've been trying to get you to do since I met you.") Mack's questions and doubts lead Henry to doubt all he has been taught. In the pre-Runner Mack days Henry was typified as a person constantly concerned with how he was getting across, particularly to whites. Now, in the days after-Runner Mack, he comes to a new awareness: "Mack says we must overcome or die trying to overcome. He says to die for the revolution is nothing." This metamorphosis of Henry from rather typical "Negro" to all-out revolutionary, while obviously not undesirable, is a bit too obvious, and herein lies the major fault of the novel. Beckham has attempted to carefully lay the groundwork for the change by picturing Henry at the outset as a man on a search; this is fine, except that the pattern of change seems too neat and compact.

In addition to the emotional growth of Henry, the main point of the Alaskan War episode seems to be a satirization of the Vietnam War. Everything in Alaska seems a ridiculous perversion of what could happen in a real war: For example, Henry and Mack and the other soldiers are not fighting humans, but are fighting animals! "Nobody said the enemy was human. Nevins (John Wayne) just calls them ginks, sloop-eyes. Those eyes look a little slanted, too. Don't tell me the enemy is not human . . . all this time we've been fighting against . . ., no, that can't be. . . . 'It's a bear,' whispered Mack, 'a polar Bear.'"

The end of the novel speeds up fantastically. Henry finds himself part of a large revolutionary movement to bomb the White House; Henry and Mack steal a copter, escape from Alaska, and make their way across the country to meet up with their comrades, only to find that nearly everyone has deserted the cause. Runner Mack, the man who has been so strong and forceful, disintegrates and in despair, hangs himself. Thus, the prop of Henry's new life is torn away and he finds himself somewhat where he was at the beginning of the novel, again searching for meaning in his life; "There has to be an answer, he told himself. He couldn't give up, not after all this. It has to make sense, but only if we keep trying." Earlier in the novel, Henry was struck by a truck, but lived. Now, again searching for meaning, he is struck and presumably killed by another truck, as he runs away from Runner Mack and toward some meaning in his life. Seemingly, he never finds the answer that he has searched for so long.

By all means, read this novel. You will enjoy it, in spite of its obvious weakness—the second half of the novel. The language will captivate you, and that is certainly a large part of what writing is all about—enchantment (as well as enlightenment). (pp. 62-4)

> *Jim Walker, in a review of "Runner Mack,"*
> *in* Black Creation, *Vol. 4, No. 2, Winter,*
> *1973, pp. 62-4.*

Barry Beckham with Sanford Pinsker (interview date 1974)

[*In the following 1974 interview, Pinsker and Beckham discuss the creation of* Runner Mack.]

[Pinsker]: *I wonder if we might begin with the seemingly allegorical nature of* **Runner Mack.** *By that I mean the resonances of specific scenes in the novel will be mute enough not to be "symbolic" in a narrow sense of the word, but the novel itself appears to be a thinly veiled allegory for something else, something larger . . .*

[Beckham]: I think I see what you mean—that ***Runner Mack*** is the kind of story that represents another story.

More open-ended, in the sense that scenes in **Runner Mack** *will correspond to movements of American history. There's an eerie quality about the book which is always pushing toward such identifications, but resisting an easy one-to-one symbolism.*

Yes. What I'm about really is the identifications pushing themselves up. On one level the book is a kind of Ellison-like journey of the black man from the South to the North. But it is also about the black man's—in this case the protagonist, Henry Adams'—awareness of himself. The character of Runner Mack makes him understand what has happened to black people, symbolically, over the years.

Let me postpone talk about Ellison for a moment and ask, instead, about the significance of the name Henry Adams. Henry Adams's "education" in your novel is very different from The Education of Henry Adams, *but both of them brood about American history and its meaning. Was* **that** *Henry Adams consciously on your mind when you chose the name for your protagonist?*

Yes, it's not very complicated. The analogy of *The Education of Henry Adams* is purposefully suggested, as a kind of American critique. You are right, of course: Henry Adams was very concerned about the republic. And Henry Adams in ***Runner Mack*** eventually becomes concerned about the republic too, especially black people in the republic.

One of the things critics worry about is how ingenious they ought to get. An easy answer might simply be—as ingenious as they can. But that can—and does—lead to all manner of silliness. Granted, Henry Adams is a consciously chosen name. But I wonder, would it be fair, as you see it, to plod on from there, suggesting that Beatrice (particularly in the seduction scene) functions as the novel's "Virgin" and that the various machines comprise the "Dynamo." I am thinking here, of course, about the most anthologized chapter of Henry Adams' book, "The Dynamo and the Virgin."

That's interesting. As a matter of fact, a professor at Wyoming made much the same observation and I played it down. Naturally the notion of the dynamo is important, but when this particular professor went on and on about Adams' chapter and my book, I pretended I hadn't read it! I think what happens is this: these "influences" work on you unconsciously. More critics talked about the similarities between ***Runner Mack*** and Ralph Ellison's *Invisible Man* and again, I think the "influence" was unconscious. The trip North, for example, is less a matter of Ellison's novel than it is a fact of black history.

But what about, say, Henry Adams' initiation into the Home Company—his abortive interview, etc.—doesn't that suggest parallels with the Liberty Paint Company section of Invisible Man? *I say this knowing that all the comparisons with Ellison must strike you as very left-handed compliments.*

Exactly, because the writer begins to feel he has written his own book 100%. The critics are going to say ***Runner Mack*** is 70% Beckham and 30% Ellison, or something like that. So, in a **sense** comparisons with Ellison are a compliment, but not as much as I would like them to be. You really don't want to be seen as someone in Ellison's country.

Yes, of course, you want to be in **Beckham** *country. And, yet, for all resonance of style which struck Ellison-like bells in my head initially, yours is a very different book. That is, at a certain point there has to be a way of sustaining the atmosphere of fantasy I associate with, say, the "battle royal" section of* Invisible Man. *Naturalism stretches there into the grotesque. But your novel, it seems to me,* **begins** *in a surrealism, however much inherited it may be. Perhaps the best way of putting it might be this: the distance between one generation of writers and another forecloses the possibility of re-doing fictional experiments in advance. And, more importantly, the experiences of life itself are so vastly different. The odyssey from the South to the North, for example, is a historical fact as you suggested earlier, but it is one Ellison experienced firsthand.* **You** *haven't lived it as have Ralph Ellison or, perhaps more spectacularly, Richard Wright. Therefore, Richard Wright will give you an initiation story that seems very different from the initiations in* **Runner Mack.** *The violence of, say* Uncle

*Tom's Children or Eight Men would look suspicious in your fiction, unless it were viewed through the lens of fantasy. For Wright, this was the naturalistic way it **was.***

I think the differences you point out are important. And, as a matter of fact, I'm after just that kind of difference. First of all, I think my book—and this is not meant to demean Ellison's accomplishment—is more hinged upon the imagination. Very little of the material in **Runner Mack** is autobiographical.

*Exactly. Certainly one of the differences between your first novel—**My Main Mother**—and **Runner Mack** has to do with what I'll call veiled autobiography. I realize* **My Main Mother** *stands on its own fictional feet, but first novels tend to be heavily endowed with autobiographical things a writer wants to get off his chest. And I think that is the case with* **My Main Mother.** *The opening of your first novel—I'm thinking here of the scene in the tilting car—was really memorable. But I saw much more of that sort of thing running throughout* **Runner Mack.**

Yes, I was much more deliberate in **Runner Mack.** And, too, the experiences from which the novel was drawn are very different. After all, I don't know personally about coming up from the South as Ellison obviously does. I did not study at Tuskegee, as he did. All this will be reflected in the writing. If only **stylistically** there is a much stronger sense of fantasy in my book, as well as the macabre, the gothic, the just plain weird.

I was almost tempted into thinking about similarities between **Runner Mack** *and William Golding's* Pincher Martin. *By this I mean, between Henry Adams' first confrontation with the truck and his final one, all the plot events are really "dream." That may not be an accurate response for a reader to make, but so much of the bulk of this novel seems to be a waking dream—or perhaps nightmare would be the better word.*

Several reviewers suggested the same thing. I must say that this was not deliberate on my part, but it seems valid enough.

Perhaps we can talk about the comic mode of **Runner Mack** *for a moment.* **Those** *choices are deliberate in ways that comparisons with other novels never quite are. By that I mean the special brand of "mumbo jumbo" which distinguishes you from Ishmael Reed. He takes inherited themes, attitudes, techniques, etc. and turns them upside down, inventing new languages and new sensibilities.* Mumbo Jumbo *is a perfect name for his new book. But you do something very different* **technically.** *The caribou count, for example, during the Alaska war scenes of your novel are outrageous, just plain funny, and, yet, they also comment on, say, the situation in Vietnam and the whole saga of American imperialism. But because it is so grotesque, because of the transference from one mode to another, the result is the sort of comic allegory I mentioned when we began talking.*

Yes. As a matter of fact it's interesting that you mention Vietnam here because other people have made the same connection. My editor wrote a book jacket blurb in which he talks about **Runner Mack** as a satire of the Vietnam War. All that might be legitimate, but what I was after more specifically had to do with the American impulse to control the world. That is, the propensity to control every waste land and I chose Alaska because it seemed to be our last great waste land—one last "forest." The Vietnam War is contemporary, of course, and much on people's minds, but in **Runner Mack** I'm talking about war in general and the American habit of waging that war even against an imaginary enemy.

*Or one like the caribou. By this I mean, if **real** enemies don't exist, America will make them up. It all reminds me of that satiric scene in Conrad's* Heart of Darkness *when the French gun-boat lobs its tiny shells against a continent and people talk about "enemies." Once again that brings up the allegorical nature of* **Runner Mack** *and the way one is encouraged toward open-ended rather than narrowly symbolic reading. For example, besides the identifications with a historical Henry Adams, there is also the mythic resonance of American Innocence. After all, Adam is the hidden name of **every** American protagonist and, sometimes, it is every part of his actual name. Hemingway's favorite protagonist for initiation stories is Nick Adams; in* **Runner Mack,** *yours is Henry Adams.*

Again what happens is a kind of spooky creativity. First I chose the name. As a matter of fact, the names for my characters sort of come to me. Runnington Mack just appeared, so to speak; it sounded right. Later, names like Henry Adams and Runner Mack began to take on other resonances, but they were planned in the strict sense of the word. At a certain point I began to be aware of certain possibilities: Adams as the first man, the Biblical Adam; Henry Adams, historical figure from a family of Presidents; the fact that Henry Adams is also a fairly common name for black people, particularly in the South. Then, too, I began to play around with certain comic possibilities: Runner Mack and the famous truck firm we all know about.

Now might be a good time to return to that well-meaning professor from Wyoming and the network of correspondences between **Runner Mack** *and Henry Adams's "The Virgin and the Dynamo." If you had such a connection* **consciously** *in mind and worked it all out in a terribly careful way, I suspect the result would be as disastrous as it would be stilted. Which is to say, I guess, that critics always labor after the creative fact.*

Exactly. That's one of the difficulties with the novel as a form. With a poem like, say, Eliot's *The Waste Land,* you can get terribly excited about making correspondences and Eliot himself has even encouraged this with his "Notes." But it is rather unseemly for a novelist to put footnotes in the back. You know, something like "For Henry Adams, please read 'The Virgin and the Dynamo.'"

But doesn't another baseball novel which comes to mind—Bernard Malamud's The Natural—*pretty much* **do** *that? I don't mean with explicit footnotes, but with a carefully worked out set of analogues to Eliot's* The Waste Land?

That's right. But I don't think it is his most successful novel, although he seems to have worked harder there than in other of his novels.

In the case of your novel, beyond the metaphorical value of baseball as the Great American Game—that is, as a structure for the flashback episodes, etc.—why baseball?

Well, I guess the first reason is the one you already pointed out—namely, that baseball **is** the American game. The novel is about America as much as anything else, a critique of American society, its values. And on a less technical level, baseball because I was very interested in it as a kid and know it pretty well.

And, yet, it seems funny to me that at a point in history when baseball attendance is at an all-time low, the number of serious novels about baseball are on the increase.

That's true. But I just **loved** baseball as a kid. At that time there were maybe 300 players in the league and it really wasn't hard to know everybody's batting average, every pitcher's earned run average, etc. And, of course, I wanted to be a baseball player. It was just a fantastic game. And, as you say, I don't translate that tremendous interest in the novel **directly.**

I suspect the real point may be that the promises associated with baseball—The American Dream, etc.—keeps people like Henry Adams hoping. And the "hoping" is metaphorically connected with "running."

Yes.

There is one scene in particular which struck me as very similar both in technique and effect to Invisible Man—*and that is the electric baseball gambit connected with Henry's tryout for the Stars. I mean here the comparisons between the grabbing for the coins on the electric rug in Ellison's novel and the reaching for the electrified baseball in yours.*

I hadn't thought of that. The novel was outlined before I even began to write it because I got the contract on the basis of the outline. And I am sure there is a chapter synopsis entitled "Henry Adams Goes For Tryout." Very often I will envision a chapter before I write it, but I never jump ahead. Everything must be chronological—that is, I never write Chapter III before I have written Chapters I and II. So in my mind I knew—even before I wrote it—that the tryout had to have a certain form. It had to have an electric sun hovering overhead, the stadium had to be domed and the tryout itself had to be a failure. And most important of all, I was going to make it as funny as I could and yet kind of sad. All the time not even thinking—at least not consciously—of the correlations between this tryout and Ellison's battle

royal scene. But now that you point it out, it makes all the sense in the world.

Yes, that's more like how writers actually work when they have their own game plan in front of them. Let me take another tack here that will hopefully put the sticky business of "influence" aside. At the end of your novel Runner Mack *sours on the revolution and hangs himself, but Adams keeps right on hoping and running—presumably into the truck which looms as the major symbol note of the book. What's the difference between the notion of revolution which ends your book and the one in, say, John A. Williams's* The Man Who Cried I Am. *Am I correct in seeing yours as more comic in tone and, emphasis?*

I'm not sure, I **meant** for it to be serious. But, then again, it's "serious" in the context of the novel being rather funny. Because I think it is possible to see **everything** as comic. For example, the Alaskan war scenes are a biting satire of the American preoccupation to control the world. That's not **funny,** but in the novel I think we have to laugh in order to correct ourselves, so to speak. In **that** sense I meant for the revolution to be taken seriously. In fact, revolution is a serious event in both my novel and Williams's. What happens, of course, is that it becomes both funny and sad. When push comes to shove, niggers just don't show up. By that I mean, we sit around and make jokes about it—God, we can't do **anything** on time, etc.—but that laughter is just a coverup for pitiful sadness.

This might be a good place to broach the very difficult business of in-group humor and white readers. I wonder, are there grounds for the notion that widely varying interpretations of specific events in a novel can be made, depending on one's experience as a white or black man? In other words, am I missing the essential context in which blacks respond to the revolution which never quite comes off?

I don't know ... I remember being with John Williams on a radio interview recently and he remarked that **Runner Mack** was so absolutely true to form at the end because nobody showed up. That's exactly what happens. When the deal goes down there's no one there, although we've had all these plans and so much enthusiasm has been shown for the project. I don't know if that supports your idea that there are things in my novel which a white reader might miss, but **he** picked it up immediately. Still the facts bear me out—black people don't show up for revolutions—and those facts are available to everyone. What I am suggesting can be translated easily enough to revolutions **per se.** We plan and plan, but at a certain point, we always back down, get cold feet.

Some final thoughts about your protagonist, Henry Adams: how much are you making him a comic butt of his own ineptness and how much the pawn of larger forces which seem to work against him systematically?

Well, again, none of these considerations were conscious ones on my part. I gave him certain idiosyncrasies. For example, when he steps into the dog shit, he has a way of wanting to smell it, because he likes to smell things. But none of this has overtones, it seems to me.

I am willing to give you all the latitude you want where the creative process is concerned, all the "mysteries" as it were, but surely some of the scenes in **Runner Mack** *are very consciously—i.e. symbolically—drawn. The train ride, for example, with such characters as the veiled figure with white shoelaces in his black shoes.*

Yes, **that** scene is. The shoelaces are only meant to suggest a kind of spooky quality about this boy. I mean, who is he? Who walks around with these kind of shoes and laces? Therefore, he must be strange and different. It's an accentuation of the novel's comic structure. The train ride itself, of course, is a mythical representation of the Underground Railroad.

While we're on this particular scene, it struck me as Kafkaesque in tone and technique—the long, confusing hallways, etc.

I enjoyed writing it. It was a purposeful attempt to move into what I think of as my style, to capture more of the macabre. You're right ... I'm aiming at something very much like Kafka. An unnatural, gothic quality. Surrealism, I suppose, is the correct term.

But if I'm right at all, the novel itself is about Henry Adams' spiritual odyssey as a kind of symbolic allegory for the black man's experience in America.

O.K.

At that point, though, I'm left with the ambivalence of his response at the end of the novel. That is, he rejects Runnington Mack's despair and suicide...

Right—and, as a matter of fact, I think that's important. He can't be despaired. Hopefully, it's a kind of irony; here's Runner Mack who is very hip and intelligent...

The **usual** *pattern—at least in proletarian fiction—is that the guide figure educates the innocent one about the prevailing ideology and then when he later gets martyred in a strike, we end with the boy picking up the fallen mantle, continuing to fight the good fight. Your version changes things radically. In* **Runner Mack,** *it is the guide who despairs and commits suicide, but Adams, in effect, who changes place with him, becomes the "runner."*

Right ... That's interesting. I called the novel **Runner Mack** almost as a deliberate irony, a kind of trick. That is, I wanted to build up tension. The reader should begin wondering: "Who's Runner Mack?" And then I think that it's appropriate. After all, here's Henry Adams who never had much awareness of what's going on and suddenly realizing that he must continue the battle. It would be quite easy for him to say: "You know I met this crazy cat and he tried to get me involved in a revolution which didn't work out and now I'm going back home." But no! The point is he **can't** go back home. He's seen too much, become too aware.

But how does that work when juxtaposed against how the novel actually ends. Just at the moment when Henry Adams gains all this awareness, he gets hit by a truck.

Well, that's a kind of Kafkaesque expectation. Again, the instilling of the macabre. Stylistically I have to do that. I've **got** to have Henry Adams hit by that truck and somehow this has got to be explained thematically. Stylistically it creates that balance between beginning and end which I think is important. You know, the continual knocking down of the striver. But the question is do we continue to strive? The novel leaves that question—like the whole matter of Henry Adams' future (does he die this time or not?)—up to the reader. I think he is the final judge of these matters—after the writer and his critics have finished talking. (pp. 35-41)

> *Barry Beckham and Sanford Pinsker, in an interview in* Black Images, *Vol. 3, No. 3, Autumn, 1974, pp. 35-41.*

Joe Weixlmann (essay date 1981)

[*In the following excerpt, Weixlmann examines the concept of "daymare" in* Runner Mack.]

The 1973 National Book Award for Fiction produced what Eric Pace, writing in *The New York Times Book Review,* called "a curious case." After a protracted period of stock-taking and vote-shifting, the Award ended up being split between John Barth, for his novella sequence, *Chimera,* and John Williams, for his novel, *Augustus.* The Award deliberations were hard on ethnic writers; not a few experts had anticipated that Isaac Bashevis Singer's *Enemies, A Love Story* or Ishmael Reed's *Mumbo Jumbo* would come away with the prize. A second Black-authored novel, Barry Beckham's **Runner Mack,** received a 1973 NBA nomination, but the book was not generally acknowledged to be among the year's top contenders and virtually no scholarly attention has been paid to the novel since the first reviewers gave it richly deserved plaudits. The remarks that follow are intended to suggest the magnitude of this neglect and to bring **Runner Mack** into critical focus.

Beckham, in a 1978 essay entitled, **"Why It Is Right to Write,"** observed that "it is necessary to give black people works that they are not accustomed to, for we as black writers have not examined our culture thoroughly enough to know yet what we are not used to." **Runner Mack** is such a work: an innovatively constructed novel no reader, regardless of race, is likely to be blasé about. True, the book's biting, satiric tone and its no-holds-barred assault on the American Dream had been anticipated by Nathanael West's 1934 novel *A Cool Million; or, The Dismantling of Lemuel Pitkin,* and Ralph Ellison, in his 1952 masterpiece *Invisible Man,* had shown that the Black novelist could effectively blend surrealistic, expressionistic, and naturalistic scenes. But neither of those books sustains so evocative a dream-reality texture as does *Runner Mack,* nor end in such total despair, with the destruction of the innocent rather than the loss of innocence, the more common American theme.

Runner Mack opens with a literal nightmare: Water dripping from a leaky apartment ceiling onto the face of the book's protagonist, Henry Adams, leads him to imagine himself being forcibly restrained in the chair of the dentist who, medicine dropper in hand, releases "tear[s] of water" that "bore into his [patient's] forehead." Similarly, the novel ends with an event that can only be construed as nightmarish: Henry's potentially fatal confrontation with a "smiling" semi, a Mack truck. In between appear repeated daydream, nightmare, and, as Henry accurately calls them, "daymare" episodes. Then, too, during much of the time that Henry is in his apartment, a TV drones on in the background, weaving its often all-too-real unreality—couples feuding on *The Newlywed Game,* for example, and the Kent State shootings—with the complexities of Henry's real and imagined interpersonal experiences. By the book's end, even by its midpoint, the reader has learned to be continuously alert to the possibility of the unexpected, for the multiplicity and chaos that so concerned the turn-of-the-century American author after whom Beckham names his protagonist has accelerated furiously since the time of the education of the historical Henry Adams'.

While the narrative fabric of *Runner Mack* is deeply textured and complex, the book's structure is not. The plot, except for some flashback episodes, is linear and is developed in two sections, the first slightly longer than the last. The first section is based on an illusion, the American dream of success brought about by the migration experience. Just as Blacks left the post-Reconstruction South by the tens of thousands with the hope of finding a better way of life in northern, urban America, only to discover there just a different form of mistreatment and squalor, Henry and his young wife, Beatrice, find themselves trapped in a blighted northern city—until, that is, Henry goes to the ultimate frontier, Alaska.

In this first section, also, are satires of the great dreams of success in business and in sports. Henry has no business experience but he is pleased to be hired by the great Home Manufacturing Company while he is waiting for his big chance in baseball. Having come to the North from Mississippi because "he had a talent that could bring him a better life, fulfillment, freedom, a chance to live, exist; breathe cleanly, comfortably," Henry does not abandon the teachings of his father in "perseverance," nor his own brand of ethics. When he reads a note hand-delivered by a bratty kid from the adjacent apartment, he responds with patriotic fervor to the note's demands: "You have been drafted to help fight the war. We are waiting for you outside. Report immediately—right now." Popping out of bed to pack some clothes in a pillowcase, he tells the distraught, two-months-pregnant Beatrice: "'I have to fight for my country—it's our country. . . . How do you expect me to play ball for a team if they know I don't want to help keep this country safe?'"

Moments later, he is out the door and into a gray military transport, and as the book's second section opens, Henry is a member of the Armed Forces, fighting in a war in Alaska. It is there that he meets the tall, hip, Black man who will so alter his political consciousness: "'The name's Mack . . . . I'm also known as Runner Mack, Runnington Mack, Runner, and the Run'.'" Having never set eyes on the enemy but having taken part in the gunning-down of a herd of caribou and the clubbing-to-death of a herd of seals, Henry is wounded during an ambush of oxen and subsequently deserts with Mack, the two returning to the lower forty-eight to help effect a revolution. Mack, having enlisted Henry in the "movement," sets out with his companion to bomb the White House, but when only eight persons attend the would-be mass rally that is to proceed the bombing, Mack hangs himself. Henry, his idol dead, returns home but his wife, grown deaf from the city's incessant noise, is not waiting for his return. He bursts out of the apartment into the path of an oncoming truck.

The version of the American Dream on which Beckham focuses his ire in part one of *Runner Mack* is well-known in literature: It is the illusion which made Horatio Alger, Jr., a best-selling novelist, which in a patently corrupt form led to Jay Gatsby's death, and which Nathanael West savaged in *A Cool Million.* Home Manufacturing Company, "a giant flag" waving from its highest tower, purports to be a realm of freedom-and-justice-for-all: "'Plenty of opportunities for our employees,'" one of the firm's three indistinguishable, pipe-smoking executives—A. L. Klein, B. J. Kind, and M. O. Baby—tells Henry. "'You can go straight to the top' [he says] . . . . The other two shook their heads stiffly." Yet, as Phyllis R. Klotman, the only previous critic to subject the book to close analysis, maintains, Henry's job interview is at once an attack on "equal opportunity" hiring and a parodic invocation of an earlier American method of adding to one's work force—the slave auction [see Further Reading]. Henry, in addition to being grilled about subjects ranging from his religious beliefs to his honesty, is, very literally, examined from tooth to penis.

The plant itself is gray, crowded, uncomfortably warm, noisy, dirty, and—at least insofar as the workers know—pointless. Henry, whose job it is to assemble spring-lock washers, check rubber rollers for smoothness of operation, and test tumbler pins in tubular mortise locks, eventually demands that Boye, a plant supervisor for thirty years, provide him with some knowledge of what the company manufactures—only to learn that Boye has no idea: "'I don't know the answers, Henry. I don't really know *what* we're doing. Or what it means. Or what I'm doing and if that means anything. I'm supervising. And I get paid for it.'"

The reader's antipathy toward Home Manufacturing amplifies with the introduction of the firm's president, Newberry Clay, since he epitomizes effeteness. Much as the literally and figuratively blind Reverend Homer A. Barbee speaks to an assembly of college students about endurance-based black success in Chapter 5 of *Invisible Man,* Clay, a cripple incapable of audible speech, meets with Home's employees to transmit—via the company's personnel manager—pat phrases designed to boost the worker's morale: *"When I started this company . . . dedicated employees . . . quality and control . . . Home is your home"* (ellipses Beckham's). Predictably the workers are not moved. But Clay's visit clarifies the full ironic impact of Beckham's having Henry work in Home's Identification and Recovery department. While one may quickly deduce that the employees, who labor behind crowded-together, identical, numbered desks, are being robbed of their identity, the word "Recovery" has little meaning until Clay prepares to present awards to the firm's most dedicated workers. Lucy Taylor, who "'reported on time three hundred and nineteen days consecutively, and was only four seconds late on the three hundred and twentieth day,'" is in the infirmary, as is Herman Anders, the other awardee. Apparently Home is where the malaise is.

Beckham's most biting assault on the American Dream of success occurs, however, as he describes Henry's tryout with the Stars baseball team. Star Stadium *is* America, and to become a Star is to be admitted into the American mainstream. This is a prize Henry cannot overlook, despite the fact that his father-in-law has questioned Henry's chances of making the team long before Henry and Beatrice have moved north: "'You actually sitting there on *my* porch taking up *my* time trying to tell *me* somebody's going to pay you to mess around with a baseball—a white baseball at that? . . . Don't make no difference no more how good you are, . . . you still black.'" There is, however, no stopping a wide-eyed optimist: "Henry never felt completely discouraged or rebellious. . . . He accepted, agreed, consented, complied, with the understanding that these disappointments and inconveniences were only temporary—were trials actually to test his mettle. . . . So one day, if he did right and acted right, as his father would say, he was positive of success."

Star Stadium, in sharp contrast to the city that surrounds it, is clean, quiet, temperate; and from its "clear, plastic-covered dome" and "gigantic" American flag to its "luminescent white" chalk lines and "red-white-and-blue chairs," it beckons to Henry. How, the protagonist wonders, could he be maltreated in such a place? "His father had insisted and insisted and insisted, that baseball was *the* American . . . he'd get a fair shake. He *had* to" (Beckham's ellipsis). But, of course, Henry does not *have* to, for the white players and officials lack his all-American belief in fair play, as Beckham dramatizes with this stingingly hyperbolic metaphor: "The national anthem blared over the stadium while Henry held his cap at his heart and the others sat on the grass, yawned, picked up and threw pebbles." Although Henry had hit

.415 in his last minor-league season, collecting sixty-three home runs in the process, and although he demonstrates almost superhuman athletic ability during his tryout, he never has a chance here.

In the tryout, Stumpy, the Stars' manager, does everything he can to make Henry look bad. Henry times the pitching machine's 150 m.p.h., throws perfectly, hitting repeated home runs and tagging one ball so hard that it cracks the dome. He catches a fly ball despite the fact that Stumpy lowers an artificial sun from the top of the dome almost into Henry's face—a trick the manager no doubt has used more than once on the Stars' opposition during league play in this most "American" of games. And the account of Henry's ability to shag a would-be home-run ball must be read in detail to be fully appreciated:

> The ball was still very high and coming down. His back was against the wall. He knew if he leaped he would still be four or five feet too short, so he began furiously to scale the wall, sticking his cleats into the wood—his glove had been thrown away for the climb—and fingernails grabbing into the tiny cracks. He would slip a foot and grab again, slip, grab some more, until he had reached the top of the wall and could climb over it, climb over the metal railing. Now he saw the ball sailing downward. There was one possibility, he thought, and balanced himself on the railing, jumped into the air toward the arc of the ball's flight, and cap in hand, stabbed at the ball. He felt it break into the cap as he plummeted down toward the grass. Dazed for an instant from the fall, he got up, raised the cap in his hand to indicate that he had caught it. Stumpy waved back.

Having asked Henry to exceed human limits, and seen the protagonist do so unerringly, Stumpy ends the tryout with a cruel joke: The pitching machine sends Henry an electrically-charged line drive. This is the way in which Beckham explains the result: "Pain sizzling through his hand and wrist, moving up to his forearm. Stumpy and the other players bending over with laughter. . . . They are still laughing, now lying on the grass, and Stumpy was jumping up and down and spinning around and shaking his stubby arms, and Henry was standing there looking at them, *wondering if he had made the team*" (italic added). Beatrice tries to make it clear to him that he has not, that the Stars have been "'just playing'" with him. But it is not until several months later, in Alaska, that Mack convinces Henry that he has been duped: "'Well, hell, my man. You'd better wake up. . . . *those* muthafuckahs are really out of their minds. How come you went for their shit for so long? What's the matter with you, Adams, don't you use your head?'"

Beckham's comment about Henry's tryout in a 1974 interview, that he had tried to make the scene "as funny as . . . [he] could and yet kind of sad," recalls critic Darwin T. Turner's recent remarks on the "blues tone" which he feels pervades Black American literature. Turner calls attention to the Afro-American writer's "unusual mixture of humor and pathos" and observes that he does not find such a mixture in most white-authored American literary works. Indeed it is this exact form of "Black Humor" which characterizes *Runner Mack* and which, according to Beckham, ultimately serves a moral function in the novel: "the Alaskan scenes are a biting satire of the American preoccupation to control the world. That's not *funny,* but in the novel I think we have to laugh in order to correct ourselves, so to speak." The book's comic element, in other words, is *not* designed to ease the reader's conscience. On the contrary, it compels us to redefine our attitudes about American society.

Henry's early days in Alaska are uncomfortable: The bitterly cold temperatures and the absurdity of slaughtering animals in lieu of fighting the enemy distress him. Yet he continues to regard military service as a duty, "a tradition, his father had called it, and this country—look what it did for us." The point is, of course, that neither his father's fighting in World War I nor his relatives' service in the Civil War improved, in any significant way, the fate of America's black populace; this is precisely the lesson that Runner Mack has to teach Henry.

Runner Mack's first task is to persuade Henry that he should ignore the pseudo-gutsy, patriotic mumbo jumbo of their commanding officer, Captain Nevins, whose penchant for cant relates him to the glib president of Home Manufacturing, Newberry Clay:

> "Gentlemen, we don't have time to train you. We're here to fight. . . . Gentlemen, our mission is to destroy these ginks, these sloop-eyes, or the next thing you know they'll be in our fuckeen backyards. Now, gentlemen, do you want that for your wives and children? . . . I know hundreds who would give their right ball to be in the situation we're in. We're where the action is, gentlemen, and this is a *beaucoup* assignment. You have the opportunity to make your wives and children proud, very proud of you, gentlemen, remember that, please. . . . Now, gentlemen, you are about to be processed. Print, don't write, in the space allotted, then hand in your cards as soon as you can. After that, gentlemen, you will write a card to your old lady and tell her you are very happy up here and having a nice time and so forth. That's all, gentlemen, carry on."

Mack tells Henry that it is one thing to be stuck in Alaska, but under no circumstances will Runner Mack fight "'for that John Wayne muthafuckah. The muthafuckah's sick just like the rest of the country. Out of his mind . . . .'" Though Henry is drawn to Runner Mack's hip, street-wise demeanor from the outset, it takes him a

Dust jacket of Beckham's most successful novel.

while to accustom himself to Mack's choice of words. "Why must he use such language?" Henry ruminates. "I could never take him down home. He'd be cursing in front of everybody. Reverend would usher us both to hell."

Eventually, however, the substance of the words begins to take precedence over their form, and this leads, almost simultaneously, to Henry's rejection of blind patriotism, his dismissal of the platitudinous ways of his parents and their community, and his acceptance of Mack as his mentor. Henry's most compelling desire appears always to have been order, some seemingly rational set of beliefs by which his actions could be rendered meaningful: "That's all I want," he reflected after the tryout with the Stars, "just for things to mean something, to make sense." In Mississippi, his parents' advice provided Henry Adams with that sense of wholeness, and he continued to apply his father's expressed belief in the fairness of American democracy in the North despite his mistreatment at Home Manufacturing and at Star Stadium, and in spite of the lunatic activities of the Army in Alaska. But under Mack's tutelage, Henry *assumes* (rather than *develops*) a new set of values: "Beautiful things!" muses Henry, thinking of the caribou. "Why do we have to kill them? Now that was a rhetorical question. Because . . . [the officers are] mad, gone insane, unable to function with reason. Mack, you are fantastic! . . . Mack, where have you been all my life?"

The reborn Henry declares that he's "been asleep" all his days and, self-aggrandizingly, pronounces himself "a slumbering giant." But a cognitive giant, the reader must understand, Henry is not. Whereas Mack "knew about things—theories, doctrines, points of view," Henry's forte is smells: "A peculiar oddity, he knew, to be concerned with smells, odors, whiffs; and even stranger that this eccentricity should extend to offal. He always had to smell things." Henry, though he desires to think acutely, responds more reliably to sensation. He is principally a reactor rather than an actor. He is a follower, not too unlike Eric Hoffer's "true believer," whereas Mack is "an organizer."

What Mack believes in, and schools his pupil Henry in, is the aesthetics of Blackness. Mack rejects the timid, pallid God of Christianity; the white-controlled, mind-dulling television industry; and that form of grinning, demeaning black servitude which Henry's parents have inculcated in him. And Mack will have nothing to do with white women, preferring beautiful, sustaining black females. So alluring are these aspects of Mack's character, especially in the light of the Black Liberation Movement of the 1960s, that those commenting on the book have failed to take Runner's shortcomings sufficiently into account.

Mack, like Henry, is attempting to live out a dream—and a politically confused one at that—a militant Black nationalist dream that is to be carried out through a biracial conspiracy. Here's the way in which Mack runs it down:

> "All right, dig. We're going to bomb the White House. After that we'll take over. *Simple as that.* . . . It's all mapped out. . . . Look, I got muthafuckahs all over the country layin' for the signal. This is it, Adams. Black dudes and white dudes. We can't do anything without the paddies, they got the bread and resources. After we take over, then we can start getting our own black thing together. But we can do nothing the way the country is now, right?" (italics added)

It is a mad scheme, borne of desperation, and its ultimate failure is hinted at in Mack's next long speech:

> "You have to wake up, Henry, and understand where you been and where you must go. You must go with me. Scope yourself, Henry; scope your history and understand why you went through all that shit you told me about. Don't be like your father. Be a new black man. Wake up. Act. Go down with me, Henry Adams."

The last line is the telling one. Mack is asking Henry to join with him in the revolution, to be "'with him'" when the bombing "'go[es] down.'" But embedded in the phrase is a second, more sinister meaning: that the conspiracy will bring about Mack's demise and, possibly, Henry's.

"Perhaps," Phyllis Klotman reasons, "Beckham is saying that black men need something more than plans that are doomed to failure"; and she adds that "Henry does not make that discovery. Indeed he does not, for unlike Ellison's Invisible Man, who develops the ability to think for himself, Henry Adams never gains his psychic independence, even though he assumes at various times that he has done so. And Mack, for all his supposed genius, deludes himself—and others—by proposing a "'simple'" solution to an extraordinarily complex dilemma. That Henry should be wary of Runner is implied very early in the novel, when the protagonist, dashing to his interview at Home Manufacturing, slips on the ice and falls, injuriously, into the path of what is twice identified as a "*Mack* truck" (italics added), the same type of vehicle which is about to strike the protagonist at the book's end. . . . To me, Beckham is saying, specifically, that the revolutionary dreams of Black militants are no more likely to achieve fruition than were the more modest dreams of those who came north during the Great Migration or than is the American Dream of success in general.

Although Beckham claims that he set his war in Alaska "because it seemed to be our last great waste land—one last 'forest,'" it is probable that Norman Mailer's 1967 novel *Why Are We in Vietnam?* provided *some* impetus for Beckham's choice. By avoiding any direct linkage between his war and the Vietnam conflict, Beckham is able to attack, as he put it, "war in general and the American habit of waging war against an imaginary enemy." To accept Mack's naive solution to America's military idiocy, however, is to embrace the irrational.

Similarly, if we defer to Mack's final, pre-suicide pronouncement, "'History keeps going and we keep trying and nothing happens and somebody else says, "I'll do it," and they try and nothing really changes. There are no answers, Henry,'" then we too will cop out and help fulfill Runner's defeatist prophecy. We can be assured that Beckham does not feel that the situation is hopeless, for writing novels can scarcely be considered an act of self-annihilation.

At the close of *Invisible Man,* Ralph Ellison's protagonist is readying to end his "hibernation," to come above ground in the hope of assuming a "socially responsible" role. The reader of that novel is drawn into the fray, verbally, in the book's very last line: "Who knows but that, on the lower frequencies, I speak for you?" Henry Adams, on the other hand, faces possible extinction at the end of *Runner Mack.* But due partly to the distancing effect of Beckham's humor and partly to the self-consciousness of his narration—"'We might be characters in a book or something, for all I know,'" Mack quips to Henry—, the novelist prevents his protagonist's fate from becoming the reader's primary concern. Instead, the book projects us, situationally, into the vacuum created by Henry's death, whether as a victim of the approaching truck or as a character in a book which has no more printed pages. As a result, the reader of *Runner Mack* is left, alone, to contemplate what he or she might do to ameliorate the deplorable condition of current-day America. Beckham is not so presumptuous as to propose *the* answer, nor is he so simple-minded as to believe that a single correct answer exists. But, in *Runner Mack,* he is forceful not only in framing significant questions but also in dramatizing some of the would-be avenues of resolution which, at least presently, seem to be closed. Beckham's richly evocative novel, like the issues which it so candidly confronts, merits our consideration. (pp. 93-102)

> *Joe Weixlmann, "The Dream Turned 'Daymare': Barry Beckham's 'Runner Mack',"* in MELUS, *Vol. 8, No. 4, Winter, 1981, pp. 93-103.*

Wiley Lee Umphlett (essay date 1987)

[*In the following essay, Umphlett examines* Runner Mack *as "the first full-length portrait of the black athlete in American fiction."*]

Barry Beckham's *Runner Mack,* which was first published by Morrow in 1972, is the first American novel by a black writer to draw on organized sports experience as a means of ordering fictional meaning and purpose. As such, this work presents us with the first full-length portrait of the black athlete in American fiction. In another place [*The Sporting Myth and the American Experience* (1975)], I have discussed in some detail the literary characteristics and cultural significance of the athletic figure in American fiction; and, as we shall see, the baseball protagonist of *Runner Mack,* like all major fictional characters molded after the athletic archetype,

also conforms to the mythical pattern of the sporting hero. Accordingly, this character's literary function is controlled by an intimate relationship with sporting experience in order to suggest the ramifications of a larger, more complex issue or problem—in this case, the plight of the black man in search of a positive identity in modern America.

Because of the dominant role blacks have played in American sports since the 1960s, one might wonder why sports as a fictional setting for a black protagonist have been almost totally ignored by our black writers. When *Runner Mack* was published in 1972, it had been some 25 years since Jackie Robinson broke the color line in major-league baseball, and by this time black athletes had made their mark in all our major sports, both amateur and professional. By this time, too, reputable novelists such as Mark Harris, Bernard Malamud, Philip Roth, and Robert Coover, writing in the increasingly popular mode of baseball fiction, had produced works of favorable critical reception. Why then had black writers failed to recognize a rich literary source in not just baseball but all American sports experience?

Part of the answer may lie in the nature of the modern sports fiction tradition itself that, according to Michael Oriard [in *Dreaming of Heroes: American Sports Fiction, 1868-1980* (1982)], was established in the late nineteenth century by writers of popular and juvenile sports fiction. These were the writers, Oriard contends, who originated the sports fiction conventions "within which and against which serious authors write." Since the inception of these conventions, though, it would appear that a significant reason why black authors have been disinclined to write "within" them is simply that such writing did not allow for black athletic models drawn after the multitude of fantasized heroes in the lineage of "Frank Merriwell's Sons," to use Oriard's apt phrase.

Popular sports fiction dating from 1890s was produced primarily for an aspiring middle-class, all-white male audience conditioned to the philosophy of success that American capitalism preached. Thus, the Waspish sports hero of that day's popular fiction grew out of a general understanding that school/college-life experiences, particularly athletics, were designed mainly to prepare a young man "for the trials of a driving, materialistic American business society and world leadership" [Christian K. Messenger, *Sport and the Spirit of Play in American Fiction: Hawthorne to Faulkner* (1981)]. Unfortunately, for most black youths growing up during the heyday of the school sport hero's fictional popularity (ca. 1900-1940), the concept of making the team in organized athletics was about as remote an experience as were their chances of becoming an integral part of "American business society and world leadership." As a result, the conventional themes of our modern sports fiction tradition appear to have had little or no influence on black writers, whose overall literary intent has expressed itself in a naturalistic way in order to dramatize the frustration and anger of embittered blacks struggling to "make the team" in a racist milieu.

In such a light, then, it is little wonder that the Afro-American athlete as a significant character portrayed "within" the conventions of American sports fiction is practically nonexistent. Nevertheless, one can't help wondering why black writers, in also electing not to write "against" the conventions of the sports fiction tradition, have seemingly ignored a ripe opportunity to portray athletic characters representative of the black cause.

To date, *Runner Mack* is the single most outstanding example in this vein because of the way in which its author has inverted the conventional sports fiction theme of "making the team" in order to compel the reader to examine the harsh facts of the black condition in America. In the larger context of establishing a critical posture on the wide distance between dream and fact in American life, Barry Beckham has taken an ironically negative approach to our most traditionally revered sport in order to set it up as a microcosm of the system at large.

George Grella, in discussing our National Game's impact on American culture, has observed: "In its theory and practice, baseball embodies some of the central preoccupations of that cultural fantasy we like to think of as the American Dream." As such, he contends that "this most American of sports speaks as few other human activities can to our country's sense of itself." He goes on to remind us that to be a success at playing the game of baseball, a player must possess certain highly individualistic skills. If baseball is representative of the Dream, then, the implication is that those who are competent enough to participate in the game will be afforded the opportunity to contribute their special skills and, if successful, realize the personal rewards of the Dream, just as we all have come to look upon the larger system to offer us an open opportunity to get ahead in life. Grella's positive analysis, of course, is structured around his unique understanding of baseball's traditional, time-honored, even mythic, aspects. On the other hand, Beckham's ironic portrayal of a baseball player who possesses all of the specialized skills one needs to be successful at the game, yet is denied the opportunity to realize himself as a team player, is central to this novel's underlying intent. In fact, in *Runner Mack,* Beckham has produced a dramatic situation sufficiently negative to characterize the American Dream in black consciousness as a prolonged nightmare from which one never seems to awaken.

On a basic narrative level, *Runner Mack* tells the story of Henry Adams, an ingenuous southern black who is seeking a career in major-league baseball but who, for reasons beyond his control, is ultimately frustrated in achieving his goal. On a deeper level, *Runner Mack* is the story of Henry's painful journey from innocence to self-knowledge; from the Horatio Alger-like mindset of striving to be a part of the system and then, after being denied entry, to the radical posture of rebelling against what it is supposed to stand for. At times, his story even borders on the comic, but its overall ominous aura keeps

reminding us of an underlying serious intent. Throughout, too, baseball remains central to Henry's literary significance, because there are numerous references to the sport that enhance his dual function as fictional athlete and representative Afro-American, as both potential participant in the system at large (symbolized by the game of baseball) and ultimate rebel against the larger system.

Structurally, *Runner Mack* is divided into two major sections—the first dominated by urban experience; the second, by that of the military. Within this framework, a surrealistic atmosphere is generated that leaves the reader with an overpowering impression of the nightmarish side of the black condition in America. For example, in the opening section, it is Beckham's dream-like description of urban imagery that predominates and helps paint a vivid picture of Henry Adams' entrapment within his alien environment. Having come north to an unnamed city with his new wife, Henry rents an apartment to await a baseball tryout that, for some unaccountable reason, never seems to materialize. In the meantime, he is compelled to take a series of odd jobs, each of which presents him with a new round of humiliations. Consequently, we learn that fourteen months of urban life have had the effect of turning Henry into "a lost Southern nomad, bewildered in the big city." And as he leaves his apartment for yet another job interview, some of the reasons for his present state of mind are described:

> The streets were always crowded like this; always presented to Henry some unfathomable obstacle that had to be entered into with great reluctance. He couldn't see too far ahead. Now he was walking almost sideways having been jostled. Nor could he see behind him. He knew only that he was part of the mass of charging mass.

In addition to the crowded streets is the noise of the city:

> the ear-stunning, bellowing pandemonium of car horns; the artillery-like barrage of machines banging and echoing, banging and echoing, as if nearby some steel buildings were being dropped and hoisted, bounced continuously from a derrick: as if the city were being bombarded by drumfire.

Even the city's offensive odors add to the oppressive atmosphere, but

> the bleak grayness of the sky bothered him the most. It was cool and somber as if something had died in the air and melted, then spread, distilled itself molecularly throughout the atmosphere. No trace of sunshine. To breathe freely as he had in Mississippi was to punish his lungs.

The irrepressible street crowds, assaulting noises, and noxious odors are recurrent motifs in all the novel's city scenes, and along with the persistently gray color of the atmosphere conspire to present an alienated, desperately bleak picture of Henry's present situation. His inability to cope with this condition is brought out most graphically when, prior to arriving for his job interview, he is struck down by a truck, an incident that, in its own bizarre way, reinforces the city as an ominous symbol of depersonalized forces in this novel. Only through the athlete's self-will and perseverance does Henry recover sufficiently to hobble on to his appointment.

The Home Manufacturing Company, where he is seeking employment, comes across as no less a picture of human alienation than the city itself. After an inquisitionlike interview conducted by imperious company bureaucrats, Henry finds himself hired and directed to his office, an area "almost as large as a baseball field." But here there are

> nothing but desks—gray steel desks with men and women bent over them, green visors sticking from the tops of their foreheads. . . . And the odor was of machines—an oily, greasy, ironlike smell. . . .

Like all authority figures in **Runner Mack,** Henry's officious supervisor, who has been with the Company for some forty years, is portrayed as a grotesque character wrapped up in his own private obsessions. And even though the supervisor cunningly attempts to win his new employee's confidence, Henry instinctively realizes that this absurd figure of a man is yet another devious, enigmatic denizen of the city with whom he will never be able to establish a meaningful rapport.

Henry's failure to communicate meaningfully with hardly anyone he encounters affords Beckham still another means of dwelling on the socio-political plight of the black man in America, in particular his isolation within the mainstream of society. Paradoxically, though, the most significant person in Henry's life with whom he suffers a communication problem is his wife, Beatrice. She keeps reminding her husband that she'd like to know more about him, but whenever they make any attempt to relate to each other, interruptions inevitably occur:

> When they took walks, the streets were always too crowded for them to move together, and they could rarely hear each other's comments because of the auditory bombardment of machines, cars, subways, boats, screams, barks. The apartment wouldn't have heat and they would be too irritated to talk about anything. The neighbors—above them or to the side—would bang against the walls or play music loudly, anything not encouraging for a quiet talk.

Even their moments of sexual intimacy result mainly in frustration, and Henry is tempted to initiate trysts with women he randomly encounters, rationalizing his lustful fantasizing by convincing himself that a man "needs some adventure now and then." Such an impersonal attitude, which categorizes women as mere sexual objects, recalls on one level the fictional athlete's inherent inability to relate to the opposite sex in a meaningful, social way and on another, his father's earlier criticism of all self-centered black men who mistreat their women: "When you black men goin' to learn to take care of your own women? Why must you keep runnin', leavin' good, honest, decent black wives sufferin' for you?"

Beatrice, who stands directly in the literary tradition of the strongwilled, long-suffering black woman, professes to Henry that she'd like to write them both a poem that would provide a way out of their predicament. It would be about a "clearing" into which they could run:

> We could go into the poem, into the clearing and get away from here. We could get to know each other. We could be free. We need a clearing, Henry. We have to get out of here because there's no sun or trees, no peace or love.

Despite Henry's ironic misunderstanding of Beatrice's attempt to reach him on even this symbolic level, he intuitively recognizes in her concept of a special place something essential to his makeup as an athletic figure. Henry's reaction is, in fact, one common to the behavior of the sporting hero in American fiction when he is moved to ask himself why it is they couldn't return to such a place that "used to be":

> There definitely was one because he felt it. Maybe that was the clearing she meant. In his bones, in his memory, in a deep well of his mind, he felt that there was a place they had been lifted out of. Yes, a place . . . where there were no divisions, no interruptions, no maddening influences. No. None of that. A closeness. Peace. Trees and sun. . . .

Here, of course, Henry is identifying with the "great, good place" of the American sporting myth—that special place in idyllic nature where the fictional athlete has his natural roots and is at one with the world around him. It is a literary sensitivity that can be traced back to the primordial experience of our archetypal sportsman, Natty Bumppo, in James Fenimore Cooper's Leatherstocking Tales. In these works, the frontier or wilderness, with its special challenges to the individual, markedly contrasts with the dehumanizing demands of encroaching civilization and persists for Natty as "the great, good place, or inviolable retreat, that which becomes for the modern sportsman the sanctified areas of the hunt, the game, or the contest" (Umphlett, *Sporting Myth*). Henry Adams himself relates directly to this state of being when, after finally receiving an invitation to try out for the Stars baseball club, he arrives at the stadium and finds himself rapturously contemplating the team's baseball diamond:

> The entire field was bright from the sun, and Henry was struck motionless by the impact of its beauty. The field looked like one of those color photographs he had seen in the magazines. But never, never had he imagined that it could be this way, with its blue-green grass which was perfectly separated, trimmed away from the running paths.

Later, the field is described as a place where the "grass stays green forever" and also as a kind of retreat isolated from the city's "noise, crowded streets, red pollution, dirt, and garbage." Beckham's treatment of both the baseball diamond as a sanctified area and his protagonist's natural affinity for it represents the one time in the novel when Henry Adams comes closest to recovering the lost harmony of the sporting hero's natural heritage—his special "clearing," as it were.

Within the literary conventions of the sporting myth, then, baseball is the most appropriate game for Beckham to dramatize Henry Adams' unique condition because it is the one American sport that suggests "a pastoral vision of peace and harmony, feeds both our memories and dreams, our sense of the past and our awareness of the future" (Grella). Accordingly, this characteristic assessment of the sport reveals the presence of a growing conflict in Henry's being: whether to become an active participant in the system (as baseball represents it) and, hopefully, assure his own future, or simply to assume a role of passive resignation in the scheme of things, as his father had done all his life. This dilemma, which expresses itself mainly through the dramatic contrast between Henry's wretched situation in the city and his nostalgic affection for his Mississippi past, finds its literary basis in Michael Oriard's observation that "baseball in literature produces most often either a nostalgic remembrance of the past or a representative of the American innocent confronting complex reality . . . ." What we finally recognize in the character of Henry Adams is a composite of these two opposing states, the same dialectical makeup we discern in other significant baseball characters in our literature. So to the list of memorable figures such as Jack Keefe, Roy Hobbs, and Bruce Pearson, who are all products of the conflict between "nostalgic remembrance" and "complex reality," we can add the name of Henry Adams. Like them, Henry grows to realize that the primal innocence of his past is something he can never hope to recover. The closest he can ever come to this state is through direct identification with sporting experience. Ironically, though, the game of baseball as Henry's surrogate special place fails to provide him with the opportunity to realize himself in the way his sporting instincts would have him do.

The main reason for his breakdown is that in *Runner Mack* baseball is as much an unfathomable system as the society that has created it. During his tryout with the Stars, for example, the duplicity of those in control is represented through Henry's confrontation with the Stars' manager, a bowlegged midget named Stumpy, whose name and physical appearance personify his deceptive methods. Characteristically, he sets up an impossible series of tests in hitting and fielding for Henry, and although the eager candidate puts on an amazing display of athletic ability in heroically passing each test, the manager remains unimpressed with his efforts. As a result, Henry Adams fails as a baseball player because no one in the system will admit to how good a player he really is. By denying a highly qualified athlete the opportunity to play, then, the system of baseball condemns Henry Adams, by extension, to be an outsider within the larger system. In spite of whatever superior abilities he has to offer the system, Beckham implies, the black man in America is fated to perform on a particular level of expectations, a condition David Halberstam has categorized as the "myth of black incapability," and one which extends, of course, to areas of experience other than to just the American sports scene. In *Runner Mack,* then, a significant factor con-

tributing to the effectiveness of Barry Beckham's literary method lies in the special attitude he has fomented toward an established American sport, an attitude whose very ambivalence helps raise the larger questions that spring from the one basic question of why the "myth of black incapability" should actually exist in our society.

In the characteristic manner of the fictional athlete, though, Henry continues to profess feelings of self-esteem, even after five weeks of waiting to be called by the Stars. Thus, when Beatrice criticizes his attitude of stoic acceptance, he retorts: "look, this is the American pastime, they've got to be fair to me. . . . They have to judge me on my ability only. That's all." And even when Henry does admit to doubts about his future, he stubbornly clings to his personal dream of making the team by countering the questioning attitude of his company supervisor as follows: "All I want to do is play baseball. That's all I want to do in my life—play ball." In other words, Henry Adams is confident enough that he has a great deal to offer the system if ever given the opportunity, yet naive enough to believe that his day of opportunity will surely come. Ultimately, though, it is the nagging thought of an abortive future with a company like Home Manufacturing and a life as dead-ended as his supervisor's that undermines his idealistic outlook and causes him to ponder what would become of himself if somehow the Stars never did bother to call. And although it had been his father who originally encouraged him to pursue a baseball career, he begins to wonder, if he were to fail, how he would be able to assume "his father's ubiquitous tranquil temperament in the face of all discord"—which amounts essentially to the black man's conditioned response of passive resignation that Henry had found naturally abhorrent.

Upon being drafted into the army, Henry's burst of patriotism reveals both his distaste for passivity and his persistent desire to be a part of the system. When his wife insists that he not report for duty, he replies:

> I have to fight for my country—it's our country. We live in it. How do you expect me to play ball for a team if they know I didn't want to help keep this country safe? I'm a man.

However, in this part of the novel centering around Henry's military experiences, his basically conservative stance undergoes a dramatic change, one which, in fact, results in the loss of his naturally innocent state.

The main catalyst for this transformation is a black soldier whom Henry meets at his post in Alaska. Known variously as Runnington Mack, Runner, or the Run, Mack not only exists as a refreshing oasis in the desert of military authoritarianism, but he also functions as Henry's alter ego, the kind of person Henry would like to be if he only knew how: "The Run had been a lot of places and seen a lot of things, Henry could tell, and he was certain of himself, sure, positive, unhesitant. . . ." In short, the worldly-wise Mack is everything that Henry is not.

So with the advent of Runner Mack, self-styled revolutionary, whose athletic-sounding name seems to epitomize action itself, Henry's real education in discovering who he is in relationship to the larger system begins. A major step in this process occurs when Mack tells Henry that he will never amount to anything until he realizes himself as "the new black man," that is, as an individual who is neither a lackey to the system, as a baseball player is, nor a submissive person like his father: "You have to wake up, Henry, and understand where you been and where you must go." In taking this advice to heart, Henry soon grows in the understanding that

> Mack had changed his life, opened his eyes, brought him around to *thinking,* and although he didn't believe everything, he was positive that there was a shared destiny of some sort between them.

Henry's special understanding of what this "shared destiny" might be is more clearly defined in his mind after Mack points out a contradiction between societal values and "the reality of what he saw every day, which was an absence of those values." Henry finds Mack's observation particularly true of organized Christianity, whose institutionalized values his conservative father had always held so dear. Because his father had never really questioned the existing order, Henry now concludes that his father's "way won't work anymore." In finally turning his back on that part of the past his father represents, then, he acknowledges his "shared destiny" with Mack as one that demands active participation in his companion's proposal to desert the army, overthrow the government, and ultimately set up the ideal black society.

Although Mack advocates violent revolution, a course of action antithetical to the sporting hero's basic nature, Henry does eventually cast his lot with Mack's plan, but only after he is wounded in combat and imagines a direct confrontation with the fictional athlete's most formidable opponent—death itself. The final step in Henry Adams' self-education occurs after he leaves the army to help organize Mack's movement. Returning to the sordidly familiar environs of the same city he had left for the military, Henry is shocked to discover his wife totally deaf and unable to converse with him. Her unfortunate condition not only serves as another reminder of blacks' isolation within the mainstream of society but also suggests a congenital weakness to unite among themselves in support of a mutual cause. Thus, the stage is set for the novel's final scene in which Mack's call to revolution fails before it can even get off the ground, mainly because of black apathy. Convinced now that "there are no answers," a disenchanted Runner Mack commits suicide. The novel then ends with Henry's decision not to reflect on the meaning of Mack's death but rather to assert himself in his most athletic manner: "he had to run, search, look, fight—but more than anything, not give up." Even so, the reader is left to ponder the underlying meaning of Henry's fate in the light of Mack's death, when once again, as in the novel's beginning, a truck suddenly appears out of the city's traffic bearing down on Henry Adams.

The ambiguous, enigmatic ending, which structurally and thematically brings the novel full circle, seems to imply that the plight of Henry Adams is representative of all Afro-Americans in their search for a positive socio-political identity; that in seeking to become a part of the system, or even in attempting to rebel against it, they risk losing their unique natural identity. Because everything related to organized, systematic control and behavior in Henry's world has failed, in particular baseball (and, of course, by extension the larger system), we may conclude that the only avenue left for him to secure a positive identity lies in trying somehow to locate and return to the natural environs of Beatrice's poetic "clearing"—the idealized world of the sporting hero, which in its own innocent way is representative of all our Edenic dreams.

It has been suggested [by Mel Watkins] that **Runner Mack** lends itself to an allegorical interpretation of the Afro-American experience because, when one recalls the mood of the socio-political setting that inspired this novel (i.e., the turbulent times of the late 1960s and early '70s), many of its scenes appear to symbolize actual events from Afro-American history. However, the contention of this essay is that a richer understanding of **Runner Mack** derives from the way in which the resources of the American sporting myth have been placed in the context of a fictional setting that is at once general and specific. In developing his narrative around the ironically negative experiences of a superior athlete on a metaphorical level, Barry Beckham has compelled the reader to confront directly on another more literal level the consequences of a painfully real but often overlooked side of American social experience. (pp. 73-83)

> *Wiley Lee Umphlett, "The Black Man as Fictional Athlete: 'Runner Mack', the Sporting Myth, and the Failure of the American Dream," in* Modern Fiction Studies, *Vol. 33, No. 1, Spring, 1987, pp. 73-83.*

FURTHER READING

Babinski, Hubert. Review of *Runner Mack,* by Barry Beckham. *Library Journal* 97 (August 1972): 2639.
    Briefly summarizes *Runner Mack,* viewing it as "an emblem of contemporary black frustration in America."

Coombs, Ordie. Review of *My Main Mother,* by Barry Beckham. *Negro Digest* XIX, No. 4 (February 1970): 77-9.
    Concise overview of *My Main Mother,* analyzing it as "a parable for our times."

Donahugh, Robert. Review of *My Main Mother,* by Barry Beckham. *Library Journal* 94 (1 December 1969): 4447.
    Examines the character of Mitchell Mibbs in *My Main Mother,* maintaining that "the cumulated impres-

sions" in the book "do not give dramatic validity to Mitchell's actions."

Klotman, Phyllis Rauch. "The Runner as Defector." In her *Another Man Gone: The Black Runner in Contemporary Afro-American Literature,* pp. 127-48. Port Washington, N.Y.: Kennikat Press, 1977.
   Summarizes *Runner Mack* and examines protagonist Henry Adams as a "runner" who rejects society's values and "literally takes flight."

Review of *Runner Mack,* by Barry Beckham. *The New York Times Book Review* (3 December 1972): 78.
   Brief review of *Runner Mack,* "an allegory of the Afro-American experience cunningly disguised as a novel."

O'Connell, Shaun. "American Fiction, 1972: The Void in the Mirror." *The Massachusetts Review* 14, No. 1 (Winter 1973): 200.
   Briefly considers the metaphorical meaning of *Runner Mack,* noting: "It is all done perhaps too easily, too heavily, but not without wit and style."

Pinsker, Sanford. "A Conversation with Barry Beckham." *Studies in Black Literature* 5, No. 3 (Winter 1974): 17-20.
   Interview with Beckham. Beckham discusses "the present state of Afro-American literature" as well as the media's portrayal of blacks in America.

Review of *My Main Mother,* by Barry Beckham. *Times Literary Supplement* (12 February 1971): 173.
   Considers the "Negro-ness" of *My Main Mother.*

Weixlmann, Joe. "Barry Beckham: A Bibliography." *CLA Journal* XXIV, No. 4 (June 1981): 522-28.
   Primary and secondary bibliography of Beckham, covering the years 1969 through 1981.

James Madison Bell

1826-1902

American poet.

Known as the "Bard of the Maumee" and the "Poet of Hope," Bell gained prominence as an outspoken author of abolitionist writings during the American Civil War. Considered a skillful orator in the tradition of such nineteenth-century rhetoricians as Frederick Douglass and William Cullen Bryant, Bell read his poems before sympathetic gatherings throughout the United States to rally support for the antislavery movement and later for the civil rights of African-Americans. His poems, though now regarded as conventional, are nonetheless respected for their inspirational qualities as well as their moral and political stands.

Born in Gallipolis, Ohio, Bell moved to Cincinnati at the age of sixteen and worked as a plasterer with his cousin while attending a high school established for blacks. In 1847 he married Louisiana Sanderline, with whom he eventually had seven children. In 1854 Bell relocated his family to Ontario, Canada. There he joined the antislavery movement and became friends with John Brown, helping the radical abolitionist organize his raid on the arsenal at Harper's Ferry, West Virginia, in 1859. Following Brown's arrest and execution, Bell left his family in Ontario and traveled to California. He stayed there for the duration of the Civil War, composing poems that he delivered as orations at antislavery rallies. In 1866 he briefly returned to Canada before establishing his family in Toledo, Ohio. Although he continued to work as a plasterer, Bell assumed the role of itinerant poet and lecturer. His literary travels took him to such cities as St. Louis, Baltimore, and Atlanta. During the 1870s he also served as a county delegate to the Republican National Convention and campaigned for various party candidates, including President Ulysses S. Grant. As he grew older, Bell gradually abandoned travel, and in 1901, a year before his death, he published his collected verse as *The Poetical Works of James Madison Bell.*

Bell's best-known writings are long poems composed to celebrate significant events in the abolitionist movement. These works, which were issued as pamphlets, include *A Poem Entitled The Day and the War, Delivered January 1, 1864, at Platt's Hall at the Celebration of the First Anniversary of President Lincoln's Emancipation Proclamation,* which moves from slavery through the Civil War to emancipation, and *An Anniversary Poem Entitled the Progress of Liberty, Delivered January 1st, 1866... at the Celebration of the Third Anniversary of President Lincoln's Proclamation,* which chronicles the assassination of Lincoln and the beginning of Reconstruction. An admirer of such poets as Alexander Pope, Sir Walter Scott, and Alfred, Lord Tennyson, Bell emulated their styles through his regular use of iambic tetrameter as well as couplets or alternating rhymes. Bell's imagery and phrasing are generally considered prosaic, but critics acknowledge that his intent was often political rather than aesthetic. Bell's most admired work, "Modern Moses, or 'My Policy Man'," transcends conventional rhetoric in its scathing satire of President Andrew Johnson and his perceived mismanagement of Reconstruction. Several of the shorter poems collected in *The Poetical Works,* such as "The Dawn of Freedom," "The Death of Lincoln," and "The Black Man's Wrongs," reflect the sentiments of Bell's longer offerings, while others, including "Creation Light" and "Descriptive Voyage from New York to Aspinwall," address his later interest in Christianity and nature.

Bell is generally regarded by contemporary critics as too uninventive a poet to be accorded a prominent place in African-American literature. Nevertheless, he is recognized as an eloquent champion of morality and human rights. J. Saunders Redding observed: "[Bell] gave freedom and the heroes who had fought for it the poetic salvos he thought so richly appropriate, swelling the final great chorus of crude music that roared out through the dark times of preparation and through the din of the years of war."

(For further information about Bell's life and works, see *Black Writers; Contemporary Authors,* Vols. 122, 124; and *Dictionary of Literary Biography,* Vol. 50: *Afro-American Writers Before the Harlem Renaissance.*)

PRINCIPAL WORKS

A Poem: Delivered August 1st, 1862... at the Grand Festival to Commemorate the Emancipation of the Slaves of the West Indian Isles (poem) 1862
A Poem Entitled The Day and the War, Delivered January 1, 1864, at Platt's Hall at the Celebration of the First Anniversary of President Lincoln's Emancipation Proclamation (poem) 1864
An Anniversary Poem Entitled The Progress of Liberty, Delivered January 1st, 1866... at the Celebration of the Third Anniversary of President Lincoln's Proclamation (poem) 1866
A Poem, Entitled the Triumph of Liberty, Delivered April 7, 1870 at Detroit Opera House, on the Occasion of the Fifteenth Amendment to the Constitution of the United States (poem) 1870
A Discourse Commemorative of John Frye Bell, Member of Hopkins High School, Hadley (poem) 1874
The Poetical Works of James Madison Bell (poetry) 1901

Bishop B. W. Arnett (essay date 1901)

[The leader of the African Methodist Episcopal (AME) Church in Ohio during the late nineteenth century, Arnett gained distinction in 1885 as the first African-American state legislator to represent a predominately white constituency. A close friend of Bell, he encouraged the author to publish his collected works. In the following 1901 introduction to The Poetical Works of James Madison Bell, *Arnett lauds Bell's commitment to the abolitionist cause and predicts that his verse "will give light and joy to the laboring and struggling people for many centuries." Arnett also provides a biographical sketch of Bell that has since become the definitive source for information regarding the author's life.]*

The wealth of a nation does not consist alone in its bonds, gold, silver or lands, but the true wealth consists in the intelligence, courage, industry and frugality of the men, the intelligence, culture and virtue of its womanhood. Each generation produces its men and women for the times in which they live.

If it is war, warriors are produced. In case of law, judges and others are produced, so that the times, whether of an individual, family or race, very seldom calls for a man, that he is not to be found to lead on the armies, to teach its children, to encourage its people to renewed energy and effort. Our race is no exception to the general rule of history. During all of our sorrowful and sad history, we have had men and women when needed. (pp. 3-4)

When the heavens were threatening and many were faint of heart, then the bow of promise spanned the western sky, it was during the dark hours of our nation's history, it was then a new star appeared above the horizon and a new trumpet sounded, new notes were heard and the vibrations of the sound reached from ocean to ocean, it was then that the subject of our sketch came upon the stage and became a lamp to our feet and a light to our pathway.

James Madison Bell was born April 3, 1826, at Gallipolis, Ohio. He lived there until he was 17 years of age. In 1842 he removed to Cincinnati, Ohio, and lived with his brother-in-law, George Knight, and learned the plasterer's trade. Mr. Knight was one of the best mechanics in the city.

At the time of the arrival of Mr. Bell in Cincinnati, the subject of education was agitated among the colored and white people. The school question was one of the living and burning questions, and had been since 1835. Previous to that time the schools were private, taught by white men for white children, but Mr. Wing and a number of others allowed the colored youth [including Bell] to attend the night schools. (pp. 4-5)

The subject of our sketch was a busy man; he worked by day and studied by night. He worked at his trade in the summer and fall and studied in the winter, each spring coming out renewed in strength and increased in knowledge. It was in these times that Mr. Bell entered school, and at the same time was indoctrinated into the principles of radical anti-slaveryism. It was in this school, in connection with Oberlin College, that the sentiment of Uncle Tom's Cabin was born in Walnut Hills, Cincinnati, giving an impetus to the cause of human freedom. Thus imbued and thus indoctrinated, he desired a wider field to breathe a freer atmosphere where his sphere of usefulness could be enlarged, which could only be enjoyed under the British flag.

In August, 1854, he moved with his family to Chatham, Canada, where he lived until 1860.

Mr. Bell was a personal friend of John Brown, of Harper's Ferry. He was a member of his counsel in Canada and assisted in enlisting men to go upon their raid. He was his guest while the recruiting was going on in Canada and was one of the last men to see John Brown when he left Canada for the United States. He only escaped the fate of many of John Brown's men by the providence of God.

He assisted in raising money to carry on the work, and is one of the last men now living who was personally connected with the Harper's Ferry raid. All honor to the men who gave aid, counsel and support to the hero of Harper's Ferry.

It was while in his twenty-second year that he courted and married Miss Louisana Sanderline, and to this marriage a number of children were born, who became useful men and women. In Canada he pursued his trade and was very successful and accumulated some money, but having a desire for a broader field, on the second day of February, 1860, he started for California and landed at San Francisco on the 29th of the same month.

On arriving on the Pacific coast he found the leaders of his race in an active campaign against the disabilities of the children and the race in that new country. He immediately became one of them, and joined hands, heart and brain to assist in breaking the fetters from the limbs of his race in California and giving an equal opportunity for the people to acquire an education. (pp. 6-8)

While in California, some of his most stirring poems were written. The poems on **"Emancipation," "Lincoln," "The Dawn of Freedom,"** and the **"War Poems,"** were all written while living at the Golden Gate. One of his finest poems is his **"Valedictory on Leaving San Francisco."** He left California and came back to the Atlantic states in 1865, just in time to fulfill his mission to the race by encouraging the new-born freedmen in their new duties and responsibilities.

He returned to Canada to visit his family, and after remaining for a short time he removed to Toledo, Ohio, and brought his family with him. For two years he traveled from city to city and proclaimed the truth and doctrines of human liberty, instructed and encouraged his race to noble deeds and to great activity in building up their newly-made homes.

It was during this period that I met him—and to meet him is to love him—and we became warm and true friends. From that day until now I have been one of his most ardent admirers, by reason of the congeniality of the man, of his intrinsic worth and his ability as a native poet.

His poetry is like the flowing of the mountain spring, the secret of its source is unknown. It was not a well dug or bored, but a natural outflowing of the crystalline stream, which came bubbling, sparkling, leaping, rolling, tumbling and jumping down the mountain side, flowing out over the plain like a silver brook on its journey towards the sea, furnishing water for thirsty beast and man, power for mills and factories, and life for the vegetable world. So it is with the poems of Mr. Bell. They will be read by the inhabitants of the mansion and hut, studied in the school house, college and university, recited in the parlor, lyceum, on the platform, and quoted by pulpit and press.

During the years 1867 and 1868 in Cincinnati, Ohio, night after night I accompanied him in his readings; thence to Lockland, Glendale, Hamilton and other places, where I had the pleasure and satisfaction of witnessing some of the effects of his poems. He read **"Modern Moses"** or **"Andrew Johnson Swinging Around the Circle"** with telling effect.

During these years of instruction, for he was instructing the people of their political and civic duties, they needed a teacher and leader, and no one could have done it better than the manner in which he presented it. It was like the music that comes from the heavenly source. His poems were read in all of the large cities of the North and South, and many a young man who was not an honor to his race and a blessing to his people received the first spark of inspiration for true greatness from hearing the poems of our subject. In Washington, St. Louis, Baltimore, Louisville, Atlanta and Charleston, the people opened their arms and received the words after beholding the star of hope as held out by the readings of our subject.

After traveling for several years he returned to Toledo, Ohio, where his family resided. His star rested over the city on the Maumee, and from that time until now he has been known as the "Bard of the Maumee."

He would follow his trade in the summer and fall, travel and read his poems during the winter—holding the trowel in one hand and his pen in the other. He was one of the best artists in his city and neighboring towns, always busy, calls more than he could fill for artistic work, though he labored hard, yet on going home in the evenings the muse would call him and a poem was born. Many of his brightest gems of thought were born on the scaffold and cradled in his wagon.

I have known him to sit down, and in a conversation some of the most beautiful expressions would come from his lips, thoughts that were crystallized, clothed in silken language, and were marshaled like an army on the battle field. His logic was irresistible, like a legion of cavalry led by Sheridan; troop after troop he would hurl against the logical battery of his opponent, whether in debate or speech, and the conclusion was shouts of victory heard above the music of the heart and the songs of the soul. (pp. 9-11)

His life has been one of great activity; his services rendered to his race cannot be measured by any standard that we have at our command. His influences have been one of those subtle influences. Like the atmosphere, it has gone many places, and the people have felt and acted upon it; they have become better and wiser by reason of reading and hearing his speeches.

The honor of presenting an individual to a select company, or to a distinguished audience, is one privilege a man, perhaps, enjoys once in a life time, but the privilege that is now afforded me is of a very high order—the privilege of introducing an author and his book, not to a select company of friends or to a high dignitary, but to the commonwealth of letters, to the reading and thinking men, women and children of the present and future generations. The honor carries with it a responsibility for the character of the individual and the character of the book, therefore I do not fear the consequence of the introduction of so distinguished an individual or so useful a book.

I can endorse both, and feel it an honor to have the privilege of so doing, for if the book is to find its place in the reading circle of the world it will stand on its own merits; it will stand the examination of the most critical, whether friend or foe.

The book is a collection of the man—a busy man, a God-fearing man, a race-loving man, one who has spent the better part of his life in work and in study. The poems are the fruitage of his spare moments. I have long and persistently entreated my dear friend to have his poems collected and published. He has at last consented, and the work of compiling has been one of love and pleasure.

I therefore take great pleasure in introducing to the members of the commonwealth of letters, J. Madison Bell, "The Bard of the Maumee."

It was my pleasure and privilege to give a helping hand to Whitman's "Not a Man and Yet a Man," but in this introduction it gives me greater pleasure than I possess language to express.

In 1884 the general conference of the A.M.E. church adjourned its session in Baltimore and was received at the white house by the President of the United States, Chester A. Arthur. It was my pleasure to present the bishops, general officers and members to his excellency, the President of the United States, an honor enjoyed by *few. This privilege of introducing one of my own race, of my own church and political faith, a man whose poems will stand as his monument from generation to generation, and will give light and joy to the laboring and struggling people for many centuries.*

He will lighten their burden and illumine their pathway, whether in religion or politics; he will stand and present the **"Banishment of Man from the Garden of the Lord,"** and from all of its effects he will hang the star of hope over the gateway of Eden. To the many under oppression, he will stand to them the day of **"Dawn of Liberty,"** and to those who are fighting the battles of the moral, religious and educational interests, he will present them with the **"Triumph of Liberty"** or **"Creation Light."** (pp. 12-14)

> *Bishop B. W. Arnett, "Biographical Sketch of J. Madison Bell: The Distinguished Poet and Reader," in* The Poetical Works of James Madison Bell *second edition, Press of Wynkoop Hallenbeck Crawford Co., 1904?, pp. 3-14.*

J. Saunders Redding (essay date 1939)

[*A pioneering literary and social commentator, Redding is the author of* To Make a Poet Black *(1939), the first comprehensive critical study of black literature by an African-American. Although dismissed during the 1960s by Amiri Baraka and other radical critics as assimilationist, Redding has gained prominence for a complex vision that encourages black artists to transcend racial distinctions and address universal themes while affirming their unique cultural heritage. In the following excerpt from* To Make a Poet Black, *Redding dismisses Bell as an "inspirational" poet of average skills.*]

[James Madison Bell] wrote less to accomplish freedom than in praise of it after it had been won. He gave freedom and the heroes who had fought for it the poetic salvos he thought so richly appropriate, swelling the final great chorus of crude music that roared out through the dark times of preparation and through the din of the years of war.

Bell was a rover—a sort of vagabond poet, lecturer, and plasterer—living at various times in Gallipolis and Cincinnati, Lansing and Detroit, and Canada. In this latter place he became friend and counselor to the insurrectionist John Brown, and only "escaped the fate of many of John Brown's men by the Providence of God." On his wanderings, combining the practical and the ideal, he followed his trade of master plasterer, recited his poetry in public gatherings, and "proclaimed the truth and doctrines of human liberty, instructed and encouraged his race to noble deeds and to great activity in building up their new homes." With a full and active life, the "Bard of the Maumee," or the "Poet of Hope" (both of which titles he unblushingly claimed) brings to a close a full and active period.

Most of Bell's verse is of the inspirational kind. He seemed to feel it his especial duty to encourage his people through commemorating events and circumstances, men and opinions that seemed to him noble. His pages thunder with lofty references to Lincoln, Douglass, Day, Garrison, John Brown, and others. Most of his poems suffer from being too long, many of them running to more than two hundred lines and two to more than a thousand. That he had neither the skill nor the power to sustain pieces of such length is evidenced by the steady drop in emotional force and the frequent shifting of metrical form within a poem.

Bell's *Poetical Works* is unusual and therefore interesting. He had read a good many of the "popular immortals" and one can see their influence at work on him. He attempted imitations of Pope and Scott, Tennyson and Bryant. His long, expository narratives are veritable melting pots of styles and treatments:

> This is proud Freedom's day!
> Swell, swell the gladsome day,
>   Till earth and sea
> Shall echo with the strain
> Through Britain's vast domain;
> No bondman clanks his chain,
>   All men are free.
>
> Of every clime, of every hue,
>   Of every tongue, of every race,
> 'Neath heaven's broad ethereal blue;
> Oh! let thy radiant smiles embrace,
> Till neither slave nor one oppressed
>   Remain throughout creation's span,
> By thee unpitied and unblest,
>   Of all the progeny of man.

What Bell attempted in most of his longer pieces is illustrated by the introductory "arguments" of two of them:

> The Progress of Liberty is delineated in the events of the past four years—the overthrow of the rebellion, the crushing of the spirit of anarchy, the total extinction of slavery, and the return of peace and joy to our beloved country.
> The invincibility of Liberty is illustrated in the beautiful episode of the Swiss patriot, William Tell, wherein the goddess is personified by an eagle towering amidst the clouds.
> The poet claims the full enfranchisement of his race from political, as well as personal thraldom, and declares that the progress of Liberty will not be complete until the ballot is given the loyal freedman.
> The noble actions and self-sacrificing spirit of the immortal Lincoln is next sung, and in mournful strains the poet bewails his martyrdom. This concludes with a touching eulogy on our sainted martyr.
> The reconstruction policy of President Johnson is reviewed, and, while objecting, he does not wholly condemn his motives, but warns the ruling powers that unless the spirit of rebellion is wholly obliterated and every vestige swept away, it will only slumber to awake again with renewed ferocity.
> The poet laments the discord of his harp, and its disuse, until answering Freedom's call he again essays its harmony. He portrays the conflict and gives thanks to God for the dawning day of Freedom. He rejoices that Columbia is free; he eulogizes the moral

heroes, and describes how America is "Marching on" in the footsteps of the war-like "Hero John."

It is not known when Bell died, but he lived and died not without honor. In a biographical sketch of him Bishop B. W. Arnett of the A. M. E. Church praised him unstintingly, especially as the poet of liberty. Before Bell's impetuous full song the last of the Negro's bitterness against slavery was swept away, but the "sweetness of the liberty" of which he sang seemed turned to wormwood on the tongues of his successors. Had he lived beyond the first decade of the twentieth century, he perhaps would have been less sure of the uninterrupted progress of Liberty than when he wrote:

> Ride onward, in thy chariot ride,
>   Thou peerless queen; ride on, ride on—
> With Truth and Justice by thy side!
>   From pole to pole, from sun to sun!

(pp. 44-7)

J. Saunders Redding, "Let Freedom Ring," in his To Make a Poet Black, *1939. Reprint by McGrath Publishing Company, 1968, pp. 19-48.*

Joan R. Sherman (essay date 1974)

[*In the following excerpt, Sherman characterizes Bell as "the* verse propagandist for Afro-Americans in his *century."*]

The "Bard of the Maumee" was one of the nineteenth century's most articulate witnesses to racial oppression and to the black man's struggle for equality. "The burden of all our songs shall be / To Lincoln, God, and Liberty!" Bell wrote, and for forty years (1860-1900) his poetic orations dramatized the Afro-American view of slavery, Civil War, emancipation, and Reconstruction. Ohio's first native black poet was born in Gallipolis on April 3, 1826. Bishop Benjamin Arnett's lengthy panegyrical sketch of Bell in *Poetical Works,* the source of all other published biographies, remains vague about many years of the poet's life. Nothing is known about Bell's family or his first sixteen years, spent in Gallipolis. From 1842 to 1853 Bell lived in Cincinnati and worked as a plasterer with his brother-in-law, George Knight, who had taught Bell the trade. They were skilled craftsmen, for in 1851 Knight and Bell "received a contract for plastering the public buildings of Hamilton County." Bell attended a Cincinnati high school established for colored people in 1844. He studied full-time during the winter and at night in summer and fall when he worked as a plasterer.

On November 9, 1847, Bell married Louisiana Sanderlin in a civil ceremony in Cincinnati; according to Arnett, they had "a number of children." In 1854 Bell moved with his family to Canada West (Ontario), where for six years he worked at his trade. In Cincinnati, Bell had been indoctrinated "into the principles of radical antislaveryism," and now he became a friend and ally of

John Brown, "The Hero, Saint and Martyr of Harpers Ferry" to whom Bell later dedicated *The Day and the War.* Brown arrived in Chatham, Canada West, for his provisional convention on April 29, 1858, and made his headquarters in Bell's home, living with Bell during the convention, May 8-10, and possibly until he left Canada on May 29. The journal of Brown's convention lists Bell as one of five men chosen to select candidates for officers and as a signer of the revolutionary "Provisional Constitution and Ordinances for the People of the United States," adopted there in great secrecy. Subsequently Bell enlisted men and raised funds for Brown's fateful raid in October, 1859.

Leaving his family in Canada, Bell departed for California and arrived in San Francisco on February 29, 1860, after a month's journey. In this city for the next five years Bell worked as a plasterer, agitated for black educational and legal rights, served as steward of the A.M.E. Church and as a prominent lay member of their convention (1863) on the finance, ministry, and Sabbath schools committees. Meanwhile he wrote, published, and gave public readings of poetry. From 1862 until 1869 (although he left California in 1866) Bell's poetry frequently appeared in the *San Francisco Elevator* and *Pacific Appeal.* These papers also reported his poetry readings at the first "literary entertainment" of the San Francisco Literary Institute (1860), at the Bethel A.M.E. Church (1863), and at later gatherings in Ohio, Illinois, and Indiana (1867).

Bell's first poem in pamphlet form was probably the one called simply *A Poem,* which he read in San Francisco on August 1, 1862, commemorating the emancipation of slaves in the District of Columbia. Two years later he recited *The Day and the War,* published with an "Argument" by Philip A. Bell, the poet's friend and editor of the *Pacific Appeal,* at the first anniversary celebration of the Emancipation Proclamation. For the third anniversary Bell composed *The Progress of Liberty* and delivered it at Zion Church on New Year's Day, 1866. Bell celebrated the Fifteenth Amendment with another ode, *The Triumph of Liberty,* read at the Detroit Opera House on April 7, 1870.

Early in 1866 Bell returned to Canada for his family and, after a short stay there, established them in Toledo, Ohio. Bell's day-to-day movements from 1866 are sketchy, but he remained a plasterer and poet and assumed the additional roles of itinerant lecturer and politician. Through the late 1860's Bell lectured and read his poetry to freedmen in Ohio (accompanied at times by Bishop Arnett, whom Bell first met in 1866). He toured "all of the large cities of the North and South," including St. Louis, Baltimore, Louisville, Atlanta, and Charleston. In 1867, at a series of poetical readings in Washington, D.C., Bell met William Wells Brown. Brown described Bell as a handsome mulatto "of fine physical appearance" and praised his oratory, his logical, acute reasoning, and his "soul-stirring appeals" which inspired "enthusiasm of admiration" in his listeners.... In Toledo from 1870 to 1873 he also served as superintendent of the A.M.E. Sunday School under the pastorate of Bishop Arnett.

Bell entered politics in 1872 as elected delegate from Lucas County (Toledo) to the state Republican convention. This body elected him as delegate at large from Ohio to the national convention in Philadelphia which nominated Grant for President (1872). Bell may have received such recognition from the party for his satiric exposé of President Andrew Johnson, **"Modern Moses, or 'My Policy' Man"** (1868?). In any case, Bell campaigned for Grant but seems to have progressed no further in a political career.

Abandoning his traveling life about 1890, Bell rejoined his family in Toledo. In 1901, at Bishop Arnett's insistence, Bell collected and published his life's poetry in *Poetical Works.* He was seventy-five years old, and a portrait in *Works* (the only one of Bell that has survived) shows a well preserved although bald and wrinkled old man, decidedly Anglo-Saxon in features and complexion, staring with grim severity at a turn-of-the-century America which had failed to heed his repeated appeals for liberty and justice for Afro-Americans. James Madison Bell died in 1902, memorialized in his *Works,* "a collection of the man—a busy man, a God-fearing man, a race-loving man."

The Bard of the Maumee's poetry requires such spirited dramatic recitals as Bell gave it on his reading tours, for on the printed page his over-long discourses are uniformly soporific. In his three longest poems, typical of all his work, both emotional force and intellectual conviction languish in abstractions, clichés, and monotonously regular meter and rhyme. Occasionally amid the generalities references to specific events, persons, or places rouse momentary interest. Bell varies his stanza lengths among four-, eight-, and twelve-line forms, and at times he adds a fifth foot to his steady iambic tetrameter. Otherwise the poems are indistinguishable from one another.

The Day and the War (1864) takes the reader from slavery days through the Civil War to Emancipation in about 750 lines.... *The Progress of Liberty* (1866) in about 850 lines reviews the four years of war and peace from 1862, liberty's triumph, and Lincoln's martyrdom:

> Hail! hail! glad day! thy blest return
>   We greet with speech and joyous lay.
> High shall our altar-fires burn,
>   And proudly beat our hearts today.
>   . . . .
> Liberia has been recognized—
>   Also the Haytian's island home;
> And lo! a Negro undisguised
>   Has preached within the Nation's dome!
>   . . . .
> For lo! Arkansas doth rejoice,
> And Texas sings with cheerful voice,
> And Mississippi's heart doth swell,
> And hail with joy the rising knell
> Now sounding on her gulf-bound coast—
> The dirge of a departed ghost.

To discuss "the changes of the last decade," Bell's *Triumph of Liberty* (1870) requires over 950 lines. Prefaced as "a statement of facts—not fiction" (which suggests Bell's problem as a poet), the poem takes us again through slavery, John Brown's triumph, the Civil War and its black heroes, and the changing fortunes of Liberty. Frequent variations in metrical and stanzaic form here cannot redeem the narrative from dullness:

> Lift up your hearts, ye long oppressed,
>   And hail the gladsome rising dawn,
> For Slavery's night, that sore distressed
>   And tortured you, has passed and gone!
>   . . . .
> Hail! hail mighty Land with thy proud destiny!
> Enduring as time, all chainless and free!
> Hail! hail to thy mountains majestic and high,
> Reclining their heads against the blue curtained
>   sky.

The poet similarly hails valleys, prairies, streamlets, oceans, cities, and railroads of the land of liberty.... A dozen shorter poems in *Works* echo the sentiments and language of Bell's major salvos to liberty and racial justice. **"The Dawn of Freedom"** celebrates William Wilberforce and abolition of slavery in the British West Indies: two poems commemorate emancipation in the District of Columbia; and **"The Death of Lincoln,"** **"Triumphs of the Free,"** and two poems for the first of August follow suit. **"Admonition"** warns that men are lords of all creation but not of other men, and it urges humanitarianism and brotherhood. **"The Black Man's Wrongs"** appeals for consistency in judging men:

> Look on the face of men like Ward,
>   Day, Douglas [*sic*], Pennington, and then
> Tell me whether these should herd
>   With beasts of burden or with men.

In the same vein Bell champions the right of contrabands to fight "the war for Freedom"; and in **"Sons of Erin"** he warns Irish-Americans to remember O'Connell and refrain from oppressing blacks as the English had the Irish.

Very few of Bell's poems digress from racial themes. **"Creation Light"** recounts the world's creation from a "shapeless, heterogeneous mass" through the events of Genesis, "Till reason's torch illumined the mind" of man. Night and chaos will return when the world ends, but "God, Jehovah, Deity" will remain changeless. The **"Descriptive Voyage from New York to Aspinwall"** is a tedious journey; Bell's account of the sea and of Aspinwall are typical of his nature description.... Two acrostics offer philosophical advice, this to Mary Jane Wilson:

> Wisdom, bless'd wisdom, she speaks unto all
> In the summer of life, prepare for the fall.
> Like apples of silver, or pictures of gold,
> So prize the rich moments of youth as they roll.

Outstanding among Bell's poems is **"Modern Moses, or 'My Policy Man,'"** a daring, original, and lively satiric assassination of the character and policies of Lincoln's successor, Andrew Johnson. The reactionary ex-Democrat is lumped with those despised braggart knaves and brainless wights raised to power by other assassins' blows. Worse than the murderer Cain is "My liege of graceless dignity, / The author of *My Policy.*"

> But choose we rather to discant,
> On one whose swaggish boast and rant,
> And vulgar jest, and pot-house slang,
> Has grown the pest of every gang
> Of debauchees wherever found,
> From Baffin's Bay to Puget Sound.

With wit and irony Bell catalogues the treacheries of Reconstruction and lays them at Johnson's door. This modern Judas, "with arrogant unworthiness," had sworn to be the bondsman's friend and Moses. Instead he vetoed the Freedman's Bureau bill:

> He next reversed the bill of rights,
> Lest all the girls—that is the whites—
> Should Desdemonias [*sic*] become,
> And fly each one her cherished home,
> And take to heart some sooty moor,
> As Fathers did in days before.
> . . . .
> Would give the matrimonial hand
> Unto some swarthy son or other
> And some, perhaps, might wed a *brother.*

Bell observes Johnson's "blooming nose," crimson either from drink or his Policy, and his playing "the *knave and clown"* on a national tour which was "the grandest burlesque of the age." Johnson is treasonous and disloyal for his switch to support of Southerners:

> For he, to use a term uncivil,
> Has long been mortgaged to the Devil;
> But the fact which no one knows,
> Is why the deuce he don't foreclose.
> Perhaps he entertains a doubt,
> And fears that Mose might turn him out;
> Hence, *His Satanic* Majesty's
> Endorsement of *My Policy.*

This memorable political satire draws its vitality from Bell's skillful combination of the rhymed couplet form, concrete topicality, and uninhibited personal (rather than corporate) emotion.

Bell's sincere dedication to Afro-American freedom and rights is unquestioned. Oral delivery of the massive Liberty odes surely stirred audiences to enthusiastic aspiration, as Bishop Arnett claimed. But it is only in recital and to such audiences of the last decades of the century that Bells' poetry could ever seem "like the flowing of the mountain spring...bubbling, sparkling, leaping, rolling, tumbling, and jumping down the mountain side." Bells' poetry, read today, lacks the spontaneity, natural vigor, particularity, and compression of thought and feeling which communicate poetic experience without the poet's physical presence. Artistic merit aside, James Madison Bell was undoubtedly *the* verse propagandist for Afro-Americans in his century. (pp. 80-7)

Joan R. Sherman, "James Madison Bell," in her Invisible Poets: Afro-Americans of the Nineteenth Century, *University of Illinois Press, 1974, pp. 80-7.*

Eugene B. Redmond (essay date 1976)

[*A poet, critic, journalist, playwright, and educator, Redmond gained prominence during the Black Arts Movement of the 1960s. His works, including* River of Bones *(1971) and* Consider Loneliness as These Things *(1973), synthesize elements of nature, music, and African folklore to interpret contemporary African-American life. In the following excerpt from his critical study* Drumvoices: The Mission of Afro-American Poetry, *he surveys Bell's career; while characterizing the author's poetic talents as generally limited, he praises "Modern Moses, or 'My Policy' Man" as an accomplished satire.*]

[James Madison Bell's strength] lay in his "pleas" and "hope." "Fortunate" enough to witness the Civil War, emancipation, and "Reconstruction," Bell railed against injustices but primarily expressed hope in his forty years of observing the black struggle. Bell spent most of his adult life delivering eloquent and weighty poetic speeches on freedom, hope, and liberty. He was born in Gallipolis, Ohio, which he left at age sixteen to pursue the trade of plasterer and the avocation of orator-poet. A wanderer, Bell played his part in the overthrow of slavery—soliciting funds and recruiting Blacks for John Brown's 1859 raid at Harpers Ferry. Before the raid, Bell had moved to Canada, where he continued his friendship with Brown and fathered a large family. He later traveled to California, back to Canada, to various cities in Ohio and Michigan, and, finally, spent time in Toledo. During this odyssey Bell appeared at concert halls, churches, and various public gatherings to read his poetry at political and commemorative events. He also took advantage of books and gained considerable understanding of history and literature. His major themes are devotion, inspiration, love, unity, collective strength, and political change. Achieving "something of Byronic power in the roll of his verse" (Kerlin), Bell's poems are often too long, too tedious, and lacking in interest. Robinson notes:

> Not to mitigate his obvious technical flaws, it is helpful to remember that Bell is best appreciated as something of an actor, his poems regarded as scripts.

Unashamedly chronicling his journeys, Bell included the following as a full title of *Triumph of Liberty (1870): A Poem, / Entitled the / Triumph of Liberty. / Delivered April 7, 1870, / Detroit Opera House, / on the Occasion of / the Grand Celebration of the Final Ratification / of the Fifteenth Amendment to the Constitution of the United States.* Consisting of 902 lines, the poem erupts through the use of all the "flourishes and vocal modulations at his experienced command." According to Redding [see essay dated 1939], Bell "unblushingly" claimed the titles of "Bard of Maumee" and "Poet of Hope." Typical of

Bell's style is his tribute to his friend John Brown (from *Triumph of Liberty):*

> Although like Samson he was ta'en,
> And by the base Philistines slain,
> Yet he in death accomplished more
> Than e'er he had in life before.
> His noble heart, which ne'er had failed,
> Proved firm, and e'en in death prevailed;
> And many a teardrop dimmed the eye
> Of e'en his foes who saw him die—
> And none who witnessed that foul act
> Will e'er in life forget the fact.

Approaching something of the stature of Vashon's "Vincent Ogé" and Whitfield's "Cinque," Bell's tribute has all the ring of indebtedness to Scott, Byron, Pope, Tennyson, and other English popular masters with whom he was familiar. However imitative and derivative, though, Bell seemed never to be at a loss for exalting, exhortatory poetical flourishes. In **"Song for the First of August"** he sings a song for "proud Freedom's day":

> Of every clime, of every hue,
>   Of every tongue, of every race,
> 'Neath heaven's broad ethereal blue;
> Oh! let thy radiant smiles embrace,
> Till neither slave nor one oppressed
>   Remain throughout creation's span,
> By thee unpitied and unblest,
> Of all the progeny of man.

One of Bell's most ambitious works is his **"Modern Moses or 'My Policy' Man"** in which—in scalding satire—he assesses the administration of President Andrew Johnson. Johnson (1805-75), who succeeded the assassinated Lincoln in 1865, was born poor and learned to write and figure from his wife. His presidency reached its height in a showdown between a progressive Republican Congress and Johnson, a reactionary Democrat. Once in office, Johnson began reversing his harsh criticisms of the South, giving former rebels a rather free hand at things and vetoing several bills aimed at giving Blacks a better share of things. Upset by the whole thing, Bell wrote a blistering satire—which often collapses as such—wherein, with couplet-fury, he observes:

> And crowns there are, and not a few,
> And royal robes and sceptres, too,
> That have, in every age and land,
> Been at the option and command
> Of men as much unfit to rule,
> As apes and monkeys are for school.

Following poets like Clark and Whitfield, and anticipating "signifying" poets of the 1960s and '70s (such as Baraka, Crouch, Touré, Eckels: "Western Syphillization," and others) Bell compares Johnson to all manner of evils. Johnson is also contrasted to "good" or liberal whites such as Congressmen Charles Sumner and Thaddeus Stevens and abolitionist Wendell Phillips. Cynical-

ly calling Johnson "Modern Moses," Bell also uses the derisive *"Mose"* —which appears to be a way of reducing him to the level of the stereotype whites reserve for Blacks.... One must chuckle somewhat at Bell's claim that Johnson cursed in the White House:

> But choose we rather to discant,
> On one whose swaggish boast and rant,
> And vulgar jest, and pot-house slang,
> Has grown the pest of every gang
> Of debauchees wherever found,
> From Baffin's Bay to Puget Sound.

Only recently have we heard echoes of Bell from journalists, congressmen and old ladies astonished at White House tapes showing that ex-President Richard Nixon cursed in the Oval Room. We have observed, then, that Bell, though a tedious and haranguing poet, is important in a continuing chronicle of the mind and creative development of the Afro-American poet. Bell's works also include **The Day and the War** (1864), dedicated to the memory of Brown; **The Progress of Liberty** (1870), a recollection of the war, praise for Lincoln and black troops, and a jubilant greeting of enfranchisement; and **The Poetical Works of James Madison Bell** (1901), including a preface by his personal friend Bishop B. W. Arnett. Even though Bishop Arnett claimed that Bell's "logic was irresistible, like a legion of cavalry led by Sheridan," the poet recognized his own limitations when he said (**Progress of Liberty**):

> "The poet laments the discord of his harp, and its
> disuse, until answering Freedom's call he again
> essays its harmony."

(pp. 94-7)

Eugene B. Redmond, "Jubillees, Jujus, and Justices (1865-1910)," in his Drumvoices: The Mission of Afro-American Poetry, a Critical History, *Anchor Books, 1976, pp. 85-138.*

FURTHER READING

Brawly, Benjamin. "Poetry and the Arts, 1830-1865." In his *The Negro Genius,* pp. 87-9. New York: Dodd, Mead & Company, 1937.

    Cursory examination of Bell's life offering an excerpt from "The Triumph of Liberty" that extols the achievements of John Brown.

Kerlin, Robert T. "The Earlier Poetry of Art." In his *Negro Poets and Their Poems,* pp. 32-5. Washington, D. C.: Associated Publishers, 1923.

    Brief survey of Bell's career that includes an excerpt from "The Progress of Liberty."

Louise Bennett

1919-

(Also known as Louise Simone Bennett-Coverley and Miss Lou) Jamaican poet and folklorist.

Bennett is an important contemporary Jamaican poet. Writing in Creole, she relies heavily on Jamaican myths, folktales, and songs to create her humorous and often ironic dialect poetry. Although some critics dismiss her as a comedian and entertainer, she has nonetheless enjoyed a loyal literary following. *Jamaica Labrish* (1966) and *Selected Poems* (1982) are considered her best works.

Born in Kingston, Jamaica, Bennett came to love Jamaican folktales while listening to them as a child. Her love for Jamaican folklore even prompted her to leave home: "Everyone thought I was insane, and that my mother was mad for permitting it, but I went out to seek folk songs and stories in the interior of the island. There I was, still a teenager, living in a society that expected respectable girls to stay home with their mother, traveling on donkeyback into the remote towns of the Maroons, the ex-slaves who had escaped and established their own free territory."

Bennett discovered early on, however, that not everyone was enthralled with native or "black" tales. "When I was a child," she said in a 1976 interview, "nearly everything about us [blacks] was bad, yuh know; they would tell yuh seh yuh have bad hair, that black people bad... and that the language yuh talk was bad. And I know that a lot of people I knew were not bad at all, they were nice people and they talked this language." The language Bennett referred to is known today by various names: Jamaican Creole, Jamaican dialect, patois, and Jamaican talk. In school Bennett studied the works of English poets and was, in her words, "influenced by their techniques." She initially wrote her poems in Standard English, but one day while on a streetcar she overheard a conversation in Creole that sparked her imagination. Shortly after the incident she began writing in Creole, much to the delight of her friends. She performed her poetry on stage, and audiences were charmed. In 1938 she made her professional debut by appearing in a popular Christmas concert organized by Eric Coverley, whom she later married. She published her first book of poetry, *Verses in Jamaican Dialect,* in 1942. A few years later, she left for London on a scholarship to the prestigious Royal Academy of Dramatic Art. Within months of her arrival in London, she had her own BBC program; as in Jamaica, audiences in England were enamored of her performances. In 1953 she left for the United States and performed in New York, New Jersey, and Connecticut. Feeling homesick, she returned to Jamaica in 1955; she remains there today, collecting more folk stories and songs. In addition to publishing poetry books, she also produced the

records *Jamaican Folk Songs* (1954), *Jamaican Singing Games* (1954), *The Honourable Miss Lou* (1981), and *Yes M'Dear: Miss Lou Live* (1983). Recently she has hosted "Ring Ding," a weekly children's television show on Jamaican folk culture, and the top-rated radio show "Miss Lou's Views."

Among Bennett's literary works are *Dialect Verses* (1943), *Jamaican Humour in Dialect* (1943), *Lulu Sey: Dialect Verse* (1943), *M's' Lulu Sez: A Collection of Dialect Poems* (1949), and *Folk Stories and Verses* (1952). She has also written several books on the adventures of Brer Anancy, the African spider who is the protagonist of most Jamaican folktales: *Anancy Stories and Poems in Dialect* (1944), *Anancy Stories and Dialect Verse* (1957), *Laugh with Louise: Dialect Verses, Folk-Songs, and Anancy Stories* (1961), and *Anancy and Miss Lou* (1979). These collections contain humorous Brer Anancy stories as well as Bennett's own poetry. Her best-loved books are, however, *Jamaica Labrish* and *Selected Poems*. Although these works have long been popular with Jamaicans, critical acknowledgment has been slow in coming. For many years, critics regarded Bennett's works as unworthy of in-depth literary attention. Dismissing her as a performer, critics only began assessing Bennett as a poet in the early 1960s. One of the first serious studies, by Mervyn Morris, was written in 1963. Morris concluded: "I do not believe that Louise Bennett is a considerable poet. But a poet, and, in her best work, a better poet than most other Jamaican writers she certainly is. She does not offer her readers any great insight into the nature of life or human experience, but she recreates human experience vividly, delightfully and intelligently.... Louise Bennett ... is a poet of serious merit.... Hers is a precious talent...."

Recent criticism of Bennett's poetry has focused on her use of Jamaican dialect. Some critics, deeming Creole an "illegitimate" poetic language, have encouraged Bennett to switch to Standard English. She has persisted in writing in Creole, however, because "nobody else was doing so and there was such rich material in the dialect that I wanted to put on paper some of the wonderful things that people say in dialect. You could never say 'look here' as vividly as 'kuyah'." Critics Morris, Carolyn Cooper, and Rex Nettleford agree. Praising what Morris called the "dramatic monologue" of Bennett's poetry, they lauded her insight into Jamaican culture and her ability to capture the humor and irony of Jamaican life. Using the language of ordinary Jamaicans, according to Nettleford, Bennett writes "wickedly." Her "wickedness," however, is far from being malicious: "Rather, it is rooted in her developed sense of irony.... She allows certain devastating facts to speak for themselves, and like her Jamaican compatriots she can 'tek bad tings mek laugh'." Similarly, Cooper stated that "the strength of Bennett's poetry is the accuracy with which it depicts and attempts to correct through laughter the absurdities of Jamaican society." A reviewer for the *Times Literary Supplement* also suggested that to experience the full impact of Bennett's poetry, one must see it performed: "In print these ballads [in *Jamaica Labrish*] are like a phonetic libretto for performance, but they cannot recreate for us the performance itself. Not merely something, but too much, is lost ... many will wish they could hear Miss Bennett fill out the text with the richness of her voice, presence, personality and humor."

In 1968 Bennett told interviewer Dennis Scott: "... I have been set apart by other creative writers a long time ago because of the language I speak and work in. From the beginning nobody ever recognized me as a writer. 'Well, she is doing dialect'; it wasn't even writing you know. Up to now a lot of people don't even think I write. They say 'Oh, you just stand up and say these things!'" Today, whether in print or in performance, Bennett's works are "remarkable as social commentary and as works of art," scholars argue. Speaking of her wider contributions, Nettleford wrote: "Louise is Jamaica's best ambassador. She is really a very shy lady, but I have seen her go onstage in front of a foreign audience and through her gift of laughter bridge the language barrier, and—without firing a shot—capture the world."

(For further information about Bennett's life and works, see *Contemporary Authors,* Vols. 97-100 and *Contemporary Literary Criticism,* Vol. 28.)

PRINCIPAL WORKS

Verses in Jamaican Dialect (poetry) 1942; revised edition, 1957
Dialect Verses (poetry) 1943
Jamaican Humour in Dialect (poetry) 1943
Lulu Sey: Dialect Verse (poetry) 1943
Anancy Stories and Poems in Dialect (folklore and poetry) 1944
M's' Lulu Sez: A Collection of Dialect Poems (poetry) 1949
Folk Stories and Verses (folklore and poetry) 1952
Anancy Stories and Dialect Verse (folklore and poetry) 1957
Laugh with Louise: Dialect Verses, Folk-Songs, and Anancy Stories (poetry and folklore) 1961
Jamaica Labrish (poetry) 1966
Anancy and Miss Lou (folklore) 1979
Selected Poems (poetry) 1982

Mervyn Morris (essay date 1963)

[*The following essay, written in 1963 and originally entitled "On Reading Louise Bennett, Seriously," won first prize in the 1963 Jamaica Festival writing competition. Here, Morris examines a selection of Bennett's poetry, focusing on the "dramatic monologue" of "Candy Seller," "South Parade Pedlar," "Dry Foot Bwoy," "Po' Ting," and "De Bathsuit And De Cow."*]

... I do not believe that Louise Bennett is a considerable poet. But a poet, and, in her best work, a better poet than most other Jamaican writers she certainly is. She does not offer her readers any great insight into the nature of life or human experience, but she recreates human experience vividly, delightfully and intelligently. She is rarely pretentious—the most common fault in West Indian poetry; she is not derived from other poets—she has her own interesting voice; and she is invariably sane.

... The form most often chosen by Miss Bennett is dramatic monologue. This is hardly surprising in a poet who often performs her work. She writes for the voice and the ear, and when her poems are expertly performed something more, movement, is added. (pp. 137-38)

As in a Browning monologue, the entire dramatic situation [of Bennett's poem **"Candy Seller"**] is made clear without the direct intervention of the author. The whole poem convinces; it has a vitality that seems perfectly to match the imagined context. The images focus on war because the poem was written in wartime and it was perfectly natural that the first abuse that came to mind should relate to war. If anyone doubts the precise suitability of the images—wedge-heel boot like submarine, clothes like black-out, and so on—he should be disarmed by the dramatic context. This could all well be said by a candy-seller in this situation. Rhythm and rhyme are used effortlessly, the pauses coming where the dramatic sense demands them. There is no constriction, no monotony. The poem has the oneness, the wholeness, of a completely realized experience. What more does literary taste ask for?

Several other of Louise Bennett's dramatic monologues could survive detailed examination: for example, **"Street Boy"**, in which a youngster, held by a policeman for swearing, pleads with passersby to beg for him, appeals to the policeman's memory of his own young days, thanks him extravagantly when he lets him go, and then, once out of reach, gloats: 'Ah get weh doah, yuh brut!' **"Parting"**, where the situation is a platform farewell, and **"South Parade Pedlar"** are other outstanding monologues of this type.

Sometimes the situation is presented through the poet as storyteller rather than directly through characters. A good example of this is **"Dry Foot Bwoy"**, in which the affected speech of a boy just home from England is dramatically contrasted with the story-teller's Jamaican dialect.... (p. 139)

In some of her poems Louise Bennett is not just a story-teller but is herself the central character. **"Television"** is an example of this.... Perhaps there is a trace of falsity here: one is not entirely convinced of the ordinariness of this performer. The milieu is wrong. She can convince us that she is a peasant or a maid or a market-woman or a street-boy, but somehow the television studio reminds us too forcibly that Miss Bennett is a trained performer; dialect seems imposed on the situation.

... I have claimed that Louise Bennett is a very sane poet and that she has generosity of spirit. She is always attacking pretension by laughter, and sometimes by hard logic. An example of logic would be **"Back to Africa"** in which an argument is ruthlessly followed through.... It takes a shape very eighteenth-century in its careful balance, the balance helping to point the strictly logical operation of a keen intelligence. Louise Bennett's sanity takes her straight to a fact that too many intellectuals, evidently, find too simple for their acceptance: the central fact of our identity: that we are Jamaicans because Jamaica is where we come from.

Miss Bennett's irony is sometimes easy and cheap; but it is also sometimes important and illuminating [as in her poem **"Independence"**].... (pp. 140-42)

Often the pretensions attacked are minor or topical pretensions, but not always. Look for example at **"Po' Ting"** in which a common, and no doubt eternal, human

pretension is ridiculed, unwillingness to face the fact of age.... (p. 142)

There is a good deal of simple plain fun in Louise Bennett. Sometimes it is fun in the situation, as in, say, **"De Bathsuit And De Cow"**, an excellent little dialect ballad. Sometimes the fun is an intoxication with language which she manipulates or invents with infectious delight....

I think [Miss Bennett's] most central difficulty is choice of subject. Many of her poems are a sort of comic-verse-journalism....

[And] Miss Bennett is sometimes false to her medium. (p.143)

[Nevertheless, to] trace Louise Bennett's development is interesting. She develops, I think, from the high-spirited monologuist to a more purposeful thinker writing in dialect: it is not for nothing that the mature irony of **"Independence"** or the logic of **"Back to Africa"** are recent, and the best dramatic monologues are early. Or, compare the tone of **"Gay Paree"** (an earlyish poem in which there is a childlike peasant delight in the strangeness of French) with the tone of **"Touris"** (much later, in which the poet sees herself ironically, with a certain sophistication). (p. 144)

In between these two stages of development Miss Bennett spent some years in England; when she returned she wrote what I consider some of her worst pieces. The dialect was forced and untrue.... She made some metrical experiments she would have done well to keep out of print. A fair example is the internal jingle of **"Pedestrian Crossin"**, a jingle which seems to have no function. The rapidity of her normal stanza form is lost, and, it seems, nothing is gained.... (p. 145)

Living in Jamaica again, Miss Bennett seemed to grow into dialect again, though she never regained her early innocent vitality. I think that accounts for the greater pervasiveness of acute intelligence in the later poems and the decreasing inclination to rumbustious dramatic monologue. Miss Bennett's own development seems to show that her use of dialect is involved with real feeling, as is any poet's use of language.

A weakness, particularly in the early poems, is for direct and unsubtle moralising. In the later poems any sentimentality or tendency to moralise is usually redeemed by irony or wit.... [For instance, in] **"Homesickness"** Miss Bennett gives a sentimental list of things she misses while in England; the list does name things we can recognize as part of a real Jamaica: bullas, sugar and water, dumplings; but is nevertheless a sentimental selection in its total effect.... [Yet there is a final irony in the last three stanzas which] redeems the poem. It gives a guarantee that there is a mind alive behind it all. (pp. 145-46)

Louise Bennett uses dialect more or less as we can believe the normal speakers of dialect might use it, if they were skilled enough; [some of our other West Indian poets]...borrow dialect for the literary middle class. The image 'smile black as sorrow' [in Dennis Scott's "Uncle Time"] is too abstract for the eminently concrete medium of dialect. It must be said, however, that this poem has a careful exquisite beauty that I cannot claim for anything in Louise Bennett.

Louise Bennett...is a poet of serious merit, although like all poets, she has her limitations. Like most poets she is, I have tried to show, developing. And she is so much more rewarding a poet than many to whom we in Jamaica give the name, that it seems reasonable to expect more of those who claim an interest in poetry to give her more attention. She is sane; throughout, her poems imply that sound common sense and generous love and understanding of people are worthwhile assets. Jamaican dialect is, of course, limiting (in more senses than one); but within its limitations Louise Bennett works well. Hers is a precious talent.... (pp. 147-48)

> *Mervyn Morris, "The Dialect Poetry of Louise Bennett," in* Critics on Caribbean Literature: Readings in Literary Criticism, *edited by Edward Baugh, St. Martin's Press, 1978, pp. 137-48.*

Rex Nettleford (essay date 1966)

[*In the following introduction to Bennett's* Jamaica Labrish, *Nettleford discusses the language and rhythm of Bennett's poetry.*]

The work of Louise Bennett is unique. Whether in the field of the Jamaican theatre where she has found form and living purpose, or in the field of literature where she is yet an unheralded guest among some of the literary establishment, she presents problems—problems of classification and of description. This in a way is her greatest asset, for she is original and of her own kind. (p. 9)

[In a quarter of a century she] has carved designs out of the shapeless and unruly substance that is the Jamaican dialect—the language which most of the Jamaican people speak most of the time—and has raised the sing-song patter of the hills and of the towns to an art level acceptable to and appreciated by people from all classes in her country. Yet not all are agreed on just what she is or stands for on the cultural scene.... [There are some] who would feel it improper to endow her with the name of poet, though they would generously crown her as the leading entertainer in Jamaica's comedy-lore whether on stage, television, or radio. And those who indulge her rumbustious abandon and spontaneous inducement of laughter will sometimes forget that behind the exuberance and carefree stance, there are years of training—formal and informal—as well as this artist's own struggles to shape an idiom whose limitations as a bastard tongue are all too evident. Then there is the view, sometimes barely conceded, that Miss Bennett has

given to Jamaica "valid social documents reflecting the way we think and feel and live".

All these views are themselves valid and serve to delineate the role of Miss Bennett in the cultural development of the infant life of a nation. (pp. 9-10)

As poet Miss Bennett must first be seen against the background of her society. This is imperative....Miss Bennett went to the basics and grasped the fact that she lived in an oral tradition where people talked and listened, cross-talked and reported and possess, almost to a fault, a high propensity for words—"bad" words, new words, archaic words, "big", long and sonorous words. The Bible, the Sankey hymnal, the folksong and the memory gems form the background to these propensities. To Louise Bennett who had the benefit of schooling, the ballad-form, the oldest form of English poetry, would probably have come as the nearest basis of comparison and in her early years it could even have been a conscious model.... Indeed, most of Miss Bennett's stanzas do take the conventional structure of iambic quatrains with an *abab* rhyme scheme and with stresses of 4 and 3 in alternating lines. But even the iambic rhythms are natural to the Jamaican drawl. Conscious aping of a poetic form is no guarantee of success, however, and one must look to Miss Bennett's own individual use of balladic and other poetic attributes to measure her success.

Like the ballad form, Miss Bennett's writing suffers from not having had a tradition of criticism.... This is, however, not surprising. The absence of more serious literary analysis is a commentary on the prevailing ignorance that envelops the subject of the Jamaican dialect. (pp. 10-11)

[And yet it] is to the form and nature of the language that one must...turn to find explanation for some of what could be mistaken as metrical aberrations in some of [Miss Bennett's] poems.... [Frederic] Cassidy's famous example of how the word "can" can be made to mean "can't" depending on pitch is a case in point. Miss Bennett has used the flexibilities to advantage and at an early stage she departed, consciously or unconsciously, from the normal iambic rhythm to variations such as were later developed and sustained in a poem like **"Pedestrian Crosses"**. Far from being a functionless jingle, this poem illustrates the propriety of metric form, language and rhythm for a subject-matter which deals with the nervous anxieties of a pedestrian who must now co-ordinate with the newly-introduced traffic control system. The racy monologue takes on the breathless gallop of the anapaestic rhythm and conveys effectively the plight of that simple, fearful fellow on the sidewalk over there.... This [poem] is technically successful, and the form is complete. Read at the proper pace the poem becomes almost a tongue-twister, thus heightening the confusion that exists in the mind of the pedestrian. (p. 13)

Terseness and brevity of expression are...the strength of her characterisation.... The hypocrisy and lovable rascality of the character from the poem, **"Roas Turkey"**, is at once portrayed. The sturdy independence of the Jamaican spirit, sometimes regarded as aggressiveness, is neatly summed up in . . . [a single] stanza from her poem **"Independence"** . . . . She is able to make incisive comments on situations without flourish or undue explanation . . . . And Jamaica's postures as a full-fledged nation are briskly put into realistic light in the poem **"Jamaica Elevate"** . . . . (pp. 14-15)

It is in poems like [**"Jamaica Elevate"**] that Louise Bennett tells the truth about us and tells it wickedly. The "wickedness" is not at all malicious. Rather, it is rooted in her developed sense of irony, her clear insight into the limitations which are often set on any given human situation and the inevitable comedy which underlies much of the sad outcome. She allows certain devastating facts to speak for themselves, and like her Jamaican compatriots she can "tek bad tings mek laugh". When accused once of not being prepared to subject her art to the rigours of the tragic experiences which plague the human condition, Louise Bennett in one of her few "serious" moments replied, "I believe in laughter." This is borne out by the satiric content of many of her political poems and of her pieces commenting on the foibles of Jamaicans. There is in this something of an analogy with the phenomenon usually found among an emergent group like the American negro community. In seeking its identity the emergent group seems very often to explore its problems and its times through the ambivalence of a comic sense coming to grips with an essentially or potentially tragic situation . . . . The comedy contains the tragedy and even overpowers it in complex forms of expression. This is why the straightforward simplicity of Louise Bennett's iambic quatrains is often deceptive. **"Colonisation In Reverse"** is a classic of her brand of satire and the biting irony of the situation is brought out even more forcibly when Miss Bennett recites this with her peculiar relish and clean fun.

For Miss Bennett is a performer, accomplished and unrivalled. If on the printed pages her poems appear to be dated frozen jingles, in the renditions she gives of them they take on vitality and meaning—capturing all the spontaneity of the ordinary Jamaican's joys and even sorrows, his ready poignant and even wicked wit, his religion and his philosophy of life. *Miss Bennett is indeed a poet of utterance.* With her experience and skill she exploits the complex intonation contours of the Jamaican dialect and turns out pieces which are at once fresh, vital and entertaining . . . . What she sometimes does is to manipulate the tonal range of the language, setting the poems almost to music as she patters along. The punch-line technique of music-hall comedy is liberally utilised . . . . Her play on the infinite nuances of meanings of a single word or phrase reminds us that she is involved in the art of words . . . . (pp. 15-16)

But to those who believe that all that [her] poems need are stentorian vocals and tireless gusto, the truth is soon revealed. For they are capable of subtle interpretation

and demand the careful modulation of tones and pitch in order to communicate honestly and vividly. Above all, they demand an understanding of and a feel for the language. For understanding and feeling are among Miss Bennett's greatest attributes, resulting in the delightful intermingling of "those qualities of head and heart which we term wit and humour—wit which illuminates and humour which reveals", as Philip Sherlock once aptly put it. (pp. 16-17)

It is through her performances that she has proven herself relevant to the society about which she writes, and it is through her performances that the sanity and generosity of spirit which Mervyn Morris commends [see excerpt dated 1963] becomes evident. This sanity and generosity of spirit is the occasion, not the cause, of her artistry. For as a poet of utterance, she has had to be sane and generous for the nightly confrontation which a live and living audience demands of any performing artist. The safe distance of the published writer she never enjoyed. But, in any case, she was using the normally *spoken* language, not the normally *written* tongue.

What was she speaking about? The question finds an answer in her role as social commentator and as such the poems in [*Jamaica Labrish*] tell not one, but many stories. Together they bear testimony to her keen sense of observation . . . . She is at once involved in and detached from the experiences, and she uses her peculiar position to very great advantage.

City Life, the first section, vividly describes aspects of life in Kingston of an earlier period. The picturesque street scenes are enhanced by such characters as the street-peddlar in South Parade crying out her wares or the candy-seller soliciting patronage from passers-by. We come to know something about the passers-by, but most of all we come to know about the candy-seller and her kind. (p. 17)

Some of her liveliest works are . . . about the city transport. For many, Kingston of the forties was Kingston of the "old palam-pam of the tram-cars" and when these were replaced by a trans-urban bus system, Kingston seemed to be no longer the same. The city grew fast in the decade after the war and with it the traffic—hence the plight of that pedestrian in the piece **"Pedestrian Crosses"** . . . .

Her *War Time* poems will undoubtedly be dated by their topicality but she did have something to say in them. When Britain went to war, the then colony of Jamaica went to war as well. But how many of the ordinary people understood the issues sufficiently to be emotionally involved in what has now come to be regarded as the great struggle against totalitarianism? Young middle-class intellectuals and working-class leaders were more concerned with achieving the goal of the nationalist movement—self-government, or the objectives of the social revolution—better wages and living conditions. Miss Bennett comments accurately on the early non-involvement in the poem **"Perplex"**. The second poem **"Obeah Win de War"**, would suggest that neither Miss Bennett nor her countrymen took the events seriously. The third and fourth stanzas, however, indicate that Jamaicans soon developed an interest in a war which sought to defeat, *inter alia,* the excesses of racism. (p. 18)

The aftermath of war brought much suffering and countless problems. Not least among these were the war-babies—the offspring of war. With a full knowledge of attitudes in her society, Louise Bennett in **"White Pickney"** gives "sound" advice to a Jamaican on what to do with her offspring or "souvenir", as she called the little ones in another war-time poem, **"Solja Work"**.

Politics (the third section) fascinated Miss Bennett. Almost from the beginning she caught the political temper of the times and her capacity to comment succinctly on the paradoxes of politics and the whims of politicians stayed with her and even matured right down to the time of Independence. The first five poems in this section recapture the crises of the late thirties and early forties, the emergence of labour leaders, the advent of the Moyne Commission and the persistence of hard times.... (p. 19)

The fourth section represents a collection of poems dealing with a variety of topics that are of general interest and relevance to life in the Jamaican community in the past and to-day. True, there are allusions which put some in a strict historical context but they also deal with the wandering Jamaican—the migrant.... The traveling Jamaican (in these cases Louise Bennett herself) continues to be a phenomenon in his display of a capacity to cope with any situation, whether it be the endless anti-colonial conferences of well-meaning Fabians (**"Poor Gum"**) or the carryings-on of a Welsh Eisteddfod (**"Eena Wales"**).

Back home, the litigiousness of the tenement and some peasant life (**"House O'Law"**) is sometimes the result of the unending yard quarrels or "tracing-matches" between people (**"Kas-Kas"** and **"Cuss-Cuss"**). Pugnacious maidservants who defy a rising and sometimes conscienceless middle-class are a force to be reckoned with (**"Me Bredda"** and **"Seeking a Job"**), and the persistent superstitions in Jamaican folklore with its oil-o-love me, duppies (ghosts), signs of the end and rolling calves are worthy of Bennettian comment.

The poem **"Po' Sammy"** caricatures the love for pets, while the two following poems recapture the Anancy spirit everywhere evident in the ease with which people will turn someone's misfortunes to their own advantage. The street urchin and "corpie" (policeman), the exuberance of love-making and the Jamaican's predisposition to preachments are dealt with in **"Street Boy"**, **"Love Letta"**, **"Uriah Preach"** and **"Amy Son"** respectively. Then comes the series dealing with the understandably conscious acquisition of a foreign tongue or accent as a status symbol—an all too common occurrence among Jamaicans returning from "foreign" or visiting a place like **"Gay Paree"**. When one chap returns from America

with no trace of linguistic influence, Miss Bennett rues the situation in **"Noh Lickle Twang"**. Yet another status symbol, that of colour, comes in for sharp comment in **"Colour Bar"** and **"Pass Fe White"**. And for those who insist on being black, **"Back To Africa"** offers some sane advice about this particular shade of identity.

The section ends with three poems which take as their subject matter the very substance of Miss Bennett's art. **"Mash Flat"** is a commentary on the flexibility of the Jamaican language, even if it leads to confusion in communication. The poem **"Proverbs"** consciously utilises the epigrams of folk-speech, which are a distillation of a folk's collective experience. And **"Bans O'Killing"** stand on its own as a kind of declaration of Miss Bennett's belief in the strength and inner consistency of the language which she has chosen for her art.... [Jamaica has] seen many crusaders against "bad speaking" ever since it was established that a command of "Standard English" was a passport to status and class in the island. There has developed genuine academic interest in the Jamaican dialect, which has been carefully studied by reputable scholars, but it is still target of middle-class snobbery. Although it has been accepted for entertainment largely through the efforts of people like Louise Bennett, and even though its literary merit is conceded by some, it still carries with it the stigma of ignorance and nonsophistication. Louise Bennett has often been the target of attack and the fact that **"Bans O'Killing"** was written in 1944 near the beginning of her career, gives the reader some insight into Miss Bennett's early sense of purpose and literary courage. That the earlier criticisms are far less applicable today is to the credit of Louise Bennett, who has never doubted the power of the language she uses to express the essential passions of her people's hearts.

Her inspiration came, and still comes, from the everyday happenings around her. She is acutely sensitive to these occurrences and finds in them a thousand wonders—wonders easily concealed from those of us who have been too long conditioned to seeing the worth of human experience only in the deeds of kings and conquerors. She may not have bothered to ask in explicit terms about the ends of existence. Nor did she labour on the fears that men have about their inevitable mortality. Instead she concentrated on the immediacy of the task of having to survive. An uprooted, poor, but proud people are primarily concerned about surviving, having found themselves alive. They make the best of it with an intelligent optimism which is the occasion of Miss Bennett's bright-side-of-life humour. Humour becomes, as it were, the expression of a people's will to live and Miss Bennett recaptures this will with understanding, compassion and truth. (pp. 21-4)

Rex Nettleford, in an introduction to Jamaica Labrish *by Louise Bennett, Sangster's Book Stores, 1966, pp. 9-24.*

Carolyn Cooper (essay date 1978)

[*In the following excerpt, Cooper reviews* Jamaica
Labrish, *stating that the majority of the poems are "a
kind of comedy of manners."*]

In a 1968 interview with the Jamaican poet Dennis
Scott, Louise Bennett describes how her use of Jamaican
Creole as poetic language disqualified her from membership in the Jamaican Poetry League: "... I have
been set apart by other creative writers a long time ago
because of the language I speak and work in. From the
beginning nobody ever recognized me as a writer. 'Well,
she is doing dialect'; it wasn't even writing you know.
Up to now a lot of people don't even think I write. They
say 'Oh, you just stand up and say these things!'" But
the very characteristic of Bennett's style that had
alienated her from the literati—the vivacious immediacy of her Jamaican Creole rhythms—has been recognized in contemporary reassessments of her poetry as its
strength. (p. 322)

The poems in Bennett's collection *Jamaica Labrish,*
spanning approximately twenty-five years, cover a
broad spectrum of dramatic personalities and events.
The poems are classified in four groups: City Life, War-
Time, Politics, and Jamaica—Now An' Then. Some of
the subject matter is so topical that not all historical
details are easily accessible to the contemporary reader.
But the majority of poems constitute a kind of comedy
of manners in which those recurring rascals of Caribbean societies—social climbers, petty crooks, displaced
colonials, to name a few—come decidedly to grief.

One kind of social climber whom Bennett satirizes
ruthlessly—for obvious reasons—is the character who
feels impelled to deny any connections with the Creole
culture. Several poems in the collection poke fun at this
character type with varying degrees of gentleness. **"Dry
Foot Bwoy"** satirizes a Jamaican of peasant stock who
has travelled to England, perhaps to study, and has
returned with an English accent and a bad case of
linguistic amnesia. He can no longer converse with his
former acquaintances, much to their annoyance, for he
disclaims knowledge of Jamaican Creole.... (pp. 322-
23)

Similarly the poem **"Noh Lickle Twang"** makes fun of a
woman who is embarrassed because her son, newly
returned from the States after six months abroad,
doesn't have even the slightest trace of an American
accent. He cannot, therefore, be shown off to the
discriminating neighbours, who, once he opens his
mouth will think that he's merely been to "Mocho"—
the archetypal Jamaican village that epitomizes social
gaucheness. The depth of the young man's failure must
be measured against his sister's success in acquiring the
semblance of an American accent after having had only
one week's exposure to American expatriates. The fact
that her parents cannot understand her is the proof of
her sophistication. (pp. 323-24)

In some poems in which Bennett confronts the demeaning poverty of the Jamaican worker—more often, non-
worker—the comic vision seems inadequate to express
the sustained pathos of intense poverty. The pain of
deprivation cannot always be sublimated in laughter.
The pair of poems that I shall now consider, **"Me
Bredda"** and **"My Dream,"** demonstrate the differences
of tone that Bennett can employ in examining the same
subject matter. In both poems the persona is that of a
female domestic servant, who, in Jamaica, has been an
ubiquitous symbol of middle-class exploitation of cheap
peasant labour. But whereas **"Me Bredda,"** in true
comic spirit, vigorously affirms the supremacy of Good
over Evil, **"My Dream"** articulates the burgeoning
political engagement of the oppressed in colonial Jamaica.

In **"Me Bredda,"** the servant manages to outwit her
prospective employer, a middle-class housewife who, on
a whim, has threatened not to hire her for the day's work
even though she had previously arranged to do so. The
servant, refusing to be intimidated by her opponent's
adamant stance, vociferously demands that expectant
onlookers summon her brother to avenge her. The
housewife, for fear of the inevitable brawl with the irate
maid—plus her brother—succumbs to the demands of
propriety. The maid's final repartee as she smugly
departs with two week's wages and her reimbursed taxi
fare is:

> You would like fe know me bredda?
> Me kean help you eena dat
> Me hooda like know him meself
> For is me one me parents got....

The vivacious maid is the clever rogue, who both dupes
the housewife and manages to convince us of the
rightness of her actions. She is a type of Anansi-figure—
that recurring hero-rascal of Caribbean folk culture—for
whom the end—survival—justifies the means—deception.

"My Dream" is an allegorical poem in which the class
struggle of **"Me Bredda"** is transformed into the nationalistic struggles of Jamaica against colonial England.
The servant—Jamaica—is compelled by malevolent
cousin Rose—England—to launder a bottomless tub of
soiled clothes. The exploited servant, powerless to
openly antagonize cousin Rose, resorts to displacing her
aggression on the laundry.... The undercurrent of
rebellion that the action of displacement reveals is an
insidious political force—akin to the cunning of the
Anansi-figure—that is celebrated in the proverb, the
traditional repository of folk wisdom:

> Dog a-sweat but long hair hide i',
> Mout a-laugh, but heart-a-leap!
> Everything wha shine noh gole piece....

(pp. 324-25)

The strength of Bennett's poetry then is the accuracy
with which it depicts and attempts to correct through

laughter the absurdities of Jamaican society. Its comic vision affirms a norm of common sense and good-natured decorum. The limitations of the poetry are partially the inevitable consequences of having used Jamaican Creole as a poetic medium. For what the experiments in Creole—whether St. Lucian, Trinidadian, or Barbadian, for example—have indicated is that there are subtle nuances of thought and feeling that are at times best expressed in Creole, at times in English. The poet who relies exclusively on either medium reduces the expressive range of his/her art.

Louise Bennett, having chosen to write exclusively in Jamaican Creole, cannot easily answer the charge of parochialism and insularity. But what she loses in universality she gains in vivid particularity. In her own words: "You know, one reason I persisted writing in dialect in spite of all the opposition was because nobody else was doing so and there was such rich material in the dialect that I wanted to put on paper some of the wonderful things that people say in dialect. You could never say 'look here' as vividly as 'kuyah.'" (pp. 325-26)

> *Carolyn Cooper, "Caribbean Poetry in English: 1900-1976," in* World Literature Written in English, *Vol. 17, No. 1, April, 1978, pp. 312-27.*

Loreto Todd (essay date 1984)

[*In the following review, Todd explores the "creolized Jamaican speech" of Bennett's* Selected Poems.]

Louise Bennett has, for over forty years, been well known to Jamaicans and to creolists as an entertainer who delights in the exploitation of Jamaican folk speech. Her stature as a poet has taken longer to recognize, but Mervyn Morris' selection of poems allows a much wider audience to read and absorb her warmth and wit, her wisdom and artistry. Many critics may conclude that she is not a *great* poet, but few will deny her ability to delineate character or to open doors, not only into the lives of Jamaicans but into the innermost recesses of the minds of people everywhere.

[*Selected Poems* (1982)] has a seventeen-page introduction; eighty-one poems subdivided into sixteen semantically related sections; forty-five pages of notes, comments and suggestions which could stimulate discussion; an eight-page glossary and a useful three-page index. Although the poems represent, for the most part, creolized Jamaican speech, the orthography employed is based on the spelling conventions of standard English:

> Bwoy, yuh no shame? Is so yuh come?
> After yuh tan so lang!
> Not even lickle language, bwoy?
> Not even lickle twang?
>   . . . .
> An yuh sister what work ongle
> One week wid Merican
> She talk so nice now dat we have
> De jooce fi understan?

The decision to use the orthography of standard English has the advantage of not making the language appear so different from international norms as to be almost incomprehensible. Using the phonetic conventions of the *Dictionary of Jamaican English,* the last four lines quoted would appear:

> An yu sista wat wok uonggl
> Wan wiik wid Merikaan
> Shii taak suo nais nou dat wii hab
> Di juus fi ondastaan.

There are, however, two serious disadvantages inherent in the selection of standard English spellings. In the first place, Jamaican English is made to look like a substandard dialect and not a creole language with its own systematic rules and coherent logic. Secondly, the standard English conventions give a very inadequate idea of the pronunciation of Jamaican English. Since many of the nuances and a great deal of the humour hinge on pronunciation, the spelling employed involved considerable loss for the reader who is not familiar with Jamaican English.

Louise Bennett's art is essentially oral and thus, although much can be gleaned from a silent reading, the full vitality of the language can only be appreciated when the work is read aloud. If we consider the following stanza, for example:

> Good mahnin, Teacher, ow is yuh?
> My name is Sarah Pool.
> Dis is fi-me li bwoy Michal
> An me just bring him a school.

we can see that it is based on the traditional ballad quatrain, such as:

> O she was buried near the old church gate
> And he was buried near the spire,
> And out of his grave grew a red, red rose
> And out of hers a briar.

Bennett's stanza appears to be rhythmically irregular until we hear it read aloud and realize that Jamaican English is syllable-timed not stress-timed like British English. We thus have, when account is taken of liaison, complete regularity with the pattern:

> A + B   14 syllables
> C + B   14 syllables

instead of the British:

> A   4 strong stresses
> B   3 strong stresses
> C   4 strong stresses
> B   3 strong stresses

Since Louise Bennett's art is essentially oral, we find in it many of the techniques associated with oral literature: mnemonic devices like lists:

> We call him Mi, Mike, Mikey,
> Jay, Jakey, Jacob, Jack

But him right name is Michal Jacob
Alexander Black;

repetition patterns of sound, vocabulary and syntax:

Some a go weh fi vacation,
Some a go weh fi tun "high,"
Some a go fi edication,
But de whole a dem a fly!
. . . .
Me ask meself warra matter,
Me ask meself wha meck,
Is tidal wave or earthquake or
Is storm deh dah expec?;

aphorisms:

Koo omuch time him slip police!
Koo omuch blood him shed!
But no care how man seh dem bad,
Man cyaan badder dan Dead!;

and the adept use of proverbs which can lend a timeless
wisdom to her verse:

Di same sinting weh sweet man mout
Wi meck him lose him head.

It is difficult to know where to stop in a review such as
this. Every poem, almost every line is worth a comment
for its humour, satire, pathos, irony, insight, its love of
people and life. Morris has selected well and given us
the means of sharing Louise Bennett's vision. Her firm
opinions and keen insights are like maypoles around
which the language dances. It would be hard, I think, to
listen to this language without being moved to serious
thoughts by its message and to joy by its rhythms. (pp.
414-16)

*Loreto Todd, in a review of "Selected
Poems," in* World Literature Written in
English, *Vol. 23, No. 2, Spring, 1984, pp.
414-16.*

FURTHER READING

James, Louis. Introduction to *The Islands in Between:
Essays on West Indian Literature,* edited by Louis James,
pp. 1-49. London: Oxford University Press, 1968.
    Discusses Bennett's *Jamaica Labrish,* proposing that
    "her verse is a valuable aid to the social historian. Her
    selection of themes reflects the concerns of Jamaican
    life; the public ones—Federation, street peddlers,
    body-building contests, Paul Robeson's visit to Jamai-
    ca, emigration or an infuriating telephone system; and
    the private—the yard gossip or the death of a pet
    turkey watched by a hungry neighbor."

Morris, Mervyn. "Louise Bennett." In *Fifty Caribbean
Writers: A Bio-Bibliographical Critical Sourcebook,* edited
by Daryl Cumber Dance, pp. 35-45. Westport, Conn.:
Greenwood Press, 1986.
    Brief biography of Bennett. Morris also reviews Ben-
    nett's major works and summarizes critical reactions
    to her poetry.

Review of *Jamaica Labrish,* by Louise Bennett. *Times
Literary Supplement* No. 3381 (15 December 1966): 1173.
    Review of *Jamaica Labrish,* concluding: "Only the
    most devoted and nostalgic admirer will read this
    volume through, though many will wish they could
    hear Miss Bennett fill out the text with the richness of
    her voice, presence, personality and humour."

Wilmot, Cynthia. "The Honorable Miss Lou." *Américas*
35, No. 1 (January/February 1983): 55.
    Profile of Bennett and her works.

Mongo Beti

1932-

(Born Alexandre Biyidi; also wrote under pseudonym Eza Boto) Cameroonian francophone novelist, short story writer, and nonfiction writer.

Many critics regard Beti as one of the greatest francophone novelists of black Africa. His often controversial reputation began with three works published in close succession: *Le pauvre Christ de Bomba* (1956; *The Poor Christ of Bomba*, 1971); *Mission terminée* (1957; *Mission Accomplished*, 1958); and *Le roi miraculé* (1958; *King Lazarus*, 1960). In these novels Beti unleashed his Rabelaisian humor to create a series of harsh but comic indictments of French colonial rule in Cameroon. Later, in *Remember Ruben* (1974; *Remember Ruben*, 1980) and *Perpétue et l'habitude du malheur* (1974; *Perpetua and the Habit of Unhappiness*, 1978), Beti criticized the corruption he witnessed in Cameroon during the years of independence.

Born in the small Cameroonian town of Mbalmayo, Beti was educated in local French missionary schools until his expulsion for unknown reasons at the age of fourteen. He then attended the lycée in Cameroon's capital, Yaoundé. He went to France in 1951, studying first at the University of Aix-en-Provence and then at the Sorbonne in Paris. He received his *licence*, or B.A., with honors from the last-named institution. Later, Beti began teaching French literature, classical Greek, and Latin in various lycées in France—an occupation that continues to this day. With the exception of one brief visit, during which the Cameroonian security police imprisoned and interrogated him, Beti has not returned to Cameroon.

While he was a student at Aix, Beti wrote and published his first novel, *Ville cruelle* (meaning "cruel city"), under the pseudonym Eza Boto. He has since repudiated both the novel and the pseudonym. This work is generally considered weak and melodramatic, but Gerald Moore, writing in 1980, claimed: *"Ville cruelle* is a rather bad novel, but it is manifestly not the work of a bad writer."* In 1956, Beti published *The Poor Christ of Bomba*, an indictment of missionary activity in Africa. The novel consists of diary entries by Denis, a naïve African acolyte who is devoted to his patron, Reverend Father Superior Drumont. In an ingenuous but well-meaning way, Drumont has set out to convert the inhabitants of a bush village and save them from the greed and temptation that had corrupted Europeans. In time, Drumont discovers that the Africans had only embraced his religion hoping to learn the Europeans' secrets of material success, and he returns to Europe, disgusted and in despair. Apparently because of its severe and overwhelmingly negative account of the missionaries, *The Poor Christ of Bomba* was banned outright in French Africa and was controversial in

France, where critics defended the French record in Africa against Beti's account. Beti followed with *Mission Accomplished*, the story of young, Western-educated Jean-Marie Medza and his mission to retrieve the wayward wife of a relation in "primitive" Kala. According to A. C. Brench in *The Novelists' Inheritance in French Africa* (1967), "Initially, [Jean Marie] looks upon this mission as a means of parading his superior knowledge. Only later does he realize how inadequate his education and understanding of life really are.... Jean-Marie appreciates more and more, as his stay lengthens, the positive qualities [the villagers] have and which he has never been able to acquire." In *King Lazarus*, Beti's next offering, some of the clergy from *The Poor Christ of Bomba* reappear, but this time the missionary, Father Le Guen, is somewhat more zealous and uncompromising than Father Drumont of *The Poor Christ of Bomba*. In the novel, Father Le Guen persuades the polygamous tribal chief of the Essazam to convert to Christianity and give up all but one of his wives. The twenty-two former wives and their families, outraged at the breach of tribal custom as well as at the rudeness of turning the women out of their home, protest to the French colonial authorities. In the confrontation between the civil administration, the missionary, and the tribal chief, Beti exposes the vices of each party.

While Beti's early work has been called "astonishingly varied," there are at least two elements common to all the novels: humor and disdain for the colonial system. This mixture of comedy and contempt had little precedent in the history of African fiction. As Fernando Lambert maintained in a 1976 *Yale French Studies* essay, "By adopting two antithetical levels of representation—the tragedy of the fate forced upon Africans by colonization and the comedy of characters and situations made possible by such a state of affairs—Beti establishes a form of dialectic which allows the necessary demystification of colonial pretensions and also the affirmation of Negro humor . . . . Beti is the first to open this path to African literature."

Although Beti's early works were generally warmly received by critics, they made little money for their author, and Beti found it necessary to teach in order to support himself and his family. After *King Lazarus,* he stopped writing novels for more than a decade. In 1972, however, he published a political essay, *Main basse sur le Cameroun* ("The Plundering of Cameroon"). In it he criticized the Yaoundé regime for remaining under the control of the French long after Cameroon's formal liberation in 1960. For years Beti had written essays on current affairs in Africa, but with *Main basse sur le Cameroun* he shifted from a historical perspective to an essentially topical one. In 1974 Beti published two novels, *Remember Ruben* and *Perpetua and the Habit of Unhappiness.* The former work follows the life of a solitary young boy, renamed Mor-Zamba by the villagers who take him in, and a friend he makes, Abena. When Mor-Zamba is older his neighbors send him to a labor camp to prevent his marriage to the daughter of a prominent villager, and Abena goes after him. The men reunite eighteen years later, Abena having become a revolutionary and a hero, and Mor-Zamba having learned his true origin. In *Remember Ruben,* Beti emphasized the corruption of national politics through glimpses of the harshness of individual lives, a theme he explored again in *Perpetua and the Habit of Unhappiness,* a critique of the slave-like conditions of the modern woman in contemporary Africa. The novel focuses on the miserable marriage of the main character, Perpetua, to her husband, Edouard; the tender but doomed affair between Perpetua and her lover, Zeyang; and the true friendship between Perpetua and her companion, Anna-Marie. Critics have praised these novels, commending Beti's new focus on African independence. Writing in *CLA Journal* in 1976, Robert P. Smith, Jr. maintained: "Mongo Beti has broken his silence, not to criticize the colonial past as was his custom, but to accuse the present period of independence and self-government, and to attempt to pave the way to a better future for Africa and Africans."

Beti has since published a sequel to *Remember Ruben* titled *La ruine presque cocasse d'une polichinelle* (1979; *Lament for an African Pol,* 1985). A novel that "no serious reader of African literature can afford to neglect," according to N. F. Lazarus, *Lament for an African Pol* chronicles the activities of Mor-Zamba, who reappears from the novel *Remember Ruben* with two revolutionary friends to organize a resistance "against the despotic rule of a colonially sanctioned chief." In addition to writing other novels, Beti found and edited *Peuples noirs Peuples africains,* a journal of francophone black radicals. Beti, as one of the first francophone African novelists to combine humor and perceptive social criticism, is widely recognized as a master among African writers of all languages. As critic Smith concluded in *CLA Journal,* Beti is "one of the best of the contemporary black African novelists who seek to promote true liberty in Africa and to insure a lasting dignity for her."

(For further information about Beti's life and works, see *Black Writers; Contemporary Authors,* Vols. 114, 124; and *Contemporary Literary Criticism,* Vol. 27.)

PRINCIPAL WORKS

"Sans haine et sans amour" (short story) 1953; published in periodical *Présence Africaine*
Ville cruelle [as Eza Boto] (novel) 1954
Le pauvre Christ de Bomba (novel) 1956
    [*The Poor Christ of Bomba,* 1971]
Mission terminée (novel) 1957
    [*Mission Accomplished,* 1958; also published as *Mission to Kala,* 1964]
Le roi miraculé: Chronique des Essazam (novel) 1958
    [*King Lazarus,* 1960; also published as *King Lazarus: A Novel,* 1971]
Main basse sur le Cameroun: Autopsie d'une décolonisation (political essay) 1972
Perpétue et l'habitude du malheur (novel) 1974
    [*Perpetua and the Habit of Unhappiness,* 1978]
Remember Ruben (novel) 1974
    [*Remember Ruben,* 1980]
La ruine presque cocasse d'un polichinelle: Remember Ruben deux (novel) 1979
    [*Lament for an African Pol,* 1985]
Les deux mères de Guillaume Ismael Dzewatama: Futur camionneur (novel) 1982
La revanche de Guillaume Isamel Dzewatama (novel) 1984

Wole Soyinka (essay date 1963)

[*A Nigerian playwright, poet, and novelist, Soyinka has been called Africa's finest living writer. Winner of the 1986 Nobel Prize in literature, he, like Beti, has blended comedy and social commentary in many of his works. In the following excerpt from his 1963 essay*

"From a Common Back Cloth: A Reassessment of the African Literary Image," he praises Beti for creating in Mission to Kala *a "human" character, one that is unhampered by an idealization of the African literary image.*]

Compassion is the twin brother of Mongo Beti's grand iconoclasm (or perhaps what we are looking for is a word that combines the two.) **Mission to Kala,** bawdy, riotous, bursting on every page with sheer animal vitality, reads like that rare piece of studied artistry, an unpremeditated novel. In the literary effort to establish the African as, first before all else, a human being, Mongo Beti with this novel has leaped to the fore as the archpriest of the African's humanity. Mongo Beti takes the back cloth as he finds it, asserting simply that tradition is upheld not by one-dimensional innocents, but by cunning old codgers on chieftaincy stools, polygamous elders, watching hawklike the approach of young blood around their harem, by the eternal trouble-making females who plunge innocents, unaware, into memorable odysseys. Hospitality is not, as we are constantly romantically informed that it is, nearly so spontaneous. There is a mercenary edge, and this, alas, is not always traceable to that alien corrupt civilization!

Peter Abrahams, Alan Paton, Onuora Nzekwu, William Conton—like the poetasters of the cultural dilemma—one after another they fall down and fail at the altar of humanity because they have not written of the African from the dignity and authority of self-acceptance. . . . Writers like Chinua Achebe, Mongo Beti and lately the South African Alex la Guma are, however, making restoration to the human image of the African. Mongo Beti, unlike the others, has employed the medium of comedy, or as he himself puts it, "my first, perhaps my only love: the absurdity of life." It is a love that many Africans tend to spurn, for it flatly rejects inflation:

> Come and restore
> Again to us
> The dignity
> Of our ancestral past
> The charity of heart
> And benevolence of soul
> Regard for age . . .
> And readiness to use
> Our strength
> To animate the weak.

The lines of a Ghanaian poet. And pure fiction. The ancestral spirits surely enjoyed the irony, for only a few pages away in the same publication the following stage directions appear in a play, *The Council of Abura,* also by a Ghanaian. "A stalwart ruffian near-by readily obeys the command and strikes the poor blind face." New dimensions in ancestral animation.

Mongo Beti has made tradition a thoroughly viable proposition. His Kala is the entire sweep of our now familiar back cloth, interpreted faithfully through a most suspiciously exact vein of wonder and participation. He has translated the slight alienation of his hero into village terms, with no condescension, no stances;

the magnificent candor of the hero, Jean-Marie Medza, stranger to Kala, creates a vigorous clarity in characters, a precision of edges that Chinua Achebe, with no such uninhibited agent to hand, achieved in neither of his books. Sex is restored to its natural proportions, not a startling discovery made by the European every publishing day, nor a neo-Africanist venture sung by the apostles of negritude and sanctified in shrines to puberty. Beti makes sex an unquestioned attitude; the result is that he demonstrates a truly idyllic love dignified by humor, by pathos, and crucial to the novel as a major factor in the development of a young, sensitive personality.

So, it can be done. Biblical ponderosities in the mouth of black dignity prove, in the end, as unreal as gutturals in the mouth of Hollywood fantasia. And the bald imitation of European *personal* idioms is simply so much schoolboy exercise. Only through the confidence of individual art, like the early Tutuola, through the hurtful realism of Alex la Guma, the sincerity of Chinua Achebe and the total defiant self-acceptance of Mongo Beti, can the African emerge as a creature of sensibilities. These are only a few examples. Idealization is a travesty of literary truth; worse still, it betrays only immature hankerings of the creative impulse. (pp. 394-96)

> *Wole Soyinka, "From a Common Back Cloth: A Reassessment of the African Literary Image," in* The American Scholar, *Vol. 32, No. 3, Summer, 1963, pp. 387-96.*

C. H. Wake (essay date 1963)

[*In the following excerpt, Wake comments on the concept of negritude—the consciousness of—and pride in, the cultural aspects of an African heritage—in works by West African writers, particularly Beti.*]

The main theme of all West African writing in French is that of cultural conflict between Africa and Europe. Negritude tends to be regarded as the philosophy by which French-speaking Africans express this conflict, but, in fact, it is to give their writing a false bias to so regard it. There is only one major writer in French-speaking West Africa who preaches the philosophy of negritude to any extent, the well-known Senegalese poet Léopold Sédar Senghor. The remaining writers, mostly novelists, are content to express themselves on this subject in a more direct way, without the medium of a system. (p. 156)

The approach to the theme of cultural conflict is treated very differently in [West African novels than it is in the poetry of Senghor]. The novel in French-speaking West Africa is more inclined to social realism, unless one excepts certain symbolic aspects of Camara Laye's novel, *Le regard du roi* (translated into English as *The Radiance of the King*). Nor does the novel have the same vision into the future, except implicitly, that one finds in Senghor's poetry. Perhaps more in keeping with its own nature, the novel in Africa tends to deal with the situation as the novelist finds it. There is unfortunately no space to make a comprehensive study of the novel from French-speaking West Africa in this article. I shall have to limit myself to one writer. Mongo Beti is in many ways the most interesting of the novelists. He has now produced four novels, and although it is four years since he published his last one, there is no indication from what he has given us already that his creative ability is exhausted. Apart from his rather cynical inclination to see all society in terms of corruption through fornication, the central theme of his novels is the complete failure of European culture to make any impact on African society. The action of his novels usually takes place somewhere in the African bush, and his favorite approach is through the Christian missionary and his failure to convert Africa to Christianity. While he treats him harshly, he also treats him with considerable sympathy, partly because he obviously has a deep detestation of the colonial administrator, whom he sees as the missionary's enemy as much as the African's and partly because the missionary alone has tried, sincerely if inadequately, to know and to understand Africa. He has tried, but he has failed hopelessly, because of his cultural arrogance. *Le pauvre Christ de Bomba,* to take one example, is the story of a missionary, Fr. Drumont, who comes to the realization that, although he has lived in Africa for twenty years and thrown himself heart and soul into his apostolate, he has not made any genuine impression on the African. He undertakes a journey into the country of the Tala tribe whom he had left alone for two years as a punishment. He finds the Faith everywhere in ruins, symbolized by the dilapidated churches and the widespread return to polygamy and the traditional religion, which he despises. Slowly he comes to realize that he has never really known the African and that he has tried to force him into a way of life too alien from his traditions. Beti's great thesis is that African society has much deeper roots than the white man realizes. Disillusioned and broken in spirit, Fr. Drumont returns to his mission at Bomba, only to discover that there, too, everything is corrupt. The book closes with the abandonment of the mission, the final symbol of failure. Yet, although Beti aims at showing the failure of Christianity to make any impact on Africa, he seems to have little faith in traditional African society, and palm wine, polygamy and promiscuity become symbols of its decay. Perhaps this explains why he now permanently resides in Paris. (p. 157)

> *C. H. Wake, "Cultural Conflict in the Writings of Senghor and Mongo Beti," in* Books Abroad, *Vol. 37, No. 2, Spring, 1963, pp. 156-57.*

The Times Literary Supplement (essay date 1969)

[*In the following unsigned 1969* Times Literary Supplement *review, a critic offers a lukewarm appraisal of Beti's* King Lazarus.]

Mongo Beti was born in a Bantu tribe in the French Cameroons, educated at the local lycée and later studied in the arts faculties of Aix-en-Provence and the Sorbonne. *King Lazarus* was first published in Paris as *Le Roi Miraculé* in 1958 and in 1960 in this anonymous English translation. It is a satire on French colonial administration, civil and religious, in a Bantu community in 1948; and since its topicality is obsolete, it has presumably been reissued in the belief that the nature of its satire is universal.

The polygamous chief of the Essazam tribe is on the threshold of death. In spite of, or because of, his 23 wives and his prodigious intake of palm-wine, he is a pillar of the French Civil Establishment, and a thorn in the flesh of the Reverend Father Le Guen, the local Roman Catholic missionary. After more than a week of illness, in the course of which he is baptised by his antique aunt and given Extreme Unction by Le Guen, this gross old pagan recovers, or, as he himself claims, comes back to life.

This miraculous recovery precipitates disaster. Now a Christian, and given a baptismal name of Lazarus, he must abandon polygamy and take one wife in Christian matrimony. When he chooses the youngest and prettiest and orders the other twenty-two back to their villages, their relatives converge on Essazam to protest tribal custom. On their heels come the French colonial authorities, the Negro doctor who is ambitious to represent Essazam in the legislature, Lequeux the Chief Regional Administrator, and his assistant from the Antilles.

For them all except Le Guen the obvious solution is peace at any price. What could be more civilized than that the twenty-two ex-wives should continue to live in Essazam and that King Lazarus having been conspicuously converted should be allowed inconspicuously to relapse into paganism? Lequeux offers the missionary a free run of the women and children, so long as he leaves the old men alone. The Reverend Father, anticipating a mass-conversion, following the raising of King Lazarus, stands his ground, until that ground is removed from under his feet, by his transfer to another post.

King Lazarus is blend of French wit with African laughter. But it hardly achieves the universality necessary for it to stand on its own after the end of the colonial situation on which it was a comment.

> *"Dated Laughter," in* The Times Literary Supplement, *No. 3507, May 15, 1969, p. 507.*

Thomas Cassirer (essay date 1970)

[*In the following excerpt, Cassirer identifies "bearers of Western ideas"—European missionaries and African students—in Beti's novels and comments on the author's portrayal of their failures.*]

All three [of Mongo Beti's novels, *Le Pauvre Christ de Bomba, Mission terminée,* and *Le Roi miraculé],* comment, in a mixture of light-hearted farce and bitter satire, on the problems encountered in the quest for an "intellectual direction," and present us with a critical portrayal of the man of ideas, the potential guide of the disoriented African.

Mongo Beti has not been generally considered in this light. Critics have usually spoken of him as one of Africa's foremost authors, "a formidable satirist and one of the most percipient critics of European colonialism," or, like Wole Soyinka and Robert Pageard, they have stressed his realistic portrayal of African life and praised his work.... In a sense Mongo Beti himself is responsible for this one-sided appreciation of his work, for he has chosen to set his portrayal of the man of ideas in the incongruous locale of the bush village, rather than in the modern city that might have seemed more appropriate. Yet this incongruity is not introduced merely as an effective comic device. It also serves to present the universal problem of disorientation in specifically African terms.

Mongo Beti's African village is situated at the meeting point between traditional communal life and a new awareness of imminent change. Within this context he raises the problem of "intellectual direction" by introducing into the village protagonists who are bearers of Western ideas as well as actual or potential guides for the villagers in their prospective odyssey into the modern world. The novels form a loose trilogy that describes the encounter between the village and the protagonists during the last three decades of European colonial rule: *Le Pauvre Christ de Bomba* takes place in the late nineteen thirties, at a time when European colonialism is still in complete control of Africa. *Le Roi miraculé* is set in the late nineteen forties and touches on the liberalization of the colonial regime brought about by the war. In *Mission terminée,* set in the nineteen fifties, the colonial authorities no longer appear and the action takes place in an entirely African community.

This time-span of some twenty years brings only one essential change to the village. The two novels set in the post-war world highlight a situation of conflict between the generations that is not mentioned in the pre-war world of *Le Pauvre Christ de Bomba.* Apart from this development,... there is little to distinguish the earthly peasant society of one novel from that of another. It is essentially pagan society, but pagan in the popular sense of the word, with none of the animist religious tradition that we find in Camara Laye's Kouroussa or Achebe's Umuofia. Mongo Beti's peasants are fun-loving materialists, possessed of an earthy good sense and considerable physical vitality. They live in what is still a stable, at times even stagnant, village society that is tightly ruled by the conventions of African social tradition.

Into this stable peasant world Mongo Beti introduces two types of protagonists: European missionaries and African students. Both of these, as one would expect, bring with them Western ideas, but in the context of Mongo Beti's conception of a materialist and socially

conservative African society they also represent a new kind of man whose life is guided by ideas and learning, and not solely by convention or self-interest. These two protagonists follow each other in the chronological sequence of the novel trilogy's epic time. The first novel is dominated by the figure of the "Christ" of the mission of Bomba, the Reverend Father Drumont. In the novel set in the late nineteen forties, *Le Roi miraculé,* Father Drumont's former assistant, Father Le Guen, shares the spotlight with two African students, Kris and Bitama. In *Mission terminée* an African student, Jean Medza, is the sole protagonist.

The missionaries are fully rounded figures whose characterization is drawn with a mixture of empathy and critical verve. Mongo Beti avoids the facile anticlericalism that turns the missionary figures of his fellow Camerounian Ferdinand Oyono into caricatures of the most unchristian type of priest, selfish, materialist, and scornful of the black man. Mongo Beti's missionaries have come to Africa inspired by what one might call a "primitivist" Christian faith, a belief in the childlike virtues of the African which should allow him to enter the Kingdom of Heaven far more easily than the white man once he has accepted the Christian message. The missionaries are the only figures in the novels whose life is guided by single-minded devotion to a faith, and they are also the only ones who explicitly believe in a universal humanity that transcends barriers of race and culture.... Yet the missionaries' faith in universal humanity remains purely abstract because their primitivist view of the African leads them to treat him as a pure child of nature with no cultural identity of his own. They cannot even conceive of adapting Christianity to African customs, an inflexibility that seems particularly striking in the representatives of a Church that has always been known for its ability to incorporate indigenous pre-Christian beliefs and practices into its structure.

It comes then as no surprise that the Africans in *Le Pauvre Christ de Bomba* repeatedly explain the missionary's failure with the statement that "Christ was not a Black man." From the time of the novel's publication, when it provoked considerable protest in Catholic and colonial circles, this has also generally been considered to be the essence of Mongo Beti's thesis. Yet the missionaries in his novels are too complex to be merely typed as the butt of an anticolonialist and anti-Christian satire. The predicament of Father Drumont in particular does not result merely from his disregard of the vitality of African customs. He finds himself defeated as well by the pervasive influence of Western materialist civilization even in the African bush. It was his opposition to this materialism that originally brought him to Africa filled with the hope of converting the natives to the Christian faith and thus protecting them from the forces which had corrupted the Europeans. He discovers, however, that his apparent success during the early years of his mission stemmed from a complete misunderstanding between him and his African converts, who flocked to him precisely in search of the secret of

European material success.... This mutual misunderstanding between the missionary and his African parishioners comes to a head at the climactic ending to the novel when Father Drumont discovers that over the years his African assistants had turned his mission from a center of Christian piety into a hotbed of corruption. Like other Catholic missions in Cameroun the mission at Bomba included a *sixa,* a house where African girls spent some months before their marriage to be instructed in the duties of a Christian wife. Father Drumont belatedly becomes aware that his assistant, his cook, and his other acolytes have exploited the *sixa* as a ready source of labor, money, and sexual pleasure. In fact the *sixa* is revealed to be spreading not so much Christian moral as venereal disease throughout the region. Faced with this horrendous proof that he has unknowingly served as an agent for the very corruption from which he tried to protect the Africans, Father Drumont returns to Europe in despair.

There is a certain ambivalence in Mongo Beti's treatment of the missionary. While on the one hand both *Le Pauvre Christ de Bomba* and *Le Roi miraculé* are thesis novels that refuse the missionary's claim to leadership in modern Africa, these same novels also present the missionary protagonist sympathetically as the man of ideals and ideas who strives heroically to overcome conservatism and materialism. Mongo Beti treats the missionary as a comic figure yet also brings the reader into sympathy with him through such devices as having the narrative of *Le Pauvre Christ de Bomba* told by Denis, the young mission boy who is the only sincere Christian among the Africans and in a sense Father Drumont's spiritual son, or by introducing into *Le Roi miraculé* pages from Father Le Guen's letters to his mother that reveal his idealism and spirituality.

The missionaries are also the only figures in Mongo Beti's novels whose action the author characterizes as revolutionary. They are unsuccessful, wrongheaded revolutionaries, to be sure, but in both *Le Pauvre Christ de Bomba* and *Le Roi miraculé* the author introduces an analogy between missionary and revolutionary activity that seems designed to highlight the missionary's role as a catalyst of change. (pp. 223-27)

Thus Mongo Beti gives us a double perspective of his protagonist. Seen from the point of view of the uncomprehending African villagers his prestige dissolves into comedy and his downfall brings proof of the power of resistance of the African bush to an alien European way of life. The point of view of the author himself, however, goes beyond this narrow perspective. He discerns the heroic as well as the comic qualities of his protagonist. He respects and even admires the missionary's dedication to an idea even as he rejects the validity of that idea for Africa. The missionary emerges in Mongo Beti's novels as the outsider per se, the man of ideas and ideals who finds himself in conflict with the structure of society. His elimination at the conclusion of the novel is tragic as well as comic, since it signifies that the forces of inertia, represented both by the village and by the

colonial administration, have forced out the troublesome agent of change. From the perspective of the village this might be a welcome development, but from the author's point of view it still leaves the village defenseless before the encroaching influence of European civilization.

Mongo Beti's other type of protagonist, the African student, is most fully delineated in *Mission terminée....* Jean Medza, a student at the *lycée* in a nearby city, who is about eighteen, relates his experiences in the course of a summer vacation spent in a village located deep in the bush. It is again the humorous account of the adventures of a protagonist who proves inadequate to the situation in which he finds himself. In the course of this narrative Mongo Beti provides us with a half-comic, half-serious analysis of the situation of the African intellectual in Africa, and voices as well his criticism of the inadequacy of the Western-educated student. (pp. 228-29)

[The] mock-heroic tone, which is sustained throughout the book, gives a light touch and perspective to the hero's philosophical quest for paradise. Like the missionaries Medza views the village in the African bush through the illusions of primitivism. He tends to think of Kala as a happy Eden peopled by ignorant natives who have been spared the torments of a troubled intellectuality. He is very careful, for instance, in what he tells them about his studies because, as he remarks repeatedly, he wants to avoid giving them complexes. He also feels a boundless admiration for the four illiterate village youths who are his constant companions, and bemoans the fact that his education prevents him from joining fully in what he conceives to be their uncomplicated instinctual existence.... (pp. 229-30)

By the end of the novel Medza has gained a more realistic understanding of African village society and his position within it. But his development is the exact opposite of Father Drumont's experience. While the missionary arrives in the bush country of the Tala tribe convinced of the importance of his role and finds himself rejected by the African village, Medza arrives in Kala convinced that he is an insignificant failure and discovers that he is a man of great importance in the village. The inhabitants regard him as a man of learning who can initiate them into the mysteries of the modern world. His efforts to satisfy their demands keep him so busy that he scarcely has time to enjoy his summer vacation.... Medza himself is so wrapped up in the psychological problem of reconciling his position as an educated man with his sense of failure that he seems scarcely aware of the potential material benefits of his position, but they are considerable, in wealth, in social standing, and even in sexual attractiveness.

This humorous tale of the rewards that education can bring in a backwoods village is interwoven with a more serious analysis of the social structure of village society: Mongo Beti's village is divided by tradition into two mutually antagonistic groups, the old and the young, who are kept from open strife only because the older generation is the sole possessor of power, wealth, and prestige. Medza's entrance brings a new factor into this stratified society of which he himself becomes aware only after some time. Although he belongs to the younger generation his position as an educated man permits him to rise to a position of wealth and influence that is characteristic of the older generation. But there is a price to be paid for this rapid rise. Wealth and success come to Medza because he has allowed the older generation to exploit him for its own purposes. The knowledge he has brought to the village serves to buttress the status quo and in fact to reinforce the advantage which the elders hold over the youth in the village. Thus, for example, his uncle Mama profits greatly from his nephew's stay since he accumulates a large herd of goats as his share of the presents Medza receives from the villagers. The local chief also strengthens his position as he enters into an alliance with the new educated class by trapping Medza into marriage with one of his daughters, in one of the most amusing scenes in the novel.

Medza, however, refuses to pay the price of his success and decides to remain loyal to the only real friends he has made in Kala, the four young men whose carefree existence he shared whenever he could escape from his duties in the village. He can only do this through a negative act, by refusing the position, the wealth, and the wife which he has acquired thanks to his education, and setting out on a wandering quest that takes him far from the village of Kala, to other countries and other continents.

Thus Mongo Beti's student protagonist ends up in exile from Africa, as did the missionaries. Yet this is not an entirely negative ending since Medza's exile is voluntary. His mission to Kala has given him a certain awareness of the predicament of modern Africa and of his role as an educated man. For the first time in his life he is able to make a choice and does not let himself be carried along by circumstances. Although he is not capable of pursuing a positive goal, he at least refuses to compromise on material success and chooses instead the uncertainty of the quest. (pp. 230-31)

Mongo Beti's fiction is a record of failure, the failure to discern either the "intellectual direction" of the new Africa or the type of leader who can initiate the African into the mysteries of the modern world. But it is a successful record of failure. The author's ability to assume a multiplicity of frequently contradictory points of view, his capacity to bring out the humor in the contradictions and incongruities of modern Africa, as well as his realistic appraisal of African village society, indicate a critical detachment, an intellectual stance, which are rare in contemporary African literature. (p. 233)

Thomas Cassirer, "The Dilemma of Leadership as Tragi-Comedy in the Novels of Mongo Beti," in L'Esprit Créateur, *Vol. X, No. 3, Fall, 1970, pp. 223-33.*

Eustace Palmer (essay date 1972)

[*In the following excerpt, Palmer opposes claims that the character of Jean-Marie Medza in* Mission to Kala *represents Beti himself and that Beti's novel is basically an indictment of Western education and civilization.*]

Mongo Beti's *Mission to Kala* tends to elicit two responses. Some applaud the author's celebration of African rural values and his rejection of modern, urban traditions. These readers see Mongo Beti as rebelling against the French educational system and calling for the preservation of pure African traditions. On the other hand are those who see the idealization of African tribal life in the novel as phoney and affected. I intend to demonstrate, *inter alia,* that both sides are wrong, and fail to respond to the novel's complexity and irony.

The misconceptions stem from too facile an identification of the author, Mongo Beti, with the narrator-hero, Jean-Marie Medza, that silly, posturing, opinionated schoolboy. It is quite easy to see what kind of boy Jean-Marie is, but it does not necessarily follow that he is Mongo Beti. One cannot assume that *Mission to Kala* is autobiographical. Apart from the fact that both Jean-Marie and Mongo Beti were born in the Cameroons, and attended Lycées there, there is very little evidence in the book or in the details of Mongo Beti's life as we know them, which indicate without question that the novel is autobiographical.

Far from identifying himself with Jean-Marie, Mongo Beti presents him ironically, subjecting his views and actions to the most critical scrutiny.... [In *Mission to Kala*] ...the first person hero's views are not endorsed by the author. Either there is a gap between the author and the narrator-hero, or we must conclude that Mongo Beti is as irresponsible, snobbish, and deluded as his schoolboy hero. In spite of his endearing wit, there are several reasons why readers might dislike Jean-Marie. He is stupid, condescending, and untruthful. Mongo Beti must distance himself from Jean-Marie to expose these qualities in him. Accordingly, Jean-Marie... becomes not so much a spokesman, as a *persona* or mask, to be manipulated at will, to be deliberately put in a number of embarrassing situations and laughed at; at times he himself actually joins in the laughter at his own expense. Irony is the dominant mode in *Mission to Kala*. (pp. 143-4)

[The] irony is primarily reflected in the nature of the hero's language. Even a superficial analysis of Jean-Marie's style reveals that he is very much addicted to clichés and stock-phrases:

> My God, how lovely she was! Her cheekbones stood out just far enough; her nose was small and pert, her mouth proud as well as sensual. Her whole personality breathed that air of calm, detached assurance which is only to be found in those girls who know what they want and can reflect on many past occasions when they got it ...

She seemed to be waiting for something; but the longer I watched her, the less certain I became of just what it was. All women spend their lives waiting for something, I thought—probably I'd read that somewhere—and they only differ in the degree of their foreknowledge.

This is surely not Mongo Beti's own style; it is more reminiscent of tenth-rate American 'sex-and-crime' fiction. In fact Beti must be applauded for very subtly moulding the style to suit the character. Take another example:

My heart began to beat violently. I was as nervous as a partisan about to raid a strongly-held enemy position.

The truth is that Jean-Marie's style has been affected by his reading of cheap fiction, and his uncritical assimilation of random phrases from his masters' lessons and conversation; hence the clichés and stock-phrases. The clichés expose the essential hollowness of Jean-Marie's mind, a point which will be of great significance as we follow the story. This is all part of the ironic technique by which Beti manipulates the reader's responses towards Jean-Marie, even though he is himself telling the story.

Irony is also effectively indicated by the tone of voice, and the vehemence or the illogicalities of the speaker's arguments. For instance, Jean-Marie describes a meal:

This was, according to local custom, an enormous meal, chiefly because they only had two meals a day. The women went to work in the fields early in the morning, and only returned late in the afternoon...
    The table was loaded with food. My uncle was distinctly lacking in table manners: he crammed his mouth so full that a great bulge appeared in each cheek, and I was afraid he might burst. I trained myself not to catch his eye during meals, so as to avoid betraying my astonishment at his feeding habits. His son, on the other hand, shot constant glances of shame and reproach at him.

Jean-Marie's condescension towards the people of Kala is surely exposed in his contemptuous reference to their 'two meals a day' and in the obvious exaggeration about his uncle's table manners. But the author does not share it. To take another example:

Is there, as I am inclined to suspect, a kind of complicity, an unspoken agreement between even the severest examiner and any candidate? But if so, does this complicity not rest on the implied assumption (which the professor, at least, is consciously aware of) that all they both know is, in differing degrees, illusory and insubstantial? Pursuing this sour train of thought, I asked myself how many geography teachers in Western Europe and the areas under European influence, such as Central Africa, had any real or precise information about contemporary conditions in Russia? It was a depressing state of affairs if countless poor little bastards were forced to sacrifice their youth in assimilating a lot of fairy tales.

Failure to appreciate the distance between Mongo Beti and his hero in a passage such as this leads to the view that Mongo Beti is a rebel against European values. But Jean-Marie is just inventing face-saving excuses for his inability to talk about Russian conditions. The passage is full of illogicalities and *non-sequiturs*. Jean-Marie assumes that since he survived an 'extra-mural' session in Kala, he would have passed an oral in Russian geography. But, he suggests, his lecturers would have demonstrated, not only their incompetence, but also the general complicity between examiner and examinee, made necessary by the ignorance of the examiners themselves. He then concludes that most European geography teachers are ignorant of Russian conditions, and refers to the facts of geography as 'fairy tales'. And all this because he was able to deceive the people of Kala with his lies about Russia. However, the readers know that Jean-Marie has failed not only his oral, but his entire baccalauréat. It is not college learning which is being criticized, but Jean-Marie's imperfect assimilation of the syllabus.

Mongo Beti is looking at Jean-Marie with a critical eye, and so should we. It is important to establish at the outset that Jean-Marie's judgements should not be accepted at face value. We can now proceed with a detailed examination of the novel.

The first point is that **Mission to Kala** is not about a mission to recover Niam's delinquent wife. Rather it is a story of growth and discovery, during which the hero is forced to acknowledge many truths about himself, his education, and his so-called rustic cousins. As is usual with the picaresque novel, interest lies less in the hero's adventures during his travels, than in his moral, emotional, and psychological development. Like all picaresque heroes, Jean-Marie starts off in a state of innocence, and has to be exposed to external experience to learn more about life.

At the start of the novel Jean-Marie is himself under no illusions about his actual position and achievement. His full consciousness of his failure is the reason for his depression. It is his fellow Vimilians who persist in regarding him as an educated man, who possesses certificates and knowledge of the white man's secrets; 'he only has to make the trip there and put the fear of God into those savages'. This is why a sixteen-year-old boy is sent on an errand to recover the wife of a thirty-five-year-old man. Mongo Beti rises to the occasion and exploits the tremendous comic potential to the full.

At this stage of the proceedings there are only two sane people: Aunt Amou, that self-effacing but very perceptive widow, is the voice of reason and sanity, seeing with amazing clarity that the Vimilians are attributing to Jean-Marie a whole scale of values that he quite patently does not possess: 'Aren't you ashamed to drag this poor boy into your dirty lies? He's just a child.' The second is Jean-Marie himself, who is quite properly appalled at the nature of the task.

But from now on a change occurs in Jean-Marie. As soon as it becomes clear that the Vimilians are determined to send him on this mission, he becomes infected with their enthusiasm for the task, and their condescension towards the people of Kala: 'an *easy* adventure, among comparatively simple people, is the secret wish and aim of every adventurer. When you come to think of it, the very existence of adventurers is only made possible by the survival of primitive simpleminded tribes.' Jean-Marie is already demonstrating an acceptance of other people's values which will make him an unreliable narrator.

Jean-Marie now begins to have delusions of grandeur, regarding himself not just as a missionary taking light to the barbarous people of Kala, but as a conquistador, about to engage on a mission of conquest. He thinks of a means of transport in terms of a richly caparisoned horse, and he refers to his bicycle as a 'splendid machine', an 'aristocrat among bicycles':

> Occasionally I stopped, and with one foot just touching the ground while the other remained, as it were, in the stirrup, I gazed at the vast panorama lying open to my future exploits. (This 'vast panorama' was for the most part restricted to a seedy vista of tree-trunks lining the road, oppressive in the most literal sense.) Then there was this strange name of mine, Medza. If I added one tiny syllable, only one, it would be transformed into a real Conquistador's name, Medzaro!—just like Pizarro, or near enough, anyway.

Jean-Marie comes to Kala with preconceived ideas about the people, but he will gradually be forced to change them. In the first place, his arrival is unnoticed, since the village is preoccupied with its own pastimes, and he fails to get a conquistador's welcome. Here is his reaction to the game he finds in progress:

> I was astonished by the whole thing, though in the end I remembered that when we were about six or so we used to play a similar sort of game at home. But in our case it was a childish pastime, a mere survival from former times, and not taken in the least seriously. At Kala, to judge by this match, it was still going very strong indeed.

Jean-Marie's condescension is striking in this passage. In his view, the people of Kala are at the emotional and mental level of children of 'six or so'. Subsequently he sees Zambo:

> Having first taken a bird's-eye, panoramic view of the scene, I now began to examine it in detail. The first thing that caught my eye was a great hulking devil in the Kala team, who had such enormous muscles that I concluded he must have bought them on the instalment system. There was simply no other explanation possible. He was tall and flat-footed, with a disproportionately lengthy torso which, nevertheless, he carried very badly. His buttocks were incredibly slender, yet he retained the country native's slight pot-belly, due to a habitually rough and meagre diet. He was like a kind of human baobab tree . . .
> I found it hard to convince myself that this monster was really my cousin, the young man from whom old Bikokolo had promised me so wonderful a reception. By what miraculous process, I asked myself, could this man be related to me in any way?

Zambo emerges from Jean-Marie's description as a clumsy brute. But as the novel progresses, we begin to entertain doubts about the accuracy of the description, for the Zambo we come to know is no brute. Indeed, all the girls seem to be in love with him, and a little later Jean-Marie himself calls Zambo his handsome cousin; on yet another occasion he calls him a Greek demi-god. Jean-Marie's initial picture of Zambo is a cruel distortion, as we can see if we look again at the passage. First Jean-Marie makes a comment which is to Zambo's credit, but then he proceeds to denigrate him; he takes away with one hand, what he give with the other. He ridicules Zambo's impressive muscles and tries to detract from the favourable impression of his height with the contemptuous 'flat-footed'. In conjunction with his long torso and incredibly slender buttocks, we are told of his cousin's pot-belly. We may well ask how Jean-Marie knows about the country native's 'rough and meagre diet' seeing he has never been in Kala before? We ourselves are soon to see that the Kalans' diet is anything but 'rough and meagre'.

Jean-Marie is deliberately forcing Zambo to fit his preconceived image of the rustic Kalan. However, from now on the position is reversed, and Jean-Marie has to laugh at himself, as he discovers his inferiority in many respects to the Kalans. His first surprise comes with the hospitality of his welcome. His cousin Zambo, from whom he expected nothing but savagery, behaves with such marked courtesy, that he almost passes out.

At Kala, Jean-Marie discovers what had been so conspicuously lacking in Vimili—the strength and warmth of personal relationships. Those four 'irresponsibles'—Zambo, Petrus Son-of-God, Abraham the Boneless Wonder, and Duckfoot Johnny—cling to each other with an almost religious devotion. Zambo enjoys the most cordial relations with his father, who even allows him to keep his mistress in the house. (We can imagine how Jean-Marie's father would react to his son's girlfriend living with them.) Indeed the Zambo-Mama relationship is the exact antithesis of Jean-Marie's with his father, who rules his household with a mailed fist, and hardly communicates with his sons. In his family there was continual fighting: 'there was never any peace or sense of security; nothing but rows, reproaches and fear'. The father scolded everyone, the mother scolded the children, the boys beat the girls, and the elder sister bullied the younger. It was a home calculated to produce juvenile delinquents, and it is hardly surprising that both Jean-Marie and his elder brother show delinquent tendencies in the end.

In Kala Jean-Marie discovers a spontaneity he never thought existed. When, during the swimming party the other boys strip and plunge in naked, Jean-Marie, conditioned by the restrictive morality of his environment, rather self-consciously keeps his pants on, until he is shamed by the others into removing them.

In Kala Jean-Marie is first introduced to the pleasures of alcohol. But by far the most important of his discoveries is sex. Sexual experience is the watershed between youth and manhood. So it is not surprising that much of the novel consists of attempts to get Jean-Marie into bed with a girl. Here in 'primitive' Kala, the supposed experienced 'city slicker' is initiated into manhood. At the start, Jean-Marie, who is a virgin, is scandalized by his cousin's offer to find him a girl, but the urge grows on him. Yet when he is confronted by the most beautiful and sophisticated girl in the village, his feeling of inadequacy makes him frigid and impotent. Later, still pretending to be the city slicker with lots of experience, he tries to cover up his inadequacy with scandalous allegations about the girl's health. Fortunately for him, however, he is finally able to make love with the equally inexperienced Edima, the chief's daughter.

Increasingly, Jean-Marie the conquistador, finds himself at a disadvantage and is forced to admit his inferiority to the other boys: 'I'd have given all the diplomas in the world to swim like Duckfoot Johnny, or dance like the Boneless Wonder; or have the sexual experience of Petrus Son-of-God.' Despite his various set-backs, in the field of learning Jean-Marie ought to be the incontestable champion. After all he is the only person in Kala with any education worth talking about, and he had been deliberately selected for this mission by Vimili, because of his learning and his certificates. The Kalans respect him because they are convinced that he knows the white man's secrets. But this is just where Jean-Marie's inferiority is most glaringly exposed. He who had intended to bring light to the barbarous savages, finds out that he can't hold a candle to them, in knowledge of basic facts and native intelligence.

Since the Kalans, like the Vimilians, wrongly regard Jean-Marie as a scholar, they organize 'extra-mural' sessions at which he is supposed to answer their questions and talk to them about the white man's secrets. Before the first of these sessions Jean-Marie behaves with his characteristic condescension and conceit. His hostess asks him what he has been taught at school and he says:

> I wanted to be kind to this woman; she meant well enough; but how on earth was I to give her the most elementary notion of such things as geography, advanced mathematics or the social sciences?
> ... I honestly believed that the old lady was suffering from the effects of senility.

Jean-Marie later wishes he had not been so condescending and conceited:

> Scarcely was dinner over when my hostess began to fire a whole fusillade of questions at me. She sat next to me and went on absolutely ruthlessly, dragging detailed explanations out of me, and going back over muddled points with a needle-sharp clarity. She obviously was aware of all my weaknesses and shortcomings; she was equipped to give me the most humiliating oral I had ever been through in my life. To think that there are people like me whose job is passing exams all their life.

The woman is not an isolated case; the entire audience direct the most penetrating questions at Jean-Marie, probing his weaknesses and exposing his ignorance. As his embarrassment increases he wants 'to yell for mercy, to throw in the sponge, anything'. Even the 'bright definitions' he had prepared to answer possible questions fail to help him. He has to tell lies about Russian geography and the problems of New York, and is quite unable to talk about his own prospects and those of other members of his generation.

And this is not all. Far from educating the Kalans, they educate him in such matters as village economics and tribal customs during his stay in Kala. Moreover, he is hardly what one might call a bright student. Indeed, on many occasions, Zambo and his father are almost in despair at the impenetrable stupidity of the boy. For instance, this is how his uncle reacts after a characteristic howler from Jean-Marie, during the celebrated discussion on blood relationships:

> He stooped down to his work again, his face twisted into a kind of despairing grimace. It was just such an expression as is common among classics masters in the provinces, indicating that their pupils are incurably third-rate and will never be any use at anything, let alone classics. Then he stood up once more, with an air of conscientious determination. *Nil desperandum* was written all over him.

On one occasion Zambo exclaims: 'Don't you know anything in your part of the country?'

We witness the complete reversal of Jean-Marie's initial relationship to the people of Kala and, in particular, his relationship with Zambo. As we have seen, he is quite convinced at the start of Zambo's barbarity and stupidity. As far as he is concerned, Zambo is mule-headed and uncritical. But increasingly the would-be conquistador is forced to rely on the dull-witted savage for security and support. Moreover, as we get to know Zambo, we fail to see any evidence of dullness or neurosis; on the contrary, he seems a highly imaginative and resourceful young man, far more quick-witted and perceptive than his 'educated' cousin. It is Zambo who first realizes that the whole episode in which Edima and Jean-Marie are discovered in bed together, is a carefully-planned farce, designed to bolster the ego of the mother and improve Edima's matrimonial chances. When Niam's delinquent wife returns and treats Jean-Marie with studied indifference, it is Zambo who points out the real reasons for her strange behaviour, and Jean-Marie is eventually forced to admit:

> There was a good deal of common sense in Zambo's remarks: he was more level-headed about the whole thing than I was.

Although in many ways the Kalans treat Jean-Marie as a superior they also exploited him as if he was an inferior. Even Zambo uses him to bolster his prestige. Jean-Marie, in his simplicity, supposed that the four friends, Zambo, Duckfoot Johnny, Abraham the Boneless-Wonder, and Petrus Son-of-God, had invited him on their groundnut-scrounging enterprise as a mark of friendship; but it turns out that he was merely being used as a mascot: 'you've got to admit it, we've our little city mascot to thank for this haul. If he hadn't been there, no one would have taken any notice of us at all... That's why we invited him to come along.'

But it is his uncle, Mama, who exploits Jean-Marie most of all. He farms him out every evening to the highest bidder, with complete lack of consideration for his health or convenience. On one occasion Jean-Marie had spoken contemptuously of those people who were 'entirely innocent of modern notions concerning economies and capitalism', but his uncle demonstrates that he has a very good notion of both. He knows very well that he has a commodity which is in demand, and the collection of sheep and poultry (the fee for hiring out Jean-Marie) continues unabated. Subsequently, his uncle calmly proceeds to appropriate half the sheep and poultry for his own use after lulling Jean-Marie into a false sense of security.

By this time any notion of Jean-Marie as a competent negotiator who could put the fear of God into those Kalans, and recover Niam's wife, has disappeared. Not surprisingly, the negotiations are largely conducted by Mama and Zambo, and Jean-Marie, the real emissary, hardly plays a significant rôle at all.

Finally, in some brilliantly comic scenes towards the end of the novel, the 'city slicker' is tricked into marrying Edima, the chief's daughter. A dreamlike quality dominates the work at this stage; Jean-Marie has been overwhelmed by forces that have proved too strong for him. The supreme irony is that the educator has become the educated, and the conquistador has become the 'conquered'.

In the meantime, Jean-Marie is himself aware of the change in his circumstances. Bullied, exploited, tricked, exposed, and faced with the superiority of these rustic Kalans, he rebels against his background, his education and his father. He feels that it is these factors, rather than any defects in his own character, which are to blame for his débâcle at Kala:

> Looking back, I suspect Eliza had become my symbol of absolute liberty, the freedom enjoyed by country boys like Duckfoot Johnny, the Boneless Wonder, Son-of-God, and the rest. I saw this freedom as the most precious possession I could acquire, and realized at the same time that in all likelihood I should never have it. Without being aware of it, I was no more than a sacrifice on the altar of Progress and Civilization. My youth was slipping away, and I was paying a terrible price for—well, for *what?* Having gone to school, at the decree of my all-powerful father? Having been chained to my books when most children of my age were out playing games?

Similar sentiments are expressed towards the end of the novel with much greater vehemence:

> Fathers used to take their children to school as they might lead sheep into a slaughterhouse... We were

catechized, confirmed, herded to Communion like a gaggle of holy-minded ducklings... What god were we being sacrificed to, I wonder?

One might take statements such as these quite literally as part of the message of the novel, and see Jean-Marie Medza as the white-man's 'representative', who, having been exposed from an early age to Western education and civilization, is at a loss in his own tribal culture. One might feel that Mongo Beti is suggesting that being exposed to an alien system of education cuts a boy off from his roots, robs him of all that is good, beautiful, and valuable, and makes him unfit, not only for tribal life, but for any kind of life at all. But this kind of judgement simplifies Mongo Beti's meaning; identifies him wrongly with Jean-Marie; does less than justice to the subtlety and complexity of his technique; and fails to see passages such as those quoted above as the culmination of the ironic process which has been going on all along.

We have already seen that Jean-Marie's judgement is unreliable. We have seen irony also operating in another passage... in which he discusses education with characteristic vehemence. In these passages the generally vehement tone indicates irony too. Is Jean-Marie's youth really slipping away? Isn't he exaggerating in calling this freedom the most precious possession he could ever acquire, and over-simplifying in describing himself as a sacrifice on the altar of progress and civilization? Jean-Marie is just wallowing in self-pity and giving vent to personal antagonism for his father, whom he sees lurking behind all his troubles. Mongo Beti does not give him his endorsement, and must not be identified with him here.

No doubt there are valuable things in Kala society, and Jean-Marie is the worse for not possessing them. But the text does not warrant the suggestion that Mongo Beti is decrying education or Western civilization. In the first place, Jean-Marie is not the representative of the white man. The Kalans and the Vimilians, not Mongo Beti, attribute white values to him, that we can see he does not possess. In the second place, Jean-Marie is not the embodiment of Western education. In spite of all the talk about his learning and certificates, we know he has failed his baccalauréat and is only half educated. Indeed, at Kala, his inability to assimilate his teacher's lessons is all too clearly revealed. At best, Jean-Marie's attitude to his studies was perfunctory; he tells us so himself:

> I had really only applied myself to my studies at all because my father was ambitious on my behalf. He wanted me to get more and more diplomas and certificates, without bothering his head overmuch as to where they would get me. In short, I had been made to go to school, and then arranged things as best as I could to suit myself: I had turned the whole thing into a game, something to pass the time away and amuse me.

Since this is Jean-Marie's attitude to his education, how can we blame his education for his reverses at Kala?

How can we say he is made impotent at Kala because he has been transformed by Western education into the 'white man's representative'?

Partly because of his antagonism to his father, and partly because of his discomfiture, Jean-Marie comes to regard Kala society as the ideal. We said before that he is too ready to accept other people's values uncritically. Now we must question the Utopian values that he attributes to Kala. In the first place, the marvellous Kalan freedom can easily degenerate into licentiousness, as in the case of Zambo himself, who cannot go to sleep so long as 'there is a girl to screw somewhere in the world'. Moreover, death is ever-present in this society, as the case of Elias Messi proves, and there is something rather pathetic about the 'togetherness' which binds Zambo and his three friends. The orphans, Endongolo and his sister, show that life in Kala is not entirely free from misery.

Mongo Beti is much too intelligent to idealize the Kalans. They can be vulgar, like Petrus Son-of-God, or the girls who watch the boys bathing in the river, generous like Zambo, self-effacing like Zambo's mother, petty like the chief, mean and calculating like Zambo's father, friendly like Endongolo, flirtatious like Edima, and sluttish like Niam's wife. Jean-Marie mistakenly regards them as the ideal, and rebels so violently against his education and background, that he becomes a juvenile delinquent and a vagrant. *Mission to Kala* is neither an attack on education nor on Western civilization; rather, it is a brilliant satire directed against all those half-baked young men who feel that a partial exposure to Western ways makes them superior to their countrymen who still live the tribal life. Mongo Beti subjects Jean-Marie's personal weaknesses—his condescension, arrogance, and stupidity—to rigorous criticism by means of his comic art. (pp. 144-54)

> *Eustace Palmer, "Mongo Beti: Mission to Kala," in* An Introduction to the African Novel: A Critical Study of Twelve Books by Chinua Achebe and Others, *Heinemann Educational Books Ltd., 1972, pp. 143-54.*

Gerald Moore (essay date 1980)

[*In the following excerpt from his 1980 study* Twelve African Writers, *Moore surveys Beti's development as a novelist.*]

[Into the tissue of events in *Le Roi Miraculé*], Beti weaves the adventures of two highly-contrasted young men: Kris, like several of Beti's early heroes, is an angry individualist, impatient with tradition and openly contemptuous of the elders. He has already been stripped of his bursary, on the eve of taking his *baccalauréat* for opposing a white instructor. Hence he has been forced to shift for himself, and this has only increased his individualist tendencies.... (p. 208)

His friend Bitama is an idealist, both in politics and sex, who has acquired a wide knowledge of Cameroun by following his father in his civil service assignments. He is an enthusiastic supporter of the PPP (Beti's usual pseudonym for the UPC [Union des Peoples Camerounaises], the militant nationalistic party of the period). But Kris has no time for anything beyond his own affairs, as he makes clear in the following exchange with Bitama:

> 'How is it that the most intelligent of our young men, the best educated, in a word the elite, are so cold towards the PPP?... Look, here one is on this lousy planet; one is black, but looking all around one, reading the books, searching the face of the famous, well, what's the use! There isn't a single one like oneself. Then you feel yourself incredibly alone; you'd like to invent men who are black like you, whom you could see all around you, men who really exist, not so? You would make yourself God, just for that. Haven't you ever felt the same way?
>
> 'The PPP offers us, for the first time in our history, the chance to develop great men of our own. I love the PPP. Isn't that natural, Kris? If you saw your brother among a dozen long-distance runners, wouldn't you suffer if you saw him come in last?'
>
> 'Me! Oh, certainly not! I'd more likely tell him "Poor old chap, you're nothing like a long-distancer. Run and see if mother has a nice piece of porcupine for you, and enjoy the spectacle of my health." That's what I'd tell him. There are non-viable races, just as there are non-viable individuals: we have to explain why in both cases. They are not like others, they lack vitality, to put it in a nutshell...'

Beti is content here to offer us two contrasted images of the young which we may set beside the dying society of Essazam [in *Le Roi Miraculé*]. He leaves us with an uneasy suspicion that he identifies more with the cynical iconoclasm of Kris than the Bitama's bubbling enthusiasm. The irony is that his early novels appeared during the very years when the UPC, led by Ruben um Nyobé, was struggling bitterly against French plans to perpetuate the colonial presence and influence in the Cameroun. Yet the only echo this struggle finds in his work of the fifties is in this one exchange. Not until the appearance of his two major novels of 1974 did Beti's personal commitment to the UPC find reflection in his work.

The explanation might be sought in the fact that all his early novels are set in the past: *Le Pauvre Christ* in the 1930s; *Le Roi Miraculé* specifically in 1948; and the other two novels in a time of youth roughly corresponding with the 1940s. But such an explanation would be superficial, for it behoves us to ask *why* African novelists of the 1950s (one thinks also of Ferdinand Oyono and Chinua Achebe) were concerned with a redefinition of the past, almost to the exclusion of any direct statement about the present. The reason, in Beti's case, does not lie in any lack of political commitment, since he was writing militant articles for *La Revue Camerounaise* at the very period when his fourth novel appeared. The explanation must lie in the impulse behind so many early novels of the colonial period—the impulse to set the part to rights, which often smothered the more urgent task (one might think) of setting the present to rights.

The silence of sixteen years which followed *Le Roi Miraculé* was the very period in which Beti found the means to make his fiction a revolutionary instrument. It was broken by the simultaneous appearance of two novels drastically different, both from each other and from all his earlier work. But these changes of direction in his work should not blind us to the elements of continuity. The two heroes of *Remember Ruben* both bear some traces of earlier characters; Abena's ruthless impatience with an outworn rural world may remind us to some extent of Kris, despite the switch from cynicism to radical commitment; likewise, Mor-Zamba certainly has something in common with the Zambo of *Mission Terminée,* although he is so much more deeply and feelingly rendered.

But when all this has been noted, the originality of *Remember Ruben* is still astonishing. [All] Beti's earlier novels were concerned with a single episode (the tour of Tala, the mission to Kala, etc.); they were limited spatially to events covering a few villages, and temporally to anything from one day to a few weeks. *Remember Ruben,* by contrast, is a novel of epic sweep, which gives us a representative account of Camerounian experience over some forty years, culminating in the civil war and the pseudo-independence of 1960. *Perpétue,* in its entirely different style, continues the story down to the 1970s. Beti's descriptive power, always one of his most outstanding talents, reaches new heights in *Remember Ruben,* both in the rustic scenes of the first part and in the evocation of urban life of the forties and fifties which follows. A powerful new element in the structure of this novel is its vision of destiny. The destiny which moulds the contrasting, diverging and finally converging careers of Mor-Zamba and Abena is the principal element in that structure—the backbone of the novel. Mor-Zamba ('Man of God', or 'Providential Man', in the Beti language of Cameroun) first appears to us as a figure of the wild; precocious, strong and apparently dumb. His sudden appearance in Ekoumdoum has all the air of the marvellous and his youthful career there, culminating in his triumphant wrestling against the Zolo, never loses that marvellous quality. As a stranger of unknown antecedents, however, he never succeeds in gaining real acceptance, despite the consistent patronage of the 'good old man' and of the fierce young Abena. After his enforced departure from Ekoumdoum, he exchanges this champion/pariah reputation for one of relative anonymity. In the cities his only marvellous feat is the rescue of Ruben um Nyobé from his executioners. His role now is not to astonish, but to bear witness; to be the typical new citizen, uprooted from the bush, uncertain of his bearings, suffering and striving to make a living, following Ruben's brilliant leadership with more faith than understanding. His companions observe his evident goodness, his fidelity and strength, but are inclined to dismiss him as a simpleton, a 'bushman'. Yet it is these very qualities which equip him, as Abena points out in the closing pages, to return to Ekoumdoum

and begin the patient work of transformation which that decadent community cries out for. It is appropriate that his real identity (the son of a brutally deposed, long-lamented Chief of Ekoumdoum) emerges at the very moment when he is ready to assume his real task.

Abena's fate is in every respect contrasted with Mor-Zamba's. Starting in the village as the son of a respected family, he first distances himself from the community by his espousal of that unlucky prodigy's cause. To go in pursuit of Mor-Zamba, he ruthlessly breaks with his family and clan; and even his spell as the 'good boy' of Father Van den Rietter is really aimed at seizing the priest's gun. Failing to release his friend from forced labour, he embarks on a nineteen-year odyssey of colonial warfare, all aimed at preparing himself for the revolutionary struggle against the French in Cameroun. And to cap the contrast, when he finally returns to Cameroun; he does so with a new identity, that of the guerilla leader Hurricane-Viet, which has largely replaced the old Abena of Ekoumdoum.

Matching this structural innovation is Beti's new departure in narrative technique. He had previously tried the diary form (*Le Pauvre Christ*), the first person narrator (*Mission Terminée*) and the omniscient narrator who is outside the story altogether (*Le Roi Miraculé*). But *Remember Ruben* wishes to chronicle the impact of heroic conduct on ordinary sensibilities, and for this purpose Beti needs a narrator who is inside the story but somewhat peripheral to it. In Part I this narrator, who is an anonymous villager, gives us his own recollections of Mor-Zamba's mysterious appearance and all that locally followed from it. But for the rest of the tale he narrates at second-hand what he has since heard, from Abena and Mor-Zamba, about all that transpired during their long absence from Ekoumdoum. This technique has the advantage of constantly reminding us (like the narrator in classical epic) that the twin heroes are not as other men; that they have been marked out from the first for an exceptional destiny, and for each other.

Yet this deep comradeship is of a curious kind, for it is one of those complementarities whose members must remain almost always apart—*aware* of each other but not *with* each other. Only the weeks together in the forest preparing to build Mor-Zamba's house (their 'initiation') evoke the quality of immediate communion:

> After each of their journeys, we witnessed the heaps of material swell, evidence of an effort which seemed beyond ordinary men, more like that of figures in a fable. And several times a day the inhabitants of Ekoumdoum would form a circle to admire without restraint, even with cries of passionate and voluble enthusiasm, the fruits of a truly gigantic labour. The two companions became the symbol at once of energy, brotherhood, and determination, so that the city adopted this saying: 'Abena and Mor-Zamba are united; what mountain can they not lift from its base?

All this admiration, however, does not bring one finger of assistance to the pair. The community in need of redemption does not always welcome or even recognize its redeemers. We might compare with the primitive energy of this scene, that later one where, like a degenerate Virgil, Jean-Louis guides Mor-Zamba through the underworld of night-time Kola-Kola:

> They soon arrived in front of a dance-hall whose entrance was blocked by a queue waiting for tickets. The two men benefited from some privilege whose nature Mor-Zamba couldn't guess, which saved them not only from queuing but even from buying tickets. Mor-Zamba was immediately abandoned by Jean-Louis, who seized one girl after another, alternately plastering them to his stomach and spinning them round, with his teeth fixed in a dazzling smile; or else went here and there to chat with his cronies. Meanwhile Mor-Zamba, dominating the crowd and recovered from the dazzling glare of the electric lights, gazed upon the scene so totally new to him.... Ecstatic girls surrounded the platform, on which the musicians toiled in their shirt-sleeves. A tall, thin mulatto, with pomaded hair, seemed to carve at his fiddle with the bow to produce the most ravishing melody whilst, at every pause, he stooped down and offered his face and neck to a fat girl, who mopped them with a wet towel.

It will be seen at how little advantage Mor-Zamba appears in the second scene, compared with the heroic exploits of the forest. Yet it is in the obscure struggle for life and freedom in the cities that he finally proves his mettle and earns his status as a representative hero of modern Cameroun. It is as such that Hurricane-Viet despatches him on the return journey to Ekoumdoum as the agent of its renewal. This is the character whom Dorothy Blair describes as 'a shadow-hero, his misfortunes the pretext for a political tract' (her fondness for this last phrase will be noted).

The end of *Remember Ruben,* as published in 1978, gave no indication that the novel was to be continued, and the appearance of Beti's sixth novel, *Perpétue,* a few weeks later, treating in an entirely different style the years since independence in 1960, seemed to indicate an abandonment of the quasi-naturalistic, quasi-mythical style of the earlier book. But the founding of his new journal *Peuples Noirs, Peuples Africains* in 1976 has given Beti a chance to begin serializing the sequel, *La Ruine Presque Cocasse d'un Polichinelle* (The Almost Farcical Ruin of a Clown). The sequel begins exactly where the earlier novel left off, with Mor-Zamba's return journey through the forest to Ekoumdoum. He is accompanied on this journey by Joe the Juggler, the irrepressible buffoon of *Remember Ruben,* and an innocent young brother of Jean-Louis', called Evariste. The published episodes resume entirely the style, tempo and character of the earlier novel, except that the predominance of Joe the Juggler's role increases the element of ironic humour and diminishes that of the marvellous, for we are now in the Cameroun of 1960, no longer in the semi-legendary days of Mor-Zamba's forest childhood. As the giant Mor-Zamba retraces the steps of the journey which, twenty years before, brought him from Ekoumdoum to the city, we are able to measure the distance which the Cameroun itself has travelled. The countryside seems not so much in the grip of civil war as in that of petty uniformed tyrants, who make their exactions unchallenged by a peasantry still too inclined to deference and passivity. As the three travellers draw nearer to Ekoumdoum, so Joe the Juggler's exuberant cynicism and quick-wittedness are slowly eclipsed by Mor-Zamba's reappearance as the master of the forest and all its crafts. The disadvantage which always dogged him among the nimble spirits of the city now falls away and exposes his personality in all its monolithic grandeur.

The belated appearance of Beti's historical chronicle *Main Basse sur le Cameroun* in 1977 (the edition 1972 having been seized by the French government, which also attempted to strip the author of his passport and nationality) enables us to juxtapose it with his fictional treatment of some of the same events. In *Remember Ruben* we see most of these events through the eyes of Mor-Zamba, who does not always fully comprehend them. But the difference is not merely one of viewpoint; Beti has also fictionalized some of the events themselves, so that they resemble, but do not correspond with, actuality. With the exception of Ruben um Nyobé and one or two lofty actors like Generals de Gaulle and Leclerc, Beti has also changed the names of the principal figures. Although his motives for this were probably artistic, he nonetheless achieved a strategic effect, for *Remember Ruben* did not suffer the fate of his chronicle, suppressed two years earlier.

Within a few weeks of *Remember Ruben* as already mentioned, Beti published his sixth novel, *Perpétue.* Here again is one of those startling innovations of style and technique which have marked his career as a novelist. Despite the air of the marvellous which clings around the early scenes, *Remember Ruben* is in general a highly naturalistic novel, characterized by brilliant detail and evocative power. *Perpétue,* by contrast, has the slightly dream-like atmosphere of the quest. Most of the characters are presented as a type rather than filled out in detail. The object of the novel, as of Essola's quest, is to discover what has poisoned the springs of independence at their source. Essola, a former PPP militant, returns from six years in a concentration camp to discover that his beloved sister Perpétue has been sold to an official by their mother and has died an obscure and early death. The venal mother seems to stand, as the novel progresses, for Beti's vision of the Cameroun of the sixties, alike in her gross favouritism of her drunken son and in her callous indifference to virtue and integrity where they exist. Perpétue's fate becomes more than a personal tragedy, more even than an indictment of the brutal materialism to which girls like her are often sacrificed. She comes to represent that quality in the life of a nation for which Essola has suffered six years of purgatory, and which he returns to find in eclipse.

The compassionate concern of the novel, so strong in the middle chapters, is marred by the sadism with which Essola disposes of his brother at the end, sadism without parallel in any other work of Beti. This exultant cruelty, of which there is no trace in **Remember Ruben,** may be justified in terms of the novel's more allegorical and representational character, which deprives its actions of literal, naturalistic meaning. But, just as likely, it may stem from the frustration of watching two decades of political militancy, international agitation and devoted struggle come to nothing. One by one, the UPC leaders had been either murdered or executed (the latest being Ernest Ouandié in 1971), their followers horribly tortured or left to rot in one of the country's many concentration camps. As Essola himself ponders, towards the end of the novel:

> If only we had won!... The only thing which might compensate a man for time lost and for his loved ones who disappear in the most absurd way, is success; that's to say, in politics, the absolute triumph of the party to which one is devoted, of the comrades at whose side one has fought.

Essola's quest for the lost Perpétue becomes also an exploration of the petit-bourgeois society which has done well out of independence. Debauched by a police officer with the connivance of her ineffectual husband, Perpétue herself finally abandons the virtue which no one values, throws herself into a passionate affair with a young footballer and dies in pregnancy with her first love-child. There is pain and sweetness in the evocation of Perpétuc's radiant character and unhappy fate, but the novel seems to me inferior in power and scope to **Remember Ruben.** Nevertheless, the publication of two novels of this calibre and contrasted quality in a single year finally confirms Beti as a master; one who, unlike many of his contemporaries, can make the transition from the relatively innocent 'protest' novel of the 1950s to the harsh realities of contemporary Africa. (pp. 208-15)

> *Gerald Moore, "Mongo Beti: From Satire to Epic," in his* Twelve African Writers, *Indiana University Press, 1980, pp. 193-216.*

Susan Domowitz (essay date 1981)

[*In the following excerpt, Domowitz discusses the role of the orphan—"an important stock character" in Cameroonian folklore and fiction—in* The Poor Christ of Bomba.]

Folklore in African literature has been widely commented upon. Few studies, however, venture below the surface to interpret such folklore items within the literary work. As Dundes has pointed out, folklorists too often identify without going on to interpret, while literary critics and anthropologists often interpret folklore without first properly identifying it as such. If we are to come to any meaningful conclusions concerning the significance of folklore in African literature, we need both identification and interpretation; we must also look at the aesthetic and metaphysical implications of this use of oral tradition.

In the oral tradition of the Beti, Basaa, and Bulu ethnic groups of Cameroon, the orphan is an important stock character and the hero of many tales. We also find orphan protagonists in the novels of several Cameroon authors, most notably Ferdinand Oyono and Mongo Beti. Their presence in these novels is not surprising since, as Finnegan points out, "Each literary culture has its own stock figures whose characteristics are immediately brought into the listener's minds by their mere mention." Certain assumptions and attitudes are focused on the character of the orphan as he (or she) appears in traditional tales. If these attitudes carry over into written literature, as I think they do, then an understanding of the orphan's traditional role in the tales is essential to a more complete understanding of modern Cameroon writing.

In the following discussion, two Cameroon "classics"—Oyono's *Une Vie de boy* and Beti's **Le Pauvre Christ de Bomba**—are examined in relation to two dozen Beti, Basaa, and Bulu orphan tales from various printed sources. As we consider the role of the orphan in oral and written literature, two specific questions arise: how has the orphan character been transformed or adapted in the transition from oral to literary tradition? How have these authors chosen to make use of the orphan character in their novels?

The terrible difficulties faced by real-life orphans in Beti, Basaa, and Bulu society are hinted at in the many traditional insults (e.g., "galeux comme un orphelin"), and proverbs (e.g., "si ta mére meurt, puise moins dans le plat") from these groups. Other figures of speech underline the misery of the orphan's solitude: reference is commonly made, for example, to "orphan fish" or "orphan stars" that occur in isolation. The orphan is usually represented as being dirty, hungry, and victimized by almost everyone. Without parents, and especially without a mother, the orphan is thrown on his or her own resources, cut off from family support and protection. As we know from the late Abbé Tsala's recollections of his own hardships as an orphan, this is true in real-life experience as well as in the tales. In the Beti, Basaa, and Bulu cultures, being abandoned and alone is the worst catastrophe that can befall anyone.

Binam Bikoi considers orphan tales from the oral tradition to be the "hinge" between *contes sérieux* and *contes légers. Contes légers* are set in daily life and are characterized by irony, social criticism and a practical moral. *Contes sérieux,* on the other hand, are mythical, marvelous tales in which man is responsible for events, and the outcome is often tragic. Just as the orphan tale itself is a sort of hinge, the orphan hero of the tale is also a hinge, or mediator, between two worlds: "la notion de l'orphelin," as Binam Bikoi explains, "...associe immédiatement la vie et la mort." The orphan, even as he inhabits this world, is bound by strong ties of affection and loyalty to his parents in the next world.

The orphan's adventures in the tale carry him back and forth between these two worlds.

The orphan tales usually begin with the death of one or both parents or the expulsion of the child from the parent's home. The tales themselves are many and varied, but they share as their central core the journey and the impossible tasks that the orphan must accomplish along the way. These tasks, along with the journey, have been compared to the initiation rites that the young people in these societies traditionally underwent in order to become adults: the orphan in the tale is the quintessential initiate. In the tales, the orphan's choice of responses to the tests is critical; whatever solution he chooses, he never refuses the task. The outcome of the tales is usually happy, at least for the orphan hero, as completion of initiation rites is a happy event.

At this point in the discussion, the initiatory quality of the orphan tales bears closer examination. Binam Bikoi argues that the orphan's itinerary very closely resembles the itinerary of certain initiation procedures among the Beti, Basaa, and Bulu. The tales contain elements that are important in helping to explain certain aspects of the initiation rites; as Binam Bikoi explains, these elements are found in the ethical values that underlie the orphan's conflicts with the universe.

The traditional Sô initiation, for example, is a long series of rigorous trials for the initiates. The trials include, among other things, bastonnades (beatings), dangerous or impossible tasks, and running the gauntlet. The last gauntlet is the culminating point of the initiation and is particularly severe: the candidate is offered various avenues of escape but is killed if escape is attempted. Candidates who successfully complete the rites are then welcomed back into the community as adults.

Motifs from the initiation frequently appear in the orphan tales. In one tale, for example, the orphan arrives at a crossroads with nine roads going off in nine different directions, and his dead mother appears to him to show him which road to take. This motif evokes that part of the initiation in which the initiate circumambulates nine times around the crossroads and then returns home. In another tale, the orphan hero is repeatedly accosted by a talking chimpanzee who beats him, but who finally gives the orphan supernatural help in carrying out the tasks that win him a wife. The chimpanzee, as it is eventually revealed in the tale, is none other than the spirit of the orphan's dead father. The orphan hero in the folktales undergoes severe trials in which he must depend on his own abilities and on supernatural help. These tests of character finally lead the orphan to a happy ending, that is, to reintegration into the society.

The initiatory character of the novels, *Une Vie de boy* and **Le Pauvre Christ de Bomba,** is also central to their development, and this fact has not gone entirely unnoticed by scholars. The relation of the written tradition (the novels) to the oral tradition (the folktales), however,

seems to have been overlooked, even though both Oyono and Beti are natives of the region in which the orphan cycle of tales is familiar part of the oral tradition. Like the tales, the novels may be seen as hinges connecting two worlds, in this case Europe and Africa. Unlike the tales, however, in which the hero is reintegrated at the end, tragic denouements are dealt out to the novels' heroes. For Toundi in *Une Vie de boy,* it is clearly spelled out; for Denis in **Le Pauvre Christ de Bomba,** we get only menacing hints. (pp. 350-52)

Paralleling Toundi's initiation on his journey from the world of the village to the European world of the Commandant's house, Denis, in **Le Pauvre Christ de Bomba,** is partially initiated in spite of himself on a mission tour with Father Drumont. Given to the mission by his father, the motherless Denis imagines himself to be Father Drumont's son. The other Africans at the mission notice his attitude and tease him about it. One of the novel's most insistent themes is Denis's quest for a mother. He imagines that Father Drumont might have been an orphan, too: "Peut-être a-t-il perdu sa mére en bas âge tout comme moi." Denis repeatedly mourns the fact that he is without a mother. He is attracted to Catherine as a maternal figure, and even after she seduces him and opens his eyes to what has been going on in Zacharia's room all this time Denis still thinks of her as being like a mother to him.

In spite of his sexual initiation, Denis is still not truly initiated, not yet completely a man. He is not confronted with other initiatory trials—the bastonnades in the novel, for example, are reserved for the amiable scoundrel Zacharia and the two women—and the end of the novel hints that Denis's real initiation is about to begin. When the Bomba Mission finally collapses under the weight of a scandal and Father Drumont leaves, it is a second orphanhood for Denis. He is without his protector as he goes off to confront the real world of colonialism. He thinks he will get a job with a Greek merchant, but the reader is left fearing that he will more likely be conscripted into the road gang.

The tour that Denis makes with Father Drumont is a circular journey, beginning and ending at the Bomba Mission; but the Denis who returns to Bomba is not the same Denis who started out. In the interim, he has moved from being a naive, motherless little boy to being on the threshold of manhood. The folktales' orphan heroes make similar circular journeys in which their status also changes. As Binam Bikoi notes, "La route de l'orphelin est donc pavée d'épreuves, et pleine de détours; une route en spirale ou, surtout en cercle. L'itinéraire doit décrire ce cercle et nouer une boucle." These circular journeys in the tales and novels may be seen as metaphors for the initiation process in which candidates leave the village for the bush, where they are initiated before returning to the village as adult members of the community.

It is interesting to note that both Oyono and Beti have placed their orphan-heroes in the care of priests in their preinitiation periods. The priests' sexual ambiguity is emphasized in the novels by means of such epithets as "châtré" or "homme-femme blanc." In addition to their role as mediators between male and female, the priests occupy a position that is neither completely European nor African, but a bridge between the two. More Africanized than the other Europeans in Africa because they live among the people and speak their language (albeit in hilariously mangled fashion), they are nevertheless not part of the African world. They represent a first link to the other worlds of colonial cruelty—the Commandant's house or the road gang.

In the folktales, the orphan meets an old woman at the beginning of the journey. This old woman acts as a protector and guide, giving counsel to the orphan so that he may fulfill his tasks and return triumphantly to the village. Like the priests, the old woman is sexually neutral, or ambiguous. The old woman represents and imparts the traditional wisdom that enables the orphan to complete his initiatory journey and be reintegrated into the society. It is through these mediators—priest and old woman—that the orphan acquires the knowledge and skills he will need if he is to succeed in his initiation.

Unlike their folktale counterparts, however, Toundi and Denis are irrevocably alienated: the real world has changed drastically, their mentors' teachings (representing European wisdom) have been inadequate and inappropriate, and the initiation has gone awry. Orphanhood in the novels, then, becomes a vivid metaphor for colonialism. Bereft of the protection and familiar rules of traditional society, the orphans of the novels stumble determinedly toward ruin. Noting that Africans have become strangers in their own lands, one African commenting on orphan tales calls Africa itself a huge orphanage. In this sense, *Une Vie de boy* and **Le Pauvre Christ de Bomba** are metaphorical extensions of the orphan folktales from the oral tradition: as the orphan folktale is a metaphor for the initiation process, the novels, springing from the same tradition, invert the metaphor and explore some of the detours on the initiatory journey. The tragic outcome of the two novels can be traced to the heedless disdain of conventional wisdom and the inability to adapt to the colonial world, in which all the rules of the game have changed.

Alienation has been a powerful and recurrent theme in modern African literature. When Oyono, Beti, and other Cameroon writers turn to this theme in their novels, they find in the orphan a ready-made metaphor from their oral tradition. The orphan in the folktales is a stock character denoting marginality, misery, and alienation, and his sequence of adventures describes the process of reintegration. Through courage and obedience the orphan hero of the folktales triumphs, and—like the initiates—rejoins his society as an adult. The orphan heroes of the novels, on the other hand, find no such reconciliation. Toundi's disobedience and gourmandism destroy him; and Denis's naive obedience to a set

of assumptions that simply does not correspond to reality leaves him vulnerable to impending disaster.

Recognizing orphanhood as a. traditional metaphor uniting oral and written literature in the case of these two Cameroon novels, we see that oral literature, or folklore, has more to offer serious literary scholarship than has perhaps been acknowledged. An appreciation of the oral tradition from which modern African writings springs will enrich our study of African written literature: it will open provocative avenues of inquiry and suggest useful frames of reference for a better understanding of the creative writing coming out of Africa today. (pp. 354-56)

> Susan Domowitz, "The Orphan in Cameroon Folklore and Fiction," in Research in African Literatures, *Vol. 12, No. 3, Fall, 1981, pp. 350-58.*

FURTHER READING

Brench, A. C. *The Novelists' Inheritance in French Africa.* London: Oxford University Press, 1967, 146 p.
> Overview of francophone African writers, with a discussion of Beti's *Mission Accomplished* and *King Lazarus.*

Cornwell, JoAnne. "Neurosis and Creativity: Two Early Novels by Mongo Beti." *The French Review* 60, No. 5 (April 1987): 644-52.
> Applies a "patterning principle"—the interaction of neurosis with the human potential to act and react creatively—to Beti's *Mission Accomplished* and *King Lazarus.*

Flannigan, Arthur. "African Discourse and the Autobiographical Novel: Mongo Bét's *Mission terminée.*" *The French Review* 55, No. 6 (May 1982): 835-45.
> Examines Beti's appropriation of a Western genre, the novel, for the form and structure of his *Mission Accomplished.*

Lambert, Fernando. "Narrative Perspectives in Mongo Beti's *Le Pauvre Christ de Bomba.*" *Yale French Studies,* No. 53 (1976): 78-91.
> Studies narrative technique in *The Poor Christ of Bomba.*

Mickelsen, David J. "The *Bildungsroman* in Africa: The Case of *Mission terminée.*" *The French Review* 59, No. 3 (February 1986): 418-27.
> Examines Beti's *Mission Accomplished* as an African adaptation of the *Bildungsroman,* a traditionally German novel form that has as its main theme the formative years or spiritual education of a young person.

Porter, Abioseh Mike. "The Child-Narrator and the Theme of Love in Mongo Beti's *Le Pauvre Christ de Bomba.*" In

Design and Intent in African Literature, edited by David F. Dorsey, Phanuel A. Egejuru, and Stephen H. Arnold, pp. 103-07. Washington, D.C.: Three Continents Press, Inc., 1982.

Argues that the love theme evident in Beti's later novels is also present in his earlier works, particularly *The Poor Christ in Bomba.*

Smith, Robert P., Jr. "Mongo Beti: The Novelist Looks at Independence and the Status of the African Woman." *CLA Journal* XIX, No. 3 (March 1976): 301-11.

Presents *Perpetua and the Habit of Unhappiness* as Beti's indictment of the slave-like status of women in Africa.

Storzer, Gerald H. "Abstraction and Orphanhood in the Novels of Mongo Beti." *Présence Francophone: Revue Littéraire,* No. 15 (Autumn 1977): 93-112.

Studies orphanhood and alienation in Beti's novels.

Arna Bontemps

1902-1973

(Born Arnaud Wendell Bontemps) American poet, critic, anthologist, dramatist, novelist, short story writer, biographer, essayist, and author of children's books.

Bontemps is recognized as the foremost scholar and historian of the Harlem Renaissance movement. He is also considered one of the most prolific and significant black American writers. His poetry, novels, short stories, essays, and other writings highlight black American culture and stress a return to one's roots. His novel *Black Thunder* (1936) stands as his crowning literary achievement and exemplifies his concern with the past and his message of hope for fellow humanity.

Arnaud Bontemps was born in 1902 in Louisiana to Paul and Marie (Pembroke) Bontemps. His father was a bricklayer and his mother a schoolteacher who instilled in him a love of books. When he was three years old, his father abruptly moved the family to California. Years later he learned that two white men emerging from a saloon one night had threatened his father, calling out, "Let's walk over the big nigger." Hoping for a better life, the Bontemps family settled in a section of Los Angeles called Watts in 1905; they were at the time the only black family in the neighborhood. When Bontemps was twelve years old, his mother died and he went to live with his grandmother in the California countryside. There he spent his youth with his Uncle Buddy, becoming his "companion and confidant in the corn rows." Once a "young mulatto dandy in elegant cravat and jeweled stickpin," according to Bontemps, Uncle Buddy was an "old derelict" and alcoholic who loved "dialect stories, preacher stories, ghost stories, slave and master stories. He half-believed in signs and charms and mumbo-jumbo, and he believed whole-heartedly in ghosts." In short, critic Robert Bone summarized, Uncle Buddy "was the living embodiment of Southern Negro folk culture." Paul Bontemps—concerned that his son might pick up Uncle Buddy's vices—sent Bontemps to a white boarding school, admonishing him, "Now don't go up there acting colored." Recalling his father's advice in 1965, Bontemps exclaimed, "How dare anyone, parent, schoolteacher, or merely literary critic, tell me not to act *colored?*" Pride in one's color and heritage would later characterize all of Bontemps's works.

Graduating from Pacific Union College in 1923, Bontemps accepted a teaching position in New York and arrived at the heart of the Harlem Renaissance. There he met fellow writers Langston Hughes, Jean Toomer, Claude McKay, James Weldon Johnson, Countee Cullen, W. E. B. Du Bois, and Zora Neale Hurston. In 1924 Bontemps launched his literary career with the publication of the poem "Hope" in the periodical *Crisis*. His poetry met with immediate success; reviewers awarded him literary prizes for "Golgotha Is a Mountain,"

"Nocturne at Bethesda," and "The Return." Critic Minrose Gwin stated of Bontemps' verse: "[His] poetry is characterized by an intoxicating gusto, a sense of excitement, of self-discovery, of release from inhibition." In the early 1930s Bontemps shifted his attention to novels. His first novel *God Sends Sunday* (1931) tells the story of a black jockey named Little Augie. Based on the life of his Uncle Buddy, Bontemps depicted in *God Sends Sunday,* according to one critic, "the lightheartedness and the soft melancholy of the Negro race." Like Uncle Buddy, Little Augie loves women, flashy clothes, gambling, and singing the blues. When *God Sends Sunday* was first published in 1931, it received mixed reviews. One critic commented that "there is an undulating movement to this prose that is closely kin to the author's dignified, well-turned poems." Du Bois, however, called it a "profound disappointment" and criticized its negative portrayal of blacks and black life. Another reviewer asserted that it had "no great significance." *God Sends Sunday* was followed by two historical novels: *Black Thunder* in 1936 and *Drums at Dusk* in 1939.

Bontemps is perhaps best known for *Black Thunder,* a fictionalized account of the "Gabriel Insurrection" that occurred in 1800 in Virginia. Gabriel Prosser—the slave protagonist in *Black Thunder*—convinced that anything "equal to a grey squirrel wants to be free," urges other slaves to revolt against their white owners. Although the insurrection ultimately fails, Gabriel nonetheless emerges as a hero. When *Black Thunder* first appeared in 1936, Richard Wright wrote: "Covering all those skimpy reaches of Negro letter I know, this is the only novel dealing forthrightly with the historical and revolutionary traditions of the Negro people. . . . *Black Thunder* sounds a new note in Negro fiction, thereby definitely extending the boundaries and ideology of the Negro novel." Critic Sterling A. Brown, echoing Wright's opinion in 1973, declared, " . . . for what it aims at, *Black Thunder* has no peer. And for whatever Negro novelists have aimed at, I would place *Black Thunder* in the top six with: *Native Son, Invisible Man, The Marrow of Tradition, Go Tell It On The Mountain,* and *Jubilee.* None of Ann Petry, Dorothy West, Chester Himes, John O. Killens, most of whose works I am entranced by, equal Arna Bontemps' *Black Thunder.*" Benjamin Brawley likewise stated: "In spite of an occasional blemish, one is led to ask if in the whole range of Negro fiction there is a book to equal this in quality. . . . [In] all that Mr. Bontemps may do or attempt in the future, it is the standard of this work that he will have to keep in mind." A few critics, most notably Bone, were less generous in their reviews: "[The] complexity of characterization, together with a tone of restraint and a tendency to underwrite, combine to save *Black Thunder* from the worst features of a propaganda novel. What remains of protest and of race pride limits the book but does not destroy it." In general, critics lauded *Black Thunder* as one of the most significant black American novels. Although Bontemps's last novel *Drums at Dusk,* a story of a black revolt in Haiti, suffered by comparison to *Black Thunder,* scholars nonetheless welcomed it as an important addition to the field of historical fiction.

In the 1930s Bontemps also began writing books for children because, in his words, "I began to suspect that it was fruitless for a Negro in the United States to address serious writing to my generation, and I began to consider the alternative of trying to reach young readers not yet hardened or grown insensitive to man's inhumanity to man, as it is called." Collaborating with his friend Hughes, he published his first juvenilia *Popo and Fifina, Children of Haiti* in 1932. Others soon followed: *You Can't Pet a Possum* (1934), *Sad-Faced Boy* (1937), *Golden Slippers: An Anthology of Negro Poetry for Young Readers* (1941), and *The Fast Sooner Hound* (1942). Critics praised the books for their "beauty of style," "crisp humor," and "simple homelike atmosphere." Concerned with the lack of role models for black youths, Bontemps also wrote *George Washington Carver* (1950), *Frederick Douglass: Slave, Fighter, Freeman* (1959), and

Young Booker: The Story of Booker T. Washington's Early Days (1972).

Adding to his growing reputation as poet, novelist, and author of children's books, Bontemps became a respected critic and anthologist with the publications of *The Poetry of the Negro, 1746-1949* (1949), *The Book of Negro Folklore* (1958), *American Negro Poetry* (1963), and *Great Slave Narratives* (1969). He also dabbled in drama, producing the musical comedy *St. Louis Woman* in 1946, an adaptation of his earlier novel *God Sends Sunday.* Reviewing the play, a New York *Herald Tribune* critic stated that "there are moments of exciting theatrical alchemy in the script, but they are random and infrequent." Another critic found "the whole 'she-bang' quite beautiful and a great lot of fun." In contrast to the varied opinions on his play, Bontemps's short stories received unanimous praise. According to critic Jonathan Yardley, the fourteen stories in *The Old South: "A Summer Tragedy" and Other Stories of the Thirties* (1973) "occupy a territory somewhere between fiction and personal reminiscence. They are low-key, informal and chatty, but possessed of more depth than one initially realizes. Most of them are set in the Depression, which was an especially bad time for Southern blacks, yet their mood is neither despairing nor bitter . . . the stories convey genuine love for the South, its people and its land."

Despite his success as short story writer and novelist, Bontemps thought of himself as a poet first. In 1963, after publishing over twenty-five books, he returned to poetry and produced a collection of verse called *Personals.* As with the majority of his works, he completed *Personals* while a librarian at Fisk University in Tennessee from 1943 to 1965. Although he left to teach at the University of Illinois and then at Yale during the late 1960s, he returned to Fisk University in 1971 and remained there until his death in 1973. At the time of his death, he was working on his autobiography entitled "A Man's Name."

Although sometimes overshadowed by his friend Langston Hughes in literary assessments, Bontemps nevertheless distinguished himself as an important writer and critic. In a tribute to his life and many works, Sterling A. Brown wrote of Bontemps: "Nobody will replace Arna . . . . Nobody will replace Arna, I repeat. There are some men who are irreplaceable. The blues line runs: *Another good man done gone.* I enlarge the line to: *Another good man, a very good man, has left us. His name was Arna Bontemps.*"

(For further information about Bontemps's life and works, see *Black Writers; Contemporary Authors,* Vols. 1-4, 41-44; *Contemporary Authors New Revision Series,* Vol. 4; *Contemporary Literary Criticism,* Vols. 1, 18; *Dictionary of Literary Biography,* Vols. 48, 51; and *Something about the Author,* Vols. 2, 24, 44. For related criticism, see the entry on the Harlem Renaissance in *Twentieth-Century Literary Criticism,* Vol. 26.)

PRINCIPAL WORKS

"Hope" (poetry) 1924: published in periodical *Crisis*

"Spring Music" (poetry) 1925; published in periodical *Crisis*

"Dirge" (poetry) 1926; published in periodical *Crisis*

"Holiday" (poetry) 1926; published in periodical *Crisis*

"Nocturne at Bethesda" (poetry) 1926; published in periodical *Crisis*

"Tree" (poetry) 1927; published in periodical *Crisis*

God Sends Sunday (novel) 1931

Popo and Fifina, Children of Haiti [with Langston Hughes] (juvenilia) 1932

You Can't Pet a Possum (juvenilia) 1934

Black Thunder (novel) 1936

Sad-Faced Boy (juvenilia) 1937

Drums at Dusk (novel) 1939

Golden Slippers: An Anthology of Negro Poetry for Young Readers [editor] (anthology) 1941

The Fast Sooner Hound [with Jack Conroy] (juvenilia) 1942

"Who Recreates Significant Moments in History" (essay) 1944; published in periodical *Opportunity: Journal of Negro Life*

They Seek A City [with Jack Conroy] (short stories) 1945; also published as *Any Place but Here* [revised edition], 1966

We Have Tomorrow (juvenilia) 1945

"Two Harlems" (essay) 1945

"Langston Hughes" (essay) 1946; published in periodical *Ebony*

Slappy Hooper, the Wonderful Sign Painter [with Jack Conroy] (juvenilia) 1946

Story of the Negro (juvenilia) 1948

Free and Easy (drama) 1949

The Poetry of the Negro, 1746-1949 [coeditor with Langston Hughes] (anthology) 1949; also published as *The Poetry of the Negro, 1946-1970* [revised edition], 1971

"Buried Treasures of Negro Art" (essay) 1950

George Washington Carver (juvenilia) 1950

"White Southern Friends of the Negro" (essay) 1950; published in periodical *Negro Digest*

Chariot in the Sky: A Story of the Jubilee Singers (juvenilia) 1951

"How I Told My Child About Race" (essay) 1951

Sam Patch, the High, Wide, & Handsome Jumper [with Jack Conroy] (juvenilia) 1951

"Bud Blooms" (essay) 1952; published in periodical *Saturday Review*

"Chesnutt Papers at Fisk" (essay) 1952; published in periodical *Library Journal*

"Facing a Dilemma" (essay) 1952; published in periodical *Saturday Review*

"Harlem Renaissance" (essay) 1953; published in periodical *Saturday Review*

The Story of George Washington Carver (biography) 1954

Lonesome Boy (juvenilia) 1955

The Book of Negro Folklore [coeditor with Langston Hughes] (anthology) 1958

Frederick Douglass: Slave, Fighter, Freeman (juvenilia) 1959

"Evolution of Our Conscience" (essay) 1961; published in periodical *Saturday Review*

"New Black Renaissance" (essay) 1961; published in periodical *Negro Digest*

"Minority's New Militant Spirit" (essay) 1962; published in periodical *Saturday Review*

American Negro Poetry [editor] (anthology) 1963

Personals (poetry) 1963

Famous Negro Athletes (juvenilia) 1964

"Harlem: The Beautiful Years. A Memoir" (essay) 1965; published in periodical *Negro Digest*

"Why I Returned" (essay) 1965; published in periodical *Harper's Magazine*

"Harlem in the Twenties" (essay) 1966; published in periodical *Crisis*

"A Tribute to Du Bois" (essay) 1966; published in periodical *Journal of Human Relations*

"Langston Hughes: He Spoke of Rivers" (essay) 1968; published in periodical *Freedomways*

Great Slave Narratives [editor] (anthology) 1969

Hold Fast to Dreams: Poems Old and New [editor] (anthology) 1969

Mr. Kelso's Lion (juvenilia) 1970

Free At Last: The Life of Frederick Douglass (juvenilia) 1971

The Harlem Renaissance Remembered: Essays [editor] (anthology) 1972

Young Booker: The Story of Booker T. Washington's Early Days (juvenilia) 1972

The Old South: "A Summer Tragedy" and Other Stories of the Thirties (short stories) 1973

Arna Bontemps-Langston Hughes Letters, 1925-1967 (letters) 1980

*This work was dramatized by Bontemps and Countee Cullen as *St. Louis Woman* in 1946.

W.E.B. Du Bois (essay date 1931)

[*Du Bois was an American educator, poet, novelist, historian, and sociologist who helped spark interest in black writers and black writing in America. Biographer Herbert Aptheker said of Du Bois: "[He] was more a history-maker than an historian." Du Bois's best-known work,* The Souls of Black Folk *(1903), is considered a landmark in the history of black self-awareness. In the following excerpt, he offers a negative review of* God Sends Sunday, *stating that it is a "profound disappointment."*]

Arna Bontemps' first venture in fiction [*God Sends Sunday*] is to me a profound disappointment. It is of the school of "Nigger Heaven" and "Home to Harlem." There is a certain pathetic touch to the painting of his poor little jockey hero, but nearly all else is sordid crime, drinking, gambling, whore-mongering, and murder. There is not a decent intelligent woman; not a single man with the slightest ambition or real education, scarcely more than one human child in the whole book. Even the horses are drab. In the "Blues" alone Bontemps sees beauty. But in brown skins, frizzled hair and full contoured faces, there are to him nothing but ugly, tawdry, hateful things, which he describes with evident caricature.

One reads hurriedly on, waiting for a gleam of light, waiting for the Sunday that some poor ugly black God may send; but somehow it never comes; and if God appears at all it is in the form of a little drunken murderer riding South to Tia Juana on his back.

> *W. E. B. Du Bois, in a review of "God Sends Sunday," in* The Crisis, *Vol. 40, No. 9, September, 1931, p. 304.*

Richard Wright (essay date 1936)

[*An American novelist, short story writer, and essayist, Wright is the acclaimed author of* Uncle Tom's Children *(1938) and* Native Son *(1940). Of Wright, Bontemps once declared: "[He] couldn't write badly if he˙tried." In the following review, Wright favorably appraises Bontemps's* Black Thunder, *describing it as "the only novel dealing forthrightly with the historical and revolutionary traditions of the Negro people."*]

In that limited and almost barren field known as the negro novel, Arna Bontemps's *Black Thunder* fills a yawning gap and fills it competently. Covering all those skimpy reaches of Negro letters I know, this is the only novel dealing forthrightly with the historical and revolutionary traditions of the Negro people.

Black Thunder is the true story of a slave insurrection that failed. But in his telling of the story of that failure Bontemps manages to reveal and dramatize through the character of his protagonist, Gabriel, a quality of folk courage unparalleled in the proletarian literature of this country....

Black Thunder is mainly the story of Gabriel, who believes in the eventual triumph of his destiny in spite of all the forces which conspire against it. He is convinced that God and the universe are on his side. He believes he must and will lead the Negro people to freedom. He seems to have no personal fear and no personal courage. He thinks, dreams, and feels wholly in terms of Negro liberation.... When considering Gabriel solely as an isolated individual, he seems sustained by an extremely foolish belief in himself; but when one remembers his slave state, when one realizes the extent to which he has made the wrongs of his people his wrongs, and the degree in which he has submerged his hopes in their hopes—when one remembers this, he appears logically and gloriously invincible....

Gabriel believes [in the uprising], he believes even when he is caught; even when the black cowl is capped about his head, even when the ax swings, he believes. Why?

For me the cardinal value of Bontemps's book, besides the fact that it is a thumping story well told, lies in the answer to that question. Perhaps I am straying further afield than the author did in search for an answer. If I do, it is because I believe we have in *Black Thunder* a revelation of the very origin and source of folk values in literature.

Even though Gabriel's character is revealed in terms of personal action and dialogue, I feel there is in him much more than mere personal dignity and personal courage. There is in his attitude something which transcends the limits of immediate consciousness. He is buoyed in his hope and courage by an optimism which takes no account of the appalling difficulties confronting him. He hopes when there are no objective reasons or grounds for hope; he fights when his fellow-slaves scamper for their lives. In doing so, he takes his place in that gallery of fictitious characters who exist on the plane of the ridiculous and the sublime. Bontemps endows Gabriel with a myth-like and deathless quality. And it is in this sense, I believe, that *Black Thunder* sounds a new note in Negro fiction, thereby definitely extending the boundaries and ideology of the Negro novel.

> *Richard Wright, "A Tale of Courage," in* Partisan Review and Anvil, *Vol. III, No. 1, February, 1936, p. 31.*

Arna Bontemps (essay date 1965)

[*In the following biographical essay entitled "Why I Returned," originally published in* Harper's Magazine *in 1965, Bontemps discusses early influences on his literary career. He also reminisces about his father, his Uncle Buddy, the Scottsboro trials, and the social conditions that shaped his literary works.*]

The last time I visited Louisiana the house in which I was born was freshly painted. To my surprise it seemed almost attractive. The present occupants, I learned, were a Negro minister and his family. Why I expected the place to be run down and the neighborhood decayed is not clear, but somewhere in my subconscious the notion that rapid deterioration was inevitable where Negroes live had been planted and allowed to grow. Moreover, familiar as I am with the gloomier aspects of living Jim Crow, this assumption did not appall me. I could reject the snide inferences. Seeing my birthplace again, however, after many years, I felt apologetic on other grounds.

Mine had not been a varmint-infested childhood so often the hallmark of Negro American autobiography. My parents and grandparents had been well-fed, well-clothed, and well-housed, although in my earliest recollections of the corner at Ninth and Winn in Alexandria both streets were rutted and sloppy. On Winn there was an abominable ditch where water settled for weeks at a time. I can remember Crazy George, the town idiot, following a flock of geese with the bough of a tree in his hand, standing in slush while the geese paddled about or probed into the muck. So fascinated was I, in fact, I did not hear my grandmother calling from the kitchen door. It was after I felt her hand on my shoulder shaking me out of my daydream that I said something that made her laugh. "You called me Arna," I protested, when she insisted on knowing why I had not answered. "My name is George." But I became Arna for the rest of her years.

I had already become aware of nicknames among the people we regarded as members of the family. Teel, Mousie, Buddy, Pinkie, Ya-ya, Mat, and Pig all had other names which one heard occasionally. I got the impression that to be loved intensely one needed a nickname. I was glad my grandmother, whose love mattered so much, had found one she liked for me.

As I recall, my hand was in my grandmother's a good part of the time. If we were not standing outside the picket gate waiting for my young uncles to come home from school, we were under the tree in the front yard picking up pecans after one of the boys had climbed up and shaken the branches. If we were not decorating a backyard bush with eggshells, we were driving in our buggy across the bridge to Pineville on the other side of the Red River.

This idyll came to a sudden senseless end at a time when everything about it seemed flawless. One afternoon my mother and her several sisters had come out of their sewing room with thimbles still on their fingers, needles and thread stuck to their tiny aprons, to fill their pockets with pecans. Next, it seemed, we were at the railroad station catching a train to California, my mother, sister, and I, with a young woman named Susy.

The story behind it, I learned, concerned my father. When he was not away working at brick or stone construction, other things occupied his time. He had come from a family of builders. His oldest brother had married into the Metoyer family on Cane River, descendants of the free Negroes who were the original builders of the famous Melrose plantation mansion. Another brother older than my father went down to New Orleans, where his daughter married one of the prominent jazzmen. My father was a bandman himself and, when he was not working too far away, the chances were he would be blowing his horn under the direction of Claiborne Williams, whose passion for band music awakened the impulse that worked its way up the river and helped to quicken American popular music.

My father was one of those dark Negroes with "good" hair, meaning almost straight. This did not bother anybody in Avoyelles Parish, where the type was common and "broken French" accents expected, but later in California people who had traveled in the Far East wondered if he were not a Ceylonese or something equally exotic. In Alexandria his looks, good clothes, and hauteur were something of a disadvantage in the first decade of this century.

He was walking on Lee Street one night when two white men wavered out of a saloon and blocked his path. One of them muttered, "Let's walk over the big nigger." My father was capable of fury, and he might have reasoned differently at another time, but that night he calmly stepped aside, allowing the pair to have the walk to themselves. The decision he made as he walked on home changed everything for all of us.

My first clear memory of my father as a person is of him waiting for us outside the Southern Pacific Depot in Los Angeles. He was shy about showing emotion, and he greeted us quickly on our arrival and let us know this was the place he had chosen for us to end our journey. We had tickets to San Francisco and were prepared to continue beyond if necessary.

We moved into a house in a neighborhood where we were the only colored family. The people next door and up and down the block were friendly and talkative, the weather was perfect, there wasn't a mud puddle anywhere, and my mother seemed to float about on the clean air. When my grandmother and a host of others followed us to this refreshing new country, I began to pick up comment about the place we had left, comment which had been withheld from me while we were still in Louisiana.

They talked mainly about my grandmother's younger brother, nicknamed Buddy. I could not remember seeing him in Louisiana, and I now learned he had been down at the Keeley Institute in New Orleans taking a cure for alcoholism. A framed portrait of Uncle Buddy was placed in my grandmother's living room in California, a young mulatto dandy in elegant cravat and jeweled stickpin. All the talk about him gave me an impression of style, grace, éclat.

That impression vanished a few years later, however, when we gathered to wait for him in my grandmother's house; he entered wearing a detachable collar without a tie. His clothes did not fit. They had been slept in for nearly a week on the train. His shoes had come unlaced. His face was pockmarked. Nothing resembled the picture in the living room.

Two things redeemed the occasion, however. He opened his makeshift luggage and brought out jars of syrup, bags of candy my grandmother had said in her letters that she missed, pecans, and filé for making gumbo. He had stuffed his suitcase with these instead of clothes; he had not brought an overcoat or a change of underwear. As we ate the sweets, he began to talk. He was not trying to impress or even entertain us. He was just telling how things were down home, how he had not taken a drink or been locked up since he came back from Keeley the last time, how the family of his employer and benefactor had been scattered or died, how the schoolteacher friend of the family was getting along, how high the Red River had risen along the levee, and such things.

Someone mentioned his white employer's daughter. A rumor persisted that Buddy had once had a dangerous crush on her. This, I took it, had to be back in the days when the picture in the living room was made, but the dim suggestion of interracial romance had an air of unreality. It was all mostly gossip, he commented, with only a shadow of a smile. Never had been much to it, and it was too long ago to talk about now. He did acknowledge, significantly, I thought, that his boss's daughter had been responsible for his enjoyment of poetry and fiction and had taught him perhaps a thousand songs, but neither of these circumstances had undermined his life-long employment in her father's bakery, where his specialty was fancy cakes. Buddy had never married. Neither had the girl.

When my mother became ill, a year or so after Buddy's arrival, we went to live with my grandmother in the country for a time. Buddy was there. He had acquired a rusticity wholly foreign to his upbringing. He had never before worked out of doors. Smoking a corncob pipe and wearing oversized clothes provided by my uncles, he resembled a scarecrow in the garden, but the dry air and the smell of green vegetables seemed to be good for him. I promptly became his companion and confidant in the corn rows.

At mealtime we were occasionally joined by my father, home from his bricklaying. The two men eyed each other with suspicion, but they did not quarrel immediately. Mostly they reminisced about Louisiana. My father would say, "Sometimes I miss all that. If I was just thinking about myself, I might want to go back and try it again. But I've got the children to think about—their education."

"Folks talk a lot about California," Buddy would reply thoughtfully, "but I'd a heap rather be down home than here, if it wasn't for the *conditions.*"

Obviously their remarks made sense to each other, but they left me with a deepening question. Why was this exchange repeated after so many of their conversations? What was it that made the South—excusing what Buddy called the *conditions*—so appealing for them?

There was less accord between them in the attitudes they revealed when each of the men talked to me privately. My father respected Buddy's ability to quote the whole of Thomas Hood's "The Vision of Eugene Aram," praised his reading and spelling ability, but he was concerned, almost troubled, about the possibility of my adopting the old derelict as an example. He was horrified by Buddy's casual and frequent use of the word *nigger*. Buddy even forgot and used it in the presence of white people once or twice that year, and was soundly criticized for it. Buddy's new friends, moreover, were sometimes below the level of polite respect. They were not bad people. they were what my father described as don't-care folk. To top it all, Buddy was still crazy about the minstrel shows and minstrel talk that had been the joy of his young manhood. He loved dialect stories, preacher stories, ghost stories, slave and master stories. He half-believed in signs and charms and mumbo-jumbo, and he believed wholeheartedly in ghosts.

I took it that my father was still endeavoring to counter Buddy's baneful influence when he sent me away to a white boarding school during my high school years, after my mother had died. "Now don't go up there acting colored," he cautioned. I believe I carried out his wish. He sometimes threatened to pull me out of school and let me scuffle for myself the minute I fell short in any one of several ways he indicated. Before I finished college, I had begun to feel that in some large and important areas I was being miseducated, and that perhaps I should have rebelled.

How dare anyone, parent, schoolteacher, or merely literary critic, tell me not to act *colored*? White people have been enjoying the privilege of acting like Negroes for more than a hundred years. The minstrel show, their most popular form of entertainment in America for a whole generation, simply epitomized, while it exaggerated, this privilege. Today nearly everyone who goes on a dance floor starts acting colored immediately, and this had been going on since the cakewalk was picked up from Negroes and became the rage. Why should I be ashamed of such influences? In popular music, as in the music of religious fervor, there is a style that is unmistakable, and its origin is certainly no mystery. On the playing field a Willie Mays could be detected by the way he catches a ball, even if his face were hidden. Should the way some Negroes walk be changed or emulated? Sometimes it is possible to tell whether or not a cook is a Negro without going into the kitchen. How about this?

In their opposing attitudes toward roots my father and my great uncle made me aware of a conflict in which every educated American Negro, and some who are not educated, must somehow take sides. By implication at least, one group advocates embracing the riches of the folk heritage; their opposites demand a clean break with the past and all it represents. Had I not gone home summers and hobnobbed with Negroes, I would have finished college without knowing that any Negro other than Paul Laurence Dunbar ever wrote a poem. I would have come out imagining that the story of the Negro could be told in two short paragraphs: a statement about jungle people in Africa and an equally brief account of the slavery issue in American history.

So what did one do after concluding that for him a break with the past and the shedding of his Negro-ness were not only impossible but unthinkable? First, perhaps, like myself, he went to New York in the 'twenties, met young Negro writers and intellectuals who were similarly searching, learned poems like Claude McKay's "Harlem Dancer" and Jean Toomer's "Song of the Son," and started writing and publishing things in this vein himself.

My first book [*God Sends Sunday*] was published just after the Depression struck. Buddy was in it, conspicuously, and I sent him a copy, which I imagine he read. In any case, he took the occasion to celebrate. Returning from an evening with his don't-care friends, he wavered along the highway and was hit and killed by an automobile. He was sixty-seven, I believe.

Alfred Harcourt, Sr. was my publisher. When he invited me to the office, I found that he was also to be my editor. He explained with a smile that he was back on the job doing editorial work because of the hard times. I soon found out what he meant. Book business appeared to be as bad as every other kind, and the lively and talented young people I had met in Harlem were scurrying to whatever brier patches they could find. I found one in Alabama.

It was the best of times and the worst of times to run to that state for refuge. Best, because the summer air was so laden with honeysuckle and spiraea it almost drugged the senses at night. I have occasionally returned since then but never at a time when the green of trees, of countryside, or even of swamps seemed so wanton. While paying jobs were harder to find here than in New York, indeed scarcely existed, one did not see evidences of hunger. Negro girls worked in kitchens not for wages but for the toting privilege—permission to take home leftovers.

The men and boys rediscovered woods and swamps and streams with which their ancestors had been intimate a century earlier, and about which their grandparents still talked wistfully. The living critters still abounded. They were as wild and numerous as anybody had ever dreamed, some small, some edible, some monstrous. I made friends with these people and went with them on possum hunts, and I was astonished to learn how much game they could bring home without gunpowder, which they did not have. When the possum was treed by the dogs, a small boy went up and shook him off the limb, and the bigger fellows finished him with sticks. Nets and traps would do for birds and fish. Cottontail rabbits driven into a clearing were actually run down and caught by barefoot boys.

Such carryings-on amused them while it delighted their palates. It also took their minds off the hard times, and they were ready for church when Sunday came. I followed them there, too, and soon began to understand why they enjoyed it so much. The preaching called to mind James Weldon Johnson's "The Creation" and "Go Down Death." The long-meter singing was from another world. The shouting was ecstasy itself. At a primitive Baptist foot washing I saw bench-walking for the first time, and it left be breathless. The young woman who rose from her seat and skimmed from the front of the church to the back, her wet feet lightly touching to tops of the pews, her eyes upward, could have astounded me no more had she walked on water. The members fluttered and wailed, rocked the church with their singing, accepted the miracle for what it was.

It was also the worst times to be in northern Alabama. That was the year, 1931, of the nine Scottsboro boys and their trials in nearby Decatur. Instead of chasing possums at night and swimming in creeks in the daytime, this group of kids without jobs and nothing else to do had taken to riding empty boxcars. When they found themselves in a boxcar with two white girls wearing overalls and traveling the same way, they knew they were in bad trouble. The charge against them was rape, and the usual finding in Alabama, when a Negro man was so much as remotely suspected, was guilty; the usual penalty, death.

To relieve the tension, as we hoped, we drove to Athens one night and listened to a program of music by young people from Negro high schools and colleges in the area. A visitor arrived from Decatur during the intermission and reported shocking developments at the trial that day. One of the girls involved had given testimony about herself which reasonably should have taken the onus from the boys. It had only succeeded in infuriating the crowd around the courthouse. The rumor that reached Athens was that crowds were spilling along the highway, lurking in unseemly places, threatening to vent their anger. After the music was over, someone suggested nervously that those of us from around Huntsville leave at the same time, keep our cars close together as we drove home, be prepared to stand by, possibly help, if anyone met with mischief.

We readily agreed. Though the drive home was actually uneventful, the tension remained, and I began to take stock with a seriousness comparable to my father's when he stepped aside for the Saturday night bullies on Lee Street in Alexandria. I was younger than he had been when he made his move, but my family was already larger by one. Moreover, I had weathered a Northern as well as a Southern exposure. My education was different, and what I was reading in newspapers differed greatly from anything he could have found in the Alexandria *Town Talk* in the first decade of this century.

With Gandhi making world news in India while the Scottsboro case inflamed passions in Alabama and awakened consciences elsewhere, I thought I could sense something beginning to shape up, possibly something on a wide scale. As a matter of fact, I had already written a stanza foreshadowing the application of a nonviolent strategy to the Negro's efforts in the South:

> We are not come to wage a strife
>   With swords upon this hill;
> It is not wise to waste the life
>   Against a stubborn will.
> Yet would we die as some have done:
> Beating a way for the rising sun.

Even so, deliverance did not yet seem imminent, and it was becoming plain that an ablebodied young Negro with a healthy family could not continue to keep friends in that community if he sat around trifling with a typewriter on the shady side of his house when he should have been working or at least trying to raise something for the table. So we moved on to Chicago.

Crime seemed to be the principal occupation of the South Side at the time of our arrival. The openness of it so startled us we could scarcely believe what we saw. Twice our small apartment was burglarized. Nearly every week we witnessed a stickup, a purse-snatching, or something equally dismaying on the street. Once I saw two men get out of a car, enter one of those blinded shops around the corner from us, return dragging a resisting victim, slam him into the back seat of the car, and speed away. We had fled from the jungle of Alabama's Scottsboro era to the jungle of Chicago's crime-ridden South Side, and one was as terrifying as the other.

Despite literary encouragement, and the heartiness of a writing clan that adopted me and bolstered my courage, I never felt that I could settle permanently with my family in Chicago. I could not accept the ghetto, and ironclad residential restrictions against Negroes situated as we were made escape impossible, confining us to neighborhoods where we had to fly home each evening before darkness fell and honest people abandoned the streets to predators. Garbage was dumped in alleys around us. Police protection was regarded as a farce. Corruption was everywhere.

When I inquired about transfers for two of our children to integrated schools which were actually more accessible to our address, I was referred to a person not connected with the school system or the city government. He assured me he could arrange the transfers—at an outrageous price. This represented ways in which Negro leadership was operating in the community at that time and by which it had been reduced to impotence.

I did not consider exchanging this way of life for the institutionalized assault on Negro personality one encountered in the Alabama of the Scottsboro trials, but suddenly the campus of a Negro college I had twice visited in Tennessee began to seem attractive. A measure of isolation, a degree of security seemed possible there. If a refuge for the harassed Negro could be found anywhere in the 1930s, it had to be in such a setting.

Fisk University, since its beginnings in surplus barracks provided by a general of the occupying army six months after the close of the Civil War, had always striven to exemplify racial concord. Integration started immediately with children of white teachers and continued till state laws forced segregation after the turn of the century. Even then, a mixed faculty was retained, together with a liberal environment and these eventually won a truce from an outside community that gradually changed from hostility to indifference to acceptance and perhaps a certain pride. Its founders helped fight the battle for public schools in Nashville, and donated part of the college's property for this purpose. Its students first introduced Negro spirituals to the musical world. The college provided a setting for a continuing dialogue between scholars across barriers and brought to the city before 1943 a pioneering Institute of Race Relations and a Program of African Studies, both firsts in the region. When a nationally known scholar told me in

Chicago that he found the atmosphere *yeasty,* I thought I understood what he meant.

We had made the move, and I had become the Librarian at Fisk when a series of train trips during World War II gave me an opportunity for reflections of another kind. I started making notes for an essay to be called "Thoughts in a Jim Crow Car." Before I could finish it, Supreme Court action removed the curtains in the railway diners, and the essay lost its point. While I had been examining my own feelings and trying to understand the need men have for customs like this, the pattern had altered. Compliance followed with what struck me, surprisingly, as an attitude of relief by all concerned. White passengers, some of whom I recognized by their positions in the public life of Nashville, who had been in a habit of maintaining a frozen silence until the train crossed the Ohio River, now nodded and began chatting with Negroes before the train left the Nashville station. I wanted to stand up and cheer. When the Army began to desegregate its units, I was sure I detected a fatal weakness in our enemy. Segregation, the monster that had terrorized my parents and driven them out of the green Eden in which they had been born, was itself vulnerable and could be attacked, possibly destroyed. I felt as if I had witnessed the first act of a spectacular drama. I wanted to stay around for the second.

Without the miseries of segregation, the South as a homeplace for a Negro of my temperament had clear advantages. In deciding to wait and see how things worked out, I was also betting that progress toward this objective in the Southern region would be more rapid, the results more satisfying, than could be expected in the metropolitan centers of the North, where whites were leaving the crumbling central areas to Negroes while they themselves moved into restricted suburbs and began setting up another kind of closed society.

The second act of the spectacular on which I had focused began with the 1954 decision of the Supreme Court. While this was a landmark, it provoked no wild optimism. I had no doubt that the tide would now turn, but it was not until the freedom movement began to express itself that I felt reassured. We were in the middle of it in Nashville. Our little world commenced to sway and rock with the fury of a resurrection. I tried to discover just how the energy was generated. I think I found it. The singing that broke out in the ranks of protest marchers, in the jails where sit-in demonstrators were held, in the mass meetings and boycott rallies, was gloriously appropriate. The only American songs suitable for a resurrection—or a revolution, for that matter—are Negro spirituals. The surge these awakened was so mighty it threatened to change the name of our era from the "space age" to the "age of freedom."

The Southern Negro's link with his past seems to me worth preserving. His greater pride in being himself, I would say, is all to the good, and I think I detect a growing nostalgia for these virtues in the speech of relatives in the North. They talk a great deal about

"Soulville" nowadays, when they mean "South." "Soul-brothers" are simply the homefolks. "Soulfood" includes black-eyed peas, chitterlings, grits, and gravy. Aretha Franklin, originally from Memphis, sings, "Soulfood—it'll make you limber; it'll make you quick." Vacations in Soulville by these expatriates in the North tend to become more frequent and to last longer since times began to get better.

Colleagues of mine at Fisk who like me have pondered the question of staying or going have told me their reasons. The effective young Dean of the Chapel, for example, who since has been wooed away by Union Theological Seminary, felt constrained mainly by the opportunities he had here to guide a large number of students and by the privilege of identifying with them. John W. Work, the musicologist and composer, finds the cultural environment more stimulating than any he could discover in the North. Aaron Douglas, an art professor, came down thirty-four years ago to get a "real, concrete experience of the touch and feel of the South." Looking back, he reflects, "If one could discount the sadness, the misery, the near-volcanic intensity of Negro life in most of the South, and concentrate on the mild, almost tropical climate and the beauty of the landscape, one is often tempted to forget the senseless cruelty and inhumanity the strong too often inflict on the weak."

For my own part, I am staying on in the South to write something about the changes I have seen in my lifetime, and about the Negro's awakening and regeneration. That is my theme, and this is where the main action is. There is also the spectacular I am watching. Was a climax reached with the passage of the Civil Rights Act last year? Or was it with Martin Luther King's addressing Lyndon B. Johnson as "my fellow Southerner"? Having stayed this long, it would be absurd not to wait for the third act—and possibly the most dramatic. (pp. 177-82)

> *Arna Bontemps, "Why I Returned," in* Harper's Magazine, *Vol. 230, No. 1379, April, 1965, pp. 177-82.*

Robert A. Bone (essay date 1965)

[*Bone is an American authority on African-American literature. He has said of himself: "A white man and critic of black literature, I try to demonstrate by the quality of my work that scholarship is not the same thing as identity." He is the author of* The Negro Novel in America *(1958) and* Down Home: A History of Afro-American Short Fiction from Its Beginnings to the End of the Harlem Renaissance *(1975). In the following excerpt from the former work, he reviews Bontemps's* God Sends Sunday, Black Thunder, *and* Drums at Dusk *as novels that "bear the mark of both the Negro Renaissance and of the depression years."*]

Arna Bontemps is a transitional figure whose novels bear the mark both of the Negro Renaissance and of the depression years which follow . . . . A minor poet during the 1920s, Bontemps turned later to fiction, history, and books for children. He has written three novels, of which the first *God Sends Sunday* (1931), is an unadulterated product of the Negro Renaissance. The setting of the novel is the sporting world of racetrack men and gamblers, of jazz and the shimmy, of fights and razor carvings. His historical novels, however, which deal with slavery times, reflect the mood of the Depression era. By choosing slave insurrections as a basis for his plots, Bontemps stresses an aspect of slavery which was emotionally appealing to the rebellious thirties. (p. 120)

The narrative technique [of *Black Thunder* (1936)], which conveys the action by a progressive treatment of the participants, is reminiscent of the novels of Dos Passos. The plot is developed in fragments, through short chapters which open with the name of the character under consideration. From this constant shift in point of view, the reader must piece together the full panorama. It is a technique especially suited to the presentation of complex historical events, and Bontemps employs it skillfully. At its best, this technique requires deft characterization, since the action of the novel is constantly refracted through a new consciousness, which the reader must understand in its own right. (p. 121)

Arna Bontemps' second historical novel, *Drums at Dusk* (1939), is in every respect a retreat from the standards of *Black Thunder.* Deriving its plot from the Haitian slave rebellion which brought Toussaint l'Ouverture to power, the novel is unworthy of its subject. In writing of a successful rebellion, Bontemps is deprived of the dramatic power of tragedy, and he discovers no appropriate attitude to take its place. Upon a highly romantic plot he grafts a class analysis of society which is post-Marxian and flagrantly unhistorical. Frequently lapsing into crude melodrama, he embroiders his narrative with all of the sword-play, sex, and sadism of a Hollywood extravaganza. (pp. 122-23)

> *Robert Bone, "Aspects of the Racial Past," in his* The Negro Novel in America, *revised edition, Yale University Press, 1965, pp. 120-52.*

Arna Bontemps (essay date 1968)

[*In the following 1968 introduction to* Black Thunder, *Bontemps discusses the writing of the book and its critical reception in 1936.*]

Time is not a river. Time is a pendulum. The thought occurred to me first in Watts in 1934. After three horrifying years of preparation in a throbbing region of the deep south, I had settled there to write my second novel, away from it all.

At the age of thirty, or thereabouts, I had lived long enough to become aware of intricate patterns of recurrence, in my own experience and in the history I had been exploring with almost frightening attention. I suspect I was preoccupied with those patterns when, early in *Black Thunder,* I tried to make something of the old major-domo's mounting the dark steps of the Sheppard mansion near Richmond to wind the clock.

The element of time was crucial to Gabriel's attempt, in historical fact as in *Black Thunder,* and the hero of that action knew well the absolute necessity of a favorable conjunction. When this did not occur, he realized that the outcome was no longer in his own hands. Perhaps it was in the stars, he reasoned.

If time is the pendulum I imagined, the snuffing of Martin Luther King, Jr.'s career may yet appear as a kind of repetition of Gabriel's shattered dream during the election year of 1800. At least the occurrence of the former as this is written serves to recall for me the tumult in my own thoughts when I began to read extensively about slave insurrections and to see in them a possible metaphor of turbulence to come.

Not having space for my typewriter, I wrote the book in longhand on the top of a folded-down sewing machine in the extra bedroom of my parents' house at 10310 Wiegand Avenue where my wife and I and our children (three at that time) were temporarily and uncomfortably quartered. A Japanese truck farmer's asparagus field was just outside our back door. From a window on the front, above the sewing machine, I could look across 103rd Street at the buildings and grounds of Jordan High School, a name I did not hear again until I came across it in some of the news accounts reporting the holocaust that swept Watts a quarter of a century later. In the vacant lot across from us on Wiegand a friendly Mexican neighbor grazed his milk goat. We could smell eucalyptus trees when my writing window was open and when we walked outside, and nearly always the air was like transparent gold in those days. I could have loved the place under different circumstances, but as matters stood there was no way to disguise the fact that our luck had run out.

My father and stepmother were bearing up reasonably well, perhaps, under the strain our presence imposed on them, but only a miracle could have healed one's own hurt pride, one's sense of shame and failure at an early age. Meanwhile, it takes time to write a novel, even one that has been painstakingly researched, and I do not blame my father for his occasional impatience. I had flagellated myself so thoroughly, I was numb to such criticism, when he spoke in my presence, and not very tactfully, about young people with bright prospects who make shipwreck of their lives.

What he had in mind, mainly, I am sure, were events which had brought me home at such an awkward time and with such uncertain plans, but somehow I suspected more. At the age at which I made my commitment to writing, he had been blowing a trombone in a Louisiana marching band under the direction of Claiborne Williams. But he had come to regard such a career as a deadend occupation unworthy of a young family man,

married to a schoolteacher, and he renounced it for something more solid: bricklaying. Years later when the building trades themselves began to fade as far as black workers were concerned, under pressure of the new labor unions, he had made another hard decision and ended his working years in the ministry.

He was reproaching me for being less resourceful, by his lights, and I was too involved in my novel to even reply. The work I had undertaken, the new country into which I had ventured when I began to explore Negro history had rendered me immune for the moment, even to implied insults.

Had the frustrations dormant in Watts at that date suddenly exploded in flame and anger, as they were eventually to do, I don't think they would have shaken my concentration; but I have a feeling that more readers might then have been in a mood to hear a tale of volcanic rumblings among angry blacks—and the end of patience. At the time, however, I began to suspect that it was fruitless for a Negro in the United States to address serious writing to my generation, and I began to consider the alternative of trying to reach young readers not yet hardened or grown insensitive to man's inhumanity to man, as it is called.

For this, as for so much else that has by turn intrigued or troubled me in subsequent years, my three-year sojourn in northern Alabama had been a kind of crude conditioning. Within weeks after the publication of my first book, as it happened, I had been caught up in a quaint and poignant disorder that failed to attract wide attention. It was one of the side effects of the crash that brought on the Depression, and it brought instant havoc to the Harlem Renaissance of the twenties. I was one of the hopeful young people displaced, so to speak. The jobs we had counted on to keep us alive and writing in New York vanished, as some observed, quicker than a cat could wink. Not knowing where else to turn, I wandered into northern Alabama, on the promise of employment as a teacher, and hopefully to wait out the bad times, but at least to get my bearings. I did not stay long enough to see any improvement in the times, but a few matters, which now seem important, did tend to become clearer as I waited.

Northern Alabama had a primitive beauty when I saw it first. I remember writing something in which I called the countryside a green Eden, but I awakened to find it dangerously infested. Two stories dominated the news as well as the daydreams of the people I met. One had to do with the demonstrations by Mahatma Gandhi and his followers in India; the other, the trials of the Scottsboro boys then in progress in Decatur, Alabama, about thirty miles from where we were living. Both seemed to foreshadow frightening consequences, and everywhere I turned someone demanded my opinions, since I was recently arrived and expected to be knowledgeable. Eventually their questions upset me as much as the news stories. We had fled here to escape our fears in the city, but the terrors we encountered here were even more upsetting than the ones we had left behind.

I was, frankly, running scared when an opportunity came for me to visit Fisk University in Nashville, Tennessee, about a hundred miles away, get a brief release from tensions, perhaps, and call on three old friends from the untroubled years of the Harlem Renaissance: James Weldon Johnson, Charles S. Johnson, and Arthur Schomburg. All, in a sense, could have been considered as refugees living in exile, and the three, privately could have been dreaming of planting an oasis at Fisk where, surrounded by bleak hostility in the area, the region, and the nation, if not indeed the world, they might not only stay alive but, conceivably, keep alive a flicker of the impulse they had detected and helped to encourage in the black awakening in Renaissance Harlem.

Each of them could and did recite by heart Countée Cullen's lines dedicated to Charles S. Johnson in an earlier year:

> We shall not always plant while other reap
> The golden increment of bursting fruit,
> Not always countenance, abject and mute,
> That lesser men should hold their brothers cheap;
> Not everlastingly while others sleep
> Shall we beguile their limbs with mellow flute,
> Not always bend to some more subtle brute;
> We were not made eternally to weep.
>
> The night whose sable breast relieves the stark,
> White stars is no less lovely being dark,
> And there are buds that cannot bloom at all
> In light, but crumple, piteous, and fall;
> So in the dark we hide the heart that bleeds,
> And wait, and tend our agonizing seeds.

Separately and with others we made my visit a time for declaring and reasserting sentiments we had stored in our memories for safekeeping against the blast that had already dispersed their young protégés and my friends and the disasters looming ahead.

Discovering in the Fisk Library a larger collection of slave narratives than I knew existed, I began to read almost frantically. In the gloom of the darkening Depression settling all around us, I began to ponder the stricken slave's will to freedom. Three historic efforts at self-emancipation caught my attention and promptly shattered peace of mind. I knew instantly that one of them would be the subject of my next novel. First, however, I would have to make a choice, and this involved research. Each had elements the others did not have, or at least not to the same degree, and except for the desperate need of freedom they had in common, each was attempted under different conditions and led by unlike personalities.

Denmark Vesey's effort I dismissed first. It was too elaborately planned for its own good. His plot was betrayed, his conspiracy crushed too soon, but it would be a mistake to say nothing came of it in Vesey's own time. The shudder it put into the hearts and minds of slaveholders was never quieted. *Nat Turner's Confession,* which I read in the Fisk Library at a table across from Schomburg's desk, bothered me on two counts. I felt uneasy about the amanuensis to whom his account was related and the conditions under which he confessed. Then there was the business of Nat's "visions" and "dreams."

Gabriel's attempt seemed to reflect more accurately for me what I felt then and feel now might have motivated slaves capable of such boldness and inspired daring. The longer I pondered, the more convinced I became. Gabriel had not opened his mind too fully and hence had not been betrayed as had Vesey. He had by his own dignity and by the esteem in which he was held inspired and maintained loyalty. He had not depended on trance-like mumbo jumbo. Freedom was a less complicated affair in his case. It was, it seemed to me, a more unmistakable equivalent of the yearning I felt and which I imagined to be general. Finally, there was the plan itself, a strategy which some contemporaries, prospective victims, felt could scarcely have failed had not the weather miraculously intervened in their behalf. Gabriel attributed his reversal, ultimately, to the stars in their courses, the only factor that had been omitted in his calculations. He had not been possessed, not even overly optimistic.

Back in Alabama, I began to sense quaint hostilities. Borrowing library books by mail, as I sometimes did, was unusual enough to attract attention. Wasn't there a whole room of books in the school where I worked—perhaps as many as a thousand? How many books could a man read in one lifetime anyway? We laughed together at the questions, but I realized they were not satisfied with my joking answers. How could I tell them about Gabriel's adventure in such an atmosphere?

Friends from the Harlem years learned from our mutual friends at Fisk that we were in the vicinity and began dropping in to say howdy en route to Decatur or Montgomery or Birmingham. There was an excitement in the state similar to that which recurred twenty-five years later when black folk began confronting hardened oppression by offering to put their bodies in escrow, if that was required. In 1931, however, the effort was centered around forlorn attempts to save the lives of nine black boys who had been convicted, in a travesty of justice, of ravishing two white girls in the empty boxcars in which all were hoboing.

The boyish poet Langston Hughes was one of those who came to protest, to interview the teen-age victims in their prison cells, and to write prose and poetry aimed at calling the world's attention to the enormity about to be perpetrated. It was natural that he should stop by to visit us. He and I had recently collaborated, mainly by mail, on the writing of a children's story, *Popo and Fifina: Children of Haiti.* He had the story and I had the children, so my publisher thought it might work. Perhaps it would not be too much to say they were justified. The story lasted a long time and was translated into a

Dust jacket for Bontemps's 1970 children's book.

number of languages. The friendship between the two authors also lasted and yielded other collaborations over the next thirty-five years. But the association was anathema to the institution which had, with some admitted reluctance, given me employment.

As my year ended, I was given an ultimatum. I would have to make a clean break with the unrest in the world as represented by Gandhi's efforts abroad and the Scottsboro protests here at home. Since I had no connection or involvement with either, other than the fact that I had known some of the people who were shouting their outrage, I was not sure how a break could be made. The head of the school had a plan, however. I could do it, he demanded publicly, by burning most of the books in my small library, a number of which were trash in his estimation anyway, the rest, race-conscious and provocative. *Harlem Shadows, The Blacker the Berry, My Bondage and Freedom, Black Majesty, The Souls of Black Folk,* and *The Autobiography of an Ex-Coloured Man* were a few of those indicated.

I was too horrified to speak, but I swallowed my indignation. My wife was expecting another child, and the options before us had been reduced to none. At the end of the following term we drove to California, sold our car, and settled down in the small room in Watts in the hope that what we had received for the car would

buy food till I could write my book. By the next spring *Black Thunder* was finished, and the advance against royalties was enough to pay our way to Chicago.

Black Thunder, when published later that year, earned no more than its advance. As discouraging as this was, I was not permitted to think of it as a total loss. The reviews were more than kind. John T. Frederick, director of the Illinois Writers Project, read the book and decided to add me to his staff. He also commended it warmly in his anthology, *Out of the Midwest,* and in his CBS broadcasts. Robert Morss Lovett mentioned it in his class at the University of Chicago. But the theme of self-assertion by black men whose endurance was strained to the breaking point was not one that readers of fiction were prepared to contemplate at the time. Now that *Black Thunder* is published again, after more than thirty years, I cannot help wondering if its story will be better understood by Americans, both black and white. I am, however, convinced that time is not a river. (pp. vii-xv)

Arna Bontemps, in an introduction to his Black Thunder, *Beacon Press, 1968, pp. vii-xv.*

Dorothy Weil (essay date 1971)

[*In the following excerpt, Weil examines Negro folk-lore motifs in Bontemps's* Black Thunder.]

[**Black Thunder**] is a superior piece of work. Interest in the action is sustained; the minds and feelings of the blacks are made lucid and believable; and the atmosphere is unique. Bontemps accomplished these ends partly through the skillful use of various motifs from Negro folklore. Several episodes of the novel are pervaded by beliefs and customs that appear in this folklore—beliefs and customs concerning death and the spirit, the importance of 'signs' or portents, and the use of Magic and Conjure.

Early in **Black Thunder** a tyrannical slave owner whips a slave, Bundy, to death, and thus hastens the rebellion that has been on the minds of the blacks of Henrico county for some time. Bontemps' treatment of the funeral of this slave and the subsequent haunting by Bundy's spirit of a fellow slave, are rooted in narratives found in folklore that have to do with death, ghosts and spirits. (p. 1)

Bontemps is faithful in detail to folklore versions of [the funeral] custom. (p. 2)

The importance of 'signs' or portents in Negro folklore underlies Bontemps' treatment of two episodes in **Black Thunder,** the extended arguments among the rebels concerning "the stars," and the episode in which Drucilla predicts the death of another character. (p. 6)

The episode in **Black Thunder** in which the female house slaves compulsively chase a bird out of the house reflects the plethora of references in Negro folklore to birds as a sign of death. (p. 9)

Elements of Conjure and Magic appear in **Black Thunder** as they appear in folk tales and beliefs recorded by collectors. Several characters employ charms and counter charms, and one episode in the novel involves a traditional "conjure-poisoning." (p. 10)

Conjure poisoning...provides the basis for a final dramatic episode in **Black Thunder.** Pharoah, the slave whose death was foreshadowed in the incident with the bird, has betrayed the rebels. He became so frightened at the prospect of defeat that he ran into richmond screaming the news of rebellion. He then begins to feel ill and suspects that he is being "conjured."... (p. 12)

Bontemps' use of folk material in **Black Thunder** shows him to be a conscious, skillful artist. He has used this material to create a fictional world that is believable and vivid. These elements lend strength to Bontemps' depiction of the community of beliefs among the black *dramatis personae,* and at the same time serve to help characterize individual personalities. The vitality of the folk credo is important in the novel; it functions in allowing the black characters to be roused to group action, and it enlivens the inner world of the rebels which is shown to be as important as outer conditions in affecting their destinies. Characters such as Ben and Pharoah are provided with believable psychologies. The motifs from folklore fulfill other functions as well. They add colorful detail to scenes such as the funeral and the insanity of Pharoah, and serve as appropriate vehicles for achieving foreshadowing and for meting out punishment. (p. 13)

> Dorothy Weil, "Folklore Motifs in Arna Bontemps' 'Black Thunder'," in Southern Folklore Quarterly, *Vol. XXXV, No. 1, March, 1971, pp. 1-14.*

Arna Bontemps with John O'Brien (interview date 1971)

[*In the following 1972 interview, O'Brien and Bontemps discuss black writers, the Harlem Renaissance, and Bontemps's novel* Black Thunder. *In a preface to the printed text of the interview, O'Brien notes: "The interview was conducted in the spring of 1972 in Mr. Bontemps' office at the Fisk University library. He endured the four-hour session with patience and wit, a few times asking me to aid him in recalling parts of his novels which were written almost forty years ago. He now lives in Nashville, teaches at Fisk, and is currently at work on his autobiography."*]

[O'Brien]: *Mr. Bontemps, you mention in your preface to your collection of poems* **Personals** *that many young blacks were arriving in Harlem at the same time as you did and that many had the same hope of becoming writers. Did you know at the time which ones were going to be important? Were there any surprises?*

[Bontemps]: I recognized Langston Hughes, Countee Cullen, Jean Toomer, and Claude McKay immediately. All of these hit me within the first year or two in Harlem. Claude McKay's *Harlem Shadows* was the only one I had read before coming to Harlem. In 1923 I missed Toomer's *Cane.* When I went to New York in 1923 a friend of mine from Los Angeles wrote me that she had heard about *Cane* and that I should read it, so I did, and I was very shook-up by it. Cullen and Hughes—I had read both of them before their books were published and I knew that they were on their way. Wallace Thurman I knew from Los Angeles. He didn't come to New York until a year after I arrived. Actually he floundered around for about three or four years. It was not until about 1929 that his first novel and play were published. He was the man of the moment in 1929. That sort of surprised me. I found that he was so cynical about himself and others that he might not make it. Many of the things he tried between 1925 and 1929 had failed. I had known him longer than I had known any of the others and I had not felt too sure that he would make it because he distrusted himself as much as he distrusted others. Some that I had expected more of did not produce. Eric Walrond, who wrote *Tropic Death,* I thought was very promising. I had thought that Rudolph Fisher would become a giant, but the first thing he did was the best. In fact, his very first story, "The City of

Refuge," which appeared in *Atlantic Monthly* he was never able to reach again. He wrote a couple of novels after that, both of which seem almost negligible now. Zora Hurston looked promising and I anticipated that she would develop, but I did not think that she would turn out to be identified with reaction.

Are there writers who you feel still have not gained proper recognition?

There are those who feel that Zora Hurston doesn't begin to have the rank among American writers that she deserves. Others feel that Nella Larson is more important than she has gotten credit for being. There were others—as I said—who didn't develop as much as I expected. Wallace Thurman went astray, but his was a failure of health as much as it was of talent. Nothing after 1929 was up to what he had done by then, and he knew it. To some extent Rudolph Fisher was like that. Like Thurman, he died almost right during the Harlem Renaissance.

You said in that same preface that the Harlem Renaissance came close to giving America a "new aesthetic." Could you elaborate on what that aesthetic involves and how it differs from that which existed then?

Perhaps not in detail, but I can suggest what I was thinking about. First of all, the white aesthetic eliminates folk sources and sociological topics; it says that these are not legitimate material for art. If you accept that, you really eliminate the black writer's whole range of experience from serious literature, because about a third of all he knows is folk and about another third is classified—rather arbitrarily—as "sociological," and only one third comes out of the traditions of the English language which he is using. He is so inhibited that he's left out. So, if you could create another literature which employs folk motifs and which doesn't shy away from the problems of urban living and race relations, you have a new aesthetic.

Do you find a division in black literature between those writers who use folk sources and those who use sociological materials? Perhaps Toomer exemplifies the former and Ann Petry the latter?

Yes, if you work with generalities. Jean Toomer is consciously preoccupied with folk living. But when you read all of *Cane* you find that he is also involved with the sociology of inner-city living in Washington, D.C. and Chicago. You have in Toomer this poetic eye trying to resolve this mix, in his story "Kabnis." The more innovative writer would not make a clean distinction between the two. He would not accept the urban problem as being sociological alone.

Perhaps that's the artistic triumph of people like Toomer, McKay, and contemporary writers like LeRoi Jones, Clarence Major, and Ishmael Reed, because they are able to transform traditionally realistic material into another literary form.

Yes, that's it exactly.

Why do you think that writers like Toomer and McKay were so ignored in their time? Was it largely because of the innovations they were making in the novel?

The time wasn't right. Even if they had written different things, the American culture was such that it would not have accepted them. They couldn't have written anything that would have been wholly acceptable as long as they were identified as blacks. Our first attacks had to be directed against the closed doors; just as the generation of the sixties had to be preoccupied with getting into restaurants, theaters, and trains, so the writers of the Renaissance had to be concerned with trying to get published by standard publishers. Prior to that there had been a period of twenty years in which no publisher issued a serious piece of literature by a Negro. There were a few quite understandable exceptions, such as Booker T. Washington. He was unique and he really wasn't a literary man. But James Weldon Johnson wrote a novel in 1912—now treated as a classic in its field—which he couldn't get published by a major publisher. He was in New York and had plenty of entree, but it wasn't until after the Renaissance people broke through the door that a publisher brought back that old novel and it has never been out of print since. So, the Renaissance writers were trying to open doors, to get into magazines. That was the challenge for these writers. When someone would get published there was a lot of noise and this accounted for the attention drawn to them. After that they were confronted with another problem that does not face the writer today—the books didn't sell. There was the resistance of the booksellers, the resistance of white readers, and then the fact that black people didn't read novels at all. And they had good reason for not reading because all they had read in the past had been so damaging to their own feelings. The next challenge to the Harlem writers was to change the minds of blacks, to break down the resistance of booksellers, and to make some inroads into the white audience as well. None of these are confronted by the writers today. They were pretty successfully conquered during the Harlem period. After the Depression was over with, the gates were wide open. So, it was easy for Richard Wright to come in.

Do you think that McKay and Toomer realized how innovative they were being in their fiction?

I think Toomer did. Toomer was consciously trying to find new ways to write through the use of symbols. He was preoccupied with them and talked about them. But I don't think that it's possible for a writer—even a black writer—to do something that doesn't have its roots in the tradition of the language. None of these writers wanted to divorce themselves from the tradition of the language.

Did you know McKay and Toomer very well?

I didn't know them in the way I knew Cullen and Hughes. For one thing they were both about ten years

Charles S. Johnson and Arna Bontemps.

older than I was and they were not around Harlem at the same time. Toomer popped in and out. McKay was abroad for the whole of the Renaissance. I didn't see him until after he came back when the Depression was over.

Why do you think that Toomer only published the one novel? Owen Dodson suggested that Toomer just seemed to fade into oblivion.

Again, the audience and the receptivity of the publishers and booksellers were all against Toomer. Add to that his innovation. I regard that as the explanation. His time has only now come. He was so far ahead of his time. I only wish that he had lived three or four more years to see it.

Did he reach a time when he did not like to be considered as a writer?

I wouldn't say that he didn't like to be considered as a writer. He wrote all his life. He was discouraged about his writing I believe. I think more than anything else he wanted to be a writer, and he was disappointed that he

never had an audience. But the influence of Gurdjieff made him settle for another kind of recognition.

What was the influence of Carl Van Vechten on the writers of the Renaissance? Was he a center around whom many of the writers revolved?

He was a figure there but I don't think it was based upon his own writing. I don't think a single writer tried to imitate him. If any did, it was Thurman who disapproved of him most. Van Vechten was sort of a middle man. He was responsible for getting some of the younger writers published. He was excited by the upsurge in self-expression in Harlem and he promoted a lot of it. But I was not in his circle for a number of reasons. I suppose one reason was that I got married soon after arriving in New York and I was preoccupied with making a living. So, I couldn't run around as much as some of those who were unattached.

What caused the Harlem Renaissance to break up?

It was the crash of the stock market on Wall Street in 1929. It took it from 1929 to 1931 to reach uptown to

Harlem. You heard a lot of things but it was not until 1931 that you could tell that anything had happened on Wall Street. That is what ended it; it was a blow to publishing. Recovery didn't come until the New Deal. By then the black writers of Harlem were all scattered.

Why did so many black writers expatriate?

So many? I'm amazed that so few did. Nothing like the number of white writers that went abroad in the twenties. Very few blacks went and very few stayed very long. More went after World War II. William Gardner Smith, Richard Wright, Chester Himes. Wright went because he could better support himself there. Chester went a little later because he was actually doing better in France than he was in America.

Could you compare what went on among the writers of the Harlem Renaissance to what is happening among the young black writers of today? Although they do not live within a few city blocks of one another, is there a closeness and vitality among them that reminds you of the writers in the twenties?

I see more contrasts than I do similarities. There is a comparable impulse motivating this generation, but the circumstances have changed, so that the differences are conspicuous. For one thing, Harlem was Harlem because it had a locus in New York which was the cultural center of the nation. Now this impulse is dissipated throughout the whole country. I don't think that this is bad; as a matter of fact, I think that it may be very good. But it makes it *seem* different. There are many young black writers who are anxious to conceive of something similar to the Harlem Renaissance, but now everyone has his own local loyalty. I think that we are really far away from unification. And I don't think that now we have anyone writing verse that compares with Hughes or Cullen. There are more dramatists now and I attribute this to the different characteristics of our time. This is the time of the demonstration, this is the era of the visual demonstration. History is coming into it. And that is closer to drama than it is to poetry. I encourage young writers to imitate the Harlem group. If history will let them, perhaps they will make the same sort of impact.

A number of contemporary black writers still insist that publishers continue to discriminate and that there are really only superficial changes since the Renaissance.

I would say that if it's difficult to get published today, it isn't for racial reasons. They don't have that obstacle.

You have described the kinds of racism that the Harlem writers had to overcome in the publishing world and several contemporary black writers have pointed to continued racism on the part of the critics which they are having to combat. Do you think that the black writer finds it difficult to avoid becoming politically involved because he is made all the more conscious of racism when he attempts to publish? Does that political involvement help or hinder his art?

My own feeling is that modern man, the artist included, is directly affected by politics in our age. When it comes to being a doctrinaire participant in the political structure, I think that a writer can be hurt more than he can be helped by too strong an identification and too strong an allegiance. When I first knew Richard Wright and Ralph Ellison both of them were deeply involved in party-line communism and both felt that they were hurt more than they were helped by it. I always avoided it because, having grown up in an environment where my father had been a preacher, I was turned off by denominational, doctrinal infighting. So I am really speaking just about my own temperament; I don't believe that you can generalize. What each one does is a matter that is determined by his own makeup, the thickness of his skin, and all these other things over which he has very little control.

You certainly have not shied away from politics in your own novels. I wonder what the reaction was to **Black Thunder** *when it was published in 1936. Were you criticized for the obvious revolutionary sympathies in the novel?*

Black Thunder was widely reviewed and favorably reviewed, very favorably. Isabella Paterson complained in the *New York Herald Tribune* that I seemed to be dragging in the word "proletariat." I didn't agree, because actually it was a current expression in the French Revolution in which time the novel is set.

Were you accused by anyone of encouraging violent revolution?

Yes and no. There were little hints of that. It didn't keep me from getting favorable reviews from people who were not in the least radical. At the time, actually, there was more tolerance for that kind of writing than there was a few years later. It was published in the depths of the Depression and even conservative people could understand why certain writers could be taking positions that were quite radical.

Would the novel have received severer criticism today do you think?

I think so. Two things would happen. I would be accused of advocating violence because everything in the novel was in that direction. On the other hand the people who support the violent approach would pick up the book in greater numbers. And I would have been satisfied (laughing) to exchange one for the other.

Were there contemporary issues which prompted you to write the book at that time which are lost to today's readers?

Yes, definitely. I had looked into the Scottsboro case, which was to the 1930s what the Till case was to the Civil Rights demonstrations. The Scottsboro case was a prologue to what happened to my thinking and it encouraged me to go ahead with some such statement as **Black Thunder.**

When you wrote the novel, did you have in mind the kind of effect you wanted to have on your audience? Did you want some change to come about as a result of the novel?

I never felt that the kind of change a novel could bring would be instantaneous or explosive; nor did I want it to have an explosive effect. I was most impressed with novels that have a delayed action, and I had hopes that my writing would be of that kind, that it would work almost imperceptibly upon the reader's consciousness. I never felt that I could write the kind of novel I wanted to write and expect it to start a fire.

You said in the introduction to a recent edition of **Black Thunder** *that you were discouraged about reaching your generation through novel-writing, so you hoped to influence future ones. Was this the reason you stopped writing novels and turned to children's books?*

Definitely, that was the transition. I was in no mood merely to write entertaining novels. The fact that *Gone With the Wind* was so popular at the time was a dramatic truth to me of what the country was willing to read. And I felt that black children had nothing with which they could identify. As a result I tried my hand at writing for children and with immediately better results.

Would today's generation be more receptive to the novels you wanted to write?

I think that novel reading is down in this generation and I don't know how long it's going to stay down. There have been some up periods since I wrote my novels but television has reduced the number of people who depend upon fiction for whatever nourishment they need.

Both your fiction and poetry are concerned with themes of history and time. You use the image of the pendulum rather than the river to describe your sense of history.

That impressed me a long time ago and I still feel that history is a pendulum that does recur. But in each recurrence there is a difference.

And the image of the river would suggest a sense of completion?

That's right. The river is finished, it goes to its outlet. I don't think the river is a very good metaphor for time because we live in a universe that is perpetually revolving. And in our own experience we always arrive at the same point again, but when we get there we find that time has worked some changes in us.

Do you think that in your poetry you look toward the past with a desire to recapture it?

Well, there certainly is some nostalgia. I don't know whether I was consciously yearning for the past. I don't think that I ever believed that I could recapture the past. I had a yearning for something, something in my own life. Unlike most black writers I yearned for something in my past because I had something there that I could look upon with a certain amount of longing. A great many writers whom I have known have wanted to forget their pasts.

In the preface to **Personals** *you suggest that much of the writing of the Renaissance looked backward and tried to establish a link with the jungle.*

It has impressed me in black literature that the primitive is often superior to the civilized or educated man.

Of course, in the white Western mind the primitive is usually associated with disorder and perhaps violence. Many black writers seem to see it as a way of tapping some resource in man that frees him from the tyrannical norms of the existing rationalistic culture.

That's right. Spontaneity seems quite important in the black culture. The person who can act with spontaneity is the one favored by nature. One of the things I talked about a great deal when I taught at Yale was that Primitivism is often thought of as having no rationale to it. In fact, oftentimes it was actually the result of a long development that had been experimented with and proved. Some African tribes that had no written language—tribes we would take to be the more primitive ones—sometimes had the most sophisticated art. The bronzes of Benin in Nigeria which had such a great influence on modern painters like Picasso, were the work of a tribe that never had a written language. And a tribe in Eastern Africa which has given so many collections of proverbs to us had no written language either until very recently. I have deduced from this that they had some reason for not writing down their language, not that they were incapable. They were capable of things that go deeper than merely writing a language. It was a conscious choice of theirs. So I toyed with the thought that they deliberately refrained from developing written records. Because of the nature of their life, which was very fluid, it may be that tribes that had written languages were more vulnerable. This might have been part of their defense against invasion and oppression. In other words, they must have very carefully considered the disadvantages of writing. There certainly were languages in Africa long before there were Western languages. These languages existed not only in Egypt but down into mid-Africa, into that area in Rhodesia where cities were buried whose languages are known. So, I think the "book" is something they knew all about, talked about, and rejected.

In America there has always been a black literary tradition, but it has not always been a written one.

Blacks were the foremost proponents of the tale told for entertainment or instruction. And it was always oral.

This literary tradition is so strongly influenced by music. The structure of McKay's and Toomer's novels was based on musical concepts and critics attacked them for being sloppy and episodic.

That's right. They were speaking out of another context, using a different form of notation. They were attempting to free themselves from what they regarded as the limitations of this closed structure which didn't hold what they wanted it to. (pp. 4-15)

> *Arna Bontemps and John O'Brien, in an interview in* Interviews with Black Writers, *edited by John O'Brien, Liveright, 1973, pp. 3-15.*

Arthur P. Davis (essay date 1974)

[*An American writer and scholar of black literature, Davis is the author of* From the Dark Tower: Afro-American Writers 1900-1960 *(1974). In the following excerpt from this work, he explores recurring themes in Bontemps's* Personals *and in* God Sends Sunday, Black Thunder, *and* Drums at Dusk.]

Bontemps' poems [collected in *Personals*] make use of several recurring themes: the alien-and-exile allusions so often found in New Negro poetry; strong racial suggestiveness and applications; religious themes and imagery subtly used; and the theme of return to a former time, a former love, or a remembered place. On occasion he combines in a way common to lyrical writing the personal with the racial or the general. Many of these poems are protest poems; but the protest is oblique and suggestive rather than frontal. Over all of Bontemps' poetry there is a sad, brooding quality, a sombre "Il Penseroso" meditative cast. In *Personals* there are no obviously joyous or humorous pieces.

The most popular theme in these verses is that of return. There are seven poems dealing in some way with this subject. The one entitled **"Return"** has a double thrust, the coming back to an old love which takes on an atavistic coloring: "Darkness brings the jungle to our room: / the throb of rain is the throb of muffled drums. / ... This is a night of love / retained from those lost nights our fathers slept in huts." There is definitely here the kind of alien-and-exile comparison found in these New Negro poems; the highest joy of lovers (real or imagined) can have is the remembered ancestral love in an idyllic Africa.

In a different way, **"Southern Mansion"** is also a return poem because for the speaker "The years go back with an iron clank...." Two waves of remembered sound come to him: music from the house and the clank of chains in the cotton field. Because of the latter, only ghosts and the poplars "standing there still as death" and symbolizing death—only they—remain.

"To a Young Girl Leaving the Hill Country" is a return poem with a Wordsworthian slant. The speaker tells the girl that she has ignored the hills of her native place, and she will therefore come back a bent old lady "to seek the girl she was in those familiar stones." He continues: "then perhaps you'll understand / just how it was you drew from them and they from you." For Bontemps, one seemingly finds his identity in a return to his remembered past (p. 85).

What is this concern with the past—with old loves, old places, ghosts of yesterday? Is there for Bontemps ... greater joy in the backward glance than in the living experience? Is he simply a late romanticist with a yen "For old unhappy far-off things, / And battles long ago"? The answer is not evident in these poems. Perhaps the answer is what each reader finds in them ....

[In] **"Nocturne at Bethesda,"** one finds the contemporary loss-of-faith theme joined with the alien-and-exile theme: "The golden days are gone ... / And why do our black faces search the empty sky?" There is a suggestion here of a double loss for the black man "wandering in strange lands"—the loss of religion and of a homeland. If there is "a returning after death," the speaker tells us to "search for me / beneath the palms of Africa." In some respects this poem reminds one of Cullen's "Heritage," but as is characteristic of Bontemps, it is a much quieter poem than Cullen's masterpiece.

"Golgotha Is a Mountain," too, employs an atavistic theme. "Some pile of wreckage," we are told, is buried beneath each mountain. "There are mountains in Africa too. / Treasure is buried there," and black men are digging with their fingers for it. "I am one of them," the speaker admits. One day, however, he seems to say, I will crumble and make a mountain. "I think it will be Golgotha." One notes the joining of the personal religious thought with the racial. The return to one's ancestral roots is suggested, but, as in all of these poems, the black man's return is pointed out as being somehow different. In this particular poem there is a hint of future hope for the Negro.... There is also homage to the black man's strongest virtue: endurance.

In **"A Black Man Talks of Reaping"** one finds the closest approach to direct protest in these poems from *Personals:* "yet what I sowed and what the orchard yields / my brothers' sons are gathering stalk and root" whereas my children "feed on bitter fruit." This is the kind of muted protest expected of a controlled poet like Bontemps.

The poems of Arna Bontemps lack the clear, unambiguous statement of those of his contemporaries: McKay, Cullen, Hughes. There is modern obscurity in these verses, and the so-called meaning often eludes the reader. Their craftsmanship, however, is impressive. The reader somehow feels a certain rightness in Bontemps' lines, that what he has said could not be expressed otherwise. There is a quiet authority in these poems. (p. 86)

Bontemps' first novel, *God Sends Sunday,* was published in 1931.... Bontemps managed to get over a little of the spirit and atmosphere necessary to make the novel plausible. But the work is a young man's work. The touch of the beginner is everywhere apparent. For example, the author evidently did not feel up to the task of rendering Little Augie's decline from affluence and power to poverty-stricken old age, and he simply jumps to the last years.... It gives a picture of a segment of Negro life that no other novelist has touched. And though there is not much depth here, it is an entertaining and dramatic work....

Bontemps' second novel, *Black Thunder*..., is a much better book in every way than his first; in fact, it is perhaps the author's outstanding publication. (p. 87)

Black Thunder tells the story of the 1800 uprising led by Gabriel Prosser and it gives a convincing account of the actions and thinking of this heroic black. Although the account is fictional, it impresses the reader as being *psychologically* true, and that is *the* important thing in a work of this sort. Bontemps does not make Gabriel too brave or too clever. He describes him as a powerful black man with a gift for organization and leadership. He has no visions, is not unusually superstitious, and is not particularly religious. His driving force is a deep conviction that "anything what's equal to a grey squirrel wants to be free." Stubbornly loyal to his followers, he refuses to inform on them....

Unfortunately, Gabriel is developed so much better than the other characters in the work that we tend to forget them, especially the whites, both slave masters and sympathetic "Jacobins." But the story of Gabriel and his sexy girlfriend, Juba, of the house servants Ben and Pharoah who "sing" to the white folks, and of the other minor leaders of the insurrection is well told. Bontemps has a gift for storytelling and for making his characters talk convincingly. Moreover, he knew well the Virginia folk speech he utilized, and this gives a certain authority to his narration. Symbolically, the novel speaks for the modern Negro. One wonders why the present-day militants have not made better use of it in this respect. Incidentally, Bontemps' Gabriel impresses the Negro reader as being more *authentic* than William Styron's Nat Turner.

In his third novel, *Drums at Dusk* (1939), Bontemps again tries historical fiction, but the work suffers by comparison with the superior *Black Thunder.* A story of the uprising in Haiti, the one that Toussaint would eventually lead, *Drums at Dusk* is more a "costume piece" than an historical novel. (p. 88)

Drums at Dusk of a necessity deals with violence, but Bontemps really has no taste for violence, and he gives as little of it as possible in this work.... The action in *Black Thunder* was much more congenial to Bontemps' temperament because it concerns threatened rather than actual violence. (pp. 88-9)

> *Arthur P. Davis, "First Fruits: Arna Bontemps," in his* From the Dark Tower: Afro-American Writers 1900-1960, *Howard University Press, 1974, pp. 83-9.*

FURTHER READING

Bone, Robert, "Arna Bontemps." In his *Down Home: A History of Afro-American Short Fiction from Its Beginnings to the End of the Harlem Renaissance,* pp. 272-87. New York: G. P. Putnam's Sons, 1975.
Overview of Bontemps's short stories, focusing on tales from *The Old South: "A Summer Tragedy" and Other Stories of the Thirties.*

Braxton, Jodi. "Asserting Selfhood." *The New Republic* 167, No. 17 (4 November 1972): 27-30.
Reviews Bontemps's *The Harlem Renaissance Remembered,* concluding: "*The Harlem Renaissance Remembered* is uneven, but the originality and excellence of a few of the essays, together with its fine bibliography, make it a real achievement."

Brown, Sterling A. "Arna Bontemps: Co-Worker, Comrade." *Black World* XXII, No. 11 (September 1973): 11, 91-7.
Discusses Bontemps's life and works, focusing on his novel *Black Thunder.* The critic also summarizes Bontemps's contributions to the wider literary world and pays tribute to his "co-worker" and "comrade."

Canaday, Nicholas. "Arna Bontemps: The Louisiana Heritage." *Callaloo* 4, Nos. 1-3 (1981): 163-69.
Discusses *God Sends Sunday* as a mirror of Bontemps's experiences in Louisiana.

Mitchell, Louis D. Review of *The Old South,* by Arna Bontemps. *Best Sellers* 33, No. 17 (1 December 1973): 385-86.
Examines *The Old South* as a reflection of Bontemps's "relations to both Negro and white life in the thirties." The critic writes: "[In *The Old South*] there is all the while that delicate melancholy that goes with thoughts of bygone days, with chips of light from the past. Family, church, school—from a Negro attitude—are folksily blended in with glimpses of the exotic fleshpots and the eccentric figures that spot the memory of everyone's childhood."

Streator, George. Review of *They Seek a City,* by Arna Bontemps and Jack Conroy. *The Commonweal* XLII, No. 14 (20 July 1945): 337-38.
Evaluates Bontemps and Conroy as writers of black history, concluding: "The authors are not totally free from errors of interpretation...our writers do best with plain research, holding to the past.... In short, where the authors are not too earnest in writing history from presentday pamphlets, they are at their best."

David Bradley

1950-

(Full name David Henry Bradley, Jr.) American novelist.

Bradley is the acclaimed author of *The Chaneysville Incident* (1981). Winner of the prestigious 1982 PEN/Faulkner Award, the novel blends historical fact and fiction in its representation of a rural Pennsylvania community marked by slavery and touched by the legacy of the Underground Railroad. Upon its publication in 1981, critics lauded the work as one of the most important books ever written by a contemporary black author.

The only son of Rev. David Henry Bradley, Sr., and Harriet Jackson Bradley, Bradley was born in 1950 in Bedford, Pennsylvania. Growing up in the predominantly white farming community of Bedford was "not that hospitable for blacks—or that comfortable," he recounted to Mel Watkins: ". . . I grew up feeding chickens, but there were always books around our house. . . . [My father] was probably most responsible for my becoming interested in writing, but writing was my second choice. I wanted to be an astronaut. Can you imagine being black and telling people in Bedford that you wanted to be an astronaut? They must have thought I was deranged."

Bradley excelled at local public schools and later at the University of Pennsylvania, garnering numerous awards and honors upon his graduation in 1972. Of his college experience, he recalled: "I got to the university at a very tricky time. It was during the middle of the civil rights movement, and there were many students who were activists. Most of them were from urban areas, and they were flexing their muscles on campus. I was a rube from the country. I knew more about cows than anything else. . . . A lot of them had the illusion that black people had power. But I had grown up in a rural white society, and I knew damn well we have no power. . . . Then, one evening while I was in Philadelphia, I went to a bar on South Street. . . . I fell in love with these people and with that street. I listened to them, and my first published novel came from that experience." His first work, *South Street* (1975)—written while Bradley was an undergraduate—received generally positive reviews upon its publication. "*South Street* is not simply another grim, naturalistic litany of the anguish of the downtrodden," Watkins commented. "Without blunting the pathos of this tale, Mr. Bradley has infused what could have been a standard story and stock characters with new vigor. Probing beneath the sociological stereotypes, he portrays his characters with fullness that amplifies much of the lusty irony of ghetto life. . . . It is Bradley's unerring depiction of the vitality that rears itself even within this despairing setting that distinguishes this novel."

As with *South Street,* Bradley conceived the idea for his second novel, *The Chaneysville Incident,* while still in college. Although he grew up hearing stories about the Underground Railroad in Bedford County, in 1969 his mother told him a story he had not heard before: While writing an article for Bedford's bicentennial, she had discovered thirteen unmarked graves in a burial plot on an area farm. Her findings confirmed a local legend about the personal heroism and sacrifice of a group of thirteen runaway slaves. Bradley was intrigued by his mother's discovery: "I knew my second novel would be about those 13 runaway slaves. . . . I tried to write the story as a straight narrative at first—you know, a typically nice commercial plantation tale with interracial sex and scenes with slaves being boiled in oil. I couldn't do it. I tried, but it was too sensational and, despite the violence and tragedy, it was funny." What has resulted—after four different drafts written during a period of eleven years—according to Patricia Holt, "is a complicated book. . . with long historical passages that are so readable they go down like cream."

The Chaneysville Incident is about a black man's confrontation with his personal past, his family history, and the living legacies of racism and slavery. The protagonist, John Washington, is a history professor who hides his feelings by talking in "little lectures"—"all neat and logical and precise." When the novel opens, he is awakened by a phone call; he learns that his boyhood mentor—Jack Crawley—the man who taught him woodsmanship, hunting, and whisky-drinking, is dying. John promptly leaves for his hometown in western Pennsylvania. Indeed, "old Jack" is perilously close to death, but with Jack's help, John begins to explore his own father's death many years ago. As the novel progresses, he comes to realize that his father's mysterious death is somehow linked to "the Chaneysville incident," an event that involved thirteen runaway slaves who, upon being captured, chose death over a return to slavery. At first John is an interested, though detached, historian, but he quickly becomes obsessed with these runaways who valued freedom over death. In the climactic scene, he relinquishes his cool, intellectual detachment and imagines what really happened in Chaneysville and to his father, at last allowing his "human" faculties to emerge. He "gets out of his skin," as one reviewer noted, and begins to claim not only his family's history, but also the history of all black people in the United States.

The Chaneysville Incident was thunderously applauded by critics when it first appeared in 1981. *Los Angeles Times* book editor Art Seidenbaum called the novel "the most significant work by a new male black author since James Baldwin." Similarly, Bruce Allen claimed that it "rivals Toni Morrison's *Song of Solomon* as the best novel about the black experience in America since Ellison's *Invisible Man*." "Whatever else may be said," Vance Bourjaily enthused, "[Bradley's] a writer. What he can do, at a pretty high level of energy, is synchronize five different kinds of rhetoric, control a complicated plot, manage a good-sized cast of characters, convey a lot of information, handle an intricate time scheme, pull off a couple of final tricks that dramatize provocative ideas, and generally keep things going for 200,000 words. . .; his novel deserves what it seems pretty sure to get: a lot of interested and challenged readers."

Bradley is acknowledged as a writer of considerable stature. "*The Chaneysville Incident,* acclaimed by fiction writers and by popular and scholarly writers alike," Smith observed, "place[s] Bradley in the vanguard of contemporary novelists." Bradley currently teaches at Temple University and is at work on other novels.

(For further information about Bradley's life and works, see *Black Writers; Contemporary Authors,* Vol. 104; *Contemporary Authors New Revision Series,* Vol. 26; *Contemporary Literary Criticism,* Vol. 23; and *Dictionary of Literary Biography,* Vol. 33: *Afro-American Fiction Writers after 1955.*)

PRINCIPAL WORKS

South Street (novel) 1975
The Chaneysville Incident (novel) 1981

Jerome Charyn (essay date 1975)

[*In the following excerpt, Charyn briefly reviews* South Street, *concluding that it is a "deeply felt book with an unfortunate amount of flab."*]

South Street is an ambitious, scraggly novel with deep pockets and vast, bumping corners that reach into the "limbo between the Schuylkill and the Delaware," for a long, bitter look at the corrugated country of black Philadelphia. Its gifted young author, David Bradley, doesn't take us into the heartlands. South Street, with its "elephantine cockroaches and rats the size of cannon shells," exists at the border of the ghetto. . . . Rubbing against Lombard Street and white Philadelphia, South Street in Mr. Bradley's book becomes a kind of haunted wasteland with "softening tar," gap-tooth buildings, and its own disturbing life.

The locus of the novel seems to be Lightnin' Ed's bar, where Mr. Bradley's characters leak out their existence. (pp. 30, 32)

The tension of the novel is generated by Adlai Stevenson Brown, a mystery figure from outside the ghetto who enters Lightnin' Ed's and shames [numbers king] Leroy Briggs in front of the bar's steady customers. Leroy, whose hold on South Street is beginning to slip, has to avenge himself, but he's afraid that Brown might be tied to the Mafia of white Philadelphia. . . . Brown, we discover, is a young black poet who came to South Street to shuck off his middle-class baggage and feed on ghetto life.

It's Adlai Stevenson Brown who gets the author into trouble; a thin creation, predictable in his language and his suffering, Brown can't carry the structure of the novel on his back. *South Street* collapses the more Brown is revealed to us. Still, he doesn't destroy the legitimacy of Lightnin' Ed's; the preachers, whores and hoodlums claw at us with their vitality and the harsh power of their voices. Despite Brown, *South Street* remains a deeply felt book with an unfortunate amount of flab. (p. 32)

> *Jerome Charyn, "Black Philly," in* The New York Times Book Review, *September 28, 1975, pp. 30, 32.*

Mel Watkins (essay date 1975)

[*In the following excerpt, Watkins reviews* South Street, *noting that despite its flaws, it "is a fine first novel."*]

[Philadelphia's "South Street"] is one of the gutted bastions of the down-and-out, the hopeless, the poor, and of the predators who feed on them. In this exceptional first novel [*South Street*], David Bradley takes us on a guided tour. We are ushered behind the dingy facade of "burned-out boarded-up bashed-in storefronts" dotted with bars, liquor stores and transient hotels; a facade that we've all hurried past, probably with a twinge of disgust and a small dose of cold fear. More important, Mr. Bradley introduces us to the street people who thrive in these cramped spaces, and brings them vividly to life. . . .

South Street is not simply another grim, naturalistic litany of the anguish of the downtrodden. Without blunting the pathos of this tale, Mr. Bradley has infused what could have been a standard story and stock characters with new vigor. Probing beneath the sociological stereotypes, he portrays his characters with a fullness that amplifies much of the lusty irony of ghetto life. His characters are trapped in their vermin-infested tenements but they are not overwhelmed. . . . It is Bradley's unerring depiction of the vitality that rears itself even within this despairing setting that distinguishes this novel.

Still, *South Street* has its flaws. Mr. Bradley's narratives on South Street and the surrounding geography are sometimes overextended and tiresome—like the loquacious drone of a facile tour guide delivering his spiel. And Adlai Stevenson Brown, the intellectual observer, is not drawn with the surehanded conviction demonstrated with lesser characters. Also, the novel's plot is exceedingly thin: Brown faces down Leroy Briggs in Lightnin' Ed's bar, challenging his authority and setting off ripples that are felt throughout Briggs's domain. And this simple plot structure provides the occasion for a series of set pieces about the various inhabitants of South Street.

It is, however, within these set pieces that Mr. Bradley's talent shines brightest. Some of them. . . are remarkably well-crafted vignettes. In these instances and throughout much of the novel, Mr. Bradley uses satire, burlesque and a perfectly pitched ear for ghetto dialect to establish a narrative tone that is both delightfully humorous and poignantly revealing.

In fact, throughout most of the novel, as when listening to some of the best of the comedian Richard Pryor's routines, one is poised on the finely tuned edge of Bradley's comic thrusts and the bitter reality that he is exposing. . . .

South Street then, despite its flaws, is a fine first novel. . . . David Bradley displays a versatile fictional talent within which control and technique are matched with an incisive eye for detail and an oblique viewpoint both refreshing and entertaining. It is to his credit that in his debut he has risked depicting some very familiar stereotypes and managed to cast them in a unique mold. He is a writer to watch.

Mel Watkins, "Old Winos, New Bottle," in The New York Times, *October 4, 1975, p. 25.*

Vance Bourjaily (essay date 1981)

[*In the following essay, Bourjaily examines theme, characterization, and rhetoric in* The Chaneysville Incident.]

Whatever else may be said, and there's apt to be a lot said about David Bradley and his second novel, **The Chaneysville Incident,** the man's a writer.

What he can do, at a pretty high level of energy, is synchronize five different kinds of rhetoric, control a complicated plot, manage a good-sized cast of characters, convey a lot of information, handle an intricate time scheme, pull off a couple of final tricks that dramatize provocative ideas, and generally keep things going for 200,000 words. That's about two and a half books for most of us.

Lyrical prose is one of the five kinds of rhetoric that Mr. Bradley uses, and with it the book opens:

"Sometimes you can hear the wire, hear it reaching out across the miles; whining with its own weight, crying from the cold, panting at the distance, humming with the phantom sounds of someone else's conversation. You cannot always hear it—only sometimes; when the night is deep and the room is dark and the sound of the phone's ringing has come slicing through uneasy sleep."

The wakened sleeper is John Washington, the book's narrator, and, like the book's author, he is young, black and a college professor. John Washington teaches history and lives in Philadelphia with a white psychiatrist named Judith.

The phone call that awakens him is from his mother, a woman of bourgeois propriety who works as a legal secretary in the small town in western Pennsylvania where John grew up. She calls to tell him a disreputable old man named Jack Crawley is dying and has asked for him. It's the second such summons. When John was 12 and his father, Moses Washington, had just been buried, "old Jack" first asked for the boy. After the funeral, the respectable members of the town's black community were gathered at the Washingtons' home when old Jack, who shined shoes for a living, came in drunk, found young John and said: "Mose tole me. . . to come for this here boy. An' I come."

Young John becomes old Jack's pupil in woodsmanship, hunting and whisky-drinking; he also becomes the chief listener to Jack's stories, and from them learns a great deal, much of it about trouble between the races. The principal character in Jack's stories is Moses Washington. John's father was a legendary moonshiner and eccentric; feared by many for his violence and cunning, he accumulated wealth and influence during his lifetime and died a mysterious death.

It is one of the interesting switches in the book that the black man, one of whose forebears was an Indian chief, gains power over the white community by dealing illegally in the firewater it craves.

When John returns home he finds that Jack is near death, and, as John sits with the old man in his shack on the wrong side of the hill, he becomes obsessed with solving the mystery of his own father's death. This solution, though, depends on the solution of a far older mystery, that of "the Chaneysville incident" from which the novel takes its name. The incident took place in the time of the underground railroad, when 13 runaway slaves, about to be recaptured, were shot instead—at, so the tale goes, their own urgent request—and buried in 13 tenderly laid-out graves.

By this point in the book, John Washington has taken over old Jack's role as storyteller, and the listener now, tensely enough, is the white woman, Judith. And here let's illustrate two more of Mr. Bradley's varieties of rhetoric. (The ones that will go unillustrated are a straightforward first-person narrative manner and a pretty fair descriptive one.)

When old Jack tells his stories—and there are dozens of pages during which we hear him do it—David Bradley renders Jack's speech in a country vernacular that is different from either Southern or ghetto dialect but no less colorful: "Mose wasn't 'xactly human when it come to coverin' ground in a hurry. . . .that night was like the Goddamn trottin' races at the county fair. . . .I won't say the trees went flyin' by, but there sure wasn't no time for carvin' your name into the bark." And again: "The bear come chargin' out of a thicket maddern Joseph after Mary said she was interfered with by an angel."

If you gather from that second quote that Mr. Bradley's more favored characters display an anti-Christian bias, you're right. It begins, deceptively enough, as a minor enough matter and becomes basic to the expression of a concept about death that is one of the book's two major themes.

The other theme involves Mr. Bradley's conception of history. It is, as a matter of fact, mirrored in the change in John Washington's storytelling manner, which is the other rhetorical device to be illustrated. At first, quite expectedly, John is professorial; he tends to talk, as Judith points out, in little lectures. They even incorporate verbal footnotes. As he walks along Richard Street to an important appointment, for example, John takes time to tell us that many streets in small Pennsylvania towns were named, like this one, after obscure members of the William Penn family: "That naming, no doubt was a function of provincial sycophancy."

As the book goes on, John becomes more an involved storyteller and less a detached historian. He is saying, indirectly, that a historian cannot really be detached. By the climactic part of the book, he is relying on narrative imagination, not research, to understand what really happened in Chaneysville and to his father. Truth in history, we are invited to consider, may not be determined by facts. Though they come first, what really happened—as old Jack demonstrated to John, and John now demonstrates to Judith—can only be learned by creating from those facts a story that satisfies them all.

From this notion about history, the book's other central theme emerges. It is introduced halfway along, when John Washington is still talking and writing like a professor, if by now a rather impassioned one. "That is what the Slave Trade was all about. Not death from poxes and musketry and whippings and malnutrition and melancholy and suicide: death itself. For before the white man came to Guinea to strip-mine field hands. . . . black people did not die. . . the decedent. . . took up residence in an afterworld that was in many ways indistinguishable from his former estate."

The tragedy, in this view, for American blacks was Christianization, with its teaching that "death is cold and final," that the body becomes dust and the spirit may be subject to eternal torture—certainly so, as blacks understood it, in the case of oppressive white masters. What made this intolerable was that often these oppressors were for blacks ancestors as well.

What blacks must do, John Washington feels, is recover belief in a religion, and particularly a view of death, suited to their African natures. The voodoo beliefs of Haiti perhaps come closest. It is just such a recovery of belief that explains both Moses' death and the Chaneysville incident, but you must follow the beautifully rendered and wildly adventurous chase that is part of John Washington's climactic narrative reconstruction to learn how.

On the way to this revelation, there are many sequences, mostly well done, some a bit Victorian in their plotting, to carry the reader along: a hunt, an intricate will, the exposure of a crooked lawyer, an attempted lynching, the wasteful death of John's brother. There has also been a fair amount of white-baiting of the rather standard kind (cf. Malcolm X and the Ayatollah), which only those white readers far gone in guilt and masochism will find gratifying or even interesting. This, we understand eventually, is a product of John Washington's attitudes, not David Bradley's. But it may be that we perceive an ironic distance between author and narrator too late in the book—on Page 431 of the 432, to be exact. For here occurs the most dramatic possible surprise, the surprise of John's forgiveness and apparent willingness to become reconciled.

Let's maintain that the establishment of this distance between John Washington and David Bradley needed earlier preparation; it's not the easiest thing in writing to manage anyway. But the author has managed so many of the other things—and none of them especially easy either—that his novel deserves what it seems pretty sure to get: a lot of interested and challenged readers. (pp. 7, 20)

Vance Bourjaily, *"Thirteen Runaway Slaves and David Bradley,"* in The New York Times Book Review, *April 19, 1981, pp. 7, 20.*

Bruce Allen (essay date 1981)

[*In the following essay, Allen appraises* The Chaneysville Incident, *claiming: "[It] rivals Toni Morrison's* Song of Solomon *as the best novel about the black experience in America since Ellison's* Invisible Man *nearly 30 years ago."*]

[Truculence and passion are integral to *The Chaneysville Incident.*] Bradley employs a sophisticated past-present structure, built on a sequence of sometimes interlocking flashbacks. The pace is slow, the digressions frequent, and John Washington's professorial sedulousness and hauteur are often grating.

All the material in the book is exposition, really—discovered, then painstakingly communicated: it represents nothing less than a triumph that this basically undramatic material is almost always suspenseful and fascinating.

This is a book that knows exactly what it's doing. Even the literary echoes (of Faulkner, Baldwin, Ralph Ellison, Warren's *All the King's Men,* among others) ring mockingly, exude a bracing irony.

John Washington's complaints about the limitations of history perfectly express the conviction that black people *must,* by virtue of their experience and their suffering, perceive the world differently than do whites. And, when we finally reach it, the many-layered dream of Africa that lies at the heart of the book is entirely convincing as religious mystery—which we have to work our way into knowing, because it was not, could never have been, a part of us.

That seems to me the ultimate challenge, in a novel that is filled with them and powerfully enriched by them. For me, *The Chaneysville Incident* rivals Toni Morrison's *Song of Solomon* as the best novel about the black experience in America since Ellison's *Invisible Man* nearly 30 years ago.

Bruce Allen, *"Well-Made Novel Sifts Black History,"* in The Christian Science Monitor, *May 20, 1981, p. 17.*

Thomas M. Gannon (essay date 1981)

[*In the following excerpt, Gannon offers a negative assessment of* The Chaneysville Incident, *stating: "The novel's problems are not limited to its structure; there are serious flaws in plot and characterization as well."*]

David Bradley gambled that he could work the historical experience of black people in this country into a successful novel without writing a conventional histori-cal novel. As it turns out, Bradley lost his gamble, for *The Chaneysville Incident* is not successful, at least not as a novel. Too much of it is thinly disguised history, rather than deeply felt, imaginatively transformed experience. . . .

Bradley filters his historical material through the consciousness of the novel's narrator, a 30-ish black histori-an named John Washington. . . . The novel's principal action is Washington's . . . immersion in his family's history in an attempt to solve the mystery of his father's suicide and complete the historical research that had preoccupied his father in the years before his death. Large quantities of data on the situation of black people in America, from the origins of the slave trade until the present, are or become part of Washington's understanding of the world around him, but they are never fully assimilated into the structure of the novel. Again and again, the data is presented in large, undifferentiated chunks, through overly precious expository passages or in the virtual lectures that Washington delivers to his lover, a white psychiatrist named Judith Powell. For long periods, the novel stands still for the recitation of the history within the story.

The novel's problems are not limited to its structure; there are serious flaws in plot and characterization as well. Washington and his lover belong to the next generation of racial stereotypes. He is the standard variety superblack, a Renaissance man from the other side of the tracks, a brilliant scholar, an accomplished woodsman, a mighty hunter. . . . Powell, with her enormous capacity for hanging around, putting up with Washington's moody silences and trying to "share" and "understand," is a strong contender for the title of Ms. White Liberal Guilt of 1981. Finally, the novel's ending creaks with contrivance. The major complexities of the plot, including the mystery of the suicide of Washington's father and the truth about the original Chaneysville incident, are resolved in a single drunken vision. It is all too easy, an abdication of responsibility on the author's part.

Bradley writes most effectively about Washington's boyhood, vividly recreating the richly textured experience of a black boy growing up in the 1950's in a small Pennsylvania town where racial distinctions, though unofficial and unsanctioned by law, were suffocatingly real. A novel more narrowly focused on this experience (which is Bradley's own, of course), though less ambitious than *The Chaneysville Incident,* would probably have been more successful.

Thomas M. Gannon, in a review of "The Chaneysville Incident," in America, *Vol. 144, No. 21, May 30, 1981, p. 449.*

David Bradley with Susan L. Blake and James A. Miller (interview date 1983)

[*In the following 1983 interview, Bradley, Blake, and Miller discuss* South Street *and* The Chaneysville

Incident, *focusing on the characters John Washington and Judith from the latter work.*]

[Miller]: *We were talking earlier about what it meant to travel as a black person, back home, to the South, before the age of the super highway. How did those experiences affect you? We're talking about how relationships changed once you crossed the Mason-Dixon line. What did you gather there? How did it shape your perception of the South, of Bedford?*

[Bradley]: I always liked the South because you knew what was happening there. Nobody ever said this stuff—this is the amazing thing—nobody ever said "This is the South, now." But if you place somebody who doesn't know what they're doing in a context where everybody knows what to do, they start knowing what to do. Bedford had the same racist structures, but nobody would acknowledge it. And so, for the first time in my life, for three weeks in the year, I knew what to do. Another thing; I never saw any white folks. Except in gas stations. Dinwiddie was sort of an old plantation. You were back in there and you never saw anybody. You camped out basically. Racism: I didn't know that word. That was before Martin Luther King was on TV. Later on, I found out. My father would carefully avoid anyplace where we might get into trouble. Anywhere. We'd be low on gas, and he would look for a *big* gas station. The more pumps, the safer he felt.

[Miller]: *How did that experience shape your view of Bedford? Coming back, did you have any conscious awareness that those forays into the South were shaping your social, political perspective toward life in Bedford at all?*

[Bradley]: Well, you see, I'm stupid. I'm slow. I didn't know what was going on until after I left. All I knew was that it was different. What happened was—and this is bizarre—I would go down South and I would meet these girls, and would write these passionate letters, all the rest of the year. Mostly I'd never see them again. I'd go back the next year and there would be different girls. But, see, there were only fifty black people in Bedford and only one black girl who was about my age who had somewhat similar interests, and she didn't do it.

[Miller]: *They never do.*

[Bradley]: It was a logical match to everybody but her. And this was a very important thing to me, 'cause this meant that the South was associated with every kind of release that there was. So I always loved those trips. And Bedford was just hell.

[Blake]: *You've said in another context that you felt alienated at the University of Pennsylvania. What exactly did you feel alienated from?*

[Bradley]: Not alienated in the common sense, or the sociological or whatever sense, of the term. It was simply this: I came from a rural background. It was black, rural, less black than rural. At this time the image of blacks that was acceptable to that sort of institution was urban black, and so it wasn't that I got to a place where they were not prepared to have black people, but where they were prepared to have a particular kind of black people, and where the black people were prepared to have a particular set of problems in dealing with white institutions. I didn't have any problem like that because I had been dealing with white institutions all my life. My problem was people would say, you know, we had rats at home. Well, we didn't have rats, we had field mice. We had chickens. So they couldn't deal with that. And it meant that the kinds of programs that were set up to make black people welcome—which weren't doing that anyway, but which were set up for that—didn't apply to me, and nobody really understood what I was doing. It was not so much that I was alienated, but that I didn't fit into the mold of what I was supposed to do, and how to satisfy my contract with the institution—because they gave me money. And being raised as a Protestant, I believed if people give you money, that means you have a job, and there's something you're supposed to do. And it took me a while to figure out what I was supposed to do. Eventually, I did; I was supposed to fuck up, but I didn't do that.

[Miller]: *What did you find on South Street that constituted an alternative to the style you found at Penn in the late sixties?*

[Bradley]: First of all, it was a small town—South Street was a small town. People related to each other, people had histories, people knew each other's mothers, you know, that sort of thing. Secondly, nobody was an intellectual. People were not prepared to intellectualize their experience all the time, and that's what went on at the university. Even the black people went around mouthing rhetoric; these people on South Street were dealing with real problems. The other thing was that the rhetoric of the time was that the horrible experience of being black in America, of being poor, of being oppressed had irrevocably damaged black people to the point where they were dehumanized, incapable of love, only capable of anger, and directing it towards each other. I didn't feel that way—and these people on South Street demonstrated love for themselves, as people. They didn't know they were dehumanized. And that was incredibly comforting. The other thing was they didn't care I went to college. I remember going to a bar once where there was this beautiful barmaid named Leola. She leaned over to me one day—and I was wearing jeans and a T-shirt—she leaned over, and she said, "You go to college, doncha?" And I thought, O.K., Penn, this is going to impress the hell out of this woman; I'm going to get over. I said "Yeah," I said, "Yeah." And she said, "That's all right, I won't tell nobody." When you're a dumb kid, who is scared to death you're going to flunk out—which I was—and somebody says, "Hey, I won't tell anybody you're in college," it's an incredibly liberating kind of thing. You drink your gin, you pay your money.

[Miller]: *The character Brown in* **South Street** *is a model of a kind of aspiring artist who is also attracted to the values of this community. He's trying to come to terms with South Street. At some levels he does; at some levels he doesn't. How complete is the fusion?*

[Bradley]: Brown was really a plot device. That book was written in a particular kind of way. The first third of it was written in a writing workshop.

[Miller]: *With whom?*

[Bradley]: Hiram Haydn. But also three other people—three other students and myself. With only four people, every four weeks, you had to come up with stuff. And so the first three chapters of **South Street** were done almost like Charles Dickens would have done it. O.K., it's time for me to come up with forty pages for the folks. And I did. It was submitted. . . What I would do was write out a rough draft, throw away pages that I didn't want, cross out stuff with a black felt-tipped marker, so nobody could see the mistakes, and xerox it, and hand it in and get reactions. Those people were into the characters; me, I'm into plot. But there was an influence that propelled the first part of that novel—somebody'd constantly say,"Gee, I liked that; gee, I liked him; gee, I liked her." So, when I left that group, and wrote the end of the book, it was *entirely* different. It was all about Brown, Brown coming from the country, Brown. . . It shifted to the first person at one point. And when I sold it, I had to write a letter telling how I was going to revise it. And I looked at it and said the best thing to do is to continue this thing. In a way, you know, it's the outsider theme. And I realized that Brown was really a plot device; he's the one that make all these other things hold together; he's the impetus.

[Miller]: *There's a relationship in the novel that interests me between Brown and the old wino Jake. Jake seems to embody a certain kind of wisdom, a certain kind of understanding of experience, and it occurred to me that the relationship seems to prefigure the relationship between John Washington and Jack Crawley later on in* **Chaneysville.**

[Bradley]: O.K., but there's something else you gotta remember, and that's that I wrote the beginning of **Chaneysville**—and particularly that old Jack Crawley and John Washington existed—before **South Street.** They were both characters in this other novel that will never see the light of day—it was really a collection of short stories. The tale-telling, in fact the story of the Chaneysville incident was part of that.

[Blake]: *Did you ever know anybody like Jack Crawley?*

[Bradley]: Yes. Three people. My own father—see my own father was forty-five years old when I was born. By the time I was old enough to start understanding what a man was, my father was sixty, and was starting to get—a little crusty. And it was difficult to see him as a father. At the same time, while I was very young, there was a man named Dan Harris, an old guy who, when I was

four or five years old, was basically my playmate. And my Uncle John, who always was crusty; he was the black sheep of the family. Did nasty stuff. But also I was always around old preachers, and, you know, a seventy-year-old preacher, having been a preacher for some time, has given up most of the vices, or is beyond most of the vices, and what he's left with is the ability to tell lies. And they sit around and they lie. And preaching is sort of lying anyway. And I would sit listening to these guys for days. And it was amazing to hear how a pious preacher, without ever using profanity or anything else, could suggest almost every funky human interaction. These were men who'd seen life. Readers respond to that, too. I don't know whether they respond to it because I respond to it or just, you know, love old men.

[Blake]: **Chaneysville** *is a historical novel—*

[Bradley]: That's what you say!

[Blake]: *Well, it has this historical incident at the core. How much of it is researchable history?*

[Bradley]: The further back you get, and the more objective you get, the more researchable it is. There was never a C.K. Washington. There was never a C.K. Washington's father, Zack. There was a rebellion in Louisiana at that time, and they did place heads on stakes. There was a man named Lewis Bolah, who betrayed that rebellion, who did serve with Commodore Perry, did petition the legislature of Virginia for permission to live in Virginia. There was a Cherokee nation that had slaves, and experienced difficulties because gold was discovered on their land. There were the things C.K. Washington supposedly wrote. They were usually listed as anonymous.

[Blake]: *So you picked out some anonymous things that fit the character of C.K.?*

[Bradley]: I decided I wanted him to have written some things, and I wanted him to be able to speak in that way. I needed things that pushed him forward. I needed documents, and so I found documents that were anonymous. There was a character named Pettis, who did advertise in southern newspapers. There were rebellions in Kentucky, although there was no evidence Pettis was involved with them. Basically what I did was I found the beginnings of lines in history, and I sort of filled in the dots.

[Blake]: *You've said that the gravestones are there near Chaneysville.*

[Bradley]: Not in that pattern.

[Blake]: *Are they associated in the legend with the escaped slaves?*

[Bradley]: O yeah, yeah. They're right next to the family graveyard. It's very clear where the Iiames family starts and these people stop. The gravestones are of a different character.

[Blake]: *So you have John Washington in the novel making that connection imaginatively, but actually in local legend, the connection between the escaped slaves and the stones is there—something John discovers when he's kicking at the stones.*

[Bradley]: Well, what he discovers is the pattern, which allows him to reconstruct the family structure and everything else, but the stones are there.

[Blake]: *You said last night that the material was "so wonderful." What was "so wonderful" about it? Why did it appeal to you?*

[Bradley]: It bothered me as a person. It appealed to me as a fiction writer. Here you've got a story of thirteen people who take a dramatic act. O.K., so you tell somebody this story—my mother wrote it, and she wrote it in two sentences. The questions that sprang to my mind when I read it were, Who were these people? Where did they come from? Why did they do this? That's a novel. Characterization: who were they? Background: where did they come from? Motivation: why did they do it? It's *all* right there. All you have to do is invent the beginning; you've got the end. Everything else in that book is a means to that end. All those characters—Old Jack, John Washington, all those things—came *after* the story.

[Miller]: *You said your mother wrote it in two sentences. Was that because the legend was so pervasive in the community?*

[Bradley]: No, it wasn't pervasive; she discovered it. Well, she didn't discover it; she was told it. But I've never seen it written anywhere else. She was told it by a guy in a store in a town called Clearville, about fifteen miles from Chaneysville. He told her to go there and look for these graves. She says that when she first went there, the guy, Iiames, who was then alive, told her that, yeah, yeah, the graves were up there. When I went there, he either had forgotten or had changed his mind and said that he hadn't known the story until my mother came and told him. He possibly just knew the graves were there and didn't know the story. But she's the one who brought those two things together.

[Miller]: *How did she respond to it? I mean what was her sense of. . .*

[Bradley]: To the story?

[Miller]: *Yes. . . discovery?*

[Bradley]: My mother is a lot like John Washington. Nobody knows what the hell she thinks about anything. She's the kind of person who would have stood there and cried her eyes out and not told anybody. So I really don't know. I know she never asked me why I was doing this, and I know she called me up and told me the story. She found out a lot of things about the county. She was doing research for a local history. It was the county bicentennial. They wanted a black person to write the history of the black community.

[Miller]: *This was Bicentennial?*

[Bradley]: Well, it was the county bicentennial, which preceded the U.S. Bicentennial by three or four years or so. It was late 1969 when she did it—'71 was the bicentennial. And first, they thought of my father, who was a trained historian, but they decided that his writing style was rather dry, and they asked me, and I wanted as little to do with Bedford at that time as possible. So they asked my mother, and she just went crazy. She went to my father, she said, "what do I do?" He said, you go to the graveyards and the courthouse. And that's what she did. She looked at these records and slavery transactions. Because these little courthouses preserve everything, and this one never burned. And the graveyards, the old graveyards. I think those are the two places that people don't lie.

[Miller]: *That suggests another issue—that is the predominance of images of fire in **Chaneysville**. There are so many other things in **Chaneysville** that do burn. Records burn, and files burn. Part of the process that seems to be going on in the novel is that a lot is being burned away to get at the real stuff.*

[Bradley]: That's too critical. The only explicit thing about fire in there is about fire and power. At that point fire is the means to an end, because the power had to be the power to destroy. Call it death if you want to. That fire image started out as an antithesis to the cold. 'Cause if you're cold, you build a fire. That was something I stole from Jack London. I think, of all the things I ever read, that short story made the most impression on me. Just at a real visceral level, 'cause, man, I hate the cold. I really hate it.

[Miller]: *To go back to the question of history, there are some very, very complex evaluations being made about history and how we look at history and what's the appropriate thing to do within history. For example, C.K. is very involved in the Abolitionist movement, and then he drops out. . .*

[Bradley]: You see, I hate it. I hate history on account of my father because my father refused to have any fun with the stuff. And it's, you know, it's a style of black history, *name* history; you read a bibliography or a book, it consists almost entirely of names, no faces, no events, and you don't know what's going on. I mean it's boring. It was boring to me. I like stories. So, that's when I decided that John had to be a historian; I figured, O.K., I'm gonna let the guy talk about history.

[Blake]: *You said this morning, in answer to a student's question, that the reason there were historical lectures in the novel was that Americans, black and white, didn't know history, and needed to know some things in order to understand the* story *that you wanted to tell. Does that imply that the history you have John say in these lectures is history* you *want people to understand? Your interpretation of events?*

[Bradley]: No, it's history that's necessary to understand the incident, understand what those people did on the Hill.

[Blake]: *But, essentially what you're giving John to say there is what you would say, too.*

[Bradley]: Sometimes. I mean John is a little extreme about a lot of things. John is extreme about his detachment. I mean, John's concept of an incident—that you take an event, and you put it on a card, and you can tear it away from everything else—is totally bullshit. But, yeah, he says things that are historical. For example, the dissertation about the slave trade—all his facts are true. The little philippic about minority set-asides—that's sort of funny, or it's supposed to be sort of funny. Is that interpretation or fact? I'd say fact. There are other things I wouldn't say that of. I don't worry that much about knowing the truth about things, as he does in the book. In a word, he's a historian, I'm not.

[Blake]: *You told Mel Watkins that one of the reasons you abandoned your first approach to the* **Chaneysville** *material was that, despite the violence and tragedy, it was funny. It seems to me that this evaluation fits Jack Crawley's story of the near-lynching of Josh White and most of* **South Street**. . .

[Bradley]: I said that?

[Blake]: *Well, he claims you did. And I wonder how you would characterize the relationship between humor and tragedy.*

[Bradley]: Well, I don't know if I do. In **South Street**, I had no problem because I could always get the jokes in. **South Street** conforms to a Shakespearean comedy. Low comedy, low characters, lots of bawdy jokes, Falstaffian people, whores, the whole business. **Chaneysville** is a tragedy. The problem with **Chaneysville** is getting any jokes in there, getting any humor in there at all. And that's one of the reasons that Old Jack stayed. After the lynching story—all the jokes are over. You get a couple of them here and there, you get a couple of ironic twists, but John is not a funny guy. And I knew I had to relieve that first-person narration some way, because nobody was going to listen to that guy for nine chapters or whatever there are unless I put some funny stuff up front. So that's why I had to keep Old Jack's voice. I don't know if that answers your question, but that's the way I approach the problem. Some of John's dissertations are there for that reason, too.

[Blake]: *In a broad sense, you and John Washington have gone through similar processes; that is, you've both taken a historical situation, researched it, and told a story about it. Are there any similarities in the two experiences? Did you go through any of the processes you have John going through?*

[Bradley]: I would like to say no, but there is one very important one.

[Blake]: *What's that?*

[Bradley]: He doesn't think he can do this thing; he goes through the whole thing maintaining he can't imagine anything. And, I would like to say that all the way through I knew I could, but in fact I could tell you almost, to the minute, the moment I knew that I was going to be able to pull this off—and it was extremely late; it was in March of 1980.

[Blake]: *A year before the book came out.*

[Bradley]: It was a year before the book came out, but what's more it was about three months after the book was due to be delivered. I mean, I was three months late on the contract and I still did not know I could pull this off. So, there is that; there is certainly a parallel in that sense. And there's the process of going through anger—which he denies and I never denied. Other things like that. There's duplication, but he's reluctant to imagine and I just do it all the time.

[Blake]: *How would you explain Judith's role in the novel?*

[Bradley]: I wouldn't. . . I would actually. Judith is one of the latest structures in the whole business and she's peripheral in this sense, that it's not about her. . . Let me just tell you how she came about. I knew that John had to have someone to tell this to, because I didn't want him just telling it to a reader—there was no point—and there would be no reaction to direct him in the right ways. So the questions she asks move him to talk to the topic, and so forth and so on. I also knew that I needed some reason for him to have to come to terms with all this because he's been sitting on this stuff for years. Why, all of a sudden, does he have to deal with this? Well, there's the whole thing that she's going to leave him. I started out with Judith being a black woman. Then I realized that black people don't talk about this stuff. Once every three weeks, you know, and they'd agree with each other. Who wants to hear two niggers sitting around complaining about white folks? So she had to be white. Which opened up the door to miscegenation, and all that other stuff—and it did. Then I needed a job for her. . . because I think people should have jobs; John had one and I thought she should have one, too. Because he's not the kind of guy who. . . I mean he's not going to have a white lover and *keep* her. I knew they couldn't be married because marriage implies that he has accepted her totally, and he wasn't going to do that. So what's she going to do? She had to be a professional of some sort, because if she were an academic she would be inclined to approach things in the same way he did, and she doesn't; she's more practical. O.K., so she's a professional. A lawyer? She can't be a lawyer because law is basically history. Anybody who knows the law knows history. She can't, she's got to be ignorant of that stuff. So she's got to be a doctor.

[Blake]: *There're only two alternatives?*

[Bradley]: Or she could be a dentist, but, I mean, come on, a dentist didn't make it, you know? Although talking to John Washington is like pulling teeth. So now we're down to doctor. Well, what kind of doctor? Now, this guy's crazy. What kind of person would be willing to sit there and say, "Uh huh, and how long have you felt this way?," be capable of listening to somebody say "I raped a woman just like you" and conceal her reaction to this? So that's how she became a shrink. But that was late. In fact, John Washington didn't exist until 1978.

[Blake]: *I was wondering, when we were talking earlier, about the novel and its development and culmination as though it were the story John discovers and tells rather than the framework. . .*

[Bradley]: I didn't know. . . John existed because of that earlier novel but I didn't know I was going to use him until real late. And then he was a kid. At one point it was in the third person and it started as sort of cinematic thing with this cabin and this one kid coming down and the old man telling him stories. And, at that point, he didn't really have an identity, and he was going to grow up and then he was going to start to talk, and I decided that that was hokey as hell and it took too damn long. And, so, he didn't become a historian until much later either, when I realized I had to get all this history in, and how was I going to do that unless this guy was a historian. So all these things came about as a result of wanting to tell the old story. Essentially, the old story existed first, then Moses Washington, as a bridge. Then I realized the generations wouldn't work out, so I needed C.K. C.K. was real late, too. C.K. came along about 1978. By the time it ran to contract, by the time it was submitted, there were two proposals, and I don't think the first proposal mentioned C.K. Washington at all; the second one did. So, somewhere in there, all these things developed.

[Miller]: *To go back to the relationship between John and Judith for a minute, one of the things that becomes clear is that John is reluctant to apply his imagination to. . .*

[Bradley]: He doesn't have one.

[Blake]: *Well, he obviously has one, doesn't he? It develops toward the end.*

[Miller]: *And John finally learns to apply his imagination to this incident and therefore unlocks that key to the history that's been tormenting him. Although Judith is very, very practical and has these qualities of a trained professional, Judith also has to learn to be able to imagine John's situation.*

[Bradley]: I'm not sure she doesn't all along. Like he says, he underestimated her. . .

[Miller]: *What does that imply? John has to change, right? John, as an individual, as a professional, John as a historian has to learn how to get rid of all that academic apparatus that stands between him and his ability to imagine, imaginatively re-create history.*

[Bradley]: I wouldn't put it that way. I would put it that he has to learn to do both things at the same time. You know, in the funeral chapter, what he's talking about is not choosing one or the other but applying both of them. It's the fact that he knows all these things that allows him to imagine. And the fact of imagining does involve the use of names and places and people that he knows. I mean, he doesn't. . . he still doesn't make anything up.

[Miller]: *But he has to go through this process. You said that Judith is really an auditor, she has a certain structural role, a certain. . .*

[Bradley]: She changes, too, though; she changes; she starts to drink. All right, you guys, I'm going to be a literary critic, too. There is a theme of drinking together in this novel.

[Miller]: *Yes. . .*

[Bradley]: With coffee with the mother. . .

[Miller]: *As ritual?*

[Bradley]: All right. At the beginning he says there would have been more Wild Turkey, although Judith didn't drink, implying that she doesn't. By the end of the novel, she too drinks a toddy. But before that, she's drinking coffee, they drink water together, and there's a progression. First, she makes him toddies, she's willing to become complicit to that extent, and then she wants one herself.

[Miller]: *Are you suggesting that the ritual of drinking really requires two acts of complicity: that John has to learn how to recreate his imagination and, simultaneously, Judith has to learn how to participate in those rituals that bond them together?*

[Bradley]: Yeah, well she wouldn't let him drink; she didn't like his drinking. She didn't understand it, she thought it was weakness, and, you know, she gave him a hard time about it. And, you know, by the end of the novel, she's willing to say: "O.K., maybe the guy has reason to drink; maybe I need a drink, too." The reason I can talk about that is because I put that one in.

[Blake]: *Well, to get back to Jim's question, it seems as though her learning to drink a toddy is an indicator of another kind of change. . .*

[Bradley]: A symbol.

[Blake]: *Yes, well I thought I would avoid that terminology.*

[Bradley]: No, you can use it, you can use it, I just can't.

[Blake]: *O.K., a change that's expressed when Judith asks who buried the fugitives and John says it was Iiames and Judith says, "why would a white man or why would you think a white man. . ."*

[Bradley]: She says both.

[Blake]: *Yes. And that indicates an absorption into John's point of view there. And John's analysis indicates a kind of ability to trust a white person. But, as you've suggested in the novel, the fundamental changes are John's. Judith learns to see John's point of view, but she's been willing and ready all along, it's just that John hasn't given her any opportunity. To the extent that these two individuals represent black and white—and both of their personal histories seem to represent general history and the whole problem in their relationship has been related to race—*

[Bradley]: No, I don't think so. I think, first of all, they're very atypical. John Washington, for sure, is not the typical black.

[Blake]: *It's not typicality: it's that their personal identities, their family histories, are linked to general racial history. Judith comes from a genteel Southern family that is connected to what John has learned about the history of the area, for example. John is preoccupied with his relationship to ancestors who were slaves, fought against slavery, escaped from slavery, and so forth.*

[Bradley]: One's black and one's white, all right? I mean, that's what it comes down to.

[Blake]: *At any rate, what does the fact that John is the one that has to change imply?*

[Bradley]: Nothing. I'll tell you what it *doesn't* imply. His changing is not something that has to do with race; it's something that has to do with his point of view; and her changing has something to do with her point of view.

[Blake]: *And are their points of view strictly individual?*

[Bradley]: I wouldn't say they're strictly individual, but. . . certainly everything somebody is grows out of something else. If you want to you can, but I would not generalize it to some sort of grand message about who should change and who should not change from the point of view of society.

[Miller]: *This is another question about the meaning of history and historical pattern, coming from a different angle. Does the novel suggest that John must confront his history, not as Moses has—to reduplicate or re-enact a historical pattern—but to overcome it, to change it, transform it, to get rid of it?*

[Bradley]: I can tell you what I believe about that in the abstract. History to me is raw material, the past is raw material. We can't be governed by it. Now, I stole half, or a third, of the book from Robert Penn Warren, and he ends *All the King's Men* with "out of history, into history, and the awful responsibility of time." O.K.? That's it.

[Miller]: *One thing that's clear to me is that you tend to resist interpretations of the novel that propose it as a metaphor for the broadscale racial agonies of America in the seventies, eighties. . .*

[Bradley]: It's not that I resist it; it's that I haven't thought about it, and didn't conceive it that way. It's not

an allegory. And, I think, certainly a novelist gets in trouble when he gets himself into the process of making an allegory. (pp. 20-33)

[Blake]: *Do you imagine an audience as you write?*

[Bradley]: *Me.* Me. I write things that please me. See, I'm into form and plot. The details that make a character alive for a reader are fully arbitrary; you can juggle a character around a lot more easily than you can juggle the plot because there's no causality in the character. Once you're locked into a plot sequence, you make maybe three decisions having to do with the plot, and that's *it*; everything else is logical. Some student today asked something about the bus passage, and the reason that I kept the bus passage in—apart from the fact that I liked it—was that I had a character who was going to have to sit on a bus for four hours, and so had to convey to the reader the passage of time. I couldn't say, "four hours later." So I put in something that takes up a little time. The solutions to those problems are what please me. And I don't worry about whether people get it. I know for a fact that most readers aren't going to understand why that section's there, anymore than when you start your car up and you drive down the road, you think about the valves and the pistons. Maybe the mechanic does and maybe the guy who works on the assembly line does, but you don't. All you know is, your car goes. So, I'm a mechanic, I'm a guy on an assembly line. (p. 34)

David Bradley with Susan L. Blake and James A. Miller, in an interview in Callaloo, *Vol. 7, No. 2, Spring-Summer, 1984, pp. 19-39.*

FURTHER READING

Campbell, Jane. "Ancestral Quests." In her *Mythic Black Fiction: The Transformation of History*, pp. 137-53. Knoxville: The University of Tennessee Press, 1986.
Compares Toni Morrison's *Song of Solomon* with Bradley's *The Chaneysville Incident*, commenting: "Without question, *Song of Solomon* and *The Chaneysville Incident* represent the culmination of the Afro-American historical romance tradition spanning the years between 1853 and 1981. The similarities between these two works mark them as companion pieces focusing on a theme of extraordinary magnitude: the African-American must acknowledge and explore the complexity of black history and culture that is symbolized by the term 'Afro-American.'"

Ensslen, Klaus. "Fictionalizing History: David Bradley's *The Chaneysville Incident*." *Callaloo* 11, No. 2 (Spring 1988): 280-96.
Examines *The Chaneysville Incident* as "fictionalized history." The critic writes: "[In his work] Bradley is trying to fuse not only black and white narrative

traditions, . . . but also more fundamentally the documentary and imaginative reconstruction of the black experience in America, while at the same time raising positive questions about the interrelation of history and fiction."

Gliserman, Martin J. "David Bradley's *The Chaneysville Incident*: The Belly of the Text." *American Imago* 43, No. 2 (Summer 1986): 97-120.

> Discusses "the belly" motif in *The Chaneysville Incident,* noting: "Although the motif appears only eighteen times in a quarter of a million words, it is central to the layers of psychological patterning in the novel."

Holt, Patricia. "David Bradley." *Publishers Weekly* 219, No. 15 (10 April 1981): 12-14.

Bradley recounts the writing of *The Chaneysville Incident.*

McDowell, Edwin. "Black Writers Gain Readers and Power." *The New York Times* (12 February 1991): B1, B3.

> Examines the upsurge of public interest in black writers, including Bradley, and their works.

Sadler, Lynn Veach. "The Black Man's Burden: The Pursuit of Nonconformity in David Bradley's *The Chaneysville Incident.*" *West Virginia University Philological Papers* 32 (1986-87): 119-27.

> Presents an overview of *The Chaneysville Incident,* focusing on John Washington's rebellion against racial stereotype.

William Stanley Braithwaite

1878-1962

American poet, critic, editor, anthologist, essayist, biographer, and prose writer.

An American editor, anthologist, and literary critic, Braithwaite is credited with helping revitalize American poetry in the early twentieth century. Although a poet himself, he is best remembered and admired for editing the annual *Anthology of Magazine Verse* from 1913 through 1929. Chiefly through this series, he reviewed and promoted the works of various American poets, including Robert Frost, Amy Lowell, James Weldon Johnson, Carl Sandburg, and Edgar Lee Masters. Summarizing Braithwaite's contributions to American poetry, a 1915 editorial in the *Boston Evening Transcript* stated: "He has helped poetry to readers as well as to poets. One is guilty of no extravagance in saying that the poets we have . . . are created largely out of the stubborn self-effacing enthusiasm of this one man. In a sense their distinction is his own. In a sense he has himself written their poetry."

Braithwaite's literary career divides neatly into two distinct facets, poet and anthologist. Braithwaite was born in Boston in 1878, the second of five children in a family that was racially mixed on both sides. According to his own testimony, he developed his love for poetry at age 15 after reading John Keats's "Ode on a Grecian Urn" one day while working at a publishing company. Charged with excitement—he called this experience "a day of annunciation"—he began reading voraciously and writing his own poetry. In the late 1890s he tried repeatedly to get work as a journalist in New York. He was rejected again and again, but never before being questioned about his race. This early exposure to racism led Braithwaite to a crucial resolution. As he recounted in the 1940s in his unfinished autobiography "The House under Arcturus," "[I resolved] to express myself on the common ground of American authorship, to demonstrate, in however humble a degree, that a man of color was the equal of any other man in possession of the attributes that produced a literature of human thought and experience, and to force a recognition of this common capacity. . . . And I resolved, with equal determination, not to treat in any phase, in any form, for any purpose, racial materials or racial experiences, until this recognition had been won, recorded, and universally confirmed . . . ."

In 1904 Braithwaite published his first collection of verse, *Lyrics of Life and Love,* followed by *The House of Falling Leaves with Other Poems* in 1908 and, years later, *Selected Poems* (1948). Like his literary idols, Keats and Percy Bysshe Shelley, Braithwaite wrote poems on romantic themes—life, death, love, and beauty. Reviews of these poems were generally unfavorable, however. As noted by Braithwaite scholar Philip

Butcher, commentators assailed Braithwaite's poetry as "unintelligibly esoteric" and "thin in substance." Critics levied their harshest judgment, however, on Braithwaite's "failure" to incorporate racial themes in his poetry, accusing him of trying to deny his Negro-ness. Jay Saunders Redding, writing in 1939, cited Braithwaite as "the most outstanding example of perverted energy that the period from 1903 to 1917 produced." He further remarked that Braithwaite's poems "might just as well have been written by someone with no background in the provocative experience of being colored in America." Writing in 1973 in his *Black Poets of the United States,* Jean Wagner echoed Redding's view, describing Braithwaite's lack of devotion to racial matters as a "rejection of his blackness." He added: "Braithwaite had not the least desire to be identified with the black world and what it stands for." Denying the contention that Braithwaite rejected his racial heritage outright, James Weldon Johnson stated in *The Book of American Negro Poetry* (1931) that "as an Afroamerican poet [Braithwaite] is unique; he has written no poetry motivated or colored by race.... It is simply that race has not impinged upon him as it has upon other Negro poets." Similarly, Kenny Williams argued in 1987 that Braithwaite was neither ashamed of being black nor ambivalent about injustices committed against blacks. Rather, as indicated in the poem "White Magic," published in *The House of Falling Leaves,* Braithwaite's refusal to explore racial themes and concerns was based on his belief that sociopolitical issues had nothing to do with the aesthetics of poetry. Thus poetry should be written for its own sake, and one's race need not motivate or influence the creative process.

When Braithwaite began the *Anthology of Magazine Verse* series in 1913, he had already established his reputation as an anthologist, having edited three poetry collections: *The Book of Elizabethan Verse* (1906), *The Book of Georgian Verse* (1909), and *The Book of Restoration Verse* (1910). Commentators who earlier criticized Braithwaite as a poet now praised him as a new force in American literature. In prefatory essays and critiques in each anthology volume, Braithwaite introduced the general public to literary trends and issues, thereby helping increase the audience for contemporary poetry. Noting Braithwaite's personal stance on the role of race and politics in poetry, some commentators have expressed surprise that he so deeply admired the works of other black writers who celebrated their blackness. Through his anthologies, he promoted works by Harlem Renaissance writers Langston Hughes, James Weldon Johnson, and Countee Cullen. Equally, Braithwaite introduced works by imagist writers who held strong anti-black attitudes, insisting that each work be judged on merit alone, regardless of the writer's color or creed.

Perhaps because of his critical objectivity and generous encouragement of young writers, Braithwaite saw his reputation as editor and anthologist grow with each new edition of *Anthology of Magazine Verse.* Referring to Braithwaite's power and influence in the literary world, rival Harriet Monroe dubbed him "Sir Oracle" and "the Boston Dictator." Poets strove to appear in Braithwaite's anthologies. A writer in the *Saturday Review* remarked: "Happy was the young poet to learn that he had won the approving eye of Braithwaite." Despite his popularity with the poets, a few adversaries, most notably Conrad Aiken, challenged Braithwaite's competence as anthologist and editor. Contending that Braithwaite lacked the ability to discriminate between "good" and "mediocre" works, Aiken declared that Braithwaite had "no standards whatever: merely a blind pervasive unreflecting ecstasy." Similarly, a 1921 review in the *Boston Evening Transcript* stated: "No one who is intellectually honest in the matter can deny the integrity of his effort, but unfortunately it is also true that the effect of his over-catholic enthusiasm for all American writers of verse is to make it increasingly difficult for the best and most significant poetry to achieve recognition out of the jungle of bad verse which he has distinguished by critical encouragement and republication...." For every detractor, however, there were numerous admir-

ers who praised Braithwaite and his work. W.E.B. Du Bois, for example, acknowledged him as "the most prominent critic of poetry in America." Glenn Clairmonte, in two recent tributes to Braithwaite, "He Made American Writers Famous" and "The Cup-Bearer: William Stanley Braithwaite of Boston," asserted that some of today's popular poets owe their success to Braithwaite. After launching the *Anthology of Magazine Verse* series in 1913 and overseeing it for some years, Braithwaite turned increasingly to business interests. In 1921 he founded and became president of B.J. Brimmer Publishing Company. Although he and his partner, Winifred Virginia Jackson, successfully published several novels, including *Confusion* by James Gould Cozzens, the company declared bankruptcy in 1927. According to Butcher, the demise of Braithwaite's business struck a severe blow to his finances. Under pressure to support his wife and children, Braithwaite accepted a professorship at Atlanta University in 1935 and remained there for the next ten years. Before his death in 1962, Braithwaite published his final collection of poetry, *Selected Poems,* a biography of the Brontes, *The Bewitched Parsonage* (1950), and the final *Anthology of Magazine Verse.*

Whatever their opinion of Braithwaite as an anthologist and critic, few commentators deny his role in shaping twentieth-century American poetry. After publishing nearly thirty anthologies, Braithwaite summarized his literary career by stating: "For twenty-five years, I gave my best for the poets and poetry of America...." Today, the literary world acknowledges him as a vital contributor to American literature.

(For further information about Braithwaite's life and works, see *Dictionary of Literary Biography,* Vols. 50, 54.)

PRINCIPAL WORKS

Lyrics of Life and Love (poetry) 1904
The Book of Elizabethan Verse [editor] (anthology) 1906
The House of Falling Leaves with Other Poems (poetry) 1908
The Book of Georgian Verse [editor] (anthology) 1909
The Book of Restoration Verse [editor] (anthology) 1910
Anthology of Magazine Verse for 1913 [editor] (anthology) 1913
Anthology of Magazine Verse for 1914 and Year Book of American Poetry [editor] (anthology) 1914
Anthology of Magazine Verse for 1915 and Year Book of American Poetry [editor] (anthology) 1915
Anthology of Magazine Verse for 1916 and Year Book of American Poetry [editor] (anthology) 1916
Representative American Poetry [coeditor with Henry Thomas Schnittkind] (anthology) 1916
Anthology of Magazine Verse for 1917 and Year Book of American Poetry [editor] (anthology) 1917
The Poetic Year for 1916: A Critical Anthology [editor] (anthology) 1917
Anthology of Magazine Verse for 1918 and Year Book of American Poetry [editor] (anthology) 1918

The Golden Treasury of Magazine Verse [editor] (anthology) 1918
Anthology of Magazine Verse for 1919 and Year Book of American Poetry [editor] (anthology) 1919
The Book of Modern British Verse [editor] (anthology) 1919
The Story of the Great War (essays and juvenilia) 1919
Victory! Celebrated by Thirty-Eight American Poets [editor] (anthology) 1919
Anthology of Magazine Verse for 1920 and Year Book of American Poetry [editor] (anthology) 1920
Anthology of Magazine Verse for 1921 and Year Book of American Poetry [editor] (anthology) 1921
Anthology of Magazine Verse for 1922 and Year Book of American Poetry [editor] (anthology) 1922
Anthology of Massachusetts Poets [editor] (anthology) 1922
Anthology of Magazine Verse for 1923 and Yearbook of American Poetry [editor] (anthology) 1923
Anthology of Magazine Verse for 1924 and Yearbook of American Poetry [editor] (anthology) 1924
Anthology of Magazine Verse for 1925 and Yearbook of American Poetry [editor] (anthology) 1925
Anthology of Magazine Verse for 1926 and Yearbook of American Poetry [editor] (anthology) 1926
Anthology of Magazine Verse for 1927 and Yearbook of American Poetry [editor] (anthology) 1927
Anthology of Magazine Verse for 1928 and Yearbook of American Poetry [editor] (anthology) 1928
Anthology of Magazine Verse for 1929 and Yearbook of American Poetry [editor] (anthology) 1929
Our Lady's Choir: A Contemporary Anthology of Verse by Catholic Sisters [editor] (anthology) 1931
"The House under Arcturus: An Autobiography" (unfinished autobiography) 1941-42; published in periodical *Phylon*
Selected Poems (poetry) 1948
"A Tribute to W. E. Burghardt Du Bois" (essay) 1949; published in periodical *Phylon*
The Bewitched Parsonage: The Story of The Brontes (biography) 1950
"Alain Locke's Relationship to the Negro in American Literature" (essay) 1957; published in periodical *Phylon*
Anthology of Magazine Verse for 1958 and Yearbook of American Poetry [coeditor with Margaret Haley Carpenter] (anthology) 1959
The William Stanley Braithwaite Reader (criticism, autobiography, reminiscences, and letters) 1972

Conrad Aiken (essay date 1916)

[*An American man of letters best known for his poetry, Aiken was deeply influenced by the psychological and literary theories of Sigmund Freud, Havelock Ellis, Edgar Allan Poe, and Henri Bergson, among others, and is considered a master of literary stream of consciousness. In reviews noted for their percepti-veness and barbed wit, Aiken exercised his theory that "criticism is really a branch of psychology." His critical position, according to Rufus A. Blanshard, "insists that the traditional notions of 'beauty' stand corrected by what we now know about the psychology of creation and consumption. Since a work of art is rooted in the personality, conscious and unconscious, of its creator, criticism should deal as much with those roots as with the finished flower." The following essay, "Looking Pegasus in the Mouth," originally appeared in the* Poetry Journal *in 1916. It rebuts two earlier articles, one by Braithwaite and the other by Amy Lowell, that were themselves written in response to Aiken's November 1915 essay titled "Prizes and Anthologies." Therein Aiken criticized the practice of awarding distinction to "mediocre" magazine poems by anthologizing them. Here, Aiken clarifies his original intentions and challenges Braithwaite's competence as editor and anthologist.*]

Mr. Braithwaite and Miss Lowell, in their replies to my article on *Prizes and Anthologies,* have rather ingeniously managed, through *argumentum ad hominem* and evasions of the main points at issue, to discredit me. Mr. Braithwaite, in his opening paragraph, represents me as attempting 'to prove that no appreciative notice should be taken of contemporary American poetry'—an attempt which I have not only no-where made, but which I should not even dream of making; it is ridiculous; it is the precise opposite of my belief; and I must confess to some amazement at Mr. Braithwaite's ability to twist it out of anything I have said. Because I remarked a year ago in *The New York Times Review* that, Mr. Braithwaite to the contrary, magazine verse was in the main mediocre, because I presumed to think at the time (before the advent of Messrs. Frost and Masters,) that our poetry could not favorably be compared to the poetry of Gibson, Masefield, Davies, Brooke and Abercrombie (and I might have added Hodgson) and because I have now again repeated my assertion that magazine verse is, as a whole, mediocre,—Mr. Braithwaite leaps to the conclusion that I am opposed to any recognition of American poetry, and even implies that I do not wish an American poetry. Like the lady referred to by Holmes, Mr. Braithwaite would argue that because I like salt water bathing I should like to be pickled in brine.

Miss Lowell is more ruthless. She accuses me of trying "to knock my way into the Temple of Fame": in other words, of insincerity. This is a curious charge. For two paragraphs later Miss Lowell speaks of the foolish idealism of "aspiring youth"—as regards the commercialization of art. Now if I am an unpractical idealist I can hardly also be insincere: Miss Lowell must perceive the inconsistency. And as she proceeds to take my article very seriously, and at great length, it is perfectly obvious that Miss Lowell accuses me of "knocking" simply out of (I say this softly) spleen. This becomes even plainer when one notices that at the heart of Miss Lowell's article is a candid confession of agreement with one of my main contentions,—that the giving of prizes is wrong. She also appears to agree with me in my other contention, that the Anthology is not sufficiently selective. Now if Miss Lowell's views are so (comparatively) in accord with mine it is a little perplexing to see why she has written at all this elaborate, heated, and it must be said, somewhat personal reply. Can it be that Miss Lowell's reference to Imagism, among other 'phobias' of mine, furnishes the clue? If I have a 'phobia'—has Miss Lowell a 'complex'?

However, to take up point by point the nimble tactics of Mr. Braithwaite and Miss Lowell would be both useless and dull. I need only refer to Mr. Braithwaite's devotion of a page or so to my supposed ignorance of the meaning of the word "blacklist"—and advise Mr. Braithwaite to look for irony in that word: the implication being that his list of the best was in fact (hyperbole!) a list of the worst. And in Miss Lowell's article I content myself with pointing out that a great part of her labor is devoted to proving that art can exist quite happily in a flourishing commercial era—which is merely to beat the wind, controversially speaking, inasmuch as I have nowhere stated or implied the contrary. In fact, on this point, I quite agree.

But what lay implicitly at the bottom of my whole article, and what Mr. Braithwaite and Miss Lowell have, by accident or design, entirely overlooked, was the belief that the prime necessity in this country at this moment is an enforcement of high and severe critical standards. Prizes are not, and in the arts, never have been, associated with the highest standards. A prize must be awarded by a committee, and it is the least common denominator of a committee that governs the decision. In ancient Greece it was precisely those poets whose works have not survived the test of time who won the prizes,—not Euripides, or Sophocles. It has been true ever since. To give a prize is almost certainly to attach importance where importance is not due. It is to advertise the inferior as the best. If it is desired to ameliorate the working conditions of the poet—very well, pay him better! That's the answer; pay not only a specially selected poet, but every poet whose works are printed.

The same theory applies equally well, or better, to the question of criticism. In a sense, though perhaps he would not admit it, Mr. Braithwaite and I are agreed. It is desirable that good poetry should be recognized and appreciated. What Mr. Braithwaite and I do not agree on is the method by which this may be done. Mr. Braithwaite believes in a sort of protective tariff for American poetry. In effect he says, 'Let us not compare the works of our poets with the poetry of contemporary England, let us not keep in mind the best poetry that the world has given us, but let us judge this poetry by its *own* background.' In other words, when Mr. Braithwaite hedges as to the meaning of his phrase 'poems of distinction' (and he does hedge) he is merely substituting a relative value in the meaning of that word 'distinction' for an absolute value; or for what to all intents is an absolute value. He now even denies having attempted to choose the 'best'—though his 'five best poems' mutely defy him from the pages of the Tran-

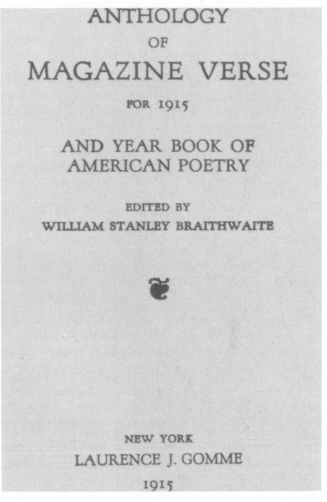

ANTHOLOGY
OF
MAGAZINE VERSE
FOR 1915

AND YEAR BOOK OF
AMERICAN POETRY

EDITED BY
WILLIAM STANLEY BRAITHWAITE

NEW YORK
LAURENCE J. GOMME
1915

Title page for the third of Braithwaite's annual anthologies, which includes poems by Wallace Stevens, Amy Lowell, Vachel Lindsay, Robert Frost, James Weldon Johnson, and Edgar Lee Masters.

script. It therefore becomes a question whether in judging poetry it is better to use absolute or relative values: whether it is wiser to make an anthology of a hundred poems (let us say) which are 'of distinction' as compared with the magazine verse of a single year, and to lend such poems 'distinction' by so labelling them, or to make an anthology, of, say, twenty poems which will stand up reasonably well by comparison with the very best. But, reduced to this, the question is a question no longer. It is obviously in the interests of poetry to select not what is merely better than the bad, but what is generally good. Mr. Braithwaite and his defenders admit that his principle in compiling *The Anthology of Magazine Verse* is the better-than-the-bad principle. But candidly, Mr. Braithwaite and Miss Lowell, does the better-than-the-bad (which is mediocrity) deserve annually a volume of one hundred and eighty pages? Does it deserve the descriptive phrase 'poems of distinction,' if one bears in mind that nine people out of ten understand the word distinction in its normal and (relatively) absolute sense? Is that not, in fact, to defeat and delay the recognition and appreciation of the genuinely good?

Let us turn to the critical parts of Mr. Braithwaite's **Anthology;** these, and Mr. Braithwaite's reviews in the Transcript, were quite as much in my mind when I wrote my article as the **Anthology** itself. It is here that one finds at its worst Mr. Braithwaite's belief in the critical protective tariff. For 1915, for example, Mr. Braithwaite has chosen some thirty-five volumes of poetry as being 'of distinction.' The principle of selection was simple: with few exceptions it consisted in a choice of the volumes published by the better known publishers. But the point of importance, here, is Mr. Braithwaite's critical attitude towards books. Superlative praise of one sort or another may be found in practically every one of these critical summaries—with four or five exceptions at the most, and with extremely few qualifications. In some cases the superlatives actually clash—in his Transcript review Mr. Braithwaite spoke of Colcord's 'Vision of War' as the most significant book of the year: in the Anthology he pairs Masters and Frost as the two most valuable contributors. But this is a trifle. Phrases like 'great vision', 'flawless technique', 'wonderful poem', 'exalted message', 'passionate idealization', 'vision of flame', 'exquisite poems', 'mystical grace', 'faultless perfection', 'poignancy of mood', 'magical substance', 'absolute genius', 'majesty and beauty', 'mental exquisiteness', 'extraordinarily graceful', 'rare power of evocable intuitions', 'impressively striking', 'austere and sombre mysticism', 'evocative vision', 'achievement of the highest order', 'lyric verse never more perfectly wrought in our day', 'magnificent verse', 'melodious muse', 'spirituality of clear flame', 'passionate', 'rapturous', 'melodious and evocative perceptions', 'one whose thought tenderly caresses the whole world', 'subtlety', 'full of spells and intuitions',—phrases like these, many of them almost meaningless, simply honeycomb Mr. Braithwaite's writings. Some of them occur again and again. And in the Transcript reviews it is even worse. If one were to take at their face value Mr. Braithwaite's remarks about most books of poetry, one could perhaps buy a new volume of 'remarkable' poetry every two weeks.

Now I contend that by so doing Mr. Braithwaite, who undeniably is poetry's well-wisher, defeats his own end. One gets tired of hearing his cry of 'genius, genius!' every week or so. And after a time, when Mr. Braithwaite has marshalled such a cohort of great poets in his train, one beings to suspect that his standards of admission are somewhat low. Does he mean 'great' when he says it, or does he mean 'fairly good'? Does he mean 'profound' or 'exquisite', when he so speaks, or does he only mean to tell us that his poet is reasonably intelligent or turns his phrases prettily? When he speaks of somebody's 'faultless perfection' does he mean it,— or does he merely mean that the poet is possessed of a deft technique? Those are some of the questions that we begin to ask. We cease to believe in Mr. Braithwaite's superlatives—with the result that when somebody genuinely good comes along Mr. Braithwaite has no way of persuading us of it. He has been crying 'Wolf! Wolf!' too long. And we have at last come to believe, so unflaggingly, so indiscriminately catholic are his tastes, and everlastingly enthusiastic, that he has no standards whatever: merely a blind pervasive unreflecting ecstasy.

No, Mr. Braithwaite, no, Miss Lowell,—let us dogmatize,—this is not the right way. Anthologies of graceful mediocrity,—puffs, pap, and prizes,—these are the methods of mediocrity itself, this is Mediocrity press-agenting the Mediocre. I have no objection to the selling of poetry to the magazines, nor to the selling of it for good sums of money,—the more the better,—for a magazine buys poetry because its readers *like* a certain kind of poetry, not because the magazine thinks it is the best; but the giving of a prize publicly postulates on the giver's part, and willy-nilly, a knowledge of good and bad,—a postulate seldom justified by the facts. And, fortunately, moreover, the time has passed when such mistaken tactics are even justified by necessity. Poetry is already, thanks to Mr. Braithwaite and Miss [Harriet] Monroe, too much rather than too little recognized in this country. There is a dead level of praise and recognition abroad which confounds issues, which obliterates all distinctions, which makes it difficult, almost impossible, for the genuinely good to make its way in the chaos. The time has come for high standards, for fewer principles of selection. Downright honest analytical criticism, even if it is sometimes mistaken, is far better in the long run than a baseless and insincere catholicity. Let us hit hard, Let us tell the truth. Let us oppose: opposition is healthy. Let us see the faults of even the best. Let us put behind us all personal collusion and nepotism, all string-pulling, all critical soft-heartedness, and all personal animus toward professional rivals; and always measure by the very highest standards, as we conceive them, and report the results faithfully. The selective process which enables the good to find the top must be helped, not thwarted. It is only in that way that we can establish the good in American poetry. (pp. 20-8)

> *Conrad Aiken, "Looking Pegasus in the Mouth," in* The Poetry Journal, *Vol. 5, No. 1, February, 1916, pp. 20-8.*

Newman Ivey White (essay date 1924)

[*In the following excerpt from the introduction to the 1924 collection* Anthology of Verse By American Negroes, *White reviews Braithwaite's* Lyrics of Love and Life *and* The House of Falling Leaves, *praising the author's "highly sensitive estheticism."*]

William Stanley Braithwaite is the Negro poet who unquestionably stands next to Dunbar. Dunbar found entrance into Stedman's American anthology; Braithwaite, who came upon the stage a little too late for this, is represented in Jesse B. Rittenhouse's *Little Book of Modern Verse.* Braithwaite is even better known for his critical work than for his poetry. In addition to editing anthologies of Elizabethan verse, Georgian verse, and

Restoration verse, he has, since 1913, collected and edited yearly anthologies of magazine verse that have been of great service to all people interested in contemporary poetry. These books, together with his yearly reviews of contemporary poetry, have undoubtedly helped create a larger and more appreciative audience for contemporary American poets. His own poems have appeared in a number of the best magazines and have been collected in two volumes, *Lyrics of Love and Life* (1904), and *The House of Falling Leaves* (1908). A highly sensitive estheticism is the keynote of his poetry. In this sense, as well as in lyric ability, he suggests Sidney Lanier. In finish and grace his poems are superior to those of Dunbar; they are superior also in another and less important respect—literary allusiveness. Braithwaite has a superior *savoir faire* in handling literary background that is probably due to his longer and more intimate associations with books and writers. His poems have grace, but he is too idealistic for humor. He has a sense of human fate and the seriousness of life, but he falls far short of the knowledge of life and the sympathetic interest in human types that Dunbar possessed. Like Shelley (his principal master, along with Keats), he is idealistic to a fault. His poetry is too much "out of time and out of space"—there is too much seclusion from the problems and men of his own day. His genuine and obvious refinement affords a pleasant contrast to much that is crude and raw in the more controversial writers but does not fully compensate for a deficiency in definite, tangible substance. His poems, some of which have been set to music, have a fine lyric quality, and the idealism of such poems as "**Nympholepsy**," "**A Song of Living**," and "**The Eternal Self**" is both sincere and inspiring. The poems, especially in the first volume, are often slight, and of no particular individual weight or ethical value, but his second volume shows a considerably greater depth of feeling and widening of interest. "**In a Grave Yard**," "**A Little Song**," "**By an Inland Lake**," and "**It's a Long Way**" are lyrics from the first volume that would be no discredit to the best contemporary poets. Among the best poems in the second volume are "**From the Crowd**," which describes a poignant lyric impression, "**A Song of Living**" and "**The Eternal Self**." His later poems show a still higher technical finish and a mystical tendency that sometimes oversteps the bounds of rational comprehension, as in "**Sandy Star and Willie Gee:**"

> Sandy Star and Willie Gee,
> Count 'em two, you make 'em three:
> Pluck the man and boy apart
> And you'll see into my heart.

Whether Mr. Braithwaite derives this tendency from his reading of Blake or from certain obscure strains in recent British and American poetry, it is one of the factors that sharply differentiates him from most of the other poets represented in this book. He himself objects, justly, to having his poems classed indiscriminately as "Negro" poetry. Just as the Caucasian really predominates in the poet's racial inheritance, so the non-racial is the striking characteristic of his verse. His poems have

no more of the Negro race in them than the poems of Longfellow or Bryant; in fact, paradoxically, they have less, by reason of their remoter connection with the substantial realities of ordinary life. There is very little real passion in Braithwaite's poetry; on the contrary there is an exquisite restraint which seems rather to avoid vigorous emotional expression and prefers instead a fine lyric suggestiveness. That this produces poetry of a high order may be seen from "**In a Graveyard**."

> In calm fellowship they sleep
> Where the graves are dark and deep
> Where nor hate nor fraud, nor feud
> Mar their perfect brotherhood.
>
> After all was done they went
> Into dreamless sleep, content
> That the years would pass them by,
> Sightless, soundless, where they lie.
>
> Wines and roses, song and dance,
> Have no portion in their trance—
> The four seasons are as one,
> Dark of night and light of sun.

(pp. 14-16)

Newman Ivey White, in an introduction to An Anthology of Verse By American Negroes, *edited by Newman Ivey White and Walter Clinton Jackson, 1924. Reprint by The Folcroft Press, Inc., 1969, pp. 1-26.*

Benjamin Brawley (essay date 1937)

[*Along with Alain Locke and Sterling Brown, Brawley is considered one of the most influential critics of the Harlem Renaissance. An educator, historian, and clergyman, he is best known as the author of the 1937 study* The Negro Genius: A New Appraisal of the Achievement of the American Negro in Literature and the Fine Arts. *In the following excerpt from this work, he explores literary influences on Braithwaite's poetry.*]

The work of William Stanley Braithwaite belongs not so much to Negro literature as to American literature in the large. With singleness of purpose he has given himself to books and the book world, and it is by this devotion that he has won the success he has achieved. (p. 202)

Lyrics of Life and Love brought together the best of the poet's early work. The little book contains eighty pages, and no one of the lyrics takes up more than two pages, twenty being just eight lines in length. This appearance of fragility, however, is a little deceptive. While Keats and Shelley are constantly present as the models in technique, the yearning of more than one lyric reflects the deeper romantic temper. The bravado and the tenderness of the old poets are in the two Christmas pieces, "**Holly Berry and Mistletoe**" and "**Yule-Song: A Memory**."

December comes, snows come,
  Comes the wintry weather;
Faces from away come—
  Hearts must be together.
Down the stair-steps of the hours
  Yule leaps the hills and towers—
Fill the bowl and hang the holly,
  Let the times be jolly.

"The Watchers" and the lines "To Dante Gabriel Rossetti" show the influence of the Pre-Raphaelites, the former also suggesting Kingsley; and the poet's handling of the sonnet may be seen from the following:

My thoughts go marching like an armed host
  Out of the city of silence, guns and cars;
Troop after troop across my dreams they post
  To the invasion of the wind and stars.
O brave array of youth's untamed desire!
  With thy bold, dauntless captain Hope to lead
His raw recruits to Fate's opposing fire.
  And up the walls of Circumstance to bleed.
How fares the expedition in the end?
  When this my heart shall have old age for king
And to the wars no further troop can send,
  What final message will the arm'stice bring?
The host gone forth in youth the world to meet,
In age returns—in victory or defeat?

After a year or two Mr. Braithwaite began to strike a new note of mysticism in his verse, and through this to influence the poetry of his day. It was first observed in "Sandy Star," that appeared in the *Atlantic* (July, 1909). It was also in "The Mystery" (or "The Way," as the poet prefers to call it) in *Scribner's* (October, 1915):

He could not tell the way he came
  Because his chart was lost:
Yet all his way was paved with flame
  From the bourne he crossed.
He did not know the way to go,
  Because he had no map:
He followed where the winds blow,—
  And the April sap.
He never knew upon his brow
  The secret that he bore—
And laughs away the mystery now
  The dark's at his door.

It would take an independent study to do justice to the critical introductions placed by Mr. Braithwaite in the successive issues of the *Anthology of Magazine Verse*. The books increased in size from the thin collection of eighty-seven pages for 1913 to the stout Sesqui-Centennial volume for 1926 running to nearly a thousand pages and containing a number of special articles. Clement Wood, writing in *Hunters of Heaven*, said of the editor: "He may be over-catholic in his inclusions, but he has shifted his emphasis from echoes to real poetry. He is an admirable anthologist, and his books are indispensable to a grasp of modern poetry." The *Transcript* said (November 30, 1915), after a special reception had been accorded the critic in New York by the authors of America: "He has helped poetry to readers as well as to poets. One is guilty of no extravagance in saying that the poets we have—and they may take their place with their peers in any country—and the gathering deference we

pay them, are created largely out of the stubborn, self-effacing enthusiasm of this one man. In a sense their distinction is his own."

The method of the critic has been to find out about any author's work that quality which is original or enduring, and so he has endeavored to do in occasional articles about Negro writers in the *Crisis* or *Opportunity*. So generous has he been and so catholic his taste that a reader once told him there was too much perfume in his ink. He holds, however, that few are likely to be injured by a little praise, while it would be fatal not to recognize even one deserving spirit. Thus one young writer after another he has encouraged rather than chastened, and all he has beckoned to the nobler heights of song. (pp. 203-06)

> *Benjamin Brawley, "Protest and Vindication," in his* The Negro Genius: A New Appraisal of the Achievement of the American Negro in Literature and the Fine Arts, *Dodd, Mead and Company, 1937, pp. 190-230.*

J. Saunders Redding (essay date 1939)

[*Redding was a distinguished American critic, historian, novelist, and autobiographer. His 1939 study* To Make a Poet Black *is considered a landmark in criticism of black writers. In the following excerpt from this work, he discusses theme and style in Braithwaite's poetry.*]

[William Stanley Braithwaite] attained prominence as critic and anthologist. His leading reviews for the *Boston Transcript,* his anthologies of magazine verse, published yearly from 1913 to 1928, and a collection of Elizabethan verse mark him as a critic of great sensibility. Braithwaite's poetry, however, is of greater pertinence to this study. He is the most outstanding example of perverted energy that the period from 1903 to 1917 produced.

Various explanations have been given for the oddity which a study of certain Negro poets like Braithwaite presents, but not one takes into account the pressure of the age. It is not considered that the expression of certain thoughts, feelings, and ideas was denied if they wished the hearing of an important audience. No one of the explanations mentions that all but one of these poets wrote better verse on material that in the very nature of things was (rather than is) Negro material. Braithwaite is the exception. On this general head, Countee Cullen has something to say in the preface to *Caroling Dusk:* "Since theirs [Negro writers] is also the heritage of the English language, their work will not present any serious aberration from the poetic tendencies of their time... for the double obligation of being both Negro and American is not so unified as we are often led to believe." Also, and apparently by way of explanation, Braithwaite's autobiographical sketch has this to say: "I inherited the incentives and ideals of the intellect from

Portrait of Braithwaite used as frontispiece for Lyrics of Life and Love *(1904.)*

an ancestry of British gentlemen." Further, it might be pointed out that he was born in Boston and has lived most of his life in Massachusetts. These remarks are definitely offered in the nature of excuses for divergence from the racial norm of creative ends.

Most of the Negro poets who from nearly the beginning of the century to the middle years of the World War turned their talents toward traditional poetic material—love, birth, death, beauty, grief, gladness—without any thought of their racial background developed a sort of dilettantism, a kind of love of display of poetic skill, and experience, and knowledge. In this their verse is comparable to the tricky poetics of the Cavaliers. It is bright and light, but without substance—Chinese fireworks.

> Lolotte, who attires my hair,
> Lost her lover. Lolotte weeps;
> Trails her hand before her eyes;
> Hangs her head and mopes and sighs,
> Mutters of the pangs of hell.
> Fills the circumambient air
> With her plaints and her despair.
> Looks at me:

> "May you never know, Mam'selle,
> Love's harsh cruelty."

Now this is pretty and skillful poetry, but it is not poetry afire with the compelling necessity for expression. No passion (even slightly remembered in tranquillity) of pain or joy, no spring of pure personal knowledge or conviction justifies it. It is just "lines expressing something or other."

Mr. Braithwaite set the pace for this particular school. It is not enough, however, to say that he seems to be merely a dilettante. He is both much more and much less than that—but it is not quite clear what or how much. In the *Poetic Year* for 1916, he wrote: "All this life that we live, this experience that we have of the world, are but footnotes to reality.... Ever since the beginning man has tried to translate the language of the spirit—the invisible, immaterial character of another existence that is as real as our own." Despite his brave, plain words, his translation of the language of the spirit leaves much to be desired in the way of clarity, and he seems never to have understood the "footnotes to reality." His poems mark the path of his steady progress into the rare atmosphere of the spiritual world, until at last he wrote, **"Sandy Star and Willie Gee,"** a poem in five titled parts, exclusive of the introduction:

> Sandy Star and Willie Gee
> Count 'em two, you make 'em three:
> Pluck the man and boy apart
> And you'll see into my heart.

> III
> Exit
> No, his exit by the gate
>   Will not leave the wind ajar;
> He will go when it is late
>   With a misty star.

> V
> Onus Probandi
> No more from out the sunset,
>   No more across the foam,
> No more across the windy hills
>   Will Sandy Star come home.

> He went away to search it
>   With a curse upon his tongue
> And in his hand the staff of life
>   Made music as it swung.

> I wonder if he found it,
>   And knows the mystery now—
> Our Sandy Star who went away
>   With the secret on his brow.

And none but a few of the now declined esoteric cult understood him. (pp. 89-92)

J. Saunders Redding, "Adjustment," in his To Make A Poet Black, *1939. Reprint by Cornell University Press, 1988, pp. 49-92.*

The Saturday Review of Literature (essay date 1949)

[*In the following 1949 review of Braithwaite's* Selected Poems, *a critic favorably appraises Braithwaite as a "sleuth of rhyme" but notes that "[his] scope as a poet is limited."*]

An older generation remembers the large annual anthologies of poetry collected by William Stanley Braithwaite of Boston. A veritable sleuth of rhyme, he read every publication large or small, near or remote in which a poem was published. He loved poetry and his attitude toward the new writer was generous and encouraging. Happy was the young poet to learn that he had won the approving eye of Braithwaite. It is fitting that Braithwaite should be given his just rewards as a poet as well as for his labors as a servant of the muse. His anthology selections are too inclusive to win lasting approval but they are a valuable reference. He is a more discerning taskmaster of his own poems than he was of the work of the poets he gathered in the highways and byways.

Braithwaite is a versatile craftsman, who can open his tool box and fashion a good sonnet, quatrain, or couplet with an admirable deftness. His talent as story-teller is shown in **"Fugue in Gardenia,"** and the philosophic ballad **"Sandy Star."** One of his most effective poems is the psalm **"Off the New England Coast"** an eloquent prayer which concludes with the affirmative plea—

> Not an inch of thy Beauty to perish,
>   not an ounce
>   thy Might to be lost.

Mr. Braithwaite's scope as a poet is limited, and his rhetoric shows no electric images, nor dramatic power. His gift is as quiet and consistent as the pleasure it evokes. To Braithwaite, noble servant of the muse and occasional rider of Pegasus, all lovers of poetry should give thanks.

> A. M. S., *"Versatile Craftsman," in* The Saturday Review of Literature, *Vol. 32, February 12, 1949, p. 31.*

FURTHER READING

Barton, Rebecca Chalmers. "William Stanley Braithwaite." In her *Witnesses for Freedom: Negro Americans in Autobiography,* pp. 93-100. New York: Harper and Brothers, 1948.
    Summarizes Braithwaite's unfinished autobiography, "The House under Arcturus," focusing on the author's account of his early childhood.

Butcher, Philip, "William Stanley Braithwaite and the College Language Association." *CLA Journal* XV, No. 2 (December 1971): 117-25.
    Discusses Braithwaite's career as a teacher at Atlanta University and documents his contact with the College Language Association.

———. Introduction to *The William Stanley Braithwaite Reader,* by William Stanley Braithwaite, edited by Philip Butcher, pp. 1-7. Ann Arbor: University of Michigan Press, 1972.
    Biographical sketch, emphasizing Braithwaite's literary career.

Clairmonte, Glenn. "He Made American Writers Famous." *Phylon* XXX, No. 2 (Summer 1969): 184-90.
    Recounts Braithwaite's contacts with Alain Locke, Amy Lowell, and other literary figures.

———. "The Cup-Bearer: William Stanley Braithwaite of Boston." *CLA Journal* XVII, No. 1 (September 1973): 101-08.
    Assesses Braithwaite's contributions to American literature, praising him as "the cup-bearer to countless striving poets as well as the means of their recognition."

Unger, Leonard. "Poets: Non-Modern, Neo-Modern, and Modern." *The Sewanee Review* LVI, No. 3 (Summer 1949): 509-21.
    Brief review of Braithwaite's *Selected Poems.* Unger states: "[*Selected Poems*] is . . . a book which I would have scruples against circulating. Its publishers say that it is 'in the classic tradition' and this turns out to mean that the poet affects the modes of Wordsworth, Keats, Browning, etc., as if he had been set to performing such exercises."

Williams, Kenny J. "An Invisible Partnership and an Unlikely Relationship: William Stanley Braithwaite and Harriet Monroe." *Callaloo* 10, No. 3 (Summer 1987): 516-50.
    Explores the "invisible" literary partnership between rivals Braithwaite and Monroe, charting their careers as poets, editors, and critics.

Gwendolyn Brooks

1917-

American poet, novelist, editor, autobiographer, and author of children's books.

A major contemporary poet and the first black American writer to win a Pulitzer Prize, Brooks is best known for her sensitive portraits of ordinary urban blacks who encounter racism and poverty in their daily lives. In her early work, Brooks avoided overt statements about the plight of blacks in America, prompting critics to define her poetry as "universal." During the late 1960s, however, her writing underwent a radical change in style and subject matter. Inspired by the black power movement and the militancy of such poets as Amiri Baraka (LeRoi Jones) and Haki R. Madhubuti (Don L. Lee), Brooks began to explore the marginality of black life through vivid imagery and forceful language and to recognize rage and despair among black people as her own.

Brooks was raised in Chicago, the eldest child of Keziah Wims Brooks, a former schoolteacher, and David Anderson Brooks, a janitor who did not achieve his dream of becoming a doctor because he lacked the funds to finish school. According to George Kent, as a child Brooks "was spurned by members of her own race because she lacked social or athletic abilities, a light skin, and good grade hair." Brooks was hurt by such rejection, and she found solace in her writing. Stunned by the quality of her early poems, her mother proclaimed: "You are going to be the lady Paul Laurence Dunbar." Brooks received compliments on her poems and encouragement from James Weldon Johnson and Langston Hughes through correspondence and visits to their readings in Chicago. By the age of sixteen she had a substantial portfolio, including some seventy-five published poems. After graduating from Wilson Junior College in 1936, she worked briefly as a maid and then as a secretary to Dr. E. N. French, a "spiritual advisor" who sold potions and charms to residents of the Mecca, a Chicago slum building. Brooks found both experiences humiliating and painful. But she participated in poetry workshops at Chicago's South Side Community Art Center in 1941 and 1942, producing poems that would appear in her first volume of poetry, *A Street in Bronzeville* (1945).

At the request of publishers, Brooks concentrated on her experiences as a black American in writing poems for *A Street in Bronzeville*. The work chronicles the aspirations and disappointments of citizens living in Bronzeville, a black district in Chicago that serves as the setting for many of her poems. The first part of *A Street in Bronzeville* provides a realistic picture of the neighborhood; the second section, a sequence of twelve sonnets entitled "Gay Chaps at the Bar," explores the unequal treatment of blacks in the Armed Forces during World

War II. This work introduces her major thematic concerns of the next two decades: family life, war, the quest for contentment and honor, and the hardships caused by racism and poverty. Brooks's second collection, *Annie Allen* (1949), is an experimental volume for which she received the Pulitzer Prize in poetry. Similar in structure to a prose narrative, the poems in *Annie Allen* focus on the growth of the title character from childhood to adulthood in an environment replete with indigence and discrimination. Critics generally praised Brooks for her subtle humor and irony, her skillful handling of conventional stanzaic forms, and her invention of the sonnet-ballad, a verse structure integrating colloquial speech and formal language. Although she relished writing "The Anniad," the "heroic epic" of her protagonist, critics often panned the poem because of its complexity. Brooks drew on her experience as a maid for her next work, *Maud Martha* (1953). This, her only novel, depicts a young, dark-skinned black woman's struggle to maintain dignity amid discrimination by both blacks and whites. Brooks's next major collection of poetry, *The Bean Eaters* (1960), details the attempts of ghetto inhabitants to escape from feelings of hopelessness. New pieces included in *Selected Poems* (1963) evidenced Brooks's growing interest in social issues and the influence of the early years of the civil rights movement. Although many critics praised the "universality" of Brooks's early poetry, in retrospect many others have characterized these poems as "establishment," "safe," and "conservative."

Brooks experienced a change in political consciousness and artistic direction after witnessing the combative spirit of several young black authors at the Second Black Writers' Conference at Fisk University in 1967. She later explained her revelations in her autobiography, *Report from Part One* (1972): "I—who have 'gone the gamut' from an almost angry rejection of my dark skin by some of my brainwashed brothers and sisters to a surprised queenhood in the new Black sun—am qualified to enter at least the kindergarten of new consciousness now.... I have hopes for myself." With *In the Mecca* (1968), which most critics regard as her transitional volume, Brooks abandoned traditional poetic forms in favor of free verse and increased her use of vernacular to make her works more accessible to black readers. The work, based on the slum building where Brooks had earlier worked, chronicles Mrs. Sallie's search for her missing daughter Pepita. Mrs. Sallie discovers that her youngest child has been murdered by a fellow resident of the Mecca. Brooks switched to a black publisher with *Riot* (1969) and *Family Pictures* (1970), in which she evoked the revolutionary legacy of such slain black activists as Medgar Evers, Malcolm X, and Martin Luther King, Jr. and examined the social upheavals of the late 1960s with a mixture of objectivity and compassion. While her concern for the black nationalist movement and racial solidarity continued to dominate her verse in the early 1970s, the energy and optimism of *Riot* and *Family Pictures* were replaced with disenchantment resulting from the divisiveness of the civil rights and black power movements. In *Beckonings* (1975) and *To Disembark* (1981), Brooks urged blacks to break free from the repression of white American society and advocated violence and anarchy if necessary. Critics are divided in their judgments of Brooks's work following her artistic and ideological transformation. Some believe that she sacrificed formal complexity and subtlety for political polemic. According to D. H. Melhem, however, Brooks "enriches both black and white cultures by revealing essential life, its universal identities, and the challenge it poses to a society beset with corruption and decay."

Now holding over fifty honorary doctorates and having served as Consultant in Poetry to the Library of Congress in 1985-86, Brooks continues to travel tirelessly and read her works throughout the United States. She has established and provides funding for the Poet Laureate Awards, a competition for young writers in Illinois. Brooks undertakes such projects in her desire to bring poetry to all black people. As she revealed in a 1974 interview, she wants "to develop a style that will appeal to black people in taverns, black people in gutters, schools, offices, factories, prisons, the consulate; I wish to reach black people in pulpits, black people in mines, on farms, on thrones." Kent determined that Brooks is "a poet for many people and many generations; her stature will surely continue to grow."

(For further information about Brooks's life and works, see *Authors in the News*, Vol. 1; *Black Writers; Concise Dictionary of American Literary Biography, 1941-1968; Contemporary Authors*, Vol. 1; *Contemporary Authors New Revision Series*, Vols. 1, 27; *Contemporary Literary Criticism*, Vols. 1, 2, 4, 5, 15, 49; *Dictionary of Literary Biography*, Vols. 5, 76; and *Something about the Author*, Vol. 6.)

PRINCIPAL WORKS

A Street in Bronzeville (poetry) 1945
Annie Allen (poetry) 1949
Maud Martha (novel) 1953
Bronzeville Boys and Girls (poetry) 1956
The Bean Eaters (poetry) 1960
Selected Poems (poetry) 1963
In the Mecca (poetry) 1968
Riot (poetry) 1969
Family Pictures (poetry) 1970
Aloneness (poetry) 1971
The World of Gwendolyn Brooks (poetry and novel) 1971
Report from Part One (autobiography) 1972
The Tiger Who Wore White Gloves: or, What You Are You Are (poetry) 1974
Beckonings (poetry) 1975
A Capsule Course in Black Poetry Writing [with Keorapetse Kgositsile, Haki R. Madhubuti, and Dudley Randall] (prose) 1975
Primer for Blacks (poetry) 1980
Young Poets Primer (prose) 1980
To Disembark (poetry) 1981
Mayor Harold Washington and Chicago, the I will City (poetry) 1983
Very Young Poets (prose) 1983
The Near-Johannesburg Boy, and Other Poems (poetry) 1986
Blacks (poetry and novel) 1987
Gottschalk and the Grande Tarantelle (poetry) 1988
Winnie (poetry) 1988

Gwendolyn Brooks (essay date 1971)

[*In the following excerpt from her 1972 autobiography* Report from Part One, *Brooks discusses the change in her thinking after participating in the Fisk University Writers' Conference in 1967. This portion of the autobiography was originally published in* McCall's *in December 1971.*]

Everybody has to go the bathroom.
That's good.
That's a great thing.

If by some quirk of fate blacks had to go to the bathroom and whites didn't I shudder to think of the genocidal horrors that would be visited on the blacks of the whole world. Here is what my little green *Webster's New World* has to say about a world-shaking word:

> black (blak), adj. (A S *blaec*) 1. opposite to white: see color. 2. dark-complexioned. 3. Negro. 4. without light; dark. 5. dirty. 6. evil; wicked. 7. sad; dismal. 8. sullen. n.1. black pigment; opposite of white. 2. dark clothing, as for mourning. 3. a Negro. v.t. & v.i., to blacken.—black-out, to lose consciousness.—blackly, adv: —blackness, n.

Interestingly enough, we do not find that "white" is "opposite of black." That would "lift" black to the importance-level of white.

> white (hwit), adj. (A S hwit). 1. having the color of pure snow or milk. 2. of a light or pale color. 3. pale; wan. 4. pure; innocent. 5. having a light-colored skin. n.1. the color of pure snow or milk. 2. a white or light-colored thing, as the albumen of an egg, the white part of the eyeball, etc. 3. a person with a light-colored skin; Caucasian.—whiteness, n.

Until 1967 my own blackness did not confront me with a shrill spelling of itself. I knew that I was what most people were calling "a Negro;" I called myself that, although always the word fell awkwardly on a poet's ear; I had never liked the sound of it (Caucasian has an ugly sound, too, while the name Indian is beautiful to look at and to hear.) *And* I knew that people of my coloration and distinctive history had been bolted to trees and sliced or burned or shredded; knocked to the back of the line; provided with separate toilets, schools, neighborhoods; denied, when possible, voting rights; hounded, hooted at, or shunned, or patronizingly patted (often the patting-hand was, I knew, surreptitiously wiped after the Kindness, so that unspeakable contamination might be avoided.) America's social climate, it seemed, was trying to tell me something. It was trying to tell me something Websterian. Yet, although almost secretly, I had always felt that to be black was good. Sometimes, there would be an approximate whisper around me: *others* felt, it seemed, that to be black was good. The translation would have been something like "Hey—being black is *fun."* Or something like "Hey—our folks have got stuff to be proud of!" Or something like "Hey—since we are so good why aren't we treated like the other 'Americans?'"

Suddenly there was New Black to meet. In the spring of 1967 I met some of it at the Fisk University Writers' Conference in Nashville. Coming from white white white South Dakota State College I arrived in Nashville, Tennessee, to give one more "reading." But blood-boiling surprise was in store for me. First, I was aware of a general energy, an electricity, in look, walk, speech, *gesture* of the young blackness I saw all about me. I had been "loved" at South Dakota State College. Here, I was

coldly Respected. Here, the heroes included the novelist-director, John Killens, editors David Llorens and Hoyt Fuller, playwright Ron Milner, historians John Henrik Clarke and Lerone Bennett (and even poor Lerone was taken to task, by irate members of a no-nonsense young audience, for affiliating himself with *Ebony Magazine,* considered at that time a traitor for allowing skin-bleach advertisements in its pages, and for over-featuring light-skinned women). Imamu Amiri Baraka, then "LeRoi Jones", was expected. He arrived in the middle of my own offering, and when I called attention to his presence there was jubilee in Jubilee Hall.

All that day and night, Margaret Danner Cunningham—another Old Girl, another coldly Respected old Has-been—and an almost hysterical Gwendolyn B. walked about in amazement, listening, looking, learning. *What was going on!*

In my cartoon basket I keep a cartoon of a stout, dowager-hatted, dowager-furred Helen Hokinson woman. She is on parade in the world. She is a sign-carrier in the wild world. Her sign says "Will someone please tell me what is going on?" Well, although I cannot give a full-blooded answer to that potent question, I have been supplied—the sources are plural—with helpful materials: hints, friendly *and* inimical clues, approximations, statistics, "proofs" of one kind and another; from these I am trying to weave the coat that I shall wear. In 1967's Nashville, however, the somewhat dotty expression in the eyes of the cartoon-woman, the *agapeness,* were certainly mine. I was in some inscrutable and uncomfortable wonderland. I didn't know what to make of what surrounded me, of what with hot sureness began almost immediately to invade me. *I* had never been, before, in the general presence of such insouciance, such live firmness, such confident vigor, such determination to mold or carve something DEFINITE.

Up against the wall, white man! was the substance of the Baraka shout, at the evening reading he shared with fierce Ron Milner among intoxicating drum-beats, heady incense and organic underhumming. Up against the wall! And a pensive (until that moment) white man of thirty or thirty three abruptly shot himself into the heavy air, screaming "Yeah! *Yeah!* Up against the wall, Brother! KILL 'EM ALL! KILL 'EM *ALL!"*

I thought that was interesting.

There is indeed a new black today. He is different from any the world has known. He's a tall-walker. Almost firm. By many of his own *brothers* he is not understood. And he is understood by *no* white. Not the wise white; not the Schooled white; not the Kind white. Your *least* pre-requisite toward an understanding of the new black is an exceptional Doctorate which can be conferred only upon those with the proper properties of bitter birth and intrinsic sorrow. I know this is infuriating, especially to those professional Negro-understanders, some of them so *very* kind, with special portfolio, special savvy. But I cannot say anything other, because nothing other is the truth.

I—who have "gone the gamut" from an almost angry rejection of my dark skin by some of my brainwashed brothers and sisters to a surprised queenhood in the new black sun—am qualified to enter at least the kindergarten of new consciousness now. New consciousness and trudge-toward-progress.

I have hopes for myself. (pp. 82-6)

> *Gwendolyn Brooks, "Report from Part One,"*
> *in her* Report from Part One, *Broadside*
> *Press, 1988, pp. 37-86.*

Houston A. Baker, Jr. (essay date 1972)

[*Baker, a poet and critic, has examined a "vernacular" theory of black American cultural expression in his critical work* Blues, Ideology, and Afro-American Literature *(1984). In the following excerpt from an essay originally published in a slightly different form in* CLA Journal *in 1972, he argues that Brooks's poetry is an example of "white style and black content."*]

Gwendolyn Brooks, like W. E. B. Du Bois, seems caught between two worlds. And both she and Du Bois manifest the duality of their lives in their literary works; Du Bois wrote in a beautiful, impressionistic style set off by quotations from the world's literary masters. Brooks writes tense, complex, rhythmic verse that contains the metaphysical complexities of John Donne and the word magic of Appollinaire, Eliot, and Pound. The high style of both authors, however, is often used to explicate the condition of black Americans trapped behind a veil that separates them from the white world. What one seems to have is white style and black content—two warring ideals in one dark body.

This apparent dichotomy has produced a confusing situation for Gwendolyn Brooks. The world of white arts and letters has pointed to her with pride; it has bestowed kudos and a Pulitzer Prize. The world of black arts and letters has looked on with mixed emotion, and pride has been only one part of the mixture. There have also been troubling questions about the poet's essential "blackness," her dedication to the melioration of the black American's social conditions. The real duality appears when we realize that Gwendolyn Brooks—although praised and awarded—does not appear on the syllabi of most American literature courses, and her name seldom appears in the annual scholarly bibliographies of the academic world. It would seem she is a black writer after all, *not* an American writer. Yet when one listens to the voice of today's black-revolutionary consciousness, one often hears that Brooks's early poetry fits the white, middle-class patterns that Imamu Baraka has seen as characteristic of "Negro literature."

When one turns to her canon, one finds that she has abided the questions of both camps. Etheridge Knight

has perfectly captured her enduring quality in the following lines:

> O courier on Pegásus, O Daughter of Parnassus
> O Splendid woman of the purple stitch.
> When beaten and blue, despairingly we sink
> Within obfuscating mire,
> O, cradle in your bosom us, hum your lullabies
> And soothe our souls with kisses of verse
> That stir us on to search for light.
> O Mother of the world. Effulgent lover of the Sun!
> For ever speak the truth.

She has the Parnassian inspiration and the earth-mother characteristics noted by the poet; her strength has come from a dedication to truth. The truth that concerns her does not amount to a facile realism or a heavy naturalism, although "realism" is the word that comes to mind when one reads a number of poems in *A Street in Bronzeville* (1945).

Poems, or segments, such as "kitchenette building," "a song in the front yard," and "the vacant lot," all support the view that the writer was intent on a realistic, even a naturalistic, portrayal of the life of lower-echelon urban dwellers:

> We are things of dry hours and the involuntary
>   plan,
> Grayed in, and gray. "Dream" makes a giddy
>   sound, not strong
> Like "rent," "feeding a wife," "satisfying a man."
>
> My mother, she tells me that Johnnie Mae
> Will grow up to be a bad woman.
> That George'll be taken to Jail soon or late
> (On account of last winter he sold our back gate.)
>
> And with seeing the squat fat daughter
> Letting in the men
> When majesty has gone for the day—
> And letting them out again.

These passages reinforce the designation of Brooks as a realist, and poems such as **"The Sundays of Satin-Legs Smith," "We Real Cool," "A Lovely Love,"** and the volume *Annie Allen* can be added to the list. If she had insisted on a strict realism and nothing more, she could perhaps be written off as a limited poet. But she is no mere chronicler of the condition of the black American poor. Even her most vividly descriptive verses contain an element that removes them from the realm of a cramped realism. All of her characters have both ratiocinative and imaginative capabilities; they have the ability to reason, dream, muse, and remember. This ability distinguishes them from the naturalistic literary victim caught in an environmental maze. From the realm of "raw and unadorned life," Satin-Legs Smith creates his own world of bright colors, splendid attire, and soft loves in the midst of a cheap hotel's odor and decay. The heroine of **"The Anniad"** conjures up a dream world, covers it in silver plate, populates it with an imaginary prince, and shores up magnificent fragments against the ruins of war. And Jessie Mitchell's mother seeks refuge from envy and death in a golden past:

> She revived for the moment settled and dried-up
>   triumphs,
> Forced perfume into old petals, pulled up the
>   droop,
> Refueled
> Triumphant long-exhaled breaths.
> Her exquisite yellow youth . . . .

Gwendolyn Brooks's characters, in short, are infinitely human because at the core of their existence is the imaginative intellect.

Given the vision of such characters, it is impossible to agree with David Littlejohn, who wishes to view them as simplistic mouthpieces for the poet's sensibility; moreover, it is not surprising that the characters' concerns transcend the ghetto life of many black Americans. They reflect the joy of childhood, the burdens and contentment of motherhood, the distortions of the war-torn psyche, the horror of blood-guiltiness, and the pains of the anti-hero confronted with a heroic ideal. Brooks's protagonists, personae, and speakers, in short, capture all of life's complexities, particularly the complexity of an industrialized age characterized by swift change, depersonalization, and war.

In **"Gay Chaps at the Bar,"** the poet shows her concern for a theme that has had a great influence on twentieth-century British and American art. In one section, "my dreams, my works, must wait till after hell," she employs the food metaphors characteristic of her writing to express the incompleteness that accompanies war:

> I hold my honey and I store my bread
> In little jars and cabinets of my will.
> I label clearly, and each latch and lid
> I bid, Bc firm till I return from hell.
> I am very hungry. I am incomplete.

In another section, "piano after war," she captures the mental anguish occasioned by war. The rejuvenation the speaker has felt in the "golden rose" music feeding his "old hungers" suddenly ends:

> But suddenly, across my climbing fever
> Of proud delight—a multiplying cry.
> A cry of bitter dead men who will never
> Attend a gentle maker of musical joy.
> Then my thawed eye will go again to ice.
> And stone will shove the softness from my face.

In **"The Anniad"** and the **"Appendix to the Anniad,"** the poet deals once again with the chaos of arms: War destroys marriage, stifles fertility, and turns men to creatures of "untranslatable ice." Her work, therefore, joins the mainstream of twentieth-century poetry in its treatment of the terrors of war, and her message comes to us through, as I have mentioned, the imaginative intellect of characters who evoke sympathy and identification.

War, however, is not the only theme that allies Gwendolyn Brooks with the mainstream. One finds telling and ironical speculation in "the preacher: ruminates behind the sermon":

> Perhaps—who knows?—He tires of looking
>   down.
> Those eyes are never lifted. Never straight.
> Perhaps sometimes He tires of being great
> In solitude. Without a hand to hold.

In **"Strong Men, Riding Horses,"** we have a Prufrockian portrait of the anti-hero. After his confrontation with the ideals of a Western film, the persona comments:

> I am not like that. I pay rent, am addled
> By illegible landlords, run, if robbers call.
>
> What mannerisms I present, employ,
> Are camouflage, and what my mouths remark
> To word-wall off that broadness of the dark
> Is pitiful.
> I am not brave at all.

In **"Mrs. Small,"** one has a picture of the "Mr. Zeros" (or Willie Lomans) of a complex century, and in **"A Bronzeville Mother Loiters in Mississippi. Meanwhile a Mississippi Mother Burns Bacon,"** we have an evocation of the blood-guiltiness of the white psyche in an age of dying colonialism. Brooks presents these themes with skill because she has the ability to endow each figure with a unique, individualizing vision of the world.

If they were considered in isolation, however, the characters and concerns of the verse would not mark the poet as an outstanding writer. Great poetry demands word magic, a sense of the infinite possibilities of language. In this technical realm Brooks is superb. Her ability to dislocate and mold language into complex patterns of meaning can be observed in her earliest poems and in her latest volumes—*In The Mecca* (1968), *Riot* (1969), and *Family Pictures* (1970). The first lines of **"The Sundays of Satin-Legs Smith"** are illustrative:

> Inamoratas, with an approbation,
> Bestowed his title. Blessed his inclination.)
>
> He wakes, unwinds, elaborately: a cat
> Tawny, reluctant, royal. He is fat
> And fine this morning. Definite. Reimbursed.

The handling of polysyllabics is not in the least strained, and the movement is so graceful that one scarcely notices the rhymed couplets. Time and again this word magic is at work, and the poet's varying rhyme schemes lend a subtle resonance that is not found in the same abundance in the works of other acknowledged American writers. It is important to qualify this judgment, however, for while Brooks employs polysyllabics and forces words into striking combinations, she preserves colloquial rhythms. Repeatedly one is confronted by a realistic voice—not unlike that in Robert Frost's poetry—that carries one along the dim corridors of the human psyche or down the rancid halls of a decaying tenement. Brooks's colloquial narrative voice, however, is more prone to complex juxtapositions than Frost's, as a stanza from **"The Anniad"** illustrates:

> Doomer, though, crescendo-comes
> Prophesying hecatombs.
> Surrealist and cynical.
> Garrulous and guttural.
> Spits upon the silver leaves.
> Denigrates the dainty eves
> Dear dexterity achieves.

This surely differs from Frost's stanzas, and the difference resides in the poet's obvious joy in words. She fuses the most elaborate words into contexts that allow them to speak naturally or to sing beautifully her meaning.

Brooks is not indebted to Frost alone for technical influences; she also acknowledges her admiration for Langston Hughes. Although a number of her themes and techniques set her work in the twentieth-century mainstream, there are those that place it firmly in the black American literary tradition. One of her most effective techniques is a sharp, black, comic irony that is closely akin to the scorn Hughes directed at the ways of white folks throughout his life. When added to her other skills, this irony proves formidable. **"The Lovers of the Poor"** is unsparing in its portrayal of ineffectual, middle-age, elitist philanthropy:

Brooks at age nineteen.

> Their guild is giving money to the poor.
> The worthy poor. The very very worthy
> And beautiful poor. Perhaps just not too swarthy?
> Perhaps just not too dirty nor too dim
> Nor—passionate. In truth, what they could wish
> Is—something less than derelict or dull.
> Not staunch enough to stab, though, gaze for gaze!
> God shield them sharply from the beggar-bold!

Hughes could not have hoped for better. And the same vitriol is directed at whites who seek the bizarre and exotic by "slumming" among blacks in **"I love those little booths at Benvenuti's":**

> But how shall they tell people they have been
> Out Bronzeville way? For all the nickels in
> Have not bought savagery or defined a "folk."
> The colored people will not "clown."
>
> The colored people arrive, sit firmly down,
> Eat their Express Spaghetti, their T-bone steak,
> Handling their steel and crockery with no clatter,
> Laugh punily, rise, go firmly out of the door.

The poet's chiding, however, is not always in the derisive mode. She often turns an irony of loving kindness on black Americans. **"We Real Cool"** would fit easily into the canon of Hughes or Sterling Brown:

> We real cool. We
> Left School. We
>
> Lurk late. We
> Strike straight. We
>
> Sing sin. We
> Thin gin. We
>
> Jazz June. We
> Die soon.

The irony is patent, but the poet's sympathy and admiration for the folk are no less obvious (the bold relief of "We," for example). A sympathetic irony in dealing with the folk has characterized some of the most outstanding works in the black American literary tradition, from Paul Laurence Dunbar's "Jimsella" and the novels of Claude McKay to Ralph Ellison's *Invisible Man* and the work of recent writers such as George Cain and Louise Meriwether. All manifest a concern with the black man living in the "promised land" of the American city, and Brooks's *A Street in Bronzeville, Annie Allen,* **"The Bean Eaters,"** and **"Bronzeville Woman in a Red Hat"** likewise reveal the employment of kindly laughter to veil the tears of a desperate situation. In her autobiography, *Report from Part One,* she attests to having been in the situation and to having felt its deeper pulsations: "I lived on 63rd Street [in Chicago] . . . and there was a good deal of life in the raw all about me. You might feel that this would be disturbing, but it was not. It contributed to my writing progress. I wrote about what I saw and heard in the street."

Finally, there are the poems of protest. A segregated military establishment comes under attack in both **"The Negro Hero"** and "the white troops had their orders but the Negroes looked like men." The ignominies of lynching are exposed in **"A Bronzeville Mother Loiters in Mississippi. Meanwhile, a Mississippi Mother Burns Bacon."** And in poems like **"Riders to the Blood-red Wrath"** and **"The Second Sermon on the Warpland,"** Brooks expresses the philosophy of militant resistance that has characterized the black American literary tradition from the day a black slave first sang of Pharaoh's army. The poet, in short, has spoken forcefully against the indignities suffered by black Americans in a racialistic society. Having undertaken a somewhat thorough revaluation of her role as a black poet in an era of transition, she has stated and proved her loyalty to the task of creating a new consciousness in her culture. Her shift from a major white publishing firm to an independent black one (Broadside Press) for her autobiography is an indication of her commitment to the cause of black institution-building that has been championed by a number of today's black artists. One might, however, take issue with her recent statement that she was "ignorant" until enlightened by the black activities and concerns of the 1960s. Although she is currently serving as one of the most engaged artistic guides for a culture, she is more justly described as a herald than as an uninformed convert. She has mediated the dichotomy that left Paul Laurence Dunbar (whose *Complete Poems* she read at an early age) a torn and agonized man. Of course, she had the example of Dunbar, the Harlem Renaissance writers, and others to build upon, but at times even superior talents have been incapable of employing the accomplishments of the past for their own ends. Unlike the turn-of-the century poet and a number of Renaissance writers, Brooks has often excelled the surrounding white framework, and she has been able to see clearly beyond it to the strengths and beauties of her own unique cultural tradition.

Gwendolyn Brooks represents a singular achievement. Beset by a double consciousness, she has kept herself from being torn asunder by crafting poems that equal the best in the black and white American literary traditions. Her characters are believable, her themes manifold, and her technique superb. The critic (whether black or white) who comes to her work seeking only support for his ideology will be disappointed for, as Etheridge Knight pointed out, she has ever spoken the truth. And truth, one likes to feel, always lies beyond the boundaries of any one ideology. Perhaps Brooks's most significant achievement is her endorsement of this point of view. From her hand and fertile imagination have come volumes that transcend the dogma on either side of the American veil. In their transcendence, they are fitting representatives of an "Effulgent lover of the Sun!" (pp. 21-8)

> *Houston A. Baker, Jr., "The Achievement of Gwendolyn Brooks," in* A Life Distilled: Gwendolyn Brooks, Her Poetry and Fiction, *edited by Maria K. Mootry and Gary Smith, University of Illinois Press, 1987, pp. 21-9.*

George Kent (essay date 1982)

[*Kent was one of the foremost authorities on Brooks's life and works; he completed her biography,* A Life of Gwendolyn Brooks, *prior to his death in 1982. In the following essay, completed two weeks before his death, he explores the development of Brooks's syntax and language in her poetry.*]

The consciousness producing *A Street in Bronzeville* (1945) was one making its first compassionate outreach to the broad range of humanity. On the one hand, it represented the mastered past: [Brooks'] old neighborhood and youth. On the other hand, it represented an intense getting acquainted with the present which was pressurized by the raw currents of Chicago's racial practices, and by World War II. Optimism prevailed, however, since the war situation had produced both threatening violence and some evidence that a broadened democracy would be born from it. In the poet's early work, one result is a deceptively simple surface. Syntax is most often either in close correlation with the usual subject plus verb plus object or complement pattern of a familiar prose sentence or within calling distance. Wielding this syntax is a friendly observer giving one a tour of the neighborhood or quick views of situations. Thus abrupt beginnings sound pretty much the way they do in our communications with friends with whom we share clarifying reference points. The observer [in **"The Old-Marrieds"**] begins: "But in the crowding darkness not a word did they say." Joining the group in "kitchenette building," the observer-narrator pitches at us a long question but one so well ordered that it is painless: "But could a dream send up through onion fumes / Its white and violet, fight with fried potatoes / And yesterday's garbage ripening in the hall, / Flutter, or sing an aria down these rooms . . . ?" At the end of three more lines we complete the question, and are then given quick relief through a series of short declarative statements whose brevity drives home the drama and the pathos of the situation.

There are poems with much simpler syntax within this group and one sonnet with a far more complex syntax. The simplest derive from closeness to conversational patterns, from reproduction of speech tones, and from the already mentioned patterning upon simple prose statements. A form such as the ballad also has conventions which allow for great simplicity of syntactical structure. The more complex structure which probably puzzles on a first reading actually derives . . . from exploitation of one of the more complex rhetorical but conventional structures—the periodic sentence. (pp. 89-90)

In terms of the relationship to conversational language and actual speech tones one will find in the style a range running from "folk" speech (the Hattie Scott poems) to that which is more self-consciously literate and affected by formal traditions (**"The Sundays of Satin Legs Smith"** and the sonnets, for example). Brooks is also alert to the richness provided by bringing contrasting traditions into strategic conjunctions or, by movement, into a very formal eloquence; again, examples of both may be seen in **"Satin Legs Smith."** And finally there is the colloquial and hip level provided by such a poem as **"Patent Leather"**: "That cool chick down on Calumet / Has got herself a brand new cat...."

For the most part imagery goes beyond the simple functions of representing an object or pictorializing, activities characteristic of the most simple poems, and manages to do so quietly. "Pretty patent leather hair" obviously has its total effect in the literal picture it creates and the comment it makes upon the judgment of the cool chick. But Brooks expanded the range and function of the realistic image in several ways: attaching to it a striking descriptive term ("crowding darkness"), combining it with a figurative gesture ("could a dream send up through onion fumes / Its white and violet"), contrasting realistic and symbolic functions (crooked and straight in **"Hunchback Girl..."**), presenting expressionistic description of a condition ("Mabbie on Mabbie with hush in the heart"), and emphasizing the figurative role of a basically realistic or pictorial expression ("wear the brave stockings of night-black lace," and "temperate holiness arranged / Ably on asking faces").

Perhaps the foregoing elements may be allowed to stand for other devices making up the total struggle with language meant by the word *style*. I have tried to suggest that the central trait of most of the language devices is that they convey the impression of actual simplicity and thus offer the appearance of easy-going accessibility. It is certainly not a total accessibility, in several cases. On one level people and their life stories appear in sharply outlined plots presenting easily recognized issues from the daily round of existence, and move to definite decisive conclusions. However, recognizing certain devices or reading at the tempo required not only by the story but by imagery and language changes will, at times, take us to another level. **"Southeast corner,"** for example, seems interested in the artistry, as well as the vanity, of the deceased madam of the school of beauty, an interpretation suggested by the vivid image of shot silk shining over her tan "impassivity." **"Satin Legs"** has meanings which reveal themselves in the imagery, language shifts, and mixture of narrative attitudes, which go beyond the basic story, and so on.

But there is no question that in *A Street in Bronzeville* (and in individual poems over the body of her work) there is a general simplicity which seems easily to contain specific complexities. The fact makes Brooks a poet speaking still, not merely to critics and other poets, but to people.

It is probable that nearly all the stylistic developments of Brooks' subsequent works are embryonically present in *A Street in Bronzeville*, since, with its publication, she was emerging from a very long and earnest apprenticeship. Some clear foreshadowing of more complex stylistic developments is in the sonnets, and in **"The Sundays of Satin Legs Smith."** Whereas, for example, the full capacity of the narrator of the Hattie Scott poems may

be shaded in the background, the sophistication and perception of the narrator of the sonnets and the life of Smith are clearly those of the narrator of *Annie Allen*. Yet it is understandable that people found the stylistic developments in this second work startling and complex.

If the opening poem of *A Street* makes things seem easy by providing a friendly narrator using language in seemingly customary ways, the opening poem of *Annie Allen*, **"the birth in a narrow room,"** makes the reader feel that the narrator's assumption is that he is to the poetic manner born. The poem demands the reader's absolute commitment, an acceptance of the role of a tougher elliptical syntax, and a comprehension of imagery which functions both realistically and mythically. Actually, the syntax is difficult largely because for several lines the infant remains the *unnamed* subject of the poem. The sources for imagery are the fairy and timeless world and the "real" objects of the "real" world, both of which function to sustain temporarily complete freedom for the young child in an Edenic world. Thus the first poem warns the reader to expect to participate in complex struggles with language.

The style of *Annie Allen* emerges not only from the fact that the poet of the highly promising first book naturally expects to present greater mastery of craft in the second but also from a changed focus in consciousness. In her first book Brooks' emphasis had been upon community consciousness. In [*Annie Allen*] her emphasis is upon self-consciousness—an attempt to give artistic structure to tensions arising from the artist's experience in moving from the Edenic environment of her parents' home into the fallen world of Chicago tenement life in the roles of young wife, mother, and artist. Her efforts, however, were not an attempt to be confessional but an attempt to take advantage of the poetic form to move experiences immediately into symbols broader than the person serving as subject. A thoroughgoing search of the territory and the aspiration for still greater mastery of craft called for a struggle with language, a fact which would require the reader to make also a creative struggle.

One device is to play conventional and unconventional structures against each other, and, sometimes, to work apparently conventional structures for very special effects. In **"the parents: people like our marriage, Maxie and Andrew,"** the reader abruptly confronts the synecdochial opening lines: "Clogged and soft and sloppy eyes / Have list the light that bites or terrifies." Afterward the poem gradually settles into the more conventional approach, though it demands that the reader absorb its realities from simple symbols instead of editorial statements. In such poems the reader's creative participation is sustained by other devices: unusual conjunctions of words, shifts in pace and rhythm, reproductions of speech tones at the point of the colloquial and at varying distances from it, figurative language, challenging twists in the diction, and others. (pp. 90-2)

The long poem on young womanhood entitled **"The Anniad"** has the task of taking Annie into maturity by carrying her from the epic dreams of maidenhood into the prosaic and disillusioning realities provided by the married life. More concretely, having inherited the romance and love lore of Euro-Americans and disabilities imposed upon Black identity, she is, at once, the would-be heroine of song and story and the Black woman whom "the higher gods" forgot and the lower ones berate. The combination of the realistic and romantic portrays the flesh and blood person and the dreamer. (p. 94)

To express the climax of accumulated problems, storms, and confusions of Annie's young life, Brooks turns completely to expressionistic imagery:

> In the indignant dark there ride
> Roughnesses and spiny things
> On infallible hundred heels.
> And a bodiless bee stings.
> Cyclone concentration reels.
> Harried sods dilate, divide,
> Such her sorrowfully inside.

The last stanzas return to the language of the realistic scale, although the language itself is not simply mimetic or pictorial. Annie is described as salvaging something of the more usual day-to-day fruits from her experiences: "Stroking swallows from the sweat. / Fingering faint violet. / Hugging gold and Sunday sun. / Kissing in her kitchenette / The minuets of memory." (p. 95)

On the level of telling the Annie Allen story, Brooks was thus able to experiment extensively with stylistic devices and license herself to move beyond realistic imagery. She did so by retaining realism as the base of conception and the norm for the behavior patterns the personalities must ultimately adopt. Thus the form includes devices for humor and pathos which register, in the world of the possible, Annie's excess of idealism, dreaminess, or self-absorption: intense pictures of imbalance, rhythms suggesting frenetic behavior, and a vocabulary suggesting the occupation of worlds which must prove incompatible. In short, the kindly satiric pat appears to halt unrealism, though the unrealism if it could be transformed into "reality" might make a richer world.

Annie Allen represents Brooks' most energetic reach for simply a great command of the devices of poetic style. Having developed this command, she could now wield the devices at will and make them relate more efficiently to form and intention. With this mastery of numerous devices came also the power to achieve originality by making variations in the contexts in which they were used and in the relationships one device makes with another. Then, too, a device which in the earlier stages of the artist's career could be completely summed up in the term *conventional* or *traditional* could, at times, now be put into innovative roles. In such a poem as **"Beverly Hills, Chicago,"** for example, the very precision of a syntax based upon the simple declarative sentence drives home the tension of the rest of the structures: "It is only natural, however, that it should occur to us /

How much more fortunate they [the rich] are than we are." (pp. 95-6)

In *The Bean Eaters* (1960) and certain of the new poems of *Selected Poems* (1963), developments in style, for the most part, are responses to experimentations with loosened forms and the mileage one can gain from very simple statements. In *Annie Allen* Brooks had loosened up the form of the sonnet in **"The Rites for Cousin Vit,"** with the use of elliptical syntax, the pressures of colloquial speech, and the cumulative capacity of all the poetic devices to create the impact of hyperbole. Cousin Vit was simply too vital to have died; thus Brooks interjects into the language of the sonnet the idiomatic swing and sensuality of the street: that Vit continued to do "the snake-hips with a hiss . . . ." In *The Bean Eaters* she again loosened up sonnet form in **"A Lovely Love"** by adapting the Petrarchan rhyme scheme to the situation of the tenement lovers, intermingling short and long complete statements with elliptical ones, and managing a nervous rhythm which imposes the illusion of being a one-to-one imitation of the behavior of the lovers. The diction of the poem is a mixture of the romantic ("hyacinth darkness"), the realistic ("Let it be stairways, and a splintery box"), and the mythically religious ("birthright of our lovely love / In swaddling clothes. Not like that Other one"). Although the elliptical structures are more numerous and informal in **"Cousin Vit, "** the rhythm of **"A Lovely Love"** seems to make that poem the more complex achievement.

Another technical development is the poet's bolder movement into a free verse appropriate to the situation which she sometimes dots with rhyme. The technique will be more noticeable and surer in its achievement in the next volume, *In the Mecca*. But the poem **"A Bronzeville Mother Loiters in Mississippi. Meanwhile, A Mississippi Mother Burns Bacon"** gives the technique full rein, except for the rhyming. The lines frequently move in the rhythms of easygoing conversation or in the loose patterns of stream of consciousness, as the poet portrays the movement from romantic notions to reality in the consciousness of the young white woman over whom a young Black boy (reminiscent of the slain Emmett Till), has been lynched by her husband and his friend. The dramatic situation determines the length of lines, and the statements vary in form; short declarative sentences, simple sentences, phrase units understandable from their ties to preceding sentences, and long, complex structures. Additional sources of rhythm are repetition, parallel structures, and alliteration.

One of the more interesting techniques of the poem is that of playing romantic diction against the realistic. Thus a stanza containing such terms as "milk-white maid," "Dark Villain," "Fine Prince" and "Happiness-Ever-After" precedes one containing the following lines:

Her bacon burned. She
Hastened to hide it in the step-on can, and
Drew more strips from the meat case. The eggs
   and sourmilk biscuits
Did well.

Two new poems in *Selected Poems,* "To Be in Love" and "Big Bessie Throws Her Son into the Street," have lines and a use of rhyme closer to the method of the poems in *In the Mecca* in their tautness. "To Be in Love," a portrait of that state of being, leans as close as possible to direct statement. "To be in love / Is to touch things with a lighter hand." The next one-line stanza: "In yourself you stretch, you are well." Rhymes then dot several areas of the poem and, near the end, combine with more complex diction to provide the emotional climax. "Big Bessie," a portrait of a mother encouraging her son to seize his independence, has similar strategies, although it is less realistic and moves toward the impressionistic. (pp. 96-7)

In the Mecca is comprised of the poem "In the Mecca" and several under the heading "After Mecca." The long poem "In the Mecca" has for setting a famous Chicago apartment building, half a block long, located between State and Dearborn streets, one block north of Thirty-fourth Street. The title poem in the company of the others marks Brooks' turn from Christianity and the hope of integration to that of nationalism. Obviously the situation means that motives different from those of the preceding works will place at the foreground the necessity for new stylistic developments. The language must emphasize Blacks developing common bonds with each other instead of the traditional "people are people" bonding. For a poet who has so intensively devoted herself to language, the situation means a turn to ways of touching deeply an audience not greatly initiated into the complexity of modern poetry and yet retaining a highly disciplined use of language. The challenge would seem all the greater since to acquire such brilliant command over so wide a range of poetic devices as Brooks had done over the years was also to build a set of reflexes in consciousness which, one would think, would weight the balance toward complex rendering. (pp. 97-8)

[*In the Mecca*] represents, on the one hand, the poet at the very height of her command and utilization of complex renderings. On the other, it represents change of concern and expansion of the use of free verse. Actually, the poem "In the Mecca" required complex resources and rendering. Its unifying story line is simple. Mrs. Sallie, a domestic worker, returns from work to find that she has lost her courageous battle to support and rear nine "fatherless" children. Her missing child Pepita, who seemed, at first, astray in the slum-blasted building, turns out to have been murdered and hidden under the bed of the mentally twisted murderer. However, the total story is complex: the rendering of the Mecca universe and what is happening to the holiness of the souls of nearly thirty people, if one counts only those characterized either by extended treatment or by the single incisive line or phrase. Obviously, all the re-

sources the poet had accumulated over the years were needed.

The older stylistic resources seem, at times, to have received further growth. Mrs. Sallie leaves the repressive environment of her employer: "Infirm booms / and suns that have not spoken die behind this / low-brown butterball." The imagery, strategic repetitions, ritualized and moralizing lines—some of which are rhymed for special emphasis—give further revelation of Mrs. Sallie's strength, complex responses, and dogged determination. Imagery and unusual conjunctions of words make each child memorable and his or her situation haunting. Yvonne of "bald innocence and gentle fright," the "undaunted," once "pushed her thumbs into the eyes of a thief." Though given a touch of irony, her love story has something of the direct style of the poem "To Be in Love." (pp. 98-9)

The language usage extends from the realistic to the expressionistic, from actual speech tones to formal eloquence. It is a language which must extend itself to engage the balked struggle and melancholy defeat of Mrs. Sallie; the embattled but tough innocence of the children; the vanities, frustrations, insanity, futility, and ruthlessness of certain characters—and the pathos of others; and, finally, the desperation, philosophies, and intellectual reaches of the young hero intellectuals seeking a way out. It also is a language which unites the disinherited of the Mecca Building with the disinherited across the universe. (p. 99)

[The] wide range of achievement in free verse is further tested by the varied functions it was required to serve in the remaining poems of the book. The function of "In the Mecca" was to continue deep definition, to lay bare, and to foreshadow. Though it contains rage, its central emotion is compassion, and Mrs. Sallie is bound within a traditional mode of responding and does not undergo a change of consciousness. Except for "To a Winter Squirrel," the succeeding poems are largely about new consciousness and the raw materials of the Black community. "The Chicago Picasso" is technically outside such a conclusion judged in its own right, but it is also present to highlight the communal celebration represented by "The Wall," since it represents individualism and conventional universalism.

The two sermons on the warpland represent the high point in the poet's struggle to move to the center of the Black struggle, with the first urging the building of solid bases for unity and communion and the second urging Blacks to bear up under the pains of the struggle and to "Live! / and have your blooming in the noise of the whirlwind." Parts I, III, and IV seem the more effective, since their style better combines the abstract and the concrete and their language moves more easily between the areas of formal eloquence and the colloquial. Effective poems addressing the communal concerns of Blacks are also in the pamphlet *Riot* (1969).... [The directness of "Riot"] and, above all, its satire regarding the privileged John Cabot are effective when read to a

Brooks at work.

Black audience. The satiric approach was both an older device of Brooks' and a feature of the new movement. The last poem, **"An Aspect of Love, Alive in the Ice and Fire,"** reproduces the directness and simplicity of the earlier **"To Be in Love."**

Gwendolyn Brooks' subsequent poetry has seen the observer of the poems evidence more easily and casually membership in the group. As part of her mission to help inspire the bonding of Blacks to each other, she wished to write poetry which could be appreciated by the person in the tavern who ordinarily did not read poetry. This ambition required some additional emphasis upon simplicity. She had already had the experience of writing prose of poetic intensity in her novel *Maud Martha* (1953) and in the short story **"The Life of Lincoln West."** ... Making minor revisions she was able to rearrange **"The Life of Lincoln West"** in verse lines, and it became the lead-off poem in *Family Pictures* (1970), whose title signified the intimate relationship between the observer-writer and the community. It is the story of a little boy who is disliked because of his pronounced African features and who becomes recon-

ciled to his situation when he learns that he "is the real thing." In style it creates an imagery, a syntax, and a diction which do not press greatly for meanings beyond the requirements of its narrative line and development. It moves close to what the poet would shortly be calling verse journalism in referring to her piece **"In Montgomery,"** in which she evoked the current situation and mood of the survivors and descendants of the Montgomery Bus Boycott. (pp. 100-01)

In the long poem **"In Montgomery,"** ... [Brooks employs] realism but also ranges, extending from direct, prosy statement to a heightening produced by some of the older but simple approaches to diction in poetry.... The poet also clearly evidences the fact that she is visiting Montgomery as a concerned relative, a definite part of the family. In the opening passages she continuously announces her presence.

> My work: to cite in semi-song the
> meaning of Confederacy's Cradle.
> Well, it means to be rocking gently, rocking
> gently!
> In Montgomery is no Race Problem.

257

There is the white decision, the white and pleas-
    ant vow
that the white foot shall not release the black
    neck.

In phrases which serve as structuring devices in parallel form, she continues to present the evidence of her presence, kinship, and role in the historical continuum . . . . (pp. 101-02)

Such poems as those devoted to Lincoln West and to Montgomery display many qualities of post-*In the Mecca* style, and they should be added to from other poems in *Family Pictures, Beckonings,* and *Primer for Blacks* and from new poems as they arrive. Some stylistic qualities can be listed: use of various types of repetition, alliteration, neologisms (crit, creeple, maki-teer), abstract terms gaining depth of meaning from reference to the group's shared experiences, epithets ("whip-stopper," "Treeplanting Man"), variations in expressional patterns usually associated with the simple ballad, ritualistic echoing of childhood-game rhythms and rhyme, gestural words, and simple words forced to yield new meanings from dramatic context. To these one might add the creation of sharp contrasts, and become inclusive by stating that the repertoire involves all the traditional resources provided for simplicity by free verse.

But such a list does not say as much as it seems to, since many of the above devices were already used in the more complex style, and the true distinguishing point is the new combination made of many of them in the later poetry. Under the caption Young Heroes in *Family Pictures* is a poem devoted to a young African poet, **"To Keorapetse Kgositsile (Willie),"** which illustrates the new simplicity and some carry-over of older devices in a somewhat simpler pattern . . . . The poem is an introduction to Kgositsile's book *My Name Is Afrika!,* and concludes simply, "'MY NAME IS AFRIKA / Well, every fella's a Foreign Country. / This Foreign Country speaks to You.'" Certainly, the use of capitals and lower-case expressions, unusual word conjunctions ("pellmelling loneliness," "lenient dignity"), and repetition can be found in the more complex style, but here, for the most part, the usage adapts to the creative capacity of an audience not drilled in poetic conventions.

In the same work, **"To Don at Salaam"** retains simplicity throughout and creates a warm portrait suggestive of disciplined intensity. The first stanza creates a symbolic picture of a person who poises himself easily amid forces that are usually overwhelming, and is notable for depending almost entirely upon monosyllabic words . . . . The third stanza notes his affectionateness, the fourth registers his definiteness in an indefinite world, the fifth brief stanza points to his harmo-niousness and capable action, and the sixth, a one-line stanza, ends simply but dramatically: "I like to see you living in the world." Part of the style is the structuring of stanzas according to function and place in the dramatic whole.

Poems dealing with persons or fraternal situations within the family of Blacks tend to be the more successful, especially those dealing with specific persons. But the sermons and lectures contain effective passages and, frequently, longer and more complex movements. In *Beckonings,* **"Boys, Black"** admonishes the boys to develop health, proper Blackness, and sanity, in their approach to existence, and urges heroic struggle.

The dramatic opening gives a sense of the positive direction suggested by the poem, and is noteworthy for drawing images and figures made simple by having been first validated by traditional usage . . . . The poem also gives an example of a distinctive use of repetition in the first line, and, in the first and second lines, the creative use of alliteration. As it proceeds, it accumulates an in-group set of references. Aside from such expressions as the opening one and the second address ("boys, young brothers, young brothers"), there is the stanza offering caution:

> Beware
> the easy griefs.
> It is too easy to cry "ATTICA"
> and shock thy street,
> and purse thy mouth,
> and go home to "Gunsmoke." Boys,
> black boys,
> beware the easy griefs
> that fool and fuel nothing.

The ending is one of love and faith and admonition: "Make of my Faith an engine / Make of my Faith / a Black Star. I am Beckoning." Much revised and addressed to Blacks in general, **"Boys, Black"** appears in a new collection of poems entitled *To Disembark* . . . . (pp. 101-04)

With the publishing of *To Disembark* it is apparent that Gwendolyn Brooks' change in outlook and consciousness has crystallized in an altered and distinctive style that offers the virtues of its own personality without denying its kinship with an earlier one. Most dramatic are the speaker's position in the center of her kinship group and the warmth and urgency of her speech. As indicated, the tendency of the language is toward a new simplicity. It can be seen in poems which, on the surface, remain very close to a traditional style of poetic realism but always evidence the fact that they proceed from an artist who is choosing from a wide range of resources. It can be seen in poems which will still, in particular passages, place language under great strain. Such patterns create also a recognizably new voice in the poetry. Thus the always-journeying poet sets the example of doing what she asks of others in the new poem **"To the Diaspora."**

> Here is some sun. Some.
> Now off into the places rough to reach.
> Though dry, though drowsy, all unwillingly a-
>   wobble,
> into the dissonant and dangerous crescendo.

Your work, that was done, to be done to be done
   to be
done.

(pp. 104-05)

George Kent, "Gwendolyn Brooks' Poetic Realism: A Developmental Survey," in Black Women Writers (1950-1980): A Critical Evaluation, *edited by Mari Evans, Anchor Press/Doubleday, 1984, pp. 88-105.*

Gary Smith (essay date 1983)

[*In the following excerpt, Smith, a critic and poet, examines* A Street in Bronzeville.]

The critical reception of *A Street in Bronzeville* contained, in embryo, many of the central issues in the scholarly debate that continues to engage Brooks's poetry. As in the following quotation from *The New York Times Book Review,* most reviewers were able to recognize Brooks's versatility and craft as a poet:

> If the idiom is colloquial, the language is universal. Brooks commands both the colloquial and more austere rhythms. She can vary manner and tone. In form, she demonstrates a wide range: quatrains, free verse, ballads, and sonnets—all appropriately controlled. The longer line suits her better than the short, but she is not verbose. In some of the sonnets, she uses an abruptness of address that is highly individual.

Yet, while noting her stylistic successes, not many critics fully understood her achievement in her first book. This difficulty was not only characteristic of critics who examined the formal aspects of prosody in her work, but also of critics who addressed themselves to the social realism in her poetry. Moreover, what Brooks gained at the hands of critics who focused on her technique, she lost to critics who chose to emphasize the exotic, Negro features of the book....

The poems in *A Street in Bronzeville* actually served notice that Brooks had learned her craft well enough to combine successfully themes and styles from both the Harlem Renaissance and Modernist poetry. She even achieves some of her more interesting effects in the book by parodying the two traditions. She juggles the pessimism of Modernist poetry with the general optimism of the Harlem Renaissance. (p. 35)

Because of the affinities *A Street in Bronzeville* shares with Modernist poetry and the Harlem Renaissance, Brooks was initiated not only into the vanguard of American literature, but also into what had been the inner circle of Harlem writers. Two of the Renaissance's leading poets, Claude McKay and Countee Cullen, addressed letters to her to mark the publication of *A Street in Bronzeville.* McKay welcomed her into a dubious but potentially rewarding career:

> I want to congratulate you again on the publication of *A Street in Bronzeville* and welcome you among the band of hard working poets who do have something to say. It is a pretty rough road we have to travel, but I suppose much compensation is derived from the joy of being able to sing. Yours sincerely, Claude McKay. (October 10, 1945.)

Cullen pinpointed her dual place in American literature:

> I have just finished reading *A Street in Bronzeville* and want you to know that I enjoyed it thoroughly. There can be no doubt that you are a poet, a good one, with every indication of becoming a better. I am glad to be able to say 'welcome' to you to that too small group of Negro poets, and to the larger group of American ones. No one can deny you your place there. (August 24, 1945.)

The immediate interest in these letters is how both poets touch upon the nerve ends of the critical debate that surrounded *A Street in Bronzeville.* For McKay, while Brooks has "something to say," she can also "sing"; and for Cullen, she belongs not only to the minority of Negro poets, but also to the majority of American ones. Nonetheless, the critical question for both poets might well have been Brooks's relationship to the Harlem Renaissance. What had she absorbed of the important tenets of the Black aesthetic as expressed during the New Negro Movement? And how had she addressed herself, as a poet, to the literary movement's assertion of the folk and African culture, and its promotion of the arts as the agent to define racial integrity and to fuse racial harmony?

Aside from its historical importance, the Harlem Renaissance—as a literary movement—is rather difficult to define.... Likewise, the general description of the movement as a Harlem Renaissance is often questioned, since most of the major writers, with the notable exceptions of Hughes and Cullen, actually did not live and work in Harlem. Finally, many of the themes and literary conventions defy definition in terms of what was and what was not a New Negro poet. Nonetheless, there was a common ground of purpose and meaning in the works of the individual writers that permits a broad definition of the spirit and intent of the Harlem Renaissance. Indeed, the New Negro poets expressed a deep pride in being Black; they found reasons for this pride in ethnic identity and heritage; and they shared a common faith in the fine arts as a means of defining and reinforcing racial pride. But in the literal expression of these artistic impulses, the poets were either romantics or realists and, quite often within a single poem, both. The realistic impulse, as defined best in the poems of McKay's *Harlem Shadows,* was a sober reflection upon Blacks as second class citizens, segregated from the mainstream of American socio-economic life, and largely unable to realize the wealth and opportunity that America promised. The romantic impulse, on the other hand, as defined in the poems of Sterling Brown's *Southern Road* (1932), often found these unrealized dreams in the collective strength and will of the folk masses. In comparing the poems in *A Street in Bronzeville* with various poems from the Renaissance, it becomes apparent that Brooks agrees, for the most part, with their prescriptions for the New Negro. Yet the unique contributions she brings to bear upon this tradition are extensive: 1) the biting ironies of intraracial discrimination, 2) the devaluation of love in heterosexual relationships between Blacks, and 3) the primacy of suffering in the lives of poor Black women.

The first clue that *A Street in Bronzeville* was, at the time of its publication, unlike any other book of poems by a Black American is its insistent emphasis on demystifying romantic love between Black men and women. The **"old marrieds"**, the first couple encountered on the walking tour of Bronzeville, are nothing like the youthful archetype that the Renaissance poets often portrayed:

> But in the crowding darkness not a word did they
>   say,
> Though the pretty-coated birds had piped so
>   lightly all the day.
> And he had seen the lovers in the little side-
>   streets.
> And she had heard the morning stories clogged
>   with sweets.
> It was quite a time for loving. It was midnight. It
>   was May.
> But in the crowding darkness not a word did they
>   say.

In this short, introductory poem, Brooks, in a manner reminiscent of Eliot's alienated *Waste Land* characters, looks not toward a glorified African past or limitless future, but rather at a stifled present. Her old lovers ponder not an image of their racial past or some symbolized possibility of self-renewal, but rather the overwhelming question of what to do in the here-and-now. Moreover, their world, circumscribed by the incantatory line that opens and closes the poem, "But in the crowding darkness not a word did they say," is one that is distinctly at odds with their lives. They move timidly through the crowded darkness of their neighborhood largely ignorant of the season, "May," the lateness of the hour, "midnight," and a particular *raison d'etre,* "a time for loving." Their attention, we infer, centers upon the implicit need to escape any peril that might consume what remains of their lives. The tempered optimism in the poem, as the title indicates, is the fact that they are "old-marrieds": a social designation that suggests the longevity of their lives and the solidity of their marital bond in what is, otherwise, an ephemeral world of change. Indeed, as the prefatory poem in *A Street in Bronzeville,* the **"old marrieds,"** on the whole, debunks one of the prevalent motifs of Harlem Renaissance poetry: its general optimism about the future.

As much as the Harlem Renaissance was noted for its optimism, an important corollary motif was that of ethnic or racial pride. This pride—often thought a reaction to the minstrel stereotypes in the Dunbar tradition—usually focused with romantic idealization upon the Black woman. (pp. 36-8)

In *A Street in Bronzeville,* this romantic impulse for idealizing the Black woman runs headlong into the biting ironies of intraracial discrimination. In poem after poem in *A Street in Bronzeville,* within the well-observed caste lines of skin color, the consequences of dark pigmentation are revealed in drastic terms. One of the more popular of these poems, **"The Ballad of Chocolate Mabbie,"** explores the tragic ordeal of Mabbie, the Black female heroine, who is victimized by her dark skin and her "saucily bold" lover, Willie Boone. . . . Mabbie's life, of course, is one of unrelieved monotony; her social contacts are limited to those who, like her, are dark skinned, rather than "lemon-hued" or light skinned. But as Brooks makes clear, the larger tragedy of Mabbie's life is the human potential that is squandered:

> Oh, warm is the waiting for joys, my dears!
> And it cannot be too long.
> O, pity the little poor chocolate lips
> That carry the bubble of song!

But if Mabbie is Brooks's parodic victim of romantic love, her counterpart in **"Ballad of Pearl May Lee"** realizes a measure of sweet revenge. In outline, Brooks's poem is reminiscent of Cullen's *The Ballad of the Brown Girl* (1927). There are, however, several important differences. The first is the poem's narrative structure: Pearl May Lee is betrayed in her love for a Black man who "couldn't abide dark meat," who subsequently makes love to a white girl and is lynched for his crime of passion, whereas Cullen's "Brown Girl" is betrayed in her love for a white man, Lord Thomas, who violated explicit social taboo by marrying her rather than Fair London, a white girl. Moreover, Cullen's poem, "a ballad retold," is traditional in its approach to the ballad form . . . . Brooks's ballad, on the other hand, dispenses with the rhetorical invocation of the traditional ballad and begins *in medias res:*

> Then off they took you, off to the jail,
> A hundred hooting after.
> And you should have heard me at my house.
> I cut my lungs with my laughter,
>   Laughter,
>   Laughter.
> I cut my lungs with my laughter.

This mocking tone is sustained throughout the poem, even as Sammy, Pearl May Lee's lover, is lynched:

> You paid for your dinner, Sammy boy,
> And you didn't pay with money.
> You paid with your hide and my heart, Sammy
>   boy,
> For your taste of pink and white honey,
>   Honey,
>   Honey,
> For your taste of pink and white honey.

Here, one possible motif in the poem is the price that Pearl May Lee pays for her measure of sweet revenge: the diminution of her own capacity to express love and compassion for another—however ill-fated—human being. But the element of realism that Brooks injects into her ballad by showing Pearl May Lee's mocking detachment from her lover's fate is a conscious effort to devalue the romantic idealization of Black love. Furthermore, Pearl May Lee's macabre humor undermines the racial pride and harmony that was an important tenet in the Renaissance prescription for the New Negro. And, lastly, Pearl May Lee's predicament belies the social myth of the Black woman as *objective correlative* of the Renaissance's romanticism. (pp. 39-41)

For Brooks, unlike the Renaissance poets, the victimization of poor Black women becomes not simply a minor chord but a predominant theme of *A Street in Bronzeville.* Few, if any, of her female characters are able to free themselves from the web of poverty and racism that threatens to strangle their lives. The Black heroine in **"obituary for a living lady"** was "decently wild / As a child," but as a victim of society's hypocritical, puritan standards, she "fell in love with a man who didn't know / That even if she wouldn't let him touch her breasts she / was still worth his hours." In another example of the complex life-choices confronting Brooks's women, the two sisters of **"Sadie and Maude"** must choose between death-in-life and life-in-death. Maude, who went to college, becomes a "thin brown mouse," presumably resigned to spinsterhood, "living all alone / In this old house," while Sadie who "scraped life / With a fine-tooth comb" bears two illegitimate children and dies, leaving as a heritage for her children her "fine-tooth comb." What is noticeable in the lives of these Black women is a mutual identity that is inextricably linked with race and poverty. (pp. 43-4)

Brooks's relationship with the Harlem Renaissance poets, as *A Street in Bronzeville* ably demonstrates, was hardly imitative. As one of the important links with the Black poetic tradition of the 1920s and 1930s, she enlarged the element of realism that was an important part of the Renaissance world-view. Although her poetry is often conditioned by the optimism that was also a legacy of the period, Brooks rejects outright their romantic prescriptions for the lives of Black women. And in this regard, she serves as a vital link with the Black Arts Movement of the 1960s that, while it witnessed the flowering of Black women as poets and social activists as well as the rise of Black feminist aesthetics in the 1970s, brought about a curious revival of romanticism in the Renaissance mode.

However, since the publication of *A Street in Bronzeville,* Brooks has not eschewed the traditional roles and values of Black women in American society; on the contrary, in her subsequent works, *Annie Allen* (1949), *The Bean Eaters* (1960), and *The Mecca* (1968), she has been remarkably consistent in identifying the root cause of intraracial problems within the Black community as white racism and its pervasive socio-economic effects. Furthermore, as one of the chief voices of the Black Arts Movement, she has developed a social version, in such works as *Riot* (1969), *Family Pictures* (1970), and *Beckonings* (1975), that describes Black women and men

as equally integral parts of the struggle for social and economic justice. (p. 45)

Gary Smith, "Gwendolyn Brooks's 'A Street in Bronzeville', the Harlem Renaissance and the Mythologies of Black Women," in MELUS, *Vol. 10, No. 3, Fall, 1983, pp. 33-46.*

D. H. Melhem (essay date 1987)

[*Melhem is the author of the 1987 study* Gwendolyn Brooks: Poetry and the Heroic Voice. *Brooks noted her approval of this work in a 1989 interview. "She was meticulous," Brooks said of Melhem. "She went through everything with me for years, ten years or more. But even there I was rather sorry that that tack was taken—that 'here is this lost little lorn thing, and she has not had much attention.'...I have really had a lot of attention from the time that my first book came out in '45." In the following excerpt from this study, Melhem discusses Brooks's poetry and her influence as a poet.*]

In contemporary poetry, the world of the poem is often conceived as a beleaguered fortress against the real world; to enter one is to depart from the other. This limits the material of reality for the work and requires a choice between the two as means or end. Whether weighted toward solipsism or manipulation, the tendency results in an exclusive poetry, usually offered with matching poetics and criticism. The art of Gwendolyn Brooks makes no such dichotomy. It includes the world, its poetic emblems, and us. We are not merely to be ranked and shaped with the raw data of existence. We matter, in the vital properties of our thought, feeling, growth, and change, so that the poem becomes an interaction in a mutual process, socially resonant. (p. 236)

[Brooks's] work cries out against the subjugation of blacks, which may have inflicted more physical than spiritual damage, while it has hurt whites spiritually. Brooks embodies caritas, expressed in the poetic voice as it articulates a racial and communal vision. Hers is a unified sensibility, pragmatic and idealistic, shaped, in part, by the needs which it ventures to meet. This kind of artistic courage, risking "the highest falls," is shown by a poet of the first rank, a major poet.

Brooks meets the criteria for major status on all four levels: craft and technique; scope or breadth; influence of the work in style, content, or productivity, upon others; and influence of the poet upon others. Technically, we have examined her mastery of form and cultivation of new and renewed forms. She has extended language itself, as Whitman did, by imaginative compounding, word-coinage, and use of black English vernacular. She belongs to that select category Pound called "the inventors," the highest classification of poets who create and expand formal limits and, thereby, taste itself. Development toward a genre of contemporary heroic poetry, offering distinctive style and language, may be considered Brooks's outstanding achievement. Various types of heroic, exemplified by several other black poets, are examined elsewhere. Yet Brooks's heroic, direct though subtle, comprehensive in sensibility and range, whether "grand" or "plain," socially responsive and evangelically fused, makes her work a paradigm of the genre. The unique authority with which she speaks to her people is based in mutual affection and esteem and a historically viable sense of kinship. Her call to Black pride, even when chiding or dismayed, has a familial intimacy. This kind of rapport hovered over the Fireside Poets who supported the Union during the Civil War. For the earlier tradition of literature in English, the configuration is Miltonic and Romantic, the poet as artist and activist. For the native tradition of the American and African American folk preacher, it is sermonic and communal.

A further complex of antecedence has been suggested: the Homeric bard, the Anglo-Saxon scop, the African griot, the balladeer. We have noted Black roots in African and African American culture: religion, religious and secular music (the latter emphasizing blues

Brooks with her husband and son.

and jazz), language, and the legacy of oral tales and verbal artistry. Yet even here, we have chiefly studied formal intersection with content: visual, aural, semantic, and psycholinguistic elements that absorb and transcend boundaries of time and place. At what point or line do we separate blues from ballad? Where do we locate the ancestral balladeer: in Britain? New Orleans? Harlem? When does gut become "the slipping string" of a Stradivarius? And what of the sonnet—when it becomes a "sonnet-ballad"? Can we usefully ghettoize our cultural traditions?... Brooks is now. "Bees in the stomach, sweat across the brow. Now." She *is* our multiethnic, multiracial American artistic heritage. (pp. 237-38)

While examining Brooks's heroic style in terms of "contemporary fact," the background of African and African American culture, and the British and American poetic tradition(s), we should also bear in mind its relation to the American democratic impulse. Brooks's work, like that of the entire genre, shares idealistic strains of the culture, notable, for example, in the early Emerson and Whitman, and in Thoreau. Observe the continuity with Whitman, who wrote in 1888: "One main genesis-motive of the 'Leaves' was my conviction (just as strong to-day as ever) that the crowning growth of the United States is to be spiritual and heroic." The words call our subject, her art infused with the historic, communal quest for emancipation and leadership.

Brooks participates in the Black Rebellion, identified by [historian Lerone Bennett, Jr.] as "one of the longest and most varied upheavals by black people in the twentieth century." Her life and work illustrate his claim that "Blackness is the real repository of values Euro-Americans proclaimed and never lived," or—in the word rightly popular among blacks—repository of the American *soul.* Beyond Blackness, therefore, and the growing sense of a pan-African heritage, we arrive at spirituality, emphasized by Du Bois and more recently by Chancellor Williams. Speaking of Africa, the latter notes:

> our land, rather than any other land, was called the *spiritual* land, the land of the Gods by the non-African world.... So that we have been a very religious people, a very humble people. What reason for it overall is kind of difficult to understand because the same religion—which is an admirable quality, in our world—turned out to be that by which we were victimized.

Brooks's ambivalence toward Christianity stems partly from its very compatibility with the African tradition of humility and acceptance. One recalls Whitman's apt prediction: "There will be soon no more priests. Their work is done...the gangs of kosmos and prophets en masse shall take their place."

It is Brooks's fundamental humanism that prevents her from being trapped either in the Victorian conflict between religion and science or in the twentieth-century dilemma of reconciling spirit, idealism, and optimism with science, determinism, and pessimism. For Brooks, ideals are the given of existence, whether or not supernaturally endowed, and the task is to create a humane society in the benign image of an extended family. She is sophisticated enough to understand the vicissitudes of progress, and determined enough not to submit to a weary pessimism. Her gentle, amused mien accompanies a fervent seriousness. The prophetic role, once assumed, is not to be put aside. In periods of confusion or disintegration, it orders vision. Since the prophet traditionally expects little or no honor in his or her own country, neither appreciation nor recognition are prerequisites for the task.

Perhaps Gwendolyn Brooks's most important contribution to the philosophy of literature is the challenge of her work to the cul-de-sac of the antiheroic ironic mode, as defined by Northrop Frye, retaining its intellectual virtues while moving toward reentry into the mythic/heroic. In this process, she also gathers historical strands of romantic and mimetic or realistic modes along with the ironic, into the heroic abode of epic genre. Frye's definition of epic is useful here. He writes, "The function of the epic, in its origin, seems to be primarily to teach the nation, or whatever we call the social unit which the poet is addressing, its own traditions." Madhubuti perceptively refers to *In the Mecca* as Brooks's "epic of black humanity." (pp. 239-40)

Brooks has not codified her transition to heroic as an "Adamic" celebration of the individual, to use the terminology of Roy Harvey Pearce. In his useful study, Pearce distinguishes an Adamic mode, embodied in Whitman and culminating in Stevens, and a mythic mode, also historically continuous, realized in Eliot. It would seem, however, that the political impulse of Whitman is distant from Stevens's detachment. Brooks is Whitmanic in a way she cannot be Stevensian. Faith in self, projected nationally, politicizes awareness. This diverges radically from poetic faith as a commitment to art, ultimately one's own. Nor can she be Eliotic, with a mythos based on stabilizing a society that she is bent upon altering. In her quest of heroic and its prosody, Brooks transforms the aristocratic concept of the hero or heroine from the conventional status of super-being—as Frye accepts the perspective for his heroic/mythic historical mode—toward redemption of that which is more compatible with the Judeo-Christian tradition of humble origins of beauty and power.

The creative by-product of Brooks's local and national efforts has been to encourage the making of poems. She has personally established a prodigious number of prizes and awards for poetry, funded student trips to Africa, anthologized, subsidized, and promoted student work. Her readings and workshops, undertaken on regular, cross-country travels, convey her to prisons and reformatories, as well as to schools, universities, and other environments. Whether journeying or at home in Chicago, she communicates the drama of current affairs with a concern that begins in the spirit. Her faithful representations of black experience define the nature of its white context. She enriches both black and white cultures by revealing essential life, its universal identities, and the challenge it poses to a society beset with corruption and decay.

Beyond critical analysis, we decide that we like a work, or we don't; we like a poet, or not. We care about the poetry of Gwendolyn Brooks in great measure because it cares about us and the existence we share. It does not lose us in a labyrinthine psyche, or make us claustrophobic to get out of life, or tax our patience with chronic self-pity. Its warmth is more immediate, for the most part, than that of Eliot, Pound, Williams, or Stevens. A social act, it hones an art of utility and beauty, at home in the world.... Its human terrain recalls John Dewey's observation that Williams found so compelling: "The local is the only universal, upon that all art builds." At the same time, Brooks's travels, her span of interests and enterprise, give her work a cosmopolitan breadth. She contributes a beauty of wholeness, of a fully articulated human being whose compassionate intelligence, wit and humor and anger transcend their tragic awareness.

It is especially just that Brooks's familial perspective on the Black Nation renders her animating quality. As we read her poems, we feel their indivisible affection, their cohering power. Acknowledging them, "an essential sanity, black and electric," we recognize a national resource, needed now. (pp. 240-42)

> *D. H. Melhem, in her* Gwendolyn Brooks: Poetry and the Heroic Voice, *The University Press of Kentucky, 1987, 270 p.*

Norris B. Clark (essay date 1987)

[*In the following excerpt, Clark traces the evolution of a unique concept of a black aesthetic in Brooks's volumes of poetry.*]

The evolution of the poetry of Gwendolyn Brooks from an egocentric orientation to an ethnocentric one is directly related to her advocacy of a black aesthetic and to the shifting aesthetic criteria in modern America. "For one thing, the whole concept of what 'good poetry' is is changing today, thank goodness... I'm just a black poet, and I write about what I see, what interests me, and I'm seeing new things."

Although she has always written poetry concerned with the black American experience, one that inheres the diversity and complexity of being black and especially being female, her poetics have primarily undergone thematic developments. Her emphasis has shifted from a private, internal, and exclusive assessment of the identity crises of twentieth-century persons to a communal, external, and inclusive assessment of the black communal experience. That change not only corresponds to the fluctuating social, political, and ideological positions of the national black American communities during the sixties and seventies, but it also correlates with the evolution of aesthetic humanism's fundamental concerns about the nature of reality, our relationship to it and its vast variety. (pp. 83-4)

Brooks's latest poetry, *Riot* (1969), *Family Pictures* (1970), *Aloneness* (1971), and *Beckonings* (1975), clearly incorporates a pronounced humanistic concern for a collective black America as well as accepting a black aesthetic ideology in terms of aesthetic relativism. Her transitional text *In the Mecca* (1968) clearly advocates and represents a turning point in her conception of art and of a black aesthetic, an artistic position in which she continues to use language as "our most faithful and indispensable picture of human experiences, of the world and its events, of thoughts and life . . . ." It is a position that remains attentive to the needs and the energetic struggle of the oppressed, as all writers of a black aesthetic persuasion maintain.

Gwendolyn Brooks's poetry, as black aestheticians have advocated, has always been committed to depicting the "simple" lives of black Americans in the medium of black language, black rituals, black experiences; it has always been reflective of the multiple values inherent in the black community. Brooks's earliest poetry, for which she is most noted in academia, *A Street in Bronzeville* (1945), *Annie Allen* (1949), *The Bean Eaters* (1960), and *Selected Poems* (1963), equally depicts, as does her latest poetry, the basic uncertainty of black people living amid the physical turbulence and psychic tensions of American society—the whirlwind of stasis within flux of twentieth-century America. One merely needs to look at Brooks's **"The Sundays of Satin-Legs Smith"** or **"Gay Chaps at the Bar"** to see her concern for the dilemma of the oppressed minorities' identity struggle. (pp. 84-5)

Critics suggest that Brooks's poetry, whether an extension of herself as an artist or as a black artist, can be divided into three groups: (1) *A Street in Bronzeville* and *Annie Allen,* primarily devoted to craft and exhibit an "objective and exquisite detachment" from the lives or emotions of individuals; (2) *The Bean Eaters, Selected Poems,* and *In the Mecca,* also devoted to craft but exhibit a strong awareness of black social concerns; and (3) *Riot, Family Pictures, Aloneness,* and *Beckonings,* less devoted to craft and more concerned about pronounced statements on a black mystique, the necessity of riots (violence), and black unity. Those categories can also be characterized in political language as traditional, prerevolutionary, and revolutionary; or in the language of sociologists as accommodationists, integrationists, and black nationalists; or in racial language as white, colored, and black. Regardless of how one chooses to classify Brooks's poetry, if one must, her corpus remains as an undeniable statement about the condition humane. More precisely, it is a statement about the myriad black American experiences as it communicates the feeling of brotherhood and love. In each phase, arbitrarily defined or not, Brooks has clearly been committed to, as black aesthetic advocates desire, black people.

Although the central theme of Gwendolyn Brooks's poems does not essentially change—to reveal the black person's presence and participation in the complexities of life—as her changing sensibility about the objectives of art evolves, the formal poetic techniques used to create art "to mean something, [that] will be something that a reader may touch" remain "technically proficient." A different emphasis between the thematic content of her earlier poems—self, motherhood, tenements, war heroes, racial ambivalence, joblessness, pretensions, poverty, religion—and her later "black" poems—a black aesthetic, black unity, black consciousness, contemporary black heroes, overt racism, riots—is noticeable. Yet, her poetry still continues to characterize not only the subtleties of racial tensions and to exhibit an intense and brilliant craftsmanship, a propriety of language in ordinary speech, but it also maintains the traditional reliance on rhetorical devices that elicit ambiguity, irony, paradox, tension and contrast . . . .

It should constantly be remembered that "she knows the ways in which Shakespeare, Spenser, Milton, Donne, Keats, Wordsworth juxtaposed intense emotion . . . creating patterns of pull and push among its elements . . . the ways in which moderns like Pound, Eliot, Yeats and Frost break traditional poetic patterns." Brooks's varied use of the traditional formal elements of poetry: rhyme, meter, couplets, quatrains, sonnet forms, ballad forms, elegies, mock epics, figures of elocution—anaphora, assonance, dissonance, enumeration, gradation, isocola, prolepsis; combined with folk elements derived from the black community: jazz and blues rhythms, black speech patterns (only determined by idiom)—slurred rhymes, slant rhyme, sprung syntax, jarring locution—and black folk heroes give Brooks a distinction as a unique modern black poet. She continuously "dislocates language and molds words into complex patterns of meaning . . . ," as in "fume of pig foot," "wrapped richly, in right linen and right wool," or "careening tinnily down the nights/across my years and arteries." Her formal concerns with poetry—to avoid clichés, to balance modern influences with intuitional phrasing, to unify rhythm with tonal effect, to discover and to create order, to avoid imitation, to use traditional forms as well as nontraditional forms, to use colloquial speech, rhyme, quick rhyme, to "blacken" English—give Gwendolyn Brooks a distinction among the ranks of contemporary modern American writers and among the ranks of most black American writers, especially advocates of a black aesthetic.

Clearly, Brooks's poetic sensibility, as a poet or as a black poet, is both modernist and traditionalist in style, form, language, and theme, rather than political. Not only does she combine in her poetic artifacts the formal, European, and American traditions, but she also infuses them with her point of view, that which any artist must do, and makes them uniquely American, modern, and black. Unlike many of the poets of a black aesthetic ideology, Brooks displays a unique individualism in her work that is devoid of racial polemic or black rhetoric.

Despite her present attentiveness to a black audience and her conscious linguistic strategies, as in **"My Name is Red Hot. Yo Name Ain Doodley Squat,"** she is neither a protest poet nor a practitioner of a popular cultural aesthetic. Whether her poems are of a dramatic nature or a narrative nature as in **"The Boy Died in My Alley"** or **"The Life of Lincoln West,"** respectively, or of song or elegy as in **"Steam Song"** or **"Elegy in a Rainbow,"** respectively, or not associated directly with "blackness" as in **"Horses Graze,"** Brooks remains a poet first, one who expresses her blackness through art. She does not, as Houston Baker suggests, have a white style and black content [see essay dated 1972].

Brooks's continuous use of nontraditional technical elements, black English, or idioms of the street indicate that Brooks's poetic style is not white, rather it is black American—one which incorporates poetic techniques from a dual heritage. One should also keep in mind that some black Americans do not speak in the idiom or linguistic structure of black English. Indeed, W. E. B. Du Bois's assessment of a dual consciousness is what Brooks's poetry has always been about: "this longing to attain self-conscious [person]hood, to merge his double self into a better and truer self. In this merging he wishes neither of the older selves to be lost."

Although Brooks's poetry is modern, American, and black, some critics think her latest poetry has lost its "universality" because it deals with social themes or exhibits a conscious concern for the political, social, and economic circumstances that stultify the lives of black people. One critic, Daniel Jaffee, condescendingly objected to Brooks's definition of her art as black poetry rather than poetry: "The label 'black poetry' cheapens the achievement of Gwendolyn Brooks. It recommends that race matters more than artistic vocation or individual voice." Despite an opinion that Brooks's achievements are cheapened because of race, such critical sensibility points not to the dilemma of her changing concept of poetry, but to the inherent dilemma of artistic evaluations that do not view race as a significant aspect of aesthetic, social, and moral judgments. To uncritically assume that "black" cheapens art denies, a priori, unbiased aesthetic evaluation, artistic integrity to black art forms and the artist, consciously or subconsciously. Moreover, such views minimize the notion that literary style is the bridge that unifies the artistic sensibility, literature, and the cultural environment into a dynamic historical and social experience. It further stigmatizes and stereotypes that which is deliberately, and potentially beautifully, created in an historically accurate and representative manner. In addition, it denies validity to Brooks's black consciousness or poetic voice as well as her magnificent poetic sensibility that has always given credence to race as significant and thus important as thematic material.... (pp. 85-8)

As George Kent suggests, Gwendolyn Brooks's "dilemma" points to the dilemma of all black artists. On the one hand, critics want to acknowledge that artifacts transcend race, while on the other paradoxically empha-

sizing that an art construct tells or shows the reader what it has meant to be a black American. As Brooks has stated, emphasized from *In the Mecca* to *Beckonings,* her art is to be more committed not only to recreating artistically the lives of black people, but also to using technical devices that permit black people to see reflections of themselves and to feel the dynamics of those reflections in her poetry. Brooks's recent artistic sensibility and criteria for art are akin to those to which many advocates of a black aesthetic adhere: to speak as a black, about blacks, to blacks. (p. 88)

Although Brooks's *The Bean Eaters* indicates a thematic change from general themes such as personal aspiration, motherhood, marriage, dreams, isolation, and birth, *In the Mecca* (1968) is Brooks's transitional text. *The Bean Eaters* illustrates that her increased social awareness began with **"A Bronzeville Mother Loiters in Mississippi. Meanwhile a Mississippi Mother Burns Bacon,"** **"The Last Quatrain of the Ballad of Emmett Till,"** and **"The Chicago *Defender* Sends a Man to Little Rock"** or the exquisite and subtle condemnation of racism in sonnet form, **"Gay Chaps at the Bar."** In contrast to those earlier poems, in *In the Mecca* Brooks makes explicit statements about how blacks should think, the ideology of Negritude, a black aesthetic, and black power. In essence, those "political" statements evolve from her reawakened and redirected artistic consciousness and reflect the black cultural milieu of the 1960s and 1970s. Even though there is an emphasis on "blackness," Brooks, importantly, continues to explore the universal qualities—social and psychological—of blacks, as they *survive* in an interracial and intraracial society. *In the Mecca* isn't solely about black nationalism or a black aesthetic; rather, it is primarily a testimony to the undisputed fact that black persons are not curios, that they do have values, that there is dignity among the uncertainties of their lives. *In the Mecca* is actually a tribute to black existence, one that avoids castigating "Whitey" to emphasize liberation of those ordinary lives that blossom and wilt among "hock[s] of ham," "hopes of heresy," "roaches and gray rats." For Brooks as indicated by *In the Mecca,* "Life sits or blazes in this Mecca./And thereby—tenable. /And thereby beautiful."

In the Mecca also clearly indicates, via the character of Don Lee, who "wants a ·new nation...new art and anthem," Brooks's leanings toward a black aesthetic as suggested by Haki Madhubuti (Don L. Lee), whom Brooks regarded as a stimulus for a new renaissance. Yet the true significance of *In the Mecca* is not so much Brooks's advocacy of a black aesthetic or Alfred's ability to finally act (rebel) or Pepita's ignoble death—"a little woman lies in dust with roaches." The true aesthetic significance, thematically, is that the black lives, whether Way-out Morgan's, Alfred's, Darkara's, or Pepita's, are meaningful and reflect an "ultimate reality" in formal juxtaposition to expectations. It symbolically represents the existential dilemma of twentieth-century humankind—the province of art and especially the province of "black art." People living or dying in the

Mecca exhibit the existential tensions confronting any people with human limitations and possibility. That epic poem reflects our madness, our helplessness, our pain and feelings of rejection. It represents the universal nature of oppression, self-imposed or externally imposed. Not to know and cherish the tragedy of our own lives is not to know the joy of being here.

Gwendolyn Brooks's later poetry after *In the Mecca* also does not only reflect a specific black aesthetic in which all black persons are "beauti-ful"; rather her art, from advocating militant resistance in **"Riders to the Blood-Red Wrath"** (1963) to wishing "jewels of black love" in **"A Black Wedding Song,"** thematically suggests a range of "ways"—"The Ways of the Mecca are in this Wise"—in which blacks can, should, and do respond to oppression. Although there is a stronger sense of a black nationalist perspective in **"Boys. Black.,"** it is one that extends the black nationalist perspective of action as suggested by Alfred's role in *In the Mecca* rather than scathe white America. Clearly, unlike the poetry of many young black writers of the sixties, especially those whom Arthur P. Davis regards as the poets of "black hate," Brooks's poetry is neither irrational nor propagandistic. She does not use devices such as incendiary polemics, militant slogans, four-letter expletives, fused words, slashed words, or phonetic spellings. Instead there is a clear use of language with some hip talk, some street talk and idiom to make her poetry less "obscurantis" to blacks in an attempt to advocate a sense of communal and individual responsibility for the spiritual and physical death of blacks.... (pp. 89-90)

In essence, Gwendolyn Brooks's thematic concerns, the tense and complex dimensions of living through the paths of petty destinies, have changed but have not eliminated an acceptance of those who choose to live and to love differently. Unlike the more radical black aesthetic poets, she does not condemn the "Intellectual Audience" as Nikki Giovanni has done, or equate Negroes with repulsive beasts as does Welton Smith in "The Nigga Section," or curse white people, as in Carolyn Rodgers's "The Last M. F." Brooks's later works, *Riot, Aloneness, Family Pictures,* and *Beckonings,* instead, emphasize a need for black unity by using "the exile rhythms of a Black people still seeking to establish at-homeness in America," but not to the exclusion of universal themes and subjects such as "brotherly love," literary critics, heroes, music, love between man and woman, false ideals, friendship, beautiful black blues. Nor like the more radical or political black poets of the sixties and early seventies such as Imamu Baraka, Sonia Sanchez, the "radical" phase of Nikki Giovanni, Welton Smith, or other black aesthetic advocates does Brooks create racist, propagandistic, and taciturn poems that advocate violence as therapeutic (Fanon's dictum), exhort whites to bring about equality, castigate or demean others. Instead, she depicts black realities without brutally frank language via her black voice, a voice that emanates a conscious humanistic concern for others. Similar to "great masters," Brooks's poetry does not tell us that there is evil, corruption, oppression,

futility, or racism; rather, she shows us the tragedy and its relationship to individuals in hopes that we may learn a moral insight from the juxtaposition of beauty and horror, death in life as in **"The Life of Lincoln West."**

Brooks's unique voice in her latest poetry is one that not only ideologically varies from a narrowly defined black aesthetic, but also thematically deviates from its total reliance on obscure African references or Africa as a source of inspiration or upon a doctrine of how to live, as in Ron Karenga's Kawaida Doctrine, or a pro-Muslim religious orientation as some black aestheticians advocate:

> Blackness
> is a going to essences and to unifyings.
> "MY NAME IS AFRIKA!"
> Well, every fella's a Foreign Country.
> This Foreign Country speaks to you.

Not surprisingly, Brooks's voice which contrasts the American ideals and practices—W. E. B. Du Bois's "Veil Metaphor"—especially the insensitivity and ignorance of whites toward blacks, as in *Riot,* is not filled with private symbolism or biting satire. Rather, self-identity in Brooks's poems leads to group-identity. She does not, as Baraka has done, only focus on a black nationalist, black Muslim, black power, or blacker-than-black perspective. Rather, her voice is one that recreates the feelings and thoughts of the unheard, as riots do, rather than merely languish in a black aesthetic of polemics devoid of lyricism. Even though Brooks's poetry calls for a black dignity and a black pride, erstwhile symbolized by Africa, she acknowledges that blacks "know so little of that long leap languid land [Africa]" and suggests that enacting "our inward law"— unity (community, family) among black Americans—is more important than any external reliances upon a leader, a god or God(s) or the heat of "easy griefs that fool and fuel nothing." Her attempt to create black unity is not to establish a bond among third-world peoples but to establish a bond between those oppressed black Americans who "are defining their own Roof...." Consequently, her content is not only specifically American but is, more so than many writers of a black aesthetic persuasion, also reflective of the attitudes, aspirations, and concerns of black Americans as they *historically* have been confronted with the denial of American ideals, racism, and pathos of human choice.

Unlike the black writers of polemics and propaganda or the rhetoricians of hate and violence, Brooks doesn't attempt to impose her personal philosophy upon others; she does not demean or denigrate blacks whose psychological mechanism to survive leads them to be "Toms" or race traitors. (In fact, some critics have questioned her attitudes or personal voice as not being strong enough on issues such as abortion.) Brooks's poetry remains one of love and affirmation, one that accepts some hate and perhaps some violence as necessary without condemning or castigating those who have been pawns to interracial and intraracial forces. Adequately reflecting the hopes and aspirations of the black community, Brooks displays a love for her brothers and sisters regardless of psychosocial or socioeconomic position. In doing so, she clearly embraces "blackness" and the values of liberation, and thus the values of all humanity. That quality, despite an emphasis on embracing blacks first, is one that is universal in literature of self-affirmation and self-identity; the universal is revealed through the particular. As her sensitivity to the spirit of social revolution emanates from her sense of "love," Brooks advocates a sense of self-love and compassion while reflecting the tensions of her time period, a tension due to racial oppression: "On the street we smile./We go/in different directions/down the imperturbable street."

Thematically and imagistically, Brooks's poetry after *In the Mecca* reflects a social sensibility that incorporates, as her earlier work has done, especially war poems, the expressive and mimetic aspects of a black experience rather than an arbitrary, political black aesthetic. An art form that has aesthetic qualities related to the black experience should, by definition, incorporate a sense of what it is like to face life's multitude of complexities as a person affected by racial values (Afrocentric and Eurocentric) pertaining to the black communities. Regardless of the ideological or social position the writer has, the genre should render that representation in a manner that is most particular, although not necessarily unique, to an existence as a person confronted with the issues of "blackness." This is not meant to imply that the central theme must be about blackness; rather it is to suggest that the world view that the art conveys, in theme as well as in image and structure, should provide a sense of what it is like to see historically, culturally, and psychologically through the eyes of a black person. The tensions of living as a black person—whether in blackness or whiteness—should be illustrated and discernible. To that end, Brooks's poetry extends. If one considers her multidimensional themes combined with her conscious attempt to fuse the traditional with the colloquial or common, it is evident that Brooks's later poetry is not thematically "more black" than her earlier poetry. Her poetry, despite her diminished reliance upon formal diction, continues to be an expression of her craftsmanship as well as an expression of her black voice as expressed in 1950. "Every Negro poet has 'something to say.' Simply because he is a Negro he cannot escape having important things to say."

The technical proficiency with which Brooks creates those meaningful lives, whether heroic, mock heroic, or parody, is what poetry is about. It is to that specific end, exposing the truth of human existence in forms meaningful to the black community, that Brooks's poetry leads. Despite the extension of Gwendolyn Brooks's poetry to a new black consciousness of the late 1960s and 1970s, her formal devices remain as alive in her later poetry as they are in her earlier poetry. She does continue to pay attention to craft, to the neat turn of phrase: "Now the way of the Mecca was on this wise," "as her underfed haunches jerk jazz," or "In the

precincts of a nightmare all contrary...." She "blackens English": "That Song it sing the sweetness/like a good Song can,...", "Unhalt hands," or uses extensive alliteration: "These merely peer and purr/and pass the passion over." She continues to infuse the traditional standard American English not only with her intuitional phrasing and coinage of words, but also with the "common folk phrasing" as exhibited in songs and folk sermons. In doing so, Brooks's poetry is more reflective of aesthetic relativism while maintaining some elements of traditional "white" culture as in **"Que tu es grossier!"** or **"death in the afternoon."** That relativism related to the black experience can be observed in her use of black folk heroes, or in **"The Wall,"** a poem in which art for art's sake is not a valid concept whereas the wall allows celebration and commitment (i.e., it is communal and functional as "Negritude" advocates). Specific references are made to black literary heroes as in **"Five Men Against the Theme, 'My Name is Red Hot. Yo Name ain Doodley Squat,'"** or musical heroes as in **"Steam Song"** (Al Green) or **"The Young Men Run"** (Melvin Van Peebles). Combined with the sounds and sense of sermons, jazz, blues, and double entendre, these references help to bring ghetto life alive and to enhance the significance of an idea and its "metaphysical function" as in **"Elegy in a Rainbow."** In addition, Brooks continues to exhibit irony, a complex sense of reality, a sensitivity to traditional line and beats, metered as well as in free verse. She juxtaposes lines that appear to move rapidly with those that tend to slow the reader down, as in **"The Boy Died in My Alley."** Furthermore, she uses sudden contrasts or repetition to make each word bear the full measure of weight and suggestion. "I don't want to stop a concern with words doing good jobs...." Whether extravagant overstatement or understatement as in **"A Poem to Peanut,"** all of those elements not only exist in black literature, but have always been a part of Brooks's concept of polishing her technique. (pp. 90-4)

Although the forms of Gwendolyn Brooks's poetry contribute to and enhance an understanding of the content—move it from the simple, mundane, and colloquial to a complex, eternal, and universal—her recent poetry does achieve aesthetic beauty and historical truth. It fails functionally in her terms only. Her latest objective: "I want to write poetry that will appeal to many, many blacks, not just the blacks who go to college but also those who have their customary habitat in taverns and the street...." is not, as she acknowledges, achieved because it doesn't reach those "taverneers." Brooks acknowledges her failure of *Riot*—"It's too meditative"—and *Beckonings* has a dual impulse (a self-analytic commentary on the nature of her own poetry). She also states that only two love poems (songs), **"When you've forgotten Sunday"** and **"Steam Song,"** can be well received in tavern readings. Similar to some of the "Broadside poets," as well as other black writers who desire to write for the black masses—as Walt Whitman and Ralph Waldo Emerson had also advocated—Gwendolyn Brooks falsely assumes that her task is to create art for those who don't appreciate formal art.

Brooks with Jerome Sachs, president of Northeastern Illinois State College in Chicago, where Brooks taught poetry.

As with most poetry, even that which infuses informal folk elements with formal literary elements, undereducated or subeducated persons—those to whom the fourth-to-sixth-grade reading level of newspapers appeals—cannot or choose not to be subjected to it. Rarely do they appreciate the subtlety and interrelationships of finely turned phrases or understand, reflectively or meditatively, the appeal of formal alliteration and repetition to a complex meaning or abstract idea. The unsophisticated generally expresses an emotional understanding or appreciation of rhythm or meter by nodding or tapping his or her foot; the sophisticated generally searches, from an objective distance, for rhetorical and metrical relationships or correlations to history, psychology, religion, or culture. Ironically, it is precisely because Brooks's poetry fails to appeal to the black masses that it appeals aesthetically to the "blacks who go to college" as well as those *littérateurs* who can and will reflect upon the "sound and sense" of a poetic artifact. (p. 95)

The aesthetic success of Gwendolyn Brooks's later poetry, and her sense of its failure, reflects the historical literary dilemma of cognitively and emotively appreciating the truth and beauty of a black experience and art per se. To create art reductively, only for one group, limits the art; to create art without letting it organically or ontologically exist limits the number of persons who have the faculties with which to appreciate it. Formal art can never be truly functional; folk art is always functional. To infuse, as Gwendolyn Brooks has, the informal with the formal, in a medium designed to be formal, subsumes the informal component, especially when it evolves from a self-conscious literary formalism. Thus attempting to reach those in taverns, the origins of some folk traditions, alters and negates the ontological component of art. It necessarily extends it beyond the folk to the formal by making it solely functional in a "literary" sense. What Brooks does with words, forms, and content—not consciously imitating anyone—is the essence of the aesthetic imagination unifying disparate elements into a coherent whole—structurally, semantically, and phonetically. As a spokesperson of the black masses, Brooks is literally different from those for whom she writes; consequently, she is the "seer and the sayer," the Emersonian poet, who articulates the needs, ideas, and aspirations of others. In doing so, she can only create, to make clear in terms she knows and understands, her perception of the raw material. Her quest, then, is to create works of an aesthetic nature and of "black origin"—whether critics appreciate it or not. To do so, as she has, is not "to be content with offering raw materials. The Negro poet's most urgent duty, at present, is to polish his technique, his way of presenting his truths and beauties, that those may be more insinuating, and therefore, more overwhelming." (p. 96)

Norris B. Clark, "Gwendolyn Brooks and a Black Aesthetic," in A Life Distilled: Gwendolyn Brooks, Her Poetry and Fiction, *edited by Maria K. Mootry and Gary Smith, University of Illinois Press, 1987, pp. 81-99.*

FURTHER READING

Dawson, Emma Waters. "Vanishing Point: The Rejected Black Woman in the Poetry of Gwendolyn Brooks." *Obsidian II* 4, No. 1 (Spring 1989): 1-11.
Explores the transition of the black woman in Brooks's poetry from a figure struck by her "inferior" physical beauty to her ultimate rejection of those feelings.

Kent, George E. *A Life of Gwendolyn Brooks.* Lexington: University Press of Kentucky, 1990, 287 p.
Kent, a leading scholar on Brooks's life and works, completed this unauthorized biography just prior to his death in 1982. Another biographer of Brooks, D. H. Melhem, added an afterword to Kent's work, updating the reader on Brooks's life after 1978.

Mootry, Maria K., and Smith, Gary, eds. *A Life Distilled: Gwendolyn Brooks, Her Poetry and Fiction.* Urbana: University of Illinois Press, 1987, 286 p.
Collection of essays treating Brooks's career and analyzing her works, in particular her novel and poetry for children.

Ryan, William F. "Blackening the Language." *American Visions* 3, No. 6 (December 1988): 32-7.
Interview with Brooks and overview of her career developments.

Satz, Martha. "Honest Reporting: An Interview with Gwendolyn Brooks." *Southwest Review* 74, No. 1 (Winter 1989): 25-35.
Brooks discusses her poetry and how she sees herself as a black woman and a poet.

Shaw, Harry B. "Perceptions of Men in the Early Works of Gwendolyn Brooks." In *Black American Poets Between Worlds, 1940-1960,* edited by Harry B. Shaw, pp. 136-59. Knoxville: University of Tennessee Press, 1986.
Categorizes and examines Brooks's portrayals of men as examples of "the citizen in relation to the larger society, the family member in relation to the personae and to the reader, and the love object."

Whitaker, Charles. "Gwendolyn Brooks: A Poet for All Ages." *Ebony* XLII, No. 8 (June 1987): 154, 156, 158, 160, 162.
Profile of Brooks's life at the age of seventy.

Claude Brown

1937-

American autobiographer and prose writer.

American author Claude Brown, who left his life of thievery and drug dealing in Harlem and became a successful writer and lecturer, is best known for his autobiographical account of that very transition, *Manchild in the Promised Land* (1965). Many critics consider this work the definitive depiction of life in a black American ghetto. In it Brown clearly and objectively portrayed the brutalities of living in Harlem—an aspect that was applauded by commentators who sensed a need for a full-length account of the situation of urban blacks.

Born in Harlem in New York City, Brown had been struck by a bus, chain-whipped, tossed into a river, and shot in the stomach by the age of thirteen. He underwent these ordeals while living on the streets of Harlem. Brown early gained a reputation as a thief; at ten he was a member of the "Forty Thieves" division of the notorious Buccaneers Gang. In an effort to get their son off the streets, Brown's parents sent him to live in the South for a year. When he returned, he was promptly sent to the Wiltwyck School for emotionally disturbed and deprived boys. There Brown made lasting friends, particularly Dr. Ernest Papanek, the school psychologist. Brown, however, was soon back on the streets, and he began to sell and use marijuana. He served three terms in reform school, running con games and dealing hard drugs when not imprisoned. Brown was not an addict, however; he had almost died from his first experience with heroin, and that prevented his dependency. Brown thus found it easier than others to break with the ghetto. He attended night school and Howard University, receiving a bachelor's degree from the latter in 1965. During his first year at Howard, Brown was urged by Dr. Papanek to write an article about Harlem for a magazine. The article attracted the attention of a publisher, who encouraged Brown to write an autobiography. Brown submitted a 1,500-page manuscript, and after considerable trimming, it was published as *Manchild in the Promised Land.*

Brown opened *Manchild in the Promised Land* with an image of himself at thirteen, unable to run away because he has just been shot while trying to steal bedsheets from a clothesline. He wrote of the doomed lives of his friends and family—only a few would escape like himself. Critics lauded *Manchild in the Promised Land* for its graphic, realistic depiction of ghetto life, and many praised the absence of sermonizing in Brown's narrative. Romulus Linney noted that *Manchild in the Promised Land* "is written with brutal and unvarnished honesty in the plain talk of the people, in language that is fierce, uproarious, obscene and tender, but always sensible and direct. And to its enormous credit, this youthful autobiography gives us its devastating portrait

of life without one cry of self-pity, outrage or malice, with no caustic sermons or searing rhetoric." The book also apparently aided the civil rights movement. Brown said in a 1965 interview: "I'm trying to show more than anything else the humanity of the Negro. Somebody has to stop problemizing and start humanizing the Negro."

Brown's next work, *The Children of Ham* (1976), is about a group of young adults in Harlem who help each other rise above the squalor of their environment, principally by avoiding the "monster" heroin. Critical reception was mixed. In a favorable review, Arnold Rampersad wrote that the book "invites comparison with the most successful of those books that record, fictionally or factually, the crusades of children against the world of their fathers and mothers." Yet Anatole Broyard faulted the work heavily, writing of Brown's use of slang in dialogue: "*The Children of Ham* suffers from a monotony of negatives and oversimplifications, and these do not sound any better when they are ungrammatically phrased."

Although Brown has not published a major work since *The Children of Ham,* he has contributed articles to magazines. In *The New York Times Magazine* in 1984, he offered his impressions of modern day Harlem. Despite what he perceives to be worsened conditions, Brown concluded: "The manchild... must be convinced that there is reason for hope. He must be made to understand that the quality of life actually does improve as he grows older, that everything falls into place as adults approach 'the age of enlightenment' some time in their 40's, and that most of the major mysteries are solved by life's two greatest detectives, time and experience. The true currency of life is time, which means that all the healthy young people on the face of the earth, including the manchild, are the richest folks in the world."

(For further information about Brown's life and works, see *Black Writers; Contemporary Authors,* Vols. 73-76; and *Contemporary Literary Criticism,* Vol. 30.)

PRINCIPAL WORKS

Manchild in the Promised Land (autobiography) 1965
The Children of Ham (prose) 1976

Eliot Fremont-Smith (essay date 1965)

[*In the following review, Fremont-Smith praises Brown for writing without excessive anger and resentment in* Manchild in the Promised Land.]

The scene [in *Manchild in the Promised Land*] is Harlem, the street, the trap, and the first word of Mr. Brown's narrative is the imperative, "Run!" But at the moment he could not run. He was 13 years old, a veteran of the street, and he had just been shot in the stomach while trying to steal some bedsheets off a clothesline. (Later, much later, after he had moved downtown, he would twice be nearly killed again, by policemen who could not believe a Negro was merely living in a white man's building, not robbing it or raping someone or shooting dope.)

Run! But first he fought, which is how a boy grows up in Harlem: he talks tough about "the Man," the whites, and fights other Negroes. When he was nine, Claude Brown was a member of the élite thieving section of the Harlem Buccaneers, a notorious bopping gang. At 11 he was sent to the Wiltwyck School for "emotionally disturbed" boys, for a two-year stay. Back on the street, he turned to pushing marijuana and cocaine. At 14 he was sent to the Warwick Reform School for the first of three stays. Again he returned to Harlem, and always to the street, the place of growing up.

And then, eventually, he did run; he escaped the street. He went to school; he learned to play the piano; he

graduated from Howard University; he wrote this book; he is now studying for a law degree.

What was different about Claude Brown? How did he escape? Most of his generation, most of the "cats" he knew, did not. Instead, they died, in spirit if not in body. They died, he reports—and no doubt are dying still—from dope and jail and prostitution, from never having found a sense of person or of purpose, from hopelessness, from being the garbage of the street and knowing it, from growing up in Harlem.

Mr. Brown offers a few clues to his survival, and gives credit to a few individuals who cared enough to help at certain crucial moments. More important, however, as this book testifies, he somehow found, or perhaps was born with, the right combination of inner resources to survive; early courage and tenacity were somehow tempered with intelligence and insight. He is now able to write, with immense control, about the debasement and self-abasement and destruction of his friends. He can record their (and his own) bitter, piteous and doomed attempts to escape the street through further loss of self-esteem—through pointless challenge and violence, through the masquerade of hipness and exotic argot that substitutes for the sense of masculinity denied to Negro men (his younger brother's name is Pimp), through cult-religions, through turning homosexual, through symbolic weapons and irrelevant, useless goals (to own a Cadillac), through drugs. All this he can write about in detail, and without the anger or resentment that he shows is justified, but blinding all the same.

Somewhere near the middle of his book, this report from hell, Claude Brown tells of running into a girl he once knew and loved and yearned for. Now, no longer beautiful, she wanted to borrow money, would pay him back by "turning a trick or two." He declined the offer, but gave her the money, and watched as she got the heroin to take her to her private "promised land." The passage sums up the quiet terror of this book, and the fate of a generation of Negroes who came of age in Harlem.

> *Eliot Fremont-Smith, "Coming of Age in Harlem: A Report from Hell," in* The New York Times, *August 14, 1965, p. 21.*

Houston A. Baker, Jr. (essay date 1971)

[*Baker is a noted American authority on African-American literary aesthetics. In the following essay, he looks at the environment of Harlem as Brown's enemy in* Manchild in the Promised Land.]

The concept of the environment as enemy is far from new; Zola and the naturalistic school of the nineteenth century took the concept as a starting point. Moreover, the concept is not new to black literature, for the Chicago of Bigger Thomas and the New York of the "invisible man" bring about the fall of the protagonists in *Native Son* and the *Invisible Man* just as surely as the mines in *Germinal* and the gin shops in *L'Assomoir* bring about the fall of the protagonists in those works. Like Zola and other naturalistic writers, Wright and Ellison have portrayed the vast web of forces surrounding man as inexorable; the environment ultimately brings either death or degradation to their respective protagonists. To deal with the environment as an injurious or hostile force in Claude Brown's *Manchild in the Promised Land,* therefore, is not to enter a world of strange literary conventions. However, the conventions here are somewhat modified. In *Manchild in the Promised Land,* there is no ineluctable march of naturalistic events; there are no long and bitter tirades against a hostile universe, and no scenes where the protagonist is portrayed as the mangled and pitiable victim of negative forces. Brown's work, therefore, can neither be rigidly classified as "naturalistic" nor as an "angry" autobiography in the manner of the narrative of William Wells Brown. Brown has not only portrayed the negative aspects of the environment, but also the positive aspects: not only the defeats brought about by the antagonistic environment, but also the victories won and the beneficial changes that resulted from the battle.

Manchild in the Promised Land presents the struggle of one black male child to escape from the throes of a colonial system; Harlem, or the initial environment, is the colony whose codes and inimical effects the protagonist has to escape. The protagonist's struggle is defined in terms of various shifts in environment, and the reader emerges with a balanced view of his struggle due to the combination of romantic nostalgia and clinical realism in the narrator's technique of description. This *philos-a-philos* relationship between the narrator and the environment gives Brown's work a critical objectivity that makes the book useful for socio-historical purposes; moreover, the changes in environment that define the protagonist's struggle reflect a historical process with a degree of accuracy that also makes the work valuable as social history. An examination of the struggle presented in the work, therefore, will reveal not only how Brown's use of the environment as enemy constitutes a modification of a literary convention, but also will show what the work tells about the struggle of blacks in a recent epoch.

The picture of the environment as a hostile force begins to emerge in the first lines of *Manchild in the Promised Land;* the protagonist at the age of thirteen is fleeing an unknown assailant, and lodged in his stomach is a bullet, "trying to take my life, all thirteen years of it." And the narrator's earliest memory is of the Harlem riot in 1943 when the population rebelled against the inimical environment surrounding it. The dark picture continues to unfold when the narrator reveals that his father has killed a man, and the landlord of the building in which he lives has clubbed a man to death for urinating in the hall. Both his father and the landlord represent the "old order" to the narrator, and the legacy of the old order consists of "liquor, religion, sex, and violence." In fact, the narrator says that "the Harlem tradition [of violence] had come from the backwoods," and he continues with the following reflection on the members of the old order: "They didn't seem to be ready for urban life."

The environment then is one conditioned by a violent past and overseen by men—both black and white—who do not understand the generation to which the narrator belongs. This lack of understanding made life at home unbearable, and as a result, the protagonist took to the streets. He defines his early habitat in the following passage:

> I always ran away [from youth shelters] to get back to the streets. I always thought of Harlem as home, but I never thought of Harlem as being in the house. To me home was the streets. I suppose there were many people who felt that. If home was so miserable, the street was the place to be.

The life of the streets consisted of fighting, stealing, smoking marijuana, and learning the "code" of the gang. The narrator says: "Throughout my childhood in Harlem, nothing was more strongly impressed on me than the fact that you had to fight and that you should fight." The things he and his contemporaries fought for were "manhood, women, and money"; the code was simple, with its emphasis on violence drawn from the quality of life:

> By the time I was nine years old, I had been hit by a bus, thrown into the Harlem River (intentionally), hit by a car, severely beaten with a chain. And I had set the house afire.

It is the meaning of this violence, however, that is of significance in any consideration of the environment as enemy, and that meaning is given in the words of the narrator. When he is urged to join the Black Muslim movement in order to rebel against white society, the narrator says:

> The revolution that you're talking about, Alley, I've had it. I've had that revolution since I was six years old. And I fought it every day—in the streets of Harlem, in the streets of Brooklyn, in the streets of the Bronx and Lower Manhattan, all over—when I was there stealing, raising hell out there, playing hookey, I rebelled against school because the teachers were white. And I went downtown and robbed the stores because the store owners were white. I ran through the subways because the cats in the change booths were white.

The street life, therefore, is revealed as a form of rebellion against the environment, an environment which, in effect, constitutes a colony held in check by white society "downtown." The accuracy of the narrator's estimation is reinforced by a statement from John Henrik Clarke's *Harlem, A Community in Transition.* Clarke says:

> Harlem is not a self-contained community. It is owned and controlled by outsiders. It is a black community with a white economic heartbeat. Of the major retail outlets, national chains and local merchants, only a handful are Negro-owned. In the raging battle for integration and equal job opportunities for Negroes, little is heard about the Negroes'

long fight to gain control of their community. A system of pure economic colonialism extends into politics, religion and every money-making endeavor that touches the life of a Harlem resident.

Through violence, stealing, indeed all aspects of the street life, the protagonist pits his skill against the pressures of the environment, but so conceived, the rebellion is destined to failure: "It was doomed to fail, right from the word go."

Indeed the inevitable failure of rebellion against the antagonistic environment can easily be seen; it takes the form of a deterministic pattern through three changes of environment that occur in the early part of *Manchild in the Promised Land.* The first change occurs when the narrator is sent to the South for a year because he has refused to attend school; the second change occurs when he is sent to Wiltwyck, a correctional institution for boys; and the third when he is sent to Warwick, another correctional institution. By the time he was fifteen, the narrator had suffered "exile" or incarceration three times for his rebellious activities against the initial environment. If the battle was indeed between the narrator and his environment, clearly, the environment was the early victor.

And yet the paradox of the penal system does not fail to operate in *Manchild in the Promised Land,* for in all of the "secondary" environments the protagonist became more skilled in the techniques of waging a battle against the initial environment. In the South, he learned to lie with proficiency; in Wiltwyck, he met companions who engaged in criminal activities with him on home visits; and in Warwick, he learned something new about crime from everyone he met. The irony of the penal system is captured by the narrator's statement that "We all came out of Warwick better criminals." The initial environment was thus a fiendishly insidious antagonist, for not only did it punish the rebel, but it also embodied the punishment in a form that made further sins unavoidable. The first three secondary environments, therefore, are little more than adjuncts—additional arms, if you will—of the enemy, and this can be seen in the code that characterized Wiltwyck and Warwick: it was the code of the streets from which the protagonist was sent. And the adverse effects of these secondary environments can be seen in the romantic nostalgia of the narrator.

The secondary environments bring about a mode of perception that proceeds out of the imaginative rather than the rational faculty, and this mode of perception conditions the nostalgia of the protagonist. For example, on returning home from the South, he says:

> When I came out of the subway at 145th Street and St. Nicholas Avenue, I thought there had never been a luckier person in the world than me. . . . I was so happy to see them, to see it, to see it all, to see Harlem again.

There is a certain pathos in these lines when one reflects on what the environment actually means—what the "blood and vomit" that the narrator sees on his arrival at home actually mean; and the pathos of the romantic vision is seen again when the narrator speaks of Harlem on his return from Wiltwyck. He says: "Oh, Lord, Harlem, let me git to you! It was an exciting feeling—going home." Finally, the same romantic nostalgia is seen just before the narrator's return from Warwick:

> All I wanted to do was get back to Harlem. I wanted to get back to Jackie and pot and the streets and stealing. This was my way of life. I couldn't take it for too long when I was there, but this was all I knew.

The already low aspirational level is further lowered by the secondary environments and these environments simply increase the protagonist's desire to continue his futile rebellion. On leaving Wiltwyck, his only desire is to get high on heroin, and on leaving Warwick, his only desire is to get back to stealing and smoking marijuana. When the end result of the return to the place so nostalgically yearned for is considered, only the narrator's desire to return can be seen as romantic. Yet this romanticism helps to preserve a balanced point of view, for it keeps the book from falling to the level of a puerile denunciation of the environment. The romanticism, in other words, acts as the *philos* that removes *Manchild in the Promised Land* from the category of the "angry" autobiography. Moreover, this romanticism functioned as one motivation for the actions of the narrator's youth, and as such it has a place in his story and quite possibly in the stories of others of his generation. The world of the Harlem streets was glorious because it stood in contrast to the miserable homes and the correctional institutions, which seemed to be the only alternatives.

Nonetheless, the ultimate effect of romantic nostalgia was adverse, for it led the narrator to give up the idea of school altogether, to move out of his parents' home, and to adopt the code of the Hamilton Terrace environment at the age of sixteen. At the age of sixteen, therefore, he was dangerously close to being destroyed by the environment. He was living in the area where the worst criminals in Harlem lived, and he was selling drugs. He says, "I was going the crime way. That's all there was to it." The next stops that life held out to him at the time were Coxsackie, Woodburn, and then Sing Sing. Clearly the environment was the victor at this point, and it had taken its toll in human lives and suffering. As the narrator says, "Most of the cats I came up with were in jail or dead or strung out on drugs."

But it is at this point of ultimate despair, at this point of the "everlasting nay," that the advantage in the battle begins to shift to the protagonist, and it is this shift that removes *Manchild in the Promised Land* most decisively from the naturalistic category. Heretofore, there has been no linear development, only the inexorable pendulum of the narrator's moves from an antagonistic initial environment to equally antagonistic secondary environments and back again; the expansion has been simply vertical as the protagonist has become more deeply involved in the life of crime. Now, at the age of seventeen, the first horizontal expansion of the book occurs as the narrator moves to Greenwich Village. In effect, the movement is equal to a movement from the colony to the mainland; the narrator starts on the road to development outside the ghetto. The horizontal expansion is not only defined in terms of the physical move, but also in terms of the narrator's point of view toward life. In commenting on the change, he says:

> I was free. For the first time in my life I didn't have the feeling that I had to go to Coxsackie, to Woodburn, and then to Sing Sing. I had the feeling now that anything could happen, anything that I decided to do. It seemed a little bit crazy, but I even had the feeling that if I wanted to become a doctor or something like that, I could go on and do it.

For the first time the narrator has a feeling of freedom and a higher aspirational level. Moreover, he is now able to reflect objectively on the enemy. There is no romantic nostalgia in his clinically realistic descriptions of the drug "plague" that swept through the community in the fifties, and he is far from romantic as he describes the lesbians, the homosexuals, the poor police protection, and the poor politicians who went to make up the colony.

In chapter eight he sees that the type of hero the community set up was a criminal such as Jim Goldie, and in chapter nine the narrator makes his first analysis of the "black reflection" that began in the early fifties. In chapters ten, eleven, and twelve, the narrator reflects on the old order of the Southern black man, on the effects of drugs on the community, and on his own future as well as the future of his younger brother, who started taking drugs at an early age. All of these chapters reach a new high in objectivity; all of the inimical aspects of the Harlem environment are seen critically as the narrator adjusts his perspectives and grows to maturity. In chapter thirteen, there is a marvelous description of what Saturday night means to blacks, and in chapter fourteen, the narrator's view of the early era of "black reflection" continues as he describes the rise of the Muslim movement in Harlem. He concludes the chapter by saying: "If they [the Muslims] don't do any more than let the nation know that there are black men in this country who are dangerously angry, then they've already served a purpose."

Finally, in chapter fifteen, the point of farthest horizontal expansion occurs. The narrator's move to Greenwich Village has allowed him to withdraw from the hostile environment for a time, and he has been relatively successful in the white world. But when he pursues his retreat to its limits and attempts to have an affair with a Jewish girl, he is defeated by the white world. This defeat provokes a retreat to the initial environment, but that initial environment can no longer be as injurious as previously, since the narrator has adjusted his perspectives and matured. He says, "It was as though I had found my place and Harlem had found its place. We were suited for each other now." The narrator is surely the victor at this point; in chapters seventeen and eighteen, his victory is confirmed by his discovery of the beneficial forces in the initial environment. He meets Reverend James, and through the funds of a church council, he gets away from the environment altogether. The last chapter deals with the changing nature of the community, the new luxury apartment buildings, and the new brand of policeman who is interested in protecting the community. By the end of the last chapter, it not only seems as though the protagonist has escaped a hostile environment, but also that the environment itself is a tame and beneficent place. One is almost tempted to ask if the environment had ever been hostile, or if the environment was indeed the enemy. And it is precisely at this point that one can see just how superb a work the author has managed to produce for the social historian, for he has presented an unimpassioned, objective, and factual account of an epoch. By maintaining a balance between romantic nostalgia and clinical realism, by keeping the *philos-aphilos* relationship in balance, the author has been able to present a work that neither succumbs to the ideological rigidities of naturalistic conventions nor the subjective distortions of angry autobiography.

That the environment is the enemy, however, can clearly be seen by a statement made near the end of the book: "It seemed as though most of the cats that we'd come up with just hadn't made it. Almost everybody was dead or in jail." By the end of the work Alleybush, Kid, and K.B., all childhood friends of the narrator, are in jail; Jackie, Debbie, and Trixie, three of the main women in his life, are prostitutes, while a fourth, Sugar, is a drug addict. Butch and Tony, two of his best friends in youth, have died as a result of drug addiction; and Pimp, the narrator's younger brother, is in jail on an armed robbery charge. The price exacted by the environment is thus a monumental one, and if any message emerges clearly, it is that only the exceptional, only the few made it—many met death at an early age. Danny, one of those who made it out of the environment, was a man capable of miracles, for he was "strung-out" on drugs, accomplished his cure, and came back to the same environment where he had met his downfall. Turk, the fighter who is the number two contender for the heavyweight crown at the end of the book, is also an exceptional figure, a person capable of the philosophical reflections seen throughout the last of the book. But the most exceptional figure of all is, of course, the narrator himself. The fact that he was able by an act of will to turn around and follow the straight road after ten or eleven years of crime is truly remarkable. And even if allowance is made for a certain amount of egocentricity and exaggeration, yet clearly the narrator was ahead of a great number of his companions. In innumerable instances throughout the work, his leadership potential and above-average abilities are revealed. Danny, Turk, and Sonny (the narrator)—these are the only ones left when *Manchild in the Promised Land* closes on a note of nostalgia with the narrator at five years of age describing the sights of the streets to his unbelieving father.

And one can sympathize with the father because it is hard to believe that in the ultra-civilized, twentieth century city such an environment could exist; yet it does exist, and one can only marvel at the restrained manner in which the author has presented his story. Though the environment described by the work is clearly the enemy, its landscapes are not totally bleak, and the possibility of victory exists. The tactics of Brown's victory should be of ultimate concern not only to the social historian, but to mankind in general. (pp. 53-9)

> *Houston A. Baker, Jr., "The Environment as Enemy in a Black Autobiography: 'Manchild in the Promised Land',"* in PHYLON: The Atlanta University Review of Race and Culture, *Vol. XXXII, No. 1, Spring, 1971, pp. 53-9.*

Arnold Rampersad (essay date 1976)

[*Rampersad is an American academic and scholar who has written widely on black life and culture. He is especially known for his biographies of W.E.B. Du Bois and Langston Hughes. In the following review, he comments on the principal themes of* The Children of Ham—*youth, self-preservation, and death—focusing on Brown's depiction of some children's struggle to survive.*]

Harlem is once again on Claude Brown's mind, and it should be on ours. With **Manchild in the Promised Land,** and now **The Children of Ham,** he has established himself as the true epic poet of modern Harlem. **Manchild** chronicled his escape from disaster there; **Children of Ham** is his testimony that no such escape is totally possible, that one *must* go home again or live and die a traitor. Brown brings the survivor's guilt to his reportage; this is the story of other menchildren and womenchildren left behind in his escape though born after his time. The manic humor of **Manchild** is gone. Harlem is an apocalypse and the story is revelation itself. Though the autobiographer of **Manchild** was part Poor Richard, part Horatio Alger hero, and part con man, with the work itself his most sophisticated and lucrative hustle, Brown's best instincts are toward the rational, the moral and the prophetic, and between the first book and the second he has had much time to think of his fate and that of his people. . . .

His literary method is simple. Armed with a tape-recorder and, perhaps, some means of inducing his subjects to relax, he allows them to tell their stories, transcribing their remarks verbatim, filling in the empty spots with impressions, explanation and facts. Of the 13 stories, four focus on the women of the group; one is about its youngest member, 14-year-old Snooky; another is about Stretch, who is close to 50 and a friendly outsider. In essence, though, they tell one tale.

The religion of this community is survival. The armor of their creed is unity and compassion for one another. Each child has been abandoned, more or less, by his or her family. . . . The Devil in their creed is "scag," "the white boy"—heroin; the devil's angels are the junkies,

who must be terrorized to keep their distance, unless, as in the case of Lee, the group decides to make an exception. The prime force of these children's lives is fear—fear of becoming a worshiper, fear of becoming a wino (lower in status than a junkie in Harlem), fear of being overtaken by the Harlem fate. The greatest compliment is to be called "swift"—a "swift dude" or a "swift chick"; speed is of the essence, and flight the better part of valor.

In the most harrowing section of that book, the narrator of **Manchild in the Promised Land** related how heroin destroyed his brother Pimp. In **The Children of Ham,** all lives have been warped by its power. . . .

If it has any impact at all, this work should ice, once and for all, the myth of Harlem propagated so assiduously since Harlem's brassy age in the early '20s, during the years when, as Langston Hughes put it, "the Negro was in vogue." The grotesque irony of Harlem as Promised Land in the title of Brown's first book is attenuated, then reversed in **The Children of Ham.** The myth of Canaan persists for these youths, but the promised land is now anywhere but Harlem. (p. 25)

Ancient as a ruin, these cave dwellers are as childlike as their most recent fantasy, illusion or dream. Their urge to rational intellection is constant and intense, if predictably inchoate, and their desire for learning heartbreaking in its misdirection. Dee Dee writes poetry, and Hebro the muscle man, seeing Nita turning in the sunlight by a window, thinks of eternal beauty, but visions and ideals live fitfully in this foul air. Snooky wants a gun and a Cadillac; Mumps, a gifted thief, wants a legitimate cover for his hustle and intends to go to college to find it; Jill dreams of being an actress. Lee, with a BA in sociology, wants to go home to Florida, but a fix keeps getting in the way. Hebro, the athlete, intends to lift himself up into the world of high salaried ballplayers. They do not see the white world as now more sympathetic or understanding, only as more vulnerable to black force.

A familiar term at the end of the last century among certain liberal reformers concerned the "unconscious moral heroism" of the poor. Perhaps it is fatuous to apply such a term to juvenile delinquents, but if self-preservation is a moral duty, then these are moral heroes of the first order. Though the book is about youth and death, its human subjects are short on self-pity. Indeed, the only pathetic character in the book is its narrator. I do not mean Claude Brown, but his persona, who visits the scene of disaster with an open notebook and a closed mouth. He exemplifies the predicament not of the author but of the reader, the person of education and means from whom the accusations of neglect and abuse in the book demand response. The book itself, of course, is the supreme act of intervention in the tragedy of these lives, but that is to Claude Brown's credit, not to ours. Nor, paradoxically, to his narrator's. Intending to be distant and scientific, an empirical sociologist gathering facts, he tries in vain to conceal his insecurities within a laconic style. But occasional pious moralizings, hip expressions, ripples of self-conscious, nervous humor and crass judgments flesh out a picture of a human being that every sensitive reader should recognize at once. Consciously or unconsciously, Brown reveals his deep discomfort in dealing with his material; this is a glaringly honest book.

The Children of Ham invites comparison with the most successful of those books that record, fictionally or factually, the crusades of children against the world of their fathers and mothers. From this perspective and in the context of the rise of the American city, it is alike in its power, if not in its art, to Stephen Crane's first novel, *Maggie, A Girl of the Streets;* as a book about those young people whose primary gift is a determination to live, it reminds one of the diary of another tenement prisoner struggling for the right of survival, Anne Frank. In any event, *The Children of Ham* is among the more important books published in recent years. (pp. 25-6)

> Arnold Rampersad, in a review of "The Children of Ham," in The New Republic, Vol. 174, No. 19, May 8, 1976, pp. 25-6.

Ishmael Reed (essay date 1976)

[*Novelist and poet Reed is a leading figure in contemporary black American literature. In the following review, originally published in* The Washington Post *in 1976, he pans* The Children of Ham, *charging that Brown has become too distant from Harlem.*]

In case you haven't heard, scag is another name for heroin. Substitute the word devil for scag and *The Children of Ham,* Claude Brown's new book, becomes a medieval mystery in which scag has supernatural power over people. They come under its influence because of bad homes, society, and one fellow says he became addicted because he was from the country instead of the city.

A few years ago, a burglary ring of clever Miami teenagers was ready with all of the sociological jargon concerning the responsibility for their actions when they were captured. That jargon is in this book of narratives by anti-junkies who've formed a "family" and live together in "spots" (apartments) of abandoned Harlem buildings.

No one seems to have ever been drawn to scag, "a monster," because it made them feel good and powerful, and gave the kind of confidence which led them to steal, and indulge in other risky adventures.

Scag is a turn-on for those who can't afford to import a California swami. The book goes on like that, all about scag and the evil it makes people do.

The children of Ham don't use it and hold views about junkies which lend credibility to a recent New York *Times* article reporting a shift in attitudes among blacks regarding black criminals. One Hamite, Herbo, proposes a Judgment Day for junkies. "You have countdown signs every day, just like the newspapers show for Christmas that you got twenty-one more shoppin' days to Christmas." If this doesn't deter addicts, Herbo proposes that when Judgment Day arrives prisoners, armed with baseball bats, be encouraged to commit mayhem upon the incorrigible junkies. Each prisoner would have a kill quota.

When I met Claude Brown at Notre Dame, I expected to meet Mr. Ghetto coming at me like a swaggering ostrich handing out all kinds of jive, you dig? Instead, I found someone who talked like the host for "Masterpiece Theatre," and who ordered in French. The author of *Manchild in the Promised Land* had gone to etiquette school. "You're the first black Wasp, Claude," I remarked.

Occasionally, the black Wasp comes through in lines like: "The old feisty dowager surely would have expired sooner had she not been too concerned about her family to relinquish life, despite the agony of its extension."

Claude Brown means well. His conclusion is that if you care for each other as the children of Ham care for each other you won't need heroin. *All you need is love!*

I wonder how the mothers and fathers of those suburban junkies who've received more care and love than any generation in history with the exception, perhaps, of some child emperors, would say about that. All you need is love. Claude means it.

But even Claude Brown can't breathe life into an image like "the rats were as big as cats." Claude has returned to his old stomping grounds, only this time he's a tourist. His predictable glossary, "cops . . . blow . . . dudes," are from an old rock record which provides background music at a suburban bar-b-cue. From time to time the tourist abandons his subjects and addresses the liberal audience this book is intended for: "The common tragedy among these youngsters is that by the time they reach the age of nineteen or twenty they are thoroughly and irreversibly demoralized."

I wanted to say, they know that already, Claude. They've been told that for twenty years through reports, fiction, non-fiction, poetry, motion pictures, documentaries, etc. Through every conceivable media and from every point of view, yet the heroin problem is worse, claiming four hundred thousand victims. There are more white addicts than black and the addict population of Los Angeles exceeds that of New York.

The liberal of ten years ago is now indifferent to these problems and with a new phony Zen Buddhism entering national politics indifference will now seem aesthetic. The liberal can't do anything about his own addicts much less about the condition of an addict in Harlem. Heroin is big business, and in the present United States big business is above the law and often owns it.

In midst of Mr. Brown's eloquent, futile pleas, and interesting, often poetical, testifying from his subjects concerning politics (colorful), and their values (flashy cars and clothes), there's a considerable amount of homosexual rape, lesbianism, thievery, murder, and whoring, and shooting gallery material.

Mr. Brown meant for his book to be an earnest illustrated sermon directed at arousing the American conscience, but the book will be read as a peep show.

For four hundred years Americans have made entertainment from blacks squirming, biting each other's ears off, roasting, and hanging. Crowds used to witness these affairs in a picnic atmosphere. Placing blacks in lurid situations, despising them, dehumanizing them, has always been a national sport.

The standard hack busing speech is probably descended from the barker's pitch in some hideous ancient American medicine show.

Claude Brown had the best intentions, and some of the children of Ham might be touched by the magic wand of publicity and rescued from their plight. But for every bright, and ambitious Hamite there are thousands who won't be rescued. The book will be liked for the wrong reasons. A peep show under the guise of sociology, just as Public Television's shoddy "Harlem Voices" was presented under the guise of freedom of information, or freedom of the right to know, etc. Of course, if the media were so interested in the public's right to know, they'd show the whole range of black life as they do with white life; from the Bowery to the White House. Only the Bowery parts of black life are portrayed.

The author of **The Children of Ham** meant for the book to be about some extraordinary people of ambivalent morality who transcended the situation in which they were thrust. But the book will become popular because of the Bowery parts. Claude Brown is best at writing about himself in the first person. That book will be a classic and it will be post-Harlem.

You can't go home again. (pp. 249-51)

> *Ishmael Reed, "The Children of Ham," in his* Shrovetide in "Old New Orleans," *Doubleday & Company, Inc., 1978, pp. 249-51.*

Claude Brown (essay date 1984)

[*In the following excerpt from an essay originally published in* The New York Times Magazine *in 1984, Brown compares the contemporary Harlem "manchild" with the one of his youth.*]

One mesmerizingly beautiful late summer day, while I was hanging out in my old Harlem neighborhood, I ran into two of my boyhood running partners, Arthur Dunmeyer and Douglas Jones. Twenty years ago, I had written about both in **Manchild in the Promised Land,** giving them the pseudonyms of Dunny and Turk and

myself the name of Sonny. That day, each of us had been independently overcome by an irresistible urge to reconnect with his roots.

Although we hadn't seen one another in a long while, we are still close friends who have kept in touch over the years. But a serendipitous encountering of two childhood chums when you have some lollygag time and can thoroughly enjoy their company is one of life's very special blessings. It is bestowed only on the manchild who is fortunate enough to attain the improbably old age of 46 in a culture and life style where the vast majority of his teen-age peers are dead, killed before they reached 30.

Since the hell-raising days of our youth, Jones had had a very promising career as a heavyweight prizefighter. He had been the No. 2 heavyweight; he clearly beat Cassius Clay, now known as Muhammad Ali, in 1963, but was robbed of the decision and is now a liquor salesman who would like a different job. Dunmeyer is a construction worker in Harlem, and I continue to write.

While enjoying our summer pilgrimage, we found ourselves comparing the present-day Harlem to the Harlem of our youth, and attempting to understand and appraise the most obvious changes. We spent the better part of the afternoon observing the current crop of teenagers, the contemporary Turks, Dunnys and Sonnys. What has a decade and a half wrought for them in this festering and corroding "promised land"?

Harlem is no longer the promised land—it never was for today's manchild. Harlem was a promised land only for his grandparents. He had not known the wretched semibondage they were subjected to under the regimes of Theodore Bilbo, James Eastland, John Sparkman, Strom Thurmond and other Southern politicians, tyrannical Pharoahs who ruthlessly ruled the cotton patch region during the 1920's, 30's and 40's.

The present-day manchild is a human paradox. Compared to Turk, Dunny and Sonny, he is a considerably more sophisticated adolescent. He is more knowledgeable, more sensitive, more amicable—and more likely to commit murder.

● ● ● ● ●

Harlem is no longer a solitary geographical section of New York City. It is all of black urban America— Boston's Roxbury, Chicago's Southside, Los Angeles's Watts, San Francisco's Fillmore district, Cleveland's Hough and various sections of Detroit, Philadelphia, Washington and Baltimore. Harlem U.S.A. is defined by a common culture. In all of these black communities can be found the same soul-food dishes on the menus in the local restaurants; the neighborhood juke boxes and the local disk jockeys play the same popular rhythm-and-blues and disco songs; the youth do the same dances and use the same slang; the clothing styles are a variation on a common theme, and there are ample churches, bars, liquor stores, numbers spots, Cadillacs, junkies and dope pushers.

Today's manchild is a teen-ager between the ages of 13 and 18, probably a second-generation ghetto dweller living with his unskilled, laboring mother and three or four sisters and brothers, maybe one or two cousins, all sharing a tiny three-, four- or five-room apartment in a dilapidated tenement or low-income, city-owned housing development commonly called "the projects."

The popular nicknames of today's manchild still reflect the current community values and aspirations—King Ben, Baldy Locks, Jimo and Eddie the Fox. Shaft, Super Fly, Godfather and Applejack, after the popular cab, were monikers of the late 1960's and early 1970's, graffiti on the walls of subway cars, public schools and abandoned buildings. The later proliferation of Omars, Hassans, Abduls and Maliks represented the "Muslimizing," or zealous "blackening," of the American Negro, but they are now obsolescent, having served their purpose—the emphatic repudiation of the stereotypical labels and derogatory Western definitions of black Americans. The Moslem name-change epidemic also indicated the indelible impression made by Malcolm X.

In my estimation, Malcolm X and the Muslim organization of 20 years ago were probably the second-greatest losses the black urban community has suffered in recent history; second only to the privation of the Warren Court. Under the leadership of Elijah Muhammad and the supervision and eloquent proselytizing of his minister, Malcolm X (who later adopted the name El-Hajj Malik El-Shabazz), the Muslims became the most positive socioeconomic force ever to captivate and stimulate the consciousness of black Americans in this country; ever more so than Jesus Christ and Christianity. It is much easier and more practical to be a black American Muslim than a black American Christian.

Urban America of two decades ago was abundantly populated with genuine, deeply devout Muslims. And they were an extremely constructive presence, despite the espousal of a few absurd doctrines. They were consistently neatly attired, well-mannered and industrious, and comported themselves in an exemplary manner that demanded respect and admiration.

The articulate and exceptionally well-disciplined Fruit of Islam, the security arm of the Nation of Islam, was highly influential, and its membership expanded rapidly with recruits from the ranks of the discarded, neglected and rejected pariahs—thieves, prostitutes, drug addicts and other debased street people. One of the most appealing features of the Muslims' message was that it was conveyed in very basic, unsophisticated language.

● ● ● ● ●

The motivations, dreams and aspirations of today's young men are essentially the same as those of the teen-agers of their parents' generation—with a few dramatic differences. They are persistently violent. They appear driven by, or almost obsessed with, a desperate need for pocket money that they cannot possibly obtain legally. They possess an uncompromising need to be able to "rock" (wear) a different pair of designer jeans at least twice a week, or even a different pair of ordinary pants twice a week. As one 16-year-old Harlem teen-ager said: "Man, it's a bring-down to have to wear the same pants, the same shirt, to school three or four times a week when everybody else is showin' fly [coming to school dressed to the nines]. This is somethin' Moms can't understand. You don't have to have a pair of Nikes, a pair of Ponys, a pair of Pumas and a pair of Adidas, but it's embarrassin' not to have a pair of one of 'em."

Nobody is more cruel or more ruthless in his relationships with his peers than the poor child. He has so few possessions of any material value that he cannot afford the additional insult that being deprived of these very commonplace symbols of "being somebody" inflicts upon him. ("Everybody wants to be a somebody; if just a little somebody," this same teen-ager said. "Nobody but a fool wants to be a nobody; or somebody who don't count, right?") Conceivably, this paradoxical American creature called manchild—pathetic and simultaneously terrifying—is an extreme human manifestation of brand-name madness in a society severely afflicted with materialism.

Like his progenitor, manchild 1984 seeks the answers to life's "unknowable whys" through informal mysticism and mind-altering media collectively called getting "high." He, too, would solve the ancient and infinitely complex philosophical mysteries of man and his place in the universe, two of life's most baffling existential and metaphysical riddles, by simply lighting up a joint. He does not yet know that one can never recapture the deep-down, through-and-through euphoria of a first high; that it's as irretrievable as one's virginity. Ah, what a blissfully simplistic existence is this brief time we know as adolescence.

Yet, the unimaginably difficult struggle to arrive at a productive manhood in urban America is more devastatingly monstrous than ever before. All street kids are at least semi-abandoned, out on those mean streets for the major portion of the day and night. They are at the mercy of a coldblooded and ruthless environment; survival is a matter of fortuity, instinct, ingenuity and unavoidable conditioning. Consequently, the manchild who survives is usually more cunning, more devious and often more vicious than his middle-class counterpart. These traits are the essential contents of his survival kit.

Three decades ago, manchild's style, manner of attire, hip walk, utter comportment accentuated by three to four inches of a white handkerchief corner dangling from a rear pocket of his pants told the world in no uncertain terms: "There is no gravity. The world, life, the earth, stinks." Today, the same message is imparted by a very similar style, emphasized by the "dew rag."

The term dew rag had originally been given to any ordinary handkerchief, stocking cap or piece of cloth used to cover the head and protect hair from rain and perspiration—"dew." Wearing a dew rag, and preserving one's "marcel" (wavy hairstyle) when "processing" (straightening) the hair with a pasty, caustic compound called Konkoline, had been a common practice among American black men in the entertainment world and street life.

The current version of the dew rag, worn because "It makes you look like a player" (in street life), is usually black and is fashioned after the Arabian *kaffiyeh*. That this popular fad of wearing the dew rag to emphasize hipness, boldness and rebelliousness originated in prison intensifies the significance of manchild's message. Prison, and doing "bits" (time), has strangely ambivalent, perhaps even pervertedly romanticized appeal to poor black teen-agers. It is viewed as an inevitability, or at least a probability, accompanied by nothing more than the mild apprehension or anxiety that attends, for instance, a bar mitzvah, joining the Marines or any other manhood initiation ritual in any normal society. One goes into the Marines as a young boy and comes out a "real man." It is the same with going into the "joint," as prison is called.

The dew rag announces loudly and clearly that the wearer is ready for whatever it takes to become a man.

• • • • •

Manchild 1984 is the product of a society so rife with violence that killing a mugging or robbery victim is now fashionable.

"That's what they do now," the 16-year-old Harlemite said.

"That's what who does now?" I asked, not understanding.

"You know, you take their stuff and you pop [shoot] 'em."

"You mean shooting the victim is in style now like wearing a pair of Pony jogging shoes or a Pierre Cardin suit?"

"Yeah, it's wrong to kill somebody. But you gotta have dollars, right?"

For more than a year, I was thoroughly baffled by the apparent senseless and often maniacal, rampant killings of mugging and robbery victims. According to what I had gathered from newspaper reports, television newscasting and victims who had survived, it was as though shooting the victim had become an integral part of the crime. Sometimes, it seemed to occur with the incredible casualness of an insignificant afterthought, an "Oh, I forgot to shoot him" bang.

I had been talking to young men in the prisons and on the ghetto streets—prisons with invisible bars—but I wasn't comprehending what they were telling me. Perhaps what I was hearing was too mindboggling, too

ghastly to understand: "Murder is in style now." (pp. 36, 38, 40, 44)

Reformatory and prison bits are still an accepted, often anticipated and virtually inevitable phase of the growing-up process for young black men in this country. They have no fear of jail; most of their friends are there. They are told by the returning, unsung, heroic P.O.W.'s of the unending ghetto war of survival that even the state joints are now country clubs.

Today's manchild has fewer choices than my generation, and those choices are more depressing. As a final desperate recourse, we could always resort to enlisting in the armed services. Manchild 1984, unable even to pass the written exams for the services, can go into a life of crime or become a drug addict (both of which almost invariably involve spending a significant portion of one's life in jail); go to an early grave (which occurs with alarming frequency), or be most fortunate and evade all of the foregoing eventualities.

There are several reasons why 1984 Harlems and their young are more violent than they were 20 years ago. The primary reason is probably the most obvious one: This nation has grown progressively more violent over the past three decades. To paraphrase a cliché, as the country goes, so go its parts and miscreants.

Fretting parents and educators can no longer accuse television writers of influencing the behavior of inner-city teen-agers. The violence of day-to-day urban reality far exceeds any cruelties, atrocities or mayhem depicted in the current crop of television crime and adventure series, with the sole exception of the 6 o'clock news, which dramatically portrays the horrors of urban living. What is the most immediate consequences of a vicious murder committed by a young mugger, who is subsequently apprehended? The answer is instant stardom by way of the 6 o'clock news and the evening headlines. Regardless of the severity of the ensuing punishment, he had his moment of infamous glory.

It is disturbing to consider that murder is the style among young muggers and that the style among the New York political establishment is anticapital-punishment liberalism, and how well the two styles complement each other.

Another plausible, not so obvious, explanation for the stupendous wave of violent crime perpetrated by today's young is that many of them were eye-witnesses, at a very tender and impressionable age, to modern-day "Dodge City" shootouts and the broad-daylight slayings so typical of the urban drug wars of the 1970's.

When they were 6, 7, 8 or so, they saw friends, neighbors, relatives and total strangers brutally murdered, and seldom heard of anyone even being arrested for any of the slayings. In the mid-1970's, these kids were sneaking out of the house in utter calculated defiance of their parents' commands. For them, it had become a compulsion. This reality tends to exert a considerably more lasting impression on the very young than movies and television.

Since the mid-1970's, a Dodge City epoch has occurred in several major municipalities. One of the most tragic ramifications of these real-life episodes of wanton violence is that they were allowed to persist long enough to seem like normal behavior to youthful spectators. Consequently, immense and probably irreparable damage had been inflicted on them, prior to the armistice. In response to some continual sensational and outraged front-page news coverage (which cited the number of victims killed on Eighth Avenue between 144th and 154th Streets within the preceding six months), an embarrassed police department finally acted to pull down the curtain on the long-running show. But, alas, the die has been cast. (pp. 44, 54)

● ● ● ● ●

Contrary to the cliché, the more things change in Harlem, the worse they appear to get.

The movie theaters are gone from Harlem, replaced by a profusion of after-hours joints, video-game/smoke-and-dope shops; more violence; more crime, and more violent crime than at any other period in its history.

Despite the vertigo-inducing proliferation of churches, the impact of religion on the young has waned drastically in the face of youth's street-learned cynicism.

Loving parents and concerned family members, an efficacious educational system, community cultural institutions, constructive entertainment and recreational centers, positive adult guidance and supervision and responsible political leadership—essential components in the normal support system of teen-agers—seem all too scarce.

The prospect of children surmounting the formidable obstacles of their circumstances becomes highly improbable.

The few remaining cultural and edifying institutions reach and influence no more than a minute minority. Perhaps this situation partially explains why we have the concomitant occurrence of a rapidly expanding black middle class in America's Harlems and increasing crime.

Contrary to the popular defeatist rationale, it is not the unavoidable price of socioeconomic progress in a morally and ethically bankrupt urban society. A more plausible explanation considers the problem of class alienation, which continues to plague this nation's Harlems as it does the entire planet, but with a considerably more divisive and socially detrimental result.

Although the intellectual and academic chasm between the upwardly mobile black middle class and the stagnant or downwardly mobile black masses is probably at least 80 percent imaginary, it is sufficient to delude the former and alienate and infuriate the latter. Admittedly, a significant percentage of this country's young black men are too bitter, too cynical or, for various other reasons, too intractable. And some are definitely incorrigible. Yet most of them possess a hunger for guidance and advice so profound it would be too humiliating to express even if they could.

Compounding the problem of class alienation is the more serious matter of apathy among the adults and community leadership. One youngster told me he lost interest in school when the teachers had no obvious interest in instructing him. "It's all about knowing somebody cares," he said. "That's what makes you care." This same manchild knows murder is wrong, but says, "Everyday poverty is hard to take."

Among today's young black men are many who prefer prison and possible death to abject poverty. They dare the middle class, lower-middle class and leadership class not to care, and an ostensibly sophisticated society continues to ignore the challenge, with tragic consequences. (pp. 76-7)

> *Claude Brown, "Manchild in Harlem," in* The New York Times Magazine, *September 16, 1984, pp. 36, 38, 40, 44, 54, 76-7.*

FURTHER READING

Daniels, Guy. "Claude Brown's World." *The New Republic* 153, No. 2653 (25 September 1965): 26-8.
    Laudatory review of *Manchild in the Promised Land* praising Brown for his objective portrayal of life in Harlem.

Goldman, Robert M., and Crano, William D. "*Black Boy* and *Manchild in the Promised Land:* Content Analysis in the Study of Value Change Over Time." *Journal of Black Studies* 7, No. 2 (December 1976): 169-80.
    Analyzes and compares Richard Wright's autobiography, *Black Boy,* with *Manchild in the Promised Land,* focusing on the "social pressures which might operate in influencing the attitudes and personality characteristics of an author."

Sterling Brown

1901-1989

(Full name Sterling Allen Brown) American poet, folklorist, editor, critic, and essayist.

An important American poet and critic, Brown was one of the first writers to infuse his poetry with black folklore. In his first collection, *Southern Road* (1932), he wove elements of ballads, spirituals, worksongs, and the blues into narrative poems generally written in a southern black dialect. Although Brown published little poetry after this collection, many critics believe that his work was significant in the development of black writing. Robert B. Stepto wrote of Brown's place among other important black writers: "Brown's blues poems are superior to Hughes's; his *Southern Road* rivals Toomer's *Cane* as a presentation of Negro American geography; his portraits of the folk, rural and urban, and his renderings of their speech, have no match."

Brown was born in Washington, D.C., the son of Sterling Nelson and Adelaide Allen Brown. Henry Louis Gates, Jr., described Brown's childhood: "Brown had all the signs of the good life: he was a mulatto with 'good hair' whose father was a well-known author, professor at Howard [University], pastor of the Lincoln Temple Congregational Church, and member of the D.C. Board of Education who had numbered among his closest friends both Frederick Douglass and Paul Laurence Dunbar." After being graduated from Williams College in 1922, Brown enrolled at Harvard University and received an M.A. in English in 1923. According to Joanne V. Gabbin, however, Brown "claimed that he received his finest education from the semiliterate farmers and migrant workers of the rural South." After graduation Brown taught in the rural South—despite his contemporaries' attempts to dissuade him. In a 1973 interview he described the impact of these experiences on his writing: "For the first time, I found something to write about. I found a world of great interest, and it was a world of people, and the poetry of the time—the poetry that I was reading—was a people's poetry." In Virginia, Missouri, Tennessee, and other parts of the South, Brown gathered the material for *Southern Road*.

Brown published *Southern Road* after leaving the South and taking a teaching position at Howard University, where he would remain for forty years. His first volume of poetry includes poems like "Sam Smiley," in which the World War I veteran returns home to find his woman in prison for having killed the baby she conceived by a rich white man in Sam's absence. Sam is lynched for murdering the man. Brown looked humorously at race relations in other poems, particularly in a series featuring the character Slim Greer. In the poem "Slim in Atlanta," the protagonist discovers that blacks are forbidden to laugh in public: "Hope to Gawd I may die / If I ain't speakin' truth / Make de niggers do deir

laughin' / In a telefoam booth." Slim finds the situation so laughable that he jumps to the front of the line, seizes a telephone booth, and proceeds to laugh for four hours, much to the dismay of the three hundred blacks in line. *Southern Road* was a critical success, prompting James Weldon Johnson to change his mind about dialect poetry. Johnson, who had previously said that dialect verse could only depict humor and pathos, now saw a greater depth with Brown's poetry, which he praised in the introduction to *Southern Road*. Despite Brown's success with his first work, however, his publisher rejected his second volume of poetry, *No Hiding Place*, and declined to issue a second printing of *Southern Road*. These decisions had a devastating effect on Brown's reputation as a poet; because no new poems appeared, many of his admirers assumed he had stopped writing. Brown subsequently turned his attention to teaching and to writing criticism, producing several major works on African-American studies. He also edited an anthology entitled *The Negro Caravan* (1941), of which Julius Lester wrote in the introduction

281

to the 1970 revised edition: "It comes as close today as it did in 1941 to being the most important single volume of black writing ever published."

Brown gradually grew depressed over the lack of attention accorded his writing, and he suffered deteriorating relationships with his colleagues. Shunned by several fellow English professors at Howard who scoffed at his "lowbrow" interest in jazz and the blues, Brown nevertheless remained dedicated to Howard. Offered a full-time teaching position at Vassar College in 1945—an offer so extraordinary for a black man at the time that it made national news—Brown politely declined. "I am devoted to Howard," he explained to *Ebony* some twenty-four years later. "These are my people and if I had anything to give they would need it more." In 1971 Howard University granted Brown an honorary degree. It was an award long overdue in the minds of students participating in the Black Arts Movement of the late 1960s, who demanded recognition for the favorite teacher at Howard. A republication of *Southern Road* and a new volume of poetry, *The Last Ride of Wild Bill and Eleven Narratives* (1975), followed. In 1980 American poet Michael S. Harper collected Brown's poems (including many from *No Hiding Place*) and published them in *The Collected Poems of Sterling A. Brown*. These actions rejuvenated interest in Brown during his final years. He died in January 1989.

Although critics often cite Brown as one of the most neglected poets of the twentieth century, they have also undertaken to correct that notion. Brown, now called the bridge between black folk culture and literature, has now received the attention he lacked in his lifetime. Gates proclaimed Brown a seminal figure in black literature: "Such a prolific output in a life that spans the era of Booker T. Washington and the era of Black Power makes him not only the bridge between 19th– and 20th-century black literature, but also the last of the great 'race men,' the Afro-American men of letters, a tradition best epitomized by W. E. B. Du Bois.... A self-styled 'Old Negro,' Sterling Brown is not only the Afro-American Poet Laureate, he is a great poet."

(For further information about Brown's life and works, see *Black Writers; Contemporary Authors,* Vols. 85-88, 127; *Contemporary Authors New Revision Series,* Vol. 26; *Contemporary Literary Criticism,* Vols. 1, 23, 59; and *Dictionary of Literary Biography,* Vols. 48, 51, 63.)

PRINCIPAL WORKS

Outline for the Study of the Poetry of American Negroes (criticism) 1931
Southern Road (poetry) 1932
The Negro in American Fiction (criticism) 1938
Negro Poetry and Drama (criticism) 1938
The Last Ride of Wild Bill and Eleven Narrative Poems (poetry) 1975
*The Collected Poems of Sterling A. Brown [edited by Michael S. Harper] (poetry) 1980

*This work includes many of the poems in Brown's unpublished *No Hiding Place*.

James Weldon Johnson (essay date 1932)

[*Johnson was a newspaper editor, lawyer, U.S. consul to Nicaragua and Venezuela, and a Broadway songwriter. His best-known song, "Lift Every Voice and Sing," has been adopted as the American black national anthem. Although he did not make his living as a writer, he was in fact a successful novelist; he wrote both conventional and experimental poetry, literary and social criticism, histories, and an autobiography. Johnson had earlier claimed that dialect poetry was limited because it contained "only two full stops, humor and pathos," but here in the introduction to Brown's* Southern Road, *he relents, praising Brown's poems that have a basis in black folk life and speech.*]

[Sterling A. Brown] has been instrumental in bringing about the more propitious era in which the Negro artist now finds himself, and in doing that he has achieved a place in the list of young American poets. Mr. Brown's work is not only fine, it is also unique. He began writing just after the Negro poets had generally discarded conventionalized dialect, with its minstrel traditions of Negro life (traditions that had but slight relation, often no relation at all, to *actual* Negro life) with its artificial and false sentiment, its exaggerated geniality and optimism. He infused his poetry with genuine characteristic flavor by adopting as his medium the common, racy, living speech of the Negro in certain phases of *real* life. For his raw material he dug down into the deep mine of Negro folk poetry. He found the unfailing sources from which sprang the Negro folk epics and ballads such as "Stagolee," "John Henry," "Casey Jones," "Long Gone John" and others. (p. xxxvi)

[But he] has made more than mere transcriptions of folk poetry, and he has done more than bring to it mere artistry; he has deepened its meanings and multiplied its implications. He has actually absorbed the spirit of his material, made it his own; and without diluting its primitive frankness and raciness, truly re-expressed it with artistry and magnified power. In a word, he has taken this raw material and worked it into original and authentic poetry. In such poems as "**Odyssey of Big Boy**" and "**Long Gone**" he makes us feel the urge that drives the Negro wandering worker from place to place, from job to job, from woman to woman. There is that not much known characteristic, Negro stoicism, in "**Memphis Blues**" and there is Negro stoicism and black tragedy, too, in "**Southern Road.**" Through the "**Slim Greer**" series he gives free play to a delicious ironical humor that is genuinely Negro. Many of these poems admit of no classification or brand, as, for example, the gorgeous "**Sporting Beasley.**" True, this poem is Negro, but, intrinsically, it is Sterling-Brownian. In such poems as "**Slim Greer**," "**Mr. Samuel and Sam**" and "**Sporting Beasley**" Mr. Brown discloses the possession of a quality that could to advantage be more common among Negro poets—the ability to laugh, to laugh at white folks as well as at black folks.

Mr. Brown has included in [*Southern Road*] some excellent poems written in literary English and form. I feel, however, it is in his poems whose sources are the folk life that he makes, beyond question, a distinctive contribution to American Poetry. (pp. xxxvi-xxxvii)

> *James Weldon Johnson, in an introduction to* Southern Road: Poems *by Sterling A. Brown, 1932. Reprint by Beacon Press, 1974, pp. xxxv-xxxvii.*

Alain Locke (essay date 1934)

[*Locke was a major figure in the Harlem Renaissance; his anthology,* The New Negro: An Interpretation *(1925), is recognized as the first to present this period in depth. In the following excerpt from a 1934 essay, he argues that Brown brings to literature "a new dimension in Negro folk-portraiture" with* Southern Road.]

Many critics, writing in praise of Sterling Brown's first volume of verse [*Southern Road*], have seen fit to hail him as a significant new Negro poet. The discriminating few go further; they hail a new era in Negro poetry, for such is the deeper significance of this volume.... Gauging the main objective of Negro poetry as the poetic portrayal of Negro folklife true in both letter and spirit to the idiom of the folk's own way of feeling and thinking, we may say that here for the first time is that much-desired and long-awaited acme attained or brought within actual reach.

Almost since the advent of the Negro poet public opinion has expected and demanded folk-poetry of him. And Negro poets have tried hard and voluminously to cater to this popular demand. But on the whole, for very understandable reasons, folk-poetry by Negroes, with notable flash exceptions, has been very unsatisfactory and weak, and despite the intimacy of the race poet's attachments, has been representative in only a limited, superficial sense. First of all, the demand has been too insistent. "They required of us a song in a strange land." "How could we sing of thee, O Zion?" There was the canker of theatricality and exhibitionism planted at the very heart of Negro poetry, unwittingly no doubt, but just as fatally. Other captive nations have suffered the same ordeal. But with the Negro another spiritual handicap was imposed. Robbed of his own tradition, there was no internal compensation to counter the external pressure. Consequently the Negro spirit had a triple plague on its heart and mind—morbid self-consciousness, self-pity and forced exhibitionism. Small wonder that so much poetry by Negroes exhibits in one degree or another the blights of bombast, bathos and artificiality. Much genuine poetic talent has thus been blighted either by these spiritual faults or their equally vicious overcompensations. And so it is epoch-making to have developed a poet whose work, to quote a recent criticism, "has no taint of music-hall convention, is neither arrogant nor servile"—and plays up to neither side of the racial dilemma. For it is as fatal to true poetry to cater to the self-pity or racial vanity of a persecuted group as to pander to the amusement complex of the overlords and masters.

I do not mean to imply that Sterling Brown's art is perfect, or even completely mature. It is all the more promising that this volume represents the work of a young man just in his early thirties. But a Negro poet with almost complete detachment, yet with a tone of persuasive sincerity, whose muse neither clowns nor shouts, is indeed a promising and a grateful phenomenon.

By some deft touch, independent of dialect, Mr. Brown is able to compose with the freshness and naturalness of folk balladry—"**Maumee Ruth**," "**Dark O' the Moon**," "**Sam Smiley**," "**Slim Green**," "**Johnny Thomas**," and "**Memphis Blues**" will convince the most sceptical that modern Negro life can yield real balladry and a Negro poet achieve an authentic folk-touch. (pp. 88-9)

With Mr. Brown the racial touch is quite independent of dialect; it is because in his ballads and lyrics he has caught the deeper idiom of feeling or the peculiar paradox of the racial situation. That gives the genuine earthy folk-touch, and justifies a statement I ventured some years back: "the soul of the Negro will be discovered in a characteristic way of thinking and in a homely philosophy rather than in a jingling and juggling of broken English." As a matter of fact, Negro dialect is extremely local—it changes from place to place, as do white dialects. And what is more, the dialect of Dunbar and the other early Negro poets never was on land or sea as a living peasant speech; but it has had such wide currency, especially on the stage, as to have successfully deceived half the world, including the many Negroes who for one reason or another imitate it.

Sterling Brown's dialect is also local, and frankly an adaptation, but he has localised it carefully, after close observation and study, and varies it according to the brogue of the locality or the characteristic jargon of the *milieu* of which he is writing. But his racial effects, as I have said, are not dependent on dialect. Consider "**Maumee Ruth**":

> Might as well bury her
> And bury her deep,
> Might as well put her
> Where she can sleep....
>
> Boy that she suckled
> How should he know,
> Hiding in city holes
> Sniffing the "snow"?

If we stop to inquire—as unfortunately the critic must—into the magic of these effects, we find the secret,

I think, in this fact more than in any other: Sterling Brown has listened long and carefully to the folk in their intimate hours, when they were talking to themselves, not, so to speak, as in Dunbar, but actually as they do when the masks of protective mimicry fall. Not only has he dared to give quiet but bold expression to this private thought and speech, but he has dared to give the Negro peasant credit for thinking. In this way he has recaptured the shrewd Aesopian quality of the Negro folk-thought, which is more profoundly characteristic than their types of metaphors or their mannerisms of speech. They are, as he himself says,

> Illiterate, and somehow very wise,

and it is this wisdom, bitter fruit of their suffering, combined with their characteristic fatalism and irony, which in this book gives a truer soul picture of the Negro than has ever yet been given poetically. The traditional Negro is a clown, a buffoon, an easy laugher, a shallow sobber and a credulous christian; the real Negro underneath is more often an all but cynical fatalist, a shrewd pretender, and a boldly whimsical pagan; or when not, a lusty, realistic religionist who tastes its nectars here and now.

> Mammy
> With deep religion defeating the grief
> Life piled so closely about her

is the key picture to the Negro as christian; Mr. Brown's **"When the Saints Come Marching Home"** is worth half a dozen essays on the Negro's religion. But to return to the question of bold exposure of the intimacies of Negro thinking—read that priceless apologia of kitchen stealing in the **"Ruminations of Luke Johnson,"** reflective husband of Mandy Jane, tromping early to work with a great big basket, and tromping wearily back with it at night laden with the petty spoils of the day's picking. . . . It is not enough to sprinkle "dis's and dat's" to be a Negro folk-poet, or to jingle rhymes and juggle popularised clichés traditional to sentimental minor poetry for generations. One must study the intimate thought of the people who can only state it in an ejaculation, or a metaphor, or at best a proverb, and translate that into an articulate attitude, or a folk philosophy or a daring fable, with Aesopian clarity and simplicity—and above all, with Aesopian candor.

The last is most important; other Negro poets in many ways have been too tender with their own, even though they have learned with the increasing boldness of new Negro thought not to be too gingerly and conciliatory to and about the white man. The Negro muse weaned itself of that in McKay, Fenton Johnson, Toomer, Countee Cullen and Langston Hughes. But in Sterling Brown it has learned to laugh at itself and to chide itself with the same broomstick. (pp. 90-1)

There is a world of psychological distance between this and the rhetorical defiance and the plaintive, furtive sarcasms of even some of our other contemporary poets—even as theirs, it must be said in all justice, was

miles better and more representative than the sycophancies and platitudes of the older writers.

In closing it might be well to trace briefly the steps by which Negro poetry has scrambled up the sides of Parnassus from the ditches of minstrelsy and the trenches of race propaganda. In complaining against the narrow compass of dialect poetry (dialect is an organ with only two stops—pathos and humor), Weldon Johnson tried to break the Dunbar mould and shake free of the traditional stereotypes. But significant as it was, this was more a threat than an accomplishment; his own dialect poetry has all of the clichés of Dunbar without Dunbar's lilting lyric charm. Later in the *Negro Sermons* Weldon Johnson discovered a way out—in a rhapsodic form free from the verse shackles of classical minor poetry, and in the attempt to substitute an idiom of racial thought and imagery for a mere dialect of peasant speech. Claude McKay then broke with all the moods conventional in his day in Negro poetry, and presented a Negro who could challenge and hate, who knew resentment, brooded intellectual sarcasm, and felt contemplative irony. In this, so to speak, he pulled the psychological cloak off the Negro and revealed, even to the Negro himself, those facts disguised till then by his shrewd protective mimicry or pressed down under the dramatic mask of living up to what was expected of him. But though McKay sensed a truer Negro, he was at times too indignant at the older sham, and, too, lacked the requisite native touch—as of West Indian birth and training—with the local color of the American Negro. Jean Toomer went deeper still—I should say higher—and saw for the first time the glaring paradoxes and the deeper ironies of the situation, as they affected not only the Negro but the white man. He realised, too, that Negro idiom was anything but trite and derivative, and also that it was in emotional substance pagan—all of which he convincingly demonstrated, alas, all too fugitively, in *Cane*. But Toomer was not enough of a realist, or patient enough as an observer, to reproduce extensively a folk idiom.

Then Langston Hughes came with his revelation of the emotional color of Negro life, and his brilliant discovery of the flow and rhythm of the modern and especially the city Negro, substituting this jazz figure and personality for the older plantation stereotype. But it was essentially a jazz version of Negro life, and that is to say as much American, or more, as Negro; and though fascinating and true to an epoch this version was surface quality after all.

Sterling Brown, more reflective, a closer student of the folklife, and above all a bolder and more detached observer, has gone deeper still, and has found certain basic, more sober and more persistent qualities of Negro thought and feeling; and so has reached a sort of common denominator between the old and the new Negro. Underneath the particularities of one generation are hidden universalities which only deeply penetrating genius can fathom and bring to the surface. Too many of the articulate intellects of the Negro group—including sadly enough the younger poets—themselves children of opportunity, have been unaware of these deep resources of the past. But here, if anywhere, in the ancient common wisdom of the folk, is the real treasure trove of the Negro poet; and Sterling Brown's poetic divining-rod has dipped significantly over this position. It is in this sense that I believe **Southern Road** ushers in a new era in Negro folk-expression and brings a new dimension in Negro folk-portraiture. (pp. 91-2)

> *Alain Locke, "Sterling Brown, The New Negro Folk-Poet," in* Negro: An Anthology, *edited by Nancy Cunard and Hugh Ford, revised edition, Frederick Ungar Publishing Co., 1970, pp. 88-92.*

Robert B. Stepto (essay date 1985)

[*Stepto is an American critic and educator. He coedited, with Robert O'Meally, The Collected Papers of Sterling Brown, Volume I (1981). In the following essay, originally presented in 1985 at a conference titled "Heritage: A Reappraisal of the Harlem Renaissance," he evaluates Brown's role in the Harlem Renaissance, an arguably undefined period of black creativity in the early twentieth century.*]

One of the most useful activities Afro-Americanist literary historians have been engaged in recently is reassessing the Harlem or New Negro Renaissance. This work has been useful both in terms of shedding new light on the Renaissance and in terms of revealing the subtle processes involved in composing historiography. Let me offer several examples.

In deciding whether to call the Renaissance the "Harlem," "Negro," "New Negro," or "Black" Renaissance, and in choosing whether to employ the term "Renaissance" or "Movement," historians are making major decisions about the Renaissance's literal and symbolic geographical siting. "Harlem" denotes a community, a city that can be alternately referred to, largely for rhetorical purposes, as a "metropolis" or a "mecca." "Negro" and "New Negro" expand the geographical limits further, suggesting something of a national scale, perhaps the Negro nation within the American nation, a nation that is paradoxically as substantial demographically as it is elusive geographically. "Black" is the least used of these terms, principally because it was used least by Renaissance participants. But the phrase "Black Renaissance" helps make an essential point that others . . . are exploring: the Renaissance was international in scale both in terms of where its contributors came from and in terms of its being merely the North American component of something larger and grander that embraced the *Negritude* and *Negrismo* movements as well.

In choosing to employ one or more of these terms, historians are also making a choice about the extent to which they wish to portray the Renaissance as a cultural and/or political phenomenon, this being in part an assertion of how interdisciplinary they and we must be in researching, teaching, and writing about the Renaissance. "Harlem," "Negro," "New Negro," "Black," "Renaissance," and "Movement" are all interdisciplinary terms, but some conventions are being established and the terms are no longer interchangeable. Addison Gayle, for example, has felt the need to yoke "Renaissance" and "Movement" together in order to stress that the activities were both cultural and political, sometimes simultaneously so. (This, of course, allows him to assert more easily than he might otherwise that the Renaissance is epitomized by both Jean Toomer and Marcus Garvey). In contrast, Robert Bone years ago established the phrase, "Negro Renaissance," mainly, I believe, to channel our historiography in the direction of placing the Renaissance in a series of other, primarily literary, American renaissances, beginning with that of the American 1840s and including the New Orleans renaissance of the 1890s, among others.

Within the ranks of historians emphasizing literary activities, periodizing the Renaissance has been more important than naming it. Of greatest interest here has been the role that literary genre has played in steering scholars to their respective formulations. Among the historians of fiction, for example, Robert Bone, Amritjit Singh, and Addison Gayle illustrate the range of opinion that can be seen. Writing thirty years ago, Bone, in his *Negro Novel in America,* adopts what is essentially a non-literary formulation of the period, focuses exclusively on writing of the 1920s, and sees everything ending not with the publication of a certain text or some other literary event, but with the stock market crash of 1929. Singh also adheres to the idea that the Renaissance was roughly a decade, but creates a literary decade, not a cultural-historical one, arguing basically that something began in 1923 with the publication of Jean Toomer's *Cane* and ended in 1933 (years *after* the market crash) with the printing of Jessie Redmon Fauset's *Comedy: American Style* and Claude McKay's *Banana Bottom.* Addison Gayle, is, to say the least, the most expansive in his formulation. He argues, in *The Way of the New World,* that you have to see the period beginning in the 1890s with the militant fictions of Sutton Elbert Griggs, and ending with those of the later 1930s and early 1940s of Richard Wright, the latter including especially *Native Son.* This argument is especially useful to Gayle, since it allows him to historicize the Renaissance while writing history "according to Wright," which is often his goal.

All of these period definitions have their merits, but part of what is fascinating about them is that historians of Afro-American poetry, for example, would probably find them unuseful. The later French Afro-Americanist, Jean Wagner, is, for instance, greatly interested in Toomer's *Cane* but not as the point of departure for Renaissance poetry, and he certainly has little use for the poorly written though politically interesting novels of Sutton Griggs. For him, the Renaissance begins in 1906 with the death of Paul Laurence Dunbar and the completion of DuBois's "Litany at Atlanta" and reaches

Brown, Dorothy Maynard, and W.E.B. Du Bois at Fisk University, 1941.

its zenith in the 1920s *and* 1930s, with the publication of three books, Langston Hughes's *The Weary Blues,* Weldon Johnson's *God's Trombones,* and Sterling Brown's **Southern Road.** Albeit to different ends, the American Gloria Hull also has little interest in the definitions of the fiction historians, her argument being that all such definitions that emphasize one genre or another tend to exclude women writers, and that any focus on Harlem results in the exclusion of all writers outside Harlem, but especially those women poets such as Georgia Douglas Johnson who were active in workshops and writing circles in cities including Chicago, Cleveland, and Washington, D.C.

It seems clear that our understanding and definition of the Harlem or New Negro Renaissance are very much in flux, partly because we are beginning to realize just how much scholarly interests and emphases affect the formulation of its history, and partly because figures as various as Claude McKay, Jean Toomer, Zora Neale Hurston, Georgia Douglas Johnson, and perhaps especially Sterling Brown, both do and do not fit in even the most contemporary assessments of the Renaissance.

Brown is a special problem, chiefly because he has asked in a variety of ways to be left out of *Harlem* Renaissance histories. This he has done in conversation, as when he responds to the charge that he wasn't on the "Renaissance boat" by saying, "I didn't go down to the pier." And he has done so in print, as when he questions the *Harlem* Renaissance in his essay, "**The New Negro in Literature, 1925-1955**," arguing:

> The New Negro is not to me a group of writers centered in Harlem during the second half of the twenties. Most of the writers were not Harlemites; much of the best writing was not about Harlem, which was the show window, the cashier's till, but no more Negro America than New York is America.

There are several ways to receive this pronouncement. One is to conclude that Brown is simply valorizing the term "New Negro" over that of "Harlem," as other historians have done. Another is to appreciate how Brown, before Gayle, Singh, and Hill, was creating space in literary history for writers much like himself who did not confine themselves to Harlem or to Harlem subjects. A third matter here is Brown's assessment, however slight, that the Renaissance was, in terms of literature, more of a publisher's "happening" (congruent, more than we would like to think, with the "happenings" in galleries and "happy hours" in bars and clubs) than an actual renaissance—the "cashier's till" being perhaps the same one that chimed in the 1960s with the "discovery" of black male writers and that rings today now that black women writers have been "unearthed." We don't have to choose; all three responses to Brown's statement are valid. With them in mind we can better understand the place of Brown's work in Renaissance writing, and not surprisingly, we can find poems which suggest that he found a middle ground, one in which he contributed mightily to the Renaissance while going his own way.

I see Brown inside the Renaissance in these terms. To begin with, he is easily as much a part of the Renaissance as is an uncontested figure like Zora Neale Hurston, chiefly because his early published works, like Hurston's, were published in New York during the 1920s and were contextualized in the Renaissance, especially when they received awards from chief Renaissance publishing outlets such as *Opportunity* magazine. (Recall here that Brown's first published poem, **"When de Saint Go Ma'chin' Home,"** was printed by *Opportunity* in 1927 and received its poetry prize for 1928.) Moreover, while Brown's poems do not appear in the pages of Alain Locke's *The New Negro,* which is too often seen as *the* anthology of Renaissance writing, they do appear in Countee Cullen's *Caroling Dusk* (1927), Charles S. Johnson's *Ebony and Topaz* (1927), and V.F. Calverton's Modern Library volume, *The Anthology of Negro American Literature* (1929). When one adds to this the fact that Brown reviewed about a half dozen books for *Opportunity* in the late 1920s (including novels by Julia Peterkin, Roark Bradford, DuBose Heyward, Howard Odum, and Langston Hughes— Brown's review of *Not Without Laughter* actually appeared in October, 1930), it is clear that Brown was part of the Renaissance literary scene, no matter how infrequent his "stopovers" (his term) in New York actually were.

But a more substantive point can be made. Brown *wrote* himself into the Renaissance, in his contribution to blues poetry and in his two major sequences of what I am persuaded to call Renaissance poetry. In the field of blues poetry, Brown matched Langston Hughes step by step, or, innovation by innovation, when he duplicated classic blues forms in poems such as **"Tin Roof Blues,"** and when he successfully simulated entire, communally contextualized blues performances in poems including **"Ma Rainey."** Where he went beyond Hughes was in his singular creations of blues quatrains.

Hughes, for the most part, was content to take the first and third lines of a classic blues stanza (the opening and closing lines), to break each line into two at its caesura, and to call the whole a quatrain. This may be illustrated as follows. The opening stanza of "Sylvester's Dying Bed," in classic blues stanzaic form, is probably something like.

> I woke up this mornin', 'Bout half-past three,
> Woke up this mornin', mama, 'bout half-past three,
> All the womens in town was gathered round me.

Hughes's variation is

> I woke up this morning',
> 'Bout half-past three.
> All the womens in town
> Was gathered round me.

With this he has a quatrain, formed upon the first and third lines, one that is effective but which, as the late George Kent would argue, does not constitute the "real opportunity" for the Afro-American writer. In contrast to Hughes, Brown seeks the "real opportunity" in more poems than one.

Consider, for example, the opening and closing stanzas of **"Riverbank Blues,"** which are blues quatrains of new order.

> A man git his feet set in a sticky mudbank,
> A man git dis yellow water in his blood,
> No need for hopin,' no need for doin,'
> Muddy streams keep him fixed for good.
>
> *"Man got his sea too lak de Mississippi*
> *Ain't got so long for a whole lot longer way,*
> *Man better move some, better not git rooted*
> *Muddy water fool you, ef you stay . . . ."*

The lines are blues lines, certainly in mood, virtually in meter; the stanzas are especially remarkable in that they exhibit anticipated blues features of repetition and call-and-response (see especially the first stanza) while modifying those features (in the second stanza, for example, the repeating line is the third line, not the second, and this breaking of blues form in and of itself communicates that one should move on and out of "muddy-water"—away from blues situations and circumstances.

While it can be said that Brown was outside the Renaissance in that he was in college at Williams when it began and either teaching at Negro colleges or in graduate school at Harvard later on, he was really only outside in the sense that his experiences in the South were more important to him and to his art than those he had in the North. It was in the South that he heard the folk expressions and cadences, the tales and the humor, that pervade his poetry; it was there that he met unforgettable figures like Big Boy Davis and Sister Lou, who are forcefully and lovingly portrayed in poems such as **"Odyssey of Big Boy," "Long Done," "Sister Lou,"** and **"Virginia Portrait".** Brown's Southern odyssey, like Jean Toomer's for him, was a turning point in his life. But we should not overemphasize the place of the resulting poems in Brown's canon any more than we should read just the Southern sections of Toomer's *Cane.* Indeed, ***Southern Road*** and ***No Hidin' Place,*** like *Cane,* offer a careful orchestration of rural and urban images, and Brown's urban settings, unlike Toomer's, include Harlem.

Brown was inside the Renaissance in that he, like Hughes, declared, "I, too, sing America," and outside in that, unlike Hughes, he really meant what he said. How he went his own way is best seen in the fact that this art was far more affected by the flood of 1927 than by cabaret life or Marcus Garvey (though he wrote of cabarets and Garvey, too). In this regard, he was more like Ma Rainey and Bessie Smith than like the average Renaissance writer, and that probably was to his benefit.

The Renaissance gains in stature when our definitions of it allow a place for Sterling Brown, and if our definitions do not offer him a place then they need to be changed. Brown's blues poems are superior to Hughes's; his **Southern Road** rivals Toomer's *Cane* as a presentation of Negro American geography; his portraits of the folk, rural and urban, and his renderings of their speech, have no match. (pp. 73-80)

> *Robert B. Stepto, "Sterling A. Brown: Outsider in the Harlem Renaissance?" in* The Harlem Renaissance: Revaluations, *edited by Amritjit Singh, William S. Shiver, and Stanley Brodwin, Garland Publishing, Inc., 1989, pp. 73-81.*

Henry Louis Gates, Jr. (essay date 1987)

[*Gates, an American critic and educator, is best known for his discovery of Harriet Wilson's* Our Nig, *the first published novel written by a black woman. He also developed the concept of "signifying," a black tradition carried from Yoruba culture to American and Caribbean black culture. He has applied this theory to the poetry of Sterling Brown, among others. In the following excerpt from a 1987 revision of an essay first published in 1981, Gates discusses Brown's impact on the development of twentieth-century black poetry.*]

> "Nigger, your breed ain't metaphysical."
> Robert Penn Warren, "Pondy Woods," 1928

> "Cracker, your breed ain't exegetical."
> Sterling Brown, interview, 1973

By 1932, when Sterling Brown published **Southern Road,** his first book of poems, the use of black vernacular structures in Afro-American poetry was controversial indeed. Of all the arts, it was only through music that blacks had invented and fully defined a tradition both widely regarded and acknowledged to be uniquely their own. Black folktales, while roundly popular, were commonly thought to be the amusing fantasies of a childlike people, whose sagas and anecdotes about rabbits and bears held nothing deeper than the attention span of a child, à la Uncle Remus or even *Green Pastures*. And what was generally called dialect, the unique form of English that Afro-Americans spoke, was thought by whites to reinforce received assumptions about the Negro's mental inferiority.

Dorothy Van Doren simply said out loud what so many other white critics thought privately. "It may be that [the Negro] can express himself only by music and rhythm," she wrote in 1931, "and not by words."

Middle-class blacks, despite the notoriety his dialect verse had garnered for Paul Laurence Dunbar and the Negro, thought that dialect was an embarrassment, the linguistic remnant of an enslavement they all longed to forget. The example of Dunbar's popular and widely reviewed "jingles in a broken tongue," coinciding with the conservatism of Booker T. Washington, was an episode best not repeated. Blacks stood in line to attack dialect poetry. William Stanley Braithwaite, Countee Cullen, and especially James Weldon Johnson argued fervently that dialect stood in the shadow of the plantation tradition of Joel Chandler Harris, James Whitcomb Riley, and Thomas Nelson Page. Dialect poetry, Johnson continued, possessed "but two full stops, humor and pathos." By 1931, Johnson, whose own "Jingles and Croons" (1917) embodied the worst in this tradition, could assert assuredly that "the passing of traditional dialect as a medium for Negro poets is complete."

As if these matters of sensibility were not barrier enough, Johnson believed, somehow that until a black person ("full-blooded" at that) created a written masterpiece of art, black Americans would remain substandard citizens.

Johnson here echoed William Dean Howells's sentiments. Howells wrote that Paul Laurence Dunbar's dialect verse "makes a stronger claim for the negro than the negro yet has done. Here in the artistic effect at least is white thinking and white feeling in a black man.... Perhaps the proof [of human unity] is to appear in the arts, and our hostilities and prejudices are to vanish in them." Even as late as 1925, Heywood Broun could reiterate this curious idea: "A supremely great negro artist who could catch the imagination of the world, would do more than any other agency to remove the disabilities against which the negro now labors." Broun concluded that this black redeemer with a pen could come at any time, and asked his audience to remain silent for ten seconds to imagine such a miracle! In short, the Black Christ would be a poet. If no one quite knew the precise form this Black Christ would assume, at least they all agreed on three things he could not possibly be: he would not be a woman like feminist Zora Neale Hurston; he would not be gay like Countee Cullen or Alain Locke; and he would most definitely not write dialect poetry. Given all this, it is ironic that Brown used dialect at all. For a "New Negro" generation too conscious of character and class as color (and vice versa), Brown had all the signs of the good life: he was a mulatto with "good hair" whose father was a well-known author, professor at Howard, pastor of the Lincoln Temple Congregational Church, and member of the D.C. Board of Education who had numbered among his closest friends both Frederick Douglass and Paul Laurence Dunbar. Brown, moreover, had received a classically liberated education at Dunbar High School, Williams College, and Harvard, where he took an M.A.

in English in 1923. Indeed, perhaps it was just this remarkably secure black artistocratic heritage that motivated Brown to turn to the folk.

Just one year after he had performed the postmortem on dialect poetry, James Weldon Johnson, in the preface to Brown's *Southern Road,* reluctantly admitted that he had been wrong about dialect. Brown's book of poetry, even more profoundly than the market crash of 1929, truly ended the Harlem Renaissance, primarily because it contained a new and distinctly black poetic diction and not merely the vapid and pathetic claim for one.

To the surprise of the Harlem Renaissance's "New Negroes," the reviews were of the sort one imagines Heywood Broun's redeemer-poet was to have gotten. The *New York Times Book Review* said that *Southern Road* is a book whose importance is considerable: "It not only indicates how far the Negro artist has progressed since the years when he began to find his voice, but it proves that the Negro artist is abundantly capable of making an original and genuine contribution to American literature." Brown's work was marked by a "dignity that respects itself.... There is everywhere art." Louis Untermeyer agreed: "He does not paint himself blacker than he is." Even Alain Locke, two years later, called it "a new era in Negro poetry." *Southern Road'*s artistic achievement ended the Harlem Renaissance, for that slim book undermined all of the New Negro's assumptions about the nature of the black tradition and its relation to individual talent. Not only were most of Brown's poems composed in dialect, but they also had as their subjects distinctively black archetypal mythic characters, as well as the black common man whose roots were rural and Southern. Brown called his poetry "portraitures," close and vivid detailings of an action of a carefully delineated subject to suggest a sense of place, in much the same way as Toulouse-Lautrec's works continue to do. These portraitures, drawn "in a manner constant with them," Brown renders in a style that emerged from several forms of folk discourse, a black vernacular matrix that includes the blues and ballads, the spirituals and worksongs. Indeed, Brown's ultimate referents are black music and mythology. His language, densely symbolic, ironical, and naturally indirect, draws upon the idioms, figures, and tones of both the sacred and the profane vernacular traditions, mediating between these in a manner unmatched before or since. Although Langston Hughes had attempted to do roughly the same, Hughes seemed content to transcribe the popular structures he received, rather than to transcend or elaborate upon them, as in "To Midnight Man at LeRoy's": "Hear dat music... / Jungle music / Hear dat music... / And the moon was white."

But it is not merely the translation of the vernacular that makes Brown's work major, informed by these forms as his best work is; it is rather the deft manner in which he created his own poetic diction by fusing several black traditions with various models provided by Anglo-American poets to form a unified and complex structure of feeling, a sort of song of a racial self. Above all else, Brown is a regionalist whose poems embody William Carlos Williams's notion that the classic is the local, fully realized. Yet Brown's region is not so much the South or Spoon River, Tilbury or Yoknapatawpha as it is "the private Negro mind," as Alain Locke put it, "this private thought and speech," or, as Zora Neale Hurston put it, "how it feels to be colored me," the very textual milieu of blackness itself. Boldly, Brown merged the Afro-American vernacular traditions of dialect and myth with the Anglo-American poetic tradition and, drawing upon the example of Jean Toomer, introduced the Afro-American modernist lyrical mode into black literature. Indeed, Brown, Toomer, and Hurston comprise three cardinal points on a triangle of influence out of which emerged, among others, Ralph Ellison, Toni Morrison, Alice Walker, and Leon Forrest.

Brown's poetic influences are various. From Walt Whitman, Brown took the oracular, demotic voice of the "I" and the racial "eye," as well as his notion that "new words, new potentialities of speech" were to be had in the use of popular forms such as the ballad. From Edward Arlington Robinson, Brown took the use of the dramatic situation and the ballad, as well as what Brown calls the subject of "the undistinguished, the extraordinary in the ordinary." Certainly Brown's poems "**Maumee Ruth,**" "**Southern Cop,**" "**Georgie Grimes,**" and "**Sam Smiley**" suggest the same art that created Miniver Cheevy and Richard Cory. From A. E. Housman, Brown borrowed the dramatic voice and tone, as well as key figures: Housman's blackbird in "When Smoke Stood Up from Ludlow" Brown refigures as a buzzard in "**Old Man Buzzard.**" Both Housman's "When I Was One and Twenty" and Brown's "**Telling Fortunes**" use the figure of "women with dark eyes," just as Brown's "**Mill Mountain**" echoes Housman's "Terence, This Is Stupid Stuff." Housman, Heinrich Heine, and Thomas Hardy seem to be Brown's central influence of tone. Robert Burns's Scottish dialect and John Millington Synge's mythical dialect of the Aran Islander in part inform Brown's use of black dialect, just as Robert Frost's realism, stoicism, and sparseness, as in "Out, Out—," "Death of the Hired Man," "Birches," "Mending Wall," and "In Dives' Dive" inform "**Southern Road,**" "**Memphis Blues,**" and "**Strange Legacies.**" Brown's choice of subject matter and everyday speech are fundamentally related to the New Poetry and the work of Amy Lowell, Vachel Lindsay, Edgar Lee Masters, and Carl Sandburg, as well as to the common language emphasis of the Imagists. In lines such as "bits of cloud-filled sky... framed in bracken pools" and "vagrant flowers that fleck unkempt meadows," William Wordsworth's *Lyrical Ballads* resound. Brown rejected the "puzzle poetry" of Ezra Pound and T. S. Eliot and severely reviewed the Southern Agrarians' "I'll Take My Stand" as politically dishonest, saccharine nostalgia for a medieval never-neverland that never was. Brown never merely borrows from any of these poets; he transforms their influence by grafting them onto black poetic roots. These transplants are splendid creations indeed. (pp. 225-29)

Rereading Brown, I was struck by how consistently he shapes the tone of his poems by the meticulous selection of the right word to suggest succinctly complex images and feelings "stripped to form," in Frost's phrase. Unlike so many of his contemporaries, Brown never lapses into pathos or sentimentality. Brown renders the oppressive relation of self to natural and (black and white) man-made environment in the broadest terms, as does the blues. Yet Brown's characters confront catastrophe with all of the irony and stoicism of the blues and black folklore. Brown's protagonists laugh and cry, fall in and out of love, and muse about death in ways not often explored in black literature. Finally, his great theme seems to be the relation of being to the individual will, rendered always in a sensuous diction, echoing what critic Joanne Gabbin calls "touchstones" of the blues lyric, such as "Don't your bed look lonesome / When your babe packs up to leave," "I'm gonna leave heah dis mawnin' ef I have to ride de blind," "Did you ever wake up in de mo'nin', yo' mind rollin' two different ways—/ One mind to leave your baby, and one mind to stay?" or "De quagmire don't hang out no signs." What's more, he is able to realize such splendid results in a variety of forms, including the classic and standard blues, the ballad, a new form that Stephen Henderson calls the blues-ballad, the sonnet, and free verse. For the first time, we can appreciate Brown's full range, his mastery of so many traditions.

In the five-poem ballad cycle "**Slim Greer**," Brown has created the most memorable character in black literature, the trickster. In "**Slim in Atlanta**," segregation is so bad that blacks are allowed to laugh only in a phone booth:

> Hope to Gawd I may die
> If I ain't speakin' truth
> Make de niggers do their laughin'
> In a telefoam booth.

In "**Slim Greer**," the wily Greer in "Arkansaw" "Passed for white, / An' he no lighter / Than a dark midnight / Found a nice white woman / At a dance, / Thought he was from Spain / Or else from France." Finally, it is Slim's uncontainable rhythm that betrays:

> An' he started a-tinklin'
> Some mo'nful blues,
> An' a-pattin' the time
> With No. Fourteen shoes.
>
> The cracker listened
> An' then he spat
> An' said, "No white man
> Could play like that....
>
> Heard Slim's music
> An' then, hot damn!
> Shouted sharp—"Nigger!"
> An' Slim said, "Ma'am?"

Brown balances this sort of humor against a sort of "literate" blues, such as "**Tornado Blues**," not meant to be sung:

> Destruction was a-drivin' it and close behind was
> Fear,
> Destruction was a-drivin' it hand in hand with
> Fear,
> Grinnin' Death and skinny Sorrow was a-bringin'
> up de Rear.
>
> Dey got some ofays, but dey mostly got de Jews
> an' us,
> Got some ofays, but mostly got de Jews an' us,
> Many po' boys castle done settled to a heap
> o'dus'.

Contrast with this stanza the meter of "**Long Track Blues**," a poem Brown recorded with piano accompaniment:

> Heard a train callin'
> Blowin' long ways down the track;
> Ain't no train due here,
> Baby, what can bring you back?
>
> Dog in the freight room
> Howlin' like he los' his mind;
> Might howl myself,
> If I was the howlin' kind.

In "**Southern Road**," Brown uses the structure of the worksong, modified by the call-and-response pattern of a traditional blues stanza:

> Doubleshackled—hunh—
> Guard behin';
> Doubleshackled—hunh—
> Guard behin';
> Ball an' chain, bebby,
> On my min'.
>
> White man tells me—hunh—
> Damn yo' soul;
> White man tells me—hunh—
> Damn yo' soul;
> Get no need, bebby,
> To be tole.

Brown is a versatile craftsman, capable of representing even destruction and death in impressively various ways. In "**Sam Smiley**," for example, he describes a lynching in the most detached manner: "The mob was in fine fettle, yet / The dogs were stupid-nosed; and day / Was far spent when the men drew round / The scrawny wood where Smiley lay. / The oaken leaves drowsed prettily, / The moon shone benignly there; / And big Sam Smiley, King Buckdancer, / Buckdanced on the midnight air." On the other hand, there is a certain irony in "**Children of the Mississippi**": "De Lord tole Norah / Dat de flood was due / Norah listened to de Lord / An' got his stock on board, / Wish dat de Lord / Had tole us too."

Brown also uses the folk-rhyme form, the sort of chant to which children skip rope: "Women as purty / As Kingdom Come / Ain't got no woman / Cause I'm black and dumb." He also combines sources as unlike as Scott's "Lady of the Lake" and the black folk ballad "Wild Negro Bill" in his most extended ballad, "**The Last Ride of Wild Bill**." Often, he takes lines directly from the classic blues, as in "**Ma Rainey**," where three lines of Bessie Smith's "Backwater Blues" appear. Perhaps Brown is at his best when he writes of death, a subject he treats with a haunting lyricism, as in "**Odyssey of Big Boy**":

> Lemme be wid Casey Jones,
>   Lemme be wid Stagolee,
> Lemme be wid such like men
>   When Death takes hol' on me,
>   When Death takes hol' on me . . . .
> Done took my livin' as it came,
>   Done grabbed my joy, done risked my life;
> Train done caught me on de trestle,
>   Man done caught me wid his wife,
>   His doggone purty wife.

He achieves a similar effect in "**After Winter**," with lines such as "He snuggles his fingers / In the blacker loam" and "Ten acres unplanted / To raise dreams on / Butterbeans fo' Clara / Sugar corn fo' Grace / An' fo' de little feller / Runnin' space."

When I asked why he chose the black folk as his subject, Brown replied:

> Where Sandburg said, "The people, yes," and Frost, "The people, yes, maybe," I said, "The people, maybe, I hope!" I didn't want to attack a stereotype by idealizing. I wanted to deepen it. I wanted to understand my people. I wanted to understand what it meant to be a Negro, what the qualities of life were. With their imagination, they combine two great loves: the love of words and the love of life. Poetry results.

Just as Brown's importance as a teacher can be measured through his students (such as LeRoi Jones, Kenneth Clarke, Ossie Davis, and many more), so too can his place as a poet be measured by his influence on other poets, such as Leopold Senghor, Aimé Césaire, Nicolas Guillen, and Michael Harper, to list only a few. Out of Brown's realism, further, came Richard Wright's naturalism; out of his lyricism came Hurston's *Their Eyes Were Watching God*; his implicit notion that "De eye dat sees / Is de I dat be's" forms the underlying structure of *Invisible Man*. In his poetry, several somehow black structures of meaning have converged to form a unified and complex structure of feeling, a poetry as black as it is Brown's. This volume of poems, some of which are recorded on two Folkways albums, along with his collected prose (three major books of criticism, dozens of essays, reviews, and a still unsurpassed anthology of black literature) being edited by Robert O'Meally and a splendid literary biography by Joanne

Gabbin, all guarantee Brown's place in literary history. Brown's prolific output coupled with a life that spans the Age of Booker T. Washington through the era of Black Power, makes him not only the bridge between nineteenth- and twentieth-century black literature but also the last of the great "race men," the Afro-American men of letters, a tradition best epitomized by W. E. B. Du Bois. . . . A self-styled "Old Negro," Sterling Brown is not only the Afro-American poet laureate; he is a great poet. (pp. 230-34)

> *Henry Louis Gates, Jr., "Songs of a Racial Self: On Sterling A. Brown," in his* Figures in Black: Words, Signs, and 'Racial' Self, *Oxford University Press, Inc., 1987, pp. 225-34.*

FURTHER READING

Allen, Samuel W. "Sterling Brown: Poems to Endure." *The Massachusetts Review* XXIV, No. 3 (Autumn 1983): 649-57.

> Praises the 1980 republication of Brown's three collections of poetry, edited by Michael Harper and entitled *The Collected Poems of Sterling A. Brown*.

Gabbin, Joanne V. *Sterling A. Brown: Building the Black Aesthetic Tradition*. Westport, Conn.: Greenwood Press, 1985, 245 p.

> Comprehensive analysis of Brown's influences and legacy, including a discussion of his years at Howard University, his work with the Federal Writers' Project, and his poetry and criticism.

Smith, Gary. "The Literary Ballads of Sterling A. Brown." *CLA Journal* XXXII, No. 4 (June 1989): 393-409.

> Appraises Brown's black American folk ballads, determining that "Brown's achievement clearly overshadows his contemporaries, Jean Toomer, Countee Cullen, Langston Hughes, and Claude McKay, all of whom, in their poetry, were important architects of the New Negro but who did considerably less than Brown to restore the ethnic identity of black Americans."

Wright, John S. "The New Negro Poet and the Nachal Man: Sterling A. Brown's Folk Odyssey." *Black American Literature Forum* 23, No. 1 (Spring 1989): 95-105.

> Explores Brown's use of folklore in his poetry.

William Wells Brown

1816?-1884

American novelist, dramatist, autobiographer, editor, essayist, and historian.

Brown is well known for two works: *Clotel; or, The President's Daughter: A Narrative of Slave Life in the United States* (1853) and *The Escape; or, A Leap for Freedom* (1858), respectively the first novel and the first drama published by a black American. Brown was also an internationally recognized historian and lecturer, known especially for his works on the African-American experience.

The son of a slave mother and a white slaveholding father, Brown was born and lived the first twenty years of his life on a plantation near Lexington, Kentucky. As a bondman, young William was often "hired out" by his various masters, providing him with opportunities not normally afforded a slave. In 1830, after working for several years in hotels and on steamboats, he began working for Elijah P. Lovejoy, an abolitionist newspaperman who was later murdered by a pro-slavery mob. Under Lovejoy's direction, William acquired a rudimentary education, though he remained functionally illiterate for some time. After six months with Lovejoy, the young man was again hired out as a steward on a steamboat. William escaped to freedom from this ship, the *Chester,* while it was docked at a small town on the Ohio River on New Year's Day, 1834. While a fugitive, William was befriended by an Ohio Quaker named Wells Brown. The young man was so grateful for the assistance he received that he honored his benefactor by taking his name. The ex-slave was known thereafter as William Wells Brown.

Brown first settled in Cleveland, Ohio, where he met and married Elizabeth Schooner, a free Negro. (Elizabeth died in 1851; nine years later he married his second wife, Annie Elizabeth Gray.) In Cleveland, Brown worked as a handyman while continuing to teach himself reading and writing. He then moved to Monroe, Michigan, where he set up his own barbershop and established a small bank, both of which were profitable. Despite these successes, he decided to hire on as a steward on a Lake Erie steamboat. During this period, Brown became an important link on the Underground Railroad, helping other escaped slaves to reach freedom in Canada. He eventually moved to Buffalo, New York, where he met William Lloyd Garrison, who enlisted him as a lecturer in the abolitionist cause. Brown became a tireless speaker on behalf of reform, temperance, and antislavery, delivering literally thousands of lectures both in the United States and abroad.

Brown's first publication, *Narrative of William W. Brown, a Fugitive Slave, Written by Himself* (1847), is a vivid account of the author's life, trials, and escape to freedom. The work was a great success; it went through four printings in two years and established Brown as an important social reformer. Brown was encouraged by the success of the *Narrative,* and in 1848 he collected a group of antislavery songs and published them under the title *The Anti-Slavery Harp: A Collection of Songs for Anti-Slavery Meetings.* Because of his ability as a speaker, Brown was chosen by the American Peace Society as its representative to the Paris Peace Congress of 1849. He was to remain in Europe for the next five years. Warmly received in European intellectual circles, Brown became friends with the English statesman Richard Cobden, the French writers Victor Hugo and Alexis de Tocqueville, and other notable figures of the day. These activities, as well as his extensive travels as an abolitionist lecturer, are chronicled in his next publication, *Three Years in Europe; or, Places I Have Seen and People I Have Met* (1852). At this time Brown was still a fugitive slave, and he did not become legally free until several English friends raised the money to pay his indenture.

While in England, Brown released the novel *Clotel; or, The President's Daughter: A Narrative of Slave Life in the United States*, a work that proved to be a popular success and something of a scandal. Drawing on the legend that Thomas Jefferson had fathered many children by his slave mistress, Brown cast his heroine, Clotel, as the slave daughter of the former president. Brown sought to depict the horror and irony of the "peculiar institution" of slavery, a system that would allow the daughter of a president to be sold into bondage. W. Edward Farrison wrote of the critical reaction to *Clotel*: "Coming within eighteen months after the first British edition of Mrs. Harriet Beecher Stowe's *Uncle Tom's Cabin,* with which it could be compared to no advantage, *Clotel* attracted no especially remarkable attention in England, and this version of the story was never published in America." Brown issued a revised version, which some critics consider an improvement, in the United States titled *Miralda; or, The Beautiful Quadroon.* This appeared in New York as a newspaper serial in 1860-1861. Three years later he published another version, this time with the title *Clotelle: A Tale of the Southern States.* The work was again reissued in 1867 as *Clotelle; or, The Colored Heroine.* For these American versions Brown chose not to suggest presidential parentage for his heroine, concentrating instead on the heroism of his black characters in their fight for freedom.

By 1856 Brown had also written a drama, *Experience; or, How to Give a Northern Man a Backbone.* This work was never published and is now lost. Numerous synopses and reports of Brown's readings of it do survive, however. These accounts indicate that audiences admired the play warmly. Within a year, Brown had composed a second play, *The Escape; or, A Leap for Freedom.* Although *The Escape* was never performed on stage, Brown gave many readings of the play, chiefly to antislavery gatherings in the North, and his recitals were enthusiastically received. Nevertheless, it is perhaps as a historian of the African-American experience that Brown is now best remembered. In such works as *The Black Man: His Antecedents, His Genius, and His Achievements* (1863), *The Negro in the American Rebellion: His Heroism and His Fidelity* (1867), and *The Rising Son; or, The Antecedents and Advancement of the Colored Race* (1874), Brown illustrated the importance of blacks in American culture. In his last work, *My Southern Home; or, The South and Its People* (1880), Brown presented essays of a nostalgic nature, combining his political and social concerns in a reminiscence of the South.

Critical reaction to Brown's works has varied over time. Although *The Escape* was praised by contemporary audiences, J. Saunders Redding later found the drama to be "loosely constructed according to the formula of the day and marred by didacticism and heroic sentimentality." Commentators have also been critical of Brown's role as both a writer and social activist; some have regarded his works as questionable mixtures of fact and fiction and have often termed them "propaganda."

Others have objected to Brown's treatment of blacks. Addison Gayle, Jr., accused Brown of creating unrealistic, almost white characters for a white audience. "To call Brown the first novelist of the black bourgeoisie is not too far wrong," wrote Gayle of Brown's novel. "Given her choice of several worlds in the novel, Clotel retained a more than casual affinity for the white." Despite the varied critical response to his works, however, Brown's place as a pioneer in the development of African-American literature is undisputed.

Brown was a passionate, committed writer and speaker who was, as he himself seemed to suggest, more concerned with the content than the form of his works. Nevertheless, critics agree that Brown strove in his works to offer more than merely an informational lecture. By exploring serious issues through humorous or thrilling action, he sought to move his listeners as well as persuade them, to entertain as well as inform. How successful he was remains the subject of critical debate. What is certain is that Brown was a dedicated fighter for the abolitionist cause who devoted his life and his work to the freedom and dignity of his people. Self-educated and strong-willed, he defied the barriers of racial prejudice to contribute the first novel, the first play, and some of the first notable works of history by an African-American.

(For further information about Brown's life and works, see *Dictionary of Literary Biography,* Vols. 3, 50; *Drama Criticism,* Vol. 1; and *Nineteenth-Century Literature Criticism,* Vol. 2.)

PRINCIPAL WORKS

A Lecture Delivered before the Female Anti-Slavery Society of Salem (essay) 1847
Narrative of William W. Brown, a Fugitive Slave, Written by Himself (autobiography) 1847
The Anti-Slavery Harp: A Collection of Songs for Anti-Slavery Meetings [editor] (songs) 1848
Three Years in Europe; or, Places I Have Seen and People I Have Met (travel essays) 1852; also published as *The American Fugitive in Europe: Sketches of Places and People Abroad,* 1855
Clotel; or, The President's Daughter: A Narrative of Slave Life in the United States (novel) 1853; also published as *Miralda; or, The Beautiful Quadroon* [revised edition] 1861-62; also published as *Clotelle: A Tale of the Southern States* [revised edition], 1864; also published as *Clotelle; or, The Colored Heroine* [revised edition], 1867
St. Domingo: Its Revolutions and Its Patriots (essay) 1855
The Escape; or, A Leap for Freedom (drama) [first publication] 1858
The Black Man: His Antecedents, His Genius, and His Achievements (history) 1863
The Negro in the American Rebellion: His Heroism and His Fidelity (history) 1867
The Rising Son; or, The Antecedents and Advancement of the Colored Race (history) 1874

My Southern Home; or, The South and Its People
(narrative essays) 1880

J. Saunders Redding (essay date 1939)

[*Redding was an American educator, critic, historian, and author. His 1939 work* To Make a Poet Black *has been highly praised as a landmark study of African-American literature. In the following excerpt from the 1939 study, he surveys Brown's life and writings, conceding that Brown's importance is undeniable, but dismissing much of his writing as propaganda.*]

The most unusual figure in the literary history of the American Negro is William Wells Brown. A great deal of the interest which attaches to him is, perhaps, artificial, growing out of the confusion and variety of the stories he told about himself. At one time or another he put forward at least three versions of his parentage and early childhood. In what seems to be the first autobiographical account, he tells us that he was born in Kentucky of slave parents, and that as a child he learned to work in the field and in the house. In the second account he sheds no further light on his ancestry, but tells us that he was stolen by a slave trader shortly after birth. Finally, in the second revised edition of his *Narrative,* he divulges that he was born on an undetermined date in Lexington, Kentucky, of a white father (scion of the family to which his mother was slave) and a mother whose father, "it was said, was the noted Daniel Boone." All accounts agree on two circumstances: that he was born in Kentucky, and that later, while still a boy, he escaped into Ohio.

The discrepancies in the stories of Brown's birth and his early life may be due to one of three things: Brown himself may have been untruthful; unscrupulous publishers, seeking to dress an old tale in more attractive colors, may have been responsible; and last, the white-father, Daniel Boone-grandfather version may have been invented by abolitionist editors in an effort further to stigmatize slavery. White (and generally aristocratic) paternity was certainly a favorite propagandic device in the fictional stories of slaves. It was used to show the demoralizing effect of slavery upon the master class. Many so-called biographies and autobiographies of "escaped slaves" were pure inventions of white writers of the period.

When Brown escaped into Ohio he was befriended by a Quaker, Wells Brown, from whom he took his name. Later he seems to have been recaptured, and through various changes in his ownership he became a cabin boy on the Mississippi, a confidential assistant to a slave trader, and finally a printer's devil in (and this is his own unestablished story) the news office of Elijah P. Lovejoy, an abolitionist journalist in St. Louis who was later killed for his liberal views. Brown tells us that it was in his capacity as printer's devil that he learned to read. Later he went into Canada.

Brown earned his living as he could and spent most of his spare time in study. Certainly in western New York State, to which he eventually made his way, there was abroad enough of the spirit of freedom and democracy to encourage him. An impressionable man all his life, he was touched by nearly everything he heard and saw, absorbing much that was odd and valueless along with that that was solid and worthwhile. His autobiographies are full of his early impressions as an escaped slave. Finally, "impressed with the importance of spreading anti-slavery truth, as a means of abolishing slavery, I commenced lecturing as an agent of the western New York Anti-Slavery Society, and have ever since devoted my time to the cause of my enslaved countrymen." Though this work engaged him for fifteen years, and though it has been estimated that he delivered in England alone a thousand speeches during a stay of five years from 1849 to 1854, Brown's speeches are lost for the most part. This apparently studied neglect of his own speeches seems to indicate that he was interested chiefly in writing.

William Wells Brown was the first serious creative prose writer of the Negro race in America. Three editions of the *Narrative of William Wells Brown,* his first considerable work, appeared under the sponsorship of the Massachusetts Anti-Slavery Society between 1847 and 1849. *The Black Man, St. Domingo,* and *Three Years In Europe,* were published before the close of the Civil War, and though the first two of these were attempts at objective historical writing and the third was a travel account, Brown was so dominated by "the cause of my countrymen" that his facts are garbled to serve the ends of propaganda.

When the slavery controversy had settled into well-defined patterns and the cause for which he had begun his career was no longer so pressing, Brown launched his purely imaginative efforts. This period from about 1850 to 1865 was productive of two novels, *Clotel; or The President's Daughter* (1853) and *Miralda; or The Beautiful Quadroon* (1867) and a play, *The Escape* (1858). These are the first pieces of fiction and the first play by an American Negro. After the war Brown did his more reasonable and most ambitious works, two histories and a group of narrative essays. *The Negro in the American Rebellion* was published in 1868, *The Rising Son* in 1874, and *My Southern Home* in 1880.

In facility of expression, in artistic discrimination, and in narrative skill Brown advanced steadily from the *Narrative* to the essays which comprise his last work. Historically more important in the development of Negro literature than any of his contemporaries, he was also the most representative Negro of the age, for he was simply a man of slightly more than ordinary talents doing his best in a cause that was his religion. Frederick Douglass was too exceptional; Remond too selfish. Almost without forethought, like an inspired prophet,

Brown gave expression to the hope and despair, the thoughts and yearnings of thousands of what he was pleased to call his "countrymen."

Brown had the vital energy that is part of the equipment of all artists. He wrote with force, with clarity, and at times with beauty. There is in his work, however, a repetitive amplification that is not altogether accountable to a desire for perfection. His autobiography, first published in 1847, had been spun out to twice its original length by the time of its publication in London two years later. *St. Domingo,* originally a speech and later a pamphlet, finally became the basis for several chapters on the West Indies in *The Rising Son.* Certain episodes from his *Narrative* were used as starting points for pieces in *My Southern Home. Three Years in Europe,* came to America as *Sketches of Places and People Abroad. Clotel* was attenuated (by deleting the unseen antagonist, Thomas Jefferson, and by making various lengthening changes) into *Clotelle; a Tale of the Southern States.* If Brown's play, *Doughface,* mentioned by William Simmons, ever comes to light, it is likely that it will be found to be merely an earlier sketch of the drama, *The Escape, or A Leap for Freedom,* published in 1858 and read in many parts of the country prior to that. Even *Miralda* got mixed up with *Clotel,* but this time it was *Clotelle, The Colored Heroine.*

Brown was driven by the necessity for turning out propaganda in a cause that was too close to him for emotional objectivity and reasonable perspective. He had power without the artist's control, but in spite of this his successes are considerable and of great importance to the history of Negro creative literature. First novelist, first playwright, first historian: the list argues his place. It is doubtful that in the writing of his novels, plays, and histories he saw beyond "the cause." Even in the later years of his life, when it seems he would have been free to focus artistically, he did not change too appreciably. *The Rising Son,* done with an eye to fact, to cause and effect, and to arriving at logical conclusions, is undoubtedly an advance over *The Black Man,* but it is also a deliberate plea in behalf of the Negro race. *My Southern Home* is a vastly better book than the *Narrative,* but less in the sense of artistic objectivity than in craftsmanship. All his days Brown was first a Negro and then a writer.

At its best Brown's language is cursive and strong, adapted to the treatment he gives his material. When he held his bitterness in check, he was inclined to lay on a heavy coating of sentimental morality. Often his lack of control did hurt to an otherwise good passage. A slave-auction scene in *Clotel* illustrates his fault. After a racy and realistic description of a Richmond slave market in which a beautiful quadroon girl was struck off to the highest bidder, Brown ends thus:

> This was a Virginia slave-auction, at which the bones, sinews, blood and nerves of a young girl of eighteen were sold for $500: her moral character for $200; her superior intellect for $100; the benefits supposed to accrue from her having been sprinkled

and immersed, together with a warranty of her devoted christianity, for $300; her ability to make a good prayer for $200; and her chastity for $700 more. This, too, in a city thronged with churches, whose tall spires look like so many signals pointing to heaven, but whose ministers preach that slavery is a God-ordained institution.

Though it is possible that Brown was true to fact in the following passage, there is nevertheless a loss of force. This loss is due to his failure to see *truth* beyond mere fact. It may be that his mother did talk and act as he has her talk and act in the following passage of the *Narrative,* but she is not real to us either as an individual or a type.

> At about ten o'clock in the morning I went on board the boat and found her there in company with fifty or sixty other slaves. She was chained to another woman. On seeing me, she immediately dropped her head on her heaving bosom. She moved not, neither did she weep. Her emotions were too deep for tears. I approached, threw my arms around her neck, kissed her, and fell upon my knees, begging her forgiveness, for I thought myself to blame for her sad condition . . . .
>
> She finally raised her head, looked me in the face, (and such a look none but an angel can give!) and said, "My dear son, you are not to blame for my being here. You have done nothing more nor less than your duty. Do not, I pray you, weep for me. I cannot last long upon a cotton plantation. I feel that my heavenly master will soon call me home, and then I shall be out of the hands of the slaveholders!"

Like many of Brown's shortcomings, the fault of sacrificing truth to fact is the result of the necessity of yielding to the demands of propaganda. He never entirely rid himself of this fault, but in *My Southern Home,* his last book, he does have southern field Negroes talk and act like southern field Negroes.

The play *The Escape,* in five acts and seventeen scenes, shows clearly that Brown knew nothing of the stage. Loosely constructed according to the formula of the day and marred by didacticism and heroic sentimentality, its chief characters are but pawns in the hands of Purpose. The heroine Melinda is the identical twin of Miralda; and Clotel might have been their mother. Except the pronounced black type, all Brown's women conform to the character pattern set by Charles Brockden Brown and the ancestral pattern established by Fenimore Cooper's Cora Munro. William Brown's women are all octoroons, quadroons, or, at the very least, mulattoes. The unconscious irony in creating such characters is very sharp, whispering his unmentionable doubt of the racial equality he preached. His characters are no more representative of the Negroes he was supposed to depict than are Eliza and Uncle Tom. His women are beautiful and charming, finely mannered, appealing. What did the women of the master class have that Melinda or Cynthia lacked?

> Poor Cynthia! I knew her well. She was a quadroon, and one of the most beautiful women I ever saw. She was a native of St. Louis, and had there an irre-

proachable character for virtue and propriety of conduct. Mr. Walker bought her for the New Orleans market, and took her down with him on one of the trips I made with him. Never shall I forget the circumstances of that voyage! On the first night that we were on board the steamboat, he directed me to put her in a stateroom that he had provided for her, apart from the other slaves. I had seen too much of the workings of slavery not to know what this meant. I accordingly watched him into the stateroom, and listened to hear what passed between them. I heard him make his base offers and her reject them . . . . Neither threats nor bribes prevailed, however, and he retired disappointed of his prey."

Brown's work as historian and commentator is far more substantial than his work in the purely creative field. Two of his earlier historical works, **The Black Man** and **The Negro in the American Rebellion,** were but as notes for **The Rising Son,** a work comprehending not only the ancient history of the Negro race in Africa, but treating successively the great epochs in the racial career down to Brown's own day. Using key episodes and men as the basis for historical narratives of more than ordinary interest, **The Rising Son** is an outline of history rather than a detailed relation of it. In this work Brown's blunt prejudices are shown softened into calmer rationalism: the swords he usually ground are here beaten into crude ploughshares. It should not be expected that after fifty years he could change precipitantly and wholly, but there is no doubt that in the end the artistic core of him rose up to assert itself.

Even more evident of the victory of his artistic consciousness over his social consciousness is his last work, **My Southern Home.** He came at last to the recognition of permanent literary values over the ephemeral sensational. He is a composed Brown in **My Southern Home,** writing charmingly and interestingly of experiences close to him and of people who are *people.* Humor and pathos, sense and nonsense are skillfully blended in pieces that show his narrative skill at its best. He does not avoid propaganda altogether, but he administers it sparingly and in sugar-coated doses. The warmth and sunshine of the South glows over his pages. It is completely right that **My Southern Home,** his last book, should be also his best.

Brown died in 1884 in Cambridge, Massachusetts, after a full life of devotion to the cause of freedom. His prose adds ballast to the whole mass of antislavery writing. His place in the social history of America and in the literary history of the American Negro is assured. The first Negro writer of the drama and the novel, he was also the first American man of color to earn his living by his pen. Undoubtedly Brown stands high in the impressive list of Americans of Negro blood. (pp. 23-30)

J. Saunders Redding, "Let Freedom Ring," in his To Make a Poet Black, *1939. Reprint by Cornell University Press, 1988, pp. 19-48.*

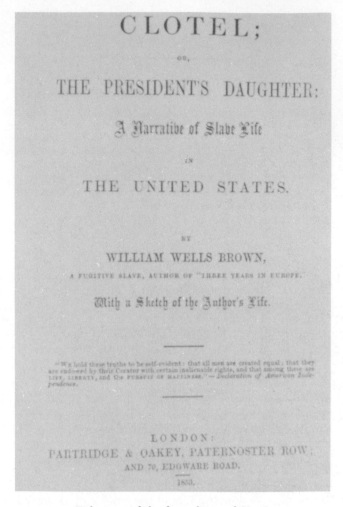

CLOTEL;

OR,

THE PRESIDENT'S DAUGHTER:

A Narrative of Slave Life

IN

THE UNITED STATES.

BY

WILLIAM WELLS BROWN,

A FUGITIVE SLAVE, AUTHOR OF "THREE YEARS IN EUROPE."

With a Sketch of the Author's Life.

LONDON:
PARTRIDGE & OAKEY, PATERNOSTER ROW;
AND 70, EDGWARE ROAD.
1853.

Title page of the first edition of Clotel.

Arna Bontemps (essay date 1966)

[*A prominent figure of the Harlem Renaissance, Bontemps was a poet, critic, dramatist, historian, novelist, and writer of children's books. In the following excerpt, he argues that Brown "was the first creative prose writer of importance produced by the Negro race in America."*]

The period in which the slave narrative flourished was, of course, the period in which the Negro spiritual reached its flowering. One was poetry, the other prose. Indeed, words from the spirituals are often quoted in the narratives. But the connection between the narratives and the subsequent literary expression they stimulated is more direct and immediate than that between the spirituals and the music they came eventually to influence.

William Wells Brown is the link. One of the three men who, in Saunders Redding's judgment, best reflected "the temper and opinion of the Negro in those years," Brown is elected as "the most representative Negro of the age" [see excerpt above]. Of the other two, Charles

Remond and Frederick Douglass, Remond's otherwise brilliant career as an antislavery exponent was marred by jealousy of Douglass, and Douglass seemed too exceptional to stand as "representative." All three devoted their lives to the cause of abolition, and only Remond did not leave an autobiography. All three could write effectively when the need arose, but only Brown's writing evolved into what might be called a literary career. Here his place among American Negroes is secure.

Like many Negroes before and since, indeed like many writers, Brown made maximum use of his personal history as literary material. Some of this can only lead to confusion if the truth is sought, because he gave at least three versions of his parentage and early childhood. In successive versions the details he gave became more exciting. Whether this reflects burgeoning professionalism in letters or merely the shedding of early reticence as he developed, the fact remains that contradictions exist.

First, he records that he was born of slave parents in Kentucky and grew up as a slave child working in the fields and the house. His second account introduces a bit of drama which reappears, interestingly, in all the biographies of George Washington Carver. He speaks of being stolen by a slave trader shortly after his birth. Then, in the second revised edition of his *Narrative,* he really lets the chips fall. He was born, he states, here, of a white father, scion of the family which owned his mulatto mother in Lexington, Kentucky. The father of his slave mother, "it was said, was the noted Daniel Boon," according to this account.

The frequent references to white paternity in autobiographical narratives like Brown's as well as in fictional stories of slaves in that period, have sometimes been branded as propaganda devices by abolitionists wishing to stigmatize slavery by showing the demoralizing effect of the institution on the master class. Photographic evidence, in Brown's case, as in many others, would seem to support the disclosure at least to the extent of the mixed parentage, and apparently no one offered to dispute it while he lived. (pp. 867-68)

In addition to three successful versions of the *Narrative of William Wells Brown* his abolitionist years yielded also for the cause *Three Years in Europe: or, Places I Have Seen and People I Have Met,* London, 1852; *St. Domingo: Its Revolutions and Its Patriots,* Boston, 1855. But in this period he also wrote and published two novels and a play, the first pieces of fiction and the first drama by an American Negro. As such they may be read either as period pieces of literary Americana or as lineal antecedents of the works of Richard Wright and Lorraine Hansberry.

The first novel, when it appeared in London in 1853, was called *Clotelle; or, The President's Daughter.* Its heroine was a beautiful near-white girl, and there was an implication that it was based on truth, making a tie-in with gossip that was then current. This became a bit more restrained in the Boston edition published almost a decade later with a new subtitle: *A Tale of the Southern States.* According to Saunders Redding, "Brown was driven by the necessity for turning out propaganda in a cause that was too close to him for emotional objectivity and reasonable perspective. He had power without the artist's control, but in spite of this his successes are considerable and of great importance to the history of Negro creative literature. First novelist, first playwright, first historian: the list argues his place." [see essay dated 1939].

A quotation from *Clotelle* suggests the mixture. Following a description of a Richmond slave market where a beautiful quadroon girl is offered to bidders, Brown summarizes:

> This was a Virginia slave-auction, at which the bones, sinews, blood and nerves of a young girl of eighteen were sold for $500; her moral character for $200; her superior intellect for $100; the benefits supposed to accrue from her having been sprinkled and immersed, together with a warranty of her devoted Christianity, for $300; her ability to make a good prayer, for $200; and her chastity for $700 more. This, too, in a city thronged with churches, whose tall spires look like so many signals pointing to heaven, but whose ministers preach that slavery is a God-ordained institution.

The second novel appears to have run in the New York *Anglo-African* as a serial, 1860-61. Its titles seem sufficiently descriptive: *Miralda, or, The Beautiful Quadroon. A Romance of American Slavery. Founded on Fact.* Meanwhile, *The Escape: or, A Leap for Freedom, Drama in Five Acts,* was published in Boston in 1858. Brown's writings after the Civil War have been described as "more reasonable." With the campaign over and tensions relaxed, he settled down and began to produce histories and narrative essays that still do him credit, nearly a hundred years later. *The Negro in the American Rebellion,* 1868, *The Rising Son,* 1874, and *My Southern Home,* 1880, are representative.

Another first, possibly as significant as those he established in fiction, drama and historical writing, was also recorded by William Wells Brown. He was the first Negro in the United States to earn a living by his writing. (pp. 868-70)

> *Arna Bontemps, "The Negro Contribution to American Letters," in* The American Negro Reference Book, *edited by John P. Davis, Prentice-Hall, Inc., 1966, pp. 850-78.*

Doris M. Abramson (essay date 1968)

[Abramson was one of the first critics to treat The Escape *as a serious work of art. In the following excerpt, she defends the drama and argues that Brown's public readings of the piece were universally praised.]*

THE DEATH OF CLOTEL. *Page* 218.

Illustration from Clotel.

In J. Saunders Redding's book, *On Being a Negro in America,* published in 1951 and reissued with "no updating needed" in 1962, that distinguished Negro scholar and teacher observed:

> Negro scholars have written thousands of dissertations, theses, monographs, articles, essays and books in a gigantic effort to correct the multiple injuries done the race by white writers. Five great collections—at Howard, Hampton, Fisk, Yale, and the Harlem Branch of the New York Public Library—house thousands of volumes and hundreds of magazine and newspaper files, but few except Negroes bother to disturb their dust. Whites show little interest in this Negroana. They seem to feel that they do not need to know about the Negro; they seem to feel that the basic truths about him were established long ago.

Whether or not Redding would revise these statements in view of recent scholarship and changing social attitudes is not the issue here. The fact remains that too much dust has been gathering on the manuscripts and scrapbooks and volumes housed in the great collections he mentions and in less likely ones where Negro materials have managed to land by chance or whim—

the Theatre Collection of the New York Public Library at Lincoln Center or the Harvard Theatre Collection or even the Boston Athenaeum, all of which contain some Negroana.

As a preface to an analysis of the earliest extant play written by an American Negro, and in order to suggest the difficulty as well as the satisfaction that comes with finding such a document, I want to detail briefly my search for William Wells Brown's *The Escape.* Having read that William Wells Brown was the first American Negro to write a novel and also the first to write a play, I looked for his works among the many old and rare volumes at the Schomburg Collection, the Harlem branch of the New York Public Library. His novels were there but not his plays, although there were references to the latter in several secondary sources. I then went to Yale University's James Weldon Johnson Collection and, finding no William Wells Brown plays there, moved on to Boston. There was nothing of his in the Harvard Theatre Collection, but I happened to go to the Boston Athenaeum, an old library near the State House, at the top of Beacon Hill, and there I found *The Escape;*

Or, A Leap for Freedom: A Drama, In Five Acts by William Wells Brown, published in Boston in 1858, probably the first play of Negro authorship published in America. It turned out to be a fascinating literary and social document.

William Wells Brown was born a slave and later, after his escape from bondage, became a professional lecturer. He was also the author of novels, plays, travel accounts, and of a history of the Negro's contribution to the Civil War. In all these literary forms he was a pioneer as a Negro writer. Between roughly 1830 and 1865, Negro leaders worked closely with Northern abolitionists; Brown, along with Frederick Douglass, lectured for New York and Massachusetts antislavery societies. The lectures were occasions for the reading of his dramas, which were probably never performed on stage but only on platforms.

A review [on 1 August 1856] in William Lloyd Garrison's abolitionist paper, *The Liberator,* praised an antislavery play by William Wells Brown that was probably **Experience, or How to Give a Northern Man a Backbone** (1856):

> On Tuesday evening Mr. Brown read his Drama, written by himself. The scene is played in a Boston parsonage, the pastor is a Northern man with Southern partialities. The author takes him South on a pleasure tour, and by a strange turn of events, the pastor is sold into slavery, and undergoes the frightful "breaking-in" process applied by planters to refractory slaves. He is kept there long enough to convince him that his views of slavery were taken from a wrong standpoint, and he is brought back by his friends with opinions thoroughly changed on the subject. The Drama closes by introducing to the pastor a fugitive slave seeking aid to escape to Canada. There are many vivid, graphic and thrilling passages in the course of the reading, and they are brought out by Mr. Brown with telling power.

The Escape; Or, A Leap for Freedom has been characterized [by Sterling A. Brown in his *Negro Poetry and Drama*] as "a hodge-podge with some humor and satire and much melodrama." It would be difficult to defend the play against these charges, but it is fair to say that such charges could be brought against most plays by white playwrights of the period. And **The Escape** did carry a message of importance to abolitionist audiences. In his preface the author stated that many incidents in the play came from his experience of eighteen years "at the South"; the characters were based on real persons then residing in Canada. There is something admirable in the concluding sentence of the preface: "The play, no doubt, abounds in defects, but as I was born in slavery, and never had a day's schooling in my life, I owe the public no apologies for errors."

The Escape, a drama in five acts, is set in the Mississippi valley, a clearing in the forest, a Quaker home in a free state, and finally at the Canadian border. Clearly it is autobiographical. Just as clearly it is nineteenth-century melodrama. Boucicault, with all his education in the theatre of England and France, would have been pleased with the plot and might have written some of the dialogue.

The chief antagonists are a white couple, Dr. and Mrs. Gaines, who mouth Christian sentiments while threatening to whip their slaves. When a clergyman, Reverend John Pinchen, visits Mrs. Gaines, he recounts a dream he has had of Paradise and of old friends he visited there. The slave Hannah asks Him, "Massa Pinchen, did you see my ole man Ben up dar in hebben?" The ensuing dialogue may be rather blatant in its humor; it is, nevertheless, telling:

> MR. P.: No, Hannah; I didn't go amongst the niggers.
>
> MRS. G.: No, of course, Brother Pinchen didn't go among the Blacks, what are you asking questions for? Never mind, my lady, I'll whip you well when I am done here. I'll skin you from head to foot. (*Aside*) Do go on with your heavenly discourse, Brother Pinchen; it does my very soul good, this is indeed a precious moment for me. I do love to hear of Christ and Him crucified.

Hero and heroine of the piece are Glen and Melinda, two young slaves. Their dialogue is not the "darky" dialect used by the other slaves. Presumably they have had a chance for some education. We know that their creator, William Wells Brown, was chosen to be the playmate of his master's son and thereby gained some advantages early in life. Slaves who were chosen to work in the household rather than in the fields had a chance to acquire literacy and perhaps to learn a craft. Often their light skins moved slaves from field to parlor. Since Melinda is described by Dr. Gaines as a "yellow wench," lightness no doubt helped her to gain refinement of speech as well as of sentiment.

A speech from Act I, scene 3, reveals Glen's special quality of language in contrast to that of other slaves. Notice, too, the comments on marriage among slaves and the Negro woman's special position in a slaveocracy.

> GLEN: How slowly the time passes away. I've been waiting here two hours, and Melinda has not yet come. What keeps her, I cannot tell. I waited long and late for her last night, and when she approached, I sprang to my feet, caught her in my arms, pressed her to my heart, and kissed away the tears from her moistened cheeks. She placed her trembling hand in mine, and said, "Glen, I am yours; I will never be the wife of another." I clasped her to my bosom, and called God to witness that I would ever regard her as my wife. Old Uncle Joseph joined us in Holy Wedlock by moonlight; that was the only marriage ceremony. I look upon the vow as ever binding on me, for I am sure that a just God will sanction our union in Heaven. Still, this man, who claims Melinda as his property, is unwilling for me to marry the woman of my choice, because he wants her for himself. But he shall not have her. What he will say when he finds that we are married, I cannot tell; but I am determined to protect my wife or die.

Marriage among slaves, except by the kind of pledge exchanged by Glen and Melinda, was unknown. William Wells Brown's mother gave birth to seven children, no two of them having the same father. Frederick Douglass saw his own mother only a few times during his lifetime, for they were separated during his infancy; nor did he know who his father was. Psychologists Kardiner and Ovesey have observed that, since a slave was no more to his master than a horse, something to be exploited for his "utility value," all cultural practices which might harm that value had to be suppressed. Slaves were allowed sexual activity, even entertainment after working hours, but *not* family organization. "Neither paternity nor permanent marriage could be recognized, for this would interfere with the free mobility of the slave for sale purposes."

Melinda's position in the household of Dr. Gaines is the special one that could be attained by sexual attractiveness, something that "can never be contained within the limits of utility." It is common knowledge that the white plantation owners took attractive Negro women as concubines. It is also true that the white master or his son often discriminated in favor of the Negro mistress' offspring, even to the point of freeing some of them. This sort of situation has provided many a playwright with a plot. In **The Escape,** Mrs. Gaines tries to sell Melinda because her husband is overly fond of the slave.

Another of the Gaines's slaves, Cato, speaks so-called "darky" dialect. He has been trusted by Dr. Gaines to "doctor" other slaves.

> CATO: I allers knowed I was a doctor, an' now de ole boss has put me at it. I muss change my coat. Ef any niggers comes in, I wants to look suspectable. Dis jacket don't suit a doctor; I'll change it. (*exit Cato—immediately returning in a long coat.*) Ah! now I looks like a doctor. Now I can bleed, pull teef, or cut off a leg. Oh! well, well, ef I ain't put de pills stuff an' the intment stuff togedder, by golly, dat ole cuss will be mad when he finds it out, won't he? . . . Ah! yonder comes Mr. Campbell's Pete an' Ned; dems de ones massa said was coming. I'll see ef I looks right. (*goes to the looking glass and views himself.*) I em some punkins, ain't I?

His comic speeches are the stuff of minstrelsy and, like Topsy in *Uncle Tom's Cabin,* he even has songs to sing. (One song, a long list of wrongs done to Negro slaves on Southern plantations, must have been very popular with abolitionist audiences.) Cato, like so many other "happy slaves," has a longing to go to Canada. One critic has wondered, in view of how many carefree blacks are described in literature and pictured in art, "why Frederick Douglass fled Maryland to the North, or why the Underground did not go brankrupt like a modern railroad" [Sidney Kaplan, in his *Portrayal of the Negro in American Painting*].

The Escape is a message play from beginning to end. Sometimes the action stops for a soliloquy, sometimes for a song. This soliloquy by Glen is particularly moving, especially when one remembers that William Wells Brown declaimed it from abolitionist platforms:

> Oh, God! thou who gavest me life, and implanted in my bosom the love of liberty, and gave me a heart to love, Oh pity the poor outraged slave! . . . Oh, speak, and put a stop to this persecution! What is death compared to slavery? Oh, heavy curse, to have thoughts, reason, taste, judgment, conscience and passions like another man, and not have equal liberty to use them! Why was I born with a wish to be free, and still be a slave? Why should I call another man master?

A Quaker who helps the escaping slave, sings "The Underground Wagon" to the tune of "Wait for the Wagon."

> Oh, where is the invention
> of this growing age,
> Claiming the attention,
> Of statesman, priest, or sage,
> In the many railways
> Through the nation found,
> Equal to the Yankees'
> Railway underground?
>
> *Chorus* No one hears the whistle,
> Or rolling of the cars,
> While Negroes ride to freedom
> Beyond the stripes and stars.

Glen and Melinda, as well as the good Cato who knew how to please while despising his master, escape to Canada with the help of Northern abolitionists. When Mr. White, a citizen of Massachusetts, tells the men in a Mississippi bar that he thanks God that he is from a free state and thinks slavery the worst act a man can commit, he is accused of talking treason. The answer Mr. White receives from a barkeeper when he claims that the Constitution gives him the right to speak his sentiments is one we sometimes hear even today—from Congressmen as well as barkeepers: "We don't care for Constitutions nor nothing else. We made the Constitution, and we'll break it."

This crude yet effective play ends with a rousing fight in which Mr. White of Massachusetts fends off the Mississippi villains—with his umbrella. Glen, Melinda, and Cato, leaping into the boat just as it pulls away from the shore, are shouting loudly for freedom as the curtain falls or, more exactly, as the reading ends.

Opinions of the press in Philadelphia and in various New York towns are quoted at the end of the published version of the play. A critic from the Philadelphia *Morning Times* was of the opinion that "the Drama is instructive, as well as very laughable." One can agree with him on both points and add that the play is a remarkable statement of the evils of slavery by a man who learned in bondage how to please and lived to be a free man who could instruct other free men.

When he was in England on a lecture tour, delivering over a thousand abolitionist lectures between 1849 and 1854, William Wells Brown may very well have seen plays by Dion Boucicault and other melodramatists of the period. In London nothing would have prevented a black man from attending the theatre, and Boucicault's plays were being presented in many London theatres at the time. Many of the stage effects suggested in Brown's plays are similar to those employed in Boucicault's.

Although reviews of Mr. Brown's play readings praised his message and fervor rather than his skill as a playwright, it is true that *The Escape* is a well-made play by standards of the period. Written in five acts, the play has variety of characterization, careful exposition, a well-designed if obvious plot, and spine-chilling scenes of seduction and revenge. The last-minute escape in the boat is not the only stage effect familiar to readers and viewers of English and American plays of the period. A striking example of melodrama occurs in Act III, scene 5. Dr. Gaines, having imprisoned the lovely slave, Melinda, tries to force his attentions on her. She protests that the doctor would be committing a double crime: outraging a woman and forcing her to be false to her husband. The doctor is enraged at the idea of her being married. He goes off to find Glen "and roast him at the stake." On the heels of the doctor's departure, Mrs. Gaines arrives with a proposition that could be anticipated by any audience familiar with nineteenth-century melodrama.

> MRS. G.: I know that your master loves you, and I intend to put a stop to it. Here, drink the contents of this vial—drink it!
>
> MELINDA: Oh, you will not take my life,—you will not!
>
> MRS. G.: Drink the poison this moment!
>
> MELINDA: I cannot drink it!
>
> MRS. G.: I tell you to drink this poison at once . . . or I will thrust this knife to your heart! The poison or the dagger this instant!

William Wells Brown turned the drama of his own experience into the melodrama acceptable in the theatre of his day. That his plays were not produced may have been due to his being a Negro. On the other hand, as a militant reformer he may have chosen the platform over the stage. The combination of his overwhelming anti-slavery bias and what he learned of dramaturgy from playwrights of his time make *The Escape; Or, A Leap For Freedom* an interesting document both from a social and a theatrical point of view. (pp. 370-75)

Doris M. Abramson, "William Wells Brown: America's First Negro Playwright," in Educational Theatre Journal, Vol. XX, No. 3, October, 1968, pp. 370-75.

William Edward Farrison (essay date 1969)

[*Farrison, a leading Brown scholar, produced numerous essays on the writer, prepared editions of* Clotel *and* The Negro in the American Rebellion, *and wrote a full-length biography,* William Wells Brown: Author and Reformer. *In the following excerpt, taken from the last-named work, he analyzes* The Escape *in detail.*]

If Brown returned to Boston before the end of 1857, he either went away again soon after the beginning of the new year or remained inactive in the city for a month or more. For a short time he was expected to participate in the annual meeting of the Massachusetts Anti-Slavery Society on January 28-29, 1858, but the *Liberator*'s report of the meeting does not refer to his being present.

Late in February a resident of Cortland, New York, informed Garrison concerning the antislavery lecturers who had recently visited that town. He said that in addition to Wendell Phillips,

> Charles C. Burleigh and Wm. Wells Brown have also been with us, and done good service, each in his own way, for the Anti-Slavery movement. Mr. Burleigh's lectures were, of course, admired for their logical, rhetorical and critical ability; and Mr. Brown's Dramas have compared favorably with the most attractive Lyceum entertainments of the season . . . . Mr. Brown is still hereabouts, working industriously, and, I think, profitably, both for himself and the cause of the slave. I saw him yesterday at the Academic Exhibition of Central College, McGrawville, which was, by the way, a fine affair, and very creditable to the students and institution—nearly a thousand persons being present as spectators. Mr. Brown gave one of his Dramas, in the evening, to a large and appreciative audience in the College Hall.

The statement concerning Brown's working industriously and profitably for himself as well as for the cause of the slave probably implied that he was then working, not as an agent for any antislavery society, but independently as a lecturer and dramatic reader.

During most of the following spring, Brown was more or less active in Boston and its vicinity. He had an engagement to lecture in the Joy Street Baptist Church on Sunday evening, April 11, on "The Great Men of the St. Domingo Revolution." Obviously this was to be his old lecture on Haiti somewhat remodeled. The next day he wrote to William Lloyd Garrison, Jr., who was then in Lynn, saying, "You will see by the hand bill I send you, that I am reading my new drama, which I consider far superior to the one I gave in Lynn." The new drama was *The Escape,* and Brown inquired about the possibility of reading it in Lynn. Garrison, Jr. must have replied favorably as well as promptly, for on April 17 Brown wrote him another letter, along with which he sent three hundred handbills for distribution. It appears from this letter that Brown was to read the drama in Sagamore Hall in Lynn on the evening of the nineteenth. In the letter he requested Garrison, Jr. to make some of the final arrangements for the reading, explaining that he would not get to Lynn "till six or seven o'clock," and that "I shall drive back the same night, as I shall have a lady with me that must be returned." The lady Brown had in mind was probably Annie Elizabeth Gray of Cambridgeport, who became his second wife two years later.

Late in the spring, the public having been apprised that it was forthcoming, Brown's new play entitled *The Escape; or, A Leap for Freedom: A Drama in Five Acts* was published by Robert F. Wallcut of Boston. This, of course, was not Brown's first play and was not, therefore, the first play written by an American Negro, as it has been frequently said to have been. Until evidence to the contrary is discovered, however, it may still be considered the first play by an American Negro author to be published.

The Escape is an octavo pamphlet of fifty-two pages. Brown said in his preface that he wrote the play "for my own amusement and not with the remotest thought that it would ever be seen by the public eye," that he read it "privately, however, to a circle of my friends, and through them was invited to read it before a Literary Society. Since then," he continued, "the Drama has been given [presented as a dramatic reading by himself] in various parts of the country. By the earnest solicitation of some in whose judgment I have the greatest confidence, I now present it in a printed form to the public." With unnecessary bluntness he explained that never having aspired to be a dramatist, he had "little or no solicitude" for the fate of the work, but was content to let it stand on whatever merits it might have. He also attested that "The main features in the Drama are true," that his hero and heroine—Glen and Melinda—were still living in Canada, and that "Many of the incidents were drawn from my own experience of eighteen years at the South." With something less than good grace, he ended his preface with the assertion that he owed the public no apology for the defects in the drama, because as he had reminded his audiences on many occasions, "I was born in slavery, and never had a day's schooling in my life."

Apparently Brown was prone to forget that not everyone who had been formally educated either spoke or wrote well, and that some of the celebrated authors he had read and admired had had but little formal education. Otherwise he might have recognized the fact that there was not necessarily any direct causal connection between his want of formal schooling and the imperfections in his works.

Whatever might have been his original purpose in writing *The Escape,* Brown made it primarily an anti-slavery argument. The subject matter of the drama belonged to the same department of the "peculiar institution" as did much of the subject matter of *Clotel*—the department of romances between masters and beautiful slave women, usually mixed breeds. The course reviewed in the drama, however, was successful only in reverse. The master-professor flunked, and the unwilling slave-student passed, but without the usual grade—a mulatto or quadroon offspring.

The time of the action in the drama might have been any time after the 1830's—after the Underground Railroad began doing a remarkably large amount of business. In addition to being a physician and politician,

Dr. Gaines of Muddy Creek and Poplar Farm, Missouri, was a connoisseur of beautiful slave women. In the opinion of Mrs. Gaines, his wife, he had long ago succeeded embarrassingly well in at least one master-slave romance. For on his first visit to the Gaineses' home, a certain Major Moore noticed the striking resemblance between Dr. Gaines and Sampey, a mulatto house slave in his teens. Moore assumed that the boy was the son of both Mrs. Gaines and the physician and complimented him accordingly to Mrs. Gaines, very much to her annoyance.

Dr. Gaines was now enamored of Melinda, one of his mulatto slaves—not without being suspected by Mrs. Gaines. Melinda, nevertheless, had bravely withstood his blandishments. For some time she had been in love with Glen, the property of the physician's brother-in-law, and had recently been secretly married to him in a moonlight ceremony conducted by "Old Uncle Joseph," the plantation slave preacher.

Meanwhile, when Walker, a slave trader, visited Muddy Creek, Mrs. Gaines insisted that her husband sell Melinda, as Wildmarsh, a neighbor who happened to be present, admitted to Dr. Gaines that he had sold his own mulatto daughter a week earlier because of his wife's jealousy of him. Instead of selling Melinda, however, as he led his wife to believe he had done, Dr. Gaines hid her in a cottage on Poplar Farm. A night later he went to the cottage and again importuned Melinda to become his mistress. The frigid style with which her replies were invested, of which the following is representative, must have been as devastating as their content:

> Sir, I am your slave; you can do as you please with
> the avails of my labor, but you shall never tempt me
> to swerve from the path of virtue.
> (act 3, scene 5)

In less artificial language Melinda finally told the physician about her marriage to Glen four weeks earlier, whereupon he went away determined to get even with both her and Glen—with the young woman for spurning him and with the young man for successfully rivaling him. The means by which he chose to get even was to have Glen imprisoned and whipped.

Dr. Gaines left the cottage just in time to avoid being caught there by Mrs. Gaines, who, like a horsewoman of the Apocalypse, descended upon the place bent on destruction. She had decided to terminate her husband's pursuit of Melinda by putting the young woman beyond pursuit forever. In soap opera fashion—whether intentional on Brown's part or not—she tried in vain to compel Melinda to commit suicide by drinking poison. Then in a frenzy of anger she attempted to stab Melinda with a dagger. The soap opera now reduced itself to slapstick comedy. In the ensuing battle far from royal between the two women, Melinda's weapon of both defense and offense was a broom with which, according to Brown's stage directions, she "sweeps off Mrs. Gaines—cap, combs and curls" as the scene ends.

A day or two later, while Glen was in prison soliloquizing about the wrongs he had suffered at the hands of Dr. Gaines, Sampey came and informed him of Melinda's whereabouts. When soon after Sampey's visit, Scragg, the overseer, arrived to flog Glen as Dr. Gaines had requested him to do, Glen overpowered him and escaped. The following night, while he and Melinda were searching for each other, they fortuitously met in a forest (act 4, scene 3) and immediately set out together for Canada. In telling Melinda about his escape from prison, Glen said in English more colloquial and more natural than he ordinarily used, "I pounded his [Scragg's] skillet well for him, and then jumped out of the window. It was a leap for freedom. Yes, Melinda, it was a leap for freedom. I've said 'master' for the last time."

Brown did not develop his plot involving Dr. Gaines, Melinda, and Glen as rapidly as the synopsis of it thus far may lead one to suppose. From the beginning he introduced a variety of characters and incidents which he did not fuse into subplots, but which he obviously intended to exemplify the brutalities and grotesqueries of slavery. There was Cato, the clownish slave who assisted Dr. Gaines in his office and practiced medicine on fellow slaves. There was the occasion on which Mrs. Gaines entertained the Reverend Mr. Pinchen in her dining room and pretended to saintly piety while planning to whip the slave Hannah for no good reason. There was the appallingly ignorant Big Sally, whom Dr. Gaines sold to Walker. At the same time the doctor sold Hannah's husband to the slave trader, thus separating the husband from his wife forever. There was Tapioca, whom Cato described as a "mulatter gal," and who was a refinement of Topsy in *Uncle Tom's Cabin.*

Near the beginning of a kitchen scene, Cato, who was indeed no less knave than fool, belied the belief that he was a contented, happy-go-lucky slave by soliloquizing about his wish to escape to Canada. He ended his soliloquy with a part of "A Song of Freedom," one of the selections in all of the editions of Brown's *Anti-Slavery Harp.*

Ignorant of Cato's real attitude towards his situation, as Price [Brown's master] was of Brown's in December, 1833, Dr. Gaines took Cato along with himself and Scragg in pursuit of Glen and Melinda. One night in a hotel in a town in Ohio, while Dr. Gaines and Scragg were asleep, Cato dressed himself in the doctor's clothes and escaped. Cato's scheme was not new in Brown's writing. Brown had already told in *Clotel* about a fugitive slave who escaped from his captors in southeastern Ohio by the same scheme. Cato joined Glen and Melinda, apparently by chance, in the home of a Quaker in northern Ohio, whence after being refreshed, all three of the fugitives were sped on their way to freedom. But they were not yet completely out of danger. Their pursuers caught up with them at noon one day just as they were about to be ferried across the Niagara River to Ontario. At the ferry there was a fight between Dr. Gaines and his official slave catchers on the one hand and the fugitives and their friends, including two comical peddlers, on the other. The latter group won, and amid cheers the fugitives were ferried across the river to a haven in Canada.

One of the contributions to *The Liberty Bell* for 1858, which was actually published by the middle of December, 1857, was Mrs. Lydia Maria Child's *The Stars and Stripes,* an antislavery melodrama in eight scenes. There are obvious similarities between Brown's drama and Mrs. Child's in characterizations and plots, though in neither setting nor style. Dr. Gaines, Melinda, Glen, and Cato have their counterparts respectively in Mr. Masters, Ellen, William, and Jim in *The Stars and Stripes.* The action in Mrs. Child's drama began on Mr. Masters' plantation in South Carolina and ended at a ferry at Detroit. The time of the action was fixed by Mr. Masters' reference in scene one to how "our brave Brooks served that miserable traitor Sumner."

With regard to the similarities in the dramas; if Mrs. Child was not indebted to Brown, it is not likely that Brown was indebted to her. By the end of 1856 *The Escape* existed in a more or less complete version, and early in 1857 Brown began presenting it in dramatic readings, some of which Mrs. Child might have witnessed. On the contrary, even if Mrs. Child's drama already existed in manuscript when Brown began reading his publicly, it is hardly any more probable that Brown had seen her manuscript than it is that she had seen his. The similarities between the dramas could have resulted, of course, from the writers' drawing upon a common stock of antislavery literature, as Mrs. Child seems to have drawn upon the story of William and Ellen Craft not only in choosing names for her hero and heroine but also in having them escape from slavery disguised as a servant and his master. Brown himself had contributed much from his own experience to the stock of antislavery literature and was familiar with it, therefore, from personal experience as well as from reading.

The similarity between the last scenes of the dramas is traceable to the kind of incident which had become a part of the stock of antislavery literature. This was the vain attempt of slave catchers to recapture slaves at an American-Canadian ferry. One such incident had been related by Alvan Stewart of Utica, New York, at the annual meeting of the American Anti-Slavery Society in New York City in May, 1836. A similar incident, it should be remembered, had been related by Brown himself in the fourth American edition of his *Narrative.* The last scene in Mrs. Child's drama is obviously an adaptation of the incident related by Stewart. The last scene in *The Escape* was doubtless based on the incident related by Brown himself.

By the time Brown wrote *The Escape,* the subject matter of which he composed it had become so familiar and indeed so stereotyped that it needed a newer and more original treatment than he gave it. All of the principal characters in the drama are stock characters. Their being such is not a fault in itself, but it is a fault that there is little or no character development as the action proceeds except in one instance. That is the one involving Mrs. Gaines, who at first tried to appear as the very soul of piety, but who appeared more and more as the termagant she really was. Among the numerous dramatic situations in the play, those most effectively realized are the farcical ones—the kind most easily portrayed. Much of the dialogue in the comical scenes consists of the speech of illiterate slaves, which Brown represented by what has traditionally become known as dialect writing. His representations are more or less typical of that kind of writing; this is to say, they are as much mutilated English as anything else.

By far the worst defect in the drama is the artificial dialogue in which it abounds. In many places in this work, as in many places especially in the latter half of *Clotel,* Brown seems to have made special efforts to write beautifully instead of simply and effectively; and like others who have indulged in such misdirected efforts, he succeeded in writing much worse than he otherwise might have written. In act I, scene 3, for example, and again in act 3, scene 4, he seems to have tried, although vainly, to model Glen's soliloquizing after Hamlet's first two soliloquies; and in act 3, scene 5, he tried to make Melinda soliloquize about sleep somewhat as Macbeth talked about it. In all of these instances he doubtless would have written less artificially and more convincingly had he tried to make his hero and heroine talk like themselves rather than like Shakespearean characters. In spite of its defects, however, *The Escape* is indeed distinctive as an authentic and vivid portrayal of slavery because of its human-interest appeal, and as a pioneering effort among Negro authors in the writing of dramas. (pp. 295-304)

> *William Edward Farrison, in his* William Wells Brown: Author and Reformer, *The University of Chicago Press, 1969, 482 p.*

Addison Gayle, Jr. (essay date 1975)

[*Gayle is an American educator, critic, and biographer. He is best known as the editor of* The Black Aesthetic *(1971), a collection of essays by prominent black literary figures and artists in which he stated that "the serious black artist of today is at war with American society." In the following excerpt, he condemns Brown's treatment of blackness in* Clotel, *calling the author an "unconscious propagator of assimilationism."*]

Brown may be immediately dismissed as a novelist of style, one who observed people well enough to portray them without reliance upon old stereotypes. In neither version of the novel, *Clotel,* does he improve in technical efficiency, is he capable of singularity of plot, organizational unity, or apt characterization. Like his successor, Sutton Griggs, his novels are marked by nothing so much as structural chaos. This chaos bears resemblance to the chaotic life of an ex-slave, one of

little organization, where people and incidents too often assume the guise of the grotesque. Brown, the ex-slave, was forced to learn of man on the run, to live a disorganized existence; it is not surprising that being forced to come by ideas secondhand, secondhand ideas proliferate in his works.

To speak of him as the great borrower is not to defame him, nor to denigrate his accomplishment, though one of the most important factors in his work is his ability to borrow from whatever source he deemed necessary. From the eighteenth-century neoclassicists, he borrowed diction; from the nineteenth-century English and American Romantics, he borrowed sentimentality and a sense of the Gothic. The nuances of plot he borrowed from American history. What he did not borrow, what he came upon firsthand, was his belief in the perfectability of man, a belief that led him to conclude, with Copernicus, that man was the center of the universe. (pp. 5-6)

At a crucial time for black people, when the novelist should have been engaged in redefining definitions, in moving to rebut both Mrs. Stowe and her detractors, Brown is found lacking. His solution to the problem of images is to offer counterimages, more appealing to whites and the black middle class than to those on the slave plantation who bore the brunt of the Southerners' attacks. *Clotel,* the octoroon heroine of his novel, is no less a romantic image than that concocted by the imagination of Mrs. Stowe and Grayson. The only difference is that the former was acceptable to many Blacks while the latter was acceptable only to whites. Thus after Brown's pen falls silent in 1874, the black novelist must reap the fruit of the bitter harvest which he helped to plant, must turn to confront a world constructed along lines which he did not oppose, must do battle with a society in which Blacks join whites as the major upholders of Anglo-Saxon values. He is not to be censured because he was a poor novelist, because he did not match his white contemporaries in mastery of the fictional form. Censure must be leveled against him for his failure, as a black novelist, to undertake the war against the American imagists. The struggle for man's freedom begins with the mind and Brown's inability to recognize this fact was his major drawback as a novelist. (pp. 6-7)

Brown recognized no dichotomy between propaganda and art. Living in an age of tumult and chaos, he would have championed the argument that art must be instrumental in liberating the people. This objective, prevalent in each version of [*Clotel*], depicts him as the moral propagandist. Any device that damages the institution of slavery—sentimentality, melodrama, contrived plots, or stolen phrases—is to be used by the writer. In this regard, sexual license granted the owner and his family over black women are singled out for special concern. For Brown, illegitimacy, the result of the ravaging of black women, which leads to the breakup of the familial structure, is the foundation of corruption inherent in the institution of slavery. Arguing Sewall's point in *The Selling of Joseph,* with more factual evidence than the former author possessed, Brown notes that the Pharaohs are in reality selling their own children. To give this thesis validity, therefore, he peoples his novel with those like Clotel, who "was not darker than other white children."

She inhabits what might be called the world in between, one populated by octoroons, quadroons, and mulattoes, and, at least in the final version of the novel, is allowed to escape the fate of the outcast—the total isolation assigned the mulatto in fiction by whites—and evidences her ability to move freely between the white and black worlds by marriage to first a white man, then a Black. Her life ends in philanthropy, her "trials and tribulations" rewarded by service to others. For those freed Blacks, now beginning to constitute the hierarchy based upon color, she is a heroine, who for all practical purposes has the skin color, morals, and ethical values of white people. To call Brown the first novelist of the black bourgeoisie is not too far wrong; despite the apologia of his biographer, each version of *Clotel* singles him out as the conscious or unconscious propagator of assimilationism. Given her choice of several worlds in the novel, Clotel retained a more than casual affinity for the white. (pp. 8-9)

> *Addison Gayle, Jr., "Paradigms of the Early Past," in his* The Way of the New World: The Black Novel in America, *Anchor Press, 1975, pp. 1-24.*

Robert B. Stepto (essay date 1979)

[*In the following excerpt, Stepto surveys Brown's writing techniques and his process of "authenticating" his narratives and* Clotel.]

In an authenticating narrative, represented . . . by William Wells Brown's *Narrative of the Life and Escape of William Wells Brown* (not to be confused with Brown's 1847 volume, *Narrative of William Wells Brown, a Fugitive Slave, Written by Himself*), the narrator exhibits considerable control of his narrative by becoming an editor of disparate texts for authentication purposes, far more than for the goal of recounting personal history. The texts Brown displays include passages from his speeches and other writings, but for the most part they are testimonials from antislavery groups in both America and England, excerpts from reviews of his travel book, *Three Years in Europe* . . . , selections from antislavery verse, and, quite significantly, letters to Brown's benefactors from his last master in slavery, Mr. Enoch Price of St. Louis. Brown's control of his narrative is comparable to Douglass's, but while Douglass gains control by improving upon the narrative failures of authors like Henry Bibb, Brown's control represents a refinement of the authenticating strategies used by publishers like Bibb's Lucius Matlack, who edited and deployed authenticating documents very much like those gathered by Brown. In this way, Brown's narrative is not so much a tale of personal history as it is a conceit upon the authorial mode of the white guarantor. Control

and authentication are achieved, but at the enormous price of abandoning the quest to present personal history in and as literary form.

Brown's "**Preface**," written notably by himself and not by a white guarantor, is peculiar in that it introduces both his narrative and the text authenticated by the narrative, *Clotel; or, The President's Daughter.* By and large, the tone of the "**Preface**" is sophisticated and generally that of a self-assured writer. . . . Brown does not skirmish with other authenticators for authorial control of the text, nor is he anxious about competition from other literary quarters of the antislavery ranks. . . . That Brown introduces a personal narrative and a somewhat fictive narrative *(Clotel)* with language and intentions commonly reserved for works of history and journalism constitutes his first admission of being motivated by extraliterary concerns. His second admission emerges from his persistent use of the term "memoir." In contrast to a confession or autobiography, a memoir refers specifically to an author's recollections of his public life, far more than to his rendering of personal history as literary form or metaphor. This former kind of portrait is, of course, exactly what Brown gives us in his narrative.

The narrative is, as I have indicated, bereft of authorship. Brown rarely renders in fresh language those incidents of which he has written elsewhere; he simply quotes himself. His posture as the editor and not the author of his tale disallows any true expression of intimacy with his personal past. This feature is reinforced by certain objectifying and distancing qualities created by third-person narration. Brown's 1847 narrative begins, "I was born in Lexington, Ky. The man who stole me as soon as I was born, recorded the births of all the infants which he claimed to be born his property, in a book which he kept for that purpose . . . ." Thus, it inaugurates the kind of personal voice and hardboiled prose which is Brown's contribution to early Afro-American letters. In contrast, the opening of the 1852 narrative is flat, without pith or strength: "William Wells Brown, the subject of this narrative, was born a slave in Lexington, Kentucky, not far from the residence of the late Hon. Henry Clay." These words do not constitute effective writing, but that is not Brown's goal. The goal is, rather, authentication, and the seemingly superfluous aside about Henry Clay—which in another narrative might very well generate the first ironic thrust against America's moral blindness—appears for the exclusive purpose of validation. In this way Brown commences an authentication strategy which he will pursue throughout the tale. (pp. 26-8)

The Enoch Price letters are undoubtedly the most interesting documents in Brown's compendium, and he makes good narrative use of them. While the other assembled documents merely serve the authenticating strategy. Price's letters, in their portrait of a slaveholder ironically invoking the dictates of fair play while vainly attempting to exact a bargain price for Brown from his benefactors, actually tell us something about Brown's circumstances.... As the editor of his résumé—his present circumstance—Brown must acknowledge slavery's looming presence in his life, but he can also attempt to bury it beneath a mountain of antislavery rhetoric and self-authenticating documentation. Through the act of self-authentication Brown may contextualize slavery and thereby control it. In these terms, then, the heroic proportions to Brown's editorial act of including and manipulating Enoch Price's letters become manifest.

Brown's personal narrative most certainly authenticates himself, but how does it also authenticate *Clotel?* The answer takes us back to Brown's "**Preface**," where he outlines the extraliterary goals of both narratives, and forward to the concluding chapter of *Clotel,* where he writes:

> My narrative has now come to a close. I may be asked, and no doubt shall, Are the various incidents and scenes related founded in truth? I answer, Yes. I have personally participated in many of those scenes. Some of the narratives I have derived from other sources; many from the lips of those who, like myself, have run away from the land of bondage.... To Mrs. Child, of New York, I am indebted for part of a short story. American Abolitionist journals are another source from whence some of the characters appearing in my narrative are taken. All these combined have made up my story.

Brown's personal narrative functions, then, as a successful rhetorical device, authenticating his *access* to the incidents, characters, scenes, and tales, which collectively make up *Clotel.* In the end, we witness a dynamic interplay between the two narratives, established by the need of each for resolution and authentication within the other. Since *Clotel* is not fully formed as either a fiction or a slave narrative, it requires completion of some sort, and finds this when it is transformed into a fairly effective antislavery device through linkage with its prefatory authenticating text. Since Brown's personal narrative is not fully formed as either an autobiography or a slave narrative, it requires fulfillment as a literary form through intimacy with a larger, more developed but related text. *Clotel* is no more a novel than Brown's preceding personal narrative is autobiography, but together they represent a roughly hewn literary tool which is, despite its defects, a sophisticated departure from the primary phases of slave narration and authentication. (pp. 29-30)

> *Robert B. Stepto, "I Rose and Found My Voice: Narration, Authentication, and Authorial Control in Four Slave Narratives," in his* From Behind the Veil: A Study of Afro-American Narrative, *University of Illinois Press, 1979, pp. 3-31.*

FURTHER READING

Brawley, Benjamin. "William Wells Brown." In his *Early Negro American Writers: Selections with Biographical and Critical Introductions,* pp. 168-70. Freeport, N.Y.: Books for Libraries Press, 1968.
    Summary of Brown's life and career.

Farrison, W. Edward. "Phylon Profile XVI: William Wells Brown." *Phylon* IX, No. 1 (First Quarter 1948): 13-23.
    Biographical portrait of the writer by the foremost Brown scholar.

————. "Brown's First Drama." *CLA Journal* II, No. 2 (December 1958): 104-10.
    Assembles the information known about Brown's first play, *Experience; or, How to Give a Northern Man a Backbone,* a work now lost.

————. *William Wells Brown: Author and Reformer.* Chicago: University of Chicago Press, 1969, 482 p.
    Definitive, full-length study of Brown and his works.

Moore, Alonzo D. "Memoir of the Author." In *The Rising Son; or, The Antecedents and Advancement of the Colored Race,* by William Wells Brown, pp. 9-35. 1874. Reprint. New York: Negro Universities Press, 1970.
    Appreciation of Brown by one of his contemporaries.

Sekora, John. "William Wells Brown." In *Fifty Southern Writers Before 1900: A Bio-Bibliographical Sourcebook,* edited by Robert Bain and Joseph M. Flora, pp. 44-54. New York: Greenwood Press, 1987.
    Includes a brief biography of Brown, a discussion of the major themes of his writing, a survey of the criticism of his works, and a bibliography of works by and about him.

Trent, Toni. "Stratification among Blacks by Black Authors." *Negro History Bulletin* 34, No. 8 (December 1971): 179-81.
    Examines the role played by African-American writers in establishing and maintaining "Blacks' own acceptance of color distinctions as bases for judging each other's value." Brown was, Trent states, "obsessed with the obvious distinctions between dark and light Blacks."

Yellin, Jean Fagan. "William Wells Brown." In his *The Intricate Knot: Black Figures in American Literature, 1776-1863,* pp. 154-81. New York: New York University Press, 1972.
    Documents the different heroes and heroines in several versions of *Clotel.*

Dennis Brutus

1924-

(Also wrote under pseudonym John Bruin) Zimbabwean-born South African poet and essayist.

Brutus is regarded as one of the most distinguished contemporary South African poets. He employs traditional forms and rich language in his poetry to detail without self-pity or bitterness the physical and mental anguish he has suffered as a political prisoner and an exile. Brutus is well known for his involvement in the anti-apartheid movement and has opposed apartheid in his works. In *Aspects of South African Literature,* R. N. Egudu deemed Brutus's poetry "the reaction of one who is in mental agony whether he is at home or abroad," adding that this agony is "partly caused by harassments, arrests, and imprisonment, and mainly by Brutus's concern for other suffering people."

Brutus was born in 1924 in Harare, Zimbabwe, which was then called Salisbury, South Rhodesia. His parents, teachers Francis Henry and Margaret Winifred Brutus, were South African "coloureds" who raised their son there in Port Elizabeth. After receiving a B.A. in English at Fort Harc University College in 1946, Brutus taught English and Afrikaans in several South African high schools. In the late 1950s Brutus began to protest apartheid actively, concentrating on the conflict of races in sports. He was later instrumental in the exclusion of South Africa from Olympic games, and some commentators hold him primarily responsible for the barring of South Africa's segregated sports teams from most international competitions. In 1961, however, the South African government removed Brutus from his teaching position and forbade him to write because of his protest activities. Brutus was arrested in 1963 at a sports meeting for defying a ban on associating with any group. Although he fled to Swaziland after his release on bail, the Portuguese secret police later apprehended him in Mozambique and surrendered him to the South African secret police. Fearing he would be killed in Johannesburg, Brutus again tried to escape but was shot in the back by police in pursuit. He was subsequently sentenced to eighteen months of hard labor at Robben Island Prison, a notorious escape-proof facility off the South African coast. Brutus found his internment there unbearable; after five months of solitary confinement, he tried to commit suicide by cutting his wrists with sharp stones. During his imprisonment his first volume of poetry, *Sirens, Knuckles, Boots* (1963), was published, and South African officials interrogated him about his poetry. In 1965 Brutus was released and allowed to leave South Africa on condition that he never return.

Sirens, Knuckles, Boots includes love poems as well as poems protesting South Africa's racial policies. These poems, like many of Brutus's later pieces, are highly personal and meditative, interweaving personal refer-

ences while developing such themes as love, pain, and anger. Brutus's work was awarded an Mbari Prize from the University of Ibadan, Nigeria. Because Brutus was forbidden to write poetry in prison, he instead wrote letters, an activity that was not prohibited. In his next collection, *Letters to Martha and Other Poems from a South African Prison* (1968), published after he left South Africa for England in 1966, Brutus recounted his prison experiences through letters to his sister-in-law. These poems, which describe the deprivation and fear of prison life, were praised for their objectivity and lucidity. Myrna Blumberg contended that in parts of *Letters to Martha,* Brutus "has grace and penetration unmatched even by Alexander Solzhenitsyn—or perhaps Brutus is just less shockable and less verbose about the levels of degradation and joy, the nature of human nature, he has seen and felt." Other critics noted that the poems in this volume are different in style from those in Brutus's first collection; Brutus acknowledged that he altered his technique in favor of simpler idioms that make his verse more accessible to the average reader. Although these works remained officially banned in South Africa, Brutus's *Thoughts Abroad* (1970), published under the pseudonym John Bruin, circulated widely in the country. A collection of poems about exile and alienation, *Thoughts Abroad* was an immediate success in South Africa, and it was even taught in several colleges there. When the government discovered that Brutus was the author, all copies were confiscated.

Brutus lived in London until 1970, when he moved to the United States and became a member of the English faculty at Northwestern University. Brutus's first volume of poetry published after leaving England, *A Simple Lust* (1973), includes his earlier work concerning prison and exile as well as new poems. Tanure Ojaide described Brutus's characteristic persona, which becomes most prominent in *A Simple Lust,* as "a troubadour who fights for a loved one against injustice and infidelity in his society." In the new poems in this collection, Brutus wrote with passion of the homeland for which he yearns and of his compatriots who remain behind. His anxiety over their suffering is intensified by the contrast between his life as a free individual and their restricted lives. In *Stubborn Hope: New Poems and Selections from "China Poems" and "Strains"* (1978), Brutus again wrote about his prison experiences and the inhumanity of apartheid. Endurance and hope are dominant themes in this volume, as Brutus extends his concern with the oppressive conditions of his homeland to a universal scale and assumes the role of spokesperson for all suffering people.

Brutus has continued to write poetry while in America, including the volume *Salutes and Censures* (1984), and he has undertaken to educate the American people about apartheid in South Africa. In his sustained opposition to the government there and to repression in general in his poetry, Colin Gardner maintains that Brutus "has found forms and foundations which dramatize an important part of the agony of South Africa and of contemporary humanity."

(For further information about Brutus's life and works, see *Black Writers; Contemporary Authors,* Vols. 49-52; *Contemporary Authors New Revision Series, Vols. 7, 27; and Contemporary Literary Criticism,* Vol. 43.)

PRINCIPAL WORKS

Sirens, Knuckles, Boots (poetry) 1963
Letters to Martha and Other Poems from a South African Prison (poetry) 1968
Poems from Algiers (poetry) 1970
Thoughts Abroad [as John Bruin] (poetry) 1970
A Simple Lust: Selected Poems Including "Sirens, Knuckles, Boots," "Letters to Martha," "Poems from Algiers," "Thoughts Abroad" (poetry) 1973
Strains (poetry) 1975; revised edition, 1982
China Poems (poetry) 1975
Stubborn Hope: New Poems and Selections from "China Poems" and "Strains" (poetry) 1978
Salutes and Censures (poetry) 1984

Paul Theroux (essay date 1966)

[*Theroux is an American novelist who frequently depicts conflicts between Westerners and Third World inhabitants in his works. He has taught in several African nations, first teaching English in Malawi as a member of the Peace Corps. He was deported, however, when he was arrested for spying and attempting to overthrow the dictator of Malawi. In the following excerpt, Theroux explores Brutus's role as an artist under a repressive regime.*]

To say, as John Pepper Clark does in connection with the South African writer, Dennis Brutus, that a 'little less shouting for more silence and mime might not only make for manly dignity, but also command attempts at rescue and action' is something less than frivolous. Under the circumstances silence might mean a kind of patient acceptance.

A man of honour might fight humbly, silently, but he will fight; it is the artist's job to articulate the struggle of these silent ones. . . . Brutus lives in a country which is only one of many that oppress him. He must fight against mining corporations in South Africa as well as investors on foreign soil who continue their windy chorus: 'We have faith in the future of South Africa. It is the only country on the continent with a reliable government . . . . .' (this is a direct quotation from an American businessman who, in this American phrase, 'puts his money where his mouth is', and recently invested £75,000 in an industry in Johannesburg). It cannot be disputed that the South African government is reliable; they can be relied upon to invoke every act of tyranny, brutality and madness to ensure the future of a white-dominated South Africa.

It would have to be a particularly irresponsible artist to ignore the tortures and inhumanities of the South African police, to choose silence over open condemnation. 'I believe there is a place for the man who yells "FIRE" and points to the smoke, without dragging the hose to the spot', said Nathanael West, the American satirist whose novels are now classical pieces. This could be the epigraph to **Sirens, Knuckles, Boots** by Dennis Brutus. What probably disturbs J. P. Clark is that Brutus appears to celebrate nothing; Brutus is constantly nagging, condemning, lamenting.

He says in one of his opening poems:

> A troubadour, I traverse all my land
> exploring all her wide-flung parts with zest
> probing in motion sweeter far than rest
> her secret thickets with an amorous hand:
> and I have laughed, disdaining those who banned
> inquiry and movement, delighting in the test
> of will when doomed by Saracened arrest,
> choosing, like unarmed thumb, simply to stand.

But reading through the book we find that, however lovely it is to think of oneself as a troubadour, laughing at the grossbooted policemen, proving in flight injustices with beautiful gestures, this is not what happens in the poems which follow. There is very little that can be called 'amorous' in the lines:

> So here I crouch and nock my venomed arrows
> to pierce deaf eardrums waxed by fear
> or spy, a Strandloper, these obscene albinos
> and from the corner of my eye
> catch glimpses of a glinting spear.

Amorousness is something that is dear to Brutus, but something that is out of reach. So Brutus concentrates on the emotion that will lead to amorousness—the way is through tenderness, to love:

> Somehow we survive
> and tenderness, frustrated, does not wither
> ....
> most cruel, all our land is scarred with terror,
> rendered unlovely and unloveable;
> sundered are we and all our passionate surrender
>
> but somehow tenderness survives.

The tenderness, the faith that Brutus places in it, may be a result of the terrible rage of the previous poem quoted above with its bowman spying on the 'obscene albinos'. . . . J. P. Clark is right in saying that Nigerian poets do not write lines like 'obscene albinos', but also the Nigerian poets are not now murdered or imprisoned because they are black; they are not considered the black stinking lubrication that helps the huge cogs of the economy to run smoothly. Brutus is whipped and he lashes back furiously. It is true that sometimes his punches are wild, sometimes his misses (he is imprecise, for example, in telling us who he is or what he is doing; he is not a troubadour, he is a victim, bleeding), but he swings enough times for us to see what he is aiming at. The man being stretched on a rack will be more concerned with his own pain than with the ingenious construction of the instrument of torture.

Brutus, speaking for the millions of black South Africans, has been frustrated and turned away and confined and shot at and still nothing has changed. And so he continues to rage. Other poets in other places may write poems about their wives to celebrate their beauty and their wonderous functions. Brutus, separated from his wife, speaks of her as if she were dead. There is a fat white hand between him and his wife; that, and many miles:

> It is your flesh that I remember best;
> its impulse to surrender and possess
> obscurely, in the nexus of my flesh
> inchoate stirrings, patterns of response
> re-act the postures of our tenderness.

Here is tenderness without rage, but more often it is a mixture of rage and tenderness that prevails in Brutus's poems. The poems are not easy to read, his book cannot be taken in one gulp—it would hurt too much. Here, as an example, is another of Brutus' love poems:

> A common hate enriched our love and us:

> Escape to parasitic ease disgusts;
> discreet expensive hushes stifled us
> the plangent wines became acidulous.

> Rich foods knotted to revolting clots
> of guilt and anger in our queasy guts
> remembering the hungry comfortless.

> In draughty angles of the concrete stairs
> or seared by salt winds under brittle stars
> we found a poignant edge to tenderness,

> and, sharper than our strain, the passion
> against our land's disfigurement and tension;
> has gouged deeper levels for our passion—
> a common hate enriched our love and us.

Here is the rebuttal to all who clamour for silence; the 'discreet expensive hushes' will undo the poet or the lover. It is piteous, the view of the lovers loving within the system of hate and even enriching themselves by it. But this is also one of Brutus' most brilliant poems, for in it he combines all the themes of love, rage and tenderness, and all the stark ugliness and terror of living in a bitter land. The poem is not a commitment to hate but to rage—rage in love and in living. The nine poems which follow this one are similar in tone. Sex in these poems is frightening, images of love-making are contrasted with images of death and dying:

> . . . you pressed my face against your womb
> and drew me to a safe and still oblivion,
> shut out the knives and teeth; boots, bayonets and
>   buckles . . .

Or:

> Desolate
> Your face gleams up
> beneath me in the dusk
>
> abandoned:
>
> a wounded dove
> helpless
> beneath the knife of love.

There is horror in these poems, but it is not the horror of a man skittering in a high wind away from white ghosts stalking him with Sten-guns. It is rather the horror of a man seeing love nourished in bad soil, in a country made ugly by hatred. Perhaps Brutus likes to picture himself in flight, but I read these poems differently. He is not moving (living furiously does not mean bobbing around); he is staying, suffering the phantasms, and he is recording them faithfully. This takes great strength and dedication; he has escaped the decayed language of revolt, the cliches of the man oppressed. If the poems are manic-depressive in their raging tenderness it is because Brutus is being hammered from within his soul and from without: the sirens in his ears, the knuckles and boots against his body.

One cannot survive long spending these precious emotions on enemies as demonic as those who plague Brutus. But Brutus will continue as long as the tyrannical governments continue, even if it means that his limp shape will be added to the already large heap of spent bodies. In the end, a hush would be far more expensive.

It is hard to refuse to detach and to descend from metaphysics to exist among the most miserable and unhappy in his country, identifying with all the injustice and lust and criminality; yet Brutus makes the descent, a descent which is the only means of resurrection:

> Under me
>   your living face endures
>   pools stare blindly
>   muddied by ageless misery:
> descending to you
>   in a rage of tenderness
>   you bear me
>   patiently.

> (pp. 42-5)

Paul Theroux, "Voices Out of the Skull," in Black Orpheus, *No. 20, August, 1966, pp. 41-58.*

Gessler Moses Nkondo (essay date 1981)

[*In the following excerpt, Nkondo surveys traditional influences—particularly those of the Western Latin tradition—in Brutus's poetry.*]

Those who know South Africa, particularly certain places like the coastal city of Port Elizabeth, overwhelmed by the sky which is so dominant a feature of the landscape, will have been struck by the Mediterranean quality of the light. I am reminded of this when I think of the work of one of the most distinguished of contemporary South African poets, Dennis Brutus. Brutus is learned, passionate, skeptical—and in his work there is an insistent, almost fierce sense of a Western Latin tradition. Perhaps one is misled by the analogy of the Latin light. It may be that the creative impulse is discrepancy, an aching consciousness of the dissimilarity between the decorative density of Europe and the native splendor of the country. More probably both impulses work together in the South African English sensibility, work together and work on one another, sharpening into positive existence the Latin elements—not just the linguistic ones—latent in the English language. Certainly Brutus is concerned in a most unusual way, for those currently writing in English, with order and coherence of feeling and with lucidity and precision in presentation. This preoccupation is a constant presence in the poetry—not always successfully realized, of course—and we have no need to go outside the verse to find a sanction for the claim I have made. (p. 32)

"**The rosy aureole of your affection**" is a remarkably contained poem, each verbal edge firmly finished off and each syntactical contour exactly defined. Two bold images, "our focussed shaped projection" and the "ancient foetus-hungry incubus" are separately drawn out and then drawn together. The tranquil, mellowed richness of the love scene, "the rosy aureole of your affection," is put into opposition and balance with the awe-inspiring aura of "older mouths from oozy shores." Together the images, locked at once in antagonism and passion, produce the strength and scent of sexual encounter. The actual tension and embrace of love are poised above and sustained by the profound processes of organic life: "The rosy aureole of your affection / extends beyond our urban bounded knowledge / to tangled undergrowths of earlier time."

The poem, keeping its varied complexities in place and in connection along a lucid descriptive line, grasps first at the physical basis of life and experience, at the flesh and the earth and the calm sagacity it generates, and then touches the quick of human experience at its exquisite crisis in the mysterious meeting of love. The mystery is an essential part of the experience which the poem offers. It includes not only the joyful, physical energy of sexual love, "the ancient foetus-hungry incubus," but also a tissue of social memories and images. These are both serene ("bright labyrinths of the mind") and terrifying ("older mouths from oozy shores"). In the poem the act of love appears as a model of all human experience which has its ancient sources buried in the earth, but which is also immediate and adapted to the light and further transformed by the imagination, itself always a carrier of a more than merely personal cargo, a conductor of both compulsion and aspiration, honor and grace.

Sexual love is a recurrent theme in Brutus's work. Occasionally he celebrates it as the beneficent completion of life and personality. More frequently he is concerned with its Lawrentian vigor and aboriginal vitality. [In the poem] "**Nightsong: Country**," . . . love is seen restoring the warmth and purity of the ancient earth and in which Brutus's energy of articulation is given a singing, aspiring quality . . . . The sense of unalloyed delight in love, spiritual as well as physical, is almost always present in Brutus's poetry. It is true that whenever he writes of love he conveys in a masterly way the pleasure of the senses and the richness and beauty of the body. But there is almost always something breaking in, something sinister or ugly or mean. Monstrous and cogent fears about the police, who supply many of the fictions in Brutus's verse, intrude on the enclosed world of lovers—sirens, knuckles, boots: "over our heads the monolithic decalogue / of fascist prohibition glowers / and teeters for a catastrophic fall; // boots club the peeling door." This stanza from "**Somehow we survive**," contrasting sharply and yet following naturally on the informal and casual opening (the brilliant twist of mood is completely logical), is an example of Brutus's supple virtuosity in modulation from the casual and throwaway to the stately and measured. It calls up the great name of Yeats, for whom Brutus has made no secret of his admiration.

But while Yeats is clearly a vital (and absorbed) influence in Brutus, his idiom is his own, being at once less gorgeous and Byzantine when full out and more flatly contemporary in the lower register . . . . [An] example of this calculatedly flat manner, and one . . . thoroughly charged with the macabre—the attraction of which for Brutus suggests a certain nauseated disgust with ordinary life as part of his response to experience—is the last stanza of "**When last I ranged and revelled**":

> When last I ranged and revelled all your length
> I vowed to savour your most beauteous curves
> with such devout and lingering delight
> that they would etch themselves into my brain
> to comfort me throughout the prisoned night.
>
> But waking early in the frowsty dawn
> and finding you deshevelled and unkempt
> my heart arose as though you showed your best
> —and then I wryly knew myself to be
> the slave of an habituated love.

Having said this—that the appeal of the macabre for Brutus testifies to some perverse disrelish for common experience—I am immediately conscious of the need to correct or qualify it. There is something nasty, an occasional gratuitous reveling in the garbage bin and perhaps the puritan self-hatred to which this is often the clue, in a few of Brutus's poems. . . . But more often some quality in the tone, a quaver of amusement, a glint of wit, a touch of self-mockery, even a cry of innocent astonishment, shows that the macabre is being put to a more complicated and controlled use. It becomes an instrument instead of a dead end, another gateway through which the poet's imagination can enter an odd, disturbed but somehow valid world. (pp. 32-4)

I have referred . . . to Brutus's writings in the formal Yeatsian mode, to his flatter, more contemporary manner and to work of the kind I call "macabre-grotesque," although I recognize the infelicity of the term, which misleadingly suggests some Gothic thrill-inducing intention on the part of the poet, when the most notable thing about these poems is the control and application with which the genre is put to serious, indeed somber, purposes. Use, management, the employment of a style for purposes beyond what it seems capable of is even more strikingly evident in another set of poems which look immediately to be more than deliberate imitations. Two members of this series are "**At a funeral**" and "**Gaily teetering on the bath's edge**." These poems are strongly reminiscent of certain religious poems of the English seventeenth century.

What in the seventeenth century Brutus fastens on is a composite sensibility made up of the passionate subtleties and the intellectual sensuousness of the metaphysical poets and the masculine, ironic force of Donne. *Why* the seventeenth century should be looked to as the source has to do with the congruence between Brutus's own poetic nature and the adult, ardent, almost mathematical reasoning habit of the metaphysicals: a balance further modified by another, the symmetry between Brutus and his admired Donne's gift of sensitive manliness, his way of being at once independent and level with his experience, however intricate; and modified yet again by Brutus's sympathetic understanding of

Donne's skill in calling upon a range of poetic resonance within a strictly defining, disciplining pattern. Nor should we overlook that Brutus had to make his choice of exemplar at a particular time and from within a certain literary tradition, not only the wider one grounded in the English language and the English tradition, but within the local African one based on the altered language of his own country. It could not be a purely personal choice, although it had to be primarily a personal one, answering to the need felt in the poet's own nerves. The poet as poet is not engaged in any explicit mission to renovate a literary tradition. But of course he is involved in such an undertaking, and the more significant a poet he is, the more profound is his involvement. Brutus's "conservatism" in fact is truly radical. His poetry has to be freed from the influence of home, from a tradition still too much domesticated within the nineteenth century in which British gentility and blandness were curiously reinforced in their parochialism by an unambitious—and suspicious—South African philistinism. The seventeenth century, so different from the nineteenth in its inclusiveness and in the very assurance of its skepticism to which poets in Britain earlier directed their attention, could be the same cleansing, tonic influence for South Africa, above all if the connection were made by a South African poet. (pp. 34-5)

"**So, for the moment, Sweet, is peace**" [is] a sardonic extrapolation from "The Canonization," and "**The sounds begin again**," a grim evocation of inner turmoil which is Roman in the strength of its despair. Both these poems are written in vigorous conceits which have something of Donne's wit and force: Donne's because the medium, handled by Brutus with remarkable naturalness, is used as the instrument of strength rather than delicacy. Indeed the conceit, employed in an easy, open way, is splendidly adapted to communicate the peculiar quality of Brutus's poetry which one is aware of even in his earliest, lightest pieces. This is its powerfully, almost physically energetic character. It is muscular, quick and solid, with the relaxed poise of the gifted athlete who brings all his force to bear rhythmically and without strain. Brutus is the least neurotic of poets, and even when he is scrutinizing his own romantic love, as in one of his best poems, "**Nightsong: City**," his regard is gravely objective without the least touch of narcissistic droop or any suspicion of anxious self-interest. Right from the start of Brutus's poetic career, the reader is aware of the formed personality beneath the finished literary character. It is positive, independent and radical in an un-South African manner; the accepted South African literary convention lacks precisely this very virtue. It is free of the fog of middle-class pretension and gentility: sharp where that was bland and harsh where that was cozy. At the same time Brutus's poetry asserts a profound commitment to the great constitutive works of the Western—not just the British—tradition, and not only in poetry but also in thought and morality. It accepts and asserts, namely, the principles of intellectual integrity, and in doing so avoids, or ignores, the clogging dangers of South African parochialism. The result is a powerful and unfashionable maturity which joins a naked freshness of original response to a richly realized conception of an ideal order.

This is a conjunction which appears in . . . "**Kneeling before you in a gesture**," the fable of which seems to be taken from *Antony and Cleopatra* or some of Donne's crabbed, more passionate outbursts. The despair which is implicit in the situation and the grimness of a passionate love call to powers deep in Brutus's nature and are transformed in his treatment to become the implacable conditions of tragic human life itself. It is written in language which very much obeys the prescription Brutus lays down: that the language of poetry should be concrete, lucid, coherent, logically connected, syntactically exact and firmly based in current idiom and usage. It begins with sharp, plaintive, clearly effective phrases, in a rhythm and in a voice which has nothing in it but tenderness. . . . The poem, mingling sadness and sensuousness in a strange, dry way, manages unfalteringly to convey at once the coldness of present misery and the radiance of remembered passion. Not that the effect is at all romantically intimate or soft. The logical structure, the carefully worked-out syntax, both of grammar and feeling, generalize the experience into something highly organized and impersonal, so that the love passages, luminous and distant in the memory, have the refinement and the deadliness of expert swordplay, abrasive and bleakly affecting. Here is the conclusion, in which we see the particular aspiring through the lucidity of form toward a larger, general order:

> and answering, you pressed my face against your
>   womb
> and drew me to a safe and still oblivion,
> shut out the knives and teeth; boots, bayonets and
>   knuckles:
> so, for the instant posed, we froze to an eternal
>   image
> became unpersoned and unageing symbols
> of humbled vulnerable wonder
> enfolded by a bayed and resolute maternalness.

"**Kneeling before you in a gesture**" is a statement—but more than a mere "statement"—about the ideal order which is implicit in, and which by means of poetry can be extracted from, the grubby detritus of life. But of course the poet could be, and is, as concerned with the other side of the duality, with the disordered elements in their chaos. In another poem, "**Erosion: Transkei**," he speaks of that preoccupation. . . . The "ravaged land" describes very well the form under which society and the modern world appear to this tough-minded, independent poet. "**My possessing**" describes the general, bracing aim which keeps his observations tart, the fervent steps, the self-confidence of the approach. The tone of these social poems, which include some of Brutus's most effective and personal work, is better seen in "**Let not this plunder be misconstrued**."

> Let not this plunder be misconstrued:
> This is the body's expression of need—

> Poor wordless body in its fumbling way
> Exposing heart's-hunger by raiding and hurt;

>> Secret recesses of lonely desire
>> Gnaw at the vitals of spirit and mind
>> When shards of existence display eager
>>   blades
>> To menace and savage the pilgriming self:

> Bruised though your flesh and all-aching my arms
> Believe me, my lovely, I too reel from our pain—
> Plucking from you these your agonised gifts
> Bares only my tenderness-hungering need.

The tone here, untensed and self-mocking, is a recognition that we are all, not excluding the poet himself, "poor wordless bodies" gnawed by "lonely desire," in the same cage, and an almost amused confession of innocence, in that whatever is wrong—and so much is, both in the lover and the beloved—derives from a common impersonal fault. It is the classical Western awareness—but light, wry and quite without guilt—that everything issues from a single, tainted source, an original flaw or sin.

Yet at other times the poet collects himself into a more feline and separate contempt. "**Off The Campus: Wits**" spits at the mass-communicating world, "**The Mob**" at the malevolently stupid mob, "**Our aims our dreams our destinations**" at the formal cruelties of religion, and "**Longing**" straight into "Science's logistics." Sometimes the tone is harsh and disgusted. The poet squarely rejects those with all the answers. . . . ["**Mirror Sermon**"] mocks at "sensual intellection."

> This cold reflection
> of our interlocking nudity
>   moralizes ascetically
> on sensual intellection
>   or mortality.

The poem makes solemn, wicked fun of the reductive habit of the contemporary mind, of its technique at getting beneath the delusive surface in the interests of uttering some pure abstract truth. Brutus combines a gravely ironic parody of psychiatric investigation with a medievally gruesome pondering on the horrors of the body, including "twitching strings of lust." Clothes, skin, flesh are peeled off until the sage lays bare the "body's aberrations.". . . The Swift-like gravity of procedure, simultaneously recommending and undermining the modest monstrous proposal, and the hideous exposure of the skinned body are devices used in the service of a serious intention but one which can express itself in a less ferocious, more bantering species of ridicule than the master of devastation would ever allow himself. The touch of tolerant lightheartedness is confirmed by the crisply humorous conclusion. It holds out a small hope that a sense of reality is perhaps recoverable, but only as the issue of total absurdity. . . . I come now to what I see as the peak of Brutus's achievement, not a great one in bulk, but still substantial enough and unusually even in quality. It is made up of a handful of poems written at intervals over the period 1960-73, a fact of composition in keeping with my feeling that

Brutus already had a fully formed literary personality when he began to publish. The poems I have in mind are "**Blood River Day**," "**Nightsong: City**," "**On the Road**," "**In the greyness of isolated time**," "**On a Saturday afternoon in summer**," "**The inherent impulse to good**," "**Landscape of my young world**" and "**In the night, in the mind**." There are others in the cluster, but these are the main lights.

"**Blood River Day**" is a powerfully meditative poem on the theme of man's sacredness and of our kinship with nature. It makes the characteristically solid impact of Brutus's best poems, seeming to have behind it the weight of personal experience which has been grasped and deeply pondered.

> Each year on this day
> they drum the earth with their boots
> and growl incantations
> to evoke the smell of blood
> for which they hungrily sniff the air:
>
> guilt
> drives them to the lair
> of primitiveness
> and ferocity:
>
> but in the dusk
> it is the all pervasive smell of dust
> the good smell of the earth
> as the rain sifts down on the hot sand
> that comes to me
>
> the good smell of the dust
> that is the same
> everywhere around the earth.

This is sheer ballet music. Its rhythm, a perfect dismissal of the daytime political dust and turmoil, alone suggests a secret, derisive sensation. Whispering, hissing sounds accentuate the secrecy which the first five lines, by contrast, set into relief. The sand is "sifted"— innocent of footprints. Tiptoeing onto it comes Brutus in the intimacy of a lover, as if his entry into this hallowed ground were a ceremony, the prelude to an innocent but uncanny bacchanal of dance and song, of which the "earth," charmed to silence, is the only audience.

It is a nocturnal ritual, one which defies the disciplines and restrictions of the politically-dominated day, for the fading of the Afrikaner "incantations" signals the withdrawal of "law," "order" and other humdrum things. The third part of the song pokes a fairy's scorn at the dullness and solemnity of the human scheme of things. Contrast the soapbox rhetoric of the opening with the delicate fluting of the next two stanzas, and the music itself should make its meaning clear; but to make it doubly and trebly clear, the auditory and kinetic images of the last eight lines are touched with a mystic grace and those of the first five with bestial clumsiness: "sifting rain" on the one hand, "growls" on the other.

The song therefore, slight though it is, is a symbol of the poet's rebellion against political disciplines, and against the social and moral disciplines that they forge. Perhaps it is charged with a deep moral. The poet is, in every sense of the word, an enchanting creature. Perhaps he symbolizes that part of the human soul which rebels against everything orderly and humdrum, violent and inhuman, and which does right to rebel. At any rate, there is no suggestion of evil in the creature, while there are many suggestions of clumsiness and ugliness in the scheme of things against which he rebels. The human race would be an antlike horror if it docilely accepted every fascist tyranny and never once conspired with golden moonlight, with music or the rain to set the prosaic, daylight, penny-snatching world at defiance.

The meaning of Brutus's song is almost all in its music. Never were words so devoid of melancholy; never was their sound so heavily charged with tenderness and sorrow. It is impossible to gabble the lines. They are woven of the longest vowels and the most difficult consonants in the language, consonants which prohibit the slurring of one word into another and which force the voice to give each bar of verbal music its full value: "... pervasive smell of dust ... rain sifts down ... that is the same ... everywhere around the earth"—attempt to say these phrases quickly, and you will be puffing and hissing like a hysterical Italian; the noises you make will certainly not sound like English.

Yet such melancholy as Brutus here expresses is free of all taint of sniveling and self-pitying lamentation. The poet, for the nonce, seems to have a fairy's immunity from human sorrow. While the sound of his words may have a mournful quality, their sense is anything but so. The poet's retreat into the woods, they imply, is the beginning of a transubstantiation into "the smell of the earth." To allow the mind to dwell on the merely visual transformation which the song suggests must be, in the end, to transcend the visions of the eye and attain a glimpse of the truth about the aboriginal spiritual reality of man, a truth which annihilates grief. In its final effect, I think, this song of Brutus's is as rich a consolation as the most elaborate dirge, elegy or funeral march. In its very dissimilarity from all clumsy, human attempts to embrace and sniffle and moan the edge off sorrow, in its apparently naïve fantasies about "the smell of dust," it offers comfort of a kind superior to that which emanates from the melancholy chords of a Miriam Makeba, a Nina Simone or the sobbing arpeggios of a John Coltrane. If it transcends human grief, it transcends death too. And just as the existence of the speaker in the song—Brutus's protagonist, if you like—is proof positive of man's power to rise superior to his own existence, so Brutus's song is a token of the human spirit's triumph over death. By this I do not mean that his pretty words prove there is a pair of wings and a harp within the reach of us all, but only that rain glimmers in the dust of the warm earth, and that Brutus's song reminds us of this at the same time as it reminds us of man's sacredness and of our kinship with the dust and the earth.

"**Blood River Day**" is a strongly objective poem, written in a mood of dry, almost grim composure, in which the settled author, unfrayed by his own situation and its pathos, stares at what is the case: namely, the twin realities of bloodthirsty Afrikaner patriots and the perfume of the earth. Much of the intensity of the poem's effect comes from the simultaneous and equal treatment of the two themes, not in a way which uses the political figure as a simple analogy or parable but as an exercise in positive ambiguity. South Africans are sometimes thought to be fustily conformist—it is a criticism the South Africans often make of themselves—but there is also in the South African psychology a quality of lissome independence corresponding, perhaps, to the marvelous bodily suppleness generated by a regimen of sun, protein and sport. Only a South African, and one with Brutus's gifts—only Brutus himself, I suppose—could use the antiquarian vocabulary in the last nine lines of "**In the greyness of isolated time**" (from the *Letters to Martha* sequence) with such unembarrassed lack of self-consciousness. There the words are, his attitude seems to imply, still with a quirky flair of life not yet quite snuffed out, as well as with a degree of dubious charm. Let me use them therefore, taking advantage of their antique attractiveness and consciously manipulating them in a new direction, like a batsman who makes not simply an unorthodox but an astonishingly original stroke, staying all the time strictly within the rules.

> Coprophilism; necrophilism; fellatio;
> penis-amputation;
> and in this gibbering society
> hooting for recognition as one's other selves
> suicide, self-damnation, walks
> if not a companionable ghost
> then a familiar familiar,
> a doppelgänger
> not to be shaken off.

There is a checked or controlled comic impulse at work here which enables Brutus to use a set of superannuated terms as though they were colloquialisms, and to employ what could easily be units of rhetoric as terms of slang. Two modes of discourse, rhetorical and familiar, run together through the poem. At one point, as in the first few lines, the rhetorical is more strongly present; at another, as in the closing five lines, the casually colloquial is emphasized. The half-amused, shoulder-shrugging tolerance keeps the rhetorical from becoming fustian while it gives a sardonic edge to the slang. (pp. 35-8)

In "**Under House Arrest**" the stony, stoical quality and the almost regular edge of the verse match the author's notation of the "screaming tensions" between artistic form and the raw material of experience. In "**Our aims our dreams**" a milder but equally critical regard is turned upon the myth of Gethsemane. In cool, almost strict verse the poet questions the grandeur of splendid Gethsemane. He registers the humanity of the myth and the irony by which evil is supposed to be brought out of good. Some critics may find metaphysical complexities in this poem, a view of the world and a sense of sin; but to me the poem seems most remarkable for its di-

rectness and simplicity. A tranquil, pagan eye, not by any means without humor, is turned upon the Judeo-Christian story. This itself makes for freshness. And it is the naturalness of the event in the fable which the poet suggests, and the human incongruity of the story; the theological implications are somewhat suppressed.

If one wanted a Mediterranean but more intimately personal and self-involved poem, one would go to "**Landscape of my young world**," where the poet travels into his interior life in search of a meaning and uses again, in keeping with that scientific habit which is part of his sensibility, the reductive method he employed in "**The rosy aureole of your affection**." But while there the poet was the evolutionary biologist, here he is the genetic psychologist. The difference between Brutus and the psychologist, however, is that Brutus brings to bear upon his enigmatically impalpable subject, the vaguely glimmering beginnings of his existence, not external measuring instruments but the most refined and disciplined of faculties, the matured poetic consciousness. The glimpse of, the hint about, the beginning of his life has a poetic definition and actuality of being, and the whole poem itself has the solidity of an event. He registers first his point of entry, the memory which is triggered as much by his immediate as by his total situation. The Browningesque reminiscence reminds us not to forget Brutus's characteristic and wholly unaffected daring. But such nerve is justified by the naturalness with which the poem starts, and the propriety and evenness with which the body of it flows from the opening. He next hints at the location, Port Elizabeth, where the "soft" hills and the aloes together with the dreaming firs and the green slopes combine the genius of South Africa and Britain, that particular blend of sensibility which is the poet's genius too. This place, the product of two national sources, is not just an enclosing context but an inward condition of the child's psychology. Implicit in that is a powerful sense of distance, of distance as a positive and creative dimension of imagination.

Brutus is a remarkable poet, one of the most distinguished South Africa has produced. His very positive literary character is both grainily individual and strongly in the main Western literary tradition to which he adheres: for accretions, whether modish or cliquish, he has no use, and indeed considerable scorn. The lucidity and precision which he is at pains to develop in his work are qualities he admires from artistic conviction, as a humanist opposed both to romantic haze and conventional trends. But they also testify to a profound cultivation of spirit, a certain wholeness and harmony of nature, as they do too to a fine independence of literary fashion. (pp. 39-40)

Gessler Moses Nkondo, "Dennis Brutus: The Domestication of a Tradition," in World Literature Today, *Vol. 55, No. 1, Winter, 1981, pp. 32-40.*

Colin Gardner (essay date 1984)

[*The following excerpt is taken from a slightly edited version of a paper entitled "Brutus and Shakespeare." Gardner delivered the paper at a conference of English teachers in South Africa, where Brutus's poetry is banned. Gardner explained: "I didn't want to give advance notice of my intentions or involve the conference organizers in the calculated (but not really very daring) act of 'illegality' that I was planning; so I decided to entitle the paper 'Brutus and Shakespeare.' It was quite a good joke—and ... it wasn't merely a joke. The paper seemed to go down well—partly, no doubt, because breaking that law was a kind of liberation. I got away with it, I may add...." Here, Gardner presents some of Brutus's poetry and explores the poet's traditional influences.*]

The problem with Dennis Brutus, of course, is that his writings are banned in the Republic of South Africa. Brutus as a writer exists, as far as the Pretoria government is concerned, as a vacuum, an absence; in the firmament of South African literature, such as it is, Brutus could be described as a black hole. But it is necessary to find him and read him, to talk and write about him, to pick up the light which in fact he does emit, because he is at his best as important as any other South African who has written poetry in English.

One of the many difficulties that have been created by the bureaucratized obscurantism to which he has been subjected is that it is hard for a person who wishes to consider him and his work briefly to know where to begin, how much to take for granted. Officially Brutus's poetry is unknown in South Africa, and one has to recognize that to a large extent the government's banning procedures do work: it seems likely that many well-read South Africans, even some of those with a distinct interest in South African poetry, are wholly or largely unacquainted with his writing. On the other hand, some people know Brutus and his work well and have known it and the critical debates that have surrounded it for a number of years. What is a new leaf to some will be old hat to others. I have drawn attention to these problems partly to highlight the awkwardness of my task, but partly also to emphasize the degree to which governmental inhibitions and prohibitions have caused disarray not only in South African society but also in our mental world, of which we sometimes imagine ourselves to be in control. And I need hardly add that Brutus is by no means the only important South African writer whose work is officially proscribed. (p. 354)

Brutus began to write in the 1950s; and his first volume of poems, *Sirens, Knuckles, Boots,* was published in Nigeria in 1963 while he was on Robben Island. He is therefore in one sense a poet of twenty years ago, though he has continued to write, often very successfully, while he has been in exile. I am conscious that, in directing an appreciative spotlight on Brutus's poetry and its methods and implications, I might be accused in some quarters of wearing a cloak of mild boldness in order to mask a critical intention which is in fact profoundly conservative, if not positively retrogressive. The truth is that while I recognize that Brutus's writing, especially that of the early 1960s, belongs to a particular moment in South African sensibility and South African history, I do not believe that his finest poems are confined to their period, although they express it so well: achieved art never dates in any simple sense. This does not mean that I deny or call into question the striking developments that have taken place in the direction and practice of verse in South Africa, particularly among black writers, in the last twelve or fifteen years. It is nevertheless often dangerous to insist that one stream of literary development, no matter how creative and dominant it may be, is the only valid and valuable current. It may be even more important for us to remember that Dennis Brutus, even though he is in exile, is still alive and writing and still a figure in contemporary South African literature. (p. 355)

The four poems which follow are all from the 1963 volume.

1
"Nightsong: City"

Sleep well, my love, sleep well:
the harbour lights glaze over restless docks,
police cars cockroach through the tunnel streets;

from the shanties creaking iron-sheets
violence like a bug-infested rag is tossed
and fear is immanent as sound in the wind-swung
    bell;

the long day's anger pants from sand and rocks;
but for this breathing night at least,
my land, my love, sleep well.

2

The sounds begin again;
the siren in the night
the thunder at the door
the shriek of nerves in pain.

Then the keening crescendo
of faces split by pain
the wordless, endless wail
only the unfree know.

Importunate as rain
the wraiths exhale their woe
over the sirens, knuckles, boots;
my sounds begin again.

3

A common hate enriched our love and us:

Escape to parasitic ease disgusts;
discreet expensive hushes stifled us
the plangent wines become acidulous

Rich foods knotted to revolting clots
of guilt and anger in our queasy guts
remembering the hungry comfortless.

In draughty angles of the concrete stairs
or seared by salt winds under brittle stars
we found a poignant edge to tenderness,

and, sharper than our strain, the passion
against our land's disfigurement and tension;
hate gouged out deeper levels for our passion—

a common hate enriched our love and us.

4

It is the constant image of your face
framed in my hands as you knelt before my chair
the grave attention of your eyes
surveying me amid my world of knives
that stays with me, perennially accuses
and convicts me of heart's-treachery;
and neither you nor I can plead excuses
for you, you know, can claim no loyalty—
my land takes precedence of all my loves.

Yet I beg mitigation, pleading guilty
for you, my dear, accomplice of my heart
made, without words, such blackmail with your
    beauty
and proffered me such dear protectiveness
that I confess without remorse or shame
my still-fresh treason to my country
and hope that she, my other, dearest love
will pardon freely, not attaching blame
being your mistress (or your match) in tenderness.

Reading these poems today, one is struck by the degree to which they are different from recent black verse: one thinks of the tangy and sometimes epigrammatic irony of the early Mtshali, who lets the carefully handled "facts" appear to speak for themselves; of the vigorous, impassioned, but subtle and sensitive, almost communal voice of Serote; of the sophisticated, seemingly relaxed but half-despairing deadpan joking of Sepamla; and of the various modes and moods of sharp indignation, analysis, and resoluteness in the more memorable of the *Staffrider* and *Wietie* poems.

The world evoked by Brutus—both the internal and the external world—is quite other. The poems are quiet, peculiarly personal, meditative. We are introduced to, or rather into, a persona, which is capacious, generous, observant, anxiously dedicated, morally and intellectually scrupulous. Everything that the poems touch on is translated or transformed to become a part of the landscape or the furniture of this inner world—not that there is anything egocentric or solipsistic about the effect that the poems achieve. . . . [For example] "The sounds begin again," has become, by the end of the poem, "*My* sounds begin again." What is happening here is of course not merely a process of internalization, of compassionate appropriation: the poet indicates, by a subtle shift, that he himself physically participates in the suffering of which he writes.

This production of a meditating persona, a richly presented working mind and sensibility into which we are drawn by the strong, spiderlike threads of the poetic structure, is a phenomenon which has been very common in Western and perhaps particularly in English poetry, from Eliot back through Wordsworth and Shakespeare to Wyatt and Surrey. And of course Brutus is a traditional poet, nourished in the classic English tradition, in a way that is largely foreign to the poets of

Soweto. ("Traditional" may seem a dangerous word to apply to anyone, in the present climate of innovation, but let me draw attention to Eliot's view that a certain kind of traditionality may be highly original.) It is at this point that I introduce my reference to Shakespeare. "It is the constant image of your face" might almost have been the opening line of a Shakespearean sonnet; so might "A common hate enriched our love and us," except that the circumstances are rather special. It is significant that Brutus has described himself as a lyrical poet and has added that "'protest elements' are only incidental, as features of the South African scene obtrude." He has said that his favorite poets are Donne, Hopkins, and Browning. In some of his work one can sense the influence of those three writers and of others, but the quietly dramatic unfolding of a delicate pattern of feeling and thought seems to me to owe most—if "owe" is quite the right word—to the Shakespeare of the sonnets. But of course those sonnets are themselves related to the soliloquies in the plays, and there are perhaps a few minor links with Brutus there too. It may not be wholly fanciful, indeed, to invoke the other Brutus, the central character in *Julius Caesar*—troubled, self-analytical, caught between the love of his wife, Portia, and his allegiance to what he feels to be essential justice and values in Rome.

This brings me back to the poet's subject matter. I think Brutus was right to see himself as primarily a lyrical poet, but he seems to me to have misinterpreted his work when he described "protest elements" as "incidental." The phrase "protest elements" is inadequate and was probably designed merely to suggest a contrast with some of the more strident forms of black American verse. But the distinctive qualities of the four poems we are considering depend entirely on the poet's particular response to a specific sociopolitical situation. In the first poem he addresses his love, inviting her to enjoy what momentary peace she can have in a situation of violent emotions and antagonisms, and he then reveals, in the last line, that his love is the land itself—the land and its peoples, clearly. In the third of these poems, the poet's love for the woman he addresses is defined in terms of, has indeed been given its identity and richness by, the surrounding political tension and horror. The interaction between personal and political, between the inward and the outward, is complete, even though it involves a paradox: "hate gouged out deeper levels for our passion." What is suggested is that the hate and the love meet at a newly discovered depth, in an impulse which is both violent and generous. In the fourth poem the structure of the love relationship is differently depicted: the loved woman and the loved land are in a state of rivalry, and the poet tries, urgently but with affection and good humor, to reconcile his two allegiances.

The sensibility that Brutus displays in these poems is clearly his own, but at the same time it offers us something of the feeling of the early 1960s, what Raymond Williams would call that period's "structure of feeling." The poet is aware that he has comrades in his political campaigns and struggles, but under intense government pressure, there is no real sense of a mass movement. The fight for liberation will be a long one, and a sensitive participant cannot but feel rather isolated. This isolation is an important aspect of the poet's mode and mood. (By the late 1960s and early 1970s, on the other hand, blacks, particularly those in the larger urban townships, were beginning to develop a corporate confidence of a wholly new kind. (pp. 356-59)

Brutus's sense that he was largely alone in his efforts can be seen in retrospect to have prepared him for his tragically long exile. New situations, new movements of thought and feeling, have produced new types of verse in South Africa. But the struggle for radical social change is of course far from over. Some of the euphoria of the mid-1970s has died away or been transmuted into newer directions, and it would be difficult to argue that the voice of isolated resolve and of exile has lost its relevance. Are we not all, black and white, if we have any awareness of what and where we are, to some extent exiles within the borders of this alien or alienated land? Brutus's best poetry has a resonance which both articulates and generalizes his specific themes; he has found forms and formulations which dramatize an important part of the agony of South Africa and of contemporary humanity. (p. 360)

> *Colin Gardner, "Brutus and Shakespeare,"*
> *in* Research in African Literatures, *Vol. 15,*
> *No. 3, Fall, 1984, pp. 354-64.*

Tanure Ojaide (essay date 1986)

[*In the following excerpt, Ojaide examines Brutus's persona of a troubadour in his poetry.*]

[Dennis Brutus] is consistently represented as a troubadour [in his poetry] and this persona unites all of Brutus's poems. Brutus acknowledges in an interview:

> . . . there recur in my poetry certain images from the language of chivalry—the troubadour, in particular. The notion of a stubborn, even foolish knight-errantry on a quest, in the service of someone loved; this is an image I use in my work, because it seems to me a true kind of shorthand for something which is part of my life and my pursuit of justice in a menacing South Africa.

The troubadour was a medieval knight "who was also a poet and who dedicated his life to the service of a lady (usually called a mistress) and whose unattainable love he praised in poetry. Often his service entailed fighting in order to rescue the mistress from monsters and other unfaithful knights." This mask of a troubadour who loves and fights for his mistress is transplanted from medieval European times to the modern world to represent the non-white poet in the apartheid society of South Africa.

The troubadour mask is extended and complicated after *Sirens Knuckles Boots, Letters to Martha,* and early exile poems. The later poems present an alienated exile, still a troubadour in his being a poet of the open road. There is

a close correlation between the poetic personality and the man in Brutus's poetry. The poet is familiar with his country and the world and speaks of human suffering because of socio-political injustice from the wealth of his individual experience as a sage and philosopher in his struggle to free the oppressed. Brutus uses this mask of a troubadour with ambivalence, but his position remains a valid poetic standpoint.

The opening poem of *A Simple Lust* establishes the poet as a troubadour:

> A troubadour, I traverse all my land
> exploring all her wide-flung parts with zest
> probing in motion sweeter far than rest
> her secret thickets with an amorous hand:
>
> and I have laughed, disdaining those who banned
> inquiry and movement, delighting in the test
> of will when doomed by Saracened arrest,
> choosing, like unarmed thumb, simply to stand.
>
> Thus, quixoting till a cast-off of my land
> I sing and fare, person to loved-one pressed
> braced for this pressure and the captor's hand
> that snaps off service like a weathered strand:
> —no mistress-favour has adorned my breast
> only the shadow of an arrow-brand.

In the poem the troubadour is represented in diverse ways. The upturned thumb, drawn from the salute of the African National Congress, is also an image of the troubadour who is hiking, hitching. According to Brutus, Don Quixote also in the poem is a variation of the troubadour, "the man who travelled across Europe, fighting and loving and singing. It's the combination of conflict and music in the troubadour which interests me—the man who can be both fighter and poet, and this is a kind of contradiction which is also present in Don Quixote." The poet wears the mask of this romantic knight on the road fighting in defence of his mistress.

The poet is a troubadour who fights for a loved one against injustice and infidelity in his society. He is the spokesman for his oppressed people and exposes the brutality of the oppressors, South Africa's white minority. The poet takes the side of the majority but oppressed non-whites against the perpetrators of apartheid, the monsters the knight has to fight for the security of his mistress. It is a case of "we" against "them." The poet establishes his spokesmanship for the oppressed by varying his use of pronouns to show himself as both individual and representative. The "I" and "me" of the poems show the poet as one of the many oppressed. In "**Nightsong: City**," when the poet exhorts "my land, my love, sleep well," he is talking about the country at large. It is in the same light that "my sounds begin again" should be seen. In "**The sounds begin again**" the poet speaks not only for himself but for all "the unfree" against "their woe." The representative voice is clear in the poet's use of the first person plural. His "we" and "us" identify the poet's group—the oppressed non-white people of South Africa—and create the tone of a spokesman. (pp. 55-7)

In addition, Brutus often uses "one" to express both personal and representative experiences. . . . Also the poet uses "one" mainly in the prison and exile poems to avoid self-centredness by distancing himself from the experience to avoid sentimentality. In any case, "one" succeeds in portraying the poet's experiences as representative of the black inmates'. This representative voice creates a sense of solidarity among the oppressed and establishes the poet as a prime mover in his society.

Conversely, the whites are referred to as "they," as in "**Blood River Day**":

> Each year on this day
> *they* drum the earth with their boots
> and growl incantations
> to evoke the smell of blood
> for which *they* hungrily sniff the air:
>
> guilt
> drives *them* to the lair
> of primitiveness
> and ferocity.

> (emphasis mine)

And in "**Their Behaviour**," the contrast is clear as "Their guilt / is not so very different from ours." The contrast of the two socio-political groups which causes tension in real life also brings tension to the verse. Besides, the poet stands out as taking the side of justice, for he is satirical and critical of the apartheid oppressors.

As spokesman, the poet speaks about South Africa to South Africans and all of humankind. He speaks of the brutality of the apartheid system . . . . As spokesman the poet explains the state of the oppressed and imprisoned to the outside world. Because he has been a victim himself, the poet understands the oppressive situation and tells others the true state of things. This helps to make outsiders view the oppressed sympathetically. . . . The poet thus explains things to outsiders so that they will be able to understand the predicament of the non-whites.

The role of the poet as a fighter is manifested in diverse ways. To discredit and embarrass the establishment on the one hand and inspire the oppressed non-whites on the other, the poet acts as a reporter and chronicles the atrocities of the "monsters" so that history will confirm the guilt of the oppressors. "**For a Dead African**" is about "John Nangoza Jebe: shot by the police in a Good Friday procession in Port Elizabeth 1956." He thus gives the correct but unofficial account of things in South Africa. The fight is not physical but mainly psychological—making "them" feel guilty and embarrassed so as to stop the inhuman policies of apartheid. (pp. 58-60)

As part of the struggle for justice, the poet encourages his people. He believes that despite their current plight the oppressed will be free. As a singing troubadour, he instills hope in his people, thus contributing positively to the psychological upliftment necessary for a successful struggle. . . .By fighting for and encouraging his people, the poet is his brother's keeper as he continues the fight even after his release from jail. He believes that as long as others are in jail or suffering, he is himself not free.

The troubadour has his mistress whom he loves. Brutus subtly symbolizes South Africa—his land and his country—as the mistress; hence his personification of the land:

> exploring all her wide-flung parts with zest
> probing in motion sweeter far than rest
> her secret thickets with an amorous hand.

Besides, "my land takes precedence of all my loves." It is in pursuing the motif of the troubadour in defence of his mistress that the poet laments that "—no mistress-favour has adorned my breast / only the shadow of an arrow-brand." In other words, unlike the troubadour who is rewarded for his service by his mistress, the poet receives wounds from the South African regime. Therein lie the irony and ambivalence of the poet in the apartheid state—that this "Dear my land" should evoke "love and pain." The poet loves the country but hates the inhumanity practised in it. This tension runs through the poetry of Brutus. The poet fights for his mistress to achieve justice which in the social context of the poems involves condemning apartheid and embarrassing its perpetrators. The poet thus fulfils his troubadour roles of lover and fighter in the poems. (p. 61)

The troubadour motif also dominates the poems after exile. Exile itself is a journey, a quest which corresponds to the wanderings of the troubadour. However, different facets of the poet's personality emerge. The poet acknowledges:

> I *am* the exile
> am the wanderer
> the troubadour.

The poet gives the impression of lack of confidence, of fighting a losing battle in this post-exile stage. Despair is immanent in the ineffectual role the poet sees himself playing. He can only

> remouth some banal platitudes
> and launch-lodge some arrows
> from a transient unambitious hand,
> a nerveless unassertive gripe.

> (p. 63)

Perhaps the poem that best expresses the wandering nature of the poet in the post-exile stage is "**And I am driftwood.**" The repetition of "I am driftwood" emphasizes the wandering nature of the poet who drifts from place to place not of his own volition, but as an act of destiny:

> For I am driftwood
> in a life and place and time
> thrown by some chance, perchance
> to an occasional use

a rare half-pleasure on a seldom chance

and I grate on the sand of being
of existence, circumstance
digging and dragging for a meaning
dragging through the dirt and debris
the refuse of existence
dragging through the diurnal treadmill of my life.

Here the purpose of the wandering is spelt out: a quest for meaning to human existence. The meaning the poet looks for is socio-political justice that will free the victimized non-whites of the apartheid system. All "the restlessness, the journeyings, the quest, / the queryings, the hungers and the lusts" are towards social justice.

In the quest two things stand out about the poet. He is both an alienated being and a spokesman for his people. He is an "alien in Africa and everywhere," a state exacerbated by Brutus's mixed blood. He is dogged by the burden of responsibility and imagination so that even in exile, he thinks of those suffering in Robben Island, "the men who are still there crouching now / in the grey cells, on the grey floors, stubborn and bowed." As in earlier poems, the poet's plight is representative of the suffering group in South Africa. It is for this that he is spokesman telling the world of the plight of the victims of apartheid:

only I speak the others' woe:
those congealed in concrete
or rotting in rusted ghetto-shacks;
only I speak their wordless woe,
their unarticulated simple lust.

So far the poet is still a troubadour, a poet of the open road in his exile and a fighter in his protest. The troubadour image is reinforced by quester-related metaphors. In *Stubborn Hope* different quest metaphors describe the poet in his exile. Most of *Stubborn Hope* are travel poems, since the poet is in flight, "one more wide range on a troubadour's earth." The poet is still on the road and this time the whole world is the setting of his poems and the experiences are universalized. . . . And he is a pilgrim who shuffles "through the waiting rooms / and the air-terminals of the world." The pilgrim as a metaphor for the poet has the same role as the troubadour; the pilgrim quests for an ideal. The poet is thus a Christian knight and the shrine is symbolic of the romantic mistress he seeks and defends. To the knight the mistress meant adoration, and the implication that the mistress could be a Christian saint is significant. (pp. 63-5)

The pain and suffering the poet witnesses are not restricted to South Africa as in the early poems but are a world-wide phenomenon. So intense is universal suffering that

Sirens contrail the night air:

Images of prisons around the world,
reports of torture, cries of pain
all strike me on a single sore
all focus on a total wound:

Isle of Shippey, Isle of Wight,
New Zealand and Australia
are places with a single name
—where I am they always are:

I go through the world with a literal scar,
their names are stitched into my flesh,
their mewedupness is my perennial ache,
their voice the texture of my air.

Sirens contrail the London air.

So wherever the poet finds himself, he lives with the burden of the suffering people; he always thinks of "those who toss on coir mats amid stone-walls / and writhe their restless loneliness." The Sharpeville massacre, the epitome of apartheid's inhumanity, is an intensification of what obtains elsewhere:

Nowhere is racial dominance
more clearly defined
nowhere the will to oppress
more clearly demonstrated

what the world whispers
apartheid declares with snarling guns
the blood the rich lust after
South Africa spills in the dust.

It is in the same "wounded land" that there exists "the unquenchable will for freedom."

As a result of general suffering, the poet praises endurance and stoicism. The title poem, "**Stubborn Hope**," is an ode on endurance:

Yet somewhere lingers the stubborn hope
thus to endure can be a kind of fight,
preserve some value, assert some faith
and even have a kind of worth.

This is the undaunted will of the troubadour in his relentless struggle. To him, "Endurance is the ultimate virtue," a shield against despair. Other poems such as "**The beauty of this single tree**" and "**At Odd Moments**" emphasize the poet's extolling the resolve to endure oppression with hope. By doing this, the poet does not give the oppressors the opportunity to rejoice in defeating the oppressed.

The poet is a humble fighter against injustice in the vein of the medieval knight. Though he is like every other person human, having "no amulet against despair / no incantation to dismiss suicide," he struggles against apartheid in sports: "Indeed I flog fresh lashes across these thieves! / And they bleed . . . ." In "**Dear God**," he prays as a Christian soldier to God to fight the evil of injustice. It is for this preoccupation with the ideal that he says: "my continental sense of sorrow drove me to work / and at times I hoped to shape your better world." And he admits: "I am a rebel and freedom is my cause." (pp. 65-7)

A Simple Lust and *Stubborn Hope* clearly present the poet who is a fighter for justice at home and abroad, struggling to realize his poetic aims. The troubadour image is consistent in all of the poetry of Brutus. The poet is variously a wanderer, an exile, a dreamer, a bird, a sea-voyager and in all these aspects he is pursuing an ideal. The poet is committed to his struggle and leaves no one in doubt as to which side he stands for: he fights as a spokesman and a representative of the oppressed and the victims of injustice in South Africa and elsewhere. As a troubadour he uses movement and the road to establish his wealth of experience and give credibility to his sayings. He is thus a witness and a victim of the injustice he fights against. The idea of being on the road has universal meaning as the road involves the quest for an ideal. The road also makes the experiences of the poet universal and human as it designates life. The poet's exile brought him the realization that there is evil everywhere, but there is an intensification of it in his country which he loves in spite of the apartheid system.

The poet in the poems and Brutus the man are inseparable, since his experience forms the basis of his poetic personality: his being a half-caste, his alienation in Africa and Europe, his detention, his being shot at while escaping from jail, his exile, his role in keeping South Africa out of international sports, and his travels are all materials for poems that sometimes look highly confessional. In times of harsh realities, as in the apartheid regime of South Africa, the poet and the man are rarely inseparable because of the compulsive experiences. The poems of Brutus are journalism by other means.

His choosing the persona of the troubadour to express himself is particularly significant as the moving and fighting roles of the medieval errant, though romantic, tally with his struggle for justice in South Africa, a land he loves dearly as the knight his mistress. The movement contrasts with the stasis of despair and enacts the stubborn hope that despite the suffering, there shall be freedom and justice for those *now* unfree. (pp. 67-8)

Tanure Ojaide, "The Troubadour: The Poet's Persona in the Poetry of Dennis Brutus," in Ariel: A Review of International English Literature, *Vol. 17, No. 1, January, 1986, pp. 55-69.*

FURTHER READING

Elimimian, Isaac I. "Form and Meaning in the Poetry of Dennis Brutus." *The Literary Half-Yearly* XXVIII, No. 1 (January 1987): 70-8.
> Explores the themes of love and hate in Brutus's poetry.

Ndu, Pol. "Passion and Poetry in the Works of Dennis Brutus." *Black Academy Review* 2, Nos. 1 and 2 (Spring-Summer 1971): 41-54.
> Examines the reconciliation of two passions, passion of sorrow and passion of joy, in Brutus's poetry, concluding that the author has not yet "resolved his passions well enough to press out from his mills the relevant imagery and symbolism he needs to produce great poetry."

Onuekwusi, Jasper A. "Pain and Anguish of an African Poet: Dennis Brutus and South African Reality." *The Literary Criterion* XXIII, Nos. 1 and 2 (1988): 59-68.
> Delineates "aspects of South African reality and in each case examine[s] its espousal" in Brutus's poetry.

Ed Bullins

1935-

(Also wrote under pseudonym Kingsley B. Bass, Jr.) American dramatist, short story writer, anthologist, and essayist.

A contemporary black American playwright, Bullins is considered one of the most significant figures to emerge from the Black Arts Movement of the 1960s. Winner of three Obie Awards, a Black Arts Alliance Award, and the New York Drama Critics Circle Award, he is the author of *Clara's Ole Man* (1965), *In the Wine Time* (1968), *The Duplex* (1970), *The Fabulous Miss Marie* (1971), and *The Taking of Miss Janie* (1975). Bullins's works are acclaimed for their realistic, sometimes controversial depictions of black ghetto life. In 1971, after producing over twenty-five plays, Bullins declared of himself: "In the area of playwriting, Ed Bullins, at this moment in time, is almost without peer in America—black, white, or imported."

Describing his life in 1973, Bullins stated: "the urban-black-ghetto thing is not a new and fascinating thing to me. I been on the streets most of my life.... I learned how to survive. I'm a street nigger." Bullins was born in 1935 and grew up in the streets of North Philadelphia in a section then known as "The Jungle" and later known as "The Pit." He belonged to the street gang "Jet Cobras" and, in his words, spent his youth drinking wine, making it with the girls, and selling bootleg whiskey. He attended Ferguson Junior High, a school outside Cobra turf, and hence, "most times I had to fight my way to school and fight my way back. You were always in danger of getting done in." Dropping out of school—he later called schools "freak factories"—he joined the United States Navy at seventeen. After a few years in the Navy, he returned to Philadelphia in 1955 but left abruptly because "If I had stayed, I would have been six feet under." He moved to Los Angeles in 1958. There he enrolled at Los Angeles City College and began writing seriously, mostly short stories and poetry. A collection of this early prose appears in *The Hungered One: Early Writings* (1971). In 1965 he began writing plays because "I found that the people I was interested in writing about or writing to—my people—didn't read much fiction, essays, or poetry."

Among Bullins's best-known early plays are *Dialect Determinism* (1965), *How Do You Do?: A Nonsense Drama,* (1965), *The Game of Adam and Eve* (1966), and *Clara's Ole Man.* With the exception of the last-named work, the plays received a cool reception; critics objected to Bullins's "obscene" language and unconventional style. Although discouraged by the lack of acceptance of his work, Bullins resolved to keep writing, especially after seeing productions of Imamu Amiri (then known as LeRoi Jones) Baraka's *The Dutchman* and *The Slave.* Recalling Jones's plays, Bullins said, "I could see that an

experienced playwright like Jones was dealing with the same qualities and conditions of black life that moved me. It's the greatest inspiration I've received in my career."

Influenced by Baraka's works and his call for black identity, Bullins joined the Black Panther Party, along with Eldridge Cleaver and Huey P. Newton, and served as its Minister of Culture in 1966. He quickly found himself in the midst of an ideological conflict, however. Opposed to some Party members' position of using art as a political weapon, Bullins left the Party in bitter disagreement. Soon after his departure in 1967 he became involved with New York's New Lafayette Theatre, becoming its resident playwright for the next several years. Bullins wrote most of his plays here, and, as he noted, his work "flourished as it probably would have in no other situation." Later serving as the associate director, Bullins remained with the New Lafayette until its demise in 1973. Since then, he has

321

continued to write and produce plays and has also taught at various colleges and universities.

Bullins's works fall into two general categories: cycle and noncycle plays. The "Twentieth-Century Cycle" is a projected series of twenty plays on the black experience in America. As of 1988, Bullins had completed seven of the twenty cycle plays. *In the Wine Time, In New England Winter* (1971), *The Duplex,* and *The Fabulous Miss Marie* are the best known of the series. According to Bullins, the cycle plays "chronicle a sense of the century for black people in this country." Through these plays he hoped to "touch the audience in an individual way, with some fresh impressions and some fresh insights into their own lives—help them . . . consider the weight of their experience." The cycle plays focus on a group of characters linked by blood or association. The non-cycle plays, such as *Goin' a Buffalo* (1968), *The Pig Pen* (1970), and *The Taking of Miss Janie,* on the other hand, focus on individual characters and their dealings with people around them. Critic Leslie Sanders has observed that the cycle plays tend to "allude to race relations, if they mention them at all," while the non-cycle plays give "detailed treatment of race relations." But as critic Richard Scharine noted, Bullins does not write "protest" plays. Similarly, Jervis Anderson maintained that Bullins's plays "are almost totally devoid of political or ideological content." Thus, commentators assert, while race is always an issue and a presence in Bullins's plays, Bullins does not exploit or provide answers to racial problems. Instead, commentator Don Evans observed, Bullins merely "hits us with a mirror that shows us the ugly, hoping that the image will lead into patterns of change."

In the late 1960s and early 1970s, Bullins produced a series of plays from his "Twentieth-Century Cycle" collection. In 1968, Bullins's first cycle play, *In the Wine Time,* debuted, followed by *In New England Winter* in 1971. These plays introduce Cliff Dawson, first as a disillusioned black drifter who goes to jail to protect his nephew in *In the Wine Time* and then as an ex-convict in *In New England Winter.* In the latter play, the character Steve Benson, often regarded as Bullins's alter ego, is introduced as Cliff's half-brother. Bullins's third cycle play, *The Duplex,* shifts focus from Cliff to Steve's ill-fated love affair with Velma, a married landlady. Steve reappears in the fourth cycle play, *The Fabulous Miss Marie,* a story, according to Scharine, "about people who have traded their pride for things." This work won an Obie Award in 1971. Although critical reactions to the cycle plays were generally favorable, some viewers complained that they are too violent and offer an unflattering picture of black life. Responding to these objections, critic Don Evans argued: "The Bullins theater is the theater of confrontation. We are forced to look at ourselves and that part of our specific community which troubles us in our quiet moments. His is not to say that we are all junkies, petty crooks and pimps, but that we must deal with our own streets, with the choices we continue to make and the dreams we trade for truth. The sounds we hear and the movements we see on the stage disturb us because they are rooted in truth."

One of the earliest non-cycle plays to be produced was *Clara's Ole Man* in 1965. The play depicts the lives of three women, Big Girl, Clara, and Baby Girl, and their relationship with one another as seen through the eyes of Jack, a suitor who visits Clara while her "ole man" is at work. Acknowledging *Clara's Ole Man* as one of Bullins's finest works, Sanders stated: "In *Clara's Ole Man,* Bullins's greatest work is foreshadowed. Its characters, like those in many of his later plays, emerge from brutal life experiences with tenacity and grace. While their language is often crude, it eloquently expresses their pain and anger, as well as the humor that sustains them . . . . Bullins regards his people unflinchingly, revealing their deformities, and their beauty, as well as their strength." The characters of Jack and Big Girl, according to Scharine, are "spiritual ancestors" of Miss Janie and Monty, the main characters in Bullins's most famous non-cycle play, *The Taking of Miss Janie.* Winner of the New York Drama Critics Circle Award for Best American Play, it is perhaps Bullins's most controversial play to date. Contending that *The Taking of Miss Janie* is symbolic of race relations and conditions in America, Bullins remarked, "Most black men would like to take a white broad at least once." This view is reflected in the play's action: Monty, a young black man, rapes Janie, a white woman clad in star-spangled bra and slip. Bullins viewed the rape as an expression of "supreme black liberation from white oppression," causing an uproar among his viewers. Reacting to such controversial statements, audiences, both black and white, angrily criticized Bullins. Responding to their outrage, he stated: "I don't care how they feel or what they think—whether they agree or disagree—just so it makes them examine themselves." Despite Bullins's having won the New York Drama Critics Circle Award for the play, people were at first reluctant to see *The Taking of Miss Janie*—a fact mentioned by Bullins in his 1975 journal: "I won the N. Y. Drama Critics Circle Award the other day. Or rather *Janie* did. It didn't do anything for business last night. I can't figure out what's wrong. Maybe the whites are threatened and the niggers are embarrassed."

The general public wasn't alone in being slow to accept Bullins's works. While a few black critics objected to Bullins's portrayal of blacks, numerous white critics gave Bullins's plays negative reviews. Walter Kerr, for example, criticized Bullins's dramas for structural flaws and "disconnected" dialogue. Critic Bernard F. Dukore, reviewing *The Duplex,* argued that the author failed to challenge his audience intellectually: "By the time the play's single intermission came, I was not only unconcerned as to how things would turn out, I was unsure what was to turn out, since no issues had been raised, and uninterested in any of the characters, since Bullins showed only their surface. With no reason to return to my seat, I left." Black critics, on the other hand, rallied to defend Bullins and attacked white critics for using "white" notions of good drama to evaluate black art.

Bullins, for the most part, remained ambivalent to critical opinions, especially those of white critics. He dismissed them by saying, "It doesn't matter whether [whites] appreciate it. It's not for them. They believe niggers come from the moon and don't have a message."

On the whole, reviews of Bullins's work have been favorable, with at least one critic acknowledging Bullins as "the playwright of the black experience" with "his hand on the jugular vein of people." In the early 1970s, New Lafayette Theatre director Robert Macbeth declared of Bullins, "There's no better playwright in the American theatre today." Similarly, Geneva Smitherman stated in a 1974 issue of *Black World,* "Ed Bullins is one of the baddest brothers in the New York Theater Movement." More recently, critic Genevieve Fabre concluded, "Next to LeRoi Jones, Ed Bullins is probably the most important black dramatist of the last twenty years."

Today, Bullins is recognized as one of the leading black playwrights in America. Commentators agree that his plays, devoid of political or revolutionary rhetoric, force viewers to examine themselves and the conditions surrounding them. Bullins has written over fifty dramas, and he continues to write because he has a story to tell: "See, when I was young, I was stabbed in a fight. I died. My heart stopped. But I was brought back for a reason. I was gifted with these abilities, and I was sent into the world to do what I do because that is the only thing I can do. I write."

(For further information about Bullins's life and works, see *Contemporary Authors,* Vols. 49-52; *Contemporary Authors New Revision Series,* Vol. 24; and *Dictionary of Literary Biography,* Vols. 7, 38.)

PRINCIPAL WORKS

"The Polished Protest: Aesthetics and the Black Writer" (essay) 1963; published in periodical *Contact*
Clara's Ole Man (drama) 1965
Dialect Determinism (or The Rally) (drama) 1965
How Do You Do?: A Nonsense Drama (drama) 1965
The Game of Adam and Eve (drama) 1966
It Has No Choice (drama) 1966
A Minor Scene (drama) 1966
"Theatre of Reality" (essay) 1966; published in periodical *Negro Digest*
The Theme is Blackness (drama) 1966
"The So-Called Western Avant-Garde Drama" (essay) 1967; published in periodical *Liberator*
"Black Theatre Notes" (essay) 1968; published in periodical *Black Theatre*
The Corner (drama) 1968
Drama Review [editor] (anthology) 1968
The Electronic Nigger and Others (dramas) 1968
Goin' a Buffalo (drama) 1968
In the Wine Time (drama) 1968
"Short Statements on Street Theatre" (essay) 1968; published in periodical *Drama Review*

"What Lies Ahead for Black Americans" (essay) 1968; published in periodical *Negro Digest*
Five Plays: Goin' a Buffalo. In the Wine Time. The Electronic Nigger. A Son, Come Home. Clara's Ole Man (dramas) 1969; also published as *The Electronic Nigger and Other Plays* [revised edition], 1970
The Gentleman Caller (drama) 1969
New Plays from the Black Theatre [editor] (anthology) 1969
We Righteous Bombers [as Kingsley B. Bass, Jr.] (drama) 1969
Death List (drama) 1970
The Devil Catchers (drama) 1970
The Duplex: A Black Love Fable in Four Movements (drama) 1970
The Helper (drama) 1970
It Bees Dat Way (drama) 1970
The Man Who Dug Fish (drama) 1970
The Pig Pen (drama) 1970
A Ritual to Raise the Dead and Foretell the Future (drama) 1970
Street Sounds (drama) 1970
The Fabulous Miss Marie (drama) 1971
The Hungered One: Early Writings (short stories) 1971
In New England Winter (drama) 1971
Four Dynamite Plays: It Bees Dat Way, Death List, Pig Pen, Night of the Beast (dramas) 1972
Next Time... (drama) 1972
The Psychic Pretenders (A Black Magic Show) (drama) 1972
Ya Gonna Let Me Take You Out Tonight, Baby? (drama) 1972
The House Party, a Soul Happening (drama) 1973
The Reluctant Rapist (novel) 1973
The Theme Is Blackness: The Corner, and Other Plays. Dialect Determinism, or The Rally. It Has No Choice. The Helper. A Minor Scene. The Theme Is Blackness. The Man Who Dug Fish. Street Sounds. Black Commercial No. 2. The American Flag Ritual. State Office Bldg. Curse. One-Minute Commercial. A Street Play. A Short Play for a Small Theatre. The Play of the Play. (dramas) 1973
The New Lafayette Theatre Presents the Complete Plays and Aesthetic Comments by Six Black Playwrights [editor] (anthology) 1974
The Taking of Miss Janie (drama) 1975
Home Boy (drama) 1976
I Am Lucy Terry (drama) 1976
Jo Anne! (drama) 1976
The Mystery of Phyllis Wheatley (drama) 1976
DADDY! (drama) 1977
Sepia Star (drama) 1977
Storyville (drama) 1977
C'mon Back to Heavenly House (drama) 1978
Michael (drama) 1978
Leavings (drama) 1980
Steve and Velma (drama) 1980

Ed Bullins with John O'Brien (interview date 1973)

[*In the following 1973 interview, O'Brien and Bullins discuss black writers and black writing in America, focusing on Bullins's plays* Goin' a Buffalo, In the Wine Time, The Electronic Nigger, Clara's Ole Man, *and* It Has No Choice.]

[O'Brien]: *What writers have influenced your writing?*

[Bullins]: Recently, of course, Imamu Amiri Baraka. He read one of my first plays. Since then, since coming to New York, I've worked in the New Lafayette Theatre. The writers around me, you know. Writers who have been developing in my workshop. And the young writers. Like Richard Wesley and J. E. Gaines, and writers I know. And the ones I see.

What about non-literary influences?

Non-literary?

Essayists, maybe...

Well, I read them, you know. Sometimes. But I can't attribute any present influences. Maybe five or six years ago. Everyone was reading Malcolm. A large part of the black community, including myself, were influenced by Elijah Muhammed. That kind of thing.

The black writer seems to be experiencing a certain crisis because of commitments to his art and politics...

What writers are you speaking of?

Well, Jones pretty much has given up writing, or at least the kind of writing that he once was doing in the Sixties, which perhaps was more artistic...

Well, no, they may not have been seen on Broadway or off-Broadway, but to my understanding he's still writing. He's still writing for his theatre in Newark. And he's just had a book come out. A book of essays. But he's also had books of poetry come out too in the last year.

The things that have come out recently have been more like political statements. It's very, very different from what he was doing in the Sixties. Now he wouldn't write something like Tales *and* The System of Dante's Hell.

Well, all artists evolve. All artists evolve. They go through periods.

Then you think it possible to reconcile politics and literature? To use the theatre or one's fiction to achieve political ends?

Oh, yes, if that is what you wish to do.

Is there a danger in this kind of literature becoming propagandistic, in which the artistic merit of the work is lost?

The only danger for the artist is confusing his purpose. If he intends to write propaganda then he should write the best propaganda he can. I'm a very good propaganda writer. And I'm somewhat of a fairly good artist. If either "propagandist" or "artist" is a valid term in today's world with ever-shifting values and realities. I have no qualms about writing propaganda. And I have no qualms about putting art in propaganda.

Does art ever get in the way of what you are trying to say? Do you ever find yourself realizing that artistically something should be there, but you know that you will be losing part of your audience if it is there?

Well, you know, aesthetics is what I make it. As the creator I determine the aesthetic range. As for readers or viewers, ... The New Lafayette Theatre, where we put on our plays, is never empty. Each time we put on a play there's people there. So, when the theatre's empty, then I'll wonder why.

What kind of thing do you want to achieve by your art?

I don't know. I wish to write certain works. I wish to continue my work in building a theatre and creating...a continuing art form. But I imagine the real value will be somewhere in the future. I may not be there. But I continue to work.

Who does a writer have responsibilities to?

First, he has a responsibility to himself. If he has any talent or genius, he must first be able to master himself, to exploit these gifts. And it follows that if he's living true to himself, and doing what's true to himself, then the people around him, his co-workers, his group, his nation, will benefit from these gifts. Or the work he's doing. But, you know, unless a person can help himself he can't help anyone else.

What peculiar problems does the black writer face in America?

I don't have any problems.

What about with publishers?

That work I can't get published by what's known as "publishers," I'll publish myself. That work which won't be produced in the commercial or noncommercial white theatre, I'll produce in my own theatre.

Do you think publishers have been and are still reluctant to publish black writers?

Of course. Of course. There's a directive that's going around publishing houses this year that they're not going to publish so many black books this year. Or we're not going to publish any black books or... It's a business. It's a machine. They take in manuscripts, put them in one end and out the other end comes money. If it doesn't come out then they don't use...they change the factors in equation. My relation to a publisher is whether or not he will publish my book, distribute my book, and send me back some money for it. I need to live and maintain myself. A secondary relationship I have to a publisher is whether he'll publish other works by the people around me that I feel should be published. Outside of that . . . it's academic. I wouldn't get hung-up in New York publishing.

What are your feelings about black writing in America? Is it distinct from the rest of American literature?

Certainly. The black American culture is distinctive. And as Jenny Franklin says, the expression of art is the internal energy of the artist. And if you take it farther, it's just the internal energy of people. So, when you have a culture that is oppressed, that has been enslaved, that has been deprived, their expression will be different from any other culture around. Especially the culture that is oppressing them. So, black literature, black art is different.

What contemporary black writers do you think are important?

There's myself (smiling). I don't know. I could give you a long list. Important in what sense?

The ones who will find a permanent place in American literature at large.

Well, I don't know whether there will be an America in the '80's and '90's. Some of the writers who are having an impact now are as we mentioned before, LeRoi Jones (Imamu Amiri Baraka). Good, young, strong black playwrights are coming along . . . and in literature, this's where the action is, in the theatre. It's influencing poetry—that's getting more dramatic. The ideas of the day are being exchanged in the theatre, the situation of the life of the people is being presented, and the artists are coming together. Some of the playwrights who are coming on the scene who are going to have an impact (I think I've mentioned some of their names) are Richard Wesley, Sonia Sanchez, J. E. Gaines. Jenny Franklin does interesting work. There's a lot of promising ones.

Are black playwrights doing more important things than white playwrights, or least different things?

The black playwrights are the only ones I've seen around who are writing with conviction, passion, and with a sense of duty and truth and with a forward vision of tomorrow. Tomorrow for themselves, tomorrow for black people. They have a sense of building something, not only the black theatre, but the black nation and the black future. So, you who are looking at these kinds of things, I wish that you would examine the theatre very closely.

What do you think of white critics being involved in the criticism of black literature?

I try not to be concerned with that. It's just a phenomena, you know. It's nothing I should get my energy into, whether a white critic criticizes black literature.

Is drama the best medium for the black artist to express himself in?

Well, at the moment, there's almost unlimited freedom in the black theatre. You can see anything you want, you can do anything you want in any way you want to do it. Black theatre for the most part, in the seventy-five theatres across the country, happens mainly within the black community. And is mainly supported through the efforts of black people, however they get the resources to support and maintain it. And consequently, anything can be said. There's no such thing as patterning something to the whims and dictates of a white, Broadway-Off-Broadway audience, or regional or college theatre. I mean there's nothing like that. A novelist, if he wishes to get out into the big world, generally has to go through a white publisher. If he wishes, but he doesn't have to. But that is the route. So, consequently, there'll be restrictions. If I had not been an established playwright, and if I didn't have the ability to say "no," then the books that have been published by me through white publishers would have been tailored, would have been cut, would have been altered. But I've gained my independence through black theatres. So, I don't owe allegiance to anyone except myself and people who are with me in the theatre and my audience, which is black on the whole.

Do you think of yourself as belonging to a revolutionary theatre and what does that mean to you?

What does that mean to me? "Revolutionary" in what sense? In Marxist-Lenin sense? Pan-African sense? What do you mean because I don't think the word "revolution" is clear any more. You find General Motors using it in selling their cars, and women's undies because they don't have a certain pleat that shapes their ass holes. That's "revolutionary." So, you know . . . What does it mean?

Well, guess the way I'm using it, something's revolutionary if it tries to create radical social and political changes.

Well, I guess you can say that. Yeah. That all the arguments, and the discussions, and the fights, and the gossip, and everything else, of the revolutionary minded people can be found within black theatre. If there's one play that epitomizes this it's Richard Wesley's play, the *Black Terror*. It's quite an experience for white people, as well as black.

How does this kind of drama differ from other, more traditional American drama?

I don't know. I don't know that much about traditional drama. I've only been to one Broadway play. And that wasn't a very traditional American Broadway play. And any other drama I've encountered didn't interest me that much. But when I started thinking about drama and started reading it, it was the Europeans who interested me. There's nothing happening in American drama.

What European writers?

Well, I read the absurd people. And a few of the British people.

Are there any dramatists in America, going back over the last century, that you may feel yourself in a tradition with?

I learned a few things from O'Neill. He seemed to have the biggest voice of any of the Americans. But, no, I don't connect myself with any of them. He's from an Irish background, and I'm from where I'm from. His father was a matinee idol and my father was a cook in a Chinese restaurant. There's just no connection.

What about formally? That you may both have written naturalistic drama?

Is that what you think my work is?

I think that there's a number of elements of naturalism in it, especially perhaps in the constant theme of characters being unable to escape from their environment. But there're also elements of absurd drama.

How much of my work have you read?

All that's been published.

Well, there's some that hasn't been published. I can see why you say that then. What was the question again?

Whether your work is naturalistic? And in what way are you an absurdist?

Well, those are terms that are yours. I show the truth of black reality, some black life, if that's "naturalism," or if you want to call it "realism." Who am I to say that you shouldn't or can't? Some of the tragedy and some of the nightmare quality in black people's reality, who am I to say that you can't call it "absurd"? It can all be found there.

Do you think that perhaps the major, pervasive theme in all your work is that of the conflict between imagination and environment? In The Wine Time *might be an example. A character with a sensitive imagination is stifled by his environment.*

Well, when you say most of my works, . . . most of my known works, yes. Well, I imagine so, yeah.

Does it differ in the things I haven't seen?

I don't know because I don't look for things like that. If that characteristic is evident, then it must be there.

Is that conflict between the imagination and the environment the result of the characters being black or is it a universal problem?

Well, I don't know, because I can't jump into your shoes or any other white person's shoes. It would be nice if I could look at it through blue eyes, but I can't. I learned that early. So, that type of identity crisis I got over with. When black people grow up in this society there are many things to rob them of their manhood, their spiritual quality, their intelligence, their humanity. The white people themselves and the things white people do,

their big machines, their unnatural way of life, . . . and this being the center of that part of the world, the European-Christian world, that has victimized, exploited, and . . . destroyed the world. Destroyed humanity.

What do you think is the function of the artist in a society like ours? Is it something different for the black artist?

To do his art. If he doesn't do his art, there's no place for him.

In regard to your themes again. Several of your characters seem to be in search of at least one other person they can trust or have faith in. And they're continually disappointed. **Goin' A' Buffalo** *may be an example of this.*

Well, if that's what's in there, I guess it's in there. That's the truth of that story.

You called **Goin' A' Buffalo** *a "tragi-fantasy," I think I understand the tragic dimension in the play. What is the "fantasy"?*

Well, the lives they lead are fantasy.

Does the tragedy result from the fantasy?

The entire thing is a tragedy.

Is Ray in **In The Wine Time** *an autobiographical character?*

I guess that you could say all my characters are.

Is "Mr. Jones" in **The Electronic Nigger** *permanently affected by what is going on in the class? Is he going to change?*

I don't know, but he's not coming back.

Is this "Mr. Jones" related to any other "Jones," a more famous one?

(laughing) Well, there's a lot of Joneses.

Not any certain playwright and poet?

No.

It struck me that about the time that the play was written LeRoi Jones was undergoing something similar.

I guess you can say that many Joneses were going through a similar crisis.

In **Clara's Ole Man,** *one character says, "It just happened that way, B. G. We didn't have any choice." Is this lack of choice caused by the fact they are black?*

Well, he said that. I guess that's true, yeah. There's no choice.

Does that lack of choice pretty well extend to your other characters?

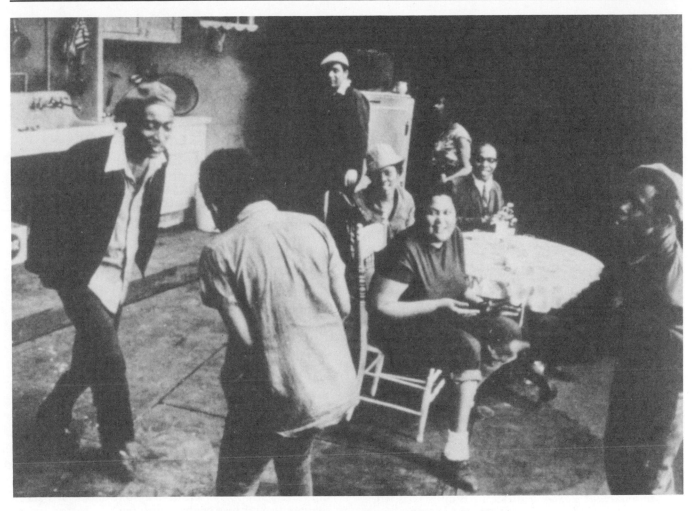

A scene from the first New York production of Clara's Ole Man.

Yes, to some of them. I mean, as characters they're deliberately deterministic types. One of them is in a play called **It Has No Choice.** It's going to be done next month.

Has that been in print yet?

No.

Is this determinism related to your own personal philosophy?

Mine is just to keep breathing in and out. (laughing) I do that with a passion.

What play do you think has been your best one?

I guess, . . . I don't know. I could say, but it wouldn't be completely true.

What would you call **The Hungered Ones?** *Was it a novel? A collection of short stories? Are the pieces interrelated? Or are they just random things you collected?*

Just pieces.

Are you trying to do something different in your fiction than you are in the drama or is it a continuation of the drama?

You can do things in fiction that you can't do in the theatre, just as you can do things in a play that you can't do in fiction. It's just a form that I work in.

One of the more interesting stories was called **"The Real Me,"** *which seems to be a satire on "the new black." At one point the character says, "I made my problem pay." Did you have anyone in mind when you wrote this or was it a certain type of people?*

I wrote it over ten years ago. It's not that new. The type exists.

You mentioned the "black future" earlier. What do you think it's going to be like over the next several years for blacks in America?

Dismal.

The distant future?

Well, I guess we who are around, as writers, we'll be writing about how dismal it was. (laughing)

Do you think that the racial situation in America will change radically in the next few decades?

I don't see the nature of the enemy changing. Until the nature of the enemy changes, the struggle will be the same. (pp. 108-12)

> *Ed Bullins and John O'Brien, in an interview in* Negro American Literature Forum, *Vol. 7, No. 3, Fall, 1973, pp. 108-12.*

Jerry H. Bryant (essay date 1973)

[*In the following excerpt, Bryant reviews Bullins's novel* The Reluctant Rapist, *describing it as "a novel of the felt texture of living, especially of living black."*]

In the title story of Ed Bullins' *The Hungered One,* there is a weird beast, a cross between a featherless bird and a rodent. It slashes and tears with its razor-sharp claws and beak. Fiercely aggressive, always hungry, it is maddened by blood. But it does not bleed itself. Even when its skull is split and its brains begin to ooze out, it retains its dangerousness and its yellow eyes keep their malevolent glitter. In his plays, Bullins is like the "hungered one." It is not conventional revolution that we find in dramas like *Goin' a Buffalo* or *In the Wine Time* but wounds laid open in black as well as white flesh by those pitiless slashing claws.

In *The Reluctant Rapist,* a different Bullins is at work, one who is strongly autobiographical and reminiscent, personal, quietly honest. The novel has the tone and the content of the 19th-century *Bildungsroman,* in which the youthful protagonist—in this case Steve Benson—is educated from innocence to experience. In the classic tradition, Steve is a loner, an outsider, and finally an outlaw. He rapes, dimly off in the background to the main action, but is "reluctant" to rape a woman he cannot love. Indeed, the reader is asked to believe that a mystical union is effected by that violation of another person's will, and that some of the women are bound to him for life.

Bullins is an earnest, even humble quester here. He has Steve Benson wander from his South Philadelphia ghetto to the eastern shore of Maryland, then to Los Angeles and San Francisco. He goes to sea and journeys through Europe, the Mediterranean countries, South America. But nothing he learns is unequivocal. He feels his aloneness, his anomalous position in America and in the world. He discovers that blacks become unfeeling out of a need to protect themselves and in doing so turn their backs upon their own people, cheat and lie to one another. The only solution to this state of mind is a kind of personal apocalypse. "One must lose faith, for faith is never quite enough. One must throw away belief, for belief is held by every black fool. One must be blown apart by all that one has been taught and reassembled in the vacuum of ignorance to form the vessel of new experience."

This is the closest thing to a working thesis that Bullins has formulated. *The Reluctant Rapist* is a handbook to the plays. As a playwright, Bullins rips, tears, rapes; he blows apart black life. As a novelist, he explains what the ripping, tearing and raping are all about. They are the acts of a lover in deep need of blasting away the conventional laws and customs, the traditional faiths and beliefs to expose the truthful, irreducible center so that he and his beloved may at last be free. Steve Benson the rapist is a metaphor of Ed Bullins the playwright. And Steve's story is a reassembling of the bits from the exploded bombs and tearing beak. It is done through a reconstitution of time and a renewal of sex. Time unrolls and unwinds in this novel, opens out and folds back on itself, stops and starts. Pieces of Steve's life loom up before us as if cut loose from chronology. But the conventional order of events is one of those beliefs that has to be destroyed. And Bullins is successful in destroying it, in fusing the past with the present, in giving us the feeling of living the past again from the standpoint of the present and seeing the future infuse the past.

Sex pervades the novel. It is lazily pleasurable, even the rapes. And in spite of the prurience of the setting, the sex seems innocent rather than lewd or lascivious. Sex, indeed, seems to be the first stage of the new experience. But the notion of sex embraces more than intercourse. It takes in the whole range of sensation. Bullins' attention is focused upon the details of consciousness, of waking—the sensation of erotic play, the shock of fists in the mouth and feet in the groin, the smell of sperm in pubic hair, the feel of wind in the evening, the taste of cheap wine drunk in an alley. There are long passages of reflection, and there are references to books and authors. But this isn't a philosophical novel. It is a novel of the felt texture of living, especially of living black. This is what we get back to after the holocaust. (pp. 502, 504)

> *Jerry H. Bryant, "The Outskirts of a New City," in* The Nation, *New York, Vol. 217, No. 16, November 12, 1973, pp. 501-2, 504.*

Harold Clurman (essay date 1975)

[*Director, author, and drama critic, Clurman was an important contributor to the development of modern American theater. In 1931, with Lee Strasberg and Cheryl Crawford, he founded the Innovative Group Theater, which produced works by such budding playwrights as Clifford Odets, William Saroyan, and Elia Kazan. He also wrote several books on the theatre, including his acclaimed autobiography* All People Are Famous *(1974). In the following essay, he offers a favorable review of Bullins's* The Taking of Miss Janie, *describing it as a "portrait" of the elements that "play upon the consciousness of articulate black people."*]

The Taking of Miss Janie . . . is a forcefully telling play. It begins with a "flash" of Janie, a white woman who weeps in desperate complaint that she has been raped by Monty, a black man whom we see with her. By the end of the play we have learned that she and Monty met in a poetry class at CCNY where she was struck by his literary talent. Her connection with him is also prompted by the fascination black people arouse in her. She withholds herself from him sexually in an effort to keep their relationship wholly friendly. Monty's feeling for her is perhaps more than desire; there is also rage at her callowness and ignorance of the black world she has entered and her resolve to keep herself chaste with him. The two sentiments mount to physical violence which she, still unenlightened by all she has witnessed and gone through with Monty, terms "rape."

Still, this is not the crux of the play. It is a dramatic portrait of those social elements which gave the 1960s their special stamp. The play focuses on the effect of all those external circumstances—the war, the student demonstrations, the resentments as well as the hopes for radical change—as they play upon the consciousness of articulate black people in particular. . . . But the play's meaning is broader than its specific ethnic background.

What we see is a people—black, white, Jew and gentile—hung up and driven nearly mad by the fearful contradictions between ragged remnants of the American "dream" and the shameful realities of actual existence. There is a strong though fitful will to overcome the resultant disaster but no one is honest, clearheaded, steadfast, informed and disciplined enough to do so. . . Ploys of escape escape nothing, drugs obliterate reality and lead to nonbeing, diverse brands of racism serve for slogans. Rabid affirmations and hysterical protests eventuate in frustration rather than relief. Nearly everyone is lost in a miserable flow of turbid emotion with no beneficent outlet. All are in the dark and no one is "saved"—not even those who have settled into unquiet compromise or stagnant surrender.

The play, despite its disturbing revelations, is neither mournful in tone nor tendentiously raucous. Vigorously humorous, it does not whine; it growls with a savage grin. Without pleading any special cause, it has sinew and muscle. Bold in its courageous objectivity, it is by no means depressing.

The picture is overcrowded or may only seem so because of the numerous characters and places. . . . At moments it is difficult to distinguish one person from another, but that in part is due to the fact that all are equally, though differently, "in trouble." The audience laughs, shouts and stamps in recognition of the types and situations depicted. It is itself the material of what it beholds and is puzzled on that account. It, too, does not *know*. It finds it impossible "to take sides" and it constantly veers in its sympathies because Bullins does not seek to direct it to any firm conclusion. He is demonstrating, not preaching. His voice here, for all its explosive resonance, is essentially poetic. (pp. 83-84)

Harold Clurman, in a review of "The Taking of Miss Janie," in The Nation, *New York, Vol. 220, No. 13, April 5, 1975, p. 414.*

Ed Bullins (journal date 1975)

[*In May 1975, Bullins won the New York Drama Critics Circle Award for* The Taking of Miss Janie. *In the following excerpt from his "Playwright's Journal 1975," published in the periodical* Confrontation, *he recounts viewers' reactions to the play. Bullins headed his journal with this motto: "The future is found in the past."*]

[*April 29, 1975*]

The day is dull but in my heart passions blaze with silent intensity. America waits poised before the future, uncertain, like a virgin bride, while the world strokes its meat, ready for the mating.

In these days of uncertainty the black thinker is turning inward or toward the past. Socialism and communism in the form of Marxist-Leninism is being adopted wholesale by former middleaged Black Nationalist spokesmen. The Muslims are talking about integration. So-called traditional Pan-Africanists are talking to themselves in esoteric mumbles. . . the 70s are here!

If George Wallace is the devil incarnate to black people and he gets elected President of the United States, then a whiteman's heaven will truly be a blackman's hell.

Something is shaping up. The KKK is rising—the old South is rising. And black people are debating and writing position papers. Sad, the black thinker is involving himself in endless white papers.

I must write a play where I capture the new black marxists, the black nationalists and where they came from, or how they developed. The contradictions, the despair and defeat, and the turn-about.

Ideas are surfacing. The occult fad has receded, if not passed, and the dialectical age is upon us.

It is time for me to arise. It is time for me to use my mind and write with a vengeance.

I am winning an audience. And that's what I need—a loyal, supportive audience. But I must write great works. I must. This is only the beginning. There's so much to do. So much to say and show . . .

[*May 2, 1975*]

Things are pressing ahead. Many of the critics will be at tonight's performance of *Janie* Sunday (5/4) is the official opening and the show is shaping up. I look forward to favorable reviews, but will the public respond? The preview audience has been so small. I'm doing a mailing out of my own pocket. If it's successful, I'll get the money back ten-fold from my royalties. But things will have to start clicking. If *Janie* dries up now

I'll have my future plans cut off. I want to fix the house up for my ole lady Trixie, and myself and kids; and I want to do some traveling this summer and begin paying off all my bills in earnest and start to live and breathe. I can write more and better when I don't have bills, taxes and expenses I can't meet pressing on me. I'm freer. I want to get more into my writing. Have been slacking off for the past six months. That's because my last several works have been turned down by the very people who commissioned them. That's a drag when that happens. I originally wrote *Janie* for Gordon Davidson at the Mark Taper Forum in Los Angeles, and the chump turned it down, after I spent nearly a year in writing it, for the little bit of money he advanced me. I really felt screwed after that. But it was finally picked up by Woodie King, then Joe Papp, and has proven such a success by getting more attention than anyone imagined . . .

I'm reading some of the revolutionary Chinese who write on art again. I remember I first read them in San Francisco, at The Black House, where Marvin X, Eldridge Cleaver and myself ran a revolutionary (Black) politico-cultural-artistic center. The forerunner of that type of thing for many, though the Black Arts Theater preceded it. That seems so long ago. I'm going to tackle a big subject soon. That's how one gets the necessary attention that one needs to do his work—take on big, public subjects. Maybe it will be the Attica play that Gilbert Moses and I have been talking about. But whatever, I won't abandon the 20th century cycle. I have the 7th play scheduled as soon as I complete this Lucy Terry play I've been researching. Either that or the Attica play will be next. I don't want to take on any commissions or TV or movie schemes. No. I have to work on my own things. If only *Janie* holds up through the summer, so that I can get this work done and pay my bills. My bills, my bills, and the things I want and need for myself and my family. Sun Ra and Ameena are especially bright and sensitive. They should go to special schools which will develop them. That takes money. I have to get this house fixed up for Trixie or her depressions will destroy us. God forbid that I should get depressed. I can't write in that state; that's why I'm always trying to keep an optimistic frame of mind. For me, a playwright, to be depressed too long is to lose everything, but ultimately, my life. If my marriage breaks up I know I'll be an emotional wreck for a number of months; I know I won't get any writing done then until things settle down inside my head. That's one of the reasons I resent marriage, I guess. It's such a prison. But I'm a matrimonial recidivist. That kind of trauma seems almost too much of a price to pay. My wife's a good woman; and I really love her, so I'm going to try and satisfy her, if I can, while satisfying myself. Because if it ain't good to me, it ain't worth going through. I don't believe in ain't worth going through. I don't believe in doing anything I don't like to do, at least, not for long. I got to make enough bread to support this family shit. And it's got to be through my income from my work, whatever I deem it; I'm not taking on any outside jobs if at all possible. Not unless

I'm doing something I want to do. No more unemployment, drug program gigs, college/university hustles, none of that bull. I hate all that. Really hate it. And that cuts off all my writing things. My head gets turned around. I'm tied up in such knots about my various outside homes that I can't get down to business. Trying to teach dumb ass college students about the craft of drama and theater when they know they know all they need about being a nurse or gym teacher is the limit. And that drug program, Elmcor, almost did me in. And that was only two hours a week. But getting myself ready for that was pure weekly pain and torment. It would take me a day to get ready and two days afterwards to recover. No more of that. I can understand those people who sell dope or rob banks rather then go on welfare. I'd do the same rather than take any job which fucks me up for writing.

[*May 7, 1975*]

Well, *Janie* is off and running. Went by the theater last night and there was an audience of paying people. Such is the power of reviews, I guess. I'm the fair-haired boy in some circles. I'm even invited to a meeting this morning with Joe Papp. Hold onto your hat, guys. Here we go.

Am up earlier. Have to do this to write more. I have to get back to my writing. I have so much writing to do. I'm corny enough to be telling people that I am attempting to fulfill my potential. And I am. I have to stay away from the play for a while and start working more on my writing. Get my head into my work, which will take some time to do. But I'll do it. Have to stop having my time taken up by unnecessary things and start giving priorities to my creative work . . .

[*May 9, 1975*]

Things seem to be looking up. *Miss Janie* is picking up more audience. This weekend will tell its story. The show has to make so much money in that little theater (The Newhouse). But if Woodie and Papp's people got off their asses, they could get people in. I know that Papp's organization is behind the production, but I think, almost know, that Woodie is shamming. Why wouldn't either of them listen to me when I told them they need a full-time audience development person for this show, someone who would concentrate on black and school and group audiences. Shit! It's all about bucks with them. For me, it's my life on the line everyday the curtain raises on one of my creations.

I'm trying to get into some writing. It's a bitch. Getting up is a fight. Discipline and concentration are hard to maintain. Finding the stimulation to do the work is difficult. I'll just have to hang-in there. And work work work work work. But I keep my mind filled with extraneous things: women, speculations on other productions, lack of money money money, my children, my wife . . .

Dreamt the other night about a duel that I got involved in, or rather, demanded. Dick Gregory, whom I've never met, made some very cruel remark about my mother. It seems, she had become a television evangelist with a following and had endorsed something that was potentially infuriating to certain people, Gregory especially. I became angry at the way he treated mother, but instead of taking a contract out on him or kicking his ass myself, I went into a duel thing. Pistols. A large part of the dream was about the loading of guns, getting instructions from our seconds, etc. Interesting dream. Might make something of it in a future play...

[*May 29, 1975*]

I won the N. Y. Drama Critics Circle Award the other day. Or rather *Janie* did. It didn't do anything for business last night. I can't figure out what's wrong. Maybe the whites are threatened and the niggers are embarrassed. But no matter, I'm working. Mostly reading. *Mein Kamp.* Doing research on my little Lucy Terry play. Reading African tales so that I can blend the images in with the American Indian and Terry legends. I got to start writing it soon. And then write other things. That's all I've got really, my writing. Trixie's either sick or wishing she was a thousand miles away. All my kids have their own mind. I guess I have to admit that I'm a bit different from other people and whatever happens, whoever/however I surround myself with family and people I'm going to be lonely and independent. At almost forty I can face that, can't I? My mother has been alone for so long. She's got her religion. Her church. And I have my writing, my art. And I'm working for my theater that I'll one day own. There's so much reading that I have to do. And I've been engaged in body/flesh pursuits for so much of my life. Maybe these next twenty years I'll catch up on my reading and studies. And maybe get some of this writing done. Picasso did his work. That's all a man can do. Do his work. As Himes sez: "A writer writes, a fighter fights." Okay. maybe. let's see.... (pp. 269-73)

> *Ed Bullins, "Playwright's Journal 1975," in* Confrontation, *Nos. 33-34, Fall-Winter, 1986-87, pp. 269-73.*

Robert L. Tener (essay date 1976)

[*In the following review essay, Tener examines a selection of Bullins's plays, focusing on the "spatial environment" of* The Duplex, In New England Winter, The Pig Pen, Clara's Ole Man, Goin' a Buffalo, *and* The Night of the Beast.]

The fictive universe of Ed Bullins' dramatic writings is like Pandora's box set within the larger compass of white American cities. Filled with the hunger and absurdity trapped in the Black life style, the dramatic scene presents a complex and powerfully delineated social landscape carefully related to its fictive personalities. Their daily world is ordered by man, chance, and change; their dreams are determined by their frustra-

tions. To some extent, James R. Giles in his discussion of tenderness and brutality attempts a study of that relationship in three of Bullins' dramas. ["Tenderness in Brutality: The Plays of Ed Bullins," *Players* XLVII, No. 1 (October-November 1972).] Beyond Giles' article, however, no one, to the best of my knowledge, has studied in any detail the characteristics of the social setting in Bullins' plays.

The elements of the social compass in Bullins' vision are the conceptual spatial environment, the nature of order within that space, and the operating fictive values. In one sense the spatial environment of the plays swings across the country from California in *The Duplex, The Pig Pen, Electronic Nigger,* and *Goin' a Buffalo* to Harlem in *Night of the Beast* and *It Bees Dat Way,* and then moves down to Philadelphia in *Clara's Ole Man* and *A Son, Come Home.* At other times it is a nameless metropolitan city as in *Death List, In New England Winter,* and *In the Wine Time.*

But the specific territory may be an apartment, small, clean, and sharply hued in *Goin' a Buffalo;* neat but impoverished in *Clara's Ole Man;* rented rooms for a day or two *In New England Winter;* a series of apartment rooms in *The Duplex;* or one room, large and well furnished in the affluent American manner in *The Pig Pen* and *The Gentleman Caller.*

While most exterior scenes are restricted to narrow streets, compressing the action by narrowing its possibilities, all the interior spaces are even more confining of action and character with their strong box-like qualities. In *Goin' a Buffalo,* Curt and Pan move back and forth from their red and white living room where they hope for a new life in Buffalo, to an unreal and fantastically colored, semi-dark arena in Deeny's night club where Pan dances. The action and their lives are restricted to both areas.

In *The Duplex* the effect is much the same for Steve Benson and Velma Best. Varying its focus and its scenes, the play gathers unity from the passion of Steve and Velma. A college student on vacation, Steve is staying with his good friend Marco in a third floor room of the duplex. Velma Best, who owns and rents out the duplex rooms, is married to O. D. Best who beats her and takes the rent money. In his third floor room Steve is as trapped as when he is in Velma's place on the ground floor. We see them as lovers only within small rooms, never in association with the unlimited expanses of the outdoors. Indeed there appears to be no room for their love. They mount each other, not in Velma's bed (where Velma feels uncomfortable with her thoughts), but in the hallway on the floor where Tootsie Franklin, a boarder and friend, sees them. Clearly the hallway, a public area designed for movement from one room to another, cannot meet the needs of their private feelings. For Steve and Velma the private resonance of their love cannot develop in box-like structures which lack the fixations of happiness and the memories of their happy protection.

Steve Benson appears again and again in Bullins' plays. Always associated with him is the reverberation of his anguish, compressed and held in lest it explode. *In New England Winter* presents a Steve hungry to return to his woman Liz who lives in New England. Needing money for that dream, Steve plans the holdup of a finance company with his half-brother Cliff. The action occurs both in the present and in the past. The present takes shape in the small room where Steve, Cliff, Bummy, and Chuck rehearse for the robbery, their feelings at the time being explosively delimited by their memories and fears; the past, as back flashes, provides the center of Steve's tight dream, a former winter in Liz's New England apartment. That warm winter past contains Steve's memories of happiness in association with the enclosure of her apartment, the protection of his love, and the surge of his frustrations. He moves from the cage of those memorable fixations to the present of the rented room without emotional satisfaction. His life, thus proscribed by the dialectic of apartments so different in their emotional relations, seems to be held by walls from which he cannot escape.

There are no external activities like country walks or Sunday drives to expand the horizons and feelings of the inhabitants of the dramatic boxes and to relate to the natural world. The images and metaphors of the earth are not descriptive of their relationships. The dramatic volume surrounding the agents seems to hold or trap them, not in the sense of a barrier preventing movement in a specific direction, but rather in the condition of being their prison. Their enclosure, however, appears to be placed within a larger spatial volume, usually never seen but sometimes referred to or implied, the all-encompassing box of the American metropolis or the gigantic impersonal "they," both of which are white.

In *The Pig Pen* the white world clearly surrounds the living nest perched on a California hill where Len and Sharon Stover share their lives in parties with the Carroll brothers who are musicians (Bobo, John, and Henry), with Margie, Ernie Butler, Carlos, Ray Crawford a poet, and Mackman a white youth. The wine bottle passes among them; the marijuana cigarettes get them high; and Sharon's body satisfies them. But all the time, isolating their partying from the rest of the world, is the white landscape just down the hill. From its confines came the white Jewish Sharon and the white Mackman who imitates the hippy life style and language habits. Both are outsiders despite the fact that Sharon is Len's wife. She is not so much a part of him as she is an object of sexual use among his friends. The center of events within the room is Len who discusses the Black Nationalist Movement and criticizes the others for merely paying lip service to it, calling their party a "ritual of communion." But it is a ritual which has no social intercourse with the white world. The one white man Mackman is a "superspade" to the Carroll brothers who reject him. It is also a ritual in which the sexual intercourse within the house suggests through parody the poverty of the relationship between the two worlds.

In *The Duplex* the other engulfing world is referred to only indirectly, yet through Steve it affects the events within the apartment complex. On vacation from his classes at a white university, Steve brings from it memories and a desire to expand his life. Although he reads Ed Bullins' short stories to Velma, he will return to the university world. He cannot remain in the confining duplex with Velma. In *Goin' a Buffalo,* the metaphor of the box within a box is more direct and resonant, the white scene almost completely engulfing the black setting. While plans and decisions and actions appear to be made by Pan, Curt, or Art, the white world reaches into their home base through its police, its jails, its prisons, and its laws. To escape from the oppression of such things is part of Pan and Curt's dream. Only in *The Night of the Beast* could one say that the two metaphorical boxes are side by side. In this play the theme is revolution, the two societies being actively opposed in terms of armed patrols in open war. Yet there remains the haunting possibility that the white territory is around Harlem and not beside it.

In some sense then the spatial volume conceptualized by Bullins contains a basic dichotomy or built in element of opposition and compression. His dramatic arena is a binary universe of engulfment rather than of simple opposition, seen as the world of black experience under the impact of a white all-engulfing mysterious outside. To understand the nature of that experience and Bullins' plays, one has to study the characteristics of their dramatic world. While some limitations of those characteristics are supplied by the image of Pandora's box, additional meaning comes from the ordering principle embedded in Bullins' vision.

Existence is ordered in Bullins' dramatic world by the agents doing what they must to survive. Their lives are the products of direct and simple contacts, not the consequences or summations of such abstractions as their dreams and desires. They are rebels and captives simultaneously. Although *Clara's Ole Man* focuses on the interaction among Jack who is a college student, Clara whom he is interested in, and her lesbian lover Big Girl, the force of the play reveals the lost innocence embedded in Clara, Big Girl, Baby Girl (Big Girl's mentally retarded sister), and ironically Jack. Big Girl no longer dreams about her sister, or herself, or Clara. Having come to accept her lesbianism, she has taught her helpless sister to be free from internal tensions by swearing. When Jack questions the results of swearing, Big Girl in anger and self pity tells her life history, the story of two sisters separated and brought up by different families. But Big Girl has survived. To have learned how to handle Clara's sexual problem, to have acquired the ability to cope with street punks like Stoogie, and to have come to accept the drunken Miss Famies and the lush Aunt Tooheys are no simple accomplishments. She has not pursued dreams or her desires. Instead she has responded pragmatically and effectively to the demands that her diminishing environment has made on her.

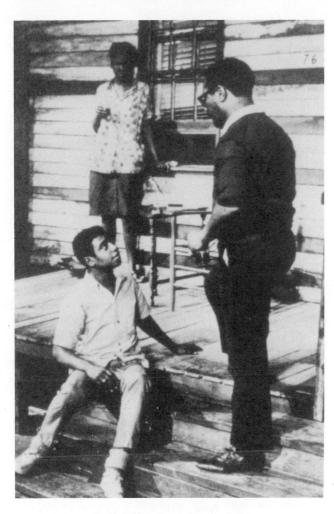

A scene from In the Wine Time.

The same principle is illustrated by *The Duplex:* the agents do what they have to to survive. In a vague way because Steve wants to help Velma and keep her as his woman, he buys a gun but never uses it. When he does try to defend her against O. D., he is badly mauled. Yet his best friend Marco does not help him. In the end Steve decides to leave without having achieved his dream. *In the Wine Time* presents Ray, Lou's nephew, joining the navy after his uncle Cliff has gone to prison for ostensibly killing Red in a knife fight to protect Ray. If Ray is to survive, he has to run away to the sea despite his love for a beautiful girl whom he has met on the avenue. If she is his first dream, he cannot follow her when she leaves. As for Cliff, his desire is to stay with Lou. But Lou is forced to choose Ray over her husband. Her uncontrollable sobs and words reflect the agony and indecisiveness of their lives, "He's all I got left, Cliff . . . He's all the family I got left." Life has become indifferent for Cliff. When he reappears as one of those planning the robbery (*In New England Winter*), he can never return to Lou. She has become part of his past, not part of his future. Cliff's dream, like the dreams which Bullins assigns his other agents, affects only a small

portion of his present life and is denied in the ordinary process of living.

Inherent in this ordering scheme is the absence of any strong social, political, or religious structures to support the characters. Each cast of agents operates outside any specific social frame needed to relate them to other persons. Nor is there a sense of a Christian God presented as an organizing principle. The few instances when Christians are used (hence indirectly implying some Christian overtones), as in *A Son, Come Home* and *In the Wine Time,* they are relatively unsympathetic. The play *In the Wine Time,* however, provides a Christian Lou whom Cliff loves and respects. But her beliefs instead of clarifying their existence add to Cliff's confused image of his role as a man. His way of life is in the fighting style of the navy; hers is based on a moral integrity which he feels ought to be admired. That response causes him to sacrifice himself because it weakens his self-image. He likes the fact that Lou tries to improve him, yet he senses his inadequacies more strongly under the impact of her Christian morality. Although she says that she made a man out of him, he accuses her of ruining Ray.

The personal ties that operate within the plays are less a function of time and family and more one of individual action and chance. Friendships are not illustrations of romantic ideals; they do not last for ever, or for that matter, for any great length of time. Friends come and go; they appear; one makes a friend. Then the friend may become an enemy. Personal ties are that carefully bound by the necessity of living.

In *Goin' a Buffalo,* because Art had helped Curt in a jail fight, when both are released from jail, Curt befriends Art and invites him to join in the plans for raising money to go to Buffalo. As the action progresses, Curt treats Art more and more like a brother. But all the time it is really Art, the outsider and archetypal betrayer, who has carefully planned to take Curt's woman by informing the white police about Curt's activities. In this play friendship appears to be a function of situation not of personalities; it suggests situational ethics instead of a Christian code. Similarly in *The Duplex,* although Marco passes as Steve's friend, the relationship is more a matter of individual need than of mutual aid because Marco refuses to support Steve against O. D. Best. One shares the good times and the wine times but not always the bad times.

In *Pig Pen,* the personal relationships are even more loosely defined. Ray Crawford the poet is apparently Len Stover's friend, yet he does not openly help Len or his wife. Indeed the three quarrel as though they were opposing elements of a triangle and were related to each other in terms of use more than in terms of feelings. The general pattern appears to be that a situation brings persons together who call themselves friends; when the situation alters, they are no longer friends. Even for *In New England Winter* Steve is not in a fixed relationship with Cliff, Bummy, and Chuck. As long as the relationship is mutually satisfactory in terms of their need to rehearse the robbery, they remain friends. But when Bummy threatens to tell Cliff that it was Steve who had fathered Lou's child, the situation has altered and Steve kills him.

If friendship is thus defined in dynamic and unfixed terms, marriage is established even more loosely. Its conception as lasting over a long period of time operates only, if at all, in the dream world. Perhaps Curt has envisioned himself and Pan as starting their business in Buffalo and living a good full life together (*Goin' a Buffalo*); during the marijuana dream that Blackman has in *Night of the Beast,* he sees Jamal and his wife happily and ideally married. But the reality of marriage in the social world is a temporary relationship filled with pathos and many turn-offs. In *Goin' a Buffalo,* Art, the dream, the narcotics, and the police separate Curt and Pan; Cliff and Lou (*In The Wine Time*) are separated by the killing of Red and Cliff's going to prison. When Bullins picks up the character of Cliff again for *In New England Winter,* we learn that Lou has no steady man and Cliff has no special woman. They never see each other again. In *The Duplex,* the only marital pattern is the brutal one between Velma and O. D. Best. *The Pig Pen* presents a special case where the marriage operating between black Len and white Sharon is the parodic wedding of the intellectual pimp and the masochistic Don Juan whore.

While some of the wives have done their tricks on the street, Pan for example, Bullins does not present them as being whores in their relations with their husbands. Whoredom is a life-style, a way of earning a livelihood before or after marriage. Only with the one wife, Sharon, who is white and hence presented derogatorily, is whoredom a part of the marital pattern.

Prison, friendship, proximity, death determine marriages and love, not dreams and ideals. Although Blackman has killed Jamal in *Night of the Beast,* within a few hours Jamal's wife has transferred her love to Blackman. Marriage and love apparently cannot afford the illusion of Platonic semi-permanences in the dramatic social setting. One loves while he can before he's boxed in further. Change in the direction of one's life separates loves and redirects the need to love within the Bullins' characters. If there is regret for the passing, there is a strength for what comes. The Cliffs and the Steves continue. There will always be an Art. It is not whom one loves that is most important; it is the necessity to love that must endure.

Even life often has a short duration in Bullins' plays. The dramatic social world is a landscape of physical and emotional violence. The particular person dies, but others live. Bummy is killed by Steve; Cliff knifes Red; Blackman stabs Jamal. But the order of the social environs does not seem to be that of the jungle. Rather the order resembles on the surface that found in the heroic age or on the American frontier. Traditionally it is based on taking what one wants and can hold on to

through individual strength, skill, courage, cunning, and intelligence. When the individual loses, it is not always because he is physically weak or stupid; sometimes he is overwhelmed by the multiplicity of events, actions, or forces developing beyond his control. For example Art is triumphant in *Goin' a Buffalo,* not through any physical or intellectual superiority over Curt but because Art's way of life is to get rid of the Cliffs before something can happen to himself. O. D. Best, on the other hand, being physically more powerful than Steve in *The Duplex,* will keep Velma. And Steve, not being able to pick the time or place or weapons of battle, must lose against simple force despite his intelligence.

As for the action in the other plays, Cliff loses Lou because there is no way for him to control the events surrounding their lives. Sometimes an agent wants what he cannot get; sometimes he cannot keep what he has. Big Girl cannot find freedom or love and must adopt a life of perpetual daily compromise. Jack cannot have Clara as his woman because Big Girl wants her. The sense of these actions is that there is always someone, or a group, or even a series of events that will deprive one of life and love which can be sustained only for the short time that one has personal power. And personal power is short-lived in Bullins' dramas. For his heroes there is no escape from the sense of daily loss and absurdity.

Something always compresses the scale of their environmental horizons. The effect is to provide a limited destiny for them. As destiny, it is not quite heroic. The intrusion of the Homeric gods into the lives of the Greek heroes tended to expand and intensify their sense of life's qualities and its essential meaningfulness. But the intrusions into the social universe of Bullins' dramas are not godlike and do not expand the psychological awareness of its inhabitants. While death and change are always immediately present, sometimes sooner than expected, heroic honor and glory are not found. The agents' lives, consequently, are restricted rather than expanded, and their scope of choice and feeling is continually narrowed.

On the other hand the lives of the characters are not necessarily dull and apathetic or filled with pathos and sorrow. The value system functioning is simply neither Platonic nor Christian. It is similar to what develops in a frontier society. What are the values in the social scene? They are drinking and sharing wine in the wine time; smoking, especially marijuana, in the dream time; talking, especially teasing talk about love, or sex, or jobs, or manhood, in the jive-time; being in the party time; playing and listening to music in the blues and jazz time; having sexual intercourse and loving in the strong delight of bodies; and especially fighting and touching body to body. Cliff, Curt, Steve fight to find their temporary place in their world; every man fights to get or keep a woman. One fights to keep from being killed or to put down those he hates; one fights as a way of life or as a ritual expression of the incoherent desire for change.

But drinking, smoking, talking, partying, having sexual intercourse, listening to music, and fighting are everyday values, short term in their effects, that get one through from night to night. Dreams are also a value, directed sometimes towards the future and usually never achieved. But Steve, Velma, Cliff, and Lou do dream just as Pan and Curt do. Perhaps the best expression of the dream as a value is caught in *The Night of the Beast.* The dream is focused on the Third World Bar and is entered when Blackman and the woman, starting to smoke their marijuana cigarette, drift into the other time and place of the bar which serves only what is good for body and mind. There all members of the Third World are brothers and sisters and the bar tender is the former leader of the revolution. But the dream remains unfulfilled. At the end of the play Blackman is killed by an insane girl and the woman is left alone to continue the revolution.

The dreams are not always gentle or pulsing with new life. Some times they are tainted with the Charley disease as in Curt and Pan's desire to acquire enough money to go into business in Buffalo. In *Clara's Ole Man,* the dream is implied as a world of lost innocence, Big Girl being corrupted by a Christian family of hypocrites and Baby Girl contracting syphilis with its attendant insanity from her family. The only reality their dream can have is a moment of reminiscence for a childhood of lost innocence which altered their lives. For *In the Wine Time* Cliff's dream to go to school on the G. I. Bill and to find himself as a man is associated with a desire to be free of some vague thing which he externalizes as women. But the major dream is Ray's, associated with the girl on the avenue. Leaving her, Ray turns to the wine times, "meeting the years which had to hurry hurry so ... [that he] could begin the search that ... [he has] not completed. It is the image of manhood in the world of the future which Ray must search for. The quest is for the discovery of the self hungry to be free of Pandora's box and filled with ambivalent hope. The dream of *In New England Winter* points backward as Steve remembers the haunting yesterdays with Liz. In her apartment she feels that she and Steve are children of the black god of the night. Her desire is to make their baby at night, or tomorrow, or some time. But misunderstandings, a drunken stupor, a covetous Crook (desiring Liz and informing on Steve), a knife, and the fact of Steve's being a deserter from the navy conspire to separate Steve and Liz from their dream. Before he flees, Steve cries out for order, form, reason, some kind of absolutes to provide something for him besides the emptiness. But such dreams are not self-fulfilling. They reflect the tension of compression in the characters and the sense of the impossibility of effecting change.

While there is no belief in a divine presence to order the world and provide meaning, there is a destiny and a drift to the agents in their fictive boxes. They live for a short time in their apartment enclosures; their enveloping environment acts or alters; and the two sets of actions through chance provide direction. The direct consequence of this drift is that the men and women have no children and are neither creative artists nor merchants of capital. They appear to be fragments of a jagged movement in time. A few remain hungry like Steve who reads stories to Velma or like Ray Crawford who writes poetry. Some of the women are or were pregnant, the Mother in *A Son, Come Home,* Velma in *The Duplex,* Clara in *Clara's Ole Man.* Their pregnancies, being neither heroic nor dignified, signal changes in the drift of their lives, causing Mother to get married or bringing Clara closer to Big Girl.

While the short term values keep the body alive, characteristically the dream value involves either freeing oneself from the box of life or creating a new society. But the ambivalent dream of manhood and the quest for self which dominates the plays as an indeterminate ideal is externalized by the idealized relationships which the men want with their women, even if the women are not the physical leaders in the revolution and most often live in a milieu of dope, jail, knives, wine, cops, fights, pregnancies, and death.

The hunger and frustration of the young men is best expressed by Steve in *The Duplex* when he explains to Marco his feelings about Velma. He says, putting his woman at the center of his delimited world,

> Nobody knows the love and beauty I find in holding my woman in my arms.... My woman...a poor little scared black girl that's even dumber than I'm supposed to be.... Nor will anybody know that she'll never know me...really know me...this black man...with this mind...they'll never understand the thoughts that flash through my head and scorch the back of my eyes...these eyes that see her being beaten and raped, these eyes that see the flames of the hell that we all live in...live our black lives in here...in our cool dark little lives...getting ready to become something we ain't now or will never be...really.... and she shouldn't be in my together program anyway 'cause I'm due for greater things. Yeah...greater things...ha ha.... Well I'm not, you know... not due, that is...not due for anything more than what I'm due for now...and that is only to be a nigger...or be black...nothing short of those two absolutes. To work in this whiteman's land...or build one of my own...to give a last ditch try to save my balls.... But where in the hell are we going, brother? Where? Into the machine maze of I. B. M.....

Perhaps it is the desire, as Steve says, to build a land of his own that reveals the ambiguity in the metaphor of Pandora's box. The desire is hope. Whether it be a vice or virtue in its context, it remains the theme of *The Duplex* and especially of *The Night of the Beast* and is part of the black compass trapped within the white American landscape. It is much of what is left for the hungered artist according to the Bullins vision. (pp. 533-44)

Robert L. Tener, "Pandora's Box: A Study of Ed Bullins' Dramas," in CLA Journal, Vol. XIX, No. 4, June, 1976, pp. 533-44.

Richard G. Scharine (essay date 1979)

[*In the following essay, Scharine examines the character of Steve Benson as he appears in* It Has No Choice, In New England Winter, The Duplex, The Fabulous Miss Marie, *and* The Reluctant Rapist. *The critic proposes that Steve's development in these plays parallels Bullins's own development as a playwright. Suggesting that Bullins is no longer a revolutionary artist, Scharine also wonders if Bullins can continue writing effectively. Bullins's rebuttal to Scharine's essay appears below.*]

Several years ago, the constant critical assumption that the character of Steve Benson was really the alter ego of Ed Bullins prompted the writer to complain: "Everybody's got him tagged as me. I'm going to kill him off." Steve's mortality aside—and he has since appeared as the title character in Bullins' novel *The Reluctant Rapist*—, the frequency of his reappearances does suggest that he and the writer see the other characters while traveling the same path. Steve is the first-person narrator of the early short story "The Messenger." A similarly told story, "Travel from Home," has as its narrator Chuckie, a nickname of Stevie Benson in yet a third story, "DANDY, or Astride the Funky Finger of Lust." The unnamed narrator of "New England Winter" becomes Steve Benson when that short story becomes the play *In New England Winter*. The unnamed narrator of "In The Wine Time" becomes Ray Crawford in a similar story-to-play conversion, but in *The Duplex* Steve Benson reads the story to Velma Best as an example of his own writing. Dramatically, Steve Benson is a central character of *It Has No Choice* (1966), *In New England Winter* (1967), and *The Duplex* (1969); a secondary character in *The Fabulous Miss Marie* (1971); and is mentioned in *The Corner* (1968). Finally, there is the aforementioned novel, *The Reluctant Rapist* (1973).

It is interesting, of course, to use the plays in which Steve Benson appears as a basis for speculation about the Bullins of the '50s. It is more interesting, however, to study them as expressions of Bullins' view of himself at the time the plays were written—that pivotal five-year period from 1966, when he was the Information Minister of the Black Panther Party in San Francisco, to 1971, by which time he was firmly established as resident playwright of the New Lafayette Theatre in New York. They are, therefore, on one level, the record of Bullins' transition from conscious revolutionary to conscious artist. Furthermore, such a study raises questions as to why—given the seeming Bullins/Benson interchangeability—Steve has never been brought forward into the time frame during which Bullins found himself as an artist, even though the successful artist with a ghetto past has been the subject of two of Bullins' most recent plays.

The other three potential Bullins alter egos also made their dramatic debuts relatively early: Art in *Goin' a Buffalo* (1966), Cliff in *In The Wine Time* (1966), and Michael in *A Son Come Home* (1968). Steve, Cliff, and Art had appeared earlier in short stories Bullins wrote for various "little magazines" in the early '60s, the best of which he grouped and published under the title *The Hungered One* in 1971. The changes that the characters underwent from the stories to the plays suggest that Bullins very early in his playwrighting career envisioned them as continuing characters, and had determined to associate Cliff with loyalty and Art with betrayal. In the short story "New England Winter," the narrator is accompanied on an armed robbery by his brother, here called Art. Inserted italicized flashbacks make it clear that the robbery is the narrator's means of making it back to the girl he left behind in New England. This story is used almost verbatim as the prologue to the 1967 play *In New England Winter,* but as the emphasis has changed from the sensitivity of the narrator's motivation to the revelation that he has betrayed his partner with his partner's wife, the narrator and accomplice-brother become Steve and Cliff respectively.

It is also clear, in retrospect, that Bullins early decided to emphasize neither the gallant losers (Cliff) or the unscrupulous takers (Art), but to follow the path of the seekers away from the numbing ghetto and the material quest.

Ray Crawford of *In The Wine Time* is an earlier version of Steve Benson. Soaking away the summers of his youth on the front stoop of his aunt and uncle (Lou and Cliff Dawson), Ray dreams of a beautiful young girl whom he sees daily on the Avenue, but who has spoken to him only once—to promise to wait for him in the outside world when he is ready to look for her. During one of these wine-filled nights, a fight erupts over a girl and another boy is stabbed to death. Cliff takes the blame for the killing, but extracts a promise from Lou that she will sign the papers that will get Ray into the Navy and out of the neighborhood.

Ray appears as a poet in the 1970 play *The Pigpen,* but by then his identity has essentially been assumed by Steve Benson. When Steve reads aloud an example of his own writing in *The Duplex* (1969), it is the first-person narrative that makes up both the short story "In The Wine Time" and Ray Crawford's prologue-monologue to the later play of the same name. Furthermore, in the short stories collected in *The Hungered One,* Steve's closest friend is an older boy named Homer—possibly the Homer Garrison who is discussed as a current Army sergeant and former nose-picker belonging to the family living next door to Ray Crawford in *In The Wine Time.* Steve Benson also lived near *Art* Garrison, if the latter's description of their childhood fights is any indication. Interestingly for the critic seeking continuity, in the 1977 production of *Daddy,* Michael Brown, the revolutionary artist turned commercially successful musician, also speaks of living next door to Art Garrison.

It is, therefore, the questing artist with whom we identify Bullins. Ray is given the opportunity to begin his search through Cliff's self-sacrifice. Michael finds fame and fortune, albeit not happiness. But it is the development of Steve Benson which holds our interest in the early plays.

The Steve Benson of *It Has No Choice* and *In New England Winter* is a pathological figure, motivated by an intense love-hate relationship with both his concept of himself and his concept of "whiteness." He exists in a constant state of racial self-betrayal, but cannot himself accept what he interprets as betrayal from anyone else. In *It Has No Choice* Steve has wooed and bedded a rather intellectually insignificant White secretary at the company where he works. At the end of what has apparently been, sexually, an extremely satisfying two-week holiday, Grace, nevertheless, wants to break off their relationship:

> You just stand around quiet and look out from behind those eyes all the time. Never saying too much. Always treating me like I'm something special when I know what you can do with your mind. What are you waiting for? When the manager is around your face is blank.... You have nothing to say but when we're alone you treat me like a pet you're pampering...an animal you're fattening up...for what, Steve?

The answer, plainly, is revenge—revenge and a desire to immerse himself in and to dominate that which he perceives as having rejected him. The title for *It Has No Choice* has been taken from the work of Franz Kafka and represents the strength of Steve's feeling about what is due to him: "The world will freely offer itself to you to be unmasked, it has no choice, it will roll in ecstasy at your feet."

The "world," in Steve's case, is patently the White world in its most mysterious and inaccessible form—a White woman. His selection of Grace, his intellectual inferior, as a means of entrance into that world is a psychological reassurance to Steve that he is entering on his terms. His devotion to her is his payment for access to that world, and her desire to be with him is to him the benchmark of his manhood:

> You entered into a contract...and you're going to keep it.... There's things you don't understand, Grace, Man is the decider in this life. Man is the creator of his situation, he, himself, is this.... My role, the role that I've made for myself, includes you...we're inseparable.... The dream of myself isn't complete without you, darling.

The inability of Steve to see himself except as the possessor of Grace eventually drives him to a desperate act of survival. He strangles her into submission, an act made doubly horrifying by the fact that its intent is neither murder nor a prelude to rape, but is rather a means of continuing their relationship: "I think I'll enjoy making love to you tomorrow, darling."

Grace is Steve's Cadillac, the "white possession" which ostensibly defines his Black manhood while in actuality betraying it. His initial seduction of Grace is no less of an act of aggression than the ropes he twists around the wrists of the blonde cashier of *In New England Winter*

"so she would never forget." In that play, Steve obsessively rehearses the robbery and binding of the girl (who had made the mistake of staring at him when they were both freshmen in high school) by making another gang member wear a dress and a pink female mask with blond wig. While obviously deriving from Genet's *The Blacks,* the image is all the more chilling because *In New England Winter* is primarily a realistic play.

In New England Winter has two times and two settings: a hot night in 1960 in Cliff's room, and Winter 1955 in an urban flat in New England. In the latter, Steve, who is AWOL from the Navy, hides out with a half-crazed girl named Liz. In the former, Steve and Cliff plan and rehearse the robbery of a finance company in order that Steve may obtain enough money to return to New England to hunt for Liz. At the end of the play, Bummie, another accomplice to the robbery, tries to tell Cliff that Steve fathered a child by Cliff's wife Lou while Cliff was in prison. Steve kills Bummie, only to have Cliff reveal that he knew about the infidelity long before Lou left him.

The revelation of Steve's unconscious subservience to White values and White symbols dominates *In New England Winter.* The fact that the "victim" in the robbery rehearsal is a Black man in disguise is not insignificant concerning Steve's true attitude toward his own race. This interpretation is further reinforced by the language he uses to describe his longstanding resentment of another gang member who years earlier knocked him down and held a gun to his head: "Cops and niggers...that's what it was.... In his monkey mind he was playin' white cop...and I was just a nigger he could...."

It is Steve, of course, who sees himself in terms of the White role:

> CLIFF. I'm not just talkin' about how you plan jobs, Steve. It's how you live...that's the part you can keep. Your bein' on time or you'll have a heart attack. Your keepin' to the schedules you make...whether it's takin' some bullshit night course, gettin' your hair cut a certain time ah month...or waitin' for years to go see the woman you love.
>
> STEVE. It's not her! I got to get myself ready to meet the future, Cliff. Don't you see?
>
> CLIFF. The future is with us right now, brother. We drown in our future each breath we take. Its phoney promises leak into our brains and turns them to shit.

It is ironic that Steve should talk of the future when his obsession is revenge for the past. Steve wants a revolution in the true sense of the word—a reversal of positions. Ultimately, he wants Black to become White. For example, he cannot accept Cliff's free flowing and improvisatory attitude toward time. Cliff lives in and enjoys the present. Steve uses the present as a means of evening the debts of the past. Unable to control what *has* happened, he recreates the past in order to revise its outcome. In one sense, the impulse to return to Liz is no different than is his strangulation of Grace, his assault on the blonde in the loan office, or eventually, his decision to become a writer. They are all Steve's means of ordering his universe so that things turn out as he wants them to be.

The whole existence of the Steve Benson of *In New England Winter* is devoted to righting the unfairness of his past. The first crime—being born Black—he attempts to rectify by thinking White. The second crime is as old as Cain and Abel—that of being the unfavored son.

> CLIFF. You've never gotten used to the idea that some other man besides your ole man made it with Brenda.
>
> STEVE. You used to call "Brenda" mom.
>
> CLIFF. You hated me for havin' Brenda all to myself five whole years before you did . . . Why are you so tight, brother? Do you doubt yourself?
>
> STEVE. You know I always win, Cliff. . . . One day even mom will like me more than you.

It is an eye for an eye revenge, however unconscious it may be on Steve's part and however undeserving Cliff may be. Certainly Steve values Cliff's love or else he would not kill to protect his secret. Certainly he feels he has betrayed Cliff—a betrayal, given Steve's almost mathematical morality, he must feel certain will end their relationship. But Cliff knows and forgives, and in so doing precipitates the change in Steve's personality that we note in the later plays: "You love me so much . . . and I hate both of us."

The negative side of the artist's ability to create his dream is his inability to accept any other view. Steve brutalizes Grace, seduces Lou, and kills Bummie, all in order to protect his own view of himself. It is Liz and the New England winter that are the true danger, however. For they represent the only means by which he can escape from his Blackness—madness and death: "You know . . . I think about her all the time. (Reminiscing.) It's snowing up there now. Snowing . . . big white flakes. Snow. Silent like death must be . . . . Death must be still and black and deep . . . . Deathly cold."

Steve takes his share from the robbery and, "praying for winter, heads north." He is never to find Liz, who—even before he left—had dissolved into a fantasy in which she bore a White baby "like the winter's face." But although he will not be immune to the act of betrayal, he will never again allow himself to be buried in the drifts of a White value system.

In a sense *The Duplex* is not Steve Benson's story at all. For he is the sought, not the seeker, and is drawn only reluctantly into an emotional relationship which nearly destroys him, body and soul. The true seeker after love and security is Velma Best, Steve's landlady while he is attending college in Los Angeles in 1961. Velma is a country girl who, anxious for a home of her own, forced her husband to bring her to L.A. There, with the help of the GI Bill, she put him through auto mechanics school.

Dust jacket for Bullin's plays produced in New York by the New Lafayette Theatre.

And there he left her, to live with another woman, returning only periodically to beat her up, rape her, and take the boarding-house money.

Bullins has subtitled *The Duplex* "A Black Love Fable in Four Movements." The four movements or acts follow the love story of Velma Best and Steve Benson from its statement of initial themes to a chord-crashing climax, followed by the briefest of codas. Each movement is introduced by a blues number which effectively sets the tone for the series of scenes to follow. For example, in the first movement, "You Gotta Be Muh Man, Man," we see Velma's quest for a "completing half," Steve's indifference to her except on a physical level, and are warned of the violence of which O.D. (a designation that surely is not accidental) is capable. In the second movement, "Party Killer," O.D. twice returns to the house to victimize Velma. In neither case is Steve able or, ultimately, willing to protect her. Thus, his commitment to Velma is to some extent sealed by his guilt. In the third movement, "Save me, save me, save me, baby," Steve comes to terms with his love for Velma, admits its irrationality, and, nevertheless, takes steps to protect her. This is "Cool blowin'," the fourth movement of the play—the events which lead up to and include the violent confrontation which resolves the action.

The idea of musical movement is carried through in the subplots involving the secondary characters. These are not given beginnings or ends, nor do they require them. They are jazz solos, colorful variations on the Steve-Velma-O.D. love-triangle theme, and form a gloss on it. The theme is love and betrayal. Some have been betrayed by time like Pops, Cliff Dawson's long ago runaway father, and his current woman Mama, the neighborhood drunk. In a moment of quiet, she speaks with regret of the life she and Pops might have had: "If we had met when we was young ... when we was strong and could depend on our backs to carry us where we was goin' and support each other on the way it might have been nice."

Some have a need for love so strong that they accept their loved ones' callousness with timid resignation. Wanda is bedded by Marco Henderson, Steve's roommate, as Steve sits brooding in a chair and Wanda's Aunt Marie snores noisily on the couch. Marco ridicules Wanda's suggestion first of marriage and later of contraceptives, and squelches her wish to go home with little tenderness: "Don't fuck up my day completely, hear?"

Oddest of all, however, is the relationship between Tootsie Franklin and his long-separated and obsessively fecund wife. Tootsie still gives his wife any money he manages to make, as well as passively accepting responsibility for her children so that she can continue to receive welfare. Marco recalls Tootsie's silent seething while another man propositioned his wife in a bar:

> Well, finally, we got ready to leave and then that cat started really workin' Lola .... he began kissin' her and tellin' her to come with him and then he said as we were puttin' on our coats, "Awww, *shit*, Lola, why don't you come with me, girl: *Damn!*" and Franklin knocked the shit out of the cat. Knocked his front teeth all over the lobby .... But listen to this. Heee heee ha ha .... "Oh, Jesus!" Franklin said after he hit the cat, "I don't let nobody cuss in front of mah wife!"

There is little nobility in Steve's early treatment of Velma. Her attraction to him is a good thing for Steve, and he takes advantage of it. She feeds him, extends his rent payments, and lends him tuition money. At the low point of his exploitation of her, he takes her on the stair landing below his room, to the eventual delight of his giggling roommates.

The second act explodes into action with O.D. kicking down the door to Velma's bedroom. Accompanied by his sidekick Crook, O.D. has come to take Velma's money back to his other woman. He does so, pausing only briefly to knock Velma down when she tries to prevent him and ignoring contemptuously the fact that Steve has responded to her cries.

At a party upstairs later that same day Velma is icily bitter about Steve's refusal to protect her. It is a small thing, however, compared to his deliberate attempt to ignore O.D.'s drunken return that night. Upstairs, the party survivors doze in a stupor while downstairs O.D. strangles Velma into sexual submission.

> (Upstairs, Steve leans forward and covers his face with his hands .... Steve stands and turns; he approaches Marie.)
>
> MARIE. Why you lookin' like that, honey? Why? ... Baby, you shouldn't do this .... I'm a married woman .... Oh, honey, I *knew* from the first time I saw you that you were the one .... you a real young man, young man .... baby, if you keep on doin' that you goin' a send me straight out that window .... (Silence, except for the sound of lovemaking which comes from the various rooms, interrupted occasionally by muffled sobs and soft whimpers.)

Steve vows never to come between Velma and her husband, but it is already too late. She is pregnant. In vain, Velma tries to get O.D. to return to her and stay with her, even to the point of blocking the door when he attempts to return to his other woman. O.D. slashes with a knife the arm with which she holds the doorknob and leaves her bleeding on the floor, but by this time Steve has already made the decision to imperil his future by combining it with Velma's:

> Don't marry anything black ... at least not as dark and down and womanly as she .... Why? Because she's nobody ... little black female nothing with babies that she don't even know how they came so fast ... and she shouldn't be in my together program anyway 'cause I'm due for greater things. That we call progress .... But she's mine and I'm not abandoning her .... I'm not leaving her with a crippled beast that would kill her because she merely loves him ... and hates her for offering herself to him ... the father of her babies.

The portrait of Steve Benson in the plays of Ed Bullins involves one long odyssey from a constricting, soul-destroying, White-oriented, consciousness to a Black sensibility, aware of its inherent problems but determined not to sacrifice humanity to them. The first key event in that transformation is the realization that despite Steve's betrayal of his brother, Cliff still loves him. The second is the decision—despite its potential consequences and, more importantly, despite the fact that she still wants her husband—to take on the responsibility of Velma Best.

It is, of course, an impossible task to achieve. Steve and Velma buy pistols for self-defense, the questionable wisdom of which is revealed when Steve (who knows nothing of firearms) narrowly misses shooting Marco by accident. Nor, when the confrontation finally does come, can Steve bring himself to use the gun:

> (O.D. enters the rear first-floor door and slams it behind him. Seeing him Steve walks calmly toward him. O.D.'s face is blank, but at the last moment he smiles slightly, before Steve punches him squarely in the face with all his might .... With a smile on her

face, Velma sits down in a chair on the other side of the room and looks on.)

Steve is a skilled boxer and for a time does well. Soon, however, the larger man's strength begins to tell, and when the fight is over, O.D. has stopped just short of killing Steve. It is Tootsie Franklin who speaks the final judgment on Steve and Velma's romance as he drags the half-conscious man up the stairs: "Man . . . that woman's wit her ole man. . . . Can't you understand that?"

The chief incident of the coda which ends the four movements of *The Duplex* is Steve's recognition of his loss of Velma, a recognition ironically counterpointed by the return of one of the revelers of the night before because "It's party time" again. For Steve, however, the coda continues through the next and last play in which he appears.

The Fabulous Miss Marie is the story of people who have traded their pride for things. It takes place entirely during a drunken party on Christmas Day 1961 at the home of Bill and Marie Horton in Los Angeles. The script is structured (complete with musical underscoring) like a series of jazz solos on a common theme—the desire for, the pleasure in, and the shortcomings of possessions and sensual satisfactions. Its climax occurs when one of the guests has a breakdown while watching the beating of Civil Rights marchers on television: "Shoot the niggers . . . shoot 'em . . . it's not fair . . . I got my rights . . . I ain't never had no trouble out of white folks." Simultaneously, Marie discovers that Art Garrison, whom she keeps around as an errand boy and sexual partner, is also dallying with yet another guest at the party. At the end of the play, Marie quietly sends Art packing and seems about to replace him with another young, down-on-his-luck Black man, Steve Benson: "Well, I'm really not in this one. I just eased through the door. Came in behind Marc. Kinda by accident. And Art's my cousin . . . and I know some of the rest of the people. So I guess I just got pulled into the middle of this."

Steve Benson is in *The Fabulous Miss Marie,* but it is not about him. His chief plot function is to replace Art so that Marie may continue her endless party, but even in this he is more passive than parasitical. He is a man in limbo, loyal enough to propose leaving with Art when Marie kicks him out, pleasurably excited by the sight of the Freedom Marchers on TV, but devoid of either of the hates that drove him in the earlier plays, and deprived of the love that he found in *The Duplex.*

When the first Steve Benson play was produced, Ed Bullins was Information Minister for the San Francisco Black Panther Party. When the last one was presented five years later, he was the Obie Award-winning resident playwright of New York's New Lafayette Theatre. In the plays Steve Benson is first defined by the intensity of his love-hate relationship with White values. Gradually he learns to accept his Blackness and the importance of his emotional commitments, a development that parallels Bullins' evolution in public posture from political

ideologist to cultural humanist. But Bullins never brings Steve Benson into his maturer periods. The Steve Benson saga ends in Marie Horton's living room on Christmas Day 1961. The later novel *The Reluctant Rapist* goes back in time to the '50s. Why?

It was Amiri Baraka who defined the role of the Black artist in the '60s with the phrase "a poem is a fist," who has the hero-victim of *The Dutchman* exclaim that, if Charlie Parker had been able to shoot the first ten White men he saw, he would never have needed to blow another note of music. Art was only an alternative to action. It was a revolution, and the purpose of Black Art was the destruction of the White Aesthetic. It was in this climate that the Steve Benson plays were written.

But the revolution never came. And in 1973, a critic [George Davis] wrote perceptively of *The Reluctant Rapist,* the novel in which Steve Benson made his last appearance: "And in this moment we sense a very careful design. We feel its human energy moving toward a collision with something unseen. Unfortunately, the collision doesn't come. We are left without the revelation we were waiting for. Steven's journey doesn't end [see Further Reading].

In a sense Steve Benson as "The Reluctant Rapist" is Bullins' best metaphor yet for the revolutionary artist. Steve assaults women, then falls asleep in the same bed, deliberately courting exposure-capture. Bullins, the artist assaults our consciousness, seeking recognition and half-expecting, half-demanding condemnation. As an artist he requires recognition. As a revolutionary he dare not be accepted. But Bullins has been accepted. Even as Steve sleeps through the night with his victim, to be greeted in the morning with a request to return, Bullins the revolutionary has received Obies, Drama Critics' Circle Awards, and Guggenheim grants. In 1968 he confidently predicted that within ten years "this reactionary racist government will have me killed." In 1976 he had to admit "I've become the establishment. At least as far as playwrighting is concerned."

In *The Reluctant Rapist* Steve Benson demands punishment and gets "I'll see you tonight, won't I honey?" But Cliff Dawson who murdered to protect his family is abandoned on an ever steeper spiral of self-destruction. And "Slicker-than-slick Art Garrison—the spiritual extension of ourselves"—is out in the cold on Christmas Day. Steve the artist (alias Bullins the playwright) has survived. But survival is not enough. As an artist he must create order and give meaning to his survival: "See, when I was young, I was stabbed in a fight. I died. My heart stopped. But I was brought back for a reason. I was gifted with these abilities and I was sent into the world to do what I do because that is the only thing I can do." If "the reluctant rapist" is not to be punished for his crime, why are Cliff and Art punished for theirs? If his art is the justification for Bullins' life, it is not surprising that he use that art to justify the events of his life.

As Bullins grows in critical acceptance, and as the distance between him and North Philadelphia lengthens both chronologically and socially, the need to reconcile the present with the past becomes a more and more relevant theme. Steve Benson is left in limbo with Cliff Dawson and Art Garrison. Re-enter Michael Brown, disco star and ex-revolutionary artist, engaged in *Daddy* in the process of setting right the mistakes of his youth.

Michael Brown first appears as the title character visiting his mother on Philadelphia's Derby Street (the setting for *In The Wine Time*) after nine years in Los Angeles in *A Son Come Home* (1968). That fence past mending, we see him in *Daddy* trying to reconcile his image of himself with his wife—who neither was faithful nor understood his music—and the children he abandoned many years earlier. *Daddy* (produced in 1977 but written in at least one version several years earlier) is resolved by the addition of a convenient foster father for the children and by Michael's decision to marry his well-born young mistress, who is already pregnant with his child. Dramatically, the choice is not a happy one—as Bullins has tacitly admitted by reworking the same material into the 1978 one-act *Michael.*

It seems likely that whatever Ed Bullins calls his alter ego in the future, he will speak with the voice of a respected artist rather than that of a drifter or a revolutionary. The real question is whether, severed from his roots and his hate, Bullins can continue to create effectively. Richard Wright is just one of those who could not. At the same time, an honest artist cannot speak with a voice that is no longer his, and whether you liked them or not, neither Steve Benson, nor Michael Brown, nor Ed Bullins ever lied to you about their feelings. (pp. 103-09)

> Richard G. Scharine, "Ed Bullins Was Steve Benson (But Who Is He Now?)," in Black American Literature Forum, *Vol. 13, No. 3, Fall, 1979, pp. 103-06, 108-09.*

Ed Bullins (essay date 1979)

[*In the following rebuttal, Bullins responds to Richard G. Scharine's 1979 article "Ed Bullins Was Steve Benson (But Who Is He Now?)" (see preceding essay). Introducing Bullins's essay, the editor of* Black American Literature Forum *stated:* "BALF's *Advisory Board felt that Scharine's essay 'Ed Bullins Was Steve Benson' deserved publication—partly due to its controversial nature. And because it is so controversial, the Board (correctly) thought that Ed Bullins might wish to respond to the critique. Printed below is the body of his letter to* BALF."]

To begin with, the author writes that I am a past Information Minister of the Black Panthers, etc. No, I was Minister of Culture for a short while. Eldridge Cleaver appointed me, witnessed by Emory Douglas, who succeeded me, as Minister of Revolutionary Culture for the Party.

I believe my characters sometimes have multiple identities, as parts of a whole, an ever-changing, interchangeable universe, as the points in a vision which expands—dreamlike.

I do not write realistic plays, no matter the style I choose.

I do not write just one style of play, if I can help it. The Steve Benson/Cliff Dawson plays are only a fragment of my work. Plays like *The Devil Catchers, The Psychic Pretenders, Jo Anne, The Mystery of Phillis Wheatley, I Am Lucy Terry, How Do You Do, Dialect Determinism, The Helper, The Gentleman Caller,* and some others, are very different from the 20th Century Cycle plays.

I was a conscious artist before I was a conscious artist-revolutionary, which has been my salvation and disguise.

In the two plays, *It Has No Choice* and *In New England Winter,* the character of Steve Benson represented some kind of a black existential archetype and credo that I was interested in at the time (early '60s writing set in '50s). Art (not Garrison, in this case, but, why not?)—the art of the civilization and society—reflects its times, and in the '50s, to me, many lives of black urban dwellers were existential indeed. And at the core of their human dilemma is the varied "love-hate relation(s)" of ghetto existence, caused by racism, hatred, poverty, disease, ignorance, and through being victims of history.

Steve's third option was Liz (mythic love and redemption), if he could ever find her.

In New England Winter should not be thought of as a realistic play—it should be stylized, in production, like a nightmare, but not so severely as to be totally surreal—it should depict the bottom of a tortured subconscious, whatever that might be, but Liz and Steve would know.

I do not feel that I am severed from my roots.

It is not always impossible to go home again—tough to stay too long—but it is the stuff that plays are made of, at least some kinds of plays.

> Ed Bullins, "Who He Is Now: Ed Bullins Replies," *in* Black American Literature Forum, *Vol. 13, No. 3, Fall, 1979, p 109.*

FURTHER READING

Anderson, Jervis. "Profiles: Ed Bullins." *The New Yorker* 49, No. 17 (16 June 1973): 40-4, 46, 48, 51-2, 54, 59, 61-2, 66, 68, 70, 72-9.

    Profile of Bullins, focusing on his career as playwright. Includes discussions of Bullins's *Clara's Ole Man, The*

Taking of Miss Janie, The Duplex, In the Wine Time, In New England Winter, and *The Reluctant Rapist.*

Andrews, W. D. E. "Theater of Black Reality: The Blues Drama of Ed Bullins." *Southwest Review* 65, No. 2 (Spring 1980): 178-90.

Characterizing Bullins's plays as "blues drama," Andrews states: "The way of viewing life, the way of feeling—the vision—that informs [Bullins's] plays is the vision of that unique form of black music, the blues. Common to both is the impulse to express the painful details of a brutal experience and yet, whatever the quantum of racial agony, to transcend it, to redeem it dialectically through the sheer force of sensuality, vitality, lyricism, and creativity into an almost exultant affirmation of life."

Blackman, Brandon R. IV. "Black Hope of Broadway." *Sepia* 24, No. 12 (December 1975): 62-8.

Discusses *The Taking of Miss Janie* as a work that "elevated Bullins to the pinnacle of theatrical fame."

David, George. Review of *The Reluctant Rapist,* by Ed Bullins. *The New York Times Book Review* (30 September 1973): 24.

Favorable review of Bullins's *The Reluctant Rapist,* labeling it a novel of "black life before black consciousness."

Elder, Arlene A. "Ed Bullins: Black Theatre as Ritual." In *Connections: Essays on Black Literatures,* edited by Emmanuel S. Nelson, pp. 101-09. Canberra, Australia: Aboriginal Studies Press, 1988.

Proposes that Bullins's plays are rooted in the "elements of traditional Afro-American oral performance." Elder explores Bullins's ability to "couch revolutionary interpretation of the black American experience in ritual form, drawing on the traditions of black oratory, narrative, street talk, myth, and especially, music."

Evans, Don. "The Theater of Confrontation: Ed Bullins, Up Against the Wall." *Black World* XXIII, No. 6 (April 1974): 14-18.

Characterizes Bullins's dramas as "theater of confrontation," citing *House Party* as one such example.

Hay, Samuel A. "Structural Elements in Ed Bullins' Plays." In *The Theater of Black Americans: A Collection of Critical Essays,* edited by Errol Hill, Vol. 1, pp. 185-91. Englewood Cliffs, N.J.: Prentice-Hall, 1980.

Contests critic Walter Kerr's assertion that Bullins's *The Duplex* lacks structure. Hay states: "Typical of non-Black critics, Kerr is not really all that concerned about the shape of Black drama.... His artistic judgments about Black drama cannot be trusted." Kerr himself presented most of his argument concerning Bullins in the *New York Times* on 19 March 1972.

Jackmon, Marvin X. "An Interview with Ed Bullins: Black Theater." *The Negro Digest* XVIII, No. 6 (April 1969): 9-16.

Interview with Ed Bullins. Marvin X (also known as El Muhajir) and Bullins discuss "black theater and some of the forces and personalities important to it."

Jackson, Kennell, Jr. "Notes on the Works of Ed Bullins." *CLA Journal* XVIII, No. 2 (December 1974): 292-99.

Reviews *The Hungered One: Early Writings,* stating: "...within this diversity and within this mixture of experimentation, the germ of the work that is later transformed into Bullins' realistic plays and stories can be discovered. Here, in this collection, we can find the early lineaments of some of his later characters waiting to be fleshed out. A few of the macabre themes that Bullins exploits later can be detected here...."

Smitherman, Geneva. "Everybody Wants to Know Why I Sing the Blues." *Black World* XXIII, No. 6 (April 1974): 4-13.

Considers Bullins's use of the blues motif as the "central mechanism for conveying his message."

True, Warren R. "Ed Bullins, Anton Chekhov, and the 'Drama of Mood'." *CLA Journal* XX, No. 4 (June 1977): 521-32.

Compares dramaturgical similarities between the plays of Chekhov and Bullins. The critic concludes: "Regardless of the vehemence with which Ed Bullins may denounce Western drama and despite his wish to divorce himself and his art from the artistic milieu derived from that drama, his plays show a skill in the management of characters and tone which, since Chekhov, is in every sense Western."

J. E. Casely-Hayford
1866-1930

(Full name Joseph Ephraim Casely-Hayford) Ghanaian novelist, biographer, and nonfiction writer.

Casely-Hayford was a staunch Ghanaian advocate of African nationalism and a leading political thinker of his day. A pioneering scholar of African studies, he expounded cultural Pan-Africanism and political nationalism in his novel *Ethiopia Unbound* (1911) and in other works. *Ethiopia Unbound*—the work on which his current reputation rests almost entirely—is recognized for its trenchant criticism of African colonial society and for its farsighted recommendations for cultural advancement in the region. The novel is therefore generally regarded as one of the most significant contributions ever made to African nationalist literature.

Casely-Hayford was the fourth son of a minister and his wife of the Anona Clan, Gold Coast (now Ghana). Educated at Wesleyan Boys' High School and Fourah Bay College, Freeport, he became a high school teacher in Accra. However, because a nationalist-oriented press was flourishing in West Africa at the time, he left education to pursue a career as a journalist. Working for his uncle, Prince Brew of Dunkwa, he advanced to the editorship of the *Western Echo* and later presided over several short-lived Gold Coast newspapers. In the 1890s he traveled to England. There he studied law at the Inner Temple, London, and Peterhouse College, Cambridge. Returning to Ghana, he combined his legal practice with a journalism career; his contributions to the weekly *Gold Coast Leader* brought him renown throughout the region for his articulate political commentary. In 1920 Casely-Hayford coordinated the meeting of the first National Congress of British West Africa. His prominence in this organization soon gained him a wide reputation as a statesman. Later, he led delegations of African leaders to London to meet with representatives of the British government. In 1927 he was elected to the Ghana Legislative Council. His support of the highly unpopular Native Administration Ordinance, which allowed the English government to retain a measure of control in Ghana, caused many of his followers to lose faith in him, believing as they did that he had compromised his ideals. Casely-Hayford continued to work in journalism until his death in August 1930.

Casely-Hayford's many nonfiction tracts reflect his fervent Pan-Africanism, which L. H. Ofosu-Appiah has defined as the aim to "[bring] together all black men in Africa and those of African descent." Calling for the political and cultural self-determination of African nations, Casely-Hayford wrote several works studying the effects of various laws and institutions on West Africa and West Africans. His only work of fiction, *Ethiopia Unbound,* has been praised by critics for its examination of African colonial society under British rule. Ostensibly the story of Kwamankra, a Ghanaian lawyer whose background closely resembles Casely-Hayford's own, *Ethiopia Unbound* presents a synthesis of its author's religious and political ideas. In this novel and other works, Casely-Hayford urged his compatriots not to imitate Europeans but to take pride in their own heritage. One of his greatest concerns was the education of African youth, and in *Ethiopia Unbound* he envisioned the establishment of a national university. According to Casely-Hayford's proposal, the university would promote African studies, language, and dress and would save parents the great sums of money that were being spent abroad to educate their children at British or American universities. He intended his novel to serve in the struggle to overcome racism. He therefore debated issues of morality, ideology, and social status. F. Nnabuenyi Ugonna has called *Ethiopia Unbound* "without a doubt the matrix of all the nationalist cultural ideas of one of the ablest African political and intellectual leaders in West Africa."

While Casely-Hayford advocated internal self-government for Ghana, he maintained that the country should remain a part of the British Empire. His popularity suffered late in his career because of that controversial view. After his death many of his works went out of print, but Ghanaian literary scholars began to reissue them in new editions in the late 1960s, reviving interest in his ideas. A beloved patriot and champion of African studies, Casely-Hayford is now considered an instrumental figure in the development of African nationalism, and his novel *Ethiopia Unbound* is praised by modern critics as one of the most important works of West African literature in the early decades of the twentieth century.

(For further information about Casely-Hayford's life and works, see *Contemporary Authors*, Vol. 123 and *Twentieth-Century Literary Criticism*, Vol. 24.)

PRINCIPAL WORKS

Gold Coast Native Institutions (nonfiction) 1903
Ethiopia Unbound (novel) 1911
Gold Coast Land Tenure and the Forest Bill (nonfiction) 1911
The Truth about the West African Land Question (nonfiction) 1913
William Waddy Harris, the West African Reformer: The Man and His Message (biography) 1915
United West Africa (nonfiction) 1919
The Disabilities of Black Folk and Their Treatment, with an Appeal to the Labour Party (nonfiction) 1929
West African Leadership (lectures) 1951
Public Speeches of J. E. Casely-Hayford (lectures) 1970

United Empire (essay date 1911)

[*In the following unsigned 1911 review, the critic argues that* Ethiopia Unbound *is essential reading for Europeans who seek to understand colonial Africa.*]

[*Ethiopia Unbound*] is a book that must be read with patience and understanding. It is always difficult for the European to understand the point of view of the educated West African native, more especially when it is articulate. Mr. Hayford, a native of the Gold Coast, has written a book that is worth careful reading and sympathetic study. There is much in it that will jar upon the European reader, and much that may even cause the incautious and rash to throw the book down unread. But if the reader will persevere to the end he will be amply rewarded. However much he may dissent from some of the author's statements or resent some of his strictures, he cannot fail to appreciate Mr. Hayford's point of view or to understand better the forces that are working slowly but surely amongst the Ethiopian peoples. It is as easy to underestimate the influence of the educated native in West Africa as it is to overestimate it. In no case can it be regarded as more than the leaven that may affect the whole. But whether the African races assimilate European culture and thought or evolve a distinct Ethiopian civilisation of their own—as Mr. Hayford desires—it would be folly for the white man to close his eyes to the progress that is being made on all sides in Africa—a progress that is not merely material. There is much sterling common-sense in *Ethiopia Unbound*. Although it is quite impossible to follow the author to the heights of idealism to which he would lead us when he preaches the doctrine of an African nationality, taking what it will of Western thought but retaining its own inherent quality, yet there can be little doubt that Mr. Hayford advances upon eminently sane lines. Thus he disapproves of the aping of European dress which is so prevalent in the coastal districts, and desires a distinct national costume for the cultured African. He would found a national university for the Gold Coast and for Ashanti, not near the influence of the coast, but at Kumasi, away from the corroding effects of a spurious Western civilisation. This should be a national university in the fullest sense, with chairs for Fanti, Hausa, and Yoruba, and the teaching in one of these languages and not through the medium of English. He would sweep away what he regards as the mock Christianity that substitutes an unholy monogamy, in which there is more immorality than is possible under polygamy, for marriage customs and laws that are the result of centuries of ingrained habit and thought. Mohammedanism is wiser in this respect. It is easy to pick holes in all Mr. Hayford's arguments. It is easy to assert that the idea of Ethiopianism is a dream incapable of achievement on a continent where races are innumerable and nations, as we understand the term, do not exist. But the really important fact remains that there are those amongst the subject races of Africa who are thinking and working, not as hewers of wood and drawers of water, but upon lines that are at present foreign to European methods of thought. It is not upon the wrongs of oppressed peoples that Mr. Hayford writes but about the question of retaining all that is good in native institutions, and preserving fundamental laws and customs that are part and parcel of the national consciousness. In fact, he is striving for a national regeneration—but not upon a prosaic Western basis. (pp 737-38)

> *A review of "Ethiopia Unbound: Studies in Race Emancipation," in* United Empire, *Vol. 11, No. 1, January, 1911, pp. 737-38.*

Robert W. July (essay date 1967)

[*An American educator and critic, July has written numerous articles and books examining African history, literature, and thought. In the following excerpt from his* Origins of Modern African Thought, *he offers a favorable appraisal of Casely-Hayford's literary style in* Ethiopia Unbound.]

In 1911 there appeared in London an unusual literary work entitled *Ethiopia Unbound.* The book was unusual primarily in its form and tone—a loosely constructed piece which appeared to be a novel but which included large portions of intellectual autobiography, of historical, philosophic and literary references, and which was spun out in such a shifting evanescent fashion as to create a dreamlike illusion of unreality. Characters drifted in and out of the loose and insubstantial narrative which was frequently interrupted by long treatises in which the author was able to set forth his ideas on matters which interested him or by dialogues conducted between idealized characters in a stilted language appropriate to their artificial aspect.

Cast as fiction, the work was in fact an attempt to rally the black people of the world in defence of their own culture, their own accomplishments, their own racial integrity. The African, it seemed to say, had to learn to be himself, not to be content with a role as counterfeit white. It was permissible for him to pursue his university study and professional training in Europe, but it was not satisfactory for him to turn into a black European. Aware of his own identity, he could take from Europe that which was useful and reject that which was inappropriate, employing the essential African soul as touchstone. Looking beyond the crudities of traditional African life he might probe the inner meaning and deeper purpose of the ancient social systems of Africa, clothing them with modern techniques and directing them towards newer contemporary objectives. In such a way could he best serve the cause of Negro independence and manhood.

The protagonist in *Ethiopia Unbound* was a Gold Coast man who had gone to London for a time to read law, and who had finally returned to his homeland only to discover heartache and ambiguity in what he saw there. One of his first visits was to the simple church of his boyhood, and when he arrived it was the hour of prayer. As he renewed acquaintance with the familiar but ageing faces, he was saddened by the inappropriateness of the scene. A Sankey hymn was being sung by the children in their Manchester homespun to the laboured accompaniment of a wheezy old harmonium. At the head of the choir stood the schoolmaster elegant in his cutaway coat, glazed cuffs, high collar and patent-leather shoes, but a bit of a fool in this costume so inappropriate to the people and the land. The minister was a white man preaching to a black congregation while outside the church a notice announced another service to be held later for Europeans only. The stranger returned home turned away in sadness and in anger. All at once he saw with a burst of insight what the mission of his life would have to be. He would dedicate himself to saving his people from the national and racial death which awaited them, practising these emasculated sentimentalities and shameless slanders proclaimed in the name of Christ. His people would have to be taught to recapture the virile religion of their past, to turn aside from a civilization which came with the Bible in one hand and the gin bottle in the other, which dismembered their tribes, alienated their lands, appropriated their goods, and drained the strength away from their time-tested authorities and institutions.

The book was to a considerable extent an exercise in autobiographical reminiscence as the vehicle for a personal profession of faith in the black race. Its author was a Cape Coast barrister and political figure, Joseph E. Casely Hayford who, like the protagonist in his story, had prepared himself in England for a legal career and returned to his home in the Gold Coast to lend his voice to the African protest against the inequities of British rule. His was to be a persistent voice over the years— intelligent and incisive in its criticism, resourceful and energetic in its proposals, sincere and courageous in its profession of patriotic faith; yet Casely Hayford, for all his insight and sensitivity, for all his liberalism and humanity, was no crusader and certainly no revolutionary. Poised against his contemporary, Attoh-Ahuma, who thundered forth his condemnation of the vagaries of British rule with bluff forthrightness, Casely Hayford was subtle, ironic, oblique. An accomplished legal practitioner and scholar like his colleague Mensah Sarbah, yet he was more at home in the political arena where his talents as writer and speaker joined with a natural flair for compromise to bring to life the master politician. A follower of the ideas of Edward Blyden, he lacked the old reformer's didactic persuasiveness, relying on indirection to achieve his objectives. *Ethiopia Unbound* was characteristic. A declaration on behalf of negritude as powerful as Blyden's best, it generated its argument through its subtleties and its sophisticated idealism, not through the purity and power of its logic. (pp. 433-35)

> *Robert W. July, "The Metamorphosis of Casely Hayford," in his* The Origins of Modern African Thought: Its Development in West Africa During the Nineteenth and Twentieth Centuries, *Frederick A. Praeger, 1967, pp. 433-57.*

F. Nnabuenyi Ugonna (essay date 1969)

[*In the following excerpt from his introduction to a 1969 edition of* Ethiopia Unbound, *Ugonna examines Casely-Hayford's social and political philosophy.*]

Ethiopia Unbound is undoubtedly one of the most important contributions to the literature of African nationalism. Although it is primarily a work of fiction and so properly belongs to the field of African literature, it contains ideas that are indispensable to all those interested in African studies.... As a contribution to African literature, *Ethiopia Unbound* combines the literary and religious function of Bunyan's *Pilgrim's Progress* with the cultural significance of Arnold's *Culture and Anarchy*. Its importance to the Africanist can hardly be emphasised. (pp. xix-xx)

The ideas of Casely Hayford about African Nationalism, colonialism and racism are easily found in his numerous works. Hayford's importance lies not only in his practical ability as a nationalist leader but in the fact that his political ideas have been immortalised in his literary works.... Between 1903 and 1929, he produced standard literary works on jurisprudence, African land tenure, indigenous institutions and Pan-Africanism or more precisely "West African Nationality." In 1903, Sweet and Maxwell of London published Casely Hayford's first work, *Gold Coast Native Institutions.* In this book Hayford discussed extensively the whole question of Native Administration, arguing that the authorities at Downing Street had better "confine themselves more to external administration, leaving the internal government of the people to develop upon the natural lines of their own institutions." (pp. xx-xxi)

In 1911 Hayford's second book *Ethiopia Unbound* was published by C. M. Phillips (London). Sub-titled "Studies in Race Emancipation" it is a veritable compendium of Casely Hayford's thoughts on politics, native institutions, race relations, African nationalism and allied subjects cast into a fictive and imaginative form. The book's literary structure will be discussed later. His two other books, *Gold Coast Land Tenure and the Forest Bill,* and *The Truth About the West African Land Question,* as their titles imply, try to explain the system of land tenure in West Africa. Although these books are of great sociological interest, they are primarily written from a legal angle, their main purpose being to argue against any scheme of land alienation in West Africa. The main theme of both books is an amplification of Mensah Sarbah's explication:

> According to native ideas there is no land without owners. What is now a forest or unused land will, as years go on, come under cultivation by subjects of the stool, or members of the village community or other members of the family ...

Gold Coast Land Tenure and the Forest Bill in particular was published, we are told in the title page, at the instance of the kings and chiefs of the central and western provinces of Ghana in conference with the Aborigines Rights Protection Society. In 1919 *United West Africa,* a pamphlet appealing to the youths of West Africa to strive towards the attainment of West African nationhood, was published in London. Some of Hayford's most memorable public speeches were collected by Magnus J. Sampson and published under the title *West African Leadership,* in 1951. Hayford's other publications include **"The Progress of the Gold Coast Native",** and *The Disabilities of the Black Folk* .... From these works one can glean the recurrent ideas of Casely Hayford.

Perhaps we can rightly say that Hayfordian philosophy is in essence based on the concept of "Ethiopianism." The idea of Ethiopianism itself is eclectic, being a crystallization of religious and political notions, associated with Ethiopia, then the only truly independent island in the sea of colonial Africa. Ethiopia thus became a symbol of African independence. He identified Africa with Ethiopia. In a slave or colonial era, Ethiopia, the only African state that had not been colonised, became a bastion of prestige and hope to thousands of Africans, especially those in America and the West Indies, who were taunted by the whites for the absence of any substantial collective achievement by their race and the inability of their people to rule themselves. (pp. xxii-xxiii)

Colonial Africa was to [Casely Hayford] Ethiopia chained. His political theory was that with Africans assuming control of their own affairs and developing their indigenous institutions, fettered Ethiopia would be unbound and eventually emerge as a giant among other nationalities. But how was this ideal to be effectively realised?

Casely Hayford believes religiously in the integrity of the African. He ridicules the idea of superior and inferior racial categories. The apparent difference between the African and the European stems from differential environmental influences and *Mutatis mutandis* the African stands on the same footing as the European. An educated man is an educated man whether he is white or black and a white nonentity is the same as a black one. To achieve greatness Africa must attain mature nationhood. Hayford advocated West African nationhood as a kind of *protasis* to African nationality. In effect he was the first African nationalist as distinct from Afro-American and Afro-West Indian nationalists, to stress so persistently the idea of what has become a pervasive theme in any discussion of African nationalism, the ideas of Pan-Africanism and African Personality. (p. xxvi)

The framework of Casely Hayford's Pan-Africanism is intrinsically cultural-nationalism. African cultural heritage, to him, is pre-eminently the index to African personality since it depicts what is unique about Africa. The emphasis on culture is not surprising. Confronted by white racists' propaganda to the effect that the African has no culture of his own, he had no choice but to prove them wrong. Unfortunately in the face of European sneers and sarcasm the contemporary African tended deliberately to suppress his culture. To combat this tendency and sustain the paramountcy of African traditional heritage, Casely Hayford ceaselessly fought for the preservation of native institutions even if in a modified form.

Advocates of African culture admit its obvious limitations and so they allow that useful western cultural patterns could be integrated into the African cultural scheme. This, from all indications, is Casely Hayford's postulate. The African should be himself. Casely Hayford deprecates all attempts to imitate closely the whites, for example, he dismisses as a "veritable fool" a school-master in his "elegantly cut-away black morning coat and beautifully-glazed cuffs and collar, not to speak of patent leather shoes." ... In his writings he consistently advocated the wearing of native dress to the extent of suggesting that academic gowns should give way, in African Universities, to traditional garbs. He contends that the question of dress and habits matters because "it goes to the root of the Ethiopian's self-respect." Because of his earnest concern for the preservation of indigenous African culture, he tends to condemn any person who preaches any form of racial integration no matter how modified. On this score, he repudiated Booker T. Washington and W.E.B. Du Bois, regarding both as provincial in their approach to racial questions while to him E. W. Blyden was universal in his approach. It is to be wondered whether Hayford was really justified in his criticism of Du Bois; for, without doubt, the problem of the Negro in American Society is far more complex. Du Bois was in fact ambivalent, for, although he insisted on integration he advocated also racial integrity—"the conservation of the races." Rightly or wrongly, however, Casely Hayford disparaged those Negroes who strive to be assimilated into American Society. He argued that "it is not so much Afro-Americans that we want as Africans" (*Ethiopia Unbound*). What he warned against was close *imitation* which could be seized upon by white racists for disparaging the black race, thus:

> How extraordinary is the spectacle of this huge race—millions of men without land or language of their own, without traditions of the country they came from, bearing the very names of the men that enslaved them.

In effect, Hayford was arguing that imitation robs the Ethiopian of self-respect because as Coleman has rightly observed, "any human relationship cast in the model imitator mould tends towards a superior-inferior stratification of attitudes. It is psychologically difficult for a model to regard an imitator as his equal." The way to project African personality is thus through the conservation of traditional cultural institutions.

African religions should be philosophically studied; this is Hayford's plea. In *Ethiopia Unbound* religious questions are broached. Christianity is constantly contrasted with indigenous religion to the disadvantage of the former. The Rev. Silas Whitely, the symbol of Christianity, is a time-serving clergyman who condones segregation and subordinates Christian principles to official policy in the West African colony. Before his ordination in England he entertained doubts about the divinity of Christ. As a clergyman in the Gold Coast he is supercilious, overbearing and vindictive. Mr. Kwaw Baidu, Whitely's African curate, is victimised and dismissed by him because Baidu dared to question the propriety of a graveyard segregation policy. In contrast, Kwamankra the so-called pagan is noble, bland, accommodating and understanding. According to his indigenous religious philosophy, he maintains, there is no reason why Christ's divinity should be doubted. From this point Hayford goes on to describe Fanti religious beliefs as an epitome of African traditional religion. (pp. xxviii-xxx)

Hayford's preoccupation with specified African institutions in his *Gold Coast Native Institutions* has been pointed out. His concern in this regard was to show that, first, Africa has a culture; second, that this culture is as rich and satisfying as any other; and third, that although there has been an inevitable diffusion of western culture in Africa, this should not be interpreted as signifying the desiccation of the cultures of Africa. In fact, the influence of western culture on African life and thought just as the effect of colonialism on the indigenous political systems, important as it may now appear, is only an historical phase in the over-all development of African culture.

In *Ethiopia Unbound*, one specific institution ubiquitously treated is marriage. In Hayford's view, the African marriage system has many advantages over the western monogamous system. The former has the advantage of fostering greater social cohesion than the latter. The African marriage system is also important for the resolution of personal and social tensions. Although Hayford does not condemn monogamy (the hero of *Ethiopia Unbound*, Kwamankra, had only one wife), he felt it was wrong for people to insist that it should supercede other forms of marriage. He observes that "any child of Eve who has deliberately become the mother of your child is worthy of your love, and to treat her as an outcast is to be unworthy of the name of a man." The reconciliation between Tandor-Kuma and Ekuba after years of separation and after Tandor-Kuma had legally married another woman and got children through this marriage, is a vindication of Casely Hayford's thesis.

A second aspect of African culture highlighted is the arts. Folksongs, the *Sankofu* (Fanti sea songs) for instance, are mentioned frequently and their deeper emotional effect as compared with Church hymns is posited. In this regard, Hayford certainly is one of the earliest African literary commentators to note the characteristic rhythm of African folk-poetry, a poetry of "drum and song," to use the expression of some contemporary critics.

Casely Hayford believed that education should be the cohesive force holding together all the strands of the great Ethiopian civilisation. Whole-sale imitation of the western form of education should be, as far as possible, eschewed. He therefore advocated in *Ethiopia Unbound* an Africanized Western University with Chairs for African History and African languages and literature. His envisaged university should primarily diffuse African culture. It is a felicitous commentary on the foresight of Casely Hayford that most African universities today are developing, though more conservatively, along his lines of thought. The distinct garb of students, male and female, Hayford tells us, amplifying his idealistic scheme for an African university, was national, with an adaptability suggestive of an advanced state of society. He stressed the need for a Faculty of Education in the university, an idea taken up seriously in West Africa only in the 1960's with the establishment of the University of Nigeria, Nsukka. G. N. Brown has remarked that "the university that is described in *Ethiopia Unbound* is astonishingly modern in conception."

Up till now, *Ethiopia Unbound* has hardly been appreciated as a work of art. This writer sees the book primarily as a fictional work comparable in certain respects to

Swift's *Battle of the Books,* Johnson's *Rasselas* or even Mandeville's *Fable of the Bees.* It has the same ironic tone as these books and is as incisive of a West African colonial community as *Gulliver's Travels,* for example, is of the eighteenth century English society. That *Ethiopia Unbound* was not immediately recognised by Hayford's contemporaries, as basically a work of art, is not so surprising. Its author was a lawyer and a politician and his publications before and after *Ethiopia Unbound* cannot be described as literary works of art, they are either legal, political or propagandist treatises. The author himself probably helped to put off the literary scent by subtitling the book "Studies in Race Emancipation." In an age of black assertiveness fostered to a large extent by the outcome of World War I and the Japanese "revolution," it was almost inevitable for readers to cling to the ideas expressed in *Ethiopia Unbound* with avowed intentions, without caring seriously about the method of communication of these ideas. (pp. xxxi-xxxiv)

In recent years, there is an increasing awareness of the imaginative potential of *Ethiopia Unbound* and students of African Literature are trying to put the work into its apropos genre—the novel, in the context of the modern trend of *littérature engagée.* L. S. Senghor has remarked, *"La littérature Africaine est une littérature engagée."* This is also true of *Ethiopia Unbound.* It is committed to a point of view. It is propagandist—a vehicle through which Hayford attempts to send his message of hope to the Ethiopians, his appeal for unity and the urgent necessity for a national regeneration.

Ethiopia Unbound is decidedly not a treatise. It is a fiction with fictive characters who live and act within a distinctly realistic social milieu, imaginatively conceived. Society is excoriated. Individuals, groups, institutions and systems are subjected to impartial criticism. The African, especially the ridiculous servile imitator of the English, is flayed alongside the vain and supercilious colonial administrator or drunken white miner who thinks he is superior to the African on grounds of colour alone. Analysing the work of destruction done by the colonialist, Hayford remarked:

> With the gin bottle in the one hand, and the Bible in the other, he urges moral excellence, which in his heart of hearts he knows to be impossible of attainment by the African under the circumstance, and when the latter fails, his benevolent protector makes such a failure a cause for dismembering his tribe, alienating his lands, appropriating his goods, and sapping the foundations of his authority and institutions.
>
> (*Ethiopia Unbound*)

The railway system is overdue for reform but there is no move to do so. It takes seven hours to cover thirty-nine miles! Other instances of satire abound throughout the book.

The language of the book is discursive, rhetorical, and allusive despite occasional quaintness and archaism.

The influence of the Bible and *Pilgrim's Progress* is evident and there are many passages from Homer. It is evident that the author had been susceptible to epical influence during the time he wrote his only imaginative work.

Ethiopia Unbound is without doubt the matrix of all the nationalist and cultural ideas of one of the ablest African political and intellectual leaders in West Africa. (pp. xxxiv-xxxvi)

> *F. Nnabuenyi Ugonna, in an introduction to* Ethiopia Unbound: Studies in Race Emancipation, *by J. E. Casely-Hayford, second edition, Frank Cass and Co. Ltd., 1969, pp. v-xxxvi.*

West Africa (essay date 1970)

[*In the following excerpt, the reviewer praises Casely-Hayford's nationalist ideas as reflected in* Gold Coast Native Institutions *and* Ethiopia Unbound.]

Outstanding among the early West African nationalists, both because of the length of his political career and because of the originality of his ideas, was Joseph Ephraim Casely Hayford....

His books are now virtually unobtainable in the original, but they are slowly being reprinted. The first to be reprinted..., was *Ethiopia Unbound,* in which Hayford's views on a variety of questions are expressed through the conversation and experiences of a Ghanaian whom we first meet as a law student in London.

Hayford's main concern always was to assert the value of African tradition and culture. Although this was not then the view of all educated Africans, he was particularly critical of Africans who aped European dress (he urged a special dress for African students) and wanted the proposed university for the Gold Coast and Ashanti to be in Kumasi, away from the coast. 60 years ago he proposed establishment of schools of African studies in the United States—for the benefit mainly of Negro Americans. He particularly admired Japan which had become strong without losing its own character. Language, polygamy, temperance, music—all are discussed in *Ethiopia Unbound.* But his student is so unracial in outlook that he delights in his meeting with his future wife at a performance of Beerbohm Tree's *Hamlet* at the Haymarket Theatre.

Today little of this may seem very interesting. In 1911, when the book was published, it was very remarkable.

Now comes, in reprint, *Gold Coast Native Institutions* Hayford's first book, published in 1903. In this he urges "an intelligent and scientific study of Native Institutions," to help a British administration directed from Downing Street to avoid mistakes like the seizure of the Golden Stool. Hayford belonged to the generation of West African leaders who were sincerely loyal to the British Crown, and never hesitated to praise British officials (he saw the fairness of British judges as being the greatest support for British rule.) He wanted the country to develop in close co-operation with Britain. Yet while in *Ethiopia Unbound* he was concerned with the preservation of African customs and local culture, in *Gold Coast Native Institutions* he was concerned to show that the British had come to the Gold Coast as "honoured guests" and should not have interfered with the existing local administration. The ideal system would be for the British to look after external matters, leaving internal self-government to Africans.

To support this case he describes in great detail the actual operation of chieftaincy in the Gold Coast, the functions of the Linguists and Councillors, the "company" system, the traditional trade, the nature of local religion, etc. He also traces the way in which British rule had been established and asserts the significance of the "Bond of 1844" as an invitation to the British to co-operate but not to dominate.

For the most part his language is elegant and restrained; it is still hard-hitting. He complains, for example, that the Governor is allowed greater power than that exercised by the King-Emperor since he was not responsible to the local tax payers but to an "over-tasked official" some 3,000 miles away "who may or may not be a capable man" and who got all his information from the Governor himself.

This has been called a lawyer's book, but it is much more. For example, Hayford is anxious for Ashanti fully to share the political life of the Gold Coast and rejects the idea that there is an inevitable division between Ashanti and the South. He recalls with approval the way in which the early British administrators had understood and co-operated with the local people. He recalls Governor Pope Hennessy's comment (1872) on the Gold Coast: "My inquiries on the spot, and an examination of the archives of the Local Government convince me that the educated natives have contrasted favourably as a body with the European residents. I was certainly impressed favourably by their tone and manner in their several interviews with me."

Hayford ranges far; what is a good newspaper; what is the effect of the West African climate on Europeans; how useful are the local herbalists? Above all, in *Ethiopia Unbound,* he shows himself to be a man proud of his country's past but in no sense racialist or reluctant to adapt customs and institutions.

> *"An Outstanding Nationalist," in* West Africa, *No. 2764, May 30, 1970, p. 585.*

O. R. Dathorne (essay date 1974)

[*Dathorne is a Guyanese-born English novelist, short story writer, and critic. Much of his fiction treats the lives of expatriate blacks in England and Africa. In the following excerpt from his 1974 study* The Black

Mind: A History of African Literature, *he offers a mixed review of* Ethiopia Unbound.]

Ethiopia Unbound, a work which takes the reader to London, West Africa, and even the underworld, is a literary expression of a wide variety of ideas. Kwamankra, the main character, is first seen in London conversing with Whiteley, a divinity student, on Christianity, a subject which is taken up time and again throughout the book. Kwamankra believes in a Black God and feels that Christ was "born of an Ethiopian woman." He is next seen in West Africa where he is helping to establish a national university. Casely-Hayford devoted many pages to discussing the implications of such a university, arguing that "no people could despise its own language, customs and institutions and hope to avoid national death." Kwamankra is then sent back to London to help translate books for the proposed university; he also becomes a law student and makes friends with another West African called "the Professor."

Education and Christianity, however, are not the only focal points of the book. Love also plays its part: one character, Tandor-Kuma, cannot marry the woman he loves because she is a maid; Kwamankra is more fortunate. After not having seen Mansa, his former girl friend, for many years, he finally meets her again. They marry and have a son, but Mansa dies when giving birth to their second child. Her death returns the author to the theme of Christianity; Kwamankra feels that through his love for Mansa "he had touched the depths of human happiness and the depths of human sorrow, and had come to know that the way to God led from one to the other." (p. 144)

He visits her in the underworld, where she is a goddess. The style alters as the author smoothly blends a biblical prose with the rhythm of classical verse in his description of the underworld: "A number of peaceful avenues, wearing a beautiful green; like unto mass, which met in one grand broadway. Each avenue was edged with luxuriant shrubs and plants whose leaves showed the most delicate tints of the rainbow in beautiful blend." Kwamankra's uncertainty about religious matters and his gesture toward Heaven are symbolized in a new structure which Mansa shows him and in which there is "unevenness in place where [there] should be uniformity." His wife gives him advice on how he should live, and the visit concludes with a promise: "Say unto the mighty that the cry of the afflicted and the distressed among the sons of Ethiopia has come up to us, and we will visit the earth.... Lo! Nyiakrapon will establish in Ethiopia a kingdom which is different therein, and an angel of light, with a two-edged sword, shall guard the gate thereof." (pp. 144-45)

When Kwamankra returns to the Gold Coast, he comes to the conclusion that he must restore the practice of indigenous religion to his people, instead of following "emasculated sentimentalities which men shamelessly and slanderously identify with the Holy one of God, His Son, Jesus Christ." (p. 145)

Abruptly scene and character again switch; Kwamankra's old acquaintance Whiteley has decided to go to the Gold Coast as a missionary. In his mission work, he proves to be an ideal imperialist; he quarrels with his Black assistant chaplain and has him dismissed over the question of segregated cemeteries.

An attempt is now made to reintroduce Kwamankra into the story; Bilcox, a Gold Coaster, Whiteley, and Kwamankra meet at a party given by the chief magistrate. During the affair, Kwamankra describes his plan for segregating by ability, rather than by race: "If you took mankind in the aggregate, irrespective of race and shook them up together, as you would the slips of paper in a jury panel box, you would find after the exercise that the cultured would shake themselves free and come together, and so would the uncouth, the vulgar, and the ignorant; but, of course, you would ignore the law of nature, and, with a wave of the hand, confine the races in separate airtight compartments." Kwamankra seems to be concerned solely with his own position, that of the privileged in an underprivileged community.

After a melodramatic meeting between Kwamankra and his son, Ekru Kwow, a meeting that has nothing to do with the development of the book, the Professor and Tandor unexpectedly re-enter the story. An amusing description is given of a train journey they take with Kwamankra in the Gold Coast. The Professor refuses to surrender his ticket, saying firmly to the ticket-collector, "I have made it a rule never to give up my ticket on this line till I have landed safely at my destination, do you understand?" The bewildered ticket-collector does not know what to make of his passengers.

Another character is then introduced and dropped: Tony Palmer is of a Sierra Leonean family and with him Kwamankra talks about marriage, asserting that any women who is worthy of his love is worthy to be his wife. Although no more is heard of Tony Palmer, this scene is juxtaposed with another, in which Tandor-Kuma, now married and ill, is nursed back to health by the mother of his child and the woman he had deserted.

Toward the end of the book, a meeting of the nations of the world on Mount Atlas is described. In this section the writer states his own opposition to colonialism and Christianity. Kwamankra is mentioned only tangentially, as giving a lecture at the African National University in America, where he puts forth his views on Edward Blyden, a pioneer African Pan-Africanist. Kwamankra is again dropped, and the author discusses the possibilities of the cultural unity of Africa, America, and the Caribbean. Kwamankra reappears as a delegate to the Pan-African Congress of 1905 where he again expounds Blyden's ideas for a unity of all Blacks. He criticizes "the African who comes to his brethren with red-hot civilisation straight from Regent Circus or the Boulevards of Paris," and identifies himself with those who "walked the banks of the Nile in the days of yore." At the end of the book, the author reinforces this idea of the equality of Africans and discusses Fanti belief and custom.

As has been seen, *Ethiopia Unbound* is a means by which Casely-Hayford attempted to express a hotchpotch of ideas. As far as action is concerned little happens, and the book vacillates between fantasy and detailed documentation. Kwamankra is allowed to disappear from the story for long periods, and either his place is taken by other characters or the author develops the ideas himself. Many of the ideas, however, lack clarity and consistency. For instance, Kwamankra goes to Britain to translate important books into his own language for the founding of the national university. Furthermore, when the author is not attacking the evils of westernization, he is advocating the study of the classics or giving his story a classical setting, as with Kwamankra's visit to the underworld and the meeting of the nations of the world on Mount Atlas.

The same vacillation is observed in his attitude toward class and Christianity. One character learns the lesson of social snobbery when he is nursed back to health by a woman he despises, but at the magistrate's party Kwamankra advocates a meritocracy. There is, however, cohesion between Kwamankra's ideas and the author's; although it is not satisfactory art when they interchange roles, it is nevertheless worth pointing out, in a book with so many deficiencies, that their ideological world is a mutual one.

If *Ethiopia Unbound* were intended as a novel, the conversations also seem unreal. Often they are stilted and in attempting to be always profound, they lack the ease which is associated with normal conversation. Pidgin English is only used once—in the train episode. This succeeds in maintaining balance, for so much of the book is serious and there are few light moments of relief.

Kwamankra has little private life. His thoughts are all concerned with the public issues of his day. One learns little about him as a person but a great deal about his attitude toward various matters. For example, in an unsuccessful scene he discusses colonialism and the "yellow peril" with his son. According to the author, "he had a call to duty, and that in the service of his race." But his race is identified with any that seems convenient at the moment—Egyptians, Greeks, Ethiopians, Chinese, Japanese, and West Indians. After a while marriage to Mansa is not treated in detail; it is as if Casely-Hayford feels that his book is one of ideas and that he must reserve the greater part for the expression of these ideas.

Archaisms predominate—"twain," "the wind blowing where it listeth," "he wot not the full meaning of what he had done"—although they are only appropriate in the description of the visit to the underworld. When Casely-Hayford aspires to a back-to-nature romanticism, the writing becomes absurd and trite. He has Mansa tell her husband: "When we arrived in England the life of the people seemed to me artificial . . . Chance took me to Germany—there in the Black Forest, I got into direct touch with Nature; the song of the birds, the bleating of the lambs, the fragrance of the fields, all seemed so natural, and I said to myself; Here is my proper place; here the atmosphere wherein my nature may expand." These seem strange sentiments coming from Kwamankra's wife, who, in the next breath, preaches world government by "Ethiopians."

Ethiopia Unbound is really a record of the author's own uncertainties and those of his generation. They were *évolués* who cherished their position, at the same time paying lip service to indigenous African beliefs. When Casely-Hayford therefore writes of a Fanti god, Nyiak-rapon, he takes pains to show that he is like the Christian God. Without knowing it, Casely-Hayford was the earliest representative of a conflict—the man with irreconcilable cultural loyalties. (pp. 145-48)

> O. R. Dathorne, "Beginnings in English," in his The Black Mind: A History of African Literature, *University of Minnesota Press, 1974, pp. 143-55.*

L. H. Ofosu-Appiah (essay date 1975)

[*A Ghanaian educator, critic, and translator, Ofosu-Appiah's works reflect his interest in African history, politics, and biography. In the following excerpt from his* Joseph Ephraim Casely Hayford: The Man of Vision and Faith, *he discusses the form and content of* Ethiopia Unbound.]

The most interesting of Casely Hayford's books is *Ethiopia Unbound.* It is a novel, but does not follow the pattern of a classical novel, since it is episodic, and in certain sections the author is merely writing speeches on politics and social injustices in Africa and America. But it appears to be a sort of autobiographical novel, and the author can be identified with the principal character, Kwamankra. The influence of John Bunyan is evident from the chapters on Love and Life and Love and Death. His wife's death affected him so much that he had to set down his feelings in those chapters. The book is also an attempt to interpret Akan Religion to a British theological student, Whitely, who eventually turns up in the Gold Coast to practise racial discrimination by insisting on separate cemeteries for blacks and whites! Apparently Whitely had not learned that there are only two things in which all men are equal by nature. All men are born naked, and all men die. The distinctions in civilisation arise after birth but end in death! Since Casely Hayford did not have much education in Fante, his Fante sentences cannot be understood without reference to his translations into English. His excursions into etymology are very odd. He claims that *Nyami* stands for *Nya oye me* or He who is I am! and *Nyiankropon* stands for *Nyia nuku ara oye pon*—He who alone is great! One can understand his desire to promote the study of African languages!

Ethiopia Unbound is also a criticism of the colonial system and the inefficiency which characterises some of its public services. The political agitator who is a lawyer appears in the person of Kwamankra, whom the white political officer dislikes; and we gather that white men who tend to sympathise with Africans have their careers cut short. His description of the 39-mile rail journey at the time sounds very much like rail travel in the 1970's. Apparently matches had to be borrowed to light the hurricane lamps in the train at night! No wonder Tandor-Kuma refused to surrender his ticket to the collector until the journey's end, for the 39 miles took seven hours to cover! He touches on the dilemma of a polygamous society and the evils of some Christian practices of the Europeans on the Coast. Racial discrim-ination is discussed by the mention of the yellow and black perils and the Black Man's burden. His interest in the Negro problem of the United States is evident from Chapter XVII, which deals with Race Emancipation. His aim in *Ethiopia Unbound* and in the *Gold Coast Native Institutions* is to impress upon Africans and Europeans that there is something good in the African way of life. But he does indulge in romanticism, for his Ethiopia which would raise its hands to God was not the ideal paradise of his dreams. It was a feudal slave-owning monarchy torn by strife and intrigues, and sunk in ignorance, poverty and illiteracy, in spite of the fact that Ethiopia has had its own script for centuries, and was known in Homeric times as the resting-place of the gods. The Ethiopians were called blameless by Homer. The romanticism was, however, meant to inculcate race consciousness, and here I think he met with some measure of success. In Africa one of the ways in which we get over our inferiority complex is to compare some features of our culture to those of the Ancient Greeks and Egyptians. Casely Hayford does that in *Ethiopia Unbound* where he makes Kwamankra discuss Nausikaa in Homer's Odyssey with his son Ekra-Ekow, and brings out the similarities between the two cultures. Perhaps if he had taken his Herodotus seriously, he could have saved himself all that trouble, since Herodotus regarded mankind as having several things in common, and most of what we now call African culture like drums and dances and the obsession with the dead have a long ancestry all over the world. (pp. 19-21)

> L. H. Ofosu-Appiah, in his Joseph Ephraim Casely Hayford: The Man of Vision and Faith, *Academy of Arts and Sciences, 1975, 31 p.*

F. Nnabuenyi Ugonna (essay date 1977)

[*In the following excerpt, Ugonna praises* Ethiopia Unbound *as an important contribution to the growth of African culture in the twentieth century.*]

Ethiopia Unbound is a remarkable story of ideas about race relations, a story whose main theme is the problem of universal human relationship. The relationship oper-ates on two distinct but related levels: on the one hand it is the problem of human relationship between the colonizer and the colonized and on the other between white and black. The two trends imperceptibly fade into each other in so far as the colonizer is white and the colonized black. This is why invariably any attack on colonialism tends to be expressed in racial terms.

Ethiopia Unbound tells the life story of Kwamankra—his experiences, first, as a student in London, and then, as a legal practitioner in Ghana; his observations of social life both in London and in various Ghanaian towns—Kumasi, Cape Coast, Sekondi and Accra; his commentary on social institutions, on education, religion, economics; and his impartial criticism of the whole concept of colonial government as applied to the West African society—the corruption, callousness and exclusiveness of colonial missionaries and political officers, the neglect and dilapidation suffered by public utilities as railways, water supplies and electricity and the general absence of sound development schemes. To this extent, the work appears to be a social documentary. But then the book has another dimension which elevates it to the status of a classic: an epic quality, characterized by heroism and a sense of deep personal tragedy and stoical triumph.

The work is certainly an exercise in African cultural projection which is a subtle and positive way of protest. The ingenious device is to present characters, that is, African characters, in such light as to belie any suggestion of their inherent inferiority. Similarly, several aspects of indigenous African culture are rationalised. Their noble, useful, serene, elegant or remarkable qualities are highlighted while their grosser traits are either ignored or glossed over. Every creative artist, of course, follows this procedure. From chunks of life—battles, hatred, fear, birth, death, quarrels, eating, drinking, marriage, endearment, he selects those combinations that will answer to his own vision of life. (pp 161-62)

Casely Hayford, in *Ethiopia Unbound,* has attempted to show that African culture is not synonymous with barbarism and cruelty, backwardness and crudity. As Mary Kinsley in a letter to the editor of the Liberian paper, *New Africa,* asked African nationalists who are conversant with their own indigenous culture to do, Hayford has indeed demonstrated that "African nationalism is a good thing, and that it is not a welter of barbarism, cannibalism and cruelty...that there is an African law and an African culture; that the African has institutions and a state form of his own."

This appeal has, as a matter of fact, been answered by other educated African nationalists in the form of treatises and newspaper articles but *Ethiopia Unbound* is clearly the first attempt to represent this idea in fiction....

Throughout his public career, Casely Hayford endeavoured to preserve what is good and admirable in his culture. All his written works tend to be lucid expositions of different aspects of the African culture involving institutions, land tenure, communal life, justice, the arts, and so on. He knew it was important for Africans

to come forward to project their culture themselves. (p. 162)

The problem was how best to demonstrate to the world that Africa has culture. Should revolutionary or violent methods be used? Casely Hayford rejected violence. Perhaps his legal education made him prefer constitutional and peaceful means. Yet he believed in action. "African manhood," he asserts, "demands that the Ethiopian should seek not his opportunity, or ask for elbow room from the white man, but that he should create the one or the other for himself." But he maintained that "the African's way to proper recognition lies not at present so much in the exhibition of material force and power, as in the gentler art of persuasion by the logic of facts and of achievements before which all reasonable men must bow." By using the words, "at present," Hayford shows that he was not after all totally against violence but that he was only being realistic and practical. Resorting to violence without adequate preparation, he surmised, would be disastrous. So his pacifism was only pragmatic. His policy was dictated by his own maxim, "Take what you get and get what you want." Rather than gain no immediate political ends, he would prefer to compromise on certain vital issues. This aspect of his character was responsible for the bitter criticism he received toward the end of his life, but he preferred a little measure of success to downright failure.

"The gentler art of persuasion"—this is the key to the general tone of *Ethiopia Unbound,* and it summarises the effect the work is designed to achieve, that is, to persuade all readers and especially whites and deracine Africans, that African culture developed independent of western culture. Hayford was aware that people are not persuaded by mere verbal protestations and unsubstantiated claims. He therefore stresses the need for resorting to "the logic of facts and of achievements." Consequently he makes his chief characters discuss different aspects of African cultural achievement with the aim of highlighting their important merits. The importance of African culture is dramatized by paralleling African cultural institutions with the corresponding western forms and then showing the advantages of the African patterns over the western.

This process begins in *Ethiopia Unbound* with the introduction in the first chapter, of two of the main characters in the book, Kwamankra and Whitely. Their personalities pervade the work but they hardly impress us as flesh and blood. They are more or less ideas personified and are used generally as mouth-pieces for expressing particular ideas. Kwamankra, in a sense, is like Samuel Johnson's Rasselas and just as *Rasselas* is a philosophical tale so is *Ethiopia Unbound* an ideological story. Kwamankra is conceived as symbolic of African personality: logical, dignified, rational, considerate, a negation of the typical western concept of the African. He believes in God, but this is after due consideration of the facts, not out of fear or superstition.

But his white foil, Whitely, a theology student, doubts the divinity of Christ. Whitely is torn between disbelief and a sense of obligation, not to God, but to his mother. To him (and he symbolizes white priesthood) belief or non-belief is not sufficiently disturbing, for, despite his doubts, he takes Holy Orders and later becomes a colonial chaplain in West Africa where he degenerates into a time-serving religious minister.

The story of *Ethiopia Unbound* opens, after a brief introduction by the narrator, with the hero Kwamankra and Whitely walking along Tottenham Court Road in London discussing ethics, religion and metaphysics. The philosophy of Marcus Aurelius, as expounded in his *Meditations,* is paralleled with the "teaching of the Holy Nazarene." The divinity of Jesus Christ is discussed, and Kwamankra, after contending that the Anglo-Saxon word from which God is derived does not in any way suggest the idea of *good,* argues that the Christian attributes of God—omnipresence, omniscience, omnipotence, are of course "borrowed from the Romans, who were pagans like ourselves, and who, indeed, had much to learn from the Ethiopians through the Greeks." Throughout the book preconceived ideas, familiar prejudices, and popular attitudes are subtly debunked by logical discussions and dialogue.

In Kwamankra's lodging the two friends continue to discuss religion.... The drift of Kwamankra's argument is that European philosophical, ethical and religious ideas were largely derived from Ethiopia, and Ethiopia ambiguously means Africa or Asia or both. By his logic Jesus Christ, Marcus Aurelius, Buddha, Confucius, Cleanthes and other stoics were Ethiopians since the idea of stoicism originated from Ethiopia.

Hayford has good reason for stressing the significance of African religious and philosophical ideas. The emphasis stems not merely from the fact that African social life is fundamentally religious but also from the feeling increasingly held at the turn of the century that Africa would have a tremendous moral influence on the rest of the world just as the West has had an unprecedented scientific impact on Africa. This is not to say that Africans envisioned a moral influence only. They also dreamt of a time when they would be (some would add, once more, implying that there was a time when Africa was) at the helm of all progress, scientific or moral (pp. 163-64)

[Casely-Hayford's] attempt in *Ethiopia Unbound* is to bring home to the Africans the truth of his conviction that only by upholding her own distinctive culture could Africa win back her self-respect and dignity. Thus he makes his hero, Kwamankra, discuss at length not only African religion and philosophy but propound a theory of African education and advocate the African system of marriage (p. 166)

The story of Tom Palmer, an ambitious youth, always dressed in "silk hat and patent leather boots" is illustrative of the cultural revolution *Ethiopia Unbound* is meant to bring about and therefore Hayford's concept of the ideal African personality. Tom Palmer is an African caught in an alien culture. At first he struts around as "leader of society" but later discovers, through the help of Kwamankra, the African sage, that love does not come only "when she is wooed in Parisian skirts and Regent Street high heels." Palmer ends up by marrying more than one wife and replacing his silk hat, etc., with sober African attire. Hayford's message here is unmistakable: return to African culture; develop it if necessary with what is edifying in the western culture. Africans should eschew a slavish imitation of the whites and should at all times maintain their cultural integrity. In this way a worthwhile, meaningful African personality would be created. (p. 168)

In *Ethiopia Unbound* Hayford has attempted to assert and define African personality. Through the character of Kwamankra he answers the question as to whether or not contemporary Africa has "collective achievement...like other nationalities." Kwamankra shows that Africa has a religion, a philosophy of life, music, art, law, etc.; that African culture though different from western culture is not inferior to it. He has also established that the African is a cultured man and is not inferior to the white man and that the only differences, psychological or mental, between a black man and a white man are "those which can be attributed solely to education and to cultural background." "It is, in fact, the social heritage, the cultural tradition, the prevailing *zeitgeist,* which differentiates the black man from the white man and not any mystical gene or hormone or any transcendental power possessed by the one and lacked by the other. (pp. 168-69)

The need for the assertion of African personality arose as a result of either and denial of the existence of African culture or the misrepresentation of the African and his way of life. *Ethiopia Unbound* has thematically demonstrated both the deep-rooted existence of different aspects of the African culture and the cultural, intellectual and spiritual capabilities of the black man. Casely Hayford in this work has therefore made a tremendous contribution to the growth of the idea of Africanness. The importance of *Ethiopia Unbound* lies, indeed, in its being the earliest known work to give an aesthetic dimension to this otherwise philosophical concept of African personality. (p. 169)

F. Nnabuenyi Ugonna, "Casely Hayford: The Fictive Dimension of African Personality," in UFAHAMU, *Vol. 7, No. 2, 1977, pp. 159-71.*

FURTHER READING

Review of *Ethiopia Unbound. African Times and Orient Review* 1 No. 5 (November 1912): 7-8.

Favorable appraisal of *Ethiopia Unbound* signed "W. F. H." According to the critic: "Through the whole story there rings the common cry of the African races who are waking. The cry of injustice from all, and the demand for equal opportunity from the educated, who claims a right to help in ruling and molding their native countries."

Eluwa, G. I. C. "Casely Hayford and African Emancipation." *Pan-African Journal* VII, No. 2 (Summer 1974): 111-18.

Introductory essay discussing Casely-Hayford's life, works, and ideas.

Jones, Eldred Durosimi. "The Development of African Writing." *Journal of the Royal Society of Arts* 122, No. 5220 (November 1974): 837-45.

Includes a brief discussion of *Ethiopia Unbound,* particularly the passage describing the meeting of the nations on Mount Atlas. According to Jones: "[*Ethiopia Unbound*], part autobiography, part allegory, part prophecy, is very modern in spirit and would certainly qualify as modern protest literature."

Hussain, Arif. "Iqbal and Casely Hayford: A Phase in Afro-Asian Philosophy." *Ibadan* 29 (1971): 45-52.

Discusses the similar philosophical beliefs of Casely-Hayford and Pakistani poet Muhammad Iqbal, his contemporary. According to Hussain: "The phase of Afro-Asian philosophy as represented by Casely-Hayford and Iqbal contains a philosophy which established the self-respect of the Afro-Asian world through faith and reason. It gave a justification for the freedom movements, a justification which is indigenous and original."

Sampson, Magnus J. "Joseph Ephraim Casely Hayford." In his *Gold Coast Men of Affairs,* pp. 160-73. London: Dawsons of Pall Mall, 1969.

Details Casely-Hayford's political career. Sampson maintains: "The career of Mr. Casely Hayford was a marvel of indefatigable application and industry, and . . . he had one of the most brilliant careers in the political history of the Gold Coast."

―――. Introduction to *West African Leadership,* by J. E. Casely-Hayford, pp. 11-36. Cass Library of African Studies: Africana Modern Library, edited by E. U. Essien-Udom, No. 10. London: Frank Cass and Co., 1969.

Summarizes West African politics during Casely-Hayford's era.

Aimé Césaire

1913-

(Full name Aimé Fernand Césaire) West Indian poet, dramatist, and essayist.

Césaire is recognized as a major Caribbean poet and dramatist. Best known for his surrealist poem *Cahier d'un retour au pays natal* (1939; *Return to My Native Land*), he is also acknowledged as "The Father of Negritude." Defining negritude as "the affirmation that one is black and proud of it," Césaire urged blacks to reject assimilation into white culture and honor instead their racial heritage. This belief strongly permeates *Return to My Native Land* and other works by Césaire.

Césaire was born in 1913 to a poor family on the island of Martinique in the French West Indies. Under the tutelage of his grandmother, he learned to read and write by age four. When he was eleven, he enrolled at Lycée Schoelcher, a leading school in Martinique's capital, Fort-de-France. There he excelled in French, Latin, English, and history. Gilbert Gratiant, a former teacher at the school, recalled: "[Césaire was] extremely nice. No difficulties. He did everything very well. Gentleness itself. The most gentle of children. Césaire was so perfect that it seemed abnormal. A very gracious little boy." According to scholar A. James Arnold, however, "[Césaire's] impeccable and genuine politeness nonetheless coexisted with a tumultuous, seething spirit that eventually expressed itself in equally genuine, if literary, violence."

Upon graduating from Lycée Schoelcher in 1931, Césaire was voted best student overall and received a scholarship to study in Paris. "Whereas the thought of exile saddened most of my classmates," Césaire later recounted, "it brought joy to me: Paris, a promise of fulfillment...." While enrolled at the École Normale Supérieure, he, along with Léopold Sedar Senghor and Léon-Goutran Damas, founded *L'étudiant noir,* a student magazine dedicated to uniting blacks and promoting pride in black culture. Although they produced only five or six issues, Césaire's involvement with the magazine was vital to the development of negritude. While working on *L'étudiant noir,* Césaire formulated the basic tenets of negritude: acceptance of one's blackness and the rejection of white assimilation. In 1939, the term "negritude" appeared in print for the first time in Césaire's poem *Return to My Native Land,* published in the Paris periodical *Volontés.* Shortly after the poem's publication, Césaire returned to Martinique.

Back home, Césaire immersed himself in politics, serving as mayor of Fort-de-France and as a member of the French National Assembly. Despite his busy political career, he continued to write poetry. In the surrealist tradition of *Return to My Native Land,* Césaire wrote *Les armes miraculeuses* (1946; "The Miracle Weap-

ons"), *Soleil cou coupé* (1948; "Beheaded Sun"), and *Corps perdu* (1949; "Disembodied"). Believing that drama would extend his audience well beyond readers of poetry, however, Césaire began writing plays in the late 1950s. *La tragédie du roi Christophe* (1963; *The Tragedy of King Christophe*), the first of Césaire's three plays, portrays Henri Christophe, the self-proclaimed Haitian king who presided over Haiti's decolonization in the early nineteenth century. According to critic Thomas Hale, "Shakespearean in tone, the play is a blend of verbal forms from several different cultures, and constitutes Césaire's message to leaders of the newly-independent states of Africa." *Une saison au Congo* (1966; *A Season in the Congo*), less successful than *Christophe,* centers on the martyrdom of Patrice Lamumba, former leader of the Republic of Congo. Césaire's last play, *Une tempête: d'après "La tempête" de Shakespeare, Adaptation pour un théâtre nègre* (1969; *A Tempest: After "The Tempest" by Shakespeare, Adaptation for the Negro Theatre*), explores the relationship between Prospero, portrayed as a decadent colonizer, and his slaves. In the late 1970s, Césaire returned to writing poetry. Unlike his earlier surreal poetry, however, poems in *Noria* (1976) and *Moi, Laminaire...* (1982; "I, Laminarian...") are considered less "extravagant." In addition to plays and poetry, Césaire also published two highly acclaimed essays: *Discours sur le colonialisme* (1950; *Discourse on Colonialism*) and *Lettre à Maurice Thorex* (1956; *Letter to Maurice Thorex*). The former work denounces colonialism, and the latter explains Césaire's reasons for leaving the Communist Party. Due to an increasingly busy political career, Césaire has written less frequently in recent years. Maintaining his mayoral office in Fort-de-France, he meets with his constituents every day. Nonetheless, "I have never stopped writing poems," Césaire said in a recent interview. "Poetry is my raison d'être, my outlet, my life buoy."

Although each of his works has received favorable reviews, none has matched the success of Césaire's first poem, *Return to My Native Land*. Many critics regard *Return to My Native Land* as a masterpiece; André Breton, for example, declared: "The poem is...nothing less than the greatest lyrical monument of our time." Consisting of three movements and covering sixty-six pages, *Return to My Native Land* is considered the original statement on negritude. The first movement surveys the demoralizing effects of colonialism on Martinique, the second chronicles Césaire's struggle to free himself from white culture, and the third celebrates negritude. In now-famous lines, Césaire proclaimed: "my negritude is not a stone, its deafness flung against the clamor of day/ my negritude is not a speck of dead water on the dead eye of the earth/ my negritude is neither a tower nor a cathedral/ it plunges into the red flash of the sun/ it plunges into the burning flesh of the sky/ it punctures the oppressive prostration of its rigid patience."

As observed by critics, Césaire's poetic language strongly shows the influence of French surrealists of the 1930s. Jean-Paul Sartre stated: "In Césaire, the great surrealist tradition is realized, it takes on its definitive meaning and is destroyed: surrealism—that supreme European movement—is taken from the Europeans by a Black man who turns it against them and gives it vigorously defined function." Like the surrealists, Césaire endeavored to free his writing from the conventions of French literature. Unlike them, however, he infused his poetry with angry images and, as noted by one writer, hurled "tongues of fire and biting irony" against Western culture. Some critics see Césaire's poetic language as a form of literary violence marked by jarring images and forceful rhythms that assault the reader. Marjorie Perloff, for example, found Césaire's language "so violently charged with meaning that each word falls on the ear (or hits the eye) with resounding force." Similarly, Alfred Cismaru declared: "Under [Césaire's] powerful, poetic eye, perception knows no limits and pierces appearances without pity. Words emerge and explode like firecrackers, catching the eye and the imagination of the reader. He makes use of the entire dictionary, of artificial and vulgar words, of elegant and forgotten ones, of technical and invented vocabulary...." In addition to admiring its literary finesse, commentators also praise *Return to My Native Land* for its "universal appeal." The poem speaks to people of all color and nationality, they contend, because Césaire's struggle for self-acceptance is a struggle shared by all people. Judith Gleason viewed *Return to My Native Land* as "a masterpiece of cultural relevance, every bit as 'important' as 'The Wasteland'." She concluded: "Its remarkable virtuosity will ensure its eloquence long after the struggle for human dignity has ceased to be viewed in racial terms." Today, Césaire's concept of negritude forms the foundation for black movements across the world. Whether consciously or unconsciously, many black leaders have adopted Césaire's negritude as their rallying cry. In the United States, for example, Eldridge Cleaver was greatly influenced by *Return to My Native Land,* prompting him to declare in his *Soul on Ice:* "Aimé Césaire [is] one of the greatest black writers of the twentieth century."

Césaire, as an opponent of white assimilation, was one of the first black leaders to promote black pride. With the words "I accept...I accept...completely, without reservation...my race that no brew of herbs and flowers could wash away," he inspired blacks to embrace their blackness and their culture. In a tribute to Césaire, James Baldwin wrote: "Césaire had spoken for those who could not speak and those who could not speak thronged around the table to shake his hand, and kiss him.... What made him so attractive now was the fact that he, without having ceased to be one of them, yet seemed to move with the European authority. He had penetrated into the heart of the great wilderness which was Europe and stolen the sacred fire."

(For further information about Césaire's life and works, see *Black Writers; Contemporary Authors,* Vols. 65-68; *Contemporary Authors New Revision Series,* Vol. 24; and *Contemporary Literary Criticism,* Vol. 32.)

PRINCIPAL WORKS

Les armes miraculeuses (poetry) 1946
Cahier d'un retour au pays natal (poetry) 1947
  [*Return to My Native Land,* 1968]
Soleil cou coupé (poetry) 1948
†*Corps perdu* (poetry) 1949
Discours sur le colonialisme (essay) 1950
  [*Discourse on Colonialism,* 1972]
Et les chiens se taisaient: Tragédie (drama) 1956
Lettre à Maurice Thorex (letter) 1956
  [*Letter to Maurice Thorex,* 1957]
Ferrements (poetry) 1960
Cadastre (poetry) 1961
  [*Cadastre,* 1973]
La Tragédie du roi Christophe (drama) 1963
  [*The Tragedy of King Christophe,* 1970]
Une saison au Congo (drama) 1966
  [*A Season in the Congo,* 1969]
State of the Union (poetry) 1966

*Une tempête: d'après "La tempête" de Shakespeare,
    Adaptation pour un théâtre nègre* [adaptor; from
    the drama *The Tempest* by William Shakespeare]
    (drama) 1969
    [*A Tempest: After "The Tempest" by Shakespeare,
    Adaptation for the Negro Theatre,* 1974]
Noria (poetry) 1976
Moi, Laminaire... (poetry) 1982
The Collected Poetry (poetry) 1983

*An incomplete version of this poem appeared in the Paris
    periodical *Volontés* in 1939.
†This work contains illustrations by Pablo Picasso.

Jean-Paul Sartre (essay date 1948)

[*A French philosopher, essayist, critic, and biographer,
Sartre is widely recognized as one of the greatest
thinkers of the twentieth century. He is chiefly remembered for his many contributions to existentialism. In
the following essay, he examines the concept of
negritude and credits Césaire with its creation. The
excerpt is from a translation of Sartre's seminal study
on negritude.* Orphée Noir, *which he wrote in 1948 as
the introduction to Léopold Sédar Senghor's* Anthologie de la nouvelle poésie nègre et malgache de langue
française. *The translation by John MacCombie first
appeared in the* Massachusetts Review *in 1965.*]

[If the poems in *Anthologie de la nouvelle poésie nègre et
malgache de langue française*] shame us..., they were
not intended to: they were not written for us; and they
will not shame any colonists or their accomplices who
open this book, for these latter will think they are
reading letters over someone's shoulder, letters not
meant for them. These black men are addressing themselves to black men about black men; their poetry is
neither satiric nor imprecatory: it is an awakening to
consciousness. (p. 7)

[Race] consciousness is based first of all on the black
soul, or, rather—since the term is often used in this
anthology—on a certain quality common to the
thoughts and conduct of Negroes which is called *Negritude....* There are only two ways to go about forming
racial concepts: either one causes certain subjective
characteristics to become objective, or else one tries to
interiorize objectively revealed manners of conduct;
thus the black man who asserts his negritude by means
of a revolutionary movement immediately places himself in the position of having to meditate, either because
he wishes to recognize in himself certain objectively
established traits of the African civilizations, or because
he hopes to discover the Essence of blackness in the well
of his heart. Thus subjectivity reappears: the relation of
the self with the self; the source of all poetry, the very
poetry from which the worker had to disengage himself.
The black man who asks his colored brothers to "find
themselves" is going to try to present to them an
exemplary image of their Negritude and will look into
his own soul to grasp it. He wants to be both a beacon
and a mirror; the first revolutionary will be the harbin-
ger of the black soul, the herald—half prophet and half
follower—who will tear Blackness out of himself in
order to offer it to the world.... In the anthology which
I am introducing to you here, there is only one subject
that all the poets attempt to treat, more or less successfully. From Haiti to Cayenne, there is a single idea:
reveal the black soul. Black poetry is evangelic, it
announces good news: Blackness has been rediscovered.

However, this negritude, which they wish to fish for in
their abyssal depths, does not fall under the soul's gaze
all by itself: in the soul, nothing is gratuitous. The herald
of the black soul has gone through white schools...; it is
through having had some contact with white culture that
his blackness has passed from the immediacy of existence to the meditative state. But at the same time, he
has more or less ceased to live his negritude. In choosing
to see what he is, he has become split, he no longer coincides with himself. And on the other hand, it is
because he was already exiled from himself that he
discovered this need to reveal himself. He therefore
begins by exile. It is a double exile: the exile of his body
offers a magnificent image of the exile of his heart; he is
in Europe most of the time, in the cold, in the middle of
gray crowds; he dreams of Port-au-Prince, of Haiti. But
in Port-au-Prince he was *already* in exile; the slavers had
torn his fathers out of Africa and dispersed them. (pp.
11-12)

However, the walls of this culture prison must be broken
down; it will be necessary to return to Africa some day:
thus the themes of return to the native country and of
re-descent into the glaring hell of the black soul are
indissolubly mixed up in the *vates* of negritude. A quest
is involved here, a systematic stripping and an "ascèse"
[the ascetic's movement of *interiorization*] accompanied
by a continual effort of investigation. And I shall call
this poetry "Orphic" because the Negro's tireless descent into himself makes me think of Orpheus going to
claim Eurydice from Pluto. Thus, through an exceptional stroke of poetic good luck, it is by letting himself fall
into trances, by rolling on the ground like a possessed
man tormented by himself, by singing of his angers, his
regrets or his hates; by exhibiting his wounds, his life
torn between "civilization" and his old black substra-
tum; in short, by becoming most lyrical, that the black
poet is most certain of creating a great collective poetry:
by speaking only of himself, he speaks for all Negroes; it
is when he seems smothered by the serpents of our
culture that he is the most revolutionary, for he then
undertakes to ruin systematically the European knowledge he has acquired, and this spiritual destruction
symbolizes the great future taking-up of arms by which
black men will destroy their chains. (p. 13)

The fact that the prophets of negritude are forced to
write their gospel *in French* means that there is a certain
risk of dangerously slowing down the efforts of black
men to reject our tutelege. Having been dispersed to the
four corners of the earth by the slave trade, black men
have no common language; in order to incite the
oppressed to unite, they must necessarily rely on the

words of the oppressor's language. And French is the language that will furnish the black poet with the largest audience, at least within the limits of French colonization.... And since words are ideas, when the Negro declares in French that he rejects French culture, he accepts with one hand what he rejects with the other; he sets up the enemy's thinking-apparatus in himself, like a crusher. This would not matter: except that this syntax and vocabulary—forged thousands of miles away in another epoch to answer other needs and to designate other objects—are unsuitable to furnish him with the means of speaking about himself, his own anxieties, his own hopes. The French language and French thought are analytical. What would happen if the black spirit were above all synthetical? The rather ugly term "negritude" is one of the few black contributions in our dictionary. But after all, if this "negritude" is a definable or at least a describable concept, it must subsume other more elementary concepts which correspond to the immediate fundamental ideas directly involved with Negro consciousness: but where are the words to describe them? (p. 14)

Only through Poetry can the black men of Tenanarive and of Cayenne, the black men of Port-au-Prince and of Saint-Louis, communicate with each other in private. And since French lacks terms and concepts to define negritude, since negritude is silence, these poets will use "allusive words, never direct, reducing themselves to the same silence" in order to evoke it. Short-circuits of language: behind the flaming fall of words, we glimpse a great black mute idol. It is not only the black man's self-portrayal that seems poetic to me; it is also his personal way of utilizing the means of expression at his disposal. His position incites him to do it: even before he thinks of writing poetry, in him, the light of white words is refracted, polarized and altered. This is nowhere more manifest than in his use of two connected terms—"white-black"—that cover both the great cosmic division—"day and night"—and the human conflict between the native and the colonist. But it is a connection based on a hierarchical system: by giving the Negro this term, the teacher also gives him a hundred language habits which consecrate the white man's rights over the black man. The Negro will learn to say "white like snow" to indicate innocence, to speak of the blackness of a look, of a soul, of a deed. As soon as he opens his mouth, he accuses himself, unless he persists in upsetting the hierarchy. And if he upsets it *in French,* he is already poetizing: can you imagine the strange savor that an expression like "the blackness of innocence" or "the darkness of virtue" would have for us? That is the savor which we taste on every page of this book.... (pp. 16-17)

[For example, throughout one of the poems,] black is color; better still, light; its soft diffuse radiance dissolves our habits; the *black* country where the ancients are sleeping is not a dark hell: it is a land of sun and fire. Then again, in another connection, the superiority of white over black does not express only the superiority that the colonist claims to have over the native: more

profoundly, it expresses a universal adoration of *day* as well as our night terrors, which also are universal. In this sense, these black men are re-establishing the hierarchy they have just upset. They don't want to be poets of *night,* poets of vain revolt and despair, they give the promise of dawn; they greet

> the transparent dawn of a new day.

At last, the black man discovers, through the pen, his baleful sense of foreboding:

> Nigger black like misery

one of them, and then another, cries out:

> Deliver me from my blood's night

Thus the word *black* is found to contain *all Evil* and *all Good,* it covers up almost unbearable tension between two contradictory classifications: solar hierarchy and racial hierarchy. It gains thereby an extraordinary poetry, like self-destructive objects from the hands of Duchamp and the Surrealists; there is a secret blackness in white, a secret whiteness in black, a vivid flickering of Being and of Non-being which is perhaps nowhere expressed as well as in this poem of Césaire:

> My tall wounded statue, a stone in its forehead;
>   my great inattentive day flesh with pitiless
>   spots, my great night flesh with day spots.

The poet will go even further; he writes:

> Our beautiful faces like the true operative power
>   of negation.

Behind this abstract eloquence evoking Lautréamont is seen an extremely bold and subtle attempt to give some sense to black skin and to realize the poetic synthesis of the two faces of night. When David Diop says that the Negro is "black like misery," he makes black represent deprivation of light. But Césaire develops and gets into this image more deeply: night is no longer absence, it is refusal. Black is not color, it is the destruction of this borrowed clarity which falls from the white sun. The revolutionary Negro is negation because he wishes to be complete nudity: in order to build his Truth, he must first destroy others' Truth. Black faces—these night memories which haunt our days—embody the dark work of Negativity which patiently gnaws at concepts. Thus, by a reversal which curiously recalls that of the humiliated Negro—insulted and called "dirty nigger" when he asserts his rights—it is the private aspect of darkness that establishes its value. Liberty is the color of night.

Destructions, *autodafés* of language, magic symbolism, ambivalence of concepts: all the negative aspects of modern poetry are here. But it is not a matter of some gratuitous game. The black man's position, his original "rending," the alienation that a foreign way of thinking imposes on him, all oblige him to reconquer his existential unity as a Negro—or, if you prefer, the original purity of his plan—through a gradual "ascèse," beyond the language stage. Negritude—like liberty—is a point of departure and an ultimate goal: it is a matter of making negritude pass from the immediate to the mediate, a matter of *thematicising* it. The black man must therefore find death in white culture in order to be reborn with a black soul.... It is not a matter of his *knowing*, nor of his ecstatically tearing himself away from himself, but rather of both discovering and becoming what he is.

There are two convergent means of arriving at this primordial simplicity of existence: one is objective, the other subjective. The poets in our anthology sometimes use one, sometimes the other, and sometimes both of them together. In effect, there exists an objective negritude that is expressed by the mores, arts, chants and dances of the African populaces.... The poetic act, then, is a dance of the soul; the poet turns round and round like a dervish until he faints; he has established his ancestors' time in himself, he feels it flowing with its peculiar violent pulls; he hopes to "find" himself in this rhythmic pulsation; I shall say that he tries to make himself "possessed" by his people's negritude; he hopes that the echoes of his tamtam will come to awaken timeless instincts sleeping within him.... The black men of Africa ... are still in the great period of mythical fecundity and French-language black poets are not just using their myths as a form of diversion as we use our epic poems: they allow themselves to be spellbound by them so that at the end of the incantation, negritude—magnificently evoked—may surge forth. This is why I call this method of "objective poetry" *magic,* or charm.

Césaire, on the contrary, chose to backtrack into himself. Since this Eurydice will disappear in smoke if Black Orpheus turns around to look back on her, he will descend the royal road of his soul with his back turned on the bottom of the grotto; he will descend below words and meanings,—"in order to think of you, I have placed all words on the mountain-of-pity"—below daily activities and the plan of "repetition," even below the first barrier reefs of revolt, with his back turned and his eyes closed, in order finally to touch with his feet the black water of dreams and desire and to let himself drown in it. Desire and dream will rise up snarling like a tidal wave; they will make words dance like flotsam and throw them pell-mell, shattered, on the shore. (pp. 17-20)

One recognizes the old surrealistic *method* (automatic writing, like mysticism, is a method: it presupposes an apprenticeship, exercises, a start along the way). One must dive under the superficial crust of reality, of common sense, of reasoning reason, in order to touch the very bottom of the soul and awaken the timeless forces of desire: desire which makes of man a refusal of everything and a love of everything: desire, the radical negation of natural laws and of the possible, a call to miracles; desire which, by its mad cosmic energy, plunges man back into the seething breast of Nature

and, at the same time, lifts him above Nature through the affirmation of his Right to be unsatisfied. Furthermore, Césaire is not the first Negro to take this road. Before him, Etienne Léro had founded *Légitime Défense*....

However, if one compares Léro with Césaire, one cannot help but be struck by their dissimilarities, and this comparison may allow us to measure the abyss that prevents a black revolutionary from utilizing white surrealism. Léro was the precursor; he invented the exploitation of surrealism as a "miraculous weapon" and an instrument for reconnaissance, a sort of radar with which one probes the depths of the abyss. But his poems are student exercises, they are mere imitations: they do not go beyond themselves; rather, they close in on each other.... (p. 21)

The purpose of surrealism is to rediscover—beyond race and condition, beyond class, behind the fire of language—dazzling silent darknesses which are no longer opposed to anything, not even to day, because day and night and all opposites are blended in them and suppressed; consequently, one might speak of the impassiveness and the impersonality of the surrealist poem, just as there is a Parnassian impassiveness and impersonality.

A poem by Césaire, on the contrary, bursts and wheels around like a rocket; suns turning and exploding into new suns come out of it; it is a perpetual going-beyond. It is not a question of the poem becoming part of the calm unity of opposites; but rather of making *one* of the opposites in the "black-white" couple expand like a phallus in its opposition to the other. The density of these words thrown into the air like stones from a volcano, is found in negritude, which is defined as being *against* Europe and colonization. What Césaire destroys is not *all* culture but rather *white* culture; what he brings to light is not desire for *everything* but rather the revolutionary aspirations of the oppressed Negro; what he touches in his very depths is not the spirit but a certain specific, concrete form of humanity. With this in mind, one can speak here about *engaged* and even *directed* automatic writing, not because there is any meditative intervention but because the words and images perpetually translate the same torrid obsession. The white surrealist finds within himself the trigger; Césaire finds within himself the fixed inflexibility of demands and feeling.... Césaire's words are pressed against each other and cemented by his furious passion. Between the most daring comparisons and between the most widely separated terms, runs a secret thread of hate and hope.... In Césaire, the great surrealist tradition is realized, it takes on its definitive meaning and is destroyed: surrealism—that European movement—is taken from the Europeans by a Black man who turns it against them and gives it rigorously defined function.... Césaire's originality lies in his having directed his powerful, concentrated anxiety as a Negro, as one oppressed, as a militant individual, into this world of the most destructive, free and metaphysical poetry at the moment when Eluard and Aragon were failing to give political content to their verse. And finally, *negritude-object* is snatched from Césaire like a cry of pain, of love and of hate. Here again he follows the surrealist tradition of *objective* poetry. Césaire's words do not describe negritude, they do not designate it, they do not copy it from the outside like a painter with a model: they *create* it; they compose it under our very eyes: henceforth it is a thing which can be observed and learned; the subjective method which he has chosen joins the objective method we spoke about earlier: he ejects the black soul from himself at the very moment when others are trying to interiorize it; the final result is the same in both cases. Negritude is the far-away tam-tam in the streets of Dakar at night; voo-doo shouts from some Haitian cellar window, sliding along level with the roadway; the Congolese mask; but it is also...[a] poem by Césaire,...[a] slobbery, bloody poem full of phlegm, twisting in the dust like a cut-up worm. This double spasm of absorption and excretion beats out the rhythm of the black heart on every page of this collection.

What then, at present, is this negritude, sole anxiety of these poets, sole subject of this book? It must first be stated that a white man could hardly speak about it suitably, since he has no inner experience of it and since European languages lack words to describe it. I ought then to let the reader encounter it in the pages of this collection and draw his own conclusions about it. But this introduction would be incomplete if, after having indicated that the quest for the Black Grail represented—both in its original intention and in its methods—the most authentic synthesis of revolutionary aspirations and poetic anxiety, I did not show that this complex notion is essentially pure Poetry. I shall therefore limit myself to examining these poems objectively as a cluster of testimonies and to pointing out some of their principal themes. Senghor says: "What makes the *negritude* of a poem is less its theme than its style, the emotional warmth which gives life to words, which transmutes the word into the Word." It could not be more explicitly stated that negritude is neither a state nor a definite ensemble of vices and virtues or of intellectual and moral qualities, but rather a certain affective attitude towards the world. (pp. 22-5)

[Here] is what Césaire tells us about it:

> My negritude is not a stone with its deafness flung
>   out against the clamor of the day
> My negritude is not a dead speck of water on the
>   dead eye of the earth
> my negritude is neither a tower nor a cathedral
> it plunges into the red flesh of the ground
> it plunges into the ardent flesh of the sky
> it perforates the opaque pressure of its righteous
>   patience.

Negritude is portrayed in these beautiful lines of verse more as an act than as a frame of mind. But this act is an *inner* determination: it is not a question of *taking* the goods of this world in one's hands and transforming

them; it is a question of *existing* in the middle of the world. (p. 25)

> Jean-Paul Sartre, "Black Orpheus," translated by John MacCombie, in The Black American Writer: Poetry and Drama, Vol. II, edited by C. W. E. Bigsby, 1969. Reprint by Penguin Books Inc., 1971, pp. 6-40.

Robert P. Smith, Jr. (essay date 1972)

[*In the following essay, Smith examines the "rejected" black hero in a selection of works by Césaire, proposing that Césaire's heroes are "very much alike and are really the same character in varying circumstances."*]

During this past decade of great social and political changes, the dramatic works of Aimé Césaire have successfully emerged, and in their own special way have helped to restore serious drama to a place of prominence in today's modern theatre. The foreign public has been made aware of Césaire's dramatic output by a number of articles in foreign periodicals like *Présence Africaine,* excerpts in literary histories, and reviews in such French newspapers as *Le Monde* and *Le Figaro Littéraire.* However a wide audience in the United States has yet to discover the theatrical creations of this Black playwright of French expression from Martinique. He is the creator of a theatre where one discovers a contemporary world in which a new Black hero finds himself liberator, father-king, outcast and sacrificial victim of his people, all at the same time. However this hero welcomes and fulfills his destiny, he analyses himself and becomes aware of the invisible and real forces which bind him to his black brothers, and he accepts the inevitable tragic consequences of his actions because he believes that there is something in life that his people must achieve, something which is more important than his temporary existence among them.

Césaire's Black hero knows that his individual destiny is and must be synonymous with the collective destiny of his people. Here we have a situation involving Blacks, which is often overlooked when one insists on the black-white confrontation in Césaire's works. Without the fanfare that has heralded his aggressive **Cahier d'un retour au pays natal** and the **Discours sur le colonialisme,** four of Césaire's plays have nonetheless made a substantial impact on contemporary French theatre: *Et les chiens se taisaient* (1956); *La tragédie du roi Christophe* (1970); *Une saison au Congo* (1967); *Une tempête* (1969). It is encouraging to know that the second and third plays mentioned above have been admirably translated into English recently by Ralph Manheim for Grove Press. While the world in these plays embraces Black Africa, the Antilles and the imaginary island of Shakespeare's Prospero, Césaire's strong and passionate cry for liberty unites them into one familiar setting where the forces of civilization are at play, and the hero is forced to undertake the superhuman task of liberating his people and teaching them how to remain free in spite of themselves, by erasing as quickly as possible and against crushing obstacles all that reminds them of the centuries of misery and degredation which they have had to endure. An examination of Césaire's plays will reveal that his heroes are very much alike and are really the same character in varying circumstances. They are interesting not only because they are black but because they are human and tragically misunderstood and rejected by those whom they would uplift, their black brothers.

Et les chiens se taisaient, written in 1946 and arranged for the theatre in 1956, is structurally a rather difficult allegorical play about a revolutionist, le Rebelle, who, before confronting a tragic death for having assasinated his slave master, looks back upon his life and relives those moments of emotional stress, conviction and violence which would give meaning to his existence. Fate has not been overly generous towards him in his fight for the recognition of the dignity of his people:

> Et le monde ne m'épargne pas . . . Il n'y a pas dans le
> monde un pauvre type lynché, un pauvre homme
> torturé, en qui je ne sois assassiné et humilié.

Consequently he will die lonely simply because he has outlived his usefulness in a sick universe, but those whom he will leave behind will now recognize and confront more successfully the creator of this world of pestilence, "l'architecte aux yeux blcus." Le Rebelle has lost the confidence of his mother, son and his friends because his executioners, "les hommes aux babines saignantes, aux yeux d'acier," have convinced them that he is a trouble maker and a traitor. He suffers injustice because they have allowed themselves to be misled but he refuses to hate, for he will not exchange roles with his executioners. His only crime was refusing to be a slave once and for all:

> Ah, oui, de cette vie que vous tous m'offrez!
> Merci. Ah c'est cela qui tous vous perd
> et le pays se perd de vouloir à tout prix se justifier
>   d'accepter l'inacceptable.
> Je veux être celui qui refuse l'inacceptable.
> Dans votre vie de compromis je veux bâtir,
> moi, de dacite coiffé de vent,
> le monument sans oiseaux du Refus.

Thus Le Rebelle is relentless in his revolt. In spite of his mother's beseeching he refuses to denounce his vengeful act of murder, and for this reason his appeals for support are rejected by those whom he loves, in the harshest and most cowardly of terms:

> Camarades c'est pour vous dire que cet homme est
> un ennemi public et un emmerdeur. Comme si on
> n'en avait pas assez d'emmerdements? bien sûr qu'on
> était pas heureux. Et maintenant, camarades, est-ce
> qu'on est heureux avec la guere et la vengeance des
> maîtres sur les bras? Alors je dis qu'il nous a trahis.

Nevertheless he faces death proudly without fear and his enemies and ungrateful brothers cannot silence his profound message of hope. He has come amongst his people like a savior, has suffered and will die for them, but not before uttering a last protest intended to rebuke

them as well as incite them to shake off the shackles of slavery:

> Accoudé à la rampe de feu
> les cris des nuages ne me suffisaient pas
> Aboyez tams-tams
> Aboyez chiens gardiens du haut portail
> chiens du néant
> aboyez de guerre lasse
> aboyez coeur de serpent
> aboyez scandale d'étuve et de gris-gris
> aboyez furie des lymphes
> concile des peurs vieilles
> aboyez
> épaves démâtées
> jusqu'à la démission des siècles et des étoiles.

Thus Le Rebelle dies in tragic solitude, but the world of his brothers will no longer be the same, for his great gesture of disapproval has shaken its very foundation.

Encouraged by the need to provide Black heroes for his countrymen, and again by the urge to dramatize the problems of newly independent Black nations, Césaire wrote *La tragédie du roi Christophe* in 1963, a powerful "tragédie de la décolonisation." The Haitian adventure of King Christophe, former slave, cook, general, statesman, evokes the collective destiny of Black Africans today, their rejection of colonialism, their civil wars and their efforts to remain free, strong and progressive:

> Pauvre Afrique! Je veux dire pauvre Haïti! C'est la
> même chose d'ailleurs. Là-bas la tribu, les langues, les
> fleuves, les castes, la forêt, village contre village,
> hameau contre hameau. Ici nègres, mulâtres, griffes,
> marabouts, que sais-je, le clan, la caste, la couleur,
> méfiance et concurrence, combats de coqs, de chiens
> pour l'os, combats de poux!

Thus after the exit of the French masters, Christophe eventually crushes his new opposition, the mulattoes and their chief Petion, and is proclaimed King Henry I. For him liberty is not an easy thing, the black man must work hard if his newly earned dignity is to be lasting.

> Peuple haïtien, Haïti a moins à craindre des Français
> que d'ellemême! L'ennemi de ce peuple, c'est son
> indolence, son effronterie, sa haine de la discipline,
> l'esprit de jouissance et de torpeur.

Therefore the Haitians have no right to be tired, and Christophe swears to save them from themselves and to govern in their best interest, happiness and glory. He hates servile imitation and encourages the development of the national genius. Revolution for him does not consist of taking the place of the white man and having business as usual. All men have the same rights but some have more duties and responsibilities than others, and suffer more than others to retain their rights:

> Et voilà pourquoi il faut en demander aux nègres plus
> qu'aux autres: plus de travail, plus de foi, plus
> d'enthousiasme, un pas, un autre pas, encore un
> autre pas et tenir gagné chaque pas! C'est d'une
> remontée jamais vue que je parle, Messieurs, et
> malheur à celui dont le pied flanche!

However the people, bourgeois and peasant, complain of too much work and wish more rest since the country is now at peace, but Christophe esteems that the national effort must be intensified. They misunderstood his noble intentions and think of themselves only as his slaves, not realizing that it is their inferiority complex and their pessimistic attitude that he detests; not comprehending that the Citadelle which he has had them build is a symbol of their strength and creativity. An insurrection breaks out against the king who now faces his destiny alone, safe for a haunting memory of his former homeland:

> Afrique! Aide-moi à rentrer, porte-moi comme un vieil enfant dans tes bras et puis tu me dévêtiras, me laveras. Défais-moi de tous ces vêtements, défais-m'en comme, l'aube venue, on se défait des rêves de la nuit... De mes nobles, de ma noblesse, de mon sceptre, de ma couronne. Et lave-moi! Oh, lave-moi de leur fard, de leurs baisers, de mon royaume! Le reste, j'y pourvoirai seul.

Therefore the feeble, paralysed but proud king commits suicide and leaves behind him the everlasting title of "homme reculeur de bornes, homme forgeur d'astres."

Césaire presents a vivid word portrait of the late Patrice Lumumba, first prime minister, hero and martyr of the former Belgian Congo, in *Une saison au Congo,* which first appeared in 1966 and was created on the stage on October 4, 1967. In the wake of the regained independence for nations in Africa, accompanied at times by unrest, revolution, clashes of cultures and political intrigue, Césaire has found it necessary to dramatize the life of one of Africa's leading political figures. In the play we see a Lumumba not unlike Christophe, for he too realizes that freedom and independence must be accompanied by responsibility, and he demands that his people work arduously for the future of their country, putting unity above all political ambition. He is a tireless worker and expects the same diligence on the part of his ministers and his followers:

> Oui, c'est ça, il paraît que je veux aller trop vite. Eh bien! Bande de limaçons, oui, il faut aller vite, il faut aller trop vite. Savez-vous combien j'ai de temps pour remonter cinquante ans d'histoire? trois mois, messieurs! Et vous croyez que j'ai le temps de ne pas aller trop vite!

Thus his countrymen, having been slaves for others, must now be slaves for themselves, for independence is no easy matter when it is threatened both from within and without. Lumumba's task is a lonely one and he is misunderstood by all: his friends, the clergy, the United Nations, and threatened by the Belgian plot:

> Congolais, c'est ce complot qu'il faut briser, comme on brise dans l'eau, les pattes de la grenouille. Congolais, allez-vous laisser assassiner notre indépendance si chèrement conquise? Et vous, Africains, mes frères, Mali, Guinée, Ghana, vers vous aussi, pardelà les frontières du Congo, nous crions. Afrique! Je te hurle!

Nevertheless he is feared by those who could serve the Congo best were they his allies. President Kala thinks of him as a goateed devil, a hothead to whom it is not easy to say no. His once trusted friend Mokutu tells him that he has been a luxury that the Congo can no longer afford. However Lumumba is the man of Africa who likes dreams. He is the man of words and he uses those words to cry out for liberty, to sing the beautiful song of Africa, to accuse the white man of having confiscated God for his own benefit, and of having robbed Africa of herself:

> C'est pourquoi je ne me veux ni messie ni mahdi. Je n'ai pour arme que ma parole, je parle, et j'éveille, je ne suis pas un redresseur de torts, pas un faiseur de miracles, je suis un redresseur de vie, je parle, et je rends l'Afrique à elle-même! Je parle, et je rends l'Afrique au monde! Je parle, et, attaquant à leur base, oppression et servitude, je rends possible, pour la première fois possible, la fraternité!

Thus he is a part of and shares the vital force of Africa with his brothers. Césaire reinforces this striking element in the hero's character by making of him finally a man of peace. Patrice no longer wants bloodshed on his account. He is not a religious man, but he is convinced that justice cannot be won by violence. He evokes the memory of Gandhi after being told by one of his loyal friends that non-violence in his situation is suicide. It is ironical that Lumumba who is now a convincingly non-violent hero, dies a most brutal and tragic death, beaten and driven through with a bayonet by the savage M'siri, and then shot by a white mercenary, all because he dared to oppose everything that stood in the way of national unity in the Congo. Before he dies however he bravely defies his political enemy M'siri, whom he considers to be an invention of the past, unlike himself, an inventor of the future. He knows that the tide of liberty cannot be stopped, and even while dying he remains the man of forceful words, the man of Africa:

> Je serai du champ; je serai du pacage
> Je serai avec le pêcheur Wagenia
> Je serai avec le bouvier du Kivu
> Je serai sur le mont, je serai dans le ravin.

Thus this alienated hero dies like a prophete of freedom whose spirit of liberty will always be among his people.

Une tempête created in 1969 for a black theatre, is Aimé Césaire's adaptation of Shakepeare's *The Tempest*. In this play the relationship between Prospero and Caliban is greatly enlarged, the former becomes a ruthless and selfish white master and the latter a shrewd and impatient black slave who wants "freedom now." Ariel becomes a mulatto slave "à patience d'oncle Tom;" and a new character is added, Eshu, a black god, "dieu-diable nègre," who amuses and then outrages assembled guests by his frankness and vulgarity. The militant black hero Caliban rejects the language, the name and the philosophy of servility which Prospero has given to him: "tu m'as volé et jusqu'à mon identité," says he to Prospero. In answer to his passive mulatto brother Ariel, who finds him too restless and impetuous and implores him to seek to change his condition through peaceful means, which include appealing to Prospero's conscience, he says:

> Mieux vaut la mort que l'humiliation et l'injustice... D'ailleurs, de toute manière, le dernier mot m'appartiendra... A moins qu'il n'appartienne au néant. Le jour où j'aurai le sentiment que tout est perdu, laisse-moi voler quelques barils de ta poudre infernale, et cette île, mon bien, mon oeuvre, du haut de l'empyrée où tu aimes planer, tu la verras sauter dans les airs, avec, je l'espère, Prospero et moi dans les débris. J'espère que tu goûteras le feu d'artifice: ce sera signé Caliban.

Consequently Caliban thinks of Prospero as an old ruffian who will never have a conscience, who lives by crushing others, and who does not know the meaning of the word fraternity. He has litte regard for the non-violent Ariel, even though they are brothers in slavery, suffering and hope, because their tactics are different. Caliban wants to take back his island from Prospero and reconquer his liberty at any cost. "Ce n'est pas la paix qui m'interéresse, tu le sais bien. C'est d'être libre. Libre, tu m'entend." Ariel has been a faithful servant to Prospero, and a party to all the master's machinations. For this he is finally granted his freedom, and he is as grateful as a child who has acquired the forbidden delicacy that he has always wanted. Caliban has failed in his loosely organized revolt against Prospero and is expected to beg for his freedom by speaking in his own defense. This he will not do: "Je ne tiens pas du tout à me défendre. Je n'ai qu'un regret, celui d'avoir échoué." He hates Prospero's condescension, his hypocricy, his world, "le vieux monde foire." He predicts that Prospero will send the other visitors back to Milan and will remain on the island to harass him, "comme ces mecs qui ont fait les colonies et qui ne peuvent plus vivre ailleurs." Prospero does not understand Caliban's impelling need to reconquer his liberty in his own way and become master again of his island. He decides to answer Caliban's violence with more violence, and this is his undoing, for the menacing words of the slave become a painful reality for the deluded master:

> Mais ta force, je m'en moque,
> comme de tes chiens, d'ailleurs,
> de ta police, de tes inventions!...
> C'est parce que je sais que je t'aurai.
> Empalé! Et au pieu que
> tu auras toi-même aiguisé!
> Empalé à toi-même!

Thus once again Caliban's song of liberty resounds throughout the enchanted island, his homeland which he can now call again his own.

In giving such intimate and at the same time grandiose portraits of his black heroes, Aimé Césaire enchants us with his powerful, poetic, captivating and thought provoking words. We witness his intense, passionate and black revolution as he presents these heroes who are more sensitive than others to the misfortunes, injustices and absurdities of life. They evoke sympathy. They cannot accept mediocrity, lethargy, cowardice, disunity,

servile imitation and lack of perseverance, and thus they become outsiders. Though scorned by their brothers they seek to inculcate in them nonetheless a spirit of unity and nationalism, and by so doing they rise above those who would oppress and reject them and they are worthy heroes to the very end. They do not run and hide from their destinies, but on the contrary they sacrifice their lives for a cause in which they believe. They protest against slavery and refuse an old and corrupt world replete with social injustice. In the words of Caliban, they reject the cruel and unjust labels which have been affixed to them from generation to generation:

> Et tu m'as tellement menti,
> menti sur le monde, menti sur moi'même,
> que tu as fini par m'imposer
> une image de moi-même:
> Un sous-développé, comme tu dis,
> un sous-capable,
> voilà comment tu m'as obligé à me voir,
> et cette image, je la hais! Et elle est fausse!
> Mais maintenant, je te connais, vieux cancer,
> et je me connais aussi!

Thus they may be physically defeated for the moment by this imperfect world, but because these heroes have unshakable faith in the future their intransigent spirit lingers on through slavery and colonialism (Le Rebelle), revolt and independance (Christophe), neo-colonialism and civil war (Lumumba), victory and total freedom in communion with nature, after a permanent rejection of all that is synonymous with the oppressor (Caliban). Aimé Césaire speaks through his misunderstood and rejected heroes and he shares their desire to modify the destiny of their people, for the author and his heroes are one in voice and spirit. Césaire himself has said of his dramatic works: "C'est un peu le drame des nègres dans le monde moderne." (*Le Monde*, 7 October, 1967, p. 14). Indeed, the theatre of this committed poet of protest is truly a commentary on the modern world, black and white.

Robert P. Smith, Jr. "The Misunderstood and Rejected Black Hero in the Theatre of Aimé Césaire in CLA Journal Vol. XVI, No. 1, September, 1972, pp. 7-15.

Alfred Cismaru (essay date 1974)

[*In the following essay, Cismaru explores the concept of negritude as it appears in* Return to My Native Land, Discourse on Colonialism, The Tragedy of King Christophe, *and* Soleil cou coupé.]

As soon as one begins to read Césaire, it becomes obvious that for him, unlike prose, poetry begins with extreme positions and espouses easily the most unexpected exaggerations. Giving himself entirely to the ancestral appeal of mother Africa, the poet often views *négritude* as virtue and whiteness as evil. His lyrical confrontation between white technology and black innocence has a quality of spontaneity about it, at once conquering and destructive. Moreover, his verbal in-candescence appears to evoke a surrealistic language saluted by André Breton himself, who saw in *Cahier d'un retour au pays natal* "the greatest lyrical monument of our time ... transcending with every line the fear that the Black have for the Black who are imprisoned in a white society, identifying with this fear and becoming one with it, causing all poets to become one with it, all artists and all thinkers, by furnishing to them the bait of his verbal genius, and by making them all aware that the condition at the basis of this fear is as intolerable as it is changeable."

"Europe is indefensible," Césaire boasted once, at a time when he was closer to the tenets of the Communist Party. His quarrel with the old Continent stemmed, then, from the fact that he equated it with Christianity, which he considered at the source of the White's mania for colonization. "What is most responsible for the situation is Christian pedantry," he stated in his now famous *Discours sur le colonialisme:* for "it advanced the dishonest equations: Christianity = civilization; pagan-ism = savagery." While admitting that exchanges be-tween continents and rapports between different civili-zations constitute the very oxygen of progress, Césaire denies that colonization did any good for the Black. Instead of human contact, what had happened, Césaire maintains, were simple liaisons of domination and of submission. To the White's statistics on roads, canals and railroads, he responds with lyrical pleas concerning the thousands of men sacrificed to the Congo-Océan and to the harbor of Abidjan dug by hand by generations of Blacks. But it is especially when he uses the device of causticity that his rebellion appears particularly effec-tive. Such sentences as: "Neither Deterding, nor Royal Dutch, nor Standard Oil will ever console me for the loss of the Aztecs nor of the Incas," are effective precisely because they tend to distract the listener and the reader from content: how can it be proved that Royal Dutch or Standard Oil had anything to do with the disappearance of ancient civilizations?

But the *Discours sur le colonialisme* is not always dubious in content, nor sarcastic in style. When violent rebellion gives way to a more sedate approach, Césaire does manage to make some very good points. For example, in answer to some detractors, such as Roger Caillois, Emile Faguet and Jules Romains, he counters with a number of indisputable facts. To the often-made charge that "The black race has not yet yielded nor will ever give us an Einstein, nor a Stravinsky, nor a Gershwin," he lists a number of achievements attribut-able more or less directly to men of his heritage: "For example, the invention of arithmetic and of geometry by the Egyptians. For example, the discovery of astronomy by the Assyrians. For example, the appearance of Rationalism in the bosom of Islam at the time when western thought was furiously pre-logical."

Nevertheless, if in the past the Blacks constituted a proud and productive race, in more recent times it bent and submitted cowardly to foreign interventions and assimilation efforts. This is a theme which constantly lards the *Discours sur le colonialisme* and which reap-pears in a number of recent plays by Aimé Césaire. It should be noted immediately, however, that the poet's switch to the theatre did not really constitute an unusual metamorphosis. In writing for the stage he conserved intact the vigor of his poetry, his predilection for lyrical outbursts, and the use of Claudelian verset. Yet, in an unusual combination at which probably the Catholic poet would shiver, Claudel joined Brecht in Césaire's theatre. Let us mention for example *La Tragédie du roi Christophe* (1964), which takes place in Haiti at the beginning of the nineteenth century, and which seizes poignantly the aspirations of a Negro leader at first hailed by his people, then abandoned by them when it becomes obvious that freedom can only be secured at the cost of blood and tears. An even more striking example of the unusual fusion between Claudel's vocab-ulary and Brecht's propagandistic exhortations occurs in *Une Saison au Congo,* a play which follows closely the events which tore apart the Congo in 1960, and which lead to the assassination of its prime minister, Patrice Lumumba. The dominating figure of the African leader captures the imagination of spectators and readers to whom he is depicted as a misunderstood and solitary savior. Listen for example to Lumumba's lyrical hymn which evokes the birth of the Congo out of the ashes of an enslaved past:

> Congolese, today is a great day because for the first time in a long time we see daylight! It is the day when the world receives, among other nations, the Congo, our mother, and especially the Congo, our child. The child of our waiting, of our suffering, of our struggle. Comrades and fellow soldiers, may each of our wounds become a breast, may each of our thoughts, each of our hopes turn into a whip ... I should like to be a *toucan*, the beautiful bird, in order to fly across the skies, and to announce, to races and languages, that our Congo has been born.

And there are, of course, numerous other examples one could select in this and other plays by Césaire in which he combines successfully a majestic and violent lyricism which re-assembles Claudelian tones, with those of the tam-tam African rhythms. Part of the attraction of this fusion, experienced even by those of different political persuasions, is in the fact that it recalls chant, mime, and dance, that is to say the traditional African culture which is essentially one based on oral and gesture communication. Moreover, this style is capable of expressing in a foreign language the divinations and the prophecies of the African temperament. The poet, synthesizing and synchronizing, manages to collect and to concretize a catching unity of great pulsations in which the *I* and the world are soldered into a mystical and quasi-erotic symbolism. In order to reach such an effect, Césaire's genius finds a heretofore unexplored poetical expression, namely that of Claudel and Brecht mingled into a single voice: the most patented, partisan politics explicated in terms of motherhood ("the Congo, our mother ... our child"); physical and spiritual inju-ries ("our wounds") evoking a most intimate part of the body ("breast") which is reminiscent of motherhood and nourishment; cogitation ("our thoughts") and expectations ("our hopes") metamorphosed into an offensive weapon ("a whip").

A Communist who could not stand the orthodoxy of the Communist Party, a Marxist who shook himself lose from Hegelian mechanisms, Aimé Césaire has always managed to hold on to his lyrical exuberance. Moreover, his separation from Europe makes it possible for him to break with clarity and description, and to become intimate with the fundamental essence of things. Under his powerful, poetic eye, perception knows no limits and pierces appearances without pity. Words emerge and explode like firecrackers, catching the eye and the imagination of the reader. He makes use of the entire dictionary, of artificial and vulgar words, of elegant and forgotten ones, of technical and invented vocabulary, marrying it to Antillean and African syllables, and allowing it to play freely in a sort of flaming folly that is both a challenge and a tenacious attempt at mystification. Witness the following little poem, [from **Soleil cou coupé**], picked at random from among dozens which are available in his various collections of poetry;

> *Another Horizon*
> night devil-like stigma
> night telegraphic bushel planted in the ocean
> for the minute love of cetaceans
> night shut
> splendid atelier of maceration
> where with all of the strength of all its savage
> colors flexes the violet muscle of the *aconitum*
> *napallus* of another sun

Its mysterious, cryptic tone notwithstanding, it is clear that the poet has communicated with Night, has identified with it, thus has managed to impart to us a most intimate and unusual experience clad in magic, powerful, and irrepressible vocabulary. Aimé Césaire's ability to convey is, therefore, not limited to topical themes, but it extends to very private and personal feelings enhanced by his genius and projected across the darkness of the world with the ease of a graceful manipulator of *chiaro-oscuros*. An exact accountant of his own suffering, Césaire is mysteriously aware of our own balance sheets on pain. He once stated in a collection, [**Cahier d'un retour au pays natal**] already quoted:

> to go.
> just as there are hyena-men and cancer-men, I
>   shall be a Jew-man
> a Black of austral Africa
> a man-Hindu-from-Calcutta
> a man-from-Harlem-who-does-not-vote
> the hungry man, the insulted man, the tortured
>   man who can be seized at any moment and
>   crushed by blows and killed—killed entirely—
>   without anyone having to give an account to
>   anybody or to apologize to anybody
> a Jew-man
> a pogrom-man
> a young dog
> a beggar . . .

> I shall find the secret of great communications
>   and of great combustions. I shall tell the storm.
>   I shall tell the river. I shall tell the tornado.
> I shall tell the leaf. I shall tell the tree.
> I shall be drenched by all the rains, humectant
>   with all the dews.

Ambitious promises, of course, but Aimé Césaire has been able to deliver. He is a poet's poet when he stays clear of political questions, a tenacious and violent propagandist when the theme requires it. His place in contemporary French letters, already recognized by Sartre and other critics, is assured in spite of the fact that not many agree with his views on Whites in general, nor with his opinions on Europe, in particular. Some have seen a certain amount of naïveté in Césaire's choice of fighting intolerance with intolerance and hate with scorn. For example, speaking of him and of others who follow in his footsteps, Pierre de Boisdeffre remarked [in *Une histoire vivante de la littérature d'au jour d'hui* (1964)]: "In acceding to the conquest of their national *I*, they continue to dream of a universal humanism of which Europe—whose grandeur they do not recognize because they have only seen its oppressive side—gave them the idea in the first place." The Everyman that he is, Césaire the Black, the Jew, the Colonized and the Freed, still uses, of course, a European language as his means of expression. That he is, at this point in history, incapable of admitting or seeing that his taste for freedom comes from the very people who have colonized and subjugated him, is of less importance than the fact that he is eminently able to become incarnated into a number of paradigms which shake the modern world and pain its conscience. Besides, unlike some Black Power advocates, Aimé Césaire sees, of course, the inadequacy of a return to what might be called the museum of African culture: the myriad languages of Africa would limit considerably the reading public of any poet, of any writer indeed. Césaire understood that African and Antillean vernaculars conserve simply an historic importance, and the only way not to have to pit one linguistic group against the other is to rely on French, which has been for so long the official administrative and scholarly language of millions of Blacks. That he does is of benefit to *aficionados* of literature everywhere. (pp. 107-11)

Alfred Cismaru, "'Negritude' in Selected Works of Aimé Césaire," in Renascence, *Vol. XXVI, No. 2, Winter, 1974, pp. 105-11.*

Thomas A. Hale (essay date 1976)

[*In the following excerpt, Hale examines structural elements in* Return to My Native Land *and praises Césaire's use of imagery and language in the work.*]

The effectiveness of **Cahier d'un retour au pays natal** lies in the poet's extremely rich and often novel vocabulary, his dazzling and occasionally surrealistic imagery, and, most importantly, the maintenance of a seemingly unstructured flow of verse and prose narrative. It is perhaps because of the lack of any divisions in the seventy-page poem . . . that critical attention has tended to sidestep to some extent considerations of structure in the work. . . . Césaire has, in fact, imposed a rather clearly-distinguishable structure on this most explosive poem [which] . . . contributes in a rather dynamic fashion to the work's almost hypnotic power. (p. 165)

[It] appears that there is a pattern of both returns and descents, and that this pattern, based on a dialectic of experience and imagination, produces the impetus for a striking metamorphosis of the narrator from observer to messiah. It is this dynamic structure which provides the vehicle for the other elements—imagery, vocabulary, rhythm, etc.—which, together, account for the tremendous impact of the work on readers today.

In the broadest sense, this pattern occurs in what we shall define as the three major parts of the poem: 1) the return to Martinique, 2) the descent into the African past and into the self in an attempt to achieve unity, and 3) the resulting synthesis of these two rather different movements which completes the metamorphosis of the narrator. (pp 165-66)

[The] experience of the first return to Martinique supplies the psychic dynamite to launch the narrator on an imagined second return, a second return which is based on the experience of a first return, but which will go beyond this experience. It is this shift from experience to imagination in the first part of the poem, this action and reaction, which produces the larger shift from the first part to the second part, from an experimental mode to an imaginary mode based solely on the poet's knowledge of an Africa he has yet to encounter.

In the second part, the same quasi-dialectical pattern which characterizes both the basic structure of the poem and the internal dynamics of its first part still holds true. One finds the same sense of action leading to reaction to produce movement towards another level of vision. But here the terms are not Europe and the Caribbean. They are instead collective and individual approaches to coincidence with self, a return through the history of the race, and a descent into the soul. (pp. 168-69)

The narrator stands naked at the end of the second part of the poem, ready for the third and concluding part. Thus, the inner dialectic of his difficulties in the imaginary world of the second part of the poem—his unsuccessful return to Africa and the consequent retreat into the self—provides the impulse to propel him into the most dramatic part of the work, where he will at last complete the metamorphosis from narrator/observer to narrator/messiah. This shift also marks the larger dialectical movement of experience in the first part of the poem to imagination in the second part which, in the third part, will produce a new mode of perception, a surreal or super imagination.

The narrator announces his transformation with a carefully-constructed reversal of the negative values ascribed to his race by the West, a reversal which echoes his earlier manipulation of the adjective white. Begin-

ning with a listing in negative terms . . . , he then goes on to praise in implicitly positive terms the values of those who live in symbiosis with nature. By combining both negative and positive perspectives, he is able to arrive at a critical transfer point, the oft-quoted definition of *négritude. . . . (p. 172)*

Having transformed these negative values into positive values, the narrator is then able to look back upon a Western world which is now in decline. . . .

From this point on, the narrator achieves what he could not do at the end of the second part of the poem. Leaving the alienations of the past behind, he takes flight, leading his people with him on the lustral vehicle of a revolted slave ship, leading them back to Africa. . . . Unlike the premature messiah of the second part of the poem who sought escape in the rhythmic chant of a tourist trade witch doctor, the nearly delirious leader of this last part literally lifts off with a vibrating, hypnotic drumbeat of more significant nature. . . . (p. 173)

The messiah who is at one with his people and their heritage is a far cry from the bitter observer of a silent and degenerating Martinique at the opening of *Cahier d'un retour au pays natal.* The pattern of this metamorphosis may not always be clear amid the rich symbolic geography of the poem. But it is there . . . , and on the broadest scale it is apparent in the quasi-dialectical relationship of experience and imagination in the first two parts which thrusts the narrator into a new mode of perception, into the super imagination of the conclusion. At another level, within each of these three main parts of the poem, the catalytic reactions of the smaller components serve to set off, to ignite these large movements.

The dynamics of this structure reflect Césaire's own violent reaction to his complex sense of alienation, and serve as the medium for his responses. No less than the poet's remarkable imagery, vocabulary, and tone, this pattern contributes dramatically to the magnetic power which has drawn generations of writers and readers to *Cahier d'un retour au pays natal* and which has made it a Third World classic. (p. 174)

> *Thomas A. Hale, "Structral Dynamics in a Third World Classic: Aimé Césaire's 'Cahier d'un retour au pays natal','" in* Yale French Studies *No. 53, 1976, pp. 163-74.*

Hilary Okam (essay date 1976)

[*In the following excerpt, Okam discusses imagery and symbolism in Césaire's poetry.*]

If Aimé Césaire's poetry is difficult to understand, as every student of his works is well aware, it appears to me that the difficulty comes principally from three basic factors. Briefly, these are Césaire's use of highly sophisticated vocabulary that bears witness to his solid literary education, his fixation for tortuous parataxic sentence structure and, what on the surface would appear to be, his cavalier penchant for discordant and disparate images and symbols as vehicles for poetic enunciation. The combination of these characteristics gives rise to poetry that is exceedingly personal in form and overtones despite the poet's avowed posture as the voice of the collective conscience of his people. Another consequence of this poetic aesthetics is that the reader emerges from Césaire's poetry with the distinct impression of having "felt" and "sensed" rather than "understood" what was intended to communicate. (p. 175)

I am strongly persuaded that Césaire's poetic idiosyncracies, especially his search for and use of uncommon vocabulary, are symptomatic of his own mental agony in the search for an exact definition of himself and, by extension, of his people and their common situation and destiny. The torments and agonies of this quest are reflected not only in the tortuous and intractable syntax of his poetry but also in the rarity of the vocabulary that attempts to capture and objectify that definition. Similarly, every image and symbol, no matter how far-fetched or seemingly unrelated but that contributes even ephemerally towards this definition by its suggestiveness and or association of ideas, is exploited to the utmost. (pp. 175-76)

From reading his poetry and contemplating his personal use of imageries and symbols one arrives at the conclusion that Aimé Césaire, among the best of our poets of French-expression, has, if I may paraphrase [Léopold Sédar Senghor, Césaire's friend and contemporary], assimilated but has not been assimilated. In other words, it is clear from his use of symbols and imagery, that despite years of alienation and acculturation he has continued to live in the concrete reality of his Negro-subjectivity. (p. 176)

It is my view that the unique qualities and seemingly disparate character of Césaire's imagery and symbols come from the role played in his poetry by his Negro subjectivity. And if his poetry attains the height of "memorable speech" the reason is to be found in the imaginative relationships he establishes between that subjectivity, defined as thought-reality, and objective reality defined as the observable and tangible phenomena of his world. (pp. 178-79)

[Césaire's subjectivity] is first and foremost black African subjectivity for as he tells us" my country is the 'night lance' of my Bambara ancestors," whose affective participation in and synthesis with the "very movement of the world" constitutes their cardinal philosophical essence. (p. 179)

Césaire's use of imagery and symbols, as vehicles for poetic expression, comes from the relationship he establishes, under the guiding hand of his synthetic Negro subjectivity (that binds and synthesizes), between the various elements that make up the socio-historical and geo-physical milieu in which he lives. To see what happens when this type of alchemy takes place we shall examine his manipulation of an object that has a kind of pervasive presence in the island, namely the sea. Césaire uses the sea as a paradigm to express various and sometimes antithetical thoughts and realities. This is understandable because, in a sense, the Caribbean sea is synonymous with Martinique since without that sea there would be no island that goes by that name. Thus literally the sea makes the island what it is and Césaire therefore exploits the sea-symbol in a variety of ways to depict in what light he sees his island-home at a given time. (p. 180)

The sea in the first part of **"Les Pur-Sang"** and **Débris"** can be seen as having suffered a decrease in its vital force and therefore has lost the power to influence the land. But when the vital force of the sea is on the ascent as in the later section of **"Les Pur-Sang"** it becomes the very symbol of the poet who sees in its largeness and clarity the vastness and purity of his love for mankind.

The essential unity of all things which is apparent in Bantu philosophy of existence permeates Césaire's imagery. In consequence, Western prosodic clichés such as metaphor, simile, allegory and personification, when seen as mere equations and transference of attributes completely fail to explain the complexity of his images . . . .

Césaire's imagery is so informed by this philosophical truth that objects considered inanimate in other cultures and philosophies arise in his poetry as animate objects full of energy and dynamism which, according to circumstances, are either on the rise or on the decline. Smoke like the sea or the sun is infused with force. (p. 184)

Through a conjuration of images drawn from the fauna and flora of his nativeland. Césaire creates the impression of a veritable revolt in which unfortunately the human population stands out as a pitiable foil. Something therefore has gone amiss if that essential unity of all things so characteristic of Negro-African philosophy and so present in Césaire's subjectivity is lacking in the people. It is then the role of Césaire, the educator of his people, to lead the people back to their true personality in order for them to see in the gestures of these plants and animals the rebellion that they should be leading against their oppressors. (p. 188)

It is within the context of the palingenesis of myths and mythology that Césaire's use of them is an apposite poetic mode to articulate the realities of the human condition of the black man. Thus, for instance, Christopher Columbus, that emblem of the triumph of European age of discovery, that personification of European spirit of adventure whose arrival at the shores of the American continent opened the new world to the old, becomes in Césaire's poetry a villain, the inaugurator of the odious slave trade . . . . Why the desecration of the apparently sacred image of Columbus? A reasonable answer is that for Césaire, as the spokesman of the black man whose ancestors were forcibly transported to the new world as slaves, the discovery of the new world was, in fact, the beginning of a calvary. (p. 193)

It is pertinent to emphasize Césaire's use of African cities, empires, legends and civilization as symbols. If in some of his symbols and imagery, Africa features subliminally because it is the source of the Negro-subjectivity that gives them their internal cohesion and relevance, in others Africa emerges concretely in response to the poems' structural and thematic imperatives. It does appear therefore that through the symbols and imagery he employs, Césaire shows himself as a man no longer torn by the agonizing imperatives of two conflicting cultures but as a man whose conscious and subconscious minds merge in their singular focus on Africa as the matrix of his poetic enunciation and source of personal definition. (p. 196)

> Hilary Okam, "Aspects of Imagery and Symbolism in the Poetry of Aimé Césaire," in Yale French Studies, No. 53, 1976, pp. 175-96.

Aimé Césaire with Philippe Decraene (interview date 1981)

[*In the following interview, originally published in French in 1981 in* Le Monde dimanche, *Decraene and Césaire discuss literary influences on Césaire's works. The interview was translated by A. James Arnold in 1983.*]

[Decraene]: *Can you describe briefly your cultural itinerary over the past fifty years?*

[Césaire]: I started with the dominant culture of my day: European culture. Thanks to my contacts with France I broadened that culture. Like everyone else of my generation I read Gide, Proust and Breton.... But to those authors I added Frobenius, let's say, to keep it short.

Like Senghor?

Like Senghor. What we hold in common is the obstinate refusal to be alienated, to lose our attachment to our countries, our peoples, our languages. Moreover, in my case it was the careful cultivation of Africans that protected me culturally. That contact counterbalanced the influence of European culture. Senghor, with whom I lived in the Latin Quarter for practically ten years before the war, held considerable sway over my personal life. Again like him, I did everything in my power to assimilate rather than be assimilated. We are both speakers of French, won over to French culture, but we want to place the **Miraculous Weapons** in the service of our peoples.

Isn't that rather complex?

In some respects I remain attached to European culture and I don't deny it. At the same time my will to put down roots remains fierce. Hegel wrote that the universal isn't the negation of the particular, since one arrives at the universal by exploring the particular in depth.... My own reference point was surrealism, because auto-matic writing allows us to go from the surface to the very depths of things. For me surrealism was the high road to Negritude, since it leads at one and the same time to freedom and to the black man. I'm talking about surrealism as a method, not as a system. And so it was by adopting a European technique—that's the paradox—that I became an African, that I achieved the hoped-for welling up of the black self....

For a young black man is that itinerary still conceivable today?

Where Africa is concerned, I don't know. But for the French West Indies, in the current state of affairs, I see no other possible one. Of course there is an awakening of West Indian identity and the defenders of the Creole language are quite militant about rehabilitating it. But let's be realistic. West Indians can neither ignore nor rewrite their history. The Amerindian, even the Indian component, the African foundation and three centuries of life in common with France, all that makes up an indivisible whole. How do you slough that off, I mean one or another of these elements, without impoverishing reality, without sterilizing it? The wealth and originality of the West Indies are the fruit of that synthesis.

Can you be more explicit about your views on the Creole language?

It is neither a patois nor a dialect. I was among the first in the French West Indies to consider it a language: at one and the same time neo-French and neo-African. Neo-French if one takes into account its fundamental vocabulary. Neo-African also and especially if one considers together its phonetics, conjugation and syntax. A white skin perhaps, but certainly a black soul. In other words, in order to shoulder his total reality the Martinican has a bilingual vocation. This must be the approach then: to proceed from the experience of using two tongues to the acceptance of a true bilingual status, over paths that have yet to be charted.

Are you more especially a poet or a political man?

I have never stopped writing poems, although I don't always publish them. Poetry is my raison d'être, my outlet, my life buoy. My deeper self, my being are expressed through poetry.... As for what's left, I consent to social posturing.... My new collection will be published by Seuil next year. It's called *I, Laminarian.* You know, the seaweed attached to the rock.

Can we talk about your political activity?

I don't consider myself basically a politican. It is more by chance than by vocation that I became a politican, and I say that with both modesty and pride. I have ideas and deeply held political convictions, of course, but I find it hard to go along with an Entertainment State or a Media State. I am not especially ambitious where material things are concerned and no Will to Power drives me really. I came to politics through a process of reasoning rather than through a deep motivation: true life is not in politics....

What do you mean?

I am a committed poet and, let's say (with a smile), "an ethnarch." I wanted—I the great-grandson of a slave—to try to lead a small people that the enormous wave of slavery had vomited up on American soil....

Poet or Chief of State? Poet and Chief of State?

I repeat: basically a poet, but a committed poet. So I don't want to disassociate poetry and action. I could not have lived as just another politician, since my political activity is part of a much larger context. Everything cultural is important in our eyes. Besides, politics wouldn't be worth a scrap of energy if it were not justified by a cultural purpose.

As a poet do you continue to owe a great deal to surrealism?

It would be a mistake to either minimize or deny it, but let's be careful about misunderstandings. I don't disown my past or those who helped me intellectually, whether they be the teachers who prepared me for the École Normale Supérieure or André Breton. But I am not an epigone of the surrealists. I don't have the temperament of a disciple, a clubman, or a sectarian. I'm not a courtier. Intellectually speaking, I consider myself to be a black rebel. You know, the ones they called the "maroons" [the name given to fugitive slaves in the West Indies]. Like them I am skittish; I belong to no group, no school, including the surrealists'.

But what about your relationship to Breton's poetry?

During the heyday of surrealism I was a student. Nonetheless, my debt to Breton is great. But when we were preparing our university entrance exams, we were thinking especially about the birth of Negritude; and we reproached Léro and his friends in the *Légitime Défense* movement for having become assimilated without admitting or even knowing it. It seemed to us that they were surrealists as their fathers had been Parnassians, by an act of cultural mimicry. As far as I was concerned, I refused to be a French surrealist, but I borrowed from André Breton a literary technique that doubled as a means of liberation. He taught me sincerity, the love of truth, and authenticity, a word that has been much abused since those days.... (pp. 63-66)

> *Aimé Césaire and Philippe Decraene in an interview, in* Callaloo, *Vol. 6, No. 1, February, 1983, pp. 63-9.*

Marjorie Perloff (essay date 1984)

[*In the following excerpt, Perloff reviews Césaire's* Collected Poetry, *focusing on the author's "violently charged" language.*]

[What] will surely be considered one of the most important translations from the French in 1983 [is Clayton Eshleman and Annette Smith's *The Collected Poetry* by Aimé Césaire].

The appeal of Césaire's poetry depends, I think, on its particular blend of a native's vitalism, a violent energy that celebrates the irrational, the strange, even the bestial, with a French sophistication, wit, and learning. If, as Eshleman and Smith note, the poetry is "a perpetual scene of dismemberment and mutilation," if it goes so far as to celebrate cannibalism as that which "symbolically eradicates the distinction between the I and the Other, between human and nonhuman, between what is (anthropologically) edible and what is not, and, finally, between the subject and the object"..., it is also a self-consciously literary poetry, full of echoes of Rimbaud (especially the Rimbaud of the *Saison en enfer*), Lautréamont, Baudelaire, and Mallarmé. Again, if Césaire's rhythms are influenced by African dances and voodoo rituals, his syntax is so Latinate and his vocabulary so esoteric, that it brings to mind the reference shelf rather than the tribal dance. (p. 43)

Césaire's is nothing if not an explosive poetry. The *Notebook of a Return to My Native Land,* for example, is a 1,055-line exorcism (part prose, part free verse) of the poet's "civilized" instincts, his lingering shame at belonging to a country and a race so abject, servile, petty and repressed as is his. A paratactic catalogue poem that piles up phrase upon phrase, image upon image, in a complex network of repetitions, its thrust is to define the threshold between sleep and waking—the sleep of oppression, the blind acceptance of the status quo, that gives way to rebirth, to a new awareness of what is and may be. Accordingly, it begins with the refrain line, repeated again and again in the first section of the poem. "Au bout du petit matin..." ("At the end of the little morning," a purposely childlike reference to dawn, which Eshleman and Smith awkwardly render as "At the end of the wee hours"), followed by a strophe that characterizes the poet's initial anguish, an anguish always laced with black humour....

Here we have the hallmarks of Césaire's style: impassioned direct address ("Va-t'en"), name-calling ("gueule de flic," "gueule de vache"), parallel constructions that aren't quite parallel ("less larbins de l'ordre et les hannetons de l'espérance"), hyperbole ("la force putréfiante des ambiances crépusculaires"), oxymoron ("dans mes profondeurs à hauteur inverse du vingtième étage des maisons les plus insolents"), violent imagery ("sacré soleil vénérien"), and above all the chant-like rhythm created by the repetition of word and sound, as in "je nourrissais...je délaçais...j'entendais" or in "de l'autre côté du désastre, un fleuve de tourterelles et de trèfles."

There is really nothing comparable to this mode in American poetry. In the long catalogue poems of Allen Ginsberg and Imamu Baraka, we find similarly impassioned repetition, parallelism, hyperbole; again, in a sequence like Galway Kinnell's *The Book of Nightmares,* we meet imagery of perhaps equal violence and stringency. But Césaire's poetry is quite different from Ginsberg's on the one hand or Kinnell's on the other in its curious conjunction of an intense realism (in the course of the *Notebook,* the topography of Martinique, its climate, architecture, and inhabitants are graphically described) with a surrealism that seems so inevitable it may almost escape our attention.

Who is it, for instance, that the poet meets "Au bout du petit matin"—a cop or a "bedbug of a petty monk"? Or both? If the former, then the paradise lost he cannot attain is one of a primitive society that had not learned the need for law-enforcement. If the latter, the enemy is primarily Christianity. These are, of course, part and parcel of the same complex for Césaire, but the point I am trying to make is that his is a language so violently charged with meaning that each word falls on the ear (or hits the eye) with resounding force. (p. 44)

What strikes me as especially remarkable [in *Cahier d'un retour au pays natal*] and in Césaire's surrealist lyrics in *Les Armes Miraculeuses* . . . of 1946 is the total absence of sentimentality or self-pity. He can see himself as [victimized] . . . without casting about for a scapegoat. For, as the "I" comes to realize in the course of the poem, "Nous vomissure de négrier" ("We the vomit of slave ships") must exorcise our own cowardice, fear, and hypocrisy before change can take place. . . . (p. 45)

*Marjorie Perloff, "The French Connection,"
in* The American Poetry Review, *Vol. 13,
No. 1, January-February, 1984, pp. 40-5.*

Hunt Hawkins (essay date 1986)

[*In the following excerpt, Hawkins offers an overview of Césaire's play* The Tragedy of King Christophe, *describing it as "a study of bad decolonization."*]

Aimé Césaire's play *La Tragédie du Roi Christophe,* generally regarded as his theatrical masterpiece, deals with events which took place in Haiti at the beginning of the nineteenth century. It is clear, however, that Césaire's concern is not strictly historical, as is evidenced by the several liberties which he takes with historical fact. Rather, Césaire obviously chose to portray the difficulties following Haitian independence because of their similarity to problems involved in the ongoing decolonization of Africa at the time the play was published in 1963. Thus, in dramatizing Christophe's unfortunate rule, Césaire's purpose was at once didactic and hortatory.

La Tragédie du Roi Christophe is the story of a bad decolonization, one in which the old colonial structures are used rather than shattered. Christophe, an ex-slave and ex-cook, became a general in Toussaint L'Ouverture's uprising against France. After L'Ouverture's death, he assumed control over the northern section of Haiti. Christophe imitates European institutions by crowning himself king, creating a native aristocracy, and turning the former colonial plantations into aristocratic estates. The oppressed, overworked peasants are left essentially the same as before. Thus in his well-intentioned but misguided, futile, and tragic attempt to establish a sense of self-worth denied by colonialism, Christophe ends up perpetuating the very colonial institutions which had been imposed by France.

It is remarkable that a number of critics have failed to see Césaire's criticism of Christophe. Like Christophe himself, they blame his failure on the recalcitrance of his subjects rather than on his own continuance of colonial methods. Thus Robert P. Smith, Jr., classifying Christophe as a "misunderstood and rejected Black hero," says that his subjects "misunderstand his noble intentions and think of themselves only as his slaves" [see excerpt dated 1972]. The Ivory Coast critic B. Kotchy-N'Guessan says that "the people do not yet understand that the construction of the citadel requires their complete abnegation." And Seth L. Wolitz [in his 1969 *Kentucky Romance Quarterly* article "The Hero of Negritude in the Theatre of Aimé Césaire"] categorizes Christophe as a "Hero of Negritude" who "as leader, or better dictator of the people, must force his people to accept the responsibility and challenge of liberty." But supposedly "the people, irresponsible, unable to perceive the future, prefer what Christophe calls 'la liberté facile' posited by their real enemies. The people, then, betray their leader and their independence."

More careful reading of the play reveals that Césaire criticizes Christophe on many counts. The failure of the people to support Christophe is not due to their "irresponsibility" and "laziness" but rather to their rightful rebellion against the perpetuation of colonial structures. Césaire's objections to Christophe may be ranged under three headings. First, the king is so obsessed with the European opinion of his people that he can only think of molding his nation according to European norms. In the play, Vastey, Christophe's minion, tells a crowd.

> Le monde entier nous regarde, citoyens, et les peuples pensent que les hommes noirs manquent de dignité! Un roi, une cour, un royaume, voilà, si nous voulons être respectés, ce que nous devrions leur montrer.

Thus Christophe does not think primarily of what actions might establish the dignity of the people in their own minds but rather now Europeans might be made to regard them as dignified. As Abiola Irele notes [in the 1968 *West Africa* article "Post-Colonial Negritude: The Political Plays of Aimé Césaire"], "Christophe's intention in establishing a monarchy . . . is not so much to identify himself with the aspirations of his own people as to justify them, with the outer forms that contemporary 'respectable' manners and opinions both offered and approved, in the eyes of the world, especially the former colonial master."

Césaire clearly mocks these strictly imitative attempts as foolish and futile. The nobles of Christophe's court are given titles such as the Duke of Lemonade, the Marquis of Downwind, the Duke of Fatso, and the Count of Stinkhole. Vastey maintains that "les Français ont bien le duc de Foix et le duc de Bouillon," but the Europeans are not likely to take this upstart nobility seriously even without its verbal silliness. Césaire's spokesman at this point is surely Magny, who says flatly of these titles: "Que signifie ce galimatias?" Even worse than their pretentiousness, these European distinctions require the suppression of the true nature of the Haitians as Césaire perceives it. Far from being a "Hero of Negritude," Christophe is shown as hindering it. When the Master of Ceremonies instructs the court how to walk, he tells them to avoid "la nonchalance désinvolte, les pieds africains et les bras créoles."

Césaire's second criticism of Christophe is more material. Under Christophe's program, the living conditions of the mass of the people stay the same as during colonialism, or even grow worse. Because there is no land reform, the peasants remain tied to their former plantations. One peasant remarks,

> Mais je me dis comme ça que si nous avons rejeté les Blancs à la mer, c'était pour l'avoir à nous, cette terre, pas pour peiner sur la terre des autres, même noirs, l'avoir à nous comme on a une femme, quoi!

Christophe's quest for dignity has no immediate significance for these workers, especially if it means the creation of a new class system in which they are again at the bottom and deprived of resources. The same peasant goes on to say, "C'est pas de l'orgueil, qu'il faut avoir . . . mais la compréhension." The peasants demand tangible land reform rather than the hollow pride offered by Christophe.

In his desire to build up his kingdom, Christophe insists that his subjects work. He fails to see that the peasants have little motivation if they are laboring on someone else's property rather than their own. Like the former French slaveowners, Christophe comes to the conclusion that his people are lazy and undisciplined: "L'ennemi de ce peuple, c'est son indolence, son effronterie, sa haine de la discipline, l'esprit de jouissance et de torpeur." He decides, again like the colonialists, that the people must be driven by force.

Césaire's criticism of Christophe at this point is remarkably similar to that made by his Martinican compatriot, Frantz Fanon, about the group he called "la bourgeoisie nationale," the ruling élite of the newly independent African countries. Although "la bourgeoisie nationale," according to Fanon, retains close economic ties with the former mother-country instead of severing relations like Christophe, this group still closely resembles the Haitian monarch in its goals and attitudes. Specifically, it insists that the recalcitrant citizenry be driven to work to build up the nation. In *Les Damnés de la terre [(1970)]*, published two years before *La Tragédie du Roi Christophe,* Fanon says:

> Le colon n'a cessé d'affirmer que l'indigène est lent. Aujourd'hui, dans certains pays indépendants, on entend des cadres reprendre cette condamnation. En vérité, le colon voulait que l'esclave fût enthousiaste. Il voulait, par une sorte de mystification qui constitue l'aliénation la plus sublime, persuader l'esclave que la terre qu'il travaille est à lui, que les mines où il perd sa santé sont sa propriété. Le colon oubliait singuliérement qu'il s'enrichissait de l'agonie de l'esclave. Pratiquement le colon disait au colonisé: 'Crève, mais que je m'enrichisse.' Aujourd'hui, nous devons procéder différemment. Nous ne devons pas dire au peuple: 'Crève, mais que le pays s'enrichisse.'

Like Césaire, Fanon insists on a "good decolonization," one which alters the former colonial attitudes and structures.

The principal work to which Christophe drives his subjects is the construction of the citadel. Even women and children are impressed to carry stones. Christophe maintains that the citadel will have defensive value: "Le rempart sans quoi il serait loisible au faucon de voler à gibier vu." But its remote mountain location would seem to render it impractical for this purpose. Rather, Christophe actually desires the citadel as an inspiring symbol of his people's ability to recover their dignity: "A ce peuple qu'on voulut à genoux, il fallait un monument qui le mît debout . . . . Annulation du négrier!" Christophe fails to realize, however, that instead of elevating his people with the glory of the citadel, he abases them with the slave labor necessary to its construction. Thus the building which is supposed to be a symbol of pride instead becomes an instrument and token of oppression.

Césaire's third, and final, criticism of Christophe is that rather than being the champion of the people as he imagines, the king becomes increasingly isolated in tyrannical egotism. His obsession with raising the people causes Christophe to become separated from them, in fact making him their most dangerous enemy. Césaire's spokesperson on this point seems to be Madame Christophe. She tells her husband that she had pictured a king as a "gros mombin sous lequel se réfugie le bétail assoiffé d'ombre" but Christophe has become "le gros figuier qui prend toute la végétation alentour et l'étouffe!" The King, however, pays no heed to this warning that he has become a fig tree rather than a mombin. In his frustration at his inability to transform his people according to his own conception of dignity, he becomes openly contemptuous of them. His frustration becomes murderous, verging on nihilism. In an odd comic scene in Act II, Christophe has his artillery blow up a peasant who is sleeping when the King thinks he should be working. The action is presented as more frivolous than cruel, but it prefigures Christophe's deliberate murders later in the play, notably that of Archbishop Brelle. At one point Christophe seems to contemplate the destruction of his kingdom as a viable alternative to building it up:

> Ah! Quel métier! Dresser ce peuple! Et me voici comme maître d'école brandissant la férule à la face d'une nation de cancres! . . . Ou bien on brise tout,

ou bien on met tout debout. On brise, cela peut se
concevoir.... Tout par terre, la nudité nue. Ma foi,
une liberté comme une autre.

Such destruction might shatter Christophe's dreams, but
it would provide nihilistic relief from his frustration.

Despite Césaire's criticisms of Christophe for his obsession with European standards of dignity, his failure to
alter the material conditions and class structure of his
country, and his demagogic, nihilistic tendencies, the
playwright does not present the king as a villain. In fact,
Césaire seems quite sympathetic toward Christophe.
Everything the king does springs from altruistic motives; nothing is selfish. One of Christophe's chief goals
is to prevent the French from taking over the country
again. He has a keen sense of this danger: "L'ocelot est
dans le buisson, le rôdeur à nos portes, le chasseur
d'hommes à l'affût, avec son fusil, son filet, sa muse-
lière; le piège est prêt, le crime de nos persécuteurs nous
cerne les talons." And in the play this fear is shown to be
quite justified, not paranoid. A French ship repeatedly
appears at the mouth of the harbor only to be turned
back. Hugonin explains: "C'est le bateau du roi de
France!... Si Monsieur a besoin de triques pour soigner
ses lumbagos, la cale en est pleine."

But while Césaire clearly sympathizes with Christophe's
desire to defend his country, he disagrees with the king's
methods. Just as Christophe has failed to build a citadel
useful for defense, so has he failed to give his people
something to fight for. In retaining the old colonial
structures, the king has merely replaced white faces with
black ones at a certain level in the system of exploitation. For the peasants, Christophe and the Europeans
are virtually interchangeable. Thus, it would not be
inconceivable for the French to return and reclaim the
slot as oppressor which Christophe has maintained. To
truly protect the country, Christophe must give his
people something to fight for by providing them with
tangible property and, more importantly, by changing
their consciousness so they see themselves as free
citizens rather than servants in their own land.

The other chief motive for Christophe's actions is his
overwhelming sense of the past humiliations inflicted
on his people. In a moving speech to his wife Christophe
says:

> A qui fera-t-on croire que tous les hommes, je dis
> tous, sans privilège, sans particulière exonération,
> ont connu la déportation, la traite, l'esclavage, le
> collectif ravalement à la bête, le total outrage, la vaste
> insulte, que tous, ils ont reçu, plaqué sur le corps, au
> visage, l'omni-niant crachat! Nous seuls, Madame,
> vous m'entendez, nous seuls, les nègres! Alors au
> fond de la fosse! ...Et si nous voulons remontrer,
> voyez comme s'imposent à nous, le pied qui
> s'arcboute, le muscle qui se tend, les dents qui se
> serrent, la tête, oh! la tête, large et froide! Et voilà
> pourquoi il faut en demander aux nègres plus qu'anx
> autres.

Christophe wants to insure that such humiliation will
never be inflicted again. He wants to guarantee that "il

n'y ait plus de par le monde une jeune fille noire qui ait
honte de sa peau et trouve dans sa couleur un obstacle à
la réalisation des vouex de son couer." And he has a
terrible feeling of urgency. Whereas other peoples have
had centuries to achieve their success, Christophe asks,
"Où est pour nous le salut, si ce n'est ce que nous feron
nous—à grands coups d'années, à grands ahans
d'années?"

Césaire surely agrees with Christophe's disire to overcome past racial humiliations, to prevent future ones.
But, as we have seen, the playwright disagrees with the
king's methods. Christophe will never be able to accomplish his ultimate goals unless he allows his people to
discover their own sense of self-worth. They will never
achieve dignity so long as he imposes European standards on them, retains the European system of property
relations, and insists that he alone is capable of rule. The
mode of Césaire's play, then, as the title indicates, is
tragedy. Christophe is not an evil man. Rather, he is a
strong, brave, and noble man, a man capable of challenging the forces of nature and the gods, a man with
good intentions who finally destroys himself. His tragic
flaw is the inability of his imagination "de briser de
manière définitive les structures coloniales." This flaw
leads him to oppress his people instead of helping them.
Consequently his supporters desert him, his mind
becomes haunted, and he finally kills himself.

While Césaire's play is a tragedy, however, it differs
from classical tragedy in that the hero's actions are not
seen as fated. While Christophe's feelings of past
humiliation and present jeopardy powerfully impel him
on the course he takes, he does have a choice. In
Césaire's next play, *Une Saison au Congo* (1966), the
playwright shows the hero, Patrice Lumumba, deciding
to break the old colonial structures even in the face of
overwhelming opposition. Lumumba declares:

> Camarades, tout est à faire, ou tout est à refaire, mais
> nous le ferons, nous le referons. Pour Kongo! Nous
> reprendrons les unes après les autres, toutes les lois,
> pour Kongo! Nous réviserons, les unes après les
> autres, toutes les coutumes, pour Kongo! Traquant
> l'injustice, nous reprendrons, l'une après l'autre
> toutes les parties de vieil édifice, et du pied à la tête,
> pour Kongo!

In contrast, Christophe "ne songe qu'à utiliser...les
structures coloniales." Césaire's lesson in *La Tragédie du
Roi Christophe* is that, however uncertain the outcome
of creating new structures might be, the choice to retain
the old colonial structures is doomed to failure and can
only result in tragedy. (pp. 145-53)

*Hunt Hawkins, "Aimé Césaire's Lesson
About Decolonization in 'La Tragedie Du
Roi Christophe'," in CLA Journal Vol. XXX,
No. 2, December, 1986, pp. 144-53.*

FURTHER READING

Arnold, A. James. *Modernism and Negritude: The Poetry and Poetics of Aimé Césaire.* Cambridge: Harvard University Press, 1981, 318p.

Discusses Césaire and his poetry, focusing on social, political, historical, and literary contexts.

Breton, André. Review of *Return to My Native Land,* by Aimé Césaire. *Hémisphères* (Fall-Winter 1943-44): 8-9.

Reviews *Return to My Native Land,* praising it as "the greatest lyrical monument of our time."

"Aimé Césaire, Caribbean Poet." *Callaloo* 6, No. 1 (February 1983): 61-136.

Special section profiling Césaire and his works. Contains essays by various authors, including a bio-bibliographical sketch by Thomas Hale and a review of Césaire's major works by Clayton Eshleman and Annette Smith.

Cohn, Ruby. "Black Power on Stage: Emperor Jones and King Christophe." *Yale French Studies* 46 (1971): 41-7.

Summarizes *The Tragedy of King Christophe,* concluding: *"La Tragédie du roi Christophe* is at once a warning and a celebration—a celebration of black independence but a warning against insidious dependence upon white admiration."

Davis, Gregson. Introduction to *Non-Vicious Circle: Twenty Poems of Aimé Césaire,* by Aimé Césaire, translated by Gregson Davis, pp. 3-28. Palo Alto, Calif.: Stanford University Press, 1984.

Brief biography of Césaire, focusing on his literary life.

Frutkin, Susan. *Aimé Césaire: Black between Worlds.* Miami, Fla: Center for Advanced International Studies: University of Miami, 1973, 66p.

Examines Césaire's careers as poet and politician. Introducing her book, Frutkin states: "This is a study of the Martiniquais, Aimé Césaire, black poet and political leader. He is an exceptional product of his race in the modern world. His influence transcends the narrow limits of his island home and reaches beyond his even wider reading public."

Gavronsky, Serge. Review of *The Collected Poetry,* by Aimé Césaire. *The New York Times Book Review* LXXXIX, No. 8 (19 February 1984): 14.

Offers a favorable review of *The Collected Poetry,* concluding: "With the publication of this collection of Mr. Césaire's poetry, his influence will no longer be limited to negritude. He has found his rightful place among the major French poets of this century."

Charles W. Chesnutt

1858-1932

(Full name Charles Waddell Chesnutt) American short story writer, novelist, essayist, journalist, and biographer.

Chesnutt was the first black American fiction writer to receive critical and popular attention from the predominantly white literary establishment and readership of his day. He is especially noted for short stories in which he conveyed implicit denunciations of slavery while appealing to readers of Plantation School fiction—fiction by white authors who wrote nostalgically of the antebellum South. Chesnutt also wrote overtly didactic short stories and novels with racial themes, advocating in particular the cause of mixed-race Americans, but the unpopularity of these perceptive works virtually ended Chesnutt's literary career.

Chesnutt was born in Cleveland, Ohio, to free parents of mixed racial heritage, and raised in Fayetteville, North Carolina. An excellent student, he became at the age of fourteen a pupil-teacher at the State Normal School for blacks. He taught elsewhere in North and South Carolina before returning to Fayetteville in 1877 to become assistant principal, and then principal, at the State Normal School. In 1878 he married; seeking more profitable employment to support his growing family, he worked briefly as a reporter for a New York newspaper before settling his family in Cleveland in 1884 and taking a job as a clerk and stenographer in the legal department of a railway company. Stimulated to study law, Chesnutt passed the Ohio bar exam in 1887 and founded a stenographic court reporting service. Although he was light-complected enough to "pass" in white society, Chesnutt never denied his black ancestry and furthermore was unwilling to accept the elitism of the nascent black and mulatto middle class that was then becoming established in the North. Subject to the inequities that befell those of mixed race, he was repudiated by many blacks as well as by whites.

Throughout his life Chesnutt considered pursuing a literary career, both as a means of making a living and with the aim of presenting racial issues from the point of view of a black person. After a few short stories and sketches appeared in local periodicals, his story "The Goophered Grapevine" was published in the *Atlantic Monthly* in 1887. Similar in structure to the Uncle Remus stories of Joel Chandler Harris, "The Goophered Grapevine" begins and ends with a frame narrative—commentary by the white narrator. A white northern couple that has moved to the South encounters Julius McAdoo, a former slave, who regales them with a "conjure tale," or supernatural folktale. An adept raconteur, McAdoo tells the story to entertain the northerners and to influence a decision they are contemplating. Claiming that the vineyard on the plantation that the

couple wishes to buy is under a dangerous "goopher," or magic spell, McAdoo hopes to persuade them not to buy; this would allow McAdoo to continue living on the abandoned plantation and profiting from his illicit manufacture of wine. Although the northerners do not believe the tale of magic, they enjoy the tale-telling and offer McAdoo employment. Similarly, each subsequent conjure story influences the couple in a way that benefits McAdoo. Capitalizing on a vogue for southern local color fiction, Houghton Mifflin published *The Conjure Woman* in 1899. The success of the volume contributed to the decision to bring out a second collection, *The Wife of His Youth, and Other Stories of the Color Line* (1899), that includes stories exploring the divided racial identity of mixed-blood Americans and the impassable racial barriers that prevent blacks from participating fully in the social, economic, and political life of the United States. This collection was less favorably received than Chesnutt's first, drawing criticism for focusing on racial issues that were commonly considered too sensitive for fictional exposition. Three subsequent novels, *The House behind the Cedars* (1900), *The Marrow of Tradition* (1901), and *The Colonel's Dream* (1905), deal at length with such controversial themes as "passing" into white society, miscegenation, and proposed solutions to the racial problems of the South. The novels were unsuccessful financially and have been evaluated by critics as less accomplished artistically than the short stories. Chesnutt encountered increasing difficulties in finding publishers, and although he wrote several novels after *The Colonel's Dream*, these works remain unpublished. While he continued to publish short stories in periodicals, as well as nonfiction essays addressing racial issues, he returned to his court reporting business in 1902 and devoted much of his time to it thereafter. His 1928 award of the Spingarn Medal by the National Association for the Advancement of Colored People was largely due to his literary achievements of several decades earlier. He died in 1932.

With Chesnutt's conjure stories, American readers were presented for the first time with authentic black folk culture. In these works, folktale motifs of magic and the traditional African folk figure of the trickster are cast against a background of the antebellum South. Often the stories are tragic, illustrating the injustice and cruelty of the slave system. The framing device rendered the protest elements of the stories less explicit and therefore, some critics contend, more acceptable to Chesnutt's white readers. The uncompromising racial themes of his second collection and his published novels are presented within no such propitiating format, and critics maintain that in his novels Chesnutt further sacrificed literary artistry to the urgency of his message. Nevertheless, these works are acclaimed for addressing the pressing social problems of race relations in the United States. As the first American author to explore the range of black experience in his fiction, Chesnutt stands at the forefront of an entire generation of black realist authors.

(For further information about Chesnutt's life and works, see *Contemporary Authors,* Vols. 106, 125; *Dictionary of Literary Biography,* Vols. 12, 50; and *Twentieth-Century Literary Criticism,* Vol. 5.)

PRINCIPAL WORKS

"The Goophered Grapevine" (short story) 1887; published in periodical *Atlantic Monthly*
The Conjure Woman (short stories) 1899
Frederick Douglass (biography) 1899
The Wife of His Youth, and Other Stories of the Color Line (short stories) 1899
The House behind the Cedars (novel) 1900
The Marrow of Tradition (novel) 1901
The Colonel's Dream (novel) 1905
The Short Fiction of Charles W. Chesnutt (short stories) 1974; revised edition, 1981

W. D. Howells (essay date 1900)

[*Howells was the chief progenitor of American Realism and one of the most influential American literary critics of the late nineteenth century. Through realism, a theory central to his fiction and criticism, he aimed to disperse "the conventional acceptations by which men live on easy terms with themselves" so that they might "examine the grounds of their social and moral opinions." In the following essay, he reviews Chesnutt's two short story collections,* The Conjure Woman *and* The Wife of His Youth, and Other Stories of the Color Line, *commenting on their literary and racial interest.*]

The critical reader of the story called "**The Wife of his Youth**" ... must have noticed uncommon traits in what was altogether a remarkable piece of work. The first was the novelty of the material; for the writer dealt not only with people who were not white, but with people who were not black enough to contrast grotesquely with white people,—who in fact were of that near approach to the ordinary American in race and color which leaves, at the last degree, every one but the connoisseur in doubt whether they are Anglo-Saxon or Anglo-African. Quite as striking as this novelty of the material was the author's thorough mastery of it, and his unerring knowledge of the life he had chosen in its peculiar racial characteristics. But above all, the story was notable for the passionless handling of a phase of our common life which is tense with potential tragedy; for the attitude, almost ironical, in which the artist observes the play of contesting emotions in the drama under his eyes; and for his apparently reluctant, apparently helpless consent to let the spectator know his real feeling in the matter. Any one accustomed to study methods in fiction, to distinguish between good and bad art, to feel the joy which the delicate skill possible only from a love of truth can give, must have known a high pleasure in the quiet self-restraint of the performance; and such a reader would probably have decided that the social situation in the piece was studied wholly from the outside, by an observer with special opportunities for knowing it, who was, as it were, surprised into final sympathy.

Now, however, it is known that the author of this story is of negro blood,—diluted, indeed, in such measure that if he did not admit this descent few would imagine it, but still quite of that middle world which lies next, though wholly outside, our own. Since his first story appeared he has contributed several others to [the *Atlantic Monthly*], and he now makes a showing palpable to criticism in a volume called ***The Wife of his Youth, and Other Stories of the Color Line;*** a volume of Southern sketches called ***The Conjure Woman;*** and a short life of Frederick Douglass, in the Beacon Series of biographies. The last is a simple, solid, straight piece of work, not remarkable above many other biographical studies by people entirely white, and yet important as the work of a man not entirely white treating of a great man of his inalienable race. But the volumes of fiction *are* remarkable above many, above most short stories by people entirely white, and would be worthy of unusual notice if they were not the work of a man not entirely white.

It is not from their racial interest that we could first wish to speak of them, though that must have a very great and very just claim upon the critic. It is much more simply and directly, as works of art, that they make their appeal, and we must allow the force of this quite independently of the other interest. Yet it cannot always be allowed. There are times in each of the stories of the first volume when the simplicity lapses, and the effect is as of a weak and uninstructed touch. There are other times when the attitude, severely impartial and studiously aloof, accuses itself of a little pompousness. There are still other times when the literature is a little too ornate for beauty, and the diction is journalistic, reporteristic. But it is right to add that these are the exceptional times, and that for far the greatest part Mr. Chesnutt seems to know quite as well what he wants to do in a given case as Maupassant, or Tourguénief, or Mr. James, or Miss Jewett, or Miss Wilkins, in other given cases, and has done it with an art of kindred quiet and force. He belongs, in other words, to the good school, the only school, all aberrations from nature being so much truancy and anarchy. He sees his people very clearly, very justly, and he shows them as he sees them, leaving the reader to divine the depth of his feeling for them. He touches all the stops, and with equal delicacy in stories of real tragedy and comedy and pathos, so that it would be hard to say which is the finest in such admirably rendered effects as **"The Web of Circumstance," "The Bouquet,"** and **"Uncle Wellington's Wives."** In some others the comedy degenerates into satire, with a look in the reader's direction which the author's friend must deplore.

As these stories are of our own time and country, and as there is not a swashbuckler of the seventeenth century, or a sentimentalist of this, or a princess of an imaginary kingdom, in any of them, they will possibly not reach half a million readers in six months, but in twelve months possibly more readers will remember them than if they had reached the half million. They are new and fresh and strong, as life always is, and fable never is; and the stories of *The Conjure Woman* have a wild, indigenous poetry, the creation of sincere and original imagination, which is imparted with a tender humorousness and a very artistic reticence. As far as his race is concerned, or his sixteenth part of a race, it does not greatly matter whether Mr. Chesnutt invented their motives, or found them, as he feigns, among his distant cousins of the Southern cabins. In either case, the wonder of their beauty is the same; and whatever is primitive and sylvan or campestral in the reader's heart is touched by the spells thrown on the simple black lives in these enchanting tales. Character, the most precious thing in fiction, is as faithfully portrayed against the poetic background as in the setting of the *Stories of the Color Line.*

Yet these stories, after all, are Mr. Chesnutt's most important work, whether we consider them merely as realistic fiction, apart from their author, or as studies of that middle world of which he is naturally and voluntarily a citizen. We had known the nethermost world of the grotesque and comical negro and the terrible and tragic negro through the white observer on the outside, and black character in its lyrical moods we had known from such an inside witness as Mr. Paul Dunbar; but it had remained for Mr. Chesnutt to acquaint us with those regions where the paler shades dwell as hopelessly, with relation to ourselves, as the blackest negro. He has not shown the dwellers there as very different from ourselves. They have within their own circles the same social ambitions and prejudices; they intrigue and truckle and crawl, and are snobs, like ourselves, both of the snobs that snub and the snobs that are snubbed. We may choose to think them droll in their parody of pure white society, but perhaps it would be wiser to recognize that they are like us because they are of our blood by more than a half, or three quarters, or nine tenths. It is not, in such cases, their negro blood that characterizes them; but it is their negro blood that excludes them, and that will imaginably fortify them and exalt them. Bound in that sad solidarity from which there is no hope of entrance into polite white society for them, they may create a civilization of their own, which need not lack the highest quality. They need not be ashamed of the race from which they have sprung, and whose exile they share; for in many of the arts it has already shown, during a single generation of freedom, gifts which slavery apparently only obscured. With Mr. Booker Washington the first American orator of our time, fresh upon the time of Frederick Douglass; with Mr. Dunbar among the truest of our poets; with Mr. Tanner, a black American, among the only three Americans from whom the French government ever bought a picture, Mr. Chesnutt may well be willing to own his color.

But that is his personal affair. Our own more universal interest in him arises from the more than promise he has given in a department of literature where Americans hold the foremost place. In this there is, happily, no color line; and if he has it in him to go forward on the way which he has traced for himself, to be true to life as he has known it, to deny himself the glories of the cheap success which awaits the charlatan in fiction, one of the places at the top is open to him. He has sounded a fresh note, boldly, not blatantly, and he has won the ear of the more intelligent public. (pp. 699-701)

W. D. Howells, "Mr. Charles W. Chesnutt's Stories," in The Atlantic Monthly, *Vol. LXXXV, No. DXI, May, 1900, pp. 699-701.*

Richard E. Baldwin (essay date 1971)

[*In the following essay, Baldwin maintains that Chesnutt explored serious racial themes in the dialect stories of* The Conjure Woman.]

In *The Conjure Woman* Charles Chesnutt analyzes with balance and subtlety the paradoxes and tensions of American racial life. The penetrating insights of these stories he never matched in his realistic fiction. Here Chesnutt avoids stifling stereotypes while criticizing the myths of white supremacy and demonstrating the range and quality of black experience. Other early black writers sought to do the same, but not until *Uncle Tom's Children* did any succeed as fully as did Chesnutt, for in **The Conjure Woman** he developed and exploited a finely balanced technique which solved the major artistic problems faced by early black writers.

The central problem was the audience. The reading public was predominantly white, and the audience that most early black writers cared most to reach was white, for it was to whites that they needed to tell the truth about the black experience in America. The need and the difficulty were one, for the problem of the black in America arose from the refusal of whites to perceive black experience accurately, and the artist's task was not simply to present the truth to white minds but to change those minds so that they could perceive the humanity of the black and the inhumanities which he suffered in America. The sentiments of white Americans could easily enough be touched, but the important and difficult task was changing their perceptions. Whites had to be trained to perceive black experience from the black point of view, for until the white man was so changed no serious black literature could receive a hearing because it would not be understood. The situation held dangers for the artist, since the task of reeducating America could not be completed quickly and the pressure of circumstances easily led writers to hasten the process by recourse to the melodramatic moral simplicity of propaganda.

Chesnutt began his career with a clear understanding of the problem and of the necessary response of the artist. In 1880, before he began writing fiction, he noted in his journal that "if I do write, I shall write for a purpose, a high, holy purpose.... The object of my writings would be not so much the elevation of the colored people as the elevation of the whites." A little later in the same entry, in an observation basic to the strategy of **The Conjure Woman,** he noted that in the struggle of the Negro to win "recognition and equality" it was "the province of literature to open the way for him to get it—to accustom the public mind to the idea [of Negro equality]; to lead people out, imperceptibly, unconsciously, step by step, to the desired state of feeling" toward Negroes.

Chesnutt aimed to modify white minds to feel the equality of the black man, and with the conjure tales he developed a perfect vehicle for his artistic needs. Chesnutt's genius shows in the certainty of touch involved in the choice of Uncle Julius as his central character. Choosing a character so close to widely current pejorative stereotypes was a stroke as significant as Wright's choice of Bigger Thomas, for only by confronting and thus destroying the stereotypes could the black artist hope to alter the public mind. Further, Uncle Julius resolves for Chesnutt the black artist's problem of creating a black character in a situation in which significant dramatic incident is possible. To

Cover for Chesnutt's first book.

demonstrate the equality of blacks and whites, a black character must be presented in dramatic conflict with whites in a situation which allows the black not only to survive but to succeed with dignity. The difficulty of imagining such situations was clearly formulated by William Couch, Jr., in an essay on "The Problem of Negro Character and Dramatic Incident" [*Phylon* XI, 1950]: "Serious dramatic situation necessitates consequential action committed by a protagonist with whom we can sympathize and admire. The assumptions of American culture, on the other hand, are not congenial to emphatic and uncompromising action on the part of a Negro. This is especially true when white interests are involved. Therefore, a dramatic situation, capable of producing a powerful effect, will usually suffer a distortion of that effect when the agent of action is a Negro character." In the face of this dilemma black artists have frequently relied on a conflict of virtuous blacks against vicious whites, thus accentuating the dilemma rather than resolving it.

Chesnutt's conjure stories, on the other hand, resolve this basic problem. The tales which Uncle Julius tells stand in the tradition of subterfuge, indirection, and subtle manipulation of whites developed by the slaves as a strategy for surviving in the face of oppression. Chesnutt's conjure stories turn the strategy of "puttin' on ol' massa" into effective dramatic action through parallels and tensions between the frames established by the white narrator and the tales told by Uncle Julius. In **"The Goophered Grapevine,"** Chesnutt's first conjure story, Julius's attempt to use the tale of the goophered grapevine to place a new "goopher" on the vineyard in order to keep the white man from depriving him of his livelihood provides the most obvious parallel between frame and tale. Julius emerges from this dramatic conflict with a qualified success, for while he loses the vineyard he gains a more stable livelihood in the white man's employment.

The limitations of his success are illuminated by another parallel between frame and tale, however. An important part of the tale centers on the experiences of Henry, a slave of Dugald McAdoo, antebellum owner of the vineyard. McAdoo purchased Henry after the success of the fatal conjure Aunt Peggy had placed on his vineyards had so increased his crop that he needed more help. Henry ate some of the grapes before he could be warned of the conjure, and his life was saved by an antidote which involved his anointing himself with sap from one of the vines. From that time on Henry's life followed the rhythms of the growing season; he became strong and supple in the spring and summer, then withered up during the winter months. McAdoo made a great deal of money exploiting Henry by selling him when he was strong and buying him back cheap when he weakened in the fall. During the winter months McAdoo coddled Henry to protect the valuable chattel. Although Henry enjoyed this comfortable life, he was more than ever at McAdoo's mercy, for his life depended on the life of the vineyards. When McAdoo's greed led him to follow foolish advice which killed the vines, Henry paid with his life for his master's folly.

Henry was about Uncle Julius's age when McAdoo purchased him, and the narrator's hiring of Julius ominously parallels that transaction. Julius had been a free entrepreneur, and although his new job may pay more than the vineyard could yield to him, it represents a new form of slavery in which Julius loses a significant measure of his freedom in return for security; Julius's love of grapes, like Henry's, places him in the power of the white man. Yet this judgment must in turn be qualified by the implied parallel between the narrator and McAdoo, for it is obvious that the narrator is in some ways a wiser man than his slave-owning predecessor, a fact which mutes the threatening potential of his hiring of Julius while the mutual service of each to the other emphasizes the ways in which the story demonstrates the inescapable connections between the lives of black and white, a central theme in much of Chesnutt's work.

"The Goophered Grapevine" gains additional richness through the complicated nature of Julius's motivation.

While he wants very much to preserve his vineyard, he simultaneously wants to strike out at the racial superiority assumed by the narrator. The tale which he tells consistently presents white men bested by blacks or acting in ways whose folly is clearly perceived by the blacks. Both in the broad outline of his tale of the goophered grapevine and in numerous minor points, such as the inability of the best white doctors to cure the goopher that Aunt Peggy has placed on Henry, Uncle Julius asserts the humanity of the black and his equality with, or superiority to, whites. Julius thus has the pleasure of effectively calling the white man a fool to his face, yet he fails to make any impression because the narrator is too blinded by racism to be able to perceive what Julius is up to. Ironically, that failure, while it underscores the truth in Julius's point, is vital to his success at preserving his livelihood, since the narrator would not likely have hired Julius had he perceived the insults. The concluding frame thus generates multiple ironies which illuminate the complex tension between the black's need to deny and attack white supremacy and the hard fact that while whites are not superior beings they nevertheless have very real power.

Chesnutt's success in dealing with this tension in *The Conjure Woman* depends not only on the complex motivation of Uncle Julius but also on the two white characters of the frame, the Northern narrator and his wife Annie. The two white people are crucial to Chesnutt's rhetorical strategy for leading white America "imperceptibly, unconsciously, step by step, to the desired state of feeling" toward blacks. The narrator, a basically decent sort of man, takes a typical paternalistic attitude towards Uncle Julius and his tales. He accepts Julius's attempts at manipulating him yet remains blinded by his own sense of superiority. His understanding of black life has been molded more by Uncle Remus and the plantation school than by Uncle Julius. As Julius begins the tale of the goophered grapevine, for instance, the narrator observes that "As he became more and more absorbed in the narrative, his eyes assumed a dreamy expression, and he seemed to lose sight of his auditors, and to be living over again in monologue his life on the old plantation." This evocation of the plantation tradition reveals the narrator's blindness to Julius's revelations about slavery, for life on the McAdoo plantation had nothing of the dreamy quality of the idyls of Harris. The statement becomes richly ironic when the conclusion shows that Uncle Julius has had his eyes very much on his auditors and the demands of the present moment. It is the narrator whose eyes are closed, and in an adumbration of the Invisible Man motif he is "beaten" by a man he never sees.

The narrator's posture has immense rhetorical value for Chesnutt, for it enables him to present his stories with detachment from the point of view of any of his characters. The framing narrative voice is that of a typical white American liberal, an unconscious racist who seems free of bigotry. In his reactions to Julius's tale the narrator is not so dull as to miss all that the black is up to, yet he misses enough that he can report the tale of slavery with no sense of the range of its meaning, especially those portions directed against him. The narrator thus appears as a mixture of sensitivity and callousness, and he can be treated sympathetically while his blindness to Uncle Julius's character and to the implications of his tales provides ironic commentary on his own character and on America's racial absurdities.

Chesnutt's technique relies heavily on irony, and like any ironic technique it runs the risk that readers will miss the point. Annie, the narrator's wife, is developed as a contrasting character in order to reduce this danger. Her permanent convalescent state underscores the feminine sensibility which leads her to respond more deeply to Uncle Julius than does her husband. When Julius announces that the vineyard is goophered, for instance, the narrator observes that "He imparted this information with such solemn earnestness, and with such an air of confidential mystery, that I felt somewhat interested, while Annie was evidently much impressed, and drew closer to me." The narrator's attitude toward his wife frequently is as condescending as his attitude toward Julius, and after the tale is finished he notes that she "doubtfully, but seriously" asked, "'Is that story true?'" His own reaction to the tale appears only in his assertion that he bought the vineyard in spite of the purported goopher. Annie's question, however, allows Chesnutt to imply the presence of metaphoric meanings through the absurd literalness of Uncle Julius's response that he can prove its truth by showing her Henry's grave. At such levels the tale obviously is not true, but the nature of the question and answer implies that other levels of meaning can be discovered by any who care to look for them.

Chesnutt seems not to have fully grasped the value of his white characters when he first wrote **"The Goophered Grapevine,"** for his second conjure story openly exploits the contrast, and when he prepared the first story for book publication he added to the opening frame several long sections which develop the narrator more fully. The opening frame of the second story, **"Po' Sandy,"** points out the difference between the narrator and Annie. When she rises eagerly to Julius's hint of a story, her husband comments that "some of these stories are quaintly humorous; others wildly extravagant, revealing the Oriental cast of the negro's imagination; while others, poured freely into the sympathetic ear of a Northern-bred woman, disclose many a tragic incident of the darker side of slavery." While the narrator has sufficient curiosity to listen to the tales with pleasure he has no patience for discovering meanings in them; rather than revelations about American life he sees only an "Oriental cast of the negro's imagination." Annie, on the other hand, instinctively leaps to at least some meanings. The resulting contrast helps Chesnutt bring a white audience to perceive events from the black point of view, for while the narrator reacts with a typical white obtuseness, Annie, by seeing through the surface of fantastic and supernatural machinery, points the reader to the vital human life behind.

Chesnutt uses this contrast most effectively in **"Po' Sandy."** Uncle Julius's tale tells of Sandy, a young slave devoted to his wife Tenie, a conjure woman. Mars Marrabo continually sends Sandy, an exceptionally good worker, to help out relatives on distant plantations, and when Sandy tires of this Tenie turns him into a tree to keep him near her. When Sandy disappears, the dogs track him to the tree, where they lose the trail. After the excitement of his disappearance passes, Tenie nightly returns Sandy to human form. But then Marrabo sends Tenie to nurse his daughter-in-law, and during her absence Sandy is cut down, and Tenie returns just in time to watch her husband sawn into lumber to build a new kitchen on the plantation. The kitchen remains haunted by Sandy's ghost, so it is eventually torn down and the lumber used to build a schoolhouse. The narrator now plans to tear down the school and use the lumber to build Annie a new kitchen.

After Julius finishes his tale, the following exchange between Annie and the narrator occurs:

> "What a system it was," she exclaimed, when Julius had finished, "under which such things were possible!"
>
> "What things?" I asked, in amazement. "Are you seriously considering the possibility of a man's being turned into a tree?"
>
> "Oh, no," she replied quickly, "not that"; and then she murmured absently, and with a dim look in her fine eyes, "Poor Tenie!"

The narrator as usual sees nothing but the surface of the tale, but with his insensitivity as a contrast Chesnutt needs no more than Annie's murmured "Poor Tenie" to alert us to the story of the pain caused by the inhuman violations of personal life and the brutalities endured by slaves. The narrator believes in the beauty of the Old South and the quaintness of Negro folktales, but through Annie we see the horrors of slavery.

Had Annie's role ended with "Poor Tenie!" the story would have verged on the sentimentality which so quickly destroys the effect of tales of pathos. But the sentimentality of the "dim look in her fine eyes" and the quiet murmur are the narrator's, not Chesnutt's. Annie has a sentimental streak, but Chesnutt nevertheless uses her to help effect a most unsentimental change of tone from the pathos and horror of the tale to the grotesquely incongruous, anticlimactic humor of the concluding frame. Through Annie's agency Chesnutt modulates the story from the grim brutalities of a man sawn into lumber to end on a note of gentle, ironic humor.

The humor of the conclusion is vital to the overall effect of the story, avoiding sentimentality and creating an impact more tautly complex than pathos. The humor of the frame relieves the pain of the tale itself, emphasizing the similar effect created by the incongruity between the horror experienced by the characters of the tales and the improbability of the conjure elements. The final effect has the complexity described by Ralph Ellison as the blues, the transcendence of pain "not by the consolation of philosophy, but by squeezing from it a near-tragic, near-comic lyricism." ["Richard Wright's Blues," in *Shadow and Act,* 1964.] At their best, Chesnutt's conjure stories require a response which sustains that type of tension between the tragic and the comic. The tension is most striking in **"Po' Sandy,"** yet Chesnutt's third conjure story, **"The Conjurer's Revenge,"** exploits it in an equally effective and perhaps more sophisticated way. In **"The Conjurer's Revenge"** the narrator needs a draught animal, and Julius hopes it will not be a mule; he hates to drive a mule for fear it may be a human being, and thereby hangs a tale. The tale tells how Primus, a slave, stole a shoat from a conjure man who revenged the theft by turning him into a mule. A large portion of the tale deals with Primus's escapades as a mule—eating tobacco in the field, guzzling a large quantity of wine, attacking the man who had taken over his woman. When the conjure man neared death he got religion, and feeling guilty about Primus summoned him in order to return him to human form. He lived long enough to turn back all of Primus except for one foot, which remained clubbed.

When Uncle Julius finishes the tale it appears that he knows a man with a horse to sell. Shortly after the narrator buys the horse Uncle Julius sports a flashy new suit, apparently purchased with his share of the money paid for the horse. Within three months, the animal dies of diseases brought on by old age, and while the entire affair makes fine comedy, the comedy has a harsh, vindictive quality unknown in the two earlier tales. The tale itself is a disconcerting mixture of the comic escapades of a man turned into a mule and the story of a slave who, to take the view of Primus's master, "'had runned erway, en stay' 'tel he got ti'ed er de swamps, en den come back on him ter be fed. He tried ter 'count fer de shape er Primus' foot by sayin' Primus got his foot smash', er snake-bit, er sump'n, w'iles he wuz erway, en den stayed out in de woods whar he couldn' git it kyoed up straight, 'stidder comin' long home whar a doctor could 'a' 'tended ter it'." Either way this tale lacks the compelling quality of the tale of Po' Sandy, and Annie's reaction to it is negative: "'That story does not appeal to me, Uncle Julius, and is not up to your usual mark. It isn't pathetic, it has no moral that I can discover, and I can't see why you should tell it. In fact, it seems to me like nonsense'."

There is a moral, although not the sort that would dim Annie's fine eyes. The moral is enunciated by the narrator when, after discovering that the fine looking animal he bought is half blind and thoroughly broken down, he exclaims, "But alas for the deceitfulness of appearances." The story underscores this point. Julius's tale is pointless by comparison with the earlier two, but his telling of the pointless tale was a deceitful appearance intentionally used to cover his own motives and set up the narrator for the sales pitch made at the end.

Chesnutt's concern reaches beyond the sales of horses and mules, though, and **"The Conjurer's Revenge"** provides a broad commentary on the American racial situation. The title suggests that Uncle Julius's intentional swindling of his employer amounts to revenge. As in the tale Primus felt the wrath of the conjure man because he stole a shoat, so in Chesnutt's story the narrator is bilked because Julius has had a valuable possession stolen—the dignity, freedom, and equality which are the components of his humanity—and works a goopher on the white man in revenge. The story focuses on "the deceitfulness of appearances" which lies at the heart of race relations, and in part on the deceitfulness of appearances in Chesnutt's earlier two stories. The earlier stories had glossed the moral turpitude of race relations by implicitly justifying Uncle Julius's behavior—in **"The Goophered Grapevine"** on grounds of practical necessity, in **"Po' Sandy"** on grounds of service to a communal group. **"The Conjurer's Revenge"** strips all romantic gloss from Southern life and presents the hard core of racial conflict, that mutual dehumanization which eliminates all moral compunctions from the black man's dealing with whites and which enables the white man to hide from himself the fact that the black man is a human being. If the white man becomes vulnerable to the deceitfulness of appearances, the appearances are his own creation, the self-delusions spawned by his denial of the black man's humanity. In this situation the black man quite naturally becomes a conjure man, using his wits to exploit and encourage the deceitful appearances which the white man has created. There is nothing moral or pathetic here, just a bald power struggle which is comically, tragically human, the deepest reality of American racial conflict.

Nearly ten years intervened between the publication of **"The Conjurer's Revenge"** and the appearance of *The Conjure Woman* in 1898. None of the additional four stories appeared previously in periodicals; so the sequence in which they were written is unknown. Each of these later stories, while it follows the original frame-tale pattern, reveals Chesnutt reaching the limits of the form's usefulness. The later four stories lack the complex balance of the earlier three. In **"Sis' Becky's Pickaninny,"** for instance, the tight relation between frame and tale is lacking. By itself the tale fails to develop significant dramatic action, and unlike the tale in **"The Conjurer's Revenge"** it is not an integral part of a larger conception. **"Hot-Foot Hannibal,"** on the other hand, has a frame and a tale technically well matched. Here, however, Julius has no significant role in either tale or frame. The parallels between tale and frame thus remain mechanical, and Chesnutt's point seems to be simply to demonstrate by the parallel that blacks feel the same pains, joys, and sorrows as whites. **"Hot-Foot Hannibal"** comes closer than any other conjure tale to the special group pleading of the propagandist.

The weakness of **"Hot-Foot Hannibal"** appears clearly when it is compared with **"The Gray Wolf's Ha'nt."** Nothing in *The Conjure Woman* surpasses Uncle Julius's tale of the gray wolf's ha'nt. This story of love, jealousy, and murder among the slaves achieves tragic stature and has no taint of propaganda. The tale is perfect in itself, but it is badly marred by being forced into a trite and irrelevant frame. The tale deals with conflict within the slave community and lacks the interracial conflict on which vital parallels between tale and frame depended in the three earlier stories. The tale does not need a frame, and its strength indicates that the conjure story could have been developed into a vehicle for exploring black culture. Interracial conflict was essential to the vitality of the form as Chesnutt initially conceived it, however, and his willingness to place this magnificent story in an unsuitable frame suggests that he was uninterested in forms which did not deal with such conflict.

The remaining conjure story, **"Mars Jeems's Nightmare,"** suggests in fact that Chesnutt had reached the limits of the form even as a vehicle for exploring racial conflict. **"Mars Jeems's Nightmare,"** which focuses on racial conflict with the unrelenting rigor of "The Conjurer's Revenge," is the only one of the later stories that creates something like the balanced tone, the intellectual strength, and the imaginative integrity of the early stories. The frame drama centers around Uncle Julius's grandson Tom, formerly employed by the narrator but fired for laziness and carelessness; Julius's aim in telling this tale is to get his grandson rehired. The tale tells how a vicious master is turned into a Negro and delivered into the hands of his own sadistic poor-white overseer until he is beaten into sympathy for his slaves. Moved by this tale Annie effects the desired change (in the concluding frame) by taking the boy back. Her act angers the narrator, but he lets the boy stay. Implicit in his acquiescence are the effects on him of the story of Mars Jeems's being turned into a slave. At the end of the tale the narrator acknowledges that the changing of a white man into a Negro was "powerful goopher," an ironic admission of the power of the tale on him and Annie, for it has in effect put them through the experience of Mars Jeems and has acted as a "powerful goopher" on them.

More than any other story, **"Mars Jeems's Nightmare"** examines the psychology which gives Uncle Julius power over the narrator. At the beginning of the story Chesnutt has the narrator characterize Uncle Julius at length in a passage which reveals more about the narrator than about Uncle Julius:

> Toward my tract of land and the things that were on it—the creeks, the swamps, the hills, the meadows, the stones, the trees—he maintained a peculiar personal attitude, that might be called predial rather than proprietary. He had been accustomed, until long after middle life, to look upon himself as the property of another. When this relation was no longer possible, owing to the war, and to his master's death and the dispersion of the family, he had been unable to break off entirely the mental habits of a lifetime, but had attached himself to the old plantation, of which he seemed to consider himself an appurtenance. We found him useful in many ways and entertaining in others, and my wife and I took quite a fancy to him.

As an analysis of Uncle Julius this passage is accurate only in its assumption that the mental habits of a lifetime could not be cast off. It is dead wrong on the nature of those habits, however. The other stories in *The Conjure Woman* reveal how little Uncle Julius sees himself as another's property, while the tales reveal how little the slaves themselves had thought that way. The narrator's error reveals the patronizing attitude which blinds him to the reality of Uncle Julius's activities and which amounts to a wish to consign the freed slave to a new subservience.

The passage also reveals how the guilt created by this attempt to create a new slavery manifests itself in a sense of responsibility for blacks. Uncle Julius understands this psychological complex thoroughly enough to be able to exploit it cynically. At the conclusion of his tale about Mars Jeems he points the moral of the tale: "Dis yer tale goes ter show . . . dat w'ite folks w'at is so ha'd en stric', en doan make no 'lowance fer po' ign'ant niggers w'at ain' had no chanst ter l'arn, is li'ble ter hab bad dreams, ter say de leas', en dat dem w'at is kin' en good ter po' people is sho' ter prosper en git 'long in de worl'." This sententious moralizing reveals Uncle Julius's awareness of the white man's guilt and his willingness to exploit that sense of guilt unscrupulously. Uncle Julius has no interest in having his grandson educated; he asks only that allowance be made for him. Uncle Julius wants the patronizing whites to pay for their sense of superiority by supporting the blacks whose shiftlessness they have created by their attitudes and actions. In this story Uncle Julius emerges as an opportunist like Ellison's Bledsoe, and his relation to the narrator in many ways resembles that of Bledsoe to Norton. The situation Chesnutt draws is virtually hopeless, a vicious circle of mutual exploitation with no will on either side to break the cycle.

Although the situation **"Mars Jeems's Nightmare"** exposes is nightmarish, the story avoids pessimism and bitterness. While it does not achieve that lyrical tension between tragedy and comedy which made **"Po' Sandy"** a prose blues, **"Mars Jeems's Nightmare"** nevertheless does balance the hopelessness of the situation with the humor of Uncle Julius's manipulation of the whites and Annie's active complicity in his success. The balance vital to the conjure stories is also threatened from another quarter, however. From the beginning Chesnutt has been the ultimate conjure man, hoping that by "wukking de roots" of black culture he might be able to work a powerful goopher on white America and lead it to accept the equality of the black. The indirection of the conjure stories enabled him to pursue his goal with consummate artistry but without sufficient power to save America from bad dreams.

His desire to deal more directly with racial problems shows in **"Mars Jeems's Nightmare"** in its concern with an issue with broad social implications, the questions of employment and education for blacks and of white responsibilities therefor. The indirection of the conjure story was ill adapted to such concerns, and **"Mars**

Jeems's Nightmare" inevitably raises questions which the limits of the form prevent it from dealing with. The crucial relation of the drama—the relation between the narrator as employer and Tom as employee—is peripheral rather than central. We can never learn about Tom, the nature of his purported laziness and carelessness, the possible causes, or the possible ways of dealing with the situation. The point of the story, of course, is that the situation precludes either party from dealing directly with these issues, and the story quite properly does not attempt to examine them. Nevertheless, such questions arise simply because the frame drama and the point of Uncle Julius's tale both enter the realm of practical social problems where these questions exist and demand attention. The grim vision of **"Mars Jeems's Nightmare"** registers the hopelessness of America's racial life and reveals the limitations of the indirect approach to racism which the conjure story provided. On the one hand, the conjure story provided a subtle instrument which could portray with a terrifying accuracy and clarity the functioning of American racial life, but it offered no imaginative way out for either author or audience. The lesson of the white narrator—that whites are too blind to perceive the truth about race—may have suggested to Chesnutt that it was not enough to show race relations in action but that what was needed was an art which would outline explicitly the white misconceptions about blacks and the forces responsible for their formation and perpetuation. In any event, Chesnutt's concern shifted from working a subtle goopher on white minds to attacking specific social problems and clearly laying bare the mechanics and consequences of racism, and the conjure story ceased to be a useful vehicle. After **The Conjure Woman** was published Chesnutt gave full attention to the realistic fiction he had been working with throughout the 1890's.

If Americans were too blind for subtle methods, they were no more amenable to direct confrontation. White Americans would not allow themselves to perceive life from a black perspective, and Chesnutt's turn from the complex art of the conjure story was unavailing. Realism did give Chesnutt room to explore additional dimensions of racial life in America, but the ultimate irony is that his realistic fiction never achieved sharper insights than those of **"Mars Jeems's Nightmare"** and the early conjure stories, while losing their balance, control, and clarity. It is through the marvelously subtle conjure fiction, which transcends the nightmare of American racism in a near-tragic, near-comic lyricism, that Chesnutt works his most powerful goopher. (pp. 385-98)

Richard E. Baldwin, "The Art of 'The Conjure Woman'," in American Literature, *Vol. 43, No. 3, November, 1971, pp. 385-98.*

David D. Britt (essay date 1972)

[*In the following excerpt, Britt examines narrative technique in Chesnutt's conjure tales.*]

A journal entry of 1880 reveals Chesnutt's strategy as a writer that is most perfectly achieved in **The Conjure Woman**; he says,

> The subtle almost indefinable feeling of repulsion toward the Negro, which is common to most Americans—cannot be stormed and taken by assault; the garrison will not capitulate, so their position must be mined, and we will find ourselves in their midst before they think it. This work is a two-fold character. The Negro's part is to prepare himself for recognition and equality, and it is the province of literature to open the way for him to get it—to accustom the public mind to the idea; to lead people out, imperceptibly, unconsciously, step by step, to the desired state of feeling.

The artistry with which Chesnutt sought to expand the awareness of white Americans constitutes one of the significant achievements in Afro-American writing. Indeed, William Dean Howells likened the skill of the conjure tales to the works of Maupassant, Tourguenief, and Henry James [see excerpt dated 1900].

But these tales are neither in the tradition of James and Maupassant nor are they parallel to the obsequious fantasies of Harris; this is not " . . . a collection of quaint tales, with an admirable Southern setting. . . ." [see Florence A. H. Morgan, entry in Further Reading]. On the contrary, **The Conjure Woman** is primarily a study in duplicity that masks or reveals its meaning according to the predisposition of the reader. All the elements of fiction—structure, characterization, language, and theme—interlock in a subtle portrayal of a black writer "wu'kin' his roots" on an unperceiving audience.

The stories are deliberately structured to allow the reader to be deceived about the more significant levels of meaning if he chooses, or needs, to be deceived. The device that initially permits misunderstanding comes through the double narrative structure: both a black and white man participate in relating each story. In each story, John, the white narrator, introduces a practical business problem to a former slave, Julius. The problems range from whether John ought to buy a particular vineyard, clear a certain tract of land, or buy a horse instead of a mule. Julius then delivers himself of a conjure tale from slavery times that serves as a parable for how John should or should not proceed. Julius's tale depicts magical transformations in nature through the "goophering" of a conjurer—men turned into wolves or trees, whites changed into slaves, boys turned into birds. The final section of each story shows the bemused John learning that Julius has some vested interest in the business venture. He owns a share in the horse, makes wine from the wild grapes in that particular vineyard, or sells honey from a tree in the land to be cleared. By sandwiching Julius's narrative in between John's sections, Chesnutt gives the first and final word to the white man, implying that the white man is the "official" interpreter of Julius's yarn. Through this structural device, Chesnutt creates a surface level of meaning that leaves the Southern caste system undisturbed.

The apparent vindication of Southern mores is furthered through the characterization of the white narrator. John comes to Patesville, North Carolina from northern Ohio, and can therefore be trusted as a disinterested observer of life in the South. He has nothing but the most effusive praise for the hospitality and generosity of the people. The mild climate, moreover, proves ideal for his wife's health and for the profitable growing of grapes. Minor things like the nine o'clock curfew in no way interfere with the social amenities; the unstated implication here, of course, is that the curfew pertains only to black people. This insensitivity to the living conditions of black people—which constitutes a dominant theme in Julius's tales—represents a central ingredient in John's characterization. From snatches of conversation in various stories it becomes apparent that his good humored condescension to black people serves as only one indicator of a thoroughgoing racist attitude. He says of Julius, for example, that "He was not entirely black, and this fact, together with the quality of his hair, which was about six inches long and very bushy, except on the top of his head, where he was quite bald, suggested a slight strain of other than negro blood. There was a shrewdness in his eyes, too, which was not altogether African, and which, as we afterward learned from experience, was indicative of a corresponding shrewdness in his character." The underlying premise of this observation rests on the notion that a black man's shrewdness derives from what is euphemistically called the benevolent infusion of white blood. On another occasion he remarks that Julius "...was a marvelous hand in the management of horses and dogs, with whose mental processes he manifested a greater familiarity than mere use would seem to account for, though it was doubtless due to the simplicity of a life that had kept him close to nature." John not only thinks of Julius's intellectual powers as more congruent with dogs and horses than men, he also believes Julius's spirit to be shackled with an abiding servility. In trying to articulate Julius's reasons for remaining on the plantation where he had formerly been a slave, John contends that Julius "...had been accustomed, until long after middle life, to look upon himself as the property of another. When this relation was no longer possible, owing to the war, and to his master's death and the dispersion of the family, he had been unable to break off entirely the mental habits of a lifetime, but had attached himself to the old plantation, of which he seemed to consider himself an appurtenance." There is a tone of lament in John's phrase, "When this relation was no longer possible," that indicates he thinks slavery, for Julius, was desirable. When these three statements are brought together—in *The Conjure Woman* they are scattered—it becomes clear that John perceives of Julius as crafty but of low intelligence and essentially servile in spirit. In other words, he subscribes to the racial biases common to most Americans. What Chesnutt does, therefore, through the characterization of John and through the structural pattern of the book is to make *The Conjure Woman* an apparently "safe" work, a reassuring collection of tales that depicts a contented, entertaining black

man working within the unchallenged framework of American social and intellectual mores. One early critic [in an anonymous review in *The Critic* 35, July 1899] even remarks on "...that peace of mind and contentment of spirit which follow hard upon these entertaining narratives of witchcraft." Arna Bontemps articulates the rationale behind Chesnutt's deceptive manipulation of his material when he says in another context that "What annoys some readers of fiction, it seems, is not so much that characters in a book are Negro or white or both as the *attitude of the writer* toward these characters. Does he accept the status quo with respect to the races? If so, any character or racial situation can be taken in stride, not excluding miscegenation. But rejection of traditional status, however reflected, tends to alienate these readers" ["The Negro Renaissance: Jean Toomer and the Harlem Writers of the 1920's," in *Anger and Beyond*, edited by Herbert Hill, 1966]. With the parameters set by John—ostensibly—who could be offended?

Chesnutt's own powers as a conjurer, though, become obvious when one sees that Julius's appearance does not correspond to his reality. Flip Wilson, that Thursday night trickster, says it well: "What you see is what you get." The most obvious technique for deception comes through Julius's language. Dialect—always quaint and humorous to the outsider—prevents the white narrator from taking Julius seriously. And operating safely from behind this language buffer, Julius is able to work on John with a considerable degree of impunity. The hustles that Julius works on John apparently revolve around picayune amounts of cash. And, given Julius's economic status, these small financial victories are not to be dismissed out of hand. But it is a mistake to view a few jugs of wine or a crock of honey as the prime objectives of Julius's maneuverings. In fact, Julius moves out of a solid economic base through being employed by John, a matter that John recognizes at the end of the first story but subsequently forgets. If this were not the case, Julius would be in terrible straits financially, for in only one of the stories, **"The Conjurer's Revenge,"** is he successful in achieving something of personal material benefit. In **"The Conjurer's Revenge"** Julius persuades John to buy a horse instead of a mule, and Julius owns part interest in the horse. He is successful in two other stories, but the gain is not strictly of personal benefit. The outcome of **"Mars Jeems's Nightmare"** secures a job for Julius's grandson, while **"Po' Sandy"** results in a meeting place for Julius's secessionist church group. Following **"The Goophered Grapevine"** and **"The Gray Wolf's Ha'nt"**, Julius has lost the income from grapes and honey. Two of the stories, moreover, **"Sis' Becky's Pickaninny"** and **"Hot-Foot Hannibal"** express not a trace of self-interest. Since in only one of the seven stories is Julius able to gain something of value to himself personally, he is either singularly unsuccessful as a hustler, or presented by Chesnutt as a "darky entertainer" in the minstrel tradition, or the stories are not about financial matters at all. My contention is that Julius's tales are not aimed at manipulating John in the way the surface narrative implies. They should be seen as elaborate metaphors, allegories really, in which the supernatural elements point toward those dread realities of the slave's life that lie beyond the comprehension of the ruling class. The black man is laying bare the nature of the slave experience, exploding myths about both masters and slaves, and showing the limitations of the white man's moral and imaginative faculties.

An extended analysis of one story, **"Po' Sandy,"** will illustrate the tension between the outside and inside narratives, establish the thematic patterns, and serve as a model for interpreting the other works. The inside narrative of **"Po' Sandy"** shows Julius telling a tall tale about the hainted character of the wood in an old school house in order to prevent John from using the lumber to build his wife a new kitchen. In the coda, Julius receives the wife's permission to use the old school house for a meeting place, temporarily. Julius's narrative, however, expresses an extended metaphor that reveals the dehumanization of the slave, the brutality of treatment afforded the slave, and the intense love that a black man and woman have for one another. Julius tells about Sandy, who is such an exceptional worker that each of Mars Marrabo McSwayne's married children asks the father to deed Sandy to him as a gift. In order to prevent family friction, however, McSwayne lends Sandy to each of them for about a month at a time. This way each gets his services without denying the others of their "rights." McSwayne, a generous man who doesn't want to give offense to anyone (white), even lends Sandy to the neighbors on occasion. During one such work trip Sandy's wife is sold to a speculator.

The recurring metaphor associated with Sandy is homelessness. His forced wandering prevents him from establishing those basic roots that nurture a sense of belonging, order, and stability. With profound understatement he says, "'I'm gettin' monst'us ti'ed er dish yer gwine roun' so much.'" Given the dehumanized state in which he lives, Sandy wishes for liberation through a magical transformation that, ironically, objectifies the dehumanization, but at the same time provides a stable existence. If he were "...a tree, er a stump, er a rock..." he tells his second wife, at least he "...could stay on the plantation fer a w'ile." Tenie wrestles momentarily with the conflict between the white man's religion (Christianity) and the powers available to her through African magic (conjuring). She has not goophered anyone for fifteen years, not since she got "religion." But now she decides that "...dey is some things I doan b'lieve it's no sin fer ter do." The preservation of the race—exemplified here in the well-being of her husband—justifies the use of whatever means are available. She conjures Sandy into a tree, after which he undergoes a series of natural disasters: a woodpecker gouges a hole in his arm and a slave, unwittingly, skins his leg while tapping the tree for turpentine. Tenie then decides to turn herself and Sandy into foxes, "...so dey could run away en go some'rs whar dey could be free en lib lack w'ite folks." The characteristics of white folks expressed in this metaphor are freedom laced with the cunning of a predator.

The brutalization of the slaves controls the next segment of the story. While Tenie is sent away to nurse a white woman, the owner decides to build a new kitchen, the lumber from which is later used to build the school house mentioned in the outside narrative. The tree into which Sandy has been transmogrified is selected for the construction. The tree, with much difficulty and groaning, is felled and hauled to the sawmill. Tenie arrives at the mill just as the saw is about to bite into the log. Her hysterical ravings prompt the mill hands to think her insane. They tie her to a post, and she is forced to watch as the log, Sandy, is cut into pieces. Thus, not only homelessness but dehumanization, mutilation, impotence, and love that drives a woman to distraction characterize the slave's experience.

This story further explodes the myth of casualness in the slaves' family structure. The fact that the slave did not have the power to keep his family together in no way diminished the intensity of love between a man and woman. When Sandy is turned into a tree, his owner cannot track him any farther than the tree itself. He questions all the slaves except Tenie about his whereabouts; not Tenie, because "...eve'ybody knowed Tenie sot too much sto' by Sandy fer ter he'p 'im run away whar she could n' nebber see 'im no mo'." She is, moreover, driven mad after watching him cut to pieces.

And what is one to make of the supernatural elements in the story? The identification of Sandy with the tree can be viewed as a comment on the status of slaves. They were simply natural resources to be used, not essentially different from cattle or timber. And the slave women's superstition that his ghost haunts the kitchen makes it possible for them to refuse, as they did, to work in the kitchen after dark. While the McSwaynes might rail against the ignorance implied in the belief in ghosts, they would not be able to force a terrified woman to work after sundown. One further suggestion arises from the belief that Sandy's spirit still inhabits the kitchen. Whether he was used as the lumber itself or was simply directed to build the kitchen, Sandy invested himself in the building process. A number of contemporary phrases come to mind at this point: "I have invested my life in that company," or "I really put myself into that—whatever." Perhaps the slave's spirit does reside in what he built. We are certainly haunted by his ghost.

The other stories in *The Conjure Woman* admit to a similar line of interpretation. The theme that unites all of Julius's narratives is the contrasting relationship of blacks and whites to the natural order, with nature serving throughout as a metaphor for the natural, moral order of the universe. The white men seek to exploit nature (cotton, vineyards, and especially other men), with a resulting atrophy of their capacity for human emotion. On the other hand, a close alliance exists between the blacks and nature. The acts of goophering show birds, animals, and even the growing seasons working in concert with black resistance against inhumane treatment. The tales accent the injustices suffered by the blacks because of enslavement and at the same time reveal their harmonious relationship with the natural order: witness, for example, their access to the powers of the conjurer, which stems directly from a compatibility with the natural order.

The themes of white dissonance and black harmony with the natural order predominate in **"The Goophered Grapevine."** Julius's tale turns, in effect, on a critique of the economics of the slaveholding system. The action begins when Mars Dugal' McAdoo has Aun' Peggy put a deadly goopher on his vineyard to keep the slaves from eating the grapes, a move designed to deny the blacks a share of what they produce while increasing his profits. A new slave, Henry, arrives on the plantation while the white folks are in the swamp with their guns and dogs looking for a slave who has broken for freedom. The other slaves on the place are too "flusterated" to tell Henry about the goopher, and he eats some conjured grapes. But because his act is inadvertent (and because he brings her a ham), Aun' Peggy puts a special goopher on Henry that cancels the original spell and allows him to eat the grapes with impunity, provided he rubs his head with first sap of the vines each year. An amazing transformation comes over Henry; he undergoes an annual rejuvenation: in the spring his hair grows long, his rheumatism leaves, his youth returns, and he chases the girls. In the fall, however, the process reverses, and the signs of age return. McAdoo, recognizing the economic potential here, begins selling Henry each spring for $1,500 and buying him back later for $500. With the profits from Henry's rejuvenation, McAdoo buys a second tract of land. His prospects for wealth increase further when a Yankee drummer promises to double the wine production through a new method of cultivation. According to Julius, Mars' Dugal' "'... des drunk it all in, des 'peared ter be *bewitch'* wid dat Yankee'" (emphasis added). The language here indicates that whites, too, are subject to a form of conjuring through their greed. The new cultivation methods, however, prove disastrous; both the vines and Henry shrivel and die. McAdoo, now ruined financially, later dies in the Civil War. Julius's tale implies that the slaveholder's exploitative greed contains the seeds of its own destruction, while the attempt to defend the slaveholding system results in death. Henry, conversely, flourishes like a plant in the regenerative cycle of nature. He possesses an immunity to the destructive goophers that the white man works on the land. He—the black man—dies a natural death, not on a battlefield defending slavery. A further oblique comment on white America emerges from this tale. **"The Goophered Grapevine,"** the first story in *The Conjure Woman,* attempts to dissuade John from perpetuating the plantation system. Hoping for profit, as did Mars McAdoo, John, however, buys the property and, as the subsequent stories make clear, remains locked into the racial and economic patterns engendered by the slaveholding system.

The themes of conflict and harmony seen in **"The Goophered Grapevine"** recur in **"Sis' Becky's Pickaninny,"** but the emphasis shifts from the acquisitiveness of the whites to their failure of human sympathy. The

whites' perception of black people as objects is dramatized here through the separation of a mother from her son. Becky, the mother, is traded by her owner for a horse, indicating the interchangeability of people for animals. This identification is completed by the horse's owner when he refuses to keep the mother and son together even though the son will cost him nothing. He says that "'... I doan raise niggers; I raise hosses.'" The son's owner becomes upset when the child falls ill following the separation from his mother, and calls a physician to look at him, not out of compassion but because "'... he wuz a lackly little nigger en wu'th raisn'.'" Julius avoids offending the white sensibilities by speaking of Kurnel Pen'leton's moral weakness only in terms of his relationship with race horses; he speculates in horses, not slaves. But the tale makes clear that the horses and slaves are interchangeable. Julius also speaks of the Colonel in the most favorable terms. The Colonel had wanted to buy Becky's husband when the neighboring plantation on which he lived was disbanded, but the Colonel was broke at the time. The Colonel, says Julius, does not like to separate children from their mothers—not, at least, "w'iles de chillun wuz little"—but he does. And this "... kin-hea'ted man" lies to Becky about selling her in order to make the separation from the child easier. Julius's protestations of the Colonel's generosity must, however, be interpreted in light of the man's actions.

The slaves in the story find recourse against the vagaries of white sentimentality and empty pocketbooks through the ministry of the conjurer. Becky's grief following the separation from her baby, Mose, is made bearable through the singing of two birds. These birds, through conjuration, are really her transformed son, sent to her by the plantation nurse. But the visitations prove ineffectual in relieving the ache of separation. And the nurse asks Aun' Peggy to reunite Becky with Mose. Aun' Peggy directs a hornet to sting the legs of the race horse that has been traded for Becky. The horse's lameness and Becky's pining make each of the traders dissatisfied with the bargain, and they swap back. Thus, nature conspires with the slaves first to bring relief then reunion.

The disruption of slave families also controls the action in another story, **"Hot-Foot Hannibal."** The actions in the outside and inside narratives parallel one another, but the lines of action move in opposite directions. Both sections of the story deal with a recurring problem in human experience: a spat between lovers. Both sections turn on jealousy toward another woman. But the consequences of the quarrels prove antithetical; the white woman achieves a reconciliation, while the black woman loses both her man and her life. Black women are not allowed the same latitude in fighting with their men. Parallels and counterpoints are also established between the male characters. Both are involved in a journey: Jeff, the slave, is sold down the river and Malcolm Murchison contemplates a trip to New York. The directions, of course, are symbolic—the North representing freedom, the South, hell—and one trip is voluntary while the other is imposed. The effect of status on emotional depth constitutes one further counterpoint in the narratives. The white woman—spoiled, petulant, confident—shows no disposition toward experiencing painful emotions; indeed, she exhibits an almost brazen insensitivity to any emotion other than fits of pique. Chloe, on the other hand, commits suicide after learning that Jeff has died on the trip South. This contrast in emotional intensity highlights the inequities implicit in the slaveholding system, and, at the same time, reiterates the crippling effect that slavery has on the white masters and their descendants.

The disparity between the black experience and the white perception of that experience is explored in **"Mars Jeems's Nightmare,"** the least original of Julius's tales in terms of basic metaphor. Here a cruel slave master is temporarily changed into a slave on his own plantation and subsequently lightens the misery of his slaves after learning from the receiving end about the brutality. The interest in **"Mars Jeems's Nightmare"** comes, therefore, not from Julius's section but from the comment it makes on the outside narrative. Julius has secured a job for his grandson even though John had "not liked his looks." John's suspicions prove correct; the grandson is trifling and inept, so John fires him. Julius's tale, however, underscores the difficulty a man has in accommodating himself to a dead-end job. Mars Jeems could not seem to get the hang of the hoe, "en could n' 'pear ter git it th'oo his min' dat he wuz a slabe en had ter wuk en min' de w'ite folks, spite er de fac' dat Ole Nick [the overseer] gun 'im a lesson eve'y day." The point is that both work habits and caste training are hard to come by. And the obvious implication of Julius's tale is the difficulty white employers have in appreciating the conditions under which black workers are supposed to learn. It seems necessary for whites to undergo the black experience (the slave experience) to appreciate the perspective that blacks bring to a menial job.

Finally, two stories, **"The Conjurer's Revenge"** and **"The Gray Wolf's Ha'nt,"** present the slaves in a totally black context, a situation designed to explode a number of stereotypes about black people. Obsequiousness, for example, drops away when no whites are present. Indeed, the black protagonists are presented as men feared by both whites and blacks. So much, then, for the notion that the slaves' retaliation against the system was limited to passive resistance (work slowdowns, broken tools), violent rebellion (Nat Turner, Denmark Vesey), or flight. Primus, the slave in **"Revenge,"** " . . . did n' min' de rules, en went w'en he felt lack it; en de w'ite folks purten' lack dey did n' know it, fer Primus was dange'ous w'en he got in dem stubborn spells, en dey'd ruther not fool wid 'im." Another myth, though—the lack of ethics among blacks—lies closer to the heart of these tales. The other stories are filled with instances of petty thefts of hams, scarves, and the like, things stolen from the whites to elicit the favors of the conjurer. These acts are presented as a matter of course by Julius, though he is careful to say that he never saw any of the slaves near the smokehouse. But **"Revenge"** and **"Gray Wolf"** deal with crimes of blacks against other blacks. Primus steals a pig that belongs to a black man and is turned into a mule, an appropriate punishment for such an action. **"The Gray Wolf's Ha'nt"** presents a more serious offense, murder, and the blood bath that follows is almost Orestian in its consequences. The point here is that internal crimes against the group are viewed as serious breaches of the norm and are dealt with accordingly. It is one thing to steal from a white man, quite another to rob a black. The ethical frames of reference are different for slaves and masters; but then who would expect the slave whose very person has been stolen to view the owner's property as the owner would? The elemental passion loosed in **"Gray Wolf"** attests to a reverence for both the marriage relationship and kinship that transcends the categories of black and white and reveals the incorruptible humanity that the slaves maintain despite their captivity. This statement of the slaves' enduring humanity despite the exploitive propensities of the whites brings the argument of the tales full cycle. The whites and blacks work from radically different moral bases, with many of the ethical premises deriving from social status.

Although the whites control the social and political realities of the world, the blacks are free to place their own interpretations on their experiences and to exert some degree of control through conjuration. Chesnutt drops conflicting clues about the approach one should take in interpreting the conjuring episodes in the stories. The African origins of goophering are explicitly stated in **"The Conjurer's Revenge,"** in which the conjurer from Guinea says, according to Julius, that " . . . his daddy wuz a king, er a guv'ner, er some sorter w'at-you-may-call-'er 'way ober yander in Affiky whar de niggers come fum, befo' he was stoled erway en sol' ter de spekilaters." But while the African influences on *The Conjure Woman* deserve serious attention, such a study is beyond my competence. Another (more western) line of interpretation, however, is provided by John's wife, Annie, who consistently demonstrates more sensitivity to Julius's tales than her husband. She views the supernatural elements as " ' . . . mere ornamental details and not at all essential. The [conjure] story is true to nature, and might have happened half a hundred times, and no doubt did happen, in those horrid days before the war'." And Julius's tales do lend themselves to metaphoric interpretation. **"The Conjurer's Revenge"** and **"The Gray Wolf's Ha'nt"** exemplify appropriate punishments for crimes within the black community, while **"Mars Jeems's Nightmare"** contains not only an appropriate punishment but a method of illumination as well. An idea fundamental to all the tales—the slaves' harmonious relationship to nature—emerges through the seasonal rejuvenation of Henry in **"The Goophered Grapevine."** Sandy's vicissitudes constitute a veiled statement of the brutality to which slaves were subjected, and Hot-Foot Hannibal's troubles result from black resistance to white domination. Julius's narrative in **"Sis' Becky's Pickaninny,"** while not essentially metaphoric, can nonetheless be seen as a specialized interpretation of natural events. In each of the stories the access to the power of the conjurer gives the slaves a sense of control over their environment, a control no more and no less efficacious than the Christian's seeking aid through prayer or interpreting events as the will of God.

If these observations about the importance of Julius to the structure and meaning of *The Conjure Woman* are sound, then the collection deserves renewed critical attention. The work should no longer be dismissed as a belated example of a minor Reconstruction genre, and similarly need not be approached as a tepid first effort in Chesnutt's increasingly militant literary career. Rather, the artistry of the tales suggests a studied control of the material that elicits multiple levels of interpretation. One begins with the literal, surface meaning suggested by the outside narratives. Julius is a hustler, and he hustles John for money. But he also, and more importantly, hustles both John and the reader by presenting the beauty and pain of his people. (pp. 269-83)

> David D. Britt, "Chesnutt's Conjure Tales: What You See Is What You Get," in CLA Journal, *Vol. XV, No. 3, March, 1972, pp. 269-83.*

Sylvia Lyons Render (essay date 1974)

[*Render is an American educator and critic with a special interest in Afro-American literature. In the following excerpt, she discusses the principal themes and literary style of Chesnutt's fiction.*]

The most recurrent themes of Chesnutt's fiction are the humanity of the Afro-American, the mistreatment of minorities—especially blacks in this country—and the universal fallibility of human nature. Chesnutt's delineation of character and manipulation of situation result in outcomes which reflect these central ideas. Thus the reader is impelled to recognize the issues inherent in the different aspects of the themes. Chesnutt also treats these themes more directly in his essays and speeches, and at greater length in his three novels—mostly from the perspective of an Afro-American.

Chesnutt treats the faulty application of our democratic principles more often than he does any other aspect of American life. His use of miscegenation suggests that he considered it one of the most deleterious of our social ills. Miscegenation is a chief motivating force in **"The Dumb Witness," "The Sheriff's Children,"** and *The House Behind the Cedars.* It is prominent though not central in *The Marrow of Tradition.* In **"The Dumb Witness"** Malcolm Murchison has no compunction about putting Viney aside. He threatens that if she continues to remonstrate, she will be punished by having to serve her former paramour's new wife in the same household where her authority had long been recognized. Intentionally or not, in the other three selections all the white fathers either permit their mixed-blood children to be born in a state of slavery or make no adequate provisions to save them from conditions little better than servitude.

In the economic sphere the black is accorded little more respect. **"The Averted Strike"** shows that race deters well-merited advancement in employment. Had Walker not saved the daughter of the plant owner and her friend from a fiery death, he would never have been accepted by less deserving white workers as their supervisor. Chesnutt was too much of a realist to let this deserved promotion take place routinely. Moreover, the climactic fire lends an additional dimension of truth and suspense to the story. That Walker is able to keep his new job attests to Chesnutt's optimistic attitude at the time.

The Colonel's Dream reflects the constantly worsening race relations in this country. When the protagonist, Colonel French, makes a proficient Afro-American the foreman of a group of bricklayers and rejects as invalid all objections to the promotion, some of the white workers walk off the job. This violation of a Southern custom sets into motion a chain of events so vicious that French leaves the South convinced that racial harmony cannot be achieved there immediately or in the foreseeable future.

Negroes suffer other injustices above as well as below the Mason-Dixon line. Installment buying is too costly in **"A Limb of Satan"** and law practices are questionable in **"The Partners."** The law is permissive in dealing with white offenders and legal services are too costly in **"Uncle Peter's House." "The Web of Circumstance"** reveals the worthlessness of such services and the vicious effects of the convict-labor system. All these abuses hit the Afro-American where he is most vulnerable—in the spheres of civil rights and economics. He has not had time to accumulate either substantial capital or sufficient understanding of legal procedures. And even when, like Ben Davis in **"The Web of Circumstance,"** he is both prosperous and respected, he cannot get justice in a court system over which he has no influence as a voting citizen. This aspect of the story is obviously Chesnutt's fictional repudiation of Booker T. Washington's theory that the Negro should forego the franchise until he had an economic foothold.

Among Chesnutt's black folk meaningful relationships outweigh economic gain. Thus the slaves suffer greatly when personal associations are ignored in favor of arrangements which their owners prefer. Hannibal in **"Hot-Foot Hannibal"** is made a servant at the "big house" and told that he may marry Chloe in the spring despite her expressed preference for Jeff. In **"A Deep Sleeper"** Cindy's mistress overrides the master's reluctance to let her leave the plantation and her husband-to-be, Skundus, for temporary service with relatives of her owners. "Cindy didn' want ter go en' said so." But "ole Miss" decided that the impending marriage

> doan' cut no figger. Dey's too much er dis foolishness 'bout husban's en' wibes 'mongs' de niggers nowadays. One nigger man is de same as ernudder, en' dey'll be plenty un 'em down ter Wash'n'ton's plantation.

Cindy and Skundus as well as Sis' Becky and little Mose in **"Sis' Becky's Pickaninny"** are among the few slaves fortunate enough to be reunited. The reason for their reunion is not their master's compassion for their grief, but his financial gain. The majority, including Tenie and Sandy in **"Po' Sandy,"** Chloe and Jeff in **"Hot-Foot Hannibal,"** and Dave and Dilsey in "Dave's Neckliss," are separated forever despite their earnest efforts to remain together.

The antipathy of whites for people of color, extending from the cradle to the grave, blights individual lives and personal ties. Miss Hohlfelder in **"Her Virginia Mammy"** unknowingly sacrifices her mother to white supremacy, and Professor Carson in **"White Weeds"** prefers to sacrifice his life to this pernicious ideal. In **"The Sheriff's Children"** Tom's belief that even father and son cannot bridge the chasm between the races triggers his suicide. Color prejudice among Negroes causes Miss Alice Clayton in **"A Matter of Principle"** and Professor Revels in **"The Sway-Backed House"** to forfeit happiness they could have enjoyed. Rose is a victim of white class prejudice in **"A Secret Ally."** Immoral behavior or unethical practices as delineated in **"The Exception," "A Soulless Corporation," "Stryker's Waterloo," "Jim's Romance," "The Kiss," "The Partners,"** and **"Walter Knox's Record"** bring sorrow and sometimes disaster to the guilty and innocent alike.

Chesnutt recognized that transgression is no respecter of race or class and gave ample evidence of this principle in the catholic manner in which he delineated his characters. At the same time, however, he recognized that blacks in the America of his time would not so often have acted nefariously had they had the same chances in life as others with whom they had to cope. Slaves, some freemen, and most freedmen had to devise unusual ways of protecting themselves and their interest. **"Mars Jeems's Nightmare"** is perhaps the author's most imaginative portrayal of such a procedure. In it Uncle Julius makes the point

> dat w'ite folks w'at is so ha'd en stric', en doan make no 'lowance fer po' ign'ant niggers w'at ain' had no chanst ter l'arn, is li'ble ter hab bad dreams, ter say de leas', en dat dem w'at is kin' en good ter po' people is sho' ter prosper en git 'long in de worl.

The slave expresses these sentiments more bluntly in **"A Deep Sleeper"** by telling Mabel, "Hit ain' my fault dat I an't able ter read de Bible." John recognizes the old man's latent ability in **"The Marked Tree"** by noting, "Had Julius lived in a happier age for men of his complexion the world might have had a black Aesop or Grimm or Hoffman."

To hasten the coming of such an age was the main thrust of Chesnutt's writings. His themes, pointing up the injustices of the system, reflect the major issues of his day—and ours.

Chesnutt's style is marked by directness, precision, forcefulness often characterized by understatement, and use of comic relief or irony. Except when striving for comic effects, he speaks solemnly about weighty matters and casually about trivial ones. His periods are sufficiently varied to avoid monotony and are marked by a restrained grace easily traceable to the Greek and Roman rhetoricians whom he read in the original as well as to his legal training and practice. His work is also distinguished by the use of the alliteration, antithesis, paradox, parallelism, puns, and repetition all approved by the classical masters and by the outstanding orators of his own time, including Abraham Lincoln. His mastery of dialect and admirable choice of diction have already been noted. Foster, who analyzed Uncle Julius's dialect, believes the former is attributable in part to Chesnutt's mastery of shorthand; the author's extensive vocabulary is certainly due to his wide reading.

Chesnutt also had the observant eye of the poet, which caught and recorded minute detail, as in the architecture of the church in which Peter Hardcase is trapped by fire in **"Wine and Water."**

Embellishment by figurative language traceable to both African and European influences lends added color and vitality to his work. In **"Wine and Water,"** for example, the fire becomes a living entity:

> The fire then burst into a little flame, slowly consuming the pile of half-dried rubbish. This only whetted its appetite. It seized a bit of carpet on the floor, and, crawling under the nearest pew, reached up to the cushions on the seats, and greedily devoured them. Then, running along the carpet in the aisle on the right, it caught the ends of the pews, and wrapping itself around the pillars, reached long tongues of flame up toward the gallery, which extended along the sides of the church.

Here and elsewhere the imagery is often symbolic. In the same story "the sparkle of liquor in a glass charmed [Peter] like the eye of a serpent," and "the fire fastened its fangs into the pulpit floor." The heart of the "U-pass" tree in **"The Marked Tree"** is rotten, appropriately suggesting the moral deterioration of the Spencer family. In **"The Dumb Witness"** Murchison sits in "a massive armchair of carved oak," but Viney occupies "a splint-bottomed chair."

Many of the early fictional pieces reflect the haste with which they were written, being obviously contrived and formulaic. A train wreck, for example, is too often the means of disposing of a character or hastening resolution of the action of a story. Some of the works are more nearly sketches than stories; the characters are flat and stereotypic, and the action pedestrian. Like many other writers of the age, he depended too much on coincidence to suit the modern reader. Chesnutt's first stories, as a whole, have too little direct discourse and too much obvious didacticism. Occasionally, too, the pathos is overdone, as in **"Aunt Lucy's Search."**

Chesnutt's strengths as a writer, however, far outweigh his weaknesses. Except for fleeting lapses in emotional control, none of the faults mentioned are apparent in the author's later and longer narratives. The Douglass biography and the expository pieces are all well done, and are highlighted by eloquent and moving passages. The stories in this volume alone are sufficient to insure Chesnutt's place as a major writer of late-nineteenth-century American fiction, as a minor writer (in terms of the comparative quality of his works) in the whole range of American literature, as a social historian, and as the first black American to receive critical acclaim for his fiction.

He is claimed by both Ohio and North Carolina, having been the most important writer to have resided in either Cleveland or Fayetteville until his death in 1932. He was the first author to give extensive treatment to the heterogeneous inhabitants of the Cape Fear area. By introducing Buckeye and Tarheel Blue Veins and by exploring their problems, he earned the title of "pioneer of the color line." Chesnutt's depiction of blacks is unquestionably superior to that of his contemporaries. For accurate, objective, and perceptive thumbnail characterizations of blacks and whites on all the social levels he explored he also deserves to be called the Jean de la Bruyère of his period.

Chesnutt was able to utilize social history as fictional material without distortion; he was the first American writer to use local Negro folk life and folklore for social purpose. Writing realistically in traditional forms carefully modified to suit his preconceived ends, Chesnutt treated current issues forthrightly. In the course of his writing he depicted the greatest variety of black characters delineated in American fiction up to that time; concurrently he treated or anticipated every important theme and tone used by Negro writers through the Second World War. He is truly the father of twentieth-century Afro-American fiction. (pp. 45-9)

> *Sylvia Lyons Render, in an introduction to* The Short Fiction of Charles W. Chesnutt, *by Charles W. Chesnutt, edited by Sylvia Lyons Render, Howard University Press, 1974, pp. 3-57.*

William L. Andrews (essay date 1980)

[*In the following excerpt, Andrews examines the relationship of the conjure stories to contemporary local color fiction and the Plantation School.*]

The literary tradition that Chesnutt followed when he wrote his conjure stories was the local color tradition, the predominant mode of the American short story during the period in which Chesnutt was primarily a writer of short stories. The 1880s in America was a "period of dialect stories, of small peculiar groups isolated and analyzed, of unique local 'characters' presented primarily for exhibition. The short story writer now thought first of materials, often only of materials" [Fred Lewis Pattee, *The Development of the American Short Story*, 1966]. Local colorists offered American readers essentially sympathetic descriptions of unfamiliar people whose quaint and often outdated

style of living had survived only in out-of-the-way places and cultural backwaters of America, or in the memories of nostalgic American writers. Readers of local color and regional fiction expected a realistic treatment of subject from their favorite authors, but the type of realism they preferred rarely took long looks at tragic or pessimistic features of American life. Fundamentally a literature of idealization and nostalgia, post-Civil War regional writing, especially in the South, sought to charm its readers' attention away from the worrisome uncertainties of the Gilded Age to a halcyon, mythical past "befo' de wah." Instead of the psychological complexity of the later realists or the environmental determinism of the naturalists, the local colorists satisfied their readers with a version of America in which superficially rendered provincial character types acted out their amusing idiosyncrasies in a setting distinguished by uniqueness and a perceptible atmospheric effect.

The setting of the conjure stories, the Cape Fear region of southeastern North Carolina where Chesnutt grew up, easily qualified as the sort of isolated, unfamiliar, and in many ways quaintly picturesque area that local color readers thrived on. The sandhills region of North Carolina did not belong to the stereotypical South of the great plantations ruled by splendid aristocrats and supported by regiments of slaves and myriad acres of cotton. It was a region of less glamorous history and much more modest economic opportunity, especially after the collapse of the rebel cause. Yet Chesnutt found "down-east" North Carolina's run-down prewar tobacco "plantations," its untouched pine and scrub oak forests, its extraordinarily sandy soil, and its little-known but reviving grape farming economy all noteworthy points of interest for a local color guide to one part of the New South. In later books about the New South, Chesnutt would probe beneath the more smiling local color appearances to some of the more sinister realities of life in post-war North Carolina. But in *The Conjure Woman,* Chesnutt's first and most uncritical book-length treatment of Dixie redivivus, his concentration simply on sandhills local color gave his frame story an authenticity and peculiarity of setting which rang true enough to the local color market. One reviewer [in the St. Paul, Minnesota *Dispatch,* 29 April 1899] summed up the appeal of the entire *Conjure Woman* in these comments:

> You are not only listening to an old negro reciting his stories of folks being 'conjured,' but it is being conveyed to you just what kind of a country North Carolina is and the character of the people and the negroes who live there. You can gather more information from this story book in regard to grape-culture and farming generally in the South than you can from many extensive works on the subject.

Satisfying the curiosity of northern readers about social idiosyncrasies and economic conditions in the New South was one of the chief purposes behind the use of a Yankee outsider, John the Ohio businessman, as narrator of *The Conjure Woman.* The distanced, at times ironic point of view through which so many regional vignettes were conveyed was almost a stock narrative device of local color, but Chesnutt, like most southern local colorists, took pains in *The Conjure Woman* to picture a bridge of acceptance and understanding between the Yankee observer and his newly adopted southern home. If reconciliation between North and South was the thematic earmark of the work of popular southern local colorists like Joel Chandler Harris and Thomas Nelson Page, then *The Conjure Woman* could easily have been read by southerners and northerners alike as part of this new "reconciliationist" trend in southern literature. One of the main themes of *The Conjure Woman,* a theme which would be contradicted vigorously just six years later by *The Colonel's Dream,* Chesnutt's last book about the New South, is the pleasant initiation of an energetic Yankee into the more unhurried, almost "somnolent" lifestyle of the South. The progressive outsider, having made his success as a grape farmer, is extolled by the local press of "Patesville," which welcomes him "as a striking illustration of the opportunities open to Northern capital in the development of Southern industries." While the New South embraces this nonsouthern entrepreneur, the Ohioan readily admits to having "caught some of the native infection of restfulness." Later his wife will succumb to the popular superstitions she once scorned as "ridiculous." In every respect, this typical northern couple becomes "southernized" as *The Conjure Woman*'s frame story develops. As a result, the book becomes indirectly a kind of advertisement for the New South (at least in the region of Patesville, North Carolina) as a quaint but thoroughly reconstructed American rural ideal. Here, according to the Ohioan, is the perfect market for the northern investor, an unsurpassed sanitarium for the sickly, an untapped agricultural field for the opportunist, and a cornucopia of regional curiosities for the reflective or the inquisitive.

Almost like a promotional guide, the frame story of *The Conjure Woman* provides random but consistently favorable commentary on the physical appearance of the countryside, its climate, the condition of its sandy soil, its hospitality, its Sunday customs, and the picturesque habits of speech of its inhabitants. Studiedly avoided are all references to the racial problems of present-day Patesville, a topic which would be aired a year later in Chesnutt's first novel, *The House Behind the Cedars.* In *The Conjure Woman,* Chesnutt adopted not only the matter but the manner of the southern local colorist. Behind the mask of a southernized northern white man he ushers his readers into the newly mythologized, "progressive" South. However, once the reader is maneuvered into the familiar and definable place and time and fellowship of the frame story, Chesnutt, janus-faced, turns to the reader behind the mask of Uncle Julius and leads him unexpectedly into the strange and disquieting world of the Old South. The same materials that are the loci of the Ohioan's mundane and rather superficial description of contemporary North Carolina rural life become in Julius' accounts the evidence of something extraordinary, something wonderful and compelling about the South. In **"The Goophered Grapevine,"** for

instance, a minor aspect of New South agriculture serves double duty, both informing the reader of postwar farming trends and introducing him into the antebellum world of Julius' memory and imagination. Thus Chesnutt adhered faithfully to his responsibility as transcriber of sandhills local color, even to the extent of ostensibly pandering to the popular notion of an accommodating, reconstructed New South. But he recognized the metaphorical possibilities of unusual and curious aspects of southern life when placed in the hands of an imaginative interpreter like Julius instead of a literal-minded reporter like John. In exploiting these differing perspectives on the South, Chesnutt made his dialect-local color collection a more complex and revealing study of southern life, past and present, than most southern local color historians engaged in.

That quality of Chesnutt's dialect tales that gave them their most obvious distinctiveness to readers of his own day, however, was the conjure motif which pervades Julius' stories. At a time when, as one reviewer put it [in the New York *Mail and Express,* 15 April 1899], "our literature of all kinds is so weighted down with dialect writing," Chesnutt seemed to demonstrate more than a facile knack for following a local color fad. He could record with apparent accuracy the speech of southern Afro-Americans, and though he realized that aural fidelity was impossible, most of his reviewers were impressed by the authenticity and readability of Julius' dialect. But, as one reviewer observed [in *Literature,* 19 May 1899], "Unlike many books with negro characters, *The Conjure Woman* was not written expressly to display its author's knowledge of dialect." Instead, the "chief aim," in this reviewer's estimation, was "to make vivid some of the superstitions current in slavery times." Insofar as this view is accurate, it helps to explain once again the success of Chesnutt's conjure stories in the local color market. The transformation of the customs of an isolated group of people into the materials for fiction was typical of regional writers. And, as Chesnutt explained in an article on **"Superstitions and Folk-Lore of the South"** [*Modern Culture XIII,* 1901] the literary preservation of such "vanishing traditions" as "conjuration" was one of his purposes in compiling *The Conjure Woman.* He hoped the book might "furnish valuable data for the sociologist, in the future study of racial development."

At the same time, Chesnutt was determined that the stories of *The Conjure Woman* not be received by the literary world as simply "folk tales," even though the tale-teller, the southern setting, and the book's cover design (which featured a balding old black man and a mischievous-looking white rabbit) was reminiscent of Joel Chandler Harris' *Uncle Remus, His Songs and His Sayings* (1880). Chesnutt did not overestimate the literary excellence of his conjure stories—if anything he understated their originality—but he was never slow to insist that they were *artistic* creations, not folklore transcriptions. Only **"The Goophered Grapevine"** had a specific folklore origin, Chesnutt maintained; the remainder of the volume was "the fruit of my own

Chesnutt at work in his study.

imagination, in which respect they differ from the *Uncle Remus* stories which are avowedly folk tales. From these remarks one can see that Chesnutt did not want to be misrepresented as a follower of Joel Chandler Harris, whom he considered a collector and skillful adaptor of the lore of another culture, not a truly creative figure in his own right. Chesnutt wanted his status among the literati predicated on his recognition as an artist, not an ethnologist. As an opening wedge into the literary world, *The Conjure Woman,* aside from its superficial local color appeal, was designed to advertise its author's imaginative capabilities in the carefully rendered style of the volume's frame story, the development of convincing characters, and the infusion of Julius' tales themselves with appropriate "morals." Thus, the particularities of the "doctrine of conjuration" did not greatly concern Chesnutt; probably his main purpose vis-à-vis the conjure materials was to endow Julius with enough knowledge of recondite folklore to make him an absorbing and believable Afro-American character. Endowing Julius with a familiarity with and propensity for talking about conjuring on the old plantation simply heightened the verisimilitude of the old man and the

tales he indulges in. It was this verisimilitude, this basically aesthetic quality and goal of fiction, which the conjure motif was supposed to augment. More fundamental, however, to the significance of *The Conjure Woman,* as Chesnutt emphasized, was not what he borrowed but what he invented, especially the three main characters of the volume and the "alleged incidents of chattel slavery" which are so constructed as to suggest a moral message to the reader. In these respects, Chesnutt aspired to more than the superficial realism of local color. (pp. 41-6)

Given the plantation tradition's identification with the "old-school Negro," the simple, self-sacrificially loyal client, and its almost exclusive exploitation of this type, it is not surprising that, to cultivate the same popular readership, Chesnutt cast Julius in the familiar livery of the Sams, Billys, Chads, Isams, Remuses, and Peter Cottons of the white plantationists. The qualities that reviewers most often praised in Julius—his loquacity, his disarming childlikeness, his ingenuousness, and his deep-down kindliness—were not unique to him. They are standard features of ex-slave characters in plantation

391

fiction. The breadth of Julius' imagination, however, is unusual. As John the Ohioan says, some of Julius' stories "are quaintly humorous; others wildly extravagant, revealing the Oriental cast of the negro's imagination; while others . . . disclose many a tragic incident of the darker side of slavery." Few of the white plantationists allowed their ex-slaves to digress beyond the "quaintly humorous" or the naïvely sentimental reminiscence. More often than not the motive behind Julius' storytelling is neither nostalgia for the old days (as is the case in Page's stories) nor a delight in entertainment (as is the case in the Uncle Remus tales) but instead the economic self-interest of the old man himself. This disingenuous self-regard is singular among characters of Julius' type in dialect fiction.

Nevertheless, though Julius does demonstrate greater capabilities than his predecessors, his most often remarked idiosyncrasy, his "shrewdness" in adapting his tales to prevent his employer's plans from clashing with his own interests, does not do violence to those qualities in Julius that were likely to stimulate the popular reader's curiosity and sympathy. Moreover, the presence of this individualized shrewdness does not make of Julius a rounded, three-dimensional character. Chesnutt does not venture Julius outside the role of storyteller, of "mouthpiece" in *The Conjure Woman.* Through his cannily crafted fictions the old man manipulates the whites in certain minor ways, but his success as a trickster depends more on their sentimental weaknesses than on his ability to deceive. John senses Julius' purposes in most of the old man's rather transparent plots, but he allows Julius to have his way in many instances because the black man has managed to ingratiate himself to Annie, the lady of the house. Only in one story in *The Conjure Woman* does Julius subvert the patron-client relationship with John and arrange to cheat his employer to his own advantage. Moreover, even though **"The Conjurer's Revenge"** diverges significantly from the norm of plantation writing in its presentation of the ex-slave "uncle" as unscrupulous sharper, Chesnutt returned to orthodoxy in **"Hot-Foot Hannibal,"** the story he chose to conclude the volume so as to leave the reader with a pleasant parting impression. In the frame of this tale, Julius shows himself a sentimentalist at heart, and he puts his trickery to a traditional end in plantation fiction, the reuniting of estranged white lovers. Thus, if Julius has a role outside that of Chesnutt's "mouthpiece" for discussion of slave life, the role is that of the petted servant whose disingenuous devices are often allowed to succeed by a forbearing employer. Julius' machinations and behavior do not upset the frame of the conventional plantation story, which posits the black man's subordination to a white patron's largess, in *The Conjure Woman.* In most respects the Uncle Julius of this collection assumes the role of the storytelling black provincial of conventional local color fiction, a functionary of some distinctive charm and interest, but essentially a static figure whose main activity outside of reciting tales is to reaffirm his endearingly mock-devious nature to an appreciative white audience.

In keeping with the point of view and tone of most southern local color which dealt with blacks, the narrator of *The Conjure Woman* presents Julius with a mixture of respect, bemusement, and condescension. John appreciates Julius' powers of narrative invention, is impressed by his employee's knowledge of the region and its history, and learns to be wary of the ex-slave's rascality and petty deceitfulness. To the white man, Julius is not a fellow to be taken seriously but rather with a kind of superior detachment reserved for the simple and unsophisticated. Julius, the reader is informed, "was a marvelous hand in the management of horses and dogs, with whose mental processes he manifested a greater familiarity than mere use would seem to account for, though it was undoubtedly due to the simplicity of a life that had kept him close to nature." In this way the obtuse Ohioan glosses over the better part of Julius' life as a slave and the effect of that life on him. John is marginally aware that Julius does possess certain limitations—he mentions the old man's "ignorance" once—which are traceable to his life in bondage. But the pervasively comic mood of *The Conjure Woman*'s frame story militates against the investigation of Julius' personal slave experience. Julius himself remembers his years as a slave without apparent rancor, and his employer complacently overlooks the whole question, content to marvel at the old man's "exhaustless store" of diverting "tales of the old slavery days."

Yet in several of the non-conjure stories of Uncle Julius that were composed after Chesnutt decided to abandon "superstition" for a greater emphasis on "feeling and passion," a view of Julius as more scarred than benefited by slavery is projected. In **"A Deep Sleeper,"** the Ohio businessman lumps Julius together with the poor whites of the region as "products of a system which they had not created and which they did not know enough to resist." In **"Lonesome Ben,"** the example of Julius causes his employer to speculate soberly "upon how many original minds, which might have added to the world's wealth of literature and art, had been buried in the ocean of slavery." And in **"Dave's Neckliss,"** the most tragic of Julius' plantation reminiscences, the frame story shows John digressing uncharacteristically on the destructive effects of slavery upon Julius' past, not on the captivating performances he can give in the present. For once, in **"Dave's Neckliss,"** the businessman sounds more like a student of abnormal psychology than a local color reporter. The result of his investigation is a drastic and unparalleled alteration of the standard type of the ex-slave narrator in Chesnutt's dialect fiction. Instead of the simple child of nature presented in *The Conjure Woman,* **"Dave's Neckliss"** displays a "curious psychological spectacle of a mind enslaved long after the shackles had been struck off." Instead of emphasizing such plantation story conventions as the "dreamy expression" in Julius' eyes and the affecting absorption of the ex-slave in his tales of the old days, the businessman in **"Dave's Neckliss"** finds a "furtive disapproval" surfacing in Julius' tone of voice when he describes the cruelty of the white masters.

There is little quaintness or humor in the Julius of **"Dave's Neckliss,"** for "centuries of repression had borne their legitimate fruit" in his truncated intellect. The "simple human feeling, and still more the undertone of sadness" which John responds to in **"Dave's Neckliss"** are the meager remnants of what was once a keen wit and a vital human understanding permanently stunted by the effects of slavery.

Clearly, the Julius of **"Dave's Neckliss"** is not the Julius of *The Conjure Woman.* The one is only a storyteller, a "mouthpiece," a depthless medium through which the old days may be viewed; the other may be delved and sounded as a human being, as a representative of the average slave himself. Looking beyond conjure lore for those more fundamental qualities considered basic to the human spirit, the narrator of **"Dave's Neckliss"** finds a void at the central being of Julius, a void which his unconscious artistry and shrewdness of mind cannot fill. The businessman doubts whether Julius "had more than the most elementary ideas of love, friendship, patriotism, religion—things which are half, and the better half, of life to us." So conditioned is Julius that his employer further doubts that he "even realized, except in a vague, uncertain way, his own degradation."

In these doubts Chesnutt revealed the crucial deficiencies of Julius as a developable literary character. More importantly, the author's honest delineation of Julius' limitations constitutes a significant rejoinder to those plantation writers who sentimentalized and extolled the "old-time Negro" as an exemplary product of the peculiar institution. The point of John's introduction to Julius in **"Dave's Neckliss"** was that at his best the ex-slave had to be recognized as still a partially blighted figure whose very picturesqueness and value as a local color raconteur depended on a sacrifice of those qualities which make up "the better half of life" to most people. As the product of the slave system, Julius pays a price for the oddities which the conjure stories celebrate, the price of a fully rounded, complex identity awakened to the ideals and opportunities of the larger world beyond his restricted mental purview. Thus in the framing commentary of **"Dave's Neckliss,"** Chesnutt hinted at least once at the tragic limitations of the local color Negro stereotype.

The Conjure Woman did not insist on the somber view of Julius given in **"Dave's Neckliss,"** most probably because such a radical departure from the dialect norm would have harmed the book's commercial chances. On the other hand, if *The Conjure Woman* did not adopt the Julius of "feeling and passion" unveiled in **"Dave's Neckliss,"** it did not pander to racial stereotypes by making him a simple "happy darkey" or "gentleman in ebony." Obviously *The Conjure Woman* was not intended, as **"Dave's Neckliss"** was, to condemn the institution of slavery and its latter-day eulogists by standing the brutalized Julius up as exhibit A in a prosecution case. Popular racial prejudice would not capitulate to discursive recitals of one slave's misfortunes, as the introduction to **"Dave's Neckliss"** offered. Chesnutt had

known for many years that the fortress of prejudice had to be mined imperceptibly, through much more artful means. He knew that ultimately his case against the plantation-dialect tradition had to come through Julius' memories, through his fictions that both enlightened and instructed his hearers. These fictions are the literary strength of *The Conjure Woman,* through which Chesnutt carried on his critique of the plantation-dialect literary tradition and the historical and racial assumptions which it perpetuated.

As has been often pointed out, the plantation tradition offered anything but a realistic and critical view of the peculiar institution upon which the agricultural economy of the Old South rested. The postwar celebrators of the Old South dismissed leftover abolitionist sentiment against the old order by showing ex-slave retainers longing for the prewar era, when life was carefree and harmonious for both races. The classic statement about the good old days comes from Sam, the narrator of Thomas Nelson Page's "Marse Chan": "Dem wuz good ole times, marster—de bes' Sam ever see! Dey wuz, in fac'! Niggers didn' hed nothin' 't all to do—jes' hed to 'ten' to de feedin' an' cleanin' de hosses, an' doin' what de marster tell 'em to do; an' when dey wuz sick, dey had things sont 'em out de house, an' de same doctor come to see 'em whar 'ten' to de white folks when dey wuz po'ly. Dyar warn' no trouble nor nothin'" [*In Ole Virginia,* 1887]. However, the point of view from which the aging ex-slaves of Page or Harris take their memories is that of the privileged servant in the plantation "big house." By contrast, Julius "never indulged in any regrets for the Arcadian joyousness and irresponsibility which was a somewhat popular conception of slavery; his had not been the lot of the petted house-servant, but that of the toiling field hand." By locating the point of view of his dialect stories in Julius, one of the large mass of ordinary field hands, Chesnutt was able to take a new look at the Old South's social and economic system, a look undistorted by the affection and nostalgia Uncle Remus and Page's uncles harbor for their erstwhile masters and former positions. The possibility lay open to examine the mundane, everyday life of the slave and his master replete with the stresses, complications, and threats which could, if handled sensitively, reveal a more reliable picture of individual black and white characters than was usually shown in the hackneyed romantic plots of plantation fiction.

The slave-master relationship in Chesnutt's dialect fiction differs significantly from the typical relationship of benevolent aristocrat and loyal retainer which dominated plantation fiction in Chesnutt's day. Accurate depiction of antebellum life in the sandhills region of North Carolina demanded a departure from the plantation norm. Unlike the Tidewater region of Virginia, which Page memorialized, and the middle Georgia farmland where Harris set his Uncle Remus tales, the part of North Carolina represented in the conjure tales possessed neither the rich soil that supported vast plantations in the deep South nor the old, established families that owned great holdings in land and slaves in

Virginia and South Carolina. The land in southeastern North Carolina around "Patesville" was cultivated by small farmers who often worked in the fields beside the few slaves they owned. As one historian has noted, the North Carolina gentry "came, in most instances, from those middle class families who by thrift and energy were able to get ahead in life" [Guion G. Johnson, *Ante-Bellum North Carolina,* 1937].

The desire to "get ahead" is what distinguishes the Mars Dugals, Mars Marrabos, and the other slaveholders of Julius' tales from the stereotyped plantation gentlemen of Page, F. Hopkinson Smith, Harry Stillwell Edwards, and their ilk. While the aristocrats in Page's stories duel and dance, court and politic, and glory in the southern cause, the parsimonious Scots in Chesnutt's conjure tales cheat each other, indulge their gambling vices, hunt down their runaways, argue with their wives, curse their slaves, and worry over their bankbooks. These are the descendants of those hard-bitten small farmers, merchants, and ruffians who enliven the work of early southwestern humorists like Johnson Jones Hooper and Augustus Baldwin Longstreet. They are not derived from the diabolic man-stealers and overseers of abolitionist fiction; their salient characteristics are not outrageous cruelty and inhumanity but meanness and selfishness. Mars Dugal of **"The Goophered Grapevine"** receives his due when Julius says of him, "it ha' ter be a mighty little hole he could n' crawl thoo, en ha' ter be a monst'us cloudy night when a dollar git by him in de dahkness'." Another conjure tale, **"A Victim of Heredity,"** describes how a planter cheats his own nephew out of his inheritance and cuts his slaves' rations by more than half . . . . There is only one harsh overseer in Julius' tales, but practically all the white people he recollects exhibit a fundamental callousness which stems from their inability to see their slaves as anything other than property to be maintained and machinery to be worked. The slave-owners in **"Hot-Foot Hannibal"** and **"Mars Jeems's Nightmare"** attain a certain liberality toward their slaves, but it is engendered out of hard-headed business sense, not humanitarian concern. They learn that to work slaves too hard or to separate children from parents or spouse from spouse produces friction, leads to diminished vitality among the slaves, and reduces work output. Thus at times the slaves abused out of the master's ignorance and insensitivity receive eventual improved treatment in some of Julius' tales, notably in **"Mars Jeems's Nightmare,"** where a master's change of heart toward his slaves occasions much "'juneseyin' en singin' en dancin'"" in the quarters at the conclusion of the story. But Chesnutt does not romanticize unduly such "reformed" white people. Mars Jeems's humane treatment of his slaves improves their lot, but it also boosts his profit margin. He got "'a finer plantation, en slicker-lookin' niggers'" as a result of his kinder attitudes; he also "'uz makin' mo' cotton en co'n, dan any yuther gent'emen in de county'."

Just as the southwestern humorists countered the infant myth of the South with realistic reports of the majority of poorer southern whites cheating and scrambling for a

place on the frontier, so Chesnutt offered his reader a picture of the representative slaveowner untinted by the rose-colored plantation myth. The whites of Julius' memory are only sketchily portrayed, but they do emanate from a more balanced view of the typical slaveholder than may be found in the picturesque, lovably eccentric aristocrats of the Page tradition. Through Julius' bland commentary, Chesnutt joined early local color depicters of the southern middle and lower classes—authors like Richard Malcolm Johnston, Mary Noailles Murfree, and Joel Chandler Harris—in their efforts to give an accurate impression of those regions of the South which did not resemble the world of most plantation fiction. Chesnutt did not focus on these aspects of the South with the thoroughness and breadth of a Johnston or a Murfree, but his efforts do represent an introduction to a seldom-discussed people in a region largely ignored by the plantation-dialect writers of his day.

If Chesnutt's conjure stories are significant because they helped to introduce the typical southern slaveholder to the post-Civil War American reading audience, they deserve even greater attention for their treatment of a type of slave unfamiliar to readers of southern local color. Within the confines of the local color tradition, Chesnutt depicted the situation of the average slave on an average plantation with greater care and sympathy than any of his white fiction-writing contemporaries. This does not mean that Chesnutt created rounded, complex black characters in his conjure stories. The brevity of his genre prevented this. Julius usually paints his slave protagonists in broad strokes; most are introduced by epithets and accompanied throughout their stories with a minimum of descriptive or analytic details. The hero of **"Po' Sandy"** is called simply a "'monst'us good nigger'" who does his work exceedingly well. The heroine of **"Hot-Foot Hannibal"** is termed "'a lackly gal en a smart gal.'" "'One nigger man is de same as ernudder,'" Julius quotes his master's wife in **"A Deep Sleeper,"** and the presumption is shared by all the slaveholders in *The Conjure Woman,* as it was, no doubt, by many of Chesnutt's late-nineteenth-century readers. To undermine this prejudice, Chesnutt constructed his conjure stories so as to bring his slave characters out of the shadows of their anonymity and separate slave status and into the light of a common humanity with the reader.

Chesnutt's strategy in promoting the idea of a common humanity between blacks and whites did not insist on the elevation of the slave protagonists of his conjure stories to the idealized plane of genteel white literature. Unlike his contemporaries in Afro-American fiction, Chesnutt did not try in Julius' tales to combat subhuman plantation fiction stereotypes with superhuman counter-stereotypes. One will find in Julius' memories no descendants of the magnificent heroic slaves who figure so strongly in the propagandistic fiction of William Wells Brown, Martin R. Delany, or Frances E. W. Harper. Instead, the reader discovers an extensive survey of black characters, ranging from Dave, the saintly slave preacher in **"Dave's Neckliss,"** to the malevolent, Iago-like conjure man in **"The Gray Wolf's Ha'nt."** Most of the slaves in Julius' stories, however, belong in the realistic middle ground of representative humanity, no better and no worse than they should be. Julius' fellow slaves are capable of great fidelity (Tenie in **Po' Sandy"**) and equal perfidy (Hannibal in **"Hot-Foot Hannibal"**), admirable self-sacrifice (Aunt Nancy in **"Sis' Becky's Pickaninny"**) and petty vengefulness (the conjure man in **"The Conjurer's Revenge"**), patient dignity (Dan in **"The Gray Wolf's Ha'nt"**) and pathetic pride (Chloe in **"Hot-Foot Hannibal"**). In most of the conjure stories, the slave protagonists demonstrate some primary character trait, predilection, or obsession which motivates them and which brings them into conflict either with white slaveholding institutions or with other black antagonists. In these conflicts, conjure practice can be used by slaves to express and preserve marriage ties (**"Po' Sandy"**), family solidarity (**"Sis' Becky's Pickaninny"**), love relationships (**"Hot-Foot Hannibal"**), and general group welfare (**"Mars Jeems's Nightmare"**). Other stories show conjuring in the service of less positive and humane purposes. In **"The Goophered Grapevine,"** Aunt Peggy, the conjure woman, accepts a white man's money for bewitching an old slave who eventually dies as a result of the spell. The employment of conjuring for more spiteful reasons is the theme of **"The Conjurer's Revenge"** and **"The Gray Wolf's Ha'nt,"** two tales concerned solely with internecine struggles between plantation slaves and free black conjure men.

The most impressive of Julius' stories from the standpoints of character development and thematic diversity are those in which conjure practice functions as the ally of slaves whose most deeply felt emotions and relationships, whose essential dignity and human identity are threatened by the inhuman slavery system. The least effective tales in *The Conjure Woman* put conjuring in the service of the depraved and selfish, leaving the reader feeling the perplexity and dissatisfaction which Annie, Julius' most perceptive listener, registers at the conclusion of **"The Conjurer's Revenge"**: "'That story does not appeal to me, Uncle Julius, and is not up to your usual mark. It isn't pathetic, it has no moral that I can discover, and I can't see why you should tell it. In fact, it seems to me like nonsense'." Actually of course, the story is not nonsensical in a practical sense. Julius' story of a slave transformed into a mule and then returned almost completely to his human shape helps to gain the old man's advantage in a horse trade at his employer's expense. However, in an aesthetic sense the story is a failure, for it lacks the twin appeals of Julius' best conjure tales—an emotionally moving, "pathetic" human situation and a "moral," a message relating to the character or situation of blacks in the South. (pp. 50-60)

In slave characters like Dave, Tenie, Sandy [in the stories **"Dave's Neckliss,"** **"Po' Sandy,"** and **"Sis' Becky's Pickaninny"**], and Becky, Chesnutt developed, if not fully rounded creations, at least characters with

black skins who exhibit incontrovertible evidence of their unstereotypical human identities. Lacking the space in Uncle Julius' tales to create complex human figures, Chesnutt concentrated on intensity of character. He stressed the slave's capacity for and motivation by familiar human passions: love, hatred, jealousy, envy, and pride. He succeeded in portraying the essential humanity of the slave beneath the accidents of his peculiar ethnic background and social status. By de-emphasizing the physical descriptions and picturesque idiosyncrasies of his characters, Chesnutt avoided the danger of local color caricature. By recounting the emotional and spiritual sufferings of Dave, Tenie, Sandy, and Becky through the words of an ex-slave himself, Chesnutt was able to expose the tragedy of the slave system as authentically and non-polemically as the white plantation writers' ex-slave narrators had glorified that system. Slavery through Julius' eyes is a condition of neither "Arcadian joyousness" nor extreme physical deprivation. In Julius' memories the most disturbing aspect of slavery is not the possibility of physical abuse, which occurs infrequently, but the likelihood of a more profound threat to the slave's dignity, his capacity to feel, and his human identity. The condition of slavery is harsh because it acts as a kind of crucible whose potentially destructive psychological pressures demand the slave's most arduous self-assertion even though he or she will be emotionally and spiritually ravaged as a result. This ravaging elevates the slaves to a tragic status, however, because in the actions of the Tenies and Beckys and Daves, profound and universal motives and emotions are revealed. Perhaps the basic relevance of **"Mars Jeems's Nightmare"** to the other stories in *The Conjure Woman* lies in the support which this story of a slaveowner transformed into a slave gives to the theme of the humanity, dignity, and tragic potentiality of the average slave. When Mars Jeems is subjected to the crucible of slavery, he reacts with the same sort of self-assertive behavior and intense emotional frustration which makes the slaves in Julius' stories sympathetic, often heroic, and occasionally tragic. The intention of Jeems's story among Chesnutt's dialect fiction seems to be the reaffirmation of the black man's humanity by showing a white man's like behavior when placed in the crucible of slavery.

Time after time in Uncle Julius' stories the exigencies of the slave condition force a particular slave into a desperate situation which elicits from him or her some kind of action. At times the slave's action may constitute a direct challenge to the authority of the master, though not all of the conjure stories may be schematized into a narrative formula pitting conventional white societal power against supernatural black conjure power. Whatever their circumstances, Chesnutt's slave heroes and heroines need not perform superhuman acts of resistance or express their superiority through daring escapes to freedom to confirm their human worth. None of the main characters in any of Chesnutt's dialect stories ever permanently escapes his or her physical bondage, but the actions of a number of slaves attest to a freedom from the enslavement of the spirit. Within the restrictions of the slave condition, Becky, Tenie, Jeems, and Dave each illustrate a realistic standard of heroism. It is not the deathless loyalty of family servants and retainers celebrated by the plantation writers before Chesnutt. Nor is it the open militancy and ineffaceable defiance of slave insurrectionists and fugitives who were the special favorites of the abolitionist writers. Whether or not the slave's reaction to his predicament is successful is less important than the fact that the action itself confirms the slave's identity in his story as a serious figure who deserves the reader's respect and empathy. What is at stake ultimately in Chesnutt's dialect fiction is not the black man's triumph over the institution of slavery (something which Chesnutt could not depict and remain true to his version of the ordinary field hand's experience). Something more important to the black man's social progress in postwar America is at stake, namely, his triumph over the attitude toward Afro-Americans that the Old South and its apologists had perpetrated.

When Charles Chesnutt first began publishing his dialect fiction, the writers of the plantation tradition had largely won the sympathy of northern reading audiences for an ideal and a social system which an earlier generation of Yankees had fought to extirpate from American soil forever. More ironically, the aristocratic ideal of the Old South resurrected by Page and his followers was displayed as more than a relic to be venerated; the idea of the aristocrat as the black man's "natural leader," patron, and "best friend" was proposed as one solution to the racial unrest of Reconstruction and its aftermath. Viewing the black man as happiest in slavery, Page and many of those who subscribed to his opinions often showed the ex-slave unfitted for life outside its confines. To these reactionaries, the erstwhile slave, though no longer his master's property, remained the white man's burden even after emancipation because he lacked the ability to deal independently and competently with the kinds of problems faced every day by whites. Stories like Joel Chandler Harris' "Free Joe and the Rest of the World" played on the long-standing stereotype of the Negro as "wretched freeman" and implied that white authority provided much-needed discipline and identity for blacks before the war. But Chesnutt's picture of blacks in slavery, by concentrating on their tenacity of purpose, their depth of feeling, their resourcefulness, strength of character, and practicality, denied this insinuation that blacks were not qualified for the responsibilities of free people. By showing slavery not as a sheltered condition tailored to meet an inferior race's needs but as a difficult and fortuitous way of life in which great determination, courage, and fortitude were needed in order to survive, Chesnutt proved once again his fundamental thesis in his dialect fiction—that in the midst of slavery's worst depredations the black man and woman had confirmed their human dignity and heroic will. Chesnutt left little doubt to the sensitive reader of *The Conjure Woman* that having endured the crucible of slavery and having been tempered by it, the Afro-American could meet and overcome the problems of a free status. (pp. 66-9)

William L. Andrews, in his The Literary Career of Charles W. Chesnutt, *Louisiana State University Press, 1980, 292 p.*

Bernard W. Bell (essay date 1987)

[*Bell is an American educator and critic. In the following excerpt, he examines Chesnutt's depiction of the social realities of the postbellum South in his novel* The Marrow of Tradition.]

Influenced by such local colorists and regionalists as Lowell, Harris, Page, Cable, and Tourgée, Chesnutt was guided in his writings by a "high holy purpose." In the journal entry for May 29, 1880, he declares:

> The object of my writings would be not so much the elevation of colored people as the elevation of the whites—for I consider the unjust spirit of caste which is so insidious as to pervade a whole nation, and so powerful as to subject a whole race and all connected with it to scorn and social ostracism—I consider this a barrier to the moral progress of the American people; and I would be one of the first to head a determined, organized crusade against it. Not a fierce indiscriminate onset, not an appeal to force, for this is something that force can but slightly affect, but a moral revolution which must be brought about in a different manner. The subtle almost indefinable feeling of repulsion toward the Negro, which is common to most Americans cannot be stormed and taken by assault; the garrison will not capitulate, so their position must be mined, and we will find ourselves in their midst before they think it.

Chesnutt's faith in God, the puritan ethic, and white Northern liberals fostered his belief that if blacks would prepare themselves for recognition and equality, literature could promote acceptance of the idea. But as he pursues these romantic moral assumptions in his two collections of short stories and three novels, we witness, especially in *The Colonel's Dream* (1905), his waning faith in the capacity of whites to advance the cause of democracy by dismantling the color bar.

Chesnutt won the acclaim of the white literary world with the publication of *The Conjure Woman, and Other Stories* (1899) and *The Wife of His Youth and Other Stories of the Color Line* (1899). On the surface, the style of the first collection resembles that of Harris and Page. But in tone and fidelity to Afro-American character, the conjure tales of Uncle Julius are a far cry from those told by Page's Uncle Sam and Harris's Aunt Fountain. Instead of being a mere mouthpiece for the glorification of the Old South, Uncle Julius, a shrewd old ex-slave whose colorful imagination and mother wit enable him to outsmart a transplanted white Northerner, spins off a series of wry wonder tales that exploit the ignorance of whites about the ways of black folk while simultaneously affirming the humanity of both. Believing that the double-consciousness of mulattoes offered him a greater challenge as an artist, Chesnutt in his second volume of short stories and three novels turned to the theme of color and caste. The main character in the title story of *The Wife of His Youth* outlines the most pressing problem of mulattoes. "'I have no race prejudice,'" says Mr. Ryder, "'but we people of mixed blood are ground between the upper and nether millstone. Our fate lies between absorption by the white race and extinction in the black. The one doesn't want us yet, but may take us in time. The other would welcome us, but it would be for us a backward step.'" A proud, conservative member of the Blue Vein society, whose membership is restricted to those of free birth whose skin is so light that their veins appear blue, Mr. Ryder wrestles with the moral dilemma of acknowledging the wife of his youth: an illiterate, toothless black woman who has selflessly helped him escape from slavery and faithfully searched for him for twenty-five years. Ryder's ultimate acknowledgment of his mate suggests the implied author's position on color and class lines within the race.

Less popular than Dunbar, Chesnutt was nevertheless the better craftsman in fiction. His stories satisfied the critical taste of subscribers to the *Atlantic Monthly,* while Dunbar's appealed to the less demanding readers of *Lippincott's.* Howells compared the "quiet and force" of Chesnutt's art to that of "Maupassant, or Tourgeunief, or Mr. James, or Miss Jewett, or Miss Wilkins" [see excerpt dated 1900]. And another critic found Chesnutt's imagination and sentiment more profound than Dunbar's. When his first novel, *The House behind the Cedars* (1900), a tragic romance on "passing," was published, it also received highly favorable reviews.

But *The Marrow of Tradition* (1901), based on the lynchings that occurred during the 1898 elections in Wilmington, North Carolina, and *The Colonel's Dream,* an attack on the peonage and convict lease labor system, ran into heavy negative criticism. Howells and Paul Elmer More headed the list of reviewers who found *The Marrow of Tradition* humiliatingly bitter. "Mr. Chesnutt," Howells wrote paternalistically in *North American Review,* "... has lost literary quality in acquiring literary quantity, and though his book, *The Marrow of Tradition,* is of the same strong material as his earlier books, it is less simple throughout, and therefore less excellent in manner" [see Further Reading]. Preferring that realism restrict itself to the more genteel aspects of life, the Dean of American Letters went on the say that Chesnutt "stands up for his own people with a courage which has more justice than mercy in it. The book is, in fact, bitter, bitter. There is no reason in history why it should not be so, if wrong is to be repaid with hate and yet it would be better if it was not so bitter." In contrast, Chesnutt considered the novel the best he had written.

Set in Wellington, North Carolina, during the Reconstruction era, the plot of *The Marrow of Tradition* is simple enough. At its center are the reactionaryism of the white aristocratic Carterets and the liberalism of the half-white middle-class Millers. The conflict between these two families, heightened by Major Carteret's belief in "the divine right of white men" and the enmity of Olivia Carteret for her half-sister Janet Miller, is dramatized in a series of confrontations in which the life of either the Carteret or the Miller child hangs in the balance. The novel reaches its climax with the death of the Miller child in a riot incited by Major Carteret's race-baiting editorials. But when the Carterets beg Dr. Miller to save their dying son's life, the Millers overcome the impulse of an eye for an eye and achieve a moral victory by agreeing to help the child. The message is clear: racial harmony depends on whether the next generation of whites will perpetuate the racist values of the Old South or create a more democratic and humanistic social order.

It is this theme that informs the novel, from the melodramatic use of names to the delineation of characters. Stressing the relative status of the children to each other and to the plot, the Carteret child is ceremoniously christened Theodore Felix but called "Dodie," while the Miller child remains nameless. Through the characters we also discover that the major cause of racial conflict in Wellington is white chauvinism. At the heart of the Southern tradition is a rigid code of social etiquette based on color and class. On one side of the color line are members of old Southern families like the Carterets, poor whites like McBane, and ineffectual intellectuals like Lee Ellis, a Quaker. On the other side are the Millers and Attorney Watson, members of the black middle class, and Mammy Jane, Jerry Letlow, Sandy Campbell, and Josh Green, poor, working-class blacks.

Arousing his white readers' interest by employing an old family retainer's trusted memory to provide retrospective narrative (a convention of Southern local color and regional writers), Chesnutt begins the novel with Mammy Jane's chronicle of the black-white love affair involving Sam Merkell, Olivia's father, Polly Ochiltree, his sister, and Julia Brown, his mulatto housekeeper and mistress. "Eve'ybody s'posed Mars Sam would give her a house an' lot, er leave her somethin' in his will," says Jane, as she recalls the Carteret family history. "But he died suddenly, and didn' leave no will, an' Mis' Polly got herse'f 'pinted gyardeen ter young Mis' 'Livy, an' driv Julia an' her young un out er de house, an' lived here in dis house wid Mis' 'Livy till Mis' 'Livy ma'ied Majah Carteret." The abuse and rejection of Julia and her daughter Janet, first by Polly and then by the Carterets, symbolize the historical relationship between white and black America. Such relations, the omniscient author-narrator interjects, "had been all too common in the old slavery days, and not a few of them had been projected into the new era. Sins, like snakes, die hard. The habits and customs of a people were not to be changed in a day, nor by the stroke of a pen." The dramatic irony here is that this reference to the Emancipation Proclamation and the Thirteenth, Fourteenth, and Fifteenth amendments of the Constitution also applies, the reader realizes, to Chesnutt's novels. Even though social realism is probably more likely to influence attitudes than laws, neither necessarily achieves this humanistic objective. This is particularly true, as Chesnutt reveals, when the lore of white racism is the marrow of the American tradition. And the most diseased aspect of this tradition for him was the prejudice and discrimination suffered by interracial middle-class families.

Plot and characterization reveal that the ethical, social, and political distance between the author-narrator and the minor characters is greater than that between him and the central character, Dr. Miller. Torn between his allegiance to color and class, the author-narrator is pessimistic about the pernicious influence of racism. Belatedly acknowledged after the tragic death of her son and the destruction of her husband's hospital, Janet bitterly rejects Olivia's sisterly recognition as coming too late and costing too much. Her warring passions and ringing rejection indicate Chesnutt's insightful displacement of the traditional stereotype of the tragic mulatto. Dr. Miller, Janet's husband, agonizes over the fact that even though he has submitted to the puritan ritual of becoming well scrubbed, well educated, and well mannered, he still suffers racial discrimination and social abuse. Nothing was more absurd to the refined doctor than the practice of Jim Crow. "Surely," he says, "if a classification of passengers on trains was at all desirable, it might be made upon some more logical and considerate basis than a mere arbitrary, tactless and ... brutal drawing of a color line." Character, culture, and class would, in his judgment, provide such a basis. Meanwhile, in the apocalyptic closing of the novel, black politicians and professionals are chased out of town; black townsmen are intimidated and murdered in the streets; and black militants are shot down defending themselves and their community from a white mob. Only in the Pyrrhic victory of the Millers is there any glimmer of hope for racial harmony in the future.

Chesnutt's aesthetics were in one respect clearly shaped by the demands of his white audience. After Richard Gilder, editor of *Century Magazine,* had rejected one of his short stories, Chesnutt expressed his disappointment in a letter to George W. Cable:

> Pardon my earnestness. I write *de plein coeur*—as I feel Mr. Gilder finds that I either lack humor or that my characters have a "brutality, a lack of mellowness, lack of spontaneous imaginative life, lack of outlook that makes them uninteresting." I fear, alas, that those are the things that do characterize them, and just about the things that might have been expected to characterize people of that kind, the only qualities which the government and society had for 300 years labored faithfully, zealously, and successfully to produce, the only qualities which would have rendered their life at all endurable in the 19th century. I suppose I shall have to drop the attempt at realism and try to make them like other folks.

In order to be published he at least had to appear to satisfy the prejudices of his white readers.

To achieve this end Chesnutt developed a highly sophisticated ironic voice. On one level, then, Mammy Jane and her grandson Jerry Letlow—whose surname symbolizes his obsequious nature—are characterized by a "doglike fidelity" to their white employers. Ancient in years and wearing a colorful frock with a red head rag, Jane exudes an undying, syrupy loyalty to her white mistress. But this image, like Chesnutt's brief yet unsympathetic portrayals of the "chip-on the-shoulder" new black generation, is a satirical slap at white interpretations of black character. Upset by the self-assertiveness of a young black nurse who rejects "old-time negroes" and considers her relationship to the Carterets as nothing more than business, Jane fumes about education spoiling young blacks: "I's fetch' my gran'son' Jerry up ter be 'umble, an' keep in 'is place. An' I tells dese other niggers dat ef dey'd do de same, an' not crowd de w'ite folks, dey'd git ernuff ter eat, an' live out deir days in peace an' comfo't. But dey don' min' me— dey don' min' me!" In addition to capturing the authentic speech of a poor black North Carolinian, Chesnutt here effectively sets up the dramatic irony of Jane's tragic death. While hurrying to aid her white folks, she is killed by those she trusts most to protect her. Jerry, who also depended on white benevolence for his personal identity and security, is another ironic victim of the white mob.

The realistic portrayals of Sandy Campbell and Josh Green also reveal the sharp eye of an intimate observer of black character and the caste system. Sandy is subtly satirized as a self-important body servant to old Mr. Delamere and a back-sliding Methodist who considers himself better than a Baptist of any degree of sanctity. Less convincingly developed is Josh Green, a militant laborer who has pledged to kill the Klansman who killed his father and drove his mother insane. As a dock worker and symbol of the revolutionary potential of the black masses, he refuses to participate in Jim Crow rituals and puts "one of dem dagoes" in the hospital for calling him a "damn' low-down nigger." When Dr. Miller and Attorney Watson refuse to lead the resistance against the white mob, Josh assumes command and shouts: "Come along boys! Dese gentlemen may have somethin' ter live fer: but ez fer my pa't, I'd ruther be a dead nigger any day dan a live dog!"

Actually, Chesnutt's black characters go beyond the demythologizing of white lore as they honestly struggle with their ambivalence as black Americans. Even though he sympathizes with the plight of the masses, Chesnutt, like Griggs, criticizes both the slavish imitation of white mores and the use of violence as a solution to racial differences. At the same time, he recognizes the responsibilities of the black middle class to the black masses. Dr. Miller, for example, is willing to devote his medical skills to the cause of his people, but he is neither ready nor willing to sacrifice his life foolishly for them. As he watches Josh and the others march off, "while entirely convinced that he had acted wisely in declining to accompany them [he] was yet conscious of a distinct feeling of shame and envy that he, too, did not feel impelled to throw away his life in a hopeless struggle."

As a member of the black bourgeoisie himself, Chesnutt realized that the vested interests of black intellectuals, professionals, and businessmen not only discouraged them from becoming revolutionaries but also frequently compromised their effectiveness as leaders in the struggle for liberation of the masses. Thus Dr. Miller's manner of resolving his double-consciousness is dictated more by class values than by ethnic solidarity or race consciousness. Social reform, not revolution, is his choice. In the last line of the novel, Chesnutt cautiously yet optimistically allows this vision of social reality to speak for itself. As Dr. Miller finally gains entry to the Carteret home, the symbol of social acceptance, to operate on the Carterets' child, he is urged: "Come on up.... There's time enough, but none to spare."

In its realistic illustration of the blood and cultural ties that bind black and white Americans together, its moral purpose of unmasking white terrorism and lore, and its ironic, more persuasive treatment of the complex influence of color and class on black character, *The Marrow of Tradition* enriches the tradition of the Afro-American novel and moves it further on the road toward social realism. (pp. 64-70)

> Bernard W. Bell, "The Early Afro-American Novel: Historical Romance, Social Realism, and Beyond," in his The Afro-American Novel and Its Tradition, *The University of Massachusetts Press, 1987, pp. 37-75.*

FURTHER READING

Ames, Russell. "Social Realism in Charles W. Chesnutt." *Phylon* XIII, No. 2 (1953): 199-206.
> Commends Chesnutt as "the first distinguished American Negro author of short stories and novels" and considers his work "the forerunner of a substantial body of fiction written by Negroes which has maintained an unusual level of social realism."

Andrews, William L. "A Reconsideration of *Charles Waddell Chesnutt: Pioneer of the Color Line.*" *CLA Journal* XIX, No. 2 (December 1975): 136-51.
> Assessment of Chesnutt's life and career based on excerpted letters and journal entries reprinted in Helen M. Chesnutt's biography *Charles Waddell Chesnutt: Pioneer of the Color Line.*

Babb, Valerie. "Subversion and Repatriation in *The Conjure Woman.*" *The Southern Quarterly* XXV, No.2 (Winter 1987): 66-75.
> Contrasts Chesnutt's use of black dialect in his conjure stories with that of Joel Chandler Harris in his Uncle Remus stories. Babb notes that dialect is used in the Uncle Remus stories to reinforce a white supremacist order, while in Chesnutt's fiction the world view of the white northern landowner (who narrates the frame stories in standard English) is consistently subverted in the dialect narrative of former slave Julius McAdoo.

Bone, Robert. "Charles Chesnutt." In his *Down Home: A History of Afro-American Short Fiction from Its Beginnings to the End of the Harlem Renaissance,* pp. 74-105. New York: Capricorn Books, 1975.
> Assesses Chesnutt's conjure stories as satiric works intended to oppose the pastoralism of Plantation School fiction.

Brooks, Van Wyck. "Eugene O'Neill: Harlem." In his *The Confident Years: 1885-1915,* pp. 539-55. New York: E. P. Dutton and Co., 1952.
> Includes mention of Chesnutt in a discussion of black writers of the period. Brooks suggests that Chesnutt's early fiction suffered from stereotyped characterizations

Chesnutt, Helen M. *Charles Waddell Chesnutt: Pioneer of the Color Line.* Chapel Hill: University of North Carolina Press, 1952, 324 p.
> Affectionate biography that reprints numerous passages from Chesnutt's journals and from correspondence to and from Chesnutt, quoting extensively from contemporary reviews of Chesnutt's published work.

Cooke, Michael G. "Self-Veiling: James Weldon Johnson, Charles Chesnutt, and Nella Larsen." In his *Afro-American Literature in the Twentieth Century: The Achievement of Intimacy,* pp. 43-70. New Haven: Yale University Press, 1984.
> Includes discussion of "self-veiling": "pulling down a mask over [the] desire for independence and an unencumbered place" by the black narrator of the conjure tales, who both entertains and manipulates the white characters.

Delmar, P. Jay. "The Mask as Theme and Structure: Charles W. Chesnutt's 'The Sheriff's Children' and 'The Passing of Grandison'." *American Literature* LI, No. 3 (November 1979); 364-75.
> Examines "the theme of the mask"—"how both whites and Blacks are constrained to hide their true personalities and, often, their true personalities and, often, their true racial identities from themselves and each other"—in the two stories, and suggests that this theme unifies much of Chesnutt's fiction.

Dixon, Melvin. "The Teller as Folk Trickster in Chesnutt's *The Conjure Woman.*" *CLA Journal* XVIII, No. 2 (December 1974): 186-97.
> Considers ways that the black narrator of the conjure stories tricks the white northerners into meeting his own needs through recounting tales that similarly depict trickery through conjuring and witchcraft.

Elder, Arlene A. "Charles Waddell Chesnutt: Art or Assimilation?" In her *The "Hindered Hand": Cultural Implications of Early African-American Fiction,* pp. 147-215. Westport, Conn.: Greenwood Press, 1978.
> Maintains that in *The Wife of His Youth, and Other Stories of the Color Line,* Chesnutt diverged from the folkloric basis of the *Conjure Woman* stories toward social realism in the portrayal of the social, economic, and political situation of black Americans.

Gayle, Addison, Jr. "The Souls of Black Folk." In his *The Way of the New World: The Black Novel in America,* pp. 25-58. Garden City, N.Y.: Anchor Press, 1975.
> Defines advocacy of the special needs and rights of the mulatto to a white audience as the major objective of Chesnutt's fiction.

George, Marjorie, and Pressman, Richard S. "Confronting the Shadow: Psycho-Political Repression in Chesnutt's *The Marrow of Tradition.*" *Phylon* XLVIII, No. 4 (Winter 1987): 287-98.

Examines unresolved tensions between the rational message of cooperation and nonviolence, and the call for resistance to and violent overthrow of the racist social and political establishment, in *The Marrow of Tradition.*

Gibson, Donald B. "Charles W. Chesnutt: The Anatomy of a Dream." In his *The Politics of Literary Expression: A Study of Major Black Writers,* pp. 125-54. Westport, Conn.: Greenwood Press, 1981.

Traces the development of Chesnutt's social and racial attitudes as reflected in his published fiction.

Hackenberry, Charles. "Meaning and Models: The Uses of Characterization in Chesnutt's *The Marrow of Tradition* and *Mandy Oxendine.*" *American Literary Realism, 1870-1910* XVII, No. 2 (Autumn 1984): 193-202.

Discusses the didactic purpose of characterization in two novels (one unpublished) by Chesnutt.

Harris, Trudier. "Chesnutt's Frank Fowler: A Failure of Purpose?" *CLA Journal* XXII, No. 3 (March 1979): 215-28.

Examines the literary and didactic function of the black working-class suitor of the light-skinned heroine of *The House behind the Cedars.*

Heermance, J. Noel. *Charles W. Chesnutt: America's First Great Black Novelist.* Hamden, Conn.: Archon Books, 1974, 324 p.

Biographical and critical overview that considers Chesnutt's accomplishment within the context of his historical times.

Hemenway, Robert. "Gothic Sociology: Charles Chesnutt and the Gothic Mode." *Studies in the Literary Imagination* VII, No. 1 (Spring 1974): 101-19.

Considers ways that the *Conjure Woman* stories both conform to and diverge from the Gothic mode.

Howells, W. D. "A Psychological Counter-Current in Recent Fiction." *The North American Review* 173, No. 6 (December 1901): 872-88.

Review of *The Marrow of Tradition* deploring the novel's bitter tone.

Jackson, Wendell. "Charles W. Chesnutt's Outrageous Fortune." *CLA Journal* XX, No. 2 (December 1976): 195-204.

Examines the reaction of the white literary establishment to Chesnutt's fiction, noting that the didacticism of his novels lost Chesnutt the small, conditional readership gained by the conjure stories.

Keller, Frances Richardson. *An American Crusade: The Life of Charles Waddell Chesnutt.* Provo, Utah: Brigham Young University Press, 1978, 304 p.

Biography that includes discussion of the contemporary reception of Chesnutt's major fiction as well as commentary on his journalism and other nonfiction writing.

Payne, Ladell. "Trunk and Branch: Charles Waddell Chesnutt, 1858-1932." In his *Black Novelists and the Southern Literary Tradition,* pp. 9-83. Athens: University of Georgia Press, 1981.

Assesses Chesnutt's career within Southern literary traditions.

Terry, Eugene. "The Shadow of Slavery in Charles Chesnutt's *The Conjure Woman.*" *Ethnic Groups* 4 (May 1982): 103-25.

Maintains that Chesnutt's purpose in writing the *Conjure Woman* stories was to discredit the benign presentation of slavery by white Plantation School authors.

Wideman, John. "Charles W. Chesnutt's *The Marrow of Tradition.*" *The American Scholar* 42, No. 1 (Winter 1972-73): 128-34.

Close examination of structure, narrative, and characterization in *The Marrow of Tradition.*

Winkleman, Donald M. "Three American Authors as Semi-Folk Artists." *Journal of American Folklore* 78, No. 308 (April-June 1965): 130-35.

Includes discussion of Chesnutt's use of folktale techniques in the conjure stories.

Alice Childress

1920-

American dramatist, novelist, prose writer, editor, and author of children's books.

Childress is considered a seminal yet critically neglected figure in contemporary black American drama. Plays like *Trouble in Mind* (1955), *Wedding Band: A Love/Hate Story in Black and White* (1966), and *Wine in the Wilderness: A Comedy-Drama* (1969), while traditional in structure, have proved to be controversial. Because Childress writes about such topics as miscegenation and teenage drug abuse, some of her works have been banned from schools and libraries in various regions. In her dramas as well as in her novels for children and adults Childress has drawn on her own experiences and featured relatively normal, everyday protagonists. She explained in a 1984 essay entitled "A Candle in a Gale Wind": "My writing attempts to interpret the 'ordinary' because they are not ordinary. . . . We are uncommonly and marvelously intricate in thought and action, our problems are most complex and, too often, silently borne."

Childress was born in Charleston, South Carolina, but grew up in Harlem in New York City. She was raised primarily by her grandmother, who was an early influence on her writing. Childress noted in a 1987 interview: "[My grandmother] used to sit at the window and say, 'There goes a man. What do you think he's thinking?' I'd say, 'I don't know. He's going home to his family.'. . . When we'd get to the end of our game, my grandmother would say to me, 'Now, write that down. That sounds like something we should keep.'" Childress attended high school for three years but left before graduation. She held several jobs while acting as a member of the American Negro Theatre in Harlem; as part of the company, she performed in *A Midsummer-Night's Dream* and in other works. Childress was also in the original cast of *Anna Lucasta* on Broadway, yet she found acting unfulfilling. She commented: "Racial prejudice was such that I was considered 'too light' to play my real self and they would not cast light-skinned blacks in white roles. I realized I had to have some other way of creating." She began to write dramas, later attributing this decision in part to her grandmother. "I never planned to become a writer, I never finished high school," she wrote in her 1984 essay. "Time, events, and Grandmother Eliza's brilliance taught me to rearrange circumstances into plays, stories, novels, and scenarios and teleplays."

In 1949 Childress's first play, *Florence,* was produced. The setting is a railway station waiting room divided into a "white" and a "colored" section. Mama sits on the colored side; she is going north to retrieve her daughter, Florence, who is trying unsuccessfully to act in New York City. Mrs. Carter is a white woman in the

other section who tries to show Mama that she is not racist. Mama finds this claim to be false when she asks Mrs. Carter to use her influence to help Florence, only to have Mrs. Carter volunteer to ask one of her friends, a stage director, to hire Florence as a domestic. Although *Florence* was produced on a small scale in Harlem, the critical praise it received launched Childress's career. She became the first black woman to achieve certain honors in American theater: with *Gold Through the Trees* (1952), she was the first black woman to have a play professionally produced on the American stage; with *Trouble in Mind*, she was the first women to win an Obie Award for best original off-Broadway play. *Trouble in Mind* is a play about a group of actors rehearsing for "Chaos in Belleville," a fictional drama with an anti-lynching message. One of the black performers, Wiletta Mayer, refuses to obey the director, who wants Wiletta's character to put her own son into the hands of a crowd that is sure to lynch him. Wiletta contends that the director is forcing her character to act illogically; thus reinforcing a negative image of blacks.

Wiletta's challenge to the director causes most of the troupe to question their own roles in "Chaos in Belleville." In one version of the drama, Wiletta leads a cast walkout and the director demands a script revision in the finale; in another, Wiletta loses her part. Although *Trouble in Mind* was optioned for Broadway, Childress would not consent to the changes that producers wanted to make in the script, and it was never produced there.

Wedding Band: which focuses on South Carolina's anti-miscegenation laws and an interracial love affair, was both controversial and difficult to produce. Despite praise accorded to the 1966 production in Michigan, *Wedding Band* did not reach a wider audience until 1973, when it was performed in New York. In the play, Julia, a thirty-five-year-old black seamstress, celebrates the ten-year anniversary of her common law marriage to Herman, a forty-year-old white baker. He gives her a wedding band to wear on a chain around her neck until they can be legally married in another state. They are never married, for Herman contracts influenza. In *Wedding Band,* Childress revealed racism in all characters, not just against black but also Germans, Chinese, and others. *Wine in the Wilderness*, Childress's next play, is about intraracial hostilities and prejudices. In it Tomorrow-Marie, called Tommy, affirms that she is not a "messed-up chick" as artist Bill would like to paint her, but the "wine in the wilderness," his image of the majestic "Mother Africa." Childress's success as a dramatist helped win her an appointment in the late 1960s at Harvard University's Radcliffe Institute for Independent Study, where she was the resident playwright and scholar.

Although Childress has devoted most of her career to drama, she is also a noted author of children's literature. She has written two plays and two novels, including *A Hero Ain't Nothin' but a Sandwich* (1973) and *Rainbow Jordan* (1981). By far her best-known work, *A Hero Ain't Nothin' but a Sandwich,* is the story of thirteen-year-old Benjie Johnson's emerging addiction to heroin. His story is told from many points of view, from his stepfather and teachers to his pusher. Despite overwhelming praise for Childress's realistic treatment of a sensitive issue, several school districts banned *A Hero Ain't Nothin' but a Sandwich,* apparently on the grounds that the theme of the work was inappropriate for young readers. Childress encountered similar resistance to her plays as well; for instance, the state of Alabama refused to telecast *Wine in the Wilderness*. Childress commented on the reception of her works in her 1984 essay: "I do not consider my work controversial, as it is not at all contrary to humanism."

Childress was instrumental in the genesis of black theater in America and remains a vital, uncompromising force in contemporary drama. Her plays and children's books have received much praise, yet many critics believe that she deserves even more attention and recognition. According to Elizabeth Guillory-Brown in *Phylon*: "Childress's twelve plays beg for scholarship. A playwright whose dramaturgical advances have paved a way for women in the theatre, Childress is that new thought, that breath of fresh air, that possibility."

(For further information about Childress's life and works, see *Black Writers; Children's Literature Review,* Vol. 14; *Contemporary Authors,* Vols. 45-48; *Contemporary Authors New Revision Series,* Vols. 3, 27; *Contemporary Literary Criticism,* Vols. 12, 15; *Dictionary of Literary Biography,* Vols. 7, 38; and *Something about the Author,* Vols. 7, 48.)

PRINCIPAL WORKS

Florence (drama) 1949
*Just a Little Simple (drama) 1950
Gold Through the Trees (drama) 1952
Trouble in Mind (drama) 1955
Like One of the Family: Conversations from a Domestic's Life (prose) 1956
Wedding Band: A Love/Hate Story in Black and White (drama) 1966
The Freedom Drum (drama) 1969; also performed as *Young Martin Luther King,* 1969
†String (drama) 1969
Wine in the Wilderness: A Comedy-Drama (drama) 1969
Mojo: A Black Love Story (drama) 1970
A Hero Ain't Nothin' but a Sandwich (novel) 1973
When the Rattlesnake Sounds (drama) [first publication] 1975
Let's Hear It for the Queen (drama) [first publication] 1976
Sea Island Song (drama) 1977
A Short Walk (novel) 1979
Rainbow Jordan (novel) 1981
Gullah (drama) 1984
Moms (drama) 1987

*This drama is an adaptation of the novel *Simple Speaks His Mind* by Langston Hughes.
†This drama is an adaptation of the story "A Piece of String" by Guy de Maupassant.

Ed Bullins (essay date 1973)

[*Bullins, a contemporary black American playwright, is considered one of the most significant figures to emerge from the Black Arts Movement of the 1960s. In the following review of* A Hero Ain't Nothing but a Sandwich, *he praises the book highly.*]

There are too few books that convince us that reading is one of the supreme gifts of being human. Alice Childress, in her short, brilliant study of a 13-year-old black heroin user, *A Hero Ain't Nothin' But a Sandwich,* achieves this feat in a masterly way by telling a real story of the victims of today's worst urban plague, heroin addiction, and it reaffirms the belief that excellent writing is alive and thriving in some black corners of America.

Benjie Johnson is a hero and a victim in this story, though he would be the last to see himself as either. In Benjie's ghetto world there are few recognizable heroes; everyone there is a victim of the life that numerous black people experience daily; even childhood is almost nonexistent for him. Let Benjie begin his story: "Now I am thirteen, but when I was a chile, it was hard to be a chile because my block is a tough block and my school is a tough school. I'm not trying to cop out on what I do or don't do cause man is man and chile is chile, but I ain't a chile no more."

Though Benjie is vulnerable, he is not innocent, and the story tells of those who are affected by his near addiction to "skag"—most severely, his mother and his stepfather, Butler, who is a hero in his own right. Butler explains to a social worker: "Benjie once told me a hero ain't nothin but a sandwich—and you say a hero is a celebrity! Listen to my credentials; then maybe yall can pin me on a hero button. I'm supportin three adults, one child, and the United States government on my salary. . . . So, explain me no heroes."

This is a family whose members suffer in turn, for dope has changed Benjie into its enemy in their midst. The other characters of the book encounter the family in its sorrow and near dissolution and are more or less concerned by the tragedy and speak of it—a black and a white teacher at Benjie's school, the principal, Benjie's once-ace boon buddy, neighbors and friends.

Even the stone-hearted pusher, Walter, is allowed his say: "Alla these crying-Emma social workers rap out lyin jive bout the 'poor addict.' Dig it, ain't nobody ever held down nobody else and shot him in the vein." This superfly explains why he sells death to youngsters: "You may's well sell to kids cause if you don't they get some grown junkie to get it for them, and he's gonna take a cut outta they bag for hisself."

Walter is cold and tough, like the streets he stalks each day. Benjie knows the hardness of the pavement and people, knows that it grinds away the tenderness of youth and innocence. Yes, in Benjie's Harlem a hero ain't nothin but a sandwich. In the black sections of Philly a sandwich is a hoagie; in other places its a submarine, grinder or po' boy. But the analogy is national in scope and extremely apt. An identity crisis stalks the children of the black community to their very graves!

This surprisingly exciting, entertaining book demystifies the pusher and the problem he sells by centering on the unwitting victim, Benjie, and the disintegration of a black family. With their own voices the people in this story tell the truths of their lives. The writer uses her considerable dramatic talents to expose a segment of society seldom spoken of above a whisper; she exposes the urban disease that hides behind the headlines of drug abuse, the child junkies, drug rehabilitation pro-

grams and the problem of sheer survival in the black urban community.

There is a suggestion of hope in this book, but there is also the unconcealed truth. This truth is well-known but up to now has been a well-kept secret. You don't even have to be heroic to discover it. Just read. (pp. 36, 38, 40)

> *Ed Bullins, in a review of "A Hero Ain't Nothin' but a Sandwich," in* The New York Times Book Review, *November 4, 1973, pp. 36, 38, 40.*

Samuel A. Hay (essay date 1984)

[*In the following essay, Hay argues that while Childress is a traditionalist in the structure of her dramas, she substitutes theme for character in the works* Florence, Trouble in Mind, Wine in the Wilderness, *and* Mojo.]

> A Drama is a play about man and his fate—a play in which God is the spectator. He is a spectator and no more; his words and gestures never mingle with the words and gestures of the players. His eyes rest upon them; that is all.
>
> *Georg Lukács,* Soul and Form

Put God in a crowded Harlem theater in 1950. Put Alice Childress's first play, **Florence,** on the stage. Make sure that "the railway station waiting room" set prominently displays a rail and the signs "Colored" over one doorway and "White" over the other. The signs are important because they are both signs and symbols. They are signs because they "serve to make us notice the situation"; they are symbols because "they help us understand the situation." The situation, known already to God and the spectators, begins when a middle-age Black woman enters, "crosses to the 'Colored' side and sits on a bench."

God knows the woman's troubles: Mama is leaving her "very small town in the South" for New York to bring back her daughter Florence, a struggling and starving actress. Mama is investing even her rent money in this trip, a symbol of its importance. When a white woman enters, God knows that her liberal words and gestures warrant watching. "You don't have to call me Mam. It's so southern. These people are still fighting the Civil War." Mama's reply, "Yes'm," indicates that Mama perceives these words to be possibly false signs of Mrs. Carter's claim to know, love, and respect Black people:

MRS. CARTER: Last week . . . Why do you know what I did? I sent a thousand dollars to a Negro College for scholarships.

MAMA: That was right kind of you.

MRS. CARTER: I know what's going on in your mind . . . and what you're thinking is wrong. I've . . . I've eaten with Negroes.

"Eating together" has been for Mama and many Blacks the symbol of equality, not only because of the biblical references but also because the Southern oligarchy made it so by outlawing "breaking bread together." However, to Mrs. Carter, "eating together" is by no means a one-to-one representation of equality, but a sign of equality. Since signs simply draw attention to the situation, the attempt to use them to make judgments invites deception, as is the case with Mama. Childress points to the sign-symbol confusion and presents the constituent idea as early as 1950 that the fight of the forties and fifties to eat with whites was assigned too much importance. Childress uses the episode to motivate Mama's temporary change of heart and to test that change:

> MAMA: Do you really, truly feel that way, mam?
>
> MRS. CARTER: I do. Please . . . I want you to believe me.
>
> MAMA: Could I ask you something?
>
> MRS. CARTER: Anything.
>
> MAMA: You won't be angry?
>
> MRS. CARTER: I won't. I promise you.
>
> MAMA: *(Gathering courage):* Florence is proud . . . but she's having it hard.
>
> MAMA: I'm sure she is.
>
> MAMA: Could you help her out some, mam? Knowing all the folks you do . . . maybe . . .

Knowing the request was for help to get Florence onstage, Mrs. Carter offers to help by getting a friend who is a director to hire Florence: "I'll just tell her . . . no heavy washing or ironing . . . just light cleaning and a little cooking . . . does she cook?"

In two ways, *Florence* is typical of Alice Childress's seventeen plays: (a) Childress is interested in a well-crafted situation about an essentially good person who is hurt by Blacks or whites because the person mistakes (false) signs for (true) symbols; and (b) Childress changes her dramatic structure according to whether a Black or a white person creates the hurt. The first typicality places Childress in the William Wells Brown tradition of writing well-structured plays which aim to show how things ought to be, or where they have gone wrong. Childress is one of four prominent Black dramatists of the fifties who carry on the Brown tradition: William Branch, with his *A Medal For Willie* (1951); Louis Peterson, *Take a Giant Step* (1954); and Loften Mitchell, *A Land Beyond the River* (1957).

What sets Childress apart is the second typicality: Childress switches the protagonist-antagonist functions and creates several other revolutionary changes in order to support her political and ethical concerns. The changes are best understood by analyzing the dramatic structure of two interracial plays (*Florence,* 1950, and *Trouble in Mind,* 1955) and two of her intraracial plays (*Wine in the Wilderness,* 1969, and *Mojo: A Black Love Story,* 1970).

Childress can be classified as a traditionalist in structure because she (a) treats her episodes as the building blocks of her play, (b) distinguishes one episode from another

by the appearance of a new character or by a principal character's leaving the scene or retiring from participation in the action, and (c) avoids improvisational and experimental structural devices altogether. Nevertheless, Childress designs her episodes for quite different purposes than the usual psychological characterization popularized by Eugene O'Neill during the forties and fifties, and adopted by such newcomers in the fifties as Tennessee Williams and Arthur Miller. Instead, Childress keeps the traditional beginning, middle, and end, and she substitutes theme for character. The substitution strains the traditional structure because Childress does not reveal the theme through characterization but through argumentation. Therefore, each episode develops not only the usually slim Childress story but, more importantly, the Main Idea. Because the constituent ideas simply repeat the Main Idea, the purpose of each episode, then, is to represent another "circumstantial detail" of the Main Idea. Elder Olson explains:

> If I remark that the news of the day includes a murder, a robbery, a fire, a suicide, a bank failure, and a divorce, you respond with simple ideas of these: but if I go into circumstantial detail, you frame very complex ones. By "circumstances," I mean the doer of the action, the act, the purpose, the instrument with which it was done, the manner in which it was done, the person or object to which it was done, the result, the time, the place, and all similar matters.

To understand fully the substitutions of the idea for character and of circumstantial detail for the Main Idea development, the concerns must be to identify which circumstantial detail develops which constituent idea of the Main Idea. For example, the Main Idea in *Florence* is: "Black people—not white liberals—must struggle if there is to be real political and economic equality." The Main Idea is detailed through seven episodes: three in the beginning, two in the middle, and two in the end.

The three episodes of the beginning quickly develop the story and establish sympathy for the protagonist. However, instead of the middle episodes further developing the story, they all but ignore the story and present circumstantial details of the Main Idea. The end summarizes the constituent ideas, presents again the Mains Idea, and concludes the story. At the *incitation to action* (which usually ends the beginning), Childress opens the argument, which is divided into two subepisodes. The design is:

1. Mrs. Carter presents the claim that she—the symbol of white liberals—loves, respects, and knows Black people.

2. Mama dismisses these words as signs. She reinforces the dismissal by going into her "humble slave" act.

3. Mrs. Carter mistakes Mama's act as symbol and tried to convince Mama of her claim by offering her brother as evidence (he publishes on Blacks and helps Blacks get published).

Cover of Childress's best-known novel for young adults.

4. Mama refutes the brother's authenticity because he thinks that "light skin" Blacks want to be white so bad that they kill themselves from the frustration. Mama now knows that Mrs. Carter's words are but signs.

5. Mrs. Carter offers her "having eaten with Negroes" as a symbol of her feelings.

6. Mama accepts the words as the symbol of Mrs. Carter's true feelings, although she still has some strong reservations about the full claim.

Childress separates the two subepisodes with a "silence," preceded by a subclimax.

> MRS. CARTER: Tears roll down her cheeks as she says almost! almost white . . . but I'm black! And then she jumps and drowns herself.
>
> MAMA: Why?
>
> MRS. CARTER: She can't face it. Living in a world where she almost belongs but not quite. Oh, it's so . . . so . . . tragic.

MAMA: That ain't so! Not one bit it ain't! My cousin Hemsley's as white as you, and . . . and he never . . .

MRS. CARTER: *(Flushed with anger . . . yet lost . . . because she doesn't know why):* Are you losing your temper? Are you angry with me?

MAMA: *(Stands silently trembling as she looks down and notices she is on the wrong side of the railing. She looks up at the "White" sign and moves back to the "Colored" side):* No *mam.* Excuse me please. *(With bitterness)*
I just meant Hemsley works in the colored section of the shoe store . . . He never once wanted to kill his self.

Childress opens the second subepisode with an apology by Mrs. Carter, her prelude into resuming the story, and Childress's prelude into shaping the seven details of this episode into a climax. The constituent details found in the middle are:

1. Mrs. Carter asks Mama the reason for her trip.

2. Mama tells her about Florence.

3. Mrs. Carter advises Mama to bring Florence home because only the most talented succeeds.

4. Mama offers hometown Black drama coach as proof that Florence is talented.

5. Mrs. Carter dismisses Black coach.

6. Mama asks Mrs. Carter for help in locating acting work for Florence.

7. Mrs. Carter offers to find Florence a maid's job, creating the climax.

> MAMA: *(Reaches out, clutches Mrs. C's wrist, almost putting her off balance):* Child!
>
> MRS. CARTER: You're hurting my wrist.
>
> MAMA: *(Looks down, realizes how tight she's clutching her, and releases her wrist):* I mustn't hurt you, must I.
>
> MRS. CARTER: *(Backs away rubbing her wrist):* It's all right.
>
> MAMA: You better get over on the other side of that rail. It's against the law for you to be here with me.

Childress designs the climax so that it occurs during a tragic recognition. Mama recognizes the truth about Mrs. Carter. But more importantly, she recognizes the truth of *her* having to make a greater sacrifice if Florence is to be given a fair chance to compete. Mama's recognition—which psychologist William E. Cross calls "encounter"—is more than usual anagnorisis it is the symbol for the heightened importance Childress assigns to recognition. It is the symbol of Main Idea.

To ensure that the spectator does not miss *this moment,* Childress underscores it by having Mama sit quietly and stare straight ahead. This moment is made tragic by its inevitability. God could have warned Mama not to mistake signs for symbols of truth. But he was strapped by the very definition of Drama to remain a spectator. Any of the spectators could have warned Mama, but the warning would have interrupted the Drama. In fact, not even Childress could have protected Mama, because the protection would have irrevocably become a new drama. Mama *has to suffer* this tragic "encounter."

The Childress climax is so intense that the end is necessarily short and soothing. Mama soon comes to her wits, and she sends Florence the money, with the note "Keep trying." The end consists of a summary of the constituent details and the departure of Mama, who is now a wiser and stronger woman.

Childress wrote such a structurally sophisticated first play that the play obviously benefitted from her acting and politicking experience in commercial theater during the forties. But not even that experience accounts for the fact that *Florence* is a finely structured drama. The fact that it is an overnight work shows Childress to be a playwright with a pretty solid understanding of the structure and power of Drama.

Trouble in Mind (1955) could have been the continuation of Florence's story some twenty years later. Now a seasoned, middle-aged actress named Wiletta Mayer, this protagonist mirrors Mama in thought as much as *Trouble* mirrors *Florence* in structure. Like Mama, Wiletta suspects that whites (this time in American theater) are racist hypocrites. The plot is equally thin: Black and white actors rehearse a play *Chaos in Belleville);* they quarrel about an episode where a mother, while suspicious, permits her fugitive son to go for "safekeeping" with a Southern sheriff to his certain death. Wiletta is fired for demanding changes in the script, arguing that it suggests a stereotypical gullibility.

Childress's first structural change in *Trouble* occurs in the beginning, where she adds a "chorus-episode." In it, Wiletta shares the symbols of her ego with Henry, an elderly Irish doorman and former revolutionary fighter. The episodes open and close Act I, and they close Act II. Childress uses the "chorus-episodes" to tell the spectator what he should have noticed.

Childress arranges the seventeen episodes comprising the middle in such a way that Wiletta slowly reveals herself as a Harriet Tubman of the theater, the second major change. Each episode facilitates her development through a continuous chain of cause and effect. For example, episode five shows the antagonist Manners to be threatened by the subject matter of the white-authored play he is directing, a play with a theme on the Black struggle for political and economic equality. The threat comes from his own suppressed racial prejudice, which Wiletta recognizes but decides to tolerate. Under the guise of helping Wiletta with her characterization— of a Black Mama, no less—Manners continually attacks Wiletta, who in alternating episodes counterattacks:

> WILETTA: You don't ever listen to me. You hear others, but not me. And it's 'cause of the school.

> 'Cause they know 'bout justifying and the . . . antagonist . . . I never studied that, so you don't want to hear me, that's all right.

> MANNERS: Wiletta, dear, I'm sorry if I've complicated things. I'll make it as clear as I can. You are pretending to act and I can see through your pretense. I want truth. What is truth? Truth is simply whatever you can bring yourself to believe, that is all. You must have integrity about your work . . . a sense of . . . well, sense.

This well-designed attack-counteract leads to the climax, which differs from the climax in *Florence* in one very important way: There is no tragic recognition or change by the protagonist, but by her foils (the other Black members of the cast, especially John). Wiletta reverses the advice given to John (in the second episode of the beginning) that he should "do the Tom" and "laugh, laugh, laugh" at all of Manners' antics and jokes. Such behavior, Wiletta assures John, endears him to the director (symbol of the white theater establishment) and ensures him continued employment. However, when Wiletta can no longer stand Manners' putting her down, Wiletta reverses the advice: "John, I told you everything wrong." Childress designs here not so much a reversal in character as in the character's tactics for fighting racism. Childress pulls off Wiletta's grinning mask and makes her confront Manners not by openly attacking him but by prodding him into a racist outburst:

> MANNERS: I've heard you out and even though you think you know more than the author . . .

> WILETTA: You don't want to hear. You are a prejudiced man, a prejudiced racist. *(Gasp from company.)*

> MANNERS: I will not accept that from you or anyone else.

Childress gives the edge at this point to Manners, by giving him the obligatory speech so familiar in Black drama. Childress uses the speech to make Manners more than a one-dimensional racist. She does this by having Manners raise their right above race to class:

> MANNERS: You think we belong to one great, grand fraternity? They stole and snatched from me for years, and I'm a club member! Ever hear of an idea man? They picked my brains . . . My brains milked, while somebody else climbed on my back and took the credit.

The cast appears ready, as are most Blacks, to buy Manners' reasonable argument that he is as much a victim of what Oliver C. Cox calls "a political class" as is Wiletta. Since members of a political class are "a power group which tends to be organized for conflict," Childress has Wiletta win back the Blacks by inviting Manners to become one of the political class:

> WILETTA: Would you send your son to be murdered?

> MANNERS: *(So wound up, he answers without thinking.)* Don't compare yourself to me! What goes for my son doesn't necessarily go for yours! Don't compare him *(points to John.)* . . . with three

strikes against him, don't compare him with my son, they've got nothing in common . . . not a Goddam thing! *(He realize what he has said, also that he has lost company sympathy. He is utterly confused and embarrassed by his own statement.)* I tried to make it clear.

(Manners quickly exits to dressing room).

JOHN: It is clear.

By shirting the reversal to the protagonist's foils, Childress avoids weakening her heroine, another important convention of traditional Black drama. Like Mama in Branch's *Medal for Willie* and Rev. Lane in Mitchell's *Land Beyond the River,* the hero suffers but does not weaken or reverse moral stands.

The most significant difference between *Trouble* and *Florence* is that the end in *Trouble* consisting of three episodes, really does not return the play to a semblance of balance. When Manners storms out, the actors attempt to resolve the conflict and are interrupted with a message from the director dismissing the cast. The final "chorus-episode" leaves little doubt that Wiletta will probably be fired, an event which clearly violates Childress's label on the play as a "comedy drama in two acts." For this reason, Childress later added a third act. According to Doris E. Abramson, in this act, Wiletta and Manners exchange apologies after Wiletta has made him repeal her firing by threatening to notify all the papers. "The play ends on a note of optimism," says Abramson about this unpublished act.

Trouble and *Florence* are assaults against racial prejudice. The criticism that Childress "would have not sacrificed depth of character had she not assaulted race prejudice at every turn" misses the mark. For Childress is interested both in depth of character and in depth of message. She clearly has something on her mind, and she clearly lets the spectator know what it is.

The structure in Childress's interracial plays differs in three ways from the traditional structure in *Florence* and *Trouble.* The first is that the middle in the intraracial plays, *Wine in the Wilderness* and *Mojo,* functions as an exposition agent, not as the argumentation agent found in the interracial plays. The reason is that the author teaches by explaining how the apparent protagonist has come to his present condition. For example, Bill in *Wine* and Teddy in *Mojo* separate themselves from their communities. Bill lives and paints above a riot; Teddy brings white dates to his room, filled with "all the expensive junk and gadgetry that money can buy." Childress develops these characters and her Main Idea by having the apparent antagonists (Tommy in *Wine* and Irene in *Mojo*) "encounter" and change them.

The second major difference is the variety of constituent ideas found in the middle. While the ideas in the interracial plays are connected through cause and effect, the ideas here are mentioned and left, as is the case in *Wine:*

TOMMY: *(Looks at a portrait on the wall).* He look like somebody I know or maybe saw before.

BILL: That's Frederick Douglass. A man who used to be a slave. He escaped and spent his life trying to make us all free. He was a great man.

TOMMY: Thank you, Mr. Douglass. Who's the light colored man?

BILL: He's white. That's John Brown.

And the lesson goes on, citing several prominent figures in Black American history. This structural device permits Childress to place in the spectator's mind those heroes so often not found in history texts. Simultaneously, Childress justifies these citations by later using Bill's knowledge of history as an indictment for his lack of caring about *living* Black Americans. Needless to say, the lengthy citations outscope that constituent idea itself. However, Childress's traditional tendencies demanded the justification, and Childress gladly complied because she could supply even more generous doses of history and politics.

The doses of history and politics needed some structural device to make the information hold as the middle of a theater piece. Therefore, Childress created the third major structural difference between the intraracial and interracial plays: suspense. She creates her suspense by separating the point of the character's recognition by several episodes from the climax, the point where the characters act—or decide not to. Let me illustrate: The single-episode middle in *Mojo* contains ten subepisodes, each revealing the story of how Teddy comes to distrust Black women: Irene had asked him to marry her, but she then abandoned him. She has come to tell him why:

IRENE: The reason I asked you to be my husband was . . . I wanted to have a baby . . . and I wanted you for the father. . . . I didn't want the child to be outta wedlock. I didn't think it was too much any of our business . . . because you didn't seem to love me like I loved you . . . I went off and had the baby . . .

(Dead silence for a few seconds.)

TEDDY: I don't believe you.

IRENE: It's true. We got a daughter.

Like Mama in *Florence,* Teddy hurts: "Sorry . . . sorry to my heart. I'm sorry." Teddy's point of recognition differs from that in *Florence* only in placement: in the latter, Mama's recognition occurs *during* the climax; in Teddy's, recognition is followed by subepisodes of both characters' histories, by Irene's correctly stating that her personal problems stem from economic discrimination. While Irene shares her fears of an upcoming cancer operation and philosophizes like one scared to death of her condition, the spectator wonders how and when Bill is going to act decisively about the recognition. This device arouses the spectator's expectations and makes the spectator considerably more tolerant of sermonizing exposition.

Childress again uses this device in *Wine,* where the apparent antagonist, Tommy, discovers that Bill is exploiting her to get her to model for his painting. In a preparation episode, Childress makes Tommy overhear Bill's telephone description of one of his previous models: "This gorgeous satin chick is . . . is . . . black velvet moonlight . . . an ebony queen of the universe. . . ." Tommy mistakes the signs to be symbols, his true feelings about *her*. She later hears the truth from Bill's trusted friend:

> OLDTIMER: *(Unveils picture.)* And this is "Wine in the Wilderness" . . . The queen of the Universe . . . the finest chick in the world.
>
> TOMMY: That's not me.
>
> OLDTIMER: No, you gonna be this here last one. The worst gal in town. A messed up chick that— that—*(He unveils the third canvas and is face to face with the almost black canvas, then realizes what he has said. He turns to see the stricken look on Tommy's face.)*
>
> TOMMY: The messed-up chick, *that's* why they brought me here, ain't it? That's why he wanted to paint me! Say it!
>
> OLDTIMER: No, I'm lyin', I didn't mean it. It's the society that messed her up. Tommy, don't look that-a-way. It's art . . . it's only art . . . he couldn't mean you . . . it's art. . . .

By letting the spectator in on the sign-symbol confusion, Childress lets the spectator see beyond each of Bill's exploitative actions. The result is that the dramatic irony again makes the spectator a more suitable subject for the Main Idea: "Stop acting toward your people in the dark, with all head and no heart." Consequently, the audience more easily accepts both Bill's and Teddy's conversions following the climaxes.

Childress's final structural difference between her interracial and intraracial plays is that in the latter, she reverses the traditional convention that the spectator meet the protagonist before the antagonist. Because Childress observes the convention in **Florence** and **Trouble,** the spectator develops an understanding of any sympathy for Mama and Wiletta before the entrances of Mrs. Carter and Mr. Manners, the antagonists. On the other hand, if the spectator develops a sympathy and understanding of Bill and Teddy, and if he makes them the protagonists, the spectator becomes increasingly confused as he finds himself pitying and loving the apparent antagonist more than the apparent protagonist. Childress evidently *wants* this confusion so that she is able to make the structural device *itself* a carrier of the Main Idea: The Black middle class is not living up to its responsibility to less well off Black neighbors. Both plays hammer the point. For example, Bill and Teddy are satisfied to exploit a Black for purely selfish reasons. Bill wants to sell paintings of the Black struggle to survive. Teddy removes himself geographically and fills his space with the cultural "gadgets" of his white girlfriend's culture. By having the apparent antagonist cause the surfacing of the protagonist's profoundly unethical traits considerably after our attachment to the apparent protagonist, Childress catches *us* nodding. She has created a familiar cultural model, has made us love

him/us, and then has exposed him/us to be the shams we should not be.

For Childress, the God in each spectator gives Drama its definition and form. The definition as usual pits humans against their fate; more specifically, it pits a Black man against the ungodliness in whites *and* Blacks. Godliness is the heart of the definition because of the high purpose assigned the drama—not the religiosity that is such an important ingredient of traditional Black drama. In fact, Childress religiously avoids religiosity; even her traditional mama, who bakes for church bazaars, confronts Mrs. Carter on her own terms without "calling on the Lord." Nevertheless, Mama is as godly as *the* mama, and godliness is a constant theme.

The variations on the theme reflect the artistic and political phases of that time in the Black community. Each play documents Childress's progressive ideas concerning Black well-being for that particular time. For example, Mama in 1950 was simply asking Mrs. Carter to help Florence survive. But in 1955, Wiletta demands that Manners let Black people control their own projected images. By 1969, Tommy, ignoring integration causes, demands that the Black man live up to his responsibilities. By the next year, which ends this brief study, Irene comes home to Teddy to get things straight between them. This evolution, one immediately recognizes, stays ahead of the ideas which later become a staple of Black thought.

The Childress dramatic form, unlike her thought, does not reflect the contemporary forms prevalent in Black theater circles. Childress remained a traditionalist even during the sixties, when Amiri Baraka and others experimented freely with Antonin Artaud. Childress simply rearranged the traditional form to serve her purposes. Childress's rearrangements, along with her significant body of works, make American theater indebted to her. (pp. 117-27)

> *Samuel A. Hay, "Alice Childress's Dramatic Structure," in* Black Women Writers (1950-1980): A Critical Evaluation, *edited by Mari Evans, Anchor Press/Doubleday, 1984, pp. 117-28.*

Alice Childress with Kathleen Betsko and Rachel Koenig (interview date 1987)

[*In the following excerpt from an interview published in Kathleen Betsko and Rachel Koenig's* Interviews with Contemporary Women Playwrights *(1987), Childress discusses her works and her writing process.*]

[Childress]: I wrote my play **Wedding Band** as a remembrance of the intellectual poor. The poor, genteel and sensitive people who are seamstresses, coal carriers, candymakers, sharecroppers, bakers, baby caretakers, housewives, foot soldiers, penny-candy sellers, vegetable peelers, who are somehow able to sustain within themselves the poet's heart, sensitivity and appreciation of pure emotion, the ability to freely spend tears and laughter without saving them up for a rainy day. I was raised by and among such people living on the poorest blocks in Harlem and have met many more on the boundary lines of the segregated life—the places where black, white, brown, yellow and red sometimes meet— in bus stations, train and plane waiting rooms, on lines where we pay gas, light and telephone bills.

Wedding Band kept coming at me from hidden, unexpected places, the characters called on my mind while I was trying to write something else, demanding attention, getting together, coming into being. It was a play I did not want to write, about people few others wanted to hear from . . . I thought. It somehow seemed to be answering back all the stage and screen stories about rich, white landowners and their "octoroon" mistresses.

Such stories meant nothing in my life. I am a black woman of light complexion, have no white relatives except on the other side of slavery, and have experienced the sweetness, joy and bitterness of living almost entirely within the Harlem community. I really did not wish to beat the drum for an interracial couple and yet there they were in front of me, not giving a damn about public opinion of this or that past day. It was like being possessed by rebel spirits, ideas clinging, taking over and starting my day for me. Instead of a joyous experience, writing the play became a trial, a rough journey through reams of paper. Characters know; they won't be fooled, not even by their medium, the writer. They *allow* you to write them, pushing you along until they're satisfied that they've done their thing to the utmost of your ability.

I was born in Charleston, South Carolina, and raised on 118th Street between Lenox and Fifth avenues in Harlem, New York City. My grandmother and her friends were not ashamed of living: "Got it to do!" they said. When people were ill, neighbors rallied and brought various home remedies to the bedside, seldom a doctor. Those days are almost gone, thank God. Who wants to live with one foot in hell just for the sake of nostalgia? Our time is forever now! Today our youngsters can freely discuss sex. Soon they will even be able to openly discuss one of the results of sex—life. I also remember death, funerals, just before it went out of style to have the last service within the home instead of at the undertaking parlor. In one corner of the kitchen, a big truckdriver of a man wept tears into a large handkerchief, his shoulders shaking with grief: "Why did she leave us? Only last week I was talking to her and answered real short: 'Shut up.' I said that to her . . . and now she's gone." And those there gathered answered him with healing words of comfort: "Well, God knows you loved her, don't take it so hard, you did your best." They brought him through that day. Other men, richer and smarter, had to go through three years of therapy to find the reasons why and why and why . . . and to know there's always another way. On our block there was prostitution, but we were so damned blind until even the prostitutes were called "Miss" Margaret or "Miss"

Beatrice or whatever. And they did not beckon to men until our backs were turned, most of the time. Heroin was not yet King of the Ghetto and a boy would not dream of killing his grandmother or hurting his mama or her friends in order to pour cooked opium dust through a hole in his arm. But they weren't "the good old days." The only good days are ahead. The characters kept chasing me down. Men in love with "nothing to offer." Women who couldn't or wouldn't hold back their emotions "for the sake of the race." They tap at the brain and move a pen to action in the middle of the night. They are alive, they really are, pushing and shoving interfering creators out of the way. Now, in this slot of time, they return singing old songs about inner discovery. Other characters keep knocking at our doors, pushing, pulling, tearing at seams of life. Poets, novelists, painters, playwrights stand around shifting from foot to foot, trying to keep score. Ordinary people know more about how to live with love and hate than given credit for . . . even though they're never seen on talk shows.

[Interviewer]: *There was a difference between the white criticism of* **Wedding Band** *[a play whose central characters are an interracial couple; it premiered in 1966] and what the black critics had to say, wasn't there?*

The white criticism was that the interracial couple needn't have stayed [in a Jim Crow state], that they could have gone away; they felt the male character, the white baker, should have turned his back on his mother and sister and escaped. Now, that's a very hard thing for poor people to do. It's easier for wealthy people. They can leave *and* send money home to their dependents. This baker *is* his family's livelihood. His mother contributed all of her money to his small bakery shop. For him to walk away from family and debts is almost unheard of in poor communities.

The black critics' objections were: Why talk about this interracial issue at all? Why couldn't I just write about a black couple? It may have sounded as though I were praising interracial love but, in fact, this was not my objective. In almost everything I write there are black couples, and there is also one in *Wedding Band.* But this was a true story my grandmother had told me, about a black woman named Miss Julia, who lived across the street from her in South Carolina and who "kept company" with a white butcher. I made him a baker in the play because I thought it would be more palatable for the audience than butchering. Black critics felt that the character I based on Miss Julia should not have wanted to marry a white man, no matter that this situation often occurs in real life. The black audience would have been more comfortable if Julia had rejected her white lover. That was true even of the last production of the play at Joe Papp's theater. [The New York Shakespeare Festival, Public Theatre, 1972]. It had been done earlier at the University of Michigan at Ann Arbor [1966] and in Chicago, where we had our greatest success. Black audiences in Chicago really liked the play. They sold out the whole six weeks, standing room only; you couldn't get tickets. (pp. 62-5)

Did you find less resistance to your artistic vision in the publishing world?

Yes I did. I didn't have to fight and struggle as in the theater because, almost by accident, an editor [at Coward McCann] came to me who knew of my playwriting—the late Ferdinand Monjo, who was also a noted children's author. He said, "Alice, you've said so much about drugs in your writing, why don't you really put some time into it and do a book?" That's how I came to write *A Hero Ain't Nothin but a Sandwich.* He told me it had to be a young adult book because he was a young adult book editor, and young adults needed such a book.

In **A Hero** . . . *each chapter represents a different character's point of view: the boy on drugs, the boy's mother, the boy's teacher, and so on. Is this an instance of your playwright's training overlapping into your fiction?*

Yes—theater and film. I was very impressed by the film *Rashomon* [by Kurosawa]. A woman was raped; she tells her story and the other characters tell their stories. Each one's version of the event is reenacted within the film. But all were *lying* except one, who was observing from a distance. And when he tells what happened, you understand why all the others lied. But I do an opposite thing. In my writing, all the stories differ, but I see that you can get ten *different* stories out of people *all telling the truth.* We don't all view things the same way, each perspective is different. Many-leveled narration is something I do well. It's true to theater. When I'm writing a character that I see as a villain, I try to take the villain's side and believe in the righteousness of the villainous act. In *A Hero* . . . we pondered long about cutting out the drug pusher's side of the story.

Because it was a book for young people?

Yes. The drug pusher is so convincing about the rightness of the acts and the reader feels for him. Monjo was very helpful. After a great deal of talk about it, we decided to leave the character in.

A Hero *went as far as the Supreme Court in a book-banning case, along with books by eight other authors. Will you discuss censorship?*

Nine books got to the Supreme Court, and mine was one of them. I don't know if I'm the first or only woman whose book got to the Supreme Court on a banning. They also banned Hawthorne's *The Scarlet Letter* because it was sympathetic to an unmarried pregnant woman. In one school, the authorities banned *Romeo and Juliet,* saying the Nurse was a poor role model because Juliet's parents had hired her to take care of their daughter, and there she was passing notes and arranging liaisons, covering up that Romeo and Juliet were seeing each other. Another school banned all of Shakespeare's plays *except Romeo and Juliet.*

Some people say, "I like this book, such a beautiful book shouldn't be banned." But they don't mind it when a book they *don't* like is banned. I feel we must be against banning regardless of whether we like a book. We do not have to accept its content and quality, we do not have to read or accept a book at all—but to ban it is wrong.

Do you have any particular criteria you use to judge what is bad and what is helpful in criticism?

Yes. I weigh it and think about it. If ten people read or see a play at different times and they all zero in on the same trouble spot, the problem might not be *exactly* what they are expressing, but the playwright knows that there is *something* there that needs to be cleared up. I have an instinctive feeling when someone is giving me "wrong" criticism. I'm wary when I've labored over something for five years and someone comes over and tells me in five minutes, "Do this, do that, change this . . ." Well, you can't just trust and do what you are told. But at the same time, you must be open to "good" criticism. You have to get off by yourself and find out if it's merely your ego that is suffering. The viewer of a film or play doesn't have to spend all the years you've spent to know the ending is upsetting to them.

Do you care if your endings are upsetting to the audience?

No, I don't, but I do care if the audience feels something is unbelievable or a lie. All fiction is tampering with the truth, but it bothers me if something seems like it's been thrown in just to make the script "work." I can't make a character do or say something that I don't think this character would do or say just because the audience would prefer it. But I do have to listen to a director or producer on whether a scene is too long, whether the progression of the play is being held up because of it. It's not only what the play has to say, but how it flows. If it's too long, it's too long. I don't care for lengthy plays—four, six, eight hours long. I don't want to go back the next night to see how it ends. I want to sit in one session, and see and hear a play all the way through, I want it all to fit, there and then. Some people criticize the "well-made" play, but it is not to be knocked. If you buy a suit you want it to be well made. You don't want the tailor to experiment; we want something dependable; well, *I* do. (pp. 65-7)

You've published several novels. Have they influenced your playwriting? Have you mastered something in your fiction that helps you to create the "well-made" play?

It's the other way around. The theater influences my novel writing. I feel each chapter is a scene. But when writing novels, I find description difficult. With plays, after we've described the set, we're free of that. We don't *have to* describe the sun rising or the sound of rain. Someone else brings lighting, set, costumes and sound to life for us. Playwrights are specialists in dialogue, situation and conflict; and they must make it all happen within a limited time and space. The novel is more permissive. When I'm writing a book, I visualize it all on a stage. I'm very pleased when critics say my novels feel like plays. I've learned to lean on theater instead of breaking with it. I came to theater first, acted for eleven years with the American Negro Theater and started writing out of that experience. When writing a novel or a play I act out all the parts. I've actually gotten up, walked around and played out a scene when I've run into difficulty with the writing . . . moved through all the entrances and exits. Making theater is more than how you feel and speak, it's how you move. You have to work it out, act it out, think it out, as if on a stage. I also think that way about a book.

You were an actress first . . .

Oh, yes. I was in the original cast of *Anna Lucasta* [1944] on Broadway. I've also worked a little in television and movies. But racial prejudice was such that I was considered "too light" to play my real self and they would not cast light-skinned blacks in white roles. I realized I had to have some other way of creating. I love acting, the art of acting, but not the business of acting and auditioning. Most of the time, I didn't like the parts they wanted me to play. Unless one is lucky enough to get a lot of stage work, creativity is cut off or underexercised. I decided I'd rather create from the start, create good roles I'd like to play by writing them. I found, however, I wasn't interested in writing parts for myself. I've never written anything for me—though I've been tempted. When my work is presented, I feel I belong out front. I want to be the beholder, the audience.

What exactly bothered you about the roles you played as an actress?

They were stereotypes, "packaged" situations. I don't necessarily mean derogatory stereotypes, but too predictable. "The black" would do one thing, "the white" another thing, and, of course, by the end they would all come together and resolve their differences—packaged solutions.

It's all very well to just take any old play and cast it from different races with no further comment—a nice exercise in democracy, a social service to one another—but I think there is something very particular about different races and religious backgrounds in America that has yet to be fully explored.

Do you mean that in the effort to be "universal," we are losing something about the parochial?

Yes. Some of the greatest plays have come from Sean O'Casey, *Irish* playwright, who wrote *about* the poor Irish, *for* the Irish. Look at the works of Sholem Aleichem and [Isaac] Peretz—out of the blood and bones of Jewish tradition. The black poet, Paul Laurence Dunbar, works the same sort of magic about particular people.

You're working on a novel about Dunbar now. Did you research extensively?

Yes. Writing about New York City in 1895, I have to find out what it was like here at that time, what products

were being used, what clothing was in style. You try to get the underlying feel of the times. . . . My writing stops when I don't know what my characters would have done in certain situations. . . what they did in houses without bathrooms. . . . This often entails reading articles and books that have nothing to do with your story but which reveal the ambience of the period. I'm writing about African-Americans, but in my research have fallen headlong into the Jewish life of the late eighteen hundreds, immigrants coming from Europe, the teeming streets of the Lower East Side. All of these details help a story to bloom. Also, I try not to write in the past tense.

Another feature of your theater training perhaps?

It's more theatrical to write in the present tense, and more interesting. I have Paul Laurence Dunbar and his sweetheart walking across the Brooklyn Bridge when it was two years old, when people were afraid to cross it. I have them talking about the newness of it.

How did your interest in Dunbar evolve?

I'm writing about Paul and his wife, Alice—their personal relationship. I read many published papers and correspondence they exchanged. I went down South and visited with their niece, and saw hundreds of original letters in faded ink. I decided to write about the four years they were married. Their union was turbulent. . . . Frightening. They were obviously in love but also tried to destroy one another. I liked the drama of it all . . . and the historical aspect. (pp. 67-9)

If someone had offered you a stage for the Dunbar story, as Coward McCann offered to publish a book [**A Hero. . .**], *would you have written it as a play?*

That would have been delightful . . . but a play would have been more difficult. A book is more lenient than the stage, which has such space and time limitations I'd have to throw out half of my story.

Why did you put your piece **Gullah** *on the stage instead of into a novel?*

It would have been simpler to write it as a novel, I felt moved to write a play. I started once on it—a big long thing—but it didn't hang together well. Then I tried again and that didn't work either. Sometime later, the South Carolina Commission of the Arts wanted a play specific to South Carolina. They only wanted a hour-long piece so that it could tour schools all over the state. Well, I said I'd boil down what I had, and make a short version. My husband, Nathan Woodard, composed music for it. We were quite pleased with the result and stopped worrying about it being full-length.

Gullah is a name for a language, isn't it? A very musical language specific to certain islands off the coast of South Carolina. How did this language evolve?

It's a poetry of the people, and embodies their poetic expression and poetic feeling. During the time of slavery, Africans were often sold in mixed lots of different nationalities and languages, because their owners didn't want them to communicate with on another. You see, there were about seven hundred fifty different tongues spoken throughout Africa. So the slave traders hit upon the idea of forming groups, "parcels," by selecting one slave from each nationality. The various groups were sold for labor on different islands off the South Carolinian coast, and a language evolved from the many African languages mixed with English and even a little German. Some people think the word *Gullah* came from people trying to say *Angola.* They became known as Gola or Gullah people. Island isolation helped preserve the Africanisms that blacks on the mainland soon lost through assimilation. My stepfather was born on one of those islands. After he died (on Edisto Island), some of his people came to visit us in New York. I could hardly understand a word. Now, of course, there are bridges, businesses have opened, property has been bought for homes and resorts. The South Carolina Commission on the Arts didn't want us to use the title **Gullah.** The word is sometimes spoken in a prejudicial way to mock country people and the way they talk. The play was called **Sea Island Song** down there but it sounded too Hawaiian, misleading, I

thought. When we came back North I went back to the original **Gullah.**

What's happening to the people and their culture?

They are being scattered and shattered. That's partly what **Gullah** is about. Their way of life is ebbing away. Their African baskets take weeks to weave. We live in an age of plastic and metal. They can't make a livelihood working with their hands. That's the problem.

Is that true of all the arts these days, do you think?

It feels that way. The longer you take to make something, the less you are paid. If a publisher pays you an advance and it takes you six months to write something, that's what you make for six months' work. If it takes three years to write it, you still make the same amount of money. So some writers do tend to think about what they can whip together fairly fast. It's not satisfying; sometimes you have to let the work go with regret. I don't think I've ever really "finished" anything to my satisfaction . . . no matter how long I've worked on the material.

Childress and her husband Nathan Woodard, composer of the music for Sea Island Song.

You've said the less a writer understands the faster he or she can write . . .

Yes. And you're forgiven for what you don't know. But when you understand your material, you can't shove it along at great speed. When you "know," there is a pleasure in taking time, in stopping yourself, in choosing another direction. As my present editor, Refna Wilkins, once said to me, "Alice, you always pick the hard way." I ask myself if it's healthy, choosing the more difficult road. I guess the bottom line about writing is that it's a torturous process, but the beautiful part is there's a deep, indescribable, inexplicable *satisfaction* in having written. A feeling of elevation and joy afterward that is greater than the despair of sitting there and doing it. I don't enjoy the writing process. I like writing when I have completed it. (pp. 69-71)

> *Alice Childress, in an interview in* Interviews with Contemporary Women Playwrights, *edited by Kathleen Betsko and Rachel Koenig, Beech Tree Books, 1987, pp. 62-74.*

FURTHER READING

Austin, Gayle. "Alice Childress: Black Woman Playwright as Feminist Critic." *The Southern Quarterly* XXV, No. 3 (Spring 1987): 53-62.
> Explores the feminist themes of *Trouble in Mind* and *Wine in the Wilderness,* asserting that Childress was ahead of her time as an advocate of women's issues.

Brown-Guillory, Elizabeth. "Images of Blacks in Plays by Black Women." *Phylon* XLVII, No. 3 (September 1986): 230-37.
> Argues that Childress has made "monumental contributions to black women's playwriting in America" and that her heroine in *Wine in the Wilderness* "survives whole, just as Childress has, regardless of seemingly impenetrable barriers."

————. "Alice Childress: A Pioneering Spirit." *SAGE* IV, No. 1 (Spring 1987): 66-8.
> Interview with Childress, focusing on her childhood, her writing process, and her dramas.

————. "Black Women Playwrights: Exorcising Myths." *Phylon* XLVIII, No. 3 (Fall 1987): 229-39.
> Examines a selection of works by Childress, Lorraine Hansberry, and Ntozake Shange—"crucial links in the development of black women playwriting in America."

Curb, Rosemary. "An Unfashionable Tragedy of American Racism: Alice Childress's *Wedding Band.*" *MELUS* 7, No. 4 (Winter 1980): 57-68.
> Surveys Childress's career as a dramatist, placing emphasis on *Wedding Band,* "her finest and most serious piece of literature."

Govan, Sandra Y. "Alice Childress's *Rainbow Jordan:* The Black Aesthetic Returns Dressed in Adolescent Fiction." *Children's Literature Association Quarterly* 13, No. 1 (Summer 1988): 70-4.
> Explores the concept of a black aesthetic in *Rainbow Jordan.*

Harris, Trudier. "'I Wish I Was a Poet': The Character As Artist in Alice Childress's *Like One of the Family.*" *Black American Literature Forum* 14, No. 1 (Spring 1980): 24-30.
> Studies Childress's combining of oral and written forms of the African-American tradition in *Like One of the Family.*

Miller, Jeanne-Marie A. "Images of Black Women in Plays by Black Playwrights." *CLA Journal* XX, No. 4 (June 1977): 494-507.
> Examines female characters in works by black dramatists, profiling Childress's strong, black female characters.

Sloan, James Park. Review of *A Short Walk,* by Alice Childress. *The New York Times Book Review* LXXXIV, No. 45 (11 November 1979): 14, 46.
> Praises *A Short Walk,* calling it "a stately achievement."

Tyler, Anne. "Looking for Mom." *The New York Times Book Review* LXXXVI, No. 17 (26 April 1981): 52-3, 69.
> Review of *Rainbow Jordan,* proclaiming it "a beautiful book."

Wilson, Geraldine L. "A Novel to Enjoy and Remember." *Freedomways* 20, No. 2 (1980): 101-02.
> Laudatory review of *A Short Walk,* praising Childress's ability to write dialogue and create believable characters.

John Pepper Clark

1935-

Nigerian poet, dramatist, essayist, critic, and scriptwriter.

Along with Wole Soyinka, Clark is one of Nigeria's foremost anglophone dramatists and poets. Although he writes in English in order to reach the widest possible audience, African images, themes, settings, and speech patterns are at the center of his work. Clark describes himself as "that fashionable cultural phenomenon they call 'mulatto'—not in flesh but in mind!" Critics note a wide range of influences in Clark's work, from ancient and modern Western sources to the myths and legends of Clark's people, the Ijaw.

Born in 1935 in Nigeria, Clark became interested in poetry while a student at University College in Ibadan. Before his graduation in 1960, he founded *The Horn,* an undergraduate magazine that published poems, reviews, and articles by young African writers. In 1962 he traveled to the United States to study at Princeton University; two years later he produced *America, Their America,* a collection of poems and prose that took a "satirical swipe at the USA," according to one critic. After returning to Nigeria, he worked briefly at the *Daily Express* and coedited *Black Orpheus* with Abiola Irele. In addition to writing several volumes of poetry and plays, Clark has also produced two documentary films: *The Ozidi of Atazi* and *The Ghost Town.* Since 1968 he has taught African literature and English at the University of Lagos and is currently the director of the PEC Repertory Theatre in Lagos.

Clark's first two plays, *Song of a Goat* (performed in 1961) and *The Masquerade* (performed in 1965), contain elements of classical Greek and Shakespearean drama, the poetic plays of T.S. Eliot, and the folk literature of the Ijaw people, which, according to Clark, has much in common with classical drama. In the first play, a barren woman consults with a masseur and conceives a child by her husband's brother. Unable to accept this situation, both the husband and his brother commit suicide. The child, grown to manhood and unaware of the circumstances of his birth, is the tragic hero of *The Masquerade.* He travels away from his native village and becomes engaged to a beautiful, strong-willed girl. When the young man's background is revealed, the girl's father forbids her to marry, but she refuses to abide by his decision. In the violent denouement, all die. Both plays are written in verse and share a relentless aura of doom; neighbors function as a chorus, commenting on the tragic happenings. *Song of a Goat, The Masquerade,* and *The Raft* (performed in 1966) were first published in the volume *Three Plays* (1964). *The Raft* concerns the misadventures of four men on a raft who attempt to bring logs downstream to be sold. Critics generally viewed the play as an exploration of the

human condition or as a character study, although some have interpreted it as an allegory of the political situation in Nigeria.

Ozidi: A Play (performed in 1966), Clark's first full-length play, was adapted from an Ijaw saga, the performance of which traditionally takes seven days and involves mime, music, and dance. Clark retained many of these elements in his version and also used masks and drums for the first time in his work. *Ozidi* is a revenge drama which, like the author's earlier plays, involves a family curse and a series of violent actions.

A Reed in the Tide (1965) was Clark's first volume of poetry to be published internationally. Besides new poems, the volume also includes many pieces from Clark's first poetry collection, *Poems* (1962) and some from *America, Their America* (1964). Most of the poems are "occasional verse," inspired by the poet's immediate surroundings. Such poems as "Agbor Dancer," "Fulani Cattle," and "Girl Bathing" are based on Nigerian scenes; others are based on Clark's trip to the United

States: "Three Moods of Princeton," "Two Views of Marilyn Monroe," and "Times Square." Two of Clark's most famous poems, "Ibadan" and "Night Rain," describe the Nigerian landscape. Many of his poems, however, go beyond concrete description to take on symbolic value. For example, in "Agbor Dancer," Clark reflects on how he as a writer has moved away from his native culture in his art, in contrast to the dancer.

Stylistically, Clark's early verse reflects his study of English poetry, particularly that of Gerard Manley Hopkins; one of Clark's poems is entitled "Variations on Hopkins." Like Hopkins, Clark used complicated metrical patterns and rich, sensuous language. Critics noted, however, that Clark moved away from this style in the later poems of *A Reed in the Tide*. They applauded this simpler style and contended that his most beautiful and effective lines are those filled with nature imagery. *Casualties: Poems 1966-1968* (1970) is a book of verse devoted to the Nigerian-Biafran conflict, during which Clark supported the Nigerian government. The role of the artist during war is an underlying theme throughout the book.

Clark's most recent books, *State of the Union* (1985) and *Mandela and Other Poems* (1988), are collections of verse that have been praised for their simple and clear language. In the former work, the author examines the moral and social deterioration of Nigeria, and in the latter he studies the wider demise of Africa. "A Letter to Oliver Tambo," "The Beast in the South," "Mandela," and "News from Ethiopia and the Sudan" have been cited by Nigerian critic J. O. J. Nwachukwu-Agbada as some of Clark's best work in *Mandela*: "The lines here are highly evocative, with an evenness of metaphoric freshness. Clark, it seems, has bid a final good-bye to the esoteric and recondite imagery of prewar Nigerian poetry. . . ."

Clark is recognized as one of the most sophisticated and polished writers in Africa today. Although his more recent poems have taken on a simpler tone, his works continue to reflect the richness of Africa's peoples and cultures. Of the poet, critic, and playwright, Bruce King has observed: "Among the second generation of Nigerian writers, J. P. Clark is perhaps the best example of an all-round man of letters."

(For further information about Clark's life and works, see *Black Writers; Contemporary Authors*, Vols. 65-68; *Contemporary Authors New Revision Series*, Vol. 16; and *Contemporary Literary Criticism*, Vol. 38. For related criticism, see the entry on Nigerian Literature in *Twentieth-Century Literary Criticism*, Vol. 30.)

PRINCIPAL WORKS

Song of a Goat (drama) [first performance] 1961
Poems (poetry) 1962
America, Their America (satire) 1964
Three Plays: Song of a Goat, The Masquerade, The Raft (dramas) [first publication] 1964

The Masquerade (drama) [first performance] 1965
A Reed in the Tide (poetry) 1965; also published as *A Reed in the Tide: A Selection of Poems*, 1970
Ozidi: A Play (drama) [first performance] 1966
The Raft (drama) [first performance] 1966
Casualties: Poems, 1966-68 (poetry) 1970
The Example of Shakespeare: Critical Essays on African Literature (essays) 1970
A Decade of Tongues: Selected Poems 1958-1968 (poetry) 1981
State of the Union (poetry) 1985
Mandela and Other Poems (poetry) 1988

Anthony Astrachan (essay date 1964)

[*In the following excerpt, Astrachan compares* Song of a Goat *and* The Masquerade *to Sophocles's* Oedipus *plays, contending that Clark's plays can "compete as equals on the stage of world literature without losing a cowrie's worth of their African qualities."*]

John Pepper Clark is in an unusual position for any playwright, much less a young playwright in a young country: his plays must be reviewed as literature by critics who have not seen them performed. This is the condition in which one often writes about Sophocles, Shakespeare, Racine. Fortunately, Clark can stand the comparison. At his weakest, he is more competent than many dramatists more widely known outside Africa; at his strongest, he is magnificent. His *Three Plays* can compete as equals on the stage of world literature without losing a cowrie's worth of their African qualities.

Lest the gods of tragedy deem the drawing of such praise *hubris,* let us ward off nemesis with a close, even a carping look. My doubts and disturbances, where they arise, do not detract from my opinion that Clark is a first-rate dramatist; great quality produces great expectations, and expectations should be examined.

Song of a Goat . . . and *The Masquerade* are a related pair of tragedies that make one look to the *Oedipus* plays for analogy. The language and feeling of both are so rich in action that the reader is compelled to stage them in the theatre of his interior vision, and not having seen them becomes less of a handicap. The third play, *The Raft,* is not strictly speaking a tragedy and is less brilliant than the others, but as we shall see, it has something in common with them.

Song of a Goat tells of the fisherman, Zifa, who has become impotent after the birth of his first child. He and his wife Ebiere ask a masseur for help, but the masseur can neither cure nor remove the curse and suggests that Zifa make over Ebiere to his brother, Tonye. All three reject the notion, but the idea has been planted, and eventually Tonye and Ebiere make love but without ceremony. When discovered, Tonye hangs himself before Zifa can kill him, and Zifa drowns himself. Clark lists neighbours as chorus in this tragedy, but to me half the function of chorus is exercised by Orukorere, Zifa's half-possessed aunt. (pp. 21-2)

The language evokes the pity and terror which are the prime aims of tragedy, and the dramatic construction has an aura of doom.... Orukorere evokes the terror of the offense that is still to come, in her half-crazed nightmare:

> I must find him, the leopard
> That will devour my goat, I must
> Find him....

These and other lines are so rich in myth that again and again they bring to mind the Oedipus plays. And this speech of Orukorere's hints at a development by unveilling, a tragedy of revelation that is the keynote and the vehicle of action in *Oedipus Tyrannos.* Yet this is what in fact is missing in **Song of a Goat.** There is no development, no suspense, nothing like the change of Oedipus from saviour of Thebes to ruler to investigator to prosecutor to transgressor and victim. There is no change, growth or degeneration in Tonye and Ebiere to bring them to sin, nor are we sure their coming together is a sin.... If Clark means that adultery without ceremony is a sin, he does not make it clear.

And indeed the basis of the tragedy is not clear. Is Zifa's impotence after he has fathered one child punishment for an offense? An offense of Zifa's and one by his father are hinted, but never given enough emphasis to bear the burden of tragedy. Perhaps impotence is an offense in itself in a society where fertility is all; the sexual and agricultural imagery strengthens this suspicion. But there is no action on Zifa's part that brings him low. He even fails in his attempt to kill his offending brother— and it seems to me to ask too much of the reader or spectator to think that Tonye's suicide is caused by Zifa's pursuit of him. Tonye kills himself because he has offended his brother or dishonoured his family, not because—at least not only because—he is afraid of Zifa's wrath. Zifa's tragedy is a tragedy without cause. Tonye and Ebiere too, though they have done something, have had their act predicated from the beginning in Zifa's impotence so that they too seem victims of external forces.

The Masquerade is not only a sequel to **Song,** but a tragedy of the same kind, a tragedy without *hubris.* A young man, Tufa, has won the heart of Titi, a girl who has previously refused all suitors. There is some mystery about Tufa. In mid-play it is revealed that Tufa is the offspring of the accurst union of Tonye and Ebiere (who is now said to have died giving birth to him, though in **Song** she is merely said to have miscarried), and Diribi, Titi's father, drives him forth. When Titi follows him, Diribi pursues and kills her. Tufa goes off to kill himself, and Diribi, spiritually emasculated by his vengeance, is left to punishment in Forcados.

Pity and terror are again present in language and plot, the more so in the contrast between the lyrical love passage between Tufa and Titi in the first scene and the grim destruction of the last. There is more suspense, more development in the dramatic construction—the revelation does not come at the beginning and the characters react more strongly when it does come. Titi, for instance, rejects the idea that marrying Tufa necessarily means pollution.... But Titi also rejects the chance to elope with Tufa, which might mean eluding the curse, because she wants to finish her bridal pageant. By insisting on the fulfilment of one custom, she lays herself open to the nemesis of another. This strengthens the myth qualities of the play.

So, perhaps, does the curse pursuing the family of Zifa, but again the curse is not brought down by action on the part of the tragic hero-victim. Diribi implies that Tufa transgressed by concealing his birth—the masquerade of the title. But how can it be a masquerade when Tufa does not know the circumstances of his birth until they are revealed in the market place? The curse on the house of Laius is renewed by a fresh act in each generation, witting (Antigone's burial of her brother) or unwitting (Oedipus's slaying of Laius and marriage with Jocasta). Similarly with the curse on the house of Atreus. But the curse on the house of Zifa depends on no act. It is an external force whose victims are helpless against it.... (pp. 22-3)

The Raft, too, is a play of victims, though it is no tragedy. It is the story of four men on a timber raft drifting down the Niger. They get caught in a whirlpool and rig a sail so a storm will blow them out, but the raft breaks up and Oloto is carried off on the part with the sail. There three survivors drift until a steamboat comes up; Ogrope, trying to swim to the boat to ask a rescue, is beaten off by its crew and caught in its sternwheel. Kengide and Ibobo drift on toward Burutu but become lost in the fog while trying to make a landfall by night. There is no why and wherefore—only the showing of four fairly well differentiated characters falling victim in different ways to a hostile environment. There is no apparent connection between a character and his particular misfortune.

The language is not so rich as in the other two plays; there are fewer metaphors, and the strengths lie in the evocation of life on the river and of Ijaw proverbs and customs rather than in the virtue of the words themselves. **The Raft** lacks the qualities of myth that make the other plays so intense.

One might say that the characters have too little action and the raft too much. When I read the play I thought it would be difficult to stage.... Clever staging cannot make great theatre out of a piece that has too little dramatic action. (pp. 23-4)

Still, producing all three plays at once on the interior stage, I am excited by the pity and terror of the two tragedies, by the vividness of their language and their myth-like qualities. I am more quietly pleased by the apparent accuracy of the dialogue and the unveiling of character in *The Raft*. I am also depressed by the fact that in all three plays, the protagonists are victims of punishment without cause, or punishment beyond their desserts, whether from society, gods or nature....

I can imagine someone saying, "Well, this is the way of Ijaw tragedy, and you cannot expect it to be like Greek tragedy." I would not be satisfied. Greek tragedy set the canons for world tragedy, and if Clark is good enough to be mentioned in the same breath with Sophocles, he owes us and himself a better strophe. The novels of Achebe and the plays of Soyinka show that individuals can assert themselves against society and environment and gods, in the most traditional cultures of Africa. I wonder if the things I find missing in Clark's plays are entirely deliberate omissions, left out in accordance with the dictates of a philosophy, a world view or a culture. These plays are all quite short. If Clark had to write a three-hour play as rich and intense as these, he might be forced to a degree of plot development and character assertion that he has not yet achieved.

Despite these dissatisfactions, John Pepper Clark has already achieved a great deal.... Despite *and* because of Aristotle's canons of tragedy, Clark's plays are good plays, and if his best work is still to be written, Nigerian drama has a truly exciting future on which to raise the curtain. (p. 24)

> *Anthony Astrachan, "Like Goats to Slaughter: Three Plays, by John Pepper Clark," in* Black Orpheus, *No. 16, October, 1964, pp. 21-4.*

LeRoi Jones (essay date 1964)

[*Jones, who changed his name to Amiri Baraka in 1968, is a seminal figure in the development of contemporary black literature in the United States. His works, which cover a variety of literary genres, focus on the oppression of blacks in white society; he is perhaps best known for the plays* Dutchman *and* The Slave. *In the following excerpt, he briefly praises the "gentle and lyrical" language of Clark's* Song of a Goat.]

John Pepper Clark, in the few poems he has in the [Langston] Hughes anthology [*Poems from Black Africa*], but more so because of his verse play **Song of a Goat,** convinces me that he is one of the most interesting Africans writing, English or French. Mr. Clark is a Nigerian, born in 1935, though I understand he is now in the graduate school at Princeton. For sure, nothing he could ever learn at Princeton would help him write so beautiful a work as **Song of a Goat.** It is English, but it is not. The tone, the references (immediate and accreted) belong to what I must consider an African experience. The English is pushed, as [Léopold Sédar] Senghor wished all Africans to do with European languages, past the immaculate boredom of the recent Victorians to a quality of experience that is non-European, though it is

the European tongue which seems to shape it, externally. But Clark is after a specific emotional texture nowhere available in European literature or life.

Masseur:	Your womb Is open and warm as a room It ought to accommodate many.
Ebière:	Well, it seems to like staying empty.
Masseur:	An empty house, my daughter, is a thing Of danger. If men will not live in it Bats or grass will, and that is enough Signal for worse things to come in.

The play is about a traditional West African family split and destroyed by adultery. And the writing moves easily through the myth heart of African life, building a kind of ritual drama that depends as much on the writer's insides for its exactness and strength as it does on the narrating of formal ritualistic acts. The language is gentle and lyrical most of the time, but Clark's images and metaphors are strikingly and, I think, indigenously vivid, enabling lines like:

1st Neighbour:	It should be easy to see a leopard If he were here. His eyes should be Blazing forth in the dark.
3rd Neighbour:	So I hear. I have heard them likened To the lighthouse out on the bar.
2nd Neighbour:	And its motion is silent as that big house, We must be careful.

These are African lines, in tone and reference, securing for any reader a sense of "place", and in this sense Senghor's ideas of *négritude* become easier to work with. The image of the leopard, that "its motion is silent as that big house" must be African. Houses in Africa, not of the European variety, do sway gently in any breeze, if they are huts. The most powerful way to deal with an image is to make sure it goes deeper than literature. That it is actually "out there". (pp. 399-400)

> *LeRoi Jones, "A Dark Bag," in* Poetry, *Vol. CIII, No. 6, March, 1964, pp. 394-401.*

Paul Theroux (essay date 1967)

[*Theroux is an expatriate American novelist, critic, and travel writer. He has traveled extensively in Africa, and several of his novels and short stories are set in Kenya and Malawi. In the following excerpt from an essay originally published in* Black Orpheus *in 1967, he appraises Clark's poetry, concluding that "there is a thin line between Clark's good poems and his bad ones."*]

Affected language and precious syntax work to John Clark's advantage in his plays. The tense atmosphere of **Song of a Goat** and **The Raft** profits by the convolutions of language, lends a brittle quality to the movement. But language can be an irritant and, where the whole edifice of a play stands up because of the brittleness, the tiny structure of a poem is not enough to support it. (pp. 120-21)

As long as poets continue to write good poems using traditional forms it is foolish to say that the metrical rhyming poems is out-moded. One of the great *villanelles* of all time was written by Dylan Thomas ('Do not go Gentle into that Good Night') and some of Robert Frost's best poems are fractured sonnets. Clark cannot be criticised for using the forms—he must be criticised for misusing the forms or for not meeting the demands of the forms he appears to be attempting.

T.S. Eliot, writing on Pound, says, 'In *Ripostes* and in *Lustra* there are many short poems of a slighter build . . . equally moving, but in which the "feeling" or "mood" is more interesting than the writing. (In the perfect poem both are equally interesting as one thing and not as two.)' It is the writing that intrudes in the early poems of Clark. If the writing does not openly irritate, it distracts. (p. 121)

Clark's best poems either crush us or lift us up with simple words, as in **"Streamside Exchange"**:

> Child: River bird, river bird,
>   Sitting all day along
>   On hook over grass,
>   River bird, river bird,
>   Sing to me a song
>   Of all that pass
>   And say,
>   Will mother come back today?
>
> Bird: You cannot know
>   And should not bother;
>   Tide and market come and go
>   And so has your mother.

The poem asks a simple question with simple words; the reply is a crushing statement of the loneliness that men must bear. Also the rhyme is not intrusive. It is a quiet poem but leaves us with a mood that cannot be shaken off.

Despite the many exclamation marks that Clark uses in his poems, he still seems to be a writer of extremely quiet poems. The effects are heightened by the simplicity and quietness and, as in **"Streamside Exchange"**, there is often great intensity in the writing. Usually, Clark is content to set a scene, make a picture or describe a drama without acting in it or having a 'dramatic movement'. It is a brilliant stroke to have the 'bird' end the poem above; the child may or may not be silent, but his further questions must be our own. The dramatic action takes place after the poem has ended; the reader is responsible for the drama. In setting the scene well Clark has given us all the ingredients of the drama without telling us what we should think, how we should act our part. It must be difficult for a writer of dramas to leave off so early; it may also be the reason for his failure in other poems where, by trying to create dramatic action, he loses control and founders in his own language. (pp. 122-23)

In the often-anthologised **"Ibadan"** the scene is set delicately:

> Ibadan,
>   running splash of rust
> and gold—flung and scattered
> among seven hills like broken
> china in the sun.

Poets compare cities to women (Paris, the raped whore; New York, the long-legged neon blonde, and so forth). Clark's poem on Ibadan presents an image that is both vivid and new. Ibadan flashes before us. I have never seen Ibadan, but when I read this poem a city materialized before me, a city of dazzling light, of both randomness and order. The sun stands out in the poem and dominates as it must in that city. The poem is interesting as one distinct visual experience, the mood and the writing fused.

I think John Clark's best poem is **"Night Rain"**. There is a natural rhythm in **"Night Rain"** which the subject demands. . . . Not only does the subject, rain, demand rhythm, it also gets it in the best possible way. There is no metrical pattern in **"Night Rain"**, yet there is metre; there is no regular rhythm, yet there is the rhythm of rain, irregular as the rain's rhythms are . . . . The images of the sleeper conscious of the rain and waiting, of the rain joining with the sea-water to rise and purify are deftly handled . . . . Read in its entirety this poem sets a mood that lulls with a peacefulness and acceptance that is very rarely matched in modern poems. The rain that soothes also makes people move, that washes clean also washes things away. It is a prayerful poem but cannot be called a strictly religious poem; it is peaceful but not monotonous. It is difficult to place this poem in correct thematic relation to Clark's other poems. It can be said, however, that the most successful poems in **Poems 1962** are the ones in which the narrator is unmoving, observing the patterns that exist in nature and in man's nature. Clark writes on many themes, not all of them consistent with the efforts in his best poems. Fulani cattle bother him because they appear inscrutable; but in describing the exterior of the cattle he has given us enough information to lead us to the place where conjecture must begin.

There is a thin line between Clark's good poems and his bad ones. The poor poems are obscured by the use of pyrotechnic and imprecise language. The good poems are illuminated by simple and direct language. Ambiguity exists in both kinds, although it is hard to take in the poor poems. If Clark has a 'general theme' it has escaped me. This is not a weakness in Clark. It shows him to be a far more curious and hungry individual than one might suppose. There is something to be said for the poet giving in to every impulse and indulgence in his poems, but it must be admitted that neither randomness alone nor symmetry alone makes art out of the substance of the poet's impulse. (pp. 123-25)

Paul Theroux, "Six Poets: Dennis Brutus, Lenrie Peters, Okogbule Nwanodi, George

Awooner-Williams, John Pepper Clark, Christopher Okigbo," in Introduction to African Literature: An Anthology of Critical Writing from "Black Orpheus," *edited by Ulli Beier, Northwestern University Press, 1970, pp. 110-31.*

John Ferguson (essay date 1968)

[*In the following excerpt, Ferguson assesses the strengths and weaknesses of* Song of a Goat, The Masquerade, *and* The Raft.]

[*Song of a Goat*] is a powerful play. The debt to Greek drama is large, but the result is in no sense imitative or derivative. The theme of the curse suggests the curses on the house of Laius or Atreus, and their working out in *Oedipus* or *Agamemnon.* Greek plays often begin or end with a divine figure, and the masseur here serves that purpose.... Orukorere plays the part of Cassandra in *Agamemnon,* though the comparison with Tiresias in *Oedipus* has also been drawn. The neighbours form the chorus, but Clark does not attempt to link his movements with song and dance sequences; there might be scope here. The movements are taut, and the characters economical in number and conception. Like Greek drama, the play is religious in tone. Some of the devices and approaches of the Greek playwrights are used with great skill; for example the concept of the Messenger's Speech is beautifully adapted to describe Zifa's self-immolation in the sea. Aristotle claimed that the most moving constituents of tragedy are *peripeteia* (when a course of action designed to serve one end lends to diametrically opposite results), and *anagnorisis* or recognition. It would be hard to find a better *peripeteia* than Ebiere's attempt to remove the curse of sterility through her relations with Tonye, an attempt which leads to the death of Zifa, Tonye, and (through miscarriage) the child she has conceived. There are two moments of recognition—perhaps even three. The first is Zifa's recognition of the truth about Ebiere and Tonye. The second is Zifa's recognition of the truth about himself. The third is perhaps Orukorere's recognition that the destruction of the goat had come not, as she had feared, through a leopard (from outside, openly), but through a snake (from inside, secretly). The numinous close reminds us of the end of Oedipus in *Oedipus at Colonus,* and the closing words "Come away, tomorrow is a heavier day" are Greek in mood.

The play is poetic drama, and must be judged as poetry as well as on its dramatic merits. The verse is free; the basic line is unusually short for so sustained a piece of writing. The effect is, so to speak, to bring the play nearer to lyric and further from epic. This has its dangers. On the one hand there is the danger of overwriting, and Clark has not altogether avoided this. Lines like

Or sports him no spoors?

are hard to stomach even from Orukorere, and the animal symbolism seems overpainted—goat and leopard and snake, fish and bird and chick.... On the other hand the inevitably prosaic lines like....

And I'm sure my son is no goat.

become more bathetic than they need. There is by compensation much of great beauty. (pp. 14-15)

I have stressed the comparison with Greek tragedy; it is a tribute to the work that the comparison can be made. But it is not Greek tragedy; it can stand on its own two feet as Ijaw tragedy. *Song of a Goat* is in many ways the most remarkable play to emerge from Nigeria. Clark's other plays need not delay us so long. *The Masquerade* is a companion piece to *Song of a Goat;* it is a not unworthy companion, but inevitably its impact is less powerful. Here the curse has passed to a new generation. (pp. 15-16)

The Masquerade has both qualities and defects from which *Song of a Goat* is free. The verse-writing is more certain but less memorable; there is less climax and less anticlimax. The finest writing is in the love-talk of the first act, which recalls some of Christopher Fry's more mellifluous passages. Its lightness contrasts well with the sombre gravity of the final scene. The handling of plot is untidier, less taut, less controlled, though one critic has argued that there is more suspense and more development in the dramatic construction. But the play's great merit is the character of Titi's father Diribi (and, though less strikingly, of her mother Umuko). The characters of *Song of a Goat* are elements in a plot, but Diribi lives. If *Song of a Goat* was Clark's *Oedipus, The Masquerade* is his *Antigone,* and it turns out to be the tragedy of Creon-Diribi. The ending is majestic....

The third play *The Raft* is very different. Four lumbermen, Olotu, Kengide, Ogro and Ibobo, are taking a raft down the Niger. The raft drifts from its moorings, out of control. The four are cut off from all except one another, and left to face hunger and danger together. (p. 16)

In many ways this is a very good play, and it is excellent to see Clark striking out in a fresh vein. This is a fresh variation of the theme of a limited number of people shut up together; Fry's *A Sleep of Prisoners* comes to mind. Clark's originality lies in conceiving a setting in which he can combine the element of restriction, confinement and limit with the element of unlimited openness. This means that he can work together the character-conflicts of the limited situation with the ageless theme of the quest, in this case for landfall, and the end of the play, with Ibobo and Kengide calling in the fog, and answered by steamer sirens and shouts of fear, is masterly.

Not that there is nothing to criticize. The language is good, easier and firmer, less overdrawn. Similes and metaphors are fewer and less fantastic; the comparison of the untravelled Kengide to a wall-gecko remains in the mind. The play is marked for its judiciously direct descriptive writing.... But though the language is good, the themes are not always relevant, and the long conversations between Ibobo and Kengide as they coast down to Burutu seem used by the author to air his views on a miscellany of subjects, including women, homosexuality, politics, economics, colonialism and many other incidentals. They are well-presented—there is a delightful description of three types of women, the log, the placid stream and the tossing wave—but the author's personality obtrudes upon his characters. Furthermore, the closed-room theme demands a sharp differentiation of character. (Sartre's *Huis Clos* is a good example.) Clark is more interested in words and ideas than people, and the differences, though real, need exaggeration for effective drama. Finally the play is exceedingly difficult to produce. The first episode is and must be largely in darkness, and in general, by definition of the situation, too little happens, and the more dramatic moments are not easy to stage convincingly. This is clear in reading; it was clearer still in performance. (pp. 17-18)

> *John Ferguson, "Nigerian Drama in English," in* Modern Drama, *Vol. XI, No. 1, May, 1968, pp. 10-26.*

Obi Maduakor (essay date 1984)

[*In the following excerpt, Maduakor evaluates the "war poems" in* Casualties—*Clark's most controversial work devoted to the Nigerian Civil War—and notes that in most of the poems, "the poetic flame is hardly allowed to go beyond a given flicker."*]

There is not much of sentimental self-pity in Clark's **Casualties** but the collection suffers from what would have seemed to [W.B.] Yeats as serious rhetorical blemishes. The first originates from Clark's conscious effort not to be sentimental. He is aware of the need to establish a correct distance between him and his material, and the question of distance is all the more urgent because of the public character of the material that Clark is dealing with. It is indeed to distance himself from his subject that Clark wrote in verse in the first instance. He had half a mind, he said, to write in prose 'this personal account of some of the unspeakable events that all but tore apart Nigeria'; but he chose poetry because the 'paths of poetry are not open to many'. One of the means by which he hoped to escape from topicality is to use animal personae as his objective correlatives—squirrels, cockerels, rats and vultures. The presence of these animals lends the poems an aura that is African: but it is not enough that the poems should be African. They should also move the reader, and retain a mood that is appropriate for the tragic theme. Clark's animals recall the animal characters of folk tales. In their poetic context they frequently diffuse rather than reinforce the tragic mood. The overall atmosphere is folksy. In **"Vulture's Choice"**, the tragic impact is dissipated by the vulture's casual attitude to serious issues. Perhaps the tone of nonchalance is intentional, but it is not appropriate for the subject. And, of course,

the poem irritates by the prosaic flatness of the vulture's replies to his unnamed interlocutor:

> Then I shall eat it for breakfast.
> Then I shall eat her for lunch.
> Then I shall eat both for the night.

Of these folksy poems only two, **"What the Squirrel Said"** and **"The Cockerel in the Tale"**, are aesthetically satisfying. **"What the Squirrel Said"** is successful in form as a note of warning sounded by a morally conscious village sentinel, the squirrel, who had sensed some danger in the air. The poem seeks to recapture the strident cry of an agitated sentinel by means of repetition and structural uniformity of the opening couplets which are antithetically and morally balanced against each other.

> THEY KILLED the lion in his den
> But left the leopard to his goats.
> They killed the bull without horns
> But left the boar to his cassava.

The poem **"The Cockerel in the Tale"** relies for its effects on the rhetorical devices and the verbal structure and phraseology of Yoruba traditional poetry, especially hunter's song (*ijala*):

> he who woke up the lion
> And burnt down his den over his crest,
> He who the same night bagged
> A rogue elephant, not sparing his brood,
> He who in the heat of the hunt
> Shot in the eye a bull with horns
> They say never gored a fly, hooves
> That never trod on cocoa or groundnut farm,
> Stood,
> Alone on the trembling loft of the land.

Clark's squirrels, cockerels, and rats, whether they function as poetic personae or as protagonists are inadequate as vehicles for a tragic experience. They do not convincingly sustain the weight of the tragic experience that inspired the poems. They fail, in this regard, as vehicles for poetic emotion. Clark has heroic animals such as lions, bulls, and elephants, but they are frequently caught up in passive roles in their contexts which add nothing to the dramatic effect. The effect is different in Okigbe's *Path of Thunder,* for instance, where elephants pound the earth and magic birds dive through the air. Only in the poem **"The Beast"** did Clark endeavour to give vigour to his verse by placing his symbolic animals in a context of action:

> Wind from the dragon takes possession
> Of masks; dung from the dragon
> Makes catacombs of cities and farms;
> With mere drippings the dragon sets
> Rivers on fire, flames of this lick
> Mangroves to salt.

That verse, however, does not sound good enough as poetry; the rhythm is somewhat mechanical and too easily predictable because of Clark's tendency to enumerate or itemize, but the verse moves forward even if on stilts.

The verse foreshadows a technical weakness that is more fundamental in *Casualties:* that is, Clark's descriptive technique. His language is frequently descriptive, affirmative and declamatory and does not evoke a mood, or order emotions. He has dispensed with the allusive, the suggestive technique that renders the poetry of *Song of a Goat* so powerful. In *Casualties*, language is neither given a fresh exploration nor exploited for its emotive responses. The poems possess, as a result, a narrative flavour which diminishes their effects as lyrical songs. **"The Burden in Boxes"** and **"The Reign of the Crocodiles"** read like allegorical tales. This is so because certain key words in these poems such as 'box' and 'gifts' have been shorn in their context of their potency as processional images; their meaning in the poem is so obvious that they have become allegorical metaphors rather than poetic images. It is not, however, Clark's allegorical tendencies alone that are disquieting; his mode of address is tactless. In **"The Burden in Boxes"** one encounters such disappointing lines as

> *Open the boxes* was the clamour
> Of monkeys above tides. *Open them all!*
> *or*
> Bring us the bearers of the gifts
> The gifts left us in boxes at
> The crossroads, bring them out, we say,
> So we may see them in the market place.

"Leader of the Hunt" and **"Return Home"** have an interest that is more important to the historical researcher than to a lover of poetry. **"July Wake"** has a good beginning. Clark starts the poem off with the technique of juxtaposing without what Marshall McLuhan calls 'the copula of logical enunciation': 'Glint of SMG, flare of mortar, tremor/Of grenades occupying ministry/And market', but six lines later he resumes his narrative tone signalled with a modified version of the conventional folk formula for beginning a story. From this moment onwards the verse slackens and loses much of what has been gained by the juxtapositional technique of the beginning.

"Conversations at Accra" has some dramatic vitality; the poem reads like a scene in a play. Language is used to suggest gesture and action, and to mark variations in tone in a conversational dialogue; but to be dramatic is not to be lyrical, and sometimes the dramatic flights descend to the level of melodrama; and above all, the entire poem has its own share of the general descriptive taint that diminishes the poetic effects of most of the poems in *Casualties.* At one point in the conversation, Character A bursts in on the reader with the following statement:

> You mean tie a thorough hound
> To a tree and set a common cur
> As guard over him? Oh, boy, oh boy
> Before you rush to the next post
> There would be reversal of roles, and you
> At the end of the leash.

The poem **"Season of Omens"** underscores what must be seen as Clark's major problem in *Casualties,* that is, the problem of transmuting the events of a political occasion into art. The original intention to write *Casualties* in prose was deep-rooted. **"Season of Omens"** is a straightforward reproduction of a piece of journalistic information that has not been transformed by the personality of the artist. In the poem, a political occasion overwhelms personality rather than personality subduing the occasion. As a result we have objective reportage rather than a subjective reshaping of an event:

> WHEN CALABASHES HELD petrol and men
> turned faggots in the streets
> *Then came the five hunters*
> When mansions and limousines made
> bornfires in sunset cities
> *Then came the five hunters*
> When clans were discovered that were not in the
> book
> and cattle counted for heads of men
> *Then came the five hunters.* (pp. 69-72)

Clark is unable to weave into the texture of his verse implications that go beyond his immediate concerns. His poetry generally lacks breadth. Images with resourceful potential are not explored beyond the attractions of their initial appeal. Emotions are not charged to a high pressure point where they can explode themselves into cathartic resolution. Even sorrow is not allowed to yield the fullest possibilities of its impact. The absence of breadth is remarkable in **"Song, Skulls and Cups"**, **"Vulture's Choice"**, **"The Usurpation"**, to name only a few examples. The question of breadth is less related to the length of the poem than to the sweep of thought and the curve of emotion within the poem itself. Even the relatively longer poems than those just mentioned rush hurriedly to a close, like **"Death of a Weaver Bird"**, **"Exodus"**, **"Aburi and After"**. Clark's poetry does not always move us because it has no heave and swell. This point is not to be taken personally against the poet; it is merely a permanent feature of his poetic temperament. Clark is not capable of giving a poetic subject-matter a sustained treatment. It is for this reason that Ulli Beier thinks of him as a 'spontaneous poet'. In most of the poems in *Casualties* the poetic flame is hardly allowed to go beyond a given flicker. What Clark needed to do was compress the whole experience that informed *Casualties* into one or two lyrics of some length, but in devoting nearly a book of poetry to the Nigerian Civil War he diversified his feelings, thereby weakening the power of his verse.

There are, however, some poems in the volume that tend to salvage Clark's poetic credibility. The poems **"Dirge"**, **"The Casualties"**, and **"Night Song"** are exempted from the general blemish that weakens the aesthetic merit of most of the poems in *Casualties.* These poems possess a compactness of structure and a tone that matches Clark's tragic theme. In **"Dirge"**, for instance, the emotional intensity is sustained through the repetition of the initial words 'tears' and 'fear' and by a conscious parallel in the structure of the lines; both devices enhance the tragic mood while lending speed and vigour to the verse:

> Earth will turn a desert
> A place of stone and bones
> Tears are founts from the heart
> Tears do not water a land
> Fear too is a child of the heart
> Fear piles up stones, piles up bones
> Fear builds a place of ruin
> O let us light the funeral pile
> But let us not become its faggot.

Clark comes closer in lines such as these to Wole Soyinka and Christopher Okigbo who also wrote about the Nigerian Civil War or anticipated it. It is their tough diction, their non-declamatory use of language, their surer sense of tragic emergency that make Soyinka and Okigbo more successful than Clark as war poets. These two poets do not possess to the same degree Yeats' technical expertise, nor do their images match the all-inclusive allusiveness of Yeats' poetic images, yet their poetry is likely to outlive their time as Clark's *Casualties* might not. (pp. 74-5)

> *Obi Maduakor, "On the Poetry of War: Yeats and J. P. Clark," in* African Literature Today, *No. 14, 1984, pp. 68-76.*

Isaac I. Elimimian (essay date 1988)

[*In the following review essay, Elimimian identifies and discusses the three stages of Clark's lyrical development: the apprenticeship stage, the imitative stage, and the individualized stage.*]

Clark's first poetic work, *Poems,* contains 40 pieces which explore various themes and subjects, some amateurish, others sophisticated in tone and execution. The amateurish poems—e.g. **"Still a Song Shall Arise"** and **"Darkness and Light"**—fail, because, to a greater or lesser degree, they dwell on abstract phenomena rather than on particularized experience. Sometimes where the reader expects to be presented with an unobtrusive, spontaneous experience, he is offered a contrived, imitative picture. Conversely, the successful ones—e.g. **"Night Rain"**, **"Fulani Cattle"**, and **"Ibadan"**—are remarkable for their compact, vivid imagery which is often rooted in African culture.

His second volume *A Reed in The Tide,* which embodies 34 poems in all (of which the large majority had previously appeared in *Poems*), is important because of its fusion of divergent experience. Almost the first half of the poems in the collection deal with the author's African background, while the others highlight the events of his travel to various countries, including the U.S. which he acidly satirizes. Here most of the opaque poems which first appeared in *Poems* are either reworked or omitted altogether in *A Reed in The Tide.*

In *Casualties,* Clark, much like a chronicler, records and delineates the events of the Nigerian civil war. The work is grouped into two parts: the first part, which contains 28 poems focuses entirely on the events culminating in the civil war; the second part, which has 11 poems, deals with occasional pieces addressed to several people and places. The success or failure of *Casualties* is a matter for judgment by posterity. All that is certain however is that, except perhaps *America Their America,* it is the single most important work that has earned Clark the title of the controversial artist that he is: For while some rebuke him for betraying the "Biafran revolution", others praise his sense of patriotism. (pp. 31-2)

Whatever the *furor-poeticus* generated by *Casualties,* it is Clark's work that is most talked about, that is perhaps most misunderstood and that is obviously the most tasking to approach (especially in its employment of animal imagery). But if nothing else is satisfying about the work, the objective reader, no doubt, is moved by the degree of commitment which Clark's publisher says inspired it: "*Casualties* carries the cry of a man of unmistakable courage and humanity in the face of . . . the unspeakable events that almost tore apart Nigeria. It is a lament for the casualties, living and dead, of a war that has bewildered the world, relieved at last by hope that reaches across the barriers erected by brother against brother".

Clark's fourth book of poetry *A Decade of Tongues,* contains 74 poems altogether, 73 of which come from his first three volumes as follows: *Poems,* 21; *A Reed in The Tide,* 13; and *Casualties* 39. The only new poem in the anthology, **"Epilogue to Casualties"**, is a dedication to Michael Echeruo. The title, *A Decade of Tongues,* symbolizes for the poet and perhaps for the Clark critic, the ten-year period during which the poems in the collection were nurtured and composed. But the book is important not only because it is the first of its kind in the life of a major African poet (in the sense that it gathers in a capsulate form his major poems within a set period), but because it reflects the ideal in Clark, that is to say, it is an embodiment of those poems which the poet holds dear, and would probably like his critics to take into consideration in any meaningful assessment of his poetic career.

If one must speculate on the future direction which Clark's poetics would take, it is in *State of the Union,* his most recent book, that one can find it. Unlike in *Poems,* where Clark is the private poet mostly engulfed in his own sensibilities, here in *State of the Union* he is the public poet concerned with national cum universal issues. The volume is a work of satire which the author had written in anticipation of the collapse of the Second Civilian Republic of Nigeria. But by an irony of fate, what would have been a prologue to that development has turned out to be its epilogue. The poems in the collection are grouped into three sections: section one, titled "State of the Union", has 25 poems; section two which is titled "Postscript" has a single poem, **"The Playwright and the Colonels"**; while the third and last section titled, "Other Songs on Other States", has 14 pieces. Obviously, the work highlights the hopes and aspirations of a people who, having attained nationhood, are disappointed by the greed, hypocrisy and high-handedness of those who wield the levers of political power. As is the case in *Casualties,* the poet does not intend to take the place that legitimately belongs to the soldier by carrying his gun, nor is he the die-hard politician, campaigning, propagating party programmes and manifestoes. Rather he is the watchdog of society, silently but consistently articulating its successes and failures. Consequently, the work enacts a standard of mores through its didacticism while at the same time it embodies a sense of awareness of what the role of the poet is and should be in society—a role which, by the very nature of his professional calling, he must play despite all odds. Clark explains in the *Preface* to the work:

> . . . there are some who will find the title of the sequence and the collection somewhat presumptuous, the poet being no elected president or acknowledged legislator of any state that they know of. I would be the first to sustain their objections. But let them remember well that while the poet is still allowed a place in the state, he will also have his say, if not as seer, clown, plain corrupter of youth or whatever, then simply like an ordinary member of the state.

But what kind of poet is Clark? He is essentially a lyric poet; this fact is generally acknowledged by critics. For example, Paul Theroux observes that "Clark's . . . good poems are illuminated by simple and direct language" [see excerpt dated 1967]. O. R. Dathorne notes that "Each poem of Clark's is self-contained." K. E. Senanu and Theo Vincent agree that "His poetry is noted for its artistry, descriptive power and the way in which it draws on his locality for its imagery and ideas." And S. H. Burton and C. J. H. Chacksfield say "His poetry sings. His words are fresh and most memorably ordered."

More than what the critics say, however, it is possible to distinguish three stages of Clark's lyrical development: namely, the apprenticeship stage, the imitative stage, and the individualized stage. This demarcation is determined not by any time configuration but by the degree of maturity and the level of sophistication which inform his verse.

By the apprenticeship stage I refer to the body of poems in which Clark is trying to find his bearing; that is, poems which seem to have been composed through a process of trial and error and, consequently, are juvenilia in structure. Although it is fairly possible to grasp the message which Clark seeks to convey, on the whole, the verse (though promising) is marred by syntactical and metrical flaws.

The imitative stage is one in which the young Clark not only borrows extensively from the Western literary conventions (e.g., the couplet measure and the sonnet form), but is fascinated by the style of the "masters"— most notably Shakespeare, Donne, Blake, Hopkins, T.S. Eliot, Yeats, Auden and Pound. Here, Clark treats his subject matter with sophistication, and even where his style falls below that of the "masters"—as it sometimes does—it is however evident to the serious reader the direction in which his wit is moving.

At the individualized stage Clark cultivates his own poetic idiom: his thinking is fresh and clear; his imagery and rhythm are not only distinctively unique, and often intensely dramatic, but mature to reflect the subject matter he develops. Perhaps it is this aspect of Clark's verse that prompts Dan Izevbaye to comment, thus:

> For the student of Nigerian literature J. P. Clark is interesting not only for the quality of his poetry but for his historical importance as one of the first poets to begin writing the type of verse that should eventually lead to the foundation of a national tradition of Nigerian poetry . . . although the new poets showed, like the pioneers, an occasional tendency to lean on conventional English poetic models because of the absence of a clearly defined written tradition in English, they represented not merely a more fundamental approach but an altogether new direction. Clark's verse was an example of this new fundamental approach.

At this individualized stage, too, Clark addresses himself to every concern that interests him, and, like a sage, he is sometimes didactic and sometimes philosophical in tone and language. We shall now examine each of these lyrical developments in some detail.

One of Clark's poems which falls within the rubric of the apprenticeship stage in his lyrical development is the dedicatory and opening piece, **"Still A Song Shall Arise"**:

> Still a song shall arise
> In my heart! Out of this pit
> Of ash and dust they trampled it
> A flame shall arise
> Like leaves on tree, tip on tip
> To burn on every lip.
> Yam tuber too late for prize
> Or price will, buried piecemeal,
> At fall of flood rise again whole,
> Turn out a hundred fold
> But enough, oh enough! For how can pestle
> Sound in mortar a song
> When Babylon of old
> As yet unbroken into odd tongue
> Poured on a bush flaming gold
> Derision and dung.

This may be regarded as a meditative, even a prayer poem, in that while the poet ruminates over the difficulties he faces—chaos, insecurity, solitude, grief— he is optimistic that he will ultimately emerge triumphant. The metaphor, "this pit/Of ash and dust", symbolizes the obstacles which confront man right from primordial birth until death.

On the surface it might appear that Clark is here concerned with his private predicament; but at bottom, he is the "representative" poet, in the sense that the problems he delineates constitute a universal phenomenon. It is only through dogged determination, and possibly through attenuation of being, he says, that the individual can hope to surmount his difficulties and achieve his life ambition.

Another subject which surfaces here is that of artistic struggle. Through the image, "Yam tuber too later for prize", the poet suggests that he has a yearning for artistic success of which, apparently, he is a late comer. Although the poet, naturally, faces despairing conditions, he too can through a combination of talent and hard-work, compose verse which will not only "burn on every lip" but immortalize him ("As yet unbroken into odd tongue").

The words "song" and "prize" are significant: as poetic metaphors they suggest Clark's growing awareness of his own vocation and the values he anticipates. The road to artistic fame (of which he has a sure place) may be rough, even late in coming, but it is one which must be tenaciously sought and followed if one must arrive at the "bush flaming gold".

In terms of technique it can be said that the poem is enriched by a host of significant contrasts: symbolized, for example, by the rising again of that which hitherto was "trampled" upon, by the re-surgence of that which was "buried piecemeal", and by the soothing effect which "song" offers a depressed heart. But, on the other hand, the attempt to rhyme "pit" and "it", "tip" and "lip", "hole" and "fold", and "tongue" and "gold" reduces the poem to a miniature. So also do the quaint sounds produced by "tip on tip", "At fall of flood", and "But enough, oh enough" and "Derision and dung" have touches of dullness.

Another of Clark's juvenile verse which achieves success in the development of its subject matter but is flawed in its styling is **"Darkness and Light"**. The poem parallels **"Still a Song Shall Arise"** in a number of ways. Here, too, the poet evolves a mode of experiencing a double vision: the perennial confrontation between death and existence, sadness and exhilaration, oblation and transformation. (pp. 32-7)

["**Iddo Bridge**", "**To A Learned Lady**", and "**The Fallen Soldier**"] depict Clark's ability to respond with his total being to a dramatic, spontaneous experience. They employ images which impress by their immediacy, speed, the here and now. And their language, cast in simple syntax of direct statements, anticipates the aesthetic temperament of a formidable poet. Finally, they are time lyrics: of now and then, and of eternity, *sub specie aeternitasis.* (p. 39)

In discussing the imitative stage of Clark's lyrical development, it is important to emphasize the fact that this is an area which has attracted the attention of a great many critics. It would be preposterous therefore either to ignore it on account of this or to suggest that the subject no longer arouses any critical interest. Two aspects of Clark's imitativeness can, however, be distinguished: the first of these has to do with the poet's employment of the Western literary forms and tech-

niques; the second centers on the influence on his verse of some of those whom he calls the "masters."

Of the Western literary forms and techniques which Clark explores, one can easily identify the quatrain, a four line stanza with varying rhyme patterns. Clark manages the respective varieties of this variant with notable success.... (p. 40)

Perhaps taking a cue from such modern poets as Robert Frost, W. H. Auden, E. E. Cummings, Richard Eberhart and others who often break from the rigid iambic pentameter pattern, Clark, in such pieces as **"Friends"**, **"Why should I Rage"** and **"Outside Gethsemane"** writes sonnets which, although in free verse with unconventional rhetorical and rhyme patterns, have infused modernity and freshness into the old, conventionalized sonnet form.

"Friends" contrasts the relationship between the loss of friends *vis-a-vis* the loss of **"Kin"** and concludes forcibly that the latter is a more serious tragedy. It is this antithetical note that gives the poem its structural intensity and counterpoint. The drastic and uneven shortening of the poem's lines (e.g., "Our loss, large as the fellowship/We kept") is innovative, and suggests Clark's skill to devise a poetics which appropriately conveys his feelings.

"Why should I Rage" laments the devastating effect which futile love exerts on the human psyche. As a sonnet the poem combines elements of modernism (suggested by its taut and ringing lines, e.g., "The fire I strove with fame/To light in your heart/Has not come to flame?") with those of traditionalism (suggested by its rhyming couplets, e.g., "I, blind with smoke,/ choking with smoke") to produce a kind of hovering quality. Besides, Clark's employment of the couplet measure in the concluding lines ("Am unable in despair/To stifle a tear?") reminiscent of Shakespearean sonnet ending, suggests both his contribution to as well as his indebtedness to this major sonnet form.

In **"Outside Gethsemane,"** Clark's rhetoric is one of sober reflection over what, apparently, he considers the futility of indulging in acts of lamentation over the Crucifixion, since, accordingly, Christ's death—which is the poem's subject—is itself a fulfilment of the Scriptures. The sonnet, arranged into three quatrains and a couplet, is structurally Shakespearean but its irregular rhyme scheme and the clear-cut demarcation of the quatrains (into stanzas) show Clark's penchant to be experimental and innovative. It also establishes the fact that, for him, the sonnet as a genre, is essentially a framework within which one can order one's experience as one considers appropriate. The poem deserves a fuller consideration because it leads us into the second part of Clark's imitativeness:

> Have you all day wandering on the moor
> sought impaling fluff-balls,
> and not known the vanity
> of chasing the wind by her skirts

O have you all day skipping on the shore
blown billowing bubbles,
and not breathed rank mortality
in million-splinter'd spurts?

Had you hearken'd to the thunder's roar
and not drowned his rumbles,
in the gross garrulity
of your tooth; you would not since birth

Have sought pollution of the flood
with vain tears of blood!

The poem's argument is organized around one principal religious image which dominates other images like a symbol. This image-symbol is "Gethsemane," the setting of Christ's betrayal and death. The significance of the other religious images in the poem—"blood" and "tears"—is clear enough: respectively they connote the Crucifixion and the subsequent lamentations. Also contributing to the tone of the poem's argument, although in a less dramatic and significant way, is the word, "Outside". It suggests that the poet, obviously distressed by Christ's suffering and humiliation, decides to keep off from the scene of the action. Here the poem invites comparison with Donne's "Good Friday", where Christ's death is a tragedy which the poet would "not see/That spectacle of too much weight for mee".

In terms of other fundamental aspects of the poem—which now leads us into the influence of poets on Clark—one finds echoes of [Gerard Manley] Hopkins' coinages and verbal intensity: "impaling fluff-balls", "blown billowing bubbles", "million-splinter'd spurts," and "gross garrulity".

Like Hopkins' poetry, the poem offers an interesting challenge to the imagination, sometimes to repudiate earlier assumptions or to discover underlying meanings and paradoxes against a backdrop of a comprehensive world view. First, for instance, one notices that the poem's four-part division is tailored to reflect an important thematic development associated with the four elements. Thus, "chasing the wind by her skirts" in stanza one highlights the element of air; the "shore" upon which one skips in stanza two suggests *earth;* the "thunder's roar" and the accompanying "rumbles" in stanza three conjures lightning or *fire;* while the "flood" in the concluding couplet recalls the element of *water.* (pp. 42-4)

Clark's affinity for Hopkins is evident, at least from the somewhat dedicatory pieces, **"Variations on Hopkins on the Theme of Child Wonder"** and **"Ibadan Dawn—After Pied Beauty."** In the first of these poems, the presence of such literary devices as assonance, consonance, internal rhyme, and euphonious alliteration in such expressions as "pity plenished", "So dry cut up, self-finished", "sick, soulful sick", "Worse, would worst live live on loan", "When puppies foul'd on filth turn out tyke", and "churlcasual" evinces Clark's conscious desire to write after the fashion of Hopkins.

In terms of argument and tone, Clark's **"Ibadan Dawn— After Pied Beauty"** parallels Hopkins' "Pied Beauty":

both are variations on the theme of passing time. The only significant difference, between them, however, is that while Clark's poem celebrates (with astonishment) the changing turn of the morning into day and then night, Hopkins' piece visualizes the changing seasons in light of the grandeur and greatness of God—which cannot but evoke appeal. Hopkins' presence can be felt in other Clark's poems (e.g., **"The Year's first Rain"** where Clark employs a string of compound words, "With-kestrel-together-leaf flaps") but I think that it is in the above poems that the younger poet can be said to have chiefly benefitted from Hopkins' poetic legacy.

T. S. Eliot is another poet that Clark is indebted to. Both poets employ the first person pronoun "I." Although Eliot (as in *Prufrock*) creates a persona who articulates his personal sensibilities while Clark is often his poem's persona (as in the last segment of *Ivbie*), the similarities in their use of this literary device are so obvious that one cannot but be persuaded to think that Clark adapts from Eliot. For instance, Eliot's Prufrock laments: "I grow old . . . I am old . . . " (possibly as a way to rationalize his shortcomings); while Clark in *Ivbie* says: "The night is old/And I am cold" (apparently to justify his lack of motivation). The important thing here is not so much that the individuals they project are identical but that both poems, rendered in interior monologues, are sharp and witty in their disclosure of private predicaments.

Similarities can also be drawn between the two poets in other areas. For instance, the whole *Ivbie* sequence which is made up of six disparate "movements", recalls the fragmentary form of *The Waste Land*. Both poets also employ satire: Eliot criticizes the malaise of contemporary civilization; Clark lampoons the "missile-hurled" "west". Eliot's Madam Sosotris warns the poem's persona to "fear death by water". Clark's Oyin employs the word "fear" more than half a dozen times, to caution against the evil forces of disruption and destruction. Eliot's *The Waste Land* draws from Christianity, history, science and technology and classical mythology. Clark's *Ivbie* echoes all these sources.

Although no distinct parallels have been established between the poetic style of [William Butler] Yeats and that of Clark, the latter's citation of Yeats' line, "We have no gift to set a statesman right" as a preface to *Casualties,* suggests, albeit tangentially, his belief in the poetic philosophy of the older poet. Furthermore, Clark's adoption of titles (e.g., **"Easter 1976"**, **"Friends"**, **"Two seedlings"**, and **"Song"**) which suggest or echo the Yeatsian mode (respectively "Easter 1916", "Friends", "The Two Trees", and "A Song") is too obvious to function simply as a mere aesthetic correspondence.

Another poet whose influence is paramount in Clark's poetry but which is less generally emphasized by critics, is Ezra Pound. Pound (in 1912) was one of the founders of the imagist movement whose philosophy included, among other things, the principle that, "As regarding rhythm", the poet should "compose in the sequence of the musical phrase, not in the sequence of the metronome". In his *Make It New* doctrine, Pound was later to add some twig to the musical possibilities of verse, by distinguishing three varieties: *melopoeia,* "wherein the words are charged, over and above their plain meaning, with some musical property, which directs the bearing or trend of that meaning"; *phanopoeia,* "which is a casting of images upon the visual imagination"; and *logopoeia,* "the dance of the intellect among words . . . it employs words not only for their direct meaning, but it takes count in a special way of habits of usage, of the context we *expect* to find with the word, its usual concomitants, of its known acceptances, and of ironical play." In Clark's poetry, facets of *melopoeia, phanopoeia* and *logopoeia* can be found respectively in **"Two Views of Marilyn Monroe"** . . . . (pp. 45-6)

Clark's poetry has also been influenced by Negritude, the literary-ideological movement which, as Senghor defines it, is "the awareness, defence, and development of African cultural values". The degree of Clark's involvement with Negritude has stimulated critical interest, with some critics suggesting *Ivbie*—the poem in which he attacks colonialism—as his most typical and representative of the movement's philosophy. Whatever the debate, the fact remains that Clark, being the highly sensitive poet that he is, could not have been indifferent to or unaffected by the spirit and mood of a literary movement which sought to promote the ideals of the black race. As he himself defines it: "Negritude . . . stands for . . . that new burning consciousness of a common race and culture that black men in America, the West Indies and Africa are beginning to feel towards one another". Of its objective he opines that it is "to preserve our heritage." Apart from *Ivbie,* other Clark's poems which echo the philosophy of Negritude include: **"Olokun"** in which he says that "we crumble in heaps" to worship the "good maid of the sea"; **"Agbor Dancer"** in which he celebrates black beauty and womanhood; and **"Abiku"** in which he discusses the African myth of the child "born to die".

Besides the poets and literary movements already discussed above, there are other influences which have their impact on Clark's verse, although in a less conspicuous way. First, for instance, are the echoes of other poets, such as: Clark's direct reference to Shakespeare's *Hamlet* in *Ivbie;* the frank confessions of **"Pub Song"** which evoke the spirit of Walt Whitman's "Native Moments"; the mock-bitter solicitous style of **"To A Learned Lady"** quite reminiscent of W. H. Auden's "Lady, Weeping At The Crossroads"; the moralistic tone of **"Passion is a Fuel"** which recalls E. A. Robinson's "Passion is Here a Soiler of the Wits." And secondly, there are classical allusions and Biblical apocalypse—symbolized by "Poor castaways to this darkling shore," "I wandered as Io," "A man of faith/With lightning strike the cruel," "Fate will have old curses fulfilled" and "Easter". The important thing in all of these literary echoes, sources and influences is not so much that they enrich Clark's poetry, invest it with meaning and significance, not only that they serve as an

index to the dimensions in which his mind is ready to adapt, create and transform antiphonally or contrapuntally as the case may be, but perhaps more importantly, through them he seems to be able to come to grips with the deepest springs of his conviction.

Coming finally to the third stage of Clark's lyrical development, it is important to emphasize the point that here we find the authentic Clark, pure and complete in his own poetic idiom. The diction, the metre, the rhythm are now uniquely Clark's. Here the bard tops not only his innate talents and vision, but also, the corpus of "experience" which Henry James says should inform every well-conceived literary artifact . . . . Many of Clark's best poems derive from his growing awareness of typology, his sense of place and the particularities of "experience". To this category of poems belong **"Song"**, **"Night Rain"** and **"Out of the Tower (For Derry for his Festschrift)"**.

"Song" was inspired by the thirty-month Nigeria/Biafra civil war in which lives and properties were lost or destroyed. Because the poem inaugurates the entire *Casualties* sequence, it underscores its aesthetic significance:

> I can look the sun in the face
> But the friends that I have lost
> I dare not look at any. Yet I have held
> Them all in my arms, shared with them
> The same bath and bed, often
> Devouring the same dish, drunk as soon
> On tea as on wine, at that time
> When but to think of an ill, made
> By God or man, was to find
> The cure prophet and physician
> Did not have. Yet to look
> At them now I dare not,
> Though I can look the sun in the face.

In this poem Clark ponders over the glorious past in which he ate and drank with "friends" and "shared with them/The same bath and bed", in contrast to the gloomy present in which the cold hands of death have eliminated his "friends" and ushered in deprivation and loneliness. But even though his "friends" are dead, he is consoled by the all-beholding "sun" which here resuscitates his inner strength and hopes. It is this antithetical handling of the vicissitudes of life that gives this poem its ironic vistas.

Because the poet's mind radiates between past and present in a glinting network of despair and hope, the piece has a note of reminiscence, daring and poise which is not easily found in any of Clark's poems. Indeed, the poem has several lyric insights. The metaphor "The cure prophet and physician/Did not have" highlights the strong bond of unity which existed between the poet and his erstwhile "friends". The metaphor "God or man" suggests the correlatives of life. The "sun" on whose "face" the poet "can look" is a metaphor for the Creator upon whom depends human salvation. Through these metaphors Clark shows that Nature embodies complex states of values. Nor can one fail to note the poet's use of specific symbols which influence man's daily preoccupations: "prophet", "physician", "sun", "friends", and "God". These universal symbols, no doubt, enlarge our sympathies and deepen our appreciation of the poem. (pp. 48-50)

From the technical point Clark employs various devices to create dramatic effect and to convey meaning. The last word of the poem's first line is "face". The last word of the poem's concluding line is "face". This repetitive employment of the same word enhances the sense of agony *vis-a-vis* soberness which the poet feels. The repetitive use of words in the first three lines and the last three lines not only produces a musical crescendo-diminuendo effect but unifies the poem's structure by echoing earlier sounds. The near-inversion of expression (exemplified in "I dare not look at any" and "Yet to look/At them now I dare not") corresponds with the alternations of attitudes, the paradoxical tragicomic blend of life's ups and downs which the poem espouses. And the poem's free-flowing lines and simplicity of language are the best and maturest ways to articulate the private-public experience which is the poet's primary concern.

"Night Rain" as I have earlier said, is a fine example of Clark's mature poetry. The piece has been widely praised by critics. For example, Robert Wren calls it "beautiful"; Dan Izevbaye says the poem's "pictures are more than just realistic"; Paul Theroux describes it as "Clark's best poem" [see excerpt dated 1967]; and O. R. Dathorne, one of Clark's most censorious critics, considers the poem, along with **"Fulani Cattle"**, **"Agbor Dancer"** and **"Ibadan"** as "Clark's best descriptive poems" in which he "gives accurate and personal observations."

There are several reasons for the poem's wide appeal. First, its imagery is evocative; it mirrors Housman's apt observation that the business of poetry is "to transfuse emotion." "Poetry is not the thing said, but a way of saying it." Thus, for instance, the water imagery imminent in the poem—e.g. "fish", "stream" "water drops", "run of water", "sea"—is not so much to convey idea but feeling. Secondly, the poem challenges the audience, especially the African audience, to reminisce on the good old days in which he witnessed rain falling on thatched houses at night. Thirdly, the piece highlights the vitality of the evanescent indigenous culture: Here one lives in the moment and the moment is inextricably foreshadowed in the past and future.

More than the above, the poem is remarkable for its use of irony and the devices of contrast and unexpectedness: for example, the contemplative serenity of the night as contrasted with the torrential downpour; the bust "mother" *vis-a-vis* the sleeping children; the dreadful and bizarre night of owls and bats as opposed to the approaching dawn and "the drumming all over the land". (pp. 51-2)

"Out of the Tower":

> That air and light may come again
> Clean and free into the chambers
> Of my heart, I give up, perhaps
> In folly, my tenure in a tower,
> Built upon a place of swamp.
> I had thought, standing in the cesspool,
> Head, shoulders and trunk above
> The stench, the rot around could not
> Infect my life. But feet in boots
> Over years of no reclamation
> Grew fetid, and lungs that were clear
> Before so much congested,
> It would have been suicide
> To stay any day longer,
> Believing one might as well accept
> The conditions, since they were
> After all endemic to the country.

deals with Clark's voluntary retirement from his chair as Professor of English at Lagos University, just when he was 45. It is a hard and painful thing to do, to have to retire from one's vocation at such an early age, especially since the official limit stipulated for University teachers in Nigeria is 60 years.

Clark's reason for his early retirement is, however, on health grounds. The contrast between "That air and light..../Clean and free into the chambers/Of my heart" and "....feet in boots/Over years of no reclamation/Grew fetid, and lungs that were clear/Before so much congested" precipitates the poet's sudden exit from the ivory tower. To have failed to shake the dust from the feet, he says, "would have been suicide."

It is a deeply reflective and "philosophical" poem whose success depends in part on its deft employment of irony. Man lives but is daily trapped in his own feelings of inadequacies. Everything is in a state of flux. Nothing ultimately satisfies. The "Clean and free" air which lures and invites, and which acts as catalyst to the creative impulse as well as to effective teaching and research, is soon submerged by the "stench, the rot". In this poem, perhaps more than any other, Clark documents his emotional state with utmost candour and dignity.

The poem also derives most of its force from the quest between space and time, from deciding between the apparently dark watershed that characterizes academic life and the independent, somewhat re-assuring retirement life. In opting for the latter, the poem gains contemporariness and realism: contemporariness in the sense that it is increasingly becoming the pre-occupation of many an academic, especially in Africa, to ruminate on when to take their exit from the profession; and realism in the sense that it is the imperatives of the mind, rather than anything else, that inspire the poet's ultimate retirement from his university job.

The "conditions" to which Clark alludes at the end is a metaphor for not only the filthy and unhealthy state for which the country has got a poor reputation, but essentially, it underscores the poet's quest for the ideals of art. True, the poet relinquishes his ivory tower job but the challenge of life remains: the creative impulse must be fostered. Consequently, he sets up the Pec Repertory Theatre which today is a symbol of his contribution to the common enterprise of art.

From the stylistic level, the lines glide smoothly and expressively, unencumbered by the poet's acquaintance with, or knowledge of, poetic conventions which impinge on his "imitative" verse. Besides, the dominance of such cadenced words as "chambers", "tenure", "cesspool", "reclamation", "congested" and "suicide" invites us to think of the entire poem as a musical composition which evokes elegiac pathos.

In conclusion it can be said that the last three poems discussed above—**"Song"**, **"Night Rain"** and **"Out of the Tower"**—are remarkable accomplishments which any careful assessment of Clark's enduring value as a poet must take into consideration, not only because they enhance our understanding and appreciation of his life and art but because they constitute the best examples of his mature poetry. (pp. 54-6)

> *Isaac I. Elimimian, "J. P. Clark as a Poet," in* The Literary Criterion, *Vol. XXIII, Nos. 1 & 2, 1988, pp. 30-58.*

J. O. J. Nwachukwu-Agbada (essay date 1989)

[*In the following essay, Nigerian critic Nwachukwu-Agbada reviews* Mandela and Other Poems, *noting that "the poems of* Mandela *are better realized than those of* State of the Union."]

Mandela and Other Poems is J. P. Clark's sixth volume of poetry. He is also a playwright and literary critic of note. The Mandela poems come after **State of the Union** (1985), in which he examined with a sense of anguish the deteriorating state of the moral and civic stance of the Nigerian life-style. In **Mandela** Clark's frustration goes beyond the Nigerian borders to hint at the various forms of deprivation in the African continent, which are encapsulated in the twenty-five-year imprisonment of South Africa's nationalist freedom fighter Nelson Mandela. In the title poem Clark asks, "Sitting or asleep on his bed of stone / what does he see, what does he dream / In the dark of day so slow to break?" His wonder is heightened by the apparent equanimity exhibited by both the prisoner and his wife. He asks for "cameras in space" to reveal "the thought of an old man kept in a cage / Away from wife / Away from life!" Other poems having to do with the South African impasse include **"A Letter to Oliver Tambo," "The Beast in the South,"** and **"The Death of Samora Machel."**

"News from Ethiopia and the Sudan" laments the famine that is now ravaging the lands that "once feasted Pharaohs and emperors." These are countries with a rich history of affluence, which they had achieved through hard work. The poet-persona calls attention to the legend that "also spoke of the ruler / who acted upon

a dream, and turned / seven lean years into a festival." Today such rulers are no more; what one finds now are those "briefly touched / By the string of troubadours" and sycophants, who, though they "hear and see all right," are only interested in "their arms and skin alone."

Part 2 of the collection comprises "death" poems entitled "Ceremonies for Departure." These poems, even when dedicated to the memory of certain friends, combine to make a statement on the various stages of falling ill, dying, and departing. Each of the poems underscores the futility of life, the difference between reality and mirage, the vagueness of existence. Part 3, "Departures," contains further poems on the dead as well as on the metaphor of passage. In **"Leaves Falling"** the fallen leaves "speak to us all return / to earth that spring from dust." In **"A Mother's Story"** the poet remarks on the fate of womanhood in the hands of an irate husband. Ironically, in old age, and in death especially, "the old man of the house / With many wives cannot breathe or take / A blow unless one old woman is at his side."

The poems of **Mandela** are better realized than those of **State of the Union,** in which the poet allowed his verse to slide through his fingers into total prose. The lines here are highly evocative, with an evenness of metaphoric freshness. Clark, it seems, has bid a final good-bye to the esoteric and recondite imagery of prewar Nigerian poetry, in which he was a participant. When we take the **State of the Union** and **Mandela** poems together, we cannot but arrive at the conclusion that Clark has embraced the call for a more limpid language by our poets, all the more so when their themes are social and civic.

> *J. O. J. Nwachukwu-Agbada, in a review of "Mandela and Other Poems," in* World Literature Today, *Vol. 63, No. 3, Summer, 1989, pp. 523-24.*

FURTHER READING

Elimimian, Isaac I. "The Theme of Violence and Protest in J. P. Clark's Poetry." *Concerning Poetry* 17, No. 2 (Fall 1984): 73-87.
  Examines the theme of violence in Clark's *Casualties,* in the poems "Ivbie" and "Agbor Dancer," and in *America, Their America.*

———. "The Rhetoric of J. P. Clark's *Ivbie.*" *World Literature Written in English* 27, No. 2 (Autumn 1987): 161-73.
  Discusses "Ivbie" as a "rhetorical tour de force." The critic concludes: " . . . I think [that "Ivbie"] will perhaps best be remembered as a work whose rhetoric centres around the poet-persona's patriotic struggle to

salvage the indigenous culture from the shattering effects of colonialism."

Nwabueze, P. Emeka. "J. P. Clark's *Song of a Goat:* An Example of Nigerian Bourgeois Drama." *World Literature Written in English* 28, No. 1 (Spring 1988): 35-40.

Contends that *Song of a Goat* is a "Nigerian bourgeois drama."

Soyinka, Wole. "A Maverick in America." *Ibadan* 22 (June 1966): 59-61.

Reviews *America, Their America,* noting: "I confess readily that like everyone else (except perhaps the American) I had enjoyed the crude vigour of *America their America* . . . . [It] will prove a useful book to present to any American we particularly wish to insult."

Austin Clarke

1934-

(Full name Austin Ardinel Chesterfield Clarke) Barbadian novelist, short story writer, essayist, autobiographer, and scriptwriter.

Clarke is recognized as one of the most prominent contemporary novelists in Canada. In his work he portrays the plight of impoverished blacks in Barbados and the problems encountered by Barbadian immigrants in Canada. While his writing is suffused with humorous observations, his social commentary is often scathing and pessimistic, reflecting the anger and frustration of victims of economic, political, and racial oppression. Clarke is especially praised by critics for his skill in rendering the nuances and rhythms of Barbadian dialects.

Like most of the characters in his fiction, Clarke was born on the West Indian island of Barbados. His father was an artist and his mother a hotel maid. Clarke excelled at his primary school, the predominantly black St. Matthias Boys School, and was given a scholarship to attend Combermere, one of the best secondary schools on the island. Unlike at St. Matthias, most of the students at Combermere were white and from well-to-do Barbadian families—a situation that made Clarke feel estranged and isolated. His sense of alienation sharpened even further when he transferred to Harrison College in 1950; a bitter account of this experience, entitled "Harrison College and Me," appeared in the periodical *New World Quarterly* in 1966. In 1955 Clarke left Barbados for Canada. Soon he began writing poems and articles for various Canadian literary magazines and newspapers. After publishing several novels and a collection of short stories, he returned to Barbados in the mid-1970s to work for the Caribbean Broadcasting Corporation, a government-owned radio and television station. He left abruptly in 1976, however, because of disagreements with Prime Minister Errol Barrow. Clarke considers himself in exile and refuses to return to Barbados under the present government. He now lives in Toronto and is at work on an autobiography.

Clarke's early novels, *The Survivors of the Crossing* (1964) and *Amongst Thistles and Thorns* (1965), depict life among indigent residents of Barbados. The former work centers on the unsuccessful efforts of a plantation laborer to organize a strike for better wages. The protagonist of *Amongst Thistles and Thorns* is an illegitimate nine-year-old boy who tries to find his father after receiving cruel treatment from his headmaster and his mother. Clarke's next three novels, *The Meeting Point* (1967), *Storm of Fortune* (1973), and *The Bigger Light* (1975), collectively known as the "Toronto Trilogy," chronicle the experiences of a group of Barbadian immigrants in Canada. The first two novels dwell mostly on Bernice Leach, a live-in maid at a wealthy

Toronto home, and her small circle of fellow immigrants. The third novel, *The Bigger Light,* explores the life of Boysie Cumberbatch, the most successful of this immigrant group, and his wife, Dots. Boysie has at last realized the dream that compelled him to leave Barbados: he owns a prosperous business, his own home, and an expensive car. However, in the process of acquiring material wealth, he has become alienated from his wife and his community. Now he searches for a greater meaning to his life—a "bigger light." "*The Bigger Light* is a painful book to read," David Rosenthal observed. It is "a story of two people with many things to say and no one to say them to, who hate themselves and bitterly resent the society around them.... Certain African novelists have also dealt with the isolation of self-made blacks, but none with Clarke's bleak intensity." Critic James Dale also noted: "*The Meeting Point* is of major importance and marks Clarke's emergence as a novelist of depth and force because of the way in which it obliges the reader to confront the tragic and comic complexities of human nature." Clarke's short stories, collected in the volumes *When He Was Free and Young and He Used to Wear Silks* (1971), *When Women Rule* (1985), and *Nine Men Who Laughed* (1986), further examine the indignities and alienation experienced by Canada's West Indians.

Growing Up Stupid under the Union Jack (1980), Clarke's autobiographical memoir, is considered by some critics to be the author's best work. It is narrated by Tom, a young man from a poor Barbadian village. Everyone in the village is proud that Tom is able to attend the Combermere School, for it is run by a "real, true-true Englishman"—an ex-British Army officer who calls his students "boy" and "darky" and who flogs them publicly. The students eagerly imitate this headmaster's morals and manners, for to them he represents "Mother England." Appraising this work, critic Anthony Boxill commented: "In this book, which deals with his life up to the time he left Combermere School, Clarke is once again at his best. Full of humour and vigor, it recreates the world of his boyhood with much affection but without glossing over the injustice and brutality with which the society treated the poor and the black. One has the feeling that far from forcing his material into a predetermined rigid mold, the author has allowed this book to grow organically." Dan Hilts was less impressed with the work: "[*Growing Up Stupid under the Union Jack*] is not compelling reading. It's a bit like looking at someone's random collection of childhood photographs.... There is also a curious lack of emphasis; most of the vignettes are presented in the same desultory manner. The lack of chronological or emotional structure combined with a point of view that is firmly placed in the past are limitations the book does not overcome." Nevertheless, this work won the Casa de las Americas Literary Prize in Cuba in 1980 and was later serialized in *The Nation*.

On the whole, Clarke's work has received positive reviews. "His [work] is bursting with vitality," B. Pomer wrote, "alive with pictures that fairly leap off the page, and bubbling with streams of natural dialogue in a West Indian idiom...." Clarke's novels—which examine the problems experienced by West Indian immigrants in Canada—are considered among the best in West Indian-Canadian literature.

(For further information about Clarke's life and works, see *Black Writers; Contemporary Authors,* Vols. 25-28; *Contemporary Authors New Revision Series,* Vol. 14; *Contemporary Literary Criticism,* Vols. 8, 53; and *Dictionary of Literary Biography,* Vol. 53: *Canadian Writers Since 1960.*)

PRINCIPAL WORKS

The Survivors of the Crossing (novel) 1964
Amongst Thistles and Thorns (novel) 1965
"Harrison College and Me" (essay) 1966; published in periodical *New World Quarterly*
The Meeting Point (novel) 1967
When He was Free and Young and He Used to Wear Silks (short stories) 1971
Storm of Fortune (novel) 1973
The Impuritans (novel) 1974
The Bigger Light (novel) 1975
The Third Kiss (novel) 1976
The Prime Minister (novel) 1977
Growing Up Stupid under the Union Jack: A Memoir (prose) 1980
The Singing Men of Cashel (novel) 1980
Short Stories of Austin Clarke (short stories) 1984
When Women Rule (short stories) 1985
Nine Men Who Laughed (short stories) 1986
Proud Empires (novel) 1986

James Dale (essay date 1968)

[*In the following essay, Dale reviews* The Meeting Point, *describing it as a novel "primarily about people, not about a racial or social situation...* The Meeting Point *is of major importance...."*]

Mr. Clarke's first two novels, **The Survivors of the Crossing** (1964) and **Amongst Thistles and Thorns** (1965), were interesting examples of a genre, the West Indian Novel. They were tidily constructed, capably written, and, inevitably, marked by racial bitterness and insularity of outlook. Now that Mr. Clarke has written himself out of his Barbadian childhood and youth he has escaped from the constrictions of fiction which is neatly labelled and categorized; **The Meeting Point** [1967] is primarily about people, not about a racial or social situation even though many of the people in the novel happen to be West Indians living in Toronto. The earlier tidiness has gone, and the novel sprawls chapterlessly, wanders back and forth in time, and breaks spasmodically into long passages of interior monologue. The simple four-legs-good-two-legs-bad morality has gone as well; the white man is no longer seen as merely the patronizing exploiter of the black, for the races are partners in misery, mutually exploiting, hating and loving in a world where nothing is simple any more.

At the centre is Bernice Leach, who has come to Canada from Barbados to work as a domestic for the Burrmanns, a Jewish family living in Forest Hill. Mrs. Burrmann comes from "a very rich and respectable Jewish home", and is "heiress to a million dollars in slum-house real estate", but she and her husband, who graduated from Trinity with first-class honours and has become a successful lawyer, are only a jump away from the ghetto and immigrant parents. The safety of their prosperity needs to be bolstered, and the West Indian maid can be safely patronized and underpaid, an object of oppression for the recently oppressed. The irony is amplified when Bernice's sister Estelle comes to stay with her for a holiday and is seduced by Mr. Burrmann, who exercises a kind of *droit de seigneur* not dissimilar to that of the plantation overseer in *The Survivors of The Crossing* who "slept with any of the women labourers he wanted." But the oppressors are also sufferers; Bernice resents her mistress and pities her too, with her endless pointless parties and her desperate search for refuge in alcohol and in "culture", and Sam Burrmann the bold seducer is really the sexual failure who tries to assert his manhood by taking Estelle as a mistress.

In seducing Estelle, Sam is taking himself back to a devastating encounter, in the days before his marriage, with "a large vulgar-laughing black woman named A-Train, who roared in and out of the El Mocombo Tavern, like an express train, singing rhythm-and-blues." It was A-Train who had given him complete sexual satisfaction, and A-Train who had rejected him as well, with: "Get to hell out, Sammy. And don't you ever come back till you's a *man*!" Sam Burrmann's attempt to recreate the past with Estelle and to compensate thereby for his failure in sexuality and essential manhood serves as a paradigm for the other black-white relationships in the novel, which function in an atmosphere of mutual resentment and desire, largely, though not exclusively, on the sexual level. Boysie Cumberbatch, a character carried over from *The Survivors of the Crossing,* is closely akin to Sam Burrmann in his resentment of his wife and his attempt to find satisfaction in women of another race. Bernice's friend Dots, who works for a doctor in Rosedale, in her loneliness and need brought Boysie from Barbados to marry her. He says: "I is not such a blasted fool that I don't know it is loneliness and *not* love, that signed my passport and turned me into a landed immigrant.... But it pains my arse to think o' myself, as a man sponsored, and sponsored, gorblummuh, by a woman at that!" So Boysie ignores his wife and goes in search of an "outside-woman", preferably white. And his friend Henry, who has lived in Canada for many years, has a curious liaison with a white woman, a Jewish girl who is a graduate student at the University of Toronto; as with Estelle and Sam, one sees in the relationship the attraction-repulsion mechanism at work between the two groups of the persecuted, Jews and Negroes.

Henry and his girl Agatha ultimately break up, and Sam rejects and discards Estelle, who dies after trying to bring on an abortion. The white has been merely using the black, failing to achieve any meaningful personal contact because of a fear of real commitment, seeking for experience rather than love. But there is guilt on the other side, too. Estelle originally intends nothing more than a cold-blooded exploitation of Sam, Henry enjoys the prestige conferred by his association with Agatha, and Boysie is all too eager to profit from the tradition which ascribes greater sexual potency to the Negro. And Bernice alternately despises and pities, hates and loves her employers, just as her attitude towards white people fluctuates: at times she is forced to admire them and their institutions and practices, at times she sinks back into the dumb acceptance of her lot which harks back to her enslaved ancestors, and at times she is outraged—she even goes through a Black Muslim phase.

The great achievement of *The Meeting Point* is this very avoidance of the simplistic, this awareness of the oddity and variety in human nature which defies neat sociological pigeonholing. The vivid dialogue and the striking insights into social and racial attitudes would, though valuable, not be enough to raise the novel above the level of entertaining competence; *The Meeting Point* is of major importance and marks Austin Clarke's emergence as a novelist of depth and force because of the way in which it obliges the reader to confront the tragic and comic complexities of human nature. (pp. 19-20)

> *James Dale, in a review of "The Meeting Point," in* The Canadian Forum, *Vol. XLVIII, No. 567, April, 1968, pp. 19-20.*

Dan Hilts (essay date 1980)

[*In the following excerpt, Hilts offers a negative review of* Growing Up Stupid under the Union Jack, *concluding: "Despite some interesting aspects ... the book is not compelling reading."*]

Most of us find our own lives an endless source of amusement and fascination. We are often all too eager to share these feelings with others. Sometimes, however, we will relinquish time to one whose life seems particularly adventurous, well-connected, or profitable, especially if it is told with charm and wit. Austin Clarke's memoirs [*Growing Up Stupid under the Union Jack*] have some of these ingredients. Their concern is one pivotal year between 1944 and 1945 when the author came of age in his native Barbados.

The details of family life, the smells and sounds of the island, are caught in sharp focus. The basis of fundamentalist religion is revealed as a search for moral superiority and as an outlet for creative energies. Clarke recalls both the pride in and resentment about being taught in an imitation English private school in a colony that prided itself on being known as "Little England." Even discounting the natural tendency to exaggerate childhood traumas, the schools he attended sound dreadful. Arbitrary and heavy-handed corporal punishment was common. Learning by rote British history, Latin, and French without any reference to local culture was hardly calculated to make education anything but painful drudgery.

The long-range view of the Second World War from a peaceful tropical island is evocative....

Despite some interesting aspects, however, the book is not compelling reading. It's a bit like looking at someone's random collection of childhood photographs. Most of the individual pictures are composed well enough and some are even arresting, but they lack any sort of unity or coherence. There is also a curious lack of emphasis; most of the vignettes are presented in the same desultory manner. The lack of chronological or emotional structure combined with a point of view that is firmly placed in the past are limitations the book does not overcome.

Dan Hilts, "Little England Made Him," in Books in Canada, *Vol. 9, No. 6, June-July, 1980, p. 23.*

Austin Clarke with Terrence Craig (interview date 1983)

[*In the following 1983 interview, Clarke and Craig discuss influences on Clarke's novels, focusing on the creation of Boysie Cumberbatch, who appears in* The Survivors of the Crossing, The Bigger Light, *and* The Prime Minister.]

[Craig]: *I would like to begin by considering the autobiographical elements in your fiction. You have produced one volume of autobiography,* **Growing Up Stupid Under the Union Jack,** *and have another almost finished. Your first work seems very autobiographical. Did you see it as such at the time, when you were writing* **Amongst Thistles and Thorns**?

[Clarke]: No, I did not see the novel *Thistles and Thorns* as autobiographical. One reason is probably that it was the second thing I'd written and I didn't think that my own life was significant enough to deliberately be the characterization of a novel. But since I had nothing to write about, nothing to rely upon except my own experiences, my own life, and even though I may have camouflaged some of the purely autobiographical material of my own life, I still wouldn't say that the novel is autobiographical. The novel is interesting in the sense that it is nostalgic, that I was groping back to a situation in Barbados, and a meaning of Barbados, at the time I used to live there. The novel was written in 1963, and I had left Barbados in 1955. I suppose if I knew at the time that I was going to become a writer, then perhaps I might have been more prepared in dealing with the material from an autobiographical point of view. But certainly in 1960, when the novel was planned, I did not know that I was going to be a writer. So I was really groping for a subject to deal with in this book.

It is true that the main character in the book is a little boy, and it is true that some of the things he experienced in the book I perhaps did experience in life. But I was not thinking of myself; I was thinking of myself as a kind of prototype. This, of course, is arrogance. I don't know if one could call it the arrogance of the novelist. But, I thought that the life I led in Barbados might have coincided with the lives of other boys my age. This of course may be a contradiction. Perhaps I'm saying that it is in fact autobiography, but I don't see it that way . . . I did not decide at the outset to write about myself and camouflage it. I decided to write about all the little boys whom I knew at the time. And it so happened that life at the time might have been very dull and commonplace, so that some of the things mentioned about that little boy naturally would have happened to other boys other than me.

But you see I feel that a writer has very little material that is not primary in its source, that is to say, in his own life, so perhaps I am really evading the truth in the question when I say that I did not see *Amongst Thistles and Thorns* as autobiographical. Perhaps I am trying to escape from admitting that everything that a writer writes is autobiographical, in the sense that it is his own experience. The subjects he chooses may not be based on himself but certainly there's an argument to suggest that the aspect of the autobiographical in the novel is perhaps greater than the aspects of research and history.

I suppose I asked that question because of your character, Boysie Cumberbatch, who has always seemed to be such a real character, with so much vitality. **Survivors of the Crossing** *introduces this character. What experiences did that novel come from, if your work does come out of personal experience to some extent?*

To answer the first part of the question first, Boysie Cumberbatch, now that I am pressed in academic circles to give his origin and his roots, I would have to say that Boysie is based on a man I used to know when I was a little boy. My family had a piece of ground, we call it— you would call it a small farm—we had a piece of ground, and we hired a man to work this ground. He was a beautiful man, he was an exceptional man in that he did not allow his poverty—and he would have been poor to be working for a poor family—he did not allow his poverty to be the definition of his pride and his dignity. He was an odd man also in the sense that he was about twenty-five when I knew him—I would have been twelve—and he was living with, in a common-law arrangement (of course we did not call it by those euphemisms), he was living with a woman who was about twice his age. And I always thought it was odd, and we used to say behind his back that he was living with his mother—of course she was not his mother. This is the man whom I saw every day of my life before I left Barbados. He was a strong man. He was a man who I think understood that there was a kind of biblical honour and dignity to his working the ground. I am saying that now not to be facetious, but to try and explain why he in fact did not kill my stepfather with a fork, knowing of course that his wages were extremely small. Of course, wages in the whole island were small, but when I look back, this was a man, say, who could be given sixpence or a shilling, and during the harvestime, about five shillings, a week, and yet he was able to organize a way of living which could certainly not be called deprived, and certainly could not have rendered him as an inhabitant of a ghetto as we know ghettos in North America.

The labour situation is invented to show the position of these workers in canefields for small landowners and for the big sugar plantations, because I have always felt that there was some injustice in that arrangement. Of course, this injustice I'm talking about is idealistic, because I know, having studied economics, there have to be workers, and workers have to be paid a certain proportion of the cost of producing this. So I know that you can't pay a sugar cane labourer the amount of money you pay a manager. There was no real labour situation. But it *could* have happened. It seemed to me that if these labourers were more revolutionary in spirit, and more educated, that they could have exacted much more as wages from, say my own stepfather, and from the large sugarcane plantation owners. But I felt that to have introduced that near riot or revolution was justified because of the inculcation or the injection into the society of one man who, say, operating in the terms of Frantz Fanon, which is to say the colonized man versus the colonizer, this man Boysie would feel that in time he had as strong a right to be operating the plantation as the owners of the plantation. And of course the history of Barbados, the political history of Barbados, tells us that Boysie Cumberbatch would in fact have behaved the same way as the white plantation owner. I'm saying this because of my close experience of politics in Barbados which finds the situation of the Boysie Cumberbatches who have now been educated, who have got money from their professions, from stealing, whatever, but who have now become the new owners of the island, and one cannot draw any great moral distinction between their attitude to poorer people in their time and the attitude of the white plantation owners to themselves when they were poor.

To pick up on that, when you say that the original for Boysie found an honour and dignity in working in the ground, that is something that appears fairly often in Canadian literature, the sense of one's value being derived from one's labour. Is the Boysie of that book and fictional situation the same Boysie who comes to Toronto and expects not to have to work very hard?

No, he's not. The arrangement of labour in a canefield is chauvinistic to the extent that the men use the fork and the women use the hoe. The men cut the canes, the women load the canes....

And in Canada the domestic situation reverses that. But what I mean is that Boysie just doesn't seem willing to work when he comes to Canada.

OK. It is the structure of that society, of that time in Barbados, that Boysie Cumberbatch who worked in the canefields would get more money than his woman regardless how industrious she was. If they were working in the canefields—and even at other jobs—the man would always get more money. The man had a certain control over her. He was head of the family. The fact of emigration has certain psycho-racial implications. By that I mean that the history of racism, in America certainly, always extracted the black woman from her environment and placed her in the white or segregated society as a domestic servant exposed to a higher standard of living, from which she may derive certain conclusions, from which she may derive certain vicarious influences, arrogances, and it was always easier for the woman to be more continuously employed than for the men, the men being regarded as a threat because of their black manhood. So that when Boysie Cumberbatch

came here, he came here with a status below that of his wife because she had been asked to come here as a domestic, with a guaranteed income. Here was a situation which, had he emigrated to America, which was the normal channel of emigration, he would have sent for her, or he would have sent money back to her in order that her socio-economic status might be improved.

When Boysie came to Canada, he found himself at a status below that of the woman he used to control a short time before in Barbados, and this accounts for that imbalance, and this accounts also for the systematic draining of his manhood.

We're talking about Boysie here as if he were a real person, so I can't help asking, what happens now to him? Are you finished with him after **The Bigger Light,** *after he drives offstage, or will he re-appear again? Would you ever take him back to Barbados as the successful exile?*

Well, all those possibilities are feasible, I'd just like to go over the scene of Boysie's exit from Canada.

He leaves in a new car. He has his favourite music. Even though he had insisted that he had stripped himself of the more conspicuous appendages of the materialism in which he lived and which he enjoyed for a while, he was going to America—the land of opportunity—in a new car.

The car, so far as I am concerned, is a new womb in which he finds himself. It is also a mechanized coffin. It is a journey, it seems to me, into an aspect of his past and at the same time into an aspect of his future that may engulf him. Now, I say that all those possibilities are feasible. I am in fact writing about Boysie in the second part of **The Prime Minister,** in the sense that I am tracing Boysie from the time he was going to school in Barbados to when he comes abroad, as a student this time, but it's the same Boysie, because the feelings, the psyche, the emotions, the traumas are all Barbadian boys', the "boys-ies." So that he would come to Canada in a different capacity and with a different self-assurance. Because he would be a student, he would be in a higher social class, he would be an intellectual.

The point is, when he goes back to Barbados, would he be, as you have suggested, a successful exile, and I think from my own personal experience that while he may bring his success back, I could not say at this point that he would become successful in Barbados. (pp. 116-19)

When Graeme Gibson interviewed you for Eleven Canadian Novelists [*see Further Reading*]*, you spoke of being influenced by jazz musicians, including Coltrane, and by Christopher Frye and Ridout. Who is Ridout? Have there been any other literary influences since? What effects have the various writers you've been exposed to in the States had on you?*

Ridout is the author of the textbooks in English which we did in Barbados when I was going to Combermere School. I thought that this was the most comprehensive

English textbook that I have come across. As a matter of fact, some friends of mine teach at universities and at Ryerson in Toronto and sometimes when we're drinking I ask them questions from those books. In particular, Book Three.

Now, to talk of my friend Mailer. I like him as a man, I like him at parties, and I like him when we sit down and talk, when we get the chance, which is not very often. Mailer affected me adversely before I met him. I had read some things that he had written during the Beatnik days about blacks. Mailer took it upon himself to be the white interpreter of black consciousness. He did it very well because of his very influential use of the language, his way of putting words together, which has always impressed me. Sometimes I would think that content is less important than the way the words are put together.

When he was involved in political activity of the civil rights, when as one may say he became a political writer and wrote about the Vietnam war, I think it was a kind of essay, or a kind of journalism which had just the required amount of objectivity but also was imbued by his personality and his vast knowledge and his ability to relate things that happened, say, on the road to Washington and the burning of the draft cards of Vietnam, with life itself. It reminds, me, his writing, *Of a Fire on the Moon* and other books, it reminds me of Jean Genet. I remember reading a copy of *Esquire* magazine, it must have been 1969 when everybody in America, white and black, thought that there was going to be a civil war. Well, that was the feeling we all got at that time, and I remember Genet was brought over from France to write his impressions of that time, that very violent time— violent in expectation—tough, concrete time when you smelled almost every day guns, and that stuff that they shoot off that makes your eyes burn. And he described the policemen standing up in never-ending lines, with their pistols and their batons. And Genet said, well, the baton is like a penis, and they're using this on the blacks in the way I suppose that the slavemasters used it on the blacks, meaning the women, and in some cases on the men. So it was a kind of lifting of the everyday prose of reporting and injecting into it the creative, imaginative touch of the writer that impressed me in Mailer's non-fiction work.

Now, the other people in America who influenced me. There was a very charming man, and I am very pleased and honoured and proud to have met him. This was C. Vann Woodward, who is regarded as the Southern historian. It was a very interesting thing that happened to me when I was at Yale. I was a fellow of Calhoun College, but I used to eat at Berkeley College because it had the best food. And I met the master there, who was a Southerner, an engineer, and we got along very well because we shared a kind of obsessive liking for Dylan Thomas. And when I tried to take this back to the students, and in particular the black students, they could not see how I as a West Indian, and in their terms, as a black man, could sit down and have a pleasant social afternoon with a white man who was a Southerner. They said even *his accent* disturbed them.

When I got close to C. Vann Woodward, we could talk about a lot of things, in the same way too that Robert Penn Warren and I used to have lunch often at the Yale Faculty Club, which was like a kind of exclusive restaurant in the South, because there were lots of professors at Yale who were Southerners. And you could sit down in the afternoons and you would think from the accents around you and the conversations that you were in the South, particularly when C. Vann Woodward and Penn Warren drank bourbon and branch water, having lazy lunches that lasted three hours. Well—I had known their work and naturally to have met them then I had to go back and see whether there was the sincerity in their work that I had experienced across the table as we drank.

I'd always liked Saul Bellow's *Henderson the Rain King* and *Herzog,* because I was at that time trying to solve many of the things that Bellow had in fact solved in *Herzog.*

Such as...

The ability to have the story go forward not on one plane but on several planes, and the injection into the narration of the thinking of the man—one calls this interior monologue—and that sort of thing. I am very sorry that I never got the chance to meet William Faulkner, even though his reputation insofar as the black/white situation is concerned may have been tarnished by the position he took when James Meredith was trying to get into the University of Mississippi. But, you know, I remember once reading a comment made by a colleague of mine, the great novelist George Lamming, who said—and this was very startling to read in 1968-69—he said there is more in common between the West Indian writer and the Southern writer, and I think he did not even think of the black Southern writer, because there were not many good black Southern writers; he was thinking of Faulkner and those people. And when I read Faulkner again recently, I realized what Lamming was saying, because of that kind of engulfing darkness, and the sensuousness of the day and the evening, the smell, the heat, the pace of life, of thinking, of expectation, the pace of sexuality which seemed to be determined by the weather, the ingrowness of the society, the incestuousness of the society, the music in the society, the religious aspect of the society, and the dignity of the most undignified man. All those things I grew up seeing. And it may be that Barbados and the South are two slave societies of various intensities, but I could understand that. So those are the writers who would have some effect on me.

To jump from the States over to England, you must often find people comparing your work with Sam Selvon's. What do you think of the comparison?

It is not an unnatural comparison, although the older we both get I do not think we are so close. But I would give you a story. When I was working at the *Globe and Mail,* after I came down from Kirkland Lake, the *Globe and Mail* in their unwisdom fired me. This then would have been the fifteenth job from which I was fired. I joined the ranks of other famous novelists who contend that they are unemployable. So I said there is no point in my going out to work for the last two weeks of this tenure at the *Globe and Mail,* why not sit down and write some short stories? Which I did. I wrote six short stories in the two weeks, one of which is "I Hanging on Praise God," the story that has brought me more money than even novels, since it is so often reproduced in anthologies. I wrote these things in dialect without realizing the obvious influence of Sam Selvon. I think that one of the most beautiful books I have read is The Lonely Immigrants.

The Lonely Londoners?

The Lonely Londoners. Sorry. I said "the lonely immigrants" thinking really of two titles, because of George Lamming's book on the same phenomenon of West Indians going to London in the 50s, and Selvon's book deals with that. Sam Selvon the Trinidadian. I had read *The Lonely Londoners* at that time, and I used to read it at parties, but I was not a writer at the time. I had not been published. But the effect was so powerful and I said, well, here's a man who is writing about Trinidadians in the way that Trinidadians speak. And I thought this was almost impossible to do because I was brought up in a very formal and classical tradition. And it never occurred to me that one could use the flavour of Barbadian or Trinidadian or Jamaican language to write about these people, without, say, writing a calypso or a comedy. What I'm saying is that it had never been done before except for making jokes, and I didn't think that that writing could be taken seriously.

Then, of course, Sam had been in my ears for years before I came to Canada, when he and Lamming and John Hearne and V.S. Naipaul and some of the West Indian poets used to broadcast from the BBC in London, on a program called "Caribbean Voices." And that was the first time we heard, coming from this established medium of the BBC, things about ourselves, and so we said, well, this is another aspect of the revolution. We are now important people, our works are being taken seriously, and they are coming from the fountainhead.

I do know Sam's novels. We are both looking at a stratum of society and describing that stratum in the way we know it, without making a statement. I am glad to have this opportunity, because I am thinking now of an interview published recently in *Canadian Literature* in which Sam Selvon is interviewed by the West Indian critic Kenneth Ramchand, who is spending quite a lot of time trying to pin Sam down to accepting that in his early novels he is dealing with the confrontation of the blacks in Trinidad and the Indians in Trinidad, and whether in fact he was making a racialistic statement. But Sam said, and as I agree and believe, that he was

just writing about people with whom he grew up, people he knew.

The Prime Minister *is a book that seems out of place in your work as a whole. What were you aiming at with it? Because of what you said earlier, now I begin to think of it as an instrument of revenge. Is that too strong?*

It may be regarded as an instrument of revenge in that I was trying to scrape up with a very ineffectual tool the remnants of my psyche, which had been smattered and smashed in my own backyard by people I had trusted and loved. It was an instrument of revenge in the sense that I was trying to spit out the bitterness of the experience and the naiveté in my own character. It was an instrument of revenge in the sense that I was trying to prove—and I don't know if it can be proven—that the pen is mightier than the sword.

But it was also an instrument of a more positive function. I thought that I could say things about power in the Caribbean, which could possibly not have been said so effectively in another medium. Because, you see, for years we have had the Calypsonians saying the same thing about power. So, here was I, close to power, tasting power, using power, and then this tragic collapse of the equation. Because I was functioning in Barbados as a politician, I had minimized the artist in myself. When I was no longer a politician, I had to convince myself that it was absurd in the first place to have wanted to be a politician and secondly that all the instincts I had to rely upon was my being an artist.

Now, you ask whether I agree that it seems out of place in the body of the work I'd done at the time. The way the book is published, it does in fact tend to be that. But, you see, the book published is, I think, exactly one half of the manuscript, and the manuscript was pared down in that way because the editor and the publisher very idiotically felt it was a kind of political thriller, so they took out what I would call the idiosyncracies of my style and the feeling for language, and so on. So it comes out as a kind of hard, polished not in a sense of improvement, but hard, concentrated work.

I was trying also to say in the novel that no matter how powerful a prime minister is, or a political leader is, because of the requirements of the job and because of the job itself, he cannot really see the people, over whom he is ruling, *as a society*; and he cannot see the society in the same way as the artists amongst the people can see it as a society. So that perhaps that is why the politician will never be able to solve the very obvious and crying problems of the people over whom he is lording.

That is a very pessimistic view of politics, isn't it?

It is a pessimistic view, perhaps, but it is a very practical one, because I have been there and I have seen it and it is happening now under a different prime minister.

What do you yourself consider the strengths, the best aspects of your work?

Well, again this exposes me as an arrogant person, which I am not...

I'm going to ask you about the weaknesses next!

[Laughter] Well, then I would say there are no weaknesses!

But the strengths of my work I would consider to be my love of the language, my insistence that it is not sufficient to describe the bare bones of a character even if that description is graphic enough, but that one should be able through the arrangement of words to describe to some extent how the person feels, what the person loves, how the person walks, and so on. And characterization, I would think would be one of my strengths. Editors and publishers may disagree.

And the other thing I would consider is my love of people talking. So that what I have said really is one thing because if I spent time in reproducing conversation, I therefore would have to understand the nuances of the character who is talking. And then too, my way of seeing things. I would look at, suppose—not to be personal—suppose I were to describe your secretary. I have never had a conversation longer than one minute with her. But I have watched her. So I would make her fidget with her hair, make her run her hands on her slacks. I would give the impression that this is a woman who is concerned with her appearance. Now if one took into consideration the avoirdupois of the lady in question, then one could easily translate that heaviness from the body to the speech. So that a person reading ought to know from this treatment that the character tends to be slightly burly, that the character is sensual. That is what I mean, to give an example we can appreciate.

Now, you ask about the weaknesses. I would say, as they would appear to a Canadian critic, they are plot and repetition. But, you see, in an earlier question you mention my being influenced by jazz musicians, and if you think of jazz music, which is to some extent an improvisation on African music—the chants—then of course you understand that you would get this repetition. For instance, Coltrane, in one of his classical pieces, "My Favorite Things," which is a standard [hums], he was able to "re-treat" and repeat the theme and each new layer of paint that he spreads on this musical canvas contains a new, sudden interpretation of the previous one. So that one then is confronted with the accumulated effects which it seems to me would make the thing more powerful. Then, of course, I tend to regard life as circular, and if life is circular I cannot see a conclusion to any of my actions. And if it is circular, perhaps I am saying that life is a groping through this darkness of knowledge in order to arrive at a certain situation which makes one comfortable in dealing with the present and in understanding the past. And prepared for the inconsistencies or the unknowns of the future, if that is not a tautological statement.

So far as plot is concerned, if I say that I consider life to be circular, then certainly I can have no plot. I don't think that plot is so important.

Would that explain the "ling" that turns up in the trilogy?

Yes. "Ling" is just the way we in Barbados say "ring." We have always used the word "ling" to mean a circle.

My last question is a somewhat precocious one. In your fiction and in your personal life you often seem to be acting the role of a middleman between white Canada and the West Indian immigrants. What do you feel West Indians have to teach white Canadians, and vice versa?

I think West Indians could teach Canadians about what I would call the enjoyment of life. And they can do this simply because in the West Indies that is all you can do. [Laughter] You can only enjoy your life because there is no great point in killing yourself, or as we say, in "breakin' your ass" to accomplish this, because the supply is limited. You do this killin' yourself when you come abroad.

Now it seems to me that this is the whole irony of the thing, that you are no longer really West Indian, you see. Because if a man has lived here for ten years I think he ceases to be a West Indian. So he is really talking as another Canadian to Canadians who were born here. So that to insist then that he is preaching means that you are still relegating him to the position of the outsider, and therefore you would say that his contribution perhaps is less valuable than the contributions of the other one. The enjoyment of life, he could teach.

He could teach too that West Indians are no different from Canadians. They may have a different colour, and they may come from a different climate, but they are both colonials. So I think that the West Indians who live here have less of a traumatic adjustment to the society than is the case, say, of a European who comes from a country of a different language and culture.

The Canadians could teach the West Indians order. I don't mean law and order. Most of us who go back to the West Indies come back and say things like "Jesus Christ, man, I went to buy a postage stamp and it took me half an hour in the line," or "I went to catch the bus and people are pushing!" [Laughter] Whereas he would have lived all his life doing that, now he sees the futility in that kind of disorder. In other words, if we could get a good mix of the Canadian structure and the West Indian non-structure, I think we would be arriving at Elysium. (pp. 121-27)

Austin Clarke and Terrence Craig, in an interview in World Literature Written in English, *Vol. 26, No. 1, Spring, 1986, pp. 115-27.*

Keith S. Henry (essay date 1985)

[*In the following excerpt, Henry presents a critical overview of Clarke's novels and short stories.*]

Of the four gifted and established West Indian-North American novelists, Frank Hercules, Paule Marshall, Rosa Guy, and Austin Clarke, Clarke is the only West Indian-Canadian. The very small native black population in Toronto, the locale of his North American novels, has allowed his to be the most single-minded focus on the exploration of the special West Indian experience in North America. (p. 9)

[Clarke's] first work, *Survivors of the Crossing,* deals with the lives of men and women in a post-mid-twentieth-century Barbados village dominated by a sugar plantation. The plantation regime here is brutal enough and omnipotent enough for at least some of the prevailing realities here to seem anachronistic for their time. The armed overseer on his horse, for example, well deserves his reputation for bloodthirstiness. The civil government in Bridgetown is of no apparent importance, except as helpful auxiliaries to the plantation in the form of police "interrogators" and merciless judges. The villagers mostly live in destitution, relieved only by an uncertain access to sex and rum and sometimes a resort to religion. However, a letter from a former laborer recently emigrated to Canada sets off an unexpected chain of events. His reports of a superior quality of life for black people in his new home inspire in the fevered mind of laborer Rufus an attempt to organize a revolutionary strike. The author's scene-setting in the early pages, dense, grim, humorous, pathetic, full of subtle personal exchanges and brutal ones, heavy with portents, may be the most brilliantly variegated pages of his entire corpus. The attempt at revolution fails. The apathy and treachery of the villagers and the vigilance of the plantation management are serious impediments, and Rufus' inadequacies are too severe to surmount them.

Many of the lasting characteristics of Clarke's work are apparent in this novel. His humor is sly and, as in most of his works, very effective. Humor is often, in Clarke, a brief and unexpected, not necessarily happy, turn amidst disquieting proceedings. ("Swing low sweet clubbio" is the author's refrain in a later work as police truncheons sail into black Henry White's body—the beating itself partly the result of a serio-comic misunderstanding.) His humor is also commonly a byproduct of his exceptionally subtle observation of interpersonal relations between close acquaintances. In the early pages of *Survivors of the Crossing,* we see a number of examples of the troubling humor Clarke extracts from relationships between "friends." Illiterate Rufus, for example, urgently asks Boysie to read to him a letter from his old political comrade, Jackson. Jackson had left for Canada six months earlier, and Rufus feels certain the letter contains momentous news about the means to a better social order in Barbados. But Rufus has to stand impatiently while Boysie chooses only to read the letter silently to himself and without comment.

Clarke is remarkably skilled also in the creation of simple, uneducated characters, women no less than men. In later novels they retain our attention even when they are not merely poverty-stricken but also often unperceptive, even stupid, and leading very physically confined lives. Clarke's use of the "Bajan" (Barbadian) dialect is extensive and effective. His recall of the minutiae of Bajan social detail and rural custom is impressive and, over the body of his work, even dazzling. These alone lend a formidable authenticity to the portrayal of his characters.

In Clarke, unlike in Paule Marshall, we never quite achieve a vivid sense of physical presence in the characters or, for that matter, in the landscapes and artifacts. Its absence is not a major failing, however.... Clarke exploits this very characteristic in his writing to achieve a second and distinctive artistic success. This absence notwithstanding, Clarke's characterizations are without doubt very successfully achieved as amalgams of textually evolved and textually elucidated personality, verbal style, and accoutrements. In this first novel, we think easily of Rufus and his fork, Clemmie and her salty religiousness, Mr. Whippetts and his slyness, Biscombe and his cunning and cowardice. But they lack an enriching physiognomic resonance. The rare treatment in Clarke of physical encounters, of combat or lovemaking, may, to some extent, explain this neglect. It also helps to explain how little we miss this quality in his novels.

We learn also from *Survivors of the Crossing* that Austin Clarke is very skilled at developing suspenseful plots and that, indeed, he has a predilection for suspense and mystery. From this penchant for suspense flow several characteristics of his novels, some happy, others undoubted failings. (pp. 10-12)

There is a mild irresolution at the end of the novel, a half-closing of ranks over free drinks as Rufus' fate is sealed. This ambiguity is satisfying, in fact, in this novel. For despite their desperate poverty, the ultimate advantage to the villagers of what Rufus crudely envisioned remains as evident as does the weight—to which they have clearly succumbed over their free liquor—of immediate temptation and opposing power. And although the villagers clearly need a respite, the potential for upheaval is patently too great for present conditions to endure. But as our familiarity with Austin Clarke grows, it is easy to suspect that other considerations, along with his artistic instinct, may have induced him to close the novel on this inconclusive note. Clarke has [a] predilection for tension and unpredictability in his plots and an aversion to imposing special teleological meaning on human events. Usually detectable in his work is an implicit moral condemnation of the rich white world, but no expectation of a righteous chastening of that world is encouraged.

In essence, Clarke's second novel, *Amongst Thistles and Thorns,* is a narrative by nine-year-old Milton Sobers, punctuated by reveries, revealing the state and progress of his life over a few hours in his native corner of Barbados. In Milton's company over these few hours, we are in effect taken on a comprehensive tour of daily semirural life in black Barbados. The fundamental characteristic of that life is a deadly poverty scarcely distinguishable from destitution. A grown man begs a loan of one penny.

The main thread of Milton's narrative is his growing resentment of the quality of life, both at school and at home. In both, a sustained lack of interest, even cruelty, is only rarely interrupted by a passing, sometimes feigned, concern. By the end of the tale, Milton's mother's lack of interest in him becomes fully evident as she endeavors to ensnare an old flame. Milton's distaste for his mother, Ruby, previously unarticulated, grows correspondingly great. Her superstition, empty religious obsessions, cowardice, gullibility, feeble maternal concern, and her responsibility for his father's death disgust him.

As in *Survivors of the Crossing,* much remains unresolved, appropriately unresolved, at the close of the work. Milton's final flight is imminent but to what? And it is unlikely, despite her efforts, that Ruby's uncaring paramour will tarry in her leaky shack beyond the morrow.

We have observed that in Clarke's fiction there is little moral judgment beyond the singular implicit moral condemnation of the rich white world. The observation remains true of this novel, as it is of Clarke's later work, with the exception of *The Prime Minister.* There are few enhancing attributes among the lowly or the victimized, and there is certainly no hint of unfolding purpose, of misfortune justly befalling the rich or powerful.... There are no genuine compensations for being poor or black.

By the end of *Amongst Thistles and Thorns,* Clarke's command of the major novelistic skills seen in *Survivors of the Crossing* is confirmed. The distinctive achievement of Clarke's second novel, however, is his special evocation of atmosphere throughout the work. Our fugitive glimpses of the figures and landscape are gained, it seems, through muslin. It is an achievement not entirely absent in some of Clarke's later works, but it is certainly most sustained in this novel. He takes brilliant advantage of what is often, elsewhere in his work, a minor failing, i.e., a lack of physical profile. The half-lit, half-submerged, helpless figures of Ruby and Milton, of Nathan and Willy-Willy, seem to share the texture and color of their landscape, a landscape that is, like them, without much definition or substantiality. (pp. 13-15)

By the end of the novel, we also begin to detect what may be some sources of concern regarding Clarke's work. Foremost among them is an occasional willingness in this writer to go to the very edge of credibility, usually for no compelling reasons. In this novel, semiliterate or thieving teachers, including a headmaster, reappear, a reappearance that does violence to the reputation of West Indian teachers. And in school-conscious Barbados, adult Willy-Willy regales a nonplussed Milton (who, we recall, is nine years old) with a lengthy exaltation of sexual debauchery: "Come outta [headmaster] Blackman' school, and help me breed the womens in this village...." (p. 16)

The Meeting Point, Storm of Fortune, and *The Bigger Light* form a trilogy progressively exploring the lives of a small circle of Barbadian migrants in Toronto. In *The Meeting Point,* whose events take place in the mid-1960s, we encounter all the main characters. There are Bernice and Dots, two live-in domestics approaching middle age. There is Estelle, Bernice's younger, more attractive, more intelligent, and self-reliant sister, staying in Bernice's cramped apartment. Boysie is Dots's wayward husband. Henry, unlike the others who together have fewer than ten years in Canada, left Barbados some twenty years ago, but, like Boysie, is apparently now among the permanently unemployed. Henry's girlfriend is Agatha, a wealthy, liberal Jewish graduate student. Bernice's employers are the discordant couple, Sam and Gladys Burrmann. Sam and Estelle carry on a mutually exploitative affair, Estelle seeking Sam's influence to enable her to acquire landed immigrant status.

Although a novel, *The Meeting Point* is clearly meant to be a social document as well. It provides us with a substantial tour of black Toronto's haunts and makes lavish use of the real names of many of Toronto's personalities, places, and institutions. Many incidents in the unhappy lives of the characters replicate ones mentioned in Clarke's published view on race relations in the same city in the same years. In addition, many incidences of antiblack racism are simply mentioned in passing by characters in the novel where it would overburden the novel to insert them as ongoing events. We are spared little of the degradation black Toronto is forced to endure even in the bountiful and relatively enlightened midsixties. We witness discrimination, unemployment, scorn, and self-hatred. (pp. 17-18)

The fact of ethnicity is all-pervasive in *The Meeting Point,* and it is the first identification both author and reader assign to every character and to every event. The work is also in fundamental respects a political novel in that we are constantly made aware of unequal power relations between racial groups expressing themselves regularly and unequivocally. Yet, *The Meeting Point* is much more than a fictionalized political tract or sociograph. For one thing, the characters in the novel are fully aware of the unequal power relations, and this awareness is employed to impart a good deal of added but unspoken tension to human relationships which are already sufficiently freighted with other difficulties. For another, the novel is skillfully constructed and developed, proceeding to a number of simultaneous resolutions, some unexpected and even exciting. The black characters have the ring of authenticity, as does the immigrant experience. Clarke's major achievement in this novel, indeed, may well be his successful depiction of his unpromising main character, Bernice Leach.

Bernice is physically unattractive, of small intellectual means, and living a physically highly monotonous and constricted life. But Clarke utilizes the few live, thin elements in her existence, without unconvincing drama or artifice, to construct a character that retains our interest permanently.

Of some interest is the novel's suggestion that a West Indian upbringing is a very slender moral resource among these migrants in a white world, an idea contrary to what we have learned to expect from sociologists and economists like Ira Reid and Thomas Sowell or a creative writer like Paule Marshall. Both Boysie and Henry have apparently suffered total defeat. And Bernice's weapons are puny and even contemptible. They range from crying and vain religiosity to morbid self-delusion about conditions in both Barbados and Toronto.

Of some interest is the novel's suggestion that a West Indian upbringing is a very slender moral resource among these migrants in a white world, an idea contrary to what we have learned to expect from sociologists and economists like Ira Reid and Thomas Sowell or a creative writer like Paule Marshall. Both Boysie and Henry have apparently suffered total defeat. And Bernice's weapons are puny and even contemptible. They range from crying and vain religiosity to morbid self-delusion about conditions in both Barbados and Toronto.

By the end of *The Meeting Point* we begin to wonder whether Clarke's vision may be essentially misanthropic. Except perhaps for Estelle, who is hardly a winning personality but who is commendably calculating, not a single major character in any of his first three novels possesses lasting appeal. Of the likeliest candidates, Agatha and Milton, the former is ultimately too naive. And the life of nine-year-old Milton is largely without engaging qualities of childish innocence, charm, and possibility. His life is too brutalized for that. Moreover, Clarke consciously magnifies our difficulties. On the same page that we hear Milton being told that learning is the only escape from his deadly village existence, we also discover that he is apparently also backward at school. Finally, his flight—undoubtedly into swift adulthood and, despite his dreams of Harlem, quite conceivably into delinquency—is imminent at the close of the novel.

Misanthropy of a limited nature, such as we seem to see in early Clarke, is of course a valid literary perspective, one whose proper test is artistic functionality. In Clarke's first two novels, it is an enhancing perspective, and its insistent hold approaches the disagreeable perhaps only in *The Meeting Point*. In his last works, it has clearly ceased to be a ruling passion. Clarke's touching and affectionate portrait of his own grandmother in her declining years, in the memoir *Growing up Stupid under the Union Jack,* is a telling example of the change. She is mildly vagrant, dependent (even mendicant), and a trifle uncomprehending, but these aspects of her life are,

with her love, all part of the allure of the portrait. (pp. 19-21)

In *The Meeting Point* we encounter again the nagging problem of credibility. Admitting her romantic attachment to "blackness," it remains difficult to see attractive, very wealthy, highly intelligent, and educated Jewish graduate student, Agatha, a woman of twenty-nine, being in love over a period of years with Henry White. Henry is black, over fifty, long unemployed, penniless and without prospects, uneducated, is neither handsome nor especially considerate, is indeed thoroughly feckless. Agatha later marries Henry, cheerfully accepting manifold rejections from friends and family that her liaison with Henry initiated and that her marriage multiplied.

The Meeting Point, although by no means a failure, is not Austin Clarke in the fullness of his powers. It is perhaps too unrelievedly distressing, too much a social document, too much in harness to political and social fact. Noticeably, Clarke's comic gift is a great deal less in evidence, his comic moments less successful, than in his earlier novels or his next.

We follow the lives of these Barbadian immigrants in *Storm of Fortune,* an absorbing sequel where lives evolve and develop with less reference to the claims of the power structure. There is certainly social comment but the social documentation is more relaxed, less consistently emotionally involving. All the same, the major revelation of the novel's closing pages is an unmistakable social insight. We are by now very familiar with how straitening and emotionally exhausting it is to be a live-in domestic. But the liberated feeling, following their departure from domestic service, of Dots and even of Bernice—who is a little self-dependent and who has been quite abruptly dismissed and been forced to live on her rapidly dwindling savings—is still surprising and is emphatic. The lives of Boysie and Henry remind us equally, however, that black life is lived under siege, even when domestic service is not involved. (pp. 22-3)

As the novel opens, Estelle lies in a hospital ward recuperating from an attempted abortion, the results of her liaison with Sam Burrmann. She is befriended during her few days there by a fellow-convalescee, a white northern Ontario woman, Gloria Macmillan, who invites her home to the town of Timmins to mend her life. Mrs. Macmillan is friendly, down-to-earth, and brilliantly persuasive. After leaving the hospital, she even sends money from her slender purse to Estelle to assist her in coming north. Estelle takes up the offer and travels north at great expense only to discover, by the most astonishing of coincidences, that Gloria Macmillan lives at North Bay, a town very far away from Timmins. This Macmillan episode is so bizarre, so much without further consequence in the novel, Gloria Macmillan so strangely unembarrassed during their accidental encounter at being revealed as a liar, Estelle so unembittered—she is still pregnant and now very out-of-pocket—that we wonder what Clarke's motive could be in developing it. Mrs. Macmillan is apparently an otherwise normal personality, but her lying is aggressive, sustained, motiveless, profitless, indeed costly. Grateful as we are for Clarke's brilliant demonstration of his facility with working-class characters, male or female, black or white, and for the entree provided by the Macmillan episode into Estelle's essentially reclusive personality, the reader is left with the feeling that the excursion is pointless. The reader fears that any new coincidences of the magnitude seen in this episode will at once deprive the novel of any further credibility. It should be said that the excessive autonomy of the Macmillan affair and its ancillary scenes (notably Estelle's eventful journey to North Bay) being conceded, this particular excess rather strangely belies one of *Storm of Fortune*'s main virtues. For in this, the most cinematic of Clarke's immigrant novels, an integrated development of the plot is on the whole very happily combined with an impressive succession of varied and independently arresting dramatic scenes. Those involving Henry are especially interesting and important: by their dramatic character, by their air of progressive desperation, and by their tranquil capitulation, they impart to the novel an element of tragedy beyond the larger one of black immigrant life in Toronto. This more closely visible tragedy is an undoubted embellishment to the work.

The explanation for the Macmillan cul-de-sac in *Storm of Fortune* is partly, it seems, that Clarke's confidence in his powers is now so great—justifiably great—that he becomes a trifle careless and gratuitous. There are other small signs of these tendencies in the novel. Inconsistencies and improbabilities begin to creep into Clarke's world. Of thematic importance are Boysie's great prosperity in his new janitorial business and his new ambition: they are decidedly unexpected in view of what we have seen of Boysie's personality, but they are, above all, implausibly sudden. So is Henry's devotion to poetry. We have already noticed Agatha's unfathomable marriage to Henry.

We begin to recognize also some features of Clarke's novels as clichés, recognizing also, however, that no prolific novelist will escape clichés. The semiliterate and unbelievable Barbadian schoolteacher, this time a headmistress, is again present: "'One buns billing!' the headmistress screamed... 'One bag o' buns missing! Who thiefed a bag of buns?'" She is remembered by Bernice in one of those reveries that we are now familiar with, reveries lightly triggered by events and in which lonely characters frequently converse with themselves. We now know, too, that the unsettling letter or newspaper article is a favorite Clarke device. It is now possible to think, too, that Clarke's relentless pursuit of his characters, to visit them in their bathrooms, even to notice Dots's discarded dirty underclothing, is not only in the service of realité. It is a technique chosen, it seems, to enable us to feel total familiarity with his characters. It fails. For, as we saw, Clarke's characters do not acquire the physical presence they easily could, considering how effective he commonly is in construct-

ing their personalities. Except for very limited descriptions of major female characters, Clarke in fact rarely takes any trouble to leave us with lasting physical images. It may be added, finally, that despite the sunlight of the last few pages of *Storm of Fortune,* the voids, viciousness, and fecklessness we encounter remain numerous. Interestingly, some disconcerting examples come near the close of the novel.

The Bigger Light concludes the trilogy on Bajan immigrant life in Toronto. The focus is now very much on Boysie's and Dots's prosperous household and on Boysie's mental state. Thematically, Boysie's mental drift away from and again towards mostly the former West Indians, his wife, Barbados and Barbadian memories, his difficult early days in Canada, is the novel's core. The techno-structural device to suggest Boysie's faltering grip on his environment, his mental sclerosis and narrowing yet blurred vision, is the *idée fixe,* a tightening cycle of recurrent and essentially trifling thoughts and events. (pp. 24-6)

The Bigger Light obviously differs much from the earlier novels of the trilogy. The social environment is a great deal less oppressive and intrusive. The lessons of Boysie's life and his fading marriage may well suggest the perils of attenuated ethnic links in an isolated community, but they are intelligible also well beyond the imperatives of ethnic and racial conflict. For the first time we have concluded one of Clarke's novels without feeling that most of the major characters are, at one time or other, repulsively vicious, brutish, stupid, or juvenile. Bernice's new employer is excellent. Bernice herself is almost vivacious. Gladys Burrmann is absent and Sam Burrmann is behaving admirably, supporting and welcoming his and Estelle's child. The Boysie of *The Meeting Point* is now unrecognizable.

The resolution of *The Bigger Light* is, as we now expect, not very final and, as we also expect, not quite what Clarke carefully prepares us for. Regrettably, Clarke succeeds in not being predictable at the cost of being anticlimactic. Boysie's impulsive crossing of the American border in his powerful car, instead of dying in the suicidal car crash he appears to be courting, simply does not seem to resolve very much. Clarke's habit in the trilogy of raising people and events to centrality, making them seem to be auguries of major events, then letting them slide into nullity, is finally largely wasteful. It is disappointing even in this novel where typically sterile developments do help to demonstrate Boysie's failing hold on reality. Such are, notably, Boysie's peculiar relationship with his neighbor, Mrs. James, and his hunger for the sight of the mysterious woman trudging to the subway every morning.

The collection of short stories *When He Was Free and Young and He Used to Wear Silks* and the autobiographical memoir *Growing Up Stupid under the Union Jack* display Clarke's familiar skills in heightened form and constitute some of his most brilliant and unblemished work. They are thematically an integral part of the body of work already treated. Some of the short stories are, in fact, with only the minutest changes, passages in the novels. Others, such as the title story, are in part, subtle intimations of themes developed in the novels. And Clarke, in any case, seems to be at pains to emphasize the thematic relationship of his stories to much of the rest of his work: old characters from the novels reappear, or new ones with old names, such as Nathan, Henry, and Lonnie. The observations above notwithstanding, Clarke does on occasion explore minor themes and moods absent or rare in the novels. In Calvin and in Jefferson Theophillis Belle, for example, we encounter single-minded and ferociously hardworking male immigrants, driven, admittedly, by ambitions that we are not permitted to regard as wholly admirable. And the very first tale, "**An Easter Carol,**" the relatively innocent forerunner to the later stories of more complex, usually grimmer, temper, has an almost impishly funny climax. Omitting the title story (where most of the classical attributes of the short story are deliberately forsaken for the more chaotic vigor of twentieth-century consciousness), the collection confirms Austin Clarke's mastery of the traditions of this genre. Economy, control, irony, moral distance from the action, expectancy, surprise, and climax are all enviably present.

In the memoir, it becomes evident that much in Clarke's fiction about Barbados life recalls his own life or that of his neighbors and acquaintances. This memoir, the first volume, we are told, of the author's autobiography, is suspended as Clarke enters the Classical Sixth Form of Barbados' prestigious Harrison College. It is a wide-ranging remembrance of a milieu judiciously viewed through the lens of maturer perception and a remembrance of young "Tom" Clarke's evolving place in it .... The memoir is at once literarily felicitous and socially alert.

Growing Up Stupid under the Union Jack supports the view, despite the many fine literary moments in his immigrant Toronto, that Clarke's art is surest and subtlest in his treatments of semirural Barbados. The richer dialect, thicker custom, more universal cast, and deeper access to the recesses of life and landscape allow him to weave a tapestry especially dense in atmosphere, action, and nuance. It must immediately be said, nonetheless, that many of the memorable passages and scenes in his Toronto novels and stories have no parallel in his Barbados tales. And it should be added that the Toronto work marries—successfully on the whole and brilliantly in places—artistic ambition and artistic opportunity, which would be unavailable to the self-limiting Bajan storyteller.

The Prime Minister stands apart from the rest of Clarke's corpus. It, too, is heavily autobiographical, the fruit of his two-year stint as General Manager of the Barbados Government's Broadcasting Company, a position from which he was unceremoniously terminated in 1976. Condemned as "vindictive" by some Caribbean critics, ***The Prime Minister*** was written, as Clarke himself concedes, in the "bitter" days following that

experience, written about "real people," he points out. It is a work very uncomplimentary about the official elite. The locale is, of course, Barbados.

As a Caribbean novel, ***The Prime Minister*** is unusual in several ways. It is a suspense and mystery novel, for one thing—its most uncharacteristic feature—and its action takes place indoors. Its focus is almost exclusively middle-class. The sexual attachments are not designed to have a primary sociological meaning. Finally, it is a novel also of political intrigue in the postcolonial world. Clarke's novel is faithful, nonetheless, to the traditional passion of West Indian novelists for explicit or implicit social commentary. (pp. 27-30)

The novel is replete with social commentary on the new, independent Barbados, pertinent and pointed, rarely flattering, but smoothly integrated. Even the romantic interludes are far more effective, it turns out, in recording the collapse of shade consciousness in John Moore's light-skinned lover than in fulfilling their more technical, novelistic objectives. The reader is left to make the important deduction, crucial to an understanding of modern West Indian history and sociology, that her experiences as a secretary in New York are the probable source of this liberation. For "the woman's" confidences to John Moore are not important and could just as easily have been provided by a maid or a male friend. Their bedroom encounters are not engrossing enough to be more than a makeweight: at best they help to maintain the controlled pace of the novel.

The Prime Minister is a final testimony to Austin Clarke's versatility and assurance as a novelist. The imaginative recall of his own and proximate experience is undoubtedly the sustaining resource in much of his work. But this resource is of unusually great range and is enriched by an outward vision and a genuine artistic, poetic sensibility. It is a final testimony, too, to his place as a West Indian intellectual, able to reflect productively on that region outside its established intellectual conventionalities. (pp. 31-2)

> *Keith S. Henry, "An Assessment of Austin Clarke, West Indian-Canadian Novelist," in* CLA Journal, *Vol. XXIX, No. 1, September, 1985, pp. 9-32.*

Paul Wilson (essay date 1986)

[*In the following excerpt, Wilson compares* Nine Men Who Laughed *with Clarke's earlier works, claiming that "Clarke's new book of nine short stories is to his earlier work as bitter lemon is to sugar cane." He asks: "What has gone wrong? What is at the root of such a fundamental and disturbing change in such a skilled writer?"*]

In his heyday ... Austin Clarke was a true pioneer, one of the few writers around dealing with the life and times of Caribbean immigrants in Toronto. His earlier work crackles with an energy, an inventiveness, and a sly, ironic humour that still reads freshly today. (I recommend *When He Was Free and Young and He Used to Wear Silks*). His characters—mostly Bajans, or Barbadians like himself—were lovable, roguish, marginally honest, upwardly mobile people trapped in a society and a subculture from which they sought, in ways both devious and direct, to escape. (p. 20)

Though it apparently inhabits the same territory, Clarke's new book of nine short stories [*Nine Men Who Laughed*] is to his earlier work as bitter lemon is to sugar cane. His characters are older, more worldly wise, more cynical. His men, most of them from the upper classes of their own societies, tend to have unrealistic and thwarted ambitions. They have got so used to blaming the world for their misfortunes they have lost the power to reflect upon themselves. Several are engaged in elaborate con-games directed against women, and the women themselves are almost invariably seen either as objects of sexual desire, financial advantage and security (Clarke says that the "system" is a woman), or disgust and loathing (they are frequently seen scratching their scars, wiping their eyes and picking their noses). Love is absent, calculation has filled the void, and relationships have dwindled to empty routine. Where Clarke once attacked real problems, like police violence, that have real solutions, he now seems to have given up, and given in to a kind of vague, catch-all condemnation of "the system" that leads to a "what's the use" attitude. And even when his characters do show normal human emotions and perceptions, they still can't behave in significant ways. It is not just that they feel helpless—they actually decline to act. When the female bank teller who narrates one of the stories receives a panic-stricken phone call from a colleague she is desperately trying to befriend, she makes no effort to help, with tragic consequences.

Clarke's literary universe—Toronto seen through Bajan eyes—has apparently undergone a deep and disturbing change. Once a world of magic newness, where wonder combined with pain and laughter, he now shows us a place that is more akin to Graham Greene's noxious portraits of fading Third World capitals. The pain has become chronic, the laughter hollow, and the primary emotions are disgust, hatred, self-loathing. His humour—the title notwithstanding—has soured. And where there was once lilt and lyricism in the speech—a melodic representation of Bajan English—there is now a duller, clunkier, and far less consistent tone.

What has gone wrong? What is at the root of such a fundamental and disturbing change in such a skilled writer? Is it the world that has altered so radically, or has something tainted the inspiration Clarke originally found in the life of the people around him?

Clarke has written an introduction that provides a few clues, some more revealing than others. He says, for instance, that the stories were written "as a means of escaping the physical and mental torment skeined by the prepossessiveness of the new culture," but that could be said of his earlier work too. He also says that the nine

men of the title are, metaphorically, himself. That makes more sense, and helps to explain the sensation of being thrust into a series of dark, brooding self-portraits that mirror a state of mind more than any "objective reality." But Clarke obviously intends those metaphors to stand for a reality outside himself, for he says that he wrote the stories "to destroy the definitions that *others* have used to portray so-called immigrants, black people . . . ." (pp. 20-1)

His vision is certainly crueller and less palatable, but is it really clearer? In his earlier work one felt the author's deep love for his characters; now one feels a sense of ennui and impatience, as though they had become less important to him than some message that—as metaphors—they were meant to convey. Somewhere in this "clear vision," Clarke's middle ground has collapsed, leaving only polarized, paralysed extremes. Even the best story in the collection, **"The Smell"** (a gripping and skillfully told tale of incest), is crippled by an abrupt and inconclusive ending, as though the author, having broached the subject, declined to go into it any further.

Clarke is clearly going through a troubled period in his creative life, and it may not be too fanciful to suggest that the author's public position in our society may have something to do with it. As a vice-chairman of the Ontario Censor Board, Clarke has assumed over his fellow citizens a position of power which, I believe, contains the seeds of corruption. In a recent interview with *Now* magazine in Toronto, he had this to say about his work:

> Censorship is not just snipping the films. It is making the decision to state that a scene should not be shown because [it] represents a skewed representation or characterization of a group or a class.

To my mind, Clarke's view of his job goes far beyond his mandate, but in any case, I don't believe a writer should ever have anything to do with censorship, period.

Scissors can be an honourable tool of the writer's trade, but only when they are used to cut and rearrange his own work. Could it be that Clarke's power as an official censor is playing havoc with his power and integrity as a writer? If it were, it would certainly not be the first time in the history of modern literature. After all, suppression and creation are irreconcilable forces, and though they are constantly at war within us all, the illusion that they have nothing to do with each other or, even worse, that they can somehow be made to co-exist peacefully, is dangerous and debilitating. Clarke clearly believes that political censorship is justified, and though he couches his views in the rhetoric of social concern, his attitude is arrogant and elitist. It is also proto-totalitarian. As George Orwell once pointed out, the effect of such an attitude on literature is almost always bad. (p. 21)

Paul Wilson, "Hollow Laughter," in Books in Canada, *Vol. 15, No. 7, October, 1986, pp. 20-1.*

FURTHER READING

Brydon, Diana. "Caribbean Revolution & Literary Convention." *Canadian Literature* 95 (Winter 1982): 181-85.
Reviews Margaret Atwood's *Bodily Harm* and Clarke's *The Prime Minister,* noting of the works: "These novels not only decry the political naiveté of tourists in the Caribbean,... they also challenge the linguistic naiveté of those who would ignore the political volatility in the region to write of it in an inappropriate language."

Garebian, Keith. "Lies and Grace." *Canadian Literature* 90 (Autumn 1981): 136-38.
Compares Clarke's *Growing Up Stupid under the Union Jack* with William Kurelek's *Someone with Me,* commenting: "Clarke's is superior in style, texture, and incident and maintains a balance between fleeting notes of anger or condemnation and those of sturdy endurance or lyrical celebration."

Gibson, Graeme. "Austin Clarke." In his *Eleven Canadian Novelists,* pp. 33-54. Toronto: House of Anansi Press Limited, 1973.
Interview with Clarke. Gibson and Clarke discuss the latter's early literary career and influences on his work.

Ryan, Frank L. Review of *When He Was Young and Free and He Used to Wear Silks,* by Austin Clarke. *Best Sellers* 33, No. 19 (1 January 1974): 434-35.
Appraises "The Motor Car" and "Griff" in Clarke's short story collection *When He Was Young and Free and He Used to Wear Silks.*

Review of *The Meeting Point,* by Austin Clarke. *The Times Literary Supplement,* No. 3402 (11 May 1967): 404.
Briefly reviews *The Meeting Point,* focusing on the character of Bernice Leach. The critic writes: "She is a character of impressive but rather bovine complexity...."

Eldridge Cleaver

1935-

(Full name Leroy Eldridge Cleaver) American essayist and editor.

One of the most significant figures of the black protest movement in the United States during the 1960s, Cleaver is best known as the author of *Soul on Ice* (1968). This work, a collection of essays written while the author was in prison, contains autobiographical sketches and commentaries on history, politics, and popular culture. As one critic wrote of *Soul on Ice,* "Cleaver, black man, ex-convict, rapist and rebel, probes an accusing finger into the sensitive areas of American racial injustice.... For white America, Cleaver is neither easy nor pleasant reading, but it is reading that needs to be done."

Cleaver was born in Wabbaseka, Arkansas, to Leroy Cleaver, a waiter and piano player, and Thelma Cleaver, an elementary school teacher. He and his family later moved to Watts, an all-black district of Los Angeles, where his parents separated. His mother supported herself and him by working as a janitor. While in his teens, Cleaver spent time in various reformatories for petty thefts and narcotics sales. In 1954 he was convicted of marijuana possession and sentenced to two and a half years in the California State Prison at Soledad. Later, in one of the essays in *Soul on Ice,* Cleaver stated that in 1954, the year the United States Supreme Court outlawed segregation, he began to form "a concept of what it meant to be black in white America." Cleaver completed his high school education in Soledad, studying the works of Karl Marx, W. E. B. Du Bois, Voltaire, and Thomas Paine. Shortly after his release from prison, however, Cleaver was convicted of rape and assault with intent to commit murder; he was sentenced to a term of two to fourteen years. He served the bulk of his term at Folsom Prison, where he became a member of the Black Muslims and took Malcolm X, a leader of the Black Muslims and a former prisoner himself, as his role model. In 1965 Cleaver, still in prison, began writing the essays that would later be collected in *Soul on Ice.* With the help of his attorney, he managed to get several of them smuggled to the leftist magazine *Ramparts,* and in June 1966 *Ramparts* published "Notes on a Native Son," Cleaver's now-famous literary attack on James Baldwin. As a result of this publication, Cleaver found support from prominent members of the American intellectual community, notably Maxwell Geismar, Norman Mailer, and Paul Jacobs. With their help and the guarantee of an editorial job at *Ramparts,* he won parole in November 1966. Released and living in California in 1967, Cleaver met Bobby Seale and Huey P. Newton, cofounders of the Black Panther Party for Self-Defense. The party was originally formed to protect black citizens from police brutality and harassment in the San Francis-

co Bay area, but F.B.I. director J. Edgar Hoover would come to call the party the nation's "greatest threat." Cleaver was impressed with the party's militant ideology and politics; he joined the Black Panthers and began touring America as their Minister of Information.

Cleaver gained national attention in 1968 with the publication of *Soul on Ice.* The artful prose and bitter frankness of Cleaver's essays were widely praised, but some critics contended that his perception of American race relations was extremely narrow. Many were shocked by Cleaver's use of profanity in the work and dismayed at the aforementioned "Notes on a Native Son." In this essay Cleaver criticized the theme of homosexuality in Baldwin's works, considering it a "racial death-wish," and attacked Baldwin personally for his sexuality and alleged hatred of black people. Gertrude Samuels, in *Saturday Review,* accused Cleaver of finding "a sexual reason for hating virtually all social and political aspects of American life." Most critics, however, praised Cleaver for his passionate insight into the state of American race relations and hailed him as a promising and powerful writer.

In April 1968, two days after the assassination of Martin Luther King, Jr., Cleaver was charged with a parole violation following a shoot-out between Black Panther members and the San Francisco police. Support for him came from around the world—many people, including writer Susan Sontag and actor Gary Merrill, demonstrated in New York, and in Europe, French film director Jean-Luc Godard urged his audience to donate to Cleaver's defense fund. Cleaver's wide liberal support became more apparent when he was chosen as the presidential candidate of the Peace and Freedom Party, an organization of both black and white radicals. Rather than face charges over the gun battle with police, Cleaver fled the country in late 1968. His *Post-Prison Writings and Speeches* (1969) was published while he was a fugitive in such places as Cuba, Algeria, and France. The work offers a detailed statement of the Black Panthers' political ideology and attempts to dispel public conceptions of the Panthers as a violent hate-group. Some critics appreciated Cleaver's candor, but most charged that the book contains too many revolutionary clichés and that Cleaver had ill-advisedly adapted his language to meet political fashions.

In 1975 Cleaver became a born-again Christian and returned to the United States, rejecting the countries he had formerly held as ideal revolutionary models. He became a Mormon and explained his general metamorphosis, especially his conversion to Christianity, in *Soul on Fire* (1978). He wrote that in a vision he saw his own face on the moon, then the faces of "my former heroes...Fidel Castro, Mao Tse-tung, Karl Marx, Friedrich Engels.... Finally, at the end of the procession, in dazzling, shimmering light, the image of Jesus Christ appeared. I fell to my knees." Critics were generally disappointed with *Soul on Fire*. Nevertheless, some welcomed Cleaver's new position and praised the work as a mature compromise with the forces of authority he had previously damned outright. Since his return to California, Cleaver has become a Republican and made an unsuccessful bid for the 1986 Republican nomination for a seat in the U.S. Senate. He hopes one day to make another run for the U.S. presidency. Some ex-Panther members have denounced his new stance and accused him of acting as an F.B.I. informant in exchange for leniency in the courts, but Cleaver ultimately blames the media for his image as a confused radical. "They try to make it look like I'm doing flip-flops all over the ocean," he explained in a 1988 *Ebony* profile. "I have a very good track record of being ahead of other people in understanding certain truths and taking political positions far in advance of the crowd and turn out to be vindicated by subsequent experience."

(For further information about Cleaver's life and works, see *Black Writers; Contemporary Authors,* Vols. 21-22; *Contemporary Authors New Revision Series,* Vol 16; and *Contemporary Literary Criticism,* Vol. 30 and *Dictio-*nary *of Literary Biography Documentary Series,* Vol 8: *The Black Aesthetic Movement.*)

PRINCIPAL WORKS

"Notes on a Native Son" (essay) 1966; published in periodical *Ramparts*
Soul on Ice (essays) 1968
Eldridge Cleaver: Post-Prison Writings and Speeches (essays) 1969
Eldridge Cleaver's Black Papers (essays) 1969
Soul on Fire (essays) 1978

Maxwell Geismar (essay date 1968)

[*Geismar, a former senior editor of* Ramparts, *championed Cleaver's cause and helped bring about his parole in 1966. In the following excerpt from an introduction to* Soul on Ice, *he applauds Cleaver's skill and vision.*]

[*Soul on Ice*] is one of the discoveries of the 1960s. In a literary epoch marked by a prevailing mediocrity of expression, a lack of substantial new talent, a kind of spiritual slough after the great wave of American writing from the 1920s to the 1940s, Eldridge Cleaver's is one of the distinctive new literary voices to be heard. It reminds me of the great days of the past. It has echoes of Richard Wright's *Native Son,* just as its true moral affinity is with one of the few other fine books of our period, the *Autobiography of Malcolm X,* and as it represents in American terms the only comparable approach to the writings of Frantz Fanon.

In a curious way Cleaver's book has definite parallels with Fanon's *Black Skin White Masks.* In both books the central problem is of *identification* as a black soul which has been "colonized"—more subtly perhaps in the United States for some three hundred years, but perhaps even more pervasively—by an oppressive white society that projects its brief, narrow vision of life as eternal truth. (p. xi)

Cleaver is simply one of the best cultural critics now writing, and I include in this statement both the formal sociologists and those contemporary fictionists who have mainly abandoned this province of literature for the cultivation of the cult of sensibility. (I am aware also of what may be considered excessive praise in this introduction; in that case I can only beg the reader to stop reading me and start directly with Cleaver.) As in Malcolm X's case, here is an "outside" critic who takes pleasure in dissecting the deepest and most cherished notions of our personal and social behavior; and it takes a certain amount of courage and a "willed objectivity" to read him. He rakes our favorite prejudices with the savage claws of his prose until our wounds are bare, our psyche is exposed, and we must either fight back or laugh with him for the service he has done us. For the "souls of black folk," in W. E. B. Du Bois' phrase, are the best mirror in which to see the white American self in mid-twentieth century.

It takes a certain boldness on Cleaver's part, also, to open this collection of essays with the section not merely on rape but on the whole profound relationship of black men and white women. There is a secret kind of sexual mysticism in this writer which adds depth and tone to his social commentary; this is a highly literary and imaginative mind surveying the salient aspects of our common life. There follow the Four Vignettes—on Watts, on the Muslims, on Catholicism and Thomas Merton, and on the heroic prison teacher called [Chris] Lovdjieff. Here we begin to feel the reach and depth of Eldridge Cleaver's mind on emotional and philosophical issues as well as historical and social ones—and yes, "heroic," a note barely sounded in contemporary fiction, is not inappropriate for certain parts of this deeply revolutionary collection of essays. (pp. xii-xiii)

But it is the part of the book called **"Blood of the Beast,"** and such pieces as **"The White Race and Its Heroes,"** that I find of primary importance, and of the greatest literary value. Describing himself as an "Ofay Watcher," Cleaver describes this historical period and this American culture in terms of the most astringent accuracy, the most ruthless irony, and the most insistent truthfulness. He reminds us of all the simple verities that decades of Cold War distortion and hypocrisy have almost wiped from our historical record—our historical consciousness.

The book is a handsome account of those years in the early sixties when the Civil Rights campaign stirred up a national psyche that had been unnaturally comatose, slothful, and evasive since the McCarthyite trauma. There is an atmosphere of turbulence in these essays, moving from the advent of the Beats and Jack Kerouac's *On The Road* to LeRoi Jones' revolutionary verses and then back to the Abolitionists (so scorned and despised by the Southern revisionist historians of the modern epoch), to Harriet Beecher Stowe and to that famous Fourth of July peroration for the slave race by Frederick Douglass in 1852.

In the concluding part of this book it seems that Eldridge Cleaver has reached his own spiritual convalescence, his healed spirit (no longer racist or narrowly nationalist), and his mature power as a writer—and how those pages do sparkle!... **"Notes on a Native Son"** is the best analysis of James Baldwin's literary career I have read; and while Cleaver calmly says things that no white critic could really dare to say, there is not a trace of petty artistic jealousy or self-vanity in his discussion—such as that, for example, which marked Baldwin's own repudiation of his former mentor, Richard Wright. The essay called "Rallying Round the Flag" gives us the plain, hard, truthful Afro-American view of the Vietnam war which Martin Luther King, just lately, has corroborated—it is in fact the world view of our

aberrant national behavior in southeast Asia. But just as this volume opens on the theme of love, just as Eldridge Cleaver never misses the sexual core of every social (or racial phenomenon, so it closes on it. (pp. xiii-xv)

I had forgotten to mention the wonderfully ironic descriptions of the Twist as the social symptom of the new age of dawning racial equality. Here, as with the Beatles and Rock n' Roll, when Eldridge Cleaver moves into the area of mass entertainment in the United States, he is as close as he ever comes to an open laughter at the white man's antics; just as in the concluding apostrophe from the Black Eunuch to the Black Queen—to the fertile black womb of all history— he reminds us how civilization has always mocked human gaiety. (p. xv)

> *Maxwell Geismar, in an introduction to* Soul
> on Ice *by Eldridge Cleaver, McGraw-Hill*
> *Book Company, 1968, pp. xi-xv.*

Robert Coles (essay date 1968)

[*Coles, a noted psychiatrist, is recognized as a leading authority on poverty and racial discrimination in the United States. In the following excerpt from a review originally published in* The Atlantic Monthly *in 1968, he faults aspects of* Soul on Ice *and harshly criticizes Maxwell Geismar's introduction to the book (see excerpt dated 1968) but acknowledges that Cleaver is a powerful and gifted writer.*]

All the essays [in *Soul on Ice*] deal with racial hurt, racial struggle, and racial pride. Mr. Cleaver is a black man, and he is not going to let either himself or anyone else forget that fact—in case it is possible for an American of either race to do so. Ralph Ellison and even James Baldwin want above all to be writers, and Cleaver says no, that is impossible, that is foolish, and certainly that is wrong.

I am with Ellison and Baldwin all the way, but the author of a book with the stark, unrelenting title *Soul on Ice* would expect that of me, a reasonably unharassed white middle-class professional man who, really, in many ways had it made from birth. I don't at all like the nasty, spiteful way Mr. Cleaver writes off *Invisible Man* or *Another Country*. I don't like the arrogant and cruel way he talks about Baldwin's life and his personality. I don't like the way he lumps white men, all of them, indiscriminately together, and I'm sick and tired of a rhetoric that takes three hundred years of complicated, tortured American history and throws it in the face of every single white man alive today. Mr. Cleaver rightly wants to be seen for the particular man *he* is, and I don't see why he should by the same token confuse the twentieth-century traveling salesman with the seventeenth-century slave trader. If he wants us to understand American history, and in fact see its economic and political continuities, all well and good; but it is really stupid to tell today's white people that they caused what in fact gradually and terribly happened. What can anyone do with that kind of historical burden, "do" with it in the sense of coming to any personal or psychological resolution?

I suppose one thing that can be done is what Maxwell Geismar does in his short and thoroughly surprising introduction [see excerpt dated 1968]. Mr. Geismar has abandoned himself without qualification to Mr. Cleaver's scorn and outrage. The black man cries out, and the white man says yes, yes, no matter what. Eldridge Cleaver is a promising and powerful writer, an intelligent and turbulent and passionate and eloquent man. But Geismar ironically treats him with the ultimate condescension of exaggerated praise, and even worse the cruelty that goes with using a man as an irrelevant foil. (pp. 106-07)

[If] I were Eldridge Cleaver I'd watch out. Praise is like power; there is nothing as corrupting (and yes, insulting) as absolute praise, particularly when one's very humanity is denied. (Which writer is without a "trace" of "self-vanity"?)

Nevertheless, apart from the introduction to this book, and apart from its black nationalism, there are some really lovely and tender and even exquisite moments to be found—when the author becomes a writer, not a pamphleteer and not a propagandist and not a devious, cruel literary critic, but a man who wants to struggle with words and ideas and tame them. There are ostensibly four parts to the relatively slim volume, but actually it is split in two. **"Letters from Prison"** and **"Prelude to Love—Three Letters"** show how one inmate of a jail becomes something much more, a literate, sensitive, and intelligent human being. There are white millionaires who have failed where Cleaver has succeeded.

How did he succeed? *Why?* We ought to ask such questions, even as we do with Malcolm X, Cleaver's great hero. People like me can tear Cleaver and Malcolm to shreds. We can discover the bad "background" they come from. We can find pathology everywhere—mental illness, physical disorder, social chaos, cultural disintegration . . . .

Yet at times he writes vivid, compelling prose. He has a sense of humor. He knows how to be astringent one minute, ironic the next. He can be tolerant and compassionate, far more so in my opinion than the man who wrote the introduction to this book. He is full of Christian care, Christian grief and disappointment, Christian resignation, Christian messianic toughness, and hope. He loves his lawyer, a white woman, and pours out his love to her in three beautiful, incredibly subtle and blunt and unsparing and unforgettable letters. How did he do it—learn to write, learn the really impressive theological subtleties that are addressed to his lawyer? . . .

Of course he also learned the other things, the handy political and sociological clichés that have blinded black and white men everywhere in every century. But above

all we must notice what he has done: begun (and only begun) to master the writer's craft. For that achievement Eldridge Cleaver deserves our unashamed awe, our admiration, and our insistence that like every other writer he work harder, rid himself of unnecessary baggage, and put to word the startling ironies that he knows from real life but sees and comprehends out of his mind's life. He ought to spare us nothing, but he ought to spare himself very little either. Inside a developing writer there is, there has to be, a kind of ice that somehow uses but also transcends the weather, the scene, the hot and cold of the outside world. (p. 107)

> Robert Coles, "Black Anger," in The Atlantic Monthly, *Vol. 221, No. 6, June, 1968, pp. 106-07.*

Eldridge Cleaver with Nat Hentoff (interview date 1968)

[An acclaimed author and journalist, Hentoff is known for his twin passions of jazz music and social reform. In the following excerpt from an interview he conducted for Playboy *magazine in 1968, he and Cleaver discuss the Black Panther party and issues of racism and redress in America.]*

[Hentoff]: *You have written [in* **Soul on Ice** *] that "a new black leadership with its own distinct style and philosophy will now come into its own, to center stage. Nothing can stop this leadership from taking over, because it is based on charisma, has the allegiance and support of the black masses, is conscious of its self and its position and is prepared to shoot its way to power if the need arises." As one who is increasingly regarded as among the pivotal figures in this new black leadership, how do you distinguish the new breed from those—such as Roy Wilkins [of the NAACP] and Whitney Young [of the Urban League]—most Americans consider the established Negro spokesmen?*

[Cleaver]: The so-called leaders you name have been willing to work within the framework of the rules laid down by the white establishment. They have tried to bring change within the system as it now is—without violence. Although Martin Luther King was the leader-spokesman for the nonviolent theme, all the rest condemn violence, too. Furthermore, all are careful to remind everybody that they're Americans as well as "Negroes," that the prestige of this country is as important to them as it is to whites. By contrast, the new black leadership identifies first and foremost with the best interests of the masses of *black* people, and we don't care about preserving the dignity of a country that has no regard for ours. We don't give a damn about any embarrassments we may cause the United States on an international level. And remember, I said the *masses* of black people. That's why we oppose [New York Congressman] Adam Clayton Powell. He's not militant enough and he represents only the black middle class, not the masses.

Since you consider yourself one of these new leaders representing the masses, what are your specific goals?

Our basic demand is for proportionate participation in the real power that runs this country. This means that black people must have part of the decision-making power concerning all legislation, all appropriations of money, foreign policy—every area of life. We cannot accept anything less than that black people, like white people, have the best lives technology is able to offer at the present time. Black people know what's going on. They're aware of this country's productivity and they want in on the good life.

So far—apart from your willingness to resort to violence in achieving that goal—you haven't proposed anything specific or different from the aims of the traditional Negro leadership.

OK, the best way to be specific is to list the ten points of the Black Panther Party. They make clear that we are not willing to accept the rules of the white establishment. One: We want freedom; we want power to determine the destiny of our black communities. Two: We want full employment for our people. Three: We want housing fit for the shelter of human beings. Four: We want all black men to be exempt from military service. Five: We want decent education for black people—education that teaches us the true nature of this decadent, racist society and that teaches young black brothers and sisters their rightful place in society; for if they don't know their place in society and the world, they can't relate to anything else. Six: We want an end to the robbery of black people in their own community by white-racist businessmen. Seven: We want an immediate end to police brutality and murder of black people. Eight: We want all black men held in city, county, state and Federal jails to be released, because they haven't had fair trials; they've been tried by all white juries, and that's like being a Jew tried in Nazi Germany. Nine: We want black people accused of crimes to be tried by members of their peer group—a peer being one who comes from the same economic, social, religious, historical and racial community. Black people, in other words, would have to compose the jury in any trial of a black person. And ten: We want land, we want money, we want housing, we want clothing, we want education, we want justice, we want peace.

Peace? But you've written that "the genie of black revolutionary violence is here."

Yes, but put that into context. I've said that war will come only if these basic demands are not met. Not just a race war; which in itself would destroy this country, but a guerilla resistance movement that will amount to a second Civil War, with thousands of white John Browns fighting on the side of the blacks, plunging America into the depths of its most desperate nightmare on the way to realizing the American Dream.

How much time is there for these demands to be met before this takes place?

What will happen—and when—will depend on the dynamics of the revolutionary struggle in the black and white communities; people are going to do what they feel they have to do as the movement takes shape and gathers strength. But how long do you expect black people, who are already fed up, to endure the continued indifference of the Federal Government to their needs? How long will they endure the continued escalation of police force and brutality? I can't give you an exact answer, but surely they will not wait indefinitely if their demands are not met—particularly since we think that the United States has already decided where its next campaign is going to be after the war in Vietnam is over. We think the Government has already picked this new target area, and it's black America. A lot of black people are very uptight about what they see in terms of preparations for the suppression of the black liberation struggle in this country. We don't work on a timetable, but we do say that the situation is deteriorating rapidly. There have been more and more armed clashes and violent encounters with the police departments that occupy black communities. Who can tell at which point any one of the dozens of incidents that take place every day will just boil over and break out into an irrevocable war? Let me make myself clear. I don't dig violence. Guns are ugly. People are what's beautiful; and when you use a gun to kill someone, you're doing something ugly. But there are two forms of violence: violence directed at you to keep you in your place and violence to defend yourself against that suppression and to win your freedom. If our demands are not met, we will sooner or later have to make a choice between continuing to be victims or deciding to seize our freedom. (pp. 90-1)

Have you considered the possibility that you could be wrong about the chances of waging a successful guerilla war? Don't you run the risk that all your efforts toward that end—even if they don't escalate beyond rhetoric— could invite a massive wave of repression that would result in a black bloodbath and turn the country's ghettos into concentration camps?

It seems to me a strange assumption that black people could just be killed or cooped up into concentration camps and that would be the end of it. This isn't the 1930s. We're not going to play Jews. The whole world is different now from what it was then. Not only would black people resist, with the help of white people, but we would also have the help of those around the world who are just waiting for some kind of extreme crisis within this country so that they can move for their own liberation from American repression abroad. This Government does not have unlimited forces of repression; it can't hold the whole world down—not at home *and* abroad. Eventually, it will be able to control the racial situation here only by ignoring its military "commitments" overseas. That might stop *our* movement for a while, but think what would be happening in Latin America, Asia, and Africa. In that event, there would be a net gain for freedom in the world. We see our struggle as inextricably bound up with the struggle of all oppressed peoples, and there is no telling what sacrifices

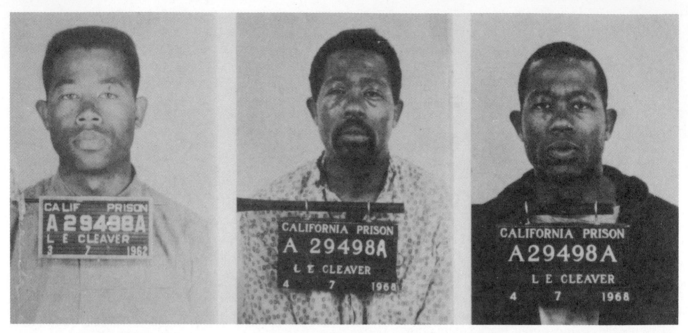

Prison mug shots of Eldridge Cleaver. The second picture shows him immediately after his 1968 arrest in Oakland, California, and the third shows him as he appeared after a shave and shower the same day.

we in this country may have to make before that struggle is won.

Do you think you have any real chance of winning that struggle—even without Government repression—as long as the majority of white Americans, who outnumber blacks ten to one remain hostile or indifferent to black aspirations? According to the indications of recent public-opinion surveys, they deplore even nonviolent demonstrations on behalf of civil rights.

At the present stage, the majority of white people are indifferent and complacent simply because their own lives have remained more or less intact and as remote from the lives of most blacks as the old French aristocracy was from "the great unwashed." It's disturbing to them to hear about Hough burning, Watts burning, the black community in Newark burning. But they don't really understand why it's happening, and they don't really care, as long as *their* homes and *their* places of work—or the schools to which they send their children—aren't burning, too. So for most whites, what's happened up to now has been something like a spectator sport. There may be a lot more of them than there are of us, but they're not really involved; and there are millions and millions of black people in this country who *are*—more than the census shows. Maybe 30,000,000, maybe more. A lot of black people never get counted in the Census. It's not going to be easy to deal with that large a number, and it won't be possible to indefinitely limit the burning to black neighborhoods— even with all the tanks, tear gas, riot guns, paddy wagons and fire trucks in this country. But if it does come to massive repression of blacks, I don't think the majority of whites are going to either approve it or remain silent.

If a situation breaks out in which soldiers are hunting down and killing black people obviously and openly, we don't think the majority will accept that for long. It could go on for a while, but at some point, we think large numbers of whites would become so revolted that leaders would arise in the white community and offer other solutions. So we don't accept the analysis that we're doomed because we're in a minority. We don't believe that the majority in this country would permit concentration camps and genocide. (p. 94)

Suppose you're right in claiming that most whites, for whatever reason, would not support massive repression of blacks in this country. These same whites, however, don't want black violence, either—but as you point out, most don't fully grasp the dimensions of the injustices against which that violence is a rebellion, nor do they understand why it continues in the wake of several milestone civil rights laws and Supreme Court decisions. The familiar question is: "What more do they want?" How would you answer it?

I can only answer with what Malcolm X said. If you've had a knife in my back for 400 years, am I supposed to thank you for pulling it out? Because that's all those laws and decisions have accomplished. The very least of your responsibility now is to compensate me, however inadequately, for centuries of degradation and disenfranchisement by granting peacefully—before I take them forcefully—the same rights and opportunities for a decent life that you've taken for granted as an American birthright. This isn't a request but a *demand,* and the ten points of that demand are set down with crystal clarity in the Black Panther Party platform.

Many would doubt that you're serious about some of them. Point four for instance: "We want all black men to be exempt from military service."

We couldn't be *more* serious about that point. As a colonized people, we consider it absurd to fight the wars of the mother country against other colonized peoples, as in Vietnam right now. The conviction that no black man should be forced to fight for the system that's suppressing him is growing among more and more black people, outside the Black Panther Party as well as in it. And as we can organize masses of black people behind that demand for exemption, it will have to be taken seriously.

Are you equally serious about point eight, which demands that all black prisoners held in city, county, state and Federal jails be released because they haven't had fair trials; and about point nine, which demands that black defendants be tried by all-black juries?

We think the day will come when these demands, too, will receive serious attention, because they deserve it. Take point eight. All the social sciences—criminology, sociology, psychology, economics—point out that if you subject people to deprivation and inhuman living conditions, you can predict that they will rebel against those conditions. What we have in this country is a system organized against black people in such a way that many are forced to rebel and turn to forms of behavior that are called criminal, in order to get the things they need to survive. Consider the basic contradiction here. You subject people to conditions that make rebellion inevitable and then you punish them for rebelling. Now, under those circumstances, does the black convict owe a debt to society or does society owe a debt to the black convict? Since the social, economic and political system is so rigged against black people, we feel the burden of the indictment should rest on the system and not on us. Therefore, black people should not be confined in jails and prisons for rebelling against that system—even though the rebellion might express itself in some unfortunate ways. And this idea can be taken further, to apply also to those white people who have been subjected to a disgusting system for so long that they resort to disgusting forms of behavior. This is part of our fundamental critique of the way this society, under its present system of organization, molds the character of its second-class citizens.

Have you considered the consequences to society of opening the prisons and setting all the inmates free? Their behavior may in one sense be society's fault, but they're still criminals.

We don't feel that there's any black man or any white man in any prison in this country who could be compared in terms of criminality with Lyndon Johnson. No mass murderer in America or in any other country comes anywhere close to the thousands and thousands of deaths for which Johnson is responsible.

Do you think that analogy is valid? After all, Johnson has been waging a war, however misguidedly, in the belief that his cause is just.

Many murderers feel exactly the same way about *their* crimes. But let me give you another example: Compare the thieves in our prisons with the big businessmen of this country, who are in control of a system that is depriving millions of people of a decent life. These people—the men who run the Government and the corporations—are much more dangerous than the guy who walks into a store with a pistol and robs somebody of a few dollars. The men in control are robbing the entire world of billions and billions of dollars.

All the men in control?

That's what I said, and they're not only stealing money, they're robbing people of life itself. When you talk about criminals, you have to recognize the vastly different degrees of criminality.

Surely no criminality proved in a court of law should go unpunished.

As you know, the poor and the black in this country don't seem to make out as well as the rich and the white in our courts of "justice." I wonder why.

You still haven't answered our question about the social consequences of releasing all those now behind bars.

Those who are not in prison could be put through a process of real rehabilitation before their release—not caged like animals, as they are now, thus guaranteeing that they'll be hardened criminals when they get out if they weren't when they went in. By rehabilitation I mean they would be trained for jobs that would not be an insult to their dignity, that would give them some sense of security, that would allow them to achieve some brotherly connection with their fellow man. But for this kind of rehabilitation to happen on a large scale would entail the complete reorganization of society, not to mention the prison system. It would call for the teaching of a new set of ethics based on the principle of cooperation, as opposed to the presently dominating principle of competition. It would require the transformation of the entire moral fabric of this country into a way of being that would make these former criminals feel more obligated to their fellow man than they do now. The way things are today, however, what reasons do these victims of society have for feeling an obligation to their fellow man? I look with respect on a guy who has walked the streets because he's been unable to find a job in a system that's rigged against him, but doesn't go around begging and instead walks into a store and says, "Stick 'em up, motherfucker!" I prefer that man to the Uncle Tom who does nothing but just shrink into himself and accept any shit that's thrown into his face. (p. 95)

One of the passages in **Soul on Ice** *had particular impact on many young white people who felt that they had been* *drummed out of "the movement." You wrote: "There is in America today a generation of white youth that is truly worthy of a black man's respect, and this is a rare event in the foul annals of American history." Having since worked in collaboration with the Peace and Freedom Party, do you still think as highly of the new generation of white youth?*

I'm even more convinced it's true than when I wrote those lines. We work with these young people all the time, and we've had nothing but encouraging experiences with them. These young white people aren't hung up battling to maintain the *status quo* like some of the older people who think they'll become extinct if the system changes. They're adventurous: they're willing to experiment with new forms; they're willing to confront life. And I don't mean only those on college campuses. A lot who aren't in college share with their college counterparts an ability to welcome and work for change.

Do you agree with those who feel that this generation of youth is going to "sell out" to the status quo *as it moves into middle age?*

I expect all of us will become somewhat less resilient as we get into our 40s and 50s—if we live that long—and I'm sure that those who come after us will look back on us as being conservative. Even us Panthers. (p. 100)

> *Eldridge Cleaver and Nat Hentoff, in an interview in* Playboy, *Vol. 15, No. 12, December, 1968, pp. 89-108, 238.*

Shane Stevens (essay date 1969)

[*Stevens, a white author and critic, has been widely praised for writing sensitively and expertly about black issues. In a May 1968 review published in* The Progressive, *he lauded* Soul on Ice, *calling it "a collection of essays straight out of Dante's* Inferno. *The hell is there, and its name is America" (see Further Reading). Here, however, he dismisses* Post-Prison Writings and Speeches *as mere propaganda and charges Cleaver with sacrificing the Panthers' cause out of self-interest.*]

[Cleaver's] volume of "post-prison" writings and speeches (a phrase stamped on the book jacket and used as part of the title on the title page, no doubt to squeeze out every last drop of sensationalism) . . . is sheer polemics. Even worse, it is mere propaganda. Manifestoes, diatribes, threats, exhortations—the whole bag of propagandist tricks is here. Ostensibly to fill a political need. In actuality, to fulfill a simple economic greed: money. No, I'm not blaming Cleaver, although there is much that he can, and will, be blamed for. He apparently did not have much to do with it, now that he is [living in exile in Algiers]. Those who should be blamed know who they are . . . .

During the past years I have talked with Cleaver, sitting with him one night into the small hours of the morning in the offices of *Ramparts* magazine. I was a sponsor of

the International Committee to Defend Eldridge Cleaver. In my review of *Soul on Ice* in the May, 1968, issue of *The Progressive,* I wrote that "this book is important . . . this book is extraordinary." I asked America to give the book a hearing because it had a freshness and insight and a power of conviction. I believed it then, and I believe it now. Eldridge Cleaver is a soul brother, and I don't like what has been happening to him. Sadly, it must be said, *Post-Prison Writings* does no one any service, least of all Cleaver. Many of the writings have appeared elsewhere, mainly in the pages of *Ramparts.* For the most party they should have remained there, for in this last year of his American life Cleaver was devoting himself exclusively to the political situation. In many respects it was akin to the last year of Lenny Bruce's life, wherein he addressed himself solely to his legal efforts. A pattern of paranoia emerged that was to hamper Bruce in his work and in his ability to view the world. As the shouting increases, conviction lessens. And when this is applied to writing, the power disappears.

The articles in Cleaver's new book are flabby; some are mere exercises. To pick several at random: **"The Decline of the Black Muslims," "My Father and Stokely Carmichael,"** and **"The Land Question and Black Liberation."** All heat, no light. All polemical, none convincing. All

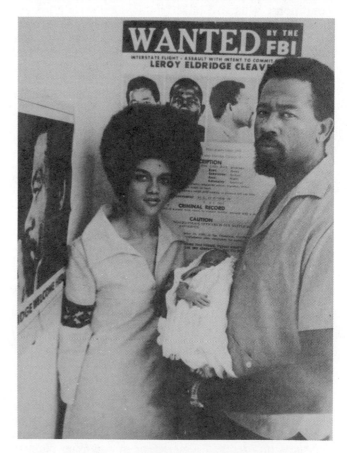

Cleaver with his wife Kathleen and infant son Maceo in Algiers in 1968.

the power gone. Perhaps only in **"Shoot-out in Oakland"** are there traces of the writer using words to convey real feeling rationally arrived at. As for the speeches, well, speeches are always best being spoken. And Cleaver is a good speaker, very good indeed. Perhaps, as is recognized now with James Baldwin—that he is a fine essayist and not a novelist—Cleaver will be seen to be a better speaker than writer. (p. 28)

So much for the book. I cannot find words strong enough to condemn the cheapness of this sordid affair. If Cleaver were just another self-styled revolutionist out for a little personal power, I would say nothing. Let them publish anything for a fast buck, and be damned. But Cleaver is more than that. Unfortunately, because of the notoriety, the book will have wide circulation. His reputation as a writer deserves better than that.

What went wrong? Where did Cleaver fail, and where did America fail him—even beyond the fact that it bore him into a racist society as a second-class citizen and made him never forget it? Toward the end of my review of *Soul on Ice* in *The Progressive* I asked the question: "Where does Cleaver go from here?" And I answered it by suggesting that what happens to him as a writer depends on what happens to him as a man: "The urge to be a full-time revolutionary in a country so desperately ill is overwhelming. Yet the writer must always retain a certain part of himself on the periphery of events if he is to be most effective."

Unfortunately, tragically, Cleaver became that full-time revolutionary; at least in his own mind. He devoted all his energies to his cause and thereby lost the very existence without which a writer can not function. He became a purveyor of propaganda, a writer of tracts, a maker of speeches. All his thoughts were channeled to one end, and the true writer that perhaps existed within slowly smothered and died. There is a world of difference between a propagandist and a writer of conviction. A world as wide as the difference between *Soul on Ice* and the present collection.

But even beyond that, Cleaver failed himself because of his total commitment to the Black Panthers. At the outset, the Black Panther Party had some semblance of revolutionary zeal in that it subscribed to the traditional revolutionary doctrine of alliances among all oppressed groups. The Black Panthers saw, or pretended to see, their role as leaders in a class struggle. (pp. 28-9)

Now, however, with each passing day the Black Panthers are veering more and more toward a racist-based ideology of a black liberation struggle. Whites will still be "used," but only in subordinate roles. And then, only when needed. Racism is in the saddle, regardless of the honeyed words being spoken. Cleaver, for all his spoken and written protestations as a people-lover, cannot be excused from sharing in this guilt.

Further, Cleaver has allowed himself to become a focal point of a "cult of personality" syndrome, which is death to any revolutionary attitude. He, among the

Black Panther leadership, is not alone in this, yet he has done nothing to negate this tendency. His—and the Black Panthers'—adoration of Che Guevara labels the present attitude for what it is: sheer romanticism....

The Black Panthers have scuttled their claim to any revolutionary fervor that could amount to anything, and they are being co-opted and nullified into just another hostile group that will be handled militarily. For this, Cleaver is as guilty as anyone else.

Finally, where did White America fail Cleaver? I mean beyond the harassment, the injustices, the debilitating hatred from known enemies. I am talking about the white liberals who bought and paid for Eldridge Cleaver—C.O.D. Almost from the time he left prison they looked upon him as Jesus Christ returned. They gave him the heady wine of instant fame: He was good copy. They gave him golden robes of green paper: He then shared in their guilt at amassing their wealth. And they crucified him on the altar of politics: Resurrecting him as long as he wrote what they wanted to read. They put him up for President in the cruelest joke since the Hunchback of Notre Dame was jeered as king.

From a writer who wrote what he wanted to say to a publicist who wrote what they wanted to hear. All in one easy stage. Harry Golden had it right: It could happen only in America.

There are 200 million stories in this sick country. This has been one of the sickest of them. (p. 29)

> *Shane Stevens, "Eldridge Cleaver: 'A Soul Brother' Gone Wrong," in* The Progressive, *Vol. 33, No. 7, July, 1969, pp. 28-9.*

Bayard Rustin (essay date 1976)

[*As head of the War Resisters' League and special assistant to Dr. Martin Luther King, Jr., Rustin had a long and distinguished career as a civil rights activist. His resistance to black political violence estranged him from more radical elements of the civil rights movement, however. In the following excerpt, he appraises Cleaver's stances on social and political issues since his return to the United States.*]

The political transformation of Eldridge Cleaver is one of the most profoundly interesting human dramas of our era. However, tracing his evolution is less my concern than the content and clarity of his thinking. Cleaver is saying many things that badly need saying and that are either not being said or not being said so well.

Cleaver's message is to remind us just how revolutionary the democratic idea really is. His emphasis on the importance of democracy may seem commonplace, but his views are powerful because they are the result of both theory and experience. His passionately felt beliefs have caused him to perceive the importance of turning the clichés of democracy back into ideals.

Cleaver, who once denounced the United States as "evil," "criminal," and "crazy," now describes himself as a patriot. He is certainly that, but at the same time he is both more and less. Unlike some previous refugees from totalitarian ideologies, Cleaver has not gone over to an opposite and equally extreme doctrine. Instead he is a radical democrat, who sees in the United States the best embodiment of the democratic ideal. (p. 20)

To those who would attempt to stereotype Cleaver as a right-wing superpatriot, he has himself provided the best answer: "The greatest mistake we have made as a nation is to allow our shining principles to lapse so far into disuse that we misname them clichés." Thus, Cleaver's patriotism is not narrow chauvinism but a sophisticated attempt to merge national pride with the fuller implementation of the American principles of democracy, equality, and justice. Cleaver's analysis is remarkably reminiscent of that of George Orwell, perhaps the most astute political observer of the twentieth century. Orwell criticized the British left for denigrating nationalism as necessarily reactionary and provincial. It was the patriotism of the British working class, he

argued, that saved Britain from defeat at the hands of Hitler. In a letter to the *Los Angeles Times* Cleaver advanced the concept of a progressive and democratic patriotism that recognizes that "admitting our weaknesses does not negate our strengths. And glorifying in our strengths, as we rightly should does not necessitate covering up our weaknesses."

Cleaver has not abandoned his belief in the necessity of fundamental social and economic transformations. He now insists that the method to achieve change is through democratic processes and not by violent revolution. Unlike some American radicals who have recently made a purely tactical endorsement of democracy because revolution is not likely to succeed in the United States, Cleaver has a profound appreciation of the human significance of democracy. Cleaver judges that political democracy is more important than economic democracy. It is easier, he contends, to add economic democracy to political democracy than to add political democracy to the sham economic democracy of the Communist states or the third-world dictatorships.

Cleaver finishes a ceramic pot in his Berkeley, California, studio, circa 1988.

In the process of altering his views about democracy, Cleaver's feelings about the black struggle in America have also changed. From his experiences abroad he has concluded that the United States is far ahead of the rest of the world in solving its racial problems. In a recent interview, Cleaver outlined his perspective on black progress in the United States thusly: "Black people need to realize very fundamentally that they are full and equal citizens of the U.S. We can no longer afford to 'fence straddle' about where we are going. We can no longer afford to ask: Are we going to stay here and be integrated, or are we going to go back to Africa, as we have been saying since slavery? Are we going to separate into five states like the black Muslims used to talk about? . . . We are as much a part of the United States as any Rockefeller, and we can no longer afford to ask such questions." Not surprisingly, Cleaver has grown much closer to those mainstream black leaders he used to denounce. He has said, "I want particularly to apologize to Martin Luther King on some points. I now appreciate his awareness that the basic relationship between communities of people has to be one of love."

Cleaver's defense of democracy is all the more persuasive because he has not only lived in totalitarian countries and third-world dictatorships, but he was also once an adherent of those regimes. Indeed, Cleaver's most valuable function may be to dispel the myths about these societies. His idea of proletarian internationalism was but a concentrated version of the still persistent romanticism about the third world and a too common naïveté about the nature of Communism. Having lived in the third world, Cleaver is uniquely qualified to communicate the truths that the third world is "an empty phrase," that there are "incredible differences" in the third-world countries, and that many third-world countries are tyrannies.

The analysis that Cleaver makes of Communism is penetrating and insightful. He observes that "communists strap onto people the most oppressive regimes in the history of the world. Regimes that are dictatorships, dictatorships in the name of the proletariat, not by the proletariat." Cleaver criticizes Détente for propping up the Soviet regimes and concludes that if the United States is truly to be a force for democracy in the world "we have an obligation to help in the disintegration of the Soviet regime." That is a harsh judgment, to be sure, but it flows naturally from Cleaver's commitment to democracy. (pp. 20-1)

I do not know how many on the left will listen to Cleaver. Certainly they will make every effort to avoid confronting his challenge to their uncritical acceptance of political myths. Sympathizers with the radical currents of the past decade cannot help but be made uncomfortable by Cleaver's proposition that it is time to sum up the questioning process, to abandon mistaken notions, and to come to some conclusions. I suspect that, nonetheless, the intensity and intelligence of Cleaver's views will force the confrontation whether or not it is desired.

Cleaver, I am convinced, is capable of speaking to a far larger audience than his former followers and sympathizers. He may well have to endure a long apprenticeship to redeem himself in the eyes of those who still suspect him or cannot yet forgive his past. Cleaver recognizes that it may be a long time before many people will agree with him.

The return of Eldridge Cleaver to the United States is a summing up of the decade of the sixties and a sign of new possibilities. In the sixties Cleaver became an almost mythical figure for thousands of young blacks and whites; but today, I believe, he is an authentic hero . . . .

Even in Cleaver's early writings there was a strongly humanistic strain. Unfortunately, his desire for a better world was so strong and consuming that he condemned a system that was unable to immediately meet his stringent demands for perfection and justice and embraced an ideology that was destructive of human values. It is to Cleaver's credit that he had the strength and intelligence to reevaluate his beliefs and to avoid the temptations of despair and cynicism. His change is best reflected in his comment: "Somehow, man is less grand than I would have thought. He's still OK, but he's less grand." This attitude of realism, responsible optimism, and genuine humanism undergirds Cleaver's political views. (p. 21)

> *Bayard Rustin, "Eldridge Cleaver and the Democratic Idea," in* The Humanist, *Vol. 36, No. 5, September-October, 1976, pp. 20-1.*

Richard Gilman (essay date 1979)

[*In the following excerpt from an essay originally published in* The New Republic *in 1979, Gilman reconsiders his 1968 review of* Soul on Ice—*a review that was later slightly revised for inclusion in his 1969 work* The Confusion of Realms—*in light of* Soul on Ice, *which he finds profoundly disappointing.*]

A little over 10 years ago I reviewed Eldridge Cleaver's **Soul on Ice** . . . . I said then (and on rereading the book still think) that Cleaver was a gifted writer but one whose particular qualities of rage, resentment and quasimystical aspiration in a context of racial struggle put him outside many of our literary canons. The review led to an agitated discussion . . . in which I tried to refine and clarify the distinctions I had drawn in the first piece.

The chief one was between what I called writing of a more or less traditional kind that happened to be by blacks (or "Negroes" at the time; that usage still held sway) and writing of a political and ideological cast that was intended mainly as a source of morale for blacks. My point was that the former could and ought to be judged the way we judge any sort of writing, but the latter, a provisional, tactical sort of thing, resisted—

legitimately, I thought—our cultivated, humanistic, "white" standards.

Whatever the virtues or defects of this argument, it's been rendered academic, in Cleaver's case at least, by his new book. *Soul on Fire* has none of the sense of urgency of its predecessor, none of its intelligent participation in crucial issues of the mind and of politics. A slipshod, ill-written, spiritless piece of work from any point of view, its only virtue is that it provides some information, for those who might feel the need of it, on Cleaver's years in exile, after fleeing the United States while under indictment, in Cuba, Algeria and finally Paris. (p. 29)

In any case, his rationale for being in political exile eroded, his hopes for a solution to his problems with the law raised by the advent of a new administration in Washington, Cleaver negotiated for his return and in the late fall of 1975 left Paris for the States. He had gone into exile as a dramatic and even charismatic figure and returned as a footnote to the history of his times.

Along with his growing patriotism, he tells us, he had experienced while abroad a rising impulse toward religion, which culminated, shortly before his departure from France, in an abrupt and unconditional surrender. Thus the change in the titles of his books from "Ice" to "Fire," reflects, as he says, his movement from the status of a prison inmate to that of a born-again Christian. When it was revealed a year or so after his return that he had become heavily engaged in evangelical activity the general reaction was, understandably, skepticism, while that of his former associates was compounded of fury contempt. These things being so, [*Soul on Fire*] is in large part an effort to establish his sincerity.

Well, such matters aren't properly subject to judgment, except perhaps from a long perspective in which a life may be seen in relation to a credo, and I for one am disposed to grant Cleaver what he asks. He's sincere, then, but the trouble is that he's become entirely uninteresting.

What's most surprising about Cleaver's change of heart and mind is the complete loss of eloquence it seems to have brought about. *Soul on Ice* was streaked with bad writing, but that stemmed I think from impatience or an excess of vitality and was more than atoned for by the many passages of sharp, accurate, often lyrical description and observation.... (pp. 30-1)

Soul on Fire has none of this fineness and originality. The account of his Paul-like conversion, for example, is doubtless honest but it makes for bad literature and probably bad theology too. He is sitting in his vacation apartment near Cannes gazing out on a beautiful night sky. He is depressed, thinking about committing suicide. Suddenly he sees an image of himself, a profile that had been used on Black Panther posters, in a shadow on the moon, and starts trembling. "As I stared at this image it changed, and I saw my former heroes paraded before my eyes. Here were Fidel Castro, Mao Tse-tung, Karl Marx, Friedrich Engels, passing in review—each one appearing for a moment of time, and then dropping out of sight, like fallen heroes. Finally, at the end of the procession, in dazzling, shimmering light, the image of Jesus Christ appeared ... I fell to my knees."

The book is filled with clichés and platitudes, as well as with an astonishing naiveté about what educated readers might or might not be expected to know. When Cleaver talks about going to bed as a child he thinks it necessary to print the entire prayer that begins "Now I lay me...." He says that "it must have rained for forty days and forty nights" and that "American violence is homemade like apple pie."...

When his writing isn't obvious and simpleminded it's gnarled and pretentious.... (p. 31)

It is all very sad. Whether or not Cleaver had the capacity to sustain an intellectual career of any kind at the center of political or cultural issues is debatable, but what's beyond dispute are the losses implicit in this book. The question isn't one of religion in itself but of the peculiar likelihood in America that if one gains faith one has to relinquish thought. Perhaps Cleaver's erratic and wayward talent thrived on a transient conjunction with the pressures and dramas of the period; but at least he was connected to it and was able to see and judge.

Now he rejoices in meetings with Billy Graham, and is happy to have [Watergate conspirator and born-again Christian] Charles Colson as his "brother" and the admiration of one Art DeMoss, president of the National Liberty Corporation of Valley Forge, who describes "Eldridge ... and the Lord" as "a great combination." These people too are of our time, but at the cock-sure, self-righteous edge of it where there is no space to turn, to "maneuver" the way Cleaver once so brilliantly did. (pp. 31-2)

Richard Gilman, in a review of "Soul on Fire," in The New Republic, *Vol. 180, No. 3, January 20, 1979, pp. 29-32.*

FURTHER READING

Cooke, Michael. "Eldridge Cleaver: Humanist and Felon." *The Yale Review* LVIII, No. 1 (October 1968): 102-07.
    Analyzes *Soul on Ice*, describing Cleaver as a satirist of black American culture.

——. "Kinship: The Power of Association in Michael Harper and Eldridge Cleaver." In his *Afro-American Literature in the Twentieth Century*, pp. 110-32. New Haven: Yale University Press, 1984.
    Examines the theme of kinship in Michael Harper's works and in Cleaver's *Soul on Ice*.

"Whatever Happened to...Eldridge Cleaver?" *Ebony* XLIII, No. 5 (March 1988): 66-8.

Profiles Cleaver's life since his return to the United States. The anonymous critic writes: "Except for a recent cocaine-possession charge, life has been fairly quiet for Cleaver over the last few years. He lives alone in Berkeley, Calif., and earns money by lecturing and by making and selling ceramic objects.... While he is cautious and distrustful of many around him, Cleaver is still optimistic and eager about his future.... In spite of the setbacks he's experienced in his life, he says, "in this heart of mine, hope always springs eternal'."

Jensen, Richard J., and Hammerback, John C. "From Muslim to Mormon: Eldridge Cleaver's Rhetorical Crusade." *Communication Quarterly* 34, No. 1 (Winter 1986): 24-40.

Probes the contention that Cleaver is an "ideological turncoat and rhetorical weathervane," determining that his conversion to Mormonism was not at all illogical because his discourse had always been "religious in nature" and his spiritual goals had not changed.

Larrabee, Harold A. "The Varieties of Black Experience." *The New England Quarterly* XLIII, No. 4 (December 1970): 638-45.

Locates *Soul on Ice* within the context of black political writing of the late 1960s.

Lockwood, Lee. *Conversation with Eldridge Cleaver: Algiers.* New York: McGraw-Hill, 1970, 131 p.

Interview with Cleaver in Algiers. Lockwood and Cleaver discuss the Black Panthers, as well as Cleaver's theories of revolution and his travels as a fugitive.

Simon, Jacqueline. "Interview with Eldridge Cleaver." *Punto de Contacto* 1, No. 1 (1975): 34-56.

Interview with Cleaver at his Paris apartment in 1975. Simon focuses on Cleaver's current political views, his wish to return to America, and his efforts to design and market "revolutionary" trousers for men.

Stevens, Shane. "Quest for Dignity." *The Progressive* 32, No. 5 (May 1968): 44-5.

Praises *Soul on Ice,* calling it "a collection of essays straight out of Dante's *Inferno.* The hell is there, and its name is America."

White, Ray Lewis. "Eldridge Cleaver's *Soul on Ice:* A Book Review Digest." *CLA Journal* XXI, No. 4 (June 1978): 556-66.

Collects forty-two reviews of *Soul on Ice* from periodicals across the United States. Virtually all the reviews hail the work as important and necessary reading.

Lucille Clifton

1936-

(Born Lucille Sayles) American poet, autobiographer, and author of children's books.

Highly praised for her strong affirmation of African-American culture, Clifton is a prolific author whose work conveys concern for the welfare of black families and youth. She writes in a simple, unadorned style that often echoes black speech and music. Although she has been named Poet Laureate of Maryland and her literary awards include a nomination for the Pulitzer Prize and two grants from the National Endowment for the Arts, commentators assert that her work has not received the level of popular and critical attention it deserves. Marilyn Hacker stated: "Clifton mythologizes herself: that is, she illuminates her surroundings and history from within in a way that casts light on much beyond. She does this with a penetrating brevity in a verse that mirrors speech as a Japanese ink drawing mirrors a mountain."

Clifton was born in Depew, New York, where her father worked in the steel mills and her mother in a laundry. In a 1976 interview she described her family as " . . . poor. But not downtrodden. We didn't have much money, but we had a lot of love." She explained that although neither of her parents graduated from elementary school, they both valued literature. According to Clifton, her mother wrote poems, which she read to her four children: "A lot of feelings went into her poetry. From Mama I knew one could write as a way to express oneself." Clifton's father often told stories about his ancestors, particularly his grandmother Caroline, who was abducted from her home in the Dahomey Republic of West Africa and brought to New Orleans, Louisiana, as a slave. At the age of eight, Caroline completed an 800-mile walk from New Orleans to Virginia. In Clifton's prose autobiography, *Generations* (1976), "Ca'line" appears as a woman of almost mythical endurance and courage, reflecting Clifton's characteristic portrayal of women as both strong and deeply nurturing. The memoir was praised for its celebration of the survival of a black family. In *Generations* Clifton asserts: "Things don't fall apart. Things hold. Lines connect in thin ways that last and last, and lines become generations made out of pictures and words just kept."

In 1953 Clifton attended Howard University in Washington, D. C., where she associated with such writers as LeRoi Jones (Amiri Baraka), A. B. Spellman, Owen Dodson, and Sterling Brown. A drama major, she acted in the first performance of James Baldwin's *The Amen Corner*. Clifton left Howard after two years (she "forgot to study") and attended Fredonia State Teachers College, where she often read and performed plays with a small group of black intellectuals and further developed her voice as a writer, using sparse punctuation and a

lyricism reflecting spoken words. Describing her writing style, she commented: "I use a simple language. I have never believed that for anything to be valid or true or intellectual or 'deep' it had to first be complex . . . . I am not interested if anyone knows whether or not I am familiar with big words, I am interested in trying to render big ideas in a simply way. I am interested in being understood not admired." Her submission of poems to Robert Hayden, a respected black poet, resulted in her receipt of the YW-YMHA Poetry Center Discovery Award in 1969—an event that was followed by the publication of her first poetry collection, *Good Times: Poems* (1969). The work was cited by the *New York Times* as one of the best books of the year. Since then Clifton has been a highly productive poet and children's author, and she credits her six children with inspiring much of her work: "They keep you aware of life. And you have to stay aware of life, keep growing to write."

In *Good Times* Clifton focused on the hardship and poverty pervading much of urban life, yet she also evoked a sense of strength and celebration in the face of adversity: "My daddy has paid the rent / and the insurance man is gone / and the lights is back on . . . / and they is good times . . . ." Critics admired the collection's portraits of dignity and strength in the face of suffering and praised its rejection of negative sociological stereotypes. In "in the inner city," Clifton juxtaposed affection for one's home with the reality of an urban wasteland made up of "houses straight as / dead men." Reviewers stressed Clifton's theme of the importance of family, and many contrasted her characterization of black men as integral family members with the tendency of contemporary writers to depict black males as unwilling to take on domestic responsibilities. Acclaimed poet Haki Madhubuti asserted: "At the base of her work is concern for the Black family, especially the destruction of its youth. Her eye is for the uniqueness of our people, always concentrating on the small strengths that have allowed us to survive the horrors of Western life."

Some critics associate Clifton with the Black Arts Movement of the 1960s and 1970s, which promoted African-American arts as tools to overcome racial oppression. Many of Clifton's poems castigate racist attitudes: "pity this poor animal / who has never gone beyond / the ape herds gathered around the fires / of Europe . . . / his mind shivers against the rocks / afraid of the dark . . . ." Clifton's poetry, as well as her juvenile literature, is recognized for its cultivation of black identity and pride through awareness of black history. Her second collection of verse, *Good News About the Earth: New Poems* (1972), contains poems dedicated to black leaders Malcolm X, Eldridge Cleaver, Bobby Seale, and Angela Davis. Her political conscience is also revealed in her collection *Next: New Poems* (1987), which laments broken promises in the political poems "at gettysburg," "at nagasaki," and "at jonestown."

Clifton often explores African-American experience from a female perspective, presenting women who are simultaneously fierce, heroic, and loving. For example, the trilogy of "Kali Poems" in *An Ordinary Woman* (1974) reveals a metaphysical and forceful image of femininity in the form of an aboriginal Indian goddess associated with blood, violence, and murder. Andrea Benton Rushing stated: "[In the "Kali Poems," Clifton] frees herself from the feminist tendency to see women as hapless victims and explores the psychic tensions of an introspective modern woman negotiating the dramatic changes in contemporary attitudes about culture, race and gender at the same time that she juggles the roles of daughter, sister, artist, writer, and mother." Clifton's next collection, *Two-Headed Woman* (1980), reveals a more personal exploration of womanhood: "the light that came to lucille clifton / came in a shift of knowing / when even her fondest sureties / faded away . . . ."

Many reviewers have noted strong tenets of Christianity in Clifton's poetry, particularly a faith in the deliverance of an oppressed people. Biblical imagery appears in much of her work; the Virgin Mary is frequently depicted as an earthly mother chosen for a miraculous experience. Written in a lower-class Caribbean dialect, the poem "holy night" portrays Mary as an uneducated young girl: "joseph, i afraid of stars, / their brilliant seeing. / so many eyes, such light . . . ." Critics have linked Clifton's Christian optimism with her strong faith in the power of human will. According to Greg Kuzma, "[Clifton's poems reveal] an implicit conviction that there is evil in the world because people allow it, and that life would be infinitely better, even perfect, could we but forgive each other and truly love."

(For further information about Clifton's life and works, see *Black Writers; Contemporary Authors*, Vols. 49-52; *Contemporary Authors New Revision Series*, Vol. 24; *Contemporary Literary Criticism*, Vol. 19; *Children's Literature Review*, Vol. 5; *Dictionary of Literary Biography*, Vols. 5, 41; and *Something about the Author*, Vol. 20.)

PRINCIPAL WORKS

Good Times: Poems (poetry) 1969
The Black BCs (juvenile fiction) 1970
Some of the Days of Everett Anderson (juvenile fiction) 1970
Everett Anderson's Christmas Coming (juvenile fiction) 1971
Good News About the Earth: New Poems (poetry) 1972
All Us Come Cross the Water (juvenile fiction) 1973
The Boy Who Didn't Believe in Spring (juvenile fiction) 1973
Don't You Remember? (juvenile fiction) 1973

Good, Says Jerome (juvenile fiction) 1973
Everett Anderson's Year (juvenile fiction) 1974
An Ordinary Woman (poetry) 1974
The Times They Used to Be (juvenile fiction) 1974
My Brother Fine with Me (juvenile fiction) 1975
Everett Anderson's Friend (juvenile fiction) 1976
Generations: A Memoir (prose autobiography) 1976
Three Wishes (juvenile fiction) 1976
Amifika (juvenile fiction) 1977
Everett Anderson's 1 2 3 (juvenile fiction) 1977
Everett Anderson's Nine Month Long (juvenile fiction) 1978
The Lucky Stone (juvenile fiction) 1979
My Friend Jacob (juvenile fiction) 1980
Two-Headed Woman (poetry) 1980
Sonora Beautiful (juvenile fiction) 1981
Everett Anderson's Goodbye (juvenile fiction) 1983
Good Woman: Poems and a Memoir, 1969-1980 (poetry) 1987
Next: New Poems (poetry) 1987

Harriet Jackson Scarupa (essay date 1976)

[*In the following excerpt, Scarupa recounts a visit to Clifton's Baltimore home, noting elements of Clifton's family history and describing the personal philosophies behind the author's writing.*]

Browsing through a volume of Lucille Clifton's poems or reading one of her children's books to my son always makes me feel good; good to be black, good to be a woman, good to be alive. **Generations,** her newest book and first prose work for adults, makes me feel like joining with her in a song of celebration to family and heritage and survival.

Still, something about Lucille Clifton irritated me. It was the title of her respected poetry collection, **An Ordinary Woman,** and what that title seemed to imply. It bothered me that this woman whose latest book has been called a "lyrical rapture" in the *New York Times Book Review,* who has written three other well-received books of poetry and a dozen children's books, and who has acquired a good handful of literary awards—all within the last seven years—persisted in calling herself "ordinary." What, I wondered, did that make all of us— me, for instance—with so many lesser accomplishments? So when I went to see Lucille Clifton, I think I expected to meet some kind of superwoman, despite all her claims to the contrary.

It was a weekday evening when I dropped by the big, rambling old house she shares with her husband Fred, an administrator for community development, and their six children in a predominantly black, middle-income Baltimore neighborhood. Lucille Clifton settled back on a worn, comfortable loveseat in her large living room.

She is a tall, soft-spoken woman with a smooth round face set off by a gray-speckled Afro.

"One of the things I was saying in the title is that the extraordinary woman *is* the ordinary one," she explains. "Take the woman with eight kids and a small income, who manages to feed them, keep sane, even have fun. It's very ordinary to do what a woman can do." As for herself, she adds, "It isn't that hard to have six kids. The things you care about you can do."

Lucille Sayles Clifton was born 40 years ago in Depew, New York, a little town outside Buffalo. (*I entered the earth in a woman jar*— from *Generations*.) Her father worked in the steel mills; her mother, in a laundry. There were four children in the family. "We were poor. But not downtrodden. We didn't have much money, but we had a lot of love."

Her father would tell her of the history of his family in this country, starting with Caroline, "born among the Dahomey people in 1822," who walked from New Orleans to Virginia when she was eight years old. And he would repeat Caroline's legacy, passed down through the years—through slavery and struggle and survival: *Get what you want, you from Dahomey women* (from *Generations*.)

Although neither parent was graduated from elementary school, both valued books. "And they both loved to read about all kinds of things," she remembers. "For instance, China, for some strange reasons. I saw reading as a natural part of life and grew up loving books and words. How I do love words!"

Her mother loved words too and set them down in poems—in straight iambic pentameter—which she read to her children. "My mother was a rather sad person," she recalls now. "She had epilepsy and died, too young, at forty-four. A lot of feelings went into her poetry. From Mama I knew one could write as a way to express oneself." (*Oh she made magic, she was a magic woman, my Mama. She was not wise in the world but she had magic wisdom*—from *Generations*.)

In 1953, Lucille Sayles went to Howard University on a full scholarship. It was her first time away from home, and she felt homesick and a little out of place in the cosmopolitan Howard world. "I went to college with my clothes in my grandmother's wedding trunk held together with rope, and here were all these kids with matching luggage." But it was a good time for a budding writer to be at Howard—people like Leroi Jones (now Amiri Baraka), A. B. Spellman, Owen Dodson, and Sterling Brown were there, writing and reading their works. She gravitated toward them and majored in drama, playing in the first performance of James Baldwin's *The Amen Corner.*

She left Howard after two years ("I forgot to study," she says wryly). Besides, as she told her disappointed father: *I don't need that stuff [college]. I'm going to write poems. I can do what I want to do. I'm from Dahomey women!*

(from *Generations*). While attending Fredonia State Teachers College near Buffalo, she joined a small group of black intellectuals who got together to read plays and perform them wherever they could. One member of the group was the novelist Ishmael Reed. Another was Fred Clifton, then teaching philosophy at the University of Buffalo. In 1958, Fred and Lucille were married.

"It was in Buffalo that I began finding my own voice as a writer," Lucille Clifton recalls. "But I still never thought about publishing. What I was writing was not like the poems I'd been reading." But Ishmael Reed showed some of her poems to Langston Hughes, who selected a few for the anthology, *Poetry of the Negro, 1746-1970*. In 1969, she sent poems to Robert Hayden, a respected black poet then teaching at Fisk University, who took them to Carolyn Kizer, another well-known poet. She, in turn, sent them along to the YW-YMHA Poetry Center in New York City. That year Lucille Clifton received the prestigious Discovery Award from the Poetry Center, given annually to promising but undiscovered poets, and Random House published her first book, *Good Times*. *The New York Times* cited it as one of the 10 best books of the year. Since then, her books have flowed with regularity.

These days Clifton writes either on the dining room table or on a cluttered desk in a sunlit room at the back of the house. "I write in spurts," she says. "I'm completely undisciplined. I never do all the things you're supposed to do, like write at a set time every day. And I can't write if it's quiet." So she sits in front of her electric typewriter, having worked out a lot of things in her head beforehand, with Aretha on the stereo if she's in the mood and the children wandering in and out. Every time she makes a mistake, even an innocent typing error, she dramatically rips paper from the typewriter. "One of the kids say something like, 'Look at all the paper mama's wasting.' I yell, 'How can I do anything with you kids? . . . '" The whole scene brings to mind her words from *Good Times:*

> children
> when they ask you
> why is your mama so funny
> say
> she is a poet
> she don't have no sense

"They get on your nerves sometimes," Clifton says of her children, her smile, almost, but not quite, betraying her words. "It's important for my children to know there are some things I need to do for myself, for them to know I'm a woman who's thinking things, that I have days when I get tired of them. But they actually help with my writing, especially the children's books." As an example, she cites the time one of her sons threatened to run away from home—and got as far as the bottom step. She used the experience in *My Brother Fine with Me*. And when her children referred to Africa as "the dark continent," she included many positive images about Africa in the book *The Black BC's* to counteract that stereotype.

But Clifton's children have helped her as a writer in a larger way than by suggesting specific ideas for stories. As she puts it, "They keep you aware of life. And you have to stay aware of life, keep growing to write." And, she adds ironically, "They also keep me sane." She continues: "I did this reading at the Library of Congress once. It was a great honor. Next day, I was ironing and I said, 'What is this great *poet* doing ironing?' The kids laughed, said, 'Are you crazy?' and I came back to earth."

Clifton gets ideas "by staying awake to things. Sometimes something hits me, 'That's it.' It's not like I really think about it. It's more intuitive. You just know when something will poem up."

When Clifton began to meet many a child with an African name, she decided to focus on one in *All Us Come Cross the Water*. In the story, a boy named Ujamaa (Unity) worries that he can't pinpoint where his ancestors come from in Africa. A friend at the Panther bookstore helps him see that black Americans have roots in all African countries; *All us crossed the water. We one people, Ujamaa. Boy got that name oughta know that.*

All Lucille Clifton's works have a lot to say about blackness and black pride, as in the poem "**after Kent State**" from *Good News About the Earth:*

> . . . oh
> people
> white ways are
> the way of death
> come into the
> Black
> and live

Some critics reading such lines have concluded that Clifton hates whites. She considers this a misreading. When she equates whiteness with death, blackness with life, she says: "What I'm talking about is a certain kind of white arrogance —and not all white people have it— that is not good. I think airs of superiority are very dangerous. I believe in justice. I try not to be about hatred."

Generations is a virtual celebration of the survival of the black family. Clifton looks back at her parents and her father's ancestors, at their struggles and their joys, and she draws strength . . . .(pp. 118, 120, 123)

> And I could tell you about things we been through, some awful ones, some wonderful, but I know that the things that make us are more than that, our lives are more than the days in them, our lives are our line and we go on. I type that and I swear I can see Ca'line standing in the green of Virginia, in the green of Afrika, and I swear she makes no sound but she nods her head and smiles.

Clifton also writes about being a woman, but in many ways she's on a different wavelength from the Women's Movement. "I believe the smartest one in the family should be deferred to, and in most cases my husband is the smartest one. Yet he's never tried to keep me from being myself.

"The Movement is helpful to some women," Clifton acknowledges. "It's good for them to realize they can be something or do something and not have to follow some prescribed role." But as a black woman, with a long history behind her, she feels she has some good reasons to be wary. In *An Ordinary Woman,* she writes about them in the poem "**To Ms. Ann**":

> i will have to forget
> your face
> when you watched me breaking
> in the fields,
> missing my children . . .
> and you never called me sister
> then, you never called me sister
> and it has only been forever and
> i will have to forget your face.

Clifton also faults the Movement—and too many people today—with not paying enough attention to love. "When people love each other, they'll accept a lot of things they wouldn't otherwise. They can deal with things they couldn't deal with otherwise. It has to do with the nature of love."

One of her early poems in *Good Times* is about what concerns her most—as a woman, as a writer—and is also her favorite:

> Here we are
> running with the weeds
> colors exaggerated
> pistils wild.
> embarrassing the calm family flowers
>   Oh
> here we are
> flourishing for the field
> and the name of the place
> is Love.

(p. 123)

Harriet Jackson Scarupa, "Lucille Clifton: Making the World 'Poem-Up'," in Ms., *Vol. V, No. 4, October, 1976, pp. 118, 120, 123.*

Lucille Clifton (essay date 1984)

[*The following essay first appeared in the critical work* Black Women Writers (1950-1980): A Critical Evaluation. *Here, Clifton describes her views of her role in society and the ideology and methods behind her poetry.*]

I write the way I write because I am the kind of person that I am. My styles and content stem from my experience. I grew up a well-loved child in a loving family and so I have always known that being very poor, which we were, had nothing to do with lovingness or familyness or character or any of that. This doesn't mean that I or we were content with whatever we had and never hoped tried worked at having more. It means that we were quite clear that what we had didn't have anything to do with what we were. We were/are quite sure that we were/are among the best of people and not having any money had nothing to do with that. Other people's opinions didn't influence us about that. We were quite sure. When I write, especially for children, I try to get that across, that being poor or whatever your circumstance, you are capable of being the best of people and that best, as a human, does not come from the outside in, it comes from the inside out.

I use a simple language. I have never believed that for anything to be valid or true or intellectual or "deep" it had to first be complex. I deliberately use the language that I use. Sometimes people have asked me when I was going to try something hard or difficult, as if my work sprang from my ignorance. I like to think that I write from my knowledge not my lack, from my strength not my weakness. I am not interested if anyone knows whether or not I am familiar with big words, I am interested in trying to render big ideas in a simple way. I am interested in being understood not admired. I wish to celebrate and not be celebrated (though a little celebration is a lot of fun).

I am a woman and I write from that experience. I am a Black woman and I write from that experience. I do not feel inhibited or bound by what I am. That does not mean that I have never had bad scenes relating to being Black and/or a woman, it means that other people's craziness has not managed to make me crazy. At least not in their way because I try very hard not to close my eye to my own craziness nor to my family's, my sex's, nor my race's. I don't believe that I should only talk about the beauty and strength and good-ness of my people but I do believe that if we talk about our room for improvement we should do it privately. I don't believe in public family fights. But I do think sometimes a good fight is cleansing. We are not perfect people. There are no perfect people.

I have been a wife for over twenty years. We have parented six children. Both these things have brought me great joy. I try to transmit the possible joy in my work. This does not mean that there have been no dark days; it means that they have not mattered. In the long run. I try to write about looking at the long run.

I have been writing things down all my life. I was first published in 1969 due to the efforts of Robert Hayden and Carolyn Kizer among others. I did not try to be published; it wasn't something that I thought that much about. I had had a short short story published in an issue of *Negro Digest* magazine earlier in the sixties. That had been my try.

When my first book was published I was thirty-three years old and had six children under ten years old. I was too busy to take it terribly seriously. I was very happy and proud of course, but had plenty of other things to think about. It was published by Random House and that seemed to bother some of my friends. At first my feelings were a little hurt that anyone would even be

concerned about it but I got over that. I decided that if something doesn't matter, it really doesn't matter. Sometimes I think that the most anger comes from ones who were late in discovering that when the world said nigger it meant them too. I grew up knowing that the world meant me too but that was the world's insanity and not mine. I have been treated in publishing very much like other poets are treated, that is, not really very well. I continue to write since my life as a human only includes my life as a poet, it doesn't depend on it.

I live in Baltimore and so I do not have sustained relationships with many of my peers. I am friends with a lot of the people who do what I do but my public and private lives tend to be separate. At home I am wife and mama mostly. My family has always come first with me. This is my choice due to my personal inclination. As the children have grown up I have been able to travel more and I enjoy it. I very much enjoy the public life and I also very much enjoy the private.

My family tends to be a spiritual and even perhaps mystical one. That certainly influences my life and my work. I write in the kitchen or wherever I happen to be though I do have a study. I write on a typewriter rather than in longhand. My children think of me as a moody person; I am shy and much less sunny than I am pictured. I draw my own conclusions and do not believe everything I am told. I am not easily fooled. I do the best I can. I try. (pp. 137-38)

> *Lucille Clifton, "A Simple Language," in* Black Women Writers (1950-1980): A Critical Evaluation, *edited by Mari Evans, Anchor Press/Doubleday, 1984, pp. 137-38.*

Haki Madhubuti (essay date 1984)

[*Madhubuti (formerly Don L. Lee) is an educator, editor, and the author of several volumes of poetry, criticism, and essays. In the essay excerpted below, he discusses the language and cultural sensitivity of Clifton's poetry.*]

In everything she creates, this Lucille Clifton, a writer of no ordinary substance, a singer of faultless ease and able storytelling, there is a message. No slogans or billboards, but words that are used refreshingly to build us, make us better, stronger, and whole. Words that defy the odds and in the end make us wiser. (p. 150)

Lucille Clifton is a woman of majestic presence, a full-time wife, over-time mother, part-time street activist and writer of small treasures (most of her books are small but weighty). That she is not known speaks to, I feel, her preoccupation with truly becoming a full Black woman and writer. Celebrity,—that is, people pointing you out in drugstores and shopping malls—does not seem to interest her. When she was almost assured of becoming the poet laureate of Maryland, she wrote Gwendolyn Brooks (poet laureate of Illinois) asking if she could consider such a position. I suggest that she really wanted to know: (1) Are there any advantages in the position for her people? and (2) Would she significantly have to change her life by accepting the honor? Brooks' response was, "It is what you make of it." Clifton accepted.

The city of Baltimore, where she and her family reside, does not figure heavily in her work. The "place" of her poetry and prose is essentially urban landscapes that are examples of most Black communities in this country. Clifton's urge is to live, is to conquer oppressive and nonnatural spaces. Her poetry is often a conscious, quiet introduction to the real world of Black sensitivities. Her focus and her faces are both the men and the women connected and connecting; the children, the family, the slave-like circumstances, the beauty, and the raw and most important the hide-outs of Black people to Black people.

Her poetry is emotion-packed and musically fluent to the point of questioning whether a label on it would limit one's understanding. Her first book of poetry, *Good Times* (1969), cannot be looked upon as simply a "first" effort. The work is unusually compacted and memory-evoking.

There is no apology for the Black condition. There is an awareness and a seriousness that speak to "houses straight as / dead men." Clifton's poems are not vacant lots; the mamas and daddies are not forgotten human baggages to be made loose of and discarded. Much of today's writing, especially much of that being published by Black women writers, seems to invalidate Black men or make small of them, often relegating them to the position of white sexual renegades in Black faces.

No such cop-out for Clifton. There is no misrepresentation of the men or women. And one would find it extremely difficult to misread Clifton. She is not a "complicated" writer in the traditional Western sense. She is a writer of complexity, and she makes her readers work and think. Her poetry has a quiet force without being pushy or alien. Whether she is cutting through family relationships, surviving American racial attitudes, or just simply renewing love ties, she puts something heavy on your mind. The great majority of her published poetry is significant. At the base of her work is concern for the Black family, especially the destruction of its youth. Her eye is for the uniqueness of our people, always concentrating on the small strengths that have allowed us to survive the horrors of Western life.

Her treatment of Black men is unusually significant and sensitive. I feel that part of the reason she treats men fairly and with balance in her work is her relationship with her father, brothers, husband, and sons. Generally, positive relationships produce positive results.

> my daddy's fingers move among the couplers
> chipping steel and skin
> and if the steel would break
> my daddy's fingers might be men again.

Lucille Clifton is often calling for the men to be Black men. Asking and demanding that they seek and be more than expected. Despite her unlimited concern for her people, she does not box herself into the corner of preaching at them or of describing them with metaphors of belittlement. Clifton has a fine, sharp voice pitched to high C and tuned carefully to the frequency of the Black world. She is a homeland technician who has not allowed her "education" to interfere with her solos.

The women of *Good Times* are strong and Dahomey-made, are imposing and tragic, yet givers of love. Unlike most of us, Clifton seemed to have taken her experiences and observations and squeezed the knowledge from them, translating them into small and memorable lessons:

> . . . surrounded by the smell
> of too old potato peels
>   . . .
> you wet brown bag of a woman
> who used to be the best looking gal in Georgia
> used to be called the Georgia Rose
> I stand up
> through your destruction
> I stand up

Standing up is what *Good Times* is about. However, Clifton can beat you up with a poem; she can write history into four stanzas and bring forth reaction from the most hardened nonreader. Listen to the story of Robert:

> Was born obedient
> without questions
>
> did a dance called
> Picking grapes
> Sticking his butt out
> for pennies
>
> Married a master
> who whipped his head
> until he died
> until he died
> the color of his life
> was nigger.

There is no time frame in such a poem. Such poems do not date easily. Robert is 1619 and 1981, is alive and dying on urban streets, in rural churches and corporate offices. "Niggers" have not disappeared; some of them (us) are now being called by last names and are receiving different types of mind whippings, mind whippings that achieve the same and sometimes greater results.

Clifton is a Black cultural poet. We see in her work a clear transmission of values. It is these values that form the base of a developing consciousness of struggle. She realizes that we do have choices that can still be exercised. Hers is most definitely to fight. From page to page, from generation to generation, the poems cry out direction, hope, and future. One of the best examples of this connecting force is from her book *An Ordinary Woman* (1974); the poem is **"Turning."**

Turning into my own
turning on in
to my own self
at last
turning out of the
white cage, turning out of the
lady cage
turning at last
on a stem like a black fruit
in my own season
at last.

It is the final voyage into oneself that is the most difficult. Then there comes the collective fight, the dismantling of the real monsters outside. But first we must become whole again. The true undiluted culture of a people is the base of wholeness. One way toward such wholeness is what Stephen Henderson calls "saturation," the giving and defining of Blackness through proclaiming such experiences as legitimate and necessary, whereas the Black poetic experience used often enough becomes natural and expected. Clifton "saturates" us in a way that forces us to look at ourselves in a different and more profound way. For every weakness, she points to a strength; where there are negatives she pulls and searches for the positives. She has not let the low ebbs of life diminish her talents or toughness. She is always looking for the good, the best, but not naïvely so. Her work is realistic and burning with the energy of renewal.

Clifton is an economist with words; her style is to use as few words as possible. Yet she is effective because, despite consciously limiting her vocabulary, she has defined her audience. She is not out to impress, or to showcase the scope of her lexicon. She is communicating ideas and concepts. She understands that precise communication is not an easy undertaking; language, at its root, seeks to express emotion, thought, action. Most poetry writing (other than the blues) is foreign to the Black community. It is nearly impossible to translate to the page the changing linguistic nuances or the subtleties of body language Blacks use in everyday conversation; the Black writer's task is an extremely complicated and delicate one. But understand me, Clifton does not write down to us, nor is she condescending or patronizing with her language. Most of her poems are short and tight, as is her language. Her poems are well-planned creations, and as small as some of them are, they are not cloudy nor rainy with words for words' sake. The task is not to fill the page with letters but to challenge the mind:

What I remember about that day
is boxes stacked across the walk
and couch springs curling through the air
and drawers and tables balanced on the curb
and us, hollering,
leaping up and around
happy to have a playground

nothing about the emptied rooms
nothing about the emptied family

Her originality is accomplished with everyday language and executed with musical percussion, pushed to the limits of poetic possibilities. Lucille Clifton is a lover of life, a person who feels her people. Her poems are messages void of didacticism and needless repetition. Nor does she shout or scream the language at you; her voice is birdlike but loud and high enough to pierce the ears of dogs. She is the quiet warrior, and, like the weapons of all good warriors, her weapons can hurt, kill, and protect.

Language is the building block of consciousness. To accurately understand the soul of a people, you not only search for their outward manifestations (e.g., institutions, art, science and technology, social and political systems), but you examine their language. And since the Black community, by and large, speaks a foreign language, the question is to what extent have we made the language work for us, i.e., build for us? All languages to some degree are bastards, created by both rulers and the ruled, king and proletariat, masters and slaves, citizens and visitors. The greatness and endurance of a people to a large degree lies in their fundamental ability to create under the most adverse conditions using the tools at hand. Language is ever growing and a tool (weapon) that must be mastered if it is to work for us.

Language used correctly (communicating and relating at the highest) expands the brain, increase one's knowledge bank, enlarges the world, and challenges the vision of those who may not have a vision. *One of the most effective ways to keep a people enslaved, in a scientific and technological state which is dependent upon a relatively high rate of literacy, is to create in that people a disrespect and fear of the written and spoken word.* For any people to compete in the new world order that is emerging, it is absolutely necessary that study, research, and serious appraisal of documentation that impact on people's lives become second nature. Fine poetry is like a tuning fork; it regulates, clears, and challenges the brain, focusing it and bringing it in line with the rest of the world. Therefore, it is a political act to keep people ignorant. We can see that it is not by accident that Black people in the United States watch more television than any other ethnic group and that more of our own children can be seen carrying radios and cassettes to school than books. The point is that it is just about impossible to make a positive contribution to the world if one cannot read, write, compute, think, and articulate one's thoughts. The major instrument for bringing out the genius of any people is the productive, creative, and stimulating use and creation of language.

Lucille Clifton has expanded the use of small language. Very seldom does she use words larger than four syllables. She has shaped and jerked, patched and stitched everyday language in a way that few poets have been able to do. In her book *An Ordinary Woman* she fulfills her promise of greatness. The book is a statement of commitment and love. The songs are those that stretch us, and in this final hour mandate the people immortal. Her nationalism is understated, yet compelling, with short stanzas and fistlike lines.

The imposing images in *An Ordinary Woman* are bones. Bones are used as the connecting force of Black people. The word is used fourteen times in a multitude of ways throughout the volume. The image is profoundly effective because bones represent strength . . . The bones are connectors and death, lineage and life.

> More than once
> I have taken the bones you hardened
> and built daughters
> and they blossom and promised fruit
> like Afrikan trees.

She is what John Gardner describes as the moral writer and what Addison Gayle, Jr., refers to [in *The Way of the New World*] as a writer's writer in the Black nationalist tradition: "The Black writer at the present time must forgo the assimilationist tradition and redirect his (her) art to the strivings within . . . to do so, he (she) must write for and speak to the majority of Black people; not to a sophisticated elite fashioned out to the programmed computers of America's largest universities."

Clifton's nationalism is sometimes subtle and bright, sometimes coarse and lonely; it is fire and beaten bodies, but what most emerges from the body of her work is a reverence for life, a hope for tomorrow, and an undying will to live and to conquer oppressive forces.

By customary standards she *is* no ordinary woman. In another time and place, that might have been the case, but here in never-never land, the make-believe capital of the world, she exemplifies the specialness we all need to be. However, the ordinariness she speaks of is an in-group definition between sister and sister:

> me and you be sisters
> we be the same
> me and you
> coming from the same place.

She too is the mother who has had sons and brothers, uncles and male friends, and seems to have learned a great deal from these relationships. I am excited about her work because she reflects me; she tells my story in a way and with an eloquence that is beyond my ability. She is sister and mother, lovingly fair; her anger controlled, her tears not quite hidden. She knows that mothers must eventually let sons and daughters stand on their own; she also knows that the tradition and politics of the West conspire to cut those sons and daughters down before they are able to magnify their lives:

> those boys that ran together
> at Tillman's
> and the poolroom
> everybody see them now
> think it's a shame
> everybody see them now
> remember they was fine boys
>
> we have some fine Black boys
> don't it make you want to cry?

Her tears are not maudlin, however: she strides, face wet with a fierce and angry water. And she keeps getting up from being down, keeps stealing future space. She is the woman of "long memory" coming from a long line "of Black and going women / who got used to making it through murdered sons." Clifton is an encourager, a pusher of the sons and daughters; a loving reminder of what was, is, must be.

She brings a Black woman's sensitivity to her poetry—brings the history of what it means to be a Black woman in America, and what she brings is not antagonistic, not stacked against Black men. When she speaks of the true enemy, it is done in a way that reinforces her humanity yet displays a unique ability to capture the underlying reasons Europe wars on the world. Speaking of the "poor animal" and the "ape herds" of Europe, she says of them:

> he heads, always, for a cave
> his mind shivers against the rocks
> afraid of the dark
> afraid of the cold
> afraid to be alone
>
> afraid of the legendary man creature
> who is black
> and walks on grass
> and has no need for fire . . .

For the Buffalo soldiers and for the Dahomey women, the two images that flow throughout the body of much of her work, she sees a bright and difficult future. And she knows how to hurt, and she knows how to heal:

> me and you be sisters
> we be the same
> me and you
> coming from the same place.
> me and you
> be greasing our legs . . .
>
> got babies
> got thirty-five
> got black . . .
> be loving ourselves
> be sisters
> only where you sing
> i poet.

Indeed, she poets. An understatement, she is like quality music; her works make you feel and care. She is also a folk historian, dealing not in dates and names but concepts. She is the original root woman, a connector to trees, earth, and the undestroyables, as in "**On the Birth of Bomani**":

> We have taken the best leaves
> and the best roots
> and your mama whose skin
> is the color of the sun
> has opened into a fire and
> your daddy whose skin
> is the color of the night
> has tended it carefully with
> his hunter's hands and
> here you have come, Bomani,

an Afrikan Treasure-Man,
may the art in the love that made you
fill your fingers
may the love in the art that made you
fill your heart.

Clifton's style is simple and solid, like rock and granite. She is a linear poet who uses very little of the page, an effective device for the free and open verse that she constructs. She is not an experimental poet. She has fashioned an uncomplicated and direct format that allows great latitude for incorporating her message.

She writes controlled and deliberate lines moving from idea to idea, image to image, building toward specific political and social concepts. She is at her best when she is succinct and direct:

Love rejected
hurts so much more
than Love rejecting;
they act like they don't love their country
No
what it is
is they found
their country don't love them.

To conclude, Europeans put up statues for their dead poets or buy their homes and make them into museums. Often, they force their poets into suicide or nonproduction. Neglect for any writer is bitter, bitter salt, and Lucille Clifton's work has not seemed to take root in the adult segments of the Black reading community. Is it because she does not live in New York, may not have "connections" with reviewers nor possess Madison Avenue visibility? Is it that she needs more than a "mere" three books of poetry and a memoir? Is it that the major body of her work is directed toward children? Is it that her expressed moral and social values are archaic? All these possibilities are significant because they speak to the exchange nature of the game played daily in the publishing world; the only business more ruthless and corrupted is the Congress.

Clifton without doubt or pause is a Black woman (in color, culture, and consciousness); a family woman whose husband, children, and extended family have represented and played roles of great importance in her life and work, and a superb writer who will not compromise. She is considered among some to be *a literary find;* she is widely published and talked about, but, like most Black women writers, not promoted, and again, like most, her work can often be found in remainder bins less than a year after publication. (I bought fifty copies of **Generations** from a used-book store.) Finally, she is serious about revolutionary change. Most writers that "make it" in this country have to become literary and physical prostitutes in one form or another. Clifton's work suggests that if she is to sell herself, it will be for benefits far greater than those which accrue from publishing a book. In recent Black literature, she is in the tradition of Gwendolyn Brooks, Mari Evans, and Sonia Sanchez. She will not compromise our people, is not to be played with, is loved and

lover (" . . . you are the one I am lit for / come with your rod that twists and is a serpent / I am the bush / I am burning / I am not consumed"), is revolutionary, is, all beauty and finality, a Black woman . . . . (pp. 150-59)

When we begin to rightfully honor the poets, Clifton will undoubtedly be gathering roses in her own community and miss the call. She is like that, a quiet unassuming person, yet bone-strong with vision of intense magnitude. She is *new bone* molded in Afrikan earth, tested in Western waters, ready for action:

Other people think they know
how long life is
how strong life is / we know.

To be original, relevant, and revolutionary in the mouth of fire is the mark of a dangerous person. Lucille Clifton is a poet of *mean* talent who has not let her gifts separate her from the work at hand. She is a teacher and an example. To read her is to give birth to bright seasons. (p. 160)

Haki Madhubuti, "Lucille Clifton: Warm Water, Greased Legs, and Dangerous Poetry," in Black Women Writers (1950-1980): A Critical Evaluation, *edited by Mari Evans, Anchor Press/Doubleday, 1984, pp. 150-60.*

Thema Bryant (essay date 1985)

[*In the following interview, Clifton discusses her writing techniques and personal interests with sixth-grader Bryant.*]

Hello! My name is Thema Bryant. I'm in the 6th grade at Mt. Royal Elementary Middle School. When I get older I would like to be a teacher and to write poetry. After hearing some of my poetry I was asked to do an interview with the great Lucille Clifton. In case you don't know, Lucille Clifton is a poet and also writes children's books. If you would like to know more about her, read the following interview and get her books.

This year I had the pleasure of interviewing a great Black woman writer by the name of Lucille Clifton. When she first answered the phone I told her my name and how honored I was to give the interview. She said how honored she was to be interviewed. The first question I asked her was, "How old were you when you first became aware of your talent as a writer?" She needed no time at all. "Well, when I first became interested I was ten but I never thought my books would be published."

After this question I asked, "Did you have an opportunity to read many Black women poets and writers during your childhood?" Again she needed no time. She just plain out said, "No." Then after a moment of silence she said, "I'd never ever heard of them."

After this answer I needed to know, "Who gave you the most encouragement during your childhood?" She said,

"My mother. She told me that nothing was impossible and she encouraged me to try." I said, "Do you have a favorite time to do your writing?" This time she waited a second and then she said, "Not much. When I first started writing, I had a lot of little children and whenever I got a chance I would write, but now I mostly write at night."

Then I asked her, "We know what your writing does for others; what does it do for you?" She replied, "Oh! it's very satisfying. It makes me satisfied with myself and what I'm doing." Then I said, "What authors' books do you enjoy reading?" She replied, "Lots of them . . . lots . . . of . . . them." She said, "I like reading children's books, even though I'm not a child, and Black women's books."

Later I asked her, "Does listening to music help?" She replied gaily, "Yes.. Yes." I then asked her which did she prefer. She said, "All kinds, especially classical. I like the composer Bach, Aretha Franklin, and Gladys Knight and the Pips." After that answer we both laughed. Then I asked her, "Are you writing something special now?" She replied with a sign, "Well, I'm working on a book *New and Old Selected Writings,* where new and old poems will be together, and I may be also writing a children's book because I have an idea."

Afterwards I asked her, "What recommendations do you have for someone who would like to follow in your footsteps?" She replied, "I think I would recommend that they write a lot, don't get discouraged, have patience." Then I said, "When you are not writing how do you enjoy spending your time?" She replied, "Well right now I teach at the University of California, I read, and I like to sit by the ocean."

I asked her, "Do you ever get writer's block, and if so how do you get rid of it?" She said unashamedly, "Yes! Sometimes I do, but when I do I just remain patient and relax, and it goes away." Then I said, "Which book that you have written do you enjoy the best." She again replied without a pause, "Um, well, let's see, I most enjoy what I am working on now." Then I asked her, "What is the most challenging thing you think someone who is a writer will come up against?" She said, "One challenging thing is when you think that being a writer is more important than writing."

For my final question I asked, "What is your advice to children." She said, "I would like for all children to remember, especially Black children, that all that you want to be you can be and just because you are not doing well on the outside doesn't mean you can't do good on the inside." After that we said our good-byes.

Thema Bryant, "A Conversation with Lucille Clifton," in SAGE, *Vol. II, No. 1, Spring, 1985, p. 52.*

Greg Kuzma (essay date 1988)

[*Kuzma is the author of several volumes of poetry. In the following excerpt, he examines the style and themes of Clifton's* Next.]

Lucille Clifton solves the problem of seeing continuity in life by never asking for it. Her poems do not pretend to be all-inclusive or to reconcile inhospitable realities. They are instead brief encounters, small disturbances of idea or language which over a few lines find a resolution and conclude. They seem oral, very much the product of doing poetry out loud, and they seem particularly dependent upon what one can safely absorb and bear in mind over a few moments, hearing them, without a text. No loose ends are allowed. Everything is neatly tucked into place, properly subordinated, arranged, and pointed toward the punch line.

Clifton too is a poet in middle age, but she seems protected from disillusionment and despair by having had children and by the patterns of changes and growth that envelop people in families, and by her blackness and her sisterhood. The very source of her grief and pain, in the collective history of her race and in her identification with the weak and the oppressed, is the source of her strength. She is rooted in many ways, and even in her poems of loss and grief, personal or cultural, she speaks always as a rooted person. We always know that someone of a large and multiple identity is speaking, and as we read through the poems we are not so much learning more of her depth and variousness as we are witnessing this same woman alive in the world. The poems are strong; they emanate from a collected and whole personality, one that is at home with itself, but they do not quest or question against absurdities. There is instead an implicit conviction that there is evil in the world because people allow it, and that life would be infinitely better, even perfect, could we but forgive each other and ourselves and truly love.

The danger with this vision is that things will be resolved too quickly, or that the treatment will seem simplistic. In **"winnie song"** [in her collection *Next*], we hear "a dark wind is blowing / the homelands into home"—which sounds good, and might even serve as a slogan, but this poem does little to address the complex and almost impossible realities of South Africa. In another South Africa poem, **"there,"** she seems to penetrate to an essential level of reality and irony, where a white woman smiles at her own child on the lawn and at her husband "home from / arresting children." Regarding her own children, Clifton is amazingly sensitive to how they have become different from herself and different from each other:

> i am the sieve she strains from
> little by little
> everyday.
>
> i am the rind
> she is discarding.
>
> i am the riddle

she is trying to answer.

something is moving
in the water.

she is the hook.
i am the line.

("**4 daughters**")

Clifton works well in images that become metaphors of conditions and that are also open-ended and mysterious. The above poem is small, but it seems to embrace an essential truth about human experience: for all our complexity, our dilemmas are often explicable in simple terms. Elsewhere these same daughters defy her expectations:

> how they bewitch you into believing
> you have thrown off a pot that is yourself
> then one night you creep into their rooms and
> their faces have hardened into odd flowers
> their voices are choosing in foreign elections and
> their legs are open to strange unwieldy men.
>
> ("**here is another bone to pick with you**")

Memorable phrases abound in the poems. Writing what is closely cropped, Clifton is conscious of the need for economy but also of how much can be achieved with the carefully drawn or apt phrase. In "**at creation**" she rises with "the dusky beasts" and a few lines later concludes with "all life is life / all clay is kin and kind." In "**at gettysburg**," she experiences the "bloody voices" of the ghosts, and remembers the battles as "this clash of kin across good farmland." In "**my dream about the cows**" she discovers "how all despair is / thin and weak and personal . . . " In "**morning mirror**" she remembers her mother, "whose only sin was dying, whose only / enemy was time . . . whose only strength was love . . . ." Clifton's language carries a high degree of authority. Where the poems sometimes seem fragmented or enigmatic we work to understand them, so well do they usually understand themselves.

In part two of the book there are a number of death poems, or rather a number of poems devoted to each of a number of deaths. A different poet might have grouped all the poems about Joanne's death from leukemia together in one or two longer poems, but Clifton leaves them to make what seems a casual assortment. Where each of the poems as we read might well be the last, we become unusually alert and attentive, only to find on the next page another Joanne poem taken from a slightly different perspective. Here is one of the poems:

> the death of joanne c.
> 11/30/82
> aged 21
>
> i am the battleground that
> shrieks like a girl.
> to myself i call myself
> gettysburg. laughing,
> twisting the i.v.,
> laughing or crying, i can't tell
> which anymore,
> i host the furious battling of

> a suicidal body and
> a murderous cure.

Other poems are "**leukemia as white rabbit**," "**incantation**," and "**chemotherapy**" with its haunting and powerful line, "my mouth is a cave of cries." There are nine in all, or perhaps ten, running from page 54 through 63, all of them brief, and though each is compact and tidy, together they make a ragged sequence. The method is a strange one, unsettling and unnerving. We go from page to page not knowing if Joanne is still alive, or what the last word might be, or whether it will all add up or make sense once it is over. Clifton in effect re-creates some of the anxiety and tension that accompany any long terminal illness. Life progresses day by day from terror to remission, from moments of anguish to moments of calm and insight and a suspension of hostilities. Any day offers a fresh perspective, or may, or holds out hope for the kind of seeing that may bring an ultimate and healing knowledge. Clifton's technique with these poems makes us aware of these realities, however painful they are, however frustrating it is to read her. Some readers may come away longing for a poem of monumental design and address, one that might through eloquence and sweep of gesture put to rest these many uneasy and desperate cries, one that will make death seem orderly and neat in its lessons and meanings. Clifton offers us, wisely, only fragments. (pp. 628-30)

> *Greg Kuzma, in a review of* Next, *in* The Georgia Review, *Vol. XLII, No. 3, Fall, 1988, pp. 628-30.*

FURTHER READING

Johnson, Joyce. "The Theme of Celebration in Lucille Clifton's Poetry." *Pacific Coast Philology* XVIII, Nos. 1 & 2 (November 1983): 70-6.

> Discusses Clifton's rejection of negative stereotypes in her portrayals of black neighborhoods.

Jong, Erica. "Three Sisters." *Parnassus: Poetry in Review* 1, No. 1 (Fall-Winter 1972): 77-88.

> Examines Clifton's representations of the African-American experience in *Good News About the Earth.*

Laing, E. K. "The Voice of a Visionary, Not a Victim." *The Christian Science Monitor* 80, No. 49 (5 February 1988): B3.

> Analyzes the style and themes of poems in *Good Woman: Poems and a Memoir, 1969-1980* and *Next.*

Lazer, Hank. "Blackness Blessed: The Writings of Lucille Clifton." *The Southern Review* 25, No. 3 (July 1989): 760-70.

> Explores the political content and aesthetic accomplishments of Clifton's poetry and children's literature.

McCluskey, Audrey T. "Tell the Good News: A View of the Works of Lucille Clifton." In *Black Women Writers (1950-*

1980): A Critical Evaluation, edited by Mari Evans, pp. 139-49. New York: Anchor Press/Doubleday, 1984.

Discusses optimism in Clifton's poetry and juvenile literature.

Plant, Deborah. Review of *Good Woman: Poems and a Memoir, 1969-1980,* by Lucille Clifton. *Prairie Schooner* 63, No. 1 (Spring 1989): 115-17.

Overview of verse collected in *Good Woman: Poems and a Memoir, 1969-1980.*

Rushing, Andrea Benton. "Lucille Clifton: A Changing Voice for Changing Times." In *Coming to Light: American Women Poets in the Twentieth Century,* edited by Diane Wood Middlebrook and Marilyn Yalom, pp. 214-22. Ann Arbor: University of Michigan Press, 1985.

Examines Clifton's relationship to the Black Arts Movement and comments on her poetic representation of women.

Joseph Seamon Cotter, Sr.

1861-1949

American poet, dramatist, and short story writer.

Cotter is best known as the author of *Caleb, the Degenerate* (1901), one of the earliest dramas by a black American. Throughout his career he also wrote sonnets, folk ballads, and black dialect poems. In these works he frequently praised black leaders such as Frederick Douglass, Booker T. Washington, and W. E. B. Du Bois for their efforts to overcome racial prejudice. Although not considered a major author, Cotter is regarded as representative of turn-of-the-century black writers who dedicated their work to overcoming the kinds of negative stereotypes of black Americans that were perpetuated by such white authors as Thomas Dixon and Thomas Nelson Page. Frequently serving as a form of counter-propaganda, Cotter's work reflects his strong moral and philosophical convictions.

Cotter was born near Bardstown, Kentucky, the illegitimate son of a Scotch-Irishman and his employee, Martha Vaughn. His mother, the freeborn daughter of an American slave, significantly influenced Cotter by sharing her appreciation of literature with him. He described her as "a poet, a story-teller, a maker of plays," and under her guidance Cotter learned to read by the time he was four years old. Cotter's formal education was interrupted when, at the age of eight, he left school and found work in order to contribute financially to the household. In his youth he developed a talent for storytelling and later utilized this skill to encourage black children to read. While employed over the next decade as a manual laborer, Cotter continued to educate himself, reading works by John Milton, Alfred Tennyson, Edgar Allan Poe, and Paul Laurence Dunbar. Cotter returned to school as an adult and eventually became a teacher in an impoverished Kentucky school district, an experience that is believed to have provided the inspiration for his poem "Description of a Kentucky School House." Viewing education as a means of social betterment for black Americans, Cotter wrote: "He who steals or kills may be reformed behind prison bars, but he who fails to educate his children libels posterity."

In 1891 Cotter founded a black community near Louisville that was known as "Little Africa." He described the community as "part of the city where the word 'segregation' breeds no terror and conjures up no lawsuits." In 1893 he founded a school he named after the black poet Paul Laurence Dunbar, who visited him the following year and who praised the "ease and beauty" of Cotter's poetry. Cotter's conviction that social and economic reform for black Americans depended on self-determination found expression in "Dr. Booker T. Washington to the National Negro Business League," a poem published in his collection *A White Song and a Black*

One (1909). In the poem Cotter supported Washington's promotion of the work ethic as a means to economic independence for black Americans. In other didactic poems directed at black readers, such as "Ned's Psalm of Life for the Negro," "The Negro Woman," and "The Negro's Educational Creed," Cotter advocated self-reliance, racial pride, personal initiative, and an optimistic outlook. Cotter's only drama, *Caleb, the Degenerate,* was published in 1901 but was never given a stage production.

On assuming the position of principal of the Samuel Taylor Coleridge school in 1911, Cotter instituted a storytelling contest, an effort that brought him recognition when by 1919 it had become a national movement. About this time, Cotter praised W. E. B. Du Bois, Booker T. Washington's ideological adversary, in the poem "The Race Welcomes Dr. W. E. B. Du Bois as Its Leader." In opposition to Washington's emphasis on vocational training as the key to social advancement for black Americans, Du Bois stressed the right of black

Americans to pursue a professional degree based on a liberal arts education. Defending Du Bois's position, Cotter now wrote: "To work with the hands / Is to feed your own mouth / And maybe your neighbor's; / To work with the mind / Is to unleash the feet of millions." Cotter retired from his position as principal in 1942 and published his last collection of miscellaneous work in 1947. He died at the age of eighty-eight.

While some critics have regarded Cotter's work as conciliatory to white Americans, others have evaluated it in terms of the black American literary tradition in which messages of social protest were often disguised to avoid antagonizing white readers. In particular, James Hatch and Betty Cain, writing in the 1970s, found that earlier critics overlooked the irony or double meanings by which Cotter disguised his real theme in *Caleb, the Degenerate*. Both Hatch and Cain viewed the drama as an indirect attack on Booker T. Washington's belief that industrial training was sufficient to overcome the obstacles to racial betterment. Hatch contended that "although the surface features of the play were meant for the white and black readers who already believed [in Washington's advocacy of industrial training], there is a subsurface that commands the attention of those aware of the black experience." Epitomizing the modern reassessment of the drama, Cain wrote: "Nothing quite like it has been seen in Afro-American drama before or since."

Cotter's work is considered important for its examination of race relations and its foreshadowing of the interests of later black writers such as James Weldon Johnson, Mary McLeod Bethune, and Langston Hughes. Praising Cotter's exploration of the nature of racial relations, Eugene B. Redmond wrote in 1976: "Brilliant, precocious, and enduring, Cotter pursued the complex side of life, daring to examine the often over-simplified phenomena of race relations in America."

(For further information about Cotter's life and works, see *Dictionary of Literary Biography*, Vol 50: *Afro-American Writers before the Harlem Renaissance*.)

PRINCIPAL WORKS

A Rhyming (poetry) 1895
Links of Friendship (poetry) 1898
Caleb, the Degenerate: A Study of the Types, Customs and Needs of the American Negro (drama) [first publication] 1901
A White Song and a Black One (poetry) 1909
Negro Tales (short stories) 1912
Twenty-fifth Anniversary of the Founding of Colored Parkland or "Little Africa" (nonfiction) 1934
Collected Poems of Joseph S. Cotter (poetry) 1938
Sequel to "The Pied Piper of Hamelin," and Other Poems (poetry) 1939
Negroes and Others at Work and Play (poetry and short stories) 1947

Joseph S. Cotter (essay date 1901)

[*In the following excerpt from a preface written for the first edition of* Caleb, the Degenerate, *Cotter explains his intentions in writing this drama.*]

The aim [of *Caleb, the Degenerate*] is to give a dramatic picture of the Negro as he is to-day. The brain and soul of the Negro are rising rapidly. On the other hand, there is more depravity among a certain class of Negroes than ever before. This is not due to anything innate. It is the result of unwise, depraved leadership and conditions growing out of it.

Rahab represents this unwise, depraved leadership. Caleb is his pupil, and represents the depraved class of Negroes referred to. Some may claim that the picture is overdrawn, but both leader and led are with us to-day and speak for themselves.

The Bishop and Olivia represent the highest types of cultivated Negro manhood and womanhood. The Dude represents the so-called educated young Negro politician, of whom something may be made if the right steps are taken in time.

The Negro needs very little politics, much industrial training, and a dogged settledness as far as going to Africa is concerned. To this should be added clean, intelligent fireside leadership. Much of any other kind is dangerous for the present.

I am a Negro and speak from experience.

> *Joseph S. Cotter, in a preface to his* Caleb, the Degenerate: A Study of the Types, Customs, and Needs of the American Negro, *The Bradley and Gilbert Company, 1903, p. v.*

Robert T. Kerlin (essay date 1940)

[*Kerlin was an American poet, educator, and critic. In the following excerpt, he praises Cotter for the technical skill and lyrical quality of his work.*]

In many of Cotter's verses there is a sonorous flow which is evidence of poetic power made creative by passion. Didacticism and philosophy do not destroy the lyrical quality. In **"The Books' Creed"** this teacher-poet makes an appeal to his generation to be as much alive and as creative as the creed makers of other days were. The slaves of the letter, the mummers of mere formulas, he thus addresses:

> You are dead to all the Then,
>   You are dead to all the Now,
> If you hold that former men
>   Wore the garland for your brow.
>
> Time and tide were theirs to brave,
>   Time and tide are yours to stem.
> Bow not o'er their open grave
>   Till you drop your diadem.

Honor all who strove and wrought,
　Even to their tears and groans;
But slay not your honest thought
　Through your reverence for their bones.

Cotter is a wizard at rhyming. His **"Sequel to the Pied Piper of Hamelin"** surpasses the original—Browning's—in technique—that is, in rushing rhythms and ingenious rhymes. It is an incredible success, with no hint of a tour-de-force performance. Its content, too, is worthy of the metrical achievement. I will lay the proof before the competent reader in an extract or two from this remarkable accomplishment:

The last sweet notes the piper blew
　Were heard by the people far and wide;
And one by one and two by two
　They flocked to the mountain-side.

Some came, of course, intensely sad
And some came looking fiercely mad,
And some came singing solemn hymns,
And some came showing shapely limbs,
And some came bearing the tops of yews,
And some came wearing wooden shoes,
And some came saying what they would do,
And some came praying (and loudly too),
And all for what? Can you not infer?
A-searching and lurching for the Pied Piper,
And the boys and girls he had taken away.
And all were ready now to pay
Any amount that he should say.

So begins the **"Sequel"**. Another passage, near the end, will indicate the trend of the story:

The years passed by, as years will do,
　When trouble is the master,
And always strives to bring to view
　A new and worse disaster;
And sorrow, like a sorcerer,
　Spread out her melancholy pall,
　So that its folds enveloped all,
And each became her worshipper.
And not a single child was born
　Through all the years thereafter;
If words sprang from the lips of scorn
　None came from those of laughter.

Finally, the inhabitants of Hamelin are passing through death's portal, and when all had departed:

—a message went to Rat-land....

And lo! a race of rats was at hand....

They swarmed into the highest towers,
And loitered in the fairest bowers,
And sat down where the mayor sat,
And also in his Sunday hat;
And gnawed revengefully thereat.
With rats for mayor and rats for people,
With rats in the cellar and rats in the steeple,
With rats without and rats within,
Stood poor, deserted Hamelin.

Like Dunbar, Cotter is a satirist of his people—or certain types of his people—a gentle, humorous, affectionate satirist. His medium for satire is dialect, inevitably. Sententious wisdom, irradiated with humor, appears in these pieces in homely garb. In standard English, without satire or humor that wisdom thus appears:

What deeds have sprung from plow and pick!
　What bank-rolls from tomatoes!
No dainty crop of rhetoric
　Can match one of potatoes.

The gospel of work has been set forth by our poet in a four-act poetic drama entitled **Caleb, the Degenerate.** All the characters are Negroes. The form is blank verse—blank verse of a very high order, too. The language, like Shakespeare's—though Browning rather than Shakespeare is suggested—is always that of a poet. The wisdom is that of a man who has observed closely and pondered deeply. Idealistic, philosophical, poetical—such it is. It bears witness to no ordinary dramatic ability.

"Best bard, because the wisest," says our Israfel. Verily. "Sage" you may call this man as well as "bard." (pp. 77-80)

> *Robert T. Kerlin, "The Present Renaissance of the Negro" and "Dialect Verse," in his* Negro Poets and Their Poems, *third edition, The Associated Publishers, Inc., 1940, pp. 51-138, 234-60.*

Doris E. Abramson (essay date 1969)

[*Abramson is an American educator and critic. In the following excerpt, she discusses* Caleb, the Degenerate *as a response to negative stereotypes of black Americans.*]

Booker T. Washington mapped out a course for his people to follow when he gave a speech at the Cotton States' Exposition in Atlanta, Georgia, in 1895. In this speech he urged his fellow Negroes to cultivate friendly relations with white men. He recommended that Negroes devote themselves to agriculture, mechanics, domestic service, and the professions. He placed more value on acquiring industrial skill than on attaining a seat in Congress. He assured members of the white race that they could rely on eight million Negroes, "whose habits you know, whose fidelity and love you have tested in days when to have proved treacherous meant the ruin of your firesides." His people, he reminded the whites, had tilled the fields and cleared the forests "without strikes and labor wars." The audience cheered when Booker T. Washington said, "In all things that are purely social we can be as separate as the fingers, yet one as the hand in all things essential to mutual progress."

Joseph S. Cotter's play, **Caleb, the Degenerate,** with the amazing subtitle *A Study of the Types, Customs, and Needs of the American Negro,* is one Negro's way of expressing appreciation of Booker T. Washington's point of view. It is a slight, pretentious play, written in blank verse. The author—at the time of publication principal of the Colored Ward School in Louisville,

Kentucky—could read, we are told in the Preface, before he was four years old but had little opportunity for schooling. At twenty-two he went to a night school for colored pupils. It is significant that the Preface was written by Thomas G. Watkins, financial editor of the *Courier-Journal*. The benevolent white man was pleased to praise the wholly self-taught Negro who advocated that Negroes mind the teachings of Booker T. Washington.

Joseph Cotter states the purpose of his play in the Author's Preface:

> The aim is to give a dramatic picture of the Negro as he is today. The brain and soul of the Negro are rising rapidly. On the other hand, there is more depravity among a certain class of Negro than ever before. This is not due to anything innate. It is the result of unwise, depraved leadership and conditions growing out of it.... The Negro needs very little politics, much industrial training, and a dogged settleness [*sic*] as far as going to Africa is concerned. To this should be added clean, intelligent fireside leadership.

There is no doubt that Cotter listened attentively to Booker T. Washington's "Atlanta Compromise."

Caleb, the Degenerate, which is in four acts, is filled with unbelievable characters spouting incredible lines. There is no moment when they touch reality, even to the extent of... early melodramas by white authors writing about Negro characters. There is no minstrel type here, no Cato or Topsy. The characters, forced to speak in blank verse that tries to soar no matter how the vocabulary would pull it down, are merely vessels for ideas. Here Caleb, who is described in the cast of characters as a pupil of a "depraved leader," is speaking to an undertaker who wishes to know if he wants to buy a coffin for his deceased father.

> A thirty-dollar coffin! I say no!
> Five dollars for a robe? No, death-worm, no!
> Four carriages? No, undertaker, no!
> Think you a son must curb his appetite
> Because a pauper father breathes no more?
> The living must have money! I'm alive!
> Cold dignity is all the dead require.

None of the characters in the play seem to exist as men but rather to represent types. Caleb and his leader, Rahab, represent wicked types, the degenerate Negroes. Goodness is personified by Olivia and her father, the Bishop. Olivia, in the course of the play, establishes an industrial school for the children of Negroes her father has described as "a people, friendless, ignorant, / living from hand to mouth, from jail to grave." Olivia and the Bishop rise to such an emotional pitch in their enthusiasm for industrial training that they give it credit for "health, wealth, morals, literature, civilization." Somehow one senses that even Booker T. Washington would not have made such extravagant claims.

Two minority views expressed by depraved characters are that Negroes should vote and that they might

consider going back to Africa. The playwright did not consider either viewpoint worth much attention. The Bishop refers to his people as "primitive people" and seems to conclude that suffrage is beyond them at the moment. He recognizes, however, that they are Americans—"And this our land shall be our paradise"—not Africans.

The degenerate Caleb is found dead of his profligacy in the woods on the grounds of Olivia's industrial school. His death is represented as being horrible because he followed the wicked Rahab who professed to lead, not to love, his race. Had Caleb listened to Olivia and the Bishop, he might have reaped the benefits of the school, which Olivia says was built with gifts from millionaires. He might at least have been able to go to war with Dude, who at the very end of the play announces:

> I go to war. Some say the Negro shirks
> The tasks of peace. Who says he will not fight?
> I go to war.

Joseph Cotter set out to write a moral tract that would show the dangers of depravity and the values of industrial training over mere book learning—"Go, cage life's life before you pause to read." He put into the play good and bad characters, drew his message, killed off the wicked, rewarded the virtuous, and even, in conclusion, waved the American flag.

Though never performed, *Caleb, the Degenerate* was published and probably read by a number of civic and religious leaders of the period. The copy of the play at the Schomburg Collection was once owned by the Unitarian minister Edward Everett Hale, who became chaplain to the United States Senate in 1903. Joseph Cotter's message on the flyleaf to the Reverend Mr. Hale was: "If you can say a good word for *Caleb*, please do so." Anyone who believed in the Atlanta Compromise probably had a good word to say for *what* the play said. It is difficult to believe that anyone had a kind word for *how* it was said. (pp. 14-18)

The theatre of Joseph Cotter's time was made up of minstrelsy, melodrama, and the beginnings of musical comedy. (Bob Cole's *A Trip to Coon Town*, in the 1898-99 season, is thought to have been the first Negro musical comedy with a story line and something more than skits.) It is unlikely, however, that Cotter visited the theatre. His play, for all that it denounces book learning, reflects only that and not experience in the live theatre of his day. He had probably read Shakespeare and the nineteenth-century English poets, hence the use of blank verse.

When we look for the wellsprings of *Caleb, the Degenerate,* it is not in the theatre but in the fiction of the day that we find them. Between 1890 and 1914, American fiction was extremely race conscious. White writers like Thomas Dixon, Thomas Nelson Page, and Robert Hilliard wrote novels of the hate in which they pictured the Negro as half animal, half child, a threat to the United States. Many Negro writers and some white ones answered their propaganda by glorifying the Negro and exposing those who exploited him. Of these writers of counterpropaganda, Hugh Gloster observed:

> In their counterpropaganda Negro fictionists usually portrayed educated and well-mannered colored characters... who often engage in long discussions of racial and political issues and are almost invariably presented as teachers, clergymen, physicians, lawyers, politicians, or journalists. A favorite practice is the depiction of these individuals attending lectures, literary societies, political councils, and institutions of higher education.

Gloster goes on to say that Negro writers were determined in their fiction to call their audiences' attention to the various repressions experienced by Negroes and to write of their time from a Negro's point of view. If Joseph Cotter's play seems to keep step with the counterpropaganda, it is well to be reminded that he was not with the majority of Negro writers when he took Washington's side in the Booker T. Washington-W. E. B. Du Bois debate. According to Gloster, this controversy received a great deal of discussion, and the majority of the writers indicated, either through implication or direct statement, a preference for the militant Du Bois rather than for the pragmatic and conciliatory school of race leadership espoused by Washington. Cotter's play did share one thing with most of the turn-of-the-century polemical fiction: melodrama. (pp. 19-20).

> *Doris E. Abramson, "Beginnings," in her* Negro Playwrights in American Theatre: 1925-1959, *Columbia University Press, 1969, pp. 5-21.*

James V. Hatch (essay date 1974)

[*Hatch is an American poet, dramatist, and critic. In the following excerpt, he argues that* Caleb, the Degenerate *may be read as both conciliatory to white readers and to followers of Booker T. Washington and as a satirical protest against these groups.*]

In the tradition of many self-made men, Joseph Cotter, Sr. gave over much of his writing to urging others to emulate his own success. The first of **"The Negro's Ten Commandments,"** he wrote, is "Thy fathers' God forsake not and thy manhood debase not, and thou shalt cease to say 'I am a Negro, therefore I cannot.'" And toward this end he published poems, stories and, in 1901, one full-length play: *Caleb, the Degenerate: A Study of the Types, Customs, and Needs of the American Negro.*

Caleb, the main character, is a degenerate and a villain by the standards of 1900. He sells his father's corpse to medical students; he pushes his mother to her death; he smokes, drinks, bullies, lies, steals, and takes cocaine. He raves against God and church:

> They rather worship god whose cruel laws
> are made up wholly of mistakes and flaws.
> The time shall be when they will cease to follow

> Views that are so disgusting and so hollow.
> Let blinded Christians, ere they think or stir,
> Confer with me, their great philosopher.

Caleb's philosophy is to vehemently spurn the Establishment in all its aspects. There is something in his perpetual anger, his bitter wit, his hopelessly destructive life, that makes him a rebel in the modern sense—much as Johnny Williams in *No Place To Be Somebody* becomes a hero as antihero.

Opposed to Caleb's satanic nature are the Bishop, his stepdaughter, Olivia, and the faculty and children of the Industrial School. These "good Negroes" represent the true course the race is to take—learn a trade, save money, be Christian, and don't get involved in any Back-to-Our-African-Homeland movements. From this simplistic interpretation, it is no wonder that most critics—among those who have bothered to read the play—have not many good words to say for it.

They attack Mr. Cotter's verse: "It is dull in the writing," says Fannin S. Belcher, Jr., "chaotic in treatment and unactable." They attack Cotter's characters: "*Caleb* ... is filled with unbelievable characters spouting incredible lines. There is no moment when they touch reality," comments Doris Abramson [see excerpt dated 1969].

When the play has been praised, it is often in a tone of condescension. Alfred Austin, poet laureate of England, responded by letter when the play was sent to him: "It affords yet further evidence of the latent capacity of your long maltreated race for mental development." Author Israel Zangwill did not manage much better: "I do not profess to understand it all, but I desire to express my appreciation of the passages of true poetry in which you express the aspirations of the Negro race for salvation by labor."

Before these evaluations are accepted, a question needs to be answered: what audience was Mr. Cotter writing for? Was he simply showing his black brothers a pathway toward economic salvation? Was he showing his white brothers that they need not fear the black man? Finally, was Mr. Cotter writing two plays, an overt and a covert one?

The answer to all these questions is "Yes." Yes, Mr. Cotter is urging the black man to follow Dr. Washington's work ethic. As has been suggested, the race virulence of America was at a crest in Cotter's time. Solutions for survival had to be found. Yes, the play was written with an eye to the white reader. The preface to the play was composed by Thomas Watkins, financial editor of the Louisville *Courier-Journal*, who wrote, "The author is one of a race that has given scarcely anything of literature to the world." How pleased Mr. Watkins must have been to help a good nigra. But although the surface features of the play were meant for the white and black readers who already believed, there is a subsurface that commands the attention of those aware of the black experience.

The failure of the critics to find much merit in *Caleb* is a failure to recognize this subsurface of black experience, a powerful intensity created out of Joseph Cotter's own growing up in America. Nowhere is this intensity greater than in the character of Caleb.

For the reader who is attracted by the emotional drive of Caleb, it is intriguing to note the author's belated attempt in the fourth act to explain Caleb's degeneracy by shifting the blame to another man.

> DOCTOR. ...His mother sinned ere he was
>   born.
>   This tainted him, therefore his wicked
>   course.
> BISHOP. No! No! She did not sin. Caleb was led
>   To that belief.
> DOCTOR. Was led?
> BISHOP. Rahab's the man!

The blame is Rahab's, but the motivation for the crime has only been pushed back, not explained. The nature of the "mother's sin" is not clear. Ten years later, Mr. Cotter made it more explicit when he published a collection of short stories. The lead story is entitled **"Caleb,"** and follows the plot of the play in many respects—except that the mother and father of Caleb were married twice: once before and once after emancipation (the slave marriage presumably was not sanctified by church and state). Caleb was born between the marriages, ergo a bastard. When Caleb learns this in the story, he strikes his father "violently over the heart." The father falls dead.

This story of patricide is followed by a tale entitled **"Rodney."** Mr. Cotter writes:

> Rodney was an illegitimate child. He knew not what this meant, but the sting of it embittered his young life.

The Negro has as much prejudice as the white man. Under like conditions the Negro would make the same laws against the white. This crept out in the treatment of Rodney. His worst enemies were always Negroes. The Anglo-Saxon blood in his veins made scoffers of some and demons of others.

To be pitied is the boy who has never framed the word "father" upon his lips. Rodney attempted it once, but failed, and never tried again. He stood before his father bareheaded and with the coveted word on his lips.

> "You have a fine head of hair," said the father.

> "That's what people say." replied Rodney.

> "Are you proud of it?"

> "Should I be, Sir?"

> "Well, my little man, it's a disgrace to you."

This was the first and last meeting of Rodney and his father. Joseph Cotter himself was the bastard son of a black mother and her "employer," a Scotch-Irishman,

"a prominent citizen of Louisville." The fact that young Joseph was not sent to school but put to menial work at the age of ten suggests that the "prominent citizen" did not rejoice in his Negro son. It is fair to speculate that Cotter's black experience as the bastard black son of a white father speaks through both Rodney and Caleb.

There are three fathers in the play: Grandison, who is dead when the play opens; the Bishop, Olivia's adopted father, a man who has a lecherous itch for his ward; and Noah, whose beard Caleb pulls out. Speeches are given over to the value of mother love, but no praises are given to fathers—nor is one ever allowed to merit praise. The Industrial School is saved by Olivia. Joseph Cotter hated his Anglo-Saxon father, and by extension, the country he attempts to praise in act three. A comparison of the Old Man's speeches, as he urges his followers to leave "a country that is one ignoble grave," with those of the Bishop, who is defending America as a paradise, makes the latter appear vacuous. The Back-to-Our-African-Homeland section is powerful. It is of small consequence that the Old Man is slipped into the final tableau to show that he has acquiesced to the Bishop's America.

> In his own preface to the play, the author states: The Negro needs very little politics, much industrial training, and a dogged settledness as far as going to Africa is concerned. To this should be added clean, intelligent fireside leadership. Much of any other kind is dangerous for the present. I am a Negro and speak from experience.

This is hardly a denunciation of those who wish to return to Africa. Militancy is not rejected: it is rejected "only for the present."

How much Mr. Cotter is aware of his own dual attitude regarding white America must be left to the reader—with one final hint. What is the real allegory of the scene in act two between the Bishop, Olivia, and the ministers? Is this a "realistic" scene, or did Mr. Cotter write a surrealistic scene of associative visual and aural images? If the scene were transferred to *Alice In Wonderland* (and it could easily be done), would it not become "significant?"

Perhaps the case that the author was consciously disguising his material can never be proved. Indeed, it may not be possible to show that some of the best scenes of the play sprang "unintended" from his unconscious. However, a fair and sensitive reading will reveal that Joseph Cotter is a black man whose total being is writing out the anguish of his life. It may be enough that he saw early that for the black man to have power he must own the means of distribution and production. And perhaps the fairytale ending was Mr. Cotter's final note of satire on what might be expected from the great white fathers. (pp. 61-3)

James V. Hatch, "Yes We Must, Yes We Can: 'Caleb, the Degenerate' (1901), Joseph S. Cotter, Sr.," in Black Theater, U.S.A.: Forty-Five Plays by Black Americans, 1847-

1974, *edited by James V. Hatch and Ted Shine, The Free Press, 1974, pp. 61-99.*

Joan R. Sherman (essay date 1974)

[*Sherman was an American novelist, editor, and critic. In the following excerpt, she examines the subject matter of Cotter's poetry.*]

During five decades of poetry-writing, Cotter's interests range from industrial education in the 1890's to the "zoot suit" and atom bomb in 1947. In both dialect and standard English verse he urges social and moral reform, sectional reconciliation, and brotherhood. He satirizes the foibles and frailties of blacks but also praises their strengths and accomplishments; he philosophically examines God's ways and mysteries of human nature; he comments on historical events and pays homage to notables like Frederick Douglass, William Lloyd Garrison, Cassius M. Clay, Presidents McKinley, Taft, and Roosevelt, Booker T. Washington, and W. E. B. Du Bois; he extols good literature and his literary idols: Shakespeare, Milton, Tennyson, Riley, Holmes, Swinburne, Poe, and his close friend Dunbar. Finally, Cotter writes story ballads and light verse enlivened by wit and striking imagery.

Cotter's major concern is race advancement, to be gained by a mixture of race pride, humility, hard work, education, and a positive, optimistic outlook. He chides lazy, aggressive, extravagant, and parasitical blacks who will never succeed in **"The Loafing Negro," "The Don't-Care Negro," "The Vicious Negro," "I'se Jes' er Little Nigger,"** and **"Negro Love Song."** He praises those who are moving upward in **"Ned's Psalm of Life for the Negro"** in **"The Negro Woman,"** which charges the female "To give the plan, to set the pace, / Then lead him in the onward race"; and in **"The True Negro"**:

> Though black or brown or white his skin,
> He boldly holds it is no sin,
> So long as he is true within,
>   To be a Negro.
>   . . . .
> He loves his place, however humbling,
> He moves by walking, not by stumbling,
> He lives by toiling, not by grumbling
>   At being a Negro.

Devoted to the ideology of Washington, Cotter advocates self-help, money-getting, and accommodation in verses like **"Tuskegee," "The Negro's Educational Creed,"** and **"Dr. Booker T. Washington to the National Negro Business League"**:

> Let's spur the Negro up to work,
>   And lead him up to giving.
> Let's chide him when he fain would shirk,
>   And show him when he's living.
>   . . . .
> What deeds have sprung from plow and pick!
>   What bank rolls from tomatoes;
> No dainty crop of rhetoric
>   Can match one of potatoes.

. . . .

> A little gold won't mar our grace,
>   A little ease our glory.
> This world's a better biding place
>   When money clinks its story.

Caleb, the Degenerate a four-act play in blank verse subtitled, "A Study of the Types, Customs, and Needs of the American Negro," dramatizes the credo of Cotter's preface: "The Negro needs very little politics, much industrial training, and a dogged settledness as far as going to Africa is concerned. To this should be added clean, intelligent fireside leadership."

Cotter introduces the characters as archetypal Negroes: Caleb, a money-hungry atheist, murders his father, philosophizes in pun-ridden Elizabethan diction, goes mad, and dies; Rahab, an amoral politician and emigrationist, corrupts everyone. Caleb and Rahab typify "unwise, depraved leadership." In contrast, the "highest types" are a magniloquent Bishop and his daughter Olivia, who teaches in the industrial school and unwisely loves Caleb. The Bishop sprinkles abstruse theological arguments with homilies: "Industrial training is the thing at last," "God's love and handicraft must save the world," "Work is the basis of life's heritage." Olivia, who has written a book, *The Negro and His Hands*, idealizes "hewers of wood and drawers of water" and the true religion:

> Hope is the star that lights self unto self.
> Faith is the hand that clutches self's decree.
> Mercy is oil self keeps for its own ills.
> Justice is hell made present by a blow.

Although ***Caleb*** is poor drama and mediocre poetry, it is probably the most original tract supporting Washington's policies and as such has considerable sociohistorical interest.

In later years Cotter recognized the value of Du Bois's "Talented Tenth" doctrine in **"The Race Welcomes Dr. W. E. B. Du Bois as Its Leader"**:

> To work with the hands
>   Is to feed your own mouth
> And maybe your neighbor's;
>   To work with the mind
> Is to unleash the feet of millions
>   And cause them to trip
> To the music of progress;
>   We welcome you, prophet,
> You who have taught us this lesson of lessons.

"We welcome you," the poem continues, "Race-called leader of Race . . . Christ-called saver of souls . . . God-sealed brother and prophet." In his subsequent work Cotter supports the combined doctrines of Washington and Du Bois.

Cotter's didactic verse, which appears in every volume, is usually trite in sentiment and style. . . . Using a variety of verse forms which complement their subjects, Cotter's tributes to those he admires are often successful. **"William Lloyd Garrison"** communicates the militancy, courage, and altruism of the "God-like" abolitionist; a tender eulogy, **"To the Memory of Joseph S. Cotter, Jr."** asks with simplicity whether the poet and his son will meet in eternity; and in **"Algernon Charles Swinburne,"** Cotter parodies Swinburne's themes and versification to show his admiration:

> Thy gift was a yearning
> That paradised learning,
> And ended in turning
>   All seasons to Junes
> Through death that caresses,
> Through hatred that blesses,
> And love that distresses,
>   And words that are tunes.
>
> A Milton may ghoul us,
> A Shakespeare may rule us,
> A Wordsworth may school us,
>   A Tennyson cheer;
> But thine is the glory,
> Star-sprung from the hoary,
> Flame-decadent story
>   Of the munificent ear.

Such facile rhyming, musicality, and unorthodox word coinage and word usage distinguish some of Cotter's tales in verse like **"The Tragedy of Pete"** and **"Sequel to the 'Pied Piper of Hamelin'."** The latter, a lively narrative in thirty stanzas of from four to twenty-one lines, recounts the search of the people of Hamelin for their children, lured away by Robert Browning's "Piper." After many years the childless adults of Hamelin die, and "a race of rats" occupies the town:

> They swarmed into the highest towers,
> And loitered in the fairest bowers,
> And sat down where the mayor sat,
> And also in his Sunday hat;
> And gnawed revengefully thereat.
> With rats for mayor and rats for people,
> With rats in the cellar and rats in the steeple,
> With rats without and rats within,
> Stood poor, deserted Hamelin.

Cotter's nursery-rhyme tone and rhythms in this **"Sequel"** are especially effective. A poem of later years, perhaps his most original effort, is reminiscent of Lewis Carroll's lyrical nonsense verse. The twenty-four-stanza **"Love's Tangle"** fascinates as it perplexes, and the tangle escapes definition. The poem begins:

> As Simile to myth and myrrh
>   She led gruff care to slaughter,
> And saw the moonlight vow to her
>   In dimples on the water....

Added to this great variety of poems are several unpretentious observations of human nature from a personal point of view, like Cotter's casual appreciation, **"On Hearing James W. Riley Read (From a Kentucky Standpoint)"** and his colloquial greeting, **"Answer to Dunbar's 'After a Visit'."** Although the aesthetic quality of Cotter's verse is extremely uneven, his catholic tastes and techniques, and his consistent race-consciousness combined with sympathetic regard for the needs, joys,

and aspirations of all people, give him well-deserved celebrity among the black poets. (pp. 166-70)

> *Joan R. Sherman, "Joseph Seamon Cotter, Sr.," in her* Invisible Poets: Afro-Americans of the Nineteenth Century, *University of Illinois Press, 1974, pp. 164-71.*

Betty Cain (essay date 1978)

[*Cain is an American educator and critic. In the following excerpt, she examines* Caleb, the Degenerate *as disguised social protest.*]

Caleb in the Bible got to the Promised Land because he did not fear the giants in the walled cities and "wholly followed the Lord" (Deuteronomy, 1:25-26). Another Caleb, the protagonist of a strange, enigmatic four-act verse drama by Afro-American poet Joseph S. Cotter Sr., is called in the title "the Degenerate." He is given actions and speeches to show "degeneracy," but other elements in the play strongly suggest the militant power of the Biblical Caleb. This question of intended thematic effect is explored in the following discussion of Cotter's *Caleb, the Degenerate: A Study of the Customs, Types, and Needs of the American Negro,* first published in 1901, and recently anthologized in 1974 in *Black Theater, U.S.A.,* edited by James Hatch and Ted Shine. These editors introduce the play [see excerpt dated 1974] with the suggestion that there may be a hidden message under the surface theme, which is that American blacks of the time needed to turn away from "degeneracy" and devote themselves to the Booker T. Washington work ethic.

That there should be a play with at least two levels of interpretation, with meanings which contradict each other in itself dramatizes the uneasy situation of Black intellectuals at the turn of the century, especially in the South. The Ku Klux Klan was powerful; voting was forbidden to Blacks; Jim Crow laws were stringent—and the only way to exist in peace seemed to be the way of Booker T. Washington. Yet the founder of Tuskegee had set limits on the growth of Black freedom in the so-called Atlanta Compromise, his address at the Atlanta Exposition of 1895:

> Our greatest danger is that in the great leap from slavery to freedom we may overlook the fact that the masses of us are to live by the productions of our hands, and fail to keep in mind that we shall glorify common labor and put brains and skill into the common occupations of life; shall prosper in proportion as we learn to draw the line between the superficial and the substantial, the ornamental gew-gaws of life and the useful. No race can prosper till it learns that there is as much dignity in tilling a field as in writing a poem.

The enthusiasm with which whites accepted this speech made Booker T. Washington the most influential Black person in America, with the power of effectively blocking other potential leaders.

It is logical then to assume that Joseph Cotter, Sr., the largely self-educated child of a slave and her white owner, for most of his long life a teacher and school principal in Louisville, should feel the necessity of writing in ways that Washington would approve. Certainly the surface plot of *Caleb, the Degenerate* fits that requirement. (pp. 37-8)

[The play's] reception since its first publication shows that it is a riddle that has never yet been solved. Cotter first asked a white patron, Cale Young Rice, to read *Caleb* in 1898. It was later published in 1901 and 1903 editions, appeared in a little-noticed 1973 reprint from the original publishers, Bradley and Gilbert of Louisville, Kentucky, and was given one public reading. Research so far has not uncovered any evidence of the play being staged. The text apparently circulated, however, because Hatch and Shine give quotations of critical opinions from three diverse sources in their introduction:

> The play brings into sharp contrast the ideas of the cultivated Negroes.... a unique and interesting addition to the dramatic literature of America.
> —*New York Dramatic Mirror*

> ...further evidence of the latent capacity of your long-maltreated race for mental development.
> —Alfred Austin, then Poet Laureate of England

> I do not profess to understand it all, but I desire to express my appreciation of the passages of true poetry in which you express the aspirations of the Negro race for salvation by labor.
> —Israel Zangwill, Jewish-American novelist

In the fifties and sixties some brief comments about *Caleb* in histories of Afro-American literature dismiss it as a "problem play" (with no discussion of the problems) [Margaret Just Butcher, *The Negro in American Literature*]; as "terribly inept blank verse" with "incidents and dialogue frequently laughable" but "the closest thing to a folk play ever turned out in the United States"; and as a "slight, pretentious play" with "unbelievable characters spouting incredible lines," reflecting none of the conventions of the live theater of the day [see excerpt by Abramson dated 1969].

In an article in *Negro Digest* "First Afro-American Theater" [see Further Reading], playwright and critic Carlton W. Molette III objected to Doris Abramson's disparagements, pointing out that in the oral tradition out of which the Afro-American theater springs, plays can be mixtures of sermons, stories, pageants, and whatever else the theme calls for. Molette does not, however, make any attempt to discuss the puzzle of theme in *Caleb.*

Hatch and Shine, calling Cotter a "disciple" of Washington, may be missing a clue in the playful irony in Cotter's doggerel lines on **"Dr. Booker T. Washington to the National Negro Business League."**

> What deeds have sprung from plow and pick!
> What bank-rolls from tomatoes.

> No dainty crop of rhetoric
> Can match one of potatoes.

In the tone of this verse and from the play *Caleb* itself, there is hardly a warrant for identifying Cotter as a "disciple" of Washington.

Another proof that Cotter was capable of using poetry for social criticism was given in a poem of his printed in 1898:

> **"To Kentucky"**
> Make not a law to rule another
> That you yourselves would not obey;
> In this, as in the ancient day,
> Man is the keeper of his brother.
> Let not the states about you see
> That you are great in all that goes
> To banish friends and harbor foes
> Around the base of freedom's tree.

The ambiguity begins with the Preface to the 1903 edition of the play. Cotter himself notes the puzzling use of elevated and often witty Shakespearean blank verse in most of the play. Why did he use the poetry that Booker T. Washington had implied is one of "the ornamental gewgaws of life," in a play seeming to promote manual labor as the panacea for Negro problems? Cotter says, "An author puts poetry into the mouths of his characters to show the possibility of individual human expression." Although somewhat cryptic, this statement seems to indicate human possibilities far beyond Washington's limited accommodationism and hints that we will find these potentials in the play's poetic speeches. Cotter, however, goes on to say, "The Negro needs very little politics, much industrial training, and a dogged settledness as far as going to Africa is concerned." That seems pretty clear, so perhaps we should look no further, and take the surface message of the play at its face value. But that future generations were *not* intended to do that, is strongly suggested by the last two sentences of the Preface: "Much of any other kind is dangerous for the present. I am a Negro and speak from experience" [see excerpt dated 1901]. In 1901, in the long period after the Reconstruction, with white power manifest in the form of lynchings and terror and the legalization of Jim Crow, Cotter, I believe, is telling us that the Negro actually *has* much of another kind of need, but to express it openly might mean persecution and even death. His play *Caleb,* I am convinced, is in the tradition of hidden messages in spirituals; Cotter is thus also a precursor of playwrights like Marcel and Sartre, who concealed anti-Nazi propaganda in seemingly neutral plays written and staged during the occupation of France.

From the first scene of the play, *Caleb, the Degenerate,* odd juxtapositions of characters, actions, and dialogue remind us more of the Expressionistic dramas of Strindberg than of any melodrama or tragedy written for the American stage before 1901. The Bishop, "adopted father" to Olivia, inveighs against "Caleb, this hell-builder upon earth" in Shakespearean blank verse. When he stops for breath, Olivia plays a violin, after first getting her bow back from the Bishop, who has seized it. The Bishop speaks of his dead wife, and then says, "I have one more! 'Tis you, Olivia!" We wonder why Olivia needs an "adopted father," when she has a real one, Noah, and sense something slightly sinister in the Bishop's more than fatherly interest in her and in his jealousy of Caleb: "You wed a brute, my child?"

"Caleb's the man!" is Olivia's impudent reply, and she goes out, playing the violin softly. The Bishop calls her back. She responds from offstage, taunting him, as she does throughout the play: "What profits it? A child is never grown." Then she "breaks chord on violin" and says: "A broken chord! Chords break so easily." The "broken chord" is immediately followed by news from Olivia's friend Frony, who is also part of the Bishop's household, that Caleb, in the company of the "libertine" preacher Rahab, has killed his father in an argument. Olivia turns pale, but talks with Frony of love and of hope for Caleb's soul.

In the second scene, in Caleb's cottage, Rahab, called "Caleb's devil's man," is hypocritically preparing a funeral sermon. Caleb strides in "with whip and spurs in hand" and shouts: "No sermon! . . . . Money! Money! Money!", and soon arranges the sale of his father's body to a medical student.

Even though Caleb's "degeneracy" is thus from the outset laid on heavily, Olivia, the idealistic young teacher, holds to him through the rest of the play—not sexually, not romantically, but intellectually and spiritually. Many long interchanges with the Bishop in later scenes express her perception of Caleb as a hero for future generations. And yet Olivia and Caleb never speak to one another on stage, and meet only once, and then briefly, the directions reading, "As Olivia enters Caleb looks abashed and runs out." Obviously there is some deeper theme here than sentimental romance. Caleb is ambivalently presented as "a hero as antihero," as Hatch and Shine suggest in their introduction. The epithet "the Degenerate" may thus be meant as heavily ironic. Blacks accused of rape were categorized as "degenerate," and therefore, their lynching was justified. Cotter here gives us a man who does not respect his father's body, his mother's love, or his sweetheart's father's white hairs—but his evil is confined to his own people and his acts may be symbolic. Further, he is motivated by a belief that his mother was guilty of adultery, that he himself was not of legitimate birth, sub-themes which were predominant in an earlier crude prose tale, **"Caleb,"** included in a collection, *Negro Tales,* all by Cotter, although the contrast between the early pathetic tale and the full-length play in style and conception is striking.

From the first scenes of *Caleb* referred to above, to the end of the play, the reader is continually intrigued and baffled by tension between the surface story and the dreamlike scenes of symbolic action, the whole effect compounded by the dialogue in archaic blank verse. Nothing quite like it has been seen in Afro-American drama before or since. Certainly the story seems as ridiculous, pretentious, and crude as some critics have said it is. But even in the above skeleton form, strange elements and combinations are apparent, which have no counterparts in the conventional melodramas of the day. Conventionally there were stock characters, action progressing through the machinations of the villain, pathos, sentimentality, "serious" action intended to create suspense, good rewarded, evil punished, and hero and heroine united at the end. *Caleb* departs from all these characteristics in complex and interesting ways.

Close study of the interrelationships of actions and characters and of the long poetic "sermons" in *Caleb* reveals a coded structure that could convey a hidden message to alert readers and audience. The two main characters, Olivia and Caleb, are the keys to the hidden structure. Olivia is central; the others can all be interpreted as they relate to her. Her actions and speeches reveal her to be much like the Shakespearean Olivia. She is brave and determined:

> OLIVIA. 'Twas horrible! 'Twas horrible! Caleb
> Did prove a demon! 'Tis my sober thought
> Great God will hear no prayers that he will make.
> FRONY. You should have seen! You should—
> OLIVIA.   I heard enough.
> FRONY. Are satisfied?
> OLIVIA.   That I should strive the more.

She is intelligent and imaginative, speaking in the elevated blank verse Cotter defended in his Preface:

> OLIVIA. Past ages toyed with man. He knew it not,
> And made their jest the altar of his praise.
> They thorned his soul with fear, yet asked him why
> He was so slow to sniff the rose of life.
> They dulled his sight by bringing Hell so close,
> They scorned him for not seeing Heaven afar.

She is witty and wily—very much a Shakespearean heroine:

> OLIVIA. As Frony says, your sermons cling to me.
> BISHOP. As you to Caleb?
> OLIVIA. I have no mind to make comparisons.
> Besides the ancient rule of courtesy
> Forbids that you bring up a second point
> When I have introduced a sober first.
> BISHOP. 'Tis true! Go on!

She is compassionate. As she exposes the politician Rahab's falseness, she asks him:

> OLIVIA. You love the race?
> RAHAB.   I love the race? I lead.
> Others may do the loving. I look up.
> OLIVIA. I love Rahab. (He turns toward her.) I love Rahab.
> RAHAB.   Woman,
> That spurs me on to action.
> OLIVIA.   That's your speech
> Upon yourself. It spurs you on—

BISHOP.   To death.

Olivia is a powerhouse of a woman, directing, manipulating, always taking the initiative, setting the philosophical tone, and always more aware of what is going on than any of the other characters. For instance, although she loves Caleb for his intelligence and rebellious assertiveness, she has no illusions of being able to save him. She knows he is doomed—

> OLIVIA. Caleb shall soon find his reward.
> ...He is the man to expiate his crimes.
> He is secure in the coils of retribution.
> His reward shall be death.

Booker T. Washington's name is nowhere mentioned in the play, although ostensibly the drama appears to promote Washington's philosophy. If Washington is represented at all, however, it is by Olivia, who is running, promoting, and raising money for a trade school for blacks. Why did Cotter make the industrial school principal a woman? We might speculate that this choice made the character so different from Washington himself that no one could claim the two are similar; thus it enabled Cotter to make his idealistic figure a complicated one, pointing beyond industrial training for the Negro and accommodationism. Many accounts of Washington's career indicate, however, that he was not so simple either; some see him as the clever trickster covering up an inner militance in order to get what blacks needed to survive in the white post-Reconstruction world. Cotter's character Olivia does this too, as she implies when she tells how she got money for the school:

> OLIVIA. Chance threw me with a group of
>   millionaires.
>   I doubted, fretted, feared. At last I spoke.
>   The speech was short and simple. See the
>   checks!
> BISHOP. They lost no time in writing them?
> OLIVIA.   A tale
>   Our folks oft slumber o'er drew tears from
>   them.

Olivia's relationships with the other characters show, however, that she is much more than a female Booker T. Washington. Her having two fathers seems odd, but can be seen as significant. Her natural father, Noah, is a ridiculous, ineffectual figure; in relation to both Caleb and Olivia, he may represent the backward older generation that the young people must break away from. As for the Bishop, in whose home she lives, we can perhaps assume that he adopted her to give her the education she could not otherwise have afforded. Thematically, Olivia's close relationship to a high church official shows the need to convert a stagnant black clergy interested only in preaching hell fire, to acting for the progress of the Negro. Evidently Cotter is trying to show that the black church can be aroused and lead the race much further than Washington considered possible during his lifetime. The closing lines of the play indicate that the Bishop has come quite far:

> BISHOP. Failure? 'Tis a misfit. Success is what?

> 'Tis a measurement of self. 'Tis measurement of all the forces that encounter self.
> 'Tis fitting these together day by day.
> 'Tis seeing goals with eyes that never blink.
> 'Tis finding desert spots and tending them
> So that their fruitage stars man's ancient lot
>   and links his freedom with the linked
>   spheres.

But why, throughout the play, is Olivia so disrespectful to an august Bishop? Why does she taunt him, mock him, and play tricks on him? Strange behavior for a proper young woman in any age, but especially in the 1890s! Even more strange is the Bishop's desire to marry his foster daughter. Not so strange, however, in terms of the hidden message, is Olivia's *not* marrying the Bishop or showing any romantic interest in him at all. The members of the younger generation, represented by Olivia, are to arouse the clergy, but they are not to be too closely allied to the church's traditional nonmilitant teachings.

In addition to providing Olivia with two fathers, Cotter has three other women in the play who may be seen as *other selves* of Olivia. One is Caleb's mother, Patsy, a good woman, who was Olivia's early teacher. Her belief in Caleb's potential, which she relates in a dream story, parallels Olivia's. After Caleb kills his father, Olivia commits herself to Patsy's role to regenerate him. Then there is Frony, Olivia's confidante, who abhors Caleb's deeds, but sympathizes with Olivia and expresses the sisterhood of feminism—

> FRONY.   I like not Caleb, but I'll help you out.
>   We women must be women! Men are
>   men!

A third variant of Olivia, introduced in Act III at the school, is simply called A Woman. That this mysterious Woman and Frony are both aspects of Olivia's personality becomes apparent in some amazing scenes using surrealistic techniques. First we see Olivia/Frony, in Act II, Scene One, as three ministers are waiting to "say goodbye" to the Bishop. Who they are, where they are going, or why, is not told. Two of the ministers are shown in by Frony. She then brings in Noah, Olivia's natural father. The Bishop asks him to stay, and the following dreamlike ritual takes place—

> (*The MINISTERS stand on either side of table and toss ball to each other. OLIVIA and FRONY let their hair so fall that it covers back of head and face. They stand with arms around each other's neck and rock to and fro.*)
> OLIVIA.   Ball! Ball!
> FRONY.   That means a little game. Ha! Ha!
>
> (*They continue to rock and measure first hands and then feet. Ball rolls under table. MINISTERS upset table in getting it. BISHOP's hat falls. FIRST MINISTER rubs his head with one hand and hands hat to SECOND MINISTER, who does same and hands hat to NOAH. NOAH takes it and wipes it reluctantly. MINISTERS whisper again.*)
> BISHOP. My hat! Is this a game of ball? My hat!

NOAH. Stay, Bishop, stay! You see just what you
    see!
BISHOP. I Stay! Is this a trick? Then let me learn!
    Even a sober man may smile at whims.
FIRST MINISTER. (*lays ball on table*) Here,
    Bishop!
SECOND MINISTER. (*puts down doll-shoes*)
    Here, Bishop!
THIRD MINISTER. (*enters hurriedly, lays on
    table doll-toys and loaf of bread*) Bishop, look
    well!
FRONY. The game! The game!
OLIVIA. Who'll live to see it out?

(*FIRST and SECOND MINISTERS run to OLIVIA
and FRONY and fan them with their beavers. NOAH
puts BISHOP's beaver on table and goes to door*)
BISHOP. Noah, you go?
NOAH. My wits won't let me stay. (*exit NOAH*)

(*OLIVIA and FRONY put up their hair*)
BISHOP. Things seem to say: "Be philosophical."
    You'd have a game? Let each one take a part.

(*FIRST and SECOND MINISTERS give their hats to
THIRD MINISTER to hold. He bows and holds them
with dignity*)
    Draw near! (*all draw near*) Olivia, take you
      the ball!
    Good Ministers, take each a little shoe!
    The loaf of bread, Frony! (*to THIRD MIN-
      ISTER*)
    Some of the toys?
THIRD MINISTER. Bishop, I'm toying now with
    this headwear
    That wears so well a score of years might fail
    To see its gloss in need of hatter's aid.
    Suppose my grandfather had owned these hats;
    Suppose they came to me as his estate;
    Suppose I brought them to a place like this;
    Suppose I fanned two ladies, side by side;
    Suppose I gave them to a friend to hold;
    Suppose he held them in his sturdy left; (*holds
      them so*)
    Suppose he drew his right and poised it thus;
    (*he draws as though to strike*)
    Suppose—
MINISTERS. We take our beavers back again.
    (*They take them and lay them aside*)
    (*to THIRD MINISTER*) What would you
      have?
    We would not slight you, sir.
THIRD MINISTER. (*walks to FRONY and points
    to bread*) A slight division of the honors here.
OLIVIA. I'll squeeze. (*she squeezes the ball.
    FIRST MINISTER points to SECOND MINIS-
    TER's feet and to little shoes*)
FIRST MINISTER. How many pairs will make a
    pair?

(*FRONY looks at bread as though she would eat it*)
FRONY. My teeth are many years younger than I.
THIRD MINISTER. (*aside*) I do not ask for a
    division there.

The Bishop then admits that—

    These trinkets seem to tell a sober tale.

He launches into a sermon on how his "misguided"
people need to learn handicrafts.

But what is the significance of Olivia's and Frony's
letting their hair fall over their faces and rocking to and
fro together? They seem in this action to be prophetesses
who know more than they are willing to tell, hiding
secrets of the future and also refusing to watch the
childish game of the ministers. They know, perhaps,
that it is far from the whole story.

Nevertheless, Olivia encourages the Bishop in his interpretations: the ball is progress; the little shoes show
"how scant our footing is"; the doll-toys are "the many
things we need to learn to make." But Olivia is surely
being ironic when she says: How far we looked to learn a
truth that's taught by jingling pots and pans. After the
ministers and Noah have gone, "OLIVIA holds the
BISHOP's beaver and motions him to toss the ball. He
does. She catches it in hat."

    OLIVIA. My hat! Is this a game of ball? My hat!
    BISHOP. Olivia my child, it is a game
      Of progress that I riddled out for you.

    (*She puts hat on table*)

Then Olivia and the Bishop exchange opposing views of
Caleb, and Olivia describes her ideal man, with strong
implications that Caleb, at least potentially, has these
qualities. The Bishop laughs scornfully and picks up his
hat to go. As he puts it on, the ball falls out—so the
Bishop really does not have the ball of progress in his
hat after all.

This strange scene in Act II Is perhaps the most
revealing key to a hidden message running counter to
the flag-waving glorification of good old American hard
manual labor in the final act. That simple solution is
here made to seem ridiculous. Yet later Olivia herself
espouses it when the Bishop visits her school. Several
thematic levels are thus interwoven throughout, as we
have seen, and their puzzling juxtaposition was very
likely intended to conceal a militance that Cotter hinted
in his Preface would be "dangerous."

In another surrealistic, expressionistic scene at Olivia's
school in Act III, Frony and the mysterious Woman
come in with Olivia's book entitled *The Negro and His
Hands* and go through actions that seem to signify
something quite opposed to Olivia's official enthusiasm
in the same scene for her pupil's learning useful trades.

    (*Enter FRONY and WOMAN with OLIVIA's book.
    They sit back to back and search books....*)
    FRONY. (*to WOMAN*) What seek you?
    WOMAN. What seek you?
    FRONY. A laugh.
    WOMAN. Find it!
    (*They search books*)

The pupils go on working and Olivia directs them,
paying no attention to her other selves, Frony and the
Woman. Then—

    FRONY. Ha! Ha!
    WOMAN. You found the laugh? Where?

FRONY. Nowhere! I laughed to cheer me up to
find the laugh.
WOMAN. You might have made me laugh a real
laugh.
FRONY. Do laugh! A real laugh! 'Twill bring
again the bloom—
FRONY. And WOMAN (*pointing to each other*)
You lost some twenty years ago.
FRONY. (*holds up book*) The laugh is here.
WOMAN. How know you that?
FRONY. The book
Was written by Olivia.
WOMAN. (*Holds up book and strikes it*) 'Tis here.
(*Drops book, laughs, and runs out*)

This "laugh" Frony and the Woman are looking for
could have several interesting meanings. It could be
making fun of the simplicity of the handiwork ethic. It
could signify the ridiculousness of the intelligent Olivia's having written a simpleminded book about that
ethic. It could stand for the free enjoyment of life that
the dull industrial training is squashing. It certainly
shows ambivalence in the Olivia/Frony/Other Woman
character.

Caleb is, of course, the other main character, and, in
spite of his "degeneracy," comes through as a tragic
hero, not quite in the ancient Greek sense, but in many
ways close to it.

But what kind of hero is this, who begins by killing his
father and then heartlessly sells the body? He says to the
undertaker who has come to offer his services:

CALEB. A thirty-dollar coffin! I say no!
Five dollars for a robe? No, deathworm, no!
Four carriages? No, undertaker, no!
Think you a son must curb his appetite
Because a pauper father breathes no more?
The living must have money! I'm alive!
Cold dignity is all the dead require.
The living must have money! Hear you that!

Caleb's behavior is so outrageous and Olivia's belief in
him so unbelievable that we must look for a subtler
signification. In the above speech, Caleb may be symbolically asserting the right of the living, new generation
to have their needs met, because they will be the doers
for the future. It might seem selfish, but it is necessary.
After his mother dies later in the play, Caleb repeats this
theme by simply saying, "She's dead? Then bury her."
Further, can we not see Caleb's killing of his father as
not a real murder but a symbol of the need for a
courageous young generation to overthrow tradition and
the unproductive ways of their fathers?

A parallel, although not so drastic, symbol reinforcing
the same theme appears when Caleb pulls off Noah's
beard. It is as though the old patriarch, the rescuer and
then founder of his people, has lived too long. Caleb
deprives him of his strength, just as Samson's strength
was in his hair. When Noah cries, "My beard is being
wasted," Caleb replies, "My strength is not."

Another motive for Caleb's "degeneracy" is his belief in
the teachings of the false prophet, Rahab, who is

collecting funds to lead Blacks back to Africa. He is
exposed as a scoundrel by Olivia and her followers, and
he too dies in what Cotter presents as a well-merited
death.

Caleb's self-awareness is expressed in his last speech
before he tries to stab himself:
CALEB. O, God, if I have sinned because the
blood
Thou gavest me was tainted ere my birth,
Whose is the wrong? Whose is the reckoning?
Master, I leave it all with thee—with thee.
Men sneer and say: "Be guided by your will!"
I have no will! I never had a will!
Thy fate, O god, did rob me of my will!

Here Caleb is of course still the rebel, flinging the blame
at God, but he recognizes that a lack of will power was
his fated and fatal flaw. Here in an interesting variation,
is the Greek tragic hero's hubris and his fated punishment for it. Caleb is certainly not a villain of the
melodramas popular when this play was written. Neither is he a true Greek tragic hero, but in many ways a
full-blooded Shakespearean one with all his complications.

Although the title of the play names Caleb, we earlier
identified Olivia as the central character and suggested
that all others can be interpreted in relation to her. As
we should expect, Olivia's direct and indirect speeches
about Caleb give us the strongest indexes to what Cotter
wanted to convey in the construction of the complex
character of Caleb.

Olivia sets the tone of her feeling about Caleb in the first
act, by saying firmly, both before and after the Bishop's
objections: "Caleb's the man! Caleb's the man!" Even
after she hears he has killed his father, she persists in her
plans to marry him. Yet, as observed earlier, there is no
real romance between Olivia and Caleb, and only the
one brief wordless meeting on stage. Their relationship
is an expression, rather, of a significant idea about the
"Needs of the American Negro" of the subtitle. That
idea is made clear in Act II, when Olivia describes her
ideal man to the Bishop. He senses that she is speaking
of what Caleb might have been had he not misused his
gifts. But she is also describing an ideal man quite
different from Booker T. Washington's ideal humble
manual laborer—

BISHOP. Your ideal man?
OLIVIA. I have him.
BISHOP. Let me hear.

First the sassy Olivia answers with a series of ridiculous
paradoxes, but the Bishop persists—

BISHOP. That character's impossible! Again!
OLIVIA. His is an eye that runs compassion's
length.
His is a tongue that snares the simplest words
Round simplest thoughts in beauty's fadeless
mesh.
Such art as his the soul of man endears
Through all the silences of all the years.

Right-fettered and full-faced he halts him by
Each column wrong has builded to the sky.
He flaws each flaw until proof-laden runs
Faith's highest hope past earth and stars and
    suns.
BISHOP. That is not Caleb—
OLIVIA. Well you know 'tis not.
BISHOP. Again!
OLIVIA. How many think you I possess?
BISHOP. What think you of his creed—his
    atheist's creed
He thundered it into his mother's ears.
He blurted it above his father's corpse.
OLIVIA. I think not of it now. I do not wish.
Accept the creed of strenuous modern life?
BISHOP. Of strenuous modern life? Well, let me
    hear.
OLIVIA. God makes a man. Conditions make his
    creed.
When reason's torch has once been kindled
    by
the vicious fancies of the ignorant
And fueled by the greed and soullessness
That stamp eternal vengeance everywhere,
The human in us often scoffs and says:
"There is no God nor Heaven to be found."
Hope is the star that lights self unto self.
Faith is the hand that clutches self's decree.
Mercy is oil self keeps for its own ills.
Justice is hell made present by a blow.
Conditions, therefore, make this creed I hold:
"God-like I strive, but man-like I rebel!"
Man is most man, and, therefore, most like
    God
When he does weigh life's actions in such
    scales
As balance not for his sufficiency,
But quiver till the All-intelligence
Applies a power whose name is very truth.
Great men, not creeds, will have the right of
    way.
BISHOP. (*he calls as to one far off*) Caleb! Caleb!
You have the right of way.
A great man, you? Ha! ha! . . . .
(*bows to* OLIVIA) Ha! ha! . . . .
OLIVIA. Great men, not creeds, will have the
    right of way.
They clash in every age; and clashing strip
Some worn-out garment from the limbs of
    Truth.
Should one put forth his eager hand and touch
Truth's perfect robes they would entangle it
And hold it captive till God's reckoning time.

This "creed of strenuous modern life" is militant and revolutionary. And above it, having "the right of way," are great men, who clash with creeds "in every age." In Olivia's eyes, Caleb could have achieved that kind of greatness.

These brave words are in the Second Act; Caleb's death (as Washington-imago), the most moving scene in the play, comes much later. Olivia has saved her School for Industrial Arts, but she has lost the "great man" she had sought as her mate. A strong wild man became degenerate, was defeated, then died.

In *Caleb, the Degenerate* Cotter attempted in dramatic form the same strategy that his friend and fellow Afro-

American poet Paul Laurence Dunbar wrote of so movingly:

We wear the mask that grins and lies,
It hides our cheeks and shades our eyes,—
This debt we pay to human guile;
With torn and bleeding hearts we smile,
And mouth with myriad subtleties.

That the mask Cotter donned was this strangely beautiful and complex drama, *Caleb, the Degenerate,* is an answer to Dunbar's cry, because, as we have seen, it is a mask we can see through, if we will. It is "beauty's fadeless mesh" spoken of by Olivia in her lines about her ideal man—

His is a tongue that snares the simplest words
Round simplest thoughts in beauty's fadeless
    mesh,
Such art as his the soul of man endears
Through all the silences of all the years.

(pp. 39-52)

Betty Cain, "Wearing the Mask: Joseph S. Cotter Sr.'s 'Caleb, the Degenerate'," in MELUS, *Vol. 5, No. 3, Fall, 1978, pp. 37-53.*

FURTHER READING

Jones, Paul W. L. "Two Kentucky Poets." *The Voice of the American Negro* III, No. VII (July 1906): 583-88.
Descriptive sketch of Cotter's life and work.

Kerlin, Robert T. "A Poet from Bardstown." *The South Atlantic Quarterly* XX, No. 3 (July 1921): 213-21.
Survey of Cotter's poetry and fiction that finds philosophical, didactic, and lyrical qualities in his work.

Molette, Carlton W. "The First Afro-American Theater." *Negro Digest* XIX, No. 6 (April 1970): 4-9.
Argues that *Caleb, the Degenerate* has been unfairly dismissed by critics who evaluated it without taking into account the particular traditions and cultural milieu out of which it arose.

Redmond, Eugene B. "Jubilees, Jujus, and Justices." In his *Drum Voices: The Mission of Afro-American Poetry*, pp. 83-138. Garden City, N.Y.: Anchor Press, 1976.
Contains a brief overview of Cotter's work. Redmond states: "Cotter . . . it must be said, was among the first black poets to represent, without shame and minstrelsy, authentic black folk life . . . . He achieves 'rushing rhythms and ingenious rhymes' when he is at his best; and a quiet, reflective perseverance when he writes introspectively."

Shockley, Ann Allen. "Joseph S. Cotter, Sr.: Biographical Sketch of a Black Louisville Bard." *College Language Association Journal* XVIII, No. 3 (March 1975): 327-40.
Overview of Cotter's life and works.

Thompson, R. W. "Negroes Who Are Doing Things: Joseph Seamon Cotter." *Alexander's Magazine,* No. 1 (15 August 1905): 25-6.

> Sketch of Cotter's life and literary career. Thompson states: "Cotter was a 'born poet' and a happy storyteller. Every sentiment, incident, or chain of events illustrative of human nature, appeals to his sensitive mind, and is gathered up by his constructive genius into a finite tale or verse."

Watkins, Thomas G. "The Author." In *Caleb, the Degenerate,* by Joseph S. Cotter. Louisville: Bradley and Gilbert Co., 1903.

> Biographical sketch. Watkins praises Cotter for surmounting personal and social obstacles "undreamed of by Burns and other sons of song who struggled up from poverty, obscurity, and ignorance to glory."

Countee Cullen

1903-1946

(Full name Countee Leroy Porter) American poet, novelist, critic, and dramatist.

Cullen was one of the foremost poets of the Harlem Renaissance, a cultural movement of unprecedented creative achievement among black American writers, musicians, and artists centered in the Harlem section of New York City during the 1920s. While Cullen strove to establish himself as the author of romantic poetry on such universal topics as love and death, he also wrote numerous poems treating contemporary racial issues, and it is for these that he is best remembered.

The facts of Cullen's early years are uncertain, and Cullen himself maintained a lifelong reticence about his youth. Scholars have determined that he was born in Louisville, Kentucky, and then raised in New York City by his paternal grandmother. Following her death in 1918, he was adopted by the Reverend and Mrs. Frederick Cullen of the Salem Methodist Episcopal Church in Harlem. In the home of his adoptive parents, Cullen was exposed to religious concerns and political issues of the day, as Reverend Cullen had helped found the National Urban League and served as president of the local chapter of the National Association for the Advancement of Colored People (NAACP). An excellent student, Cullen attended DeWitt Clinton High School, then New York's premier preparatory school, before enrolling at New York University in 1922. During high school and college Cullen placed poems in campus and national publications and won numerous literary prizes, beginning with second place in the Witter Bynner Poetry Contest for undergraduates for *The Ballad of the Brown Girl. Color,* Cullen's first volume of poetry, was published in 1925, the same year he graduated from New York University. After completing a graduate degree at Harvard University, Cullen returned to New York, where he was already considered a leading literary figure of the Harlem Renaissance, and began writing a column on literary and social issues for *Opportunity,* the journal of the National Urban League. He published several volumes of poetry and edited *Caroling Dusk: An Anthology of Verse by Negro Poets* (1927). During the late 1920s and early 1930s Cullen's poetic output declined, and critics maintain that the poems of this period do not fulfill the potential he had demonstrated in his earlier works. Turning his attention to other forms of writing, he published *One Way to Heaven* (1932), a novel that was praised for its accurate portrayal of Harlem life, and stories and verse for children. In the mid-1940s Cullen began preparing a definitive collection of those poems he considered his best: *On These I Stand: An Anthology of the Best Poems of Countee Cullen* was published in 1947, the year after his death.

Believing that good literature transcends race, Cullen stated that he wanted to be recognized as a poet, not a "Negro poet." Nevertheless, critics have asserted that he often seemed uncertain about the purpose of his poetry, and Alan R. Shucard has suggested that Cullen often appeared "to vacillate between playing the pure aesthete and the racial spokesman." Cullen himself reflected in an interview, "In spite of myself...I find that I am actuated by a strong sense of race consciousness. This grows upon me, I find, as I grow older, and although I struggle against it, it colors my writing, I fear, in spite of everything I can do." Among his best-known poems are "Yet Do I Marvel," which focuses on the perceived contradiction between his status as a member of an oppressed race and his poetic skill; "Incident," which relates the experience of an eight-year-old child who is the object of a racial slur; and "Uncle Jim," in which a young man is warned by his uncle of the differences between blacks and whites in American society. In other poems Cullen combined racial and religious issues. "The Black Christ," for example, recounts the lynching and resurrection of a Southern black man. Such poems as "Heritage" reflect the tension Cullen felt between his identification with Christian values and tradition and his desire to claim an African heritage. Although occasionally criticized for displaying Cullen's ignorance about Africa, "Heritage" is widely considered his finest poem. The issue of racial identity is also raised in some of Cullen's love poems, notably "A Song of Praise," in which Cullen considered differences between loving a black woman and loving a white one. Cullen reworked a traditional English verse in *The Ballad of the Brown Girl* (1927), the story of Lord Thomas, who must choose between a white maiden and a "brown girl." While Cullen's interpretation of the story has occasionally been questioned because critics disagree whether the original ballad signified racial or social differences, the poem was one of his first major successes.

Cullen believed that poetry consisted of "lofty thoughts beautifully expressed," and he preferred poetic forms characterized by dignity and control. He wrote a number of sonnets and used quatrains, couplets, and conventional rhyme, frequently incorporating religious imagery and classical allusions. While some critics have praised Cullen's skill at traditional versification, others suggest that his style was not suited to the treatment of contemporary racial issues and that his adherence to conventional forms resulted in poems that are insincere and unconvincing. Despite the controversy surrounding his traditional poetic style and his ambivalence toward racial subject matter in art, Cullen remains an important figure in black American literature.

(For further information about Cullen's life and works, see *Black Writers; Concise Dictionary of American Literary Biography, 1917-1929; Contemporary Authors,* Vols. 108, 124; *Dictionary of Literary Biography,* Vols. 4, 48, 51; *Something about the Author,* Vol. 18; and *Twentieth-Century Literary Criticism,* Vols. 4, 37. For related criticism, see the entry on the Harlem Renaissance in *Twentieth-Century Literary Criticism,* Vol. 26.)

PRINCIPAL WORKS

Color (poetry) 1925
The Ballad of the Brown Girl: An Old Ballad Retold (poem) 1927
Caroling Dusk: An Anthology of Verse by Negro Poets [editor] (poetry) 1927
Copper Sun (poetry) 1927
The Black Christ, and Other Poems (poetry) 1929
One Way to Heaven (novel) 1932
The Medea, and Some Poems (poetry and drama) 1935
The Lost Zoo (A Rhyme for the Young, but Not Too Young) (poetry) 1940
My Lives and How I Lost Them (juvenile fiction) 1942
On These I Stand: An Anthology of the Best Poems of Countee Cullen (poetry) 1947
My Soul's High Song: The Collected Writings of Countee Cullen, Voice of the Harlem Renaissance (poetry, novel, and essays) 1991

Babette Deutsch (essays date 1925)

[*In the following 1925* Nation and Athenaeum *review, Deutsch explores race-consciousness in Cullen's first volume of poetry,* Color.]

[The lyrics in **Color**] by the youngest of the Negro poets—Countee Cullen is just past his majority—are likely to be considered less as the work of a gifted individual than as the utterance of a gifted, and enslaved, people. And indeed Mr. Cullen's poems are intensely race-conscious. He writes out of the pain of inflamed memories, and with a wistful harking back to the primitive heritage of his own folk. The peculiar flavor which the book gets from the fact that it was written by a colored man is to be had most sharply in the first section, from which the volume takes its title. This tang is the essence of such pieces as **"Atlantic City Waiter," "Fruit of the Flower,"** and **"Heritage,"** with their insistence on the savage past; it is the essence, too, of the lovely **"Song of Praise,"** and of that shrewd lyric "To My Fairer Brethren." ... (p. 763)

Again and again Mr. Cullen strikes the harsh note which carries the scorn of the oppressed, the arrogance of the insulted and injured. He is engaged by the somber power and terrible brilliance of Africa as a Jew might be engaged by the purple days of Solomon's glory, or as the Gael is moved by the bright bloody history of his island. The poem by which Mr. Cullen is perhaps best known, **"The Shroud of Color,"** could have been written only by a Negro. It is a piece which, in spite of its sad lack of concision and its many cliches, yet abounds in true spiritual vigor.

But though one may recognize that certain of Mr. Cullen's verses owe their being to the fact that he shares the tragedy of his people, it must be owned that the real virtue of his work lies in his personal response to an experience which, however conditioned by his race, is not so much racial as profoundly human. The color of his mind is more important than the color of his skin. The faint acridness that gives an edge to many of these lyrics is a quality which one finds in Housman, or even in the minor strains of Herrick and of Horace. There is, for example, the song **"To a Brown Girl"**; and the same pungency is felt in the companion piece, **"To a Brown Boy,"** or in **"Wisdom Cometh with the Years."** The twenty-eight rhymed **"Epitaphs"** have, almost without exception, a pure Gallic salt, as witness the one **"For a Lovely Lady"**:

> A creature slender as a reed,
>   And sad-eyed as a doe
> Lies here (but take my word for it,
>   And do not pry below).

And even in what might be called his African poems it is Mr. Cullen's endowment of music and imagery and emotional awareness that matters, over and above the presence of jungle shapes and shadows.

These excellences—fantasy, lyricism, and fine sensitiveness—the book undoubtedly has. It has also faults, the faults of youth. The poet does not shrink from such rubber-stamp phrases as "costly fee," "crimson vintage," "ensanguined mead," "coral lips." He clutches at stars and clings to dreams like any neophyte, and lives in the pleasant reassurance that after death he will return to talk to his love "in liquid words of rain." But there seems little doubt that he will shed these puerilities before his youth is over, that he will discipline and develop his unquestionable gift. (pp. 763-64)

> *Babette Deutsch, "Let It Be Allowed," in* The Nation and the Athenaeum, *Vol. CXXI, No. 3156, December 30, 1925, pp. 763-64.*

Mark Van Doren (essay date 1926)

[*Van Doren was one of the most prolific men of letters in twentieth-century American writing. His work includes poetry (for which he won the Pulitzer Prize in 1939), novels, short stories, drama criticism, social commentary, and the editing of a number of popular anthologies. In the following 1926 review, he assesses the strengths and weaknesses of* Color.]

There are numerous things which Mr. Cullen as a poet has not yet begun to do, and there are some which he will never do, but in this first volume he makes it clear that he has mastered a tune. Few recent books of poems have been so tuneful—at least so tuneful in the execution of significant themes. Probably that accounts for the almost instantaneous success of Mr. Cullen when he began not long ago to appear in the magazines. He had something to say, and he sang it.

What he had to say was nothing new even in his own generation. Edna Millay had said as much and more, and she had employed something like the same melodies. Mr. Cullen's **"The Shroud of Color"** could be referred back, if one wished to treat it that way, to "Renascence"; **"Saturday's Child"** and **"Fruit of the Flower"** have also their counterpart in Miss Millay's most piquant and interesting pieces—those sketching a spiritual heritage. But Mr. Cullen is not seriously damaged by the reference; first, because he obviously means what he sings and, second, because he has an accent of his own.

Mr. Cullen's skill appears in the clarity and the certainty of his song. Those who have tried to do a similar thing will be in the best position to appreciate the success of the following lines from the poem which prefaces the volume:

> Soon every sprinter,
>   However fleet,
> Comes to a winter
>   Of sure defeat:
> Though he may race
>   Like the hunted doe,
> Time has a pace
>   To lay him low.

> Soon we who sing,
>   However high,
> Must face the Thing
>   We cannot fly.
> Yea, though we fling
>   Our notes to the sun,
> Time will outsing
>   Us every one.

The theme of this poem is the shortness of life—a sacred theme for lyric poets always—and Mr. Cullen is so full of it that there is actually something joyous in the cadences with which he pays it his respects. The paradox is not surprising, perhaps, but it is attractive—the paradox of youth declaring that Time is a terrible enemy, and yet declaring this gayly, as if there were something delicious in the terror which the thought of death had inspired. The theme appears again and again in *Color,* in forming the love poems with that doctrine which we know best through the two words *carpe diem,* and imparting vitality to whatever pieces assert the preciousness of the present moment.

> Now I am young and a fool for love,
>   My blood goes mad to see
> A brown girl pass me like a dove
>   That flies melodiously.

> Let me be lavish of my tears.
>   And dream that false is true;
> Though wisdom cometh with the years,
>   The barren days come, too.

The prefatory poem, from which the first quotation was taken, is too long; ten further stanzas do little more than repeat the thought and beat it thin. If Mr. Cullen faces any danger it is this—that he shall call facility a virtue rather than the aspect of a virtue. Other poems here are too long for their content, and certain poems should not be here at all. It seems important both for Mr. Cullen and for the race which he so admirably represents that he should not hurry his next book into the world.

> *Mark Van Doren, "Countee Cullen Commences," in* New York Herald Tribune Books, *January 10, 1926, p. 3.*

James Weldon Johnson (essay date 1931)

[*Johnson was one of the most versatile and accomplished black writers of the twentieth century. As critic, poet, essayist, editor, autobiographer, teacher, consul, and civil rights activist, he championed major black causes of his day, strongly emphasizing race pride. One of his best-known poems, "Fifty Years," published in 1913 on the fiftieth anniversary of the Emancipation Proclamation, sums up his views: "This land is ours by right of birth,/This land is ours by right of toil;/We helped to turn its virgin earth,/Our sweat is in its fruitful soil." In the following excerpt from the 1931 revision of his* Book of American Negro Poetry, *he evaluates claims that Cullen is not "a Negro poet."*]

One of Cullen's earliest poems, **"I Have a Rendezvous with Life,"** reveals him as an adventurer in spirit. Even as a boy he had a lively and penetrating curiosity about life, and this quality in him is the mainspring of nearly all his poetry. It is the chief reason that the body of his poetry, young as he is, constitutes a "criticism of life." It does this more completely than the work of any other of the major Negro poets.

Cullen is a fine and sensitive lyric poet, belonging to the classic line. The modern innovators have had no influence on him. His models are Keats and Shelley, and he might be called a younger brother of Housman. He never bids for popular favor through the use of bizarre effects either in manner or subject matter. He would disdain anything approaching sensationalism. All of his work is laid within the lines of the long-approved English patterns. And by that very gauge a measure of his gifts and powers as a poet may be taken. These old forms come from his hands filled with fresh beauty. A high test for a poet in this blasé age.

Some critics have ventured to state that Cullen is not an authentic Negro poet. This statement, of necessity, involves a definition of "a Negro poet" and of "Negro poetry." There might be several definitions framed, but the question raised is a pure irrelevance. Also there is in it a faint flare-up of the old taboo which would object to the use of "white" material by the Negro artist, or at least, regard it with indulgent condescension. Cullen himself has declared that, in the sense of wishing for consideration or allowances on account of race or of recognizing for himself any limitation to "racial" themes and forms, he has no desire or intention of being a Negro poet. In this he is not only within his right; he is right.

Yet, strangely, it is because Cullen revolts against these "racial" limitations—technical and spiritual—that the best of his poetry is motivated by race. He is always seeking to free himself and his art from these bonds. He never entirely escapes, but from the very fret and chafe he brings forth poetry that contains the quintessence of race-consciousness. It is through his power to deepen and heighten these inner experiences that he achieves his finest work. It is pardonable for me to repeat here that the two most poignant lines in American literature, lines that surged up from the vortex of these experiences, are in the sonnet of his in which he expresses the faith that God can explain all the puzzling paradoxes of life; then gathering up an infinity of irony, pathos and tragedy in the final couplet, says:

> Yet do I marvel at this curious thing
> To make a poet black and bid him sing.

Cullen's poetry demonstrates high lyric quality, sure artistry, rich imagination, and intellectual content. He has, too, the gift for witty and the power for epigrammatic expression. Pessimism is, perhaps, the pervading note in his poetry—it is in this note that he often sings of the ephemeral quality of love—but rarely does he fail to give it a sudden ironic turn that raises it above pathos or peevishness. (pp. 219-21)

James Weldon Johnson, "Countee Cullen," in The Book of American Negro Poetry, *edited by James Weldon Johnson, revised edition, Harcourt Brace Jovanovich, Inc., 1931, pp. 219-31.*

The Times Literary Supplement (essay date 1932)

[*In the following 1932 review of* One Way to Heaven, *the anonymous critic argues that the novel is structurally flawed.*]

Mr. Countee Cullen's **One Way to Heaven** opens with Sam Lucas, professional religionist, "tricking God" at a Methodist revival: his pretended conversion makes a devout convert of Mattie Johnson. It closes with the dying Sam, who has married, deserted and attempted to murder Mattie, tricking his wife from worthier motives into the belief that he has found a way to Heaven. It would not be true to say that this novel—the first by a writer with an established reputation among the coloured poets of America—has two plots: it scarcely has one. But there are two moods, corresponding to the two scenes in Harlem in which the action is laid, and to the two social classes of the actors. On the one hand are Sam, ticket-chopper in a movie-house; Mattie, a domestic servant who prefers a coloured mistress, however eccentric, to a white; and Aunt Maudy, an odd blend of devotion, shrewdness and negro credulity; on the other the refined and cultured circle revolving round polysyllabic Mrs. Brandon, her *soirées* and her more social than literary Booklovers' Society. Constancia Brandon's *salon,* as the "tall, fair-haired, imbibing Englishman" was astonished to find, was the one place in America where freedom of speech was a reality: it was "like a patch of Hyde Park." Yet this Englishman was not alone in his embarrassment when Constancia arranged for a fierce and bitter white professor to lecture to her coloured friends on "The Menace of the Negro to our American Civilization."

The freedom from race-consciousness of the social booklovers is unreal because Mr. Cullen is gently satirical, kindly sceptical, in his treatment of the "movements" of the *intelligentsia* of Harlem. The religion of Mattie, of Aunt Maudy, of the revivalist preachers, is real enough to themselves; but, because the author of **"The Black Christ"** wishes—or so it seems—to avoid expressing in his novel the intimately personal experiences which his poetry expresses, there is an unreality compounded of unwillingness to interpret the scenes and emotions described and uncertainty of presentation. In the result, though particular incidents are very poignantly related, there is no cohesion in at least those portions of the book that deal with the lower of the two social strata. Either by itself would have presented a self-sufficient model; together they require a far larger canvas than Mr. Cullen has allowed himself, and a more clearly defined attitude—whether practical or satirical—towards the sociological problems involved.

A review of "One Way to Heaven," in The Times Literary Supplement, *No. 1612, December 22, 1932, p. 976.*

Blyden Jackson (essay date 1946)

[*In the following excerpt from an essay first published in* The Journal of Negro Education *in 1946, Jackson discusses the effect of Cullen's aestheticism on his depiction of Africa and presentation of racial themes in his poetry.*]

Cullen's passing is lamentable. He was in many good ways an exceptional individual, and he was, beyond any caviling, one of the very best artists yet to emerge from our American Negro community. But he was not good enough. He fell too far short of epic achievement. He himself said in *Caroling Dusk* that he wished "any merit that may be in ... my work to flow from it solely as the expression of a poet—with no racial consideration to bolster it up." As a writer, or as a champion of a minority group, he could not, of course, have taken any other stand and been respectable. People who oppose segregation, as Cullen did, and everyone of us should, must fight it all down the line. As a poet, therefore, it was important to Cullen that his race should not bar him from a universal audience on universal terms. He who also once said of some apparently Tory folks— " ... they do not know that you, / John Keats, keep revel with me too"—was right in his consciousness of our desperate need to think in absolutes. That way, and that way alone, lies the only road that can establish Negro artists upon significant positions in an enduring culture. For commercial success or for transient celebrity we can produce picturesque vignettes of what too many people would like to suppose our whole life is—a cute, though rather savage, exoticism. But in so doing we are guilty of high treason to our best, indeed, our only, hope. Or we can press, as Cullen did, toward the mark of a high calling, and be, at the very worst, as Cullen was, a failure whose constructive elements, particularly in his youth, justify sympathetic and attentive regard by subsequent artists with irreproachable aspirations.

What then has Cullen to teach us? Surely his grand strategy was a campaign against cultural isolationism, for he saw very clearly that the interaction of art and society was a fact, and an important fact. Moreover, on the issue of integration he did not reason too simply. He had grasped the distinction, given wide currency by Howard Odum, between regionalism and sectionalism, between local emphases that act centripetally, strengthening even while they diversify a cultural unity, and local emphases of centrifugal, and, consequently, separatist, effect only. Thus reasoning, therefore, he could quite properly identify cultural isolationism with sectionalism and define genuine regionalism as a desirable factor in a well-rounded national literature. His major premises, then, left apparently nothing to be desired. But his operations did; and the reasons, probably, are not far to seek.

To begin with, Cullen as a person was a paradox—indeed, with master irony, he was the very sort of paradox that proved most bitterly his central credo that segregation is not a law of creation. Largely reared in New York City as the foster son of a minister, schooled there, graduated Phi Beta Kappa from New York University, with a Master of Arts degree from Harvard, Cullen was—in spite of his insistence that "his chief problem has been that of reconciling a Christian upbringing with a pagan inclination" and his sincere, in so far as he was aware, nostalgia for what he considered African moods—a well-bred American Aryan with a bourgeois background. All his life, without being conscious of his affectation, Cullen was trying to pass for a Negro. One illustration will here have to suffice.

Cullen, there is no need for anyone to suppose with guile, was much preoccupied with the paganism he considered so much a part of himself that, as he put it:

> God's alabaster turrets gleam
> Too high for me to win
> Unless he turns his face and lets
> Me bring my own gods in.

Moreover, Cullen thought of this paganism as African, as an atavism that unmistakably determined his cultural descent. But the truth is that Cullen's paganism was no more African than Visigothic, both of which it was far too sophisticated to have been. His Africa was a seventeenth-century pastoral; his paganism, Pan in a witch-doctor role. As Granville Hicks, thinking of E. E. Cummings and his fellows, has pointed out, the college generation to which Cullen belonged produced in its artists aesthetes—gentlemen who, if the one of them quoted by Hicks to support his thesis can be believed, "had no interest in social problems ... read Casanova in French and Petronius in Latin, discussed Pater's prose, and argued about the voluptuousness of the church and the virtue of prostitution." How Cullen encountered Casanova and Petronius, if he tarried with them at all, I do not presume to know (although, curiously enough, the number of Magdalens he romanticizes in his verse is one form of documentary evidence fitting him to Hicks's formula and allying him with Hicks's dilettantes), but that Pater would hardly have been distressed by the Africa configured within the "copper sun and the scarlet sea" can hardly be doubted. For this synthetic continent lay in an aesthete's realm, discernible, with appropriate vagueness only, through a misty atmosphere of neo-Hellenism. The spicy grove, the cinnamon tree, the throbbing drums, the "cruel padded feet treading out, in the body's street, a jungle track," how pleasant the sensations they could set atingle in the blood of an Oxford don sipping tea between snatches of easygoing talk in his tranquil study, or how sweet the shocks they could start in the nerves of a pale student pining, in his imagist's ivory tower beside the Harvard Yard, to be consumed in a hard gem-like flame.

By the 1920s the real black man's Africa was no secret. Marcus Garvey had too many bright uniforms, but still a closer view of it than any aesthete. He at least saw it, though with a tragically illiterate concept of economics and politics and in terms primarily rooted in its exploitation. But whoever looked at Africa clear-eyed could see it plainly for what it was, with its leprosy, its elephantiasis, its human and animal filth, its harsh native codes in the diamond mines of South Africa, its ghastly memories of Leopold's "free state" and of the older Goering's wholesale extinction of a people in the quondam German colonies, its lack of sanitation, of machinery, of capital, of leadership, of power, of knowledge, but not without hope and not, for all its want of an Isles-of-Greece or Land-of-the-Lotos glamour in itself or in anything it had ever been, without a past that could be reliably, yet movingly, interpreted.

But Cullen's paganism had no source in any Africa, present or past. Substantially there was no difference between it and the vision of the dark continent that a kindly disposed white man of Cullen's temperament would have concocted. Yet while Cullen's romantic glorification of a non-Nordic universe demonstrated in its terms how white he was, it did psychologically answer other purposes as a means of defense and escape. As a defense it was part of Cullen's answer to the extravagant code of insult directed by his own social order against any Negro's self-respect. Cullen's environment bombarded him with its derogations of everything black, studied affronts to his dignity, Jemimas on the billboards, Gold-Dust twins in the magazine advertisements, Stepin Fetchits on the movie screen, a scornful silence in the history books. So Cullen fought back. He found "pride in clean, brown limbs," and "a brown girl's swagger" giving "a twitch to beauty like a queen." Once at least he flailed out too blindly:

> Who lies with his milk-white maiden
> Bound in the length of her pale gold hair,
> Cooled by her lips with the cold kiss laden,
> He lies, but he loves not there."
>
> Who lies with his nut-brown maiden,
> Bruised to the bone by her sin-black hair,
> Warmed with the wine that her full lips trade in,
> He lies, and his love lies there.

Some men do feel that the blacker the berry, the sweeter the juice. On the other hand only in a moment when he was perplexed to the extreme could Cullen have forgotten that, if anything in this world is unpredictable, it is the way of a man with a maid. The hapless savagery of Cullen's denial that anyone could love a white woman is merely a crescendo note in his rebellion against racism's debasement of everything not white. It was just an obvious example of his defensive instinct operating not wisely, but too well. It was, that is to say, part of the pattern of resistance for the service of which he had invoked his curiously treasonable reproduction of the African past. And it was, under keen analysis, only a little less felicitous. For, like his creation of pre-colonial Africa, it represented emotion run riot.

Cullen's intellect was not on guard when he blasphemed the efficiency of white women as lovers. Neither was his

vigilance as acute as one could wish in the business of making real and meaningful his nonwhite heritage. Yet here one must remember the strength of a vicious circle before he condemns too harshly. It would have required on Cullen's part no *tour de force* to find pregnant and localized symbols for the Western culture whose departure Eliot laments in "Gerontion." Who were the heroes Cullen could name? Theseus, Ulysses, Jason, Aeneas, Siegfried, Beowulf, Roland, Arthur, Galahad, Tristram, Robin Hood, William Tell. What places chimed rich echoes in his legend-making memory? The Troad, the isles of Greece, *Mare Nostrum* and imperial Rome, Camelot, Lyonnesse, perhaps a northern castle ringed with fire. The white man's myths were, willy-nilly, an integral part of Cullen. Could he match the names he had learned in New York, at Harvard, in Europe, with similar symbols from African tradition? Why is his Africa no closer to the Congo than Sicily? Why are the terms in which he seeks its recapture so lacking in concreteness? Why are they the stock images only of the literary artificer? When Robert Frost mends a wall or picks apples in New England the right touch is there, the particular conclusive detail, putting the signature of authenticity upon this Yankee world, but whatever tricks Puck might try upon Shakespeare's groundings they were not fooled. They knew they were in English Arden, not in an Attican grove. And, in spite of Cullen's noble purpose, name his world what he will, it, too, is still his cultural homeland, a province built, like Keats's "realms of gold," from the matter of bards who reign in fealty to Apollo.

The revolt in Cullen's paganism is, then, a revolt in name only. As such it leaves much to be desired. It is an ironic debacle, a case of fighting fire with fire. As a defense mechanism it is hoist upon its own petard, and as an escape device it ends, like all escapist literature, demobilized in a *cul de sac.* Of course, however, to charge Cullen with escapism, or more precisely, with undue escapism (since, obviously, a certain amount of release from this world is an inevitable gratification of artistic enterprise) is to raise something of an issue. For Cullen was an earnest worker. He was no poseur, and, let it never be forgotten, he was not, despite anything that might be said against him, a disreputable artist. Along with a felicity in graceful phrasing and a knack for endowing his verse with an elegant tone, he had high purposes of great value. He wanted Negroes accepted into the human family as casually as other people. As a part of that program he wanted to point up the fact that Negroes, too, have dignity and other favorable qualities. Yet he did not want Negroes stereotyped only as objects of noble pathos either. Quite deliberately he kept these intentions in the forefront of his consciousness. And so the Topsys and the Emperor Joneses are not typical of Cullen's work. Indeed much of his poetry is not "racial" at all. A decade before Frank Yerby's *The Foxes of Harrow* (in 1935, to be exact), Cullen had published his **The Medea and Some Poems;** and in 1940 his delightful little fancy, **The Lost Zoo,** with its Squilililigees, Lapalakes, Ha-Ha-Has, Pussybows, Hoodinkuses-With-the-Double-Head, or Just Hoodinkuses, and their extinct associates, reminded the reading public that even Negroes are capable of pure, pointless, winsome fun. His themes also had the catholicity which his opposition to cultural isolationism implied. If he wrote of brown girls' love he also wrote of love as Robert Herrick or Sir John Suckling would have done; indeed, with even less of local color than these unregenerate Britishers, he pleigned of desire and the sense of loss, of the delights lovers find in being together, of the praise of love and of the anguish that accompanies the recognition of its cruelty. It is true that his long poem, **"The Black Christ,"** is a poem of racial protest, but his equally ambitious **"Medea"** is no more a case of special pleading than its name suggests. In many ways, therefore, Cullen's impulses and his achievements were both estimable. Withal, it should not be overlooked to what extent Cullen was a pioneer and, as such, a person of resolution, integrity, and independence. Surely in doing many of his pieces he was intending to crack a tradition—the same tradition that says, for example, that all Negro sociologists must be experts on the black belt, or that all Negro singers must close their programs with a group of spirituals. In other words, in one respect at least, Cullen was a literary statesman rather than a literary politician, for the politician would have considered his market with a crafty callousness beyond Cullen. All these endearing qualities Cullen had. Yet he also had a taste for beauty as beauty, and this returns us to the escapist element in his poetry.

The aesthetic bias in Cullen is perhaps less noticeable because, according to the calendar at least, he belongs to our generation. Actually, although he probably thought of himself as having preeminent affinities with Keats, Cullen's milieu seems a curious blend of the seventeenth and eighteenth centuries (in England, not Africa or America). Poetry, as Elizabeth Drew and John L. Sweeney persuasively outline its history in their *Directions in Modern Poetry,* appears to alternate between periods of social and individual emphasis. The full-blooded Elizabethan Age was a time when literature was a highly social product. The seventeenth-century reflex was a poetry equally individual, in which the great preoccupations were love and religion, both matters primarily personal. Neo-classicism reflected the corporate disposition of its age. The Romanticists returned again to a major concern with the isolated ego. What were Cullen's abiding interests if they were not love and religion? Sometimes the love might take the form of hate; sometimes the religion might be paganism or aestheticism. Love and religion they still are. Again, did not Cullen prefer the tested diction, the familiar rhythms? Does he not also have his evidences of sensibility and sentimentality? These date his lyricism closer to Samuel Johnson's standards than to the Romanticists, though this might not be a judgment in which Cullen himself would concur. Be that as it may, however, the fact remains that the aesthetes of Cullen's generation are, by and large, experimentalists in radical styles. Whereas Cullen's sense of form is altogether orthodox, their craving after sensations enjoyable to themselves often shows itself in arresting patterns. The

poetry of E.E. Cummings, for instance, is the poetry of a man whose aesthetic predispositions have much to do with the organization of his expression in a manner disturbingly revolutionary to conventional people. The dialogue of Ernest Hemingway is famous for its preoccupation with form, its concern for squeezing into the way the thing is said every possible characteristic overtone, and famous also for its marked stylistic departure from the old school. It would be a gross reader, indeed, who did not immediately become aware of Cummings' spectacular deviations from the norm in his handling of punctuation, word arrangement, typography itself, or of the simplicity *sui generis* of Hemingway's dialogue and his narrative style. Yet that same reader might never think of Cullen as a writer whose appetite for form got the better of him to a degree in which it did not ultimately damage the output of these other two.

The plain truth is that Cullen never had too much to say. Measure him as he himself has suggested, with an absolute yardstick. Try him against the major poet with whom he connected himself, with Keats, and cast up the account. Keats's absorbing preoccupation was with an issue as old as the hills—truth, beauty, mutability, reality, epistemology, ontology. State it how you may, men have been puzzling over this question of the real versus the specious since memory runneth not to the contrary. They still are, of course, and even now, as any sympathetic reader of Wallace Stevens will hasten to testify, continue to say important things about it. Nevertheless "La Belle Dame Sans Merci," though it has fallen on the evil days of dutiful classroom *translation* into literally true vernacular, remains a major attack upon the cult of glamour, just as its concomitant "Ode to a Nightingale" remains a major affirmation of the values beyond glamour's futility. Cullen's **"Heritage"** is an attack on racism. But does it argue against racism as effectively as "La Belle Dame Sans Merci" attacks false standards? It does not. It lacks the plurisigns in which Keats spoke. Keep rereading it and it shrinks. The bitter-edged satire of its closing couplet is the right kind of a *coup de grace, corto y derecho,* short and straight. It stands up under pressure, but the rest of the poem largely goes bad, leaving nothing in the couplet's support. "Sweeney among the Nightingales" is a poem famous for the success with which T. S. Eliot creates and maintains throughout it the required atmosphere of foreboding, so that when, at its end, through the agency of the nightingales Eliot links together the vulgar nonentity, Apeneck Sweeney, with the great Agamemnon in a brilliant play upon the colonel's-lady-and-Judy-O'Grady theme, the effect is tremendous. The whole short lyric is a mighty unit, all the pieces of the orchestra preparing the final consummation. And in "La Belle Dame Sans Merci," also, Keats does not release a word in error. His problem is to build up in his reader's consciousness, more through overtones than otherwise, a sense of the sort of beauty that ought to be repudiated. He wants his reader to have the intimate, absolute knowledge of this treasonable beauty that comes out of feeling it, not by definitions. So Keats's poem is a perfect metaphor made up of subsidiary metaphors all directed to one end, to make real in the terms of art, through a blending of sound with imagery and movement, Keats's concept of the nature of the loveliness that deceives.

But in **"Heritage"** the parts hardly fit. The images resolve themselves, upon analysis, into the pretty and irrelevant confections that they are. There is no way to make them tonally acceptable to the mood of the satire that the situation demands. And just as there is no logic by which the moods of this poem can be synthesized, so is there also a fatal schism in the argument. Cullen, in his use of the African background, seems to be saying essentially, "Look out. I am savage. At any time the real me may burst through this veneer and run amok." But, to say that the heathenism in America is dangerous because it challenges the heathenism in his past is not merely to cheapen the terms of his theme, but also to blunt the appeal of his satire. His "strong bronzed men" and "regal black women" at least are in the right church, for his success as a polemicist. They are obviously meant to imply a fineness, a self-respect, and a self-sufficiency in the African culture that would properly explain and justify his rebellion against the white man's attempts to degrade Cullen for his black ancestry. They build Cullen up properly as a creature of royal lineage for whom only royal treatment is mete. But far too much of the material in **"Heritage"** will neither in sound nor in sense support this good motif. A considerable portion of the poem, on the other hand, is a technicolored jungle that bears substantially the same relation to the real Africa of slave-trading days as Longfellow's delightful Indian preserve—another literary kingdom in which, to borrow Van Wyck Brooks's apt characterization, there is only "the vague myth of a sunset land, a paradise in the West, where the mountains and forests were filled with deer and the lake swarmed with fishes"—bears to the actual pre-Columbian America.

Over Longfellow's happy hunting ground blew the Indians' gentle south wind, Shawondessa, a perfect symbol, not only in its zephyrous image, but even in its delicate luxuries of phonetics, for Longfellow's own genteel aestheticism. And it is Shawondessa, not the sand-bearing, throat-burning harmattan with its harsh implication of life's frequent rigor, which ripples ever so tenderly the pastel vegetation in Cullen's Watteau thickets. It is Shawondessa which passes "Where young forest lovers lie / Plighting troth beneath the sky." It is, indeed, this same Shawondessa, not true, unlearned, aboriginal, violent savagery that Cullen describes himself as feeling in

> ...my sombre flesh and skin
> With the dark blood dammed within
> Like great pulsing tides of wine
> That, I fear, must burst the fine
> Channels of the chafing net
> Where they surge and foam and fret

or as moving

> Through my body, crying, "Strip!

> Doff this new exuberance.
> Come and dance the Lover's Dance!"

So when Cullen asks and answers: "Africa? A book one thumbs / Listlessly, till slumber comes—" he has been honest about his own reaction. Africa has lulled him into sleep, an aesthete's trance, for ultimately the deliciousness of small sensations has captured everything in this poetry. If **"Heritage"** proposed to say something serious or important, or to develop moods consonant with the nature of its theme, those *desiderata* have in the act of realization been, surely unwittingly, forsaken. Cullen has escaped into the enchanted wood whence, undiverted, he can be rapt by the song of the nightingale. These verses cannot be justified by a reader searching in Cullen's poetry for the bread of life, but their tone-coloring is so sensuously worked in and the pictures that they make are such exquisite dreams. They are as escapist as that quatrain of his (in **"Colored Blues Singer,"** not in **"Heritage"**):

> Such songs the mellow-bosomed maids
> Of Africa intone
> For lovers dead in hidden glades,
> Slow rotting flesh and bone,

where the swooning of the sound goes hand-in-glove with the pasteurization of the maids' bosoms and the euphemism of the corpses decomposing inoffensively in the fecund tropics. But escapism, even when it is as relatively innocuous as Cullen's aestheticism, has, in final terms, no positive values for the artist. The aesthetic surrender in **"Heritage"** constitutes a flight, not only from the real world with its complicated pattern of good and bad, its stench and maggots, as well as its "gentle flesh that feeds by the river brink," but also from the technical problems of the poem as a poem, its fusion of voices, its unity of context, its resolution of theme. So it indicates the general manner in which Cullen's aestheticism operated to his detriment, weakening his will, confusing and diluting his effects, turning him astray from the ends toward which he started. So also it leads us, together with his misconstrued paganism, into an understanding of the fact that neither intellectually nor artistically did Cullen possess the mastery without which an artist can never be truly sufficient. So it reminds us that Negro artists may fail on the universal world of art because of individual inadequacies as well as racial vendettas. And thus it carries us as a point of departure toward the consideration of an issue that leads beyond a concern with Cullen only or, for that matter, with any single writer, into a generalization which, sound or not, is certainly evangelical.

The disparity between Cullen's conscious aspirations and his real achievement is all too clear. What he most sincerely desired was a thing in itself right and good. He wanted to write poetry of such quality that it would be read and regarded highly as poetry, not charitably dismissed as "racial" literature. Yet Cullen had neither the intelligence nor the power to speak with superlative effectiveness either as Everyman or as "The Negro." (pp. 43-55)

Blyden Jackson, "Largo for Adonais," in his
The Waiting Years: Essays on American
Negro Literature, *Louisiana State University
Press, 1976, pp. 42-62.*

William Stanley Braithwaite (essay date 1947)

[*Braithwaite was a leading black American editor,
anthologist, autobiographer, and poet. In the following
1947* Opportunity *review of Cullen's posthumously
published* On These I Stand, *he views Cullen as the
most "complete and spontaneous" master of poetic
technique "we have as yet produced."*]

[What] did Countee Cullen stand for as a poet, and as a
poet who was also a Negro? He has given a partial
answer to this question in that famous and often quoted
couplet closing the sonnet **"Yet Do I Marvel."**

> Yet do I marvel at this curious thing:
> To make a poet black, and bid him sing.

Now some critics have demanded that because a poet is
black he must sing always with a social and ethnical
implication, and that his importance lies in the degree to
which his propaganda is vital and colorful rather than in
the quality of his work as an artist. A recent review of
[*On These I Stand*] in an important publication, though
not by a particularly discerning reviewer, made this
demand, and not being satisfied that Countee Cullen
was painfully social or histrionically ethnical denied
him the full accomplishment as a poet to which he is
entitled. Such a mind, and others like it, miss wholly
both the ideas and evocative emotions of poems like
"Heritage" and **"The Black Christ,"** to name but two
poems where the triumphant nature and power of the
poet transcends racial limitations while at the same
time, in treating a racial theme, bestows upon it a
universal significance.

Countee Cullen as a poet was a traditionalist in line with
the great English poets, and an apostle of beauty with
the fountainhead of his inspiration in the poetic philosophy of John Keats. If his imagination was scorched by
the injustice and oppression of a people with whom his
lot was thrown, like Keats whose sensitive nature was
also wounded, he soared, not by way of escape, but by
precept and counsel, into the abstract realm of the
spirit . . . .

No poet we have as yet produced was so complete and
spontaneous a master of the poetic technique as Countee Cullen. His octosyllabic line has not been more
skilfully handled by any modern poet. He has used the
sonnet for many moods and themes and carved its
fourteen lines of varied temper and structure with a
lyrical unity that earns him a place in the company of
Wordsworth, Rossetti and Bridges. He possessed an
epigrammatic gift and turn of wit that gave uncommon
delight as witnessed in the series of **"Epitaphs"** among
which the one **"For a Mouthy Woman"** is a masterpiece.
His translations from Baudelaire, especially the sinuous

felinity of cats, rank with those of Swinburne, Arthur
Symons and George Dillon, in the rendering of that
feverish and fantastic French poet into English. The
fantasy of the **"Wakeupworld"** from the mythical narrative of **"The Lost Zoo,"** established his poetic kinship in
imaginative humor to the delightful foolery of Richard
H. Barham's "Ingoldsby Legends."

No one will deny that Countee Cullen escaped the aches
that come to a sensitive spirit aware of racial prejudice
and insult, but he did not allow them to distort or
distemper the ideals and visions which endowed him as
an artist and poet. He had as deep a sensibility for the
human denials and aches, which absorbed the lesser
racial ones, and strove through the exquisite creation of
imagery and music to evoke and communicate the spirit
of Beauty as a solacing and restorative power. Time will,
I think, accept him on the spiritual terms he set for
himself in the poem **"To John Keats, the Poet at Spring
Time,"** and know that though he could sing a **"Ballad for
a Brown Girl"** and make a **"Litany of the Dark People"**
the blood and soul of mankind were alike in its passions
and aspirations.

> *William Stanley Braithwaite, in a review of
> "On These I Stand," in* Opportunity, *Vol.
> XXV, No. 3, July-September, 1947, p. 170.*

Jean Wagner (essay date 1962)

[*A French author and critic, Wagner is an expert on
the works of black and Southern writers of the United
States and an authority on American slang and
dialects. In the following excerpt from his* Les poètes
nègres des États-Unis *(1962;* Black Poets of the
United States, *1973), he discusses Cullen's "inner
development" as it is reflected in* Color *and* The Black
Christ.]

Together with Claude McKay, Countee Cullen was the
black poet gifted with the most intense inner life, but he
was also a most tormented personality. The particular
circumstances surrounding his youthful years, an intellectual preparation acquired almost entirely outside his
racial milieu, and, furthermore, particularly haunting
personal problems—these were some of the influences
that help to explain the strange note sounded by his lyric
poetry. Its tone constituted a seemingly impassable
barrier between the poet and the people of his own race.

Cullen, for them, soon became a great, misunderstood
figure, and he found their lack of comprehension a
burden hard to bear. But his direct experience of
suffering was, for his inner life, a source of extraordinary enrichment.

His lyric gift was incontestable and, indeed, exceptional.
But his poetry has none of McKay's fiery virility, and
the treasures it encloses are, rather, those of a soul that
at times indulged in an excess of sensibility and preferred to express itself in the half-tones and nuances of a
high scrupulousness. (p. 283)

[The] real substance of his lyric gift came from his individual experience at least as much as, if not more than, from the experience of the racial group to which he belonged and against whose encroachments he never ceased to defend himself with vigor. Even at those moments when the poetic élan is most directly inspired by his color, his individual voice always dominates that of the group.

Thus it is hardly possible to treat him fairly unless one takes good care to allot its proper share to each of these two elements. (pp. 292-93)

[What] an excessive burden the shame of his origins was for him: the shame of his birth, which diminished him in his own eyes; the shame of the sin which, as he envisaged it, surrounded the circumstances of his adoption, and which exposed him to God's judgment; and especially the shame he felt at his color, which debased him in the eyes of other men and bent him beneath a weight he longed to shake off in death. (p. 293)

Nor can there by any doubt that his feeling of inferiority is also derived, by a more direct route, from his partial or total inability to lead a normal sexual life. Where he sees a sin committed before God, in the physical reality there is also a humiliating defeat before the love of woman. His marriage demonstrates this, and the poet is not oblivious of the fact. (p. 295)

The sense of inferiority that overwhelmed him did not have a purely racial cause, and one must take fully into account the other emotional perturbations we have noted if one wishes to understand why Cullen, unlike the other poets of the Negro Renaissance, did not regard his race primarily as an object of pride. (pp. 295-96)

An examination of the tendencies manifested in the evolution of his poetic themes enables one to distinguish, in Cullen's work, two different periods marked off by the moment of reassessment represented in his life by the year 1927.

In his inner development, the primacy of race is scarcely noticeable after an early extroverted phase, during which his behavior tended to seek an adjustment to the surrounding environment. This reaction to racial tensions is an instinctive phenomenon, on a par with the attitude of most of his racial brothers. There is no point in looking elsewhere for any deeper reason that would explain the success of *Color* . . . from the moment of its publication. When he sang of the burden of color and of its nobility. . . . and above all when he nostalgically evoked the memory of the African homeland, black America had no difficulty in recognizing its own states of soul in those of the poet. (p. 302)

Despite surface appearances, his racial experience was indeed but one factor in what might be called his problem, and the basic urge behind his poetry must be sought in his scruples of conscience . . . .

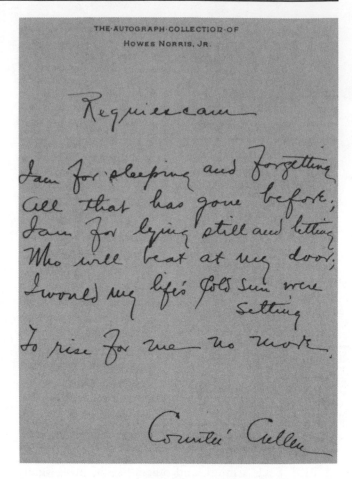

Fair copy of Cullen's "Requiescam."

Even while Cullen was exploring the dimensions of his color, there occurred an imperceptible shift in its value. Its significance, which had been a collective one, now shrank until it corresponded to the limits of the poet's individual consciousness. As the demands of the spirit grew more insistent, color itself became spiritualized and amounted, in the end, to no more than an array of symbols that swirled around Cullen's reflection on his destiny.

This tenuous thread of symbolism, whose purely inner relevancy was not at first appreciated, enabled the racial community to maintain for some time longer the illusion that, through a shared loyalty to color, it was in communication with the poet. But they were no longer speaking a common language. The poet's eyes, raised above the contingency of race, were already turned toward the Creator who bore the ultimate responsibility and to whom he, the black poet-prophet, sought to lead his whole people. Unfortunately, his own followed him not on the rugged paths of the spirit. Little by little, a gulf widened between them and him, so that the poet found himself a stranger in the midst of his own people. His lonely itinerary to the heights then became an actual Calvary on whose summit he, like another Christ, was crucified between the exigencies of his color and his loyalty to his individual ideal.... Thus the first period is followed by one characterized by introversion, during which Cullen retreats ever further within himself. He has not severed all contacts with the external world, but this world is ever more often experienced as a cause of suffering for which he seeks a balm in his mystic dialogue with Christ.

It need scarcely be said that there is no absolute rupture between these two phases of his inner development. The last echoes of the African theme still resound faintly in ["The Black Christ"], and the colloquy with Christ had been inaugurated in *Color.* From one end of his work to the other, and more markedly than in the case of any other black poet, color and spirituality are inextricably intertwined. But as the former loses importance, his spiritual preoccupations take on ever clearer shape and soon outrank all else.

It is a change of course that happens rather early in the poet's career, and by the time *Copper Sun* was published... it may be considered an established fact. The critics were quite taken aback by that volume. Meeting with hardly any of the racial hyperboles they had noted in *Color,* they reached the conclusion that the writer "has borrowed the temperament of his poems," and that his verse no longer had its source in his own inner experience. In a word, the blunt indictment was that his lines lacked sincerity.

Cullen is already a much more characteristic product of the black bourgeoisie, having been exposed to all its pressures as he grew up in the Harlem home of a Methodist minister. The whole course of his education took place in schools and universities with a majority of whites, and theirs were the standards and prejudices he unconsciously absorbed. He had scarcely any close associations with the people of his own race, and he had no sense of communion with them. The people, as a result, make no genuine contribution to his work in verse, and popular Negro themes and forms are entirely absent from it.

It would even seem that Cullen always sensed the existence of some incompatibility between restrictions of any kind that might be imposed on the poet because of his color, and the universality that is the distinguishing mark of poetry.... In any event, up to the very end Cullen will maintain his determination to be independent of his racial group, even at the risk of being called a traitor by his own.... (pp. 307-08)

Among the religious themes of which Cullen's poetry has an unusual abundance, exceptional importance is given to Christ's figure, which haunted the poet throughout his life. Every volume of his poetry, except perhaps *The Medea,* turns to the theme which, in his mind, was to have found its culmination in his longest poem, "The Black Christ," published three years after his visit to Jerusalem. (p. 329)

Even at those moments when Christ appeared to him most hostile, Cullen thirsts for the Christian ideal of perfection and self-transcendence, and no one could have suffered more than he did from the sense of guilt that awareness of his sinfulness aroused in him. But since he found himself on hostile terms with Christ on the spiritual plane because of his sin, and on the racial plane also because Christ seemed to have abandoned the black race, it was tempting to unite the two terms on either side of the barrier—to promote the urges of the flesh to the rank of a positive value, indeed, of a black value that had been consecrated by the African gods who thus came to challenge the place held in his soul by the white Christ.... (p. 332)

In the Negro folk tradition that predated Cullen, blacks had become accustomed to recognizing themselves in the Hebrew people, the chosen of God, whereas white people, especially southern whites, were equated with the Egyptians and their Pharaoh, who held captive the people of Israel. The choice of the crucified Christ to symbolize the lynched Negro was a new idea, and it appears that its originator was indeed Cullen. (p. 335)

The poet, after making Christ black, shows his dexterity by treating his color as worse than a crime....

But not only in the person of the lynched Negro is Christ's sacrifice undergone once more. His Calvary prefigures also that of the whole black people, crowned with thorns and crucified on a cross of the same color as the oppressors, for this people, after having foresworn the ancestors' African gods, had entrusted itself completely to Christ, for better and for worse.... (p. 336)

His mystic intimacy with Christ finds its culmination in "The Black Christ." This great poem is also his spiritual testament, where all the fundamental themes of his poetic achievement are taken up once more and placed in their ultimate perspective. (p. 341)

[The scope of "The Black Christ"] would be lost if one paid attention only to the narrative aspect, for with Cullen this is also, ultimately, a way of activating symbols so that they may confront one another. In this perspective, "The Black Christ" is a masterly reconstruction of the poet's inner drama. It retraces the long debate, already launched in "Heritage," whose protagonists are incredulity and faith, each of these parties to the confrontation being endowed with its entire accompaniment of racial and personal overtones, which in this poem are orchestrated into an imposing *da capo.*

In this internal confrontation, in which the poet functions not only as the narrator but also as the moderator whose role it is to synthesize the opposing elements, the mother stands for the people's unshakable Christian faith. She is one of the humble who believe without having seen and to whom, for this reason, the Lord has revealed mighty things he keeps hidden from the proud and the argumentative.

The voice of the mother, as she speaks to her son in the humble setting of a southern cabin, at the same time is clearly that of faith speaking to the poet within his own heart. But the mother represents more than faith. She also symbolizes the people and, beyond them, the doubly ungrateful southern soil from which they draw their deep roots.

Thus Countee Cullen discovers...the perennial strength of the trinity made up of earth, folk, and faith, all irrational values against which the young intellectual had revelled in fiery protest in the days when he was winning his first triumphs as a poet.

Standing over against the values represented by the mother is the figure of Jim, who in many respects might well be looked on as the incarnation of the "New Negro." His whole being breathes pride of race and intolerance of any yoke. He also symbolizes the religious skepticism that sprang up in the heart of a whole race that had to witness unpunished injustice. (pp. 343-44)

One is reminded of Keats in reading the celebration of spring that is placed at the beginning of Jim's speech, as he is about to tell how the white man came upon him unawares. From the narrative point of view, this forms too lengthy a parenthesis, but because of its symbolic value it rounds out the portrait of Jim. It cannot be doubted that in it Cullen sought to depict everything within himself that represented an obstacle on the path that ultimately led him to God.

The arguments advanced by the mother and by Jim do battle, throughout the poem, in the poet's own heart, and doubt appears to be on the point of winning when, after the lynching has been carried out and the mother and her surviving son abandon themselves to their grief inside their cabin, Jim suddenly manifests himself in the glory of his resurrection. Before this revelation of divine power and mercy, doubt finally is routed forever and the poet, another Doubting Thomas, falls to his knees. He is overcome with remorse at the thought of all the blasphemies he had hurled at god, and which have been answered by the Divine mercy.

It is easy to understand why this long poem of 963 lines finally lost Cullen the sympathies of the black public. For the poem, with its mystical character, and despite the title and the theme of the narrative, is not essentially Negro in any way. Its very mysticism was condemned as childish, and one critic actually reproached the author for having dated the poem from Paris. (pp. 345-46)

"The Black Christ" must be read as a poem of thanksgiving for the bestowal of the light of faith, as well as the translation into words of a contemplative experience. The religious exaltation that dictates the poem's entire structure bears the marks of the neophyte's sense of wonderment and his whole touching naïveté. With such characteristics, however, "The Black Christ" was inevitably inaccessible to all but a handful of readers.

It must be confessed that the poem has all the defects that correspond to its virtues. A mystical experience always retains a certain incommunicability, and in the present case the reader has to make a considerable effort

of self-adaptation to remain attuned to the poet who, in his exaltation, sometimes leaves all trammels so far behind that he falls into incoherence and neglects the external form. The tetrameter, which he had always favored and which he uses throughout the poem, may be appropriate for the narrative passages, but the prolonged meditations, which occupy an important place, might have moved more freely in a less constricting meter. The presence of rhyme, too, disposed with impenetrable arbitrariness, awakens a vague malaise and does injury to the sobriety of the whole. (pp. 346-47)

These reservations made, it must be avowed that this most sustained effort of Cullen's poetic inspiration finds, to the very end, accents of a deeply moving sincerity, and the undeniable beauty of a number of scenes within this great poetic fresco bespeaks the writer's quality of soul no less than his genius....

[While] he appears to have discovered the permanent value embodied by the people, it is less likely that his sympathy went beyond the strictly spiritual. He had grown up apart from the people, and to the very end the people seem to have remained an abstraction for him.

All in all, and in spite of its extraordinary density, his poetic achievement will stand less as a mirroring of the black soul than as a living testimony to the great spiritual adventure of a poet named Countee Cullen. (p. 347)

Jean Wagner, "Countee Cullen," in his Black Poets of the United States: From Paul Laurence Dunbar to Langston Hughes, translated by Kenneth Douglas, University of Illinois Press, 1973, pp. 283-347.

Stephen H. Bronz (essay date 1964)

[*In the following excerpt, Bronz discusses themes of race and religion in* Color *and* Copper Sun.]

Chauvinism, atavism, and the paradox of racial hatred in a divinely created world pervade the most important poems in *Color*. Thus, for example, "A Song of Praise (For One Who Praised His Lady's Being Fair)":

> You have not heard my love's dark throat,
> Slow-fluting like a reed,
> Release the perfect golden note
> She caged there for my need.
>
> Her walk is like the replica
> Of some barbaric dance
> Wherein the soul of Africa
> Is winged with arrogance...
>
> My love is dark as yours is fair,
> Yet lovelier I hold her
> Than listless maids with pallid hair,
> And blood that's thin and colder...

Besides demonstrating Cullen's mastery of the white man's classical verse forms, "A Song of Praise" boldly asserts the inevitable superiority of the darker lady, and cheerfully accepts the stereotype of a sexually torrid Negro race. Also, the poem refers to Africa, that previously unknown continent in which Negroes were beginning to adopt a new but still superficial interest, as a racial homeland. **"A Song of Praise,"** then, offered much to the Negro readers of the 'twenties in bolstering their self-pride. To whites Cullen asserted that Harlem, with its new poetry and exotic women, had something to offer besides jazz.

"Atlantic City Waiter" well demonstrates Cullen's abstractness when dealing poetically with the Negro's lot in America. For Cullen the Atlantic City waiter is less an individual than a stimulus to the poet's own racially-oriented mental meanderings. The poem reads:

> With subtle poise he grips his tray
> Of delicate things to eat;
> Choice viands to their mouths half way,
> The ladies watch his feet
>
> Go carving dexterous avenues
> Through sly intricacies;
> Ten thousand years on jungle clues
> Alone shaped feet like these.
>
> For him to be humble who is proud
> Needs colder artifice;
> Though half his pride is disavowed,
> In vain the sacrifice.
>
> Sheer through his acquiescent mask
> Of bland gentility,
> The jungle flames like a copper cask
> Set where the sun strikes free.

By glorifying the waiter as a proud African nobleman Cullen by implication glorifies every Negro. Here, as in **"A Song of Praise,"** a new racial stereotype replaces the old one. Instead of the kindly servant ever anxious to please, we have an austere, ennobled savage.

One of the longest and most frequently quoted of Cullen's poems probes the meaning of Africa to twentieth century Negro-Americans, and emerges with no clear answers. The refrain to **"Heritage"** states the question:

> *One three centuries removed*
> *From the scenes his fathers loved,*
> *Spicy grove, cinnamon tree,*
> *What is Africa to me?*

The first part of **"Heritage"** depicts stirringly the Africa which the speaker, try as he might, cannot keep from surging up in his blood. Africa does not mean the precolonial African art, philosophy, and state-craft being rediscovered in the 'twenties in America and France, but an exotic jungle and plains Africa of "wild barbaric birds," "juggernauts of flesh," "cats / Crouching in the river reeds," "silver snakes," and "leprous flowers." From the pen of Countee Cullen, Northern-bred, college educated, these images, with their smooth sounds and vague pictures, ring false. Nonetheless, despite its inaccuracies, such as placing the Ceylonese cinnamon tree in

Africa, the poem presents a far more favorable view of Africa than did Vachel Lindsay's bombastic "Congo," which had been published in 1914.

Exotic Africa served a distinct purpose. History to the Negro was not the national pageant of exploration, settlement, independence, western expansion, and wars to preserve the union and democracy, but a story of bondage, physical freedom, and Jim Crow. The Negroes' need for a past of which to feel proud produced a growing interest in the 'twenties in Negro history; it also produced Cullen's **"Heritage."** Africa was a heritage no white man could claim, a link with savage splendors so different from the more intellectual heritage of Western Europe. If Cullen's poem seems artificial, so, as he recognized, was the African heritage somewhat artificial, and a product more of the pen than of the blood.

After his excursion into atavism, Cullen turns in **"Heritage"** to a subject closer to his heart, the meaning of Christianity for the Negro.

> Quaint, outlandish heathen gods
> Black men fashion out of rods,
> Clay, and brittle bits of stone,
> In a likeness like their own,
> My conversion came high-priced;
> I belong to Jesus Christ,
> Preacher of humility;
> Heathen gods are naught to me.
>
> . . . although I speak
> With my mouth thus, in my heart
> Do I play a double part.
> Ever at Thy glowing altar
> Must my heart grow sick and falter,
> Wishing He I served were black . . .
> Surely then this flesh would know
> Yours had borne a kindred woe.

Note that Cullen decries not so much the white man's control of organized religion or the unchristian acts of white men, as the meaning of Christ's suffering itself. The poem ends in self-contradiction:

> Not yet has my heart or head
> In the least way realized
> They and I are civilized.

One does not emerge from the latter part of **"Heritage"** with clear, provoking theological argument, but rather with an ill-defined but strongly expressed feeling that somehow all is not right with the world and Christianity. The popularity of the poem does not attest so much to the strength of agnosticism among Negroes in the 'twenties, as to the appeal of Cullen's own conception of poetry—"lofty thoughts beautifully expressed." For Cullen, beauty seems to have meant beauty of sound and, in keeping with the title of the volume, beauty of imagery of color. In these, the poem abounds; in the concreteness of imagery and economy of language that can make poetry meaningful and powerful it is sorely lacking.

More directly concerned with God and the American Negro is **"Shroud of Color."** However wordy it may be, **"Shroud of Color"** seems more powerful and sincere than **"Heritage"** because Cullen deals with the problem in a grand and imaginative fashion, so that we find it easier to overlook the persisting absence of concreteness. The first part of the poem presents a despairing Negro speaker, disillusioned with a life in which prejudice puts "a hurt / In all the simple joys which to a child / Are sweet." His dreams of joy, and even of truth itself are damned to frustration and distortion, the speaker laments. Has God hidden some special lamb, some special reward and relief for him? The speaker doubts that God has, but resolves to live intensely regardless. He lives, he struggles, and at last, "all passion spent, [he] lay full length / And quivered like a flayed and bleeding thing." From this exhausted despair, the speaker is "lifted on a great black wing," as if in a dream, and permitted, by God, to view great proofs of the value of life and man's passion for it. The speaker witnesses animals' and plants' tenacious struggles for life, but remains unconvinced: "Than animated death," he asks, "can death be worse?"

Next, the speaker watches, in addition to animals, all of mankind struggling for life. "Well, let them fight," he replies, still skeptical, "they *can* whose flesh is fair." Even seeing the great heavenly war between the good and bad angels does not suffice: "Why mock me thus? Am I a God?" Finally, God shows the speaker a panorama of the history of the Negro race: the "strange wild music" of Africa and the "bitterness and death" of slavery, in spite of which "there ran / Through all a harmony of faith in man. / A knowledge all would end as it began."

> ... I had no further claim to urge
> For death; ...
> "Lord, not for what I saw in flesh or bone
> Of Fairer men; not raised on faith alone;
> Lord, I will live persuaded by mine own
> I cannot play the recreant to these; ...

Returned by the black wing to earth, the speaker looks up, and sees the rising sun.

Here, in the same volume of poetry, we have an answer to the question posed in **"Heritage,"** but an answer that does not seem altogether to have satisfied Cullen. His faith seems weak, and in need of repeated reassurance. But, as with so many of Cullen's poems, the personal statements and conflicts are less notable than the poem's place in the Harlem Renaissance. Christianity served dramatically as a consolation for the Negro slave, and for the slowly rising Negro under Jim Crow. Life on earth plainly had much that was wrong with it; some promise of a golden future was a near necessity for any sort of earthly happiness. And the understandable antagonisms towards the master and, later, towards a white society, needed some outlet. This, religion had helped to provide.

But Cullen, in **"Heritage"** and **"Shroud of Color,"** questions the validity and relevance of religion for the Negro. He demands, in effect, that greater attention be turned to the here and now. This life must not be quietly accepted as a vale of sorrows. It must be changed or the Negro will cease struggling, as in **"Shroud of Color,"** and, by killing himself, mock God's chief gift to man. Cullen demanded not only an equal place for the Negro in American society, but, concomitantly, an equal place for the Negro in the eyes of God. It would have been surprising to find such a poem written twenty years earlier—Dunbar never indulged in such speculations. And twenty years later, Negro intellectuals, and more and more the Negro people as a whole, were much more concerned with actively improving the Negro's lot through specific measures, or in venting the Negro's suppressed fury at an unjust society and the white race.

Again concerned with the Negro and God, though with a somewhat different emphasis, is **"Yet Do I Marvel."** In this poem, reminiscent in form of some seventeenth century metaphysical poetry, Cullen lists a series of paradoxes of seeming evil in a divinely created world. The speaker says he does not doubt God's ability to explain these paradoxes—why the mole is blind, why men must die, why Tantalus and Sisyphus must endure interminable tortures. Cullen concludes the poem with the final paradox, perhaps his most famous line: "Yet I do marvel at this curious thing: / To make a poet black, and bid him sing!" This paradox, to be sure, had been blunted by the success among whites of the Harlem Renaissance by 1925. Still, though a Negro poet was not such a strange phenomenon in the cosmos, it was a fairly radical notion to Negroes and whites before the Harlem Renaissance. The Sambo stereotype of the Negro was fading, and Cullen's own writings both stressed and exemplified that change.

Among the other racially oriented poems in *Color*, many of which assert the ultimate equality of the races or elegize beautiful though unnamed brown girls (the word *Negro* apparently did not meet Cullen's criteria for elevated poetry), one poem stands out as direct, concrete, and popular. It is entitled **"Incident."**

> Once riding in old Baltimore,
> Heart-filled, head-filled with glee,
> I saw a Baltimorean
> Keep looking straight at me.
>
> Now I was eight and very small,
> And he was no whit bigger,
> And so I smiled, but he poked out
> His tongue, and called me, "Nigger."
>
> I saw the whole of Baltimore
> From May until December;
> Of all the things that happened there
> That's all that I remember.

The lightness, subtle directness, and quality of drama of **"Incident"** are reminiscent of the poems of Emily Dickinson. In all of *Color,* only in this small poem, with its diminutive title, does Cullen place a moving, credible picture before the reader's eyes. It is with disappointment that one reads Cullen's insistent statements that this "incident" did not in fact happen to him, but that he only imagined it. Still, the poem remains, whatever the story of its making, and serves as a precursor to such works as Richard Wright's bitter and terrifying autobiography, *Black Boy.*

Cullen's second published volume, *Copper Sun,* has far fewer poems on racial themes than *Color.* More of an established poet by 1927, Cullen turned towards more universal subjects: love and death. The racially oriented poems that are in *Copper Sun* repeat, usually in more stilted and vague terms, the ideas expressed in *Color.* There are exceptions, however, and those exceptions imply that Cullen was becoming more aware of the day-to-day lives of Negroes. In the poem entitled **"Colors,"** the "Red" section describes a scene concretely enough to make us feel Cullen had witnessed it himself. An "ugly, black, and fat" woman went to buy a hat, and the salesladies, mockingly, sold her a bright red one, "And then they laughed behind her back / To see it glow against the black." But the black lady, unperturbed, "paid for it with regal mien, / And walked out proud as any queen." In its content, if not in its expression, this is one of Cullen's most successful poems. He creates a dramatic situation, with credible characters, and combines a racial with a universal theme. The black lady could be seen to represent any unsophisticated woman who maintains her human dignity before a condescending attack.

"Uncle Jim," with more plausible characters than most of Cullen's efforts, reveals much of the contradictory nature of Cullen's own views on race and beauty.

> "White folks is white," says uncle Jim;
> "A platitude," I sneer; . . .
>
> His heart walled up with bitterness,
> He smokes his pungent pipe,
> And nods at me as if to say,
> "Young fool, you'll soon be ripe!"

The speaker, however, while with a friend whose interests coincide with his own, perplexedly finds his mind straying from "the Grecian urn / To muse on uncle Jim." It is not altogether clear what uncle Jim meant by "White folks is white," whether he was calling attention to the lower position granted Negroes in American society, or to the unremitting hostility of whites towards Negroes. But he does, in any event, represent the voice of experience, warning the young idealist to lay aside his Keatsian musings on universal beauty, and come to terms with life and race problems. Like the speaker in the poem, Cullen's own first instincts were towards thinking and writing of what he saw as universals. And like the speaker in the poem, he found himself, despite first instincts, dealing in life and poetry with racial questions. (pp. 48-56)

> *Stephen H. Bronz, "Countee Cullen," in his* Roots of Negro Racial Consciousness, the 1920's: Three Harlem Renaissance Authors, *Libra Publishers, Inc., 1964, pp. 47-65.*

Nathan Irvin Huggins (essay date 1971)

[*Huggins is an American historian and critic who specializes in African-American studies. In the following excerpt, he argues that in literary matters Cullen was a conservative idealist.*]

By the end of his life, Countee Cullen had acquired all of the marks of a poet. He had published five books of original poetry, not including **On These I Stand** (1947), which collects his already published work. In addition, Cullen had edited a book of Negro verse, written a novel and two books about his cat, and collaborated on two theatrical works. He had won prizes: The Witter Bynner award for the best poetry by a college undergraduate, the *Opportunity* magazine contests, the Harmon Foundation competition, and a Guggenheim Fellowship. From the writing of his earliest verse, in high school, to the end of his life, he had always received favorable critical comment, pointing to him as exemplary of one whose art had transcended race.

This kind of judgment was especially pleasing to Cullen, because he believed that art—especially poetry—should transcend the mundane, the ordinary; be elevating. His view of art was quite conventional—indeed conservative—in the postwar years. He believed poetry should deal with higher emotions and ideals; it should avoid sensuality—its language more pure than ordinary speech, more elevated than prose. While this convention had been under attack in the United States since before the war—many of Cullen's white contemporaries had long since thrown over their obedience to it, and were experimenting not only with form but with poetry's proper subject and common diction—Cullen, himself, held quite tenaciously to the genteel tradition.

This conservative idealism was educated into the poet. In high school and college, Cullen took the traditional path to the art of poetry: languages, classics, English literature. He helped to edit as well as contributed poetry to the DeWitt Clinton High School literary magazine, *The Magpie.* While an undergraduate at New York University, Cullen published in several literary magazines, including *Bookman* and *Poetry,* and in his senior year Harper contracted to publish his first book of poems, *Color* (1925). His acclaim in his college years was for poems which varied in subject if not style: **"Simon the Cyrenian Speaks"** as well as appreciations of John Keats. His *Ballad of the Brown Girl* won the Witter Bynner award and was considered by Harvard's Lyman Kittredge to be the finest literary ballad by an American he had read. So Countee Cullen was already published and praised (a Phi Beta Kappa graduate) when he went to take his Master's degree at Harvard. He found Robert Hillyer's seminar in versification just to his liking. Hillyer had asked for exercises in various traditional forms of English verse; that poet-professor later was to publish one of Cullen's exercises as a rare American example of the Chaucerian rime royal. Cullen was forever committed to the formalism that this education implies. His biographer attributes to him the assertion that his poetry just "came out" in metered lines and rhyme. In any case, he never experimented with anything else, and that is quite remarkable considering what other poets were doing in the 1920s.

Formalism was not the only mark of Cullen's conservatism. He understood Art to be a slave to Beauty (he would capitalize those nouns). Poetry more than prose was the pure essence of the literary art; as essential beauty it should allow the human imagination to soar, to live with the gods. He was encouraged in this by the influence of Alain Locke, and by W. E. B. DuBois, whose views on art and uplift would vie with any other New England Yankees for gentility and conservatism. Furthermore, Countee Cullen had tied himself spiritually to the Romantics, particularly John Keats, who continued to serve as models for his verse as well as inspirations for his vision. He cultivated in himself that emotional temperament that expected to find poems in graveyards and palm-pressed palpitations on hillsides, and which saw the body and human condition as inconvenient harness to the spirit; the muse, genius, the imagination, and art transformed man into a kind of immortal, into a kind of god. He visited Keats's grave in Rome and read the epitaph that Keats had chosen for himself: "Here lies one whose name was writ in water." Later Cullen wrote his own.

"For John Keats, Apostle of Beauty"

Not writ in water, nor in mist,
    Sweet lyric throat, thy name.
Thy singing lips that cold death kissed
    Have seared his own with flame.

One could hardly find a more perfect example of a twentieth-century poet marching to a nineteenth-century drummer: the subject, the title, the diction, the stiff period of the first two lines, the conceit of the poet, the "lyric throat" and the kiss of "cold death." Like most of Cullen's poetry, this epitaph leaves the reader with little doubt about what it is. It looks like a poem, it sounds like a poem, and it is about what poems are supposed to be about.

With all of his sense of idealized art, Countee Cullen was, nevertheless, very conscious of the obligation that race placed on him as a poet. Given his view of the art of poetry, his race consciousness was quite a dilemma. The problems of Negroes were real, too real. They were a part of this world, the mud, guts, and stuff of life. Lynchings, murder, discrimination, poverty inevitably would be the subjects of Negro life. Yet how could this be translated into verse that would be elevating and truly poetic? Furthermore, Cullen believed that the art of poetry, like all art and true culture, was abstracted from race or any other condition of life. It was Cullen who told Langston Hughes that he wanted to be a poet, not a Negro poet. For him, there was no such thing as Negro poetry. How, then, could he remain true to his sense of art and, at the same time, to his strong racial feelings? His conservative critical judgment told him that he must write poems that were at least once removed from the source of his strongest emotions. No

wonder that he thought God had done a curious thing: "To make a poet black and bid him sing."

Cullen also was never free from his sense of being exemplary. Like so many Negroes whose achievement catapults them into the public eye, he was a public Negro. He was not merely a poet, he was a "credit to his race." No matter how much he achieved or how little it depended on race, it was inevitable that his blackness would mark him. Of the ten initiates into New York University's Phi Beta Kappa chapter, it was Countee Cullen who was singled out for extensive press coverage—an example of Negro achievement. While he consciously wrote to ensure his acceptance as a good American poet, and while critics often remarked that his true achievement was as a poet and not as a Negro poet, he never could avoid being defined by race. *The New York Times* of January 10, 1946, amplified the irony with its headline: "Countee Cullen, Negro Poet, Dead." Nor can one say that the poet would have really wanted it otherwise. Langston Hughes's simplistic logic did not recognize that the motive to write like a poet (a white poet) could be indeed quite the opposite from wanting to be white. Cullen wanted to be acknowledged as a poet so that he would not be condescended to as a Negro, so that he could be an example of Negro potential, successfully competing on the white man's ground. As an exemplar, he could point the way to others, he could be a symbol of possibility, and he could turn other black boys' eyes to poetry and art so that the muse might allow them to transcend their condition as he had. Such a conception was problematic, yet Cullen was sustained by important Negroes—Booker T. Washington, W. E. B. DuBois, James Weldon Johnson—in this view of racial uplift through culture, achievement, and example.

In writing love poems it was easy enough for Cullen to handle the problem of race and art. In his art, love, like spring, was color-blind, and for the most part those poems could be addressed to a lady of any hue. Cullen sometimes wrote poems about brown girls and brown boys, but for the most part the color was only in the title; the poems themselves were characteristically devoid of concreteness and specificity. In **"A Song of Praise,"** Cullen answers a poet who praises his lady for being fair, by alluding to African beauty. The same theme is suggested in **"Brown Boy to Brown Girl."** But, as with most of his poems, the reader is left in the realm of idea, far from palpable reality. *Ballad of the Brown Girl,* however, does point to the difficulty of emulating, for racial purposes, works of an alien era and culture. Cullen mistakenly thought the brown girl in the medieval ballad was Negro, whereas, in fact, the balladeer meant a peasant girl. This tale of a struggle for the affections of a handsome lord by a country girl and a fair London maiden had different meaning from what Cullen intended. Tied as he was to the story as well as to form, the poem is only slight and confused comfort to the Negro reader who might hope to be elated by it.

When Countee Cullen wanted to write seriously about Negroes, his aesthetic forced him to couch his meaning and intent in classical or religious context. The reader would have to infer the racial significance, and it was thought that the classical context would elevate the particular to the universal. He wrote **"Simon the Cyrenian Speaks"** to show the courageous dignity of a humble black man's answer to the Christian call. He obliquely wrote about prostitutes in **"Black Magdalens,"** thus dignifying Harlem whores with biblical reference. The predicament of the black man, deprived of justice and possibility, is worked out in **"Shroud of Color,"** a poem of passion in which the narrator challenges God to tell him why he must go on living. God gives him a series of visions, but it is the final chorus of all black men's hopes and aspirations that gives him courage, will, and determination to live as one of these.

> And somehow it was borne upon my brain
> How being dark, and living through the pain
> Of it, is courage more than angels have.

Lynching is the subject of **"Black Christ,"** his long narrative. Whereas the same subject moved Claude McKay to bitterness and James Weldon Johnson in "Brothers" to expose the brutality of murdering mobs and their kinship to the victim, Cullen characteristically chose another statement. Bitterness was not beautiful or elevating, neither was the bestiality of men; these could not be the voice or theme of a poem. Cullen used the lynching as a test of faith. The brother of the lynched man lost his faith in God, despite his mother's unswerving devotion. But the lynched brother rises from the dead, redeeming his doubting brother. The resurrection also, completing the analogy to Christ, ennobles the murdered man and the murder. And even when Cullen wanted to explore the question of his African heritage, he chose in **"Heritage"** to bind the problem to the religious question of pagan vs. Christian belief.

These were never very satisfactory ways of dealing with the themes that prompted the poems. Sometimes, one suspects, the work would have been more successful as prose. Always the reader—the modern reader at any rate—wonders why the poet does not say what is on his mind. The obliqueness surely does not help. Yet Cullen, forever true to a genteel straightjacket, seldom if ever ventured to tell it as it was, or better yet, to tell it as he felt it.

I quote here the four stanzas of **"Harsh World That Lashest Me"** because it illustrates Countee Cullen's persistent Romantic vision, and it serves as a sharp contrast to Claude McKay's treatments of the same themes in "America"... and "Baptism."

"Harsh World That Lashest Me"

> Harsh World that lashest me each day,
>   Dub me not cowardly because
> I seem to find no sudden way
>   To throttle you or clip your claws.
> No force compels me to the wound
>   Whereof my body bears the scar;
> Although my feet are on the ground,
>   Doubt not my eyes are on a star.

> You cannot keep me captive, World,
>   Entrammeled, chained, spit on, and
>   spurned.
> More free than all your flags unfurled,
>   I give my body to be burned.
> I mount my cross because I will,
>   I drink the hemlock which you give
> For wine which you withhold—and still
>   Because I will not die, I live.

> I live because an ember in
>   Me smoulders to regain its fire,
> Because what is and what has been
>   Not yet have conquered my desire.
> I live to prove the groping clod
>   Is surely more than simple dust;
> I live to see the breath of God
>   Beatify the carnal crust.

> But when I will, World, I can go,
>   Though triple bronze should wall me round
> Slip past your guard as swift as snow,
>   Translated without pain or sound.
> Within myself is lodged the key
>   To that vast room of couches laid
> For those too proud to live and see
>   Their dreams of light eclipsed in shade.

There is, here, no real evidence that the poet is black, yet one has to know that fact to have the romantic sentiment make any sense. Cullen like McKay speaks of torment in the world (McKay calls America a "cultured hell"). Cullen and McKay alike echo the late Victorian stoicism of W. E. Henley and Kipling which finds comfort in an indomitable soul.

Countee Cullen had a genuine talent for lyric verse, and he did manage to write pretty lines. William Grant Still put **"If You Should Go"** to music.

"If You Should Go"

> Love, leave me like the light,
>   The gently passing day;
> We would not know, but for the night,
>   When it has slipped away.

> Go quietly; a dream
>   When done, should leave no trace
> That it has lived, except a gleam
>   Across the dreamer's face.

There is a prettiness here that wants to live in all of Cullen's work. He liked softness and liquid sounds. Seldom did he write anything harsh. **"Incident"** is the one exception. For in this poem a white boy of about eight years calls the narrator "Nigger"; nevertheless, the tone is plaintive and innocent.

Countee Cullen liked form, he liked words, and he liked rhyme, but he never experimented with any of them. One looks in vain in his poems to find departures from convention. The rhymes are regular, and the reader is never startled by a strange or new one. He never forgot his formal exercises from his Harvard seminar. He was content to be good at them, so his poetry remained exercises in verse, never experiment or play. And the same for words. Cullen did not serve that function of poetry which molds the language into something new.

Surely, he would never write in vernacular, and even his precious diction is never marked by freshness of usage. Poetry was a very serious business to Countee Cullen; he might be light but never funny. Significantly, he left his slight poetic humor for short verse epitaphs.

In 1935, just ten years after his first book of poems, Countee Cullen published *The Medea and Some Poems,* which was to be his last book of new poetry. He did write some children's stories and two books about his cat, but to all intents his life as a poet had ended. He taught in the New York City public schools, working very hard to interest young boys in poetry. This was time-consuming, but it fails to explain why a young man who was dedicated to poetry early in his youth should have lost the will to write. Since his days in high school nothing else had mattered. But, despite what he told himself, his dedication was not to the art; he did nothing toward advancing the art. As he told Langston Hughes, he wanted to write poetry, not Negro poetry; he wanted to be a poet, not a Negro poet. It was akin to his wanting to be first in his class, and being Phi Beta Kappa (which he was). It was a means of excelling and being exempla-

Cullen in 1941, photographed by Carl Van Vechten.

ry. Having several volumes of poetry to his name, several awards, and critical recognition as a poet among Negroes, the real incentive was gone. He already had what he wanted. Of course, his health began to deteriorate; he was troubled with ulcers and hypertension—common ailments of exemplars. Remarkably, in 1945, when he was just forty-three, Cullen began to arrange with his publisher for a collection of his poetry. He did not plan to publish another book of verse, and he wanted a single volume to contain the work on which his reputation should rest. *On These I Stand* appeared in 1947, just about a year after Countee Cullen's death. (pp. 205-14)

> *Nathan Irvin Huggins, "Art: The Ethnic Province," in his* Harlem Renaissance, *Oxford University Press, Inc., 1971, pp. 190-243.*

Arthur P. Davis (essay date 1974)

[*Davis, an American scholar of black literature, has contributed articles, short stories, and book reviews to magazines, anthologies, and professional journals. He also coedited* The Negro Caravan *(1941) and* Cavalcade: Negro American Writers from 1760 to the Present *(1971). In the following excerpt, he discusses the "alien-and-exile" theme in Cullen's works and provides a positive assessment of Cullen's contribution to modern poetry. An early version of this essay was published in* Phylon *in 1953.*]

The work of Cullen is found in nine major publications: one novel, two children's books, a version of *Medea* which also contains poems, and five volumes of verse. Though he wrote effectively in other genres, Cullen is pre-eminently a lyrical poet. As a poet, he admits to being "a rank conservative, loving the measured line and the skillful rhyme." Though he rebelled against being labeled a "Negro poet," he is, if not the finest, certainly one of the best poets of the New Negro Renaissance.

In each of his publications Cullen grouped his racial poems under the heading "Color." Many of the pieces in these sections fall into the alien-and-exile category. Most of the early New Negro poets use this theme, but Cullen used it more persistently and effectively than any of the others.

In poem after poem he states or implies that the American Negro is and can never be other than an alien here, an exile from his African homeland. As such he suffers from the insults and discriminations that unassimilated foreigners of all kinds endure, as well as a few additional ones because of his color. The Negro has not only lost an idyllic mother country, he has also lost his pagan gods, gods which, unlike the pale Christian deities, would be sympathetic to his peculiar needs. The religious loss is stressed more in Cullen's poems than in those of other Renaissance poets. In all probability he used the theme to express poetically some of his own religious concerns, as we shall see below.

In these poems Africa is not actually a real place. It is a symbol, an idealized land in which the Negro was once happy and free. The Harlem Renaissance poets used it to accentuate the differences between the Negro's harsh American existence and that he once led in this legendary "dusky dream-lit land." This subconscious contrast is never absent from the alien-and-exile's thoughts, and it puts a tremendous pressure on him. The best example of the alien-and-exile theme, Cullen's **"Heritage,"** describes dramatically this atavistic "pull":

> What is Africa to me:
> Copper sun or scarlet sea,
> Jungle star or jungle track,
> Strong bronzed men, or regal black
> Women from whose loins I sprang
> When the birds of Eden sang?
> *One three centuries removed*
> *From the scenes his fathers loved,*
> *Spicy grove, cinnamon tree,*
> *What is Africa to me?*

Neither night or day can the speaker find peace or a release from the pull of *Africa* drumming in his blood. Twisting and writhing like a "baited worm," he wants to strip and dance "in an old remembered way." Though he fights against it, he also longs for "quaint, outlandish heathen gods / Black men fashion out of rods...." And he wishes God were black, believing that if He were, He would suffer as the Negro suffers and therefore be more sympathetic to black misery. The poem ends on a note of doubt concerning his ability to fight the pull of the motherland:

> *All day long and all night through,*
> *One thing only must I do:*
> *Quench my pride and cool my blood,*
> *Lest I perish in the flood.*
> *Lest a hidden ember set*
> *Timber that I thought was wet*
> *Burning like the dryest flax,*
> *Melting like the merest wax,*
> *Lest the grave restore its dead.*
> *Not yet has my heart or head*
> *In the least way realized*
> *They and I are civilized.*

Although, as **"Heritage"** suggests, there is no way of escape for the black exile, there are means of alleviating the pain. One is to glorify the differences between the two groups, making attractive those which the enemy would deride:

> My love is dark as yours is fair
>   Yet lovelier I hold her
> Than listless maids with pallid hair
>   And blood that's thin and colder.

(This is an early variant of the present-day "black is beautiful" slogan.) Another means of alleviating the condition is to rise superior to it through the wisdom and courage that suffering brings:

> How being black and living through the pain
> Of it, is courage more than angels have.

Suicide is still another way out for the black sufferer, and in one of Cullen's longer poems, **"The Shroud of Color,"** the speaker considers this means:

> "Lord, being dark," I said, "I cannot bear
> The further touch of earth, the scented air;
> Lord, being dark, forewilled to that despair
> My color shrouds me in, I am as dirt
> Beneath my brother's heel; there is a hurt
> In all the simple joys which to a child
> Are sweet; they are contaminate, defiled
> By truths of wrongs the childish vision fails
> To see; too great a cost this birth entails.
> I strangle in this yoke drawn tighter than
> The worth of bearing it, just to be man.
> I am not brave enough to pay the price
> In full; I lack the strength to sacrifice."

A final means of alleviating the exile's agony is to acquire a mystic faith in a new world and a better day for the oppressed. One of Cullen's best sonnets, **"From the Dark Tower,"** considers this hope:

> We shall not always plant while others reap
> The golden increment of bursting fruit,
> Not always countenance abject and mute,
> That lesser men should hold their brothers
>   cheap; . . .
> We were not made eternally to weep.

As stated, Countee Cullen stressed the religious aspect of the alien-and-exile theme, and the last section if **"Heritage"** is a brilliant poetic reflection of both the speaker's and the author's divided loyalties. Writing his own biographical sketch in *Caroling Dusk,* Cullen makes the following revealing statement: "Born in New York City... and reared in the conservative atmosphere of a Methodist parsonage, Countee Cullen's chief problem has been that of reconciling a Christian upbringing with a pagan inclination. His life so far has not convinced him that the problem is insoluble." This was written in 1927. Several poems in his first volume, *Color* (1925), reflected, as did **"Heritage,"** his "pagan inclination," among them **"Pagan Prayer"** and **"Gods."**

In his second volume, however, we find signs of a change in the poet's attitude. Although there is a hint of skepticism in **"Epilogue,"** the poem **"In Spite of Death"** suggests a faith in the existence of an afterlife, and **"The Litany of the Dark People"** is almost a direct repudiation of the earlier pagan stand:

> Yet no assault the old gods make
> Upon our agony
> Shall swerve our footsteps from the wake
> Of Thine toward calvary.

In short, *Copper Sun* (1927) prepares the reader for the complete reversal the poet expresses in *The Black Christ and Other Poems* (1929).

The title poem in the *The Black Christ* not only repudiates Cullen's earlier religious position, it also repudiates the whole alien-and-exile attitude as expressed in **"Heritage"** and other verses on this theme. *The Black Christ,* modeled on a medieval saints' legend, is actually a strong affirmation of faith in Christianity and in the Negro's place in America ("This ground and I, are we not one?"). It may be approached as a *débat* between the Cullen of *Color,* paganistic yet seeking, and the Cullen of *The Black Christ,* who tells us in **"Counter Mood"**:

> I who am mortal say I shall not die;
> I who am dust of this am positive
> That though my nights tend towards the grave, yet
>   I
> Shall on some brighter day arise and live.

With *The Black Christ* volume, the poet took leave of racial writing, of the type of poems he placed under the heading "Color." (We note that in his first volume there are twenty-three poems in this category; in *Copper Sun,* seven; in *The Black Christ,* four, including, of course, the long title poem. *Medea and Some Poems* contains twenty pieces in all, but only one is related to racial matters, and the relationship is oblique.) In one of these "Color" pieces in *The Black Christ,* pointedly entitled **"To Certain Critics,"** Cullen leaves us in no doubt concerning his position:

> Then call me traitor if you must,
> Shout treason and default!
> Say I betray a sacred trust....
> I'll bear your censure as your praise,
> *For never shall the clan*
> *Confine my singing to its ways*
> *Beyond the ways of man.* [italics inserted]

From now on, he seems to be saying, no "racial option" will confine me; I shall write as a poet, not as a "Negro poet." And he stuck to his decision. As stated above, *Medea and Some Poems* (1935), has only one race poem. In 1940 and 1942, with the "aid" of Christopher Cat, he published first *The Lost Zoo* and later *My Lives and How I Lost Them,* both charming and imaginative children's works.

Why did Cullen stop writing racial poems after *The Black Christ*? One answer the poet has given us. Indirectly, he probably gave us another, found also in *The Black Christ.* In a poem called **"Self Criticism"** the author writes:

> Shall I go all my bright days singing
>   (A little pallid, a trifle wan)
> The failing note still vainly clinging
> To the throat of the stricken swan?

And in another, entitled **"A Wish,"** he says:

> I hope when I have sung my rounds
>   Of song, I shall have the strength to slay
>   The wish to chirp on any grounds,
> Content that silence hold her sway,
> My tongue not rolling futile sounds
> After my heart has had its say.

Perhaps Cullen felt that he had *written out* on racial themes and elected to be silent. The race problem, to a sensitive person, can be an intolerable bore and a great weariness to the soul.

In addition to the "Color" grouping in each volume (except *Medea and Some Poems*), Cullen used the following divisions: In *Color,* "Epitaphs," "For Love's Sake," and "Varia"; in *Copper Sun,* "The Deep in Love," "At Cambridge," "Varia," and "Juvenilia"; and in *The Black Christ and Other Poems,* "Varia" and "Interlude." The poems in these sections, as one deduces from the titles, concern themselves with the subjects that lyric poets from the time of the Greeks have written about: love, the joys of nature, the transitoriness of life, and death.

For some reason Cullen was morbidly concerned with death and death-imagery. He uses funereal allusions oftentimes in poetry in which, when first read, they seem out of place. One expects to meet skull-and-crossbones references in poems like **"A Brown Girl Dead,"** **"Requiescam,"** and **"Two Thoughts on Death,"** but they appear just as frequently in other poems, **"The Love Tree,"** **"Advice to a Beauty,"** and **"The Proud Heart."** The poet, for some reason, was also morbidly concerned with suicide. For example, **"The Wise,"** **"Suicide Chant,"** **"The Shroud of Color,"** **"Mood,"** and **"Harsh World That Lashest Me"** are all suicide poems, and there are others. In the last-named poem the poet catalogues ominously the several ways to go:

> I think an impulse stronger than my mind
> May someday grasp a knife, unloose a vial,
> Or with a leaden ball unbind
> The cords that tie me to the rank and file....

It is always dangerous to confuse the author with the speaker in a poem, whether the subject is suicide or love, but one notes that Cullen's love poems *after* his unfortunate first marriage take on a bitter tone. A good example of the type is **"Song in Spite of Myself"**:

> Never love with all your heart,
>   It only ends in aching;
> And bit by bit to the smallest part
>   That organ will be breaking.

Cullen is excellent as a writer of "Epitaphs." These short, closely packed verses have a bite and a sting uncommon in Renaissance poetry. One of the best known and most often-quoted of these little poems is **"For a Lady I Know"**:

> She even thinks that up in heaven
>   Her class lies late and snores,
> While poor black cherubs rise at seven
>   To do celestial chores

Cullen's protest poetry, as exemplified in the above epitaph, was seldom, if ever, a frontal attack. He preferred the oblique, the hinted, the ironic approach. In one of his late poems, **"Scottsboro, Too, Is Worth Its Song (a poem to American poets),"** he points out that the

Sacco-Vanzetti case brought forth a flood of poetic protest. Thinking about the precedent set:

> Surely, I said,
> Now will the poets sing.
>   But they have raised no cry.
>   I wonder why.

One of the most brilliant of Cullen's poems in this vein, a piece that has become a protest classic, is entitled **"Incident"**:

> Once riding in old Baltimore,
>   Heart-filled, head-filled with glee,
> I saw a Baltimorean
>   Keep looking straight at me.
>
> Now I was eight and very small,
>   And he was no whit bigger,
> And so I smiled, but he poked out
>   His tongue, and called me, "Nigger."
>
> I saw the whole of Baltimore
>   From May until December;
> Of all the things that happened there
>   That's all that I remember.

Cullen had the skill of McKay, but not the intensity. He preferred the suggestion to the blunt statement. He pricked rather than slashed.

The verse forms of Cullen, like those of McKay, are traditional: quatrains, couplets, stanzas of varying lengths, and sonnets. He has been criticized for using too slavishly these tried forms, for never, as did Langston Hughes, venturing out into the forms made popular by the New Poetry Movement or forms derived from folk literature. This brings up a foolish question: Would he have been a better poet if he had abandoned his classic models? The trouble with writing like Keats and other nineteenth-century greats is that they are difficult men to follow. Even though Cullen was by no means an unworthy follower of such poets, their greatness tends in some measure to dwarf by comparison his accomplishment. Cullen, however, had a motivation Keats never had. Cullen unlike Keats knew what it meant to be called a *"nigger."*

As a poet Countee Cullen will probably outlast his century. Measured by any standard, his work, particularly the "Color" pieces, will be read as long as protest poems have meaning in America. There are critics who believe that **"Heritage"** is the best poem published during the Harlem Renaissance. (pp. 75-81)

> *Arthur P. Davis, "First Fruits: Countee Cullen," in his* From the Dark Tower: Afro-American Writers, 1900 to 1960, *Howard University Press, 1974, pp. 73-83.*

Houston A. Baker, Jr. (essay date 1974)

[*A poet and educator, Baker has contributed essays on black literature to numerous anthologies and periodicals, including* Phylon, Black World, *and* The Virginia Quarterly Review. *In addition, he has edited critical volumes on African, Caribbean, and black American literature. In the following excerpt, he surveys themes and techniques in Cullen's poetry.*]

In a headnote in **Caroling Dusk,** Cullen states that one of his chief problems was "reconciling a Christian upbringing with a pagan inclination." The poems in **Color** reveal the accuracy of his comment, for a dichotomy pervades the volume. Faith and doubt, hedonism and reverence, innocence and experience, white and black, life and death are constantly juxtaposed, and the tensions that result often lead to striking poems. In the dedicatory poem, for example, the brevity of existence is set against the implied immortality of the poet, and the germination of spring is seen as a foil for the destructiveness of winter:

> When the dreadful Ax
>   Rives me apart,
> When the sharp wedge cracks
>   My arid heart,
> Turn to this book
>   Of the singing me
> For a springtime look
>   At the wintry tree.

("To You Who Read My Book")

And in **"Tableau,"** Cullen uses nature imagery to demonstrate the contrast between black and white, the natural and the artificial:

> Locked arm in arm they cross the way,
>   The black boy and the white,
> The golden splendor of the day,
>   The sable pride of night.
>
> From lowered blinds the dark folk stare,
>   And here the fair folk talk,
> Indignant that these two should dare
>   In unison to walk.

The boys are outside, joined in the natural camaraderie of youth, while their elders—both Black and white—gossip about their friendship behind lowered blinds. Bertram Woodruff has commented aptly on the bifurcation in Cullen's poetry between a cynical realism and a subjective idealism—a materialistic and a theistic conception of life [see Further Reading]—and James Weldon Johnson noted the poet's sudden ironic turns of thought [see excerpt dated 1931]. These are essential characteristics of the canon and grow, in part, out of the conflicts occasioned by Cullen's aesthetic stance. The poet who did not want his work bolstered by racial considerations begins **Color** with twenty-four racial poems. The artist who adopted the romantic mode is pulled continually toward the darker side of this realm, and his work abounds in pessimism and despair. Divided into four sections—Color, Epitaphs, For Love's Sake, and Varia—**Color** expresses the major themes of the canon.

The racial poems in the volume range from the somewhat bombastic **"The Shroud of Color"** to the magnificently sustained and accomplished **"Heritage"** with a variety of noble sentiment, libertinism, atavism, fine description, and "initiation" filling out the middle range. Arthur Davis has demonstrated [see excerpt dated 1974] that one of the chief subjects of the opening section is alienation and exile:

> For Cullen, the Negro is both a geographical and a spiritual exile. He has lost not only an idyllic homeland; but equally as important, he has also lost understanding pagan gods who would be far more sympathetic to his peculiar needs than the pale Christian deities.

One finds this sense of displacement in poems such as **"Atlantic City Waiter," "Near White," "Brown Boy to Brown Girl," "Pagan Prayer,"** and **"Heritage."** In these poems, the Black man is conceived as a deracinated individual pulled abruptly from some edenic place and set amidst strange gods. But there are also poems that show no sense of alienation; they simply enjoin a hedonistic existence. **"To a Brown Girl,"** for example, offers the following comment:

> What if his glance is bold and free,
>   His mouth the lash of whips?
> So should the eyes of lovers be;
>   And so a lover's lips.

And **"To a Brown Boy"** gives similar advice:

> That brown girl's swagger gives a twitch
>   To beauty like a queen;
> Lad, never dam your body's itch
>   When loveliness is seen.

There are poems, moreover, that have more to do with a specific social situation than with a feeling of exile. **"A Brown Girl Dead"** and **"Saturday's Child"** are both ironical protests against economic oppression:

> Her mother pawned her wedding ring
>   To lay her out in white;
> She'd be so proud she'd dance and sing
>   To see herself tonight.
> (**"A Brown Girl Dead"**)

> For I was born on Saturday—
>   "Bad time for planting a seed,"
> Was all my father had to say,
>   And, "One more mouth to feed."
>
> Death cut the strings that gave me life,
>   And handed me to Sorrow,
> The only kind of middle wife
>   My folks could beg or borrow.
> (**"Saturday's Child"**)

The dominant feeling of the racial poems, however, is (in the words of Claude McKay) one of being "born, far from my native clime, / Under the white man's menace, out of time."

"Yet Do I Marvel" and **"Heritage"** capture the irony and ambiguity of this situation. The former is devastating in its restrained cynicism:

> I doubt not God is good, well-meaning, kind,
> And did He stoop to quibble could tell why
> The little buried mole continues blind,
> Why flesh that mirrors Him must some day die.

The list of incongruities moves to the assertion that God's ways are too grandiose for the simple human mind; then with a swift stroke of genius, come the concluding lines:

> Yet do I marvel at this curious thing:
> To make a poet black, and bid him sing!

The *angst* of Cullen's aesthetic is summed up in this couplet. By association, the Black poet takes on the burdens of the disinherited and is doomed to the tortures of Sisyphus and Tantalus; the persona exposes both his own skepticism and the awesome task of the Black artist.

"Heritage" displays the same sense of irony and skepticism. The poem opens with what turns out to be a rhetorical question:

> What is Africa to me:
> Copper sun or scarlet sea,
> Jungle star or jungle track,
> Strong bronzed men, or regal black
> Women from whose loins I sprang
> When the birds of Eden sang?

The text reveals that Africa is not only the spirit realm to which the narrator feels most allied, but also a land in fierce opposition to his present home. As in McKay's **"Flame-Heart,"** the narrator of **"Heritage"** makes a claim that is not justified by the poem itself:

> Africa? A book one thumbs
> Listlessly, till slumber comes.
> Unremembered are her bats
> Circling through the night, her cats
> Crouching in the river reeds,
> Stalking gentle flesh that feeds
> By the river brink . . . .

The vivid descriptions of its fierce flowers and pagan impulses show that Africa is much more than bedtime reading for the narrator. Moreover, when he states that he is trying to move beyond the call of heathen deities, the text leaps forth in refutation. Some critics have faulted Cullen for **"Heritage,"** stating that he makes topographical mistakes and perpetuates the idea of the Black man as a "noble savage." Such responses can carry one only so far, however, with a poem as thoroughly ironical as **"Heritage."** While it is true that there is an undue enthusiasm recurrent in the passages of Africa, it is also true that Cullen was interested in a blatant contrast between the benign and unsmiling deities of the new land and the thoroughly initiated gods of the old. The entire poem is placed in a confessional framework as the narrator tries to define his relationship to some white, ontological being and finds that a Black impulse ceaselessly draws him back. The italicized concluding lines read like the penance exacted from an unregenerate schoolboy:

All day long and all night through,
One thing only must I do:
Quench my pride and cool my blood,
Lest I perish in the flood,
Lest a hidden ember set
Timber that I thought was wet
Burning like the dryest flax,
Melting like the merest wax,
Lest the grave restore its dead,
Not yet has my heart or head
In the least way realized
They and I are civilized.

"Heritage" is a longer and more comprehensive statement of the message contained in **"Pagan Prayer,"** and it reveals the sharp line that Cullen saw dividing two cultures. The poet's "paganism" reveals itself in the end as a repudiation of the white man's religion.

A poem like **"Incident"** reveals why such a rejection is necessary:

Once riding in old Baltimore,
    Heart-filled, head-filled with glee,
I saw a Baltimorean
    Keep looking straight at me.

Now I was eight and very small,
    And he was no whit bigger,
And so I smiled, but he poked out
    His tongue, and called me, "Nigger."

I saw the whole of Baltimore
    From May until December;
Of all the things that happened there
    That's all that I remember.

The sense of irony and the dichotomized world-view that appear throughout Cullen's work are skillfully captured here. There is a movement from gay innocence to initiation, which is repeated in the seasonal reference ("May until December"), and at the time of recounting the speaker has not forgotten the incident. Not only the vistas of Baltimore, one suspects, but the whole of his life has been clouded by the sudden realization that the norms of the larger society do not work for him. Adjustment often involves the type of repudiation seen in **"Heritage"** and **"Pagan Prayer."**

The two themes that stand out in *Color*'s nonracial poems are love and mortality. The second section consists of twenty-nine epitaphs written in the manner of Edgar Lee Masters's *Spoon River Anthology*. Cullen, however, is not interested in showing what the restrictions of the village do to the human psyche. He is concerned with the many types that make up society, and thus the poems display subtle irony, tender feeling, and adept portraiture. **"For a Lady I Know"** captures in miniature the type of woman whom the poet's atavistic **"Atlantic City Waiter"** might have served:

She even thinks that up in heaven
    Her class lies late and snores,
While poor black cherubs rise at seven
    To do celestial chores.

"For My Grandmother" demonstrates Cullen's ability to set forth mild sentiments:

This lovely flower fell to seed;
    Work gently, sun and rain;
She held it as her dying creed
    That she would grow again.

There is fine irony in both **"For a Virgin"** and **"For an Atheist"**:

For forty years I shunned the lust
    Inherent in my clay;
Death only was so amorous
    I let him have his way.

and

Mountains cover me like rain,
    Billows whirl and rise;
Hide me from the stabbing pain
    In His reproachful eyes.

Finally, there is the often quoted **"For Paul Laurence Dunbar"**:

Born of the sorrowful of heart,
    Mirth was a crown upon his head;
Pride kept his twisted lips apart
    In jest, to hide a heart that bled.

Though the poems as a group offer a comment on various styles of human life, the overwhelming fact of the sequence—as of all epitaphs—is the common end to which flesh is heir. This condition brings about much of the humor that resides in the individual sketches, and the same sense of mortality occasions the despair that appears in a number of the poems in the concluding sections of *Color.*

It may seem commonplace to say that Cullen's romanticism is derivative, but in the context of nineteenth-century English poetry, the statement becomes more descriptive. Though the poet chose as his ideal the second wave of British romanticism, including Keats and Shelley, his own lyrics read more like the work of Dante Rossetti, Charles Swinburne, and the authors of *fin de siècle* England. These were the romantics *manqué* who shared the same lyrical impulses but lacked the sweeping vision, the mythicizing potential, and the colossal certainties of their predecessors. The shades of Ernest Dowson and Arthur Symons appear with the first lines of **"Oh, For a Little While Be Kind"**:

Oh, for a little while be kind to me
Who stand in such imperious need of you,
And for a fitful space let my head lie
Happily on your passion's frigid breast.

The moment of contentment is brief, and though the poem ends on an ironical note, its basic assumptions are that life is fleeting and love is short. **"If You Should Go"** deals once again with the departure of the beloved, and **"To One Who Said Me Nay"** is a restatement of the familiar *carpe diem* theme. **"Advice to Youth"** follows the same pattern, while **"Caprice"** captures the heart-rending and incomprehensible ways of love:

> "I'll tell him, when he comes," she said,
>   "Body and baggage, to go,
> Though the night be darker than my hair,
>   And the ground be hard with snow."
>
> But when he came with his gay black head
>   Thrown back, and his lips apart,
> She flipped a light hair from his coat,
>   And sobbed against his heart.

The male figure here reminds one of the protagonist in **"Two Who Crossed a Line (He Crosses),"** and once again we see the contrasts that mark Cullen's verse—harmony and discontent, light and dark. Both **"Sacrament"** and **"Bread and Wine"**—as one might expect—juxtapose the sacred and the profane. In the first, the speaker is considered unworthy of the beloved; in the second, the beloved is deemed the only thing holy in a mortal world. Cullen's use of religious imagery in the two poems is in harmony with his canon as a whole, for time and again there are biblical allusions. The final poem in the third section, **"Spring Reminiscence,"** moves quite well until the final couplet, where the merger of a religious allusion with a colloquialism destroys the effect. The poem, however, has thematic significance, for it is a memory in spring of springs gone by. There is the possibility, in other words, of resurrecting the joy and beauty of the past through the agency of poetry. The poet and his experiences possess a certain immortality, and spring—the time of nature's rejuvenation—becomes symbolic of enduring spirituality.

All of this cannot be inferred from **"Spring Reminiscence,"** of course, but the stanza quoted earlier from **"To You Who Read My Book,"** combined with **"In Memory of Col. Charles Young"** and **"To John Keats, Poet: At Springtime,"** make the argument clearer. Young, the Black colonel who was retired from the army at the beginning of World War I to prevent his promotion to general, becomes one with nature in the course of the poem:

> The great dark heart is like a well
>   Drained bitter by the sky,
> And all the honeyed lies they tell
>   Come there to thirst and die.
>
> No lie is strong enough to kill
>   The roots that work below;
> From your rich dust and slaughtered will
>   A tree with tongues will grow.

And there is a similar merger and generative process in **"To John Keats, Poet: At Springtime"**:

> And you and I, shall we lie still,
> John Keats, while Beauty summons us?
> Somehow I feel your sensitive will
> Is pulsing up some tremulous
> Sap road of a maple tree, whose leaves
> Grow music as they grow, since your
> Wild voice is in them, a harp that grieves
> For life that opens death's dark door.

> Though dust, your fingers still can push
> The Vision Splendid to a birth,
> Though now they work as grass in the hush
> Of the night on the broad sweet page of the earth.

Part of Cullen's "pagan inclination" displays itself in poems like these, where he not only reminds us of the ineluctability of the spiritual, but also recalls the fact that spring (before its arrogation by Christianity) was a time of bacchanalian celebration and heady splendor in the grass. For the Poet, spring is the season when the natural man, the sensitive soul, and the germinating seed push forth in a rebirth of wonder.

Finally in *Color* are Cullen's concern for the outcast—**"Black Magdalens," "For Daughters of Magdalen,"** and **"Judas Iscariot"**—and his treatment of the idealistic dreamer. The poet achieves a masterful irony by placing streetwalkers in a biblical context:

> They fare full ill since Christ forsook
>   The cross to mount a throne,
> And Virtue still is stooping down
>   To cast the first hard stone.

and

> Ours is the ancient story:
>   Delicate flowers of sin,
> Lilies, arrayed in glory,
>   That would not toil nor spin.

Judas is viewed as a man who had to betray Christ so the vision He cherished would come true. In **"Simon the Cyrenian Speaks,"** the persona says:

> But He was dying for a dream,
>   And He was very meek,
> And in His eyes there shone a gleam
>   Men journeyed far to seek.

In **"For a Poet,"** the creative artist is also viewed as a keeper of dreams. Like other matter in Cullen's canon, therefore, Christianity is seen in a dual light. Insofar as God is cryptic or inscrutable in *Color*'s first two poems, He is the object of cynicism and repudiation; as Christ, the carrier of the dream, however, He is to be ranked among the highest idealists.

"I've kept on doing the same things, and doing them no better. I have never gotten to the things I really wanted to do," Dunbar told James Weldon Johnson as he suffered the agonies of his final illness. Some would expect a similar confession from Countee Cullen, since *Color* is his finest volume, although he went on to produce four more. If the poet had made a similar statement, he would have falsified his own accomplishments. Some things he did a good deal better as his career progressed. From his early efforts, he moved to the fine group of poems labelled "Interlude" in *The Black Christ,* and he developed his narrative voice in *The Ballad of the Brown Girl.* He not only provided a rendering of Euripides's *Medea,* but also did work as a translator. And in his final volume, he seems to counteract—through the sanity and balance of his verse—

Benjamin Brawley's charge that "there is a sophomoric note in the work of Mr. Cullen that he finds it hard to outgrow" [see Further Reading].

The overriding dichotomy in the second volume is one of stasis and change. On the one hand, the poet believes despair is enduring and death the bitter end of all. On the other, he sees a better day approaching, the possibility of regeneration and immortality, and death as an occasion for solace and wisdom. The seven racial poems in *Copper Sun* fall generally on the positive side. Though he is now battered and scarred, there is a new day coming for the Black American:

> We shall not always plant while others reap
> The golden increment of bursting fruit
> Not always countenance, abject and mute,
> That lesser men should hold their brothers cheap
> **("From the Dark Tower")**

> If for a day joy masters me,
> Think not my wounds are healed;
> . . . . .
> They shall bear blossoms with the fall;
> I have their word for this,
> Who tend my roots with rains of gall,
> And suns of prejudice.
> **("Confession")**

> Our flesh that was a battle-ground
> Shows now the morning-break;
> The ancient deities are downed
> For Thy eternal sake.
> Now that the past is left behind,
> Fling wide Thy garment's hem
> To keep us one with Thee in mind,
> Thou Christ of Bethlehem.
> **("The Litany of the Dark People")**

The metaphor of germination appears (particularly in **"Threnody for a Brown Girl"**), and the last poem in the group seems to favor an acceptance of the white man's religion as a means of salvation. Despite the laconic warning of Uncle Jim that "White folks is white," the speaker in most of the poems has adopted the attitude that improvement is a reality for the Black American. There are tones of apocalypse in both **"From the Dark Tower"** and **"Confession,"** but **"The Litany of the Dark People"** does much to soften them.

The optimism of the first section is out of harmony with the remainder of *Copper Sun,* for a note of despondency sounds with **"Pity the Deep in Love."** And while there is a contrapuntal rhythm between this and the poems that speak of the eternality of beauty and the splendor of the dream, the pervasive timbre is melancholy:

> Pity the deep in love;
> They move as men asleep,
> Traveling a narrow way
> Precipitous and steep.
> **("Pity the Deep in Love")**

> But never past the frail intent
> My will may flow,
> Though gentle looks of yours are bent
> Upon me where I go.

> So must I, starved for love's delight,
> Affect the mute,
> When love's divinest acolyte
> Extends me holy fruit.
> **("Timid Lover")**

> Of all men born he deems himself so much
>   accurst,
> His plight so piteous, his proper pain so rare,
> The very bread he eats so dry, so fierce his thirst,
> What shall we liken such a martyr to? Compare
> Him to a man with poison raging in his throat,
> And far away the one mind with an antidote.
> **("Portrait of a Lover")**

The unrequited love, dejection, indifference, *carpe diem,* and sighing in *Copper Sun* would have delighted the nineteenth-century decadent poets and would stimulate anew the pale shades of Sir John Suckling and Edmund Waller. Cullen's songs of desperation in the second volume do not seem to have a substantial base; somehow they come across as exercises in depression rather than genuine reflections of the poet's inner being. It is, of course, difficult to argue about the effect a poem has on the reader, and one should steer clear of Wimsatt and Beardsley's "affective fallacy"—contemplating a poem as though it were the ground for some ultimate emotional state. What heightens one's impression of insincerity, however, is the body of poems that state exactly the opposite point of view.

The lovers' relationship may not terminate entirely, and there is always a nagging hope in the background:

> What if you come
> Again and swell
> The throat of some
> Mute bird;
> How shall I tell?
> How shall I know
> That it is so,
> Having heard?
> **("Words to My Love")**

> Come, let us plant our love as farmers plant
> A seed, and you shall water it with tears,
> And I shall weed it with my hands until
> They bleed. Perchance this buried love of ours
> Will fall on goodly ground and bear a tree
> With fruit and flowers...
> **("The Love Tree")**

Though love departs, its beauty may either linger or be reborn. And this ambiguity is also present in the poet's treatment of death, for in **"To Lovers of Earth: Fair Warning"** he states that man's end is certain and that it goes unmarked by nature. In the following poem, **"In Spite of Death,"** however, the speaker says:

> No less shall I in some new fashion flare
> Again, when death has blown my candles out;
> Although my blood went down in shameful rout
> Tonight, by all this living frame holds fair,
> Though death should closet me tonight, I swear
> Tomorrow's sun would find his cupboard bare.

In **"Cor Cordium," "The Poet,"** and **"To Endymion,"** Cullen once again views the poet and his song as immortal and further confuses the issue with **"Hunger"** and **"At the Wailing Wall in Jerusalem,"** where he views both dreams and the holy wall as tokens of everlasting beauty.

The question is not one of arrangement in *Copper Sun*; no new scheme would alter the content of the individual poems. Cullen seems to have been confronted with the problem of choosing between alternatives. The smaller number of racial poems is an indication that he had decided to steer closer to the universal romantic ideal, but the prevailing dichotomy and the issue of "belief in poetry" that it raises give evidence that he had not found a firm base on which to stand as a romantic poet. He laments, derides, and protests the passing of love and life but never faces the issues of despair and mortality in a convincing manner. One suspects that Harvey Webster had *Copper Sun* very much in mind when he wrote: "Cullen neither accepted nor developed a comprehensive world-view. As a consequence his poems seem to result from occasional impulses rather than from directions by an integrated individual" [see Further Reading]. Of course, one knows that Cullen was anything but an "integrated individual" and that the bifurcations in his *Weltanschauung* result, in part, from his aesthetic stance. They play an important role in *Color.* In the second volume, however, the division between stasis and change is accompanied by a narrowing of range and blatant contradictions that cause one to think back on Brawley's statement with a smile of assent.

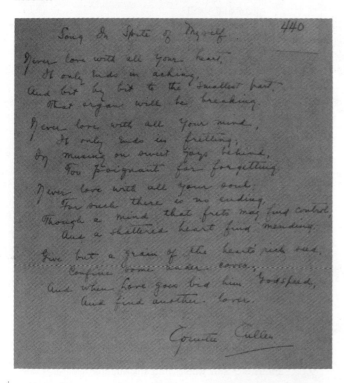

Holograph of Cullen's "Song in Spite of Myself," a poem published in the December 1928 issue of Harper's.

The Ballad of the Brown Girl: An Old Ballad Retold makes much more effective use of the divisions that are basic to Cullen's poetry. The narrator insists that the story was garnered from the grandams "in the land where the grass is blue," and it is not surprising that an English ballad should find its way into the repertoire of a Kentucky storyteller, since some regions of that state were at one time considered the finest preserves of British Elizabethan dialect. What is striking is the interpretation that Cullen places on the ballad. Rather than a story of a "dark brown" peasant contending with a fair city maiden for the heart of an aristocrat, the story is presented as a small and colorful drama of miscegenation and conflict. The leitmotif and moral involve the dangers of the acquisitive instincts, and Lord Thomas's mother is left with the burden of the guilt. Cullen shows himself a master of the ballad stanza in the poem, and his unique rendering of the tale makes it possible for him to engage in fine color imagery:

> Her hair was black as sin is black
> And ringed about with fire;
> Her eyes were black as night is black
> When moon and stars conspire;
> Her mouth was one red cherry clipt
> In twain, her voice a lyre.

or

> Her skin was white as almond milk
> Slow trickling from the flower;
> Her frost-blue eyes were darkening
> Like clouds before a shower.

There are several things that mar the poem. First, the hero is a pale and nervous spectre when the ballad opens, a man who must kneel before his mother to learn which woman to choose. At the end, he is a farseeing individual capable of an ennobling suicide. T. S. Eliot's reservations about Hamlet might well apply to Lord Thomas. Second, Cullen—after a skillful dramatic buildup and climax—relies upon description for his denouement. Finally, the ascription of guilt to the mother seems simplistic, as do the morals of most ballads. Cullen could have mined his material, however, for a more complex statement of the issues his interpretation raises. There are also several infelicities of style.

The Black Christ and Other Poems represents a marked progression in Cullen's thought. The volume closes rather than opens with a section titled "Color," and the beginning "Varia" group makes a number of definite statements about the poet and the age in which he lives. In **"To the Three for Whom the Book,"** the speaker is the committed, romantic poet—the man who dwells above the bending of an "idolatrous knee" to stone and steel. He is the individual who writes of "old, unhappy, far-off things, / And battles long ago." **"That Bright Chimeric Beast"** reinforces the point:

> That bright chimeric beast
> Conceived yet never born,
> Save in the poet's breast,
> The white-flanked unicorn,

> Never may be shaken
> From his solitude;
> Never may be taken
> In any earthly wood.

There is lost love and despondency in *The Black Christ,* but the volume also expresses a sincerity and a certainty about the artist's task that are lacking in *Copper Sun.* In "**To an Unknown Poet,**" the dreamer is removed from an unholy time, and in "**Counter Mood,**" the speaker asserts his own immortality. "**A Miracle Demanded**" comes as a surprise from the poet who marched to a pagan drummer in *Color;* he now asks for a renewal of his faith and a confirmation of the position taken in "**Counter Mood.**" Finally, there are poems like "**A Wish,**" "**Minutely Hurt,**" and "**Self Criticism**" that show a movement toward a more balanced view of life. In "**Minutely Hurt,**" there is little of the dire lamentation of the rejected lover, and the other two poems express the poet's hope that when he has had his say he will possess the wisdom and courage to stop writing. Meanwhile, the dreamer's life remains one of commitment and loneliness:

> The poet is compelled to love his star,
> Not knowing he could never tell you why
> Though silence makes inadequate reply.
>
>   ("**Tongue-tied**")

> A hungry cancer will not let him rest
> Whose heart is loyal to the least of dreams;
> There is a thorn forever in his breast
> Who cannot take his world for what it seems;
> Aloof and lonely must he ever walk,
> Plying a strange and unaccustomed tongue,
> An alien to the daily round of talk,
> Mute when the sordid songs of earth are sung.
>
>   ("**A Thorn Forever in the Breast**")

The sense of maturity and dedication in *The Black Christ* results first, from the marital difficulties Cullen was encountering when a number of the poems were written. Second, the volume was composed in France, and it is possible that Cullen felt he could be "just a poet" there:

> As he whose eyes are gouged craves light to see,
> And he whose limbs are broken strength to run,
> So have I sought in you that alchemy
> That knits my bones and turns me to the sun;
> And found across a continent of foam
> What was denied my hungry heart at home.
>
>   ("**To France,**" from *The Medea and Some Poems*)

Third, when *The Black Christ* was published, he had tentatively resolved the problem of a Christian background and a pagan inclination.

"Interlude," the section that deals with the termination of a love affair, constitutes one of the most unified and consistent groups of Cullen's poetry, and its careful style and unfeigned simplicity are akin to George Meredith's *Modern Love.* Two poems capture the spirit and the mastery of the group:

> I know of all the words I speak or write,

> Precious and woven of a vibrant sound,
> None ever snares your faith, intrigues you quite,
> Or sends you soaring from the solid ground.
> You are the level-headed lover who
> Can match my fever while the kisses last,
> But you are never shaken through and through;
> Your roots are firm after the storm has passed.
>
> I shall know nights of tossing in my sleep
> Fondling a hollow where a head should lie;
> But you a calm review, no tears to weep,
> No wounds to dress, no futile breaths to sigh.
> Ever this was the way of wind with flame:
> To harry it, then leave swift as it came.
>
>   ("**The Simple Truth**")

> Breast under breast when you shall lie
>   With him who in my place
> Bends over you with flashing eye
>   And ever nearing face;
>
> Hand fast in hand when you shall tread
>   With him the springing ways
> Of love from me inherited
>   After my little phase;
>
> Be not surprised if suddenly
>   The couch of air confound
> Your ravished ears upbraidingly,
>   And silence turn to sound.
>
> But never let it trouble you,
>   Or cost you one caress;
> Ghosts are soon sent with a word or two
>   Back to their loneliness.
>
>   ("**Ghosts**")

Cullen thus deals with the most genuine and heart-rending emotions he had ever felt, and in the volume's final poem he constructs his strongest assertion of faith.

"**The Black Christ (Hopefully Dedicated to White America)**" is the story of a lynching in which Christ mysteriously appears and offers himself for the intended victim. The poem traces the narrator's movement from doubt to faith and depicts his mother as an archetypal southern Black American who holds to the ideals of Christianity. To view the poem as simply the story of a rebellious and agnostic Jim who strikes down a white man and is condemned to death by a mob, however, is to do it less than justice. And, in a sense, to treat the poem as a simple resolution of the narrator's uncertainties is to fail to comprehend its significance in Cullen's canon. On its most fundamental level, "**The Black Christ**" fits into the tradition of Black American literature as a conversion tale; it is one of those recountings—complete with mysterious events and marvellings at the Lord's way—that characterized the Black church during Reconstruction and that can be heard today when the out-of-town guest is called upon to "testify." Cullen captures the spirit of these occasions quite well in *One Way to Heaven,* and there is little doubt that the son of a successful Harlem minister was familiar with conversion stories. If the poem is seen in this light, some of its apparent flaws turn out to be necessities, e.g., the long retelling of incidents and the sense of suspense and wonder the narrator attempts to create toward the conclusion. A man speaking to a congregation would not be remiss in accounting for every detail and strange phenomenon.

Cullen seems to adopt the form of the conversion story in a rather tentative way, however, for Jim—the agnostic badman hero—certainly appears as glamorous as the sacrificial Christ. But surely this was intentional, since the final reconciliation represents a momentary stasis in the Christian-pagan conflict. Jim, after all, commits his assault because the white man has corrupted the natural reverence for spring on the part of the Black man and white woman, and the virginal tree on which Christ is hung comes to life after the lynching. Christ (the representative of religious faith) and Jim—the sensitive, agnostic worshipper of spring—come together in a rite of regeneration. In the pagan and natural moment, Jim and the white woman are as harmonious as the boys in "Tableau." The white man intrudes, and he and the mob stand for white America. The narrator never loses his admiration for his brother, and the wonder and firmness he feels in his new faith are the results of a miracle.

Throughout the poem, Cullen seems to stand by the narrator's side, whispering that both Christ, the dreamer, and the pagan-spirited Jim are needed to unify the opposing points of his canon. To say the poet avoids some of the issues—like Christ's exoneration of a murderer and the hopelessness His crucifixion portends—is to capture the letter of the poem, but not its spirit. It was inevitable that Cullen would attempt a synthesis and that he would do so in a manner that raised the question of race. The results are not altogether satisfactory, but the strong commitment to an idealistic point of view should not be forgotten. The poet, the dreamer, the man who treasures the wonders of spring wins out in the end. If culture was not entirely "colorless" in the United States, at least it was neutral enough in France for Cullen to compose his only truly romantic volume of poetry. The book contains the poet's message "To Certain Critics":

> Then call me traitor if you must,
> Shout treason and default!
> Say I betray a sacred trust
> Aching beyond this vault.
> I'll bear your censure as your praise,
> For never shall the clan
> Confine my singing to its way
> Beyond the ways of man.
>
> No racial option narrows grief,
> Pain is no patriot,
> And sorrow plaits her dismal leaf
> For all as lief as not.
> With blind sheep groping every hill,
> Searching an oriflamme,
> How shall the shepherd heart then thrill
> To only the darker lamb?

Six years elapsed between *The Black Christ* and *The Medea and Some Poems,* Cullen's last volume of serious verse. The prose rendering of Euripides's classic play is interesting and shows a broadening of the poet's activities, but it possesses little of the grandeur of the original. Cullen added two female characters to the drama to act

as confidantes for Medea; in Euripides's version, the entire chorus acts the role. The substitution means that one of the Greek dramatist's major contentions loses much of its force; no longer is a large sector of the city-state inclined toward the irrationality and paganism represented by the heroine. There seems little possibility that the entire order will be destroyed by the kind of wild frenzy that characterizes the *Bacchae.* Cullen's work is also more maudlin than Euripides's. Medea's soliloquy over her victims and the words of one of her children before the execution—"What are you such a baby for? Mother won't hurt us. Ah!"—drip with sentimentality. Finally, Cullen's characters speak far too often in Poor-Richard slang, and his heroine is reduced to a shrew who engages in such incongruously comical exchanges as:

> MEDEA. Then you have no sons yet, Aegeus?
> AEGEUS. None. The gods have kept be barren!
> MEDEA. Have you tried a wife? That might help.

Cullen's effort precedes Jean Paul Sartre's rendition of Aeschylus by a number of years. But Sartre's *The Flies* was undertaken as an act of freedom and was first performed in occupied Paris. Hence, there is more justification for his deliberately second-rate translation; it offers an example of "engaged" literature. Cullen's play suffers by comparison, for it shifts the original emphasis on the mythic, barbarian, and fatalistic to the hard-hearted woman scorned. Certainly, this aspect is present in the Euripidean version, but it is not blatant. Cullen's flaccid prose and rhyming choruses are scarcely improvements on earlier translations.

The twenty-eight lyrics in *The Medea* make the volume readable and show a mellowing of the poet's attitudes and a refinement of his technique. There is an expansion of his humanism in verses such as "Magnets," "Any Human to Another," "Every Lover," and "To One Not There," and he rededicates himself to poetry in "After a Visit (At Padraic Colum's Where There Were Irish Poets)." His "Sonnet: Some for a Little While Do Love" and the concluding poems of *The Medea* show a movement toward a more controlled verse and a more gentle (one might almost say "senescent") point of view:

> Some for a little while do love, and some for long;
> And some rare few forever and for aye;
> Some for the measure of a poet's song,
> And some the ribbon width of a summer's day.
> Some on a golden crucifix do swear,
> And some in blood do plight a fickle troth;
> Some struck divinely mad may only stare,
> And out of silence weave an iron oath.
>
> So many ways love has none may appear
> The bitter best, and none the sweetest worst;
> Strange food the hungry have been known to bear,
> And brackish water slakes an utter thirst.
> It is a rare and tantalizing fruit
> Our hands reach for, but nothing absolute.

"To France" asks that the land of "kindly foreign folk" act as the poet's Byzantium, and "Belitis Sings (From the French of Pierre Louys)" is charming in its delicate artificiality. Finally, **"The Cat"** and **"Cats"**—both translations of Baudelaire—substitute the feline loveliness of a domestic pet for the mythical beasts and fickle lovers seen elsewhere in Cullen's canon. Cats are "quite as scholars and as lovers bold," and they sit "in noble attitudes" and dream—"small sphinxes miming those in lonelier lands." The poet thus sinks quietly into a land of domesticity with a cat for his companion.

The volume closes, however, with **"Scottsboro, Too, Is Worth Its Song,"** a protest poem on the order of **"Not Sacco and Vanzetti"** (*The Black Christ*). Though Cullen would, henceforth, live and write in collaboration with his cherished Christopher Cat, "all disgrace" and "epic wrong" still exercise their ineluctable and dichotomizing influence. The man who was born Black and bidden to sing turned to the world of children for his next two books, but his canon closes on the propagandistic note that James Weldon Johnson found "well nigh irresistible" for the Black artist. (pp. 30-52)

> *Houston A. Baker, Jr., in his* A Many-Colored Coat of Dreams: The Poetry of Countee Cullen, *Broadside Press, 1974, 60 p.*

Bernard W. Bell (essay date 1987)

[*Bell is an American critic and educator. In the following excerpt from his 1987 study* The Afro-American Novel and Its Traditions, *he discusses characterizations in* One Way to Heaven *and compares the work with two novels by Langston Hughes.*]

Divided into two major parts, **One Way to Heaven,** like [Langston] Hughes's *Tambourines to Glory,* is a sympathetic exposure of the gullibility and superstition of unsophisticated lower-class urban blacks. It is the love story of Sam Lucas, a one-armed confidence man who fakes religious conversion at black churches up and down the Eastern seaboard to satisfy his immediate physical needs, and Mattie Johnson, an attractive but desperate young domestic whose religious zeal Sam awakens with his con game. At revival meetings and watch-night services, Sam goes into his act at a dramatic moment during testimonials. Walking from the rear of the church to the mourner's bench, he would throw down a greasy deck of cards and polished razor, fall on his knees in tears, and sob for salvation. To devout Methodists and Baptists, Sam's last-minute conversion was "mystery and miracle and the confirmation of faith." As they came forward to shake hands with the converts and show their gratitude, many of the faithful would secretly slip him money, and "he had never joined church yet but it had led to an affair." In Part 1 (chap. 1-7) Sam's act in a Harlem church becomes the catalyst for Mattie's salvation, and in blind faith she marries him. In Part 2 (chaps. 8-15) her religiosity drives him into the arms of another woman. But a fatal case of double pneumonia brings them together again, and for her sake he fakes a deathbed conversion.

The author-narrator's mild ridicule of the superstitious practices of his lower-class characters is in sharp contrast to his sardonic treatment of the pretentious customs of the black bourgeoisie. Sam, for example, uses his cards and razor for both good and evil, and though an indolent, irreligious vagabond, his excessive pragmatism evokes our sympathetic laughter. Equally humorous and realistic is Mattie's Aunt Mandy, whom the third-person omniscient author-narrator describes in the sympathetic manner that characterizes the frequent commentaries on the beliefs and rituals of the lower class: "Though she was not averse to trusting serenely to the ways of Providence, she often attempted by reading tea leaves and coffee dregs, and by consulting her cards, to speed the blessings of Heaven or to ward off, if possible, some celestial chastisement." In contrast, the language used in chapters 8, 9, and 10 to describe Constancia Brandon, Mattie's well-bred but patronizing black employer, and her high-society crowd is characterized by biting wit, repartee, and hyperbole.

A Boston-born Baptist, Constancia Brandon changed her name at sixteen and rejected "the religious ecstasies of the Baptist and Methodist faiths... to scale the heavenly ramparts by way of the less rugged paths of the Episcopalian persuasion." Constancia's "tongue was her chief attraction, ornament, and deterrent." At Radcliffe she was called Lady Macbeth, not because she was unsexed and shrewd in the pursuit of her ambition, but because she never spoke in a monosyllable when she could use a polysyllable. Her monthly soirees were pompous, gala occasions. Although these innumerable gatherings were held "under the uninviting and prosaic auspices of the Booklovers' Society," it was widely known and admitted by more than half of the group itself that they never read books. Now and then, however, "they might under pressure, purchase the latest opus of some Negro novelist or poet." The core of this polyglot group of booklovers, friends, and social parasites includes Sarah Desverney, a local librarian for whom "no Negro had written anything of import since Dunbar and Chesnutt"; Bradley Norris, a radical poet "to whom everything not New Negro was anathema"; Samuel Weinstein, a caustic self-appointed Negrophile and authority on Negro life; and Mrs. Harold De Peyster Johnson, a race-conscious public school teacher on whom the author-narrator heaps more than four pages of blistering scorn: "She had, as it were, midwifed at the New Negro's birth, and had groaned in spirit with the travail and suffering of Ethiopia in delivering herself to this black *enfant terrible,* born capped and gowned, singing, "The Negro National Anthem" and clutching in one hand a pen, in the other a paintbrush." Whether humorous or witty, amused or contemptuous, Cullen's satire is generally indirect, and his motives are most clearly revealed in Constancia's explanation for inviting the Negrophobic Professor Calhoun to address the Booklovers' Society on "The Menace of the Negro to Our American Civilization." "'An irrefutable evidence of a sense of humor... is the ability to laugh at oneself, as well as at one's tormentors and defamers,'" she says,

"'If we haven't learned that in these three hundred years, we have made sorry progress.'"

Even though the chapters depicting black high society sparkle with wit, farce, caricature, and repartee, they have at best a tenuous connection to the moral theme of the narrative, which is symbolized in the bond between Sam and Aunt Mandy. For them and the ministers, Johnson and Drummond, life is ambiguous; the ways of God mysterious; and "there were more ways to Heaven than one." The moral ambiguity of Sam's life is apparent in the use of his cards and razor. In response to his question about whether cards were evil, Aunt Mandy, the moral center of the novel, replies, "'It all depends on the kind of cards you have and what you do with them.'" Although a staunch Methodist, Aunt Mandy relies on the power of conjuration as well as on the songs and emotionalism of her church to affirm her faith in love and life. During prayer service, she was as fervent in her singing, rocking back and forth, and moaning as the other "aging handmaidens of the Lord." She felt that it was all right to be lost in the inner life, "but there were things in this other life which were more important. And loving was one." When Mattie was losing Sam to another woman, Aunt Mandy advises her that "'sometimes when the angels is too busy to help you, you have to fight the devil with his own tools.'" After sleeping three nights on the cards and razor which were baptized in Madam Samantha's magic water, Mattie is suddenly reunited with Sam. Thus, the plot, characters, and style of *One Way to Heaven* point with wry humor to more than one way to heaven.

In addition to the convincing portrayals of commonplace church-going people, the novels of Cullen and Hughes provide interesting contrasts in narrative technique and the handling of time. In [Hughes's] *Not without Laughter,* a *bildungsroman,* and *Tambourines to Glory,* a low comedy, the emphasis is on dramatizing events in order to heighten immediacy and verisimilitude; represented and representational time are frequently congruent; and showing predominates over telling. In contrast, *One Way to Heaven,* a mixture of satiric comedy and comedy of manners, relies heavily on the author-narrator's commentary on plot, character, and theme to make explicit and to expand the ironic pattern of the narrative; the time-ratio is manipulated to facilitate analysis of character; and telling predominates over showing. There is little emotional but considerable moral and intellectual distance between the author-narrators and their protagonists. The relationship of the reader to the protagonists, however, is less simple. Because the authors permit Sandy and Sam to tell only part of their stories and then only in the third person, much of the reader's sympathy for them is sacrificed, which is a more serious weakness in *Not without Laughter* than in *One Way to Heaven....* Finally, because Cullen exploits irony, ambiguity, and symbolism more self-consciously than Hughes, he appeals to the reader's intellectual interests but risks more serious flaws in structure and character as he moves from the realistic to the satiric mode. (pp. 134-36)

Bernard W. Bell, "The Harlem Renaissance and the Search for New Modes of Narrative," in his The Afro-American Novel and Its Tradition, *The University of Massachusetts Press, 1987, pp. 93-149.*

FURTHER READING

Bontemps, Arna. "The Harlem Renaissance." *The Saturday Review of Literature* XXX, No. 12 (22 March 1947): 12-13, 44.
    Biographical sketches of Cullen and Langston Hughes, stressing their importance in the Harlem Renaissance.

Brawley, Benjamin. "Protest and Vindication." In his *The Negro Genius: A New Appraisal of the Achievement of the American Negro in Literature and the Fine Arts,* pp. 190-230. New York: Dodd, Mead & Co., 1937.
    Assesses *Color* as a "work of promise," adding: "The fact is that there is a sophomoric note in the work of Mr. Cullen that he finds...hard to outgrow."

Brown, Lloyd W. "The Expatriate Consciousness in Black American Literature." *Studies in Black Literature* 3, No. 2 (Summer 1972): 9-12.
    Examines Cullen's poem "Heritage," viewing it as an expression of a black artist in search of cultural roots.

Canaday, Nicholas, Jr. "Major Themes in the Poetry of Countee Cullen." In *The Harlem Renaissance Remembered,* edited by Arna Bontemps, pp. 103-25. New York: Dodd, Mead & Co., 1972.
    Studies Cullen's treatment of religion, love, death, and racial conflict in his poems.

Ciardi, John. Review of *On These I Stand,* by Countee Cullen. *The Atlantic Monthly* 179, No. 2 (February 1947): 144-45.
    Briefly assesses Cullen's place in the history of American literature, concluding: "[A] taint of artiness, an overready reliance on the poetic cliché, a weakness for bookish literary forms, and a regrettable insensitivity to the spoken language flaw too many of the poems. It is for the one poem in ten that emerges whole that Countee Cullen will be remembered."

Collier, Eugenia W. "I Do Not Marvel, Countee Cullen." *CLA Journal* XI, No. 1 (September 1967): 73-87.
    Considers Cullen in an essay praising poets of the Harlem Renaissance.

Copeland, Catherine H. "The Unifying Effect of Coupling in Countee Cullen's 'Yet Do I Marvel.'" *CLA Journal* XVIII, No. 2 (December 1974): 258-61.
    Analyzes how technical aspects of "Yet Do I Marvel" reinforce the theme Cullen intended to convey.

Dillon, George H. "Mr. Cullen's First Book." *Poetry* XXVIII, No. 1 (April 1926): 50-3.
    Positive review of *Color.*

Dorsey, David F., Jr. "Countee Cullen's Use of Greek Mythology." *CLA Journal* XIII, No. 1 (September 1969): 68-77.

Evaluates Cullen's use of classical allusions in his poetry, suggesting that "it is characteristic of Cullen's poetic technique to reverse the symbolic content of his allusions to Greek (and sometimes Christian) mythology, thereby doubling their semantic content, that is, their significance in his own contexts."

Emanuel, James A. "Renaissance Sonneteers: Their Contributions to the Seventies." *Black World* XXIV, No. 10 (August 1975): 32-45, 92-7.

Critical examination of three Cullen sonnets, explaining their racial thought.

Ferguson, Blanche E. *Countee Cullen and the Negro Renaissance.* New York: Dodd, Mead & Co., 1966, 213 p.

Biography of Cullen, with profiles of other prominent black writers and educators of Cullen's era.

Huggins, Nathan Irvin. "Art: The Ethnic Province." In his *Harlem Renaissance,* pp. 190-243. New York: Oxford University Press, 1971.

Explores Cullen's poetic style, in which the critic sees Cullen firmly grounded in the genteel tradition.

Larson, Charles R. "Three Harlem Novels of the Jazz Age." *Critique: Studies in Modern Fiction* XI, No. 3 (1969): 66-78.

Presents, largely by plot synopsis, Cullen's *One Way to Heaven,* Claude McKay's *Home to Harlem,* and Carl Van Vechten's *Nigger Heaven,* with a brief comparison of the three novels.

Littlejohn, David. "Before *Native Son:* The Renaissance and After." In his *Black on White: A Critical Survey of Writing by American Negroes,* pp. 39-65. New York: Viking Press, 1966.

Includes general criticism of *One Way to Heaven* and selected poems by Cullen.

Lomax, Michael L. "Countee Cullen: A Key to the Puzzle." In *The Harlem Renaissance Re-examined,* edited by Victor A. Kramer, pp. 213-22. New York: AMS Press, 1987.

Surveys the development of Cullen's career, suggesting that Cullen's rejection of race as a poetic theme was the major reason for his decline as a poet.

Perry Margaret. *A Bio-Bibliography of Countée P. Cullen, 1903-1946.* Westport, Conn.: Greenwood Publishing Corp., 1971, 134 p.

Valuable index to writings by and about Cullen, with a short biography.

———. *Silence to the Drums: A Survey of the Literature of the Harlem Renaissance.* Westport, Conn.: Greenwood Press, 1976, 194 p.

Comparative study of Harlem Renaissance writers, with a thematic and technical analysis of Cullen's poems and novel.

Potter, Vilma. "Countee Cullen: The Making of a Poet-Editor." *Pacific Coast Philology* XV, No. 2 (December 1980): 19-27.

Discusses Cullen's role as editor of a special issue of *PALMS,* a small poetry magazine, and of the anthology *Caroling Dusk,* suggesting that Cullen's poetic output declined as editing became a central part of his career.

Rice, Philip Blair. "Euripides in Harlem" *The Nation* 141, No. 3663 (18 September 1935): 336.

Praises Cullen's rendering of *The Medea.*

Shucard, Alan R. *Countee Cullen.* Boston: Twayne, 1984, 145 p.

Full-length critical study of Cullen's life and works.

Smylie, James H. "Countee Cullen's 'The Black Christ.'" *Theology Today* XXXVIII, No. 2 (July 1981): 160-73.

Examines Cullen's depiction in his works of the relationship between Christ's crucifixion and the lynching of American blacks. Smylie states that Cullen's "The Black Christ" "transforms the existential black experience into a universal message about Christ's passion and triumph."

Tuttleton, James W. "Countee Cullen at 'The Heights.'" In *The Harlem Renaissance: Revaluations,* edited by Amritjit Singh, William S. Shiver, and Stanley Brodwin, pp. 101-37. New York: Garland Publishing, 1989.

Describes Cullen's undergraduate career at New York University, noting the influence of Professor Hyder E. Rollins on the development of Cullen's poetry. The essay includes a reprint of Cullen's honors thesis on the poetry of Edna St. Vincent Millay.

Webster, Harvey Curtis. "A Difficult Career." *Poetry* LXX, No. 4 (July 1947): 222-25.

Briefly considers why Cullen's promise as a poet "faded into mediocre fulfillment."

Woodruff, Bertram L. "The Poetic Philosophy of Countee Cullen." *Phylon* 1, No. 3 (September 1940): 213-23.

Overview of Cullen's treatment of the themes of love, beauty, and suffering in his poems.

Young, James O. *Black Writers of the Thirties.* Baton Rouge: Louisiana State University Press, 1973, 257 p.

Contains numerous references to Cullen, contrasting the attitudes he expressed in "The Black Christ" and *One Way to Heaven* with those of other black writers of the 1930s.

Frank Marshall Davis

1905-1987

American poet, journalist, and editor.

An American poet living in Chicago during the Harlem Renaissance, Davis shunned the "Effete East" for the "raw strength of the Midwest," as he commented in a 1982-83 interview. His poetry, though not associated with that Eastern movement in black literature, nevertheless received accolades, and contemporary critics hailed him as the "Newer Negro." Others called his militant, ironic poetry "propaganda." Although Davis moved to Hawaii in 1948 and stopped publishing poems for approximately thirty years, he was "rediscovered" by publisher Dudley Randall and scholar Stephen Henderson in 1973. Since then, many critics have come to consider Davis the "father of modern black poetry."

Born in Arkansas City, Kansas, Davis experienced violent racism when he was five years old. In an incident that left him traumatized and confused, several white third graders, eager to find out how it felt to lynch someone, experimented on Davis, nearly hanging him. According to critic John Edgar Tidwell, "His early lessons about racism inculcated in Davis an inferiority complex that made him shy and extremely self-conscious; it also nurtured a consuming hatred of white people." Davis left Arkansas City for Wichita, Kansas, in 1923, enrolling in the School of Journalism at Kansas State Agricultural College in Manhattan. Given the choice of writing either an essay or a poem for an English class, Davis tried free verse because he thought it would be easier. Soon after this experience, he developed an interest in poetry. "There were only twenty-six Black students at the entire college," he recalled, "and I immediately became a curiosity, soon becoming known as 'the poet who looks like a prizefighter.'"

In 1927 Davis moved to Chicago. According to Tidwell, "Although he was well acquainted with the works of New Negro Renaissance writers Countee Cullen, Rudolph Fisher, Langston Hughes, and Jean Toomer, and although he could have gone to New York himself, Davis felt he could do for Chicago what they did for Harlem." Davis briefly moved to Atlanta in 1930 in order to upgrade the *Atlanta World;* under his leadership, it became the first successful black daily newspaper in America. Meanwhile, one of his published poems, "Chicago's Congo," attracted the patronage of bohemian intellectual Frances Norton Manning, with whose help Davis published his first collection of poetry, *Black Man's Verse,* in 1935.

Black Man's Verse was a critical success and was widely recognized as an important statement about the sociology of race pride. Several poems in the collection reveal the influence of blues and jazz, and a section entitled

"Ebony under Granite" was especially popular. Here Davis recounted the lives of fictional people buried in a cemetery, a concept first used by Edgar Lee Masters in *Spoon River Anthology.* Characters include Goldie Blackwell, a two-dollar prostitute who trades respectability for independence; George Brown, sentenced to life imprisonment for voting more than once—a crime he had seen whites commit many times without punishment; and Roosevelt Smith, a black writer who becomes a postman after continually failing to please critics sufficiently. Davis's next collection of poetry, *I Am the American Negro* (1937), generally drew favorable reviews, but most critics believed it too similar to his first work. Alain Locke asserted that *I Am the American Negro* "has too many echoes of the author's first volume.... It is not a crescendo in the light of the achievement of [*Black Man's Verse*]."

Davis accounted for the eleven-year gap between publication of *I Am the American Negro* and his next volume of poetry, *47th Street* (1948), in a 1973 interview: "I was going through a number of changes during that particular time and I had to wait for these changes to settle and jell before I produced other work.... And, of course, some critics naturally have thought that I would have been better off had I just continued to jell indefinitely." Nevertheless, several critics considered *47th Street* to be Davis's greatest poetic achievement, chiefly on account of its first-hand observations about urban black life. Other commentators, however, perceived a shift away from black nationalism toward proletarian beliefs and called *47th Street* propagandistic. Davis was confronted with a negative turn in public sentiment during the 1950s. The House Un-American Activities Committee, the Senate's Eastland Committee, and the Federal Bureau of Investigation judged his work to be politically subversive. As a result, many libraries and schools removed Davis's books from their shelves.

After publication of *47th Street,* Davis and his family moved to Hawaii. He told Dudley Randall in a 1973 interview: "I came over and liked the place so well that I have stayed here and not paid a visit to the mainland since coming here in 1948.... Since we do not have the confrontations that exist between white and Black in so many parts of the mainland, living here has been a relief, not only to me but to many whites who have been most anxious to show and prove friendship with Blacks." Randall, founder of Broadside Press, and Stephen Henderson of Howard University revived interest in Davis's poetry in 1973, when Davis gave a college lecture tour in the contiguous United States. He published some poetry and enjoyed status as a "mystery poet" who had been "twenty years ahead of his time." In 1987 Davis died in Honolulu, Hawaii.

Although critics have disagreed about the quality of Davis's poetry, few dispute the sociological and historical value of his works. And most agree that Langston Hughes, Davis's contemporary and a participant in the Harlem Renaissance, provided the best measure of Davis's achievement when he wrote: "When his poems are poetry, they are powerful."

(For further information about Davis's life and works, see *Black Writers; Contemporary Authors,* Vols. 123, 125; and *Dictionary of Literary Biography,* Vol. 51: *Afro-American Writers from the Harlem Renaissance to 1940.*)

PRINCIPAL WORKS

Black Man's Verse (poetry) 1935
I Am the American Negro (poetry) 1937
Through Sepia Eyes (poetry) 1938
47th Street (poetry) 1948
Awakening, and Other Poems (poetry) 1978

William Rose Benét (essay date 1936)

[*Benét, today remembered chiefly as the brother of poet Stephen Vincent Benét and husband of novelist Elinor Wylie, was an accomplished poet who was praised for his technical precision. In the following excerpt, he lauds Davis and* Black Man's Verse.]

A thin black book with a negro's head on it in black and silver. The black spine of it is stamped in silver, **"Black Man's Verse.** Davis." The paper is coarse and the bold-face type is blunt. And on page 19 I read:

> Tired looking houses of brown stone
> Ramshackle flats with sightless eyes
> A surface car throws a handful of white sparks at cracked red bricks
> An L train roars oaths at backyard clotheslines
> Mornings on South Parkway flats sit like silent cats watching the green mice of buses running up and down the boulevard
> And only grass has heard the secret of vacant lots

This poet can express himself! Who is he? I turn to the end of his introduction. Toward the last, after a couple of paragraphs with a humorous shrug in them, the poet ends:

> It is merely enough to say that I, *Frank Marshall Davis,* a Duskymerican born December 31, 1905, in Arkansas City, Kansas, and exposed to what is termed education at the public schools there, at Friends University in Wichita and at Kansas State College, have written this foreward [*sic*] in Chicago, Illinois, June 24, 1935.

The book is printed in Chicago at the BlackCatPress. The verse is collected from a number of small magazines and anthologies. The passage I quoted above is from the first poem entitled **"Chicago's Congo"** *(Sonata for an Orchestra).* Many of his poems refer to music, like **"Lynched,"** *(Symphonic Interlude for Twenty-one Selected Instruments)* **"Jazz Band," "The Slave"** *(For a Bass Viol),* **"Lullaby"** *(Melody for a 'Cello),* and so on. He has rhythm and music in him and fiery words and fresh phrases and images. Obviously he has read Whitman, Sandburg, Lindsay, and "Spoon River," but his voice is his own voice too. He is a realist in speaking up for his own race, in his picture of the steel mills at Gary, Indiana, in his pictures of Chicago,—and his love songs are those of a black Solomon. In **"Georgia's Atlanta"** he shows his complete awareness of the Southern white's attitude toward the negro. Yet there is not a trace of whining or maundering in this book. There is a natural dignity in the utterance, and intelligence. All this poet needs to do is to go ahead and forge a style wholly his own. As it is he can work notably in free verse.

William Rose Benét, "The Phoenix Nest," in The Saturday Review of Literature, *Vol. XIII, No. 12, January 18, 1936, p. 19.*

The Nation (essay date 1936)

[*In the following unsigned review, the critic, appreciative of the lack of "melancholy" in Davis's poetry, praises* Black Man's Verse.]

Kansas born, Mr. Davis brings a Western note to Negro expression in his first volume of verse, [**Black Man's Verse**]. With little of the melancholy in his race, little influenced by the mood or style of the spiritual, Mr. Davis accepts the raw vigor of his environment and responds to its casual aspects of beauty in a free-running verse that has something of the hard brightness of Sandburg. Yet a more complicated feeling enters as the book progresses, and the last poem is ironically aware of the many pitfalls awaiting a Negro poet in a white civilization. It tells the history of one Roosevelt Smith, "the only dusky child born and bred in Pine City, Nebraska."

> At college they worshiped the novelty of a black
> poet and predicted fame

But Roosevelt listened too conscientiously to the critics as his successive books appeared. Told that he wasn't using his racial material, he took up darky dialect. Told then that he sentimentalized the Negro, he went sophisticated. Told that sophistication was inappropriate to a Negro, he tried for classic simplicity. Told again that he was being only a black-faced white, he went to Africa. When the critics could make nothing of the resulting book, "since it followed nothing done by any white poet," Roosevelt

> traded conscience and critics for the leather pouch
> and bunions of a mail carrier and read in the papers
> until his death how little the American Negro had
> contributed to his nation's literature . . .

This book suggests a different fate for Mr. Davis.

> *A review of "Black Man's Verse," in* The Nation, *New York, Vol. CXLII, No. 3688, March 11, 1936, p. 328.*

Harriet Monroe (essay date 1936)

[*Monroe was the founder and editor of* Poetry *magazine and a key figure of the American "poetry renaissance" of the early twentieth century. In the following 1936* Poetry *review, she praises Davis for his work in* Black Man's Verse.]

There is a good deal of swinging strength in this book of a Chicago Negro, [**Black Man's Verse**], which "has been undertaken in a chance effort to reconcile the writer's bewilderment" over contrasting comments on his poems—a good deal of strength, much satirical club-bludgeoning over injustices to his race, some epigrammatic wit, and often touches of imaginative beauty. The experiments in free rhythms range from very perpendicular short-line measures with a word or two or three in a line, which remind this writer of Kreymborg's early skits, to long-line wheeling circles which plainly take

lessons from Sandburg, and sometimes, less obviously, from Lindsay. I do not mean that the poems are derivative; they have their own message to deliver in rich tunes of their own; but the melodic foundation is plainly Sandburgian.

We will pass over the bitter things Mr. Davis has to say about lynchings, and Scottsboro, and **Georgia's Atlanta** of chain-gangs, breadlines, and the Ku-Klux Klan, for the racial passion in which, heaven knows, there is reason enough. We might pause over some of the lines in **Chicago's Congo** —

> Between the covers of books lie the bones of
> yesterdays.
> Today is a new dollar,
> And my city is money-mad—

but that poem is a loosely scattered kind of second chapter to Sandburg's *Chicago,* with interludes suggestive of Lindsay's *Congo,* and too little compactness of structure. There are motives and tunes more original than these in some of the shorter poems, or in parts of certain longer ones. The poem, **Death,** for example, which its author calls an "overture for an organ," should consist of only its last fine strophe.

Here is **Failure:**

> I would sing a song
> but I have no words
> I would hum a tune
> but I have no melody
> success
> like grains of brown sand
> at the sea-shore
> slips through my nerveless fingers
> the world
> has not time
> even to laugh.

Perhaps the poem, **Cabaret,** of some fifty or sixty lines, is the best built and most successful of the longer pieces. It salutes the different instruments of the band—the saxophone, violin, tuba, cornet, trombone and ends thus with the banjo:

> But I don't think I'd talk to the banjo. We both
> suckled at Sorrow's breast and I have no more
> time for pain.
>
> Weave for me a strange garment, O Maker of All!
> Make me a jacket of silver stolen from the
> cornet's high C,
> Take the violin's tremolo and make me a shim-
> mering golden waistcoat
> Of black, O Maker of All—the piano has plenty to
> spare,
> Just a little of its bass would make a long thick
> cloak.
> I'll die some day I hope—
> Death must be a winsome hermaphrodite or men
> and women would leave those arms.
> I'd like, O Maker of All, to wear these garments
> when I take my last dance with Death.

This is enough to show that we have here a poet of authentic inspiration, who belongs not only among the best of his race, but who need not lean upon his race for recognition as an impassioned singer with something to say. (pp. 293-95)

Harriet Monroe, "A New Negro Poet," in Poetry, *Vol. XLVIII, No. 5, August, 1936, pp. 293-95.*

Nick Aaron Ford (essay date 1950)

[*Ford, author of* The Contemporary Negro Novel *(1936), published several collections of writings by black writers. In an essay published in* Phylon *in 1950, he produced a four-point "blueprint" of instructions to help black writers guide black literature to a truly elevated status: (1) Master craftsmanship, (2) continue use of racial themes, (3) use propaganda subtly, and (4) use symbolism skillfully. In the following excerpt from this essay, Ford deems Davis in violation of the third requirement.*]

Is propaganda a legitimate ingredient of literature? Albert Guerard, in *Art for Art's Sake*, says, "An artist does not suffer from being identified with a cause; if the cause is himself, a vital part of himself, it is also a fit element of his art. He suffers most from not being identified with his cause, from adopting and serving a purpose which remains alien to his personality."

In *The Great Tradition* Granville Hicks maintains, "In the whole history of American literature one can scarcely think of a writer, commonly recognized as great, who did not immerse himself in the life of the times, who did not concern himself with the problems of his age."

Tolstoi, in *What is Art?*, declares, "We know that the wellbeing of man lies in union with his fellowmen . . . . Art should transform this perception into feeling."

If one accepts the conclusions of the three critics quoted above, as I certainly do, he must also accept propaganda as a legitimate ingredient of serious literature. But I do not advocate art for the sake of propaganda. I demand a proper subordination and the observance of good taste. An example of the violation of the limitations I place upon this requirement may be seen in the poetry of Frank Marshall Davis. His propaganda, though based on sound critical analysis, is so blunt and militant that it has little chance of winning sympathetic consideration. In addition, much of it offends good taste. Such bitter iconoclasm as the following quotation from **"Christ Is a Dixie Nigger"** goes beyond the bounds which I have prescribed:

> Your pink priests who whine about Pilate and
>   Judas and Gethsemane I'd like to hog-tie and
>   dump into the stinking cells to write a New
>   Testament around the Scottsboro Boys.
> Subdivide your million dollar temples into liquor
>   taverns and high class whore-houses . . . . My
>   nigger Christ can't get past the door anyway.
> Remember this, you wise guys.

> Your tales about Jesus of Nazareth are no go with
>   me . . . . I've got a dozen Christs in Dixie all
>   bloody and black.

With his extraordinary imagination and his marvelous skills in the use of words, Davis could make a favorable impression in the world of poetry, provided he curb his bitterness and temper his cynicism with reasonable restraint. (p. 376)

Nick Aaron Ford, "A Blueprint for Negro Authors," in PHYLON: The Atlanta University Review of Race and Culture, *Vol. XI, No. 4, fourth quarter (December, 1950), pp. 374-77.*

Jean Wagner (essay date 1963)

[*A French author and critic, Wagner wrote on the works of black and Southern writers of the United States. A student of American slang and dialects, he is the author of* Les poètes nègres des Etats-Unis *(1963;* Black Poets of the United States, *1973), a critical survey of black American poets from Paul Laurence Dunbar to Langston Hughes. In the following excerpt from this work, he profiles Davis in what one critic called a "representative although especially vituperative" assessment of Davis's career.*]

More and more, on top of racial consciousness a layer of class consciousness tended to impose itself, and out of it was born at the same time an internal social critique directed on occasion against the Negro masses, to pillory their naïveté, their illusions, and their failings, and on other occasions against the black bourgeoisie, a milieu made up of social climbers and snobs, ever eager to stress their superiority to common folk (with whom they hated to be lumped together) and aping the ways of the white middle class.

Among the minor poets who gained some prominence during these years, the name of Frank Marshall Davis, the author of **Black Man's Verse** (1935), *I Am the American Negro* (1937), and **47th Street** (1948), is worthy of mention. Though Davis exhibits a certain talent in his better poems, it remains undisciplined and is too often wasted by recourse to facility. An untiring polemicist, he could not resist prosiness and verbosity, and his longer poems suffer from their patent lack of structure. But his principal defect is a sort of bad taste which his journalistic activities did nothing to mitigate. It is revealed in his search for forced or incongruous images, and in his flashy display of borrowed devices used in inappropriate contexts. All too frequently one notices the clumsily transposed influences of Vachel Lindsay, Carl Sandburg, and Langston Hughes. He is overly fond of orchestrations and indications of setting in the manner of Lindsay; these marginal scenic notations become irritating in the long run, since they so obviously are gratuitous additions. It is hard to see how a poem like **"Lynched"** gains from being subtitled **"symphonic interlude for twenty-one selected instruments,"** or why **"Hands of a Brown Woman"** needs the accompaniment of a "quartet of two guitars, a banjo and a tom-tom." In some places he becomes positively grotesque, as at the beginning of **"Modern Man—The Superman,"** with its subtitle, **"A Song of Praise for Hearst, Hitler, Mussolini and the Munitions Makers,"** and accompanied by the marginal note, "Eight airplane motors, each keyed to a different pitch, are turned on and off to furnish musical accompaniment within the range of an octave." Sandburg, too, may not have been a suitable model for a mind already so devoid of discipline as was Davis's. For it is from Sandburg, rather than directly from Walt Whitman, that Davis seems to have derived the notion of his enumerative poems, or even poem-inventories, the graveyard of genuine poetry, as is demonstrated by such poems as **"What Do You Want America?"** and **"For All Common People."**

Yet his borrowings are, at times, thoroughly judicious. In his first two volumes, the sections entitled **"Ebony under Granite"** amount to a highly successful Negro prolongation of *Spoon River Anthology*. Here he takes Negro society as his main target, scoring a number of bull's eyes with his daring naturalism. Like Masters, Davis reveals to us, behind the facade of happiness and success, the meannesses and the nauseating appetites that provide the mainspring of the social climber and, on occasion, also put an end to his climbing. From the depths of the grave, the Reverend Joseph Williams informs us that he had scattered bastards liberally throughout his parish. Benjamin Blakely, great contractor and swinger of deals,

> Would have died more content
> Had he ever learned
> From which of his mistresses
> He contracted
> That fatal social disease...

Robert Whitmore, the successful businessman who three times was the ruler of the local Elks

> died of apoplexy
> when a stranger from Georgia
> mistook him
> for a former Macon waiter.

Mrs. Clifton Townsend, who could count among her ancestors many prominent white Southerners, came of a family in which the marriages were always planned to preserve the light skin color of which she was so proud:

> It was not childbirth
> In her forty-second year
> That took the life
> of Mrs. Clifton Townsend
> But shame at bearing
> Through inconsiderate Nature
> A penny-brown son...

Ralph Williamson, editor of the weekly *News-Protest,* built his fortune and his nationwide reputation on his readiness to denounce racial injustice and discrimination. So it is easy to understand how he suddenly expires as the consequence of a frightful nightmare in which he

dreams that America has become a land without blemish, where all ill feelings between the races has vanished in a trice.

It would be minimizing Frank M. Davis's excellent qualities, were one to consider only the poems of **"Ebony under Granite."** His skill as a portraitist, his intimate understanding of racial psychology's subtle mechanisms, and his mordant irony create memorable frescoes such as that of **"47th Street,"** which admirably brings to life the humble folk of this black district in Chicago. But one is entitled to believe that poetry as a means of expression was not well suited to Davis's special talents, and that the sketch or the short story would have been a more appropriate form. (pp. 187-90)

> *Jean Wagner, "The Negro Renaissance," in his* Black Poets of the United States: From Paul Laurence Dunbar to Langston Hughes, *translated by Kenneth Douglas, University of Illinois Press, 1973, pp. 149-93.*

Helena Kloder (essay date 1971)

[*In the following essay, Kloder discusses the strong visual images in Davis's poetry.*]

It is unfortunate in this current renaissance of Negro American literature, no publishers and few anthologies have republished the work of the black poet, Frank Marshall Davis. Davis' earliest books of poetry, ***Black Man's Verse*** and *I Am the American Negro,* appeared in 1935 and 1937, respectively; his last book, ***47th Street,*** was published in 1948. Despite the contemporary popularity of African rhythms and aggressive racial pride and consciousness in poetry, neither the passage of time nor the evolution of militant philosophies invalidates or enervates Davis' work; for Davis' greatest strength lies not in his style or message, but in his creation of visual art. Davis' poetry is a force of verbal kodacolor snapshots and reels of spliced, almost always precisely edited, motion pictures.

If Davis' goal was exclusively to "take the little, pale, wan penny apiece words, weave them into gay tapestries... to step high and swiftly across a printed page," then he certainly was successful. Davis' works are an assortment of colorful, realistic portraits of Americans (black and white), their lifestyles, their visions. He manages vivid street scenes in the North and lynchings in the South; he incorporates the dialects of both areas, with an acute understanding of the connotative slang that distinguishes class as well as race. Davis' themes and style are as varied as the characters and scenes that fill his pages. The writer treats love; the frustrated black American artist; the universal heritage and relationship that bind all men, regardless of skin color; the poor and the workers pitted against the powerful rich; middle class blacks; the estrangements in the South; the superficial relations in the North; and the hypocrisy of American democracy and the myth of the American Dream. His constructions are equally variant; sometimes tiny dramas (complete with leading parts, bit players, a chorus, and a tragic hero), sometimes long monologues or clipped-verse dialogues. Davis often intertwines his verse with song lyrics, as in **"To Those Who Sing America"**:

> "My country! 'tis of thee . . . "
>
> (On the shores of this, my country, dwell Plenty in a forty-room mansion and Poverty in a one-room hovel . . . a nation turned prostitute for the fat pimps of Politicians and Captains of Industry . . . This is my country with the star spangled robe snatched away)
>
> "Sweet land of liberty . . . . "

He makes copious use of familiar history, alluding to newspaper headlines of the urban North and insidious rumors of the rural South: he names men and places.

In his eagerness to expose every ill in American society and to try to combine social comment with art, Davis determined to squeeze the range of his opinions into single, pithy phrases to attain the tightness of verse. This forced construction of stanzas results in a confusion of prose and poetry. Davis' failure, in much of his work, to distinguish between genuine prose and poetry may provide a clue to his weak critical reception. Poetry is more than abbreviated prose and whimsically measured lines. Free verse does not preclude the essential musicality that defines and elevates the genre. Davis recognized the strength of staccato succinctness when he created his brilliant portraits belonging to the **"Ebony under Granite"** collection. The crisp words and clipped lines are perfect for his satire and ironic understatement. He knew which sounds secured the desirable harsh and abrupt qualities, which produced the heavy cadence that emphasized somber, weighted dragging; he understood caressive and dreamy sounds. He often included marginal notes for musical accompaniment to his verse; and even if he never seriously intended such accompaniment, the notes induce the reader to hear that music. Consider for example, **"The Slave"**:

> **"The Slave"**
> (for a Bass Viol)
>
> Here was titanic sorrow
> condensed
> in the ebony splendor
> of a black man's verse
>
> Here was a form
> on which the mark
> of a parasite civilization
> had been branded
>
> burning deeply
> exposing a soul
> contaminating it
> with the purple of sadness
>
> should not a soul sing of joy?
> Should not a soul sing of peace?
>
> Lord, deliver me,
> You helped Daniel

> You helped David
> You helped Moses, too
> Lord, let my people go
>
> Here was a sadness . . .
> carved on a black man's soul

Even without such an introductory note, Davis has captured the exciting sensuous way of the music in the rhythmic **"Dancing Gal"**:

> Black and tan—yeah, black and tan
> Spewing the moans of a jigtime band
> What does your belly crave?
>
> A brown-sugar brown
> Slim gal sways
> Pretzel twisting
> Beneath a yellow thumb
> of steel-stiff light.
> Amid a striped rain
> Of red-note, blue-note
> Jazz-hot jazz
> Gazelle graceful
> Lovely as a lover's dream
> Silken skinned, stillwater soft
> Young girl breasts in gold encased
> Scant gold around her lower waist . . . .

But most of Davis' work just misses achieving this fine musicality.

Davis' poetic failure, when it occurs, derives from his determination to shape and include all his wealth of emotion, fact, and aesthetic perception to fit the label, "poetry." He seemed unwilling to distribute some of that wealth by working in another genre. Davis' parenthetical interjections are too often obtrusive and superfluous. Extensive mention of Scottsboro, Alabama, dissipates its impact. He often needed to eliminate excessive ideas and images to attain the sharpness of good poetry.

Poetry is more than erratic clusters of print. Great poetry soars, even when its subject is the most mundane; it stabs when it penetrates the reader; it is simultaneously gossamer and lead that the reader carries away, the blend of joy and pain that comes from experiencing great beauty.

But we cannot dismiss Frank Marshall Davis' verse by concluding that it is neither pure prose nor pure poetry, and it is our loss if his work is not drawn to critics' and editors' attention. His "impurities" are a conglomeration of talents. He is acutely perceptive in his details of color and light of faces and bodies of people on the streets. He is intelligent about history and the black man's role in it, sensitive to the poor and suffering, and keenly aware of America's most subtle hypocrisies. Furthermore, he understands the essences and relationships of painting, music, and literature. He has brilliant lines in many of his poems, and several are unforgettable, for example **"Hands of a Brown Woman"** and **"Mojo Mike's Beer Garden,"** both in *Black Man's Verse*:

> **"Mojo Mike's Beer Garden"**

Davis, 1984.

Four fat white spiders of throttled electric globes
    cling motionless to the ceiling spinning a misty
    web downward through the porous air

Soft runners of light finger the brown contours of
    a gambler's chin, a harlot's face, a pimp's
    profile then go floating on

The room is filled with the misty web, the white
    thin web four spiders spin

Two yellows gals take 'em their beer and wine and
    gin . . .
        This room is an unscored symphony of colors
        and sounds
        People sitting like geometric angles awaiting
        measurement
        Their talk is countless bubbles breaking against
        the ceiling
        Sharp scissors of a radio snip fancy cutouts in
        the thick noise
        Gray pigeons of tobacco smoke fly lazily in the
        air above
        Like a leafy tree in high winds the room moves
        its heads and hands

Two slate black men and two orange brown
    women spill low stories into four steins of beer

From her youngly rouged face fifty year old eyes
    look out like unwashed windows in a newly
    painted house . . . this woman who sits alone
    tosses a promise through her gaze to all male
    youths

Words shoot from the lips of three race track
    losers like water from a hose from the Stock-
    yards Fire

Before the long flat back of a brown stained bar
    men and women laugh, talk, drink, sweat
    swapping monotony for alcohol

From his stool by the cash register Mojo Mike
    sees nothing but faces and each face is a nickel
    beer or the price of a pint of whiskey to be put
    away and counted when his joint is emptied for
    the night

And . . . while the spiders spin . . . two yellow gals
    take 'em their beer and wine and gin . . .

The verbal art of Frank Marshall Davis, Negro poet of
the thirties and forties, is of immeasurable sociological
and historical value. **"47th Street,"** a literary painting, is
full of animation, color, meaning, the life of **"Chicago's
Congo."** Although he often chooses to tell too much for
us to absorb, ignoring the potential and the economy of
ambiguous symbols, his works deserve renewed attention. Of Davis' verse, the late Langston Hughes once
wrote, "When his poems are poetry, they are powerful."
(pp. 59-63)

*Helena Kloder, "The Film and Canvas of
Frank Marshall Davis," in* CLA Journal,
Vol. XV, No. 1, September, 1971, pp. 59-63.

Frank Marshall Davis with John Edgar Tidwell (interview date 1982-83)

[*Tidwell, wishing to probe "the thinking of one of
[Black poetry's] more prominent but neglected members," conducted an interview with Davis by mail on
July 29, 1982, and on May 27, 1983. In the following
excerpt from this interview, Davis discusses early
influences on his work, offers his opinion of the
Harlem Renaissance, and comments on the social
content of his poetry.*]

[Tidwell]: *You came of age when the New American
Poetry of Frost, E.A. Robinson, Sandburg, and Vachel
Lindsay was popular. Did these writers mean anything to
you?*

[Davis]: Very soon at Kansas State I came across the
poetry of Carl Sandburg who was far and away my
greatest single influence. Sandburg became my idol
because of his hard, muscular poetry, which turned me
on. Edgar Lee Masters, especially his *Spoon River
Anthology,* was also of great influence. I like Masters
because of his economy of words and ability to knife
through to the heart; I had no patience with his rhyme.
Lindsay's sounds, his feeling of jazz and syncopation,
pleased me. To a lesser extent I was captivated by Edwin
Arlington Robinson. I liked Robinson, but he did not
have the smashing impact of the others. e.e. cummings
and Maxwell Bodenheim also appealed to me. But I
cared little for Robert Frost. As for e.e. cummings, I felt
a kindred rebel spirit which I could not find in Frost or
Eliot. To me they seemed lukewarm.

Few, if any, Black poets writing after World War I followed Pound and Eliot into the new territory they charted for poetry, which emphasized the importance of ritual, myth, and symbol. Why did Black poets find them "lukewarm," and why did you choose a different course for your writing?

I could not relate to Ezra Pound or T. S. Eliot. Their preoccupation with myth and ritual turned me off as I believe it did other Black poets. I think that rebellion is deep in the psyche of most Black poets, and neither Pound nor Eliot and others of that type had this basic ingredient.

Did you find any Black poets useful in your own aesthetic development?

I was greatly influenced during these early years by one Black poet, Fenton Johnson of Chicago. I looked upon him as a kindred soul. I found him at a time when I needed him. This was before I was acquainted with any other Black free verse practitioneer. Because of my using Sandburg as a role model, I tended to judge all poets, whether white or Black, by their kinship to Sandburg. I came to know Fenton Johnson while we were both members of a small, short-lived writers' group early in my Chicago days. Our mutual admiration for Sandburg was a bond. Johnson was both quiet and self-effacing. Later, when I became acquainted with their work, I developed great fondness and respect for Sterling Brown and Langston Hughes. The same was true, although to a lesser extent, with Claude McKay, who, incidentally, spent a semester or two at Kansas State. Before World War II, the region's top critics often pointed out that "the state's three foremost writers are all Negroes: McKay, Hughes, and Davis." Incidentally, I found no appeal at all in Fenton Johnson's traditional, rhymed work. I felt that content was more important than technique. That is probably why I could not get into Countee Cullen. He was a superior technician but again there was the matter of rhyme. I also thought Arna Bontemps a fine craftsman, but he usually left me cold. He was also a good personal friend.

Periodically we read of creative writers who say that a particular physical locale is an important stimulus to their creativity. Ernest Gaines, for example, finds in Louisiana not only subject matter but spiritual renewal too. (He calls it that "Louisiana thing that drives me.") Chicago appears to be such a place for you. Would you comment on Chicago as a place that shapes your poetry?

I liked the tough, often brutal, image of Chicago projected by Sandburg and felt this was my city. I never liked Kansas when I was growing up—too many restrictions. Kansas City was better. But Chicago in the late 1920s and early 1930s was a complete challenge. It was big and the home of the *Chicago Defender,* at that time the nation's largest Negro newspaper; it was then the jazz capital of the nation. I wanted to paint it in verse. At this time Harlem had plenty of Black writers. But except for Fenton Johnson and possibly two or three more, when I reached Chicago in 1927, it was as barren

of Black writers as the Sahara. So I put down my roots to live in Chicago, and I think I had some success in my attempt to mirror Aframerican Chicago in particular. I believe that my verse had Sandburgian directness. I aimed to make my verse easily read and understood. This may have caused some critics to say [that] much of my poetry is actually prose. At the same time others have told me they preferred an intermix of prose and poetry; this prevented boredom. But then, what is poetry to one person can be prose to his neighbor. There is no law preventing the ancient muse from blowing a saxophone.

Your name has never been mentioned as a participant in the 1920s' New Negro Renaissance (which is often discussed as a New York phenomenon), even though you were publishing poetry in the late 1920s and early 1930s. What was your relationship to those familiar names of the New Negro Renaissance: Hughes, Cullen, Hurston, Toomer, and McKay?

By staying in Chicago, I avoided being identified with the New Negro Renaissance. I did not want to be part of the Effete East. In 1927, Harlem was the cultural capital of Black America. The nation's only two Negro magazines, *Opportunity* and *Crisis,* were published there. Chicago was rugged, possibly brutal, and unsophisticated. There were also no Black writers there of the quality of those who had flocked to Harlem, except for Fenton Johnson. New York was over-refined, lacking the raw strength of the Midwest. Of course there was jealousy in this evaluation. We sought to compensate for our lack of refinement by dubbing this section of our nation as the Effete East. However, there were so few Black writers around at that time in Chicago that our opinions were unimportant. But Chicago was the jazz capital, and Harlem was trying to reach the status of Chicago with Armstrong, King Oliver, and the others who had migrated there from New Orleans. As time passed and while at the Associated Negro Press, I did meet Zora Neale Hurston and Claude McKay and later became friends with Hughes. I also knew James Weldon Johnson. While in Atlanta from 1931 to 1934, I did meet Sterling Brown, whose poetry I have continued to admire. And I believe I was the first to publish the fiction of Chester Himes.

Did Alain Locke, who professed to be the "philosophical midwife" of the Renaissance, attempt to draw you into the fold? And what contact did you have with W.E.B Du Bois?

By the time I met Dr. Locke, the Renaissance was all but dead and buried. I believe I met Locke around 1937 on one of his occasional visits to Chicago. He was a dapper, fastidious little man who by then had become disillusioned with the Harlem Renaissance and was a little bit cynical about some of the participants. In one letter, he told me that it would have blown up in everybody's faces had it not been for free gin in the big posh apartments on Park Avenue and the personal efforts of Carl Van Vechten. When I told him of the jealousies and difficulties of trying to keep together another fledgling writers' group in Chicago, he told me of how some of the Harlem writers stayed together only because it was a way of establishing new homosexual relationships. I never had any contact with Dr. Du Bois.

Since you did not participate in the patronage system arranged by Locke, Walter White, or Du Bois, how then did you resolve the problem of getting your works published, and what interaction did you have with other writers?

It was during this period that I began taking my own poetry seriously, mainly because of intellectual prodding from Frances Norton Manning, a Chicago white woman. She was so impressed by my **"Chicago's Congo"** that she got in touch with me in Atlanta, encouraged me to write more poetry, and found a publisher, the Black Cat Press of Chicago, for my first two books. When I returned to the Windy City in 1934, I joined the staff of the Associated Negro Press, and after my first book, **Black Man's Verse** (1935), I became acquainted with a growing number of writers. The Chicago chapter of the League of American Writers, for example, was organized around 1935 or 1936. I joined at the behest of Richard Wright, whom I had met when the National Negro Congress was formed in Chicago in 1935. We became good friends. He was then a Communist, and I often kidded him about it. He was also on relief and was never too proud to admit it. As a member of the League, I attended all meetings and for the first time was thrown in contact with a number of white writers. Nelson Algren, the novelist, lived a block or so away on Chicago's South Side. I also came to know Stuart Engstrand, a novelist, and also his wife, herself a novelist; Meyer Levin, then a reporter and short-story writer who became a novelist; Paul Romaine, literary critic and collector; and Jack Conroy, editor and novelist. I prevailed upon Conroy, editor of a literary publication called *The New Anvil*, to publish Frank Yerby's first short story. Yerby was then a college student in Georgia who came to Chicago each summer to stay with relatives. We shared a mutual interest in photography. (Speaking of photography, I sold Richard Wright his first camera immediately after taking his portrait, which was then used in *Time* magazine in connection with his book *Black Boy*. Incidentally, I also read galley proofs of *Native Son*, part of which was left out by the publisher as too pornographic for that era.) Still another member of the League was Ted Ward, playwright and author of *Big White Fog*, one of the few Black-written dramas of that day.

We also had a short-lived writers' group whose members included Margaret Walker, Gwendolyn Brooks, and others. I would not consider this to be a Chicago "school" of writers. Gwendolyn Brooks had not yet reached her zenith, nor had Margaret Walker, who read us part of the historical novel she was working on. Richard read us some of his work in *Uncle Tom's Children,* his book of short stories he was then writing.

Your poetry is largely social rather than private. It often protests and even declaims in an effort to "clear space" for Black people, truth, justice, and humanity. Since some literary critics have regarded your work as propaganda, not poetry, would you please comment on what you think poetry is, including its function?

To me, poetry is a subjective way of looking at the world. All poetry worthy of the name is propaganda. Milton's *Paradise Lost* is Christian propaganda as is Joyce Kilmer's "Trees." But such works are not likely to be condemned as propaganda because the beliefs expressed in these and similar poems are shared by a majority of the population. The poetry of Edgar Allen Poe is ear candy with a propaganda message glorifying the bizarre and macabre. The poet who locks himself in his ivory tower produces propaganda depicting his inability or unwillingness to cope with the real world. Since I take pride in being considered a social realist, my work will be looked upon as blatant propaganda by some not in sympathy with my goals and as fine poetry by others of equal discernment who agree with me. But that is not to say that the craftmanship is always equal. There may be a variation in technical skill in parts of the same poem. To me, good poetry condenses and distills emotions by painting unusual—perhaps memorable—pictures with words. I know of no completely new thoughts. A poet therefore must find a different way of presenting old ideas. Since I am blues-oriented, I try to be as direct as good blues. This implies social commentary. Yet some of my work is quite private, in particular such love poems as **"To You."** This kind of poem is basically introspective emotion. Yet there are other private poems such as **"Rain"** and **"Four Glimpses of Night,"** to name two which have been widely reprinted.

Of what importance is Black history to your poetry?

Quite a bit of my poetry contains Black history. I knew nothing of our background when I finished high school in 1923 and attended college. I had to learn what I could elsewhere. I thought that with the consciousness of Black studies the last twenty years or so there would be considerable knowledge. But when I made a poetry concert tour in 1973, starting at Howard University and ending at the University of California at Berkeley, followed by two subsequent trips for appearances on campuses in Southern California, I found that Black students generally were pitifully uninformed about our past. My poems with historic references were usually well received. This work is, of course, obvious propaganda. Is this what critics object to? On the other hand, when I appeared at Howard I was told that Senghor, then president of Senegal and himself one of the world's most widely acclaimed poets, was especially pleased with my verse because of its display of Negritude. This is, I think, a basic ingredient of Black poetry which comes from the experiences of Aframericans. Such poetry often contains words and phrases termed "Black English." However, I do reject Black English when it departs too far from the norm and becomes a strange lingo, substituting the worst of washroom graffiti for imagination.

Black music, especially blues and jazz, figures prominently in your work. Would you discuss first your conception of blues? How then does this idea function as an organizing principle in much of your poetry?

When I heard my first blues and early jazz at the age of eight years, I felt the same kind of exultant kinship with this music that I felt when I read my first free verse in college. I am by nature an intellectual rebel, and I felt emotionally akin to those musicians who emancipated themselves from the rigid traditions of Western music. The improvisation and freedom from rigid rules which made the blues and jazz so revolutionary appealed immediately to me, just as did the break with tradition and the freewheeling which are basic ingredients for free verse. Originally, the twelve-bar blues required the ability to improvise with words, to make up rhymes while singing three four-bar segments. After your first statement, taking up most of the first bars, you more or less repeated the words to emphasize your statement in the second four bars while thinking up a rhyming and forceful final four bars. Since the wording rarely took exactly four bars, the rest of the rhythmic phrase was usually filled with vocal sounds or instrumental notes when the voice was accompanied. This filling out, incidentally, is the basis for the origin of jazz. Anyway, this radical departure from tradition found in the blues and jazz is the twin of the radical departure from traditional poetry found in free verse. In many respects, free verse is a similar rebellion against the tyranny of rhyme and meter found in traditional European poetry. I like to think that in my verse I show the same kind of emotional liberation and freedom associated with jazz. Although I do not borrow from the classic blues format, I think that I have the feeling. Such poets as Langston Hughes and Sterling Brown have often used more obvious blues devices. But I feel the blues walked into my life when I first heard them and have never left me. That's why I call my autobiography "Livin' the Blues." (pp. 105-08)

"Black Moods: New and Collected Poems," for which you are now seeking a publisher, documents your career as a poet. What changes have you undergone in aesthetic sensibility over the years, and how do you see your work in relation to that written by Black poets today?

Since living in Hawaii I have written poetry which I believe shows more maturity but no noticeable increase in sensitivity over my previous work. Some of these more recent poems have appeared in *Black World*. I also have a long poem on Hawaii and a series of short portraits called **"Horizontal Cameos"** about women who make their living on their backs. These poems compare favorably, in my prejudiced estimation, with what is being done by other Black poets today. But there are many more Blacks writing today. Many more are being published. I have been amazed at the sheer volume. When I came along there were very few. Some critics have dubbed me "the father of modern Black poetry" and have said I was "twenty years ahead of my time." Take that any way you wish. But with the amount of poetry being produced today by Black poets there is bound to be an abundance of superior work. My advice to young Black writers who want to become excellent writers, then, is that the only way to write poetry is to write poetry. (p. 108)

> *Frank Marshall Davis with John Edgar Tidwell, in an interview in* Black American Literature Forum, *Vol. 19, No. 3, Fall, 1985, pp. 105-08.*

FURTHER READING

Randall, Dudley. "'Mystery' Poet: An Interview with Frank Marshall Davis." *Black World* XXIII, No. 3 (January 1974): 37-48.

Randall is an American poet and founder of Broadside Press, one of the first publishing companies exclusively for black writers; he and Stephen Henderson "rediscovered" Davis and his poetry. In this interview with Randall, Davis discusses his years of anonymity as well as poetry by other black poets since the publication of his own works in the 1930s and 1940s.

Samuel R. Delany

1942-

(Full name Samuel Ray Delany, Jr.) American novelist, short story writer, critic, memoirist, and editor.

An American science fiction writer, Delany is regarded as one of the most inventive writers in the genre. He is often associated with authors who gained prominence in the New Wave science fiction movement of the late 1960s; like these writers, Delany has placed less emphasis on the physical sciences and technology in his works and has instead concentrated on the social and psychological aspects of his created worlds and characters. He has thus expanded the traditional scope of science fiction to include themes found in mainstream literature. Further, as one of the few black and bisexual writers of the genre, he has brought a different perspective to science fiction literature. Delany's pioneering efforts in the genre inspired Gerald Jonas to make this statement in *The New York Times Book Review:* "The name of Samuel R. Delany is synonymous in science fiction circles with artistic ambition."

Delany, the son of Margaret and Samuel R. Delany, Sr., was born and raised in Harlem in New York City. His father, a prosperous funeral home director, sent his son to school in Manhattan at the progressive and predominantly white Dalton School. According to Sandra Y. Govan, "The dichotomies in his daily life affected young Sam's emotional stability and his behavior; he ran away from home several times between the ages of five and seventeen, and eventually he was referred to a child-guidance center for psychotherapy because of his 'deep maladjustment.'" Although Delany was a good student at Dalton and later at the Bronx High School of Science, his undiagnosed dyslexia caused his teachers to relegate him to remedial English. In 1961, at the age of nineteen, he married a former fellow Dalton student, poet Marilyn Hacker, and enrolled in the City College of New York. He dropped out of City College the following spring, however, never to return to college as a student.

Delany's wife was largely responsible for the publication of his first novel, *The Jewels of Aptor* (1962). Hacker was an assistant editor at Ace Books and encouraged Delany to submit a manuscript. *Jewels,* Delany's only fantasy novel, is the story of the poet Geo, who, with a band of adventurers, sets out to rescue the kidnapped High Priestess of the goddess Argo. Delany published four more novels by the time he was twenty-two: *The Fall of the Towers* trilogy, called a "space opera" because of its clear division of good and evil and its use of traditional sci-fi technology, and *The Ballad of Beta-2* (1965), a novel about mythmaking featuring as its protagonist a university honors student in galactic anthropology, Joneny Horatio T'wabaga. Delany was unable to keep up with the constant output required of science fiction novelists, however, and suffered a nervous breakdown

in 1964. He changed the pace of his publishing, and two subsequent novels, *Babel-17* (1966) and *The Einstein Intersection* (1967), each won Nebula awards. *Babel-17* involves the discovery of a mysterious, powerful language—known as Babel-17—by Rydra Wong, an Asian poet. *The Einstein Intersection* is the story of Lobey, a black musician whose instrument doubles as a machete. Lobey is also a "different" one, being half-man and half-beast, and he must discover what is killing those who are "different." Many critics believe that Delany's next novel, *Nova* (1969), is the culmination of the first stage of his writing—the stage in which he adhered to fairly traditional science fiction forms. Another "space opera," it is the story of Lorq Von Ray, the mulatto hero who must obtain the rare element Illyrion from an exploding star.

For the next seven years, Delany stopped publishing mainstream science fiction novels. He lived in the Heavenly Breakfast commune in New York City and endeavored to be in a rock band; he also published a pornographic novel, *The Tides of Lust* (1973). In 1975, however, he published *Dhalgren,* the novel thought to be his most demanding work. The dyslexic, epileptic artist-hero of the book, "Kid" (he does not remember his name), enters the "autumnal city" of Bellona and becomes the leader of a predominantly black gang called the Scorpions. With the publication of *Dhalgren,* Delany became something of a cult figure. Because the novel is narrated by a dyslexic character who has severe memory lapses, it lacks a clear narrative structure and conception of time. Some critics objected to the novel's difficulty and denied that it is a science fiction novel. Others took exception to the explicit sex scenes, first found in *The Tides of Lust. Dhalgren* marked the introduction of diverse sexual relationships to Delany's mainstream fiction. According to Seth McEvoy in his 1984 work *Samuel R. Delany,* "It is in *Dhalgren* that we get closest (of all his earlier works) to Delany as a person. No longer does he hide behind the predominantly heterosexual characters that have been the focus of his earlier books." Delany had acknowledged his homosexuality since his youth, and sexual orientation and society gradually became a major part of his fiction. *Triton* (1976), Delany's next novel, is set in a futuristic "sexual utopia" where sex change operations and unconventional relationships are prevalent and widely accepted in society. In addition to his science fiction works, Delany has written several works of science fiction criticism, and he composed a "sword and sorcery" series called "Return to Nevèrÿon."

Delany is generally recognized as an innovative, if sometimes controversial, author of science fiction. He noted of himself and his works in a 1987 interview: "For a number of reasons, from my racial make-up to my sexuality to my chosen field of writing, SF—or even because, in this society, I've chosen to write at all—my life has always tended to have a large element of marginality to it .... To write clearly, accurately, with knowledge of and respect for the marginal is to *be* controversial ...."

(For further information about Delany's life and works, see *Black Writers; Contemporary Authors,* Vols. 81-84; *Contemporary Authors New Revision Series,* Vol. 27; *Contemporary Literary Criticism,* Vols. 8, 14, 38; and *Dictionary of Literary Biography,* Vols. 8, 33.)

PRINCIPAL WORKS

The Jewels of Aptor (novel) 1962
Captives of the Flame (novel) 1963; also published as *Out of the Dead City* [revised edition], 1968
The Towers of Toron (novel) 1964; revised edition, 1968
The Ballad of Beta-2 (novel) 1965
City of a Thousand Suns (novel) 1965; revised edition, 1969
Babel-17 (novel) 1966
Empire Star (novel) 1966
The Einstein Intersection (novel) 1967; corrected edition, 1968

Nova (novel) 1968
"Time Considered as a Helix of Semi-Precious Stones" (novelette) 1969; published in *World's Best Science-Fiction: 1969*
The Fall of the Towers (novel) 1970
Driftglass: Ten Tales of Speculative Fiction (short stories) 1971
The Tides of Lust (novel) 1973
Dhalgren (novel) 1975
Triton (novel) 1976
The Jewel-Hinged Jaw: Notes on the Language of Science Fiction (criticism) 1977
The American Shore (criticism) 1978
Empire [with Howard V. Chaykin] (graphic novel) 1978
Heavenly Breakfast (memoirs) 1979
†*The Tales of Nevèrÿon* (novel) 1979
Distant Stars (novel) 1981
†*Neveryóna; or, The Tale of Signs and Cities* (novel) 1983
Starboard Wine: More Notes on the Language of Science Fiction (criticism) 1984
Stars in My Pocket Like Grains of Sand (novel) 1984
†*Flight from Nevèrÿon* (novel) 1985
The Complete Nebula Award-Winning Fiction (short stories) 1986
†*The Bridge of Lost Desire* (novel) 1987
The Motion of Light in Water: Sex and Science Fiction Writing in the East Village, 1957-1965 (memoirs) 1988
Straits of Messina (essays) 1988
Wagner/Artaud: A Play of Nineteenth and Twentieth Century Critical Fictions (criticism) 1988

*These works were published as *The Fall of the Towers* trilogy in 1970.
†These works are a part of the "Return to Nevèrÿon" series.

Peter S. Alterman (essay date 1977)

[*In the following excerpt, Alterman discusses major themes in Delany's works.*]

Within the last few years, there have been additions to the anthology of science-fiction definitions which are not rooted in archetypes, themes, or emotional responses, but in the way language is used in science fiction. Whether or not they are universally applicable, these recent linguistic definitions do help shed light on one of the field's most enigmatic and controversial writers, Samuel R. Delany. A stylistic analysis of Delany's fiction does assist the reader in understanding the larger fictive concerns at work in his novels. (p. 25)

Delany's literary style is a combination of subtly derived linguistic techniques coupled with a disturbing liberation of certain structural elements. Within Delany's novels, time, logic, and point of view are cut loose from traditional literary positions, and function relativistically. Yet these free elements are rigidly controlled by the rules of a relativistic universe, thereby fulfilling Delany's comment ... [in the appendix to *Triton* (1976)] that technical possibility actualizes metaphor in science fiction.

In *Dhalgren* (1975), after Kid has made his first run with the Scorpions against Emboriky's, he retreats to the Reverend Tayler's for a meal and meets Ernest Newboy. There he corrects the galleys for his collection of poems, *Brass Orchids.* Lanya meets him and they realize that for him one day has passed, but for the rest of Bellona, five days have passed .... The issue of the linearity of time in Delany's novels is clearly shown here. In Bellona, time is not a constant.

In the relativistic universe, time is indeed not a constant, but is related to the velocity and frame of reference of the observer. This is dramatized in *Dhalgren,* and although it is a physical reality of the universe we all inhabit, we persist in viewing time as a universal and linear norm.

The uses of time in Delany's novels, here and more notably in *Empire Star* (1966), violate certain conventions of prose fiction. What seems to be a fantastic use of time is in fact a realistic use of time, because time is psychologically a function of the state of the observer and physically a function of the velocity of the observer. In more traditional fiction, the use of psychological time is well understood. But when Delany applies relativistic physical laws to time, the psychological metaphor of variable time becomes confusing, because the metaphor has been transformed into fact.

Empire Star presents much the same kind of tortured time. Comet Jo, the first "hero" of the novel, travels through a universe which is bent back on itself in a cycloid motion. Everything has already happened. He meets the same people, including himself, at various times of their lives. On one level, this is a nice manipulation of technique, showing the development of the hero's awareness of historicity and his part in it. But then Delany turns the technique on its head by showing the reader that time is, indeed, twisted in the universe. The center of the galaxy, Empire Star, gathers in time and space through a warp, bends it, and returns it in different sequence. This further confuses the reader, who has been expecting a proper linear end to the story. In fact, time and space are warped around gravity wells. And *Empire Star* is designed to be read as a sequence of perceptions of the same story .... The properties of physical space are here used to serve the aesthetic and formal needs of the novel. (pp. 25-6)

[In his book *Structural Fabulation,* Robert Scholes] points out that the modern novelist's response is to accept the impossibility of recording the real, and to create a system based upon subjectivity. This position is interestingly much like Delany's position, for he not only accepts narrative subjectivity, but he applies to the subjective presence of, say, time, a physical concept which supports his unique use of time. In this manner,

what Delany is doing by insisting upon a subjective or eccentric temporal mode is both satisfying the need of the modern novel to emphasize the impossibility of rendering the world outside, and at the same time presenting a close and scientifically acceptable vision of the world.

In a like manner, Delany deals creatively with the question of point of view, which is another shifting element. In *Empire Star,* the narrator is ostensibly a crystallized and objective point. Yet throughout the novel, we learn more and more about the point of view (not as a character, but as a force in the novel). Jewel, the narrative device, eventually unfolds enough of the plot for us to understand that the ordering of the elements is left to us. There is no attempt made to explicate or order the sequence of actions for the reader. The first reading is from the point of view of Comet Jo, learning his way from youth to maturity to an understanding of the nature of his task in life. This position leads to a second reading, of the nature of the society of the Lll, and the story of their freedom and bondage, with Jo playing a minor role. Then a third sequential reading, from the point of view of the Jewel itself, is suggested.

In each of these readings, more of the substance of the novel is revealed, and each uses a different point of view. Yet there is only one novel. The answer to this paradox is that at the end of the novel, the reader is challenged to read multi-levelly (multiplexially), with an eye on the growth of the narrator, protagonist, and universe .... (pp. 26-7)

A second example of the fluidity of the narrator is in *Dhalgren.* Kid clearly is responsible for writing the journal, and therein perhaps the novel, but there are many Kids. There is Kidd, the confused immigrant, Kid the Poet, who also may be Ernest Newboy, Kid the Scorpion leader, and finally, the Michael Henry. Which Kid is the narrator of *Dhalgren*? They all are, for as Kid ventures farther and farther into the maze of Bellona, he changes. And as he changes, the novel he writes changes. In order to understand the nature of the narrator, one must then not attempt to discover a static character, but to apprehend both a personality and the way that personality changes. Perhaps this is a major confusing element of the novel, for we read the novel through Kid's eyes, but those eyes are not the same throughout the novel.

The metaphor of a person's changing as he grows is literalized and exaggerated. But Delany has also accepted an implicit requirement of that act—his novel changes as its narrator changes. In the absence of many traditional science fiction motifs, this one stylistic element—the concretizing of a metaphor—gives *Dhalgren* the unmistakable flavor of science fiction.

A third area where Delany's fiction is unexpectedly fluid is in his use of logic. (p. 27)

Delany's non-linear, non-rational logic is predictably built upon a mathematical model: Gödel's Law .... The resultant universe is one in which traditional rational explication takes second place. It is a universe of experience and emotion. It is a world where the protagonist may not know what is going on, but will be able to act on the experience of something's happening.

This is, in fact, what Lobey does [in *The Einstein Intersection* 1967)]. He reacts with no intellectual understanding of what he is doing. Furthermore the chapter epigraphs are all related to the chapters they present, sometimes by clear logical links, but more often by non-linear relationships, which exemplify the creative link between the artist's rational experience and his non-rational translation of that experience into his art. Taken together with the text of the novel, the epigraphs form an example of the novel's concept of the relationship between experience and art. Delany seems to be trying to manipulate the textures of experiences, not the meanings of those experiences, in order to elicit emotional responses from the reader and from his protagonist . . . . Delany . . . [asserts] that his fiction is designed to elicit a range of ordered responses from the reader, generated by sequences of key orders, images, or patterns. The rational and logical form of traditional prose . . . attempts to create a pattern of purely logical, intellectual responses to a closely reasoned argument, what the novel would consider an "Einsteinian" response. *The Einstein Intersection* manipulates experiences to produce the desired sequence of emotional responses from Lobey and from the reader.

The same sequence of choreographed patterns is called for in *Dhalgren* when, for example, the giant red sun rises over Bellona. There is no rational explanation presented for it. Nor is there any causal link with it in the text of the novel. Yet the wonder it creates is a response to the wonder Kid and the reader feel at the marvelous mating of Kid, Lanya, and Danny for the first time. . . . Yet the major effect of the giant sun cannot be apprehended by looking for logical connectives, although they are present. We must read it as a symbolic response to the experience of coming awake in a new world of wonder, of making love, and being loved, for the first time.

While this concern with patterns of response may seem to be a retreat into the philosophy of communication, it is central to Delany's style—a style which baffles many readers. Once again, Delany has taken a normally static element, logic, and wrenched it into a new, fluid role. At the same time, he has founded his actions in legitimate theoretical bases. In so doing, he has reconciled the ideological problem of the modern novelist, identified by Scholes—that of the limitations of realism—with a theory of science fiction as a stylistic construct reconciling the various forms of experience within a relativistic and formal universe.

Each of the three areas broken free by Delany—time, point of view, and logic—is broken on the authority of some valid, or potentially valid, physical law or thesis. In turn, the freedom these elements lend to Delany's

novels requires close attention from the reader, lest he become confused by looking for the traditional prose forms.

Close attention is just what Delany gives to his fiction, most obviously to the very sentences out of which the novels grow. In the essay **"Thickening the Plot,"** Delany sets about to define the creative process in concrete terms. In this essay, he stresses the photographic accuracy of his imaginings, the completeness with which he visualizes his subject, and describes how he forces visual precision into his language. He also notes that the very process of converting the vision into language changes the scene being described, so that the final product is a surreal translation, a partnership between the rich word and the richer vision, the translation of the vision affecting the vision itself. This methodology implies a rigid adherence to the concrete, the sensual, the "realistic" world on one hand, and to the mythic, metaphoric elements of language on the other. Here again Delany confronts the opposing moments of force, the photographic "real" and the untrustworthy "subjective."

The practical effect of striving for the precise evocation of experience gives a unique flavor to that experience. Delany's novels display an intense sense of being in touch with the physical world. In fact, the effort of accurately rendering the physical drives Delany to confront the limits of perceived experience, the point at which language breaks down under the intensity of his gaze, and forces him toward a new use of language.

For example, the presence of multiplicity and simultaneity in Delany's mental images of reality demands that he jam multiplicity into the essentially linear and sequential form of English prose. (pp. 27-9)

The handling of simultaneous material in a necessarily linear form is a good indication of the kind of word-by-word craftsmanship in Delany's prose. In resolving the problem of rendering a "fantastic" or science-fictional sequence realistically, he visualizes the subject matter completely, rather than retreating from it into vague cubist shapes or highly mannered prose. And remarkably, by striving to describe the seams of reality, he breaks through "reality" to describe the perceiving mind as much as the perceived experience. The parenthetical statement is a good example, for it is both a pause in the exposition and a gloss on the transcribed experience without. Together, reality, observer, and language form a collage of meaning. It is like his concretizing of metaphor. The vaguely *like* becomes the solid *is*. Precision is what these two techniques share.

Delany's theoretical concern with the uses of prose appears frequently in his fiction, almost as if the work was a test-bed for linguistic theory. He considers the totality of the story, plot, character, language, etc. to be a *textus,* or web of meaning, within which the text proper resides. The manner in which *textus* translates into text he alludes to with the term metonymy, the concept of language as connotative rather than denotative . . . . It is therefore not unusual to find images of myths, meanings, and memories, as well as convoluted symbolism in Delany's fiction. His concept of language and literature implies this rich depth of layering.... That each major group of metonymic meanings has an analogue in the surface of the story is proof enough of that. What Delany does with this technique is to make the reader feel the weight of meaning and symbol around the text, i.e., invoke a *textus* for the story. This enriches the story, and charges the linear tale with alternative meanings, possibilities, and significance. It is another way of transcending the limitations of realism, of working in the subjective mind of the reader.

In other places, Delany's insistence on the perception of language as a burdened element is more baldly stated, or worked into the tale.... (p. 30)

The image of the text as a web of meaning itself is present in the body of Delany's fiction, especially in **Babel-17** [1966], which in this light can be read as an animated recitation on the nature of the relationship between language and meaning:

> She rose slowly, and the web caught her around the chest. Some sort of infirmary. She looked down at the—not "webbing", but rather a three particle vowel differential, each particle of which defined one stress of the three-way tie, so that the weakest points in the mesh were identified when the total sound of the differential reached its lowest point. By breaking the threads at these points, she realized, the whole web would unravel. Had she failed at it, and not named it in this new language, it would have been more than secure enough to hold her. The transition from "memorized" to "known" had taken place while she had been....

In this example, Rydra Wong has just learned how to think in the highly artificial language of Babel-17, which forces her to think, perceive, and react in an extremely precise and rapid way. The web is an image of the effects of language on the mind and of the mind as shaper of reality. This scene becomes symbolic of the inter-relationship of mind, language, and reality, a web like the triple-stressed web Rydra lies in, analyzes, and breaks.

The experience of the work of art transcends the language used to construct it, because of, not in spite of, the nature of Delany's use of words. The technique Delany uses is to move beyond the literal, not by a retreat from concrete reality, but by approaching the literal closely, so closely that the mind of the narrator/artist shows through. Delany's prose style is an amalgam of elements: the precise visual rendering of images coupled with a conscious use of metonymy to create a language of experience.

Complementing Delany's theoretical concern with the function of his prose is an equally obvious concern with structural issues, such as the definition of the novel in **Nova** [1968], the relationship between theoretical criticism and creative writing in **Dhalgren,** and, of course, the question of point of view in **Empire Star**.... Whereas Delany's idea of language is accretive and

Front cover for Delany's 1975 novel.

inclusive, his idea of literary forms is much more rigid and formal. (p. 31)

Many of Delany's novels...are characterized by a conscious discussion of the formal nature and function of literature and the relationship between experience and art. In every case, art is able to organize experience, bringing pattern and order to chaos. This issue manifests itself in Delany's use of language: the order of realism rests uneasily on the chaotic subjectivism of the perceiving narrator. These two stylistic elements identify a central concern of his fiction: his prose attempts to render the texture of the chaotic universe by actualizing literary metaphors with scientific theory, and the larger construct of his prose attempts to organize that chaos into intelligible, translatable forms.

For Delany, the process of artistic creation is an attempt to derive order from the chaos of experience. More precisely, it is an attempt to reconcile the contrary demands of the subjective perspective of the artist, who must admit to experiencing life from a biased point of view—the structural requirements of formal literary patterns, which can wrench meaning and order from randomness, and the restrictions inherent in language as a medium of transmitting vision. In Delany's prose, neither the subjective nor the objective—neither the chaos of the individual mind's perceiving, nor the artifice of literary device, is given primacy. Just as metaphor is solidified by fact, experience is ordered by the effect of art upon the raw material of the mind, which is able to translate the chaotic elements of life accurately into words. Delany's later novels, especially, are arenas in which life and language confront one another and come together to form a dialectic of literature. Delany's science fiction includes and capitalizes on the tension between scientific theory and linguistic potential. (pp. 33-4)

> *Peter S. Alterman, "The Surreal Translations of Samuel R. Delany," in* Science-Fiction Studies, *Vol. 4, No. 11, March, 1977, pp. 25-34.*

Jane Branham Weedman (essay date 1982)

[*In the following excerpt from her 1982 study* Samuel R. Delany, *Weedman analyzes* Dhalgren, *believed by several critics to be Delany's magnum opus.*]

In **Dhalgren,** Delany incorporates stylistic and thematic elements he experimented with in his previous works. His holistic view of society, first introduced as multiple viewpoints in **Empire Star,** is in **Dhalgren** linked more strongly to familiar themes developed in earlier works. The sexual scenes of **Dhalgren** are extensions of **Tides of Lust,** while he returns to **The Fall of the Towers** for the artist/criminal concept, to **Babel-17** and **The Jewels of Aptor** for the poet as central character, to **The Einstein Intersection** for art as a motivating force in society, and to **Nova** for the novelist as narrator. The massive **Dhalgren** is the most complete metafictional statement of Delany's works.

This discussion of **Dhalgren** will include three sections: (1) the artist observing, recording, and questioning paradigms of his society; (2) the use of multiple viewpoints to discuss the effect of different reality models in our society, and (3) the use of metafiction to explicate the novel and comment on fiction in general.

In **Dhalgren,** Delany presents "that central subject, that great event which shakes history and makes the links strike and glitter for me." It is set in the moment in history following the assassination of Martin Luther King when blacks switched from non-violent to violent protest. In this work Delany demonstrates, through his depiction of civil disruption in the city of Bellona, why the change in attitude occurred. The conflict between the prevailing idealism of the American dream and black American reality is similar to the conflict dramatized in the novel. Blacks, following the Christian precepts of nonviolence advocated by Martin Luther King, believed that with time, patience, and hard work they would achieve their goals—their American dream. The assassination, in which many believed the F. B. I.

was involved, showed them that what they believed was true was not real. They were forced to question the paradigms of their own movement as well as reassess those of the American culture. Delany is not, however, addressing a problem solely restricted to blacks. Events in our society or in our personal lives will force most of us at least to occasionally acknowledge a conflict between what we believe is true and what we observe as real.

The violence, which erupts when a group recognizes their victimization and acts upon this new consciousness, is dramatized in the civil disturbances which destroy the city of Bellona both physically and socially. Bellona becomes a burnt-out city in which people must survive in a way different than they ever had before.

Despite the misleading newspaper reporting, it is Paul Fenster's assassination, not George's rape of June, which precipitates the violence that destroys the metropolis of Bellona. George can be interpreted as representative of the desires of the Black Power movement of the Sixties. He is symbolic of their recognition that the black man must regain his sexual, economic, political, and social identity outside of the identity imposed by the white culture.

In **Dhalgren,** when Rev. Amy attempts to explain the phenomena of the huge sun and the two moons, one of which has been named after George, the people reject her mythical explanations. Instead they choose a flesh and blood god, George, to believe in. They prefer to believe in one of their own who they can know and observe rather than accept the mystical which is unobservable. George is real, and in this society the people have become aware that what they had conceived of as true simply does not apply in the world in which they find themselves living. This is one example of Delany's concentration on the perceivable interrelationships of events, not on their causes.

Nor is Calkins, the white conservative newspaperman, presented as a reliable source for a view of their city. He can be seen as a representative of our mass media that Delany attacks as hypocritical because of its failure to acknowledge what is really happening in our time in our country. Calkins doesn't want to know, as is indicated by his refusal to read Kid's poems.

Notably it is Kid, a minority member himself, who observes and records what is really happening in the society. The society that he describes is not one of great social progress. The society has changed but not noticeably for the betterment of any group. The economy of Bellona, once founded on capitalism, has collapsed. Each person is left to his own devices to survive since there is apparently little transportation of goods into or out of the city and no one earns money. Also there are no city services available. As a result, each person simply takes what he needs. And, as Tak comments, most people find they need surprisingly little.

The society that Kid describes includes: a commune whose members live in the park organizing numerous projects but seldom completing any; the Scorpions, who terrorize the town to relieve their boredom because there is no meaningful or fulfilling work to do; people who still live in the Jackson ghetto; and people, such as the Richards, who pretend that nothing has changed.

Delany does not provide a resolution of the society's problems. He indicates that the society will continue to evolve by questioning what will happen when June finds George. However, Delany does not indicate how the society will change, only that a change will take place because two of the variables (June and George) will change and this will affect other variables (other citizens will react to June's and George's actions), an affirmation of Delany's belief that societies evolve rather than progress.

The multiple viewpoints in *Dhalgren* express Kid's multiple reality models. Kid is half American Indian, half white. Because of his amnesia, he cannot even recall his own name. Although Kid becomes the leader of the Scorpions, he does not restrict himself to that group nor does he define himself through them. He plays at being a hero and an anti-hero, paradoxically helping George rescue children from a burning building and also leading destructive raids. Delany questions what happens when reality models do not conform with those of the majority of society; through Kid, Delany demonstrates that if the conflict is great, one becomes a criminal, an artist, a criminal/artist, or insane.

Kid's multiple views in *Dhalgren* also illustrate the world view of a dyslexic, complete with time, sequence, vision and left-right disorientation. These are illustrated by Kid's belief that the sun rises in the wrong direction, his loss or misplacement of time, his inability to remember what events followed or preceded each other, and his view of the constantly changing positions of things, such as the bridge. Although other characters occasionally go through disorienting experiences, they have a basic sense of time, direction, sequence, and topography. They can rely on internal stimuli to function in a disorienting world. But what if one's internal pattern is different? What if one can't function because one's reality models differ from everyone else's?

Delany is a multiple dyslexic. He has problems with right-left orientation, with visual reversal of letters and objects, with chronology of events, and with topographical disorientation. Although unable to remember the order of events, Delany is a keen observer of detail so that the incidents remain clear. As a dyslexic, Delany had to overcome these disorientations to function in the world. He also had to deal with the disorienting problems of being a black man in a predominately white society. In *Dhalgren,* Delany portrays his own experiences as a black dyslexic in a white society through the protagonist/narrator Kid. What type of a narrator is there in *Dhalgren*? The reader doesn't know who he is and the narrator doesn't know either. He is, at first

glance, unreliable, has little sense of chronological time, and has periods of amnesia. Not only does he refer to incidents not discussed previously in the novel, but more frequently he will actually tell about an incident twice and place it in a different sequence of events each time.

There are various reasons stated within the text of the novel that could explain the unreliable narrator/protagonist. Kid could be an acid-head, his mind muddled by drugs—confusing perception of time, place, and incident; he could be insane with the same result. Either condition alone could cause the physical symptoms that Madame Brown labels as anxiety attacks. Kid admits he has spent time in a mental hospital because of depression. Each of these interpretations appear valid at least on a superficial level. However, these interpretations remove Kid from the realm of believability—that is, the reader cannot relate his/her personal experience with Kid's—providing one is neither an acid-head or insane. It also removes the opportunity for social comment. If we view Kid as a multiple dyslexic with epilepsy, however, this allows the reader to understand Kid's world in a different way. That is, Kid is neither drugged nor crazy, merely different in his perceptions. His brain works differently but not unintelligibly. If Kid is to be viewed this way, can this interpretation be supported from the text and from Delany's experiences and observations? If so, then, this would explain the seemingly unreliable narrator and make his perceptions understandable.

Delany has indicated, when discussing *Dhalgren,* that he purposefully created physical attacks resembling epilepsy prior to each of Kid's periods of amnesia. Epilepsy has numerous effects depending on its location in the brain and its severity. It is not unusual for a person with epilepsy to have amnesia after a seizure. Not only will that person not remember the seizure, he may not remember what happens (depending on the severity of the seizure) for minutes, hours or even days after the seizure, even though he will be capable of behaving "normally" during that period of time.

Although there are many examples in the text, only a few are necessary to substantiate the narrator as a dyslexic epileptic. The left-right disorientation is illustrated when Kid makes a wrong turn when leaving Tak's place and ends up on the other side of the street. Delany explains the effect of this type of dyslexia: "The whole tape of reality which he had been following had somehow overturned. It still continued; he still followed. But during some moment when he had blinked days had elapsed and everything right had shifted left: Everything left was now right." This quote also indicates the time loss experienced by epileptics after a seizure. One of the many examples of sequence disorientation is illustrated by naming months in the wrong order, but is more explicit when the narrator says of his diary: "... I note the entries only ghost chronological order." Topographic disorientation is illustrated by Kid's differing perceptions of the relationship of the waterfront and the bridge:

> When I came off the waterfront, across the bridge. This place, it was like two blocks away, maybe. And then, when I first came up here, you could just see the water, as though suddenly the river was a half a mile off. It was right through there. But now I can't see . . . .

Finally, visual disorientation is shown by the reversal of letters in a word in Kid's journal: "This is the last full balnk [blank?] page left" [sic].

What then would be the artistic result of a dyslexic, epileptic narrator? For what purposes might Delany create Kid: To examine our prejudices against those who perceive things differently than ourselves? To make us realize that there is a difference between the true and the real? What does this allow Delany to say that would not be apparent from the point of view of a drug addict or a crazy person?

The epileptic interpretation is important in that it helps explain the long lapses of time that Kid doesn't remember and the physical actions which he cannot account for, such as suddenly having the orchid on his wrist without his remembering he had put it on. These periods of time cannot be accounted for as willful disrememberings, for according to others, Kid's actions are very similar whether he remembers them or not. And these periods of amnesia also account for the four different styles of handwriting in the journal. Since Kid is ambidextrous, the writings are different because he writes in an identifiable way with his right and left hand when he is fully conscious of what he is doing, and writes in another manner with his right and left hands during the periods of amnesia that follow seizures.

What does the dyslexic, epileptic narrator/protagonist allow Delany to do in this novel? Kid's characterization allows Delany the opportunity to make the reader understand the disorientation resulting from and involved in the problems which must be faced on a daily basis by minorities whose reality models differ from those of their dominant culture.

Reality models are the learned concepts we have of what something is. Each time we see a chair we do not consciously define for ourselves what a chair is because we already have a reality model of it. But what happens when something observable occurs which differs from the reality in our mind? To refer to the earlier example used in discussing reality models, if we observe a three-legged object with a seat and a back, it does not conform to our reality model of a chair. How do we react to this contradiction? We might pretend that the three-legged object does conform to our reality model of a chair. In this case we question our perception of the object rather than questioning the reality model in our mind. Or we may acknowledge the difference between the object and the model which results in our questioning the validity of the reality model.

Delany creates disorientation in *Dhalgren* to explore the problems which occur when reality models differ from reality. By illustrating these occurrences he is able to approach two problems in our society: prejudice and insanity.

Since American blacks exist in two cultures, both of which have their own reality models, they necessarily have some conflicting reality models. The reality models of both cultures may also conflict with what they actually observe. By using multiple viewpoints in the novel, Delany illustrates that, depending on one's culture and one's position in that culture, one's reality models may well vary from those of others. The importance of this perception is that new points of view are opened up and an understanding of other ways of life are made available to the reader. Naturally this provides the opportunity to break down ethnocentric concepts. Acknowledging that others do not perceive an object as you do is a step in acknowledging that values held by others, although different from your own, are as valid for them as yours are for you. This is the first step in breaking down prejudice.

The second area Delany explores is our hesitancy to accept that others perceive differently than we do. Why do we fear these differences? They challenge our own security, our faith in our perceptions, and our reality models. We are afraid to question our perceptions because we fear what will happen to our minds if we are stripped of our familiar patterns. We designate, because of our fear, that those who differ are wrong and therefore less acceptable than we are, or we label them as insane.

Through the dyslexic, epileptic narrator/protagonist Delany attempts to break down the ethnocentricity and fear which we feel when our own reality models are questioned, when we perceive that there is a variance between what we have been taught is true and what we perceive is real. Kid as criminal/artist/narrator presents a holistic view of society which would not be possible through one viewpoint. It would also not be possible for Delany to explore the effects on the mind of a person who was experiencing the world from multiple viewpoints, nor to illustrate the effects of having multiple reality models at constant conflict with one another.

The multiple viewpoint technique which Delany chooses for this work is indicative of his theme. Kid writes in first and third person, often switching in mid-paragraph. A black person experiences this same process: "Here I am in the white world, my actions defined by another culture, functioning as I must to survive. Somehow that imposed identity is partially removed from me. I have been taught that it is true, but I perceive that it is not real. I am different there within myself, but frequently in the white world, I am the only one who perceives that difference. I am the only one who agrees on the truth and reality of myself."

Delany continues his discussion of the true and the real by presenting metafictional comments from several viewpoints in *Dhalgren.* Metafiction is the discussion of writing and art and of critical literary theory within a fictional work. Delany's metafictional statements can be divided into two groups: those which explicate the novel *Dhalgren* and those which discuss literature in general.

Delany assists the reader in unraveling the massive and frequently confusing *Dhalgren* by making metafictional explanations within the work about his choice of setting, of the meaning of the prism and lens as symbols, and of the multiple viewpoints of the narrator. Through the narrator, Delany posits the significance of the setting of Bellona for his novel: "There is no articulate resonance. The common problem, I suppose, is to have more to say than vocabulary and syntax can bear. That is why I am hunting in these desiccated streets."

Delany points out that the prisms and lens so frequently mentioned in the novel are symbolic of points of view. Newboy questions Kid: "have you hunkered down close to it, [the prism] sighted through the lips of it the juncture of your own humanity with that of the race?" This is followed by a long description by Newboy of viewpoint, illustrated by the labels of lens and prisms. Delany uses this method of explaining to his readers the symbolic significance of the prisms and lens so frequently mentioned in the Scorpions' chains: the lens is described as a way of viewing things from a complex point of view; the prism affords a multiplex point of view. Newboy speaks of the artist's wound that never heals and claims that even without the complex and multiplex views of the world, the wound still would not heal, but "...that without it [the viewpoints] there plainly and starkly would have been nothing there; no, nothing at all."

It is difficult throughout most of the novel for the reader to understand the identity of the narrator. This confusion over viewpoint is part of the disorienting effect Delany creates to emphasize his theme of the effects of differing reality models. There are four groups of writing referred to within *Dhalgren*: the two different groups of entries in the journal; the book of poems, *The Brass Orchids;* and the text itself. By the end of the novel, it is clear that Kid has written all four. By writing about these writings, Delany clarifies Kid's various functions.

The first information that Delany gives the reader concerning Kid as narrator is in the opening chapter when a journal entry begins with the same wording as the opening sentences of *Dhalgren.* The reader, therefore, infers that the author of the journal entry is the narrator of the novel.

In an editor's note (this is an editor Delany invents within *Dhalgren*) at the beginning of section seven, the journal is introduced as written by the author of *Brass Orchids,* thus establishing that Kid is author of both the journal and the book of poems. Kid narrates in the text about the two writings in the journal:

> Re-reading, I note the entries only ghost chronological order.... Sometimes I cannot tell who wrote

what. That is upsetting. With some sections, I can remember the place and time I wrote them, but have no memory of the incidents described. Similarly, other sections refur [sic] to things I recall happening to me, but kne/o/w [sic] just as well I never wrote out .... Most annoying is when I recall an entry, go hunting through, and not find it [sic] find it or half of it not there ....

In this quote Delany makes it clear that Kid is the narrator of the text and author of both sets of entries in the journal. Without this metafictional inclusion, the reader would not be able to verify these functions of the character Kid.

Further clarification is given concerning these multiple viewpoints when Delany explains through Kid why the novel was written in first and third person. "Also wonder if writing about myself in the third person is really the way to go about losing or making a name." This problem of "losing or making a name" not only reaffirms Kid as the author of first and third person sections, it also supports Delany's attempt to develop Kid as a character in search of his identity.

Delany does not restrict his metafictional statements to his own work. Within *Dhalgren,* he also analyzes the functions of the arts, the difficulty of writing dialogue and of recounting experiences, and of the nature of the poet and of poetry.

Delany implies that art cannot be subjugated to or dominate over religion and psychiatry because they all interact. Through the character Lanya, he describes the interrelationships of these three self-perpetuating systems:

> All *three* of them promise you a sense of inner worth and meaning, and spend a lot of time telling you about the suffering you have to go through to achieve it. As soon as you get a problem in any one of them, the solution it gives is always to go deeper into the same system. They're all in a rather uneasy truce with one another in what's actually a mortal battle. Like all self-reinforcing systems. At best, each is trying to encompass the other two and define them as subgroups.

Here he discusses the arts to clarify one of his purposes in writing the novel: to illustrate that all systems interact in a society.

Through the character Newboy, Delany describes the past and present relationships between art and its audience:

> The aesthetic equation ... The artist has some internal experience that produces a poem, a painting, a piece of music. Spectators submit themselves to the work, which generates an inner experience for them. But historically *it's a very new, not to mention vulgar, idea that the spectator's experience should be identical to, or even have anything to do with, the artist's.* This idea comes from an over-industrialized society which has learned to distrust magic—.

This emphasizes another of Delany's themes, exposing his audience to ideas and experiences which they have not encountered.

Poetry is discussed in several contexts. Delany uses a novelist to comment on Kid's poetry to discuss one of the advantages of poetry over fiction:

> ... watching your poems gain that effect showed me some of the reasons why my prose often doesn't. That condensed and clear *descriptive* insight is something I envy you. And you wield it as naturally as speech, turning it on this and that and the other.

But Kid remarks that his poems are "... not *descriptions* of anything. They're complex names." In a journal entry, the relationship of viewpoint to poetry is discussed:

> Speech is always in excess of poetry as print is always inadequate for speech. A word sets images flying through the brain from which auguries we recall all extent and intention. I'm not a poet because I have nothing to give life to make it due, except my attention. And I don't know if my wounded sort is enough.

In a pastiche of Auden's "Calebar to the Audience," Delany defines, through Newboy's monologue, two kinds of artists: one is committed to art; the other, which he favors, is committed to life. Newboy also rationalizes how his character traits of laziness, acrimony, and lust for power make him a better poet. The thrust of these statements is that the poet, to be effective, must value himself and the true nature of his relationship to society.

The problems of writing are directly discussed several times. Kid bemoans the impossibility of totally retrieving an experience by writing it down:

> Writing, he had not thought to retrieve any of it. But the prospect of publication had somehow convinced him magic was in process that would return to him, in *tacto* (not *memorium*), some of what the city had squandered. The conviction was now identified by its fraudulance, before the inadequate objects. But as it died, kicking in his gut, spastic and stuttering, he knew it had been as real and unquestioned as any surround: air to a bird, water to a fish, earth to a worm.

The problems of writing dialogue are also mentioned: "(If I wrote her words down, Kid thought, what she's saying would vanish into something meaningless as the literal record of the sound June or George makes)." In these two quotes, Delany is emphasizing the inadequacy of simply copying verbatum conversations or meticulously describing an experience. To be successful, the writer cannot just copy or describe, he must interpret, sifting the material until he recreates its essence.

The epigraph to the novel, "You have confused the true and the real," indicates the basic paradigm which is questioned in *Dhalgren.* Kid, the narrator/criminal/artist is the medium through which Delany discusses the role of artist in society, questioning the

reality models established by society. The struggle between what we believe is true and what we perceive as real is incorporated in his character. Kid, as artist, observes and then records experience through his poems and journal. He questions his own sanity because of the differences between what he observes and what he has been taught is true. Through Kid, Delany urges the Wittgensteinian maxim that metaphysical considerations have only emotive force and that experiences must be observable to have meaning. Kid's multiple views are an excellent example of the premise that style and content cannot be separated, that expression and meaning are multiple and integrated, because the viewpoint influences the content of this novel and the content influences the viewpoint.

The crucial question presented in *Dhalgren* is "What happens when patterns of perception are changed, when we are forced to accept the fact that our reality models are different from others?" Delany tells us that you become an artist, a criminal, an artist/criminal, or insane. Delany has taken our views of insanity and illustrated them. He indicates that reality models are verified by the society. When what we perceive of as real opposes already established reality models, we may be labeled as insane by others and by ourselves. (pp. 61-9)

> *Jane Branham Weedman, in her* Samuel R. Delany, *Starmont House, 1982, 79 p.*

Sandra Y. Govan (essay date 1984)

[*In the following excerpt, Govan argues that Delany brings a black perspective to the white-dominated genre of science fiction.*]

Typically, sf is not the genre scholars and critics of Afro-American literature turn toward to see the way that black fictionalists shape a vision of black experience and character. Our critical stance has presupposed that an Afro-American author is either creating a space for him- or herself somewhere within the Afro-American literary tradition—whether one calls that tradition "protest," "nationalistic," "Neo-hoodoo," or "the literature of black affirmation"—or is jumping into the "mainstream" to play the "I-am-an-American-writer-who-happens-to-be-black" shell game with both the black and the white critical establishment. By focusing on writers who have lent themselves, conveniently, to our presuppositions and who have obliged us by creating works we review and judge according to expected patterns, we have developed a critical astigmatism which prevents us from clearly seeing black writers who work outside our established norms. This serious limitation has, until recently, prohibited us from recognizing the achievements of so gifted a writer as Samuel R. Delany, merely because he works in a popular form. Having repeatedly received both Nebula and Hugo awards (the two most coveted prizes in science fiction), Samuel "Chip" Delany is one of the field's preeminent authors. He is also a writer who, while working in a genre long dominated by whites, brings to his speculative worlds a black presence and a subtle black perspective. (p. 43)

Delany, in his fiction, is not enamored of the technical or "hard" sciences—physics, astronomy, thermodynamics, computers. His forte is the adult novel utilizing the "soft" sciences—biology, psychology, anthropology, linguistic theory. Technological gadgetry, specialized computers, or, in *Nova,* "sockets" attached to people to "plug" them into machinery are simply facets of the setting and not the prime cause for the story. One is drawn into Delany's stories because they have a complexity; an acute consciousness of language, structure, and form; a dextrous ability to weave together mythology and anthropology, linguistic theory and cultural history, gestalt psychology and sociology as well as philosophy, structuralism, and the adventure story. Frequently the hero of a Delany adventure is likely to be a violent artist who produces both beauty and death. What is ultimately appealing about Delany's work is that it is stimulating, even if one cannot entirely peel back all the intricate, sometimes enigmatic layers of meaning. Delany challenges his audience. His work is studded with epigraphs, allusions, and symbols which force a reader to stretch to make connections. *The Einstein Intersection,* for example, offers epigraphs from a Pepsi slogan . . . to John Ruskin to Emily Dickinson in order to cue us to his protagonist's development on his quest.

Delany has a clearly articulated concern for what he terms "aesthetic discipline—that which makes most accessible all the substance of a given work." Because of that obvious concern, most of the critical attention his work receives focuses on the aesthetic apparatus he uses to frame his fiction. For instance, critics examining *The Einstein Intersection* look immediately to its mythic elements. An alien from a group inhabiting Earth after humankind has vanished, Lo Lobey, the novel's protagonist, is half-man and half-animal in appearance. For critics, Lobey is Pan; he is Theseus; he is Orpheus. He is also a latter-day Ringo Starr, the Beatle who did not sing . . . . That alien Lobey has adopted, in part, the appearance of a black man—"brown face with spun brass for hair"—is unremarkable.

In *Babel-17* what impresses critics most is Delany's handling of language and linguistic theories. *Babel-17,* we're told, is about communication, verbal and nonverbal; it makes use of the Whorf-Sapir hypothesis, which suggests that "language shapes perception drastically and completely." Rydra Wong, poet and heroine, must break an enemy code, Babel-17, undecipherable to military cryptographers. The code, however, is a language by itself, one that obliterates "I"—the self—as a basic referent, one that forges linguistic traps and dangerous patterns of action, capitalizing on typical gestalt psychology. Delany's knowledge of linguistics and semiotics is everywhere apparent in the novel, as are the connections to structuralism and French symbolism (Rimbaud, the French symbolist, in a direct allusion becomes "the Rimbaud," Rydra Wong's spaceship) . . . .

Obviously, communication via language, symbol, or sign is the central element of *Babel-17.* Yet most discussions of the text wholly ignore Delany's subtle stress on ethnicity. Rydra Wong is an Asian woman. The one man she relies on when she is distressed by her own formidable powers of perception is an African man, Dr. Markus T'mwarba, her psychotherapist.

In *Nova,* a black man moves from the role of strong support to that of hero proper; but again, most of the critical response to the novel concentrates on Delany's wedding of form to theme; space opera to the mythic quests for power, for art, for meaning, for free will. *Nova* follows the adventures of Captain Lorq Von Ray and his adversaries, Prince and Ruby Red, through the galaxy to an exploding star, a nova, to bring back the rare element Illyrion . . . . The son of a Senegalese mother and a Norwegian father, Lorq Von Ray is a black man and hero clearly at the center of this novel.

Samuel Delany's vision of future and possible worlds is a vision in which race, however subtly manifested, is as emblematically significant as any of the other concerns his work treats. If in *Nova*'s Lorq, Delany has rendered one of his most commanding signs denoting the signifi-

Delany, circa 1964.

cance of black folk in his speculative future, in his other works black people are viable too. His black characters may be heroic, or they may merely assist the protagonist. What most matters is that, in science fiction worlds in which very few blacks have appeared, they are *there.* (pp. 44-5)

Delany has described his future worlds as places "where things have changed. In most of my futures the racial situation has changed and changed for the better. As a young writer I thought it very important to keep an image of such a possibility before people. I don't ever remember subscribing to the idea that 'being black doesn't matter.' I wanted to write about worlds where being black mattered in different ways from the way it matters now." In *The Einstein Intersection* and *Babel-17* Delany clearly succeeds in articulating a difference. In *Nova,* valiant as Lorq is, the sexual mythology attached to black man/white woman is sufficient to show us that being black in the distant future still matters to some in a way not so different from our present. However, that Lorq is able to pit his strength and will successfully against the Reds, rather than be lynched by them, says something different about the cycle of violence and oppression blacks of the future may endure.

Delany's recent novels *Dhalgren* and *Triton* are vastly different from either the stories in *Driftglass* (1971) or Delany's previous novels. *Dhalgren* (1975) is probably his most controversial novel; certainly it is his most challenging. Its setting is not distant stars but Earth and a contemporary city embodying urban decay. (pp. 46-7)

There is no question that *Dhalgren* is saturated with fragmented versions of Delany's own experiences. It is his retelling, through the persona of an amnesic schizophrenic artist dubbed the Kid, of his excursions through those socio-psychological barriers mentioned earlier—only this time with the violence unrestrained. For the bulk of the novel, the Kid resides in violence-torn Bellona, a wounded "autumnal city" existing in some undefined, undisclosed physical parentheses at the outer edge of the normal world. Bellona (named after the Roman goddess of war) has suffered some unmentioned cataclysmic holocaust. Most of its population has departed, yet it is not a closed city; wanderers from cities like Seattle, Washington, and Euclid, Ohio, drift in and out.... No economic, social, physical, or temporal laws apply in Bellona. Days and years are ironically designated by the Bellona *Times,* the whimsical town newspaper; it might declare 1995 the year in one issue and 1776 the year in the next. A gigantic orange sun may rise and set in the space of an hour, or twin moons may rise unaccountably. Most of the city operates on a quasi-communal model, drawn from Delany's intimate knowledge of commune and extended family life.

Kid, the psychologically wounded poet-protagonist, is a distorted reflection of Delany. Like Delany, he has been a wanderer, and he keeps a writer's journal. Like Delany, he uses poetry to distill meanings, composing *Brass Orchids* in the midst of Bellona's confusion and

becoming a celebrated Wunderkind.... Like Delany, the Kid participates in various kinds of sexual activity, all sanctioned by the social mores of the city and by its communal structure. (The novel's sexual explicitness disturbs many critics.) And, like Delany, the Kid has been a patient in a mental hospital. Both have suffered from hallucinations, disorientation, general nervous breakdown; Kid still loses huge blocks of time, measured in days and weeks, not merely hours. Unlike Delany, though, the Kid's parentage is half-Indian, half-white; he is not black, but he becomes the leader of a group/gang called the scorpions, most of whose membership, male and female, is black.

Race as an issue is unavoidable and unmistakable in *Dhalgren.* Three-fourths of the scorpions are black. Bellona is still, after the holocaust, bifurcated by race. There are fewer goods and supplies in the city's black sections than in its white neighborhoods, and there are snipers who shoot blacks from the tops of deserted buildings and arsonists who burn black neighborhoods. There is also the Reverend Amy Tayler, a black evangelical minister who directs her church's Evening Aid Program for the hungry, and who preaches vehemently about the moral state of Bellona.... Finally, there is George Harrison—rapist (according to the Bellona *Times*), hero, macho sex symbol to white women and white homosexual men alike. Obscene posters of George, displaying his genitals, abound in Bellona; his vaunted sexuality is mythic. His exploits are so famous they mask the real man. George Harrison is so much larger than life that, when a second moon inexplicably rises over Bellona, the inhabitants name it George, and after their fear subsides, they go on about their business having further mythologized his prowess.

In Delany's 1976 novel *Triton,* race and sex are entirely different concerns from those of *Dhalgren* or those of present-day America, yet more than a vestige of classic racism and sexual chauvinism is ingrained in the psyche of the chief protagonist, Bron Helstrom. *Triton* is about many things: communication, human sexuality, and bigotry among them. Bron is a narrow-minded, isolated man, so self-serving that he is incapable of reaching outside himself to love another or even understand another despite his best intentions. He abuses Miriamne, a black woman with roots in Earth's Kenya, ostensibly because her sexual preference is not his. He hates Sam Jones because Sam is handsome, expansive, and friendly to everyone, even Bron. Bron thinks of Sam as an average "type," only to discover to his great annoyance that "good looking, friendly, intelligent," oppressed-by-the-system Sam, "doing his bit as some overworked salesman/consultant," is actually "the head of the Political Liaison Department between the Outer Satellite Diplomatic Corps and Outer Satellite Intelligence; and had all the privileges (and training) of both." This news shocks Bron, but what rocks him is the discovery that black Sam, before coming to Triton, had been a "sallow-faced, blond, blue-eyed waitress... with a penchant for other sallow-faced, blond, blue-eyed waitresses who... were all just gaga over the six-foot-plus Wallunda and Katanga emigrants who had absolutely infested the neighborhood."...Complete sex change is a possibility in the outer worlds, and before the novel's end Bron makes one. However, the physical change cannot change a psychologically distorted personality, and Bron remains an alienated loner unable to make meaningful human contact. One of Delany's major white characters, he is, in the author's words, the "epitome of the unsavory WASP."

Delany's variety of black and mixed-blood characters represents his method of grappling with his own position as a black American writer. In a "multiplex" configuration that includes the metaphorical, the allegorical, the figurative (the use of the Ull in *Empire Star* is an allegorical reminder of the cycle of oppression, guilt, and responsibility that slavery begets), Delany parades black characters across the spectrum of his speculative fiction not simply to attest to black survival in the future, but to punctuate his social criticism of our present. While he does not dwell on a "black experience" as we would encounter it in familiar mainstream Afro-American literature, Delany does give us memorable black characters, and his science-fiction novels affirm the diversity and vitality of black life. Obviously, in some of the novels, Delany utilizes existing negative racial mythologies about blacks, but, in all his works, he twists the commonplace images and stereotypes to his own ends, creating a far richer and clearly pluralistic future, while at the same time ever so carefully structuring a pointed commentary on the present.... Other science-fiction writers may have tried to omit or obliterate black folk in their versions of the future, but in Samuel Delany's speculative world a black consciousness *is,* and black folk *are,* an insistent presence. (pp. 47-8)

> Sandra Y. Govan, "The Insistent Presence of Black Folk in the Novels of Samuel R. Delany," in Black American Literature Forum, *Vol. 18, No. 2, Summer, 1984, pp. 43-8.*

Samuel Delany with Charles Johnson (interview date 1984)

[*Winner of the 1990 National Book Award for* Middle Passage, *Johnson has won critical acclaim for fiction that variously incorporates elements of fantasy, the parable, folklore, and the slave narrative. In the introduction to a 1984 issue of* Callaloo, *guest editor Johnson wrote: "Samuel Delany has made a lasting contribution to the 'New Wave' fringe of science fiction (though he doesn't call it that) as a novelist and literary critic, and among black writers he stands alone.... There is no one quite like this man. He is rare." In the following excerpt from an interview Johnson conducted at the University of Washington in May 1984, Delany discusses science fiction writing. A small portion of this interview was revised by Delany especially for* Black Literature Criticism.]

[Johnson]: *Why do you think academics have not been as responsive as they should be in treating what is probably the most imaginative form of storytelling, and also the most intellectually vigorous, that is to say, in the exploration of ideas?*

[Delany]: Well, it [science fiction] simply hasn't come up by the proper provenance; it has come up in the pulp magazines, outside the traditional realms of literature, and when you go back to the nineteenth century, the same gesture that establishes literature also establishes *para*literature; you can't have one without the other. That's when literature was established as a set of texts with a certain order of value; you must therefore have certain texts that are not of that order of value, otherwise you don't have the proper spread, and science fiction grew up in those texts that were not of that order of value... (pp. 27-8)

Let me ask another question, probably one you've been asked before. When I look at Joanna [Russ's] work what I see is an interrogation of fantasy, science fiction, and horror literature for the sexist values they embody; a sort of cultural critique is happening in her work and, on another level in stories like her adventures of Alyx, she is claiming this literature for women. How do you, as a black writer, feel about this entrance of blacks and women consciously as *blacks and women into the field?*

Well, again: science fiction grows up outside this established set of literary texts and I think it's always easier to appropriate the margin; it always has been for blacks and women, for anyone who is in a marginal position. In that sense, this is what people in a marginal social position have been doing constantly, appropriating what is marginal in the rest of cultural production, so that's nothing new. What causes the problem of course, the conflict, is when people in a marginal position try to appropriate the center. And that really goes back to your first question: Why aren't people who are in the center of the spotlight looking to what is in the margins? Well, they never have, and there's not too much reason to expect them to do terribly much about it other than in a token way. (p. 29)

Back to your phrase, "paraliterature." Will you define that?

I'm using literature as a generic term; I'm referring to science fiction as a something that happens, historically, as growing up outside the realms of literature, a *para*literature, if you will.

Yet, your own work has been highly praised, especially by critics for investigating large cultural phenomena, i.e., language, and for advancing what has been called the New Wave in science fiction.

Well, some of it has sold very well, and that's always very nice. The other thing is that in a social field such as the United States you tend not to have a real center anymore. You tend to have lots and lots of centers; so talk of centers and margins becomes a more and more strained metaphor after a certain point. Nevertheless, when you realize that there are lots and lots of sub-populations, each with its own center and margin, it still has some validity.

Why did you select science fiction as your field for expression?

I don't think I really *did* select it; it selected me. I always liked to read it; it gave me a lot of pleasure as a reader, so at a certain point I started writing it.

Any particular authors that have been very influential?

I liked Heinlein. I liked Theodore Sturgeon, who has always been my single favorite writer . . . I liked Merril and Kathryn McClean, although as a kid I think I read mostly for story, for the science fiction experience, and I wasn't terribly concerned with who had written it, which I think still goes on today. Your average science fiction reader is less concerned with creating an author figure than with just reading.

You're mentioned often among the "New Wave" science fiction authors. How do you see yourself in this trend?

Well, I think New Wave is one of those over-used terms. New Wave, as a meaningful term, referred to a bunch of writers associated with the British magazine, *New Worlds* between 1965 and 1968, and I wasn't part of it, as much as I might have liked to have been. I was writing space operas with people diving through suns and things like that, and they had a more serious program that was a lot more sensitive to experimental writing. The kind of stuff I was doing wasn't and still isn't all that terribly experimental, otherwise it wouldn't be anywhere near as popular as it is, but I was very much in sympathy with what they wanted to do, and I thought it was a very good thing, and I was very excited by it as a reader. But as a writer I was just a kind of fellow traveler rather than really involved with it. The thing is, of course, that when the term moved away from that particular group in 1970 or so, it brought this whole oppositional model that says if there's a New Wave, there has got to be an *Old* Wave, somewhere; so instead of an island of production in the vaster sea of Science Fiction production, you get this notion of a sort of unlocateable set of oppositions that propogates throughout the whole of science fiction; that's the New Wave in most people's minds, and it really doesn't refer to anything. By the time you get to the mid-seventies any writer who was under forty, or with liberal political tendencies or at all aesthetically interesting, or who was writing a new book, had been called New Wave, so the term was kind of generalized out of all meaningfulness. I'm much more aware of how what I'm doing relates to what's been done in the past, than how it breaks with what's been done in the past.

Then you see no significant, large trends—new ones—in the field of science fiction?

(Laughter) No. I think a little bit more care is being paid to the sentences that construct the textual object; I think there is a lot more sensitivity to the various ideological positions that one is forced to take as soon as one picks up a pen, or sets one's fingers on a set of typewriter keys. And this I think is a good thing. One would like to see that spread outside the realm of science fiction, and become a little bit more generally the case for other fiction. (pp. 30-1)

> *Samuel Delany with Charles Johnson, in an interview in* Callaloo, *Vol. 7, No. 3, Fall, 1984, pp. 27-35.*

FURTHER READING

Collings, Michael R. "Samuel R. Delany and John Wilkins: Artificial Languages, Sciences, and Science Fiction." In *Reflections on the Fantastic: Selected Essays from the Fourth International Conference on the Fantastic in the Arts,* edited by Michael R. Collings, pp. 61-8. New York: Greenwood Press, 1986.
>   Attempts to establish a connection between Delany and John Wilkins, a seventeenth-century scientist, in regard to their theories of "artificial" languages. The critic concludes that both men "confronted the essential human activity of communication and, even though by accident, developed systems that parallel each other in their attempts to weld language more firmly and efficiently to reality."

Collins, Robert A. "Allegory in Delany's *Einstein Intersection.*" In *Forms of the Fantastic: Selected Essays from the Third International Conference on the Fantastic in Literature and Film,* edited by Jan Hokenson and Howard Pearce, pp. 87-90. New York: Greenwood Press, 1986.
>   Allegorical interpretation of *The Einstein Intersection,* arguing that Delany believes blacks "must discard the 'borrowed' culture of their adopted land, including a Christian religion, which dominates Western myth, before they can achieve a genuine sense of themselves."

Delany, Samuel R. "The Semiology of Science." *Science-Fiction Studies* 14, No. 2 (July 1987): 134-64.
>   Self-assessment by Delany of his language theories, with additional remarks by Sinda Gregory and Larry McCaffery.

Fox, Robert Elliot. "The Politics of Desire in *Triton* and *The Tides of Lust.*" *Black American Literature Forum* 18, No. 2 (Winter 1984): 49-56.
>   Examines social structures and sexuality in *The Tides of Lust* and *Triton,* novels in which "matters of sexual politics seem to be most prominent."

———. *Conscientious Sorcerers: The Black Postmodernist Fiction of LeRoi Jones/Amiri Baraka, Ishmael Reed, and Samuel R. Delany.* New York: Greenwood Press, 1987, 142 p.

Profiles the postmodernist works of Amiri Baraka, Ishmael Reed, and Delany.

Hassler, Donald M. "*Dhalgren, The Beggar's Opera,* and Georgic: Implications for the Nature of Genre." *Extrapolation* 30, No. 4 (Winter 1989): 332-38.
    Argues that Delany, in breaking "genre expectations" with *Dhalgren,* was influenced by John Gay's *The Beggar's Opera.*

Jonas, Gerald. Review of *The Motion of Light in Water. The New York Times Book Review* XCIII, No. 30 (24 July 1988): 25.
    Offers a favorable review of Delany's autobiography but worries that the work does nothing to introduce new readers to the "many pleasures" of Delany's fiction.

McEvoy, Seth. *Samuel R. Delany.* New York: Frederick Ungar Publishing Company, 1984, 142 p.
    Biography of Delany with discussions of his major works.

Nilon, Charles. "The Science Fiction of Samuel R. Delany and the Limits of Technology." *Black American Literature Forum* 18, No. 2 (Summer 1984): 62-8.

Analyzes Delany's use of technology, concluding that his novels show that "technology is always both constructive and destructive—and that technology is limited in what it can do to make man more human."

Renault, Gregory. "Speculative Porn: Aesthetic Form in Samuel R. Delany's 'The Tides of Lust.'" *Extrapolation* 24, No. 2 (Summer 1983): 116-29.
    Aims to rescue *The Tides of Lust* from the classification of "mere pornography," arguing that it is "a significant attempt by Delany to explore further the artistic possibilities of contemporary mass culture."

Tatsumi, Takayuki. "Interview: Samuel R. Delany." *Diacritics* 16, No. 3 (Fall 1986): 27-45.
    Interview with Delany, focusing on his criticism and literary theories.

Weedman, Jane. "Art and the Artist's Role in Delany's Works." In *Voices for the Future: Volume Three,* edited by Thomas D. Clareson and Thomas L. Wymer, pp. 151-85. Bowling Green, Ohio: Bowling Green University Popular Press, 1984.
    Examines the role of the artist in Delany's works, determining that it is "to observe, record, or transmit and question paradigms in a society."

William Demby

1922-

American novelist, short story writer, scriptwriter, translator, and critic.

A contemporary American novelist, Demby is chiefly known for *Beetlecreek* (1950) and *The Catacombs* (1965). Exploring themes of life, death, and love, he strives to incorporate existential issues in all his works. His novels have earned critical praise but enjoy only a modest readership. Demby's admirers maintain, nonetheless, that they are important additions to the field of black literature.

Born in Pennsylvania, Demby grew up in a coal-mining town in West Virginia and attended local public schools until enrolling at West Virginia State College. His college education was interrupted when he joined the United States Army during World War II. While on wartime duty in Italy and North Africa, he decided to pursue a writing career; following the war, he continued his education at Fisk University. He served as assistant editor of the student magazine *Fisk Herald* and published his first short story, "Saint Joey," in the periodical in 1946. He was graduated a year later and returned to Italy to study art at the University of Rome. For the next twenty years he wrote screenplays for film and television and translated scripts into English for Italian director Roberto Rossellini. Since his return to the United States, he has been teaching at Staten Island Community College in New York.

While residing in Rome, Demby completed his first book, *Beetlecreek*. Described by Edward Margolies as "a novel of defeat and death," *Beetlecreek* portrays Johnny Johnson, a black youth sent to live with his aunt and uncle in the southern backwater community of Beetlecreek. Johnny and his uncle soon befriend Bill Trapp, a white hermit living in the town's black section. Although temporarily able to surmount the prejudices of Beetlecreek through their friendship with Trapp, Johnny and his uncle are ultimately forced into betrayal by the oppressive nature of the community. The novel concludes when Johnny sets fire to Trapp's house to gain acceptance among a black gang. Although faulted for oversimplification, *Beetlecreek* received mostly positive reviews for its reversal of the conventional scenario of a black man in a white world, through which Demby transforms racial isolation into a symbol of alienation within American society. While John F. Bayliss asserted that *Beetlecreek* is best viewed as "a human document," several critics defined the novel's theme as existential. According to Robert Bone, *Beetlecreek* moves thematically "toward an existentialist definition of evil" because Johnny and his uncle prove unable to transcend the moral and spiritual vacuum of the town or to resist the negative influences of the racist community and the gang. Demby also drew praise for his realistic style and

his cinematic focus on particular objects and actions to convey the hopelessness and stagnation of Beetlecreek.

Demby's second novel, *The Catacombs*, is a self-reflexive work that blends realism and imagination in the story of fictional author Bill Demby. It tells of his sexual and spiritual relationship with Doris, a black dancer who becomes pregnant after an affair with an Italian count. Demby often interjects his authorial persona into this novel, commenting on its structure and progress or interweaving news items concerning national crises as well as personal incidents derived from letters and diaries. Reviewers were initially bewildered by *The Catacombs,* and some lamented Demby's departure from the more traditional narrative form of *Beetlecreek.* One critic noted: " ... most of this book... 'stinks'." Similarly, Maggie Rennert stated, "Reviewing this non-novel is as melancholy and fruitless a proceeding as writing a report on a miscarriage." Later commentators, however, have contended that Demby is successful in his stylistic experimentation and have placed his novel in the modernist tradition of James Joyce's *Ulysses*. Often maintaining that Demby's treatment of time is derived from cubist models, critics have also noted such influences as modern art, contemporary scientific and social theory, and the cinematic experiments of Italian film directors Federico Fellini, Roberto Rossellini, and Michelangelo Antonioni.

Demby's third novel, *Love Story Black* (1978), has been alternately regarded as an examination of the redemptive power of the archetypal black woman and a latent critique of black feminism. In this book, a middle-aged professor pursues relationships with several women, including Mona Pariss, an aging singer whom he interviews for a black journal. While largely ignored by critics, some of whom contended that the novel lacks the thematic and structural intricacies of Demby's earlier work, *Love Story Black* garnered praise for its uncommon evocation of the innocent, Edenic quality of love. Summing up, Addison Gayle commented: "*Love Story Black* is ... a novel about making love, about truth and revelation, birth, rebirth and death.... For Camus's doctrine, 'I rebel, therefore I am,' Demby would proclaim I love, therefore I am, thus raising the existential equation beyond romanticism to touch the most profound longings and utterings of the human soul."

Because of the existential nature of his books, Demby is often overlooked in assessments of black literature; Margaret Perry has observed that "[Demby] has been separated from the tradition of black literature because his novels have a universality about them." This "universality," however, distinguishes his works from those of many other black writers, thus affording him a place in the wider literary world.

(For further information about Demby's life and works, see *Black Writers; Contemporary Authors,* Vols. 81-84; *Contemporary Literary Criticism,* Vol. 53; and *Dictionary of Literary Biography,* Vol. 33: *Afro-American Fiction Writers after 1955.)*

PRINCIPAL WORKS

"Saint Joey" (short story) 1946; published in periodical *Fisk Herald*
Beetlecreek (novel) 1950
"The Geisha Girls of Ponto-cho" (prose) 1954; published in periodical *Harper's Magazine*
"They Surely Can't Stop Us Now" (prose) 1956; published in periodical *Reporter*
"A Walk in Tuscany" (prose) 1957; published in periodical *Holiday*
"Blueblood Cats of Rome" (prose) 1960; published in periodical *Holiday*
The Catacombs (novel) 1965
Love Story Black (novel) 1978
Blueboy (novel) 1979

Edward Margolies (essay date 1968)

[*An American essayist and critic, Margolies is the author of* Native Sons: A Critical Study of Twentieth-Century Negro American Authors. *In the following excerpt from this work, an essay originally entitled "The Expatriate as Novelist: William Demby," he favorably appraises* Beetlecreek *and* The Catacombs, *describing them as novels immersed in "European modes of thinking" but "conditioned by a profoundly American outlook."*]

Since the 1920's, a considerable number of Negro authors have gone abroad to live and work. Some have returned, dissatisfied and weary at what they have found. But a surprising hard core have remained overseas, determined in one way or another, to fashion a better life for themselves. As Negroes, they say, they are made constantly aware of their status in America, and race consciousness cannot help but influence the character of their work. Here, then, they write as Negroes first and artists second; hopefully, in a "raceless" milieu they might avoid such difficulties.

Unfortunately, in the vast majority of cases, they do not succeed. (p. 173)

One remarkable exception is the novelist William Demby. Demby's works [*Beetlecreek* and *The Catacombs*] reveal a thoroughly unself-conscious immersion in European modes of thinking, conditioned by a profoundly American outlook. He is, like his literary ancestors, Melville and Hawthorne, obsessed with the problem of evil, but he expresses his concerns in philosophical terms akin to Christian existentialism. He has appropriated techniques ranging from Joycean stream of consciousness to modern cinematography, and incorporated these as instruments of his philosophical quest. (p. 174)

[Biographical] data can scarcely provide any major insights into Demby's creative psychology. What does become apparent, however, are the obvious extremes of his experiences. He was brought up in the relatively confining atmosphere of the Negro ghettos of Pittsburgh and a West Virginia mining town. Even as a college student, he attended all-Negro institutions. As an adult, on the other hand, living a cosmopolitan life among film directors, writers, artists, and the like, his life assumes an altogether different character. These opposing patterns are reflected in his work, where they are pitted against one another as the central conflict of his novels.

In a very real sense the drama in Demby's works revolves around an ever-shifting battle between Life and Death. Death, or evil, is equated with the static, the inert, the stultifying qualities of existence—and judging from the allusions in his works to his American years, one would gather Demby regards this period as having been deadly and constraining. Life, for its part, implies creative evolutionary energies, love and reason. These, presumably, Demby discovered in the European phases of his career.

Although its setting is a small Negro community in a forsaken Depression mining town in West Virginia, Demby wrote *Beetlecreek* in Italy and published the novel three years after leaving Fisk. The novel is related in the third person from the point of view of four characters, each of whom is struggling to extricate himself from the death grip the community symbolizes. The story deals primarily with Johnny Johnson.... Johnny, feeling lonely and unloved, befriends a white hermit named Bill Trapp, who lives on a ramshackle farm on the edge of Beetlecreek. (pp. 175-76)

Bill is an enigmatic creature, whose presence in Beetlecreek has seldom disturbed the general torpor of the community. But after fifteen years of self-imposed silence, he determines to communicate and love the world, mainly through Johnny.... Alternately imagined in Johnny's dreams and fantasies as a saint and a shepherd, he becomes something of a martyr when Johnny, succumbing to the deathlike atmosphere of Beetlecreek, turns on him and attempts to burn down his house.

Interwoven with Johnny's relationship to Bill are accounts of David and Mary Diggs. David, Johnny's uncle, represents a somewhat older version of his nephew. He, too, as the novel opens, feel alienated and alone, but has come to accept the passive drift of his life. He is awakened momentarily by his friendship with Bill, whom he has met through Johnny. But when an old college sweetheart returns to town to attend a funeral, David forsakes Bill and decides to run away with her. In doing so, David pursues an illusion. Edith is a death figure, having been hardened and corrupted in the big-city Negro ghettos.

Mary, David's wife, is the least defined of Demby's characters. Her vitality has been drained by a loveless marriage and the stifling environment of Beetlecreek; her principal spiritual resources are the odd tidbits of gossip she gathers in the kitchen of the white folks she works for, and a driving ambition to become president of the Woman's Missionary Guild of her local church. Ironically, though, her success in gaining the latter is attended by the desertion of her husband and the murderous arson of her nephew, Johnny.

Thus *Beetlecreek* is a novel of defeat and death. Beetlecreek is itself a metaphor of death, a dreary and sluggish town whose inhabitants have lost all desire for change or hope for improved circumstances. Even its name suggests an arrested form of the evolutionary processes. (pp. 176-77)

Demby employs a kind of stark, refined realism to seize his effects—not unlike some film directors who focus on seemingly prosaic objects in order to register a meaning that might otherwise be overlooked. Johnny, standing on the swinging bridge that spans the creek, observes, in the course of a conversation with some of the gang members, "a hole in the bottom plank of the bridge and in it was a waxy beetle struggling to get off its back." Demby depends more on closely realized visual elements than most novelists. The physical atmosphere of Beetlecreek informs the moral and spiritual dilemma of Demby's characters as much as anything they say or do. Thus Demby will focus on the light that falls over the town at certain hours of the day, or the wind-swept leaves and candy wrappers as they scatter along an empty street, or the freakishly warm weather of an Indian summer night. (p. 177)

Sometimes these images will become more obvious, as when Nature appears to suggest portents that hover ominously beyond the horizon. Indian Summer weather lingers on well into autumn, out-of-season earthworms surface to the ground, birds swoop around the roofs and chimneys of houses as if "undecided what to do"—just as, in a fashion, Johnny and David remain suspended in moral indecision regarding what actions they will take concerning Bill Trapp, whether indeed they will save or betray him.

On an even more specific level, Demby will set a critical scene in a junk yard or cemetery, or he will describe a hearse as "shiny and low-slung like a super enameled beetle," or Bill Trapp's fingers "moving back and forth slowly like the antennae of insects." But these literal images are only part of the effect. The impact of the novel lies generally in the contrast between the vaguely looming violence that hangs over the town and the callowness of the townsfolk, the triteness of their talk, the superficiality of their behavior, the narrowness of their vision. In effect, Demby is saying that by the inert and passive qualities of their lives, they have chosen (by not choosing) evil for good, death for life, as revealed by the very essence of the physical atmosphere that engulfs them.

The images convey far more of the message of the novel than the dialogue. The sentences the characters utter are tired, flat and prosaic—as if the very act of expression were a spiritually exhausting experience. What the reader remembers best are scenes where scarcely any words are spoken.... Demby shifts his scenes back and forth dramatically among his characters, viewing them, analyzing them at simultaneous moments wherever they may be. (pp. 178-79)

Although *Beetlecreek* is by no means a "Negro novel" in any provincial sense, its existential themes are particularly applicable to the Negro experience. The stifling and frequently destructive atmosphere of the ghetto has been portrayed many times by the Negro authors, but here it is shown more as a kind of human condition than as a symptom of a specific social dysfunction. Moreover, such an atmosphere must intensify those universal existential feelings of dread and despair and terror that sociologists relate as being particularly prevalent among Negro slum dwellers. Demby himself recognizes as much when he represents David's thoughts of "how Negro life was a fishnet, a mosquito net, lace, wrapped round and round, each thread a pain...." The nice little paradox of Demby's novel, however, is that this view of Negro life is not particularly Negro. The white man, Bill Trapp (the name is significant), is as much a Negro as the others—a pariah, an outcast, all his life he has known shame and fear and self-contempt. And the circle becomes complete when the Negro community persecutes him *because he is a white man.* Thus Negro life in all its deathly aspects is the mirror image of white society. (p. 179)

Demby's second book, *The Catacombs,* published fifteen years later, is about a novelist named William Demby living in Rome, who is writing a novel about a Negro girl named Doris... Demby has introduced her to an Italian count with whom she proceeds to have an affair for the next two years. Doris sees Bill frequently and gives an account of herself which Demby will presumably incorporate in the novel.

In the course of her affair with the Count (who is married but living apart from his wife), she takes Bill as an occasional lover.... [At] one juncture in the novel, she does not know whether Bill or the Count is the father of the baby to whom she is about to give birth. Doris determines the child is the Count's, but the baby is born dead.... [Finally, Demby] prepares to leave for New York, where he has been offered a position in an advertising agency. In the final passages of the book, the Count has taken Doris on a tour through the Catacombs, Rome's ancient cemetery for Christian martyrs. He loses her in the gloom, and as he pursues her along the maze of cold, dark corridors, calling out her name, the novel abruptly ends.

For Demby, plot in the conventional sense is an artifice that conceals the realities he endeavors to express. The fortunes of no one person can be isolated from any other's—indeed, all of existence, animate and inanimate, bears on the essential realities of the individual portrayed; hence any attempt to project the true life of a character in a novel must attempt to project at the same time the multifaceted elements of existence that constitute that life. (pp. 179-80)

Demby construes time-existence as being cyclic—as revealed in the cycle of the seasons, as expressed in the death and resurrection of Christ on the Christian calendar, as imagined in the periodic eclipses of the sun, and as symbolized by the two-headed god Janus whose month January looks both backward on death (winter) and forward to renewed life (spring, Easter).

In order to reinforce what Demby... describes as "illusory motion, the dreamlike sense of progression and progress," images, events, colors, puns, patterns of speech, dreams, and mythological, literary, and historical allusions reappear in startlingly different contexts, as the characters proceed along their way—themselves experiencing spiritual death and rebirth. As in *Beetlecreek,* death as opposed to life is related to will-lessness, a failure of courage to act and to love. Its manifestations are violence and nonfeeling.... Life and death are thus locked in immemorial struggle as are good and evil in individuals. (p. 181)

[Demby] describes the intellectual as one engaged in the "new warfare of ideas."... (p. 182)

Demby's methods of warfare are at first mystifying, but it is warfare directed not against the reader, but against evil. The key to Demby's tactics may be found on the opening pages of the novel. It is morning and he is in his studio awaiting Doris, who will tell him about her night with the Count. The sun shines on his Rotella collages "that have begun to dance like gorgeous jungle flowers." Before Doris arrives, he will read from a number of newspapers that lie on his desk.

From here on in the novel achieves something of a collage effect in which at odd moments the newspaper accounts Demby reads and quotes superimpose themselves, however precariously, on the narrative—the effect is a hovering sense of world and time on even the most private situations. But the various strands of the novel crisscross in other places as well. Demby may intrude on his story with seemingly vagrant thoughts of his own... or more frequently he may break into any dramatic action of his principals by projecting what some of the other major or minor characters may be doing or thinking at the precise moment. This simultaneity of presentation is presumably what Demby means when he speaks somewhere of "cubistic time." It is something almost animate.... Actually, although the narrative generally unfolds in chronological order, Demby will, on occasion, shuttle back and forth in time in personal recollection or fantasy, or in a kind of Jungian race memory in which some odd newspaper item or disparate event suddenly assumes symbolic or archetypal importance. And yet the fragments do piece together. The novel begins and ends at the Easter season, and themes of death and resurrection become everywhere apparent like spirals within spirals.

If Demby's technique make *The Catacombs* sound like something of a jigsaw, it is surprising to discover what intensely good reading the novel is. Part of the reason is Demby himself, around whom all the threads of the novel are bound. The prose is informed by a passion and honesty wherein the author tries to come to grips with himself in a world wracked by violence and stress. His principal means are his two "imaginary" or fictional characters, Doris and the Count, whose life-and-death confrontation is a reflection of Demby's own inward spiritual struggle. (Real-life characters stalk in and out of this novel as well—among them Demby's wife and son.) The Count, for all his sophistication and elegance, is a death figure. Centuries of inbreeding have left him spiritually debilitated. He endeavors unsuccessfully to reach out of himself, to act toward Doris according to his feelings, but his entire conditioning inhibits him. For social reasons he is afraid to bring Doris with him to Hong Kong, and it is significant that the beginning and end of their relationship takes place in a restaurant near the Catacombs. In contrast to the will-less Count, Demby poses another aristocrat he had once regarded as "dehydrated" who, as a journalist, defied the threats of French Algerian terrorists and remained in North Africa to record the terrible struggle for freedom. Thus Demby is saying that by an act of will, of courage, it would not have been impossible for the Count to transform himself had he so desired.

If the Count represents one segment of Demby's nature, Doris represents another. When the reader first meets her, she is all energy and live.... Later Demby says there is something about her that suggests fertility.... Throughout the course of the novel, Doris stands opposed to the Count as a kind of life force. When she tells him she is going to have his baby, he is angry and terrified at the prospect.

What is perhaps most interesting about Doris is that her creative energies become intimately associated with her Negroness, her African ancestry. Demby speaks of her "forest-tapered legs," her "dream-secret Negro laughter." Beyond that, her négritude begins to assume a kind of saintly quality.... The Count's sister, a nun who has returned from the Congo, says that Africa is an "idea," a dream, where people still speak a "human language that the rest of humanity has forgotten," and that if society is to survive, it will have to become like Africa again and face "the realities of the tom-tom bed, the subtle clucking of the Bantu tongue." The Count himself admits to his wife that embracing Doris is like embracing "a girl in a dream."

Doris's symbolism is further enhanced by her Christlike sufferings. She accuses both Demby and the Count of being vampires; in drawing their sustenance from her, they suggest in involuted fashion worshippers at Communion. Doris's plight is made symbolic of the plight of all women who are used and suffer (and die) that their men might survive.... [It] is clear that Demby intends his Christian symbolism mainly for Doris. He likens her afterward to Mary, Queen of Scots, and her disappearance in the Catacombs suggests the death of another Christian martyr.

Yet Doris and the Count, for all their symbolic status, ring true as people. Doris talks and sounds like a slightly worldly, slightly exuberant American college girl who pretends to brook no sentimentality.... She manages to keep up her skeptical, vaguely amused facade throughout the novel—especially with the Count, about whom she really entertains no illusions. The Count, for his part, always maintains his aristocratic demeanor.... (pp. 182-86)

Demby casts his characters in remarkably real settings—cafés, clubs, barbershops, beaches, drawing rooms, country estates. As in *Beetlecreek*—but now with greater skill—he focuses his camera on the seemingly irrelevant to provide an authenticity that might not otherwise be caught... Demby cuts swiftly, impressionistically, in and out from one scene to the next, back to the brooding Demby who is imagining his novel—catching his characters in unguarded moments, infusing an air of reality into the dreamlike fragments of the structure.

It is a long way from the Beetlecreek of the Depression era to Europe in the 1960s, but in some respects the distance is not so great. For Doris and Demby, the entire West begins to assume the character of a Beetlecreek deathtrap.... The degradation of Europe is imaged in terms reminiscent of the primeval ooze and slime of Beetlecreek. The levels to which life has now descended are fishy and reptilian, and Demby introduces these metaphors unobtrusively. (pp. 186-87)

There is, in addition, a considerable graveyard imagery. Demby attends the funerals of the Pope and of close friends and relatives, and observes on television the stiff, unreal ceremonies following the death of the American President. Rome and Greece, the foundation stones of Western civilization, are now viewed as cemeteries. (p. 187)

But if the West is a graveyard, there remains the expectation of rebirth. Although death images predominate, there are hints of resurrection. A new Pope is elected and makes a pilgrimage to Palestine, the birthplace of Christ. There is even some hope that the Count's flight to the East may rehabilitate him. Demby himself, secure now in his faith, in the sanctity of all existence, decides to fly back to the United States on Easter Monday. (pp. 187-88)

But for all his fond hopes, Demby is aware that the life-and-death struggle will persist, and that troubled days lie ahead. His is an almost Manichaean vision of being and nonbeing locked in timeless combat, and the shifting fortunes of the combatants fluctuate like the ebb and flow of the tides. Within this eternal pattern, it is the business of men to assert their life forces so that the battle may not be lost. And it is especially in America that the battle has been very nearly lost. He tells Doris about an earlier visit to America, where the raw hatreds and underground tremors of social and racial violence portended for him the conquest of Death.

Yet Demby in the novel returns to America a fulfilled man. In part, of course, his deeply religious outlook has discovered for him the role he plays in the cosmos. But in part too, by means of his Christianity, he has recovered his identity as a black man. For Doris has provided him with the example of Christian martyrdom. And it is Africa, lush, green, and fertile, that gives him the sense of Christian life. As the nun, the Count's sister, has put it, here lies the source and redemption of the human race. In contrast, Europe, white, cold, and sterile, has all but exhausted its spirit. (pp. 188-89)

Demby's resolution is a very private one, as any spiritual conversion must be. Yet there is something beyond the privacy of his vision that makes this book so striking. Demby is one of those rare Negro Americans, immersed in the culture of the West, who has discovered himself at home in a civilization that has deeply wounded him. His acceptance of the West has not negated his Negro identity but has enhanced it. (p. 189)

Edward Margolies, "The Expatriate as Novelist: William Demby," in his Native Sons: A Critical Study of Twentieth-Century Negro American Authors, *J. B. Lippincott Company*, 1968, pp. 173-89.

Robert Bone (essay date 1969)

[Bone is an American authority on African-American literature. He has said of himself: "A white man and critic of black literature, I try to demonstrate by the quality of my work that scholarship is not the same thing as identity." He is the author of The Negro Novel in America *(1958) and* Down Home: A History of Afro-American Short Fiction from Its Beginnings to the End of the Harlem Renaissance *(1975). In the following excerpt, he reviews* The Catacombs, *praising it as an "ambitious book, whose themes are drawn from every sphere of contemporary culture."]*

> The day is not far distant when humanity will realize that biologically it is faced with a choice between suicide and adoration.

—Teilhard de Chardin

The writer who succeeds, against all odds, in expanding contemporary consciousness must be prepared for baffled readers and irascible reviewers. The unprecedented stratagems that are required create their own resistance, and the writer's audience grows restive, out of a natural desire to organize experience along familiar lines. It is precisely this familiar order that is challenged by the serious writer, and often enough the price that he must pay for innovation is indifference and neglect.

Such has been the fate of a recent novel by William Demby. Launched by Pantheon in the spring of 1965, **The Catacombs** orbited briefly, encountered a thin cultural atmosphere, and parachuted soundlessly into a deserted sea. What is now required is a search and recovery operation. For Demby's novel, which is entirely a product of the Space Age, has probed to the outer limits of contemporary consciousness. What follows is an effort to substantiate this claim. (p. 127)

[Demby's first book, **Beetlecreek**], is a young man's novel: rebellious, but thoroughly controlled in execution. The point of view is existentialist, the tone expatriate. The style, thick with images of revulsion and disgust, reveals a man in desperate retreat from the smug parochialism of mid-century America. But if **Beetlecreek** is Demby's myth of disaffiliation, **The Catacombs** is his myth of reconciliation and return.

Demby's growth, between his first and second novels, was nourished by a wide variety of intellectual and literary interests. First and foremost was his participation in the great flowering of contemporary Italian cinema. To be on the scene when Fellini and Antonioni broke through the limits of postwar neo-realism was to witness the creation of a new esthetic, hostile to naturalism and mythic in intent. The aim of these directors was to reaffirm the primacy of the imagina-

tion; their method, to require an act of collaboration from the cinematic audience. Demby's recent novel makes a comparable demand.

In his early years abroad, while still searching for his own metier, Demby studied art history at the University of Rome. He remains an ardent viewer, a collector, and a connoisseur. His interest in Italian painting and statuary, both classical and contemporary, is everywhere apparent in **The Catacombs.** (p. 128)

Given Demby's background in literature and painting, and his work in a medium where the two arts intersect, it was natural that he develop a concern with communications theory. The pioneering media studies of Marshall McLuhan appeared during the years of composition of **The Catacombs,** and there is ample evidence to show that Demby was familiar, with McLuhan's work.

To these concerns must be added an intelligent layman's interest in contemporary science. Demby is curious about the recent developments in physics and mathematics which have altered our notions of causation and hence our theories of time. . . . Time is not linear in Demby's fiction. He is fascinated by the space between the frames of a motion picture. In **The Catacombs,** he slips into that space and explores its formal possibilities.

Demby's philosophic speculations were given a direction and a form by his discovery of the writings of Pierre Teilhard de Chardin. Father Teilhard's Catholic evolutionism supplied him with a cosmic perspective from which to view the biological dilemma and the cultural crisis of contemporary man. Many puzzling passages and mystifying symbols in **The Catacombs** will be plain enough if placed in the context of Teilhard's thought. The cone, the spiral, and the Omega Point, for example, may be found on the famous medallion designed by Teilhard to illustrate his concept of convergence ("Everything that rises must converge").

One preliminary task remains: to place Demby in his literary tradition. It is not so much American as cosmopolitan and European. Above all it is modernist: *nonrepresentational* is the metaphor that comes to mind. Like the postimpressionists, Demby forgoes a surface realism, in order to create a more compelling reality. He is the direct descendant of that pioneering generation whom we associate with the origins of modern art. His esthetic is derived from the cubist painters and their literary allies.

The American writer whom Demby most resembles is Gertrude Stein. Consider the affinities: like Demby, Stein was a highly Europeanized expatriate . . . . Both writers are inclined toward radical experimentation with the novel as a form. Both abandon the conventional plot-line based on linear time and replace it with a matrix of mosaic, essentially timeless, which Stein has called "the continuous present."

Finally, in the context of literary influence, mention must be made of the works of Isak Dinesen. Demby was introduced to *Seven Gothic Tales* and *Out of Africa* by his wife, who made an Italian translation of the latter volume. He was plainly captivated, for both books have left their mark on **The Catacombs.** Between the Danish baroness, who spent some eighteen years in Kenya, and the American Negro, living abroad in Rome, the immediate affinities are obvious enough. They have to do with the poignancy of exile, a cosmopolitan world-view, and a fascination with things African. They extend, however, to include such literary matters as a penchant for pastiche and an antipathy to naturalism.

On more than one occasion, Demby describes the present epoch as a Gothic age, requiring commensurate devices to render it in fiction. *Seven Gothic Tales,* with its absurd and fantastic elements, must have struck him as a valid image of the times. From the African memoir, by way of contrast, comes the inspiration for his central situation. That fusion of primitive and aristocratic virtues which is the theme of *Out of Africa* is a principal concern in Demby's novel. It is dramatized through the love affair of an American Negro dancing girl and an Italian count. But let us turn at this point to the surface texture of the novel. (pp. 129-30)

The setting of **The Catacombs** is modern Rome. The title recalls us at once to the epoch of early Christianity and the decline of Roman power. Demby thus establishes a parallel perspective, and invites us to consider the fate of modern Europe in the light of ancient Rome. Hunted, persecuted, driven underground, the early Christians retreated to subterranean chambers where they continued to celebrate the Eucharist and the Agape. In what quarter shall we seek their counterpart: a saving remnant holding forth the promise of redemption to the modern world?

Rome, moreover, is a symbol of imperial power, of the white man's historic depredations into Africa.... In Demby's novel, contemporary Rome becomes a stage on which a great historico-religious drama sweeps to its final act. For as Africa awakens from twenty centuries of stony sleep, a crisis of staggering proportions is thrust upon the Western world.

Rome, above all, is the Holy City of Western Christendom. Insofar as Europe responds to the challenge of a resurgent Africa, that response will be manifest in the religious councils of the Roman church. Demby is therefore fascinated by what might be called the symbolic gestures of Vatican II. (p. 131)

The action of the novel takes place over a period of two years, from March 1962 to March 1964. Action must be redefined, however, to accommodate Demby's theory of cubistic time. Just as in a Picasso the artist may present us with a head simultaneously drawn in profile and three-quarter view, so Demby strives for simultaneity in the design of his novel. Along with the traditional narrative dimension he attempts to convey, through a stream-of-consciousness technique, the writer's state of mind during the period of composition, including his awareness of historical events.

The novel moves forward simultaneously through three planes of reality. Headlines, news items, and miscellaneous excerpts from a dozen newspapers provide the texture of contemporary history. Musings, free associations, and entries from a kind of spiritual diary supply the subjective dimension. Embedded in this matrix is the fractured story line which alone must satisfy our cravings for a plot. The historical and biographical materials are never merely background, but are held in metaphorical relation to the fictive episodes. The result is a series of illuminating insights, a brilliant crystallization of contemporary consciousness.

The biographical material is paradoxically an expression of the author's antinaturalism. It is precisely to demonstrate that art is *not* a slice of life that Demby introduces this material. Directly observed events from his own life are reported almost casually, only to be processed into art before our very eyes. The process is the important thing, as the writer selects and arranges from the welter of experience those elements that will enhance his theme. What it amounts to is an upgrading of the imagination. "True" facts and "fictional" facts are given equal status, out of deference to the creative act.

These are the strategies of Pirandello, adapted to the novel form. Their success depends upon a special brand of whimsy. One has to see the playfulness, for example, in Demby's approach to the technical problem of characterization. In the opening scene, a writer named William Demby is waiting in his studio for Doris, an attractive dancing girl who is to be the heroine of his new novel. It is some pages before we discover that Doris is an *invented* character, and still longer before we realize that the putative William Demby, who is after all a character in Demby's novel, is invented in precisely the same way.

The object of this playfulness is to tease the reader into an examination of his own metaphysical assumptions. When the putative William Demby invites his "fictional" mistress to have dinner with his "real" wife, the effect is to dissolve our conventional notions of reality. If the familiar categories of the actual and the imaginary are systematically destroyed, then a proposition will emerge about the nature of human existence:

> I am beginning to have the strangest feeling that we are all nothing more than shadows, spirits, breathed into life and manipulated by Pirandello's fertile mind.

The fertility of the imagination is precisely Demby's subject; throughout **The Catacombs** it is set off against contrasting images of sterility and barrenness. Man is the inventor of his own reality: that is the sum and substance of Demby's fictional technique. (pp. 131-33)

[**The Catacombs** begins in Rome] in the spring of 1962. The Algerian War is mounting to a climax, and the newspapers are filled with the terrorist activities of the European Secret Army. Against this backdrop of life-denying violence, the love affair of Doris and the Count begins.... [By August, 1962, the] world is moving toward the Cuban missile crisis, with human life itself perhaps at stake. On an isolated beach in Tuscany, Doris and Bill Demby are making love. (p. 133)

[The novel then shifts to] the month of the twin-faced Janus, 1963. Doris finds herself with "the dilemma of the century to solve."...[She] is pregnant, but cannot say whether the white man or the Negro is the father of her child. Her personal crisis is the crisis of the epoch. Just as she must choose between abortion and illegitimacy, so contemporary man must face nuclear suicide, or transcend his present moral categories. Demby sees this choice in the evolutionary perspective of Teilhard de Chardin. If we choose unwisely, all of human history may become a vast abortion.

From this point forward, the novel is concerned with birth: a birth that doesn't happen and a birth that does. The period of Doris' pregnancy is one of stasis, in world affairs, in Demby's personal life, and in the progress of his novel. The mood is one of lassitude, as we await the birth of what is ever more explicitly a symbolic child. Doris, we are told, is expecting her child in August.... [But] Doris does not give birth, at least to a literal child.

Toward the end of the novel, Doris confides to Demby:

> I wanted to name the baby John, you know, because of Pope John, and John Kennedy, for what they both did. Giving birth to whatever it was you mean by the "third thing," using the manly weapon of dialogue instead of the old womanly weapon of poison and the bargain basement gun.

The child that refuses to be born, in short, is a symbol of sanity, reason, *dialogue:* the triumph of the life force. This force was embodied in world politics by the old Pope and the young President.

In the final episode, a symbolic birth occurs. It is the Easter season, 1964.... The Count will soon abandon [Don's], having been transferred to Hong Kong on company business. Doris pleads to be taken with him, but is denied. They pay a final visit to the catacombs, and as a young priest describes the sepulture of those who have "died in the Lord," Doris vanishes from sight. It is the Count's turn now to suffer, but through the loss of Doris he is born again.... (pp. 134-35)

The Catacombs is an ambitious book, whose themes are drawn from every sphere of contemporary culture. Science and technology, art and literature, sex and race, politics, morality, religion: all are woven into Demby's tapestry. The danger posed by this diversity of theme is a lack of focus, but Demby has surmounted it. Crucial to his unifying vision is the evolutionary creed of Teilhard de Chardin. The ligature which binds together these discrete levels of experience is Teilhard's philosophy of change.

Here is Demby's poetic statement of the matter:

> Doris too must conform, must submit, to that most sacred of universal laws, that first and only law which forever has taught, shall in all eternity teach, that life is existence and existence is sacred,... the embarrassing, the terrifying, the unembalmable law of changeless change.

What Doris must submit to is the law of evolution. That law, which is grounded in a paradox, perpetuates the life force by altering its forms. Essences persist, even as forms are modified: that is Demby's fundamental insight. When lower forms give way to higher, we describe the process as evolution. To evolve is to transcend, to outgrow the old forms which once possessed survival value but now are rendered obsolete. Man's highest wisdom is the willing acceptance of evolutionary change. (p. 135)

Conversely, to refuse the evolutionary challenge is to deny the will of God. This is the embalming heresy: the attempt to preserve dead forms. All that is conservative in the social organism, all that resists change and innovation, balks at the new imperative. Forms are mistaken for essences, and the loss of cherished forms is viewed as a catastrophe. Emotional attachments to the past cannot be transcended and the organism, perversely enamored of its own dead forms, perishes. This is the crux of Demby's novel. Modern man, as a result of his atomic technology, faces an evolutionary imperative. He must grow or die. The necessity of our epoch is to dare everything, to accept whatever risk may be entailed in the next stage of human evolution.

If there is a technological threat, there is also a technological transcendence. Modern man is living through a period of transition from the age of the machine to that of cybernetics.... Through the improvement of human communications systems, the global unification of human consciousness will be accomplished. A universal language will evolve, based on the stop and go pulsations of the binary computer. (pp. 135-36)

All forms, including linguistic forms, which derive from the machine are doomed. That is the burden of an elaborate image pattern which persists throughout the novel. Machine production and the spiritual values of rationality and efficiency which it promotes are associated in Demby's prose with squares and rectangles. (p. 136)

The electronics revolution, however, which is based on circuitry and the principle of feed-back, will supplant the square with the circle. The latter form is associated in *The Catacombs* with love, art, and religion. This image-pattern, taken as a whole, amounts to an assault on Western rationalism. The square and rectangle represent the subordination of man to machinery; the circle embodies Demby's hopes for a more human world.

Nowhere in contemporary culture is the transcendence of dead forms more apparent than in the plastic arts. A tradition of five centuries, stemming from the Renaissance, is being overthrown, as representational art is superseded by non-objective forms....

Demby dramatizes this cultural revolution by juxtaposing two art objects. The first is a statue by Michelangelo; the second, a contemporary painting by Losavio.... (p. 137)

In the case of the Michelangelo, the meaning of the statue depends upon its *placing*. If we alter the spatial relations of the object to its surroundings, we alter the meaning, however imperceptibly. The object exists, in short, in a state of *contingency*. This is the result of certain preconceptions concerning space, and the conceptual model, wherein all parts of a spatial field are related to each other, is the machine.

In the case of the Losavio, however, the state of contingency is explicitly repudiated, and space is organized in a radically different way. Instead of contingency, we have ambiguity; instead of mechanical determinism, uncertainty, probability, indeterminacy.... (pp. 137-38)

The idea of indeterminacy is particularly crucial to Demby's theory of the novel. In naturalistic fiction, the hero's actions are determined by environment and circumstance. Action in the present is contingent on the past, and the role of choice in human destiny is minimized. In Demby's work, however, the element of choice is central. Neither the outbreak of atomic war nor the outcome of a novel is a foregone conclusion. The freedom of a novelist to shape his denouement is emblematic of mankind's freedom to affect the future. Man is the first organism capable of intervening by conscious choice in the evolutionary process.

What are the implications of indeterminacy for the novel as a form? They will become manifest, above all, in the novelist's treatment of time. The naturalistic novel has attempted to imitate or reproduce or represent *natural* time. Demby's "non-representational" fiction, by way of contrast, attempts to free human action from the tyranny of time. It breaks with natural time, much as the cubist painters broke with natural shapes and natural colors. It replaces natural with fictive time—that is, with time relationships entirely of the artist's fabrication.

A fiction that stresses choice and indeterminacy can exert a liberating influence upon the human psyche.... [The] function of the artist is to liberate the imprisoned memory of the race, to free man from the dead forms of the past. By his constant invention of new forms, the artist serves as an instrument of sacred evolution.

The preservation of old forms, and more precisely the forms of power, is the unifying theme in Demby's treatment of sex, race, and politics. Male supremacy, white supremacy, and the political rule of the capitalist class have everywhere been challenged in the modern world. On the sexual plane, the challenge to male power from the emancipated woman has produced a severe disorder:

The crisis of the bourgeois male of this century is a crisis of the absolute power of the man in the family. The bourgeois male, no longer "King," suffers from so-called complexes and neuroses: ... it is then that the famous crisis of the male whose crown has been taken away occurs.

Demby goes on to discuss "the vendetta of the dethroned King." The male's quest for revenge takes the form of sadism.... Having established the psychological principle, Demby proceeds to apply it to other crises of absolute power. He compares the position of the *independent woman* to that of the *independence movement* in Algeria, and discerns in the terrorism of the European Secret Army, a parallel to the vendetta of the dethroned male. By metaphorical extension, he moves from the violence and sadism of the French "colons" to that of Mississippi racists and Northern mobs participating in the white backlash.

Demby wants to isolate for our consideration a certain type of violence, grounded in hostility to change. Adherence to the old forms no matter what, a blind commitment to the past, a determination to destroy rather than accommodate have produced a mood of hysteria and a rising tempo of violence in the modern world. The name of this violence, projected on the political plane, is fascism. From his vantage point in Rome, Demby reminds us of that earlier convulsion when the European middle classes, frightened by the specter of a rising proletariat, turned to fascism as a bulwark of the capitalist order. He characterizes this act of self-betrayal as a dinosaur response—a suicidal effort to resist change even at the price of extinction.

When Demby returns to America for a few months in 1963, he is appalled by the high pitch of violence and hatred. (pp. 138-40)

[From] images of violence and criminality, the novel moves toward a definition of evil and, by implication, of God. Demby's concrete representation of the demonic principle is a total eclipse of the sun.... (p. 140)

If the Devil exists, then God exists: such are the terms of Demby's spiritual dialectic. If eclipse, or non-being, is synonymous with evil, then "life is existence and existence is sacred." Reverence for life is thus the cornerstone of Demby's values. In the eternal contest between birth and death, growth and decay, he turns in a mood of adoration to all that is life-enhancing. God becomes a kind of choreographer, inviting man to join the dance of the universe.... In responding to this invitation, Demby overcomes the skepticism which is the birthright of the modern intellectual. With religious art forms as his intermediaries, he moves toward reconciliation with the Christian faith.

The Catacombs is finally a drama of reconciliation. Neither facile nor sentimental, however, the reconciliation that Demby has in mind takes full account of man's capacity for evil. The modern world is haunted by a death-wish, a morbid fascination with non-being. Men have everywhere succumbed to the spirit of vendetta, or entrapment in the hatreds of the past. (pp. 140-41)

To break the chain of evil, to rise above his ancient animosities, and to defeat the cult of death, it is imperative that modern man assent to change..... It is on this note that Demby's novel ends. We return in the last scene to the catacombs, that dark underworld which was at once the burial vault and the womb of historic Christianity. There, in the person of the Count, the soul of Western man is reborn. The redemptive agent is a dark Madonna, in whose veins the blood of Africa still flows. (p. 141)

> Robert Bone, "William Demby's Dance of Life," in TriQuarterly, No. 15, Spring, 1969, pp. 127-41.

William Demby with John O'Brien (interview date 1971)

[*In the following 1971 interview, O'Brien and Demby discuss the structure and style of* The Catacombs *and* Beetlecreek.]

[O'Brien]: *Are there any authors who have affected your writing?*

[Demby]: Well, I think that Virginia Woolf did, for some reason.

Perhaps because of her use and treatment of time?

Yes, time. Certainly it came out in **The Catacombs,** the way she was able to slow down time, or stretch it, or treat time as though it were something that one touched, and could mold....

What about non-literary influences?

Music. (These are comparatively recent influences. I was writing my first novel over twenty years ago.) But in music, Schoenberg and Berg, everybody who was fooling around with ideas of time. I think that that was one influence that really, really profoundly influenced me in ways that I still am not sure of but which certainly influenced the whole structure of **The Catacombs.** (p. 1)

The achievement of **The Catacombs** *is that you are able to incorporate things that are happening in the outside world and mold them into some artistic framework and give them some meaning...*

That was a deliberate effort on my part, I was speaking at Rochester a couple of weeks ago, and all this came up. We were discussing all these problems of being bombarded by all these events which come into our consciousness electronically or otherwise, at a fantastic speed, almost the speed of light. How can the novelist give this somehow to,... how can he recreate this feeling? I was with some Russian writers—I belong to the European Community of Writers—this was in Florence, Italy. We were having an international meeting.... And there was a big tapestry on the wall, and a

friend of mine from Iceland and some other people were watching this and saying, "that's the way a novel should be." Not linear, not in a kind of horizontal sequence of events, but as one perceives reality looking at that enormous tapestry upon which any number of things were happening.... So that is what I tried to do. First I thought, why not try to start a novel at a certain point and, instead of going forward in time, go backwards? Why was it not possible? I never really found out. It was from that idea, that liberating idea, that I conceived of writing a novel, but without any of the controls that a novel usually would have. That is, that I would begin on a certain day and continuously go forward. Every page or every day's work would reflect what has happened to me in my personal life and the lives of the fictional characters who moved around at the same time as the so-called real characters, the people in real life. So each day should reflect all of these things: what I perceived from the newspapers that I was reading, or the things that were happening in other countries, or in the southern part of Italy. Anything. My wife's family. Anything that was going on. All of this was reflected. What astonished me that there was a real pattern that you perceived. What created this pattern, I don't know. Was it in the consciousness of the author, or was it that any event that you would see happening anywhere, were you to turn your consciousness on it, it would fall into some kind of order? I'm not sure yet how it works but I knew that it worked in **The Catacombs.** And in that novel there was never any turning back, nothing was ever rewritten. It just went forward from day to day until some instinct would tell me that that would be the end of it. That went on for two years.

This may raise the question of whether the artist imposes order or whether he reflects it. Is it resolved in **The Catacombs** *whether the order is created by you or whether it exists and you are finding it?*

I think that it gets to the deeper truth that there is no such thing as chaos perhaps. There may not be....

You try to make connections out of everything in **The Catacombs.** *You don't just try to create an individual, private order.*

I agree with that. I totally agree with that. I mean that that obviously is the function of the novelist. The novelist must have this function of seeing connections. He also has the responsibility (and this may be true for all artists,) to make some connection with the past. (p. 2)

Would **The Catacombs** *have been written had you stayed in this country?*

No. I don't think so. I was lucky to be in Europe at that time. In Rome you were always at a kind of center for ideas. I might have fallen into the naturalistic novel had I remained in this country. I might have.

Do you think of **Beetlecreek** *as being a kind of naturalistic novel?*

No. I don't think so. Not **Beetlecreek.**

I think Herbert Hill made the point that the novel tended towards naturalism.

Well, the truth is those scenes were written in Salzburg, in Austria. And what had happened was that I had fallen in love with a woman . . . . And one night she went out with somebody else and I was pissed-off. That's when I wrote that pathetic closing scene in **Beetlecreek.** So, how do we know where these inspirations come from? I know that it is not a naturalistic novel. I wouldn't call it that at all. The reality of the novel is not naturalistic. The movement that each of the characters has is much more secret than any cause and effect relationship. Johnny certainly wasn't reacting to any . . . it wasn't that he wanted to be in a boy's gang or anything like that. I think that it was the imperative to act, to do anything. I think that all the characters came into something like that. Everyone did something and we say how these doings had a pattern and I suppose you can do that with any group of people. But it is only when they do something, when they move, and the movement is on the level that is perceivable, then I guess at that moment it is worthwhile to write about it. What happened in the novel? Not very much.

Would you accept a term like "existential" to describe the novel?

I always was a little wary of that until two weeks ago. I was up in Rochester reading and talking. A young lady who had been my classmate at Fisk University and worked on the literary magazine I edited, showed me a number in which I had written a review of Camus' *The Stranger,* in which I was also discussing existentialism. Now I had thought that I had been interested in existentialism in Europe when it was fashionable at the time. I know now that I had been interested in it in college, though I had forgotten about that. It appealed to me very much, though I was not quite sure what existentialism means, and I am not sure I am now. (p. 3)

What form of existentialism affected you do you think?

What has always astonished me was how little minor movements on that great tapestry or landscape there, how minor things are interconnected. So that, if you are doing something . . . and this is how the characters in **Beetlecreek** were moving existentially. That is, the things they did seemed in themselves of no importance and yet they moved or touched other lives . . . .

*Is there any hope at the end of **Beetlecreek?***

Well, . . . hope. I think the only movement in my novels (and the novels I will be working on) will be more and more a trying to understand the relationships between small movements. That is, people think they move in a meaningful way, that they have come to a decision: they get on a bus. That is only movement without any real . . . I don't know why people expected that in the novel there should be something resolved . . . . [Hope]

means that you still have options or movement. I suppose that that is the only thing hope can be. You cannot conceive of yourself changing, because you cannot change. Not only will that character who went North on the bus . . . bring with him the experiences in Beetlecreek, but all his life he'll carry that bag around with him . . . . . Hope? I don't know. Is it desirable for the characters to change? I don't know. (p. 4)

Who does the determining, either in life or literature, as to what is to be designated as evil?

Oh, I believe in a moral universe. That is, a universe in which there is movement, where people are born and they die. These are basic things. The world we must live in has a kind of intrinsic order to it. And occasionally there will be gestures which are presumptuous in that they pretend to make things happen when the truth probably is that they are only acting in accordance with something over which they have no control . . . . If this is true, then it means that a lot of the movements, the revolutionary movements, are just expended energy. They are not leading to anything that will be a change. In one period, at least the period I try to demonstrate in **The Catacombs,** there is no change. There is only the illusion of change. It's an idea I will have to think about in the future. (pp. 4-5)

*[In regards to the structure of **The Catacombs:** had other actual] events taken place, would they have worked themselves into the novel and have influenced the outcome?*

I think so. It's a weird experience. But, yes, all these things were included in. And it seemed to me that sometimes I would be sitting down and it seemed to me that events (and this is real paranoia) were being dictated to fit in with the novel, when of course, it is the other way around. But, using this technique creates paranoia. You begin giving attention to things which didn't merit all that attention. But it occurred to me that any time that anyone gives attention to certain things . . . you get unbalanced by placing too much . . . you know, you really could.

I guess now there is a possibility that you could write a novel about how that novel was written.

In writing it, I think I said this at one point or another in the novel, I felt as though I were boxed inside the novel and would never get out. And I remember, I think there is a Zen story of a painter who painted a picture and couldn't get out of the painting. I really felt boxed in.

Is that why the real life characters worked themselves into the novel and why your fictional characters would come out of the novel and become real?

There's a lot of that. Sometimes some people who knew . . . some nutty girls who knew how I was working on this novel would try to invent things so that they would get into the novel. But, of course, I would put them in or not put them in. One of these girls committed suicide, so she was in the novel . . . .

I think that it was Joyce who had a great fear of the written word, that once it was said it would occur in life . . .

Yes. And I was sensing that too. On the other hand, if you are going to assume that type of magic, you could go to the other extreme and say that just by writing it down, it will not happen. But . . . there's ideas of magic there. (p. 5)

John O'Brien, "Interview with William Demby," in Studies in Black Literature, *Vol. 3, No. 3, Autumn, 1972, pp. 1-6.*

Jay R. Berry (essay date 1983)

[*In the following review essay, Berry explores Demby's development as a writer, focusing on* Beetlecreek, The Catacombs, *and* Love Story Black.]

Afro-American novelist William Demby has been ignored for too long by literary critics. Although he has managed to publish only three novels (**Beetlecreek**, 1950; **The Catacombs**, 1965; and **Love Story Black**, 1978), each one contains interesting and effective stylistic and structural devices that serve to focus the theme(s) he is expressing. Demby is primarily a stylist, one who is extremely self-conscious in his choice of personae and narrative points of view, and in his use of time, imagery, and language. One cannot successfully discuss Demby's work without analyzing the stylistic intricacies of his novels. His work illustrates a growth of artistic consciousness and a maturation of technical skill, and I will focus upon the development of stylistic technique in his novels.

Beetlecreek

William Demby grew up in Clarksburg, West Virginia, "in the heart of the mining region which provides the setting for [**Beetlecreek**]." He was educated at West Virginia State College for Negroes and at Fisk University, where he was graduated in 1947. Demby edited the *Fisk Herald* and wrote stories in addition to attending classes at Fisk. One of the stories, entitled **"Saint Joey,"** concerns vigilante action by a gang of white teenagers against an old recluse who betrayed the unwritten social and racial mores of the community. The characters and the actions of this story were later modified to form one of the basic plot lines of **Beetlecreek.** Following his graduation from Fisk, Demby chose to pursue his interests in art history and literature in Italy, at the University of Rome. It was during his first two years in Rome that **Beetlecreek** was written.

Beetlecreek is essentially a novel about four characters whose lives and frustrations are inextricably linked. The novel opens with Bill Trapp, an old white recluse, chasing a group of apple thieves off his farm. However, he manages to catch one of them, a boy named Johnny

Johnson. As they share cider and talk, Trapp learns that Johnny is living in Beetlecreek with his aunt and uncle, Mary and David Diggs, while his mother recovers from a protracted illness at home in Pennsylvania. For the first time in fifteen years Bill Trapp has interacted with someone on a personal level, and he begins to feel the need of becoming a social creature once again. [According to Edward Margolies in *Native Sons: A Critical Study of Twentieth-Century Negro American Authors*], "In the beginning he enjoys some success (e.g., picking pumpkins for the church festival), but he is finally met with suspicion and fear and he retreats once more to his solitude."

The frustrations of young Johnny are also played out in the novel. He is very lonely, being in a strange town without his mother or friends. His loneliness compels him to search for acceptance among his peers in Beetlecreek, a group of local toughs nicknamed the Nightriders. Johnny recognizes their behavior as reprehensible, but decides that their friendship is more important to him than opposing their immoral behavior. Ultimately, his desire for acceptance causes him to betray his friend Bill Trapp (at the behest of the Nightriders), "whom the townfolk unjustly have come to denounce as a pervert," by attempting to burn down his house.

David Diggs is merely an older version of his nephew. He is college-educated and a talented artist. He is trapped, however, in a lethargic town with a boring job and a wife who is not very important to him. He had come to accept his dreary life until he found a kindred soul in Bill Trapp and began to yearn for a fuller life. This yearning is heightened when Edith Johnson, a lover from his college days, arrives in town. He sees her as the means to his spiritual salvation, the key to a new way of life in a different town. She is a dubious savior at best. She and David have moved far apart since college, he to Beetlecreek, she to an urban ghetto where her outlook on life became hardened and cynical. By pursuing Edith, David pursues an illusion, an empty ideal that will never be fulfilled.

Mary, David's wife, is the least defined of Demby's main characters. Nevertheless, the reader knows that a loveless marriage and the stifling environment of Beetlecreek have transformed her into a nearly lifeless figure. Her tenuous hold on life seems to hinge on her advancement in the Women's Missionary Guild within her church, and on picking up and passing on gossip about local white and black families.

Thus, as Edward Margolies points out in *Native Sons* [see excerpted dated 1968], **"Beetlecreek** is a novel of defeat and death. Beetlecreek is itself a metaphor of death, a dreary and sluggish town whose inhabitants have lost all desire for change or hope for improved circumstances." Robert Bone and Edward Margolies, among others, have argued that **Beetlecreek** is an existentialist novel that treats its characters as isolated and alienated individuals living in a seemingly purposeless

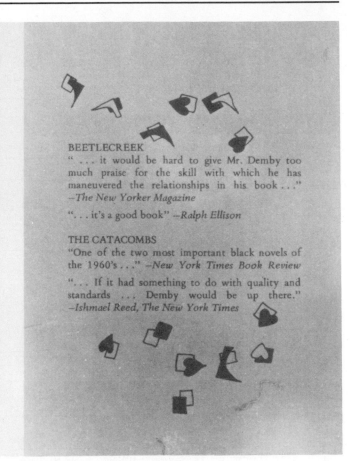

Front and back covers of Demby's third novel.

world. The characters attempt to assert themselves in a positive manner, but will resort to destruction and violence if this is not possible.

More intriguing than the theme of existentialism are the narrative and stylistic devices Demby uses to focus and dramatize the story. The novel follows a linear progression and is related in the third person, from the points of view of the four main characters. In general, each chapter is related from the perspective of a particular character. The action described is perceived and given shape by that character. Thus Bill Trapp is concerned about becoming more sociable, Johnny is tired of being lonely and yearns for peer acceptance, David plots his escape from Beetlecreek, and Mary accepts her dull life, concerned only with passing on gossip and baking the best gingerbread for the Women's Missionary Guild festival.

When the chapters are juxtaposed against one another, the shifts in perspective make the actions of the characters more forceful and dramatic than a more conventional narrative perspective would have accomplished. The juxtapositions also serve to illustrate both the alienation of the various characters and the interconnectedness of their actions, often presented ironically. The last three chapters of the book, for example,

occur roughly at the same time. The first concludes with Johnny violently expressing his profound sense of alienation by setting fire to Bill Trapp's farm. Demby then cuts to the church festival and Mary Digg's successful gingerbread booth. For the first time in the novel she is very happy and has an optimistic air about her. Finally, Demby shifts to David's and Edith's departure from Beetlecreek. They are on a bus bound for somewhere in the North. As the bus is leaving town, it is passed by a company of fire trucks heading toward Bill Trapp's farm.

Mary's momentary jubilance is ironically contrasted with John's destructiveness and David's naively idealistic attempt to escape from the town and his own sense of alienation. The novel has been building steadily toward this conclusion, and Demby's decision to juxtapose these three points of view gives the ending of **Beetlecreek** a sense of dramatic power and irony. The concluding chapters also illustrate the interconnectedness of the lives of Bill Trapp, Johnny Johnson, and David and Mary Diggs. In an interview with John O'Brien [see excerpt dated 1971], William Demby asserted:

> What has always astonished me was how little minor movements [and] minor things are interconnected... That is, the things [the characters in **Beetlecreek**] did seemed in themselves of no importance

553

and yet they moved or touched their lives. And I suppose we look at reality like that, and the relationships. We don't always see the small movements of people.

Demby is particularly effective in describing the "small movements" of his characters that lead up to the novel's climax. He achieves this less through dialogue, which is flat, tired, and dull like the lives of his characters, than through the manipulation of visual imagery that focuses on minute detail. Demby's skillful handling of visual imagery evokes moods and atmospheres, and also establishes various characters' states of mind.

Ultimately, what the reader remembers are the stark images presented in the novel. Johnny's loneliness and restlessness are reflected in images of swooping birds:

> Now there was the slanted light of sunset that made the street brilliant copper, and swarms of birds swooped screeching on every perch, restless, unsatisfied, tearing apart the space between roof and sky. It was a melancholy, fall sight and it made Johnny very sad. [The Baily Brothers' hearse] that he had seen represented everything of Beetlecreek and was like the restlessness and dissatisfaction of the birds only inside him, swarming and swooping inside him, filling him with vague fear and shame, preparing him for something . . . separating him from things that were happening around him, apart from him, pulling him along toward things he could not see or know.

Later in the novel, Johnny waits for the Nightriders to join him on the bridge. The visual image of the rhythm of the bridge moving in the wind reflects his nervousness and apprehension:

> Johnny sat on the railing of the swinging bridge looking down toward the creek. . . . The cold wind pushed the bridge back and forth, back and forth very gently and the greased cables strained against the big holes in the planks.

David Diggs's mental state is likewise presented in visual terms, compared to the current of the creek:

> Often he would sit on the railing of the swinging bridge, looking down at the creek, watching the current. He would watch floating things—boxes, tin cans, bottles. He would watch how some of these things became trapped in the reeds alongside the shore. First there was a whirlpool to entice the floating object, then a slow-flowing pool, and finally, the deadly mud backwater in the reeds . . . . This was Beetlecreek, he thought. And he knew that, like the rusty cans, he was trapped, caught, unable to move again.

In David's life, the enticing whirlpool represents his life with Mary before their marriage; the "slow-flowing pool" represents David's and Mary's early married life in Beetlecreek before frustration and boredom set in; and the "deadly mud backwater" describes his present situation. By focusing on a series of images Demby has given the reader a capsulized summary of David's life in Beetlecreek.

Demby also uses imagery to evoke mood and atmosphere. The title of the book, for example, is a powerful image of stultification, and the creek and town bear out the implications of the image. Moreover, the aura of irresponsibility that surrounds the Nightriders group is most effectively illustrated visually, as when the leader snatches a pigeon that had been trapped in the clubhouse and "took the bleating bird by the neck and began to swing it over his head in an ever increasing arc. Johnny watched horrified as drops of blood sprinkled the floor. Suddenly the body was torn from the head and smashed against the wall with a loud thud."

Eerie settings are used as a backdrop for some of the most important scenes in the book. The "romantic" scenes between David and Edith occur in the junk yard, a place of death and decay that comments ironically on their actions:

> They walked alongside the creek, past the swinging bridge until the road narrowed into a kind of path ending in the village dump. The tottering derrick of an abandoned oil well dominated the field. They sat on one of the tar-soaked timbers that formed the base of the structure . . . . Now he saw her as the girl of the college days. There, in the night of the junk yard, closed off from the Beetlecreek world, she had come back, and he recognized her and desired her.

Some of the recurring images assume symbolic proportion, and they are deftly handled by Demby, as Robert Bone correctly observes [in his *The Negro Novel in America* (1958)]:

> The frantic swooping birds provide an objective correlative to David's and Johnny's feelings of restlessness and dissatisfaction. The mirrors (each of the characters studies himself in a mirror) underscore the problem of identity, while the swinging bridge suggests the social separation becolored and white in Beetlecreek.

In the final analysis the strength of *Beetlecreek* lies in its narrative structure and in its visual style. Both enhance the theme of existentialism that dominates the novel. The problem in *Beetlecreek,* fairly minor ones to be sure, stem from the weak characterization of Mary and Edith and from a slightly shallow story line. Had the action of the novel been expanded slightly, it would have been a stronger work. *The Catacombs,* Demby's second novel, is more ambitious than *Beetlecreek* in both scope and technique, because it probes the limits of, and attempts to expand, the contemporary consciousness.

The Catacombs

Demby's artistic growth between his first and second novels was fostered by a number of intellectual interests he developed while living in Italy. Most important was his participation in the growth of postwar Italian cinema. He acted as a screenwriter and translator for neorealist director Roberto Rossellini throughout the 1950s and was on the scene when the new wave of Italian directors (e.g., Fellini and Antonioni) began their careers. These younger directors emphasized the importance of the imagination in the creation of a work of art, making a sharp break from the neorealism of the 1940s and early 1950s, and forced the audience to collaborate with them in creating and synthesizing the films. This act of collaboration is important to the success of *The Catacombs*, as is the cinematic technique of swift cutting that Demby employs—the constant imposition of image over image—that transforms the novel into a virtual collage of images.

Demby was also interested in twentieth-century art, and he studied art history at the University of Rome. Clearly his knowledge and appreciation of the cubist theory of painting is illustrated throughout the novel. His concern for the non-representational depiction of reality (i.e., reality as viewed from a number of perspectives simultaneously, just as a cubist painting presents a multifaceted view of its subject) and for nonlinear time has its artistic roots in cubism.

A third area of interest was contemporary science. In *The Catacombs*, Demby attempts to come to grips with some of the implications of modern scientific principles—particularly the Heisenberg uncertainty principle and the theory of indeterminacy—as they apply to the notion of time. As Robert Bone suggests [see excerpt dated 1969], these contemporary theories have altered our linear view of time by altering our notions of causation, and *The Catacombs* employs a nonlinear conception of time in its presentation of themes and plot.

The actual writing of the novel was no less innovative than some of its intellectual influences. The very act of writing was an attempt to capture the sense of simultaneity Demby was striving for [see excerpt dated 1971]:

> I conceived of writing a novel, but without any of the controls that a novel usually would have. That is, I would begin on a certain day and continuously go forward. Every page or every day's work would reflect what has happened to me in my personal life and the lives of the fictional characters who moved around at the same time as the so-called real characters, the people in real life. So each day should reflect all of these things: what I perceived from newspapers that I was reading, or the things that were happening in other countries, or in the southern part of Italy. Anything.

What emerges is not a linear progression of events, but a tapestry, a work that must be experienced, not from one point to another, but in its entirety, as one would experience a cubist painting by Picasso or Braque. *The Catacombs* is, indeed, a novelist's novel.

The cool reception it received from reviewers may be due to the fact that they either misunderstood or were unaware of Demby's aims in *The Catacombs*. Peter Buitenhuis, for example, simply did not know what to do with the novel: "*The Catacombs* should be labeled not as a novel but as an autobiography or pastiche or ragbag...for surely a novel has to have a guiding principle, a central idea, or at least an attitude." As I suggested earlier, Demby does have a guiding princi-

ple—a careful examination of contemporary consciousness through an experimental depiction of reality and action. Buitenhuis goes on to complain that "proportion, progression, rhythm ...must be ordered and adjusted so that the chaos we call life is given some new meaning" [see Further Reading]. Once again, I believe that Demby does impose order on the "chaos we call life," but not in the traditional sense (which is implied by Buitenhuis when he refers to "proportion, progression, and rhythm"). An examination of the structure and style of *The Catacombs* should illuminate Demby's ordering process. The plot of *The Catacombs* is linear, but it is quite fractured. It is constantly being interrupted by other aspects of the novel. It involves William Demby, an Afro-American novelist living in Rome, who is writing a novel about a girl named Doris. Doris is the daughter of one of Demby's former girlfriends in the United States, and she has called on him at her mother's behest (hoping he will introduce her to life in Rome). Soon after Doris's arrival, Demby introduces her to a count, with whom she has an affair for the next two years. During that time Doris frequently meets with Demby to relate the happenings in her affair so that they can be incorporated in his novel.

As the novel progresses, Doris occasionally takes Demby as a lover, and at one point she becomes pregnant and does not know whether Demby or the Count is the baby's father. She believes the baby is the Count's, but this is immaterial since it is either born dead, aborted, or miscarried (Demby never resolves this point for the reader). At the end of the novel, the Count informs Doris that the airline company he works for is transferring him to Hong Kong; Demby prepares to leave for New York to take a position in an advertising agency; and Doris, it is assumed, will remain in Italy, her request to accompany the Count being rejected. In the final paragraphs, the Count has taken Doris on a tour of the Catacombs in Rome. He loses her in the darkness, and as he searches for her through the corridors, the novel suddenly ends.

The plot of *The Catacombs* is intriguing and bizarre. It is not as important, however, as the narrative structure behind it. The purpose of the plot is to draw the reader into the structure and action of the novel. Action in *The Catacombs* includes more than just the plot. In a larger sense, the action revolves around Demby's cubistic conception of time and reality. In "William Demby's Dance of Life" [see excerpt dated 1969], Robert Bone states that "along with the traditional narrative dimension Demby attempts to convey, through a stream-of-consciousness technique, the writer's state of mind during the period of composition, including his awareness of historical events." The novel moves simultaneously between three levels of time and reality. Newspaper items and stories provide the historical context; Demby's own stream-of-conscious musings provide the subjective, or personal, context; and the frequently interrupted story line (the affair between Doris and the Count) tries to fulfill the narrative requirements of a plot.

Within this three-fold structure, Demby gives equal status to both "true" facts (e.g., newspaper stories) and "fictional" facts (e.g., Demby's musing and the actions of the fictional characters). The novel also includes both "real" characters, such as Demby and his wife, and "fictional" characters, such as Doris and the Count. This structural arrangement has at least three implications.

First, it is a reaction against the realistic/naturalistic tradition in literature. *The Catacombs* is not a "slice of life." It is slices of lives, if you will; an ordering of lives and actions that are seemingly unrelated. The interaction among real and fictional characters, and the arrangement of newspaper stories create connections between lives. Demby's use of the subjective stream-of-consciousness technique, coupled with the news items he comes across and the fictional plot, creates a tapestry of lives and a myriad of realities.

Second, the novel's structure blurs and distorts traditional notions of reality. When Demby and his "real" wife dine with the "fictional" Doris, a reader cannot help questioning his/her own assumptions about the nature of reality. Moreover, the factual newspaper headlines and stories are juxtaposed in a way that forces readers to reexamine their views of reality and of the proper relationship between the individual and society/world.

Demby juxtaposes a story about two Cleveland, Ohio, blacks who were beaten by a mob of whites with one that covers the nomination of Martin Luther King for the Nobel Peace Prize. Elsewhere he juxtaposes a story about the death of a shepherd with his recollection of a picture-taking session where Louis Armstrong and he (Demby) are shaking hands. The juxtapositions concern images of life and death. They show, or at least imply, the cosmic interrelatedness of human lives and actions, and the readers are left to make other connections for themselves.

Finally, the structure illustrates Demby's own idea about the role of the artist and the imagination. As Bone points out, "the fertility of the imagination is precisely Demby's subject.... Man is the inventor of his own reality: that is the sum and substance of Demby's fictional technique." Demby himself makes this point clear in the novel: "The looking glass our symbol, we dream of reinventing reality, we straddle time and space as all around the visible and invisible clash." The artist's task, therefore, is to observe and shape "the seeming mutations, the illusory motion, the dreamlike sense of progression and progress which occur when the sun's rays shifts on the eternal and timeless, the statis, the sacredly silk-threaded tapestry of lives. And this process, for Demby, involves the reinventing, or at least the reshaping, of reality.

For this reason, Demby's choice of the first person point of view is a shrewd one; it marks a sharp departure from the point of view employed in *Beetlecreek.* Despite the existentialist philosophy that permeates the earlier novel, the use of the third person implies a sense of logic and order in the cosmos. This order is external to the characters, something imposed upon them from outside the sphere of action (by the artist). Demby's use of the first person in *The Catacombs* is appropriate because he (as both writer and "character") is trying to bring order to "the chaos we call life." Here the writer-character imposes his own order on the world from within the sphere of action in the novel. But the order is not merely an individual, private one. In *The Catacombs,* Demby makes spontaneous connections between phenomena, personal connections with the help of the reader (similar to the cinematic collaboration previously mentioned). Thus the choice of narrative perspective is a very effective one that enhances both the structure and the theme of the work.

What caused Demby to write a novel in which fact and fiction, real and unreal, are blurred seemingly beyond recognition? It was probably his belief in the interconnectedness of all aspects of existence. No one can be seen in isolation; actions of one person or character have an effect on others. This concept can be related to Demby's comments on the "small movements" of the characters in *Beetlecreek,* and how they were inextricably linked. Existence, therefore, cannot be seen chronologically. It must be seen as a woven tapestry, where all life interacts against a large common background. The novelist's task is to bring together as many strands of existence as he/she is able to do:

> What I mean, though, is simply this. That everything and everybody, real or invented, characters in books or in newspapers, the "news" itself, stones and broken bottles *do* matter, *are* important, if only they are looked at, if only they are observed, just because they are composed of matter. Because everything and everybody, real or invented, characters in books, even the books themselves, even the book jacket and the colored ink on the cover design, is composed of matter and for this reason matters, must therefore breathe in harmony with a single governing law, respond according to its aliveness, its *alertness,* to the degree that it is awake or awakened, to the shifting humors of the wind-tormented involucre of our physical environment, which through Penelope's law of tapestry, Penelope's law of changeless change, can, so often as it does, become transmuted into climate and weather, weather peaceful or calm, these wild pregnant storm signals that flash ignored through our minds....

Through the particular narrative structure and point of view employed in *The Catacombs,* Demby is able to bring together a large number of strands of existence. The cubistic conception of time and reality (i.e., simultaneity) compels the reader to question his/her notions of reality and existence. In this way William Demby is able to expand the limits of contemporary consciousness and to comment upon the present state of humankind. *The Catacombs* is thus his most ambitious and satisfying novel.

Love Story Black

William Demby's most recent novel, *Love Story Black,* was published thirteen years after *The Catacombs.* While it is not as stylistically complex as its predecesor, *Love Story Black* illustrates even further growth in Demby's concerns. For the first time, he immerses his work in the Afro-American community and attempts to address some concerns of blacks.

Love Story Black is most importantly a love story, as the title suggests. Edwards—free-lance writer, professor of black literature, and narrator of the novel—is asked some very penetrating questions by a student one day. In some ways they shape the content of the novel:

> "[W]hy are our black authors—or at least the ones I've read so far—so negative," [the quiet girl asked]. "For example, how come they're always talking about Black people as though they're some kind of sociological disease?... Black people are tired of being studied under a microscope like they're some kind of social disease. Why don't Black writers write about love, for example?"

Love Story Black is a novel of a number of types of love. It depicts the passionate, yet shallow, love shared by Edwards and Hortense Schiller, a coworker at *New Black Woman* magazine; the platonic love between Mona Pariss, a once famous entertainer, and Doc, the man who discovered her and managed her musical career; and the mythic/Edenic love between Edwards and Pariss, who is the subject of a series of articles he is writing for *New Black Woman.* In addition to treating the theme of love, the novel also addresses questions of history and myth. These themes and the structure of the book will be taken up shortly.

The novel opens with Edwards—forced into free-lance writing by a pack of creditors—attempting to gain an audience with Mona Pariss. He wants to write a series of biographical articles for the *New Black Woman.* After she is satisfied that he is not a welfare inspector, Pariss asks him to return later that evening to conduct the first interview.

When Edwards returns, Pariss begins her "memorizing" about the past. She makes him take off all of his clothes and get into bed with her before she will talk. This ritual is repeated each time an interview is conducted. Pariss' story of her rise from humble beginnings to wealth and and notoriety (and, ultimately, her fall into poverty) is a "metaphor for the universal initiation myth" according to Edwards. Her story assumes important stature in his life. Her experience is transformed into a rite of self-initiation, and Edwards feels that he is to learn from her, to be initiated into experience by her.

Edwards continues his interviews with Pariss and also talks with Reverend Grooms, her wardrobe designer and longtime companion, to get a different perspective on her career. Meanwhile, Edwards becomes involved with Hortense Schiller. They plan a trip to Africa the following summer. Upon arrival, Edwards becomes very ill, and Hortense goes on without him. Before he recuperates enough to leave the hospital, he receives a letter from her. It seems that she has met an attractive young revolutionary and has decided to marry him.

Edwards, sad and bewildered, returns to New York and prepares to pick up the Pariss interviews. When he arrives at her apartment building, he sees that it is being demolished. He searches for Pariss, finds her in her apartment, and tries to get her to leave before the building collapses. Instead, she makes love with him in a ritualistic fashion, and the novel concludes at the point of penetration.

Demby's stylistic techniques have been greatly altered since the composition of *The Catacombs. Love Story Black* is not preoccupied with the concepts of cubism or simultaneity; thus the narrative has a roughly linear flow. He is also less concerned with different levels of reality that permeated *The Catacombs.* Demby's sentences are more simply structured, and the novel as a whole is far more conventional than the previous one. There are some stylistic similarities, however, that do carry over into *Love Story Black.* One can find elements of interconnectedness in the book. Mona Pariss' life for example, is viewed from three perspectives—her own, Reverend Grooms's, and that gained from memorabilia found in her old steamer trunk. Moreover, Demby's concern for themes such as life, death, and love are as important to *Love Story Black* as they are to *Beetlecreek* and *The Catacombs.*

While *Love Story Black* may be more conventional than *The Catacombs,* its structure is no less effective and compelling. Since *Love Story Black* is a love story, it is fitting that loving relationships are used to structure the book. Demby includes three levels of love that involve Edwards. The relationship between Edwards and Gracie, the aggressive editor of *New Black Woman,* is superficial and entirely physical. No rapport or intimacy exists between them. The love is superficial, casual, and therefore unfulfilling. Hortense Schiller is able to instill passion and emotional intimacy into their relationship, but this is still inadequate. While in Africa Edwards becomes ill, and she leaves him to marry a young black revolutionary. Throughout the novel, Demby depicts Hortense as somewhat fickle and immature—hardly someone able to sustain a relationship.

These two unfulfilling relationships only serve to highlight the mythic/Edenic relationship between Edwards and Mona Pariss. Their love remains on the platonic level throughout most of the novel, but it is an enduring kind of love, especially for Edwards. Edwards, the reader is told, has recently returned from an extended stay in Europe. His detractors, like Gracie (at times) and some of his students, believe that he and his novels have become Europeanized; he has lost touch with the Afro-American experience. Thus, as Addison Gayle points out [see Further Reading], "the writer must undergo his own odyssey, seek a clue to many riddles, search for classification, meaning." For this reason, Demby's use of the first person point of view is especially significant.

The point of view emphasizes the subjective quality of Edwards's odyssey.

That Edwards needs to make this spiritual journey is made evident when he reveals a nightmare that he once had. The dream is set in an African hut, far out in the bush:

> "[A]nd in the hut there is an old woman . . . a wise woman, a seer, a prophetess—and I humbly enter the hut and ask for a drink of water, a supplicant—I have come millions of miles over the desert of time with a riddle, I must know the answer, and the old prophetess tells me she will only give me the answer, the meaning of the riddle, if I make love to her."

Demby indicates throughout the book that Mona Pariss is something of a mystical prophet.

Much of Pariss' earlier life is shrouded in mystery. Some clues are provided by the contents of her old steamer trunk— hand bills, clothing, and other memorabilia— but many details are never mentioned. The reader is made aware of the fact that in her youth she was infatuated with a pullman porter named Doc. He was the first to recognize beauty and talent in Pariss, discovered her so to speak, and offered to be her manager. He started her on the road to success, but was never able to give her what she wanted most because he had been castrated years earlier by whites. Thus Pariss is a representative of a virgin myth. In a way her virginal state is a manifestation of Edenic love. She is both innocent and experienced; an Edenic figure and a repository of wisdom. She is therefore able to initiate Edwards into experience while also reaffirming Edenic love.

As **Love Story Black** closes, Edwards is trying to coax Pariss out of her apartment and into the street. Pariss sees him as Doc reincarnated. It is at this time that she consummates the previously platonic relationship with "Doc." The love scene is almost a coupling between Adam and Eve. As Pariss prepares to make love, she remembers the pastoral setting where she and Doc used to spend time together. As the building falls down around Pariss and Edwards, they couple. Edwards has become Doc; he has accepted the role thrust upon him by Pariss. And amidst the squalor of the apartment and the surrounding neighborhood, love is reaffirmed. [According to Gayle]:

> For Camus's doctrine, "I rebel, therefore I am," Demby would proclaim I love, therefore I am, thus raising the existential equation beyond romanticism to touch the most profound longings and utterings of the human soul. Such are exemplified in the life and times of Mona Pariss and the old woman herself in her quest and in her achievement, exemplifies humankind at its best.

Love Story Black is a well-written book that contains many memorable scenes; yet is is in some ways the shallowest of Demby's novels. He grapples with problems of history and myth, and he also addresses the topic of love among blacks. The novel is, indeed, a homage to love in its many forms. It is a satisfying work, but it lacks the interesting thematic complexities of his two earlier novels.

In each of his three novels, William Demby has focused upon themes that he deems important. These themes have been linked to the style and structure of the novels. His stylistic abilities have matured over a period of thirty years: **Beetlecreek** features a beautifully visual style that enhanced the book's existentialist theme; **The Catacombs** probes the limits of modern consciousness through nonrepresentational experimentation; and **Love Story Black** illustrates a subtle use of language and structure, with the various types of love framing the novel. William Demby is a writer of great skill and sensitivity, and his work merits serious scholarly attention. (pp. 434-51)

> *Jay R. Berry, "The Achievement of William Demby," in* CLA Journal, *Vol. XXVI, No. 4, June, 1983, pp. 434-51.*

FURTHER READING

Bayliss, John F. "Beetlecreek: Existential or Human Document?" *Negro Digest* XIX, No. 1 (November 1969): 70-4.
  Refutes Robert Bones's assertion that *Beetlecreek* is predominately an existentialist novel. The critic writes: "I. . . disagree with [Bone's] overemphasis on the existentialist nature of this interesting work. . . . Sufficient evidence . . . show[s] that the human content of *Beetlecreek* far outweighs the existentialist patterning that is brought in by Bone as interpretation."

Bone, Robert. "The Contemporary Negro Novel." In his *The Negro Novel in America*, rev. ed., pp. 173-212. New Haven: Yale University Press, 1965.
  Assesses *Beetlecreek* as an existentialist and expatriate novel "whose tone is dominated by pessimism and disgust, flowing from a robust rejection of American culture and of Negro life in particular."

Buitenhuis, Peter. "Doris is Always Getting Pushed Aside." *The New York Times Book Review* (11 July 1965): 4, 32.
  Negative appraisal of *The Catacombs*, stating of the work: ". . . most of this book . . . 'stinks'."

Connelly, Joseph F. "William Demby's Fiction: The Pursuit of Muse." *Negro American Literature Forum* 10, No. 3 (Fall 1976): 100, 102-03.
  Examines the theme, setting, structure, and tone of *Beetlecreek* and *The Catacombs*.

Derleth, August. "This Racial Novel Turns the Tables." *Chicago Tribune* (12 February 1950): 4.
  Reviews *Beetlecreek*, concluding: "It is skillfully done. Mr. Demby is by no means heavyhanded, nor does he belabor scenes or characterizations; his people are credible, their actions likewise, and his story has

evenness of pace, whatever it may lack in significance and depth."

Fuller, Edmund. "Hermit with Blacks." *The Saturday Review of Literature* XXXIII, No. 9 (4 March 1950): 17.
  Discusses characterization in *Beetlecreek*. Although the critic applauds their "well-realized personalities," he notes that the "richness in the book's people is scarcely tapped."

Gayle, Addison. Review of *Love Story Black,* by William Demby. *The American Book Review* 2, No. 6 (September-October 1980): 10.
  Explores symbolism in *Love Story Black.*

Lee, A. Robert. "Making New: Styles of Innovation in the Contemporary Black American Novel." In *Black Fiction: New Studies in the Afro-American Novel Since 1945,* edited by A. Robert Lee, pp. 222-50. London: Vision Press, 1980.
  Appraises *Beetlecreek* and *The Catacombs,* stating: "The two novels read very much as a diptych, linking visions of human loss and subsequent recovery."

Rennert, Maggie. "Write One, Splice Two." *New York Herald Tribune* (27 June 1965): 22.
  Review of *The Catacombs,* noting of the work: ". . . this non-novel is as melancholy and fruitless a proceeding as writing a report on a miscarriage."

Owen Dodson

1914-1983

American dramatist, poet, novelist, librettist, short story writer, and nonfiction writer.

Although critics have acknowledged Dodson to be an accomplished poet, dramatist, and novelist, his works have all but escaped serious critical attention. As a drama professor at Howard University and as a major figure among black dramatists and poets, however, he acquired a devoted following that continues to recognize him as a great writer and man.

Born to Nathaniel Dodson, a free-lance journalist for black newspapers, and Sarah Elizabeth Goode Dodson, Owen Dodson enjoyed a poor but culturally rich childhood in Brooklyn, New York. His father, director of the National Negro Press Association, introduced young Dodson to important black thinkers and artists like Booker T. Washington, W. E. B. Du Bois, and James Weldon Johnson. Receiving a scholarship in 1932, Dodson went to Bates College in Maine. There he soon became interested in classical English literature, informing his English professor that he could write a sonnet as fine as John Keats's "On First Looking into Chapman's Homer." The professor ordered Dodson to write a sonnet each week and submit it to him until he matched Keats or graduated, whichever came first. Dodson consequently was able to publish his work in the *New York Herald Tribune* and *Phylon* by the time of his graduation.

After receiving his B.A. in 1936, Dodson entered Yale Drama School on a fellowship. His first play, *Divine Comedy,* was produced there in 1938. In it he exposed the nonsense of adoring "prophets" like Father Divine, an evangelist who claimed he was God. James V. Hatch, in his 1987 essay "Owen Dodson: Excerpts from a Biography in Progress," wrote of Dodson's inspiration for *Divine Comedy:* "At ten, Owen met God, at least a man who called himself God. Owen and his brother Kenneth were taken out to Sayville, Long Island, and there they gazed upon Mother and Father Divine. Kenneth looked askance at Father Divine who kept drawing milk from a spigot on the table that never ran dry; after everyone left the feast, Kenneth looked under the tablecloth and there was a little Negro boy with a large cask of milk and a pump." Dodson greatly enjoyed this childhood revelation, and the result of this early experience has been called the finest verse drama ever written by a black writer. Dodson's next play was *Garden of Time,* produced in 1939 at Yale. It is a retelling of the Medea story in terms of American race relations, with the conflict between black Medea and white Jason shifting scenes in the midst of the play from Greece to postbellum South Carolina. Upon graduation from Yale in 1939, Dodson taught drama and speech at several colleges and enlisted in the United States Navy,

where he was charged with "raising the morale of the Negro seaman" through a series of plays about black war heroes. After being discharged from the service because of asthma, Dodson wrote and directed *New World A-Coming* in 1944; it was a widely attended pageant designed to commemorate and gain recognition for the black American contribution to the war effort. The overwhelming success of the production guaranteed Dodson's appointment to the newly founded Committee for Mass Education in Race Relations at the American Film Center, where he worked with artists like Richard Wright, Langston Hughes, and Arna Bontemps. Although he eventually became convinced of the committee's ineffectuality and resigned his appointment, Dodson continued to write plays and operas and to teach drama at Howard University and elsewhere. His years as a teacher and dramatist made him the honorary "Dean of Black Theater."

Although Dodson distinguished himself in the theater, Pulitzer Prize-winning poet Richard Eberhart once called him "the best Negro poet in the United States." Dodson's reputation as a poet was established in 1946 with the publication of his first volume of poetry, *Powerful Long Ladder.* Its epigraph expresses the work's theme: "It takes a powerful long ladder to climb to the sky/ and catch the bird of freedom for the dark." After the publication of *Powerful Long Ladder,* however, Dodson temporarily stopped writing poetry and turned to a new genre, the novel. In 1951 he published his first and most acclaimed novel, *Boy at the Window.* This poetic and semi-autobiographical work is the story of Coin Foreman, a sensitive young boy who feels that his conversion to the Baptist church should have prevented his mother's death. Dodson later resumed writing poetry, producing, among others, the work he considered his masterpiece, *The Confession Stone: Song Cycles* (1970). This collection of poetry consists of monologues about Jesus spoken by New Testament figures. Despite his accomplishments as a poet, Dodson remained inextricably tied to the theater. In his 1979 essay "The Legendary Owen Dodson of Howard University: His Contributions to the American Theatre," Bernard L. Peterson, Jr., wrote: "Although recognized as an outstanding poet whose work has been compared with that of Frost and Sandburg, it is perhaps as a drama director and playwright that Owen Dodson will be best remembered." By instructing artists like Amiri Baraka, Roxie Roker, Earle Hyman, Debbie Allen, and Ossie Davis at Howard University, Dodson tirelessly helped many in their careers until his death in 1983.

Dodson, though long recognized as exceptionally talented, never enjoyed much notoriety, evidently because he wrote in traditional, not progressive, forms and never had strong ties to black literary movements. His forced retirement at the age of fifty-six from Howard University—ironically, the place where he established his importance to black theater—explains in part the lack of attention accorded to Dodson and his works. Hatch wrote in his 1987 essay of Dodson's attempt to find a position at a university: "Repeatedly, his applications were returned to him, stamped by an invisible hand: 'Sorry, Professor Dodson. Our universities in these 1970s need your colleagues—Ralph Bunche, John Hope Franklin—to explain to us just what it is that is making black people behave in such a rebellious manner. We are also hiring the young militants Larry Neal, Amiri Baraka, Nikki Giovanni, so that our students may assimilate their idioms, their music. However, we have no need for a fifty-six-year-old black humanist to direct one more production of *Hamlet.*'" Too young to have participated in the Harlem Renaissance and too traditional to be among the angry black militants of the 1960s, Dodson escaped categorization and, consequently, attention. His proficiency in many genres makes his achievement difficult to gauge. Nevertheless, Dodson's works have been an inspiration to many people as much as Dodson himself was as a friend and teacher.

(For further information about Dodson's life and works, see *Black Writers; Contemporary Authors,* Vols. 65-68; *Contemporary Authors New Revision Series,* Vols. 24, 110; and *Dictionary of Literary Biography,* Vol. 76: *Afro-American Writers, 1940-1955.*)

PRINCIPAL WORKS

Divine Comedy (drama) 1938
Garden of Time (drama) 1939
"Someday We're Gonna Tear Them Pillars Down" (poem) 1942; published in periodical *Harlem Quarterly*
Everybody Join Hands (drama) 1943; published in periodical *Theatre Arts*
"Black Mother Praying in the Summer of 1943" (poem) 1944; published in periodical *Common Ground*
Dorrie Miller (broadcast) 1944
"Jonathan's Song" (poem) 1944; published in periodical *New Currents*
"Martha Graham" (poem) 1944; published in periodical *Theatre Arts*
New World A-Coming (drama) 1944
"Pearl Primus" (poem) 1944; published in periodical *Theatre Arts*
Powerful Long Ladder (poetry) 1946
The Third Fourth of July [with Countee Cullen] (drama) 1946; published in periodical *Theatre Arts*
"Color USA" (nonfiction) 1947; published in periodical *Twice a Year*
Bayou Legend (drama) 1948
"College Troopers Abroad" (nonfiction) 1950; published in periodical *Negro Digest*
Boy at the Window (novel) 1951; also published as *When Trees Were Green,* 1967
Cages (poetry) 1953
"The Summer Fire" (short story) 1956; published in periodical *Paris Review*
The Confession Stone (poetry) 1968; also published as *The Confession Stone: Song Cycles* [revised and enlarged edition], 1970
"Playwrights in Dark Glasses" (nonfiction) 1968; published in periodical *Negro Digest*
Till Victory Is Won [with Mark Fax] (opera) 1974
Come Home Early, Child (novel) 1977
"Who Has Seen the Wind?" (nonfiction) 1977; published in periodical *Black American Literature Forum*
The Harlem Book of the Dead [with James Van Der Zee and Camille Billops] (poetry) 1978
Freedom, the Banner (drama) 1984; published in periodical *Callaloo*

George Jean Nathan (essay date 1945)

[*Nathan has been called the most learned and influential drama critic the United States has yet produced. He is particularly known for his occasional stinging invective and verbal adroitness. In the following excerpt, he criticizes Dodson for taking on too much as a novice with* Garden of Time.]

[Owen Dodson], quondam head of the drama department at Hampton Institute, has [in *Garden of Time*] undertaken something. "I believe," he stated in the public prints, "that the modern drama is too stingy. We don't use it for all it's worth. *Garden Of Time* is told in terms of the fable of the Golden Fleece instead of hard, realistic terms. It uses music and song and dance and poetry. It begins in ancient times in Colchis off the coast of Asia Minor and ends in a graveyard in Georgia, U. S. A., at the end of the nineteenth century. It's the story of one country, Greece, the ruling country of the world, going to a smaller country, Colchis, whose people are a dark people and trying to take its emblems. Jason, the Greek, captures the Golden Fleece, aided by Medea, priestess of Colchis, who has fallen in love with him. They flee to Greece, killing Medea's brother in their flight. Two children are born to them, but eventually Jason deserts Medea. 'You're dark,' he tells her, 'I can't stand you.' Actually he is spurred on by the chance of marriage with Creusa and its promise of new wealth and possessions."

Here, continued the author, "the play switches to the end of the last century, with Georgia substituted for Greece and Haiti for Colchis, and with the main characters going on and the Greek idea of vengeance and atonement being realized through Mama Leua, a Haitian voodooist, who is like the ancient goddess Hecate." Then, elaborating, "Jason and Medea could have gotten along together, but these passions that move them—ambition, lust, greed—destroy them. They realize what has been wrong when the play comes to its end but it's too late to turn back. The play foreshadows an end of all this, however, as the nineteenth century Medea says:

> 'The rats been eating at the
>   seeds of time,
> Eaten full the gullet
> But the end's coming.'"

Since Mr. Dodson's previous demonstrations of dramatic composition consisted chiefly in an unproduced play written while at college and in one or two shows executed for amateur performances while he was in the Navy, it is not to be wondered that his ambitious plan, which would come near to frightening even a dramatist like O'Neill, who seems rarely to be frightened by anything, has been too much for him. Like various other tyros, he has attempted to enlarge the scope of the "too stingy" drama without first mastering the stingy scope of such dramatists as, say, Ibsen, Strindberg, *et al.* His process of enlargement resolves itself mainly into fancy rhetorical flights which adorn his story like so many artificial beads; in the kind of experiment, however well-intentioned, which operates upon that story to its serio-comic undoing, like a small boy's improvement upon the telephone by attaching the dinner table bell to it; and in a garrulity which, while it undeniably enlarges the script, reduces to a minimum what active drama his theme may intrinsically possess. He might have profited

by taking a cue from Charles Sebree's classical stage settings and by writing his play in equally simple terms.

The performance of a mixed company of Negroes and whites was as confused as the materials, only louder. (pp. 290-91)

> *George Jean Nathan, "The Year's Productions: 'Garden of Time','" in his* The Theatre Book of the Year, 1944-1945: A Record and an Interpretation, *Alfred A. Knopf, 1945, pp. 290-291.*

Richard Wright (essay date 1946)

[*Wright established a reputation as a leading spokesman for black Americans with his first novel,* Native Son, *in 1940. In the following excerpt from a 1946 letter to Dodson, he urges his friend to continue portraying the realities of black American life.*]

One of the reasons that compel me to write you now is my memory of your description of what you saw on your Mississippi trip. What you told me is truly important, and since I've been here in Paris I've been wondering if you really realize just how important. The French people, like ours, are also ignorant of the Negro. The forces of commerce have done a damn good job in painting the Negro as something exotic, as a race of people with something queer in them that makes them write jazz music. I wonder if American Negroes really realize the vast harm that they are doing their cause by making themselves into something unreal, something that always sings, something that is always childish? While the great body of their life experiences are untouched and unexpressed? There is no reason why the Negro point of view cannot be put over in Europe, if the right people come over here. There are thousands of Frenchmen who know of our jazz, and no one here seems to realize the great tragedy of the Negro in America, or the meaning of his life. But few could really understand your poem about the Negro mother praying ... All of this is by way of saying that I do hope and wish that you continue to dig into the rich materials of Negro life and lift them up for all to see, and you ought to know while doing it that you'll be doing more than holding up Negro life for others to see, but you will be holding up human life in all of its forms for all to see. The more we dig into Negro life, the more we are digging into human life.

My work is already being translated over here, and the astonishment, bewilderment which greets it makes me know that they have never had an opportunity to look straight at Negro life. People just do not know what to say or think. It confounds them. They had been led to look at the Negro and laugh; well, they are learning to look at him and let their mouths fall open. So far, there is no opposition here to looking at the Negro honestly. They've just never had a chance to do so before now. So you must realize that it is your duty to keep plugging. (pp. 125-26)

Richard Wright, in a letter to Owen Dodson on June 9, 1946, in New Letters, *Vol. 38, No. 2, Winter, 1971, pp. 125-27.*

John Holmes (essay date 1946)

[*In the following excerpt from a 1946* New York Times Book Review *essay, Holmes criticizes Dodson for making "too much of an issue of his race and color" in* Powerful Long Ladder.]

With the friendliest intentions, I'll risk saying that Mr. Dodson makes too much of an issue of his race and color [in **Powerful Long Ladder**]. It obtrudes, and that is bad art in any language. There is good poetry in his book, best when least self-conscious. There is awareness of the inevitable tragedy of life; there is rich, deep rhythm and feeling as in this *"Epitaph for a Negro Woman"*:

> How cool beneath this stone the soft moss lies
>   How smooth and long the silken threads have
>   kept
> Without the taste of slender rain or stars,
>   How tranquilly the outer coats have slept.
> Alone with only wind, with only ice,
>   The moss is growing, clinging to the stone;
> And seeing only what the darkness shows,
>   *It thrives without the moon, it thrives alone.*

Or in this formal Shakespearean sonnet:

> I loved the apple-sweetness of the air
>   And pines that settled slanting on the hill,
> Indians old and soft with needles there
>   Where once we stood, and both so strangely
>   still.
> We must have surely known what other days
>   Would come in other flaming autumn's flame
> And even though we walk through different ways
>   To different hills that hill remains the same,
> Watch every splendor, envy all the sky.
>   But recognize the days we knew, and hear
> The simple sounds we heard. As birds that fly
>   Southward to warmth, we shall come back one
>   year.
> The little teeth of time will make no mark
>   *On any stone, on any leaf or bark.*

Passages from longer works also indicate his power and promise. But he appears to be in some danger of falling into certain patterns somewhat expected of poets who are Negroes. Dodson uses language and rhythm in a way that I think is book-learned—slave songs, blues. It is clear from the bulk of his poetry that he can, if he will, outgrow this.

> *John Holmes, in a review of "Powerful Long Ladder," in* The New York Times Book Review, *September 29, 1946, p. 22.*

Alfred Kreymborg (essay date 1947)

[*Kreymborg, a poet, editor, dramatist, and critic, was prominent among American writers in Paris in the*

1930s and 1940s. According to biographical sketches, Dodson was a great admirer of his poetry. In the following excerpt from an essay originally published in The Saturday Review of Literature *in 1947, he praises* Powerful Long Ladder.]

A year ago, American poetry was enriched by the arrival of Gwendolyn Brooks and her thoroughly original poems, *A Street in Bronzeville*. In **Powerful Long Ladder,** our poetry is enriched once more by a compelling young man whose record in our social life is already impressive. Educated at Bates and Yale, [Owen Dodson] received a Rosenwald Fellowship, directed drama at various Negro institutions, headed a morale building program while in the Navy, won a Maxwell Anderson Verse Play Contest, and is now executive secretary for the Committee for Mass Education in Race Relations. From these factors it may be gathered that his principal medium of expression would be poetic drama. Even his lyrical poems have a dramatic tendency, notably a tragic sequence on estranged lovers, an old theme in poetry, but one now informed with fire, wisdom, and dignity.

The poems on Negro themes are composed of clear and supple images wedded to chanting cadences. Memorable lines reveal a whole race in a single strain. "Sorrow is the only faithful one." At times the tone is biblical, at others colloquial. In the title poem, a dramatic chant between a leader and a chorus of slaves, the vernacular is handled with realistic skill:

> Ma father say: Freedom a story they tell that
>   never happen.
> When, O when, ma brothers, ma sisters, will the
>   well be drained of masquerading death?
> When will the noosed rope strangle the nooser?
> It take a powerful long ladder to climb to the sky
>   an catch the bird of freedom for the dark.

Three choruses from a verse drama, **Divine Comedy,** are included, and they unfold "people in search of something to believe in when they are trapped in poverty, fear, and prejudice. They follow a false prophet for a time, but when he is killed, they turn to the strength in themselves for guidance and faith." Or, one might add, to prophets and leaders like Paul Robeson and Owen Dodson. There is only one poem in which this ardent poet assumes a satirical role. But that one suffices—a conversation on V:

> They got pictures of V stamped on letter stamps;
> Miss Eagle wear one in her lapel to her Red Cross
>   suit;
> Mr. Bigful, the bank president, got one in his lapel
>   too;
> Some of the people I do laundry with got big ones
>   in they windows;
> Hadley Brothers Department Store uptown got
>   picturs of V on they store-bought dresses,
> Even got a V ice-cream dish-girls selling them so
>   fast had to run up a sign: NO MORE V
>   SUNDAES;
> And bless God, Lucy done gone up North and
>   come back with one gleaming on her pocket-
>   book.

Now let's get this straight; what do these V's
mean?
V stands for Victory.
Now just what is this here Victory?
It what we get when we fight for it.
Ought to be Freedom. God do know that!

(pp. 32-3)

*Alfred Kreymborg, "Exiles in Black and
White," in* The Saturday Review of Literature, *Vol. XXX, No. 5, February 1, 1947, pp.
32-3.*

J. Saunders Redding (essay date 1951)

[*Redding is a distinguished American critic, historian,
novelist, and autobiographer. His first book,* To Make
a Poet Black *(1939), is a scholarly appraisal of black
poetry; as one of the first anthologies of its type to be
written by a black critic, this book is considered a
landmark in criticism of black writers. In the following
review, originally published in* The New York Times
Book Review *in 1951, he deems Dodson's* Boy at the
Window *a real achievement as a poet's first novel.*]

The delineation of a sensitive boy's growing up is the
business of *Boy at the Window.* As a poet's first novel, it
is a real achievement. It is an achievement in the kind of
writing that steers its tenuous way between the grossness
of physical reality and the too nice refinement of
emotional truth. "Clinographic" is the word Middleton
Murry applied to this kind of writing in the works of
Virginia Woolf. It is perceptive, but emotionally oblique
and indirect without being obscure.

I have called *Boy at the Window* a delineation, a portrait.
Rather, it is a series of portraits. It is as if Coin
Foreman, the subject, were caught in various attitudes
at the revealing heights of certain stages of his development. Limned carefully but in miniature around him are
half a dozen other portraits—of his mother, father,
brother, and of people in the house and on the street
where Coin lives.

There is story only in the most tenuous narrative sense.
It is not "And then. . .and then. . ." Yet this does not
mean that there are no events, no happenings. It means
only that the events, though arranged precisely in time,
do not depend upon each other in such a way as to forge
a chain of circumstances and bring about an inevitable
result. It means further that Coin is more important
than any happening.

The events are soon retold. Coin sees God; Coin gets
religion (in the church where his father has been a
deacon for twenty years); Coin's mother dies (after an
illness that began with Coin's birth); Coin goes to live
with a blind uncle in Washington. And that is all. And
these events themselves are caught in a kind of static
mobility, as in a picture, that does not exercise Mr.
Dodson's narrative powers but does prove his sure
talent in description.

Yet even this talent, it seems to me, is not the author's
most noteworthy. His best talent shows itself in what he
does with the between-events. It is a gift for total
immersion in mood and for recapturing the feel of those
deliciously painful and divine mysteries in the growing
mind and the absorptive heart of a boy.

*J. Saunders Redding, The Pains of Growing
Up," in* The New York Times Book Review,
February 18, 1951, p. 4.

Owen Dodson with John O'Brien (interview date 1971)

[*In the following excerpt from a 1971 interview
conducted at Dodson's New York apartment, Dodson
talks about his writing and gives his views of other
black writers. The unpublished novel Dodson mentions in his first response was later published as* Come
Home Early, Child *in 1977. According to the interviewer, "At the time [of the interview Dodson] was
convalescing from a recent illness and tired after about
the first hour of conversation. A year later he agreed to
expand on some of his previous answers, which he did
by mail."*]

[O'Brien]: *I know that you wrote a sequel to your first
novel* Boy at the Window. *Why wasn't it ever published?*

[Dodson]: I had proposed to do a series of novels, the
first one of which was *Boy at the Window.* What I
wanted to do was to follow the life of a little boy from
his birth on. I started with *Boy at the Window.* Then I
got a Guggenheim Fellowship and wrote the second
novel which I now have in manuscript form. But I was
told that the novel was not "black enough." Part of it
won a prize in *Paris Review* and was put in *The Best
Short Stories of* THE PARIS REVIEW. Of course, writers
from all over the world were represented there, not just
black writers. In *Soon One Morning* the first chapter of
the novel, "Come Home Early Child," was published.
So the second novel is here, but it ain't "black." It's
about the growing up and fulfillment of a little boy, and
that's why it has not been published. The book of poems
which I have here and which I will read to you from
later is not "black enough" either. They want Nicki
Giovanni poems now. You know these poems. You can
make them up in a minute. You can say: "Look, man, I
am black/Don't you see how black I am?/I'm black as
my fingernails/and I'm black to my toes/and if you smell
me/I am black/And now I want you to give me a
job/because I am black." That's the end of the poem.
You can make them up by the minute. I myself have a
sense of humor about the whole thing.

*Then you have personally felt pressure to write certain
kinds of novels and poems?*

Any writer has got to write about what he sees and what
he feels, his total observation. The black writer is no
different from any other writer. White writers or Chinese writers walk along the same street and they observe
what they observe. Then they put it down on paper. The

black writer has no obligation to "blackness." He's got an obligation to what he sees and what he feels and what he knows. They sent me a letter from Bates College where I had received my undergraduate degree and asked me to join the Black Alumni Association of Bates. I wrote one sentence back: "Did I learn black Latin?" That was the end of that. Yale did the same thing. I didn't answer them at all. I think we have to begin to realize that people are people, they're not black or white or anything. They're themselves. People. And they have their own worth. That's the only thing that we can consider. If we try to do anything else, then we're lost.

Do you have positive feelings about the work being done by young contemporary black writers, writers like LeRoi Jones and Ed Bullins?

Well, I think that the strength and power of a work like Jones' *Dutchman* is tremendous. He had a drama there, he knew about conflict, knew about all the things that were important, that make drama work. So I have a great respect for what he has written in drama but not for what he has written in poetry. I had to lecture recently on Mr. Bullins and other black writers, mostly

Dodson, circa 1933.

dramatists. I had a whole week at Lincoln University to prepare, so I read all of Bullins' things that I could get ahold of. Two weeks ago I read in the *New York Times* that Ed Bullins is one of the greatest dramatists in the world. And I said, "Bullshit!" That's what I said to myself, and that's what I meant. Here was a man who is presenting or thinks he is presenting a whole race and that race is doing nothing but cursing, fucking, and farting. And that's what he writes about. I don't see any spire of meaning, any richness of hope. I just came across a quotation which says that if you don't see any hope in the theater then flee from it. The people have fled from the New Lafayette Theater where Mr. Bullins is Playwright-in-residence. They have fled from it because there is nothing there. What he is doing is feeding garbage to people when that's what they've been brought up on. Garbage. And I know now that playwrights and writers like Richard Wright know that even in the degradation there is something golden in everybody's mind. There is gold even in those people, as you see them walking along Amsterdam, Broadway, and Lenox Avenue. They want to be something else. Richer in their spirits. But they don't know how to do it. The playwrights must say that it can be done. When people talk about praying at the table and all that, that's not important. God has given everybody an intelligence, a mind. That's what we work from. We don't work from God because God has given us what we need and we must use those gifts. You think of people like Richard Wright and Margaret Walker coming out of the depths of the South. They made themselves do it. I just wrote an article about Richard Wright and I tried to say something about this man. What education did he have? He didn't have any education at all. He educated himself. When he got to Brooklyn he wanted to know how to grow vegetables in his little yard, so he got all the books on it (laughing). I think it's ridiculous, but it's kind of wonderful too. Books about seeds and about growth and about how to make the earth fertile. And then he took up physics. And why would he do that? That man was after something. We can't excuse society but we can't excuse ourselves either. Never. We can't excuse ourselves for our behavior.

In your poetry and plays a recurrent theme is religion and history. You have an apocalyptic sense of both. Do you think this characterizes what your central concern is in your writing?

I have written three books of poetry. The first was —I would say—somewhat propaganda, but the third was filled with stories, diaries, and remembrances of Jesus. They are really framed in diaries by Mary, Martha, Joseph, Judas, Jesus, and even God. This, I believe, is my most dedicated work. But I have also been interested in history. A record company asked me to write some kind of history of black people from slavery to their entrance into the United States and now. I did this in *A Dream Awake.* It is illustrated and spoken by James Earl Jones, Josephine Premice, Josh White, Jr. and others who are dedicated to the mainstream of making the world a wide world, a blessed world, a step-in world where all races hold hands and bless God. I have written and fought somehow in my writing, but I know now that the courage and forthrightness of writers and poets will change something a little in our dilapidation. (pp. 56-9)

I know that you were acquainted with many of the writers from the Harlem Renaissance. Did any of them have a direct influence upon your work?

One writer is Langston Hughes. He presented the whole idea of Negro life. He said, "These are my people and I love them and I will live on 127*th* Street and I will grow flowers there." He wrote poems that had such thrust. Langston had a beautiful perception about people. In his will he wanted two things. He said, "Do nothing until you hear from me." And, of course, I've been writing and hearing from him. Second, he wanted a combo at his funeral. And he had a combo—ain't that nice? A combo. The combo was on a little stage. But when the combo came in, Langston had to get out because his coffin was too large for the combo. So they moved him out. Countee Cullen was another influence. He was black and lost because he made—or rather we did—his dedication to society. He wanted to be a lyric poet; that's what he wanted. He didn't want to write all these things about race, but he did. He was pushed into death. They say he died of some blood disease. No! That man was made to die, by himself and by us, because we did not recognize the universal quality of what he wanted to say. In one of his poems he wrote, "Wake up world, O world awake." That's what he wanted to write. He didn't want to write about rioting in old Baltimore. He wanted to write about the lyrical quality of life. (pp. 60-1)

Do you like talking about your novel **Boy at the Window?** *It has been about twenty years since it was first published.*

It's really difficult for me to remember specific things about the novel. Characters take over when you are writing a novel. They tell you what to do. It's very strange. It is no longer your writing. All you have to do is to sit down and begin to put things down on paper. If you want to know something about one of my characters, ask them. Of course, you will never find them. It's like when somebody asks me whether they can use such and such a poem. I say, "What poem?" They tell me the poem and I say, "Well, I didn't even remember it." It is especially difficult to talk about the protagonist, Coin, except to say that he has worked something out for himself when the novel ends. But I can't say where he will go or what he will do. Richard Wright in talking about Bigger Thomas could say a great deal, because Bigger Thomas is such a direct character and he has a direct ending. But Coin is just starting. (p. 61)

> *Owen Dodson and John O'Brien, in an interview in* Interviews with Black Writers, *edited by John O'Brien, Liveright, 1973, pp. 55-61.*

James V. Hatch (essay date 1984)

[*In the following essay, Hatch, an expert on Dodson's life and works and a personal acquaintance, reminisces about an evening he spent with the writer. In a brief preface to the essay, the editor of* Black American Literature Forum *notes: "Hopefully the tribute to Owen Dodson which follows will give readers unfortunate enough not to have met him some sense of the man behind the writing. I don't think it's an exaggeration to say that he was one of the true giants of Afro-American letters. He will, personally and professionally, be deeply missed. This second of two issues devoted to black American poetry is dedicated, with love, to Owen's memory."*]

One autumn, in truth, yesterday, a young playwright invited me to a reading of his new play. The occasion was to be held near 8th Avenue, two or three blocks from Owen's New York City apartment, so I asked him to accompany me, thinking that the playwright would benefit from the critique and that the outing might please Owen.

When I called at Owen's flat, his sister Edith opened the door. Owen, wrapped in his velvet cape with his embroidered cap on his head, sat with his steel crutches gleaming against the red plush sofa. His moustache was neatly trimmed, and he touched his new spectacles, which made his eyes large and luminous.

"Chile, ain't these something? Don't they make me look like Dr. Eckleburg from what's his name's novel? I think they're kinda wonderful, don't you? Makes me seem wide-eyed with wonderment."

He refused my offer to bring a cab and committed himself to the walk on foot. His neighborhood was not the best, and I sometimes worried that he was an easy mark for young hoodlums. As he swung along, he spoke to a sullen man who supported himself against an iron grate of a store window, and to a woman in a doorway who guarded her shopping bags of rags and memories. "How ya doin'?" Whether surprised by the greeting from an elegant gentleman, or by the sudden reminder that they still had the use of their legs, these street souls responded, "Evenin'." "Can't complain." "How you?"

When we arrived where the reading was to be, we were confronted by two steep flights of wooden stairs, no elevator. I cursed. Why hadn't I asked before dragging him here? Owen handed me the crutches. "I'll pull myself up by the hand railing." And so we began our ascent, step by step by step, with me close behind, braced if he should fall. Before we reached the halfway, two young men appeared from the top to offer assistance. Owen refused them gently and, after a moment to catch his breath, climbed on. He remained strong in his arms and even his legs, but the steel ball-joints in his hips had never worked properly. He shunned the physical therapist. When I would press him on this point, saying the exercises were necessary for his legs, lest they degenerate, he would shake his head. "It doesn't matter ... doesn't matter."

At the top, I introduced Owen to the playwright. I impressed the young man with his good fortune—he had in his audience an artist who had written over twenty produced plays, who had directed a hundred shows, and who had led many talents to the discovery of their own genius. However, the attention of this writer, as it must be in nascent talent, was absorbed with his own womb's issue. We filed into the rows of steel chairs to witness the drama, a play that harbored a curious emotional power, somehow imprisoned in an improbable story of Vietnam veterans in a bar.

When the curtain came down, the writer invited us all to make comments so that he might be guided in his rewrites. The actors spoke of their characters, the audience complained of confusion, and because I couldn't get a handle on what the problem was, I said something useless about the plot. Then Owen spoke: "This play is about love, the love of two men, one black and one white, who become as brothers in Vietnam. But once in America, they can not find a way to express this love, physically or verbally, so they fight."

The mystery revealed! I was stunned. Owen had placed his finger upon the soul of the play. I looked at the writer expecting to see revelation upon his face; there was none. He hadn't understood because the play had come from a place within him that he did not yet know.

Later, as we crept along the dark street home, I extolled Owen's insights, and apologized that my student had not responded to them. "It's all right," he said, pausing before his building to find his keys; "if he continues to write, he'll find himself. Wanta come up for a drink?"

As we rode up in the elevator, my mind went back to 1958 to Professor Reardon's playwriting workshop at the University of Iowa. There, Ted Shine, myself, and other young talents attempted our first plays. Into our workshop one day, a guest, a black writer, a professor from Howard University, a poet whom *Time* magazine had called a peer to Frost, a man without glasses, strode briskly in with an entourage of local dignitaries. That day, Owen spoke to us, chatting about people and things of the theatre. He was, at first hearing, a shameless storyteller and a gossip. He would seize upon the famous and near-great with gentle malice. He delighted in the naughtiness of people and the exposure of their vanities. He made us all feel warm and cozy in the sauce of our own laughter. I was young then and, of course, didn't need to write any of it down on paper.

After the talk, Ted introduced me to Owen, who had a way of paying each person a particular and unhurried attention, as though he searched for the wonderment in you. I sensed that Ted held this man in a special reverence, but in my ignorance and racism, I assumed Ted's respect rested upon their both being black writers. It would be many years, and after many knocks on heart and head, before I would meet Owen again and before I learned what Ted Shine had known so long before.

The elevator reached the penthouse floor, and when Owen let us into the apartment, the rooms were silent; Edith had gone to bed. "There's a bottle of champagne in the refrigerator, and glasses in the cabinet opposite. Take them to the living room. I want to read you a new poem."

I found the champagne, half a bottle that had been recorked. I poured two glasses and settled into a deep chair to wait. The room's distinction was not its floor-to-ceiling books, its square grand piano, or even the paintings crowding the walls—not even the man-high candelabra that he lent out to concerts, or the wooden horse he planned to leave to the Brooklyn Children's Museum. These treasures were not possessions. Rather, each object seemed to have chosen to live with Owen; like exotic creatures from the world over, they had come to Owen's living room to nestle there.

Presently, he rocked in on his walker, gripping two yellow legal sheets, scribbled over in a large hand. At the time he had been composing poems for **The Harlem Book of the Dead,** a collaboration with Camille Billops and James Van Der Zee. He took a long sip of champagne, put down the glass, and read the poem that would be the final one in the book. He read slowly, twisting the paper to follow his inserts and rewrites. When he concluded, he took another sip of wine and said, "I'll read it again." He loved to read his own work, especially new poems. Sometimes he would ring me late at night. I never stopped him to say that he had read that same poem to me the night before; he knew he had; he wished to read the poem again. And he read magnificently. Years of theatre had taught him how to sing.

He finished and looked up. I nodded. The poem had startled me with its images, that unique signature Owen had, his blend of classic and folk, his voice of erudition and innocence, his ambivalence between submission and defiance. "When I die," he mused, "I would like to leave some memorable line . . . like Keats and Auden." He emptied his glass and poured another.

I looked at him. Owen was in no wise a perfect man; he could be jealous, self-pitying, and even mean. Yet, he was one of nature's noblemen. He had become like an old tai chi master; the lucidity of his art had become indistinguishable from the grace he afforded lies. He nudged me from my thoughts. "Chile, listen to these lines." He sipped again, then read again. I gave him a hug and walked out into a starless New York night. All the way home, part of a poem, one of the many that reconciled Owen to his death, sang in my mind.

> We will be the good-byes never said
> The farewells fortunetellers never glimpse
> All our farewells cry to thee
> Hammer on thy house!
> A hail of farewells!
> Are you awake
> with your eyes shut?

On June 21, 1983, Owen died. We "hammer on thy house a hail of farewells," but "sorrow is the only faithful one." (pp. 3-4)

James V. Hatch, "All Our Farewells Cry to Thee: A Memory of an Evening with Owen Dodson," in Black American Literature Forum, Vol. 18, No. 1, Spring, 1984, pp. 3-4.

C. James Trotman (essay date 1986)

[*In the following essay, Trotman closely examines* Powerful Long Ladder, *Dodson's first poetry collection.*]

Except for an occasional listing here and there, Owen Dodson's first collection of poems entitled *Powerful Long Ladder* (1946) has not received any serious written attention by the intellectual community and by literary scholars. This is a strange form of neglect because, until his death in June, 1983, Owen Dodson was known for his literary, cultural and academic accomplishments, ranging from his successful novel *Boy At The Window* to a multi-media presentation of his poetry done as recently as May 3, 1982, under the auspices of Joseph Papp and The Public Theatre in New York City. Before then, Dodson had been chairman and a member of the Drama Department at Howard University from 1947 until his retirement in 1970. Moreover, the neglect is regrettable because *Powerful Long Ladder* is an important book of American poetry and, in a particular manner, it adds substantively to collections of poetry, from Phillis Wheatley to Maya Angelou, expressing the development of American and Black American poetry in the United States.

Powerful Long Ladder is divided into five sections. Each varies in mood and texture, style and technique, but it does not exaggerate a reading of the collection to say that each section is calibrated to contribute to the book's major theme suggested by the title: to climb a ladder, which is to say that to go beyond the given, one must be willing to reach out over one's head and pull one's self up. The figure evokes images of struggle, sacrifice and searching—but to what end? In Dodson's poetry, the ends are practical though the routes are spiritual and psychological; and the passions for human understanding, freedom and love are goals to replace a world of experiences in which indifference, injustice and hate prevail.

We can do better, Dodson seems to suggest in these poems, and the reassurances are there for all who are interested in improving the quality of human life. Idealism is very much a part of the pitch one hears in this volume; however, it would be a mistake to think that this is poetry which shuns genuine feelings. The range is not only wide in its vision of human life, it also offers a broad scale in which the notes are sometimes somber, sometimes humorous, encouraging us to pause and reflect on the most cataclysmic personal struggles; and then sometimes we are, I think, seemingly urged to just sit back and allow a skillful writer to promenade with the rhymes and rhythms of his chosen craft.

Part one takes its title from the book, and we hear a lyrical voice which is resolute and determined to speak for those who won't or cannot speak because experience has paralyzed them, or they lack human recognition. Readers familiar with the poetry of Robert Frost and Langston Hughes will recall through Dodson the effective use of a controlling, sometimes omniscient voice in the lyric mode. In **"Lament,"** for example, the first poem, we see something of the demands Dodson presents to his readers. The poem begins with a directive to the dead: "Wake up, boy, and tell me how you died." Responding to the grief of death, the narrator's imperative dramatizes the futility of the situation. Its chief purpose is to remind us that while we cannot actually know death (or freedom or fear, or love, or other abstractions) we can nevertheless feel its power.

Not all of the poems in this first section carry their resolve in this way. **"Guitar,"** with its uses of the ballad, and **"Sorrow Is The Only Faithful One,"** with its studied contrast between nature and human nature, are two poems which emphasize a complex vision of human nature. Not very far into reading this volume does one proceed before becoming aware of the breadth of Dodson's vision. With Frostian detachment and Hughes' social sensitivity, Dodson makes **"The Signifying Darkness"** a journey into a private and public terror where the devastations of war and the ravages of cultural racism are like bomb craters on a map of humanity too blinded by its folly to see the ruins. The darkness that Dodson describes is at once existential in its suggestion of an indifferent universe; it is cultural atrophy; and it is the personal anguish, to use the poet's words, of human "condescension, greed and charity." The psychological invisibility being addressed in the poem is a theme in Afro-American writing that has received a great deal of attention from the outstanding contemporary example of *Invisible Man,* Ralph Ellison's modern masterpiece, where symbol and myth are two of the extraordinary techniques used in the novel. In Dodson's poem, the theme of psychological invisibility has mythic overtones. Pristine imagery opens the poem ("There was an evil darkness way before / The war rose clear, a darkness before that dawn"); and the poem closes on an image of human destruction as "The black, wet face / of a dark mother staring at . . . her boy." Beside its own qualities as a poem **"Signifying Darkness"** joins **"Black Mother Praying"** as one of several poems in which the poet is writing from a viewpoint that is both ethnocentric and universal.

In *Modern Poetry and the Tradition* (1939), Cleanth Brooks wrote that "a healthy tradition is capable of a continual modification." This is a helpful comment because several of Dodson's poems focus on familiar subjects. What are we to make of **"Epitaph for a Negro Woman"** and **"Black Mother Praying"** by Dodson when we have Paul Laurence Dunbar's "When Malindy Sings" and Langston Hughes' frequently anthologized and graceful "Mother to Son" and "The Negro Mother"? The Dodson poems also appear in this first section and it is clear that they owe their inspiration to other poems and people. An analysis of styles, language and metrical techniques would lead a reader to the conclusion that Dodson, like Hughes and Dunbar before him, knows how to control the elegy and to sustain his focus, but we would still be left without a response to the similarities existing between these poems. Others have also articulated a need to know about these similarities. Wellek and Warren, for example, remind us that literacy genres never remain fixed; with each new work a category shifts as our experiences with literature (and life) modify our conception of a literary kind. An analysis might yield a "winner" in some strange sense of literary competition, but it would not tell us about the poetry in the poems.

What these poems by Dodson bring is not worn imagery but renewed vigor and insight into poetry, the role of black women in the struggle for liberation and the role of women affirming their maternal and sexual contribu-

tions to human life. **"Epitaph for a Negro Woman"** is a dirge where even in death the only true companion is growing moss. **"Black Mother Praying"** returns the reader to the more familiar struggle of the individual seeking to find personal meaning in a society tearing itself apart; "And [where] Freedom is writ big and crossed out." The fullness of these women in Dodson's poetry is due to their stature. They are heroes. They are reminders in Afro-American life of the wealth of human potential frequently lost in the depersonalized, racist patterns of modern society. They are also symbols for a larger humanity, particularly women, because of the broad social canvas Dodson presents.

The centerpiece for the first section is **"Someday We're Gonna Tear Them Pillars Down."** It deserves our attention for several reasons. It is here that we find the book's title and, because it is verse drama, it is the first time we see Dodson employing this proscenium art. This form gives the poet more freedom to explore with greater metaphorical richness the personal need to be determined and stubborn about retaining the dignity of

Dodson at the 1952 Festival of Negro Poets in Jackson, Mississippi. Standing at rear (left to right): Arna Bontemps, Melvin B. Tolson, Jacob Reddix, Dodson, and Robert Hayden. Seated: Sterling Brown, Zora Neale Hurston, Margaret Walker, and Langston Hughes.

our lives. It isn't easy; transcendence never is, since nature and circumstance usually intrude. Dodson's poem takes us back to chattel slavery, a symbolic time when the human condition was at its lowest. Men who enslave men are themselves slaves, and Dodson personifies the voices of fear, doubt, cynicism and despair in order to suggest how much hope may have existed in spite of the dark midnight of that hour. As one might expect, the poem dramatizes its conflict by taking its readers through a series of images which thematically render the distortion that accompanied this spiritual holocaust. Fire does not warn, characters shiver in the heat of mid-day, and the simple expressions of song are "poisonous." Even the very air lacks comfort and support while freedom, the poem says, is "a story they tell that never happen."

Dodson was a careful writer and a careful observer of human behavior who reminds us of the longing to overcome barriers. When the longing becomes part of our selves, and our consciousness, it appears "like a miracle bird." The ideal and real clash in the poem when the voices of those requiring some form of assurance that everything will work out are juxtaposed to others expressing with equal determination that no such promise can be given. While a symbolic leader for the downtrodden does appear in the poem, the imagery carries the message: The ladder of the title is a symbol to be used for reaching out and up for the bird of freedom. Yet there is restraint. The leader admonishes his followers not to try and grab the bird but to allow it to serve as a source of inspiration for all to take on the risky business of attempting to be free.

The pillars, like the walls of Robert Frost's famous poem, "Mending Wall," are common symbols for human barriers, but Dodson, characteristically expansive in his thoughts, may have been thinking about aesthetics and craftsmanship as pillars to demolish also in order to reach a plane of artistic accomplishment. Dodson wrote about this concept in 1980, and with similar imagery, in an essay entitled **"Who Has Seen The Wind"**:

> Beginning to master any art, especially playwriting, is an arduous, sometimes torturous task. A play is never fulfilled by one person: There are the producer, the director, the actors, designers, and, above all, the audience. But before these run interference, the writer must face the thick walls of craftsmanship, figuring how to blast until they come tumbling down and he can enter the inner city of whatever life he chooses to portray. Some don't have to use the dynamite of experimentation; they walk into their city casually, almost carelessly, by themselves, tipping their hats to acquaintances, finding friends and family, sleeping with lovers, revealing the themes surrounding them astutely. But they are rare.

Dodson's interest in freedom for the individual would of course include examples. This is the intent surrounding the poem honoring Samuel Chapman Armstrong, who founded Hampton Institute, and the two white women, Miss Packard and Miss Giles, who founded Spelman College for (to use the historical term) Negro women in Georgia.

If a reader moves through the book in the order in which the poems are presented, as I have done, one is likely to feel growth with the next two sections, "Three Choruses from a Verse Drama: Divine Comedy" and "Poems for My Brother Kenneth." The spiritual themes of transcendence from human misery and sorrow certainly recall previously mentioned poems such as **"Someday We're Gonna Tear Them Pillars Down"** and **"Sorrow Is The Only Faithful One."** The familiarity, which is not to be confused with redundancy or stale imagery, is welcomed because it allows us to enjoy the poet working in concentration.

"Divine Comedy," with its allusion to Dante's world masterpiece in the title is, like its literary forebear, a study in faith. The sensibility that pervades Dodson's work is distinctively modern, yet the tone of the poem makes it more like its ancestor than the appropriation of a famous title. Here, as in Dante, the lyrical voice of the poet is submerged into the content of the dramatization by the poet's use of multiple personae. Some, in fact most, are allegorical figures representing groups (youth, a vacillating community, the chorus, a temple priest) whose presence is not felt by what they say to one another but what they say to us as readers. They cry out for "liberty, and peace and freedom," essential goals for experiencing human potential, which is exactly the vision they lack. In rendering these empty, despairing voices the poetry elevates their condition to the level at which the pain and confusion are not only felt but can be applied universally. For example, the despair is reflected in the barrenness of speech: no one has more than several lines, and the words in the lines are stark and linguistically stripped to the most elemental expressions:

> Chorus:
> Where are the mirrors to show us normal
> To pain
> Love
> Hate
> Kindness?
> To show we love our children?
>
> Crazy Woman:
> We need a new star to live on.
> The wind is fierce here.
> I have rheumatism, arthritis, and cancer in
>   my left armpit.
> The wind is fierce here and my heart . . .
>
> One:
> Run before the wind slashes us together
>
> Another:
> Rip up the pavement and hide
>
> Another:
> Hide in the closets with automatic locks
>
> Another:
> Run into darkness for safety
>
> Another:
> Run to the attic

Another:
> The cellar

Another:
> Run!!!

Old Man:
> If you run, the city hounds are faster,
> The country hounds are more practiced.
> Stand here and lean against each other.

Chorus:
> Cancel us,
> Let doomsday come down
> Like the foot of God on us.

What moves us, however, in the verse dramatization is not the situation, because we have become conditioned to lonely voices in world and modern literatures. We are moved by the prospect of hope and the silent, powerful meditation that is called prayer.

Dodson is not proselytizing for a specific religious organization but for an awakening that is spiritual, inwardly directed and personal. The process is poetic, the symbols are recognizable (Christian, literary) and the journey is a sort of flight into feeling and moral enlightenment. This is what Dr. Johnson meant when he wrote: "The natural flights of the human mind are not from pleasure to pleasure, but from hope to hope." Dodson's poetry presents the same theme when a character at the end says to the masses:

> I know, Lord, I know the deep well side of
>   life ....
> The power and the glory.

"Poems for My Brother Kenneth," like *Divine Comedy,* is a separate section in the book, not a long one, but it stirs and touches. This section reminds one of Tennyson when he writes (from "In Memoriam"), "I sometimes hold it half a sin / To put in words the grief I feel / For words, like Nature half reveal / And half conceal the Soul within." This is the sensibility pervading this section: the struggle to find the strength to transform human pain. In addition to Tennyson, other poems and poets writing in English have brought dignity to the lyric-romantic tradition of poems about death. One hopes every school child would know Milton's "Lycidas," Donne's "Death Be Not Proud" and perhaps Gray's "Elegy in a Country Church-Yard." I mention these to acknowledge Dodson's participation in this tradition. For in spite of many social gains, the black writer remains the most oppressed figure in the publishing world because so many, many reviewers (readers of manuscripts, in particular) cannot conceive of the black writer dramatizing much that is not bare-knuckled racism. The poems for Kenneth contain some of Dodson's most beautiful writing in the collection and, like other good poems on the subject, they add something special to our vocabulary for struggling with grief and the inexorable human journey toward death. For example, in Section IV, the transformation of grief into a new enthusiasm is wrapped in child-like innocence, for memory and vividness make the poet assert that "There

is a new language to learn / And I am learning like a truant child." But it is better to see the lines in their whole:

> My chief citizen is dead
> And my town at half-mast:
> Even in speech
> Even in walking,
> Even in seeing
> The busy streets where he stood
> And the room where he was host to his friends
> And his enemies, where we erased the night to
>   dawn
> With conversation of what I had seen and he had
>   seen
> And done and written during the space of time we
>   were apart.

With Dodson scorning the image of helpless mankind, we might expect that his spirit would not yield before the image of death in human life. This is in fact what we find in Section VIII where the poet's mind declares the figure of death a charlatan leaving itself in a world without a world. The small section is worth quoting:

> Death, split-second guest, negative magician
> When will you believe you are not final?

After the Kenneth poems comes **"All This Review."** If we can appropriate the language of music for describing this section, we can call it a melody of focused themes in which the orchestration of content and craft moves closest to realizing itself in a single voice. The themes of self-reliance and self-determination are here, but the most impressive characteristic is the lyricism itself.

In **"When I Am Dead"** and **"Countee Cullen,"** an encomium for the distinguished poet of the Harlem Renaissance, the lines sparkle with reversals and ironies. From the first and last stanzas:

> Now begins the sleep, my friend:
> Where the cold dirt blanket is, you will be warm,
> Where seeds begin to root, you will flower.
>   and, ...
> Also in your brave and tender singing
> We hear all mankind yearning
> For a new year without hemlock in our glasses.

"Circle One" and **"Circle Two"** which follow are epigrams, with the trochaic foot carrying the metrical stress for these intellectual exercises. **"All This Review,"** the title piece, is a love song of lost innocence and unrequited love. Here one finds Dodson being conventional with the lyric tradition in poetry by seeking that correspondence between nature and human nature, taking imaginative flights that stimulate thought and action in order to relieve the burdens of an uneasy spirit and turning, as in **"The Verdict," "The Reunion," "I Break the Sky,"** and **"That Star,"** to the incidents of yearnings; or, as in the words from **"That Star,"** "Loves hours, only hours, never light."

"Counterpoint" is the concluding section of *Powerful Long Ladder.* It contains strong poems on established social and psychological themes; and we do not tire of them because the imagery is sharpened by exquisite phrasing. In **"Jonathan's Song,"** subtitled **"A Negro Saw The Jewish Pageant, 'We Will Never Die,'"** demonstrates Dodson's universal vision and his commitment to a spiritual view of humanity:

> I am part of this
> Memorial to suffering,
> Militant strength:
> I am a Jew.

Dodson's social consciousness, as Margaret Just Butcher has written, is also the subject of **"Conversation on V"** where race and war are Dodson's focus. But **"Iphigenia,"** because of its allusion through the title to the Greek myth of social innocence and ritualized sacrifice, has special significance. Its use of myth reminds one of Dodson's broad view of the materials capable of rendering authentically the truth of humanity; in **"The Watching"** Dodson turns to the Biblical saga of Samson to once again use material from the broadest elements of western culture to depict modern anguish and human fear.

The final four poems are compelling in their assertion of human potential and the risks involved; in fact they may be seen as lyrical refrains on the book's themes of hope and struggle, but they are presented with a vigor that derives from the craftman's growing confidence in the truth of his vision and the agility with which he is saying it.

"Definition" has an ingenuous quality about its development. The first line establishes this tone: "Everyone says: fate is a bad number, ... " Dodson's development in the poem leads to a challenge against that received perspective. In the third quatrain he writes: "Fate is ourselves awake and asleep." And to make the point more emphatic he turns to one of his favorite sources for the expression of human truth, Christianity and its rituals, by writing that:

> ...Fate is the collection plate
> Of our sins and our loves—variety of coins,
> Stored away or stolen by fakirs
> Who blame the plus or minus of our condition
> On God or Devil or the sound of the sea.

There is a sense in which what **"Definition"** begins by way of reconstructing our perceptions of human possibilities continues in the remaining three poems. In **"The Precedent"** the poem moves from a description of nature desecrated by man to the poetic assertion of a new day which is, like the inexplicable in nature, itself "A precedent: spring will come / Like fire to the snow." In other words, there will be a rebirth, it is inexorable, and it will lead to a better day.

"Martha Graham" is about doing something to improve our common lot in the face of adversity. The imagery of the poem is full of signs and symbols for our technical capabilities for making war—indeed, there is some prescience here, a wisdom in the aftermath of WW II—

that rings all too familiar to the contemporary reader, and it is born out of the poet's search for a new vision.

> There is the world chasing the world
> In the dark, in the spaceless dark
> While the moon hides terrified
> At the mechanical cannon bark.

What are we to do? We are to "Dance them out of the speechless dark / Into the talking day." This, of course, is a symbol for human action, using the name of an artist most closely identified with modernizing the dance and revitalizing its forms to mirror the signs of our times.

"Open Letter" is an anthem. It is a paean and a plea for humanity to close ranks and to permit the time "when peace surrounds us like a credible universe."

As one might expect from a poet whose work engages reality and especially the dark side of experience, there are perspectives, sometimes even philosophies, and human truths to be found in this collection. Perhaps the largest among them is the necessary struggle of the human predicament to know that there is struggle and conflict, handicap and pain. It is sometimes brought on by war, racism, poverty, loneliness and misunderstanding; but it is painful. And that human pain, Dodson's poetry suggests, not only defines our common humanity but can lead to visions of independence and spiritual wealth, to sights and sounds of the impossible made possible by each of us. That statement on human potential is not going to be accepted by all, if that matters, but what is certain is the experience of responding to the verbal orchestration, the measured steps, that brought us to the point of making that decision for ourselves. (pp. 96-107)

> *C. James Trotman, "The Measured Steps of a Powerful Long Ladder: The Poetry of Owen Dodson," in* Obsidian II, *Vol. I, Nos. 1 and 2, Spring-Summer, 1986, pp. 96-107.*

FURTHER READING

Hatch, James V. "Owen Dodson: Excerpts from a Biography in Progress." *The Massachusetts Review* XXVIII, No. 4 (Winter 1987): 627-41.

    Revised and expanded version of Hatch's article "All Our Farewells Cry To Thee: A Memory of an Evening with Owen Dodson" (see essay dated 1984).

———; Ward, Douglas A. M.; and Weixlmann, Joe. "The Rungs of a Powerful Long Ladder: An Owen Dodson Bibliography." *Black American Literature Forum* 14, No. 2 (Summer 1980): 60-8.

    Comprehensive bibliography of works by and about Dodson.

Kramer, Aaron. "Remembering Owen Dodson." *Freedomways* 23, No. 4 (Fourth Quarter 1983): 258-69.
> Reminiscence of Dodson by Kramer, a poet and friend.

North, Jessica Nelson. "Somber and Real." *Poetry* LXIX, No. III (December 1946): 175-77.
> Mildly laudatory review of *Powerful Long Ladder.*

Peterson, Bernard L., Jr. "The Legendary Owen Dodson of Howard University: His Contributions to the American Theatre." *The Crisis* 86, No. 9 (November 1979): 373-74, 376-78.
> Retrospective of Dodson's work in the theater.

Rosenthal, M. L. "Ideas Fused with Fire." *The New York Herald Tribune Weekly Book Review* 23, No. 3 (16 March 1947): 12.
> Review of *Powerful Long Ladder,* determining that Dodson has the power "to discover the best way to release a tremendous store of emotional and moral power."

Frederick Douglass

1817?-1895

(Born Frederick Augustus Washington Bailey) American lecturer, autobiographer, editor, essayist, and novella writer.

Douglass is recognized as one of the most distinguished black writers of nineteenth-century America. Born into slavery, he escaped in 1838 and subsequently devoted his considerable rhetorical skills to the abolitionist movement. Expounding the theme of racial equality in stirring, invective-charged orations and newspaper editorials in the 1840s, 1850s, and 1860s, he was recognized by his peers as an outstanding orator and the foremost black abolitionist of his era. Douglass's current reputation as a powerful and effective prose writer is based primarily on his 1845 autobiography *Narrative of the Life of Frederick Douglass, an American Slave, Written by Himself.* Regarded as one of the most compelling antislavery documents ever written, the *Narrative* is also valued as an eloquent argument for human rights. As such, it has transcended its immediate historical milieu and is now regarded as a landmark in American autobiography.

The son of a black slave and an unidentified white man, Douglass was separated from his mother in his infancy. Nurtured by his maternal grandmother on the Tuckahoe, Maryland, estate of Captain Aaron Anthony, he enjoyed a relatively happy childhood until he was pressed into service on the plantation of Anthony's employer, Colonel Edward Lloyd. There Douglass endured the rigors of slavery. In 1825, Douglass was transferred to the Baltimore household of Hugh Auld, who inadvertently provided Douglass with his first critical insight into the slavery system. In an incident that Douglass described as a "revelation," he overheard Auld rebuke his wife for teaching the boy the rudiments of reading. Deducing that ignorance perpetuated subjugation, Douglass undertook reading as an avenue to freedom. His secret efforts to educate himself—aided by *Webster's Spelling Book* and the random instruction of white playmates—were fruitful: obtaining a copy of *The Columbian Orator,* a popular collection of writings on democratic themes, he avidly studied the speeches of Richard Brinsley Sheridan, Charles James Fox, and other advocates of liberty. Douglass grew restive as his desire for freedom increased, and he was eventually sent to be disciplined, or "broken," by Edward Covey. When he refused to submit to Covey's beatings and instead challenged him in a violent confrontation, Douglass overcame an important psychological barrier to freedom. In 1838, he realized his long-cherished goal by escaping to New York.

Once free, Douglass quickly became a prominent figure in the abolitionist movement. In 1841, he delivered his first public address—a moving extemporaneous speech at an antislavery meeting in Nantucket, Massachusetts—and was invited by William Lloyd Garrison and other abolitionist leaders to work as a lecturer for the Massachusetts Antislavery Society. Sharing the podium with such renowned orators as Garrison and Wendell Phillips, he served successfully in that capacity for four years. By 1845, Douglass's eloquent and cogent oratory had led many to doubt that he was indeed a former slave. When urged by supporters to authenticate his experience, he responded with a detailed account of his slave life, the *Narrative of the Life of Frederick Douglass,* which was an immediate popular success. Liable to capture under the fugitive slave laws, Douglass fled the United States in late 1845 and traveled to Great Britain, where he was honored by the great reformers of the day. Returning to the United States in 1847, he received sufficient funds to purchase his freedom and establish *The North Star,* a weekly abolitionist newspaper.

During the 1850s and early 1860s, Douglass continued his activities as a journalist, abolitionist speaker, and autobiographer. After splitting with Garrison over the issue of disunion, he aligned himself with Gerrit Smith's conservative Liberty Party and marked the change by rechristening his periodical *Frederick Douglass' Paper.* By the outbreak of the Civil War, Douglass had emerged as a nationally recognized spokesman for black Americans and, in 1863, he advised President Abraham Lincoln on the use and treatment of black soldiers in the Union Army. Douglass then founded *The New National Era,* a short-lived newspaper, and delivered numerous addresses on the lyceum lecture circuit, but his last years were chiefly devoted to political and diplomatic assignments. When he revised his final autobiographical work, the *Life and Times of Frederick Douglass, Written by Himself* (1881), he was able to record numerous political honors, including presidential assignments as assistant secretary to the Santo Domingo Commission, marshal of the District of Columbia, and United States minister resident and consul-general to the Republic of Haiti. Douglass died at his home in Anacostia Heights, D.C., in 1895.

In his speeches on abolition, Douglass frequently drew on his first-hand experience of slavery to evoke pathos in his audience. He is most often noted, however, for his skillful use of scorn and irony in denouncing the slave system and its abettors. One of the stock addresses in his abolitionist repertoire was a "slaveholder's sermon" in which he sarcastically mimicked a pro-slavery minister's travesty of the biblical injunction to "do unto others as you would have them do unto you." His most famous speech, an address delivered on 5 July 1852 in Rochester, N.Y., commonly referred to as the "Fourth of July Oration," is a heavily ironic reflection on the significance of Independence Day for slaves. Douglass was described by a contemporary critic as being "particularly obnoxious to... those in general who mix up character and color, man and his skin—to all, in short, who have little hearts and muddy heads," and he is occasionally criticized for indiscriminate severity and humorlessness. In general, however, his polemical techniques are praised as commendable attributes of reformist oratory. Douglass's postbellum orations are regarded as more intellectual—and by many critics as less artistic—than his abolitionist addresses. In J. Saunders Redding's words, he had become a "finished public speaker" by the 1880s, "more concerned with intellectual than emotional responses."

A similar estimate has been made of Douglass's powers as an autobiographer. Critics generally agree that, in retelling and updating his life history in *My Bondage and My Freedom* (1855) and the *Life and Times of Frederick Douglass,* Douglass provided a classic American story of struggle and achievement but failed to recapture the artistic vitality of the *Narrative.* Valued by historians as a detailed, credible account of slave life, the *Narrative* is widely acclaimed as an artfully compressed yet extraordinarily expressive story of self-discovery and self-liberation. Recording his personal reactions to bondage in such unaffected yet moving passages as his apostrophe to the vessels sailing free on the Chesapeake Bay and his account of his confrontation with Edward Covey, Douglass distinguished himself from most other slave narrators, who often leaned toward embellishment.

Appealing variously to the political, sociological, and aesthetic interests of successive generations of critics, Douglass has maintained an enviable reputation as an orator and prose writer. Douglass's contemporaries, who were influenced by Garrison and other abolitionist sympathizers, viewed him primarily as a talented antislavery agitator whose manifest abilities as an orator and writer refuted the idea of black inferiority. This view persisted until the 1930s, when both Vernon Loggins and J. Saunders Redding called attention to the "intrinsic merit" of Douglass's writing and acknowledged him to be the most important figure in nineteenth-century black American literature. In the 1940s and 1950s, Alain Locke and Benjamin Quarles respectively pointed to the *Life and Times of Frederick Douglass* and the *Narrative* as classic works that symbolize the black role of protest, struggle, and aspiration in American life. Led by Albert E. Stone, Robert B. Stepto, and Houston A. Baker, Jr., Douglass's critics have become far more exacting in recent years, for they have analyzed—and usually praised—the specific narrative strategies that Douglass employed in the *Narrative* to establish a distinctly individual black identity. Stepto's recent examination of Douglass's long-neglected novella, *The Heroic Slave* (1853), testifies to the growing recognition of Douglass's narrative skills.

Distinguished by praise and diversity, the history of critical response to Douglass's works may be taken as an indication of their abiding interest. As G. Thomas Couser has observed, Douglass was a remarkable man who lived in an exceptionally tumultuous period in American history. His works are among the best mirrors of their age: lucid, probing, and analytical—strong testaments to the abolitionist spirit and humankind's ardent desire for freedom and self-expression.

(For further information about Douglass's life and works, see *Concise Dictionary of American Literary Biography, 1640-1865; Dictionary of Literary Biography,* Vols. 1, 43, 50; *Nineteenth-Century Literature Criticism,* Vol. 7; and *Something about the Author,* Vol. 29. For related criticism, see the entry on American Slave Narratives in *Nineteenth-Century Literature Criticism,* Vol. 20.)

PRINCIPAL WORKS

Narrative of the Life of Frederick Douglass, an American Slave, Written by Himself (autobiography) 1845
Oration, Delivered in Corinthian Hall, Rochester, by Frederick Douglass, July 5th, 1852 (speech) 1852
The Heroic Slave (novella) 1853; published in *Autographs for Freedom*
The Claims of the Negro Ethnologically Considered (speech) 1854
My Bondage and My Freedom (autobiography) 1855

Men of Color, to Arms! (essay) 1863
"What the Black Man Wants" (speech) 1865; published in *The Equality of All Men before the Law Claimed and Defended in Speeches by Hon. William D. Kelley, Wendell Phillips, and Frederick Douglass*
John Brown (speech) 1881
Life and Times of Frederick Douglass, Written by Himself (autobiography) 1881; also published as *Life and Times of Frederick Douglass, Written by Himself* [revised edition], 1892
The Life and Writings of Frederick Douglass. 5 vols. (letters, speeches, and essays) 1950-75
The Frederick Douglass Papers. 2 vols. (speeches and debates) 1979-82

Nathaniel Peabody Rogers (essay date 1841)

[*The following laudatory account of one of Douglass's early abolitionist addresses originally appeared on 5 December 1841 in the* Herald of Freedom. *Here, in testifying to Douglass's commanding physical presence and exceptional oratorical ability, Rogers treats Douglass as a living challenge to slavery and the notion of black inferiority.*]

The fugitive Douglass was up when we entered. This is an extraordinary man. He was cut out for a hero. In a rising for Liberty, he would have been a Toussaint or a Hamilton. He has the "heart to conceive, the head to contrive, and the hand to execute." A commanding person—over six feet, we should say, in height, and of most manly proportions. His head would strike a phrenologist amid a sea of them in Exeter Hall, and his voice would ring like a trumpet in the field. Let the South congratulate herself that he is a *fugitive.* It would not have been safe for her if he had remained about the plantations a year or two longer . . . . As a speaker he has few equals. It is not declamation—but oratory, power of debate. He watches the tide of discussion with the eye of the veteran, and dashes into it at once with all the tact of the forum or the bar. He has wit, argument, sarcasm, pathos—all that first-rate men show in their master efforts. His voice is highly melodious and rich, and his enunciation quite elegant, and yet he has been but two or three years out of the house of bondage. We noticed that he had strikingly improved, since we heard him at Dover in September. We say thus much of him, for he is esteemed by our multitude as of an inferior race. We should like to see him before any New England legislature or bar, and let him feel the freedom of the anti-slavery meeting, and see what would become of his inferiority. Yet he is a *thing,* in American estimate. He is the chattel of some pale-faced tyrant. How his owner would cower and shiver to hear him thunder in an antislavery hall! How he would shrink away, with his infernal whip, from his flaming eye when kindled with anti-slavery emotion! And the brotherhood of thieves, . . . we wish a hecatomb or two of the proudest

and flintiest of them, were obliged to hear him thunder for human liberty, and lay the enslavement of his people at their doors. They would tremble like Belshazzar. (pp. 99-100)

Nathaniel Peabody Rogers, in an extract from "'Magnificent Orator',' in Frederick Douglass, *edited by Benjamin Quarles, Prentice-Hall, Inc., 1968, pp. 99-100.*

William Lloyd Garrison (essay date 1845)

[*Garrison was a nationally recognized leader in the abolitionist movement and a key figure in Douglass's rise to public prominence. The first person to publicly acknowledge Douglass's speaking abilities, Garrison subsequently advised him early in his career as an antislavery agent and promoted his speeches and writings in his influential abolitionist newspaper,* The Liberator. *In the following essay, which was originally published as the preface to the 1845 edition of the* Narrative of the Life of Frederick Douglass, *he records his passionate reaction to Douglass's first public address, praises his influence and skill as a public speaker, and recommends the* Narrative *as an authentic and unexaggerated account of slave life.*]

In the month of August, 1841, I attended an anti-slavery convention in Nantucket, at which it was my happiness to become acquainted with Frederick Douglass, the writer of the following *Narrative.* He was a stranger to nearly every member of that body; but, having recently made his escape from the southern prison-house of bondage, and feeling his curiosity excited to ascertain the principles and measures of the abolitionists, . . . he was induced to give his attendance, on the occasion alluded to . . . . (p. 3)

Fortunate, most fortunate occurrence!—fortunate for the millions of his manacled brethren, yet panting for deliverance from their awful thraldom!—fortunate for the cause of negro emancipation, and of universal liberty!—fortunate for the land of his birth, which he has already done so much to save and bless! . . . [Fortunate] for himself, as it at once brought him into the field of public usefulness, "gave the world assurance of a MAN," quickened the slumbering energies of his soul, and consecrated him to the great work of breaking the rod of the oppressor, and letting the oppressed go free!

I shall never forget [Douglass's first speech at an anti-slavery convention in Nantucket in 1841]—the extraordinary emotion it excited in my own mind—the powerful impression it created upon a crowded auditory, completely taken by surprise . . . . I think I never hated slavery so intensely as at that moment; certainly, my perception of the enormous outrage which is inflicted by it, on the godlike nature of its victims, was rendered far more clear than ever. There stood one, in physical proportion and stature commanding and exact—in intellect richly endowed—in natural eloquence a prodigy—in soul manifestly "created but a little lower than the angels"—yet a slave, ay, a fugitive slave,—trembling for his safety, hardly daring to believe that on the American soil, a single white person could be found who would befriend him at all hazards, for the love of God and humanity! Capable of high attainments as an intellectual and moral being—needing nothing but a comparatively small amount of cultivation to make him an ornament to society and a blessing to his race—by the law of the land, by the voice of the people, by the terms of the slave code, he was only a piece of property, a beast of burden, a chattel personal, nevertheless! (pp. 4-5)

As soon as he had taken his seat, filled with hope and admiration, I rose, and declared that Patrick Henry, of revolutionary fame, never made a speech more eloquent in the cause of liberty, than the one we had just listened to from the lips of that hunted fugitive. So I believed at that time—such is my belief now. (p. 5)

As a public speaker, [Douglass] excels in pathos, wit, comparison, imitation, strength of reasoning, and fluency of language. There is in him that union of head and heart, which is indispensable to an enlightenment of the heads and a winning of the hearts of others. May his strength continue to be equal to his day! May he continue to "grow in grace, and in the knowledge of God," that he may be increasingly serviceable in the cause of bleeding humanity, whether at home or abroad! (p. 7)

Mr. Douglass has very properly chosen to write his [*Narrative of the Life of Frederick Douglass*], in his own style, and according to the best of his ability, rather than to employ some one else. It is, therefore, entirely his own production; and, considering how long and dark was the career he had to run as a slave,—how few have been his opportunities to improve his mind since he broke his iron fetters,—it is, in my judgment, highly creditable to his head and heart. He who can peruse it without a tearful eye, a heaving breast, an afflicted spirit,—without being filled with an unutterable abhorrence of slavery and all its abettors, and animated with a determination to seek the immediate overthrow of that execrable system,—without trembling for the fate of this country in the hands of a righteous God . . . —must have a flinty heart, and be qualified to act the part of a trafficker "in slaves and the souls of men." I am confident that it is essentially true in all its statements; that nothing has been set down in malice, nothing exaggerated, nothing drawn from the imagination; that it comes short of the reality, rather than overstates a single fact in regard to SLAVERY AS IT IS. The experience of Frederick Douglass, as a slave, was not a peculiar one: his lot was not especially a hard one . . . Many have suffered incomparably more, while very few on the plantations have suffered less, than himself. Yet how deplorable was his situation! what terrible chastisements were inflicted upon his person! what still more shocking outrages were perpetrated upon his mind! with all his noble powers and sublime aspirations, how like a brute was he treated, even by those professing to have the same mind in them that was in Christ Jesus! (pp. 9-10)

This *Narrative* contains many affecting incidents, many passages of great eloquence and power; but I think the most thrilling one of them all is the description Douglass gives of his feelings, as he stood soliloquizing respecting his fate, and the chances of his one day being a freeman, on the banks of the Chesapeake Bay—viewing the receding vessels as they flew with their white wings before the breeze, and apostrophizing them as animated by the living spirit of freedom. Who can read that passage, and be insensible to its pathos and sublimity? Compressed into it is a whole Alexandrian library of thought, feeling, and sentiment—all that can, all that need be urged, in the form of expostulation, entreaty, rebuke, against that crime of crimes,—making man the property of his fellow-man! (p. 11)

So profoundly ignorant of the nature of slavery are many persons, that they are stubbornly incredulous whenever they read or listen to any recital of the cruelties which are daily inflicted on its victims . . . . Such will try to discredit the shocking tales of slaveholding cruelty which are recorded in this truthful *Narrative*; but they will labor in vain. Mr. Douglass has frankly disclosed the place of his birth, the names of those who claimed ownership in his body and soul, and the names also of those who committed the crimes which he has alleged against them. His statements, therefore, may easily be disproved, if they are untrue. (pp. 11-13)

The effect of a religious profession on the conduct of southern masters is vividly described in the following *Narrative,* and shown to be anything but salutary. In the nature of the case, it must be in the highest degree pernicious. The testimony of Mr. Douglass, on this point, is sustained by a cloud of witnesses, whose veracity is unimpeachable. "A slaveholder's profession of Christianity is a palpable imposture. He is a felon of the highest grade. He is a manstealer. It is of no importance what you put in the other scale."

Reader! are you with the man-stealers in sympathy and purpose, or on the side of their down-trodden victims? If with the former, then are you the foe of God and man. If with the latter, what are you prepared to do and dare in their behalf? Be faithful, be vigilant, be untiring in your efforts to break every yoke, and let the oppressed go free. Come what may—cost what it may—inscribe on the banner which you unfurl to the breeze, as your religious and political motto—"NO COMPROMISE WITH SLAVERY! NO UNION WITH SLAVEHOLDERS!" (pp. 14-15)

William Lloyd Garrison, in a preface to Narrative of the Life of Frederick Douglass, an American Slave *by Frederick Douglass, edited by Benjamin Quarles, Belknap Press, 1960, pp. 3-15.*

Wendell Phillips (letter date 1845)

[*Like Douglass, Phillips was a renowned nineteenth-century reformist orator. Both men were associated with William Lloyd Garrison in the 1840s, and they frequently appeared together at antislavery meetings. In the letter excerpted below, Phillips discusses the soon-to-be published* Narrative *and expresses his gratitude to Douglass for recording his sense of the spiritual degradation of slavery, which Phillips regards as the most compelling argument for abolition. His letter was first published in the 1845 edition of the* Narrative.]

You remember the old fable of "The Man and the Lion," where the lion complained that he should not be so misrepresented "when the lions wrote history."

I am glad the time has come when the "lions write history." We have been left long enough to gather the character of slavery from the involuntary evidence of the masters.... [A man must be disposed] to hate slavery for other reasons than because it starves men and whips women,—before he is ready to lay the first stone of his anti-slavery life.

I was glad to learn, in your [*Narrative of the Life of Frederick Douglass*], how early the most neglected of God's children waken to a sense of their rights, and of the injustice done them. Experience is a keen teacher, and long before you had mastered your A B C, or knew where the "white sails" of the Chesapeake were bound, you began, I see, to gauge the wretchedness of the slave, not by his hunger and want, not by his lashes and toil, but by the cruel and blighting death which gathers over his soul.

In connection with this, there is one circumstance which makes your recollections peculiarly valuable, and renders your early insight the more remarkable. You come from that part of the country where we are told slavery appears with its fairest features. Let us hear, then, what it is at its best estate—gaze on its bright side, if it has one; and then imagination may task her powers to add dark lines to the picture, as she travels southward to that (for the colored man) Valley of the Shadow of Death, where the Mississippi sweeps along. (pp. 17-18)

Every one who has heard you speak has felt, and, I am confident, every one who reads your book will feel, persuaded that you give them a fair specimen of the whole truth. No one-sided portrait,—no wholesale complaints,—but strict justice done, whenever individual kindliness has neutralized, for a moment the deadly system with which it was strangely allied. (pp. 18-19)

In reading your life, no one can say that we have unfairly picked out some rare specimens of cruelty. We know that the bitter drops, which even you have drained from the cup, are no incidental aggravations, no individual ills, but such as must mingle always and necessarily in the lot of every slave. They are the essential ingredients, not the occasional results, of the system.

After all, I shall read your book with trembling for you.... They say the fathers, in 1776, signed the Declaration of Independence with the halter about their necks. You, too, publish your declaration of freedom with danger compassing you around. In all the broad lands which the Constitution of the United States overshadows, there is no single spot,—however narrow or desolate,—where a fugitive slave can plant himself and say, "I am safe." The whole armory of Northern Law has no shield for you. I am free to say that, in your place, I should throw the MS. into the fire.

You, perhaps, may tell your story in safety, endeared as you are to so many warm hearts by rare gifts, and a still rarer devotion of them to the service of others. (pp. 19-20)

Yet it is sad to think, that these very throbbing hearts which welcome your story, and form your best safeguard in telling it, are all beating contrary to the "statute in such case made and provided." Go on, my dear friend, till you, and those who, like you, have been saved, so as by fire, from the dark prisonhouse, shall stereotype these free, illegal pulses into statutes; and New England, cutting loose from a blood-stained Union, shall glory in being the house of refuge for the oppressed;—till we no longer merely "*hide* the outcast," or make a merit of standing idly by while he is hunted in our midst; but, consecrating anew the soil of the Pilgrims as an asylum for the oppressed, proclaim our *welcome* to the slave so loudly, that the tones shall reach every hut in the Carolinas, and make the broken-hearted bondman leap up at the thought of old Massachusetts.

God speed the day!

(pp. 20-1)

Wendell Phillips, in a letter to Frederick Douglass on April 22, 1845 in Narrative of the Life of Frederick Douglass, an American Slave *by Frederick Douglass, edited by Benjamin Quarles, Belknap Press, 1960, pp. 17-21.*

Rev. Samuel Hanson Cox (essay date 1846)

[*Cox's comments, which were originally published in a letter to the New York* Evangelist *in 1846, refer to Douglass's 7 August 1846 address before the World's Temperance Convention in London, England. In his address, Douglass reminded the convention that, by virtue of their bondage, slaves were effectively excluded from American temperance societies, and that black freedmen were barred from them by racial prejudice. Cox, who was a member of the American delegation, here charges Douglass with opportunism, indiscriminate severity, and condescension.*]

[The convention delegates] advocated the same cause, showed a glorious union of thought and feeling, and the effect was constantly being raised—the moral scene was superb and glorious—when Frederick Douglass, the colored Abolitionist, agitator and ultraist, came to the platform and so spoke *à la mode* as to ruin the influence almost of all that preceded! (p. 108)

What a perversion, an abuse, an iniquity against the law of reciprocal righteousness, to call thousands together and get them, some certain ones, to seem conspicuous and devoted for one sole and grand object, and then all at once, with obliquity, open an avalanche on them for some imputed evil or monstrosity, for which, whatever be the wound or injury inflicted, they were both too fatigued and hurried with surprise, and too straitened for time, to be properly prepared. I say it is a streak of meanness; it is abominable. On this occasion Mr. Douglass allowed himself to denounce America and all its temperance societies together as a grinding community of the enemies of his people; said evil with no alloy of good concerning the whole of us; was perfectly indiscriminate in his severities; talked of the American delegates and to them as if he had been our schoolmaster, and we his docile and devoted pupils; and launched his revengeful missiles at our country without one palliative word, and as if not a Christian or a true anti-slavery man lived in the whole United States. (p. 109)

> *Rev. Samuel Hanson Cox, in an extract from an originally unsigned account of Frederick Douglass's address at the World's Temperance Convention at Covent Garden on August 7, 1846, in* Frederick Douglass *by Booker T. Washington, Haskell House Publishers Ltd., 1968, pp. 108-09.*

Frederick Douglass (letter date 1855)

[*In the letter excerpted below, Douglass explains his reasons for writing* My Bondage and My Freedom, *his second autobiographical work. The letter is directed to the book's editor.*]

In my letters and speeches, I have generally aimed to discuss the question of Slavery in the light of fundamental principles, and upon facts, notorious and open to all; making, I trust, no more of the fact of my own former enslavement, than circumstances seemed absolutely to require. I have never placed my opposition to slavery on a basis so narrow as my own enslavement, but rather upon the indestructible and unchangeable laws of human nature, every one of which is perpetually and flagrantly violated by the slave system. I have also felt that it was best for those having histories worth the writing—or supposed to be so—to commit such work to hands other than their own. To write of one's self, in such a manner as not to incur the imputation of weakness, vanity, and egotism, is a work within the ability of but few; and I have little reason to believe that I belong to that fortunate few.

These considerations caused me to hesitate, when first you kindly urged me to prepare for publication a full account of my life as a slave, and my life as a freeman.

Nevertheless, I see, with you, many reasons for regarding my autobiography as exceptional in its character, and as being, in some sense, naturally beyond the reach of those reproaches which honorable and sensitive minds dislike to incur. It is not to illustrate any heroic achievements of a man, but to vindicate a just and beneficent principle, in its application to the whole human family, by letting in the light of truth upon a system, esteemed by some as a blessing, and by others as a curse and a crime. I agree with you, that this system is now at the bar of public opinion—not only of this country, but of the whole civilized world—for judgment. Its friends have made for it the usual plea—"not guilty;" the case must, therefore, proceed. Any facts, either from slaves, slaveholders, or by-standers, calculated to enlighten the public mind, by revealing the true nature, character, and tendency of the slave system, are in order, and can scarcely be innocently withheld.

I see, too, that there are special reasons why I should write my own biography, in preference to employing another to do it. Not only is slavery on trial, but unfortunately, the enslaved people are also on trial. It is alleged, that they are, naturally, inferior; that they are *so low* in the scale of humanity, and so utterly stupid, that they are unconscious of their wrongs, and do not apprehend their rights. Looking, then, at your request, from this stand-point, and wishing everything of which you think me capable to go to the benefit of my afflicted people, I part with my doubts and hesitation, and proceed to furnish you the desired manuscript.... (pp. vi-vii)

> *Frederick Douglass, in a letter to an unidentified recipient on July 2, 1855, in his* My Bondage and My Freedom, *Dover Publications, Inc., 1969, pp. v-viii.*

John Edward Bruce (letter date 1889)

[*Although he was generally revered by his contemporaries, Douglass had his detractors. One of his most outspoken critics in the 1880s was the black newspaper editor and journalist John Edward Bruce. On 11 May and 8 June 1889—apparently in reaction to remarks that Douglass had made in a speech commemorating the twenty-seventh anniversary of the abolition of slavery in the District of Columbia—he published the following comments in letters to the editor of the* Cleveland Gazette.]

Mr. Frederick Douglass, in a speech delivered [in Washington D.C.] on the 16th of April last, took occasion to advise the colored people of the United States against encouraging race pride, arguing that a solid black minority would tend to array the white people against us—intimating that we would come nearer to the solution of the problem by assimilating with the whites, etc., etc. This is Mr. Douglass' advice to the Negro. It is bad advice; it is one of Mr. Douglass' dreams, which he nor his posterity will hardly live to see realized. Mr. Douglass evidently wants to get away from the Negro race, and from the criticism I have heard quite recently of him, he will not meet with any armed resistance in his flight. (p. 118)

[Mr. Douglass] owes much of his popularity to the colored fool editors around the country whose little patent inside and outside sheets have made him something less than a god, by keeping his name continually in their columns, and in endeavoring to convince ordinary mortals that when God created Frederick Douglass, He finished His work with the exception of the sun, moon and stars to reflect their rays upon him as he walked up and down the land. Mr. Douglass has courted their attention; he has coquetted with their editors, correspondents and reporters; he has used them to the extent of his ability; he has commended them as indispensable auxiliaries in the work of lifting the race to a higher plane in the social and intellectual world. And now that he sees or imagines that they can no longer be used, the question of their utility as helps in the solution of the Negro problem is disposed of by him with a slur and a contemptuous fling at their "youthful imperfections." ...Socrates said, "He is unjust who does not return deserved thanks for any benefit, whether the giver be friend or foe." Noble words, these, and fitly spoken. Mr. Douglass may not be able to discover at this time any thing in colored journalism worthy of his support and encouragement. His own failures as a journalist and publisher may have doubtless embittered him somewhat, but all colored journals are not failures. Many of them manage to exist without the yearly subscription of Frederick Douglass some way or another. (pp. 118-19)

> *John Edward Bruce, "Somewhat Less than a God," in* Frederick Douglass, *edited by Benjamin Quarles, Prentice-Hall, Inc., 1968, pp. 118-20.*

Paul Laurence Dunbar (poem date 1896)

[*Dunbar was a late nineteenth- and early twentieth-century black American poet renowned for his skillful use of dialect, humor, and folkways. Befriended by Douglass early in his career, he published the following eulogistic ode to him in 1896 in his* Lyrics of Lowly Life.]

> A hush is over all the teeming lists,
> 　And there is pause, a breath-space in the strife;
> A spirit brave has passed beyond the mists
> 　And vapors that obscure the sun of life.
> And Ethiopia, with bosom torn,
> Laments the passing of her noblest born.
>
> She weeps for him a mother's burning tears—
> 　She loved him with a mother's deepest love.
> He was her champion thro' direful years,
> 　And held her weal all other ends above.
> When Bondage held her bleeding in the dust,
> He raised her up and whispered, "Hope and Trust."
>
> For her his voice, a fearless clarion, rung
> 　That broke in warning on the ears of men;

> For her the strong bow of his power he strung,
> 　And sent his arrows to the very den
> Where grim Oppression held his bloody place
> And gloated o'er the mis'ries of a race.
>
> And he was no soft-tongued apologist;
> 　He spoke straightforward, fearlessly uncowed;
> The sunlight of his truth dispelled the mist,
> 　And set in bold relief each dark-hued cloud;
> To sin and crime he gave their proper hue,
> And hurled at evil what was evil's due.
>
> Through good and ill report he cleaved his way
> 　Right onward, with his face set toward the heights,
> Nor feared to face the foeman's dread array,—
> 　The lash of scorn, the sting of petty spites.
> He dared the lightning in the lightning's track,
> And answered thunder with his thunder back.
>
> When men maligned him, and their torrent wrath
> 　In furious imprecations o'er him broke.
> He kept his counsel as he kept his path;
> 　'Twas for his race, not for himself, he spoke.
> He knew the import of his Master's call,
> And felt himself too mighty to be small.
>
> No miser in the good he held was he,—
> 　His kindness followed his horizon's rim.
> His heart, his talents, and his hands were free
> 　To all who truly needed aught of him.
> Where poverty and ignorance were rife,
> He gave his bounty as he gave his life.
>
> The place and cause that first aroused his might
> 　Still proved its power until his latest day.
> In Freedom's lists and for the aid of Right
> 　Still in the foremost rank he waged the fray;
> Wrong lived; his occupation was not gone.
> He died in action with his armor on!
>
> We weep for him, but we have touched his hand,
> 　And felt the magic of his presence nigh,
> The current that he sent throughout the land,
> 　The kindling spirit of his battle-cry.
> O'er all that holds us we shall triumph yet,
> And place our banner where his hopes were set!
>
> Oh, Douglass, thou hast passed beyond the shore,
> 　But still thy voice is ringing o'er the gale!
> Thou'st taught thy race how high her hopes may soar,
> 　And bade her seek the heights, nor faint, nor fail.
> She will not fail, she heeds thy stirring cry,
> She knows thy guardian spirit will be nigh,
> And, rising from beneath the chast'ning rod,
> She stretches out her bleeding hands to God!

(pp. 8-11)

> *Paul Laurence Dunbar, "Frederick Douglass," in his* Lyrics of Lowly Life, The Gregg Press, *1968, pp. 8-11.*

J. Saunders Redding (essay date 1939)

[*Redding was a distinguished American authority on African-American literature and history. He is remembered for a number of important studies of black culture, including* To Make a Poet Black *(1939),* They Came in Chains: Americans from Africa *(1950;*

revised edition, 1973), and The Lonesome Road: The Story of the Negro's Part in America *(1958). In the following excerpt from* To Make a Poet Black, *he calls attention to the artistic qualities of Douglass's works and accords him an important place in the history of American literature.*]

The 1845 autobiography, *Narrative of the Life of Frederick Douglass,* came at a time when the writing of slave narratives, real or fictitious, was popular propaganda, but Douglass's book is in many ways too remarkable to be dismissed as mere hack writing. . . . In utter contrast to the tortured style of most of the slave biographies, Douglass's style is calm and modest. Even in this first book his sense of discrimination in the selection of details is fine and sure. The certainty of the book's emotional power is due in part to the stringent simplicity of style and in part to the ingenuous revelation of the author's character. (p. 32)

The same dignity with which [Douglass's letters to the press] answered malicious attacks or set forth his arguments marked his speeches. Indeed, reading his letters now, one feels that they were written for speech, that Douglass made no difference between the written and the spoken word. (p. 33)

The speeches [that Douglass] made between 1849 and 1860 were never equaled in logic, in emotional force, or in simple clarity. His peculiarly stony denunciation, the calm bitterness of his irony, and his frequent use of the simple and emotional language of the Bible make the speeches of this period memorable examples of the oratorical art. (pp. 33-4)

In 1855 the autobiographical *My Bondage and My Freedom* was published. His style, still without tricks, proves surer. Considerably longer than his first book, its length is amply justified by its matter. Though the first part follows in general the simple plan of the *Narrative,* he acquaints us more intimately with slavery and expresses his more mature thoughts on the problems which he faced. It is evident, especially when he writes of his English trip, that his knowledge of men had grown. Equally evident in the logic and sincerity of his arguments is the growth of his knowledge of issues. . . . *My Bondage and My Freedom* is the high mark of the second stage of Douglass's career. Indeed, though for many years after 1865 he was active as both speaker and writer, and though his thoughts steadily matured, he did not exceed the emotional pitch of this second period. As his intellectual vigor increased (and became, it may be said, a little warped by the overdevelopment of his capacity for irony), his emotional and artistic powers fell off. By the 1880's he was not an orator speaking with a spontaneous overflow of emotion: he was a finished public speaker, more concerned with intellectual than emotional responses. (p. 35)

[*Life and Times of Frederick Douglass*] was published in 1881. Its interest comes authentically from the man's life and thought. It has been called properly the most American of American life stories. Unconsciously, with no fanfare of self-satisfaction, the story develops the dramatic theme from bondage to the council tables of a great nation. It is written with the same lucid simplicity that marks all of Douglass's best work, but there is still the lack of differentiation between speaker and writer. *Life and Times* is his best book. (pp. 36-7)

[The larger edition of *Life and Times,* issued in 1892,] is slow and repetitious. [Douglass's] powers had waned, but he was still aware that all was not finished. He had mellowed with only slight decay; grown into acceptance without resignation. To the last, he wrote as he spoke. (p. 37)

The literary work of Douglass is first important as examples of a type and period of American literature. Many of his speeches rank with the best of all times. . . . That at least two of his books, *My Bondage and My Freedom* and the first *Life and Times,* have not been recognized for what they are is attributable more to neglect than to the judgment of honest inquiry. Certainly no American biographies rank above them in the literary qualities of simplicity, interest, and compression of style. They delineate from an exceptional point of view a period in the history of the United States than which no other is more fraught with drama and sociological significance. By any standard his work ranks high.

That he was easily the most important figure in American Negro literature at the time of his death goes without saying. He was the very core of the For Freedom group, fitting his art more nearly to his purposes than any of the others—and suffering less intrinsically for doing it. Without him the For Freedom group would be destitute of true greatness, Negro literature would be poorer, and American literary fields of oratory and autobiography would be lacking a figure in whom they might justly claim pride. (pp. 37-8)

> *J. Saunders Redding, "Let Freedom Ring: Charles Remond, William W. Brown, Frederick Douglass, Frances Ellen Watkins, James Madison Bell," in his* To Make a Poet Black, *1939. Reprint by McGrath Publishing Company, 1968, pp. 19-48.*

Alain Locke (essay date 1941)

[*During the 1920s, 1930s, and 1940s, Locke wrote and edited several works exploring black society and art in the United States. He is best known as the editor of* The New Negro: An Interpretation, *a famous anthology in which he introduced the "New Negro" writers of the Harlem Renaissance. In the excerpt below, Locke promotes the* Life and Times of Frederick Douglass *as "the classic of American Negro biography" and reaffirms the relevance of Douglass's life and thought. His comments, which were originally published in a foreword to the 1941 edition of the* Life and Times, *are in large measure a response to Booker T. Washington's implicit repudiation of Douglass's*

relevance in his 1907 biography Frederick Douglass
(see Further Reading).]

In the lengthening perspective of the Negro's history in America the career and character of Frederick Douglass take on more and more the stature and significance of the epical. For in terms of the race experience his was, beyond doubt, the symbolic career, typical, on the one hand, of the common lot, but on the other, inspiringly representative of outstanding achievement. Its basic pattern is that of the chattel slave become freeman, with the heroic accent, however, of self-emancipation and successful participation in the struggle for group freedom. Superimposed is the dramatic design of a personal history of achievement against odds, in the course of which the hero becomes both an acknowledged minority leader and spokesman and a general American publicist and statesman. Both chance and history conspired toward this, as he himself acknowledges, modestly enough, in his autobiography, but no one can come away from the reading of it except with the conviction that in mind and character he was, in large part, author of his own destiny. This heroic cast makes the story of Fred Douglass an imperishable part of the Negro epic, and should make his *Life and Times*...the classic of American Negro biography.

Another narrative of outstanding individual achievement and group service, however,—Booker Washington's *Up From Slavery,* has long held pre-eminence in popular attention and favor. Its author, himself a biographer of Frederick Douglass [see Further Reading], gives an apt clue to at least one important reason for this.... Washington speaks of the Douglass career as falling "almost wholly within the first period of the struggle in which the race problem has involved the people of this country,—the period of revolution and liberation." "That period is now closed," he goes on to say, "we are at present in the period of construction and readjustment." So different did it seem, then, to Washington in 1906 that he could regret "that many of the animosities engendered by the conflicts and controversies of half a century ago still survive to confuse the councils of those who are seeking to live in the present and future rather than in the past" and express the hope that nothing in Douglass's life narrative should "serve to revive or keep alive the bitterness of those controversies of which it gives the history." In so saying Washington does more than reveal the dominant philosophy of his own program of conciliation and compromise; he reflects the dominant psychology of a whole American generation of materialism and reaction which dimmed, along with Douglass and other crisis heroes, the glory and fervor of much early American idealism.

That period, in its turn, is closed or closing.... A chronicle of the initial struggles for freedom and social justice is...particularly pertinent again in our present decade of crisis and social reconstruction. Without undue belittlement, then, of Booker Washington in his time and place of limited vision and circumscribed action, it is only fair and right to measure Douglass,

with his militant courage and unequivocal values, against the yardstick, not of a reactionary generation, but of all times. It is thus evident why in the intervening years Douglass has grown in stature and significance, and why he promises to become a paramount hero for Negro youth of today.

This can happen most sanely and effectively if today we read or re-read Douglass's career in his own crisp and graphic words, lest he be minimized or maximized by the biographers. There is most truth and best service in a realistic rather than a romanticized Frederick Douglass. For he was no paragon, without flaw or contradiction, even though, on the whole the consistent champion of human rights and the ardent, ever-loyal advocate of the Negro's cause. His life was full of paradoxes, and on several issues he can be quoted against himself. In the course of events, for example, the man who "unsold himself from slavery" accepted, for expediency at the hands of philanthropic Anti-Slavery friends, the purchase price of his legal freedom; he could whip his overseer and defy, physically and morally, the slaveholder and yet forgive and benefact his old master.... [In] 1850, he declared uncompromisingly for pacifism and peaceful Abolition, but in 1862 pleaded with Lincoln to enlist Negro troops and when the order finally came, sent in his two sons and started out himself as a recruiting agent. More contradictions of this sort could be cited, none more illustrative than the dilemma of intermarriage, which he had to face late in life before the bar of divided public opinion after a long and happy first marriage to his devoted wife, Anna Murray Douglass, a free Negro woman who had befriended him while he was still a slave in Baltimore and who aided him to escape from slavery. Said he to friends, in skillful but incisive self-justification, "In my first marriage I paid a compliment to my mother's race; in my second, to my father's." Whoever reads the full story will doubtless grant him in all cases the tribute of sincerity and courage, and in most instances, too, the vindication of the higher consistency. (pp. 169-72)

Douglass's long and close identification with the Anti-Slavery cause, by which he is generally known, obscures his many-sided public life and service. Perhaps his surest claim to greatness came from his ability to generalize the issues of the Negro cause and see them as basic principles of human freedom, everywhere and in every instance. We see him accordingly taking sides with land and labor reforms in England and Ireland when there on a two-year Anti-Slavery campaign. Similarly he became one of the first public advocates of woman's rights and suffrage.... His advocacy of Civil Rights legislation and of free public education...showed him far in advance of any narrowly racialist view or stand. (p. 172)

Indeed, objectives which later seem to have become rivals and incompatibles in the hands of leaders of lesser calibre were, in the conception of Douglass, allies in the common-sense strategy of a common cause. In this respect, he seems, particularly as we read his pithy prose so different from the polished and often florid periods of his orations, a sort of Negro edition of Ben Franklin, reacting to the issues of his time with truly profound and unbiased sanity. It is unusual for a campaigning advocate of causes and a professional orator to be so sane.

Witness his shrewd realistic comment that flanks, in his autobiography, his impassioned editorial **Men of Color, to Arms!**:—showing him to be by no means the dupe of his own rhetoric,—"When at last the truth began to dawn upon the administration that the Negro might be made useful to loyalty as well as to treason, to the Union as well as to the Confederacy, it then considered in what way it could employ him, which would in the least shock and offend the popular prejudice against him."

Much of his writing has upon it the timeless stamp of the sage. "No people," he says, "to whom liberty is given, can hold it as firmly and wear it as grandly as those who wrench their liberty from the iron hand of the tyrant." ... "Neither we, nor any other people, will ever be respected till we respect ourselves, and we will never respect ourselves till we have the means to live respectably." ... "My hope for the future of my race is further supported by the rapid decline of an emotional, shouting, and thoughtless religion. Scarcely in any direction can there be found a less favorable field for mind or morals than where such a religion prevails." Obviously there is much in Douglass, both of word and deed, which is vital and relevant to this present generation and to our world of today. Racially and nationally we still need the effective reenforcement of his career and personality. Youth, in its time of stress and testing crisis, needs and can benefit by the inspiring example of a crusading and uncompromising equalitarian. (pp. 172-73)

> *Alain Locke, in an extract from "The Enduring Douglass," in* Frederick Douglass, *edited by Benjamin Quarles, Prentice-Hall, Inc., 1968, pp. 169-73.*

Houston A. Baker, Jr. (essay date 1980)

[*An American academic and critic, Baker has written widely on black literature. In the following excerpt from his 1980 study* The Journey Back: Issues in Black Literature and Criticism, *he argues that Douglass never presented his "authentic self" in his autobiographies but moved instead to a "public version of the self—one molded by the values of white America."*]

[Much of **The Narrative of the Life of Frederick Douglass**] counterpoints the assumption of the white world that the slave is a brute against the slave's expanding awareness of language and its capacity to carry him toward new dimensions of experience....

For [Douglass], language brings the possibility of freedom but renders slavery intolerable. It gives rise to his decision to escape as soon as his age and the opportunity are appropriate. (pp. 34-5)

When clarified and understood through language, the deathly, terrifying nothingness around [Douglass] reveals the grounds of being. Freedom, the ability to choose one's own direction, makes life beautiful and pure. Only the man free from bondage has a chance to obtain the farthest reaches of humanity. From what appears a blank and awesome backdrop, Douglass wrests significance. His subsequent progression through the roles of educated leader, freeman, abolitionist, and autobiographer marks his firm sense of being.

But while it is the fact that the ships are loosed from their moorings that intrigues the narrator [in his famous passage describing the ships on Chesapeake Bay], he also drives home their whiteness and places them in a Christian context. Here certain added difficulties for the black autobiographer reveal themselves. The acquisition of language, which leads to being, has ramifications that have been best stated by the West Indian novelist George Lamming, drawing on the relationship between Prospero and Caliban in *The Tempest*:

> Prospero has given Caliban Language; and with it an unstated history of consequences, an unknown history of future intentions. This gift of language meant not English, in particular, but speech and concept as a way, a method, a necessary avenue towards areas of the self which could not be reached in any other way. It is in this way, entirely Prospero's enterprise, which makes Caliban aware of possibilities. Therefore, all of Caliban's future—for future is the very name for possibilities—must derive from Prospero's experiment, which is also his risk.

Mr. Auld had seen that "learning" could lead to the restiveness of his slave. Neither he nor his representer, however, seem to understand that it might be possible to imprison the slave even more thoroughly in the way described by Lamming. The angelic Mrs. Auld, however, in accord with the evangelical codes of her era, has given Douglass the rudiments of a system that leads to intriguing restrictions. True, the slave can arrive at a sense of being only through language. But it is also true that, in Douglass's case, a conception of the preeminent form of being is conditioned by white, Christian standards. (pp. 35-6)

In recovering the details of his past, ... [Douglass] shows a progression from baffled and isolated existent to Christian abolitionist lecturer and writer. The self in the autobiographical moment (the present, the time in which the work is composed), however, seems unaware of the limitations that have accompanied this progress.... One can realize one's humanity through "speech and concept," but one cannot distinguish the uniqueness of the self if the "avenue towards areas of the self" excludes rigorously individualizing definitions of a human, black identity.

Douglass grasps language in a Promethean act of will, but he leaves unexamined its potentially devastating effects. One reflection of his uncritical acceptance of the perspective made available by literacy is the *Narrative* itself, which was written at the urging of white abolitionists who had become the fugitive slave's employers. The work was written to prove that the narrator had indeed been a slave. And while autobiographical conventions forced him to portray as accurately as possible the existentiality of his original condition, the light of abolitionism is always implicitly present, guiding the narrator into calm, Christian, and publicly accessible harbors. The issue here is not simply one of intentionality (how the author wished his utterances to be taken). It is, rather, one that combines Douglass's understandable desire to keep his job with more complex considerations governing "privacy" as a philosophical concept.

Language, like other social institutions, is public; it is one of the surest means we have of communicating with the "other," the world outside ourselves. Moreover, since language seems to provide the principal way in which we conceptualize and convey anything (thoughts, feelings, sensations, and so forth), it is possible that no easily describable "private" domain exists. By adopting language as his instrument for extracting meaning from nothingness, being from existence, Douglass becomes a public figure.

He is comforted, but also restricted, by the system he adopts. The results are shown in the hierarchy of preferences that, finally, constitute value in the *Narrative.* The results are additionally demonstrated by those instances in the *Narrative* where the work's style is indistinguishable from that of the sentimental-romantic oratory and creative writing that marked the American nineteenth century. Had there been a separate, written black language available, Douglass might have fared better. What is seminal to this discussion, however, is that the nature of the autobiographer's situation seemed to force him to move to a public version of the self—one molded by the values of white America. (pp. 38-9)

[The slave narrator must] accomplish the almost unthinkable . . . task of transmuting an authentic, unwritten self—a self that exists outside the conventional literary discourse structures of a white reading public—into a literary representation. The simplest, and perhaps the most effective, way of proceeding is for the narrator to represent his "authentic" self as a figure embodying the public virtues and values esteemed by his intended audience. Once he has seized the public medium, the slave narrator can construct a public message, or massage, calculated to win approval for himself and (provided he has one) his cause. In the white abolitionist William Lloyd Garrison's preface to Douglass's *Narrative,* for example, the slave narrator is elaborately praised for his seemingly godlike movement "into the field of public usefulness" [see excerpt dated 1845] . . . . Obviously, a talented, heroic, and richly endowed figure such as Garrison describes was of inestimable "public usefulness" to the abolitionist crusade. (pp. 39-42)

The issue that such an "autobiographical" act raises for the literary analyst is that of authenticity. Where, for example, in Douglass's *Narrative* does a prototypical black American self reside? What are the distinctive

Portrait of Douglass in about 1844, attributed to Elisha Hammond. One year later, in 1845, Douglass published his Narrative of the Life of Frederick Douglass, an American Slave.

narrative elements that combine to form a representation of this self? . . . . [It] seems that such elements would be located in those episodes and passages of the *Narrative* that chronicle the struggle for literacy. For once literacy has been achieved, the black self, even as represented in the *Narrative,* begins to distance itself from the domain of experience constituted by the oral-aural community of the slave quarters . . . . The voice of the unwritten self, once it is subjected to the linguistic codes, literary conventions, and audience expectations of a literate population, is perhaps never again the authentic voice of black American slavery. It is, rather, the voice of a self transformed by an autobiographical act into a sharer in the general public discourse about slavery.

How much of the lived (as opposed to the represented) slave experience is lost in this transformation depends upon the keenness of the narrator's skill in confronting both the freedom and the limitations resulting from his literacy in Prospero's tongue. By the conclusion of Douglass's *Narrative,* the represented self seems to have left the quarters almost entirely behind. The self that appears in the work's closing moments is that of a public spokesman, talking about slavery to a Nantucket convention of whites:

> while attending an anti-slavery convention at Nantucket, on the 11th of August, 1841, I felt strongly moved to speak, and was at the same time much urged to do so by Mr. William C. Coffin, a gentleman who had heard me speak in the colored people's meeting at New Bedford. It was a severe cross, and I took it up reluctantly. The truth was, I felt myself a slave, and the idea of speaking to white people weighed me down. I spoke but a few moments, when I felt a degree of freedom, and said what I desired with considerable ease. From that time until now, I have been engaged in pleading the cause of my brethren—with what success, and with what devotion, I leave to those acquainted with my labors to decide . . . .

The Christian imagery ("a severe cross"), strained reluctance to speak before whites, discovered ease of eloquence, and public-spirited devotion to the cause of his brethren that appear in this passage are all in keeping with the image of the publicly useful and ideal fugitive captured in Garrison's preface. Immediately before telling the reader of his address to the Nantucket convention, Douglass notes that "he had not long been a reader of the 'Liberator'" before he got "a pretty correct idea of the principles, measures and spirit of the anti-slavery reform"; he adds that he "took right hold of the cause . . . and never felt happier than when in an anti-slavery meeting." . . . This suggests to me that the communication between Douglass and Garrison begins long before their face-to-face encounter at Nantucket, with the fugitive slave's culling from the white publisher's newspaper those virtues and values esteemed by abolitionist readers. The fugitive's voice is further refined by his attendance and speeches at the "colored people's meeting at New Bedford," and it finally achieves its emotionally stirring participation in the white world of public discourse at the 1841 Nantucket convention.

Of course, there are tangible reasons within the historical . . . domain for the image that Douglass projects. The feeling of larger goals shared with a white majority culture has always been present among blacks . . . . From at least the third decade of the nineteenth century this feeling of a common pursuit was reinforced by men like Garrison and Wendall Phillips, by constitutional amendments, civil rights legislation, and perennial assurances that the white man's dream is the black man's as well. Furthermore, what better support for this assumption of commonality could Douglass find than in his own palpable achievements in American society?

When he revised his original *Narrative* for the third time, therefore, in 1893, the work that resulted represented the conclusion of a process that began for Douglass at the home of Hugh Auld. *The Life and Times of Frederick Douglass Written by Himself* is public, rooted in the language of its time, and considerably less existential in tone than the 1845 *Narrative.* What we have is a verbose and somewhat hackneyed story of a life, written by a man of achievement. The white

externality has been transformed into a world where sterling deeds by blacks are possible. Douglass describes his visit to the home of his former master who, forty years after the slave's escape, now rests on his deathbed:

> On reaching the house I was met by Mr. Wm. H. Buff, a son-in-law of Capt. Auld, and Mrs. Louisa Buff, his daughter, and was conducted to the bedroom of Capt. Auld. We addressed each other simultaneously, he called me "Marshal Douglass," and I, as I had always called him, "Captain Auld." Hearing myself called by him "Marshall Douglass," I instantly broke up the formal nature of the meeting by saying, "not *Marshal,* but Frederick to you as formerly." We shook hands cordially and in the act of doing so, he, having been long stricken with palsy, shed tears as men thus afflicted will do when excited by any deep emotion. The sight of him, the changes which time had wrought in him, his tremulous hands constantly in motion, and all the circumstances of his condition affected me deeply, and for a time choked my voice and made me speechless.

A nearly tearful silence by the black "Marshal" (a term repeated three times in very brief space) of the District of Columbia as he gazes with sympathy on the body of his former master—this is a great distance, to be sure, from the aggressive young slave who appropriated language in order to do battle with the masters. (pp. 42-5)

> *Houston A. Baker, Jr., "Autobiographical Acts and the Voice of the Southern Slave," in his* The Journey Back: Issues in Black Literature and Criticism, *University of Chicago Press, 1980, pp. 27-52.*

Robert B. Stepto (essay date 1982)

[*Douglass published his only fictional work, a novella based on the 1841 revolt on board the slave ship* Creole, *in 1853. Entitled* The Heroic Slave, *the story was long neglected by Douglass's critics. In the excerpt below, Stepto, a leading authority on African-American literature, finds evidence in* The Heroic Slave *that Douglass was a sophisticated narrator.*]

The Heroic Slave is not an altogether extraordinary piece of work. I'm not about to argue that it should take a place beside, say, *Benito Cereno* as a major short fiction of the day. Still, after dismissing the florid soliloquies which unfortunately besmirch this and too many other antislavery writings, we find that the novella is full of craft, especially of the sort which combines artfulness with a certain fabulistic usefulness. Appropriately enough, evidence of Douglass' craft is available in the novella's attention to both theme and character. In Part I of *The Heroic Slave,* we are told of the "double state" of Virginia and introduced not only to Madison Washington but also to Mr. Listwell, who figures as the model abolitionist in the story. The meticulous development of the Virginia theme and of the portrait of Mr. Listwell, much more than the portrayal of Washington as a hero, is the stuff of useful art-making in Douglass' novella. (p. 360)

[The first paragraph of the novella], but especially its initial sentences, can be seen as significant revoicing of the conventional opening of a slave narrative. Slave narratives usually begin with the phrase "I was born."... In *The Heroic Slave,* however, Douglass transforms "I was born" into the broader assertion that in Virginia many heroes have been born. After that, he then works his way to the central point that a certain *one*—an unknown hero who lives now only in the chattel records and not the history books—has been born. Douglass knows the slave narrative convention, partly because he has used it himself; but more to the point, he seems to have an understanding of how to exploit its rhetorical usefulness in terms of proclaiming the existence and identity of an individual without merely employing it verbatim. This is clear evidence, I think, of a first step, albeit a small one, toward the creation of an Afro-American fiction based upon the conventions of the slave narratives. That Douglass himself was quite possibly thinking in these terms while writing is suggested by his persistent reference to the "chattel records" which must, in effect, be transformed by "the pen of genius" so that his hero's merits may be set forth—indeed, set free. If by this Douglass means that his hero's story must be liberated from the realm— the text—of brutal fact, and more, that texts must be created to compete with other texts, then it's safe to say that he brought to the creation of *The Heroic Slave* all the intentions, if not all the skills, of the self-conscious *writer*.

The other key feature of the paragraph pertains more directly to the novella's Virginia theme.... After declaring that his hero loved liberty as much as did Patrick Henry, and deserved it as much as Thomas Jefferson, Douglass refuses to name the third famous son of Virginia with whom his hero is to be compared. He speaks only of "he who led all the armies of the American colonies through the great war for freedom and independence." Of course, as any school boy or girl knows, the mystery man is Washington. And that is the answer—and point—to Douglass' funny-sad joke about the "double state" of Virginia as well: *his* mystery man is also a hero named Washington. Thus, Douglass advances his comparison of heroic statesmen and heroic chattel, and does so quite ingenuously by both naming and *not* naming them in such a way that we are led to discover that statesmen and slaves may share the same name and be heroes and Virginians alike. Rhetoric and meaning conjoin in a very sophisticated way in this passage, thus providing us with an indication of how seriously and ambitiously Douglass will take the task of composing the rest of the novella.

The Heroic Slave is divided into four parts, and in each Virginia becomes less and less of a setting (especially of a demographic or even historical sort) and more of a ritual ground ... for symbolic encounters between slaves and abolitionists or Virginians and Virginians. For example, in Part I, the encounter between Mr. Listwell, our soon-to-be abolitionist, and Madison Washington, our soon-to-be fugitive slave, takes place in a magnifi-cent Virginia forest. In accord with many familiar notions regarding the transformational powers of nature in its purest state, both men leave the sylvan glen determined and resolved to become an abolitionist and a free man respectively. Thus, the Virginia forest is established as a very particular space within the figurative geography of the novella.... (pp. 361-62)

Part II of *The Heroic Slave* takes place in Ohio. Listwell lives there and has the opportunity to aid an escaping slave who turns out to be none other than Madison Washington. This change in setting from Virginia to Ohio assists in the development of the Virginia theme chiefly because it gives Douglass the opportunity to stress the point that something truly happened to each man in that "sacred" forest, one happy result being that their paths did cross once again in the cause of freedom.... By the end of Part II, it becomes clear in the context of the emerging novella that Ohio, as a free state, is an increasingly symbolic state to be achieved through acts of fellowship initiated however indirectly before. (pp. 362-63)

Having portrayed Virginia's heaven—the forest replete with pathways to freedom—Douglass now offers Virginia's hell [in Part III]. As one might imagine, given Douglass' zeal for temperance and the abolition of slavery, hell is a tavern full of drunkards, knaves, and traders of human flesh. Hell's first circle is the yard adjacent to the tavern where slaves on their way to market are "stabled" while the soul-driver drinks a dram. Its second circle is the remaining fifteen miles to Richmond where a slave auction awaits. The third circle may be sale to a new Virginia master and a long walk to a new plantation, or it may be a horrific re-encounter with middle passage, in the form of a "cruise" aboard a Baltimore-built slaver bound for New Orleans. (p. 363)

The point to Part III is that while Washington has returned to Virginia, lost his wife in their escape attempt, and been re-enslaved, Listwell is also there and able to provide the means by which Washington may free himself—*and others.* The suggestion is that it is quite one thing to aid an escaping slave in Ohio and quite another to assist one in deepest, darkest Virginia. Listwell rises to the occasion and ... slips Washington several files for the chains binding him. What Washington and the rest do once on board the *Creole* is, of course, a matter of historical record.

One might think that the fourth and last part of *The Heroic Slave* would be totally devoted to a vivid narration of swashbuckling valor aboard the high seas. This is not the case. The scene is once again Virginia; the time is set some time after the revolt on the *Creole;* the place is a "Marine Coffee-house" in Richmond; and the conversation is quite provocatively between two white Virginia sailors.... The conversation takes a sharp turn when ... [Jack Williams, who had not shipped on the *Creole,*] makes it clear that, "For my part I feel ashamed to have the idea go abroad, that a ship load of slaves can't be safely taken from Richmond to

New Orleans. I should like, merely to redeem the character of Virginia sailors, to take charge of a ship load of 'em to-morrow."... Tom Grant, who had been on the *Creole,* soon replies, "I dare say *here* what many men *feel,* but *dare not speak,* that this whole slave-trading business is a disgrace and scandal to Old Virginia."... The conversation goes on, and before it's done, Tom Grant has indeed told the story of the revolt led by Madison Washington. (pp. 363-64)

Thus, Douglass ends his novella by creating the dialogue between Virginians about the "state" of Virginia which was effectively prefigured in the novella's first paragraph. The duality or doubleness of Virginia (and indeed of America) first offered as an assertion and then in the form of a riddle now assumes a full-blown literary form. More to the point, perhaps, is the fact that Tom Grant ... [has become something of an abolitionist] and, most certainly, something of a white Southern storyteller of a tale of black freedom. This particular aspect of Grant's transformation is in keeping with what happens to our white Northerner, Mr. Listwell. What we see here, then, is an expression within Douglass' narrative design of the signal idea that freedom for slaves can transform the South and the North and hence the nation.

This brings us to Mr. Listwell, whose creation is possibly *the* polemical and literary achievement of the novella. In many ways, his name is his story and his story his name. He is indeed a "Listwell" in that he *enlists* as an abolitionist and does *well* by the cause.... He is also a "Listwell" in that he *listens* well; he is, in the context of his relations with Madison Washington and in accord with the aesthetics of storytelling, a model storylistener and hence an agent, in many senses of the term, for the continuing performance of the story he and Washington increasingly share and "tell" together. Of course, Douglass' point is that both features of Listwell's "listing" are connected and, ideally, inextricably bound: one cannot be a good abolitionist without being a good listener, with the reverse often being true as well.

Douglass' elaborate presentation of these ideas begins in Part I of **The Heroic Slave** when Washington apostrophizes in the Virginia forest on his plight as an abject slave and unknowingly is *overheard* by Listwell. At the end of his speech, the storyteller slave vows to gain freedom and the storylistener white Northerner vows to become an abolitionist so that he might aid slaves such as the one he has just overheard. This is storytelling of a sort conducted at a distance. Both storyteller and storylistener are present, and closure of a kind occurs in that both performers resolve to embark on new journeys or careers. But, of course, the teller (slave) doesn't know yet that he has a listener (abolitionist, brother in the cause), and the listener doesn't know yet what role he will play in telling the story that has just begun. In this way, Douglass spins three primary narrative threads: one is the storyteller/slave's journey to freedom; another is the storylistener/abolitionist's journey to service; the third is the resolution or consummation of purposeful

human brotherhood between slave and abolitionist, as it may be most particularly achieved through the communal aesthetic of storytelling.

In Part II, the three primary threads reappear in an advanced state. Washington has escaped and is indeed journeying to freedom; Listwell is now a confirmed abolitionist whose references to conversations with other abolitionists suggest that he is actively involved; and Washington and Listwell are indeed in the process of becoming brothers in the struggle, both because they befriend each other on a cold night and because, once settled before Listwell's fire, they engage for long hours in storytelling. Several features of their storytelling are worth remarking upon. One is that Washington, as the storyteller, actually tells two stories about his adventures in the Virginia forest, one about a thwarted escape attempt and the resulting limbo he enters while neither slave nor free, and the other about how he finally breaks out of limbo, reasserting his desire for freedom. The importance of this feature is that it occasions a repetition of the novella's "primary" forest episode which creates in turn a narrative rhythm which we commonly associate with oral storytelling. (pp. 364-66)

Another pertinent feature is that Listwell, as the storylistener, is both a good listener and, increasingly, a good prompter of Washington's stories. Early on, Listwell says, "But this was five years ago; where have you been since?" Washington replies, "I will try to tell you," and to be sure storytelling ensues. Other examples of this abound. In one notable instance, in response to Washington's explanation as to why he stole food while in flight, Listwell asserts, "And just there you were right.... I once had doubts on this point myself, but a conversation with Gerrit Smith ... put an end to all my doubts on this point. But do not let me interrupt you."... Listwell interrupts, but his is what we might call a good interruption, for he *authenticates* the slave's rationale for stealing instead of questioning it. In this way, Listwell's remarks advance both story *and* cause, which is exactly what he's supposed to do now that he's an abolitionist.

Resolution of this episode takes the form of a letter from Washington to Listwell, written in Canada a few short days after both men have told stories into the night. It begins, "My dear Friend,—for such you truly are:— ... Madison is out of the woods at last...." The language here takes us back to the initial encounter in the Virginia forest between Washington and Listwell, back to a time when they weren't acquaintances, let alone friends—nor on their respective journeys to freedom and service. In examining the essential differences between Washington's apostrophe to no apparent listener and his warm letter to a dear friend, we are drawn to the fact that in each case, a simple voice cries out, but in the second instance a listener is not only addressed but remembered and hence recreated. The great effect is that a former slave's conventional token of freedom and literacy bound and found in Canada takes on certain indelible storytelling properties.

587

From this point on in *The Heroic Slave* little more needs to be established between Washington and Listwell, either as fugitive slave and abolitionist or as storyteller and listener, except the all important point that their bond is true and that Listwell will indeed come to Washington's aid in Virginia just as promptly as he did before in the North. In a sense their story is over, but in another respect it isn't: there remains the issue, endemic to both oral and written art, of how their story will live on with full flavor and purpose. On one hand, the story told by Washington and Listwell lives on in a direct, apparent way in the rebellion aboard the *Creole,* the resulting dialogue between the two Virginia sailors who debate the state of their State, and the transformation of one of the sailors, Tom Grant, into a teller of the story. On the other, the story lives on in another way which draws the seemingly distant narrator into the communal bonds of storytelling and the cause.

Late in the novella, in Part III, the narrator employs the phrase "Mr. Listwell says" and soon thereafter refers to Listwell as "our informant." These phrases suggest rather clearly that Listwell has told his shared tale to the narrator and that he has thus been a storyteller as well as a storylistener all along. The other point to be made is, of course, that the narrator has been at some earlier point a good storylistener, meaning in part that he can now tell a slave's tale well because he was willing to *hear* it before making it his own tale to tell. What's remarkable about this narrative strategy is how it serves Douglass' needs both as a novelist and as a black public figure under pressure. Here was a theory of narrative distilled from the relations between tellers and listeners in the black and white worlds Douglass knew best; here was an answer to all who cried, "Frederick, tell your story"—and then couldn't or wouldn't hear him. (pp. 366-68)

> *Robert B. Stepto, "Storytelling in Early Afro-American Fiction: Frederick Douglass' 'The Heroic Slave',"* in The Georgia Review, *Vol. XXXVI, No. 2, Summer, 1982, pp. 355-68.*

John Sekora (essay date 1983)

[*In the following excerpt, Sekora examines Douglass's autobiographical writings within the context of the American slave narrative tradition.*]

In the struggles of Frederick Douglass lies the intellectual history of nineteenth-century America. Douglass directly influenced much of that history and touched virtually every issue of consequence in black-white relations. Once he mounted an anti-slavery platform in the summer of 1841, neither abolition nor Afro-American writing were ever the same again. He was so prescient, his successes so many, the strength of his writing and speaking so great, we are inclined to pass quickly over many of his conflicts, confident that history has upheld the positions he took. In the best-known example of the pre-war period, later historians have indeed credited him with exposing the intellectual compromises and sheer blindness of the Garrisonian wing of the abolition movement. Yet not all features of even that quarrel have been explored, and on one aspect it is *literary* historians who must speak.

In the first of his life stories, the monumental *Narrative* of 1845, Douglass leads up to his rise to prominence in abolition circles, his association with Garrison and other leaders, and his stunning successes as lecturer and writer in the anti-slavery cause. His second narrative, *My Bondage and My Freedom* of 1855, appears well after the break with Garrison and the advent of his own, independent literary career. In a passage of arresting compression, he notes a personal dilemma—and thereby the constraint felt by a generation of slave lecturers and narrators.

> "Let us have the facts," said the people. So also said Friend George Foster, who always wished to pin me down to my simple narratives. "Give us the facts," said Collins, "we will take care of the philosophy." . . . "Tell your story, Frederick," would whisper my then revered friend, William Lloyd Garrison . . . . I could not always obey, for I was now reading and thinking. New views of the subject were presented to my mind. It did not entirely satisfy me to *narrate* wrongs; I felt like *denouncing* them, I could not always curb my moral indignation . . . long enough for a circumstantial statement of the facts which I felt almost everybody must know. Besides, I was growing and needed room. (1855 ed., pp. 361-62)

The distant occasion of this recollection is Douglass's experience as anti-slavery agent and lecturer. Blended with this is the later, more immediate memory of his trials as author and international representative of American anti-slavery societies. They are two sides of one coin. The literary history of the antebellum slave narrative is also put at issue in this passage. For we now know that other writers, before Douglass and during his lifetime, were equally distressed by the form they had unwittingly inherited. But it is he who poses the major questions—questions that American literary history has not yet addressed. What are the "facts" the people crave? Who are the "people" who crave them? Who are the "we" Collins refers to, and what is the "philosophy" "we" will take care of? Why are "the facts" equivalent to Douglass's whole "story"? Why is that story pinned down to narratives that are merely "simple"? Why does he choose the word "obey" to describe his relations with fellow abolitionists? Why is he asked to limit himself to narrating the wrongs of slavery? Was he not already denouncing them, exercising his moral indignation? Why did he feel constrained to "a circumstantial statement of the facts"? Why did he feel "almost everybody must know" those facts already? Why did not the form of the slave narrative provide him with room to grow and flourish?

Although the questions Douglass raises are intertwined, they cannot be answered fully in an essay. Why for instance does he challenge the form of the slave narrative *in* a slave narrative? So each question subdivides itself interminably. Yet tentative answers are possible if one permits a summary convergence. All of his misgivings imply that the narrative as a form has an existence prior to and beyond the narrator's control or possession. Is that implication valid? If so, *who owns the slave narrative?*

The question itself has a long history, extending to the very beginnings of the genre in the eighteenth century. As the earliest slave narrative in America, some historians cite the ten-page transcript of a trial held in Boston 3 August to 2 November 1703. *Adam Negro's Tryall* is in text and celebrity the quarrel between two very prominent men, Samuel Sewell and John Saffin, who battle one another in court over the terms of Adam's bondage. Adam is called upon to recount a small portion of his life in response to interrogation, but he is merely the proximate cause in a dispute between white figures. *A Narrative of the Uncommon Sufferings, and Surprizing Deliverance of Briton Hammon, A Negro Man*, published in 1760, is an actual personal narrative and is told in the first person. Its title page joins it to earlier and highly popular stories of Indian captivity. It also indicates the heavy burden of "facts" the slave narrative will carry. For in fourteen pages we will be given a circumstantial statement of how in negligence Hammon fled from his owner, suffered daily hardships thereafter, went to sea and was captured, then tortured by Florida Indians, endured nearly five years of captivity, and by divine providence was reunited with his owner and returned to Boston. Although Hammon's life has been filled with wonders, his preface explains why the narrative will be limited to a circumstantial rehearsal of bare facts:

> As my Capacities and Conditions of Life are very low, it cannot be expected that I should make those Remarks on the Sufferings I have met with, or the kind Providence of a good GOD for my Preservation, as one in a higher Station; but shall leave that to the Reader as he goes along, and so I shall only relate Matters of Fact as they occur to my Mind.

In this carefully wrought sentence we have the earliest instance of the distinction noted by Douglass between "facts" and "philosophy." The decisive error of Hammon's early life was his claim to too much freedom. Having endured uncommon sufferings as a result, he has learned better. He will disciple himself severely in the narrative, leaving all philosophy, all acts of interpretation to his betters. As William L. Andrews has observed [in "The First Fifty Years of the Slave Narrative, 1760-1810," in *The Art of Slave Narrative: Original Essays in Criticism and Theory* (1982), ed. by John Sekora and Darwin T. Turner], this is the first example of a black subject relinquishing all claim to the significance of his life. Because of his "very low" capacity, Hammon will be limited to mechanical recollection of "Matters of Fact," leaving the moral and literary meaning of his life to be determined by others—of *higher station*.

Even without questioning how much of Hammon's narrative is edited or dictated, the intellectual hierarchy and division of labor is sufficiently clear. A white editor

has determined that the bare incidents of an exciting Indian captivity will engage a white audience, who would not (needless to say) be concerned with Anglo-American captivity. Hammon's recollection of relevant facts will be given a proper context and a proper meaning by his audience. Hammon does seem to be left with a residue of freedom: to select from his memory the facts that are relevant and to order them as he wishes. But even that small exercise of selfhood is illusory.

Also published in Boston early in 1760 and in its third printing when Hammon's was printed was the captivity narrative of a young white man, Thomas Brown. The full title page of *A Plain Narrative of the Uncommon Sufferings, and Remarkable Deliverance of Thomas Brown*, names and dates aside, is virtually identical to Hammon's. So too is the narrative; its preface emphasizes age rather than status:

> As I am but a Youth, I shall not make those Remarks on the Difficulties I have met with, or the kind Appearances of a good GOD for my Preservation, as one of riper Years might do; but shall leave that to the Reader as he goes long, and shall only beg his Prayers, the Mercies and Afflictions may be sanctified to me, and relate Matters of Fact as they occur to my Mind.—

Brown's narrative was in all likelihood the immediate model for Hammon. If so, then the last vestige of Hammon's autonomy is exercised, for the facts of his story and their ordering are called up, not from the voluntary activity of his will, but from the involuntary pre-existence of a white model. The facts *are* the whole of his story. Neither Hammon nor Brown, it is true, is permitted to possess his own life story. One is disqualified by lowly status, the other by youth. Perhaps both are disqualified for reasons of class and education. Whatever the case, the conditions Douglass describes in 1855 are present a century earlier. And the slave narrative is born into a world of literary confinement: of simplicity, facticity, and submission to authority.

While we cannot know with conviction the overarching shape of Briton Hammon's historical life, we can doubt that it would easily fit the mold of a prodigal white apprentice. The black subject is held, as if in court, as witness to his own existence; what is to be made of that existence is left to a negotiation between sponsors and readers, who together determine the shape of the life story, its emphases and principles of ordering, and its language of expression. On the language of the narratives, the practice of interrogation, dictation, and revision became the norm for the remainder of the century and well into the next. Another captivity narrative, that of John Marrant in 1785, is "Taken down from His Own Relation, Arranged, Corrected, and Published By the Rev. Mr. Aldridge." Marrant's life story is already announced to be a collective enterprise, before Aldridge reveals more in his preface: "I have always preserved Mr. Marrant's ideas, tho' I could not his language . . . ." Moreover, the collective pattern present in such captivity tales is extended by the end of the century to all other forms of slave narrative, including those of religious conversion, criminal confession, and ministerial labor.

Whether one begins with *Adam Negro's Tryall*, the *Narrative* of Hammon, or a later narrative, the distinction persists between the "facts" provided by the nominal subject and the "philosophy" "we" as editors/sponsors/readers will supply. Precisely why this is true is not clear. Evangelical Protestantism was determined to record and inscribe the triumphal American errand into the wilderness. Fully to do so might require inclusion of at least a few examples drawn from the lowliest of the low. Perhaps the slave was for white sponsors necessarily Other. Perhaps the local treatment of (say) Hammon was later generalized into the treatment of all slave narratives. Whatever the motive, its consequence was to distance the narrative and its subject, to envelope both in the workings of institutional power. What is constant, moreover, is the institutional imperative. Here is Alridge's preface to the *Narrative* of Marrant:

> The following Narrative is as plain and artless as it is surprising, and extraordinary. Plausible reasonings may amuse and delight, but facts, and facts like these, strike, are felt, and go home to the heart. Were the power, grace and providence of God ever more eminently displayed, than in the conversion, success, and deliverance of John Marrant?

Alridge tells readers what not to expect—art, style, logic, amusement—as well as what they may look forward to—facts, extraordinary facts. He assures readers they will not be affronted by the life story of a former slave; rather they will be moved by a story of God's providential dealings. Besides constructing the "philosophy" for the narrative, he has turned Marrant inside out—from the subject of the narrative to the object. Thus while becoming the object of God's favor and the beneficence of religious institutions, the slave narrator is simultaneously the object of the sponsor and reader's condescension.

Although Foster, Collins, Garrison, and the other abolitionists of Douglass's circle did not invent the conditions of Douglass's dilemma, they did aggravate them. When he enlisted in the anti-slavery movement in 1841, five constitutive principles were already in place. First, for Garrison, Tappan, Weld and other white leaders, the goal of the crusade was action on the part of white northerners; white abolitionists would somehow compel the white majority to rise up and expunge slavery from the land. Whether of slave or freeman, black expectations were taken for granted and hence irrelevant. Second, former slaves were essential in one role—as witnesses, bodywitnesses to the horrors of bondage. Less articulate fugitives would, when identified, be interrogated, their stories transcribed and then verified and published. For articulate fugitives, the role was greater; like Douglass they would be encouraged to serve as full-time anti-slavery agents and lecturers. Speaking about their lives under slavery was their primary duty; writing was secondary, valuable insofar as it reached areas that

lecturers could not and brought in funds otherwise untapped. By the late 1830s some eighty anti-slavery societies had been formed across the Northeast into the Mid-West. More than half were formed by white groups, and of these nearly thirty took part in the printing of slave narratives.

Third, the abolitionist design for lectures and narratives alike was a collective one: to describe slavery to an ignorant northern audience, not to describe an individual life. Reviews and announcements routinely stated that "former slaves have a simple, moving story to tell," using the singular noun to suggest a collective account transcending personal variations. Titles, prefaces, introductory letters would be used to the same purpose, Fourth, all this emphasis upon facticity and collectivity converged in the demand for authenticity. Because white abolitionists sought to convert the ignorant and the indifferent, they scrutinized and investigated slave accounts with all the references available to them. Facts were useful—and verifiable. Personality and opinion—these were indispensable. Not literary authority but historical veracity was the quality demanded in a narrative.

Finally, black expression was expected to be collective in yet another sense. Each slave lecturer or narrator was normally preceded and followed by several white figures who supplied introductions, testimonials, affidavits, support, approval. When a narrative was published by an anti-slavery society, it must carry the *nihil obstat* as well as the *imprimatur* of the movement. In time white sponsors came to view their editing and introducing as causal to the narratives. In one sense they were entirely correct. For the language of the narratives—their social attitudes and philosophical presuppositions—had been formed in the 1820s and early 1830s, before blacks had been enlisted in the cause. Among other things this meant that moral indignation against the South was one thing, but against the North it was something else. Likewise the call for abolition was mandatory, the call for racial equality forbidden. Samuel May, Jr., said that William Wells Brown had no life apart from the movement and that he should be grateful for the reason for being that it gave him. Garrison of course was much more bitter toward Douglass.

Douglass came eventually to distrust all of these constraints upon black expression. Slavery is incidental to the narrative of Briton Hammon, but it is essential to the narrative of Frederick Douglass. Why cannot he and other authors be entrusted to provide the moral context for their own life stories? The short answer, Douglass came to believe, was that many of the white abolitionists he knew well did not understand blacks or black demands at all. These men and women regarded black life as little more than *what was done to blacks*; present and former slaves were basically passive victims. This false philosophy became the language of abolition, justifying a kind of cultural hegemony, and on so many issues of great moment to blacks anti-slavery societies could not reason without reasoning falsely. It is clear

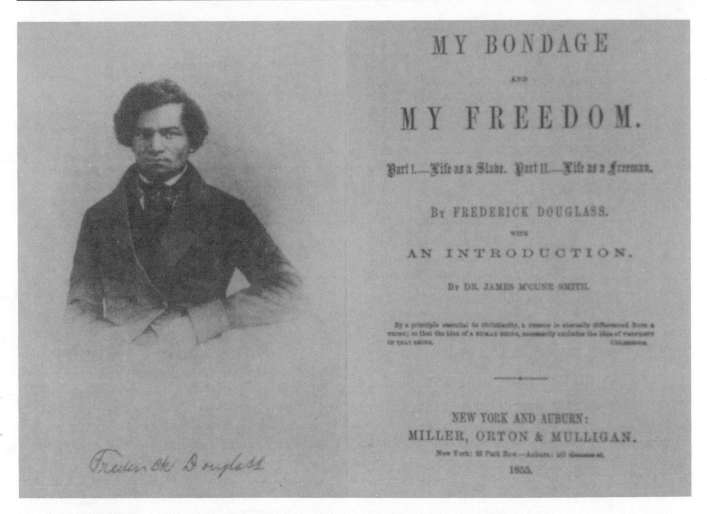

Frontispiece and title page of Douglass's second autobiography.

that the limitations of the abolitionists are inscribed upon the form of the slave narrative. It is equally true that much of the interest of the narrative derives from an author's attempts to evade or subvert white literary impositions.

After his break with Garrison, Douglass's black colleagues applauded a new stage in his struggle for black civil rights. James McCune Smith wrote of his decision to found his own newspaper: "Only since his Editorial career has [Douglass] seen to become a colored man! I have read his paper very carefully and find phase after phase develop itself as in one newly born among us." A final small portion of his dilemma can be sketched by noting a private side of Garrison certain to rankle. In his correspondence with white friends, Garrison's terms of praise for a white author are "magnificent," "powerful" and the like. When he is describing the work of a black author, however, his recognition is limited to "useful," "agreeable," or "making a very favorable impression." His abiding question is, how will a white audience respond?

For more than thirty arduous years Garrison worked at close hand with dozens of fugitives and freemen. Yet his voluminous correspondence is as silent in personal understanding of his black associates as it is effusive about his white. In his dealings with Douglass and Wells Brown, he required black leaders to be strong enough to control their followers, yet sufficiently weak not to challenge him. In his correspondence he treats black writers as though they exist in some distinct, segregated limbo, hardly in touch with the white world. On 30 July 1868 he writes to Tilton concerning a petition proposed by Horace Greeley:

Mr. Greeley suggests getting the names of "at least fifty leading, life-long Abolitionists" to the desired document. In the present divided state of feeling, I doubt whether half that number could be obtained of those who are well known to the country. Neither Phillips, nor Pillsbury, nor Foster, nor Whipple, nor any who affiliate with them, would join in any such movement. Probably Gerrit Smith, Samuel J. May, Samuel May, Jr., Samuel E. Sewall, and Edmund Quincy would sign the paper. Some colored names ought to be added—such as Douglass, Garnet, Nell, Wells, Brown, Langston, & c, & c. Perhaps these had better send an appeal of their own. Of course, Purvis and Remond would have nothing to do with the matter.

Structurally similar to several earlier ones, this letter separates his anti-slavery colleagues into white and black sentences, with the black names appended ("colored names ought to be added") as an afterthought. While most white figures are identified by full names, even initials, the blacks are referred to as examples ("such as") by last names only, followed by a sign that Garrison will not try to be exhaustive ("etc, etc").

By way of explanation, he continues: "There are so few of the freedmen who, in the nature of things, can know anything of the Abolitionists, that I am not quite sure it would amount to much if any number of names were appended to the paper proposed." This is one of the most startling sentences, public or private, Garrison ever penned. The specific nature of Greeley's petition is unknown; Garrison's editors guess it concerned amnesty or suffrage. In any case, Garrison is referring to black leaders who have known him for more than a generation, who were anti-slavery authors, lecturers, and international representatives. They include men who have been speaking and writing at length over many years about white abolitionists and the cause; Douglass alone delivered an estimated 1,000 lectures, Brown 2,000. They too called themselves Abolitionists, though now he would withhold the title. What is the mysterious "nature of things" that allows knowledge to flow but one way, to whites but not to blacks? His lament may be that the influence of freedmen, even of the stature of Douglass, would not amount to much. Yet the ignorance he finds may be his own. His final words on the subject reflect a familiar gambit—using the threat of southern retaliation to suppress black voices: "Moreover, might not such names exasperate the rebel enemies of the freedmen, and stimulate them to the infliction of fresh outrages? It is worth considering whether a calm and simple statement *per se,* as to what is the political duty of the freedmen in the coming struggle, will not be sufficient." Like Agassiz, Garrison seems preoccupied with the potential for "our detriment." In earlier campaigns black voices were considered an essential chorus; now they are not. (Calm and simple statements *per se,* it should be remembered, are the *raison d'être* of the slave narrators.) What Garrison prefers is an unequivocal announcement of white hegemony: a statement drafted by men like himself to direct freedmen to their political duty. Blacks are not needed to frame the language of such a statement, merely to fulfill it. The dilemma faced by Douglass and other slave narrators is clearer. Garrison would have important decisions made by white people talking to white people.

When he set off on his own course, several of his former sponsors charged that Douglass had betrayed the cause, some said he secretly opposed emancipation, and one said he was no longer mentally fit. On 5 June 1958 Clennon King, a black professor at Alcorn A and M, attempted to register for doctoral courses at the then-all-white University of Mississippi. From the registration line, King was taken into custody by the Mississippi highway patrol and committed to a state mental hospital. Patrolmen explained to reporters: "A nigger *has* to be crazy to try to get into Ole Miss." Douglass would have understood King's predicament. Sometimes it is as hard to break out of a white institution as to break in. (pp. 219-25)

John Sekora, "The Dilemma of Frederick Douglass: The Slave Narrative as Literary Institution," in Essays in Literature, *Vol. X, No. 2, Fall, 1983, pp. 219-26.*

William L. Andrews (essay date 1990)

[*In the excerpt below, Andrews examines voice and narrative technique in* The Heroic Slave.]

The Heroic Slave reads in some ways like a historical novel pared down to the basic plot of the slave narrative, the quest for freedom. During the decade between the slave revolt aboard the *Creole* and the publication of **The Heroic Slave,** Madison Washington did not become the sort of historical personage that usually appears in historical fiction, but the insurrection he led and its international political and economic consequences left their mark on the thinking of both defenders and critics of slavery. During the early 1840s, numerous abolitionists celebrated Washington and the "Immortal Nineteen" slaves who had participated in the revolt. But why did Douglass keep the example of Washington alive in his speeches and writing long after the *Creole* affair had lost its currency? And why did he do so in a fictionalized form largely devoted to dramatizing Washington's life *before* the *Creole* affair? To answer these questions, we must look briefly at the details of Washington's life that were available to Douglass and at their significance to the public debate generated by the revolt.

The primary resource for facts about Washington is the collection of depositions the American consul took from the *Creole* officers and a handful of its seamen and passengers soon after the slave-commandeered ship reached port at Nassau (*Senate Documents* 1-46). The captain of the brig, Robert Ensor, was severely wounded during the uprising; the first and second mates, Zephaniah Gifford and Lucius Stevens, escaped serious injury, but the victorious insurrectionists threatened them with death if they did not steer the ship to safe harbor. A third important deponent, William Merritt, a passenger, helped plot and navigate the *Creole's* course to Nassau, but also under threat of death. Obviously none of these men had any reason to speak well of Madison Washington or his cohorts in what the ship's officers consistently call the "murder" and "mutiny" perpetrated aboard their vessel. Yet even though all the deponents identify Washington as the precipitator and one of the masterminds of the revolt, the whites depict him as singularly reasonable, self-controlled, and humane, in marked contrast to the cursing, bloodthirsty "bad negroes" under him, whose violence he restrains and directs. For instance, Merritt credits Washington with "interceding" for him when one of the most menacing of the insurrectionists seemed determined to kill him. Gifford recalls that rather than leave Ensor to bleed to death in the rigging where he had taken refuge, Washington ordered that the captain be taken down in a sling and locked in the forehold with his wife, where the two remained undisturbed for the remainder of the ship's journey to Nassau.

There is no evidence in the depositions that these actions on Washington's part mitigated his criminality as far as the whites aboard the *Creole* were concerned. Only once in all the depositions is there even the slightest acknowledgment that the motive of the insurrectionists was liberation from their chains, not the murder of every white person on the ship. Moreover, this brief remark—"The nineteen [active participants in the revolt] said all they had done was for their freedom"—is followed by a comment on the refusal of the rest of the 134 slaves aboard ship to confirm or deny their allegiance to the insurrectionists, "they were so much afraid of the nineteen" (*Senate Documents* 41). Nevertheless, to American abolitionists it was the positive information about Washington that emerged from the testimony of the whites on the *Creole* that made him, unlike Nat Turner, a slave revolutionary whom whites could admire instead of fear. At a time when abolitionists were just starting to exploit the propagandistic value of the life stories of slaves who had broken their shackles in the name of freedom, Madison Washington's story seemed full of potential. Unfortunately, so few facts were known about the man that no one knew how to turn them into an authentic slave narrative or him into its hero.

In June 1842 the *Liberator* published what it called "Madison Washington: Another Chapter in His History," in which it brought a few new facts to light about Washington's activities before the *Creole* affair. The *Liberator* cited a message from a Canadian abolitionist, Hiram Wilson, who said Washington had been living in Canada for "some time" while planning a trip to Virginia to rescue his enslaved wife. There was evidence from abolitionists in New York who had given Washington money to defray his expenses on his journey south. But as to what had happened when the black man arrived in Virginia, the *Liberator* could only speculate. It inferred that in the process of trying to free his wife, Washington had been apprehended and "sold for New-Orleans," an explanation that would account for why he was part of the human cargo of the New Orleans-bound *Creole.* But what about the fate of his wife? The *Liberator* remembered from the depositions of a year earlier that the discovery of Washington in the slave women's cabin had led to the first violent acts of the slave revolt. "Might not his wife have been there among the women?" And if so, might not the entire insurrection "prove to have been but part of that great game, in which the highest stake was the liberty of [Washington's] dear wife?" Clearly, a romantic dimension to Washington's story was something the *Liberator* wanted to read into the scanty facts it had amassed about his pre-*Creole* past. This effort by the *Liberator* to infer a romantic plot underlying the *Creole* incidents testifies to the strong desire of American abolitionism for *a* story, if not *the* story, about Washington that would realize him as a powerful symbol of black antislavery heroism.

In speeches during the late 1840s Douglass did his part to keep the memory of Madison Washington alive. But it was not until passage of the Fugitive Slave Law in 1850 that Douglass became sufficiently militant on the justifiability of violence against slaveholders to treat Washington as the epitome of the "heroic slave." Still, Douglass could not write a narrative tribute to Washington without facing the problem that the *Liberator* had posed a decade before: how to make a "history" of the fragmentary information available on Washington. Ten fruitless years had passed since the *Liberator* asked that someone get the facts about Washington in the conventional way, in a narrative "from his own lips." It must have become plain to Douglass that for the example of Washington ever to be exploited in antislavery discourse, someone else would have to do Washington's narrating for him. But in order for there to be any narrating, there would have to be a story of Washington to tell. Without a story that explained and justified the climactic action on the *Creole,* that action would lose much of its power to dictate the terms of its own interpretations. Thus the task of the narrator of **The Heroic Slave** became primarily to make Washington narratable, to empower in and through an authenticating story, in a history, that which Washington truly represented—the revolutionary, not the blindly rampaging, slave.

Douglass's approach to the problem of how to make Washington a part of history was novel. He made the lack of knowledge about Washington, as opposed to the wealth of historical information about other champions of liberty from Virginia, the gambit of his text. Unlike typical slave narrators, who promised the reader facts based on the most intimate knowledge of their subjects, the narrator of **The Heroic Slave** promises his reader only "marks, traces, possibles, and probabilities" relating to a subject that "is still enveloped in darkness." The identity of the subject of **The Heroic Slave** is not specified in the opening paragraphs of the text. The only biographical fact brought out about the unnamed slave in question is that he is Virginia-born. Like the illustrious Patrick Henry, Thomas Jefferson, and George Washington, all the "great ones of the Old Dominion" whose names and deeds have been emblazoned in "American annals," this unnamed slave was "a man who loved liberty." And yet while "history has not been sparing in recording their names," the slave's name "lives now only in the chattel records of his native State."

There could be no more apt way for the first fictive narrator in African American literature to establish intercourse with his white reading audience. What sort of authority should be granted to your "history," he asks, if it celebrates as heroes of liberty slave owners like

Henry and Washington while ignoring a slave who "deserved" and "fought for" his liberty every bit as heroically as these men did? To what sources must we go to find the real "history" of the struggle for freedom in Virginia? As long as freedom-loving slaves exist only in records of chattel, they will be disqualified from their rightful place in "history," the authoritative record of people of consequence. Obviously then, the aim of the narrator of *The Heroic Slave* is first to liberate his slave hero from all the records that chattelize him and then to make him a part of history so that his real significance as a son of Virginia can be recognized.

Since the "chattel records" are necessarily commodified and hence perverse and imcomplete, the narrator who would do this service to Virginia history must "command the pen of genius." Instead of simply recording the known, he must penetrate the unknown, the "marks, traces, possibles, and probabilities" left by the fragmentary "chattel records." The narrator of *The Heroic Slave* does not go so far as to say that the "genius" he will employ will be that of the novelist, but one cannot escape this implication, nor does the narrator want the reader to miss it. If, in writing the history of a slave the narrator is compelled to create what might be called a "fiction of factual representation," he wants it clear that Virginia's "chattel records" leave him no alternative. To historicize, to *realize* this son of Virginia in history, it is necessary to fictionalize him. The entire narrative enterprise of *The Heroic Slave* rests on the reader's accepting the paradoxical necessity of the fictiveness of Washington's history.

As a storyteller, the narrator of *The Heroic Slave* plays a number of roles after justifying the fictiveness of his work. Because Robert B. Stepto has given close attention to the storytelling dimension of Douglass's text, [see excerpt dated 1982], I do not devote more of my discussion to it here. Suffice it to say that after the introduction to the story, the narrator makes no effort to authenticate any specific contention made about Washington in the rest of the narrative. The narrator offers no means of distinguishing between facts, "possibles," and "probabilities." By structuring the story around speeches that he seems merely to report verbatim to the reader, the narrator gives the narration an appearance of objectivity. As his source for most of the speeches and much of the behavior of Washington, he names a Mr. Listwell, whom he also claims as a personal acquaintance. This disclosure lends to the narration of the first three parts of the text a consistent and plausible point of view. We seem to be reading one of those narratives "told by X [Listwell] to Y [the narrator] apropos of Z [Washington]" that make up "the very fabric of our 'experience'" in the real world. In ways like these, the narrator of *The Heroic Slave* tries to make Washington's story sound objectively told without holding himself accountable for the authenticity of anything in particular said by or about Washington.

In taking these steps to objectify the narrating of *The Heroic Slave,* Douglass finesses the problem of authenticating what that narrating voice actually says. Unlike in the traditional slave narrative, which predicates the narrator's authority on authentication provided by the facts in the text or the testimonials that preface and append the text, in *The Heroic Slave* the authority of the narrator is insisted on from the start by him alone. Indeed, his right to tell his story in his own way, free from the obligation to limit himself only to the few facts available to him, is insisted on before any narrating actually takes place. Herein lies the fundamental importance of *The Heroic Slave* to the evolution of African American narrative from "natural" to "fictive" discourse: priority in *The Heroic Slave* is given to the empowering of a mode of fictive discourse whose authority does not depend on the authentication of what is asserted in that discourse. The authority of fictive discourse in African American narrative depends on a sabotaging of the presumed authoritative plenitude of history as "natural" discourse so that the right of the fictive to supplement (that is, to subvert) "history" can be declared and then exploited. (pp. 27-30)

William L. Andrews, "The Novelization of Voice in Early African American Narrative," in PMLA *Vol. 105, No. 1, January, 1990, pp. 23-34.*

FURTHER READING

Allen, William G. "Orators and Oratory." *The Liberator* XXII, No. 44 (29 October 1852): 176.
> Laudatory assessment of Douglass as orator. Allen states: "He, in very deed, sways a magic wand. In the ability to imitate, he stands almost alone and unapproachable; and there is no actor living, whether he be tragedian or comedian, who would not give the world for such a face as his."

Andrews, William L. "Reunion in the Postbellum Slave Narrative: Frederick Douglass and Elizabeth Keckley." *Black American Literature Forum* 23, No. 1 (Spring 1989): 5-16.
> Explores themes of reconciliation and reunion in the *Life and Times of Frederick Douglass.*

Aptheker, Herbert. "Du Bois on Douglass: 1895." *The Journal of Negro History* XLIX, No. 4 (October 1964): 264-68.
> Transcript of an address delivered by W. E. B. Du Bois at a memorial service for Douglass held at Wilberforce University in 1895.

Baker, Houston A., Jr. "Revolution and Reform: Walker, Douglass, and the Road to Freedom." In his *Long Black Song: Essays in Black American Literature and Culture,* pp. 58-83. Charlottesville: University Press of Virginia, 1972.
> Discusses Douglass's use of humor, verisimilitude, animal imagery, and other narrative devices in the *Narrative of the Life of Frederick Douglass.*

Blight, David W. "'For Something beyond the Battlefield': Frederick Douglass and the Struggle for the Memory of the Civil War." *The Journal of American History* 75, No. 4 (March 1989): 1156-78.
    Discusses Douglass's conception of the memory and meaning of the Civil War, both personally and historically.

Bontemps, Arna. *Free at Last: The Life of Frederick Douglass.* New York: Dodd, Mead & Co., 1971, 310 p.
    Popularized account of Douglass's life following his escape from slavery in 1838.

Burt, James. "Learning to Write: The Narrative of Frederick Douglass." *Western Humanities Review* XLII, No. 4 (Winter 1988): 330-44.
    Discusses Douglass's views of his early education, particularly his learning to write, as presented in the *Narrative.*

Chesnutt, Charles W. *Frederick Douglass.* 4th ed. The Beacon Biographies of Eminent Americans, edited by M. A. DeWolfe Howe. Boston: Small, Maynard & Co., 1899, 141 p.
    An early biography that focuses on Douglass's career as an abolitionist and civil rights advocate. Chesnutt is recognized as a pioneer in African-American fiction.

Cox, James M. "Trial for a Southern Life." *The Sewanee Review* XCVII, No. 2 (Spring 1989): 238-52.
    Places Douglass's *Narrative* within a tradition of Southern autobiographical writing.

De Pietro, Thomas. "Vision and Revision in the Autobiographies of Frederick Douglass." *CLA Journal* XXVI, No. 4 (June 1983): 384-96.
    Explores changes in Douglass's narrative intentions as evidenced in successive versions of his autobiography.

Foner, Philip S. *Frederick Douglass.* New York: Citadel Press, 1964, 444 p.
    A major biographical study. Although Foner is critical of Douglass's approach to certain issues affecting the economic welfare of blacks, he otherwise praises him as an uncompromising and effective agitator for the "full freedom" of his race.

Gates, Henry Louis, Jr. "Frederick Douglass and the Language of the Self." In his *Figures in Black: Words, Signs, and the "Racial" Self,* pp. 98-124. New York: Oxford University Press, 1987.
    Argues that Douglass was deeply concerned with presenting a public, fictive self in his autobiographies and that he himself carefully shaped the public image by which he wanted to be remembered. Gates notes: "When I choose to call these selves fictive ones, I do not mean to suggest any sense of falsity or ill intent: rather, I mean by fictive the act of crafting or making by design, in this instance a process that unfolds in language, through the very discourse that Douglass employs to narrate his autobiographies."

Gibson, Donald B. "Reconciling Public and Private in Frederick Douglass' *Narrative.*" *American Literature* 57, No. 4 (December 1985): 549-69.
    Examines authorial point of view in Douglass's *Narrative.*

Goddu, Teresa A., and Smith, Craig V. "Scenes of Writing in Frederick Douglass's *Narrative*: Autobiography and the Creation of Self." *The Southern Review* 25, No. 4 (Autumn 1989): 822-40.
    Close study of tropes in Douglass's *Narrative,* focusing on the author's "self-creation."

Holland, Frederic May. *Frederick Douglass: The Colored Orator.* Rev. ed. 1895. Reprint. New York: Haskell House Publishers, 1969, 431 p.
    The first comprehensive Douglass biography. As part of his research for the volume, Holland interviewed Douglass at his home in Anacostia Heights, D.C.

Joshi, Manoj K. "Frederick Douglass and the Emigrationist Movement." *The Western Journal of Black Studies* 9, No. 3 (Fall 1985): 135-43.
    Discusses the development of Douglass's views about schemes calling for blacks to leave the United States and settle abroad.

Leverenz, David. "Frederick Douglass's Self-Refashioning." *Criticism* XXIX, No. 3 (Summer 1987): 344-70.
    Close study of *My Bondage and My Freedom,* focusing on changes in authorial intent from the 1845 *Narrative.*

"Douglass's 'North Star'." *The Liberator* XVIII, No. 4 (28 January 1848): 15.
    Anonymous review of four issues of Douglass's newspaper *North Star,* praising Douglass as writer, editor, typographer, orthographer, and grammarian.

Logan, Rayford W. Introduction to *Life and Times of Frederick Douglass,* by Frederick Douglass, pp. 15-24. New York: Collier Books, 1962.
    Biographical and critical essay on Douglass and his *Life and Times.* Logan, who describes the work as a "classic in American literature," challenges the view that the *Life and Times* reveals only the worst aspects of slavery.

MacKethan, Lucinda H. "From Fugitive Slave to Man of Letters: The Conversion of Frederick Douglass." *The Journal of Narrative Technique* 16, No. 1 (Winter 1986): 55-71.
    Studies Douglass's works in light of "their need to act both as quests for and proofs of the entitling powers of language."

McFeely, William S. *Frederick Douglass.* New York: W. W. Norton, 1991, 465 p.
    Comprehensive overview of Douglass's life and career, focusing on Douglass's vulnerability and intellectual complexity. McFeely states: "Frederick Douglass was one of the giants of nineteenth-century America.... In an age of oratory, some judged him to have had the greatest voice. As a writer, he created an unforgettable character named Frederick Douglass; as a citizen, he struggled in a winning cause to rid his homeland of its most grievous social flaw, only to see slavery replaced with injustice and terror."

Miller, Kelly. "Frederick Douglass." In his *Race Adjustment. The Everlasting Stain,* pp. 211-20. 1908; 1924. Reprint. New York: Arno Press and The New York Times, 1968.

> An appreciation honoring Douglass as the outstanding model of emulation for black Americans. Miller's essay appears in the *Race Adjustment* portion of this volume of reprints.

Olney, James. "The Founding Fathers—Frederick Douglass and Booker T. Washington." In *Slavery and the Literary Imagination: Selected Papers from the English Institute, 1987,* edited by Deborah E. McDowell and Arnold Rampersad, pp. 1-24. Baltimore: Johns Hopkins University Press, 1989.

> Views Douglass and Booker T. Washington as Founding Fathers of a distinct African-American literary tradition that later encompassed such writers as Richard Wright and Ralph Ellison. Olney states: "[Autobiographies] and novels in the Douglass-Wright tradition are almost entirely concerned with the encounter between the races and with the efforts of black males to realize themselves or to make something significant of their lives in a world where whites rule and oppress blacks."

Piper, Henry Dan. "The Place of Frederick Douglass's *Narrative of the Life of an American Slave* in the Development of a Native American Prose Style." *The Journal of Afro-American Issues* V, No. 2 (Spring 1977): 183-91.

> Close study of Douglass's successive revisions of his autobiography.

Quarles, Benjamin. *Frederick Douglass.* Washington, D.C.: Associated Publishers, 1948, 378 p.

> The standard biography.

————. "Abolition's Different Drummer: Frederick Douglass." In *The Antislavery Vanguard: New Essays on the Abolitionists,* edited by Martin Duberman, pp. 123-34. Princeton: Princeton University Press, 1965.

> Examines the factors that contributed to Douglass's prominence as an abolitionist. According to Quarles, Douglass was distinguished by his oratorical skills, race, fundamental concern for human rights, and intransigent opposition to slavery.

————. *Narrative of the Life of Frederick Douglass."* In *Landmarks of American Writing,* edited by Hennig Cohen, pp. 90-100. New York: Basic Books, 1969.

> A general discussion of the qualities that give the *Narrative* its pre-eminent position among American slave narratives. Quarles here repeats many of the views expressed in his introduction to the 1960 edition of the *Narrative.*

Sekora, John. "Comprehending Slavery: Language and Personal History in Douglass' *Narrative* of 1845." *CLA Journal* XXIX, No. 2 (December 1985): 157-70.

> Admires Douglass's 1845 *Narrative* as the first comprehensive, personal history of American slavery.

Stowe, Harriet Beecher. "Frederick Douglass." In her *Men of Our Times; or, Leading Patriots of the Day,* pp. 378-404. Hartford, Conn.: Hartford Publishing Co., 1868.

> A contemporary memoir by the author of *Uncle Tom's Cabin.* Founding her account on Douglass's *Narrative,* Stowe perceives and presents Douglass's personal history as "a comment on the slavery system which speaks for itself."

Takaki, Ronald T. "Not Afraid to Die: Frederick Douglass and Violence." In his *Violence in the Black Imagination: Essays and Documents,* edited by Herbert Hill, pp. 17-35. New York: G. P. Putnam's Sons, 1972.

> Examines Douglass's attitude toward the use of violence in achieving black emancipation. Takaki interprets the slave rebellion in *The Heroic Slave* as an expression of Douglass's ultimate acceptance of violence as a means of black liberation.

Washington, Booker T. *Frederick Douglass.* 1907. Reprint. New York: Haskell House Publishers, 1968. 365 p.

> A biography that focuses primarily on Douglass's public life, interspersed with comments on social and political issues relevant to his career. In his preface, Washington implicitly disassociates himself from Douglass's militancy, stating: "Frederick Douglass's career falls almost wholly within the first period of the struggle in which [the race] problem has involved the people of this country,—the period of revolution and liberation. That period has now ended.... This book will have failed of its purpose just so far as anything here said shall serve to keep alive the bitterness of those controversies of which it gives the history...."

Yellin, Jean Fagan. "William Wells Brown." In her *The Intricate Knot: Black Figures in American Literature, 1776-1863,* pp. 154-81. New York: New York University Press, 1972.

> Includes an insightful critical description of Douglass's autobiographies.

W. E. B. Du Bois

1868-1963

(Full name William Edward Burghardt Du Bois) American historian, essayist, novelist, biographer, poet, autobiographer, and editor.

Du Bois was a major force in helping define black social and political causes in the United States. He was both a leader and an outcast of his race, an intellectual who espoused controversial opinions early in his life and who in time earned himself the title of "prophet." He is widely remembered for his conflict with Booker T. Washington over the role to be played by blacks in American society—an issue that he treated at length in his famous *The Souls of Black Folk* (1903). Among his important works in many genres, he is particularly known for his historiography and for his pioneering role in the study of black history. According to Herbert Aptheker, however, Du Bois was more of a "history maker," and his works and ideas continue to attract attention and generate controversy today.

Du Bois had an almost idyllic childhood in Great Barrington, Massachusetts, where his family was part of a stable community of fifty blacks in the small town of 5,000. Born with "a flood of Negro blood, a strain of French, a bit of Dutch, but, thank God! no 'Anglo-Saxon'," Du Bois escaped outright racism and segregation in this small New England town. He and his mother, Mary Burghardt Du Bois, lived a meager existence; his father, Alfred Du Bois, left his mother about the time Du Bois was born. Class and race distinctions were slight in Great Barrington, however, and the town quickly recognized Du Bois to be a youth of exceptional intelligence and ability. When his mother died soon after his high school graduation, some residents of the town gave Du Bois a scholarship on condition that he attend Fisk University, a southern school founded for the children of emancipated slaves. Du Bois, however, had always dreamt of attending Harvard University. Some biographers maintain that the residents of Great Barrington thought their high school was ill-equipped to send students to Harvard. In 1885 Du Bois traveled to Fisk in Nashville, Tennessee—his first journey to the southern United States.

"No one but a Negro going into the South without previous experience of color caste can have any conception of its barbarism," Du Bois later wrote in his posthumously published *Autobiography* (1968). Yet Du Bois was "deliriously happy" at Fisk, where he met students of his own race. There he excelled at studies and during summers taught the young blacks who lived in destitute rural areas of Tennessee. After being graduated with honors from Fisk in three years, Du Bois entered Harvard in 1888 to receive a second bachelor's degree and eventually his doctorate. Although fellow students greeted him with animosity, Du Bois found at

Harvard professors who would provide lifelong inspiration—Josiah Royce, George Santayana, Albert Bushnell Hart, and William James, who became a mentor and friend. With only his dissertation to complete to receive his doctorate in history, Du Bois enrolled at the University of Berlin in Germany; there he studied philosophy, sociology, and history for two years. Upon return to the United States in 1894, however, he promptly rediscovered "'nigger'-hating America," where the chances of a black history instructor finding a teaching position were slim. In 1895 Du Bois completed his dissertation, *The Suppression of the African Slave-Trade to the United States of America, 1638-1870*. The work became the first volume of the Harvard Historical Studies series, and Du Bois became the first black American to receive his doctorate from Harvard. In 1899 Du Bois published the sociological study *The Philadelphia Negro,* the product of interviews with 5,000 black persons living in the "dirt, drunkenness, poverty, and crime" of Philadelphia. The work, commissioned by the University of Pennsylvania, pioneered the scholarly study of black Americans. Yet the university did not give Du Bois a position on its faculty. Du Bois found this to be typical; despite his advanced degrees and important published works, he was denied key teaching positions time and again for no other reason than his color.

At the advent of the twentieth century the champion of black Americans was Booker T. Washington, then the principal of Tuskegee Institute in Alabama and the most powerful black man in America. In the preface to his *W. E. B. Du Bois: Negro Leader in a Time of Crisis,* Francis L. Broderick described Washington's accommodationist tactics as "speaking soft words to white men and careful words to colored men." Washington laid the blame for blacks' social positions on their inferior economic positions. As spokesman for his race, he was prepared to let black Americans be disenfranchised until they contributed to the economy by learning trades in agriculture and industry. Du Bois, however, could not abide by this stance. Broderick wrote of Du Bois: "Long restive under Washington's acquiescence in second-class citizenship, Du Bois ordered the Negro to be a man and demanded that white America recognize him as such." The two men, diametrically opposed in their views toward education, each found supporters, and the historic conflict began. In 1903 Du Bois published his best-known work, a collection of essays entitled *The Souls of Black Folk;* according to Arnold Rampersad, Souls became "perhaps the most influential work on blacks in America since *Uncle Tom's Cabin.*" Du Bois's critique of *Up from Slavery,* Washington's autobiography, was one of the essays in *Souls,* and with the work's publication Du Bois became inextricably involved with the fight for equality for blacks.

In 1905 Du Bois formed the Niagara Movement, the first black protest movement of the twentieth century. Twenty-nine black men met on the Canadian side of Niagara Falls and planned to dismantle segregation and discrimination while opposing Washington. Du Bois helped institute a more lasting movement in 1909 when he became the only black founding member of the National Association for the Advancement of Colored People (NAACP). Du Bois also founded and edited *Crisis,* the official publication of the NAACP; under his editorial direction, the magazine became the most important black periodical of its day. In it Du Bois wrote editorials condemning lynching and disenfranchisement, and his discussion of arts and letters in *Crisis* is considered the catalyst of the Harlem Renaissance. But in 1918 Du Bois lost credibility when he urged support for American involvement in World War I in the editorial "Close Ranks"; later, he discovered widespread racism in the armed forces in Europe. Many black Americans turned away from Du Bois's leadership at this time, for as an intellectual and member of the middle class, he seemed at a distance from many of them. For instance, Du Bois was bewildered at the widespread popular appeal accorded to Marcus Garvey, Jamaican leader of the Universal Negro Improvement Association and founder of the "back-to-Africa" move-

ment. His conflict with Garvey, whom he eventually called "the most dangerous enemy of the Negro race in America and the world," indicated his alienation from a large part of the black population in America.

"I would have been hailed with approval, if I had died at age fifty. At seventy-five my death was practically requested," said Du Bois of struggles later in his life, according to Addison Gayle, Jr. Although Du Bois continued to write great works, including his self-proclaimed magnum opus *Black Reconstruction* (1935), his popularity waned and resentment toward him grew. He was removed from the NAACP twice for ideological differences—he opposed the NAACP's idea of integration on the pages of *Crisis,* for example, and he supported Progressive party candidate Henry Wallace for president in the election of 1948 while the NAACP's executive secretary, Walter White, unofficially campaigned for Harry Truman. In 1951 Du Bois was indicted as an unregistered "agent of a foreign principal" because of his involvement in the "subversive" Peace Information Center, an organization that sought to inform Americans about international events and to abolish the atomic bomb. Although Du Bois was acquitted, his passport remained in the custody of the United States government. Gayle wrote: "The black churches, the black press, the black educational institutions, and the NAACP were mostly silent during and after the period of his struggle." Du Bois found needed support instead from the "communists of the world." Awarded the International Lenin Prize in 1958, he became a member of the Communist Party of the United States in 1961, shortly before renouncing his American citizenship. He died at the age of ninety-five in Accra, Ghana.

"The problem of the twentieth century is the problem of the color line," said Du Bois to the Pan-African Congress in 1900, and his famous statement, which became the introduction to *The Souls of Black Folk,* has been hailed as prophetic. Despite the controversy that surrounded his ideas and actions throughout his embattled lifetime, Du Bois continued to fight for equality between races. As Rampersad wrote in his 1976 study *The Art and Imagination of W. E. B. Du Bois*: "Far more powerfully than any other American intellectual, he explicated the mysteries of race in a nation which, proud of its racial pluralism, has just begun to show remorse for crimes inspired by racism."

(For further information about Du Bois's life and works, see *Black Writers; Concise Dictionary of American Literary Biography, 1865-1917; Contemporary Authors,* Vols. 85-88; *Contemporary Literary Criticism,* Vols. 1, 2, 13; *Dictionary of Literary Biography,* Vols. 47, 50, 91; and *Something about the Author,* Vol. 42.)

PRINCIPAL WORKS

The Suppression of the African Slave-Trade to the United States of America, 1638-1870 (history) 1896
The Philadelphia Negro: A Social Study (essay) 1899

The Souls of Black Folk: Essays and Sketches (essays) 1903

The Negro in the South: His Economic Progress in Relation to His Moral and Religious Development: Being the William Levi Bull Lectures for the Year 1907 [with Booker T. Washington] (lectures) 1907

John Brown (biography) 1909

The Quest of the Silver Fleece (novel) 1911

The Negro (history) 1915

Darkwater: Voices from Within the Veil (poems, essays, and sketches) 1920

The Gift of Black Folk: The Negroes in the Making of America (history) 1924

Dark Princess: A Romance (novel) 1928

Africa: Its Geography, People and Products (history) 1930

Africa: Its Place in Modern History (history) 1930

Black Reconstruction: An Essay Toward a History of the Part Which Black Folk Played in the Attempt to Reconstruct Democracy in America, 1860-1880 (history) 1935

Black Folk, Then and Now: An Essay in the History and Sociology of the Negro Race (history) 1939

Dusk of Dawn: An Essay Toward an Autobiography of a Race Concept (autobiography) 1940

Color and Democracy: Colonies and Peace (essay) 1945

The World and Africa: An Inquiry into the Part Which Africa Has Played in World History (criticism) 1947

In Battle for Peace: The Story of My 83rd Birthday (memoirs) 1952

* *The Ordeal of Mansart* (novel) 1957

* *Mansart Builds a School* (novel) 1959

* *Worlds of Color* (novel) 1961

†*Selected Poems* (poetry) 1964

The Autobiography of W. E. B. Du Bois: A Soliloquy on Viewing My Life From the Last Decade of Its First Century [edited by Herbert Aptheker] (autobiography) 1968

W. E. B. Du Bois Speaks: Speeches and Addresses [edited by Philip S. Foner] (speeches) 1970

W. E. B. Du Bois: The Crisis Writing [edited by Daniel Walden] (essays) 1972

The Emerging Thought of W. E. B. Du Bois: Essays and Editorials From "The Crisis" [edited by Henry Lee Moon] (essays) 1972

The Education of Black People: Ten Critiques, 1906-1960 [edited by Herbert Aptheker] (essays) 1973

---

*These works are collectively referred to as the *Black Flame* trilogy.

†The publication date of this work is uncertain.

William H. Ferris (essay date 1913)

[*In his 1913 work* The African Abroad, *Ferris wrote:* "I understand [The Souls of Black Folk] *because I am a Negro. White people put it down, surprised that a colored man's soul should be so sensitive to slights and insults."* *In the following excerpt from an edited version of this work, he analyzes the effect of* Souls *on himself and black people.*]

[Both Paul Laurence Dunbar and Charles Waddell Chesnutt] have artistically uncovered to our gaze the inner life of the Negro, but Du Bois has done this and something more. He has not only graphically pictured the Negro as he is, but he has brooded and reflected upon and critically surveyed the peculiar environment of the Negro, and with his soul on fire with a righteous indignation, has written with the fervid eloquence of a Carlyle. If one desires to see how it feels to be a Negro and a man at the same time, if one desires to see how a sensitive and refined Negro mentally and spiritually reacts against social, civil, and political ostracism, if one desires to see a Negro passing judgment upon his civil and political status, and critically dissecting American race prejudice as with a scalping knife, he must go to Du Bois.

I well remember the thrill and pleasure with which I read his **Souls of Black Folk.** It was an eventful day in my life. It affected me just like Carlyle's *Heroes and Hero Worship* in my sophomore days at Yale, Emerson's *Nature and Other Addresses* in my senior year, and Carlyle's *Sartor Resartus* in my graduate days.

The reading of these three books were epochs and crucial moments in my moral and spiritual life. Henceforth the world was a different world for me. They revealed to me my own spiritual birthright, showed that there was a divine spark in every soul, and that God was manifest in every human soul and breathed his own nature into every human soul. Du Bois' **Souls of Black Folk** came to me as a bolt from the blue. It was the rebellion of a fearless soul, the protest of a noble nature against the blighting American caste prejudice. It proclaimed in thunder tones and in words of magic beauty the worth and sacredness of human personality even when clothed in a black skin.

Du Bois is a literary artist who can clothe his thought in such forms of poetic beauty that we are captivated by the opulent splendor and richness of his diction, while our souls are being stirred by his burning eloquence. His style is not only graphic and picturesque, he can not only vividly describe a county, in his brilliant chapter upon the Black Belt, but there is a dreamy suggestiveness to his chapters "Upon our Spiritual Strivings," "The Wings of Atalanta," and "Alexander Crummell," a delicate literary touch, which entitles Du Bois to a place in the magic circle of prose poets. As a literary genius he ranks with Newman, Ruskin, Renan, and Taine, and he has come to a self-realization of the ideals of his own race.

What then does Du Bois lack? As Dunbar lacks a grasp of the problems that interest and perplex the modern mind, so Du Bois seems to ignore the unity of human history. He is the voice of one crying in the wilderness, "The black man has the same feelings and thoughts and aspirations as the white man." It is a voice that has caught the ear of this country, and made its appeal to the American conscience. But it is a lone, solitary voice. It is Du Bois, an individual, crying out in righteous indignation and piteous wail, because he and his race, in the valley below, are prevented by the walls of American caste prejudice from climbing to the heights of Mt. Olympus and banqueting with the other immortals there. It is a Pilgrim, goaded and hurt because his race alone is shut out from the paradise of equal civil and political rights and equality of opportunity. It is not a prophetic voice, freighted with a message from the eternal, speaking, not with human force and emphasis, but with a "Thus saith the Lord" assurance and authority.

I understand the book because I am a Negro. White people put it down, surprised that a colored man's soul should be so sensitive to slights and insults.

But suppose Du Bois had gone back to Father Abraham, and showed that Abraham, Moses, Elijah, Elisha, and Isaiah championed the idea of the sovereignty of God, that they believed that he breathed into the nostrils of man the breath of life, and that man became a living soul, and that Christ completed this conception and revelation by declaring the brotherhood of man; suppose Du Bois saw in the religious faith of the Dark Ages, in the wresting of the Magna Carta from King John, in the Protestant Reformation in Germany, in the Puritan Reformation in England, in the American Revolution and the French Revolution, nothing but stages in the practical application to life of Christ's disclosure of the sacredness and worth of human personality; suppose that he saw in the anti-slavery struggle and the Negro's emancipation, not only the recognition of the Negro as a man but the application to him of Christ's divine revelation, and the culmination of the history of fifty centuries—then Du Bois' argument would have swept the country off its feet, because the tidal wave of five thousand years of history would have backed his argument with its irresistible movement, and would have carried his argument along with its resistless roll.

Then the Americans would not have seen in Du Bois a Negro chafing because he and his people have been caged and fettered, but a Daniel who reads the handwriting on the wall, and sees the hand of the Almighty in the progressive movement of human history. Matthew Arnold, the doubter, saw in human history "an eternal power not ourselves that makes for righteousness." Yes, what is human history but man's coming to self-knowledge, man realizing his own spiritual birthright, man realizing the moral and spiritual meaning and significance of life, man realizing that the same human soul pulses and throbs in men of all ages and races and colors.

Just as we cannot explain that impulse in grass and flower and seed that transforms the world into a fairyland every spring, save as we see that it is the Divine Mind and Life breaking into expression, so we cannot understand righteous indignation at wrong, and the impulse in man toward a nobler life and a saving faith in humanity, save as we see in it the stirring within human nature of God, the World Spirit, who is constantly uttering himself in nature and human nature. If Du Bois had grasped these truths as Carlyle and Emerson and Browning did, then he could say, "It is not I, Du Bois, who speak, but God, the World Spirit, in whom I live and move and have my being, speaking in me." As it is, *The Souls of Black Folk* is the protest of Du Bois, the individual, and not the protest of the universe against caste prejudice.

But it may be that if the subjective and personal note was not so clear and strong in *The Souls of Black Folk*; if instead of having for its keynote a despairing wail, it had rung with the buoyant faith of a Browning, the book might not have caught the ear of the age in the way that it has. Perhaps just such a pessimistic view of the race question was needed to arouse the American mind out of its lethargy, awaken the American conscience to its duty to the Negro, and acquaint the world with the unrest and dissatisfaction of colored men and women, who faced a blighting and blasting caste prejudice.

That Du Bois' *Souls of Black Folk* has become the political bible of the Negro race, that he is regarded by the colored people as the long-looked-for political Messiah, the Moses that will lead them out of the Egypt of peonage, across the Red Sea of Jim Crow legislation, through the wilderness of disfranchisement and restricted opportunity, and into the promised land of liberty of opportunity and equality of rights, is shown by the recent Niagara Movement, which has crowned Du Bois as the Joshua before whom it is hoped the Jericho of American caste prejudice will fall down. In July, 1905, colored men from thirteen different states, representing graduates from Harvard and Yale Universities, professors in Howard University, Washington, D. C., and some of the most prominent colored educators, preachers, lawyers, and businessmen of the South and West, assembled at Niagara Falls, issued the declaration of Negro manhood and hailed Du Bois as the standard-bearer of Negro rights and Negro liberty. (pp. 88-92)

> William H. Ferris, "The Emerging Leader— A Contemporary View," in W. E. B. Du Bois: A Profile, *edited by Rayford W. Logan, Hill and Wang, 1971, pp. 86-121.*

J. Saunders Redding (essay date 1948-49)

[*Redding is a distinguished critic, historian, novelist, and autobiographer. His celebrated study* They Came in Chains: Americans from Africa *(1950) traces the history of black people in America. Written in a fluid style, the work has been called a creative story as opposed to a dry catalogue of historical facts—a style that closely mirrors Du Bois's own attitude toward the writing of history. In the following "portrait" of Du Bois, originally published in* The American Scholar *when Du Bois was eighty-one years old, Redding profiles the man and his thought.*]

The first time I saw W. E. Burghardt Du Bois was on an occasion when he spoke in Philadelphia back in 1922 or '23. I remember that my father, who was then secretary of the Wilmington, Delaware, branch of the N.A.A.C.P., anticipated the event for days. I think he had never seen Du Bois either. But he had read him. He had read aloud to his uncomprehending offspring passages from *The Souls of Black Folk* and from *Darkwater,* and editorials from the *Crisis.* Indeed, though we could child-handle and mistreat the *Pathfinder,* the *Literary Digest,* and the *National Geographic* without fear of reprimand, the *Crisis* was strictly inviolate until my father himself had unwrapped and read it—often, as I have said, aloud. Afterwards it was turned over to us, and we looked at the pictures of the colored babies, the handsome colored college graduates, and the famous colored college athletes, and read Effie Lee Newsome's "Children's Corner." Miss Newsome, we thought, was a fine writer. The name of W. E. B. Du Bois meant little to us as children.

But it had begun to mean something by the time I had reached my early teens. The meaning was purely emotional. We had a family friend whose sister had often danced with Du Bois in his Harvard days. In church on Sundays, the dark, passionate words of **"A Litany of Atlanta,"** which I had learned as a recitation, kept substituting themselves for the General Supplication. A speaker once told our small high-school assembly that we were of the "talented tenth," and somehow I remembered that the phrase was Du Bois'. So, when the opportunity came to see and hear this man, I was quite as eager as my father.

I did not know what to expect. Certainly, though, a man of giant stature—not the delicately structured man that Du Bois was: certainly a voice of thunder, and not merely the clear, clipped voice that Du Bois had: certainly an apostolic storm of wrath (for that is the way my father read him), and not the probing, deliberate, impersonal light that Du Bois' speech shed, like sparks struck off from tempered steel. I was disappointed. If my father was also, he did not tell me.

Dr. Du Bois, of course, is tempered steel, and it is a matter of both character and mind. The bold outlines of his character—persistence, independence and a sort of realistic idealism—take their shape from a long line of down-East ancestors who were poor but never poverty-stricken, proud and self-contained but never self-centered. There were no particular subtleties in the characters of those ancestors; there are none in Du Bois. There was nothing of radiance; nothing mercurial, magnetic, gay. There is nothing of this in Du Bois either, except rarely. He is reserved, even aloof. His personality does not light up the place where he happens to be. Until he speaks on some subject that interests him, his presence in a room half full of people might go unnoticed by all save the artist, who would see the fine mold of the copper-colored features and the beautiful head.

Du Bois at age nineteen.

The flexible sharpness of Du Bois' mind is due, at least in part, to the circumstance and experience of growing up a Negro in New England. In Great Barrington, Massachusetts, where he was born, he could cultivate the sensitiveness of perception that a town in Georgia would have dulled. There was little to stimulate emotionalism. The problem of color had some significance for him, but the tides of race ran calmly through the valley of the Berkshires, and the young Du Bois could breast them with a glorious disdain. He could be a competitor, without the beaten-in feeling of being a combatant against emotional forces too wild and unreasonable for understanding. The competition offered by his youthful associates was largely intellectual.

But the very mildness of the color problem in Great Barrington was teasing bait to Du Bois' expanding mind. Whenever he went to Albany, Hartford or Providence, he got "swift glimpses of the colored world," and had veritable seizures of awareness of that world's peculiar isolation, its slave heritage, its neurotic tensions, and its precarious clutch on the soiled hem of the economy. These things showed through the bright surface beauty and edged the gaiety with the icy lace of spiritual death. Du Bois came early to see the problem of color in impersonal terms as a matter of social condition, and this condition itself "as a matter of education, as a matter of knowledge; as a matter of scientific procedure in a world which had become scientific in concept."

Since before Fisk, which he entered in 1885, and through Harvard, the University of Berlin, and Harvard again, Dr. Du Bois has followed "knowledge like a sinking star." Now in his eighty-first year, he is still following it—not knowledge for its own sweet sake, which is a luxury of leisure his practical idealism would scorn, but knowledge purposeful, knowledge working. The pursuit has given him one of the most catholic minds of the century. It is not a difficult mind to know.

• • • • •

It is not a difficult mind to know, for it lies exposed in a dozen major books, hundreds of editorials and articles, and a thin scattering of poems. The writings of Du Bois have the lucidity of a series of anatomical drawings showing the progressive stages in the development of an organism. In this case the organism is truth—the truth of historics, which is both sociology and history. Du Bois sees this truth as a tool for the better performance of the scientific task of probing and assaying "the scope of chance and unreason in human action." That he has applied it to the limited area of race relations is partly because of the traditional "specialization" of modern scholarship, and partly because doing otherwise would have meant rejection of race and a consequent upsetting of the careful balance between intellect and emotion. Even a scientist need not be a monstrosity of sheer brain supported by the dehumanized mechanism, the body.

Certainly Dr. Du Bois is not. After *The Suppression of the African Slave Trade,* his doctoral dissertation, and *The Philadelphia Negro,* and in the midst of those Atlanta University Studies on the Negro, he published *The Souls of Black Folk.* This is perhaps as emotional and subjective a book as any written in the first decade of this century. Du Bois meant it to be that way. Four times in a long career devoted principally to investigation and research in material that *is* emotional—in material upon which he was one of the first to bring to bear the scientific method—hc has had to give himself a thorough emotional housecleaning. *Darkwater* is a book like *The Souls of Black Folk; The Gift of Black Folk* is another; and the novels, in a different way, are others.

What is remarkable is that these introspective sprees have come so seldom, and that they have not led to a pattern of introspective behavior, as with so many Negro leaders. Remarkable that his energies have not dribbled off in mere invective and condemnation, race chauvinism and apology and defense.

But the truth is that in spite of the general belief as to his purposes, Du Bois' professional commitment has been to a program of "scientific investigation into social conditions, primarily for scientific ends." One who reads his chief works must be convinced that their emotional overcast is inherent in the material, and is not a quality of the treatment. For almost twenty years Du Bois, alone among Negro spokesmen, believed that the basis for interracial change for the better was a knowledge of the facts and the broader truth they represented. Thirteen years of work at Atlanta University were posited upon this belief; this was at the heart of much that appeared in the *Crisis* and in *Phylon* under his editorship.

But Du Bois' scientific problem has been complicated in a way unknown to most professional scholars until recently. When a group of outstanding scientists came to realize the stake they had in the future application of their knowledge, atomic physics ceased to be a scientific problem merely: it became a freighted social problem too—and the physicists were social beings! Thus it has always been with Du Bois. Himself a Negro, he has been a socially responsible part of his problem; he has been concerned with the practical application of his discovered knowledge to the problem. This certainly accounts for his insistence upon a program of higher liberal education for Negroes; for his espousal of the "talented tenth" idea; for his connection with the N.A.A.C.P., and for the controversy with Booker T. Washington.

These interests and activities have been the logical consequences of Du Bois' concern. Higher education, especially for the talented tenth of Negroes, meant to him the training of leaders who could guide the race to cultural fulfillment. The controversy with Booker Washington, which increased in bitterness as it lengthened in years, started because Dr. Du Bois disdained the role of second class citizen which Washington thought the Negro ought to play. Du Bois has believed in political action, in the black world's fighting for equality "with the weapons of Truth, with the sword of the intrepid, uncompromising Spirit." Washington, who wished the Negro to remain politically passive, was a compromiser. He deplored agitation for equal rights. He was a gradualist. Du Bois has believed that the cultural contribution of the race to the nation was not less because it was different; Washington felt that the value of that contribution was doubtful. Du Bois remains certain that the autocratic power bestowed upon Washington by well-meaning but misguided whites was a danger and a thwart to Negro advancement.

Finally, Du Bois has believed in democracy, and his ultimate personal and spiritual commitment has been to this. He has never believed democracy impossible of attainment. As a social being, he has followed three paths that at one time or another seemed to lead to the ideal. The first, along which he started in his teaching days, was the path of objective Truth. He followed it on the assumption that once "the scientifically attested truth concerning Negroes and race relations" was realized, the world would act in accordance with the findings of science. The second was the path of Organization to propagandize and popularize the truth. This was in the early N.A.A.C.P. and the *Crisis* period. The third was the path of Security, to ensure "the survival of the Negro race" and the maintenance of its cultural advance, "not for itself alone, but for the emancipation of mankind, the realization of democracy and the progress of civilization." Du Bois has gone back to the first path now, and it is likely that he will remain in it until his journey's done.

The mind is not always perfectly the man and the personality. In spite of the tremendous respect which his high accomplishments have earned him, Dr. Du Bois is not generally liked. Many of the stories about him set him forth as a crusty, mordant-witted snob of both the intellectual and social varieties. He is, the stories say, a little too proud of himself. Negro and white people—and not just inconsequential people either—complain that they must be introduced to Du Bois time after time, because only the fifth or sixth introduction seems to "take" with him. Many think his preference for a certain brand of expensive cigarette an affectation, and they attribute the fact that he blends and generally brews his own coffee to a desire to maintain a social distance. Just below average in height, careful, even meticulous about his personal appearance, Dr. Du Bois gives some an impression of daintiness which does not fit into the popular concept either of scholar or dynamic leader. Yet it is the highest tribute, it seems to me, that even those who grumble about Du Bois in this wise acknowledge that he was indubitably their chosen leader, *the* Negro leader, from 1914 until the election of Franklin D. Roosevelt. He did not seek the place of leader. His intellectual honesty, his far length of vision, and a fundamental integrity destined him to it.

As a consequence of his position, Dr. Du Bois has few intimates, but these call him "Dubbie." They find him charming, witty and occasionally gay. Whatever sense of intellectual superiority he has never comes out in bombast or pomposity. When the mood strikes him, he can tell a fascinating story, though to call him a raconteur would stretch a point. His public addresses are usually brilliant and as carefully developed as works of art, but his delivery is deadpan, in-taking (as if he must reappraise his utterances), not out-giving. Because he has no oratorical flair, because he never talks down to an audience, and because audiences are what they are, he has been called a dull platform speaker. In 1931, after one of his lectures in Atlanta, where I was teaching at the time, a bright young college sophomore remarked, "The old man's lost his stride, hasn't he?" I do not remember what I answered besides the simple negative, but I know that Dr. Du Bois was not old then. He is not old now. Just three years ago, when he was resettling in New York after a long absence, I heard him talk with glowing enthusiasm about the new furnishings for his apartment and about the years that lay ahead. At eighty he has still his hope and his dream, and his faith that one day truth will make men free. (pp. 93-6)

J. Saunders Redding, "Portrait . . . W. E. Burghardt Du Bois," in The American Scholar, *Vol. 18, No. 1, Winter, 1948-49, pp. 93-6.*

Herbert Aptheker (essay date 1969)

[*In 1946 Du Bois asked Herbert Aptheker to edit his correspondence and personal papers. According to J. Saunders Redding, Du Bois's choice was controversial. "Aptheker was white," wrote Redding in* Phylon, *"and editing the correspondence of a black American of Dr. Du Bois's stature and international prominence was a job for a Negro American, they said." The fact that Aptheker is an avowed Marxist further prejudiced black scholars against him. Nevertheless, Aptheker is widely recognized as the leading editor and scholar of Du Bois's works. In the following excerpt from a speech originally delivered to the American Historical Association in 1968 and published in an expanded version in 1969, he surveys Du Bois's career and contributions as a historian.*]

Dr. Du Bois was more a history-maker than an historian. The two were intertwined, however; what interested Du Bois as a maker of History helped determine what he wrote, and what he wrote helped make history.

Du Bois was an agitator-prophet. He tore at the Veil; at the same time, behind that Veil, he had a particular perspective from which he saw this country and world, past, present, and future, differently—more truly, I think, but certainly in a manner different from the conventional and the dominant. His main formal training—fairly strong in mathematics, languages, psychology, philosophy and economics—was especially thorough in history. As historian, dedicated to the most rigorous standards of integrity, he remained, nevertheless, agitator-prophet; present was another fundamental ingredient in the man, namely, the poet. Professor Charles H. Wesley, in the course of producing perhaps the most penetrating review of Du Bois' **Black Reconstruction,** caught this aspect very well indeed when he referred to Du Bois as "the lyric historian."

Du Bois's extraordinary career manifests a remarkable continuity. From his 1890 Harvard Commencement address to his posthumously-published **Autobiography,** the *essential* theme is the beauty, rationality, and need of service and of equality, and the ugliness, irrationality and threat of greed and elitism. Because of the especially oppressed condition of the colored peoples of the earth—and particularly of the African and African-derived peoples—Du Bois believed in their capacity for compassion and comradeship, or, as he put it in the 1890 speech, "for the cool, purposeful *Ich Dien* of the African." Keenly conscious of color and of consequent discrimination, convinced of his own capacities, and wedded to the idea of service—Du Bois never shed New England—he told himself as a graduate student in Berlin, on his 25th birthday:

The general proposition of working for the world's good becomes too soon sickly sentimentality. I therefore take the world that the Unknown lay in my hands and work for the rise of the Negro people, taking for granted that their best development means the best development of the world...

These are my plans: to make a name in science, to make a name in literature and thus to raise my race.....

Our present task is to follow Du Bois as historian. How did he conceive of history? The basic answer comes, of course, from his writings, and an enormous—almost incredible—corpus they are. While not all of it by any means represents history-writing, almost all of it—including the novels—does illustrate in one way or another Du Bois' view of history; to a few of these works we shall more particularly refer in subsequent pages. In addition, Du Bois did from time to time refer rather directly to his conception of history and historiography and to this we now turn.

For Du Bois, history-writing was *writing*; one who produces a book should try, thereby, to produce *literature*. He drove himself hard on this. All authors, I think, are anxious to see their work in print; crusading authors probably feel this anxiety more than others (if there are others!). Yet, Du Bois wrote and re-wrote his massive **Black Reconstruction** three times; and after that, revised and revised and cut and cut (as much as 250 pages were cut by him in the summer of 1934). In this connection he informed Charles Pearce—the person in charge of his manuscript at Harcourt, Brace—on July 10, 1933 that he had written his Reconstruction book a second time, but that it was not satisfactory for two reasons: "Its present length would require at least two volumes"; and: "It is not yet a piece of literature. It still resembles....a Ph.D thesis, well documented and with far too many figures. I have clearly in mind the sort of thing that I want to do and I think I can accomplish it but that means writing the book again." (pp. 6-7)

Du Bois was explicit in his belief that while living behind the Veil might carry the danger of provincialism, it had the great advantage of helping disclose truth or neglected aspects of reality exactly because its point of observation differed. There was something else, too; Du Bois not only held that a new vantage point offered new insights. He held also that a racist viewpoint was a blighted one; that it could not fail to distort reality and that an explicitly anti-racist viewpoint was not only different but better. Hence, he insisted that the view— or prejudice, if one wishes—which he brought to data would get closer to reality not only because it was fresh but also because it was egalitarian. One gets a somewhat different shading in at least one passage in Du Bois' writing where he suggests that possibly something "in between" may be nearer the truth. It occurs in **Black Folk: Then and Now** and requires quotation in full:

> I do not for a moment doubt that my Negro descent and narrow group culture have in many cases predisposed me to interpret my facts too favorably for my race; but there is little danger of long misleading here,

for the champions of white folk are legion. The Negro has long been the clown of history; the football of anthropology; and the slave of industry. I am trying to show here why these attitudes can no longer be maintained. I realize that the truth of history lies not in the mouths of partisans but rather in the calm Science that sits between. Her cause I seek to serve, and wherever I fail, I am at least paying Truth the respect of earnest effort.

On this ground, too, he tended to justify—even excuse—his practice of depending largely upon published sources and graduate papers rather than upon manuscript materials; he noted, in addition, particular discriminatory problems facing Negro scholars and authors and in his own case, problems of money and time— given his myriad activities. In **Black Reconstruction,** after having told the reader in the Preface, that he meant to retell the history of the years from 1860 to 1880 "with especial reference to the efforts and experiences of the Negroes themselves," he added that he was "going to tell this story as though Negroes were ordinary human beings, realizing that this attitude will from the first seriously curtail my audience." And in the body of the text he apologized for having "depended very largely upon secondary material," named collections of Papers that he was sure would contain relevant materials, acknowledged that the "weight of this work would have been vastly strengthened" had they been consulted—for which he had had neither "time nor opportunity." Nevertheless, he wrote that, standing as he did "literally aghast" at what racist historiography had done in this field, his own effort certainly must represent a significant and needed corrective.

A generation earlier, in the preface to his **John Brown** (1909), Du Bois made a substantially similar point and added a thought which still awaits comprehension by most in the historical profession:

> After the work of Sanborn, Hinton, Connelley, and Redpath, the only excuse for another life of John Brown is an opportunity to lay new emphasis upon the material which they so carefully collected, and to treat these facts from a different point of view. The view-point adopted in this book is that of the little known but vastly important inner development of the Negro American. John Brown worked not simply for Black Men—he worked with them; and he was a companion of their daily life, knew their faults and virtues, and felt, as few white Americans have felt, the bitter tragedy of their lot.

Du Bois saw the neglect of, or prejudice against, the Negro in American historiography as an aspect of a prevailing elitism in dominant history-writing in general. Du Bois felt that the assumption linking the well-born with the able was no more than an assumption; that to insist the poor's incapacity was demonstrated in their poverty was, at best, elliptical argument. His ironic response to the way in which dominant history deplored the suffering of the elite in periods of decisive social change or challenge—as Reconstruction—and its blithe ignoring of or apologizing for the age-long crucifixion of the poor reminds one of the celebrated passage in Mark

Twain's *Connecticut Yankee*; Du Bois' image, too, comes from the French Revolution: "In all this," he wrote in ***Black Reconstruction,*** "one sees the old snobbery of class judgment in new form—tears and sentiment for Marie Antoinette on the scaffold, but no sign of grief for the gutters of Paris and the fields of France, where the victims of exploitation and ignorance lay rotting in piles."

Sometimes Du Bois made this aspect of his philosophy of history perfectly explicit; thus: "We have the record of kings and gentlemen *ad nauseam* and in stupid detail; but of the common run of human beings, and particularly of the half or wholly submerged working group, the world has saved all too little of authentic record and tried to forget or ignore even the little saved."

Du Bois in practice resolved the difficult problem of objectivity and partisanship, of truth and justice, of the moral and the scientific by affirming—perhaps assuming would be more exact, for the argument is never quite explicit—that separating morals from science caricatures the latter, that the just is the true, and that while objectivity in the sense of utter neutrality in any meaningful matter is absurd this does not rule out the describing of reality—of "telling it like it is"; that, rather, the solution to the apparent paradox has a paradoxical twist: it is intense partisanship—on the side of the exploited and therefore on the side of justice—that makes possible the grasping of truth. Or, at least, that such partisanship is the highway leading to that accumulation of knowledge which brings one closer and closer to the real but not reachable final truth.

At times, Du Bois does separate the function of description and interpretation even to affirm—in a way reminiscent of his late nineteenth-century German training—that it is necessary (and possible) for an historian to "make clear the facts with utter disregard to his own wish and desire and belief," that "we have got to know, so far as possible" the "things that actually happened in the world" and then "with that much clear and open to every reader, the philosopher and prophet has a chance to interpret these facts" (***Black Reconstruction***). Yet, in practice, he combines the philosopher and the prophet with the historian; else the latter will become a clerk rather than a scientist; indeed, few writing in the area of American history have accomplished this combination so effectively as did Du Bois.

In a book review that Du Bois published in the *American Historical Review,* in lamenting what he thought were failures, he illuminated his own views on historiography; the succinctness necessary to the review form leads to a certain clarity of expression. Du Bois regretted that in the study in question he could find,

> . . . no sense of unity or growth, no careful digestion or arrangement of his material, no conception of the inner reactions of this changing and developing group of human beings, and no comprehension of the drama involved.

In connection with "drama" Du Bois added: "Some social scientists seem to think that because the scientist may not be emotional he has, therefore, no call to study emotion. This, of course, is a ridiculous *non sequitur.*"

In ***Black Reconstruction*** a few paragraphs devoted to the Beards' *Rise of American Civilization* illuminate Du Bois' concept of history and offer penetrating criticisms of the Beards' work. Reading it, said Du Bois, one had "the comfortable feeling that nothing right or wrong is involved." Two differing systems develop in the North and the South, Du Bois continued, and "they clash, as winds and waters strive." The "mechanistic interpretation" failed because human experience was not mechanistic. Furthermore—and here we get again Du Bois' insistence on "drama" as the heart of history—in such a presentation,

> . . . there is no room for the real plot of the story, for the clear mistake and guilt of building a new slavery of the working class in the midst of a fateful experiment in democracy; for the triumph of sheer moral courage and sacrifice in the abolition crusade; and for the hurt and struggle of degraded black millions in their fight for freedom and their attempt to enter democracy. Can all this be omitted or half suppressed in a treatise that calls itself scientific?

Du Bois had a towering sense of the Right, of the Just, a basic faith in reason and a passionate commitment towards achieving the just through the use of reason. Indeed, all this together is what Du Bois meant by that word which to him was most sacred: Science. And in his lifetime and in his experience the central lie was racism; this, therefore, received the brunt of his blows. "As a student of science," he wrote (in ***Black Reconstruction***), "I want to be fair, objective and judicial; to let no searing of the memory by intolerable insult and cruelty make me fail to sympathize with human frailties and contradiction, in the eternal paradox of good and evil." What, he asked, should be the object of writing history—the history of Reconstruction, for example?

> Is it to wipe out the disgrace of a people which fought to make slaves of Negroes? Is it to show that the North had higher motives than freeing black men? Is it to prove that Negroes were black angels? No, it is simply to establish the Truth, on which Right in the future might be built.

With all this one understands that Du Bois could never accept the idea that cause and effect was nothing but a man-made myth; he caustically rejected this idea which attracted much attention early in the 1940's, especially with Charles Beard's abandonment of causation. He labelled this, indeed, "asinine frivolity" and thought it "must cease if the decadence of the age is not to become definitive and irreversible." In this same essay, Du Bois, again decrying a mechanistic outlook, insisted that for the historian causation must be "conceived in truly humanistic, dynamic terms." He repudiated the heritage of Ranke only insofar as it had "become so exaggerated as to tend to dehumanize it." The historian, Du Bois held, must believe "that creative human initiative, working outside mechanical sequence, directs and changes the course of human action and so history...it is man who causes movement and change...". Du Bois did not mean here that man functioned independently of his circumstances; rather he was created by and created them. Thus, Du Bois' work is filled with the pressure of such circumstance, notably, but by no means solely, the economic. An example from his first professional history paper—that delivered before the Annual Meeting of this Association...back in 1891—must suffice.

> If slave labor was an economic god, then the slave trade was its strong right arm; and with Southern planters recognizing this and Northern capital unfettered by a conscience it was almost like legislating against economic laws to attempt to abolish the slave trade by statutes.

As historian, Du Bois' first concern—and one he never lost—was the rigorous study of the American Negro's past. The preface to his first book...before its paragraph of acknowledgments, closes with this thought: "...I nevertheless trust that I have succeeded in rendering this monograph a small contribution to the scientific study of slavery and the American Negro."

Somewhat later he articulated another basic working hypothesis in his approach to history; he began his **Black Reconstruction** by offering its reader the opinion that the experience of Negro people "became a central thread in the history of the United States, at once a challenge to its democracy and always an important part of its economic history and social development."

His penetrating observation, first offered in 1900 and twice repeated in a significant article published the next year—"The problem of the twentieth century is the problem of the color line"—was fundamental to his vision of the unity of all African peoples (to grow, as Du Bois advanced in years, to the idea that this itself was preliminary to the unity of all the darker peoples of the earth and *that* was part of the process of the worldwide unification of all who labor) and was, indeed, first enunciated as the Call of the original Pan-African Conference. This insight forms the inspiration for and thesis of his **The Negro, Black Folk, Then and Now, Color and Democracy: Colonies and Peace, The World and Africa**; most completely in the enlarged edition of that volume published two years after his death.

How shall we sum up Du Bois' conception of history? There is the facile technique of labels, normally unsatisfactory and in the case of a man as polemical, radical and productive as Du Bois, bound to be, I suggest, especially unsatisfactory. This does not mean the labelling has not been done, of course—and not simply by a berserk government that said Du Bois was—of all things—an "unregistered foreign agent!"

Thus, two historians were not only convinced that Du Bois was a Marxist; they felt able to tell their readers just when his baptism occurred. Harvey Wish wrote that Dr. Du Bois went to the Soviet Union in 1927—which is true—and that he "emerged a confirmed Marxist." Carl

Degler puts the conversion seven years later, affirming that "by the time" Du Bois wrote **Black Reconstruction** "he had become a Marxist." On the other hand, Rembert W. Patrick writes that Du Bois was "not a Marxian" when writing that book; while Howard K. Beale suggested that "perhaps it would be fairer to Marx to call Du Bois a quasi-Marxist." Having found Du Bois described as a confirmed Marxist, a plain Marxist, a quasi-Marxist and not a Marxist we have perhaps exhausted the possibilities.

Du Bois was a Du Boisite. His political affiliations or affinities varied as times changed, as programs altered and as he changed: in his 20s no doubt a reform Republican (like Douglass); prior to World War I a Socialist; in 1912, however, urging Wilson's election; in the post-War period often voting—at least in national elections—for Thomas; in the early 30s a leader, along with John Dewey and Paul Douglas and others, in a movement for an Independent politics; after World War II, favoring the (Henry) Wallace movement and Progressive Party efforts; in the 1950s running for U.S. Senator on the American Labor Party ticket (and getting a quarter of a million votes); and at the nadir of the political fortunes of the Communist Party, with its illegality apparently affirmed by the U.S. Supreme Court, choosing that moment to announce his decision to join that Party.

These were, however, political choices and not defining marks of his philosophical approaches. All his life Du Bois was a radical democrat; this was true even with his "Talented Tenth" concept which held that mass advance depended upon leadership and service from a trained minority, and insisted that such a goal and such service were the duty of such a minority and if not accepted and performed spelled the vitiation of the minority itself.

This sketch of Du Bois' political biography and the account in the preceding pages of his views of history surely do not add up to the term Marxist in any meaningful sense. Du Bois certainly was significantly influenced by Marx and Marxism which is to say—as C. Wright Mills did say under somewhat analogous circumstances that Du Bois was an educated man; this influence, however, came in concentrated form only towards the last third of his life. For this lateness Du Bois was severely self-critical (as he was, by the way, for a neglect of Freud); he certainly did conclude that no other system of thought was as revealing as Marxism but to the end of his days he remained an idealist—philosophically speaking—in key areas of his thinking. It may be added that while he found Marx rather late in his life, he seriously concerned himself with Lenin's views even later; as late as October, 1934, he remarked in a letter: "I have a fair library of Marx, but only one or two of Lenin's works." Had this neglect not existed it is difficult to see how Du Bois could have persisted in using the term "dictatorship of the proletariat"—even in the very limited way in which he did use that term (something on which more will be said below)—as

The After=Thought

Hear my Cry, O God the Reader; vouchsafe that this my book fall not stillborn into the world=wilderness. Let there spring, Gentle One, from out its *leaves* vigor of thought and thoughtful deed to reap the harvest wonderful. Let the ears of a guilty people tingle with truth, and seventy millions sigh for the righteousness which exalteth nations in this drear day when human brotherhood is a mockery and a snare. *Thus* in Thy good time *may* infinite reason turn the tangle straight, *and* these crooked marks on a fragile leaf be not indeed

The End.

Manuscript for the concluding page of The Souls of Black Folk.

pertains to the Radical Reconstruction governments. He did affirm views on capitalism as a system and colonialism as a phenomenon that were strikingly similar to—though not fully identical with—those of Marx and of Lenin, but his attitude towards the working class, the State, Communist Parties, mass initiative and towards the entire materialist outlook were not those of Marx nor of Lenin, though again marked similarities appear. If one insists on shorthand perhaps the careful Howard Beale came closest with his term, "quasi-Marxist"; given, however, Du Bois' own genius and the monumental scope of his interests and his output and the dynamic quality of his thinking I would myself prefer the term of Du Boisite; what this lacks in imagination and in illumination it makes up for in—accuracy!

Du Bois, while personally shy and remarkably objective about himself, never suffered from self-effacement or an excessive humility. At a very early age he was persuaded—as were his neighbors and associates, black and white—that his powers were considerable. Of all his books, he knew the first was the most scholarly—in the conventional sense (he even saw this as one of its limitations). The volume which—as he once told this writer—was his favorite was his biography of John Brown, based altogether upon rather easily accessible secondary works. But in the area of historiography, he knew, as he said in a letter written while in the throes of creating it, that his "magnum opus" was *Black Reconstruction*; that book he said, in applying for funds to assist in its final revision, "will not sell widely," but "in the long run, it can never be ignored." Du Bois was right on both counts.

Black Reconstruction deserves a book in its own right: how it came to be written, its sources, the people participating in its creation, how it was funded, examining its revisions, analyzing its contents, estimating its critical and popular reception, observing its impact upon black and white opinion, upon the scientific community, upon the making of history and the making of history books and texts. Obviously this is not the occasion for the presentation of such an effort.

For purposes of brevity we choose as a theme the remarks of one among the many more recent commentators on Reconstruction; this is Professor Staughton Lynd and I select him for both what he says and what he omits. Lynd pays generous tribute to Du Bois' pioneering in denying that enfranchising the Negro after the Civil War was a "great mistake"; and in showing that the Reconstruction governments had been slandered by the profession generally. Lynd says that "liberal historians of the last generation who have sought to correct the traditional image of cigar-smoking Negro legislators voting themselves gold-spittoons have added very little," since Du Bois' paper of 1909.

Lynd writes that the main problem now and for the future should be "what strategy of planned social change might have succeeded?" He thinks that the futility of legal and military force "to coerce deep-seated atti-

tudes" is plain; that those who hold that such efforts stopped too soon offer little real help; and that a third alternative is sounder, namely: "the fundamental error in Reconstruction policy was that it did not give the freedman land of his own ... Congress should have given the ex-slaves the economic independence to resist political intimidation."

It is unclear to this writer that alternative number three should be distinguished from alternative one and/or two; giving land to the freedmen surely would have required legal action and in all likelihood rather considerable military action, too; and to see that such a transformation in the socio-economic nature of the South was actually maintained as well as begun would have surely required alertness lest both legal and military measures be terminated too soon.

Professor Lynd goes on to point out that Du Bois in his 1901 article on the Freedmen's Bureau saw the consequence of this kind of land policy. I want to add that this is one of the central themes of his *Black Reconstruction* and that in the book it is developed and documented with infinitely greater care and depth than in the limits of the 1901 essay; Lynd's failure to make this clear is noted because in the estimates of *Black Reconstruction* this significant feature of its content is normally omitted.

Many other areas of Reconstruction—some of them beginning to receive treatment only in our own day—are in *Black Reconstruction.*

The point made by Professor C. Vann Woodward—that the political rights of the Southern black population were quite tenuous, given dependence upon a single party, the political and economic motivations of Republican leaders for extending those rights, with the possibility (and, as it happened, the reality) of the motivations changing and so the attitude towards those rights changing—also is in Du Bois' book.

The relationship between the possibilities of the exploitation of the resources and labor of the South by a rising industrial capitalism and the impact this was bound to have upon Reconstruction politics also is in his work; so is the suggestion that much of the alleged corruption in Reconstruction governments would be found to originate in one or another mode of enriching the masters of that rising industrial capitalism—a central theme in Horace Mann Bond's penetrating study.

While Du Bois' book is weak insofar as it tends to ignore the former nonslaveholding whites who were landed—i.e., the yeomanry—and who therefore had class as well as racist differences with the black millions, and is weak, too, insofar as it accepts the concept of a monolithic white South from the pre-Civil War period to Reconstruction, it pioneered in a related area, for it called attention very forcefully to the neglect, then, of the history of the poorer whites in the South.

The momentous impact upon the nature of U.S. society and therefore upon world history of the failure of the effort at democratizing the South—which is what the defeat of Reconstruction meant in Du Bois' view—is emphasized in **Black Reconstruction.** The consequent turn towards an imperial career, to which Woodrow Wilson pointed with delight, was a development which Du Bois denounced and concerning which he warned in prescient terms.

Du Bois also sought to make clear that Reconstruction was an episode in the entire—and worldwide—struggle of the rich versus the poor; in this connection he emphasized not only the specifics of the land question in the South but the whole matter of property rights; indeed, he called one of the most pregnant chapters in his volume, "Counter-Revolution of Property." He saw—as had Madison a century before him—that the right to and control of property was central to problems of the state and therefore of all forms of state, including that of democracy. Indeed, Du Bois—as Madison— emphasized the special connection between democracy and property insofar as the principle of universal enfranchisement meant political power in the hands of the majority and that majority normally had been and was the non-propertied.

In this sense, Du Bois saw the story of Reconstruction— especially as it concerned the millions of dispossessed blacks—as an essential feature of the story of labor; not labor in the sense of industrial and/or urban working people, but labor in the more generic sense of those who had to work—to labor—in order to make ends meet. I think, too, that Du Bois' use of the term proletariat was more classical than Marxian; *i.e.,* the proletariat, the lower classes, as the dictionary says, and from the Latin *proletarius,* a citizen of the lowest class. (In this connection, let it be recalled that Du Bois began his teaching career as Professor of Greek and Latin and that throughout his life he would lapse into Latin phrases at frequent intervals.)

Du Bois states in **Black Reconstruction** that he had originally entitled chapter ten "The Dictatorship of the Black Proletariat in South Carolina," but that he had changed it to "The Black Proletariat in South Carolina" because "it has been brought to my attention that" the former would be incorrect. Obviously, since he made the change, he agreed with the criticism (which came from Abram L. Harris and Benjamin Stolberg and probably others). But here is the reason which he gave for the original title:

> My reason for this title is that in South Carolina, beginning in 1867, there were distinct evidences of a determination on the part of the black laborers to tax property and administer the state primarily for the benefit of labor. This was not only a conscious ideal but it would lead to heavy taxing on land, to the buying of large tracts of land to be distributed among the poor, and to many direct intelligent statements of the object of these policies.

In this same letter, Du Bois himself went on to remark that this manifested petty bourgeois influences "both among white and colored, and in a strict Marxian sense, the state and country was not ready for that dictatorship of the proletariat which might have come in a later development and on (sic) other surroundings."

When this meaning that Du Bois had in mind and when his purpose is comprehended, then perhaps one will be less apt than both contemporary and later commentators have been to simply dismiss all this out of hand. Certainly, in the Marxian sense, Radical Reconstruction represented an effort to bring a bourgeois-democratic order to the South and in this effort—given the formerly slave-based plantation economy—the idea of "land to the landless" was fundamental; this meant not the elimination of the private ownership of the means of production—a basic aim of the dictatorship of the proletariat—but rather its wider distribution. From this point of view Du Bois' choice of words and expressions was confusing—and erroneous; but his perception of the relationship of particularly exploited black masses to any effort at making democracy real and to any secure advance of the deprived of all colors—which is what he was bringing forward—was a profound one and remains a challenging one for today, not only in terms of history-writing but also in terms of history-making.

In this connection it is relevant to note that Du Bois' original title for his book was *Black Reconstruction of Democracy in America.* At the urging of the publisher the title was shortened; nevertheless, with the shortened title, Du Bois insisted that the title page (and the original dust jacket) carry this subtitle: "An Essay toward a History of the Part which Black Folk Played in the Attempt to Reconstruct Democracy in America, 1860-1880."

While spelling out the full sub-title, notice is to be taken of the dates Du Bois offered, and his book does start with the Civil War. This represented not only Du Bois' insistence upon the decisive role Negroes had played in preserving the Union and in emancipating themselves— quite new ideas in the 1930s, and still unreported in most U.S. history texts—but also his conception of the unity of the whole struggle against slavery, of the War and of the Reconstruction effort. This, too, has been urged by some later commentators (as Howard K. Beale) who have failed to note Du Bois' attempt at it decades ago. It should be added, also that in **Black Reconstruction** Du Bois denied that with its defeat, struggle and activity on the part of black people ceased for a generation; on the contrary, he pointed out that it continued and even had some successes in the late 1870s, 1880s and 1890s: this theme, too, has only recently been "discovered."

It will be well at this point to allow Du Bois himself to state the basic theme of **Black Reconstruction**; presumably he is a good authority for this. He stated this, in differing ways, several times; we shall for reasons of space, quote only one and that extremely brief:

To me, these propositions, extreme as they may sound, seem clear and true:

> 1. The American Negro not only was the cause of the Civil War but a prime factor in enabling the North to win it.

> 2. The Negro was the only effective tool which could be used for the immediate restoration of the federal union after the war.

> 3. The enfranchisement of the freedmen after the war was one of the greatest steps toward democracy taken in the nineteenth century.

> 4. The attempts to retrace that step, disfranchising the Negro and reducing him to caste conditions, are the deeds which make the South today the nation's social problem Number One.

Du Bois added that involved in the reality of Reconstruction was "the question of the equal humanity of black, brown, yellow and white people." And then he flung this question—in his prophetic way tossing out a generation ago today's most urgent problem: "Is this a world where its peoples in mutual helpfulness and mutual respect can live and work; or will it be a world in the future as in the past, where white Europe and white America must rule 'niggers'?" (pp. 7-14)

> Herbert Aptheker, "Du Bois as Historian," in Negro History Bulletin, *Vol. 32, No. 4, April, 1969, pp. 6-16.*

Arnold Rampersad (essay date 1987)

[*Rampersad is the author of the 1976 study* The Art and Imagination of W. E. B. Du Bois. *In the following essay, originally presented at the session on "Slavery and the Literary Imagination" at the 1987 English Institute and reprinted in the 1989 collection* Slavery and the Literary Imagination, *he analyzes Du Bois's concept of slavery in* The Souls of Black Folk, *noting how it differs from Booker T. Washington's in his autobiography* Up from Slavery.]

W. E. B. Du Bois's *The Souls of Black Folk* was a controversial book when it appeared in 1903, but few readers opposed to it could deny its originality and beauty as a portrait of the Afro-American people. In the succeeding years, the collection of essays lost little of its power, so that it remains acknowledged today as a masterpiece of black American writing. In 1918, the literary historian Benjamin Brawley still could feel in Du Bois's book "the passion of a mighty heart" when he hailed it as the most important work "in classic English" published to that time by a black writer. About thirty years after its appearance, the poet, novelist, and NAACP leader James Weldon Johnson judged that Du Bois's work had produced "a greater effect upon and within the Negro race in America than any other single book published in this country since *Uncle Tom's Cabin.*" With admiration bordering on reverence for the book, Langston Hughes recalled that "my earliest memories of written words are those of Du Bois and the

Bible." In the 1960s, the astute literary critic J. Saunders Redding weighed the impact of *Souls of Black Folk* on a variety of black intellectuals and leaders and pronounced it "more history-making than historical." In 1973, Herbert Aptheker, the leading Du Bois editor and scholar, hailed the text as "one of the classics in the English language."

These are fervent claims for a book of thirteen essays and a short story written by an academic who had been rigidly trained in history and sociology (especially at Harvard and the University of Berlin, where Du Bois did extensive doctoral work), and whose previous books had been an austere dissertation in history, *The Suppression of the African Slave-Trade to the United States,* and an empirical sociological study of urban blacks, *The Philadelphia Negro.* Clearly, however, *The Souls of Black Folk* was something other than academic history and sociology. If white academics and intellectuals mainly ignored its existence (although Henry James called it "the only Southern book of distinction published in many a year"), its impression was marked on the class of black Americans who provided the leadership of their race. Among black intellectuals, above all, *The Souls of Black Folk* became a kind of sacred book, the central text for the interpretation of the Afro-American experience and the most trustworthy guide into the grim future that seemed to loom before their race in America.

The main cause of the controversy surrounding *The Souls of Black Folk* was its devastating attack on Booker T. Washington. The head of the Tuskegee Institute in Alabama was already a famous man when his autobiography *Up from Slavery* was published in 1901. His epochal compromise speech at the Atlanta Exposition in 1895 had catapulted him to the position of leading spokesman for his race before the white world, a friend of rich industrialists like Andrew Carnegie and a dinner guest in the White House of Theodore Roosevelt. Nevertheless, *Up from Slavery* reinforced Washington's authority to a significant extent. Above all, he has used the skeleton of the slave narrative form (that is, the story of a life that progresses from a state of legal bondage to a state of freedom and a substantial degree of self-realization) not only to describe his rise in the world but also to dramatize the heart of the Tuskegee argument that the salvation of Afro-America lay in self-reliance, conciliation of the reactionary white South, a surrender of the right to vote and the right to social equality, dependence on thrift and industriousness, and an emphasis on vocational training rather than the liberal arts in the education of the young. To these ideas, Du Bois and *The Souls of Black Folk* were unalterably opposed.

I wish to suggest here that perhaps the most important element in the making of Du Bois's book, which drew on his previously published material but also on fresh work, derived in significant degree from his full awareness of *Up from Slavery.* While this could hardly be an altogether novel suggestion—given Du Bois's attack on Washington in his book—the crucial area of difference between them has not been adequately recognized. I

Du Bois with his wife and son, 1895.

would argue that this crucial element involved Du Bois's acute sensitivity to slavery both as an institution in American history and as an idea, along with his distaste for Washington's treatment of the subject in *Up from Slavery*. To some extent Du Bois's book functions, in spite of its only partial status as an autobiography, as a direct, parodic challenge to certain forms and assumptions of the slave narrative (in all their variety) which had so aided Booker T. Washington's arguments. While it does so mainly to refute the major ideas in Washington's influential text, at the same time its contrariness of form is made obligatory by Du Bois's peculiar attitudes toward slavery.

The resulting book can be seen as marking Du Bois's sense (and that of the many writers and intellectuals influenced by him) of the obsolescence of the slave narrative as a paradigm for Afro-American experience, as well as the beginning of a reflexive paradigm, allied to the slave narrative, that leads the reader—and the race described in the book—into the modern Afro-American world. William L. Andrews has pointed out . . . in his essay on slavery and the rise of Afro-American literary

realism, that postbellum slave narratives de-emphasized the hellishly destructive nature of slavery and offered it instead as a crucible in which future black manhood was formed. Du Bois's approach, I would argue, is in part a revival of the earlier, antebellum spirit of black autobiography and the slave narrative, but in more significant part also differs from that earlier spirit. In both the earlier and the later slave narratives there is progress for the black as he or she moves away from slavery. Du Bois's central point, as we shall see, is different.

For Booker T. Washington in *Up from Slavery*, slavery was not an institution to be defended overtly. Nevertheless, its evils had been much overstated, as he saw them, and its blessings were real. The evils, insofar as they existed, were to be acknowledged briefly and then forgotten. While this approach in some senses is to be expected of an autobiography by a man born only seven years before emancipation, it also underscores Washington's public attitude to American slavery in particular and to history in general. In Washington's considered view, neither slavery nor history is of great consequence—or, at the very least, of daunting consequence to any black man of sound character who properly trains himself for the demands of the modern world. In *Up from Slavery,* Washington writes flatly of "the cruelty and moral wrong of slavery," and he remarks conclusively about the former slaves that "I have never seen one who did not want to be free, or one who would return to slavery." "I condemn it as an institution," he adds. Tellingly, however, this condemnation springs from a need to clarify the major message about slavery in his chapter on his slave years, "A Slave among Slaves." The need itself springs from the patent ambiguity of Washington's view of slavery.

Whatever he intends to do, Washington stresses the fundamentally innocuous, almost innocent, nature of the institution. Of his white father (said to be a prosperous neighbor, who refused to acknowledge him) and of his poor, black mother (who sometimes stole chickens in order to feed herself and her children), Washington's judgment is the same. In lacking the courage or generosity to acknowledge his son, his father "was simply another unfortunate victim of the institution which the Nation unhappily had engrafted upon it at the time." In her thievery, his mother "was simply a victim of the system of slavery." Moreover, Washington's lack of hostility to his father allegedly reflected the complacent attitudes of other blacks to whites. There was no "bitter feeling toward the white people on the part of my race" about the fact that many whites were fighting as soldiers in the Confederate army to preserve slavery; where slaves had been treated "with anything like decency," they showed love and tenderness to their masters, even those in the military. The chapter "A Slave among Slaves" ends with a striking tableau of the day of emancipation. Whites are sad not because of the loss of valuable property but "because of parting with those whom they had reared and who were in many ways very close to them." Blacks are initially ecstatic, but the older freedmen, "stealthily at first," return later to the "big house" to consult their former masters about their future.

Doubtless sincere in his expressions of antipathy to slavery, Washington nevertheless emphasizes the benefits gained by blacks through the institution. "Notwithstanding the cruel wrongs inflicted upon us," he asserts, "the black man got nearly as much out of slavery as the white man did." With Afro-Americans comprising the most advanced community of blacks in the world (as Washington claimed), slavery was indisputably a fortunate act. Indeed, it was further proof of the notion that "Providence so often uses men and institutions to accomplish a purpose." Through all difficulties, Washington continues to derive faith in the future of black Americans by dwelling on "the wilderness through which and out of which, a good Providence has already led us."

For Washington, the acknowledgement of Providence piously marks his negation of the consequences of forces such as those of history, psychology, economics, and philosophy at play in the field of slavery. (Providence

does not perform a more positive function in his scheme, in which there is little room for religious enthusiasm or spiritual complexity. Of religion and spirituality in *Up from Slavery* he writes: "While a great deal of stress is laid upon the industrial side of the work at Tuskegee, we do not neglect or overlook in any degree the religious and spiritual side. The school is strictly undenominational, but it is thoroughly Christian, and the spiritual training of the students is not neglected." Willing to share in the belief that economic competition and greed had been at the root of slavery, and that slavery itself was ultimately the cause of the Civil War, he pushes no further into causes and effects even as he everywhere, as a champion of pragmatism, lauds the value of "facts" and the "need to look facts in the face." In his scheme, the mental legacy of slavery to the black freedman is not conflict, but a blank, a kind of tabula rasa on which is to be inscribed those values and skills that would serve the freedman best in the new age. Although he offers a critical view of the past of his people, "who had spent generations in slavery, and before that generations in the darkest heathenism," Washington in fact invites a vision of the Afro-American as black Adam. This Adam is, in a way, both prelapsarian and postlapsarian. He is an Adam in the Eden of the South, with the world before him. He is also Adam who has fallen. The fall was slavery itself. Slavery, as seen in this context, is a "fortunate fall"—the fall by which Africans gained the skills and the knowledge needed for the modern world. But who is responsible for the fall? Who has sinned? The answer surely must be the black slave himself, since *Up from Slavery* places no blame on the white world. The failure to investigate the origins, the nature, and the consequences of slavery has led Washington to a subtle and yet far-reaching defamation of the African and Afro-American peoples.

The black American Adam, in his prelapsarian guise, and in the simplicity of his capabilities, must be protected from the fruit that would destroy him—in this case, knowledge in the form of classical learning. Otherwise, the black man may become a kind of Satan, excessively proud. Washington denounces the idea, apparently embraced eagerly by many blacks in the aftermath of the Civil War, "that a knowledge, however little, of the Greek and Latin languages would make one a very superior human being, something bordering almost on the supernatural." Inveighing against false black pride, he dismisses passionate black claims to the right to vote. The secret of progress appears to be regression. Deploring the mass black migration to the cities, he often wishes "that by some power of magic I might remove the great bulk of these people into the country districts and plant them upon the soil, upon the solid and never deceptive foundation of Mother Nature, where all nations and races that have ever succeeded have gotten their start." His garden is a priceless source of resuscitation. There, "I feel that I am coming into contact with something that is giving me strength for the many duties and hard places that await me out in the big world. I pity the man or woman who has never learned to enjoy nature and to get strength and inspiration out of it."

This refusal to confront slavery (or even the understandable association in the minds of many blacks of agricultural work with the terms of slavery) and this black variation on the myth of an American Adam make *Up from Slavery* an odd slave narrative according to either the antebellum or the postbellum model. Nevertheless, the hero moves from slavery to freedom and into his future as from darkness to light. Holding the story together is the distinction Washington quietly makes between himself and the other ex-slaves in general. He is the hero of a slave narrative. He sheds the dead skin of slavery, seeks an education, builds on it, and emerges as a powerful, fully realized human being, confident, almost invincible (within the bounds of discretion). This is seen as a possibility also for Washington's disciples, as the graduates of Tuskegee are represented. "Wherever our graduates go," he writes near the end of his book, "the changes which soon begin to appear in the buying of land, improving homes, saving money, in education, and in high moral character are remarkable. Whole communities are fast being revolutionized through the instrumentality of these men and women." The same cannot be said of the masses of blacks who have not been to Tuskegee or who have not come under the Tuskegee influence in some other way. In *Up from Slavery,* they remain blanks. This was hardly the first slave narrative in which the central character saw great distance between himself and other blacks. In Du Bois's *The Souls of Black Folk,* however, that distance would shrink dramatically.

When *The Souls of Black Folk* appeared in 1903, slavery had been officially dead in the United States for forty years. Du Bois himself, thirty-five years of age in 1903, had not been born a slave. Indeed, he had been born on free soil, in Great Barrington, Massachusetts, in a family that had lived there for several generations. One ancestor had even been a revolutionary soldier. Nevertheless, the shadow of slavery hangs powerfully over *The Souls of Black Folk.* Thus Du Bois acknowledged that fact that his book is about a people whose number included many who had been born slaves, and a vast majority who were immediately descended from slaves. On this central point, *The Souls of Black Folk* is a stark contrast to *Up from Slavery.*

In July 1901, shortly after the latter appeared, Du Bois reviewed it in *Dial* magazine. This was his first open criticism of Washington. In 1895, he had saluted Washington's compromising Atlanta Exposition speech as "a word fitly spoken." In the following years, however, he had watched with increasing dismay as the head of Tuskegee propagated his doctrine of compromise and silenced much of his opposition through his manipulation of elements of the black press and other sources of power. Du Bois's attack on him in *Dial* was decisive. The *Dial* review, followed by *The Souls of Black Folk* (where the review again appeared, in adapted form), created "a split of the race into two contending

camps," as James Weldon Johnson later noted astutely. Cryptically noting that Washington had given "but glimpses of the real struggle which he has had for leadership," Du Bois accused him of peddling a "Lie." Surveying the various modes of black response to white power from the earliest days in America, he concluded that the vaunted Tuskegee philosophy for black self-improvement was little more than "the old [black] attitude of adjustment to environment, emphasizing the economic phase."

In *The Souls of Black Folk,* unable to fashion an autobiography to match Washington's, young Du Bois nevertheless infused a powerful autobiographical spirit and presence into his essays. From about three dozen of his published articles on aspects of black history and sociology, he selected eight for adaptation or reprinting as nine chapters in *The Souls of Black Folk.* The brief fifth chapter, **"Of the Wings of Atalanta,"** about commercialism and the city of Atlanta, was new, as were the last four chapters: **"Of the Passing of the First-Born,"** Du Bois's prose elegy on the death of his only son, Burghardt; **"Of Alexander Crummell,"** his tribute to an exceptional black man; **"Of the Coming of John,"** a short story; and **"Of the Sorrow Songs,"** an essay on spirituals. Holding these various efforts together is the central figure of Du Bois, who presents himself as a scholar and historian but more dramatically as an artist and a visionary who would not only depict the present state of black culture but also try to prophesy something about its future and the future of the nation.

Du Bois understood clearly that the representation of slavery was central to the entire task. Unlike Washington in *Up from Slavery,* he believed that slavery had been a force of extraordinary—and mainly destructive—potency. Destructive as it had been, however, slavery had not destroyed every major aspect of the African character and psychology (topics on which Washington had been silent); the African core had survived. But so had slavery. Where Washington saw opportunity on every hand for the black, if the right course was followed, Du Bois proclaimed that American slavery was not dead. In one guise or another, it still persisted, with its power scarcely diminished. The act of emancipation had been both a fact (such as Washington loved to fasten on) and a mirage: "Years have passed since then—ten, twenty, forty; forty years of national life, forty years of renewal and development, and yet the swarthy spectre sits in its accustomed seat at the Nation's feast.... The Nation has not yet found peace from its sins; the freedman has not yet found in freedom his promised land."

Although there were elements of agreement between Washington and Du Bois on the nature of slavery, *The Souls of Black Folk* portrays the institution in terms essentially opposite to those in *Up from Slavery.* Du Bois does not deny that slavery had its benign side, but in almost every instance his conclusion about its effects is radical when compared with Washington's. American slavery had not been the "worst slavery in the world," and had known something of "kindliness, fidelity, and happiness"; nevertheless, it "classed the black man and the ox together." Less equivocally, and more typical of Du Bois's view of slavery, black men were "emasculated" by the institution. Emancipation brought them "suddenly, violently...into a new birthright." The white southern universities had been contaminated by "the foul breath of slavery." Instead of the providential view of slavery espoused by Washington, for Du Bois the institution had amounted to "two hundred and fifty years of assiduous education in submission, carelessness, and stealing."

Du Bois's emphasis on slavery as a social evil is only one part of the scheme by which he measures the Afro-American and American reality. Central to his argument is his belief in the persistence of the power of slavery beyond emancipation. Many current ills had their start in slavery. The widespread tendency of white businessmen and industrialists to see human beings as property, or "among the material resources of a land to be trained with an eye single to future dividend," was "born of slavery." The "plague-spot in sexual relations" among blacks—easy marriage and easy separation—"is the plain heritage from slavery." Many whites in the South live "haunted by the ghost of an untrue dream". "Slavery and race-prejudice are potent if not sufficient causes of the Negro's position" today. Du Bois does not pretend, in the manner of a demogogue, that slavery and

neo-slavery are absolutely identical. He sometimes proposes a new slavery as only a distinct possibility. The power of the ballot, downplayed by Booker T. Washington, is absolutely needed—"else what shall save us from a second slavery?" And yet, if the black man is not actually a slave, he is actually not free. "Despite compromise, war, and struggle," Du Bois insists, "the Negro is not free" and is in danger "of being reduced to semi-slavery." Repeatedly he invokes the central symbol of enslavement to portray the status of the modern black. Today, blacks are "shackled men."

In the final analysis, black Americans live in neo-slavery. The race passed from formal slavery through an interim illusion of emancipation ("after the first flush of freedom wore off") into a new version of slavery that in many respects continues the old. The law courts were used by the white South as the first means of "reenslaving the blacks." Examining estates that once were slave plantations, Du Bois marvels at how the design and disposition of the black cabins are "the same as in slavery days." While for Booker T. Washington the Tuskegee education eradicates the vestiges of slavery from students at the institute, Du Bois sees the legacy of slavery as inescapable: "No people a generation removed from slavery can escape a certain unpleasant rawness and *gaucherie,* despite the best of training." Even the Tuskegee philosophy, as has been pointed out,

Du Bois (right) in the Crisis *office, circa 1914.*

reflects for Du Bois, in its spirit of compromise, the timidity forced on blacks by slavery.

It is vital to recognize that, far from being the result of distorting bitterness or propaganda, Du Bois's position on neo-slavery at the turn of the century, which he amply documents with vivid examples (many drawn from his personal experience), is fully supported by a wide range of leading historians. Central to their analysis were not simply the repressive local laws but the even more confining decisions of the Supreme Court in *Plessy v. Ferguson* in 1896, which held that "separate but equal" facilities were constitutionally valid, and in *Williams v. Mississippi* in 1898, which endorsed that state's plan to strip blacks of the franchise given them after the Civil War. Rayford W. Logan dubbed the period before the end of the century the "Nadir" of the Afro-American experience. "When complete," C. Vann Woodward wrote of these segregationist laws, "the new codes of White Supremacy were vastly more complex than the ante-bellum slave codes or the Black Codes of 1865-66, and, if anything, they were stronger and more rigidly enforced."

Du Bois's attitude toward slavery, the black present, and the black future is heavily dependent on his attitude toward the preslavery situation of blacks—that is, to Africa. In *The Souls of Black Folk* he does not dwell on the historical evidence of African civilization before slavery that twelve years later would form virtually the main subject of his Pan-Africanist volume, *The Negro* (1915). But where Washington writes only of heathenistic darkness in *Up from Slavery,* Du Bois concedes heathenism but also attributes to the slave a complex, dignified, and usable past. "He was brought from a definite social environment," Du Bois explains,"—the polygamous clan life under the headship of the chief and the potent influence of the priest. His religion was nature-worship, with profound belief in invisible surrounding influences, good and bad, and his worship was through incantation and sacrifice." In other words, the African lived in a stable, consistent, complex social order, complemented by strong and formal religious beliefs. Far from being a blank, the mind of the black, both in Africa and as a slave brought to the New World, was a remarkable instrument. And because of this background, the slave's natural reaction to slavery was not passivity—which was learned later—but revolt. "Endowed with a rich tropical imagination," Du Bois asserts, "and a keen, delicate appreciation of Nature, the transplanted African lived in a world animate with gods and devils, elves and witches; full of strange influences,—of God to be implored, of Evil to be propitiated. Slavery, then, was to him the dark triumph of Evil over him. All the fateful powers of the Underworld were striving against him, and a spirit of revolt and revenge filled his heart."

In ascribing to the black in Africa and in the New World a mind that in its own say is as powerful as that of any other race in the world, Du Bois does more than merely try to boost his race's reputation. He shifts the terms of the debate toward the question of the black mind and character, and introduces questions of history, psychology, myth, and art. He also introduces into his scheme at least two other elements severely downplayed by Washington in *Up from Slavery.* One is the role of imagination; the other, that of memory. Otherwise derogatory of blacks, many white racial "scientists," including the Count de Gobineau, the author of the influential *Essay on the Inequality of Human Races,* had often credited them with remarkable imaginative and artistic faculties (the "rich tropical imagination" Du Bois ascribed to the transplanted African). Du Bois allows this credit to influence not only what he wrote about blacks but also how he wrote it.

Booker T. Washington, finding little that is useful in the African and the slave past, seems in *Up from Slavery* to harbor a deep suspicion of the black imagination, or even to be unaware that it exists. Indeed, his entire attitude toward the imagination contrasts with Du Bois's. While he reads books, or advocates the reading of books, he mentions no novels or poems. He is proud of the fact that his keenest pleasures are in the practical world. "Few things are more satisfactory to me than a high-grade Berkshire or Poland China pig," he writes. "Games I care little for." Du Bois is different. From early in his life, he tells us, he has seen the development of his imagination as one possible key to simultaneous self-realization and the leadership of his race against the whites. "Just how I would do it I could never decide," he writes of his youthful dreams of racial and personal victory; "by reading law, by healing the sick, by telling the wonderful tales that swam in my head,—some way".

In fact, Du Bois's greatest cultural claims for blacks are in the areas of art and imagination. In these claims, slaves play the decisive role. He lauds them as musicians, especially when music is blended with spirituality in the "sorrow songs." In a nation where "vigor and ingenuity" are prized, rather than beauty, "the Negro folk-song—the rhythmic cry of the slave—stands to-day not simply as the sole American music, but as the most beautiful expression of human experience born this side the seas." Of the three gifts from blacks to American culture, the first is "a gift of story and song—soft, stirring melody in an ill-harmonized and unmelodious land." (The other gifts are toil and "a gift of the Spirit.")

Recognizing imagination as a source of black strength, and confirming the power of the imagination in Africa, slavery, and thereafter, also freed Du Bois as a thinker and a writer. In his previous book, *The Philadelphia Negro,* he had warned fastidiously that the scholar "must ever tremble lest some personal bias, some moral conviction or some unconscious trend of thought due to previous training, has to a degree distorted the picture in his view." This timidity is abandoned in *The Souls of Black Folk,* which is full of impressionistic writing, including occasionally startling descriptions of people and places, and clearly subjective judgments. Du Bois based the book on his scholarly knowledge of history and sociology, but the eye and mind of the artist are given almost free play.

He was well aware of the possible price of indulging the imagination and even believed that he had paid a part of that price. A year after the book appeared, in a note about it published in the *Independent,* Du Bois conceded that "the style and workmanship" of *The Souls of Black Folk* did not make its meaning "altogether clear." He was sure that the book presented a "clear central message," but also that around this core floated what he called a shadowy "penumbra" of vagueness and partly obscured allusions. Similarly, in his preface, "The Forethought," Du Bois was restrained in outlining his plans. He will sketch, "in vague, uncertain outline," the spiritual world in which the ten million black Americans live." In both pieces, Du Bois is acknowledging the "tropic imagination" of blacks, of which he is one. His elite, formal, Western education has curbed this tropic imagination for too long; now it is free.

A crucial factor here is the connection thus proclaimed between the author of *The Souls of Black Folk* and the masses of American blacks, the despised slaves they had been or were descended from, and the Africans beyond the seas. Du Bois made this connection for all to see when he said of his book, in the note in the *Independent* just cited, that "in its larger aspects the style is tropical—African." In his "Forethought," too, he had linked himself to other blacks, and to slaves: "Need I add that I who speak here am bone of the bone and flesh of the flesh of them that live within the Veil?"

By indulging his imagination, Du Bois gains for his book much of its distinction. Where Booker T. Washington stresses cold facts, and avoids metaphors and similes, imagination leads Du Bois to the invocation of keen images to represent black reality, and to major insights. Chief among the images is that of "the Veil," which hangs between the black and white races, an apparently harmless fabric but one that the rest of the book shows to be in some respects an almost impregnable wall, and the prime source of misery. In one place he even links his image of the veil to the symbol of an ongoing slavery; at one and the same time, he records "the wail of prisoned souls within our veil, and the mounting fury of shackled men." Linked to the image of the veil, but going far beyond it, and inscribed in the very title of the book, is the idea of black American "double consciousness." Taking the basic idea of double consciousness as a feature or a capability of the human brain from the reflections of leading psychologists of the time, such as his former professor William James, Du Bois applied the notion with telling force to the mental consequences of the social, political, and cultural conflicts that came with being Afro-American. Perhaps no more challenging single statement about the nature of the black American mind, about the psychological consequences of slavery and racism, has ever been offered. Both the notion of black invisibility and of innately conflicted Afro-American consciousness would

be reflected powerfully in future black poetry and fiction.

The "souls" of the title is a play on words. It alludes to the "twoness" of the black American that Du Bois initially suggests in his first chapter. America, a predominantly white country, yields the black "no true self-consciousness, but only lets him see himself through the revelation of the other world." The result is "a peculiar sensation, this double-consciousness, this sense of always looking at one's self through the eyes of others, of measuring one's soul by the tape of a world that looks on in amused contempt and pity. One ever feels his twoness,—an American, a Negro; two souls, two thoughts, two unreconciled strivings; two warring ideals in one dark body, whose dogged strength alone keeps it from being torn asunder." "Such a double life," Du Bois writes later, in his chapter on religion, "with double thoughts, double duties, and double social classes, must give rise to double words and double ideals, and tempt the mind to pretence or revolt, to hypocrisy or radicalism." Another way of seeing these two souls surely is as a contest between memory and its'opposite, amnesia. American culture demands of its blacks amnesia concerning slavery and Africa, just as it encourages amnesia of a different kind in whites. For Du Bois, blacks may not be able to remember Africa but they should remember slavery, since it has hardly ended.

"In the days of bondage," he writes of the slaves, stressing their imagination, "they thought to see in one divine event the end of all doubt and disappointment; few men ever worshipped Freedom with half such unquestioning faith as did the American Negro for two centuries.... In song and exhortation swelled one refrain—Liberty; in his tears and curses the God he implored had Freedom in his right hand. At last it came,—suddenly, fearfully, like a dream." The first decade after the war "was merely a prolongation of the vain search for freedom, the boon that seemed ever barely to elude their grasp,—like tantalizing will-o'-the-wisp, maddening and misleading the helpless host." Freedom never came, but something else did, very faintly, that "changed the child of Emancipation to the youth with dawning self-consciousness, self-realization, self-respect."

The fundamental progression of the Afro-American in history, as seen by Du Bois, is from a simple bondage to a more complex bondage slightly ameliorated by this "dawning" of "self-consciousness, self-realization, self-respect." "In those sombre forests of his striving, his own soul rose before him, and he saw himself,—darkly as through a veil; and yet he saw in himself some faint revelation of his power, of his mission." This realization, although "faint," facilitates Du Bois's shift toward what one might call cultural nationalism in the black: "He began to have a dim feeling that, to attain his place in the world, he must be himself, and not another." Cultural nationalism does not mean anti-intellectualism: "For the first time he sought to analyze the burden he bore upon his back, that deadweight of social

The founding members of the first black protest organization in twentieth-century America, the Niagara Movement.

degradation partially masked behind a half-named Negro problem."

The diminution of the myth of freedom, the elevation of the power of slavery, allows Du Bois to establish a continuum of African and Afro-American psychology. Times change and the nature and amount of data change, but the black mind remains more or less constant, for Du Bois sees it as irrevocably linked to its African origins. If that constancy is anywhere observable, it is for Du Bois in black Christian religion, which in the main is a product of slavery. For him, "the frenzy of a Negro revival in the untouched backwoods of the South" re-creates tellingly "the religious feeling of the slave." The full meaning of slavery "to the African savage" is unknown to Du Bois, but he believes that the answer is to be found only in "a study of Negro religion as a development" from heathenism to the institutionalized urban churches of the North. The black church is the key to knowing "the inner ethical life of the people who compose it." Then follows a venture in analysis that may be taken as the foundation of Du Bois's sense of the Afro-American mind, or soul.

By the 1750s, after the initial impulse to revolt had been crushed by white power, "the black slave had sunk, with hushed murmurs, to his place at the bottom of a new economic system, and was unconsciously ripe for a new

philosophy of life." The Christian doctrine of passive submission facilitated this shift in which "courtesy became humility, moral strength degenerated into submission, and the exquisite native appreciation of the beautiful became an infinite capacity for dumb suffering." A century later, black religion had transformed itself once again, this time around the cry for abolition, which became a "religion to the black world. Thus, when Emancipation finally came, it seemed to the freedman a literal Coming of the Lord. His fervid imagination was stirred as never before, by the tramp of armies, the blood and dust of battle, and the wail and whirl of social upheaval." Forty years later, with the world changing swiftly, Du Bois sees "a time of intense ethical ferment, of religious heart-searching and intellectual unrest." This leads him, looking backward and forward, into history and into the future. "From the double life every American Negro must live, as a Negro and as an American, as swept on by the current of the nineteenth while yet struggling in the eddies of the fifteenth century,—from this must arise a painful self-consciousness, an almost morbid sense of personality and a moral hesitancy which is fatal to self-confidence." These are the secondary, but almost equally binding, shackles of neo-slavery.

The authenticity of slavery as metaphor for the black experience is firmly underscored in the most "creative," or imaginative, areas of *The Souls of Black Folk.* These are the autobiographical passages of the book; the biographical chapter, on Alexander Crummell; and the short story, "Of the Coming of John." The sharpest focus of the autobiographical element occurs in "Of the Passing of the First-Born," about the death of Du Bois's son (who died of dysentery in Atlanta). In certain respects this is an almost classical elegy, in impassioned and yet formal language. But it is one in which the central mourner, as a black, can find no consolation. Thus it is in truth anti-Christian, a bitter parody of the Christian elegy such as Milton's *Lycidas.* For Du Bois, unable to believe in Booker T. Washington's Providence, doubt completely infects his vision of his son's future: "If still he be, and he be There, and there be a There, let him be happy, O Fate!" Perhaps one day the veil will be lifted and the imprisoned blacks set free, but not in Du Bois's time: "Not for me,—I shall die in my bonds." The metaphor of black life as slavery preempts the annealing possibilities of the elegy.

This chapter underscores the memorable autobiographical impressions left by the first few pages of the book, in which Du Bois discusses his first, youthful encounter with racism: "Then it dawned upon me with a certain suddenness that I was different from the others [his white classmates]; or like, mayhap, in heart and life and longing, but shut out from their world by a vast veil." Taking refuge in fierce competitiveness, he wins small victories but understands at last that "the worlds I longed for, and all their dazzling opportunities, were theirs, not mine." Many of his black friends deteriorate into sycophancy or into hatred and distrust of whites. Du Bois does not, but "the shades of the prison-house

Speakers at Harvard's 1890 commencement, at which Du Bois (seated far right) received his B.A.

closed round about us all; walls strait and stubborn to the whitest, but relentlessly narrow, tall, and unscalable to sons of night."

Thus, just as the acceptance of the idea of neo-slavery forbids Du Bois the writing of classical elegy, with its formal consolation, so does that acceptance also forbid Du Bois the writing of anything that resembles either the "classical" slave narrative—the account of a life that has passed from bondage to freedom, from darkness to light—or its white American counterpart, the rags-to-riches autobiographical tale built on the materialist base of the American Dream. Indeed, if one isolates Du Bois as the hero of *The Souls of Black Folk,* one sees the reverse pattern. He goes from light into darkness, from the freedom of infancy and childhood into the bondage of maturity. Each modern black American, he argues implicitly, re-creates this regressive journey. So too has the black race, in its New World experience, enacted a historical regression. Preslavery African manhood and womanhood have deteriorated into passivity, moral hesitancy, cynicism, and rage.

Du Bois does not see all blacks as succumbing to pressure, but in any event those who resist have no hope of a lasting triumph. The most honored single figure in *The Souls of Black Folk* is Alexander Crummell (1819-1898), who struggled against tremendous odds but succeeded in being ordained as a priest in the almost entirely white Protestant Episcopal Church, earned a degree from Cambridge University, then went on to years of diligent service in Africa and the United States. Crummell also helped to found the American Negro Academy, in which Du Bois himself was involved. Clearly he stands as Du Bois's idea of the highest achievement among black Americans. Pointedly, Crummell was born when "the slave-ship still groaned across the Atlantic." His life is one of trial and tribulation, but also of resistance to doubt, hatred, and despair. He decides early to live for his people: "He heard the hateful clank of their chains; he felt them cringe and grovel, and there rose within him a protest and a prophesy." But no great triumph followed. For all his service and achievement, Crummell's name is now barely known. "And herein lies the tragedy of the age: not that men are poor,—all men know something of

618

poverty; not that men are wicked,—who is good? not that men are ignorant,—what is Truth? Nay, but that men know so little of men." Again, the consolation of faith is impossible: "I wonder where he is today?"

The short story **"Of the Coming of John"** (in a sense, one of "the wonderful tales that swam in my head" to which Du Bois alludes early in the book) further underscores the destructive force of neo-slavery. Black John, a simple country boy, comes to "Wells Institute" to be educated. But education cannot save him from racism, and his spirit deteriorates: "A tinge of sarcasm crept into his speech, and a vague bitterness into his life." Education alienates him from his own people; he returns home only to be struck by the "sordidness and narrowness" of what he had left behind. Unwittingly he tramples on the religious beliefs of the local blacks, and he preaches democracy in the black school although it is under the control of a reactionary white judge. Dismissed from his job there, he wanders in a daze until he sees his sister tussling with a white man he had known as a boy. He kills the man. John tells his mother he is going away—"I'm going to be free." Not understanding, she asks if he is going north again. "Yes, mammy," John replies, "I'm going,—North." He is soon lynched by revengeful whites. Going north and freedom are meaningless for John and for blacks in America. Freedom does not exist, except in death.

Education is only one of the forces that, subverted by racism and neo-slavery, betray John when he should have been elevated by them. For a person of Du Bois's complicated and elite schooling, this must have been a particularly poignant aspect to the condition he describes. Education should lead to light and truth. Booker T. Washington rearranged the chronology of his life in *Up from Slavery* to end his book close to the dizzying personal height of a Harvard honorary degree awarded in 1896 to the former illiterate slave. With the invitation in hand, "tears came into my eyes." But education for John leads to darkness and death. The fate of Alexander Crummell and of the author of *The Souls of Black Folk* is not much more exalted.

The Souls of Black Folk offers no transcendent confidence in the future. Du Bois's essay on religion, **"Of the Faith of the Fathers,"** ends with an assertion of the existence of "the deep religious feeling of the real Negro heart, the stirring, unguided might of powerful human souls who have lost the guiding star of the past and seek in the great night a new religious ideal." Only in concluding the book does Du Bois appeal to the longest possible historical view. The assumption of whites that certain races cannot be "saved" is "the arrogance of people irreverent toward Time and ignorant of the deeds of men. A thousand years ago such an assumption, easily possible, would have made it difficult for the Teuton to prove his right to life." As powerful as it was, American slavery thus becomes for him, in the end, only an episode in the African people's history, not the history itself.

Before this point, however, he has engaged slavery valiantly in his text. His point of view is clear. Admitting and exploring the reality of slavery is necessarily painful for a black American, but only by doing so can he or she begin to understand himself or herself and American and Afro-American culture in general. The normal price of the evasion of the fact of slavery is intellectual and spiritual death. Only by grappling with the meaning and legacy of slavery can the imagination, recognizing finally the temporality of the institution, begin to transcend it. (pp. 104-23)

> *Arnold Rampersad, "Slavery and the Literary Imagination: Du Bois's 'The Souls of Black Folk'," in* Slavery and the Literary Imagination, *edited by Deborah E. McDowell and Arnold Rampersad, The Johns Hopkins University Press, 1989, pp. 104-24.*

FURTHER READING

Aptheker, Herbert. *Annotated Bibliography of the Published Writings of W. E. B. Du Bois.* Millwood, N.Y.: Kraus-Thomson Organization Limited, 1973, 626 p.
> Comprehensive bibliography of Du Bois's published writings, prepared by Aptheker at Du Bois's request.

———. *The Literary Legacy of W. E. B. Du Bois.* White Plains, N.Y.: Kraus International Publications, 1989, 371 p.
> Collection of essays based on the introductions to Du Bois's works.

Broderick, Francis L. *W. E. B. Du Bois: Negro Leader in a Time of Crisis.* Stanford: Stanford University Press, 1959, 259 p.
> The first book-length biography of Du Bois. Broderick made use of Du Bois's private papers at the University of Massachusetts until Du Bois closed them to the public after his 1951 indictment as an unregistered agent of a foreign power.

Brodwin, Stanley. "The Veil Transcended: Form and Meaning in W. E. B. Du Bois's 'The Souls of Black Folk'." *Journal of Black Studies* 2, No. 3 (March 1972): 303-21.
> Analyzes the essays in *The Souls of Black Folk.*

Clarke, John Henrik; Jackson, Esther; Kaiser, Ernest; and O'Dell, J. H., eds. *Black Titan: W. E. B. Du Bois.* Boston: Beacon Press, 1970, 333 p.
> Anthology by the editors of *Freedomways.* Includes tributes to Du Bois by Kwame Nkrumah, Langston Hughes, and Paul Robeson, among others; critical essays on Du Bois; and selected essays and poems by Du Bois.

DeMarco, Joseph P. *The Social Thought of W. E. B. Du Bois.* Lanham, MD.: University Press of America, 1983, 203 p.

Studies Du Bois's evolving social thought throughout his lifetime.

Diggs, Irene. Introduction to *Dusk of Dawn: An Essay Toward an Autobiography of a Race Concept,* by W. E. B. Du Bois, pp. vii-xxvi. New Brunswick, N.J.: Transaction Books, 1984.
    Brief biography of Du Bois by his former student and assistant.

Du Bois, Shirley Graham. *His Day Is Marching On: A Memoir of W. E. B. Du Bois.* Philadelphia: J. B. Lippincott Company, 1971, 384 p.
    Biography and personal memoir by Du Bois's second wife, herself a writer.

Elder, Arlene A. "Swamp Versus Plantation: Symbolic Structure in W. E. B. Du Bois' *The Quest of the Silver Fleece.*" *Phylon* XXXIV, No. 4 (December 1973): 358-67.
    Examines symbolism in *The Quest of the Silver Fleece.*

Finkelstein, Sidney. "W. E. B. Du Bois's Trilogy: A Literary Triumph." *Mainstream* 14, No. 10 (October 1961): 6-17.
    Examines Du Bois's *Black Flame* trilogy, determining "there can be no doubt of the fact that it is a work that could only have been produced by a man of genius."

Hackett, Francis. "The Negro Speaks." *The New Republic* XXII, No. 279 (7 April 1920): 189-90.
    Reviews *Darkwater: Voices from Within the Veil,* arguing that it "must be reckoned among those [books] that add not only to the wisdom but to the exaltation and glory of man."

Kostelanetz, Richard. "W. E. B. Du Bois: Perhaps the Most Important Black in American Intellectual History." *Commonweal* LXXXIX, No. 5 (1 November 1968): 161-62.
    Reviews Du Bois's third autobiography, a work informed "by the American theme of personal possibility and disciplined accomplishment in spite of racial prejudice and social disadvantage."

Review of *The Quest of the Silver Fleece,* by W. E. B. Du Bois. *The Literary Digest* XLIII, No. 21 (18 November 1911): 926.
    Favorable review of Du Bois's first novel.

Logan, Rayford W., ed. *W. E. B. Du Bois: A Profile.* New York: Hill and Wang, 1971, 324 p.
    Collection of critical essays about Du Bois's life and works.

Moore, Jack B. *W. E. B. Du Bois.* Boston: Twayne Publishers, 1981, 185 p.
    Biography concentrating on Du Bois's life and works and deemphasizing his conflicts with opponents.

Moses, Wilson J. "The Poetics of Ethiopianism: W. E. B. Du Bois and Literary Black Nationalism." *American Literature* XLVII, No. 3 (November 1975): 411-26.
    Explores the concept of Ethiopianism, "a literary-religious tradition common to English-speaking Africans, regardless of nationality," in Du Bois's works.

Review of *John Brown,* by W. E. B. Du Bois. *The Nation* 89, No. 2313 (28 October 1909): 405.

Criticizes Du Bois for relying on existing biographies of Brown for his research, thereby absorbing the errors and inaccuracies of those works.

Rampersad, Arnold. *The Art and Imagination of W. E. B. Du Bois.* Cambridge, Mass.: Harvard University Press, 1976, 325 p.
    Evaluation of Du Bois's intellectual influences and changing thought.

————. "W. E. B. Du Bois as a Man of Literature." *American Literature* 51, No. 1 (March 1979): 50-68.
    Appraises Du Bois's career as a writer of fiction.

Spero, Sterling D. "The Negro's Role." *The Nation* CXLI, No. 3655 (24 July 1935): 108-09.
    Argues that *Black Reconstruction* adds "more confusion than light" to the period of history it treats.

Stepto, Robert B. "The Quest of the Weary Traveler: W. E. B. Du Bois's *The Souls of Black Folk.*" In his *From Behind the Veil: A Study of Afro-American Narrative,* pp. 52-91. Urbana: University of Illinois Press, 1979.
    Examines the structure of *The Souls of Black Folk.*

Stillman, Clara Gruening. "Tracing the Color Line." *New York Herald Tribune Books* (25 June 1939): 12.
    Praises *Black Folk Then and Now: An Essay on the History and Sociology of the Negro Race.*

Stone, William B. "Idiolect and Ideology: Some Stylistic Aspects of Norris, James, and Du Bois." *Style* 10, No. 4 (Fall 1976): 405-25.
    Explores style and politics in Frank Norris's *The Pit,* Henry James's *The Ambassadors,* and Du Bois's *The Souls of Black Folk,* works by American writers published in 1903.

Taylor, A. A. Review of *Black Reconstruction: An Essay Toward a History of the Part Which Black Folk Played in the Attempt to Reconstruct Democracy in America, 1860-1880,* by W. E. B. Du Bois. *The New England Quarterly* 8, No. 4 (December 1935): 608-12.
    Praises *Black Reconstruction,* maintaining that it is a work written from the "enlightened point of view" that a black person is an ordinary human being and not a "distinctly inferior creation."

Turner, Darwin T. "W. E. B. Du Bois and the Theory of a Black Aesthetic." In *The Harlem Renaissance Re-examined,* edited by Victor A. Kramer, pp. 9-30. New York: AMS Press, 1987.
    Discusses Du Bois's theories on criticism of art by black artists.

Tuttle, William M., Jr., ed. *W. E. B. Du Bois.* Englewood Cliffs, N.J.: Prentice-Hall, Inc., 1973, 186 p.
    Brief biography, with essays by Du Bois, reactions from his contemporaries, and essays by scholars August Meier and Francis Broderick.

Villard, Oswald Garrison. "Darkwater." *The Nation* CX, No. 2865 (29 May 1920): 726-27.
    Villard, a founding member of the NAACP, offers a mixed review of *Darkwater* and discusses Du Bois's changing role as a spokesman for his race.

Wesley, Charles H. "Propaganda and Historical Writing: The Emancipation of the Historian." *Opportunity* XIII, No. 8 (August 1935): 244-46, 254.

Celebrated laudatory review of *Black Reconstruction,* the work Du Bois and several others considered his magnum opus.

————. "W. E. B. Du Bois the Historian." *Freedomways* 5, No. 1 (First Quarter 1965): 59-72.

Overview of Du Bois's career as a historian.

Paul Laurence Dunbar

1872-1906

American poet, short story writer, novelist, librettist, dramatist, and essayist.

Best known for his poetry written in black American dialect, Dunbar is widely acknowledged as one of the first important black poets in American literature. He enjoyed his greatest popularity in the early twentieth century following the publication of two seminal books, *Majors and Minors* (1895) and *Lyrics of Lowly Life* (1896). In these and other works, Dunbar sought first to win over his audience with the humor of his dialect verse and then to display his abilities as a serious artist in standard English forms. His non-dialect poems and stories, however, were not popular with white readers, and Dunbar found himself trapped in the undesired role of dialect poet. The dialect poems constitute only a small portion of Dunbar's canon, which is replete with novels, short stories, essays, and poems in standard English. In its entirety, Dunbar's literary body is an impressive representation of black life in turn-of-the-century America. As Dunbar's friend James Weldon Johnson noted in the preface to his *Book of American Poetry:* "Paul Laurence Dunbar stands out as the first poet from the Negro race in the United States to show a combined mastery over poetic material and poetic technique, to reveal innate literary distinction in what he wrote, and to maintain a high level of performance. He was the first to rise to a height from which he could take a perspective view of his own race. He was the first to see objectively its humor, its superstitions, its shortcomings; the first to feel sympathetically its heart-wounds, its yearnings, its aspirations, and to voice them all in a purely literary form."

The son of former slaves, Dunbar was born in 1872 in Dayton, Ohio. When Dunbar was twelve years old his father died, and he grew up with his mother, listening to stories about her life as a slave. Later, as an adult, he incorporated information from these tales into his poetry and short stories. However, because his mother had omitted the more brutal facts of slavery from her stories, Dunbar tended to glorify plantation life, an aspect of his work that has been widely criticized. The only black in his high school, Dunbar was president of his class, editor in chief of the *High School Times,* president of the high school literary club, and class poet. By 1889, two years before he graduated, he had already published poems in the *Dayton Herald* and worked as editor of the short-lived *Dayton Tattler,* a newspaper for blacks published by classmate Orville Wright, who later gained fame with brother Wilbur Wright as inventors of the airplane. Dunbar wanted to be a lawyer, but his mother's meager financial situation made a university education impossible. He consequently looked for employment with various Dayton businesses, including newspapers, only to be rejected because of his race. He finally settled for work as an elevator operator, a job that allowed him time to continue writing. Between calls, he wrote articles, poems, and short stories for various midwestern newspapers, often receiving little or no pay for them.

In 1892 Dunbar was invited by one of his former teachers to address the Western Association of Writers (WAOW), which was then convening in Dayton. At the meeting Dunbar befriended James Newton Matthews, who later praised Dunbar's work in a letter to an Illinois newspaper. Matthews's letter was reprinted by newspapers throughout the country and thus brought Dunbar recognition outside Dayton. Shortly after the article appeared Dunbar was admitted as a WAOW member and his popularity as a speaker increased. Encouraged, he privately published *Oak and Ivy* (1893), which he sold from his elevator post and after recitals. A Toledo attorney, Charles Thatcher, impressed by the book, offered to sponsor Dunbar's college education. Dunbar reluctantly refused, however, because his mother depended on his earnings for her livelihood. Thatcher, nevertheless, remained one of several white benefactors who supported Dunbar throughout his career.

In 1893 Dunbar left Dayton to work with Frederick Douglass in the Haitian Exposition of the Chicago World's Fair. On "Colored Day" he recited original compositions in standard English and was given a warm reception. Unfortunately, during the next two years Dunbar suffered career setbacks as his health, poor since childhood, worsened. Unable to support himself and his mother, he considered suicide, but Thatcher sent Dunbar enough money to sustain him and later used his influence to help publish Dunbar's poetry collection, *Majors and Minors.* Writing in *Harper's Weekly,* William Dean Howells, then the most prominent and influential critic in America, praised the dialect poems in *Majors and Minors,* noting that Dunbar "reveals in these a finely ironical perception of the negro's limitations, with a tenderness for them which I think so rare as to be almost quite new.... It is this humorous quality which Mr. Dunbar has added to our literature, and it will be this which will most distinguish him." While Howells praised the dialect verse, he was less impressed by the standard English poems: "Some of these I thought very good, but not distinctly his contribution to the body of American poetry"—a verdict that haunted Dunbar throughout his career. Initially overwhelmed by Howells's review and the fame that followed, Dunbar later confessed that he believed Howells had done him more harm than good; the favorable response to the dialect poetry and tentative praise for the standard English poems led Dunbar to believe that if he continued to please audiences and publishers by producing dialect poetry, his more serious work would eventually gain acceptance. To his dismay, however, periodicals rejected his standard English poetry, requesting dialect pieces instead.

After a trip to England, where he met and collaborated with the black composer Samuel Coleridge Taylor, Dunbar returned to New York and married a poet and school teacher, Alice Ruth Moore, with whom he had corresponded by mail for two years. During this period Dunbar completed his first novel, *The Uncalled* (1898), and collaborated with songwriter Will Marion Cook on the musical *Clorindy; or, The Origin of the Cakewalk* (1898). A huge success, the show was the first to feature syncopated music and the first in which the chorus sang and danced simultaneously. Although Dunbar had agreed to collaborate on future projects with Cook, he was quickly disillusioned with his press reception as "king of the coon shows." Moreover, he was pressured to quit by his wife and mother, who were insulted by his association with the degrading minstrel tradition. Dunbar reluctantly fulfilled his obligations and in the process became acquainted with the artists, actors, singers, and musicians who frequented Harlem's popular theaters; he later included many of these colorful characters in his short stories and in the novel *The Sport of the Gods* (1902). While in New York Dunbar con-

tracted tuberculosis and began drinking to relieve his physical discomfort. His illness worsened in the last years of his life, necessitating intermittent retreats to milder climates. At age thirty-four, separated from his wife and suffering from alcohol abuse and his lingering illness, Dunbar died at his mother's home. He had once described himself as a "black white man": he wanted acceptance as an artist, not as a representative of his race or a dialect poet, and died believing that his career had been a national joke and a failure.

Dunbar's dialect poetry has long been his most popular work. Dialect was a common literary device in the late nineteenth century, particularly as practiced by Sidney Lanier and Joel Chandler Harris, but Dunbar's work in the genre is considered especially realistic and sensitive. Like other dialect writers, Dunbar was primarily concerned with humorous situations; however, he portrayed these events with ironic tenderness that conveys the emotions and thoughts of his uneducated, inarticulate subjects. Even Dunbar's detractors admit that his dialect poetry vividly captures the folklife and beliefs of late nineteenth-century black Americans.

Dunbar's dialect poetry, however, constitutes only a small part of his creative achievement. He wrote many poems in standard English as well as four novels and several volumes of short stories. Unlike his dialect poems, his non-dialect verse is chiefly concerned with his personal pain and anguish, not with created characters and situations. Similarly, his fiction reveals his struggle with artistic honesty and commercial success. His early short stories, written for popular magazines, are romantic, sentimental tales about the lives of black Americans on the plantation. Later in his career Dunbar wrote more directly about racial problems and the injustices of white America. Although some critics assert that Dunbar failed to fully document the harshness of life for black Americans, others argue that in these later stories he displayed an awakening social conscience.

Dunbar's novels, in general, are considered failures. Critics largely rejected his first novel, *The Uncalled,* as dull and unconvincing in its portrait of Frederick Brent, a white pastor who had, in childhood, been abandoned by an alcoholic father and then raised by a zealously devout spinster, Hester Prime. His second novel, *The Love of Landry* (1900), is about an ailing woman who arrives in Colorado for convalescence and finds true happiness with a cowboy. It was likewise deemed unconvincing in its presentation of white characters. Dunbar suffered further critical setback with his next novel, *The Fanatics* (1901), about America at the beginning of the Civil War. Its central characters, from white families, differ in their North-South sympathies and spark a dispute in their Ohio community. *The Fanatics* was a commercial failure and is considered superficial and uncompelling. Among the novel's many detractors is Robert Bone, who claimed that Dunbar resorted to "caricature in his treatment of minor Negro characters" and that his stereotypic portraits of black characters only served to reinforce prejudice.

The Sport of the Gods, Dunbar's final—and most successful—novel, presents a far more disturbing portrait of black America. Written two years before his death, it is the only novel in which Dunbar depicted a black protagonist, Berry Hamilton. When Berry is wrongly charged with theft by his white employers, he is sentenced to ten years of prison labor. His remaining family—wife, son, and daughter—consequently find themselves targets of abuse in their southern community, and after being robbed by the local police they head north to Harlem. There they encounter further hardship and strife; the son becomes embroiled in the city's seamy nightlife and succumbs to alcoholism and crime; the naive daughter is exploited by fellow blacks and begins a questionable dancing career; and the mother, convinced that her husband's prison sentence has negated their marriage, weds an abusive profligate. A happy resolution is achieved only after Berry's accuser confesses, while dying, that his charge was fabricated, whereupon Berry is released from prison. He then travels north and finds his family in disarray. Matters are finally set right when, after a series of incidents, the parental Hamiltons are reunited in marriage.

Discussion of Dunbar's work has often mirrored the political and social climate of the United States. During the author's lifetime, when most of his readers were white, his humorous dialect poetry was most widely praised. Although evidently well-intentioned, many of these early critics demonstrated patronizing visions of black artists and the lives of black Americans. Similarly, race was constantly a factor—Dunbar was invariably praised as the first great modern black American poet, while his stature as simply a poet was overlooked. After his death, Dunbar was almost completely ignored by white critics, but black critics were more inclined to examine Dunbar's total achievement. Benjamin Brawley, for example, noted that many of Dunbar's standard English poems were unsurpassed by anyone of his era "in the pure flow of the lyrical verse." During the Harlem Renaissance of the 1920s and 1930s, black artists rebelled against the minstrel tradition, with which Dunbar was associated. For the next three decades, critics often depicted Dunbar as a man who caricatured his race for money and who, with few exceptions, supported white America's prejudiced view of blacks.

During the Black Arts Movement of the 1960s, critics began to pay more attention to Dunbar's achievements and, in so doing, resurrected Dunbar as an important voice in American literature. Since then, critics have made a greater effort to understand Dunbar's compromises rather than attack him as a literary Uncle Tom. Today, critics agree that Dunbar, the first black author in America to earn his living by his pen, had to write works that a predominantly white audience would be willing to purchase. Jean Wagner and Peter Revell, in particular, have helped correct misunderstandings about Dunbar's poetry and have demonstrated the true trage-

dy of his position—that of a man who hated the only work he could sell.

Dunbar is regarded as America's first great black poet. His literary career mirrors the pain and frustration he experienced while living with one race and trying to gain acceptance from another. For Nikki Giovanni and other Dunbar scholars, his work constitutes both a history and a celebration of black life. "There is no poet, black or nonblack, who measures his achievement," Giovanni declared. "Even today. He wanted to be a writer and he wrote."

(For further information about Dunbar's life and works, see *Blacks Writers; Contemporary Authors,* Vols. 104, 124; *Dictionary of Literary Biography,* Vols. 50, 54, 78; *Something about the Author,* Vol. 34; and *Twentieth-Century Literary Criticism,* Vols. 2, 12.)

PRINCIPAL WORKS

Oak and Ivy (poetry) 1893
Majors and Minors (poetry) 1895
Lyrics of Lowly Life (poetry) 1896
Clorindy; or, The Origin of the Cakewalk [with Will Marion Cook] (libretto) 1898
Dream Lovers: An Operatic Romance (libretto) 1898
Folks from Dixie (short stories) 1898
The Uncalled (novel) 1898
Lyrics of the Hearthside (poetry) 1899
Poems of Cabin and Field (poetry) 1899
The Love of Landry (novel) 1900
The Strength of Gideon, and Other Stories (short stories) 1900
Uncle Eph's Christmas (drama) 1900
Candle-Lightin' Time (poetry) 1901
The Fanatics (novel) 1901
In Dahomey: A Negro Musical Comedy [with others] (libretto) 1902
The Sport of the Gods (novel) 1902; also published as *The Jest of Fate: A Story of Negro Life,* 1903
In Old Plantation Days (short stories) 1903
Lyrics of Love and Laughter (poetry) 1903
When Malindy Sings (poetry) 1903
The Heart of Happy Hollow (short stories) 1904
Li'l Gal (poetry) 1904
Chris'mus Is a Comin', and Other Poems (poetry) 1905
Howdy, Honey, Howdy (poetry) 1905
Lyrics of Sunshine and Shadow (poetry) 1905
A Plantation Portrait (poetry) 1905
Joggin'erlong (poetry) 1906
The Life and Works of Paul Laurence Dunbar (poetry and short stories) 1907
The Complete Poems of Paul Laurence Dunbar (poetry) 1913
Speakin' o' Christmas, and Other Christmas and Special Poems (poetry) 1914
The Best Stories of Paul Laurence Dunbar (short stories) 1938
The Letters of Paul and Alice Dunbar: A Private History (letters) 1974

The Paul Laurence Dunbar Reader (poetry, short stories, essays, journalism, and letters) 1975
I Greet the Dawn: Poems by Paul Laurence Dunbar (poetry) 1978

W. D. Howells (essay date 1896)

[*Howells was the chief progenitor of American Realism and one of the most influential American literary critics of the late nineteenth century. He wrote nearly three dozen novels, few of which are read today. Despite his eclipse, he stands as one of the major literary figures of the nineteenth century: he successfully weaned American literature away from the sentimental romanticism of its infancy, earning the popular sobriquet "the Dean of American Letters." Through Realism, a theory central to his fiction and criticism, Howells sought to disperse "the conventional acceptations by which men live on easy terms with themselves" that they might "examine the grounds of their social and moral opinions." To accomplish this, according to Howells, the writer must strive to record impressions of everyday life in detail, endowing characters with true-to-life motives and avoiding authorial comment in the narrative. In addition to many notable studies of the works of his friends Mark Twain and Henry James, Howells reviewed three generations of international literature, urging Americans to read the works of Émile Zola, Bernard Shaw, Henrik Ibsen, Emily Dickinson, and other important authors. Dunbar was another writer that Howells introduced to the reading public. In the following excerpt from* Harper's Weekly, *he reviews* Majors and Minors, *praising Dunbar's dialect verse. This review proved to be a milestone in the poet's career. A year later, however, Dunbar sadly remarked: "I see now very clearly that Mr. Howells has done me irrevocable harm in the dictum he laid down regarding my dialect verse."*]

[Mr. Dunbar] is a real poet whether he speaks a dialect or whether he writes a language. He calls his little book **Majors and Minors,** the Majors being in our American English, and the Minors being in dialect, the dialect of the middle-south negroes and the middle-south whites; for the poet's ear has been quick for the accent of his neighbors as well as for that of his kindred. I have no means of knowing whether he values his Majors more than his Minors; but I should not suppose it at all unlikely, and I am bound to say none of them are despicable. In very many I find the proofs of honest thinking and true feeling, and in some the record of experience, whose genuineness the reader can test by his own . . . .

Most of these pieces, however, are like most of the pieces of most young poets, cries of passionate aspiration and disappointment, more or less personal or universal, which except for the negro face of the author one could not find specially notable. It is when we come to Mr. Dunbar's Minors that we feel ourselves in the presence of a man with a direct and a fresh authority to do the kind of thing he is doing. . . .

One sees how the poet exults in his material, as the artist always does; it is not for him to blink its commonness, or to be ashamed of its rudeness; and in his treatment of it he has been able to bring us nearer to the heart of primitive human nature in his race than any one else has yet done. The range between appetite and emotion is not great, but it is here that his race has hitherto had its being, with a lift now and then far above and beyond it. A rich, humorous sense pervades his recognition of this fact, without excluding a fond sympathy, and it is the blending of these which delights me in all his dialect verse . . . .

Several of the pieces are pure sentiment, like "**The Deserted Plantation**"; but these without lapsing into sentimentality recall the too easy pathos of the pseudo-negro poetry of the minstrel show . . . .

Mr. Dunbar's race is nothing if not lyrical, and he comes by his rhythm honestly. But what is better, what is finer, what is of larger import, in his work is what is conscious and individual in it. He is, so far as I know, the first man of his color to study his race objectively, to analyze it to himself, and then to represent it in art as he felt it and found it to be; to represent it humorously, yet tenderly, and above all so faithfully that we know the portrait to be undeniably like. A race which has reached this effect in any of its members can no longer be held wholly uncivilized; and intellectually Mr. Dunbar makes a stronger claim for the negro than the negro yet has done . . . .

I am speaking of him as a black poet, when I should be speaking of him as a poet; but the notion of what he is insists too strongly for present impartiality. I hope I have not praised him too much, because he has surprised me so very much; for his excellences are positive and not comparative. If his Minors had been written by a white man, I should have been struck by their very uncommon quality; I should have said that they were wonderful divinations. But since they are expressions of a race-life from within the race, they seem to me indefinitely more valuable and significant. I have sometimes fancied that perhaps the negroes *thought* black, and *felt* black; that they were racially so utterly alien and distinct from ourselves that there never could be common intellectual and emotional ground between us, and that whatever eternity might do to reconcile us, the end of time would find us as far asunder as ever. But this little book has given me pause in my speculation. Here, in the artistic effect at least, is white thinking and white feeling in a black man, and perhaps the human unity, and not the race unity, is the precious thing, the divine thing, after all. God hath made of one blood all nations of men; perhaps the proof of this saying is to appear in the arts, and our hostilities and prejudices are to vanish in them.

Mr. Dunbar, at any rate, seems to have fathomed the souls of his simple white neighbors, as well as those of his own kindred; and certainly he has reported as faithfully what passes in them as any man of our race has yet done with respect to the souls of his. It would be very incomplete recognition of his work not to speak particularly of the non-negro dialect pieces, and it is to the lover of homely and tender poetry, as well as the student of tendencies, that I commend such charming sketches as **"Speakin o' Christmas," "After a Visit," "Lonesome,"** and **"The Spellin' Bee."** They are good, very good ....

> *W. D. Howells, in a review of "Majors and Minors," in* Harper's Weekly, *June 20, 1896, p. 630.*

Joseph G. Bryant (essay date 1905)

[*In the following essay, Bryant offers high praise for Dunbar's poetic skill, comparing the author to the Scottish poet Robert Burns, a master of dialect poetry.*]

[The] sparkling wit, the quaint and delightful humor, the individuality and charm of Dunbar's poetry are not excelled by any lines from the pen of a Negro. No person can read his verse without being forcibly impressed that he is a remarkable man, a genius demanding attention. The New World has not produced a bard like him. Although distinctively American by birth and education, as well as a Negro, yet his prototype is on the other side of the Atlantic. Robert Burns and Dunbar, in many important particulars, are parallel poets. They seem to have been cast in the same mould; with limited educational advantages, both struggled up through poverty, and each wrote largely in the dialect of his clan. He is strong and original, and like Burns, lyrical in inspiration. Probably there never were two men of opposite races, so widely separated by time and distance, and yet so much alike in soul-qualities. With no desire and no doubt unconsciously, he has walked complete in the footprints of the eminent Scottish bard; has the same infirmity, animated by the same hope, and blessed with the same success. (p. 256)

In Dunbar there is no threnody, not even distant clouds arch the sky. Hope and joy are the dominant notes of his song. No poet more effectively warms the cold side of our life and sends sunshine into grief-stricken souls than he. He laughs sorrow away; he takes us into the huts of the lowly and oppressed. There we find, amidst poverty and illiteracy, unfeigned contentment and true happiness; a smile is on every face, and hope displays her brightest gifts. No matter how sorrowful, who can read without considerable emotion **"When de Co'n Pone's Hot," "The Colored Band," "The Visitor," "The Old Front Gate," "De Way Tings Come,"** and **"Philosophy."**

But not all his poetry bubbles with fun, at times he is a serious poet, and appeals strongly to the serious side of life, as does his **"Weltschmertz."** It is full of tender sympathy; it touches chords which vibrate throughout the poles of our nature; he makes us feel that he takes our sorrows and makes them his own, and helps us to bear up when burdened with woe. **"The Fount of Tears," "Life's Tragedy," "The Haunted Oak,"** and the fifth lyric of **"Love and Sorrow"** reveal a high order of poetical genius; he reaches the deepest spiritual recesses of our being. (pp. 256-57)

I prefer **"The Rugged Way"** to Lowell's "After the Burial." **"The Unsung Heroes"** has all the imagination and pathos of Bryant's "Marion's Men;" **"The Black Sampson of Brandywine"** will live as long as his "African Chief." Read Bryant's and Dunbar's **"Lincoln"**—the black poet does not suffer by comparison. I do not in the least wish to convey the impression that Dunbar is a greater poet than Bryant; they move in different parts of the poetical firmament. Each is a master in his respective sphere. As a writer of blank verse Bryant has no equal in America; and as a lyrical poet with a large vein of rich humor Dunbar is without a peer in the Western Continent. (p. 257)

> *Joseph G. Bryant, "Negro Poetry," in* The Colored American Magazine, *Vol. VIII, No. 5, May, 1905, pp. 254-57.*

Vernon Loggins (essay date 1931)

[*In the following review essay, Loggins surveys Dunbar's novels, short stories, and poetry, noting: "The publication in 1896 of Dunbar's* Lyrics of Lowly Life *is the greatest single event in the history of American Negro literature."*]

Dunbar's first collection of short stories, *Folks from Dixie* ..., contains some of his most characteristic and best work as a writer of fiction .... Whatever unity the book as a whole has is told by the title, *Folks from Dixie*; the characters, not all of them colored, are either still in Dixie or once lived there. Two of the stories, **"The Ordeal at Mt. Hope,"** an argument for industrial education, and **"At Shaft II,"** an indirect plea for the Negro to stay out of labor unions, were designed for more than entertainment. The rest are pure tales. **"The Colonel's Awakening,"** the scene of which is laid in Virginia, follows so closely [Thomas Nelson] Page's method of extracting pathos out of the portrayal of the love and devotion of a faithful Negro servant that it might fit well into *In Ole Virginia*. A similar blending of kindliness and romance and sentimentality is in **"A Family Feud,"** a tale of ante-bellum days on two Kentucky plantations. The majority of the stories in the volume, however, show an indebtedness to [Joel Chandler] Harris rather than to Page. Dunbar's knowledge of plantation life in Kentucky probably came from his mother, who passed her childhood and early womanhood as a slave and who was throughout most of Dunbar's life his constant companion. At any rate, he had derived from some source a penetrating understanding of the primitive Negro's superstitions, religious zeal, romance, humor, and language .... And it was his intimate knowledge of the folk ways of Negroes which enabled Dunbar to do

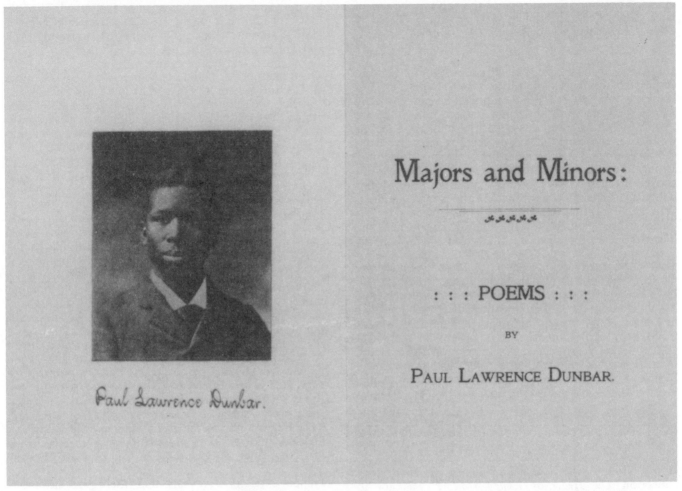

Frontispiece and title page for Dunbar's second volume of poetry. Its subsequent review by William Dean Howells launched the poet's career.

some of the strongest work found in his later volumes of short stories, [*The Strength of Gideon, In Old Plantation Days,* and *The Heart of Happy Hollow* ...].

At the time of its appearance *Folks from Dixie* was by far the most artistic book of fiction which had come from an American Negro. But it was within a year superseded by Mr. Chesnutt's *The Conjure Woman.* Dunbar was certainly more skillful than Mr. Chesnutt as a recorder of dialect, and he perhaps got closer to the real heart of the plantation Negro. However, he created no such character as Uncle Julius, and he never attained Mr. Chesnutt's mastery of treating a folk tale from a subtle and intellectual point of view. Dunbar's stories appealed to the readers of such periodicals as *Lippincott's Magazine,* while Mr. Chesnutt's met the requirements of the more critical *Atlantic Monthly* public.

Among the American writers who have been unable to judge what they could and could not do Dunbar is conspicuous. In 1898, the year of *Folks from Dixie,* he published his first novel, *The Uncalled.* It was to a certain extent autobiographical, an exposition of Dun-

bar's own ordeal in deciding whether he ought to enter the ministry. Since he was really writing about a personal experience, one cannot help wondering why he did not put himself into the story as a colored man. The action deals with the conflict in the mind of a white youth living in a small Ohio town who feels that he should not become a preacher but who is forced by circumstances into a seminary and then into the pulpit. There is not a single Negro character in the book. As a story about whites written by a Negro it introduces us to the second type of fiction which the Negro of the period attempted. Such a type Dunbar should have painstakingly avoided. All of the bubbling spontaneity which he showed in his tales on blacks is replaced in *The Uncalled* by cheap conventional story-telling, with echoes of Dickens and the popular magazine, and with an English which is often downright faulty. The book came as a great disappointment to Dunbar's admirers. Despite its weakness, it seems to have had some commercial success, and in 1900 Dunbar published a second novel in which all of the characters are whites, *The Love of Landry.* It is a story of Easterners, all treacly sentimentalists, who think that they find the sublime beauty of reality on a Colorado ranch. It was, if that is possible, even a poorer performance than *The Uncalled.* (pp. 314-17)

Dunbar's third novel, *The Fanatics* ..., is a more successful treatment of white types. While it is a romance of the Civil War, emphasis is not on battle scenes, but on how the struggle affects a small Ohio town which is made up of sympathizers for the South as well as for the North. There is exciting narrative from the beginning. However, interest does not become strong until the "contrabands" come pouring in from across the Ohio River with their queer songs and delightful dialect. Yet entirely too little is made of them. With the exception of a minor character, who provides an interesting climax for the ending of the tale, the Negro appears for no more than atmosphere. (p. 317)

Two of the stories in Paul Laurence Dunbar's *Folks from Dixie,* "The Ordeal at Mt. Hope" and "At Shaft II," have been pointed out as dealing with social problems. They belong to the ... field in which the Negro novelists and short story writers between 1865 and 1900 ventured, that of fiction offering comment on the social status of the Negro, especially in relation to the white man. It was, as we might expect, the field in which the Negro was most voluminous, and, if not most pleasing, most vigorous. It was also the field in which he was most original.

In his later collections of short stories Dunbar dwelt more and more on racial problems. (p. 320)

Happy Hollow [the fictional setting of the short story collection *The Heart of Happy Hollow*] was not to Dunbar a place for nothing more than sentimental tears and spontaneous laughter. It had its serious side, its sense of wronged justice, its tragedy. In a story of an educated colored youth's ruthless disillusionment, **"One Man's Fortune,"** included in *The Strength of Gideon,* a white lawyer is made to say:

> The sentiment of remorse and the desire for atoning which actuated so many white men to help Negroes right after the war has passed off without being replaced by that sense of plain justice which gives a black man his due, not because of, nor in spite of, but without consideration of his color.

The idea thus expressed was a guiding principle for Dunbar in writing stories on such themes as Negroes exploited by unscrupulous politicians, the economic relations existing between whites and blacks, and the effect of city life on country-bred Negroes. The deep pathos of the truth which it expresses is brought out with force in two stories on lynching, **"The Tragedy at Three Corners,"** in *The Strength of Gideon,* and "The Lynching of Jube Benson," in *The Heart of Happy Hollow.*

But Dunbar's most complete and profound study of the true reality of Happy Hollow came in his fourth and last novel, *The Sport of the Gods* .... It is at the same time

his most interesting and most imperfect novel. The title hints that Dunbar might have been reading Thomas Hardy, and the story itself more than once shows a naturalistic view of life. (p. 321)

The tragedy is attributed not so much to the wiles of the city as to the ignorant Negro's helplessness when in the clutches of circumstance aggravated by an unfair social system. The novel is structurally about as bad as it could be. A half happy ending is dragged in, and no temptation to submit to melodrama is resisted. Plausibility is in many situations strained to the shattering point. The style is nervous and uneven, typical of that which one might expect from the mind of a man who is suffering from tuberculosis. But there are many patches which are intense, serious, and telling. The description of the first evening which the country Hamiltons spend at a Negro theatre in New York is an effective blending of the Dickensian and the bitter. The horrid tinsel of life as it is portrayed in the Banner Club is saved from the nauseating and repelling only by a grim sort of humor .... [An] anonymous critic at the time of Dunbar's death [referred] to *The Sport of the Gods* as a compendium of information for the average American. If it was a revelation to white America, it was a sermon to all America. Dunbar usually lost himself as an artist when he felt strongly the urge to preach, and *The Sport of the Gods* suffers extremely as a specimen of pure fiction. But with the exception of certain perfectly executed short stories, such as **"Jimsella"** in *Folks from Dixie* and **"The Finding of Zach"** in *The Strength of Gideon,* it is of all Dunbar's work in prose the book in which the modern reader would probably find greatest interest.

Dunbar's poetry ... reveals that there was little bitterness in his nature. Moreover, he was a writer with a broad public to please. Bold and uncompromising fiction on the Negro problem was not to be expected from him. (pp. 323-24)

The publication in 1896 of Dunbar's *Lyrics of Lowly Life* is the greatest single event in the history of American Negro literature. Dunbar incorporated into the book the best selections from his earlier volumes, *Oak and Ivy* ... and *Majors and Minors* .... Although some of his short stories were thoughtfully conceived and admirably constructed, and although one of his novels, *The Sport of the Gods,* contains such material as should be an inspiration to Negro fiction writers for years to come, his verse is the work which distinguishes him as the universally recognized outstanding literary figure who had by 1900 arisen from the ranks of the American Negro. And *Lyrics of Lowly Life* is in all respects his happiest and most significant volume.

"Ere Sleep Comes Down to Soothe the Weary Eyes," the poem which opens the volume, is a song of the man who sees in the "waking world a world of lies," a theme possibly inspired by Shelley, whom Dunbar counted as his favorite poet. But the book is not a lyrical arraignment of society .... One poem after another in the volume proves that Dunbar was a master of spontaneous melody. There is never intricacy of thought nor of imagery, but there is always the song that arouses mood. It was Shelley the melodist and not Shelley the humanitarian whom Dunbar worshipped. And he was natural and sincere enough to distinguish between thoughtful influence and slavish dependence. He came as near to Shelley in **"The Rising of the Storm"** as in any poem he wrote, but . . . he was not submitting to downright imitation. . . . Most of the pieces in *Lyrics of Lowly Life* are in Shelley's English. Many of the subjects—including definitions of life, the mysteries of love and passion, the appeal of nature, and the premonitions of death—are such as one finds often treated in the lyrics of Shelley. If the volume had contained no more, it would be accounted merely a collection of gentle sentiments sung in pure melody, far superior, to be sure, to anything which any other American Negro poet had done, but not sufficiently strong to be considered a contribution of merit to American literature.

Fortunately, the volume contains a number of selections written in what Howells called the Negro's "own accent of our English." The dialect poems justify the term "lowly life" used in the title. The first which one comes upon is **"Accountability,"** a monologue of an old "darky" who has stolen "one ob mastah's chickens" and who tries to rationalize the morality of the deed. . . . Too infrequently, follow more poems in the language which the Negro's unguided habits fashioned out of English. The soul of the black laborer satisfied with little is expressed with a pure art in **"When de Co'n Pone's Hot."** . . . **"When Malindy Sings,"** inspired, we are told, by the singing of the poet's mother, is another true expression of Negro character. . . . Equally expressive of the true nature of the lowly Negro are **"Discovered"** and **"A Coquette Conquered,"** humorous love poems; **"The Deserted Plantation,"** a sentimental song of reminiscence, suggestive of the mood of Thomas Nelson Page's "Marse Chan"; **"Signs of the Times,"** a pastoral of autumn; and **"The Party,"** an hilarious descriptive poem.

The dialect poems in *Lyrics of Lowly Life* made the book the artistic, as well as the popular, success which it became. They made the reputation of Dunbar. After all, the teacher who meant most to him was not Shelley, but James Whitcomb Riley. . . . His admiration for Riley led him to include in *Lyrics of Lowly Life* **"After a Visit,"** **"The Spellin' Bee," "A Confidence,"** and a few other pieces written in the dialect of the middle western white farmer. Entertaining, humorous, and highly musical, they might easily be mistaken for Riley's own work. Therefore, there is little excuse for their existence. But in applying Riley's methods to the Negro, Dunbar achieved genuine originality. His strongest predecessors in the writing of Negro dialect verse, Sidney Lanier, Irwin Russell, and Joel Chandler Harris, were detached from their material; Dunbar was a part of his. His realism is better than theirs because it was inspired by sincere feeling and not by the search for novelty; his music appeals to us as more natural because we do not in any way have to associate it with white singers. His

Negro dialect verse is today generally accepted as the best which has been written in America. It deserves that consideration, and will probably maintain it. For the picturesque and poetic Negro language which Dunbar knew so well is rapidly passing away; he preserved a record of it at the right time.

A type of pure English verse which Dunbar should have cultivated more intensively is represented in *Lyrics of Lowly Life* by such pieces as **"Frederick Douglass,"** undoubtedly more eloquent than any memorial poem produced by any one of Dunbar's Negro predecessors; **"The Colored Soldiers,"** a stirring tribute to the colored men who fell in the Civil War; and **"Ode to Ethiopia,"** perhaps the most significant of the poems which are not in dialect. . . . The gravest charge which can justly be brought against Dunbar as the author of *Lyrics of Lowly Life* is that he too often forgot the pledge which he made to his race in **"Ode to Ethiopia."** He was endowed by nature "to sing of Ethiopia's glory," but he crowded his first important volume with songs which have little relation to himself and none to his own people. Such songs can be estimated as no more than pretty exercises.

He was twenty-four years old when *Lyrics of Lowly Life* was published, and youthfulness might have been accepted as a reason for the shortcomings of the book. But Dunbar never fulfilled its unusual promise. . . . [Recognition] as a poet prepared the way for the attainment of an ambition which he had long cherished, that for publishing prose fiction. . . . Three volumes of verse followed *Lyrics of Lowly Life: [Lyrics of the Hearthside; Lyrics of Love and Laughter;* and *Lyrics of Sunshine and Shadow]*. . . . In spite of the odds which he had to fight against in writing the verse included in these volumes, no one of them falls below the standards which he set for himself in *Lyrics of Lowly Life.* Each, containing pure lyrics, occasional verses on the Negro written in straight English, and dialect poems, is similar in arrangement to the earlier volume. While his prose fiction was being printed in the popular magazines, his verse was appearing usually in such periodicals as the *Century, Harper's,* the *Outlook, Current Literature,* the *Bookman,* and the *Atlantic Monthly.* That he held himself true to the poet within him during the hectic nine years of life which were allotted him after his first great success is a sure mark of Dunbar's genius. If he had in the first place made poets of the soil, such as Burns and Riley, his exclusive masters, and if he had turned his back against popularity, his career would possibly be one of the most singular which American literature has to record.

But it is unfair criticism to expect too much of a Negro poet who lived in the United States in the days when Dunbar lived. The more one considers his work in verse, the more one wonders at his accomplishment. (pp. 344-52)

Vernon Loggins, "Fiction and Poetry, 1865-1900," in his The Negro Author: His Development in America to 1900, *1931. Reprint by Kennikat Press, Inc., 1964, pp. 305-52.*

J. Saunders Redding (essay date 1939)

[*Redding was a distinguished critic, historian, novelist, and autobiographer. His first book,* To Make a Poet Black *(1939), is a scholarly appraisal of black poetry and is considered a landmark in criticism of black writers. In the following excerpt from this work, he evaluates Dunbar's literary canon, concluding that Dunbar "falls short in prose fiction" but was a "master" of dialect verse.*]

How tenacious, demanding, and circumscribing the dialect tradition and its concomitants had become before the turn of the century is illustrated in the poet Paul Laurence Dunbar. No Negro of finer artistic spirit has been born in America, and none whose fierce, secret energies were more powerfully directed toward breaking down the vast wall of emotional and intellectual misunderstanding within which he, as poet, was immured . . . .

[Dunbar is often noted as a poet of dialect.] Not so well known is the fact that his most serious efforts in *Oak and Ivy* and *Majors and Minors,* his second book, are given to the pieces in pure English. Scarcely known at all is the fact that all of his life he fervently sought to win recognition as a master of the pure tongue. (p. 56)

If there are times when his English pieces achieved only a sentimental pathos, there are other times when he wrought lyrics of delicate beauty. Primarily a lyrist, the music of words is one of his chief charms. (p. 58)

Not only did Dunbar use pure English for more than half his poetry, he used it for all his novels and most of his short stories. Perhaps this was a mistake. It may have been that he could have done as fine a work in the dialect short tale as Charles Chesnutt was to do. **"The Case of 'Ca'line,"** a story in the folk tradition, helps support this view. Excepting only a few of his short stories, Dunbar invariably falls short in prose fiction. His failure is twofold: he did not understand fully the extreme adaptability of folk material; and he did not study the art of prose fiction. The result of the first is that nearly all the folk stories are limited to burlesque, while the result of the second is that some very fine story stuff is hopelessly bungled.

It is, however, in his prose that Dunbar more nearly expressed the Negro, though rather as champion than as an artistically objective creator. (p. 59)

But champions are notably more effective in poetry than in prose . . . . [When] propaganda enters into prose fiction it acquires necessarily some of the broad solidity of the prosaic medium, and this firm quality immediately puts the reader on the defensive. The reader's reaction is as of one being gulled, being shown a thing for the good of his soul. These are the things one comes to feel in too many of the stories of Dunbar. Like a leaden ghost, Purpose treads the print of **"Silas Jackson," "The Ingrate," "One Man's Fortunes,"** and **"Shaft II."** Not only is the technique of the stories faulty, but plausible, character-derived motivation and convincing situation are lacking. The story that brushes aside

esthetic ends must be faultless in construction and style in order to succeed. It must captivate by sheer perfection of form. Dunbar was not aware of this. He brought to this difficult art only a zest in the message of his serious tales, and an instinctive sense of the humor inherent in certain situations in his burlesque stories. The latter are saved from failure; but a story representative of the former, **"The Strength of Gideon,"** with its powerful theme and well-defined plot, boils off in the end to a watery pottage.

The gem of Dunbar's stories is **"The Trustfulness of Polly."** In it Dunbar did not seek to express the Negro, but to recreate him. It was written in 1899, five years before his writing career ended, but he never again found such perfect focus of characterization, motivation, theme, plot, and style. It is a story of the low-life school, a type that was not to become popular until twenty years after Dunbar's death. . . . **"The Trustfulness of Polly"** is the first story of Negro low-life in New York written by a Negro. Not only is it significant as the forerunner of the long list of low-life stories from *Home to Harlem* to *Beale Street,* but it presaged the courageous, if misled, objectivity with which the postwar Negro artist was to see the life of his people.

With the exception of *The Sport of the Gods,* Dunbar's novels are as different in tone, treatment, and ideas from his short stories as it is possible for them to be. In them he carried his rebellion against the minstrel tradition to the extreme of repudiating race. But he came face to face with bitter irony. He saw clearly that even his own life story—the unfolding of his youthful spiritual struggles, his yearnings and ambitions—would not seem true to a people who knew the Negro only as a buffoon. There had been Negroes generally known to America as anything but buffoons, but they were oddities, "exceptional because of their white blood." The story of a Negro boy living through Dunbar's experiences would not win credence. Negroes simply could not have certain emotional and spiritual things happen to them. So, in the novel *The Uncalled,* Dunbar, for the sake of plausibility (so little does realism have to do with truth), characterized himself as Frederick Brent, a white youth.

In two other novels, *The Love of Landry* and *The Fanatics,* he went even further. He drew white characters in typical white environment and sought to inspire the whole with the breath of living truth. He worked on an assumption which the minstrel tradition had consistently denied. He took forcibly the stand that Dumas and Pushkin, products of entirely different milieus [and both mulattoes], had come into naturally. Fundamentally, he said, there is no difference between Negro and white: the artist is free to work in whatever material he wishes. This was more than letting an imaginary white character stand for him; this was standing for white characters. This was exchange—and of a most equalizing kind. He did not say that he was looking at white characters from a colored point of view. He simply assumed inherent emotional, intellectual, and spiritual identity with his characters. It had not been done before: except for a few scattered instances it has not been done in exactly this way since. (pp. 59-62)

That Dunbar's white novels are faulty proves only what is suggested by the faults of *The Sport of the Gods*: Dunbar was not a novelist. Because it deals with Negro characters, and because it was written after the discipline of the three other novels, *The Sport of the Gods* might be expected to be his best novel. But it is not. It is only his most interesting. As a blood and thunder tale of crime and retribution and as an analysis of the elements in the urban life of the Negro it does very well. As an artistic accomplishment it ranks below both *The Love of Landry* and *The Fanatics.*

But we must go back to Dunbar's verse, his dialect pieces, for though the necessity that drove him to dialect was bitter to him, he did his best work in this medium. His dialect pieces are not, however, most representative of his creative temper: they are merely what he had to do to win and hold his audience.

The comparison which is made so often between Paul Dunbar and Robert Burns, the Scottish poet, cannot fairly be taken further than to say that they were both singers. Burns's dialect was standard, a native tongue, understood by all the Scots, representative of them and, therefore, broad enough to give full expression to the people to whom it belonged. Burns's medium did not impose upon him the limitations to which the Negro poet was confined. On the other hand, Dunbar's dialect was not native. It was not even representative of a few Negro communities. Had he imitated the speech of the north Georgia Negro and uttered it among the Geechees of south Georgia or the Gullahs of South Carolina he would not have been understood. Dunbar, from scant knowledge of many dialects, made a language, a synthetic dialect that could be read with ease and pleasure by the northern whites to whom dialect meant only an amusing burlesque of Yankee English. Through such a bastard medium it was (and is) impossible to speak the whole heart of a people. (pp. 62-3)

At [dialect verse] Dunbar was a master. His sense of rhythm and harmony, evident in whatever he wrote, makes all the difference between his dialect pieces and the dialect of dozens of his imitators. While he was sentimental, they were vulgar and maudlin. While they bent at the knees with coarse laughter, he was content with a gentle and pathetic smile. While they blundered with dialect, he knew what could be done with it and how far it could be made to go as a poetic medium. He knew the subjects it would fit—the sweet delight of calf love, the thrill of simple music, the querulousness of old age, the satisfactions of a full stomach, the distractions of an empty one, the time-mellowed pain of bereavement. He brought to these subjects a childlike quality, a hushed wonder that is the secret of his charm in them. At times, though, something sterner crept into the dialect pieces. He was not above touches of satire, cries

of reproach, and even weary resignation to a life that at its best was extremely hard.

More often, however, he reserved the firmer tone for his pure English, going the way of challenging comparison in poetry that William Wells Brown had gone in prose, but doing it more effectively. Ignored by contemporary critics as this work was, it is principally by virtue of it that Dunbar holds the place of reverence in the hearts of Negroes. (pp. 63-4)

Such a poem as **"The Colored Soldiers"** marks him as being in one sense the spiritual father of James Weldon Johnson, Claude McKay, and a number of younger poets. But in these, as in his dialect pieces, Dunbar did not feel that he had fulfilled his larger self. He did not marvel, as does Cullen, that God had made a poet black and bade him sing. He was more concerned with singing than with blackness. He wanted to be known and remembered not as a black poet, but as a *poet*. The price he paid made his popularity among whites as dross to him. The tribute he paid to his race was in kind no different from that paid by Tennyson as poet-laureate to his queen. Time and again he expresses his disappointment at "the world's disdain" of the work which he himself held in the highest estimation.

The best of these pieces show a morbid concern with failure and death. He could not have been concerned with failure as a dialect poet. His success in that line was assured. It was the other failure he feared—and foresaw. (pp. 65-6)

How right was Dunbar's judgment as to the worth of his own poems is only partly our concern. It may be said, however, that if the poet is to be judged by his hold on the consciousness of his audience, Dunbar must rest content with the appeal of his dialect to his white audience and the grip of his eulogies on the hearts and minds of his Negro audience. Though certain of his pure English lines are frequently quoted, in general they are overlooked; not because they are poor, but because they do not distinguish him from dozens of other poets. And a poet, to succeed, must be distinguishable. Such poems as **"Life," "We Wear the Mask," "Who Knows,"** and a half dozen others must be excluded from this general criticism. (pp. 66-7)

> *J. Saunders Redding, "Adjustment," in his* To Make a Poet Black, *1939. Reprint by McGrath Publishing Company, 1968, pp. 49-92.*

Victor Lawson (essay date 1941)

[*In the following excerpt, Lawson examines Dunbar's short stories and novels, concluding: "Dunbar's prose adds up to four volumes of weak short stories, usually in the plantation tradition, and four novels, none of which is good enough to be called 'second-rate'."*]

To understand the picture of life among Negroes given by Dunbar's short stories, we have but to see how he—

softened ... whatever may have been evil; enlarged the scale of life, increased proportionately the colors, showed gentlemen perfected in courtly grace, gay girls in loveliness, and slaves in immeasurable devotion. And, we might add, life of Negroes in the North was maladjusted, full of longing for the old South, with no greater woes than those that might be encompassed by a brief range of genteel laughter and tears. (p. 82)

The most clearly and truly plantation tradition characters in Dunbar's short stories were, white: the genial, kindly overlord, the dashing belles and duelling cavaliers, and the unkind, ungentlemanly, and at least in the spirit of the thing un-southern overseers; and colored: mammy, *the proprietary;* and slave, *the contented.* There were characterizations in other trends among the whites: a scheming master educating a slave for his own gain and fuming when the slave makes his escape, or a doty septuagenarian or bereft belle stranded by a receding tidal wave of war—but the latter two are of the tradition, and the former is an exceptional character who seldom appears. Characterizations other than those named among Negroes, however, were more than exceptions. Affectionate wives and husbands, brothers loyal to each other, self-respecting church workers appeared so frequently in Dunbar's stories of plantation life as to constitute a strain of mild common man, sentimental, "genteel," but sympathetic portraiture running through the special pleading for the South. Unfortunately the sympathetic portraiture often ceases to be *that* and becomes truckling burlesque. The ministers, as much in Parker, spiritual middle-man of the Mordaunt plantation who appears in several stories of *Old Plantation Days,* as in those who appear in but one story, are quaint, funny people to a great extent rather than powerful uneducated men, purveyors of saving or betraying opiates (evaluated in relation to times and needs) that more thoughtful and frank commentators have made them.

The Negro characters *off* the plantation were human enough in their genteel way, their humanity being betrayed by the great loyalty to the South which militated against their own interest. (pp. 87-8)

Dunbar's short stories deal with Negroes on plantations, and in keeping with the plantation tradition his Negroes were proprietary, bossy and well-loved mammies, loyal slaves, comical or at least strangely unhampered banjo twaddlers and preachers. A few instances of well-placed loyalty or affection and a general tendency to make Negroes human, if piquant in fiction, shows a drawing away from some elements of the plantation tradition. It is noteworthy that the brute Negro, a favorite with some southern propagandists, was absent from Dunbar's short stories, but it is unfortunate that other elements in his work make this absence one to be commented upon.

The proprietary mammy "bossing the whole household round ..." comfortably established with special privileges, belongs to the plantation tradition, and with it, to Dunbar. (p. 97)

The house in Dayton, Ohio, where Dunbar lived from 1903 until his death in 1906.

Akin to the proprietary mammy was the contented slave.... He was so proud he didn't want to be free. Most loyal to his master of all the slaves in Dunbar's stories is Gideon, the hero of the title story in *The Strength of Gideon.* He was the perfect example of that loyalty which militated against the slaves' better interests, referred to in *The Fanatics.* (p. 100)

"Nelse Hatton's Vengeance" turns out to be the vendetta of those who will inherit the earth. Hatton certainly must have had cheek, for, when pressed, he turned the other. In this story of an ex-slave's meeting with his former master, many years after the Civil War, and his kindnesses to the former master after a moment of passionately angry remembrances, Dunbar fails fully to develop either by direct analysis or ample suggestion the dramatic possibilities—the servant's and master's recognitions, the master's possible fear, the servant's probable anger, the inner debates of the former slave—and hence fails to write the gripping story some one might do; not necessarily a melodramatic one, but perhaps one simply pathetic.... (p. 104)

Most unpardonable is Dunbar's burlesquing of the ministry, which group often expressed in sheer poetry the faith that made the black man whole in a world he could call only in small part his own. Brother Parker, the Negro minister of the Mordaunt plantation, who filled a role of ignoble lackey similar to that of rural clergymen in eighteenth century England, was the butt of several of Dunbar's joke-book stories. Off to tend the sick, Brother Parker falls in a puddle and ruins his trousers. He borrows a pair at the home of a sick woman, continues to church, delivers his sermon, and is embarrassed when a pair of cards falls from his pocket. The owner of the pants appears in time to clear Parker of the sin implied by the cards. (pp. 104-05)

Other stories, **"The Trial Sermons on Bull-Skin"** and **"Mt. Pisgah's Christmas Possum,"** are sad attempts at humour treating with buffoonery the groups which gave the world very great music, perhaps greater than that of any other religious group but the Catholics. When the religious thinker, Dunbar of *The Uncalled* and **"Weltsch-merz,"** conceived of the "Psalmist and his brethren sitting at a 'possum feast with the congregation of a rival church looking enviously on" he was sacrilegious; he made a mockery of a faith of which he could see the beauty very clearly.

Following into the rialto of the half-world such writers as Poe and Twain, Dunbar did several stories on diddling. His accounts of investment companies in which one man was the company suggest the character of business as it is among Negroes, though Dunbar is Amos 'n' Andy rather than middle-class crisis in his tendencies. There are amusing stories of conjuring and courtship, in which the Negroes' "credulity" and "mawkishness" are paraded, but in which understanding is lacking on the part of the author. Such stories are **"Dandy Jim's Conjur Scare," "The Conjuring Contest,"** and **"The Deliberation of Mr. Dunkin."** Dunbar's humour in these stories is on the side of minstrel joking. Dunbar's works "created a vogue" as one writer says. But there was waiting for them an audience which wished to welcome a quaint and curious black man whom it would not have to call "mister." To this audience Dunbar was a friend.

Dunbar wrote a few stories which broke with the plantation tradition and pseudo-gentility. Sometimes in stories truly of the tradition he introduced the unusual (that is, the generally true). Sometimes he made complete departures from mythic apology in writing of the South. Sometimes he wrote of the North without regret for the melon-patch or ire at the sinful city. In **"The Memory of Martha"** the human affection of Uncle Ben for his wife transforms the first impression one has when he reads that Ben was an excellent banjoist.... Uncle Ben stops playing when his wife dies. He takes up his banjo once more, several years later, to please his master and guests. Ending with the hymn "Hark! From the Tomb," which he played when Martha died, he himself dies. The brother-love of Jim and Joe, shown by Jim's stealing of food to feed his brother, who fled rather than be *given* (traditionally, he is not sold) to Mr. Groby (who is not quite a gentleman) and Jim's return from hiding to save Joe from a beating, command respect. **"The Wisdom of Silence,"** a very traditional story in which the master proves the freed Negro's best friend, saving him from loan sharks, admits the picture of a prosperous, talkative Negro being burned out by envious whites. Marred by "gentility" but untouched by plantation tradition is **"Viney's Free Papers,"** which tells of Ben's struggles to buy freedom for himself and his wife. Viney, the first to become free, plans to go North leaving her husband a slave, but is gripped by a gratuitous last minute repentance which rings with a hollow sound. (pp. 107-09)

Dunbar depicted the colored college graduate, the politician, the sincere and sometimes thoughtful preacher in a few stories. He showed the sparsity of positions for educated Negroes. At least once, in **"A Council of State"** as well as in a few lines of **"The Fanatics"** he touched the taboo subject of color discrimination within the Negro group. He showed by what indirect routes and spurious appeals the Negro vote was corralled. Stories such as these had factual accuracy.

The favorite stories of Dunbar, telling of happy days, hot-blooded duels, warm romance, regret in the North for happiness in the South, despite the occasional exceptional stories..., placed his work in the plantation tradition. Lacking in bare actualness, the stories also were not even clever. The stock Negro characters probably existed in kind, if not degree, but they were not the only, or the main, or the most profound characters to be found in Negro life. (pp. 115-16)

Dunbar's novels, like the short stories, were fourth-rate. They do not contain the distorted picture of Negro life which makes possible protracted, if unfavorable, criticism. But the ideas around which the stories center, partially conventional, reflect the author's ability to think independently and coherently. Literary history in a restricted sense would be interested more in the novels for completeness than for merit, but a biographer would have to consider a real religious and philosophic basis of tolerance, disconcertingly but patently distinct from Dunbar's Pollyanna optimism, revealed in the novels. The ideas expressed may not have been Dunbar's. He must have been able to grasp them, however. (p. 124)

The story [*The Uncalled*] might have been set in another town, or among Negroes rather than whites, without great change. Out of the character of strict Methodist orthodoxy, however, arises the psychological conflict which could have taken place in another town, or with Negro Methodists, but which could not have taken place without the straightjacket which Methodist orthodoxy appears as in the story.

The main characters, united in family and outward love, but bitterly opposed in outlook on life, are clearly drawn, Miss Prime's narrowness being *her's,* and not palpably that of an author who could conceive character only narrowly. Freddie Brent's rebellion, sublimated into the protest of a religious radical, results in revelation of shifting character, expressed in prose that is, in a few paragraphs, quite excellent. (p. 125)

The Uncalled is amateurish and trite in some places. The characterization of Freddie as a child is episodic, and the episodes are overworked. Freddie's arrival on a river bank to rescue his minister's daughter twenty yards ahead of everyone else is no mean feat. The coincidence by which Freddie meets his long absent, drunken, and reformed father is a possible improbability.

Yet these early incidents prepare the way for better-written climaxes.... *The Uncalled* is weakly told in many parts. Yet a few passages... reveal Dunbar as one not incapable of excellent prose or intense, independent thoughts. In essence, it is the romantic tale of Nature *versus* Art.

The Love of Landry is trivial. Unlike *The Uncalled,* it is not redeemed at all by powerful passages towards the end, or anywhere else. Dunbar wrote the book for his own amusement, using a Colorado setting which he knew, to some extent, from a visit. (pp. 126-27)

As in *The Uncalled,* the lines giving thoughts expressed by a leading character come closest to able writing.

The Fanatics tells a story of strained ties and family loyalty tested and re-examined under pressure of the State to side with it against all public enemies.... [The] "message" of the novel becomes: "The ideals of brotherhood and love are more to be followed than demands of the State." The shattering of these ideals is a greater catastrophe than defeat, and the approbation of the ideals among the enemy is greater than victory. This is the theme of *Antigone,* and while *The Fanatics* is not even a middling-good novel, Dunbar's development of the theme, presupposing a previous self-clarification, adds another hint of independent reflection already glimpsed in a few poems, and from time to time in the prose. (pp. 127-28)

The Sport of the Gods, in which Dunbar wrote of Negroes as main characters but broke with the "plantation tradition," is naturalistic. Dunbar need not have had any more definite idea of social protest than Hardy in this story of a world in which all must end ill. Nevertheless the story debunks southern "gentility." But the mishaps of Berry Hamilton's family, however Hardyan, are too close to the evils which cropped up in Dunbar's short stories of the romantic sinful town to prove he had gotten free of the old pattern entirely. (p. 130)

The novel, however much of the romantic sinful town it retained, however much it may have been a mere exercise in naturalism, gave a warranted rebuff to "that strange, ridiculous something we misname Southern honour, that honour which strains at a gnat and swallows a camel..."

Dunbar's prose adds up to four volumes of weak short stories, usually in the "plantation tradition," and four novels, none of which is good enough to be called "second-rate." Three of the novels are about white characters mainly. While it may be argued it was better to write about whites than to malign Negro character as in most of the short stories, that three out of twelve or more books is a small number for a Negro on whites, that the people of *The Uncalled* could have been made Negro by adding a word here and there, since their significant characteristic was Methodism of which Negroes could have partaken—yet Dunbar was not the great spokesman of the aspirations of Negroes he has often been called, and in spite of the apology for his defection contained in *The Fanatics* the novels are unfortunately in the direction of his shallow optimism with regard to race relations, and his repudiation of a praiseworthy canon of realists of his time: write the truth. (pp. 131-32)

Victor Lawson, in his Dunbar Critically Examined, *Associated Publishers, 1941, 151 p.*

Hugh M. Gloster (essay date 1948)

[In the following essay, Gloster offers a critical overview of Dunbar's novels and short stories.]

Catering to the demands of publishers and readers of his time, Dunbar generally evaded themes such as those presented in Chesnutt's novels and usually specialized either in the treatment of white American life or in the perpetuation of the plantation tradition. Three of his novels—*The Uncalled* (1898), *The Love of Landry* (1900), and *The Fanatics* (1901)—deal almost entirely with white characters; and the fourth, *The Sport of the Gods* (1902), though a promising naturalistic study, illustrates the plantation-school concept that the Negro becomes homesick and demoralized in the urban North. With a few exceptions, moreover, the short stories comprising *Folks from Dixie* (1898), *The Strength of Gideon* (1900), *In Old Plantation Days* (1903), and *The Heart of Happy Hollow* (1904) follow the formulas of Thomas Nelson Page.

Dunbar's first novel, *The Uncalled* (1898), appeared complete in *Lippincott's Monthly Magazine* for May, 1898, and was published in book form later in the same year. Reflecting Dunbar's contemplation of a ministerial career, the novel traces the life of Frederick Brent, a small-town orphan boy who is compulsorily educated for the clergy. Brent obtains a Methodist pastorate voluntarily relinquished by the elderly father of his fiancée but resigns rather than preach openly against a woman who had digressed from virtue. In Cincinnati, where he later obtains a clerical position, he joins the Congregational Church.

Distinctly a shallow novel, *The Uncalled* attacks the religious bigotry of the small town. Discussing Hester's determination to train Brent for the church, Dunbar writes:

> Poor, blind, conceited humanity! Interpreters of God, indeed! We reduce the deity to vulgar fractions. We place our own little ambitions and inclinations before a shrine, and label them "Divine messages." We set up our own Delphian tripod, and we are the priests and oracles. We despise the plans of Nature's Ruler and substitute our own. With our short sight we affect to take a comprehensive view of eternity. Our horizon is the universe. We spy on the Divine and try to surprise his secrets, or to sneak into his confidence by stealth. We make God the eternal a puppet. We measure the infinite with a foot-rule.

In the metropolitan environment of Cincinnati, however, Brent breathes a freer air, as the following passage from one of his letters shows:

> "I feel that I am growing. I can take good full breaths here. I couldn't in Dexter: the air was too rarefied by religion."

Dunbar also answers the small-town concept of the immorality of the large city:

> It is one of the defects of the provincial mind that it can never see any good in a great city. It concludes that as many people are wicked, where large numbers of human beings are gathered together there must be a much greater amount of evil than in a smaller place. It overlooks the equally obvious reasoning that, as some people are good, in the larger mass there must be also a larger amount of goodness.

The Love of Landry (1900), the weakest of Dunbar's novels, is a tedious and pointless account of the journey of tubercular Mildred Osborne to Colorado for her health. While in the West, Mildred falls in love with Landry Thayer, a well-born Philadelphian. The only Negro character in the story is a train porter who thinks that white people delight in "trampling on, and making a fool of, the black man." Perhaps the main importance of *The Love of Landry* is its suggestion of Dunbar's residence in Colorado and sympathy for fellow-sufferers with lung ailments. Certainly the book has no literary distinction.

Of *The Fanatics* (1901), a more successful handling of white characters, Dunbar writes: "You do not know how my hopes were planted in that book, but it has utterly disappointed me." Mirroring intersectional strife among relatives and friends in a small Ohio town during the Civil War period, the novel opens with two former friends—Bradford Waters, a Unionist, and Stephen Van Doren, a Confederate supporter—alienated as a result of conflicting ideologies. When Van Doren's son Bob joins the Southern forces, Waters insists that his daughter Mary end her courtship with the young rebel; but the girl refuses:

> She loved Bob, not his politics. What had she to do with those black men down there in the South, it was none of her business? For her part, she only knew one black man and he was bad enough. Of course, Nigger Ed was funny. They all liked him and laughed at him, but he was not exemplary. He filled, with equal adaptability, the position of town crier and town drunkard. Really, if all his brethren were like him, they would be none the worse for having masters.

Exasperated by Mary's loyalty to her lover, Waters ejects his daughter. At the close of the war, however, the Waters and Van Dorens are reconciled; and Nigger Ed becomes more than the town buffoon:

> There were men who had seen that black man on bloody fields, which were thick with the wounded and dying, and these could speak of him without tears in their eyes. There were women who begged him to come in and talk to them about their sons who had been left on some Southern field, wives who wanted to hear over again the last words of their loved ones. And so they gave him a place for life and everything he wanted, and from being despised he was much petted and spoiled, for they were all fanatics.

In his last and most promising novel, *The Sport of the Gods* (1902), which had previously appeared in *Lippin-*

cott's Monthly Magazine for May, 1901, Dunbar describes the misfortunes of a Negro family that migrates from a small Southern town to New York City. The first paragraph of the book suggests Dunbar's awareness of the repeated romanticizing of the ante-bellum South and his intention to depart from the tradition in portraying the family whose members are the main characters of the story:

> Fiction has said so much in regret of the old days when there were plantations and overseers and masters and slaves, that it was good to come upon such a household as Berry Hamilton's, if for no other reason than that it afforded a relief from the monotony of tiresome iteration.

Not all continues well with the Hamiltons, however, for Berry receives a ten-year sentence for the alleged theft of money from Francis, the irresponsible half-brother of his employer, Maurice Oakley. Because of community ill will, Fannie, Kit, and Joe Hamilton—Berry's wife, daughter, and son respectively—move to New York City. In Harlem, Joe disintegrates, and Dunbar comments as follows upon the change in his character:

> Whom the gods wish to destroy they first make mad. The first sign of the demoralization of the provincial who comes to New York is his pride at his insensibility to certain impressions which used to influence him at home. First, he begins to scoff, and there is no truth in his views nor depth in his laugh. But by and by, from mere pretending, it becomes real. He grows callous. After that he goes to the devil very cheerfully.

Becoming a frequenter of the Banner Club, "a social cesspool, generating a poisonous miasma and rocking with the stench of decayed and rotten moralities," Joe meets and later murders yellow-skinned Hattie Sterling. In contemplation of the fate of the youth, Dunbar states that "the stream of young Negro life would continue to flow up from the South, dashing itself against the hard necessities of the city and breaking like waves against a rock,—that, until the gods grew tired of their cruel sport, there must still be sacrifices to false ideals and unreal ambitions." After Joe is sent to the penitentiary, Francis confesses use of the money supposedly stolen by Berry and urges the acquittal of the Negro; but Maurice determines to protect the honor of his relative. Eventually, however, a New York newspaper reporter conducts an investigation which results in Berry's release. At the close of the novel Kit is dancing on the stage for a living, Maurice is mentally deranged because of an obsessive determination to maintain Francis' innocence, and Berry is living with his wife in their former home on the Oakley place. Of the old couple's re-establishment in the South, Dunbar writes fatalistically:

> It was not a happy life, but it was all that was left to them, and they took it up without complaint, for they knew they were powerless against some Will infinitely stronger than their own.

Though amateurish in execution, *The Sport of the Gods* is Dunbar's worthiest effort in fiction and suggests abilities which possibly did not achieve fruition because of the author's early death. Written under the influence of naturalism, which Parrington defines as "pessimistic realism," *The Sport of the Gods* follows Emile Zola's *Nana* (1880), Stephen Crane's *Maggie: A Girl of the Streets* (1893), Frank Norris' *McTeague* (1899), and other novels in which man is conceived as a powerless figure in an amoral and careless world. Showing race prejudice as an all-destructive virus, the book reveals social corruption in the South as well as in the North. In the Southern small town, interracial distrust is exposed, and the vaunted chivalry of Dixie gentlemen is debunked through the characterization of Francis and Maurice Oakley. In the New York setting, inexperienced Negro youth are pictured in a treacherous environment which deterministically produces degeneration and disaster. By treating the challenging and comparatively unworked Harlem low-life scene, Dunbar analyzed a background that was later to intrigue Claude McKay, Carl Van Vechten, and other writers of the 1920's. As a matter of fact, Van Vechten expresses the indebtedness of *Nigger Heaven* to *The Sport of the Gods* by saying that in the latter novel Dunbar "described the plight of a young outsider who comes to the larger New York Negro world to make his fortune, but who falls a victim to the sordid snares of that world, a theme I elaborated in 1926 to fit a newer and much more intricate social system."

To move from Dunbar's novels to his short stories is to enter a different field. Three of the novels sentimentally treat white characters in their conventional setting, and the fourth is a naturalistic study of a post-bellum Negro family in a small Southern town and in Harlem. However, in most of the short stories comprising *Folks From Dixie* (1898), *The Strength of Gideon and Other Stories* (1900), *In Old Plantation Days* (1903), and *The Heart of Happy Hollow* (1904), Dunbar becomes a successful imitator of the plantation school. Like other resuscitators of the legendary South, he presents "the big house," peopled by high-spirited and indulgent blue-bloods, and "the quarters," inhabited by spoiled and satisfied slaves whose lives are made picturesque by conjuration, gambling, feasting, rivalries, love affairs, mimicry, and primitive religion. In this environment move such familiar types as the proprietary mammy, the pompous butler, the pretentious coachman, and the plantation exhorter. A wide social gulf divides the slaves in "the big house" from those in "the quarters." The relationship between master and slave is idealized as one of mutual affection and loyalty, and the best masters do not buy and sell slaves unless forced to do so because of financial strain. Furthermore, the patricians generally avoid flogging by delegating this unpleasant assignment to overseers or supervised Negroes. The overseer, being in most cases a representative of "poor white trash," is not portrayed sympathetically. A purveyor of these expected themes, Dunbar avoids penetrating social analysis of the South and suggests that Negroes who migrate to the North become maladjusted and demoralized individuals who remember the years before emancipation with pitiable nostalgia.

Folks from Dixie, Dunbar's first collection of short stories, contains twelve tales treating action before and after the Civil War. The majority of the narratives conform to the postulates of the plantation tradition. **"Anner Lizer's Stumblin' Block"** presents a slave woman who will not become converted until sure of the marital intentions of her lover. **"A Family Feud"** is a story of ante-bellum days told to the author by Aunt Joshy. **"The Intervention of Peter"** shows how an old Negro prevents a duel between two Southern gentlemen. **"The Colonel's Awakening"** mirrors the loyalty of two ex-slaves to their elderly demented master who has lost his wealth and sons in the Civil War. **"The Ordeal at Mount Hope,"** **"The Trial Sermons on Bull-Skin,"** and **"Mt. Pisgah's Christmas Possum"** furnish glimpses of Negro church life. Anticipating *The Sport of the Gods,* **"Jimsella"** describes the struggles of a Negro couple in New York, where "it was all very different: one room in a crowded tenement house, and the necessity of grinding day after day to keep the wolf—a very terrible and ravenous wolf—from the door." Several stories in *Folks from Dixie,* however, tend to diverge from plantation prescriptions. **"Aunt Mandy's Investment"** treats the machinations of a Negro shyster who fleeces gullible black folk. **"The Deliberation of Mr. Dunkin"** unfolds the wooing of a teacher by an affected member of the school board. **"Nelse Hatton's Revenge"** sets forth the kindness of an ex-slave to a former master whom he had earlier vowed to kill. Veering from plantation requirements more than any other story in the volume, **"At Shaft 11"** recounts the heroic part played by Sam Bowles, a Negro foreman, in a West Virginia mine strike and race riot.

The imprint of the plantation tradition is also strong upon *The Strength of Gideon and Other Stories,* a collection of twenty narratives. The title story and **"Mammy Peggy's Pride"** depict the loyalty of ex-bondmen to their former masters. **"Viney's Free Papers,"** **"The Fruitful Sleeping of the Rev. Elisha Edwards,"** **"The Case of 'Ca'line': A Kitchen Monologue,"** **"Jim's Probation,"** and **"Uncle Simon's Sunday Out"** portray various experiences of plantation life. Illustrative of the unfitness of the Negro to cope with the inhospitable environment of the Northern metropolis are **"An Old Time Christmas,"** **"The Trustfulness of Polly,"** **"The Finding of Zach,"** **"The Faith Cure Man,"** **"Silas Jackson,"** **"The Finish of Patsy Barnes,"** and **"One Man's Fortunes."** The last-named story records the failure of a Negro lawyer who learns "that the adages, as well as the books and the formulas, were made by and for others than us of the black race." Several stories of the volume, however, break rather sharply from typical plantation subject matter. **"Mr. Cornelius Johnson, Office Seeker,"** **"A Mess of Pottage,"** and **"A Council of State"** present the Negro in politics. **"The Ingrate"** portrays a slave who yearns for freedom:

> To him his slavery was deep night. What wonder, then, that he should dream, and that through the ivory gate should come to him the forbidden vision of freedom? To own himself, to be master of his hands, feet, of his whole body—something would

clutch at his heart as he thought of it; and the breath would come hard between his lips.

Escaping to Canada, he rejoices in the work of the Abolitionists and joins the Union Army during the Civil War. A bloody tale of lynching and mob passion, **"The Tragedy of Three Forks"** is social protest that is a far cry from Dunbar's usual treatment of the Southern scene. After Jane Hunster, a white girl of a small Kentucky town, commits arson because of jealousy, her father hastily attributes the crime to a Negro:

> "Look a here, folks, I tell you that's the work o' niggers. I kin see their hand in it."

Thereafter incendiary newspaper articles result in the seizure and lynching of two innocent Negroes. In a struggle for pieces of the mob's rope to be kept as souvenirs, Dock Heaters fatally stabs Jane's fiancé; and the one-sided justice of the South is indicated in the following persuasive reply to a demand that the murderer also by lynched: "No," cried an imperious voice, "who knows what may have put him up to it? Give a white man a chance for his life."

Most of the stories of *In Old Plantation Days* follow the pattern of those in Page's *In Ole Virginia* and have their setting on the plantation of Stuart Mordaunt, a typical master of the legendary South. **"Aunt Tempy's Triumph"** shows how a proprietary mammy, who thinks she owns the "plantation with all the white folks and niggers on it," succeeds in giving away the master's daughter in marriage. **"Dizzy-Headed Dick," "A Lady Slipper,"** and **"Who Stand for the Gods"** present slaves who intervene to assist white lovers. **"Aunt Tempy's Revenge," "The Trouble about Sophiny," "Ash-Cake Hannah and Her Ben," "The Conjuring Contest," "Dandy Jim's Conjure Scare," "The Memory of Martha,"** and **"The Easter Wedding"** deal principally with the love affairs of bondmen. The old-fashioned exhorter and plantation religious life are described in **"The Walls of Jericho," "How Brother Parker Fell from Grace," "The Trousers,"** and **"The Last Fiddling of Mordaunt's Jim."** Slave loyalty is exemplified in **"A Blessed Deceit"** and **"The Stanton Coachman." "The Brief Cure of Aunt Fanny"** reveals the rivalry between two plantation cooks, while **"A Supper by Proxy"** pictures a lavish feast prepared by Negroes in "the big house" in the absence of the master. **"Mr. Groby's Slippery Gift"** unfolds the loyalty of two slave brothers and the cruelty of an overseer. The last five stories of the volume shift to post-bellum times and urban scenes. **"The Finding of Martha,"** highly suggestive of Chesnutt's "The Wife of His Youth," sets forth the successful quest of a Negro preacher for his wife of slavery times. **"The Defection of Mary Ann Gibbs," "A Judgment of Paris," "Silent Samuel,"** and **"The Way of a Woman,"** all having their locale in the Negro ghetto of a Northern city, are chiefly concerned with competition in love.

In *The Heart of Happy Hollow* Dunbar gives the following description of the setting of the stories:

> Wherever Negroes colonize in the cities or villages, North or South, wherever the hod carrier, the porter, and the waiter are the society men of the town; wherever the picnic and the excursion are the chief summer diversion, and the revival the winter-time of repentance, wherever the cheese cloth obtains at a wedding, and the little white hearse goes by with black mourners in the one carriage behind, there—there—is Happy Hollow. Wherever laughter and tears rub elbows day by day, and the spirit of labour and laziness shake hands, there—there—is Happy Hollow, and of some of it may the following pages show the heart.

Though dealing chiefly with post-bellum Negro life, many of the sixteen tales of *The Heart of Happy Hollow* do not escape the influence of the plantation tradition. **"Cahoots"** sentimentalizes the life-long devotion of a slave to his master. **"The Wisdom of Silence"** portrays an ex-slave who, having grown prosperous and boastful, is humbled and thereafter aided by his former owner. **"One Christmas at Shiloh"** and **"A Matter of Doctrine"** present Negro ministers as suitors. **"Old Abe's Conversion"** traces the transformation of an old-fashioned exhorter into a progressive pastor. **"A Defender of the Faith"** and **"The Interference of Patsy Ann"** mirror the pathos of Negro life in a big city. **"The Mission of Mr. Scatters," "The Promoter,"** and **"Schwalliger's Philosophy"** expose colored swindlers. **"The Scapegoat"** describes the craft of a Negro politician, while **"The Home-Coming of Rastus Smith"** limns a young Negro lawyer who adopts a supercilious attitude toward his mother and former sweetheart. **"The Boy and the Bayonet"** illustrates a lesson in military discipline. Misleadingly titled, **"The Race Question"** is the soliloquy of an old colored man at a race track. In **"The Lynching of Jube Benson,"** a white physician, defending his opposition to mob violence, recounts the murder of a loyal and innocent Negro friend.

In his short stories, therefore, Dunbar generally accepts the limitations and circumscriptions of the plantation tradition. Glorifying the good old days in the accepted manner, he sentimentalizes master-slave relationships and implies that freedom brings social misery to the black man. Negro migrants to the urban North are usually represented as nostalgic misfits, some of whom fall prey to poverty, immorality, or disease, and others to disillusionment occasioned by political or professional reverses. **"The Ingrate"** and **"The Tragedy at Three Forks,"** both of which are effective examples of the use of irony, are possibly the only stories in the four volumes that entirely escape the tendency to idealize Dixie. Furthermore, the narratives give an unauthentic recording of life because of their neglect of the unpleasant realities of the Southland. These considerations lead directly to the observation that Dunbar usually catered to the racial preconceptions of his publishers and readers by employing the themes and stereotypes of the plantation tradition. Nevertheless, his literary reputation itself constituted a strong argument against Negro inferiority; and he helped to prepare the American audience for succeeding authors possessing greater originality and deeper social understanding. (pp. 46-56)

Hugh M. Gloster, "Negro Fiction to World War I," in his Negro Voices in American Fiction, 1948. Reprint by Russell & Russell, Inc., 1965, pp. 23-100.

Darwin T. Turner (essay date 1967)

[In the following excerpt, Turner discusses the ironic nature of Dunbar's works, arguing that Dunbar was "far more bitter and scathing, much more a part of the protest tradition than his reputation suggests."]

[Dunbar's] image has been defaced by scholars who have censured him for tarnishing the symbol by perpetuating the derogatory caricatures of the minstrel show and the plantation tales.... His reputation has suffered also from those readers who, seeking to compress his thought into pithy phrases, have failed to reveal the significant changes in his subject-matter and attitudes. His reputation has suffered from those who have been blinded by a single work or who have failed to discern his attempts at ironic protest. The result has been the currently popular images of Dunbar as a disenchanted angel fluttering his wings against publishers' restrictions or as a money-hungry Esau willing to betray his birthright for a mess of popularity. Careful examination of Dunbar and of his works explains the reasons for his inability to write the kind of protest which some of his critics wish. Simultaneously, such scrutiny reveals Dunbar to be far more bitter and scathing, much more a part of the protest tradition than his reputation suggests.

Paul Laurence Dunbar's experiences, his political and economic philosophies, and his artistic ideals prevented his writing the acerbate criticism of the South which some readers desire. Paul Laurence Dunbar's cardinal sin is that he violated the unwritten commandment which American Society has handed down to the Negro: "Thou shalt not laugh at thy black brother" (Especially thou shalt not laugh at thy black brother who spoke dialect and was a slave). But Paul Laurence Dunbar could not identify himself with the slave or freedman about whom he wrote.... Dunbar judged the color of his skin to be a very thin bond linking him to the half-Christian, half-pagan slaves a mere two-hundred years removed from savagery, in his opinion. That bond of color was insufficiently tight to gag his chuckles about some of their ridiculous antics which his mother, an ex-slave, had narrated.

Even if Dunbar had been completely free to write scathing protest about the South, he could not have written it, or would have written in ineptly. His experiences and those of his family had not compelled him to hate white people as a group or the South as a region. After Dunbar was twenty, every major job he secured, every publication, and all national recognition resulted directly from the assistance of white benefactors. It is not remarkable that Dunbar assumed that successful Negroes need such help or that, knowing the actuality of Northern benefactors, he believed in the existence of their Southern counterparts. (pp. 1-2)

Even had his experiences prompted protest against the South, his social and economic philosophies would have militated against it. Believing that America would prosper only if all citizens recognized their interdependence, he sought to win respect for Negroes by showing that, instead of sulking about the past, they were ready to participate in the joint effort to create a new America. In the poems of *Majors and Minors* ... and the stories of *Folks from Dixie*..., he repeatedly emphasized the ability and willingness of Negroes to forgive white Americans for previous injustices.

Dunbar's noble sentiments and protagonists reveal not only a naive political philosophy but also a romantic and idealized concept of society. He believed in right rule by an aristocracy based on birth and blood which assured culture, good breeding, and all the virtues appropriate to a gentleman. He further believed that Negroes, instead of condemning such a society, must prove themselves worthy of a place in it by showing that they had civilized themselves to a level above the savagery which he assumed to be characteristic of Africa. Furthermore, having been reared in Dayton, Ohio, he distrusted big cities and industrialization. Provincially, he assumed the good life for the uneducated to be the life of a farmer in a small western or midwestern settlement or the life of a sharecropper for a benevolent Southern aristocrat. Neither a scholar, political scientist, nor economist, he naively offered an agrarian myth as a shield against the painful reality of discrimination in cities.

Artistic ideals also restricted Dunbar's protest. Even Saunders Redding, generally extremely perceptive in his study of Dunbar, has regretted Dunbar's failure to criticize his society more frequently in his poetry [see excerpt dated 1939]. Dunbar, however, regarded poetry—in standard English—as a noble language, best suited for expressing elevated ideas. Prose was his voice of protest. Protest is missing even from his first two books of poetry, which were privately printed....

Dunbar's experiences, his social and economic philosophies, and his artistic ideals limited his criticism of the South. This fact, however, should not imply, as some suppose, that Dunbar accepted the total myth of the plantation tradition. In reality, he was no more willing to assume the romanticized plantation to be characteristic of the entire South than he was willing to deny that some slaves had loved their masters or had behaved foolishly.

Nor should it be assumed that his hunger for fame and money silenced his protest against unjust treatment. Actually, he vigorously castigated [in his books and newspaper articles] conditions familiar to him in the North. (pp. 3-4)

[His] protests [in newspaper articles] had been mild. In *The Strength of Gideon and Other Stories*..., however, Dunbar slapped back. In **"A Mess of Pottage"** he pictured the Negro as an individual betrayed by both

Dunbar's bedroom. The bicycle was a gift from Orville Wright, Dunbar's high-school friend.

political parties. **"A Council of State"** is written in a similar tone. (p. 5)

Dunbar's characteristic irony occasionally seeps through the bitterness.... The irony, however, does not lighten the tone. These stories cannot be called pessimistic. The confirmed pessimist at least perceives an alternative outcome even while he positively affirms the inevitability of the undesired outcome. In these stories Dunbar, however, saw only destruction. (pp. 6-7)

In *The Strength of Gideon and Other Stories,* economic problems and injustice also harass the uneducated....

Dunbar also examined injustices in the South. The popularity of lynchings inspired the ironic **"The Tragedy at Three Forks."** (p. 8)

Dunbar wedded his social criticism of Negroes and of America in a novel, *The Sport of the Gods*.... His savage attack upon stereotypes and myths of the plantation tradition has been blunted by critics who, observing the melodramatic occurrences and the diatribes against city life, fail to perceive the abject despair suggested by the ending. (p. 9)

Some critics argue that the attack on the evils of New York and the return to the South evidence Dunbar's inability to avoid the plantation tradition. Dunbar's ending, however, is far more bitter and hopeless than that. The alternatives he offers are the restraint of the body in the South and the festering of the soul in the North....

If these two books had been published anonymously, they would be considered bitter protests and the author would be heralded as the first major ironist in literature by Negroes. Several reasons underlie the failure of many readers to recognize these qualities. Dunbar often phrased ideas ambiguously; consequently, his most successful irony is that which is heavily and fully developed. Second, some of his subtlety may have been

overlooked by critics. Finally, his dark acerbity may have been missed by readers blinded by his bright image as a comic writer. (p. 11)

A muted voice of protest... was sounded in his poetry collection, *Lyrics of Love and Laughter*.... In two poems, **"The Haunted Oak"** and **"To the New South,"** he attacked lynchings and the ingratitude of the South.

In his final two works of protest fiction, **"The Wisdom of Silence"** and **"The Lynching of Jube Benson,"** he continued his criticism of the South. (pp. 11-12)

His writings evidence Dunbar's protests against both the South and the North. His position, however, is difficult to appraise exactly because he vacillated and assumed seemingly contradictory stances. Some of his attitudes are difficult to explain. (p. 12)

Perhaps the simplest explanation which offers any consistency is that readers have demanded too much of Dunbar as a symbol. Commanding him to speak for the Negro, they forget that Negroes speak with hundreds of different voices. Dunbar is merely one. Insensitive to the implications of creating comic Negro figures, he was extremely sensitive to the insults which a Northern society might inflict upon an educated Negro. Willing to criticize injustices of Northern or Southern society, he, nevertheless, supported outmoded economic and social ideals. Occasionally conscious of the ridiculous postures of white Americans, he was even more conscious and less tolerant of ridiculous behavior of Negro Americans. Ignorant of historical truths about Africa and about slavery, he respected as fact the myths current in his time. Because he recognized distinctions between Negroes he knew and Negro stereotypes of the plantation stories, he inferred the race's remarkable progress within a generation. In short, Paul Laurence Dunbar was a talented, creative, high school graduate whose views reflect the limited knowledge of many historians, economists, and social philosophers of his day. (pp. 12-13)

Darwin T. Turner, "Paul Laurence Dunbar: The Rejected Symbol," in Journal of Negro History, *January, 1967, pp. 1-13.*

Robert Bone (essay date 1975)

[*Bone is the author of* The Negro Novel in America *(1958) and* Down Home: A History of Afro-American Short Fiction from Its Beginnings to the End of the Harlem Renaissance *(1975). A student of African-American, English, and American literature, with a special interest in Shakespeare, he has said of himself: "A white man and critic of black literature, I try to demonstrate by the quality of my work that scholarship is not the same thing as identity." In the following excerpt, he discusses "six basic story-types" that encompass Dunbar's short fiction.*]

Six basic story-types encompass most of [Dunbar's short fiction] output.... First there are the pastorals..., deriving essentially from the Plantation School. Next the travesties..., deriving from the minstrel shows. Third, protestations of loyalty..., which offer reassurance to the whites in the Washington tradition. Fourth, stories of uplift..., which celebrate the success virtues. Fifth, protest stories..., which challenge the artificial barriers of caste. Sixth, stories of illicit aspiration..., which are close in spirit to the Brer Rabbit tales. (pp. 62-3)

In his short stories and his novels, Dunbar employs three distinct varieties of pastoral. According to their basic thrust, I have called them pastorals of release, pastorals of reconciliation, and pastorals of place. The first type predominates among the Ohio pastorals; the second, among the antebellum tales; the third, among the post-emancipation stories. Each type, moreover, is associated with a particular Dunbar novel. Thus the pastorals of release may be thought of as spin-off from *The Uncalled*..., the pastorals of reconciliation, from *The Fanatics*..., and the pastorals of place, from *The Sport of the Gods*....

The pastorals of release have their source in the strict authoritarian controls of Dunbar's youth. They celebrate his liberation from the Protestant ethic of hard work and self-denial, from the competitive pressures of the Negro middle class, or in other words, from his mother's tyranny. Truancy is the central metaphor of these stories, and in this respect they anticipate the fiction of Claude McKay. Their tone is one of genial humor, deriving from a leniency and mellowness of spirit. They advocate a tolerance of human weakness, and a generous forgiveness of venial sins. These stories are designed, in short, to mitigate the rigors of the puritan tradition. (p. 63)

[The] emotional syndrome of rebellion, guilt, and reconciliation is typical of Dunbar's Ohio pastorals.

The pastorals of reconciliation have their origin in this syndrome. Revolt against maternal domination produces guilt, which in turn necessitates a reconciliation with the mother.... This motif, projected on the historical plane, accounts for most of Dunbar's antebellum tales.

Breach-and-reconciliation constitutes the plot of these plantation tales. Typically they open with a feud or bitter quarrel between two lovers or their families; between Blue-and-Grey, master-and-slave, or east-and-west plantations. In the end a reconciliation is effected, often through the intervention of a faithful servant. The moral injunction implicit in these tales is to forgive and forget. The spirit of dissension, or faction, or die-hard conservatism is condemned, while the virtues of conciliation and openness to change are celebrated.

The pastorals of place are concerned with exposing false ambition or restraining the aspiring mind. Working within the conventions of the Plantation School, Dunbar subscribes—or pretends to subscribe—to Southern agrarian values. He thus portrays the Great Migration as a moral disaster. At the same time, the Northern

movement that he condemns functions in his fiction as a metaphor of social mobility. The moral of these stories is: know your place, be content with what you have, and resist the temptation to aspire above your station. The pastorals of place, in short, subserve the Washingtonian doctrine of limited aspiration. (pp. 64-5)

A variation on the theme of false ambition is what might be called the carpetbagger theme. Here the protagonist is tempted by a get-rich-quick scheme which promises to bring success without the trouble of hard work.... The moral of these tales is Washingtonian: only through hard work and sacrifice can the black man hope to improve his lot.

Some of Dunbar's overly ambitious blacks are undone by their own pretentiousness and pride.... Such stories as **"The Wisdom of Silence," "Johnsonham, Jr."** and **"The Home-Coming of 'Rastus Smith"** warn the blacks to keep a low profile and do nothing to arouse the envy of their enemies.

Pastoral and travesty are closely related literary forms. Both employ the device of masquerade, but so to speak, in opposite directions. When a courtier pretends to be a shepherd, the result is pastoral, but when a shepherd pretends to be a courtier, the result is travesty. In travesty the masker "dresses up," while in pastoral he "dresses down." But in either case, the form depends on audience recognition that the masquerader is not what he pretends to be. (pp. 65-6)

Dunbar's travesties run true to form. They stress the imitative, or derivative, or secondhand features of Negro life. The key characters are those members of the black community—headwaiters, butlers, and body servants—who have the freest access to white culture. This dimension of Dunbar's art is closely related to the popular diversion of the cakewalk. He was familiar with the form through his efforts in the field of musical comedy. The cakewalk, in which Negro slaves parodied the elegance and formal manners of the Big House, was a standard ingredient of every minstrel show. If we recognize its equivalent in Dunbar's fiction, we cannot fail to be impressed with the affinity of his art to minstrelsy. (pp. 66-7)

"A Supper by Proxy" is a classic example of social travesty, whose comedy derives from the attempt to rise above one's station. He who imitates his betters, like Malvolio, runs the risk of ridicule.... What is really at issue in these tales is the former slave's desperate quest for a code of manners, a model of deportment, a standard of taste appropriate to his new status as a freedman. That this painful effort on the part of black folks to become "respectable" should be perceived as comical by Dunbar is a measure of his psychological assimilation to the white man's point of view.

Dunbar's religious travesties constitute a variation on the theme. Here a comic disproportion arises between saintly pretensions and human frailties. These stories contrast the high road of salvation with the low road of appetite. They move from a lofty spiritual plane to a mundane level of petty intrigue, ulterior motive, courtship rivalry, or venial sin. Thus a convert is not so much "under conviction" as in search of a husband (**"Anner 'Lizer's Stumblin' Block"**); or what seems to be a miracle turns out to be a prank (**"The Walls of Jericho"**). Often these stories have a bathetic ending which provides a naturalistic explanation for a seemingly supernatural event.

Most of Dunbar's religious travesties are antebellum tales whose common setting is the Virginia plantation of Stuart Mordaunt.... These travesties derive from the folk form of the preacher tale, in which the black preacher's alleged pomposity, greed, unchastity, or hypocrisy provides a source of deflationary humor.

A few religious travesties have post-emancipation settings. Their plots generally turn on some form of rivalry in church governance. But the tone is comic; the issues trivial or insignificant. These stories proclaim above all that the lives of black folk are lacking in high seriousness. We are presented not with Negro church life, but a parody thereof. Dramatic conflict may be present, but it is unworthy of mature minds. Of these undignified portrayals, **"The Trial Sermon on Bull-Skin"** is perhaps the most representative, while **"Mt. Pisgah's Christmas 'Possum"** is closest to the minstrel stereotype. (pp. 67-8)

Eight of Dunbar's tales are protestations of loyalty.... Some are set in the antebellum South; others follow the fortunes of a Southern family beyond the Civil War, in order to demonstrate the loyalty of former slaves through thick and thin. All reflect the house-servant orientation inherited by Dunbar from his mother. (p. 69)

Six of Dunbar's stories are concerned with the theme of moral uplift. Inspirational in tone, they seek to redeem the darker brother from his backward ways. Their origin can thus be traced to the missionary impulse of the planter class, which would not rest content until its slaves were Christianized. This impulse toward salvation has been secularized in Dunbar, and amounts to little more than the inculcation of bourgeois values. These stories are little sermonettes on the dangers of gambling, alcohol, and sex, or the vices of shiftlessness, irresponsibility, and wife-desertion. They are dedicated to the dissemination of what might be called the Booker-T virtues. (pp. 69-70)

Despite his natural inclination to accommodate, Dunbar is not entirely lacking in rebelliousness. While ordinarily his true feelings are well masked, on occasion the mask slips, and we catch a glimpse of the authentic self. Six of his stories, for example, are concerned with voicing historic grievances, protesting current injustices, and defending his race from the ravages of the post-Reconstruction, repression. (p. 70)

"One Man's Fortunes" is typical of Dunbar's protest tales. Autobiographical in origin, it reflects the young poet's bitterness, following his high-school graduation,

when he was unable to find a decent job.... Perhaps in this astringent tale Dunbar discloses what he truly feels about the Washington doctrine of limited aspiration.

If legitimate ambition is thwarted by the color line, then illicit forms of aspiration are certain to appear. A new type of hero is required to dramatize this theme. In Dunbar's early stories the heroes are paragons of virtue, as virtue would be understood by whites. In certain of his later tales, however, a hero of a different stamp appears. This is a man whose character and actions are shrouded in moral ambiguity. With his appearance, the moral certainties of melodrama are dissolved, and the outlines of a more sophisticated moral vision are revealed. Dunbar is striving to transcend the official (or white) morality of which he has been heretofore a captive, and an outlaw (or Negro) code is beginning to emerge.

Thus we have the confidence man, the racetrack tout, or the convicted felon cast in the heroic role. These are metaphors, or ritual masks, behind which lurks the elusive figure of Brer Rabbit. For it was the signifying Rabbit who first embodied this outlaw code. In a social order where the white man possesses all the power, writes all the laws, and formulates the moral code, the black man is pushed beyond the pale of conventional morality. He becomes a moral outlaw. So it is with Dunbar's disreputable heroes: the trickster with his signifying ways is a threat to the white man's moral order; the racetrack tout is a challenge to white respectability; the convict is a victim of the white man's law. (pp. 70-1)

How shall we assess Dunbar's work in the short-story form? Much of it is inauthentic, in the sense that it reflects the white man's definitions of reality. Much of what remains is parochial or topical, and does not survive its own historical epoch. Very few of Dunbar's stories escape the limitations of a facile commercialism: they were mass-produced, written to standard specifications, and packaged for a quick sale. The truth is that Dunbar was a black businessman working in the literary line.

Despite these strictures, it cannot be denied that Dunbar played an important role in the evolution of the Afro-American short story. He established a pastoral tradition that would come to fruition in the era of the Harlem Renaissance. He was the founder, moreover, of a populist and anti-intellectual tradition that descends through Langston Hughes to the revolutionary writers of the Black Power movement. Finally, in his focus on the theme of Negro aspiration he identified a subject to which generations of black storytellers would return.

On balance, however, the verdict must be negative. In the short-story field, Dunbar will be remembered chiefly as a purveyor of dead forms. Plantation tales, minstrel travesties, loyalty sagas: these were the sterile fantasies of a nation engaged in a hollow ritual of self-justification. That they survived at all in the fiction of a black

American is testimony to the coercive power of the white man's literary forms.

There is a moribund quality in Dunbar's art, attributable at least in part to the limitations of his age. To overcome those limitations, to make the most of his restricted possibilities, to stretch the imaginations of his contemporaries and thereby enlarge their moral horizons, it would have been necessary for Dunbar to adopt a sharply different literary stance. Romanticism would have had to yield to realism; loyalty to satire; pastoral to antipastoral. (pp. 72-3)

> *Robert Bone, "Paul Dunbar," in his* Down Home: Origins of the Afro-American Short Story, *Columbia University Press, 1988, pp. 42-73.*

FURTHER READING

Arden, Eugene. "The Early Harlem Novel." *Phylon: The Atlanta University Review of Race and Culture* XX, No. 1 (March 1959): 25-31.
> Discusses *The Sport of the Gods* as a forerunner of the novels of the Harlem Renaissance.

Baker, Houston A., Jr. "The 'Limitless' Freedom of Myth: Paul Laurence Dunbar's 'The Sport of the Gods' and the Criticism of Afro-American Literature." In *The American Self: Myth, Ideology, and Popular Culture,* edited by Sam B. Girgus, pp. 124-43. Albuquerque: University of New Mexico Press, 1981.
> Examines Dunbar's *The Sport of the Gods,* noting: "*The Sport of the Gods* is essentially a discourse, I think, on the fallibility of human habits of thought."

Brawley, Benjamin. *Paul Laurence Dunbar: Poet of His People,* 1936. Reprint. Port Washington, N.Y.: Kennikat Press, 1967, 159 p.

Critical biography based on the poet's letters and personal interviews with his mother, former wife, friends, and acquaintances.

Cunningham, Virginia. *Paul Laurence Dunbar and His Song.* New York: Dodd, Mead & Co., 1947, 283 p.
> Considered one of the most authoritative biographies. The book, which contains dialogue attributed to letters, scrap books, and personal reminiscences, traces the poet's life, presenting a picture of a dutiful son, loyal friend, and brilliant writer. Racial problems and controversies are given only passing mention.

Du Bois, W. E. Burghardt. "Negro Art and Literature." In his *The Gift of Black Folk: The Negro in the Making of America,* pp. 287-319. Boston: The Stratford Co., 1924.
> Brief history of black American writers. Du Bois calls Dunbar "the undoubted laureate of the race" and notes that he became a national figure by raising dialect from the "minstrel stage to literature."

Martin, Jay, ed. *A Singer in the Dawn: Reinterpretations of Paul Laurence Dunbar.* New York: Dodd, Mead & Co., 1975, 255 p.
> Lectures and memorial poems presented at the Centenary Conference on Paul Laurence Dunbar at the University of California, Irvine, in 1972. Contributors include Arna Bontemps, Addison Gayle, Jr., Nikki Giovanni, Saunders Redding, and Darwin T. Turner, among others.

Redding, J. Saunders. "American Negro Literature." *The American Scholar* 18, No. 2 (Spring 1949): 137-48.
> Discusses Dunbar as a writer who pandered to white racists' conceptions of black Americans.

Williams, Kenny J. "The Masking of the Poet." In his *They Also Spoke: An Essay on Negro Literature in America, 1787-1930,* pp. 153-215. Nashville: Townsend Press, 1970.
> Study of Dunbar's novels and short stories. The critic divides Dunbar's fiction into three types: the romantic tradition, the plantation tradition, and the naturalistic tradition, and assesses the strengths and weaknesses of each.

Cyprian Ekwensi

1921-

(Also wrote as C. O. D. Ekwensi) Nigerian novelist, short story writer, and author of children's books.

Ekwensi is a popular contemporary Nigerian novelist whose works are simultaneously praised and ridiculed. Some critics laud his "warm and vivid writing" about Nigerian city life while others lambast his mimicry of "fourth-rate Western fiction." One detractor remarked, "[Ekwensi's works] are appreciated only by those who have not been exposed to better writing," prompting Peter Nazareth to respond: "[Ekwensi] holds his audience spellbound, until he chooses to release it, while other certified African writers bore their audience to tears. Could this be a careless, fourth-rate writer? Or is there something wrong with the perceptions and values of the critics? Why does Ekwensi continue to be one of the most popular writers in Africa if he is no good?" Ekwensi has published nearly thirty books, including *Jagua Nana (1961), Beautiful Feathers (1963),* and *Survive the Peace (1976).* He maintains that he is a "popular novelist" and remains ambivalent about the controversy surrounding his work: "I think I am a writer who regards himself as a writer of the masses... I am more interested in getting at the heart of the truth which the man in the street can recognize than in just spinning words."

Born in Northern Nigeria in 1921, Ekwensi grew up in various cities and had ample opportunity to observe what one critic called the "urban politics" of Nigeria. He went to schools in Ibadan, Lagos, and the Gold Coast, excelling in English, mathematics, and science; a high school record indicates that only his "temper and occasional sullen moods" kept him from being the ideal student. In the early 1940s he enrolled at the School of Forestry in Western Nigeria; successfully completing his degree requirements in 1944, he began his work as a forestry officer. According to biographer Ernest Emenyonu, "it was... while wandering in the domains of animals and trees that Ekwensi decided to become a writer. Taking advantage of his wild and lonely environment he began to create adventure stories with forest backgrounds." Among his early works are the short stories "Banana Peel," "The Tinted Scarf," and "Land of Sani," which he published together with a collection of Igbo folk tales under the title *Ikolo the Wrestler and Other Ibo Tales* (1947). Other early works include *When Love Whispers* (1948) and *The Leopard's Claw* (1950); he also published several adventure stories for children: *The Drummer Boy (1960), The Passport of Mallam Ilia (1960), An African Night's Entertainment: A Tale of Vengeance (1962),* and *Juju Rock (1966).* Since the 1950s, he has worked as a professional writer, a pharmacist, and a teacher. Most recently he has been involved with the Nigerian Broadcasting Corporation and various newspaper and publishing organizations.

Despite his popularity as folklorist and writer of children's literature, Ekwensi's admirers contend that he is an "urban novelist par excellence." His widely read novels—*People of the City (1954), Jagua Nana, Beautiful Feathers,* and *Iska (1966)*—are all set in the city of Lagos, and according to critic Juliet Okonkwo: "[Ekwensi] revels in the excitement of city life and loves to expose its many faces of modernity. He writes about... its criminals, prostitutes, band-leaders, ministers of state, businessmen, civil servants, professionals, policemen on duty, thugs, thieves, and many other types that are found in the city.... Employing a naturalistic narrative technique reminiscent of Emile Zola, Ekwensi has been able to capture both the restless excitement and the frustrations of life in the city." *Burning Grass: A Story of the Fulani of Northern Nigeria* (1962) and *Survive the Peace* are exceptions to his "city novels." The former centers on Mai Sunsaye, a Fulani cattleman living on the grassy plains of Nigeria, and the latter on James Oduga, a radio journalist who tries to rebuild his life after a war.

Of Ekwensi's city novels, *Jagua Nana* is considered his best work. It focuses on Jagua Nana, an aging prostitute who thrives on Lagos nightlife—"They called her Jagua because of her good looks and stunning fashions. They said she was Ja-gwa, after the famous British prestige car." When the novel opens she is in love with Freddie Namme, an ambitious young teacher. She continues to sleep with other men for money, to Freddie's dismay, because she wants to "wear fine cloth": "She loved Freddie well, but his whole salary would not buy that dress. He must understand that taking money from the Syrian did not mean that she loved him less." Freddie claims to despise Jagua's lifestyle but doesn't refuse the luxuries that her income provides. Seeking consolation, Freddie has an affair with a younger woman, but before Jagua can unleash her jealous rage, he leaves for England. When Jagua and Freddie meet again, Freddie is running for office against Uncle Taiwo, a large, crass, power-hungry politician "who has chosen to absorb and use all that is worst in European ways," according to critic John Povey. The novel ends with Freddie and Uncle Taiwo both murdered and Jagua fleeing Lagos for her life. "Through Jagua, her career, her pursuits and her fluctuating fortune," Okonkwo observed, "Ekwensi reveals the common wickedness, squalor, materialism and immorality of the city, together with its crimes and violence." Since its publication in 1961, *Jagua Nana* has attracted bitter controversy. Church organizations and women's groups vehemently attacked it, prompting some schools to ban it from their libraries. The Nigerian Parliament refused an Italian studio's request to film the book. Some readers called it an "obscene artifice" and "a mere exercise in pornography," while others praised it as "a West African masterpiece." Literary critics were equally divided in their opinions: some were impressed with *Jagua Nana,* particularly by Ekwensi's use of language and depth of characterization, but others dismissed it as another "whore-with-a-heart-of-gold" story commonly found in "third-rate American movies" and "fourth-rate western fiction."

Controversy appears to follow all of Ekwensi's fiction; while *Jagua Nana* has received the most attention, his other books have also been scrutinized. Assessing Ekwensi as a writer, critic Bernth Lindfors declared: "...not one [of his works] is entirely free of amateurish blots and blunders, not one could be called the handiwork of a careful, skilled craftsman. Ekwensi may be simply too impatient an artist to take pains with his work or to learn by a calm, rational process of trial and error. When he is not repeating his old mistakes, he is stumbling upon spectacular new ones. As a consequence, many of his stories and novels can serve as excellent examples of how not to write fiction." Similarly, Douglas Killam observed: "Ekwensi's limitations as a novelist are many...we find the same kinds of hero—almost a stereotype—who, progressively lacking energy, becomes unconvincing as a character.... Ekwensi pays

little attention to his plots and his novels are full of inconsistencies and contradictions. [Moreover] Ekwensi has not mastered the rules of English and the bad English which is often used in his novels...militate against his fiction achieving the first rank in importance as art." Another critic simply noted that Ekwensi was "hired to debase literature." Ekwensi's supporters, most notably Povey, have argued otherwise. Acknowledging Ekwensi's weaknesses as a writer, Povey explained: "He often dangerously approaches the sentimental, the vulgar and melodramatic. Behind his work stands a reading of American popular fiction and paperback crime stories. Yet Ekwensi's writing cannot be dismissed with such assertions.... Ekwensi is interesting because he is concerned with the present, with the violence of the new Lagos slums, the dishonesty of the new native politicians.... Only Ekwensi has dared to approach the contemporary scene with critical satire." A contributor to *African Authors: A Companion to Black African Writing 1800-1973* likewise noted: "Ekwensi is not an accomplished stylist, but he writes with vivacity and can paint a scene quickly and convincingly. His work expresses a very warm sensuality and there is little preciosity or primness in all his work...."

Ekwensi's stature as a novelist is still debated. Emenyonu believes that Ekwensi's commitment "to portray the naked truth about the life of modern man" is the reason for the existing controversy over *Jagua Nana* and all of Ekwensi's fiction. "When one looks at his works over the past three decades," he observed, "one sees the deep imprints of a literature of social awareness and commitment, and this is Ekwensi's greatest achievement in the field of modern African writing."

(For further information about Ekwensi's life and works, see *Black Writers; Contemporary Authors,* Vols. 29-32; *Contemporary Authors New Revision Series,* Vol. 18; and *Contemporary Literary Criticism,* Vol. 4. For related criticism, see the entry on Nigerian Literature in *Twentieth-Century Literary Criticism,* Vol. 30.)

PRINCIPAL WORKS

Ikolo the Wrestler and Other Ibo Tales [as C. O. D. Ekwensi] (juvenile fiction) 1947

When Love Whispers [as C. O. D. Ekwensi] (novella) 1948

The Leopard's Claw [as C. O. D. Ekwensi] (juvenile fiction) 1950

People of the City (novel) 1954

The Drummer Boy (juvenile fiction) 1960

The Passport of Mallam Ilia (juvenile fiction) 1960

Jagua Nana (novel) 1961

An African Night's Entertainment: A Tale of Vengeance (folklore) 1962

Burning Grass: A Story of the Fulani of Northern Nigeria (novel) 1962

Yaba Roundabout Murder (novel) 1962

Beautiful Feathers (novel) 1963

The Great-Elephant Bird (juvenile fiction) 1965

The Rainmaker and Other Stories (short stories) 1965

The Boa Suitor (juvenile fiction) 1966
Iska (novel) 1966
Juju Rock (juvenile fiction) 1966
Lokotown and Other Stories (short stories) 1966
Trouble in Form Six (juvenile fiction) 1966
Coal Camp Boy (juvenile fiction) 1971
Samankwe in the Strange Forest (juvenile fiction) 1973
The Rainbow-Tinted Scarf and Other Stories (short stories) 1975
The Restless City and Christmas Gold, with Other Stories (short stories) 1975
Samankwe and the Highway Robbers (short stories) 1975
Survive the Peace (short stories) 1976
Festac Anthology of Nigerian Writing [editor] (anthology) 1977
Divided We Stand (novel) 1980
Motherless Baby (novella) 1980

Cyprian Ekwensi (letter date 1964)

[*In the following 1964 letter, Ekwensi addresses a student at Ibadan University who vehemently criticized* Jagua Nana *as an "obscene artifice."*]

Dear Sir,

My advice to you is GET OUT OF YOUR CLOISTERED HALLS AND LIVE!

It is not a coincidence that those who violently react to the absolute realism of *Jagua* are based in isolated places like the corridors of University libraries and the back doors of Christian Councils. I am not by this implying that ALL students in Universities and ALL Christians or Christian Bodies consist of such people. But the fact remains that people like you belong to a hypocritical group that simply refuses to have red blood running through your veins or sweat and dust trickling down your face. You simply have NEVER lived. Have you smelt the humus in the forests of the Mid-West, or been face to face with a leopard and looked into its eyes at night; have you ever swept a woman off her feet and experienced the pangs of love; have you ever seen children left adrift because their father has left their mother and run after another woman—usually a 'bad' woman who does him 'good'?

You must be too young to have lived. You could never even have fired a rifle or been to war.

You are not even LIVING in Nigeria, but in the pages of books, dull books written by hermits like yourself.

How can you possibly write such trash: ARE OUR ELECTION CAMPAIGNS SUCH THAT INVARIABLY RESULT IN MURDER OF CANDIDATES while in the same paper in which your silly letter appears there is this to read: OKPARA WAYLAID—POLICE ALERTED

I have never bothered to reply to any of the nonsense that has been written by the illiterate and uninformed like yourself. But I am writing to you for the simple reason that there is SOME hope. You are young, you are in a very highly respected University (hence the tragedy of it all). You stand a chance of having your erroneous views at least re-orientated. Not necessarily by me. I am too emotionally close to all this rubbish.

Let's begin at the beginning. The function of a novelist. At least ONE of them: To hold a mirror up to nature.

This particular mirror shows you naked, ashamed, exposed and bleeding. The reflection is terrifying and ghastly. Therefore, what do you do? You cry out. Throw a cloth over the mirror, it cannot be true!

How funny!

Did you cry in this manner when you read *Burning Grass, People of the City, When Love Whispers, A Stranger from Lagos, African Night's Entertainment, Drums and Voices, Glittering City, Drummer Boy, Ol' Man Forest, The Leopard's Claw, Yaba Roundabout Murder, Passport of Mallam Ilia, Beware the Bight of Benin, For a Role of Parchment*—to name only a few of my works in the past 25 years?

Or are you merely joining in the hypocritical din against *Jagua* just to be numbered among those who spoke? Or are you now—in the hypocritical manner [to] which I have since resigned my ears—going to tell me that there are NO PROSTITUTES IN NIGERIA, in Ekotedo Ibadan; or that school teachers can never fall in love with prostitutes.

Let me tell you that a Reverend Father (Catholic of course) has said that Jagua is not a sinful woman. She knows her failings, she has an inborn DESIRE to be good; she hides her acts from Freddie, because to him she wants to be represented as good. She wants motherhood, a decent home; she is a charitable person. But she has that BODY which made you destroy the book. The BODY is the story of Jagua just as the open savannah is the story of *Burning Grass* and the 'samba drum' is the story of *Drummer Boy*.

You want to know books which are on the borderline of being daubed 'obscene' but have since exonerated themselves on the grounds of artistic merit:

Henry Miller:	*Tropic of Cancer*
	Tropic of Capricorn
D. H. Lawrence:	*Lady Chatterly's Lover*
James Joyce:	*Ulysses*
Stanley Kaufman:	*The Philanderer*

Get hold of those five (if you can find the time from your cloistered exam halls) and begin your education. Your narrow young life may then begin to have some meaning.

After that, put down your books for a change: go to the Mid-West now (I keep quoting the Mid-West because it is the most topical place now). Four years ago, it could have been the Federal Territory. I can cast my mind back and see clearly now a photograph of a CUTLASS across the front page of the *Sunday Times.* I can cast my mind back and see also a picture of a prominent Western Nigerian carried shoulder high at an election rally, and held aloft in his right hand is a SHOTGUN.

May, I say it again. You are not LIVING in Nigeria. The accent is on *LIVING.*

Close your books, go out and LIVE. Then, you will be qualified to write another letter to the *Post* or to any other paper.

I am, Sir,
        Your Obedient Servant.
C.O.D. Ekwensi

(pp. 124-26)

Cyprian Ekwensi, in a letter on January 23, 1964, in Cyprian Ekwensi, *by Ernest Emenyonu, Evans Brothers Limited, 1974, 137 p.*

John F. Povey (essay date 1965)

[*Educated in South Africa and the United States, Povey is an English critic of African literature and the editor of* African Arts. *In the following essay, he appraises* Beautiful Feathers *as Ekwensi's best work to date.*]

Cyprian Ekwensi is the most prolific of the new writers of Nigeria. This fact in itself separates his work from the thinly disguised autobiographies that constitute the one-shot attempts at novel writing by the educated African amateur. Ekwensi is a professional. He was trained in England as a pharmacist but he chose to live by his writing. He thus became a figure virtually unique in African writing. If he were an American we would not have much difficulty in assessing his position. He would be a best-selling book-of-the-month-club author. But it needs little knowledge of the contemporary African scene to appreciate the significant difference between a writer such as Chinua Achebe, intellectual, classic, and a novelist who can declare, "I am a writer who regards himself as a writer for masses." With such a determination, it is easy to see where the obvious strengths and weaknesses of Ekwensi's writing will lie. He often dangerously approaches the sentimental, the vulgar and melodramatic. Behind his work stands a reading of American popular fiction and paperback crime stories. Yet Ekwensi's writing cannot be dismissed with such assertions. The very practice of writing, the developing professionalism of his work, makes us find in Ekwensi a new and perhaps important phenomenon in African writing. By constant productivity, his style is becoming purged of its derivative excess and his plots begin to take on a less picaresque structure. Ekwensi is interesting because he is concerned with the present, with the

violence of the new Lagos slums, the dishonesty of the new native politicians. Other Nigerian novelists have sought their material from the past, the history of missionaries and British administration as in Chinua Achebe's books, the schoolboy memoirs of Onuora Nzekwu. Ekwensi faces the difficult task of catching the present tone of Africa, changing at a speed that frighteningly destroys the old certainties. In describing this world, Ekwensi has gradually become a significant writer. His development can be traced through the three novels that have been published in this country. If there are disconcerting intrusions into his later work of bad writing and scenes of sheer silliness, there is also a growing understanding of what he can achieve, the description of the face of the new Nigeria which has become the new Africa. Only Ekwensi has dared to approach the contemporary scene with critical satire. For others the fact of independence seems too triumphant for the more recent changes to be recorded.

It is in his latest novel **Beautiful Feathers** that Ekwensi best exhibits those characteristics that will make him important in the African literature. His earlier books had their commendable moments, but the melodrama and the falseness of their situations make them remarkable largely for their energy and enthusiasm. In his first novel, **People of the City** (London 1954), we have a surfeit of incidents, enough for three normal books. Before the adventures of the hero, Amusa Sango, are concluded, we have women who are stripped in the street, slugged into a miscarriage, have cayenne pepper rubbed into their private parts and die of venereal disease! But for all this excess, Ekwensi's chosen hero is an ideal figure for seeing the situation of modern Lagos. His is a journalist and a part-time band leader. His is thus intelligent and sophisticated but without the narrowness and superiority that separated the "been-to's" and their European education from their compatriots. Journalism gives the hero access to the crooked politics and violence of the Lagos slums, while the band leader is the medium for exposing the frivolity of the new urbanized noveau riche. Unfortunately except for occasional scenes such as the description of the national mourning at the funeral of the old patriot de Periera, he does not allow his true and serious subject room for development. There is too much violence and crime to be reported.

By the time Ekwensi's second novel **Jagua Nana** was published in 1961 there were already promising changes. The major character is a whore with the heart of gold who only wants to find true love. This is an obvious stereotype from western fiction. But Jagua Nana has a stagey life of her own, and if not subtle, she has an urgent liveliness. Perhaps we regret what a popular film script some elements of this book will make and we learn that this is to be the first film produced with a Nigerian story. But there is a more significant element in this book than the adventures of Jagua's generous promiscuity. Jagua meets Uncle Taiwo, the secretary of the major political party. He becomes Ekwensi's most successful character. He has a tremendous power. He is grossly amorous, shamelessly venial, crass and vicious. His huge laugh roars without humor at the follies of his challengers. Perhaps he has some part of his origin in the Huey Long type of American politician but Uncle Taiwo remains African; and African who has taken from the west all its evil, its greed and corruption, its tricks of shabby political manipulation. This figure is the most sure and powerful creation of modern African fiction in spite of all the praise of Achebe's noble priests.

Ekwensi's third novel called **Burning Grass** is a tale of the Fulani tribe and outside the normal themes of his work, but with the publication of **Beautiful Feathers** in 1963, he begins to show achievement as well as potential. There are lapses in the style and the old sentimentality pushes itself in occasionally, but the moments are rarer and only emphasize the many superior sections of the book.

The story of **Beautiful Feathers** concerns Wilson Iyari who, like Ekwensi, is a druggist and is also ambitiously forming his own political party to foster the cause of pan-African solidarity. Ekwensi structures his book to balance Iyari's increasing prominence and success as a politician against his failure as a husband and a father. The literary sophistication of this construction is in total contrast to the, at best, picaresque organization of **People of the City.** A good example of this balanced confrontation in Wilson's life occurs in a scene where he is having a meeting of the party at his house. His wife, having settled their revolutionary family of children, Lumumba, Jomo, and Pandhit, is going out to meet her lover. There is Wilson, confident, authoritative, haranguing his party subordinates on the necessity of unity, solidarity, when she walks through the room ignoring him. The words of impassioned rhetoric die on his lips. It is a magnificent confrontation, but more significant is the diction that Ekwensi uses for this scene. Before there has been strain, excess, here there is assured understatement that makes the moment doubly effective.

> "Solidarity is imperative. We don't care how difficult it is . . . . " As he mentioned the word "solidarity," Wilson saw the door of the bedroom open, His wife, resplendent, came out, passed through the sitting room, and before they could rise to greet her, she was outside, leaving behind a bewitching trail of Balmain.

That concludes the incident. Nothing more has to be said. For a moment the two lives are brought against one another and with sure skill Ekwensi has had us contemplate their extremes. When the wife returns from the adultery that she commits not out of love but out of spite and revenge, she returns to no triumph, only the squawling of her baby who needs its diaper changed. There is no romance left in this necessary domesticity. Illusion is pricked as Ekwensi records the scene.

> As she put her clothes away, it seemed to her that all the furtive and tiring joy she had gone out to buy was being shed away for the reality which now confronted her: pissing children, the wrath of the outraged

husband. She touched little Jomo's napkin and found it was wet. She took it to the sink and changed it.

Just as effectively subtle and knowledgeable are the scenes of marital quarreling between Wilson and his wife. Again the incident is created without the vulgarity and excess that marked the violent battles between Jagua Nana and her lovers. There is a cold self-lacerating spite which one feels instinctively is the real tone for a marriage that is being consciously destroyed. There is no love left and no respect. She sees him as a feeble and unloving man. It is only the outsiders who can admire his political principles and so there is both desperation and pathos in Wilson's vehement cry, "Say what you like. Behave to me as you like. The fact remains, to the world outside I am something." But this fact does not allow him to reconcile his wife and they finally come to the moment where he demands that she leave him.

> She did not say a word. He waited for her to say something before he plunged deeper into the mess he had now made. She opened her mouth like one struck and closed it. But there were no words. He turned and walked slowly to his room. There was a book at his bedside. He opened it and lay on his back to read. The print swam before his eyes.

Nothing more has to be said. We are not treated to impassioned explanation. The chapter concludes at this point, but characterization is subtly rendered by this restrained description. The writing in these scenes is a measure of Ekwensi's growing confidence. When it is employed in the political scenes, his characterization is even more effective. It suggests that one day Ekwensi will write a full scale political satire of present day Nigeria; vicious, sardonic, and pointed. In this novel there is no single character with the grand solidity, the Falstaffian grossness of Uncle Taiwo, but there are others of a similar caliber. There is Wilson's brother-in-law Jacob, who exists on the fringes of politics and crime, demanding Wilson's reluctant handouts. He is a corrupt minor demagogue who "could assemble masses of people quickly and easily convert three votes to a thousand for a consideration." He boasts a shabby veneer of sophistication, western extravagances, and a taste for fat-bottomed women, but he has none of Uncle Taiwo's cheerful crudeness, the cruelty concealed under false bonhomie. Jacob is meanly vicious, more rat than lion. When Wilson tries to arrange a peaceful demonstration, it is Jacob who sees that it degenerates into violent riot; for him plunder before politics and rape before rebellion.

As if this were not enough to cope with, Wilson comes up against the high level graft; the figure of the millionaire buying votes and dictating policies. There is a profound irony when Wilson scornfully refuses his bribe and is told, "And I thought you were serious."

There is another exaggerated political figure, now full satire, in the tradition of Evelyn Waugh. This is the government official magnificently entitled the Minister of Consolation. The minister, when not ordering about his abused English male secretary, passes the time working on his public relations and looking in the mirror to find the most photogenic poses for when the reporters come. At press conferences "he showed his teeth in a manner which the mirror had told him was most flattering. The minister maneuvered the reporter till he was farther from the camera." Surrounded by his train of hangers-on all seeking the consolation of undeserved favours, the minister dominates this section of the book and becomes less humorous, more frighteningly ominous in his every act.

The satire portraits are more effective than the idealistic description of politics. The portrait of the president of the republic is too nobly wise, improbably benign, with virtues that read like the praises of Joseph Stalin some years ago. Less successful too, are the scenes where Wilson represents his country at the Pan-African Conference. Perhaps Ekwensi has little conviction about the probable efficacy of the Pan-African movement. Certainly pious platitudes take the place of sharp perception. This might determine Ekwensi on the best direction for his future writing, but one must admit that Ekwensi does not even seem very certain of what are the relative qualities of his writing. The latter part of the book has much less to recommend it and shows the ever threatening influences of bad movies and cheap magazine stories on Ekwensi. There is the incident when Wilson's friend who has been politically exiled decides to risk the probability of arrest and return to his own country to carry on the political struggle. He is shot while crossing the border and every stock incident from a dozen films of the man running through the barrier is shamelessly borrowed. "Like something out of a movie," observes one of the characters, and with a sigh we agree. And if it were not enough that the political incidents have degenerated into melodrama, the sophisticated man-wife scenes degenerate into sentimentality. Wilson's wife in a mood of masochistic guilt throws herself into the way of an assassin's knife thrust to protect her husband. With unctuous self-sacrifice she insists that he marry a worthier woman. "It is good like this. I am so happy Wilson. I am no use to you any longer, I told you so." As if this were not bad enough, she is revived for a shabbily contrived happy ending of marital reconciliation. After this crude winding up of the plot the last lines are like Dickens at his most lachrymous.

> They had truly come together now. It could be said of him that he was famous outside and that at home he had the backing of a family united by bonds of love. Wilson's beautiful feathers had ceased to be superficial and had become a substantial asset.

It is regrettable that such a promising work had to end on such a disagreeable note. There are antidotes to such writing in this book, and if one is offended by the conclusion, perhaps one has only to go back and once again read the strangely tender and compassionate farewell of Chini to her English lover, dismissed to allow the Africanization of the civil service. It has a touching dignity that exemplifies Ekwensi's new capacity.

It may seem after these comments that the total of Ekwensi's achievement is not very extensive. Some bits of *People of the City,* a character in *Jagua Nana,* several scenes from *Beautiful Feathers.* But Ekwensi is a prolific writer and each novel has shown a development in his control and creativity. Until that sloppy ending, *Beautiful Feathers* can be measured against any novel we have yet had from Africa. It may be that Ekwensi's very weaknesses will prove to be the source of his future promise. If his attempt to be popular and modern leads him into the trivial and shallow, it also saves him from the contrary threat that makes pedagogic competence and mediocrity the common flaws of some African writing. His energy and liveliness may be controlled by a more serious subject and indeed there is already evidence of this. I shall expect Ekwensi's next novel to show this increasing depth and sophistication. Some critics apparently feel that his attempt at the merely popular makes his writing unworthy of serious critical consideration. I believe that they may be missing not only a new phenomenon in African writing, but a novelist who will have the potential to create books far more profound and complex than those he has so far achieved. (pp. 63-9)

> *John F. Povey, "Cyprian Ekwensi and 'Beautiful Feathers'," in* Critique: Studies in Modern Fiction, *Vol. VIII, No. 1, Fall, 1965, pp. 63-9.*

Bernth Lindfors (essay date 1969)

[*In the following essay, Lindfors explores American and African influences on Ekwensi's works. Negatively appraising Ekwensi's novels, the critic further contends that they are "excellent examples of how not to write fiction."*]

Of all the Africans who have written full-length novels in English, Cyprian Ekwensi of Eastern Nigeria (now Biafra) perhaps best illustrates the dictum that practice does not make a writer perfect. At least nine novels, four of them still unpublished, six novelettes for schoolchildren, two collections of folktales, and dozens of short stories have poured from his pen, but not one is entirely free of amateurish blots and blunders, not one could be called the handiwork of a careful, skilled craftsman. Ekwensi may be simply too impatient an artist to take pains with his work or to learn by a calm, rational process of trial and error. When he is not repeating his old mistakes, he is stumbling upon spectacular new ones. As a consequence, many of his stories and novels can serve as excellent examples of how not to write fiction.

Part of his problem is that he attempts to write truly popular literature. Unlike other African writers who address themselves to Europe or to an educated African elite, Ekwensi prides himself on being a writer for the masses, a writer who can communicate with any African literate in English. He does not pretend to be profound, subtle or erudite; he would rather be considered entertaining, exciting, sensational. His ambition is to produce thrillers like those that first stimulated his interest in reading and writing. Unfortunately, he seems to have obtained most of his stimulation from third-rate American movies and fourth-rate British and American paperback novels, for these are certainly the most pronounced influences on what he has written. In his favour it may be said that Ekwensi possesses a peculiar talent for imitating bad models well and adapting them to fit into an African setting. He is in this respect an accomplished literary *assimilado.* If his fiction still retains a few vestigial Africanisms, they tend to be all but obliterated under a smooth veneer of slick Western varnish. Nevertheless, these immanent Africanisms should not be overlooked in any evaluation of his writing, for they help to explain some of his idiosyncrasies. This paper will explore Ekwensi's debts to Western popular literature traditions and to indigenous oral traditions and will assess the effects of such influences on his fiction.

Ekwensi's first borrowings were from fairly harmless sources. As a young schoolboy he had been thrilled by his reading of simplified editions of English popular novels: 'I was reading Rider Haggard, Edgar Wallace, Dickens, Sapper, Bates. At Government College in Ibadan we could recite whole chunks of *King Solomon's Mines. Nada the Lily* was a favourite; so was *She,* and *Allan Quartermain . . . Treasure Island* [was] unforgettable.' The impact that these juvenile classics made on Ekwensi can be discerned in one of his first attempts at long fiction, *Juju Rock,* which reverberates with echoes from *Treasure Island* and *King Solomon's Mines.* Though not published until 1966, *Juju Rock* may have been written as much as twenty years earlier. There are references to it in *The Leopard's Claw* (London 1950) and *The Passport of Mallam Ilia* (Cambridge 1960) both of which were written in 1947.

The story of *Juju Rock* is narrated by its hero. Rikku, a young Fulani schoolboy in Western Nigeria who serves as a guide to three Englishmen on an expedition to mysterious Juju Rock in the northern grasslands. The men are searching for a lost gold mine and for an old sailor who had disappeared on an earlier expedition and was thought to have located the mine. As they near their destination, Rikku, like Jim Hawkins, overhears his companions plotting to kill him as soon as the gold is found. Rikku escapes, disguises himself as a canoe boy, and bravely rejoins the evil three.

When the group arrives at Juju Rock, Robert Louis Stevenson gives way to Rider Haggard. Rikku and his companions come upon a dangerous tribal 'Secret Society' carrying out its rituals, and a fierce battle in a dark cave ensues. The tribesmen overcome Rikku and the three Englishmen and are preparing to sacrifice them when an unexpected rescue party arrives and saves them. Rikku then finds the old sailor in the cave and after a few more scuffles and narrow escapes hears him tell his side of the story. Thus, as in most school readers narrated in the first person, loose ends are conveniently tied up and mysteries efficiently explained so events can

be rapidly concluded. As might be expected, the three villains end up in prison and Rikku returns to school a national hero.

If any further proof is required to demonstrate that *Juju Rock* was written in imitation of juvenile adventure fiction, it can be found in the text itself, for Ekwensi, in his eagerness to place his story in the genre, drew very specific parallels for his readers. The first chapter begins as follows:

> Now that I have been through it all, and the whole thing seems so distant and remote, I sometimes wonder what it was that lured me into that *Juju Rock* adventure. Boyish curiosity, perhaps, an eagerness to learn more, and the influence of 'Wild West' fiction and very recent reading of *King Solomon's Mines.* In many ways *Juju Rock* was like something out of those romantic days.

Having made this point, Ekwensi apparently did not want anyone to forget it. Later in the story, when Rikku has been captured by the 'Secret Society' and fears he is about to be speared to death by the Chief Priest, Ekwensi has him say:

> I could see the eyes of the Chief Priest as he glared at me and I knew he hated me with all his might. This was certainly the end. Never again would I have the joy of reading Wild West stories, or books like *King Solomon's Mines.*

The chapter in which this occurs, it should be noted, is entitled 'Showdown at Juju Rock'. Ekwensi was doing everything he could to ensure that readers would associate his novelette with the 'thrillers' or 'real life adventure stories' that boys enjoyed reading at school.

Ekwensi's familiarity with 'Wild West' stories is most clearly displayed in *The Passport of Mallam Ilia,* another of his early attempts at juvenile adventure fiction set in the cattle lands of Northern Nigeria. Here is a scene borrowed lock, stock and barrel from stagecoach melodramas of the American Southwest:

> Mallam Usuman quickly guided his horse up the bank of the stream, and, riding slowly along, studied the transport for a time. Experience told him that they had been travelling for some time and were therefore very tired. He dug his heels into the flanks of his horse. In a moment he had drawn up beside them and levelled his gun.
>
> 'Whoever you are,' he snarled, 'you can choose.'
>
> The transport stopped and the driver turned his sunscorched face towards him. There was anger in his flaming eyes.
>
> 'Which do you choose,' Usuman went on, 'your life or your money?'
>
> 'There—there is no money,' stammered the driver.
>
> 'Don't lie!'
>
> Usuman with his quick eye had already seen the wooden box beneath the driver's seat; but now, as the

passengers began to complain and show signs of terror, Usuman noticed that there was a woman in the carriage. She was sitting tightly wedged in between the other passengers, calm and cool. She lifted her black veil for a moment and Usuman's eyes widened at the sight of her face. She was beautiful.

The driver must have been watching him, for he said in Hausa: 'You like her then? Unfortunately, she is not for you . . .'

'You rat!' snapped Usuman. 'Throw down the money and drive on.'

The driver glanced from the bore of the rifle into Usuman's face and decided to obey. He got down, fumbled for a moment, and was bringing out something from under the box when Usuman shot him in the hand and a British revolver dropped to the ground.

'Now will you put down the box?'

Cursing, the driver pushed down the box with his left hand and climbed back into his seat.

'Not yet,' said Usuman. He turned and winked at the lady. 'Open the carriage and let her step down!'

Ekwensi was apparently familiar with all the standard clichés of the Western. Whether he picked them up from fiction or from films cannot be determined, but it is clear that he had no qualms about using them, even if it meant dressing Billy the Kid in the robes and turban of a Hausa Mallam.

Burning Grass, Ekwensi's first attempt at longer fiction, also bears the imprint of the Western branding iron. In **Burning Grass,** there are cattle rustlings, stampedes, galloping horses, saloon confrontations, and ferocious battles galore. Here is an archetypal ambush:

Hodio's gallop out of New Chanka quickened as his temper mounted. He dug his heels hard into his horse's flanks, cursing the while, slashing cruelly down with his cane. Lying close to his horse's mane, his eyes darted keenly into every nook and crevice of the scrub . . .

His horse twisted and turned as it followed the crooked path before him. Shehu and his men had had too much of a start. At this rate, he might never catch up with them . . .

He slowed down. The large rock ahead of him would bear no prints. But something else seemed imminent. He could almost feel a third presence. He got down, climbed the large rock. From the top he commanded a grand view of the country behind him. It was a dead end, true enough. But somewhere behind this rock should be another path. It might take long to find, perhaps too long.

He decided to search. He turned. Like a flash, the arrows whizzed past his ear. He threw himself flat down. His horse broke away, yelping with pain. He could see the butts of at least three arrows in its flank. Slowly the horse would die of the poison in the iron tips.

He looked down the bottom of the rock and saw three men labouring up towards him. The biggest of them all was Shehu, the man he sought.

What is most remarkable about these quoted excerpts is that they are very accurate imitations. Ekwensi has an uncommonly good ear for narrative style, a gift for mimicry, and a knack for transplanting un-African events onto African soil. He can make Nigerian schoolboys imagine an impossible treasure hunt or feel at home on the range because he has mastered the conventions and commonplaces of foreign juvenile adventure fiction and knows how to domesticate them. His is a literature of imitation and adaptation, not a literature of imagination and original invention. So long as he continued to address an adolescent audience, his fiction remained as innocuous and unobjectionable as the material upon which it was modelled. It was when he began to try to reach an older audience that he turned to less innocent models and descended from the highroads of classic juvenile literature to the more pedestrian paths of earthy popular fiction.

Ekwensi's first tentative step in this new direction was taken in 1947, when he published a forty-four page pamphlet novel entitled **When Love Whispers.** This was one of the first inexpensive paperback novelettes, now commonly called chapbooks, to be issued in Nigeria. Like so many that have followed since, **When Love Whispers** was essentially the story of a maiden in distress. Beautiful, pure-hearted Ashoka, whose fiancé has just left for engineering studies in England, finds herself in continual difficulty. She is kidnapped, almost sold to an odious white man in a neighbouring French territory, and eventually seduced by her fiancé's best friend. Unable to abort her pregnancy, she marries a third man whom she doesn't love. The wages of sin are sorrow.

Appropriately enough, **When Love Whispers** is written in a style which closely approximates that found in much drugstore pulp magazine fiction. Ekwensi must have known this type of literature quite well, for he was able to echo it very faithfully. The following passage is taken from the first few pages of the novelette:

She loved him. She had promised to marry him. She was waiting now, hoping and praying for that great day when both of them would stand before the priest and say those age-old words . . . And then they would walk down arm in arm, she in her white bridal dress, he in his starched collar.

It must be remembered that at this early stage in his literary career Ekwensi was accustomed to addressing his fiction to a young audience so he had had little experience in writing passionate love scenes. This may explain why love-making is described with such reticence in **When Love Whispers.** In later novels Ekwensi grew much bolder and seemed to relish going through all the motions of a seduction scene, but during his apprenticeship he didn't dare treat sex too explicitly. Here, for example, is how Ashoka loses her virginity:

> She turned her face towards him in the moonlight, and there were points of fire in his eyes.
>
> 'You're just too beautiful for words,' he said. 'Is that not how the song goes?'
>
> She said nothing.
>
> She felt his hand on her cheeks, and then he was touching soft parts of her, and still she said nothing. Then his lips were hot on hers and she was sighing.
>
> 'Leave me!' she shouted suddenly, pushing him back. 'Let me go: you thief! You thief! I—I shall never see you again.'

In Ekwensi's later novels there was never any doubt about what the thief had stolen or which soft parts he had touched.

Perhaps it was the enormous popular success of *When Love Whispers* that prompted Ekwensi to write two full-length novels about the misadventures of liberated Nigerian women. *Jagua Nana,* probably his most successful work, records the ups and downs of an ageing Lagos prostitute who is in love with her work. In describing her affairs Ekwensi sometimes cannot suppress a vulgar smirk:

> He was beginning to regard himself as the rightful lover, always jealous. She got around him by mothering him. She went over now and sat on his knee, rubbing her thinly clad hips into his thighs. She threw one arm over his shoulder, so that her left breast snuggled close to his lips. Presently she felt his thick, rough lips close on the nipple. 'A dog with food in his mouth does not bark,' went the proverb.

In *Iska,* his most recent novel, another city girl falls into a life of sin and later comes to rue her misspent youth. Ekwensi again spices the narrative with racy details;

> He came over, gripping the body of her breasts. She did not resist. Instead she took off her clothes and stood revealed before him.
>
> He gazed at her with his eyes nearly coming off their sockets. There she was on offer, the flesh of black woman, pale and bleached by a thousand cosmetic creams, completely devastating.

Because his sinful heroines usually come to bad ends, Ekwensi can be viewed as a serious moralist whose novels offer instruction in virtue by displaying the tragic consequences of vice. But it is always quite clear to the reader that he is far more interested in vice than in virtue and that he aims to titillate as well as teach.

As Ekwensi moved from romantic love to torrid sex he also developed an interest in crime. The hero of his first full-length novel, *People of the City,* was both a crime reporter and a part-time band leader, a man in an excellent position to observe both lowlife and highlife in a Nigerian metropolis. Here is a typical scene from this stereotypical novel:

> The phone rang. Sango went over.
>
> '*West African Sensation . . .*'
>
> 'May I speak to the editor, please?' The voice was tinny, strained, very excited.
>
> Sango could feel the tension.
>
> 'The editor is not here.'
>
> 'Any reporter there?'
>
> 'Yes . . . who's speaking, please?'
>
> The office became silent. Over the wires, Sango could smell news. It always gave him a kick to smell news. Even Lajide and his debtor had frozen and were looking at him, listening intently. Sango felt proud to impress Lajide with his importance.
>
> 'Never mind who I am. If you want something for your paper, come out to the Magamu Bush, and you'll get it.'
>
> 'Where are you speaking from? Hello . . . Hello . . . Hello . . . ! Oh! He's hung up.'

Ekwensi was obviously still operating under the influence of Hollywood and popular pulp fiction.

It was perhaps inevitable that Ekwensi should eventually try his hand at detective fiction. *Yaba Roundabout Murder,* a chapbook he published in Lagos in 1962, relates how a clever police inspector catches a murderer by pretending to make advances to the murderer's wife. Many of the standard ingredients of detective fiction—the anonymous telephone tip, the trail of clues, the interrogations, the newspaper headlines, the cool-headed police inspector—can be found here, the only novelty being the African setting in which they appear. What detective novel does not have a scene something like the following:

> Inspector John Faolu walked up to the door and knocked. But he found the door open. There was no one in the room. He pressed the switch. There was no light. His torchlight showed him that there was a bulb in the ceiling, but apparently it had not been connected to the mains. The house was a new one.
>
> The room was in disorder. There was every sign that the occupants had left in a great hurry. Clothes were carelessly strewn on the bed.
>
> The books on the table had been disarranged, and beneath this was a box which though closed, had a number of clothes sticking out of it.
>
> Faolu took in the scene with deep interest.

This passage and others like it reveal that Ekwensi was familiar with the whodunit genre, knew its stock situations and cliches, and had not lost his flair for imitating bad models well.

Given Ekwensi's extraordinary susceptibility to influences from Western popular literature, what, if anything, could he possibly be said to owe to indigenous oral traditions? Can it be seriously suggested that there is something characteristically African or, more precisely, something characteristic of African oral narrative art in his fiction? The answer to this question is a tentative yes. There are at least two features of Ekwensi's novels and novelettes that resemble and perhaps derive from features of oral narrative art. Whether these are exclusively African characteristics is doubtful, but it seems more likely that Ekwensi assimilated them from traditional African narratives than from traditional European or American tales. In the late nineteen-forties and early fifties, when he was just getting started as a writer, he avidly collected and translated Ibo folktales, publishing them in local magazines and later in booklets designed for use in schools. In 1947 he also collected a long traditional tale of vengeance from 'an aged Hausa Mallam' who offered it as a story that 'would keep [his] readers awake all night.' Ekwensi published this tale fifteen years later under the title *An African Night's Entertainment.* Thus it may be said that both early and late in his writing career Ekwensi demonstrated an active interest in African oral narratives.

One of the features that Ekwensi's fiction shares with African folktales is a tendency to moralise, a tendency to use action and character to illustrate a thesis or underscore a point. Ekwensi's heroes and heroines sometimes seem like cardboard personifications of virtue or vice. They are more complex and better individualised than folktale heroes, but they give the same impression of having been created for a specific didactic purpose. They are like wooden puppets clumsily manipulated to spell out a conventional message. Ekwensi does not ordinarily state his moral explicitly at the end, as do many traditional storytellers, but he gives the reader enough nudges and winks along the way to make the moral known.

Good examples of Ekwensi's heavyhanded moralising can be found in one of his most recent novels, *Beautiful Feathers,* the title of which is based on an Ibo proverb: 'However famous a man is outside, if he is not respected inside his own home he is like a bird with *beautiful feathers,* wonderful on the outside but ordinary within.' The hero of the novel is a Pan-Africanist politician who is just beginning to win a reputation and following when his marriage starts to collapse. His neglected wife not only refuses to prepare his meals but spites him by brazenly taking a lover. Ekwensi has his hero recognise the mordant irony of his situation:

> Solidarity, where does it begin? Here, in my own home? I am the leader of the Nigerian Movement for African and Malagasy Solidarity. Wilson Iyari, good looking, famous outside. At home I am nothing. I am like a fowl with beautiful feathers on the outside for all to see. When the feathers are removed the flesh and bones underneath are the same as for any other fowl. I am not really different from other men. In fact, if only they knew how I am spited in my own

home they would despise me. They would never again listen to me talking about solidarity.

Throughout the novel Ekwensi plays upon the proverbial image of the ordinary fowl with beautiful feathers by continuing to contrast sharply Wilson's successful public life with his steadily deteriorating home life. For example, there is a splendid scene in which Wilson, while addressing a group of political leaders in his home, sees his wife go out to meet her lover.

> As he mentioned the word 'solidarity' Wilson saw the door of the bedroom open. His wife, resplendent, came out, passed through the sitting-room, and before they could rise to greet her she was outside, leaving a bewitching trail of *Balmain.*

The contrast between Wilson's public and private life is presented with graphic clarity here, but Ekwensi is not content to leave it at that. A few lines later he firmly underlines the message so no one will miss it.

> *She is going to meet her lover,* Wilson thought, *I talk about solidarity. There it is! My own family split. But how can Africa be united when such a small unit as my family is not united?*

Such heavy-handedness ruins some of Ekwensi's best effects. Even the ending of the novel is spoiled by a lack of subtlety. After having Wilson retire from politics and reunite with his wife, Ekwensi concludes:

> They had truly come together now. It could be said of him that he was famous outside and that at home he had the backing of a family united by bonds of love. Wilson's beautiful feathers had ceased to be superficial and had become a substantial asset.

Ekwensi simply cannot resist the temptation to tell his readers what the action signifies. Like a traditional storyteller, he frames his tale to illustrate a proverb.

Another feature that Ekwensi's fiction shares with many African oral narratives is a circular structure. To use Joseph Campbell's terms in *The Hero with a Thousand Faces* (New York 1949) the hero undergoes a sequence of adventures involving a departure, an initiation and a return. In the end he is usually back where he started, older and wiser for his experiences and purged of all personal excesses. He has accomplished his tasks, liquidated his lacks, and achieved a state of emotional equilibrium. Sometimes he completes his cycle of adventures by repudiating new Western ways and affirming old African values. He returns, in other words, to his African essence, to his roots, abandoning deviant foreign patterns. He is, in a sense, a modern African culture hero.

A few examples of Ekwensi's reliance on circular structures will suffice. In three of his juvenile novelettes—*Juju Rock, The Leopard's Claw,* and *The Drummer Boy*—a boy-hero rejects school life, enters a corrupt adult world where he encounters and overcomes evil, and then, having proven his courage and integrity, turns eagerly to the very life he had earlier rejected. In *Beautiful Feathers* the hero becomes embroiled in European-style politics but quits in order to save his marriage. He decides his family means more to him than fame, so he gives up his Westernised, individualistic pursuit of personal glory. In **People of the City** a young man leaves his village in the Eastern Greens for the glamour and easy money of the big city, but after being exposed to some of the city's ills, temptations and tragedies, he yearns for a cleaner life and departs for the Gold Coast to make a fresh start. In **Jagua Nana** a childless middle-aged woman leaves her idyllic village, turns to a life of prostitution in the city, and then returns home to bear an illegitimate child. In his article, '"Rebushing" or Ontological Recession to Africanism' Austin J. Shelton has persuasively argued that her return to the village is 'more than a symbol of the rejection of westernisation,' that it is in fact an act of 'rebushing' or ontological recession, 'showing that [her] very Africanism, *despite her Europeanisation,* militates against her remaining permanently in the city where she has been separated from all the truly vital forces of her people and culture.' Following 'the cyclic principle of African personality,' she first proceeds outward from the village and tradition and then returns to her African heritage. Her return is thus psychologically and philosophically fulfilling. It is perhaps significant that in his article 'The Dilemma of the African Writer' (*West African Review,* July 1956, p. 703) Ekwensi once defined African writing as 'that piece of self-expression in which the psychology behind African thought is manifest; in which the philosophy and the pattern of culture from which it springs can be discerned.' In Ekwensi's fiction it is often by means of a circular structure that the psychology behind African thought and the philosophy and African pattern of culture from which it springs are made manifest.

All this said, Ekwensi's novels are still failures. They combine some of the worst features of Western popular literature with some of the least subtle techniques of African oral narrative art. It seems that when Ekwensi is not trying to get by with cheap effects borrowed from shoddy sources, he is labouring to make an obvious point. Thus, rather like his heroes, he vacillates between complete Westernisation and reversions to his African heritage. There would be nothing wrong with mixing foreign and native narrative traditions in a literary work, if it were artfully done. But Ekwensi lacks artistic discretion, and for a popular novelist there is no more fatal flaw. (pp. 2-14)

> *Bernth Lindfors, "Cyprian Ekwensi: An African Popular Novelist," in* African Literature Today, *No. 4, 1969, pp. 2-14.*

Douglas Killam (essay date 1971)

[*In the following excerpt, Killam reviews* People of the City, Jagua Nana, Beautiful Feathers, *and* Iska, *stating that although "Ekwensi's limitations as a novelist are many," he is nonetheless "a serious novelist whose writing reflects his serious concern with*

some of the most pressing problems facing modern Nigeria."]

Ekwensi's limitations as a novelist are many and it is as well to mention them at the outset. He has often declared that he considers himself a writer of popular fiction, and if we define popular fiction to be that which pleases or is read by a class of reader commonly indifferent to literature, we understand that Ekwensi directs his work to a wider audience than, say, Achebe, Clark or Soyinka, and suggests, as well, the limitations that work may possess. His novels do not possess the unique qualities which are inherent in works of literature—a formal beauty of design and execution which lead the reader on to a new awareness of the greater potentialities of self. Rather, Ekwensi's work is concerned with the external features of modern Nigerian life, especially the life in and of the city. His heroes seek for but never make profound discoveries about themselves. Perhaps this accounts for the fact that in each of the full-length novels we find the same kind of hero—almost a stereotype—who, progressively lacking energy, becomes unconvincing as a character.

His plots suffer in the same way: just as we find the same kind of hero in each of the novels, so we find him (or her) in more or less the same circumstances. Moreover, Ekwensi pays little attention to his plots and his novels are full of inconsistencies and contradictions. The books, therefore, possess a perverse logic in terms of the art of the novel: because the motives of the characters are not explored in any depth, because their behaviour is based on the novelist's whim rather than on the circumstances of their lives about which the novelist forces them to reflect and accordingly revalue and adjust their behaviour, the plots of the novels reflect this confusion and irresoluteness, and organic unity is lacking in them. Added to this is an insistently melodramatic approach, the presentation of sensation for its own sake.

A final delimiting feature which must also be mentioned is Ekwensi's uncertain use of English. Achebe remarks on the problems which confront an African writing in English. He says the writer 'can try to contain what he wants to say within the limits of conventional English or he can try to push back those limits to accommodate his ideas', and he enjoins his fellow-novelists that, whatever method they adopt, those 'who can do the work of extending the frontiers of English so as to accommodate African thought-patterns must do it through their mastery of English and not out of innocence. . . . It is important first to learn the rules of English and afterwards break them if we wish. The good ones will know how to do this and the bad ones will be bad, anyway.' These comments are timely and relevant to all Nigerian writing, and while they nowhere relate specifically to Ekwensi's writing, they do apply. Ekwensi has not mastered the rules of English and the bad English which is often used in his novels, taken together with the inconsistencies of plot and characterization we have mentioned, and the insistent melodrama in his treatments, militate against his fiction achieving the first rank in importance as art.

Yet despite these limitations—which are considerable—Ekwensi is a serious novelist whose writing reflects his serious concern with some of the most pressing problems facing modern Nigeria. Ekwensi's fiction represents, almost exclusively, an attempt to come to terms with the chaotic formlessness and persistent flux of the modern Nigerian city—that is, with Lagos. His novels arise out of his acquaintance with and involvement in the complexities of city living and his attempt to probe with an unflinching realism the superficial delights and real terrors of the city places his work in a twentieth-century tradition of novel writing. The tension in his major novels derives from the attempts of their heroes—Amusa Sango, Jagua, Wilson Iyari and Filia Enu, all of whom live on the borderline between success and failure, triumph and collapse—to extract as much pleasure as they can from city living whilst constantly confronted by the fear of poverty and failure.

In *People of the City* are found the themes, structure, characters, style and values which characterize all of Ekwensi's attempts at serious fiction. *People of the City* is a novel of city manners. The plot is loose and episodic. It has a certain style without structure. It has a rich verbal texture without dramatic form. The novel tells the story of Amusa Sango, born in the 'Eastern Greens' of Nigeria, and, when the story opens, a crime reporter with the *West African Sensation* and, in his spare time, the leader of a dance band playing in various Lagos clubs. The opening paragraphs encompass the whole of the novel's meaning.

> Most girls in the famous West African city . . . knew the address Twenty Molomo Street for there lived a most colourful and eligible young bachelor, by name Amusa Sango.

> In addition to being crime reporter for the *West African Sensation,* Sango in his spare time led a dance band that played the *calypsos* and the *konkomas* in the only way that delighted the hearts of the city women.

> . . .

> Of women Sango could have his pick, from the silk-clad ones who wore lipstick in the European manner and smelled of scent in the warm air to the more ample, less sophisticated ones in the bigsleeved velvet blouses that feminized a woman.

> Yet Sango's one desire in the city was peace and the desire to forge ahead. No one would believe this, knowing the kind of life he led: that beneath his gay exterior lay a serious nature and determined to carve for itself a place of renown in this city of opportunities.

The two needs which Sango, and indeed all of the other characters in the book, experience—the need for success on the one hand and the need for peace on the other—are presented as a necessary condition of city living. Yet

the two things are not compatible: the need to compete and survive at one level and to succeed at another destroys the possibility of finding peace, as the novel shows through its description of Sango's career as a reporter and in revealing his affairs with various 'people of the city'. By developing those aspects of plot which relate to Sango's career as a crime reporter, Ekwensi is able to offer criticism, sometimes implied, sometimes direct, on general social issues which characterize modern Nigerian urban life. By delineating Sango's affairs with a variety of women Ekwensi is able to dramatize general problems as they are consolidated in the lives of specific individuals, at the same time broadening the scope of the novel. (pp. 79-81)

Ekwensi's limitations as an artist are plain [in *People of the City*]. The episodic nature of the plot precludes the emergence of a satisfying overall pattern in the book. Characters are not drawn in any depth—while they possess a certain individuality, they are types who represent a cross-section of the people who live in the city and seek to come to terms with it. In this respect the novel can claim an importance. Through a deliberately realistic approach Ekwensi seeks to lay bare and call attention to various evils in society—to corruption in high places and low, in politics, government, civic administration; to debased morality both public and private. The obvious polemical and reformatory purposes dominate the novel. There are passages of descriptive and dramatic power and Ekwensi does have genuine insight into the complexity of problems which attend modern urban living in Nigeria. But he is unable to develop and sustain these insights in novelistic terms and the book, in the end, is a series, however valid and worth while, of random vignettes and impressions.

Jagua Nana, Ekwensi's second full-length novel and probably his best, bears many resemblances to *People of the City* but here the author pays more attention to the formal problems of fiction writing and the effect is more satisfying and convincing than the first book. An early review of the book called Ekwensi a 'Nigerian Defoe [who] chronicles the fierce life of the city of Lagos' and describes its heroine, Jagua Nana, as 'a Nigerian Moll Flanders.' The comparison is valid in several respects. The novel has, for two-thirds of its length, the loose, episodic structure of the picaresque form with unity supplied by the central relationship of the heroine to the events described and dramatized. Jagua, like Moll in Defoe's book, is a woman who struggles for survival in a tough, competitive society which threatens to engulf her at any moment. In the first novel the hero, Amusa Sango, sought to earn his living through socially acceptable means—journalism and band-leading. But Jagua, like Moll, though she has an awareness of moral standards, will sacrifice them without hesitation to the necessities of the moment. And like Defoe, Ekwensi has a strong moral purpose (not as overtly declared as Defoe's): he displays Jagua's moral turpitude in order to expose and condemn those forces which make her behaviour necessary.

JAGUA NANA
A NOVEL BY CYPRIAN EKWENSI

"*Jagua Nana* is a West African masterpiece; it is a story all oppressed people can tell. Only Ekwensi tells it better."
— John A. Williams

Cover for Ekwensi's most popular novel.

Jagua Nana, like **People of the City,** offers a view of urbanized Nigerian life. Ekwensi evokes a convincing portrayal of the variety of Lagosian life—its poverty and squalor, existing side by side with glamour and riches; its pimps, prostitutes and politicians and their greed and lust. As Ulli Beier observes, this is not every Nigerian's Lagos but 'everybody will come into contact with this aspect of the city's life at some time or other—people from the most diverse walks of life form an integral part of it.'

The story centres on Jagua Nana—'they called her Jagua because of her good looks and stunning fashions. They said she was Ja–gwa, after the famous British prestige car. Jagua is an independent woman from eastern Nigeria, a woman of easy virtue who although no longer young when we meet her, clings to a life of drinking and dancing, fine clothes and many lovers. Though she indulges in a bewildering series of casual love affairs, living on the 'dashes' of the men she sleeps with, her real love is for Freddie, a young, idealistic and impecunious student. Eventually Freddie leaves Lagos to study in England and Jagua travels to her village in the east, where she has a brief affair with a powerful chief, Obufara, and seeks wealth in an unsuccessful venture among the market queens of Onitsha. When Ekwensi moves from the intense and familiar urban life of Lagos he is likely to go astray. It is a feature of modern Nigerian writing that at some point in the story a character returns to his village at a place remote from the city. This affords the author the opportunity of contrasting the alleged simplicity of village life with the sophistication and complexity of life in the city. Many novelists—Nzekwu, Achebe, Aluko and Nwanko—manage this with conviction. Ekwensi's account of Jagua's affair with Chief Obufara is the least successful part of the book.

At last Jagua returns to Lagos, continues her casual, immoral life, becomes involved with an unscrupulous politician, Uncle Taiwo, who in an election campaign stands against and is responsible for the death of Freddie, now returned from England. Uncle Taiwo is eventually murdered and Jagua, because of her association with him and his campaign, is forced to flee to her village, a broken woman. She loses a child born of an affair with a lorry driver and, in a contrived happy ending, finds peace (and fifty thousand pounds given, unknown to her at the time, by Uncle Taiwo and stolen from party funds).

The episodic form and picaresque treatment of the first two-thirds of the novel give way to a firm and developing narrative in the final third, the part of the novel devoted to the election campaign, a campaign centred on the two principal competitors for Jagua's affection. Whereas Ekwensi's treatment of politics in **People of the City** is ironic and flippant, here it is bitter and characterized by an invective and presented with a brutality which preclude irony or humour. Jagua says to Freddie when he announces his intention to contest the Obanla riding, held by Uncle Taiwo:

> 'No, Freddie, I no wan' you to win.' She saw him sit eagerly forward and frown. She went on. 'Politics not for you, Freddie. You got education. You got culture. You're a gentleman an' proud. Politics be game for dog. And in dis Lagos, is a rough game. De roughest game in de whole worl'. Is smelly and dirty and you too clean an' sweet. I speakin' frank to you Freddie.'

And she goes on to explain the methods by which elections are won:

> Elections in Lagos were not won by wearing smart clothes and appearing distant from the people. You had to show them what you could do for them, before you won. You must associate with everyone, particularly the lowest ones, and regard them as your friends. You must give them the freedom of your time and thought, your car and your room. In such a manner only would you learn how they thought and acted. Uncle Taiwo was working very hard indeed, she told him. Uncle Taiwo was distributing money presents to the people. She told what happened only last week. She went with him to the court in Obanla and when anyone was fined, Uncle Taiwo promptly paid up the fine.... The whole of Obanla was plastered with pictures of Uncle Taiwo and all

women had received match boxes and cooking stoves
with his portrait on them and the school children
exercise books with his portrait.

This represents Ekwensi's appraisal of contemporary
Nigerian politics and the rest of the book dramatizes the
prosecution and consequences of the campaign in which
both Freddie and Uncle Taiwo lose their lives. The story
of Uncle Taiwo's end, told to Jagua by her friend Rosa,
is presented with a starkness unmatched in contemporary African writing. (pp. 86-8)

Many Nigerians have condemned both *People in the
City* and *Jagua Nana* for presenting modern Nigeria in a
bad light. They claim that Ekwensi exaggerates events
for the sake of sensation. Present events would seem to
confirm that his evaluation of the political life of the
country in the time he describes was not far wrong.
Moreover, and more important, he convinces us that the
world of *Jagua Nana* is authentic. Jagua and the people
around her are vital and memorable. Their lives are the
legitimate material for novels. As Ulli Beier points out,
'nobody in his right senses would assume that all people
of Lagos are like Jagua' and her circle. They are,
however, a prominent feature of Lagos life, members of
the lower reaches of society, people who influence and
shape the quality of the life of the city.

Beautiful Feathers, Ekwensi's third novel, is an attempt
to provide a fictional assessment of Pan-Africanism.
The book has the same virtues (a strong sense of place, a
plethora of incident, a moral earnestness) and faults
(careless plotting and an uncertain use of language) as
the earlier books. The novel has two related plots
suggested by the title, itself taken from an Ibo proverb
which says: 'However famous a man is outside, if he is
not respected inside his own home, he is like a bird with
beautiful feathers, wonderful on the outside but ordinary within.'

Wilson Iyari, the proprietor of the Independence Phar-
macy, is the leader of the Nigerian Movement for
African and Malagasy Solidarity, a Pan-African movement formed because of Iyari's recognition that, although all of the political parties in Nigeria—the
N.C.N.C., Action Group and Northern People's
Congress—were 'Striving towards the same end, freedom from Colonial rule', the dream would not be
realised because none of the parties 'could put aside the
bitterness, frustrations and jealousies and realize that
the end in view was the same.' Iyari enjoys the respect of
the masses, and among leaders of Nigerian political
thought his name and movement have significance. But
inside his own home he has no authority. His wife,
Yaniya, rejects him, finds satisfaction in the arms of
various lovers and eventually leaves him, taking their
children with her to her father's home in the forest near
Benin. The eldest son, Lumumba (all Iyari's children are
named after leaders of anti-colonial Independence
movements), dies and she returns to Lagos where she
lives for a time on the fringes of the underworld before
becoming a hostess with Nigerian airlines.

Iyari, after leading an abortive protest demonstration on
Independence Day (the exact purposes of which are
never clearly defined) which results in a riot, is enlisted
by the Prime Minister (modelled on Nigeria's first
Prime Minister, Sir Abubakar Tafawa Balewa, to whom
the novel is dedicated) to represent Nigeria at a congress
on self-determination at Dakar. While accord is seemingly reached between whites and blacks at the conference table, the underlying enmity between races is
pointed up in a hunting episode. A shooting party
comprised of Americans, Russians, British, French and
delegates from various African countries, come upon
and kill 'a beast shaped like a rhino, but infinitely more
elegant.' An argument arises—'some of the hunters
wanted the horns, some wanted the whole beast preserved in a museum'—followed by confusion and
shooting:

> Wilson saw the white men carrying off the beast and
> running down the slope. He aimed at the retreating
> white men, but a shot struck him in the ribs and he
> fell. He lay there in a shot-riddled mist, choking for
> breath, while his body floated in endless circles,
> weightless.

The symbolism is palpable and underlined by the Prime
Minister's comments when he speaks to Iyari on the
latter's return from Dakar after spending two months in
the hospital:

> 'My dear Mr. Iyari. You are a young man.' His voice
> fell one octave. 'A very young man, and therefore
> impatient. You led a strike here because you thought
> Nigeria was this, Nigeria was that. Now you've seen
> for yourself how a very little thing can upset unity.
> But we must keep trying.'

Iyari's experiences in Dakar, together with the death of
his Ghanaian friend, a political agitator exiled in
Nigeria and significantly named Kwame Amantu, chas-
tens his enthusiasm for African and Malagasy independence and he learns that unity of the kind he envisages is
comprised of more complex factors than he at first
supposed. This leads him to seek and achieve reconciliation with his wife and family. In the end he settles for
the more modest role of successful pharmacist and
husband.

> Wilson was touched by the new attitude of Yaniya.
> He could not believe his eyes or his ears. They had
> truly come together now. It could be said of him that
> he was famous outside and that at home he had the
> backing of a family united by bonds of love. Wilson's
> beautiful feathers had ceased to be superficial and
> had become a substantial asset.

The novel reveals political concern without political
awareness. It reveals, as well, Ekwensi's desire to offer a
serious treatment of his subject. But because he fails to
define what the N.M.F.A.M.S. really stands for and
what its aims really are, the novel ultimately lacks
convincingness.

Iska, the most recent novel, is in many ways the least
satisfactory of the four books mentioned and displays in
excess the faults in Ekwensi's approach to writing

fiction. This is the story of Filia Enu, a beautiful young Ibo girl born in Northern Nigeria who, on the death of her father and her Muslim Hausa lover, Dan Kayiba, moves to Lagos, becomes involved with 'fashionable' literary and political cliques, becomes a model, attracts many lovers and eventually dies, overwhelmed and defeated by the city.

The title of the book, *Iska,* is the Hausa word for 'wind' and the symbolic analogies which this title affords Ekwensi are obvious. Filia Enu (as indeed are all of the characters in the novel) is a 'child of the wind', subject to its caprices and at its mercy. The publisher's blurb for the novel says that the wind symbolizes the change which 'blows strongly through Africa, destroying the old, preparing the way for the new.' Doubtless this is less satisfactory as a summary of his achievement.

The novel is formally divided into five parts, each named after a character with whom Filia is closely associated. Filia's story is the subject of the first section but then it is subordinated to that of each of the characters for whom the other sections are named. The movement of the novel is linear: themes are introduced and developed independently, then woven together in rather skilful counterpoint which evokes the complexity of Lagos living. The first two parts of the novel are the best because they offer, unlike the others, fresh material. Here Filia's life in Northern Nigeria is described. Here the Hausa-Ibo quarrel is an important part of the theme. Against the background of tension and rioting, the tribal quarrel is given focus in the tragic story of Filia and Dan Kayiba. The young Hausaman is killed by a group of Ibomen in a dispute over an entirely trivial matter. The convincingness of these sections of the novel is marred to some extent by the author's moralizing and his preaching of the need for national unity and federalism, a worthy enough motive in itself.

The reader, in trying to assimilate Filia's experience and assess its central meaning, is directed to the closing pages of the novel, to the musings of Dapo Ladele, Filia's latest lover, as he travels for the first time into Iboland.

> His impressions were quick and sharp. He quickly noted the industrialization and eagerness of the East. The new roads. The new progress. The impressiveness and love of the people of Eastern Nigeria. It was startling to him and quite unbelievable. Having for so long earned his living by writing articles inciting the hatred of a people, he had almost reached the stage where—temporarily at least—he was inclined to believe what he wrote. Now he knew that he had been living in a dream world. Once across the Niger he understood the background of Filia's life and struggles, her pride and independence.

The conclusion is an impasse: corruption and dissipation of human and emotional resources will continue; side by side with these, we are told, the desires of people like Filia and Dapo may ultimately be attainable.

Lokotown and Other Stories, also published in 1966, is a collection comprised of two long stories—the title story

and 'Glittering City'—and seven short pieces. Of these the longer ones are the best, although **'The Ivory Dancer'** and **'Timber Merchant'** display the control and economy of statement, and the irony in their endings, which characterize successful short-story writing. The stories here, as in the novels, deal with city life. Their plots follow the familiar theme of the innocent from the village caught up in the competition for survival in the hard, bright city, sometimes successfully, but generally disillusioned and broken. Ekwensi evokes his characters and situations with economy and precision, and the moralizing too often blatant in the longer works is here implicit in the fabric of the stories. While the characters in these stories are familiar, they possess an urgency and vitality which carry readers through the segments of their lives which the stories dramatize.

Finally, brief mention must be made of *Burning Grass.* One commentator has said that the book is of 'purely anthropological interest.' This is to do the book less than justice. This novel—perhaps tale is a better description—reveals Ekwensi's knowledge of and affection for the Fulani cattlemen of Northern Nigeria and tells the story of Mai Sunsaye, a patriarch who is afflicted with the *sokugo,* the wandering sickness, his adventures and those of his herdsmen and sons. The opening paragraphs establish the tone of the story:

> When they begin to burn the grass in Northern Nigeria, it is time for the herdsmen to be moving the cattle southwards to the banks of the great river. And the hunters, lurking on the edge of the flames with dane gun, bow and arrow, sniff the fumes and train their eyes to catch the faintest flicker of beasts hastening from their hiding places.
>
> It is time too for the harmattan to blow dust into eyes and teeth, to wrinkle the skin: the harmattan that leaves in its wake from Libya to Lagos a shroud of fog that veils the walls and trees like muslin on a sheikh.

Ekwensi's control of his materials is nowhere more secure as he blends facts and fantasy, reality and illusion. The characters suggest typical figures in the landscape and carry great conviction. The story closes on the same note as it opens. Mai Sunsaye, worn out by his long and eventual wanderings, dies, the name of his beloved son Rikku on his lips. Ekwensi records this with simplicity and tenderness:

> Sunsaye was indeed well beloved and they buried him in great pomp on the spot where his first camp had been. Then they cleared away in great haste. For legend holds that the place where a man has died is bad luck.

Burning Grass is Ekwensi's most successful book from the point of view of its achievement as art. But it is not typical. He is the chronicler of city life, of the morality of the city and its influences and effects on the lives of city dwellers. We have commented on the excesses and inefficacies apparent in his use of the novel form. His success often proceeds from his topicality—he is always up to date. The faults and excesses arise from the reflection of the chaos of life in the modern urbanized Africa the novels seek to create. We recall Achebe's comment that the novelist's duty is 'not to beat the morning's headlines in topicality'. This statement clearly specifies the difference between writing which is likely to endure and that which achieves brief popularity and then passes. Ekwensi's fiction falls within the realm of popular art. And this is not without its importance. Popular fiction is always significant as indicating current popular interests and morality. Ekwensi's work is redeemed (although not saved as art) by his serious concern with the moral issues which inform contemporary Nigerian life. As such they will always be relevant to Nigerian literary history and to Nigerian tradition. (pp. 90-5)

> *Douglas Killam, "Cyprian Ekwensi," in* Introduction to Nigerian Literature, *edited by Bruce King, 1971. Reprint by Africana Publishing Company, 1972, pp. 77-96.*

Juliet Okonkwo (essay date 1986)

[*In the following excerpt, Okonkwo examines narrative technique, language, and characterization in Ekwensi's novels.*]

Cyprian Ekwensi, with six novels to his credit, is usually regarded as the urban novelist par excellence. With the exception of **Burning Grass** (1962), and **Survive the Peace** (1976) all his novels are set in the city of Lagos. He revels in the excitement of city life and loves to expose its many faces of modernity. He writes about the cultural centres, department stores, beaches, lagoons, political organizations and campaigns; its criminals, prostitutes, band-leaders; ministers of state, businessmen, civil servants, professionals; policemen on duty, thugs, thieves, and many other types that are found in the city. Unlike Achebe and others of the African—culture school who are interested in the pre-colonial African past, Ekwensi focuses his attention on the contemporary scene. Employing a naturalistic narrative technique reminiscent of Emile Zola, Ekwensi has been able to capture both the restless excitement and the frustrations of life in the city. Many of the incidents in his novels are taken from the everyday life around him, in his country, because he believes that the function of a novelist is to reflect the social scene as faithfully as possible. Ekwensi's novels therefore follow the history of Nigeria in chronological sequence. *People of the City* (1954) is set in the last days of the colonial era; *Jagua Nana* (1961) covers the period of the election campaigns which ushered in the first independent government; *Beautiful Feathers* (1963) reflects the first optimistic years of independence with its concern for Panafricanism; *Iska* (1966) exposes the fissures in the fabric of the nation as manifested in the tribal and factional divisions and animosities that finally erupted in the Nigerian Civil War; *Survive the Peace* starts with the tail-end of the war and deals with the immediate problems of security and rehabilitation.

The first novel, **People of the City,** is a picaresque novel which focuses on one central charter, Amusa Sango, through whose progress the reader is initiated into the various kinds of life that exist in the city. Ekwensi's declared intention in this novel is to show "How the city attracts all types and how the unwary must suffer from ignorance of its ways". In order to gain this objective, the author makes Amusa Sango a crime reporter for a Lagos newspaper, and a band-leader in one of the night clubs. From these vantage positions, the protagonist is able to observe many sordid aspects of life in the city, and the author thus piles up scene after scene of urban life in all its ramifications. Readers learn about the materialistic outlook of city people, about the bribery and corruption, the squalor of the slums, the predatory secret societies; they are told of extortionist landlords and business racketeers, and, more particularly, of the utter sexual laxity which is characteristic of the new urban society. Amusa has come to the city from the Eastern Greens in order to take advantage of the opportunities it offers for material and social self-improvement, but he is drawn into the dissipating pleasures of women and the fast life. Artistically, *People of the City* is not a successful novel. Its many narrative elements have not been fused into one artistic whole. Ekwensi's handling of language is still unsure, his characterization superficial and sometimes contradictory, his exploration of the motivation of actions and their import on the deeper levels of life is shallow.

In his second novel, **Jagua Nana,** Ekwensi remains faithful to the picaresque technique, Jagua (called after the prestigious British car) has escaped from conventional married life in the Eastern Greens to the city where she has been active as a prostitute. Now, at forty, she grows anxious about her looks, which are very essential in her trade; more than this, she hankers after a life of respectability through marriage and motherhood. She has attached herself to a young teacher, Freddie, with whom she is in love, and for whom she sacrifices a great deal in order to retain his interest in her. Through Jagua, her career, her pursuits and her fluctuating fortunes, Ekwensi reveals the common wickedness, squalor, materialism and immorality of the city, together with its crimes and violence. But he also delves into the complex nature of his heroine, so that Jagua is presented in greater depth than Sango and we see her in roles of prostitute, woman and mother. Ekwensi's greater success in **Jagua Nana** is also due to his better control of language; particularly impressive in his ability to handle various levels of English expression, allotting the appropriate level to each character. Jagua, for instance, because she is illiterate, talks pidgin English; but her pidgin is different from that of her mother, who never left the village at all. When this is set against the standard English of the narrative, and the diversified speech levels of other characters, a semblance of reality is achieved.

In **Burning Grass,** Ekwensi retreats from the city to the grassy plains of northern Nigeria in which he sets his story about the adventures of a Fulani cattleman, Mai

Sunsayi and of his family. Mai Sunsayi has been struck with the *Sokugo,* a wandering disease which separates him from his family, who, for their part, try to follow his trail in order to recover him. Like the earlier two novels, this is a picaresque story; and Ekwensi's main achievement lies in the recreation of the life patterns of the Fulani. A short novel with a limited objective, *Burning Grass* might better be described as a tale. There is no attempt at in-depth presentations of characters and their motives, or any complexity in the action. The language is unexciting, though controlled.

With *Beautiful Feathers,* Ekwensi came back to Lagos. Its chief character, Wilson Iyari, a pharmacist by profession, has political ambitions and is leader of a pan-africanist political party. The theme and the title of the novel come from an Igbo proverb which says: "However famous a man is outside, if he is not respected inside his own house, he is like a bird with beautiful feathers; wonderful outside but ordinary within." Iyari has great difficulty in reconciling his responsibilities as a pharmacist and politician with those of a husband and a father in his house. The conflicts generated by this situation threaten the peace of his home and lead to a minor tragedy. In this novel, Ekwensi discards the picaresque technique and attempts to share out actions and interest among different characters. He makes a greater effort to inter-relate the various facets of his narration and bring them to bear on a central theme. There is greater in-depth exploration of character, and a probing of the cause-and-effect relations of events that is lacking in the preceding novels: Ekwensi achieves some degree of maturity in the handling of the central techniques of the novel, such as character delineation, plot construction, effective dialogue and economy that leaves nothing wasted and superfluous.

Because of the technical improvement evident in the progress from *People of the City* to *Beautiful Feathers,* a number of critics assumed that Ekwensi was gradually solving his problems of form, character and language in the art of fiction writing. Unfortunately, that optimism has not been borne out by his later novels. In his two latest novels, he has reverted to the picaresque mode with its loose episodic plots, unconvincing characterization and melodramatic excesses. *Iska* focuses on the fortunes of a young Igbo girl, Filia Enu, who was born and educated in Northern Nigeria, and who falls in love with and marries a young Hausa, Dan Kaybi. From that moment, her life becomes a series of tragedies. Having lost her husband in a pub brawl, she moves over to Lagos where she tries to give meaning to her life through education and respectable employment. As Filia is driven from one experience to another in this effort, Ekwensi is once more able to spotlight the goings on in Nigeria's capital. This time, revivalist churches, shady politics and journalism, the world of women's fashions, the inevitable prostitution, the sexual adventures of men in high places, crime on large and small scales come within his compass.

It took Ekwensi ten years to produce his next novel, *Survive the Peace* which is set in Biafra immediately after the civil war. Yet another picaresque story, the tale follows the fortunes of James Odugo, a radio journalist, as he tries to pick up the threads and resume normal life after the disruption of the war. In the dangerous state of chaos that prevailed between the crumbling of an old order and the setting up of a new, he tries to locate and bring together the various members of his family who had been separated by the war. The author thus creates for himself the opportunity to present with great vividness the state of insecurity due to the many abandoned guns that fell into ruthless hands, the rampaging soldiers from both sides of the fighting, molestations of innocent civilians, especially young women; the danger on the roads, broken homes, sexual permissiveness; the destructions of war, countless refugees and relief operations. Through a series of flashbacks, certain moments during the war itself are re-created. It is difficult to think of any aspects of life of this period which have not been incorporated, in one way or another, into this simple story.

Ekwensi's place as a novelist of stature is a subject of controversy. Most people would concede his importance in the historical development of African fiction, but only a few will grant him recognition as a serious craftsman because of a number of disturbing qualities in his work. It is, however, misguided to judge Ekwensi by standards to which he has never aspired. As he once disclosed to Lewis Nkosi:

> I think I am a writer who regards himself as a writer of the masses. I don't think of myself as a literary stylist: if my style comes, that is just incidental, but I am more interested in getting at the heart of the truth which the man in the street can recognize than in just spinning words.

Ekwensi is by choice a popular novelist and he launched himself on this career by writing the first Onitsha chapbooks: *Ikolo the Wrestler and Other Ibo Tales,* (1947), and *When Love Whispers* (1948). His art has not seriously transcended their level. (pp. 655-58)

> *Juliet Okonkwo, "Popular Urban Fiction and Cyprian Ekwensi," in* European-Language Writing in Sub-Saharan Africa, *edited by Albert S. Gérard, Akadémiai Kiadó, 1986, pp. 650-58.*

FURTHER READING

Abdurrahman, Umar. "Cyprian Ekwensi's *Burning Grass:* A Critical Assessment." *Ufahamu* XVI, No. 1 (Fall 1987-88): 78-100.
  Examines the setting, plot, and theme of *Burning Grass,* concluding: "The novel's overall merit lies in its adept mixture of fantasy and reality, of history and

sociology, which makes it enjoyable for all types of readers."

Emenyonu, Ernest. *Cyprian Ekwensi.* London: Evans Brothers Limited, 1974, 137 p.
  Biography of Ekwensi, focusing on his literary works.

Grandsaigne, J. de. "A Narrative Grammar of Cyprian Ekwensi's Short Stories." *Research in African Literatures* 16, No. 4 (Winter 1985): 541-55.
  Analysis of "textual strategies" in Ekwensi's short stories.

Lindfors, Bernth. "Interview with Cyprian Ekwensi." *World Literature Written in English* 13, No. 2 (November 1974): 141-54.
  Interview with Ekwensi. Lindfors and Ekwensi discuss Ekwensi's most popular works: *Jagua Nana, When Love Whispers, Burning Grass,* and *The Passport of Mallam Ilia.*

McClusky, John. "The City as a Force: Three Novels by Cyprian Ekwensi." *Journal of Black Studies* 7, No. 2 (December 1976): 211-14.
  Study of "Ekwensi's development of the force of the city in three of his major novels: *People of the City* (1954), *Jagua Nana* (1961), and *Beautiful Feathers* (1963)."

Nazareth, Peter. "*Survive the Peace:* Cyprian Ekwensi As a Political Novelist." In *Marxism and African Literature,* edited by Georg M. Gugelberger, pp. 165-77. London: James Currey Ltd., 1985.
  Reviews *Survive the Peace,* noting: "*Survive the Peace* is a fine political novel, one of Ekwensi's best in a long and distinguished career working for the people of Nigeria."

Okonkwo, Juliet I. "Ekwensi and Modern Nigerian Culture." *Ariel: A Review of International English Literature* 7, No. 2 (April 1976): 32-45.
  Explores Ekwensi's works as reflections of Nigerian culture. The critic observes: "Literature is a mirror of life and no other Nigerian writer to date has succeeded as much as Ekwensi in reflecting the contemporary scene with all its complications and contradictions."

Povey, John. "Cyprian Ekwensi: The Novelist and the Pressure of the City." In *The Critical Evaluation of African Literature,* edited by Edgar Wright, pp. 73-94. London: Cox & Wyman Ltd., 1973.
  Contends that Ekwensi is a writer with "potential": "In his work there is recognition and skill.... At present, too often a vulgarly emotional note intrudes, but the evidence of skill remains. It is upon this that one bases an assertion that the future may still offer the prospect of a major novel from Ekwensi."

Lonne Elder III
1931-

American dramatist and screenwriter.

An American dramatist and screenwriter, Elder is widely recognized as the author of works designed to raise audience consciousness of racial tensions in modern America. He accomplishes this goal by documenting the hardships that generations of prejudice have imposed on the black community. His works explore the question of black identity by focusing on a recurring theme: the resilience of the black family. In his 1969 play *Ceremonies in Dark Old Men,* Elder depicted a traumatized ghetto family as a microcosm of American black experience. This dynamic is also at the heart of his 1972 screenplay for the motion picture *Sounder,* an adaptation of William H. Armstrong's novel about the bigotry and prejudice faced by a black family in the Depression-era South. As Elder himself has claimed, his career shift from dramatist to screenwriter reflects his search for a wider audience for his message of social awareness. Through his continued work in motion pictures and television, Elder hopes to change the way blacks are portrayed in the media.

Born in Americus, Georgia, in 1931, Elder moved with his family to a farm in New Jersey while still an infant. His father died when Elder was ten, and his mother was killed in a car accident in 1943. Orphaned, Elder went to live with his aunt and uncle in Jersey City, where he helped his uncle, a numbers runner, by following behind him with the betting slips. After high school, Elder briefly attended New Jersey State Teachers College (now Trenton State Teachers College), withdrawing before the end of his first year. He moved to Harlem at nineteen and enrolled in nonmatriculate courses at the Jefferson School and the New School for Social Research. Drafted into the U.S. Army in 1952, he was stationed at Fort Campbell, Kentucky. At nearby Fisk University he was introduced to poet and teacher Dr. Robert Hayden, who encouraged Elder's early literary efforts by helping him structure his short stories and poems. After his discharge from the military, Elder returned to Harlem, where he held a succession of odd jobs—waiter, dock worker, poker dealer in an after-hours club—while beginning his career as a writer. Joining the Harlem Writers Guild, he came into contact with such important playwrights as Lorraine Hansberry and Douglas Turner Ward. Elder shared an apartment with Ward between 1953 and 1956—an experience that encouraged him to write for the theater. He also studied acting during this period and worked with a summer stock company directed by Alice Childress, another member of the Harlem Writers Guild. Hansberry then asked him to audition for the role of Bobo in her play *A Raisin in the Sun;* Elder held the role for two years, on Broadway and on tour, and the steady income allowed him time to

concentrate on his writing. In 1963 he obtained a job as a staff writer on the CBS television series *Camera Three.* He married Betty Gross the same year; the couple had a son, David Dubois, before divorcing in 1967.

Between 1963 and 1969 Elder produced his greatest volume of work for the theater. An early version of *Ceremonies in Dark Old Men* received its first public reading at the New Dramatists Committee in 1965 and was performed at Wagner College, Staten Island, in July of the same year. Subsequently, Elder received a series of grants and fellowships that enabled him to study drama and filmmaking at Yale University from 1965 to 1967. Around this time, the New York Mobilization for Youth commissioned him to write a play. The result, *Charades on East Fourth Street,* is a drama about a gang of black youths that holds a white policeman captive; it was first performed at Expo '67 in Montreal, Canada. Elder next obtained a job as a staff writer for the television series *N.Y.P.D.,* which allowed him to remain in New York and strengthen his ties to the theater. From

1967 to 1969 he served as coordinator of the playwrights and directors unit of the Negro Ensemble Company. His reworked version of *Ceremonies in Dark Old Men,* performed by the Negro Ensemble Company in 1969, marked Elder's professional debut as a playwright. The drama opened to critical acclaim and received several awards, including the Outer Drama Critics Award and the Los Angeles Drama Critics Award. The play also received a Pulitzer Prize nomination; it finished second in the voting. Elder married Judith Ann Johnson, a member of the Negro Ensemble Company cast of *Ceremonies in Dark Old Men,* in 1969; shortly thereafter, he moved to the West coast to concentrate on writing feature films.

Elder wrote scripts for the NBC television series *McCloud* in 1970 and 1971 before beginning work on screenplays for two motion pictures. His murder mystery *Melinda,* adapted from a screen story by Raymond Cistheri, was released by Metro-Goldwyn-Mayer in 1972. Hurriedly written in order to capitalize on a trend for black exploitation movies, this crime melodrama—which featured Elder in a minor role—was panned by the critics. *Sounder,* his adaptation of William H. Armstrong's Newberry Prize-winning novel, was released later in the year to critical acclaim. The story of a family of sharecroppers in rural Louisiana, *Sounder* marked a return to the themes of black struggle and familial love. Sounder, the family's hound dog, comes to be identified with the love and determination that hold a family together in the face of terrible hardship—even after the father is imprisoned for stealing food. Released by Twentieth Century-Fox, *Sounder* garnered two Academy Award nominations, one for best picture and one for best screenplay based on material from another medium. Elder next revised *Ceremonies in Dark Old Men* for a 1975 television production, which won a Christopher Award. Later he completed work on the 1976 release *Sounder, Part 2.* Other film work includes *Bustin' Loose,* a 1981 adaptation of a screen story by Richard Pryor about a bus driver who helps handicapped children. Elder's most recent work for the stage, *Splendid Mummer,* is the story of Ira Frederick Aldridge, a black Shakespearean actor who left America in the 1820s to pursue his career in Europe; the monodrama was first produced at the American Palace Theater in 1988. Elder currently lives with his family in Sherman Oaks, California, where he continues to develop projects for the stage and screen.

Critics hold that despite his many contributions to film and television, Elder's reputation as a dramatist is based chiefly on one work, *Ceremonies in Dark Old Men.* The "ceremonies" in the title refer to "rituals of survival," the mechanisms by which blacks try to reconcile their own personal values in a world dominated by whites. The two-act comedy-drama explores the various options facing a black ghetto family struggling for economic viability and self-fulfillment. The poverty and despair of the ghetto are evident in the setting: the virtually empty Harlem barbershop of Russell B. Parker. An ex-vaudeville dancer, Parker passes his time playing checkers

with his friend Jenkins, maintaining the charade that he is a barber because he cannot face a menial job in the white business world. The humiliation of working for "the man" also keeps Parker's two sons unemployed; Theopolis, an aspiring painter, dreams of becoming an artist, while Bobby concentrates his efforts on becoming "the best shoplifter in Harlem." The family is supported by Parker's daughter, Adele, who works as a secretary downtown. Adele precipitates the play's action by threatening to withdraw her financial support if the men in the family do not find jobs. Theo and Bobby convince their father to form an alliance with a racketeer, Blue Haven, and they turn the barbershop into a front for Haven's illegal operations. Over the objections of Adele, the men proceed to become involved in numbers running, shoplifting, and the illegal manufacture and sale of corn whiskey. The family enjoys a brief period of prosperity, but the endeavor ends in tragedy. Bobby is killed while attempting a robbery, and the shattered family must somehow find a way to carry on.

Critical response to *Ceremonies in Dark Old Men* was overwhelmingly positive. Richard Watts of the *New York Post* called it the "best play of the new season," and Edith Oliver of *The New Yorker* speculated that it was perhaps the finest first effort by an American playwright. Much of the credit for the enthusiastic response may be attributed to the highly lauded performance of the 1969 Negro Ensemble Company cast, directed by Edmund Cambridge. The acting, which featured playwright Douglas Turner Ward as Russell B. Parker, was widely praised. Several critics noted that the Negro Ensemble Company seemed particularly attuned to Elder's work, a sense heightened by the proximity of the Harlem setting. While some commentators labeled the play "overlong," "repetitious," and "predictable," these were but minor reservations about a work the same reviewers hailed as "powerful," "moving," and "important." Commentators praised Elder's realistic characters, noting that because they contained both personal weaknesses and strengths, they defy stereotypes. What some critics decried as Naturalism, Elder labeled "more akin to exalted realism"; and most critics would agree with Henry Hewes of the *Saturday Review,* who extolled Elder's "trueness of observation" and his "complete avoidance of self-pity." The greatness of *Ceremonies in Dark Old Men,* critics hold, is that it embodies the themes of love and social injustice not in symbols or vague abstractions, but in characters that exist as real people.

Elder remains committed to depicting the black struggle with a power and depth that refuses to descend to sentimentality. Despite the tragic conclusion of *Ceremonies in Dark Old Men,* the overarching theme of familial love emerges at the center of Elder's vision of black survival in America. As he once stated in an interview with Liz Gant of *Black World,* "One theme basically rides throughout my work. I'm trying to deal with Black people in the fullest sense by trying to illustrate all the ways that we've historically survived in the face of physical and psychological brutality which completely denies survival, or sanity for that matter."

(For further information about Elder's life and works, see *Contemporary Authors,* Vols. 81-84; *Contemporary Authors New Revision Series,* Vol. 25; and *Dictionary of Literary Biography,* Vols. 7, 38, 44.)

PRINCIPAL WORKS

Ceremonies in Dark Old Men (drama) 1965; performed and published as *Ceremonies in Dark Old Men* [revised version], 1969
Charades on East Fourth Street (drama) 1967
Melinda [adaptor; from a screen story by Raymond Cistheri] (screenplay) 1972
Sounder [adaptor; from the novel *Sounder* by William H. Armstrong] (screenplay) 1972
Bustin' Loose [adaptor; from a screen story by Richard Pryor] (screenplay) 1981
Splendid Mummer (drama) 1988

Edith Oliver (essay date 1969)

[*Oliver has been a drama critic for* The New Yorker *since 1961. In the following review essay, she discusses* Ceremonies in Dark Old Men, *noting: "[It] is the first play by Lonne Elder to be done professionally, and if any American has written a finer one I can't think what it is."*]

Anybody who is worried about the future of the American theatre, or of just the theatre, had better try to get tickets for *Ceremonies in Dark Old Men,* the second production this year of the Negro Ensemble Company, at the St. Marks. *Ceremonies* is the first play by Lonne Elder III to be done professionally, and if any American has written a finer one I can't think what it is. And the actors bring to life all its tragic power and beauty, its humanity and humor and wit. The company has been getting better and better over the past year or so; now the seven members of this cast, under Edmund Cambridge's remarkably firm and understanding direction, show that they are capable of the accomplished acting that a strong play demands. With a technique that always conceals itself, the performers realize the characters in all the depth and complexity of their feelings for one another—feelings that often seem to be masked by their stormy or mocking or teasing or generally comic behavior.

Ceremonies in Dark Old Men tells, in non-heroic terms, the story of a heroic adventure that ends in disaster but was worth a try. The adventurers have the brains and moral discernment and courage to realize exactly what they are doing and what they are risking, so that the disaster becomes a tragedy. They are members of a black family named Parker who live in a shabby rented house in Harlem. The father, a former vaudeville dancer, now runs a barbershop in the front downstairs room—or, at least, he makes a pretense of it. There have been no customers for years, so he is able to sneak in any number of games of checkers with his dignified West Indian friend Mr. Jenkins. Parker has two sons, both in their twenties, and a daughter, who is thirty. The older son, Theo, has been fooling around at painting and anything else he can turn his hand to in order to avoid doing degrading menial work for the white man. The younger son, Bobby, has been practicing a little light shoplifting at local stores. The daughter, Adele—the only member of the family who can face the white community—has an office job downtown, and she supports the household, as her dead mother did before her. It is Adele who precipitates a family crisis by declaring that she will no longer continue to take care of three grown men and that they must start earning some money or get out. Mr. Parker makes one humiliating try at finding a job, but the boys rebel, hating the situation as much as Adele does, and hating even more her female authority over them. Then Theo brings to light a hidden talent for making corn liquor and an idea to go with it that will free the Parkers of any dependence on the white man and allow them to work for themselves. He introduces into the household a racketeer called Blue Haven, who has a finger in every sordid and crooked pie in Harlem, and who produces a plan to turn the barbershop into an outlet for bootleg whiskey made on the premises. Mr. Parker first refuses and then agrees, partly out of a longing for the one last chance at love and living that money might give him, but mostly out of love for his family and sympathy for their hurt pride and as a token of his confidence in Theo. ("If I'm going to run a crooked house, *I'm going to run it.* . . . If being a crook is what you want to be, you're going to be the best crook in the world.") Adele, who knows that their getting mixed up with gangsters will defeat them, objects. She is right, but she is overruled.

In trying to describe plays that one has enjoyed or admired, one is often forced to say that it is the individual scenes, not the plot, that matters. The plot of *Ceremonies in Dark Old Men* matters a great deal, but the scenes, many of them very funny, give the play its richness and the tragedy its depth. The writing is beautifully controlled, with a trace of rhetoric. The Parkers are as close a family as you will ever see on a stage (which may be as much Mr. Cambridge's doing as Mr. Elder's), so responsive to one another that they barely need to speak, although they do a lot of talking. There is a delightful scene, near the beginning, in which Mr. Parker reminisces about old show-business days and how-I-met-your-mother, with his sons egging him on as his rapt, tongue-in-cheek audience, and which ends with all of them breaking into a slow dance as they whistle "Sweet Georgia Brown." There is another, near the end, in which he tells, and wildly acts out for the benefit of the same gleeful listeners, what appears to be a wholly apocryphal story of a stretch he once did on a Georgia chain gang. There are, of course, many powerful serious scenes—those in which Theo, the tragic hero of the play, takes on himself all the guilt and responsibility for the disasters that befall everyone, quietly standing up even to the sinister Blue Haven. William Jay is good in the role. As Adele, vulnerable and fiery, and accepting defeat and self-defeat, Rosalind Cash is absolutely wonderful, giving what amounts to a star performance in a non-star part. Douglas Turner is fine, too, as Mr. Parker, jovial or bossy or impatient or ardent, sometimes foolish and sometimes foxy-grandpa, and having to accept a few defeats of his own, among them that the beautiful girl he brings home is nothing but a treacherous hustler. I also admired, without reservation, Arthur French as Mr. Jenkins, David Downing as Bobby Parker, Samual Blue, Jr., as Blue Haven, and Judyann Jonsson as Mr. Parker's girl. (pp. 90, 92-3)

Edith Oliver, "The First Hurrah," in The New Yorker, *Vol. XLIV, No. 52, February 15, 1969, pp. 90, 92-93.*

Henry Hewes (essay date 1969)

[*An American drama critic, Hewes is also known as a stage director. In the following 1969 review of a recent Negro Ensemble Company performance of* Ceremonies in Dark Old Men, *he examines plot, theme, and characterization in the work.*]

It is a difficult time for those of us who look forward to an America in which mutual respect, warm friendship, and socioeconomic justice will prevail in all relationships between those of differing racial ancestry. Therefore, it is most heartening to visit the Negro Ensemble Company at their small St. Mark's Playhouse and find a play such as *Ceremonies in Dark Old Men.* For this work by Lonne Elder, 3rd, deals most realistically yet unrancorously with today's Harlem.

Furthermore, it never lets fear of possibly contributing to the perpetuation of a racist-held stereotype force it into a well meaning but patently false distortion of the characters it has chosen to depict, It is as if Mr. Elder is trusting us to think of these characters as the understandable victims of a racist society that has deprived them of virility and the incentive to become educated or even industrious. They are what any of us might be, if we had faced the same negative conditions.

The play begins a bit like *Juno and the Paycock,* with two old men in an empty Harlem barber shop, talking big but frightened to death of the woman who pays the rent and lays down the law to them. In this case, the woman is the daughter of the household, who works to support her fifty-four-year-old father and her two younger brothers. The father, a former vaudeville tap dancer whose legs gave out on him, couldn't face the indignity of taking a job with a broom and dustpan, so he had allowed his wife to go to work and support the family, and after her death the daughter assumed her mother's role. Not only has this turned the father into a weak individual, but presumably it has contributed to making his two sons shiftless, although it is again clear that they

too are rebelling against the apparent necessity of accepting a daily life of "going downtown to meet the man."

Now a diabolical agent appears in the person of "Blue" Haven. Blue is a con man who has worked out a system for exploiting the current tensions in Harlem. He has set up an organization called "The Harlem De-Colonization Association," which aims to drive "Mr. You Know Who" out of Harlem by continued robbery of stores and illegal competition. Of course, it will also make Blue rich and powerful.

To rid themselves of dependence upon their sister, the boys urge their father to accept a proposition in which the barber shop will become a cover-up for a corn whiskey and numbers game operation. The rest of the play demonstrates the comic ironies and tragic consequences of what the playwright has made seem a completely understandable choice.

Although Elder has done a great deal of television writing, this is his first play, and he often offers us sequences that, because they are not essential to the plot, make the play seem overlong. He also uses conflict too much, not trusting his characters to hold our attention with their deeper emotional involvement in the action. But ultimately we forgive him all this because of the trueness of his observation and the complete avoidance of self-pity in a situation that could very easily have played upon our guilt by indicting us for the misfortunes the play's characters suffer.

Under Edmund Cambridge's direction, the performances seem slanted toward obvious comedy, which may be a mistake. For it has the effect of making the characters seem somewhat superficial and at odds with their climatic moments of self-revelation. The role of the father is difficult because he is represented as weak and yet is called upon to show strength and fearlessness here and there. As played by Douglas Turner, the actor (who is also Douglas Turner Ward, the playwright), the father is most effective when he tells humorous stories such as the one about the ridiculous problems that attended his turning over in bed while chained to fellow inmates of a Georgia chain gang. But he is less convincing at expressing deep pain. Thus the intensely dramatic short final line of the play doesn't detonate quite as powerfully as it should.

On the other hand, Samual Blue, Jr., who is half-absurd, half-sinister as the racketeer, Blue Haven, seems to become an almost new and far more interesting character in one long speech describing his ambivalent feelings about his relationship with his wife and little boy. William Jay and David Downing play the two brothers with a credible relaxation, which makes it hard for them to suggest an underlying love for their father and for each other. And Rosalind Cash is not totally successful in her game attempt to move abruptly from being the steady head-of-the-household in the first scene to the high-living woman she later becomes.

Nevertheless, the ensemble-playing of this company achieves an overall balance between realism and entertainment that perhaps works against the dangers of artificiality and melodrama in the play. It is certainly a remarkable and unique company, and one that thoroughly deserves the Brandeis University Creative Arts Citation it is to receive in May.

> *Henry Hewes, "Harlem on Our Mind," in* Saturday Review, *Vol. LII, No. 8, February 22, 1969, p. 29.*

Harold Clurman (essay date 1969)

[*Clurman was a leading twentieth-century American drama critic and stage director. He is perhaps best remembered for drama reviews regularly contributed to* The New Republic *from 1949 to 1953 and to* The Nation *thereafter. In the following review, originally published in* The Nation *in 1969, he praises a recent Negro Ensemble Company performance of* Ceremonies in Dark Old Men.]

The only new play which has genuinely interested me for some time is Lonne Elder's *Ceremonies in Dark Old Men,* as given by the Negro Ensemble Company. When I say "play" I refer to the whole phenomenon of stage presentation: "words" in the "music" of an acting team perceived as a single experience. (*Tango,* in contrast, contains a vital text damaged by inadequate acting.) With *Ceremonies in Dark Old Men* I did not think to evaluate any of its parts (script, acting, setting, direction) separately. That is *theatre.* With Elder's play the Negro Ensemble has achieved its own proper pitch.

One may note some repetitiousness in the text and there were overfacile strokes for comedy effect. The total impression, however, is without blemish. Even the crudities in the play's texture are of a kind which appear organic with the material, part of its reality.

There is no special pleading: it proclaims no thesis, espouses no cause, appeals for no largess. *Ceremonies* is a family play whose characters are foolish, fallible, sweet, stupid, lovable, always understandable folk. They are richly human and as such not easily subject to petty compromise in humdrum jobs at paltry wages.

Russell Parker was a pop dancer till one day he no longer had the strength. He became a barber, but without any aptitude for the work, earned little in his Harlem shop and allowed his faithful wife to support him till she died of the burden. Their daughter took over her mother's task; now she supports her father who spends most of his time playing checkers with a kindly friend and recounting tall tales to the delight of his two sons, who also find indolence more convenient than work. One day the hard-driven girl, fed up with the situation, announces that either they get jobs or she will refuse to contribute her earnings to their further maintenance. Crisis!

The younger brother has already begun to amuse himself by larceny; the older one has hit upon a scheme suggested by a local racketeer, Blue Haven. Since the young idler has a talent for making bootleg whisky on the premises, they will arrange to convert the barber shop into a speak-easy. Parker balks at the proposal but, faced with the alternative humiliation of finding work "downtown," agrees to the plan.

It all ends disastrously, though the play cannot be said to have an "end." We know at the last fade-out only that the family will abandon their illegal trade after (but not because) the young brother has been killed during a robbery which is one of the activities into which he had been led by Blue Haven.

None of this gives any idea of the humor, the oblique pathos, the unsentimental pain—affecting the racketeer himself—with which the story is told. If the play were to be summarized in a bald reduction of its theme, it might be stated as an account of how poverty and other wretched circumstances in the lives of a black family force them into a tragic mess, for which there is no base motive, but only the wish to enjoy life, freely and fully. But such a summation lacks the savor of what I felt while observing the characters through what, despite elements of violence, are really little more than casual happenings in a poor black neighborhood. There is no sensationalism, not even a "problem"—only the warp and woof of ordinary living: funny, crazy, frightening and somehow strangely innocent, heartwarming as much as heartbreaking. The play, the first by a writer of 30, is a "little" comedy—much more telling than many that are ambitiously "significant."

What makes it altogether delightful and arresting is the unadorned, exciting, joyous and entirely devoted nature of the acting—the kind which not only makes one believe that he is *there* (yet happily in the theatre), but that the actors have invented their own lines, on the spur of the moment. Speech and flesh are one. It all seems so artless as to constitute the truest art.

If only one member of the cast were to be singled out, it would have to be Douglas Turner in the central role. His passion, his raciness, his vigor, his total commitment to the essence of each moment make his performance one of the memorable occasions of the year: far more expressive and *useful* than some of those exuberantly touted elsewhere in town. There are few more hilarious scenes in recent days than the one in which Turner, as Parker, tells of his travail on a chain gang—a yarn which ain't necessarily so but which he makes more vividly to the point than truth itself.

It would be a critical misdemeanor to pass over Arthur French. Parker's companion in fun, games and sorrow; he is inescapably winning. And William Jay as the older son, David Downing as the younger, Rosalind Cash as their doughty sister, Samual Blue, Jr., as the racketeer, and sexy Judyann Jonsson as Parker's fling all contribute more than honorably to the evening's success.

Harold Clurman, in a review of "Ceremonies in Dark Old Men," in The Nation, *New York, Vol. 208, No. 8, February 24, 1969, p. 253.*

Jeanne-Marie A. Miller (essay date 1971)

[*Miller is an American authority on contemporary drama. She served as editor of* Black Theater Bulletin *from 1977 to 1986. In the following essay, she examines* Ceremonies in Dark Old Men *as a realistic portrayal of black ghetto experience in America.*]

Plays of the black experience are being written by the black writer who is interested in dramatizing the nuances of black life in America. Lonne Elder's statement on black writers is worth noting:

> Black writers have a particular frame of reference. They can't avoid the ghetto or the terrible deprivation or the experience of bigotry and racism. They are in the midst of it all and they have to fight to get on top of it. There is an awful kind of purity in this kind of experience. LeRoi Jones, Ed Bullins, Ralph Ellison, Douglas Turner Ward, we all express ourselves differently as artists but we all create from the same basic need—we are men and we want to be listened to.

Elder, in *Ceremonies in Dark Old Men,* a two-act realistic comedy-drama, is concerned with the life of a black family in Harlem. Its oppressed male members try to improve their lives through a get-rich-quick scheme of selling corn liquor and dart games. Parker, the dark old man in the drama, an ex-vaudeville dancer, operates an unprofitable barber shop. After his legs grew weak and he could dance no more, he retired, a man broken in spirit, and let his wife support him. He lives off the pipe dream that the barber shop will be successful and that he will write a book of stories taken from his life. While he dreams and plays checkers with Jenkins, another dark old man, his wife sickens and dies. When the drama opens, it is Adele, his thirty-year-old daughter, who, in trying to replace her dead mother, runs the household and supports her father and two grown brothers, Theopolis and Bobby. Theopolis, the brighter of the two boys, is a painter of some talent, but has depended on a variety of schemes to prevent his having to break his back and his spirit for "the man." The common enemy in this play, although he never appears, is the white man. At one point in the drama, Parker declares: "I'm telling you, them crackers is mean—don't let nobody tell you about no communists, Chinese or anything—there ain't nothing on this earth meaner and dirtier than an American-born cracker!"

The drama is set in motion when Adele threatens to put the men out of the house if they do not find jobs. The father and brothers then get involved in a money-making racket with Blue Haven, Prime Minister of the Harlem De-Colonization Association, whose aim is to drive "Mr. You Know Who" out of Harlem. Parker is not deceived by Blue and his organization, but he allows his shop to be used to sell the corn liquor made by

Theopolis and the dart games which feature the faces of white racists as targets. Bobby, Parker's younger son, becomes a member of Blue's band of thieves, who rob white-owned stores at night. The business prospers, and several of the pilfered stores are forced to close.

The new wealth, however, does not bring happiness to the Parker family. Theopolis must work constantly in order to meet the demands for his corn liquor. His unfinished painting reminds him of his lack of free time. Mr. Parker, loaded with money appears in dapper dress and harbors a new dream that he will end his days with a soft kitten of a girl in her twenties. Adele who is not a part of their new business venture, has remained on the premises, ostensibly, to hold her family together. Their tawdry success, however, only drives her into a life of debauchery with the Avenue crowd. Theopolis unhappily watches this new prosperity tear his family apart. He explains why he has entered into such a business: "I have never been lazy—I just didn't wanta break my back for the man!" The success separates the two brothers. Bobby's recently launched career of stealing brings him a new independence. Theopolis, realizing that the business is destroying his family, wants to end it, but it is already too late. His father comes home a broken man. The woman he dreamed of marrying is only a common prostitute. The gloom deepens. Bobby, his son, is killed fleeing from a robbery.

The mood of this play, poised between comedy and tragedy, its intensity of feeling and love of language, and its under-currents of rebellion remind critic Clive Barnes of Sean O'Casey's *Juno and the Paycock.* *Ceremonies in Dark Old Men,* he writes, survives despite its straggling and changing directions.

> [Elder's] theme of a man struggling for honesty in a world where honesty is not so much a luxury as an incongruity, works wonderfully. It is moving and realistic. And it is no less moving because the honesty has an ironic, bitter aftertaste.

Ceremonies ranges out of control because Elder packs too much into it—the story of a dark old man who dreams, lives off memories, and tries to squeeze a bit of love out of life before he dies; the story of a matriarchal black woman who wants her father and brothers to be respectable; the story of a bright, black young man who wants to be successful without working for the white man; the story of the professional schemer who sets up the Parker family in an illegal business; the story of the younger brother who loses his life doing what he knows best—stealing.

In an interview with C. W. E. Bigsby, Elder states that his play is written in long scenes and depends a great deal on its language, "on the tone, innuendo and rhythm." He categorizes *Ceremonies* as being "More akin to exalted realism" than naturalism, although it is naturalistic out of necessity in areas where it has to be. Although the play is based on the daily ritual of survival in the black community, this survival, declares Elder, does not "necessarily have anything to do with

A scene from Elder's 1975 television production of Ceremonies in Dark Old Men.

black/white confrontation or any clenched fist anger." Because the last scene is total irony, completely against what has gone before, despite criticism about the length of the last act, Elder believes that he is unable to turn that final scene into a third act. Making it a third act would destroy its effectiveness.

Despite the structural problems that *Ceremonies* may have, the drama is an enjoyable one both to read and to see performed. Barnes, writing in *The New York Times,* concludes that the "white view of the black ghetto has a kind of hope tinged onto it," whereas the "black view of the black ghetto is less cheerful, even though it is full of sad laughter." *Ceremonies in Dark Old Men,* in depicting a slice of this life, contains many bitter truths. (pp. 395-97)

> *Jeanne-Marie A. Miller, in a review of "Ceremonies in Dark Old Men," in* The Journal of Negro Education, *Vol. XL, No. 4, Fall, 1971, pp. 395-97.*

Dan Sullivan (essay date 1975)

[*The following essay, "What's a Nice Black Playwright Doing in a Place Like This?", originally* appeared on the "Television" page of *The New York Times in January 1975. Here, Sullivan explores Elder's recent work as a screenwriter in Hollywood.*]

Young writer has hit play, goes off to Hollywood and is never heard from again. And if he's a *black* playwright? Lonne Elder 3d is watching out.

Elder's hit was *Ceremonies in Dark Old Men* (1969), which will be presented in a new TV production by the Negro Ensemble Company tomorrow night from 9 to 11 on ABC. *Ceremonies*—a sadly knowing study of a Harlem family trying to beat the system and instead losing a son to it—was the most successful black drama since *Raisin in the Sun.* It won Elder a Pulitzer Prize [nomination], but it was not followed by another play. Instead, in 1970, Elder moved West with his wife and young son, and he has made his living here ever since writing films (notably *Sounder*) and TV scripts.

The wraparound ranch house-with-pool in suburban Sherman Oaks says that he has made a good living. But—asks the still, small voice that equates the stage with integrity and the screen (small or big) with mealy-mouthed compromise—at what cost?

So far, the losses have been, in the military phrase, acceptable. Elder has had to adjust to what he calls "the whore mentality" that smogs the film-TV industry, the assumption that one's talent is on call to an inscrutable client who will drop you the minute you fail to give pleasure. As a black writer, he has had to deal with the particular temptations of the "blaxploitation" film and the neo-Amos 'n' Andy TV comedy series, two genres that he has little respect for but that do offer good money and, what is almost as important in Hollywood, highly visible credits.

Elder has, in fact, done one blaxploitation picture—MGM's *Melinda* (1972), a splinter off that studio's successful *Shaft.* "I went in under the delusion that I could write a crime melodrama that wouldn't just titillate. I wasn't able to do it. No, I wouldn't say I'm proud of that picture. But I'm not ashamed of it, either. There were a couple of nice things in it. What puts you in a position to do what you *want* to do out here is to be successful at what you are *doing.*"

That's the realist in Lonne Elder talking, the one who explains that the ceremonies in *Ceremonies in Dark Old Men* are ceremonies of survival and that a black artist, too, had better know how to survive if he wants to do his people any good. Elder came to Hollywood, in the first place, he says, because he was sick of having people break into his apartment in New York City, and in the second place, because film and TV send "information" into everybody's heads, not just into the relatively few heads that can be reached in the theater. Since, in Elder's opinion, most of the "information" that The Industry has passed on about black life is dead wrong, a black writer has a special reason for wanting to correct it. If that involves learning to play "the Hollywood charade," he is willing to do it. Life isn't all that pure any place.

We're sitting in Elder's study. (Elder has an office at Paramount Studios but mostly works at home.) He's talking about the old days in New York City before *Ceremonies,* when he kept body and soul together by hustling. Hustling? "It's a good word," says Elder. "It doesn't mean pimping. It means working hard; really taking care of business. Like, I used to unload trucks. I was a dealer in a gambling house until somebody pulled a gun on me. I was an actor. I did what I had to do to get the time to write. I hustled!"

At 42, Elder still hustles. He finished the TV script for *Ceremonies* months ago (cleaning up the language, expanding on the barbershop setting, no major changes). Now he's got two big projects cooking: a TV-movie based on *Sounder,* which he hopes will be the pilot for a dramatic series on television, and a feature film for Paramount about the music business, *No. 1 with a Bullet,* based on Elaine Jesmer's novel.

The *Sounder* pilot, in which a black family tries to start a back-country school, will reflect the gentle, austere tone of the original story. *No. 1 with a Bullet* (the title refers to Cashbox magazine's label for a monster-hit) will be a

tough look at a black record company devouring its own. Obviously, the two films say different things. But to Elder, both say the same thing underneath, the thing that *Ceremonies* also says, namely: Get rid of those old images in your head. Blacks aren't that simple. Never were.

TV and films haven't got this straight yet, says Elder. "It's better than in the old days. But the black man still exists in the media not as a man but as a problem. A headline. Or else a clown. Those new TV comedy shows are just a twist on Uncle Tom. None of them has any kind of black control and very few are written by blacks. An actor on one of them told me, 'I was trying to do it natural, and they kept saying, "Talk black! Be black!"' Meaning, be foolish. Swagger around."

He lights a little cigar. "What it is, no one wants to really believe that black people are human. How *dare* a young black singing group think of singing anything other than soul music? How *dare* a black writer present his people as being complex? They're always ready to make a movie about black revolutionaries with submachine guns. That's less fearsome than a black character who falls into the realm of the poetic or the profound, like the father in *Ceremonies.*

"Because if the black man did emerge as a human entity, it would mean that he should participate in the culture, that he should own a part of it. That still bothers people. There's a character in *Number One With A Bullet* who wants to own it all, and that *really* bothers them."

It also bothers many people that *Ceremonies* and *Bullet* show blacks ripping-off other blacks. "There's a feeling that we've been victims of the prevailing culture for so long, why show us using each other? But what happens to the Parkers in *Ceremonies* is inevitable in the ghetto the culture has put them in. It's a place to die in. And the people in *Bullet* also had been programmed to behave that way by some very powerful people at the top of their world—they just don't realize it.

"After *Sounder,* I made a strong decision not to do anything that would enhance the historical crimes of the predominant culture on my people. But if I'm gonna be any kind of artist, I have to concern myself with truth, which isn't simple, because people aren't simple.

"As an artist, I'm much more interested in victimizers than victims. Remember the Nazis in those old war movies? You *wondered* about them. In the same way, I'd like to write about some base racist character so as to get to the core of his beastliness. I tried that with the character called Blue Haven in *Ceremonies,* not to excuse what he does to the family but to illuminate the kind of pain *he* was in, to catch him at some private moment when no one was looking.

"So Russell B. Parker, the hero of *Ceremonies* (Douglas Turner Ward, who originated the role in the New York stage production, will re-create it on TV) is a passive father with a genuine sense of command, a loving husband who let his wife work herself to death. He's based on an uncle of mine and a lot of other people. The ceremonies in the title are rituals, ways of getting by, and the old men aren't necessarily chronologically old ones. Really it's a play about old *habits*.

"The barbershop the play is set in is symbolic of a whole lot of things in black culture. A whole lot of lies are told in barbershops. A whole lot of ceremonies happen. The things I used to hear in barbershops!

"The con man, Blue Haven—Robert Hooks plays him—is just that for the family: a haven. But not one you go to. One that comes to you. Very appealing. The message, I guess, is that what looks safest and most appealing can be most dangerous and most terrifying."

Could that apply, in Elder's case, to Hollywood?

"You mean, is my fire going out? My doctor can tell you it isn't! When somebody tells me a script is due November 12, unless Lonne Elder has got the dynamics of that script where he wants 'em, that script don't get delivered, November 12 or no! And the minute Lonne Elder feels he's not doing something out here for his people, he quits!"

Elder pounds his desk happily. If he talks to producers like that, he's O.K.

> Dan Sullivan, "What's a Nice Black Playwright Doing in a Place Like This?", in The New York Times, *January 5, 1975, p. 23.*

Chester J. Fontenot (essay date 1980)

[*Scholar and playwright Fontenot has stated: "All of my writings are an attempt to reconcile the sufferings of black people with the humanity evident in the black culture." In the following excerpt, he argues that the conflict in* Ceremonies in Dark Old Men *evidences the tension between the linear and mythic conceptions of history.*]

There are a number of ways one might approach setting criteria for evaluating Afro-American drama. We might say, for instance, that a significant number of these plays employ reversals of the American minstrel tradition, and thus move from tragedy into satire and farce (i.e., Douglas Turner Ward's *Day of Absence*). Or we could say that some plays use the mysticism of Black folk tradition as a basis for building their character types (i.e., Jean Toomer's *Balo* and Adrienne Kennedy's *The Owl Answers*). We may argue that Black music (spirituals, blues, jazz) provides the key, so to speak, which enables us to decode a large number of Afro-American drama thematically by ascertaining the point(s) where the playwrights seem to be concerned with freedom, social protest, theatre for a Black audience, and so on.

Though each of these approaches is valid in itself, in this essay I want to discuss another way of criticizing Afro-American popular drama. In many of these plays, there is a tension between the linear and the mythic conceptions of history. These two conceptions are diametrically opposed views, for the linear consciousness advocates the annihilation of the Black historical past, while the mythic consciousness threatens to keep the past alive through the social conditions of the present. The former attempts to substitute for the Black historical past a version of progress which, by its very nature, implies that the conditions Black people have had to live under are vestiges of a bygone age of disharmony. According to this theory, Black people are no longer slaves, but have been integrated as full participants in society. The extent to which Black people have not become full participants in American society indicates their unwillingness to accept the routes the larger society has created for them. Within the linear conception of history, the events which produced and continue to sustain the psychological enslavement of Black people are a set of discontinuous events linked together chronologically. But these events have no real connection to one another except that they happen along a particular part of the historical cycle. These events have no real connection to the present social conditions of Black people in the sense that Black people's present social predicament is simply the result of their lack of ability to take advantage of opportunities. The linear historical consciousness negates the past in favor of a distorted version of the present and an obscure vision of some distant future.

In contrast to the linear historical conception, the mythic view of history insists on the constant recreation of the Black historical past through the actions of white Americans against Black people. Within the mythic consciousness, slavery is not a vestige of a bygone age of disharmony but is alive in the segregation of Black people in the ghettos, in the lack of employment for Black youths, and in the aborted dreams of Black people in general and Black men in particular. This vantage point implies that there is no such thing as a distant past and obscure future, but that there is only a radical present which view threatens to destroy the linear conception, since the former is better able to substantiate its claims to truth than the latter. All one has to do to support the mythic view is to point toward the present conditions of Black people. To substantiate the linear conception, one must formulate a set of abstractions which gather strength from philosophical musings, and not from historical reality or from present social conditions. The oppression of Black people tends to create a mythic consciousness wherein "progress" is not seen as something achieved through the humanistic grace of Anglo-Americans, but is rather the product of sacrifice by Black Americans. Progress, in this sense, is not organic but is an imposed system on linear history. This is viewed within the mythic consciousness as not really progress, but as appeasement.

Since Black people, for the most part, live within the mythic consciousness, they are constantly put at odds with the linear system in their attempts to cope with American society. This conflict is presented in Afro-

Paul Winfield and Kevin Hooks star as father and son in Sounder, *Elder's portrayal of an embattled black family in the Depression-era South.*

American popular drama not as vague abstractions of massive struggles of light and dark forces, of good and evil powers, but as real tensions between characters who represent either side of the dichotomy. The tension is seldom resolved, since it would take an herculean effort to synthesize moral turpitude with pragmatic choices to bring the conflict to an end. Instead, Afro-American playwrights seem to provide the reader with an analysis of the problem and to suggest different strategies by which to resolve it. Two plays which illustrate this thesis are Joseph Walker's *River Niger* and Lonne Elder's *Ceremonies in Dark Old Men;* these show the tension between myth and history. (pp. 41-2)

The shadow of the deceased mother in *Ceremonies in Dark Old Men* looms as the manifestation of the linear consciousness. Mr. Parker's daughter, Adele, constantly reminds her father and two brothers of their failure to achieve manhood through employment. Adele, the sole supporter of the family, keeps her mother's memory alive by confronting the family with the reason for Mrs. Parker's untimely demise. In one scene Adele challenges her father's devotion to her mother: "What about

Mama? She died working for you! Did you ever stop to think about that! In fact, did you ever love her? No!!" The conflict between Adele and the castrated men produces the mythic consciousness in the play.

Adele, as the breadwinner in the family, is likewise the source of moral authority. For it is she who attempts to place limits on the illegal actions her father and brothers wish to undertake. But placing these restrictions does not resolve the source of conflict between moral turpitude and pragmatic action. Even though her father might try to keep Adele happy because she pays the rent, he still feels that his dreams have been aborted and are unreachable through the route dictated to him by history—getting a job. To Mr. Parker, a job is simply a way of aborting his dreams. In the opening scene of the play, his longtime friend, Mr. Jenkins, questions the validity of Mr. Parker's masquerading as a barber when he could "count the heads of hair you done cut in this shop on one hand." Mr. Parker replies, "This shop is gon' work yet; I know it can. Just give me one more year and you'll see . . . Going out to get a job ain't gon' solve nothing—all its gon' do is create a lot of bad feelings with everybody. I can't work! I don't know how to!"

The irony in this statement is not that Mr. Parker really doesn't know how to work, but that the kind of work he is accustomed to doing is obsolete. He was a minstrel man who has been outdated by the lack of historical consciousness of the new Black generation. He is part of a distinct age of slavery and oppression. For Mr. Parker to acknowledge this fact is tantamount to him accepting the linear view of history, which advocates the annihilation of the Black historical past. Adele intensifies this struggle by her incessant demands that her father and brothers get a job.

When faced with this dilemma, Mr. Parker, his two sons, Theopolis and Bobby, and his best friend, Mr. Jenkins, choose an alternate route to fulfillment of manhood; they accept an offer from "Blue Haven," a Black gangster, to turn the barbershop into a front for manufacturing and selling bootleg liquor. But in doing this, Mr. Parker throws into chaos the moral world Adele has sought to keep intact. Bobby puts his talents at thievery to work for Blue Haven; Mr. Parker embezzles money from the enterprise to reclaim his lost youth; and Theopolis is left to do all the work.

Blue Haven symbolizes a path through which Black men can gain access to manhood, the ability to determine one's destiny. Such an ability has been stifled by segregating Blacks, by confining them to ghettos, and by prohibiting them from entering the labor force. Blue Haven—regardless of his moral code—represents an achievement for Black men, an achievement which, in its very essence, attests to the inhumanity Black people have experienced in America. Blue Haven is able to conceal his immoral actions from Mr. Parker, Theopolis, Bobby, and Mr. Jenkins, because of the attractiveness of the route he offers them. If they participate in Blue Haven's organization, they can regain the dignity they have lost in their confinement in the ghetto. After all, they have not sought jobs actively, not because there is little chance of them finding a suitable one, but because they do not wish to work for white people. To work for white people is tantamount to acknowledging the linear historical consciousness and to participating in the destruction of the mythic conception. Blue Haven's offer acknowledges the Black historical past and provides them with a route to fulfilling their role as men without "selling out," so to speak.

Just as John Williams must die in *The River Niger* to unify the cosmos which has been thrown into chaos in his search for a battlefield, Mr. Parker's youngest son, Bobby, must die in order for the family to be shocked into reality. Bobby's death while participating in a robbery attempt for Blue Haven's gang returns Mr. Parker and the rest of the family to the moral world where they see that Blue Haven's offer was not a viable choice, but only the appearance of one. Blue Haven has simply inverted the world, overturned societal values, not for the good of Black people as a whole, but for his own selfish purposes. The route Mr. Parker and his son, Theopolis, must find to manhood cannot be defined in opposition to that dictated by history. It must be firmly grounded in the Black historical past and must contain a viable vision of the future.

Ceremonies in Dark Old Men attempts to resolve the tension between the linear and mythic conceptions, but falls short. At the end of the play, the family decides to stand on moral grounds and to reject Blue Haven's enterprise in their barber shop. They make a decision to throw the equipment Blue Haven has placed in the barber shop into the river and to confront him when he comes to collect his money. The strength the family acquires in the death of Bobby might lead one to think that they will triumph, as a family, over the efforts of Blue Haven to keep them in the business of making bootleg liquor. But this resolution is somewhat superficial. Blue Haven's character is drawn in such a way that his presence dominates the play. The tone of the play shifts when Blue Haven enters the scene—the entire moral world is overturned when he makes his offer to the family. A character with this type of appeal cannot be dispensed with in such a perfunctory manner. When the play ends, there is still the feeling that Blue Haven is going to come back to the barber shop to collect his money, only to find that the family has rejected his business and has destroyed his equipment. The family must still confront the gangster with more than moral philosophical rantings. All that is finally resolved in the play is that Blue Haven represents a facade, not the resolution to the conflict between the linear and mythic conceptions of history.

The problem that is presented in these two plays is common to a large number of Afro-American plays which are aimed at large audiences. These plays attempt to present the problem DuBois speaks of in *Souls of Black Folk*. Black people live within what DuBois called "the veil," that is, the realization that one is neither a

part of American society nor a member of a distinct ethnic group which is tied to linear history. In other words, Black people experience a double-consciousness which manifests itself in the tension between the linear and mythic conceptions. In developing criteria to evaluate these plays, one must realize that drama, unlike other literary genres, is often construed as a direct manifestation of reality and not as something remote and suspended from historical reality. Afro-American playwrights have been required to make their plays directly responsive to the needs of oppressed peoples, and they have done so by presenting the conflict in the consciousness of Black people. This can serve as a basis for developing parameters within which one can operate when discussing the subject. And it can hopefully provide the dramaturgical enterprise with the perspective with which it can categorize Afro-American popular drama. (pp. 46-9)

> *Chester J. Fontenot, "Mythic Patterns in 'River Niger' and 'Ceremonies in Dark Old Men'," in* MELUS, *Vol. 7, No. 1, Spring, 1980, pp. 41-49.*

FURTHER READING

Review of *Ceremonies in Dark Old Men,* by Lonne Elder III. *Choice* 7, No. 1 (March 1970): 100.
> Brief review of *Ceremonies in Dark Old Men* , noting: "It is a tragedy with laughs. A remarkable example of a realistic play put to good use in our time, it is more Ibsen than LeRoi Jones."

Fenderson, Lewis H. "The New Breed of Black Writers and Their Jaundiced View of Tradition." *CLA Journal* XV, No. 1 (September 1971): 18-24.
> Surveys contemporary black literature. Fenderson notes: "Lonne Elder's *Ceremonies in Dark Old Men* is a play of provocative challenges—whether a black man can resolve his problems more readily by participation in big city rackets, or by revolting against the system."

Gant, Liz. "An Interview with Lonne Elder III." *Black World* XXII, No. 6 (April 1973): 38-48.
> Interview with Elder about his development as a writer for the stage and screen. The discussion focuses on his two 1972 screenplays, *Melinda* and *Sounder*.

Jeffers, Lance. "Bullins, Baraka, and Elder: The Dawn of Grandeur in Black Drama." *CLA Journal* XVI, No. 1 (September 1972): 32-48.
> Examines realistic depictions of ghetto life in literature and drama. Jeffers holds that the Parker family in *Ceremonies in Dark Old Men* serves as a microcosm for black people as a whole.

Shepard, Richard F. "Lonne Elder Talks of Theater in Black and White." *The New York Times* CXVII (8 February 1969): 22.

Traces Elder's early life and emergence as a playwright, focusing on his portrayal of blacks in the theater.

Ralph Ellison

1914-

(Full name Ralph Waldo Ellison) American novelist, essayist, short story writer, critic, and editor.

Ellison is recognized as one of the most influential and accomplished American authors of the twentieth century. He is best known for his highly acclaimed novel *Invisible Man* (1952), a work that affirms the need for the individual to attain self-awareness. Honored with the National Book Award for fiction, *Invisible Man* is regarded as a masterpiece for its complex treatment of racial repression and betrayal. Shifting between naturalism, expressionism, and surrealism, Ellison combined concerns of European and African-American literature to chronicle an unnamed black youth's quest to discover his identity within a deluding, hostile world. Although critics have faulted Ellison's style as occasionally excessive, *Invisible Man* has consistently been praised for its poetic, ambiguous form, sustained blend of tragedy and comedy, and complex symbolism and characterizations.

Born in Oklahoma City, Oklahoma, Ellison was raised in a cultural atmosphere that encouraged self-fulfillment. After studying music from 1933 to 1936 at Tuskegee Institute, a college founded by Booker T. Washington to promote black scholarship, Ellison traveled to New York City, where he met author Richard Wright and became involved in the Federal Writers' Project. Encouraged to write a book review for *New Challenge,* a publication edited by Wright, Ellison began composing essays and stories that focus on the strength of the human spirit and the necessity for racial pride. Two of his most celebrated early short stories, "Flying Home" and "King of the Bingo Game," foreshadow *Invisible Man* in their portrayal of alienated young protagonists who seek social recognition. "Flying Home" is set during World War II and depicts a young black pilot whose obsessive desire to rid himself of stereotypes causes him to become contemptuous of his own race. After his airplane crashes, he is nursed back to health by a group of farmers who awaken his sense of cultural kinship and self-esteem. The anonymous protagonist of "King of the Bingo Game" is desperate to save his dying wife and enters a bingo tournament hoping to win enough money to hire a doctor. As the tournament proceeds, the bingo game becomes a symbol of his inability to control his destiny.

Although he originally envisioned writing a war novel, Ellison instead began work on *Invisible Man* following his honorable discharge from the United States Merchant Marines in 1945. His initial intention, to show the irony of black soldiers fighting for freedom who return to a civilian life of oppression, developed into a broader psychological study of the individual in society. Most critics consider the unspecified action of *Invisible Man* to take place between the early 1930s and 1950s. The

novel's picaresque hero is often compared to Voltaire's Candide, who remains optimistic despite enduring betrayal, manipulation, humiliation, and the loss of his illusions. Narrating his story from an underground cell, the anonymous protagonist explains in the prologue that he is involuntarily invisible because society sees his social stereotype rather than his true personality. Establishing the novel's themes of betrayal and anonymity, the narrator recalls how he was raised in the South, named valedictorian of his high school graduation class, and invited to recite a speech for the community's prominent white citizens. This episode, which critics often refer to as Ellison's "battle royal" chapter, was originally published as a short story entitled "Invisible Man" in *Horizon* magazine. Among other degradations, the protagonist and several other black youths invited to the meeting are forced to participate in blind boxing matches and to crawl for money on an electrified carpet. Only after he has suffered these humiliations is the narrator allowed to recite his speech. Although largely ignored by the drunken gathering, Ellison's hero is presented with a college scholarship and assumes that education will help overcome the racial problems he encounters. The evening's brutality convinces him that he will be rewarded if he does what white people expect, and this naive assumption provokes an identity crisis.

While attending a Southern college that strongly resembles Tuskegee Institute, the protagonist is assigned to chauffeur Mr. Norton, a white philanthropist, and innocently takes him to visit Jim Trueblood, a disreputable sharecropper whom Norton believes to be a colorful storyteller in the folk tradition of Uncle Remus. Upon hearing Trueblood's account of incest with his daughter, Norton is both horrified and fascinated by the indulgence in moral taboos that he himself has secretly considered transgressing. Many critics concur that this episode contains some of Ellison's finest dialogue and characterizations. By evoking society's reactions to Trueblood, Ellison refuted stereotypes of ethical, principled whites and decadent, unscrupulous blacks. Following Trueblood's revelation, the narrator takes Norton to a saloon called the Golden Day. The saloon's name refers to the Era of Reform between 1830 and 1860, during which many citizens entertained idealistic hopes of social reform that were later thwarted by industrialism and materialistic values. Norton's visit occurs at a time when the saloon is crowded with American veterans of World War I who, after fighting overseas for the freedom of others, were institutionalized for refusing to conform to segregation laws. One patron, a brilliant brain surgeon, later gives the narrator advice for his future: "[The] world is possibility if only you'll discover it." The narrator contemplates the surgeon's comment as he travels north, a move reminiscent of the Great Migration of the 1920s, when displaced southerners journeyed to the industrialized northern United States to obtain employment.

Expelled from college for his misadventure with Mr. Norton, Ellison's protagonist travels to the Harlem district of New York City in search of a job. He possesses sealed letters of reference from Doctor Bledsoe, president of his former university, that are later revealed to contain character defamations. The narrator nonetheless obtains employment with Liberty Paints, a company that manufactures white paint to be used in the bleaching of national monuments. As the result of an accident for which he is held responsible, the protagonist is hospitalized and given a form of electroshock therapy intended to mimic the effects of a lobotomy. Although desensitized, he vividly recalls the folklore of his Southern boyhood and emerges with a new sense of racial pride, while the superficiality of his previous experience is erased. For the first time he is unashamed of his background and asserts his disdain for servile blacks by dumping a spittoon on a man whom he mistakes for Doctor Bledsoe.

Following an impromptu speech that he delivers on a street after discovering that an elderly couple have been evicted from their home, the narrator of *Invisible Man* attracts the attention of the Brotherhood, an organiza-

tion that critics generally equate with American Communist associations of the 1930s. After briefly embracing the group's utopian ideals, he discovers that the Brotherhood merely feigns interest in civil rights while actually working to repress blacks and deny their individuality. The chaos that ensues in the black community following the frenzied exhortations of a fanatic nationalist develops into a hallucinatory treatment of the Harlem race riots of the 1940s and culminates in the protagonist's final rejection of false identities. Wright Morris asserted: "Mr. Ellison handles this surrealist evening with so much authority and macabre humor, observing the forces with such detachment, that the reader is justified in feeling that in the process of mastering his rage, he has also mastered his art." Upon escaping the uproar of the riots, the narrator accidentally falls into a coal cellar that leads to the cell where he eventually achieves self-definition. Although he succumbs to anger by stealing electricity from the local power company, he deduces that his experiences have made him a unique individual. Despite his invisibility, the protagonist realizes that he must accept social responsibility and face the world.

Although attacked by black nationalists for lacking stringent militancy toward civil rights issues, *Invisible Man* garnered laudatory reviews immediately following its publication and has continued to generate scholarly exegeses. Many critics have commented on how the book's dexterous style, dense symbolism, and narrative structure lend intricacy to its plot. The narrator, who reflects on his past experiences, is observed as both an idealistic, gullible youth and as an enlightened, responsible man who actively addresses problems that may result from social inequality. Timothy Brennan declared: "[The] language and methods of the protest tradition are wielded by Ellison with an ambiguous voice, never finally pronouncing or judging, but building to a culmination of alternating hope and bitterness, rebellion and despair."

The most controversial issue concerning *Invisible Man* involves its classification as either a work written for and about blacks alone or as a novel with universal import. Critics who insist the book strictly concerns black culture maintain that the experiences, emotions, and lifestyles described could not possibly be simulated by white authors, while supporters of the more prevalent view that *Invisible Man* transcends racial concerns contend that the protagonist's problems of illusion, betrayal, and self-awareness are experienced by every segment of society. Ellison himself asserted that *Invisible Man* is a novel that attempts to provide a portrait of the American individual who must define his values and himself despite a transitory existence. Jonathan Baumbach observed: "Refracted by satire, at times cartooned, Ellison's world is at once surreal and real, comic and tragic, grotesque and normal—our world viewed in its essentials rather than its externals. Though the protagonist of *Invisible Man* is a southern Negro, he is, in Ellison's rendering, profoundly all of us."

Ellison is also highly regarded for his accomplishments as an essayist. *Shadow and Act* (1964) collects twenty-two years of reviews, criticism, and interviews concerning such subjects as art, music, literature, and the influence of the black experience on American culture. This acclaimed volume is often considered autobiographical in intent and is noted for its lucidity and insights into *Invisible Man. Going to the Territory* (1986), which contains speeches, reviews, and interviews written since 1957, echoes many of the concerns of *Shadow and Act.* Making use of ironic humor in the manner of *Invisible Man,* Ellison here reflected on personal influences and payed tribute to such creative mentors as Richard Wright and Duke Ellington. Ellison's short stories remain uncollected but are anthologized in such volumes as *A New Southern Harvest* (1957), *The Angry Black* (1962), and *Soon, One Morning: New Writing by American Negroes, 1940-1962* (1963; published in Great Britain as *Black Voices*). The latter book contains "Out of the Hospital and under the Bar," a noted excerpt deleted from *Invisible Man.*

Ellison's influence as both novelist and critic, as artist and cultural historian, is enormous. A measure of his stature and achievement is his readers' vigil for his long-awaited second novel. Although Ellison often refuses to answer questions about the work-in-progress, there is evidence to suggest that the manuscript is very large, that all or part of it was destroyed in a fire and is being rewritten, and that its creation has been a long and painful task. Most readers wait expectantly, believing that Ellison, who said in *Shadow and Act* that he "failed of eloquence" in *Invisible Man,* won't publish his second novel until it equals his imaginative vision of the American novel as conqueror of the frontier and answers the Emersonian call for a literature to release all people from the bonds of oppression.

Eight excerpts from this novel-in-progress have been published in literary journals. Set in the South in the years spanning the Jazz Age to the Civil Rights movement, these fragments seem an attempt to recreate modern American history and identity. The major characters are the Reverend Hickman, a one-time jazz musician, and Bliss, the light-skinned boy whom he adopts and who later passes into white society and becomes Senator Sunraider, an advocate of white supremacy. As Robert G. O'Meally noted in his 1980 study *The Craft of Ralph Ellison,* the major difference between Bliss and Ellison's earlier young protagonists is that despite some harsh collisions with reality, Bliss refuses to divest himself of his illusions and accept his personal history. Says O'Meally: "Moreover, it is a renunciation of the blackness of American experience and culture, a refusal to accept the American past in all its complexity."

Like *Invisible Man,* this novel promises to be a broad and searching inquiry into identity, ideologies, culture, and history. The narrative form is similar as well; here, too, is the blending of popular and classical myth, of contradictory cultural memories, of an intricate pattern of images of birth, death, and rebirth. In *Shadow and Act* Ellison described the novel's form as "a realism extended beyond realism." What the ultimate form of the novel will be—if, indeed, these excerpts are to be part of one novel—remains hidden. But the pieces seize the reader's imagination even if they deny systematic analysis.

One thing does seem certain about these stories. In them Bliss becomes a traitor to his own race, loses his hold on those things of transforming, affirmative value. Hickman, on the other hand, accepts and celebrates his heritage, his belief in the timeless value of his history. The tone of these excerpts is primarily tragicomic, a mode well-suited to Ellison's definition of life. As he wrote in *Shadow and Act,* "I think that the mixture of the marvelous and the terrible is a basic condition of human life and that the persistence of human ideals represents the marvelous pulling itself up out of the chaos of the universe." Elsewhere in the book, Ellison argued that "true novels, even when most pessimistic and bitter, arise out of an impulse to celebrate human life." As *Invisible Man* before and the Hickman novel yet to come, they celebrate the "human and absurd" commixture of American life.

(For further information about Ellison's life and works, see *Black Writers; Concise Dictionary of American Literary Biography, 1941-1968; Contemporary Authors,* Vols. 9-12; *Contemporary Authors New Revision Series,* Vol. 24; *Contemporary Literary Criticism,* Vols. 1, 3, 11, 54; and *Dictionary of Literary Biography,* Vols. 2, 76.)

PRINCIPAL WORKS

"Flying Home" (short story) 1944; published in *Cross Section;* also published in *Dark Symphony: Negro Literature in America,* 1968
"King of the Bingo Game" (short story) 1944; published in periodical *Tomorrow;* also published in *Dark Symphony: Negro Literature in America,* 1968
Invisible Man (novel) 1952
"Out of the Hospital and under the Bar" (prose) 1963; published in *Soon, One Morning: New Writing by American Negroes, 1940-1962*
Shadow and Act (essays and interviews) 1964
Going to the Territory (essays, lectures, and interviews) 1986

Wright Morris (essay date 1952)

[*A prolific American writer who has published works in a variety of genres, Morris is best known for novels in which he focuses on such themes as the quest for identity, relationships between males and females, the effects of the past on people's lives, the relativity of knowledge, and the values associated with material success. In the following excerpt from an essay first published in* The New York Times Book Review *in 1952, he explores the concepts of "invisibility" and "the underground" in* Invisible Man.]

The geography of hell is still in the process of being mapped. The borders shift, the shore lines erode, coral islands appear complete with new sirens, but all the men who have been there speak with a similar voice. These reports are seldom mistaken as coming from anywhere else. As varied as the life might be on the surface, the life underground has a good deal in common—the stamp of hell, the signature of pain, is on all of the inhabitants. Here, if anywhere, is the real brotherhood of man . . . .

[The title character of Ellison's ***Invisible Man***] lives, he tells us, in an underground hole. To fill this dark hole with light, he burns 1,369 bulbs. He burns them free. A fine Dostoevskyan touch. In his *Notes From the Underground* Dostoevsky says: "We are discussing things seriously: but if you won't deign to give me your attention, I will drop your acquaintance. I can retreat into my underground hole."

The Invisible Man is also discussing things seriously. His report in this novel might be subtitled, "Notes From Underground America," or "The Invisible Black Man in the Visible White Man's World." That is part of his story, but the deeper layer, revealed, perhaps, in spite of himself, is the invisible man becoming visible. The word, against all of the odds, becoming the flesh. Neither black nor white flesh, however, for where the color line is drawn with profundity, as it is here, it also vanishes. There is not much to choose, under the skin, between being black and invisible, and being white, currently fashionable and opaque . . . .

[The Invisible Man's] report begins the day that rich men from the North, white philantropists, appear on the campus of a Negro college in the South. They are there for the ceremony of Founders Day. The Invisible Man, a student at the college, is chosen to act as the chauffeur for one of them. He shows him, inadvertently, the underground black world that should not be seen. Before the day is over, both the millionaire and the student have been disillusioned, and the student, expelled from the college, leaves for New York.

In the city he becomes increasingly invisible. Hearing him rouse the crowd at the scene of a Harlem eviction, a key party bigwig sees a bright future for him in the brotherhood. The mysteries of the Order, revealed and unrevealed, as they fall to the lot of the Invisible Man, have the authentic air of unreality that must have bemused so many honest, tormented men. The climax of the book, and a model of vivid, memorable writing, is the night of the Harlem riots. Mr. Ellison handles this surrealist evening with so much authority and macabre humor, observing the forces with such detachment, that the reader is justified in feeling that in the process of mastering his rage, he has also mastered his art . . . .

The reader who is familiar with the traumatic phase of the black man's rage in America, will find something more in Mr. Ellison's report. He will find the long anguished step toward its mastery. The author sells no phony forgiveness. He asks none himself. It is a resolutely honest, tormented, profoundly American book.

"Being invisible and without substance, a disembodied voice, as it were, what else could I do?" the Invisible Man asks us in closing. "What else but try to tell you what was really happening when your eyes were looking through! And it is this which frightens me: Who knows but that, on the lower frequencies, I speak for you?"

But this is not another journey to the end of the night. With this book the author maps a course from the underground world into the light. *Invisible Man* belongs on the shelf with the classical efforts man has made to chart the river Lethe from its mouth to its source.

> *Wright Morris, "The World Below," in* The New York Times Book Review, *April 13, 1952, p. 5.*

Anthony West (essay date 1952)

[*West was an English novelist, critic, biographer, and editor. In the following excerpt from a 1952 New Yorker review, he praises the vitality and depth of* Invisible Man.]

Ralph Ellison's first novel, ***Invisible Man,*** is an exceptionally good book and in parts an extremely funny one. That is not to say that it is without defects, but since they are almost entirely confined to the intolerably arty prologue and epilogue, and to certain expressionist passages conveniently printed in italics, they can easily be skipped, and they should be, for they are trifling in comparison with its virtues. What gives it its strength is that it is about being colored in a white society and yet manages not to be a grievance book; it has not got the whine of a hard-luck story about it, and it has not got the blurting, incoherent quality of a statement made in anger. What gives it its character is a robust courage; it walks squarely up to color the way seventeenth-century writing walks up to mortality and death, to look it in the face as a part of the human situation that has to be lived with. Mr. Ellison's hero is a Negro of the South who starts out with the naïve illusion that what stands between him and the whites is a matter of education. He is given a scholarship to a Southern college that has been endowed by Northern philanthropists, and he goes to it in great delight, thinking that what he will learn there will pare away all his disabilities and disadvantages. He finds that the college cannot do that for him and does not even try to do it; it is concerned only with helping him make realistic adjustments to things as they are. He gets into a mess of trouble and is expelled. Before expelling him, the dean tells him just what the facts of colored life are:

> You have some vague notions about dignity . . . .
> You have some white folk backing you and you don't want to face them because nothing is worse for a black man than to be humiliated by white folk. I

know all about that too . . . . But you'll get over it; it's foolish and expensive and a lot of dead weight. You let the white folk worry about pride and dignity—you learn where you are and get yourself power, influence, contacts with powerful and influential people—then stay in the dark and use it!

He is too young and too nobly stubborn to believe that this is the best that can be done with his life, and the rest of the book deals with his attempts to force the world to accept him on a pride-and-dignity basis, and with his final realization that he has to stay in the dark as an invisible man. This could easily be a glum and painful performance, but Mr. Ellison has the real satirical gift for handling ideas at the level of low comedy, and when he is most serious he is most funny. The technique is that of which *Candide* is the supreme example, but there is nothing archaic about the writing, which has an entirely contemporary vitality and a quite unexpected depth.

The first chapter is a little slow, but the second and third, which describe the trouble that leads to the hero's expulsion, convince one that Mr. Ellison is a writer with much more than promise. (p. 93)

A good deal of [*Invisible Man*] is concerned with penetrating to the unease and self-consciousness that underlie a great many earnest white progressive approaches to The Question. After the student is kicked out of college, he goes North to try to make his way in New York, and his adventures are told in a highly imaginative, picaresque story, but, though the storytelling is excellent, in the end the impressive thing is the analysis of attitudes that rises out of each situation; there are always such sharpness of observation, such awareness of shades of feeling, at work. The hero is caught up in what is clearly an agit-prop apparatus of the communist Party (Mr. Ellison does not, though, give it that name) that is exploiting the color situation in Harlem. He is a natural speaker and he is made use of in campaigns as a front for the white committee. There is not only perceptive writing about the feeling between Negro and white in this part of the book but there is also perhaps the best description of rank-and-file Communist Party activity that has yet appeared in an American novel . . . . At last, the hero discerns the rank stink of falsity in the Party line about color, partly through catching on to the way in which a white Comrade who has married a colored girl makes play with the fact to strengthen his hand in policy discussions of district tactics, partly through a realization that the white Comrades have used him as a lure, as a Negro gull to gull other Negroes. He sees that his district leader, Brother Jack, is just as much Marse Jack as a field boss in a white-supremacy state. The description of his disillusion with the Party, a true agon, which is also his final understanding that there is no external machine that can produce any ready-made solution either to the color problem or to his own perplexities, is as moving and vivid a piece of writing on this difficult subject as one could wish to read.

The book ends with a . . . tour de force . . . . The Party has lost control of its agitation campaign as a result of what at first seems to the hero to be a typical tactical blunder, and the mass support that it has won drifts over to a straight anti-Communist and anti-white agitator called Ras, whose wild speeches bring on a wave of rioting and looting. The drift into disorder and the spread of violence are astonishingly well described in realistic terms, and through it all Mr. Ellison never loses touch with his gift for comic invention. As the riot builds up, the hero realizes that not only have the Communists an unfriendly interest in him but that he is due for unpleasantness from Ras's strong-arm men . . . . The hero's evasions as all Harlem comes apart have a real nightmare humor. And in the middle of it all, as the riot squads and the mounted police move in and shooting begins, he suddenly sees what is happening. The Party has not made a tactical blunder at all; it has deliberately surrendered its mass following to Ras in order to provoke violence, so that colored martyrs, shot down by the police, can be exploited in the next phase of agitation in the district. The hero emerges in his own identity to warn the innocents he has helped to fool what is being done to them. But Mr. Ellison has a tight grip on his satiric comedy, and he is not going to let his buffoon hero escape into tragedy; martyrdom is not to be *his* fate. A gang of white looters chase him up a dark street, and he falls through an open manhole into a coal cellar. The whites, enraged by this surprising vanishing trick, slam the manhole cover down and leave him lying there helpless while the riot burns itself out above.

Few writers can have made a more commanding first appearance. Up to a point, *Invisible Man* resembles Céline's *Death on the Installment Plan*. Its humor recalls the jokes that hang on Céline's fraudulent scientist, with his ascents in worn-out and patched balloons, his absurd magazine, and his system of electromagnetic plant culture, but Ellison's jokes are on the whole funnier, and his satire is much more convincing because there is clearly visible behind it—as there is not in Céline—a positive alternative to the evils he is attacking, the knowledge of a better way without which all satire becomes merely an empty scolding. It is a pity that Mr. Ellison's direct statement of the better way takes the form it does in the prologue and the epilogue, since they are the two worst pieces of writing. But the ideas toward which they fumble are as dignified as they are impressive, and it is perhaps unnecessary to have this direct statement; as they are so plainly implied in the rest of the book. It is not merely the Negro who has to realize that the only escape from the rattrap of worry about what one is or is not is to abandon the constant tease of self-consciousness. The Invisible Man of Mr. Ellison's title is the unattached man of Aldous Huxley's Perennial Philosophy, the man with courage to be utterly indifferent to himself and to his place in the world, the man who is alone free to be fully a man. (pp. 94-6)

Anthony West, "Black Man's Burden," in The New Yorker, *Vol. XXVIII, No. 15, May 31, 1952, pp. 93-6.*

Ralph Ellison with Richard Kostelanetz (interview date 1965)

[*An American poet, essayist, literary critic, and novelist, Kostelanetz is best known for his studies of avant-garde writers and their works. The following excerpt is from a 1965 interview he conducted with Ellison for the British Broadcasting Corporation. In a headnote to the 1989 first printing of the text, Kostelanetz noted: "What follows is an interview that I did with Ralph Ellison for the BBC in the fall of 1965. Keep that date in mind when you hear some of these replies. His reputation as one of America's best writers is based on only one novel, which was published in 1952.* Invisible Man *received the National Book Award the following year and in 1965 a large poll of American critics and writers judged* Invisible Man *to be the best single novel of the post-war period." Here, Ellison discusses his growth as a writer, focusing on the genesis of* Invisible Man.]

[Kostelanetz]: *How did you turn to writing?*

[Ellison]: Actually, I turned to writing before I realized what had happened. Sometime during my high school days, it must've been around the eleventh grade, I had a very bad cold that just clung to me. The school nurse, Miss Waller, saw me on the street one day—I was still coughing—and she made me go to a lung clinic at one of the hospitals. I had to wait in a reception room with all these obviously ill people. I was rather horrified and I began to try to describe what was going on to some of the people who were around me. I was doing it in the style, I thought, of O. O. McIntyre, who was a syndicated columnist who used to appear in the Oklahoma City papers. I remember that as a first doodling with writing. The next thing I did was to set to verse a thing on the swamp country by the Southern writer Albion Tourgée. I took this to the American literature teacher and he looked at me as though I had gone out of my mind, because I hadn't shown too much interest in the class itself. I got passing grades but I had never tried to do any writing or shown any real interest in literature as it was being taught, although I read quite a lot; so you have that in the background. It was nothing that I did consciously or with any intensity, but those were the beginnings. The other thing was, reading the prefaces of Shaw when I was in high school. A friend's parents' library had all of Shaw and I thought those prefaces—I think the first one I read was a preface to *Candida*—most incongruous, but there it was. I remember that in my themes in school, I tried to get some of the Shavian quality in my writing but there again, no one paid any attention to it and I didn't take it seriously.

What was the point after that?

The point after that was that I became very, very much involved with modern letters after I read *The Waste Land.* I was so intrigued that I started reading all the commentaries that I could find. Among them Edmund Wilson's *Axel's Castle,* Harriet Monroe's book of criticism, and Babette Deutsch's book of criticism. I read a lot of Pound, and Eliot's essays. Evidently I was actually

trying my hand at writing poetry during those days, because years later Al Murray pointed out to me that he had found some of my attempts in a library book. I suppose I blanked that out of my mind. Incidentally, I never wrote a decent poem, but the conscious concern with writing began there at Tuskegee: again without my being conscious that it was a forecast of what I was going to do. It was a kind of innocent word-play. Then I came to New York during my junior year (1936) intending to work that summer and return. That didn't work out, but a few months after I'd been in New York I met Richard Wright. He asked me to review a book for the magazine, *New Challenge,* that he'd come to New York to edit. After my review was published, he asked me to do a short story. I had never tried to do a piece of fiction, never in my life! So I made my first attempt at a short story at Wright's suggestion. My story got to the galley proof stage, but then, thanks to a dispute between Wright and his fellow editors, the magazine was discontinued before my story could be published. Naturally, I was disappointed, but that's how I got started writing fiction.

What did you find in Eliot?

I found imagery for one thing; I found overtones of a sort of religious pattern which I could identify with my own background. I also saw a style of improvisation—that quality of improvising which is very close to jazz. Most people think I'm being pretentious when I say this but it grows out of a similar and quite American approach to the classics, just as Armstrong and any other jazz musician of that period would take a theme and start improvising. Then he would pay his respects to *Aïda,* to any number of operas, to light opera, or to religious music. All this came out in the course of the improvisation. It was these pinpoints of familiarity that made me want to solve the mystery. *The Waste Land* had the quality of a conundrum anyway, so you were really trying to trace the thing down and make it whole within your own mind.

Unlike some other Afro-American writers, you choose to live in America, indeed, near Harlem. Why?

Living here is the only living that I could do as a novelist. I lived in Italy for two years when I had the Rome Prize. But, for all of its difficulties, I had to face the challenges of the United States. Now that's one thing. Why do I live always close to other Negroes? Because I have to hear the language. My medium is language, and there is a Negro idiom, in fact there are many Negro idioms in the American language. I have to hear that sounding in my ears, I have to. A place like Harlem, or any American Negro community, has an expressiveness about it which is almost Elizabethan. Things are revealed in speech in the streets. There's a lot of humor and the language is always feeding back to the past; it's throwing up wisdom, it's throwing up patterns and I never know but when I'm going to hear something just in the street which is going to be the making of some piece of fiction that I'm trying to write.

Is it fair then to speak of Harlem as a ghetto?

I think that this is one of the most damaging misuses of a concept that has ever come about in the United States. A ghetto implies a cultural and religious distance. That's where the term came from.

It came to describe the Jewish neighborhoods...

That's right.

...on the Lower East Side...

Not only the Lower East Side but it comes from Europe, as we know, and it had a content there which obscures further the relationships between American whites and American Negroes. Language for one thing, for another the patterns of myth—of universal myths, so to speak, of Christian myth, and so on as they have been given embodiment in terms of Negro patterns. It's not too difficult to look at John Henry and see the Hercules myth. If you are aware of the connections, if you know where to look. It's not too unusual to see that the rhetoric of a Negro sermon, for instance, can be traced back to Shakespeare, if you know where to look, or to the metaphysical poets. I'm not saying that these very often unlettered ministers have read John Donne, but on the other hand they are possessors of a living tradition.

And have heard people who have read John Donne.

That's right. Actually you find now that the great tradition of nineteenth century eloquence in oratory is most alive within the Negro community. We don't find it so much in Congress anymore, but you find it among Negroes, especially right in the churches.

This is because American Negro culture is more oral?

Yes, it is still more oral than literary but it would be a mistake to look upon it as primitive, because it is informed by the usual American concerns.

By this you mean that Negro culture can't be anything but American culture?

In the United States it's a part of the general American culture, the language itself. The American English would not have the same music in it if it were not for the existence of great numbers of Negroes and great numbers of white Southerners, who have learned their English partially from Negroes. This is not true on the other hand where you have people who spoke or who speak a different language. In Harlem, in fact in most so-called Negro ghettos, a lot of Negroes do not spend most of their time there. They work outside. They work as domestics in white homes; they're cooking, they're taking care of children, they're teaching them their manners, they're changing their diapers; they are completely involved in America on that level. The music, the dances that Americans do are greatly determined by Negro American style, by a Negro American sense of elegance, by an American Negro sense of what the American experience should be, by what Negroes feel about how an American should move, should express himself. The ghetto concept obscures this. It's much better to say you have slums. It's an old term and it doesn't cause as much confusion. It's economic, not cultural.

One way in which the American tradition appears in **Invisible Man** *is the tradition of story-telling. People are telling stories about experiences.*

Yes, that's true. And I connect this with certain problems in the novel. James, for instance, had some negative things to say about the first person point of view making for loose and baggy monsters. And I happen to feel that one of the things I wanted to prove, to myself at least, was that you could write a dramatic novel using the first person.

But the blues singer sings in the first person, too.

Yes, and the blues singer is one of the most developed of existentialist poets, but we never think about it in that way. It wasn't until Sartre began to have his novels translated here that I became aware that some of the blues were much better statements of the existentialist position than he was able to embody, in *Nausea* for instance...

For example?

Well, "Troublin' Mind" is an example, any number of Leroy Carr's blues...

Would you say then analogously your book is to Western literature as jazz is to Western music? And, in effect a product of Negro American culture? Which is still American, which is still Western?`

Yes, I would just point out that they are both Western, they are both American precisely because they try to use any and everything which has been developed by great music and great literature. As for music, on the other hand, I suspect that the one body of music which expresses the United States—which expresses this continent—is jazz and the blues. What we have with Western music, with so-called classical music, is an American version of Western classical music.

What do you mean when you say that many books written by Negro writers are intended for a white audience?

Well, I think that when you examine these books you will find that in expressing Negro protest the writer directs his protest, his emotion, his plot even toward a white audience. I suppose, what I mean by this is that the books tend to be overly sociological, that they are ultimately about civil rights, about sociological conditions rather than an attempt to reveal personality living within certain conditions.

Isn't there a sense in which the white audience expects a Negro to be angry about the condition of being Negro in America?

I'm afraid so, and if the conditions were good I think that many white readers would expect the Negro writer to be angry because he wasn't white. I mean you have that thing operating underneath. More seriously, I try to use an approach which is dictated not by my anger or my lack of anger, not by my protest or any lack of feelings of protest, but by the logic of the art itself. I write what my imagination throws up to me and I must feed this back through my own critical sensibility. That critical sensibility is informed by a sense of life which grows in its immediacy out of my being part of the Negro American group. That's where I find an oral tradition, that's where I found my closest friends who are a great part of my life, that's where my parents were, that's where my friends were. That's where emotion, that is the emotional content of ideas and symbols and dreams, is to be found, where I can release myself, release whatever creative capacity that I have. There is a kind of ideal reader and that ideal reader would be a Negro who was in full possession of all the subtleties of literature and art and politics. You see what I mean? Not out of racist motives do I imagine this ideal reader, but to give my own experience, both acquired and that which I was born with, its broadest possibilities.

Is there any particular person who is your ideal reader?

No, I don't think so. The best reader of course is the person who has the imagination, regardless of what his color is. Some readers, I suspect, bring more imagination to a work than the author has put into it. And when you get that kind of reader you're very fortunate because he gives you a stature, let's say, that you haven't really earned.

Well, there are ways of misreading **Invisible Man.** *One way is to think that it's autobiographical.*

Yes, that's true. It is not autobiographical.

But the first person narrator?

Yes, I did this, as I say, as an attempt to see whether I could write in the first person and make it interesting, make it dramatic and give it a strong dramatic drive.

But there's a sense in which **Invisible Man** *might first strike a reader as a catalogue of adverse experiences of an innocent Negro in America. Is this a correct interpretation?*

I would think that it was an incorrect and sentimental interpretation inasmuch as the narrator of the book could have stopped much of his experience had he been willing to accept the harsh nature of reality. He creates much of his own fate. I don't look upon him as heroic in that way. I think that he made a lot of mistakes. But many white readers certainly are so sentimental about the Negro thing that they can's see that.

Isn't one of his more universal failures a failure of perception? He doesn't understand his own experience. He doesn't understand why he fails.

I think so. It's a failure of perception and it's a sort of wrong-headed desire to summon up, to take on an identity imposed upon him by the outside, when we know very well that each individual has to discover himself and the world for himself. Usually this is done through some sort of pain. But I must say that this is a tough guy because he goes through many, many experiences which should have driven him to himself and to his reality.

In what sense does the title apply? How is the narrator or the Negro an invisible man?

Well, I wasn't writing about *the* Negro. I was writing about a specific character, in specific circumstances, at a specific time. The invisibility, there is a joke about that which is tied up with the sociological dictum that Negroes in the United States have a rough time because we have *high* visibility.

Your color is very apparent.

High pigmentation, so the formula has it, which is true. No one will ever mistake me for white. But the problem for the narrator of *Invisible Man* is that he creates his own invisibility to a certain extent by not asserting himself. He does not do the thing which will break the pattern, which will reveal himself, until far along in the book. So he is not a victim. At least not merely a victim. He is a man who is wrong-headed.

For some years now you have been working on a second novel. Parts have appeared to critical acclaim. Why does it take so long to write a novel?

Well, it takes me a long time because I have a deep uncertainty about what I am doing. I try to deal with large bodies of experience which I see as quite complex. There is such a tendency to reduce the American experience, especially when it centers around the Negro experience. I'm constantly writing—I write a lot—but I have to put it aside. It has to gel, then I come back. If I still react positively to it, if I can still see possibilities of development, then I keep it.

As a novelist, what do you think is the ultimate purpose of your profession?

For me, I think it is to seize upon the abiding patterns of the American experience as they come up within my own part of the American nation, and project those patterns, those personality types, those versions of man's dilemmas, in terms of symbolic actions. Reduce it to eloquent form—that sounds perhaps pretentious but I think that's what the novel does—

Oh, so modest!

Oh, I don't mean to be too modest.

Do you mean that you don't assume that the novelist can have any great social reforming power or have any great expansive power or any great power as a spokesman?

I think that the good novelist tries to provide his reader with vivid depictions of certain crucial and abiding patterns of human existence. This he attempts to do by reducing the chaos of human experience to artistic form. And when successful he provides the reader with a fresh vision of reality. For then through the symbolic action of his characters and plot he enables the reader to share forms of experience not immediately his own. And thus the reader is able to recognize the meaning and value of the presented experience and the essential unity of human experience as a whole. This may, or may not, lead to social change or bring the novelist recognition as a spokesman. But it is, nevertheless, a form of social action, and an important task. Yes, and in its own right a form of social power. (pp. 2-10)

> *Ralph Ellison and Richard Kostelanetz, in an interview in* The Iowa Review, *Vol. 19, No. 3, Fall, 1989, pp. 1-10.*

David Littlejohn (essay date 1966)

[*In the following excerpt from his 1966 study* Black on White: A Critical Survey of Writing by American Negroes, *Littlejohn assesses theme, content, and motive in* Invisible Man, *labeling the novel "the supreme work of art created by an American Negro."*]

Ralph (Waldo) Ellison stands at the opposite end of the writer's world from Richard Wright. Although he is as aware of the issues of the race war as anyone else, he is no more a consciously active participant than, say, Gwendolyn Brooks or William Faulkner. "I wasn't, and am not, primarily concerned with injustice, but with art." He achieves his extraordinary power through artistry and control, through objectivity, irony, distance: he works with symbol rather than with act. He is at least as much an artist as a Negro. He accepts both roles so naturally, in fact, that he has made them one. His one novel [*Invisible Man*], the supreme work of art created by an American Negro, is essentially a Negro's novel. It is written entirely out of a Negro's experience, and reveals its full dimension, I am convinced, only to the perfect *Negro* reader. But it is not a "Negro novel." Like Gwendolyn Brooks, like Faulkner, like most serious artists, he has transmuted himself and his experience almost entirely into his art. Only by turning to his essays and interviews can one discover the degree to which his own opinions, on racial issues or any other, are implicit in *Invisible Man.*

Invisible Man (1952) was not, Ellison insists, "an attack upon white society." . . . It is not, really, a race-war novel. But as no Negro's life in America, not even in the symbolic recreation, can be entirely free of racial combat, there are elements in the book that can be legitimately read in a race-war context. (pp. 110-11)

Several instances of direct propaganda occur, although each time in so organically convincing a situation that one does not think of attributing them to Ellison directly. They are simply taken as true, dramatically and substantially. (pp. 111-12)

[This] book is, among other things, a complete story of Negro life in America. By nature something of a pacifist, a quietist, Ellison is much more free than the embattled protestors like Wright to try to tell *all* of the Negro's story. It has been the theme of his entire creative life, in fact, that there is far, far more to the Negro's story in America than oppression, suffering, and hate: "The view from inside the skin," he insists, "is not so dark as it appears to be." (p. 113)

The focus of all [his] propaganda and history and ironic sociology is the nameless hero, the Invisible Man ("invisible," that is, to white men's eyes), the Negroes' Joseph K. It is his story, really, not the race's, not the war's, except insofar as he is of the race and in the war. (His non-naming, through five hundred pages, never becomes obvious or ominous—a testimony to the subtlety of Ellison's art. It is simply never needed.) The creation and loving sustenance of this narrator-hero, with all his follies and limitations, are among the triumphs of the book.

Reaching out from the central artifice of the narrator-hero are other displays of Ellison's art. His style, the "fine texture," is exact and acute, the language (usually) at fingertip control. Hear the crisp offhandedness of wicked ironies, the cool black humor; or . . . the needle-sharp evocations of sensation and interior pain. He can manipulate language, as he can character, event, and design, for the optimum effects of irony, of a balanced double vision. Certain devices, tiny tricks, he leaves about like fingerprints: the strange selectivity of detail that leaves characters and objects and events undefinably charged, "off," ever so slightly left of real; the pre-announcement of a thing some lines before it is identified, giving to it an eerie surreality. Ellison has also, to move to items of slightly larger focus, the fullest sense of drama; he knows when to signal and advance a key moment, how to pace and position effects for the fullest buildup of artful tension or comedy or suspense: he can work up cool quiet horror like Harold Pinter, or handle the giant crescendo of effects needed for pageants like Clifton's funeral or the Harlem riots.

His rhetorical skill is prodigious, and he is not reticent about displaying its range. Not only does he indulge himself in perfect mimicry of the tall tale, the emotion-charged address, the Negro sermon; he also allows himself chances for Joycean word display, and makes his hero's hold on history a "way with words," a gift of tongues, an awesome and dangerous eloquence like his own.

Ellison's creative imagination, if such a talent can be singly regarded, is also more prolific than that of his peers. His exotic range of living characters, their vividness and magnitude; the extraordinary sequence of scenes and situations, each rendered with overflowing fullness—rooms, inner states, mob scenes, the fantasia of the hospital, the unforgettable battle royal at the Southern white men's smoker with which the novel opens: such independent creations bear witness to one of the most awesomely fertile living imaginations in American writing. (pp. 114-16)

His proper tradition *is* that of the great American novelists, as he so hoped it would be, and it is among them, rather than among the New Negroes, that he should be judged. Hawthorne and Melville, certainly, are of the family, and Faulkner and Fitzgerald: all the great ironists of the double vision, the half-romantic, half-cynical creators and retailers of the corrupted American dream. They are all symbolic artists, who charged their objects and events and effects with preternatural significance, who designed their fictions into national myths. He is not up *there,* of course; but I see no reason not to assign him a place—even for one unbalanced book—at least in the high second rank, with such other ironic idealists as Sherwood Anderson or Nathanael West. (p. 119)

> David Littlejohn, "Negro Writers Today: The Novelists I," in his Black on White: A Critical Survey of Writing by American Negroes, *Grossman Publishers, 1966, pp. 101-37.*

Edward Margolies (essay date 1968)

[*An American authority on African-American literature, Margolies has written widely on the life and works of novelist and autobiographer Richard Wright. In the following excerpt from his* Native Sons: A Critical Study of Twentieth-Century Negro American Authors, *he examines Ellison's depiction of black life in America in* Invisible Man.]

[It] was not until the 1920's that Negro authors seriously attempted to deal with the folk materials in their culture. And when they did, the authors of the Harlem school treated Negro life self-consciously, as if somehow Negroness and poverty produced a superior kind of humanity, given to song and dance, and to a primitive, noble, exotic happiness as opposed to the corruption and neurosis of the surrounding white civilization.

The stark years of the thirties forced the Negro author to take a more realistic assessment of his situation. Frequently he labored under a structured ideology not altogether suited to his problems, but in any event he was required by this kind of discipline to relate what was unique in his culture to a broader over-all concept of history. During the first half of the decade the Communists appeared to champion an independent state located somewhere in the South, but after 1934 more and more stress was laid on full-fledged assimilation and integration into American life. This forced Negro intellectuals to examine even more closely their own ambivalent assimilationist and separatist views.

One of these was a young college student, Ralph Ellison, who came to New York in 1937 and began writing under the guidance and encouragement of a confirmed Party member, Richard Wright. Wright himself had written about the problem of Negro cultural identity and its place in a pluralistic society. Ellison almost immediately took up the dilemma, and in a sense devoted all his energies to its pursuit. (pp. 128-29)

No one could have been better suited, by virtue of his training and upbringing and experience, to undertake the challenge. Born in Oklahoma City in 1914, when caste lines were not yet so rigidly drawn as in other parts of the South, Ellison enjoyed a freedom to partake of the various crosscurrents of American life that were still sweeping across that near-frontier area. Not only did he encounter in his day-to-day experiences persons of different backgrounds, but he learned their songs, dances, and literature in the public schools. Moreover, he attended films and theater and read books avidly, and none of these suggested to him the "limitations" of Negro life. (p. 129)

He knew best, of course, his Negro culture, and he projected on his vision of the outside world the specificities of a Negro outlook.... [Jazz] and especially blues provided him with the greatest sources of satisfaction. In his growing years, Kansas City jazz attained its ultimate refinement in the environs of Oklahoma City, and figures like Jimmie Rushing, Hot Lips Paige, Charlie Christian, and others became heroes to hosts of Negro boys. And if jazz was not regarded as being quite respectable in the schools he attended, he was given a rather impressive training in classical music so that he could make comparisons and perceive relationships. Thus for Ellison it was not simply a case of Negro culture standing apart, but a convergence in which Negro culture maintained its separate identity in a wider spectrum.

Not surprisingly, Ellison's understanding of his early life corresponds to his definition of Negro jazz. And ultimately it is jazz, and blues especially, that becomes the aesthetic mainspring of his writing.... [Music], however tragic its message, is an affirmation of life, a celebration of the indomitable human spirit, in that it imposes order and form on the chaos of experience.

> The delicate balance struck between strong individual personality and the group...was a marvel of social organization. I had learned too that the end of all this discipline and technical mastery was the desire to express an affirmative way of life through its musical tradition and that this tradition insisted that each artist achieve his creativity within its frame. He must learn the best of the past, and add to it his personal vision. Life could be harsh, loud and wrong if it wished, but they lived it fully, and when they expressed their attitude toward the world it was with a fluid style that reduced the chaos of living to form.

(pp. 129-31)

The hero of *Invisible Man,* in the course of a journey from the deep South to Harlem, assumes a variety of poses, most of which he believes in at the time, to fit the white man's definition of a Negro. But each of these roles fails him, and a kind of chaos ensues..., for no one of them takes into account the fluidity and complexity of his individual being. At the end of the novel, hidden away in a forgotten basement room in an apartment building, the hero comes to no true resolution of his dilemma except the realization that his humanity is invisible to most persons, Negroes as well as white, and that he must discover for himself what he thinks, feels, and is. Yet the mere act of telling his story in novel form has given order to the meaninglessness of his experiences, and has thus become an affirmation, a celebration of life. He intends, he says, to ascend to the surface soon, to have another "go" at the world.

The novel is no more than a recapitulation of the pain the hero has suffered in his twenty or so years—the telling of which is its own catharsis. No social message, no system of beliefs, no intellectual conclusions arise from his tale other than his own consolation in telling it. Yet in the telling, he cannot but see the comically absurd aspects of his existence, of all Existence—and his narration is therefore not without humor. (Ellison told one interviewer that he thought he had written a very funny book). *Invisible Man* is tragic in the sense that it celebrates the hero's capacity to endure, comic in the sense that he avers the fecundity of life, the wealth of the possibilities he may choose (and he often chooses wrongly) amidst the abundance of chaos.

Ellison has several times described this view of life as blues. In 1946 he wrote:

> The blues is an impulse to keep the painful details and episodes of a brutal experience alive in one's aching consciousness, to finger its jagged grain, and to transcend it, not by the consolation of philosophy but by squeezing from it a near-tragic, near-comic lyricism. As a form, the blues is an autobiographical chronicle of personal catastrophe....

Ellison also sees the blues as serving a ritual function.

> The blues speak to us simultaneously of the tragic and comic aspects of the human condition and they express a profound sense of life shared by many Negroes precisely because their lives have combined these modes.... This is a group experience...and any effective study of the blues would treat them first as poetry and ritual.

Invisible Man opens with a prologue in which the hero, in his secret basement room, announces he is about to recite the catastrophic events of his life.... He has been playing a Louis Armstrong record, the refrain of which runs: "What did I do / To be so black / And blue?" In a sense, this refrain implicitly follows each of the major episodes of the novel. As his attempts to play out the roles that whites have assigned him (each of them different, but all of them dehumanizing, like variations on a theme) meet with disaster, the hero in effect asks himself Armstrong's punning question. He has tried to

play the game according to the rules but has each time discovered himself more bruised. Thus each episode serves almost as an extended blues verse, and the narrator becomes the singer. The epilogue brings us back to the present; the reader is returned to the basement room, and the hero tells us that despite his psychic wounds (he has dreamt that he has been castrated), he has not yet given up on life. Hence the novel ends as it had begun, just as the last verse of a blues is frequently the same as the first.

Since the blues, according to Ellison, is by its very nature a record of past wrongs, pains, and defeats, it serves to define the singer as one who has suffered, and in so doing it has provided him with a history. As the novel develops, the hero takes on the role of a Negro Everyman, whose adventures and cries of woe and laughter become the history of a people. As a high-school boy in the South, he is a "Tom"—little better than a darky entertainer; in college, a Booker T. Washington accommodationist. When he moves North, he works as a nonunion laborer and then flirts for a while with Communism. Finally, he becomes a Rinehart, Ellison's word for the unattached, alienated, urban Negro who deliberately endeavors to manipulate the fantasies of whites and Negroes to his own advantage. But besides being a kind of symbolic recapitulation of Negro history, the blues structure of the novel suggests a philosophy of history as well—something outside racial determinism, progress, or various ideologies, something indefinably human, unexpected and perhaps nonrational.

In one sense the negro since Emancipation has telescoped the American experience, passing from an agrarian existence to a highly industrialized urban life. In another sense this history is enigmatic—not only invisible but unformed—a history in which chance and accident act as principles in a designless universe. So long as men demand predetermined patterns of their universe, in order to reassure themselves that existence is not chaotic (which it is), they will demand that Negroes play out certain roles to conform to these patterns. But there is an issue of "necessity" involved. The Negro, like any other man, is unresolved nature, mysterious and complex, and cannot by the very exuberance of his being long play out these roles. When this occurs, illusion is then momentarily stripped away and chaos is seen for what it is. But the white man, terrified at these realities, proceeds to force upon the Negro still another role to suit yet another fancied pattern of existence. Does this mean that history and life need be perceived as unmitigated purposelessness? In effect Ellison never truly resolves the question aesthetically. But he seems to be saying that if men recognize first that existence is purposeless, they may then be able to perceive the possibility of shaping their existence in some kind of viable form—in much the same manner as the blues artist gives form to his senseless pain and suffering. (pp. 131-34)

As the novel proper opens, the hero recalls his grandfather's dying words: "I never told you, but our life is a war and I have been a traitor all my born days, a spy in the enemy's country ever since I give up my gun in the Reconstruction." He goes on to advise, "I want you to overcome 'em with yeses, undermine 'em with grins, agree 'em to death and destruction, let 'em swoller you till they vomit or bust wide open." These then will be the tactics the Negro will employ for survival in years to come. He will pretend to agree to his invisibility until reality strikes down the white man for his obdurate blindness. The novel then proceeds to record the hero's various initiation rites into invisibility wherein the white man accords him several identities—none of them human. Ultimately his is a journey into self-recognition. He recognizes first that he is invisible—and second, that he is a man. (pp. 134-35)

The tone of the first half of the novel is that of an almost Gulliverlike innocence. [The hero] relates objectively how "sincerely" he attempts to fulfill his roles, how deeply he believes in them. As a high-school graduate, he is invited to deliver his valedictorian address on humility as being the "very essence of progress" to a smoker of the leading white citizens of the town.... The hero is finally allowed to give his speech (at first scarcely anyone appears to be listening), but there is very nearly an explosive situation, when, by a slip of the tongue, he mentions social equality. At the end of his speech, he is given a briefcase in which, during the course of his subsequent adventures, he will place tokens and mementos of the various identities the Negro has assumed during his history.

The second episode takes place in a Southern Negro college whose buildings and environs—magnolias, honeysuckle, moonlight—the hero describes in glowing (faintly satirical) terms. The college has been endowed in large part by Northern liberals who, since Reconstruction, have endorsed Booker T. Washington's twin principles of equality and caste submission—not only a logical contradiction, but, again, a kind of blindness to reality. But here Ellison is suggesting as well that the Northern white liberal philantropist demands the invisibility of the Negro no less than his Southern racist counterpart, in order to conceal from himself his ancestors' complicity in Negro slavery. Ellison, in this portion of the novel, employs, in addition, constant allusion to Negro history as a means of discovering the Negro's present invisibility. The hero relates, for example, the presence on the campus of a statue of the Founder, a former slave, who is removing (or placing?) a veil from (or on?) the eyes of a kneeling Negro. Was Negro enlightenment simply another guise of keeping the Negro in the dark, invisible from himself?

There are mellow scenes of students assembled in chapel singing symphonic and devitalized slave spirituals for white patrons. Or a moving and eloquent address by an ancient Negro minister rehearsing the life, trials, and achievement of the Founder. The Founder's immense sacrifices, the students are told (probably for the thou-

sandth time) in wonderful old-fashioned ringing rhetoric, have made possible the progress and happiness they enjoy today. At the close of his speech, the minister stumbles as he leaves the rostrum and the students suddenly realize that the minister is himself blind.

Some of the best passages in the novel occur when the hero, an honors student, acting as chauffeur to one of the white patrons who has been visiting the college, inadvertently drives him beyond the picturesque manicured environs of the college campus past the old slave quarters. This is a part of the countryside Mr. Norton has never before seen and he is met with reality for the first time. The habitations are unchanged since antebellum days and the Negro peasants living thereabouts are regarded as little better than barbarians by the middle-class college community. Norton talks to one of them, Jim Trueblood, who recounts the fantastic events relating to his incest with his daughter, which has made him a celebrated figure among the whites in the county. (Respectable Negroes are ashamed.)... At the close of Trueblood's story, Norton apparently suffers a heart attack, and the hero takes him to a Negro roadhouse, the Golden Day, in order to revive him with whisky. As luck would have it, they arrive at about the same time as a group of Negro mental patients, shellshocked veterans of World War I, who pay periodic visits under guard for a respite of drinks and disreputable women. A wild riot erupts and Norton is hurt and hustled out, but not before one of the veterans tells him that for all his vaunted philanthropy, the Negro is not a human being but a "thing," a cipher to satisfy his guilt and his cravings for adulation and love.

Here Ellison suggests the results of a hundred years of white liberal patrimony of the Negro. Large financial donations may afford the givers some illusion of having fulfilled their moral obligations, but failure to recognize the Negro's humanity has produced only a worsening of pain.... Although Norton would like to believe the college is a monument to his efforts, in reality the maddened rioting veterans of the Golden Day are his true fate. They represent the logical absurdity of his dream, for they are not, like Trueblood, Negro peasants bound to the soil, but testimonials to Negro progress—doctors, lawyers, teachers. Thus has Ellison married elements of the Negro's invisible past to the Negro's invisible present: slavery (Trueblood), Reconstruction (the college campus), philanthropy (Norton), and World War I (the veterans)—all resulting in a chaos called The Golden Day. (pp. 135-38)

[As the novel ensues], Ellison moves from the white-Negro Southern power structure to the Negro's Northern plight. Bledsoe has ostensibly suspended the hero for the summer months but has provided him with letters of identity to important New York capitalists who might employ him. The journey North has a blues ring, especially when the hero discovers that Bledsoe too has deluded him with false promises. But the hero does manage to find work at the Liberty Paint Company, whose motto reads, "Keep America Pure with Liberty

Paints." His first task is to infuse ten drops of a blackish substance into buckets of a white base liquid and stir, the result being a product called Optic White which is used in repainting national monuments. Here Ellison's allegory becomes a little too obvious.

The hero is next assigned to work at the furnaces of a basement, three levels underground, with a strange little Negro foreman named Lucius Brockaway. It develops that Brockaway, who has charge of all the immensely complicated machinery below ground—boilers, furnaces, cables, pipes, wires, and so on—is indispensable in running the plant. Efforts to displace him with white engineers have resulted in a total breakdown of production.... From simple allegory Ellison has moved to a more subtle kind of symbolism. Somewhere beyond the narrative level, he is saying that America has depended from the start on the unacknowledged skills and sacrifices of Negro labor.

But if Brockaway is the indispensable man, he is also the white capitalist's man as well. He is fiercely opposed to labor unions, and when he learns that the hero, during his lunch hour, inadvertently stumbled onto a union meeting (in which, incidentally, a discussion had been proceeding regarding the employment of nonunion Negro workers), he accuses the hero of treachery and betrayal. He attacks the hero and the two wrestle weirdly in the underground chamber—a Northern echo of the battle of the boys at the white citizens' smoker. Just when the hero believes that Brockaway has finally reconciled himself to his presence, a boiler explodes and the hero awakens to discover himself in the plant hospital. (pp. 138-40)

The hero is released from the hospital and dismissed from his job ("You just aren't prepared to work under our industrial conditions"), after an operation intended to produce in him a new and more docile personality.... Yet the operation does not altogether remove his identity. He remembers snatches of folklore and songs his grandmother had sung to him as a child which seem strangely applicable to his situation. The past lives on, then, in the present, and whatever else urban life and the Depression may have done to him, they have given him a greater sense of pride and an awareness of his history.

The hero now strides through the streets of Harlem somehow reassured by the swarming black life about him. He eschews the black middle class that hopelessly and ludicrously models itself on the white bourgeoisie—his first place of residence, Men's House, is a haven for such persons—and lives in a boardinghouse run by Aunt Mary, a formidable mother-earth figure who cares warmly for the lost and bewildered children of her native Southland. Nor is the hero any longer ashamed of Southern Negro foods that identify him with a slave and peasant ancestry. On one occasion he stops to purchase a yam from a Southern street vender. "I am what I am," he says as he bites in the hot buttered delicacy.

But if urban life awakens the hero to emotions of a specific Negro historical identity,...the Depression expands these feelings to include an active sense of social responsibility the hero now shares with many other city Negroes. And the latter part of the novel deals with some of the forces that endeavored to make political use of the new awakening in Negro communities.

Black nationalism, the first of these, is represented in the figure of Ras the Exhorter, an exotic West Indian extremist. The hero sees Ras violently addressing a street corner gathering when he first arrives in Harlem from the South. He pays little attention at the time but when he later involves himself with the Brotherhood (the Communist Party), Ras and his followers play a distinct role in his experiences. Ras, who suggests something of the colorful Marcus Garvey, preaches a doctrine of complete black virtue coupled with an utter distrust of the white man. (pp. 140-41)

The hero is recruited by the Brotherhood when, after witnessing the physical eviction of an elderly Negro couple from their tenement, he delivers a fiery speech protesting the injustice of it all to a gathering street crowd. Even here, Ellison suggests the specific Negro history that has ultimately placed the unhappy pair on the dreary Harlem sidewalk. He cites the pathetic paucity of personal effects they are allowed to keep, among them a small Ethiopian flag, a tintype of Abraham Lincoln, a manumission paper dated 1859, a pair of "knocking bones" used in minstrel shows, some faded and void insurance policies, and a "yellowing newspaper portrait of a huge black man with the caption: 'MARCUS GARVEY DEPORTED.'" (pp. 141-42)

Ellison perhaps devotes too much space proportionally to the Communist wooing of the Negro, but these are experiences he knew, after all, firsthand, and the marxist emphasis on Negro history as being part of a larger dialectical process must have appealed to Ellison's ingrained aesthetic sense. In any event, his hero's Communist experiences are too complicated to chronicle fully. He becomes an authentic Harlem "spokesman," but even when he is most blinded by his Marxist rhetoric, there persist in the marrow of his being some suspicions regarding the relevance of his Negro experience to the notions of history he publicly upholds. Indeed, Ras's violent and chauvinistic opposition to Brotherhood ideals is closer to what the hero knows to be true. What he finally learns in the course of his radical adventures is that even for the Brothers, the Negro is a thing, an object, an instrument of power politics and of preordained historical design, rather than a divinely complex and complicated human mystery. (p. 142).

Yet his experiences as a radical are not a total loss. For one thing, the hero, like his author, has acquired an education of sorts regarding the Negro's role in history. If what the hero learns is at considerable variance from what the Brotherhood wanted him to learn, he does nonetheless take away with himself an added sense of his own importance. Second, and possibly more important, is that in making him a Harlem leader, the Brotherhood has unwittingly given him access to his fellow Negroes on a level he had hitherto seldom achieved. He discovers to his astonishment (and to the chagrin of the Brothers) a bond of love and shared experience that the outside world can never know.

In one of his first performances for the Brothers, he addresses an assembly of Negroes on the question of rent evictions. (pp. 142-43)

As a result of his speech, his reputation is established. He begins to campaign against rent dispossessions, but then quite unexpectedly he is transferred downtown, ostensibly for further indoctrination. Upon his return several months later, he learns that the agitation he had begun so successfully has lost nearly all its momentum and that the community has become hostile to the Brotherhood for its betrayal.... His anxieties are further aroused when he learns that Tod Clifton, his closest Harlem comrade and a Brotherhood lieutenant, has vanished.... Later the hero witnesses Clifton being shot to death by a policeman who had been trying to arrest him.

On his return subway trip to Harlem, the hero ponders Clifton's death, and then as he observes a trio of zootsuited adolescent Negro boys sitting quietly in front of him, he realizes that:

> They were men out of time—unless they found Brotherhood. Men out of time, who would soon be gone and forgotten.... But who knew (and now I began to tremble so violently I had to lean against a refuse can)—who knew but they were the saviors, the true leaders, the bearers of something precious? The stewards of something uncomfortable, burdensome, which they hated because, living outside the realm of history, there was no one to applaud their value and they themselves failed to understand it. What if Brother Jack were wrong?.... What if history was not a reasonable citizen, but a madman full of paranoid guile and these boys his agents, his big surprise! His own revenge? For they were outside, in the dark with Sambo, the dancing paper doll, taking it on the lambo with my fallen brother, Tod Clifton (Tod, Tod) running and dodging the forces of history instead of making a dominating stand.

Here then is the blues theme as applied to history. The accidental, the unplanned, the unforeseen variables of history are symbolized by the presence of the Negro, who because of his invisibility should not logically exist, but who nonetheless endures and may, on some future occasion, transform events overnight. And the mere fact of his survival, despite sufferings, defeats and repressions, represents an affirmation of life that undercuts any "system" of history. Because human beings are involved, history, like blues, records only the possibilities of existence.

The hero organizes a huge procession for the dead Clifton on the streets of Harlem.... The Brotherhood at once makes plain its opposition to the hero's militan-

cy and he is now finally convinced he has once more been betrayed. He intends as vengeance to delude them as they had all along been deluding him. He will follow his grandfather's advice: "overcome 'em with yeses, undermine 'em with grins" until the entire Harlem community erupts in their faces. He will pretend to them that their more pacific plans to organize the community are eminently successful, while in reality he knows that Harlem seethes with social and racial tensions, not the least of which are aimed at the Brotherhood.

Since much of the hostility of the community is directed toward him as being an instrument of a white man's organization, the hero determines to take a new identity. He settles for a wide-brimmed white hat and dark glasses—but the disguise works only too well. He is constantly being stopped on the street by persons who mistake him for someone named Rinehart. But on each occasion they know Rinehart as possessing a different occupation.... The hero is thus reborn as Rinehart, whose "world was possibility...[a] vast seething hot world of fluidity" in which Rinehart plays many roles. For the real Rinehart had evidently perceived the Negro's world as an undesigned Chaos in which he could have as many images as he wished. Is this not the white man's world as well, the hero wonders, since no understanding of history can have any validity if it fails to recognize the Negro's existence? Here, Ellison and his hero stand at the brink of existential despair, where values such as love, honor, and integrity have no meaning.

But before he can resolve his disturbed vision, the hero is pulled back into a Harlem uprising of destruction and violence for which he is in part responsible.... [Pursued by a pair of white hoodlums he] dives into an open manhole and ultimately finds his way into the discarded basement room which will become his home.

In the basement room the hero decides that he has all along been invisible. But before he can determine who he is, Ellison makes him discard the contents of the briefcase he has been carrying ever since the night of the smoker. In the course of his life he has collected a number of objects which he has "unthinkingly" stuffed in his briefcase. In effect these represent not only his past identities but the roles the Negro has played in history. At one time or another, the briefcase has contained a small antique cast-iron bank for coins molded in the figure of a red-lipped, minstrel Negro (economic exploitation), a leg shackle (peonage), his high-school diploma (his Jim Crow education), Clifton's Sambo doll (his minstrel role), a letter from Jack identifying him as a Brother, and his dark Rinehart glasses. In jettisoning these, as it were, the hero can come to a true recognition of himself.

In isolating the historical theme of Ellison's blues, one does not, of course, begin to do justice to the novel. The narrative pace is swift and engaging, and the hero's adventures possess their own intrinsic interest. Moreover, Ellison's symbols seldom intrude as they explain, and yet are quite as original as they are functional. Nonetheless, splendid and ambitious as Ellison's novel is, it does not quite succeed. Perhaps one reason is that his hero, owning no identity or at best an invisible one, does not create in the reader any real empathy. He is not a lovable rogue, nor a goodhearted innocent, but merely a passive figure who, for the most part quite mindlessly, allows things to happen to him. This was of course Ellison's intention, but given the sustained length of the novel and the colorlessness of the protagonist, the reader is made more and more aware that he is reading a book. There is simply too much distance between the reader and the hero and one finds oneself subconsciously congratulating the author for the deftness with which he moves his character along, rather than paying attention to his troubles or his meaning. Secondly, there is a singleness of theme—the hero's invisibility—and episode after episode plays variations on this theme. It is as if one were compelled to listen to a marvelous blues extended to symphonic length. One may admire its various parts, but wish after a while for a different kind of movement—to catch oneself up in surprise or elation or another level of comprehension.

In all fairness, Ellison attempts to do this. The tone of the hero changes from that of a gullible innocent in the beginning to that of a straightforward narrator somewhere midway in the novel, to that of a somewhat more sophisticated observer of himself later on. And Ellison himself has said of his novel that it moves stylistically from naturalism to expressionism to surrealism—all of which is true. But these are, after all, effects, and the single idea still dominates. One somehow expects more, for all its richness, and the "more" is seldom forthcoming.

Which brings us once again to the thematic weakness of the novel. For Ellison's hero simply has nowhere to go once he tells us he is invisible. He does indeed, in the Epilogue, say that he intends to rise again and try his hand at life, that he has faith in democratic principles, and that life itself is its own excuse despite the blows it has dealt him. But there is no evidence in the text to fortify his beliefs. The blues singer has depths of feeling to begin with, but Ellison's hero has just begun to learn to feel as the novel ends. (pp. 143-48)

> *Edward Margolies, "History as Blues: Ralph Ellison's 'Invisible Man'," in his* Native Sons: A Critical Study of Twentieth-Century Negro American Authors, *J. B. Lippincott Company, 1968, pp. 127-48.*

F. H. Langman (essay date 1976)

[*In the following excerpt, Langman offers a mixed review of* Invisible Man, *noting especially Ellison's handling of set pieces and characterization in the novel.*]

Ralph Ellison's *Invisible Man* has suffered some fierce attacks, survived, and seems now to be taking its place as a classic. The attacks on it have been usually for bad reasons, misreading and the misapplication of dogma; but it has been defended for reasons often equally bad. Much of the dispute has shown not the irrelevance to literature of the clamour for social relevance but its sometimes stupefying shallowness and lack of focus. Critics on both sides have used the novel as a pretext to affirm their own preconceptions, slogans, and wishes. But others who have tried to lift the debate to a level more technically sophisticated, more literary in a restricted sense, have generally done no better. If anything they have done worse, because they have obscured the ways in which a concern with literary quality can show itself through serious, exacting assessment of the claim to social significance in such a work....

Like much else in the intellectual fiction of its period (1952), *Invisible Man* puts itself rather self-consciously at the service of a criticism specializing in elaborate mechanical analysis. Its reward has been high praise, but the praise seldom touches the life of the book. Thus critics have been able to trace through it a complex pattern of symbols and motifs; images of sight, of the visible and the invisible, of black and white, dark and light, have been counted through, assembled, interpreted.... To recognize these patterns has some point: they are certainly present. Yet to accept them as significant grants far too much. The kind of organization they represent is inadequate, without further development, to mediate deeper understanding, to give substance to the novel's key inter-relationships, or to pull the whole work together in a meaningful way. Beneath the intricate surface pattern, the novel may remain unrealized and incoherent. (p. 114)

Invisible Man is clearly a novel into which a good deal of impassioned thought has entered. It seeks to take a position, it formulates and reformulates a persistent problem, and by the fabling, allegorical cast of its narrative it invites interpretation in depth. Critics have pointed to the universality of the book's preoccupations. Although it tells the story of a black man's search for himself—his name is never given—it represents more than the quest for black identity. It is at once more specific, a very individual story, and more general, dramatizing the identity-crisis of a whole society. The case of the hero is seen not as unique but only as heightened by his blackness, made more dramatically explicit. He is seen as a quintessential American, trying to find his real nature through the succession of roles he is called on to play, trying to restore the traditional values his society professes but disregards, trying to reaffirm his personal innocence while caught up in the corruption of history. To recognize all this is to become aware of what the novel undertakes, of its scope and serious intent. It would be a mistake, however, to suppose the undertaking significant merely because of its scope, or to take it seriously because of its earnest ambitions. Even at the high level of generality prompted by thematic interpretation, where almost anything can be made to seem important, the novel's main conceptions may appear as facile as they are familiar. The necessary critical question is whether these conceptions are adequately realized in the novel, brought convincingly to life and mastered.

The answer is that the manifest intentions of *Invisible Man* remain largely embryonic. It is a novel of patches, a few of them brilliant, but as a whole deeply unsatisfying. Part of what makes it so unsatisfactory is the evidence it contains of how good it might have been. At its best the novel races along, vivid, funny, thoughtful, powerful; but it quickly flags, time after time. Then the meanings become forced, the comedy wilful, the judgments perverse or confused.

In form, *Invisible Man* is picaresque. That accounts sufficiently for its loosely episodic sequence, and enables it to accommodate the inset tales which provide its main strength. But it is riven by kinds of confusion and indeterminacy more fundamental than such considerations of form can explain. The narrative moves through a variety of styles, not in a controlled and cumulative development but, it seems, according to the fluctuations of merely local impulse, passage by passage. Documentary literalism alternates with surreal nightmare, farce with rather previous lyricism. The trouble is not that these modes are intrinsically incompatible, or could not be unified by ironic counterpointing: it is that the novel as a whole lacks orchestration. In addition, Ellison's success in each mode is unsustained, fragmentary. The novel reads as a succession of improvisations, often weakly derivative and eclectic in their models. Thus the abounding verbal quibbles and attempts at lyrical fine-writing carry strong but pointless (and damaging) reminders of James Joyce. (pp. 114-15)

Like the unaccountable changes in style, the passages of pastiche and imitation can be taken as signs of technical immaturity, but it is difficult to separate that from an immaturity of conception. Wavering between parody and simple attempts to emulate, they indicate an author unsure what effects he wants to produce and from what moral position he writes. Similar indications occur elsewhere, in fact almost everywhere in the texture of the prose: an uncertainty of touch is in the grain.

At its best the prose has remarkable vigour and sweep. It is contemporary, fluent, figuratively rich, rhythmically apt and various.... (p. 116)

More typical of the prose—the novel has a multitude of sentences and extended passages like it—is this passage:

> Shuddering into motion, the machine gave a sudden scream like a circular saw, and sent a tattoo of sharp crystals against my face. I moved clumsily away, seeing Brockway grin like a dried prune. Then with the dying hum of the furiously whirling drums, I heard the grains sifting lazily in the sudden stillness, sliding sand-like down the chute into the pot beneath.

This is characteristic in its fresh, vivid particularity; characteristic too in its weaknesses—the use twice in

three sentences of "sudden" (one of Ellison's most overworked words), the intrusive alliteration, the straining for effect. The sense of strain, of an attempt to force words to do what the imagination has failed to do, is endemic in the novel. It comes most often from the extended comparisons, the paradoxes, the sheer violence of expression in sentences like this:

> I had to take myself by the throat and choke myself until my eyes bulged and my tongue hung out and wagged like the door of an empty house in a high wind.

What makes that example particularly telling is its emptiness of reference in the context. The protagonist is describing the outrage done to his own feelings on the occasions when he had tried to justify and affirm the mistaken beliefs of his friends, "saying 'yes' against the nay-saying of my stomach". The realities of experience to which that would correspond are simply not in the novel. The convictions of the protagonist have been too nebulous, his conscience too opportunistic, to provide concrete instances of the self-suppression the quoted sentence lays claim to. (p. 117)

[What saves *Invisible Man* from dismissal is] Ellison's gift for writing set pieces, those self-contained episodes and passages in a special style which display his considerable gifts at their best. Some readers have found the first of such pieces, the account of the battle royal, so effective that the remainder of the novel seems one long anti-climax. But the best single sequence, the one in which the author's urbane sense of complexities and his powerfully aroused emotions are held together in full equipoise, is Jim Trueblood's story.

Faulkner provides the model here. We catch his note in the sly humour, the idiom, the long, additive, conversational sentences. But whatever Ellison has learned from Faulkner he here makes his own, and the character of Trueblood—abject, proud, calculating, naive, sardonic, stoical, loving—is created with economy, insight, compassion and zest.

Trueblood's recollection of the time in his young manhood when he would lie in bed with his girl on summer nights and listen to the moving along the river establishes the moral ground of the tale. In his evocation of sounds and sights, the sensations of encroaching sleep, the multiple blended enjoyments of repose, companionship, spectacle, there is a human reality, and a sense of the deep satisfyingness of life, which transform the raw farce of his disgrace. His shameful act itself comes to seem an outcome of his innocent capacity for the enjoyment of life, and leaves untouched the fundamental self-respect to be felt here:

> They used to have musicianers on them boats, and sometimes I used to wake her up to hear the music when they come up the river. I'd be layin' there and it would be quiet and I could hear it comin' from way, way off. Like when you quail huntin' and it's getting dark and you can hear the boss bird whistlin' tryin' to get the covey together again, and he's coming towards you slow and whistlin' soft, cause he knows

you somewhere around with your gun. Still he got to round them up, so he keeps on comin'. Them boss quails is like a good man, what he got to do he *do*.

The first-hand quality of the observation here, and above all the authenticity of the feeling—the huntsman's respect for the bird, amounting almost to empathy with a worthy opponent—warrant the idea of a standard implied in the last sentence. Trueblood's conception of what makes a good man grows directly out of experience. With this passage, his own claim to be a man becomes charged with a kind of moral force. His affirmation of that force is there in his account of responsibility: "a good man, what he got to do he *do*". (pp. 119-20)

In his frank enjoyment and his strong sense of mutuality, Trueblood possesses a more complete identity, is more fully a man, than any other figure in the book. In contrast with the puritanical self-suppression and sublimation of Mr. Norton, the white millionaire, Trueblood's self-acceptance makes him whole yet keeps him from the chaos that Norton fears. This completeness transforms his act of shame into something approaching a triumph. It happens because of the strength of life in him, not because of perversity or deprivation. And it begins in the innocence of sleep. Matty Lou, his nubile daughter, lies close beside him for warmth, and blends in his fading consciousness with the girl he has been

remembering from his long-gone youth. He falls into a dream of elemental images, unmistakably suggestive to the reader yet strange enough to keep the dreamer from seeing through their disguise to the real nature of what he is doing. Were it left here, though, were it simply a matter of something done in sleep, the act would have only the moral quality of an accident. But Trueblood wakes up, and the act isn't over. He is still, so to speak, fixed in his predicament. As he puts it, "once a man gits hisself in a tight spot like that there ain't much he can do". Either to move or to stay would be sin: "There was only one way I can figger that I could git out: that was with a knife". The scene has become farce; another page and it becomes knockabout, when his wife wakes up and has to use several kinds of violence to dislodge him. Even in the account of these wild moments, Trueblood preserves some dignity beneath the absurdity. He likes himself in that hair-raising situation to a man whom the police had besieged, and who continued to shoot at his assailants "until they set fire to the house and burned him up." "So like that fellow", he says, "I stayed, I had to fight it on out to the end. He mighta died, but I suspects now that he got a heapa satisfaction before he went". (pp. 120-21)

[While making Trueblood admirable in some respects], Ellison avoids sentimentalizing him. The comic treatment of his tale helps to ensure this, although humour in such a case could seem defensive and dishonest. Trueblood is not reduced to a clown or a grotesque. He is given a human complexity sufficient to prevent his example from being shrugged off or laughed away. The very verve with which he tells his story testifies to his integrity; and then another side to his character peeps through—he half-enjoys the story and the effect it invariably creates, and his manner of telling it is not without artifice and creative pride. (p. 121)

It would be tempting to suggest that the comic treatment is what saves this tale from the over-insistence and obscurity which mar comparable things in some other parts of the novel, but it wouldn't be quite true. Elsewhere the humour too can seem forced or disproportionate; and on the other hand some of the best things in the book occur in quite other kinds of narrative. In certain scenes of anger, fear or pain there are flashes of impressive moral insight. One of the finest is in the description of the blonde dancer at the battle-royal:

> The hair was yellow like that of a circus kewpie-doll,
> the face heavily powdered and rouged as though to
> form an abstract mask, the eyes hollow and smeared
> a cool blue, the colour of a baboon's butt.

At this stage the hero does not see the significance of this picture. He is too fiercely caught up in the turmoil of his own emotions, but the very ambivalence of his feelings—"I wanted . . . to caress her and destroy her, to love her and murder her"—indicates what she has been made into: her vulnerable humanity is at once exposed and depersonalized. She is turned into something less than human—beast, mask, object. And in this ghastly

A page of typescript from Ellison's Invisible Man.

subjection what she undergoes is a telling counterpart to the depersonalizing of the hero himself. At first he fails to see it: regarding her as an object (the definite articles instead of pronouns in the passage quoted help to indicate this—the hair, the face, the eyes), he is unable to think of her as capable of suffering. He speaks of her "impersonal eyes". Later, when she is roughly manhandled, he does make the connection: "above her red, fixed-smiling lips I saw the terror and disgust in her eyes, almost like my own terror."

Another such moment, though somewhat less persuasive, occurs during the first party of the Brotherhood's. A drunken guest makes remarks about the musicality of Negroes that sound offensively patronising. He is ejected from the party for "unconscious racial chauvinism". Afterwards, the hero is disturbed by a new reflection:

> Shouldn't there be some way for us to be asked to sing? Shouldn't the short man have the right to make a mistake without his motives being considered consciously or unconsciously malicious?

At such moments the novel cuts not only through the familiar forms of racial prejudice but also through the complementary prejudices of enlightenment. It shows how even supposedly benevolent attitudes in a polarised situation force people into predetermined roles, denying their individual humanity. These insights intimate what the novel might have achieved. They are too isolated and undeveloped, intermixed with too much that is inferior or even morally oblique, properly to justify the novel's theme. But at least they show an awareness of what might have been done with it. And in the treatment of the central character, too, there are signs of the clarifying honesty the whole conception of the book required. Invisible to others because never seen simply as himself, seen always in the garb of their own preconceptions, he is also invisible to himself. He cannot know himself because he is altogether too ready to try the roles he is offered, especially the role of leader of his people. If the character of the invisible man seems sketchy, elusive or inconsistent, this is surely part of the meaning of the novel. The absence of recognition in the world around him deprives him not only of visible identity but also of a stable inner sense of self.

And yet, granting the importance of this conception, I think we have to demur. Much in the presentation of the character troubles me, and I'm troubled still more by the willingness of critics to accept an estimate of his moral claim more generous even than his own. If he does not fully know himself, it's not clear how certainly the author knows him either. The author's attitudes and purposes waver, he treats the character sometimes as spokesman, sometimes as uncomprehending victim, and fails to create for him a distinctive voice. This happens partly because Ellison has not mastered the perils of first-person narration. The method creates peculiar difficulties in the control of distance, tone, and irony, and requires considerable definiteness of purpose and attitude. Lacking sure control, the novel frequently leaves us uncertain how far to accept the hero's valua-

tion of himself or others. In consequence, no strong sense of a central personality can be created, and it is not surprising that the novel seems to break up into fragments of variable quality.

The same kind of uncertainty appears in the novel's attempts at direct handling of its social and political materials. The hero's relationship with the Brotherhood provides the main test. Because his own values remain unclear—because it is frequently difficult to tell whether he is offered as victim or villain, satirical butt or prophetic spokesman—his hostility to the organization remains unfocused, seems merely personal and arbitrary. (pp. 122-23)

The Brotherhood is blamed for cynically manipulating the people of Harlem, and the hero indignantly tells himself that they must be made to pay for the betrayal. Yet precisely how and where the committee perpetrated this betrayal, and what they could hope to achieve by it, never appear. On the contrary, the riot in Harlem occurs only because the hero himself had chosen, without instructions and as it turns out against the committee's wish, to stir up the people. By his speech at Tod Clifton's funeral he exacerbates their feelings, but as he has neither programme nor principle to put before them it's no wonder that what they are moved to ends in bloody and pointless riot.

There is a still deeper anomaly. Although the hero is outraged by the cynicism of the Brotherhood, his own cynicism is as great. He exploits the Brotherhood without caring for its policies, and the people of Harlem without offering any tangible reforms. His own driving concern has never been the welfare of his people. It has been the fulfillment of his own ambitions. He goes to New York to prepare himself for personal success. At first, he sees himself as Dr. Bledsoe's successor .... His cynicism towards his own people is thorough: "I would have one way of speaking in the North and another in the South. Give them what they wanted down South, that was the way". As the book goes on, he modifies his ambitions but not his attitude. Instead of wanting to join Bledsoe, he hopes to succeed through the Brotherhood .... When he has worked for the Brotherhood, studied its ideology, and made himself (unbelievably) the leading figure in Harlem, his real motives remain unchanged. He seeks self-advancement: "I could reach the very top and I meant to get there" .... When he plans the public funeral for Tod Clifton, it is neither out of homage to his dead friend nor in the belief that the people of Harlem need this means of expressing their grief and outrage. He sees it as a way of restoring his own political fortunes, regaining his prestige: "I seized upon the idea now as though it would save my life." My life! Given this motive, it is difficult to accept his sense of moral betrayal when the Brotherhood refuses to endorse his action and sustain the campaign in Harlem. Still less is it possible to believe in the protestations of injured innocence he is made solemnly to utter. Of all things, he prides himself on integrity in his dealings with the Brotherhood: "I'd tried to build my integrity upon the role of Brotherhood and now it had changed to water, air."

As such examples accumulate, they prompt the question of whether the novel has been misread by a generation of admirers. Perhaps its main purpose is to satirize political demagogues and charlatans, with the nameless hero as archetype of the breed. At times such a reading does seem plausible. In the Epilogue, for example, Ellison has the protagonist confess that he finds "the utmost difficulty" in being honest. Commenting on the novel, in **Shadow and Act,** Ellison describes as "the major flaw in the hero's character" his "unquestioning willingness to do what is required of him by others as a way to success". That, however, is ambiguous testimony: it's not clear whether the "flaw" should be understood as the desire for "success" or merely as the "unquestioning willingness". It looks unhappily like the latter, since Ellison adds that "this was the specific form of his 'innocence'". And in much of the novel itself the hero is presented as naive but honest victim. This makes the moral drive of the book peculiarly disturbing.... It is not true that what he wants is what Harlem wants. He wants personal power, prestige, admiration; by the end of this very paragraph he is again shown to be concerned simply with salvaging his "career." It would be comforting to think that Ellison saw the hero's claim to be a spokesman for Harlem as a contemptible rationalization, but the novel gives no sign of that. What it shows instead, time and again, is an uncertainty about his motives and actions amounting, in places, to self-contradiction. (pp. 123-25)

The worst confusions in the novel, however, seem to me to lie in its treatment of white women. Except for the one moment of clear sight with the terrified dancer, it subjects white women to a kind of indignity essentially similar to what the hero is supposed to suffer. It sees them as stereotypes. There is something extraordinarily obtuse and unpleasant in the way they are reduced to the role of bitch in heat. By what I take to be an inadvertent though also inexcusable irony, these women are shown as projecting their fantasies of sexual fulfilment on to the black hero while the novel itself conjures them up out of fantasy just as gross and untrue. The writing in these episodes becomes intolerably trashy: "in one swift motion the red robe swept aside like a veil, and I went breathless at the petite and generously curved nude". It also becomes cruel: "she was a leathery old girl." But the ugliest quality of these scenes is their self-righteous moralizing. The hero has made up to the woman called Sybil solely in hope of extracting information about the Brotherhood from her. He is unashamedly ready to exploit, and in that way dehumanize, the sexual relationship he fully expects to have with her. When she makes an obscene proposal he is horrified. With no awareness of using a double standard, he thinks of lecturing her "on the respect due one's bedmate in our society". These scenes are meant to be comic, and the hero's ineptitude as a seducer is offered as something to smile at, but this is another way of trying to make him seem innocent.

At the end of the novel, the hero decides to come out of hibernation. He affirms his belief in the "Possibility that even an invisible man has a socially responsible role to play". It is a hollow gesture, and critics have been rightly troubled by it. But their attempts to explain what is wrong with it seem to me disastrously wrong-headed: they put all the blame on to the world outside the hero.... Marcus Klein argues that there is no positive principle on which the hero can come out and act responsibly, since "given the social facts of America, both invisibility and what he now calls his 'hibernation' are his permanent condition". Against that, one has to say "the social facts of America" are not "given". They are not given in the sense that the novel does not persuasively render and interpret them: apart from a few intense and well-realized scenes, the social setting remains vague or factitious. But in a larger sense, too, the social facts are not "given." The stultifying assumption made by both critics, and attributed by them to the novel, is far too easy. Social attitudes are not immutable, meaningful action is not inconceivable, the novel has merely failed to conceive of it, and its satire on political activists has been directed against men of straw. The invisible man's affirmation at the end is meaningless, not because the novel has shown the impossibility of responsible action but because he has no specific idea of what a responsible role might be. (pp. 126-27)

> *F. H. Langman, "Reconsidering 'Invisible Man',"* in The Critical Review, *Melbourne, No. 18, 1976, pp. 114-27.*

Phyllis Rauch Klotman (essay date 1977)

[*Klotman is a leading American writer on black history and literature. In the following excerpt from her 1977 study* Another Man Gone: The Black Runner in Contemporary Afro-American Literature, *she discusses the concept of the "Running Man" in* Invisible Man.]

The Running Man in literature is recognizable in his most simple state as the protagonist who rejects the values of the culture or society in which he finds himself by birth, compulsion, or volition, and literally takes flight. During the nineteenth century when he attempted to escape the tentacles of an inimical society, he could still run away *from* but also *to* something: from the settlement to the frontier (Cooper), from slavery to freedom (the slave narrative), from land to sea (Melville), from society to the river (Twain) or to the Pond (Thoreau). Often romantic, his flight was rarely abortive. He was, then as now, a critic of his time and place. Twentieth-century society, however, in effectively depriving him of his goal, has forced his very act of running to assume complex shades of ambiguity. (pp. 3-4)

Ralph Ellison's **Invisible Man** is the culmination of the Running Man metaphor, the electric "umbilical cord" connecting the running men of the past with those of the present. In no other single work is the metaphor as central to the meaning and significance of the artist's overall conception; in no other work is the ambiguity so consistently sustained. Indeed, running gives shape and unity to the novel. While the prologue and epilogue are static—in both sections the protagonist is immobilized, even though the epilogue intimates a change—the central section is a series of spasmodic movements in flight.

Unlike the slave, who exercised volition in his desire and decision to escape, Ellison's protagonist is essentially a runner by coercion, precipitated into flight by some unwitting but irrevocable blunder. His *faux pas,* though seemingly self-initiated, are for the most part governed by those all-but-invisible puppet strings, manipulated by the forces of power in whatever form they manifest themselves: the southern white power structure, the black college, the factory system, industrial unionism, the Brotherhood. Running, then, as revealed in the dream quotation, is a negative uncontrolled response to a metaphoric cattle prod used by others to shock the Invisible Man into random, indiscriminate movement, leaving him impotent, without control over himself or his environment (symbolized specifically in the "hospital" scene, which is ambiguously rebirth *and* the partial death of emasculation). The protagonist never controls his environment—that great Hemingway ideal—until he stops running *physically* and is alone, reflective, visible at least to himself. (p. 71)

The major part of the book is an account of the narrator's life: the first half, an escape from various unsatisfactory social identities, leading to the climactic death-and-rebirth section; the second half, the quest for a new identity, and in common with Harry Angstrom and Holden Caulfield, the search for an "environment in which he can perform at his best," the result "a painful contemporary odyssey." The epilogue rounds the work to a finish with an indication of renewed activity: "Without the possibility of action, all knowledge comes to one labeled 'file and forget,' and I can neither file nor forget." True, there is no final resolution; the Running Man metaphor remains ambiguous, because running for Ellison as for Thoreau is striving, and therefore a function of life. The narrator, like Thoreau, absents himself from society for a time, although not initially by choice—the black experience in America has a way of eliminating free will. *His* Walden is not a pond but a hole; he has not walked out to it of his own volition, but fallen *into* it while attempting to escape with his life. (pp. 72-3)

Once "Clubbed into his cellar" and losing the world, the Invisible Man learns the difficulty of looking into one's self:

> When one is invisible he finds such problems as good and evil, honesty and dishonesty, of such shifting shapes that he confuses one with the other, depending upon who happens to be looking through him at the time. Well, now I've been trying to look through myself, and there's a risk in it.

At risk may be more than being hated when trying to be honest, or liked when dishonestly affirming someone else's mistaken beliefs; the risk may be the trauma when one is confronted . . . with the specter of a formless self and the incumbent responsibility, albeit opportunity, to shape one's own identity. . . . The protean quality of Ellison's protagonist is symbolized by the namelessness of the character and is artistically related to the Running Man metaphor, for each time he takes flight his identity is subtly altered or drastically changed.

To Ellison, Proteus is both America and "the inheritance of illusion through which all men must fight to achieve reality." The writer must

> challenge the apparent forms of reality—that is, the fixed manners and values of the few, and . . . struggle with it until it reveals its mad, vari-implicated chaos, its false faces, and on until it surrenders its insight, its truth.

Isn't this also the struggle of the nameless narrator in *Invisible Man*? The forms of reality with which he struggles stubbornly refuse to reveal their truth, so that he himself takes up the masks, the false faces, that reveal only chaos. Ironically, he is both Proteus, struggling and turning into diverse shapes, and the grandson of Proteus, holding and pressing the past so that he can achieve reality in the present.

The first identity the narrator assumes is conventional for a bright southern Negro boy: he imagines himself another Booker T. Washington. . . . Only the dream, ineluctably linked to the stolid black peasantry of his past—symbolized by his grandfather—mocks his false face and sets him mentally on the road. The white-man's-black-man identity fades into unreality when his next irrevocable error threatens the myth so carefully nurtured by the southern black educator. Dr. Bledsoe makes a reality of the nightmarish dream. Because the young idealist hasn't learned "to act the nigger," Bledsoe propels him onto the road North, ostensibly because "the race needs good, smart disillusioned fighters," but actually because his own position of power depends upon the docility and blindness, or covert compliance, of the young.

Bewildered by his loss of identity—"here within this quiet greenness I possessed the only identity I had ever known, and I was losing it"—the protagonist runs North with "letters of recommendation" from Bledsoe, honorably unopened in his treasured briefcase, a gift from the good white citizens in the distant past of his white-man's black-man identity. But the letters, one for each day in the week, open no doors, and he begins to feel that he is playing a part in some scheme he cannot understand. No matter how he wrings his mind, the scheme will not reveal its truth. What is his role, his new identity? Who assigns the roles—northern whites or southern black educators? He doesn't find the answers to all of these questions but he desperately tries to prove his "identity" to the disenchanted son of his seventh and last hope. This liberal son of a northern industrialist lives in his own masquerade world and offers the confused narrator a more sophisticated role in his version of an old classic: Huck and Jim at the Club Calamus. But the young narrator doesn't understand the double entendre and keeps insisting that he has another identity. "'Identity!' 'Huckleberry' Emerson cries, 'My God! Who has any identity any more anyway?'" Then he reveals the information that impels the protagonist again to flight. "'I beg of you, sir,' Bledsoe says in his letter to Emerson the father, 'to help him continue in the direction of that promise which, like the horizon, recedes ever brightly and distantly beyond the hopeful traveler.'" Nowhere is there a more sardonic treatment of the Emersonian style of northern intellectual, the man who deals in instant self-reliance; obviously Ralph Waldo Ellison has a special antipathy for the type.

As hopeless traveler and black pariah, the protagonist blunders into the role of union scab at Liberty Paints, artfully conceived as a microcosm of both American society and the industrial complex. A neophyte laborer, he commits an unpardonable error in paint mixing by exceeding the ten black drops that assure pure American whitewash. This blunder reveals the invisible contributions of black people to America (as did his off-campus error of exposing atavistic Trueblood of the black past to the delicate white sensibility), and projects him into an abortive conflict with Brockway, who represents the black foundation on which society and industry rest. The importance of outside pressure (the gauges) is forgotten as the two men lock in a black-against-black struggle (comparable to "battle royal") while the factory explodes, at least in the protagonist's mind. "'I seemed to run swiftly up an incline and shot forward with sudden acceleration into a wet blast of black emptiness that was somehow a bath of whiteness'." He is thus projected, like human fallout, into the climactic hospital scene, which symbolizes both death and rebirth. Immaculately conceived by the machine (age), the protagonist is reborn without identity, individuality, or background—the proper moment for his re-conception, when he no longer knows his name, where he was born, who he *was*. (pp. 73-5)

One flaw mars the machinery, however; it cannot turn out a completely computerized (non)man when even the most minuscule amount of humanity remains to touch him into life. This is much better illustrated in the original section deleted from *Invisible Man* and published separately as **"Out of the Hospital and Under the Bar"** in *Soon, One Morning* (1966). In an "Author's Note," Ellison explains:

> For those who would care to fit it back into *Invisible Man* let them start at the point where the explosion occurs in the paint factory, substitute the following happenings, and leave them once the hero is living in Mary's hope.

Mother Mary of Harlem, who finds the young man staggering out of the subway, springs rather unsatisfactorily from nowhere into the novel, but she helps him achieve rebirth in the original episode . . . . Without real knowledge of the machine's complexity, she partially releases him and restores his strength with a foul-tasting home remedy: "That stuff'll make a baby strong." Through Mary and her urbanized black folk world, the protagonist moves toward an identity based on his gradual acceptance of the realities of the past: swallowing the past, no matter how galling, makes the present possible. The overtones of emasculation are still there, for it is quite clear that to Ellison this is the essence of the black experience in America.

"Out of the Hospital and Under the Bar" is one of the most effective, densely symbolic scenes Ellison has written and the exigencies of publication should not have forced its excision. It is similar but superior to the Golden Day episode and foreshadows the running riot scene that returns the narrator to his underground womb. In a Freudian serio-comic nightmare, the naked narrator runs and is chased through the labyrinthine passages of his mind, until he bursts newborn from the subterranean womb into Harlem:

> I rolled, looking into the faces of two women dressed in white.
>
> "Police! A naked man, a naked . . . . !" the woman screamed. "Police!"
>
> "Oh no! No!" called a woman who crouched against a building front. "Not naked! Is he, Sis Spencer? Let's us be sure 'fore we call the cops. Wait'll I change my glasses."
>
> "As ever he was born in the world!"

Two nurse-like women attend this birth, but the protagonist himself has been the most active, experiencing the pangs of passage, expelling himself from the symbolically ambiguous orifice—a manhole—naked into a new world of consciousness. But he has run a long way, leaving behind bodies deadened by the machine (age); shocking whites with his nakedness; encountering another basement black whose life is a perpetual gamble; and slipping away from the straitjacket-bearing attendant who tries to fit him with an adjustable identity— "It'll fit, all right, it's endlessly adjustable." The naked narrator, however, has slipped off *all* identities, theirs and his own, and is racing toward some intangible hope, the possibility of perception:

> And I was conscious of being somehow different. It was not only that I had forgotten my name or that I had been processed in the machine, or even that I had taken Mary's medicine—but something internal. My thoughts seemed to be the thoughts of another. Impressions flashed through my mind, too fleeting and secretly meaningful to have been my own— whoever I was. And yet somehow they were. It was as though I had become capable of new powers of understanding.

But the cellar of his mind is still cluttered with old memories, all of which he must traverse before he can be free . . . . (pp. 76-7)

"Out of the Hospital" is almost completely a running scene, but for the first time the protagonist has an awareness of the meaning of running. The runner is in a flight that has the dreamlike quality of double vision: standing back, he watches himself running through his own history, which is, in a sense, a history of the race in microcosm. The hospital scene in the novel has this quality, but with little of the dramatic impact of the deleted section. Ellison sustains this motion and suspense, reminiscent of the excitement of escape in the slave narrative, even to the inclusion of the pursuing hound. When the narrator finally arrives "Under the Bar," he blends into the blackness—"nigger in the coal locker"—until the dog and the men at his heels force him to thrust himself through the manhole. The section ends with the protagonist deciding to find "Old Mary," but in the meantime he has had an important encounter with a blind man in Harlem who bears a startling resemblance to his grandfather (from whom he cannot escape), and who also reminds him of Bledsoe, the briefcase, and part of his still undigested past: "Well, a young fellow has to keep moving...."

"Out of the Hospital" is an artfully executed recapitulation section that will be used later, not so much as a structural device, but as contrast. The protagonist's running in the simulated riot is realistically, almost naturalistically, described and the outcome is reversed. The runner drops back through the manhole into the womb of the earth to be born again or finally buried. In this earlier episode, however, he is reborn into the bosom of the folk with a beginning recognition of and pride in his origins—essentially a new identity reshaped from the old. The old remedy, put together from herbs and recipes of the past, has given him strength to force himself out of the mechanical womb of an automated society that seeks to make automatons of men and to exploit their strength for its perpetuation. When he finally comes up for air, from the underground of past feelings and experiences, he finds himself in Harlem, the promised land that will not yield its promise. This he has yet to experience; now he is without fear, but also without illusions. (pp. 77-8)

Ironically, the Brotherhood thinks of him as a new "Booker T. Washington," but he has already shed his illusions of ever assuming such an identity: "To hell with this Booker T. Washington business. I would do the work but I would be no one except myself—whoever I was." He finds, however, that his role of "Brother" carries with it ill-fitting masks that are repugnant to him: he is an Uncle Tom to Ras, a black stud to Emma, an opportunistic plotter to Brother Westrum (Rest Room), and eventually a traitor to the people in Harlem who trusted him. The latter mask he tries to rid himself of when Ras the Destroyer's men attempt to track him down. The Hollywood disguise he thinks he is assuming with shades "of a green glass so dark that it appeared black" metamorphoses him into Rinehart, a confidence man in the Melville tradition, a "confidencing sonafa-bitch." ... (p. 78)

Ellison sees Rinehart's nonidentity as a negative perspective for his protagonist. The epitome of the happy Proteus, his invisibility is essentially egoistic, conscienceless, asocial if not antisocial. He is a gambler, a briber, a lover (roles the protagonist will never master), a man who can cope with the shifting realities of the times because his own identity is fluid, unimpeded by the barriers of a functioning superego. Running is a way of life for him and invisibility his natural dress. (p. 79)

Running has become a way of life for the narrator, too, but its meaning remains ambiguous. Because he has neither a "smooth tongue" nor a "heartless heart," he is not at home in Rinehart's "hot world of fluidity," in the confidence game of life even though its potential seems limitless.... Knowing of Rinehart's existence, however, is a salutary experience, and the narrator even thinks for a time that he can put it to use. But the Rinehart mask he dons, fortuitously does not fit when he tries to act the role. Rinehartism, which he finally equates with cynicism and charlatanism, is not his way and eventually he rejects it. What he does learn is that "somewhere between Rinehart and invisibility there were great potentialities."

Rejecting Rinehartism as an identity does not mean that the protagonist embraces invisibility. That final role is forced upon him by the blindness of others: Bledsoe, Norton, Emerson, Kimbro, Brockway, Jack, Hambro, even Mary. It was his role in the beginning ("the end was in the beginning"), only he did not recognize it. He *was* and yet *was not,* and somehow his recognition of nonbeing moves him toward a state of definition:

> I was my experiences and my experiences were me, and no blind men, no matter how powerful they became, even if they conquered the world, could take that, or change one single itch, taunt, laugh, cry, scar, ache, rage or pain of it."

(pp. 79-80)

Ellison's protagonist has no martyr complex. He is not a godlike, heroic figure ready to sacrifice himself for the sins of humanity, black or white; he is unheroic modern man, fleeing from chaos toward a rational sense of order, which if it does not exist in the world, can exist at least in his own mind. When he returns to his underground womb (a circular journey if we include the **"Out of the Hospital"** sequence), it is to escape irrational forces in the shape of two white men armed with a baseball bat who want to wrest from him all that he has gained in experience—his briefcase. He alone can divest himself of those past identities, and he does, one by one, lighting his way to his underground future. But the underground life is not permanent: "Thus, having tried to give pattern to the chaos which lives within the pattern of your certainties, I must come out, I must emerge." His hibernation is over, the narrator tells us, the immobility that can be like death—total inaction, final invisibility. He does not know whether he will find death or life aboveground, and he is braced only by the certainty of his invisibility and the possibility of ours.

That possibility, and the narrator's sense of social responsibility, makes Ellison one of the few black writers whose Running Man most clearly reflects both positive *and* negative aspects of running, and whose protagonist epitomizes the experiences of both the black and white Running Man of the twentieth century. For Running Man *is* twentieth-century man, fleeing from invisibility (nonidentity) toward a visibility (identity) which he has at least some role in shaping. Invisibility in Ellison's novel is due not only to color, or its absence, but to the fact that such is the human condition, the fate of man impotent in the face of the powerful dehumanizing forces of contemporary society. (pp. 81-2)

If Ellison's Running Man is modern man, speaking in a generalized way for all of us, how can he also speak in a particularized way for the Afro-American, whose experiences we know are unique? For one thing, his flight is a creative recapitulation of black history in this country. His roots are in the plantation South; his aspirations move him toward the black southern college for "good niggers"; his move North parallels the Great Migration of the twenties and is fraught with disillusionment. Second, the reality of his life in America, especially his heritage of slavery, has made the experience of running not merely a gesture toward freedom but a flight for his life. This is literally true for Ellison's protagonist during the riot scene—a contemporary development—where he is hounded not only by whites but also by bellicose blacks. Third, his area of choice is severely limited. Unlike the runners in Fitzgerald, Salinger, Kerouac, and Updike, who, no matter how limited they are psychologically or monetarily, freely make the decision to run, the Invisible Man is usually precipitated into running by some "sin" he commits against the system. It is a satiric comment on the black man's experience in America, on the negative alternatives rather than clear choices with which he is usually confronted. (p. 83)

Is the ending of *Invisible Man* completely negative, as many critics have suggested? Only if we consider all flight negative. The protagonist's last venture into himself, like Thoreau's, is a successful leap into perception, a perception of his own identity and his own reality. What he has begun to learn above ground—that he could not return to Mary's, to the campus, to the Brotherhood, or home—he has assimilated emotionally during the hiatus underground. The knowledge needed to resume action has finally been exhumed to the level of consciousness, and he is ready to leave his hibernation—to return, as Ishmael does, to the shore—with his conflicts but also with his sense of humanity restored. (p. 84)

> *Phyllis Rauch Klotman, in an introduction and "Ellison: 'Keep That Nigger-Boy Running',"* in her *Another Man Gone: The Black Runner in Contemporary Afro-American Literature,* Kennikat Press, 1977, pp. 3-9, 71-84.

Timothy Brennan (essay date 1981)

[*In the following excerpt, Brennan contends that there is a fundamental solipsism in* Invisible Man.]

No black American author has been so showered in glory as Ralph Ellison. Awards, honorary degrees, and committee chairs followed the publication of *Invisible Man,* winner of the National Book Award in 1952. On the merits of this novel alone, a poll of the literary community in 1965 ranked Ellison the sixth greatest American author since the War. And yet the unprecedented acclaim has more or less based itself on the fiction of a continuous Ralph Ellison, obscuring the novel's tension between public and private, oration and dream. The clenched fist has been submerged beneath the bended knee of a spiritual suffering, distorting a perceptual ambivalence in Ellison on the nature of racism and culpability.

Only a small group of dissenting critics has hinted at the dichotomy in Ellison's career between a Wrightian protest apprenticeship and a later affinity to the ritualist and symbolic schools of Stanley Hyman and Kenneth Burke. The new emphases which surface in a comparison of a 1945 essay like **"Beating that Boy,"** and a typical post-*Invisible Man* essay like **"Hidden Name, Complex Fate,"** describe an evolution from the world of physical conflict to the world of unity in diversity. The former condemns the "ethical schizophrenia" of the white world in disregarding racism; the latter speaks of "the diversity, fluidity and magical freedom of American life." Composed between 1945 and 1952, roughly the period in which his essays show signs of the change, *Invisible Man* is in part a document of Ellison's pilgrimage from one view to the other.

The novel's stylistic virtuosity and its immense erudition have directed the attention of friends and foes alike to its unique "sophistication" among black novels, which had always more or less meant kinship with a white European literary tradition. Many enthusiastic admirers have therefore foolishly encouraged what they saw as Ellison's rejection of racial themes at the same time that they praised his high technique, seeing the one as part of the other. His detractors, on the other hand, have scoffed at Ellison's remarkable poetic finish in the apparent belief that a racial theme can be handled only with the grunts and blunts of "realistic" narrative. If one looks at American literature as a racially integrated totality (which is how Ellison saw it), neither of these views grasps the point.

On the one hand, the admirers refuse to consider Ellison's didacticism—his concern not only with portraying the black man in historical anguish and human triumph, but with a fullness demanding empathy from a white audience. For Ellison, black characterization simply had to transcend *both* the conditioned responses of the black protest school *and* the racist caricatures of its white forebears.... The enormous excitement of Ellison's admirers with his technical achievements, his employment of myth and ritual, and his incorporation of the blues is thoroughly apt, but unfortunately has been used as a shield of insulting disregard for his ambitious attempt to solve an old American literary problem: how to find a fictional form that might embody the immense diversity of American life. (pp. 162-64)

On the other hand, his detractors have been unable to move beyond the esthetic of the protest school. They have equated Ellison's "reactionary" conclusions with his sensational plot devices, his employment of various styles, and his literary allusions, all of which they have seen as commercially minded sensationalism or self-conscious snobbery. In fact, these elements are all corollaries of a symbolic elaboration of his early work which these critics, often without saying so, associate with Ellison's "cop-out."

Neither side is able to draw a connection between Ellison's eventual loyalty to a symbolic structure and his evolving views on the historical question of black liberty. They are too busy evading the half of Ellison they find offensive. So while *Invisible Man* has either been faulted on political grounds or praised on esthetic grounds, no one seems to have traced in the pages of the text a tangible flaw. This can only be done by investigating the novel's operative thematic threads. For when Ellison seeks to translate his evolving views into the form of his novel, the writing of his apprenticeship continues in a vestigial form and is forced to the surface by the nature of his material. It is this expression of the material forcing itself to the surface which is the crucial point. Consequently, the novel is unable convincingly to develop its view of the primacy of self-awareness and "possibility" as unifying factors because of its inadvertent portrayal of a specific and mutable oppression. The problems of identity, the assimilation of tradition, and social involvement are so closely patterned after the specific historical experiences of the American Negro that their claims to universality are destroyed. The bridge from black to white experience collapses with them, ruining Ellison's chances to realize his maxim, "one, and yet many." In its place, and with soggy props, is placed a bridge of solipsism. (pp. 164-65)

Invisible Man can be seen as an attempt to synthesize two "realities": a white, which represses guilt by denying the existence of the black as human; the black, which, insisting upon its separateness, cultivates it, wallowing in a blind rage against an inequality which becomes alibi. In the sphere of culture, this divergence has taken the form of two recognizable traditions which are ostensibly pure but secretly miscegenational. For Ellison, the two "realities" are surmountable, just as their two cultural strains have long since grown together, although they are never expressed with equal force, and though the two deluded sides refuse to admit the other's influence.

Among so many other damaging effects, this division in American society has created a barrier to the writing of an inclusive American novel. Although the nineteenth-century American masters had progressed in this direction by using the Negro as the symbol of Man, they could not create characters with the sensitivity required for a believably human portraiture. Ellison's answer is to symbolize black experience itself, so that the travails of the American Negro reappear as a manifestation of a larger human condition, thus creating a common ground for white and black.

Between 1945 and 1952, however, his views on the culpability of racism (the major issue of his novel) significantly shift. In the pre-1946 Ellison, the problem is that writers have pushed the issue of racial conflict underground after the Emancipation, buried it in the depths of their consciences, and subsequently ignored it. The suppression of the issue has shrivelled the writer's creative energies because it has given him the habit of "living and thinking in a culture that is opposed to the deep thought and feeling necessary to profound art." The argument is that "there is ... an inescapable connection between the writer and the beliefs and attitudes current in his culture." If one pretends that something vital in one's culture does not exist, one is doomed to produce "literary offspring without hearts, without brains, viscera or vision." (pp. 167-68)

The early Ellison mercilessly condemns the same kind of fiction he later tries to create in *Invisible Man.* In 1945, the practical result of the white writer's willful blindness to racism was an inferior literature. The so-called "Negro Problem," he says, is a "guilt problem charged with pain. Just how painful might be judged from the ceaseless effort expended to dull its throbbings with the anesthesia of legend, myth, hypnotic ritual and narcotic modes of thinking." He goes on to complain of how "serious literature ... [has] been conscripted ... to drown out the persistent voice of outraged conscience." (pp. 168-69)

In the course of the evolution from protest to poetry, two enormous efforts become congealed in a single project: to portray the black man in his human fullness and to find a common theme for white and black. On the one hand, Ellison investigates Negro history, psychology, and everyday life. In respect to the novel, this entails a treatment of the historical crises of the black past—the period of slavery, the Emancipation, the migration North after the First World War, the era of Garveyite nationalism, and the peak of Communist Party influence. In this mode, the language and methods of the protest tradition are wielded by Ellison with an ambiguous voice, never finally pronouncing or judging, but building to a culmination of alternating hope and bitterness, rebellion and despair.

On the other hand, Ellison undertakes the effort to abstract from the black experience a common ground. The black is not free, but no one is "free"; the black must hide his true emotions to advance in business, but the working world demands everyone's duplicity; the black is cut off from his African origins, but the white, too, is a loner in the New World. In this second mode, the problem becomes volitional. And the tension we referred to in the opening paragraphs arises here, pulling at either end of the major theme until the whole is placed into a box which is the human mind. (pp. 169-70)

"Invisibility," as it appears in the novel's Prologue, is an unwanted state imposed from without:

> I am invisible, understand, simply because people refuse to see me . . . . When they approach me they see only my surroundings, themselves, or figments of their imagination.

The avoidance of guilt for "the Negro Problem" which Ellison had described as a form of mental suppression is converted here into literature as visual metaphor—the black man, who is a "man of substance, of flesh and bone, fiber and liquids," is made invisible by a willful myopia. One sees a Negro; one feels then either irrational hatred ("blond man"), paternalism (Mr. Norton), myth-based and insulting admiration (Emerson), or the assumption of ingrained rebellion (Jack). But one does not see a person, as you or I are persons; one sees a member of a race . . . .

[The white] world is hostile to blacks; the protagonist, already in the hibernation with which the novel ends, appears ready to set about describing how, as a black man, he has learned to deal with this hostility. The response is sure to coincide with the prevalent feelings of indignation and resistance—of refusing to pay "outrageous rates" to a monopoly, of "striking out with your fists," of refusing to "ignore the violence of [our] days." (p. 170)

But the "invisibility" image undergoes a similar mutation. The Prologue has been speaking of the poor inner vision of others—"you often doubt if . . . you aren't simply a phantom in other people's minds." In the Epilogue, however, although in the same novel-time as the Prologue, this colloquial irony departs, and "invisibility" becomes something indeed of the mind—the evanescent "failure to assent to [one's] own humanity." The social shortsightedness of the beholders of the Negro has become the moral failing in the Negro himself, to the point where the protagonist can speak even of Mary Rambo, the shelterer and mother figure, as guilty of the blindness which has made him "invisible."

So, too, in the Golden Day episode a thematic confusion prevails. As the hero enters the bar with his white benefactor, Mr. Norton, one of a group of black war veterans grips him by the arm and coldly prophesies:

> It will occur at 5:30 . . . the great all-embracing absolute Armistice, the end of the world.

Looking around at the drunk and lascivious black veterans—insane asylum patients on leave—the hero realizes that appearances lie. The vets, whom the hero first describes as a chain gang, are actually a broad cross section of the black community:

> Many of them had been doctors, lawyers, teachers, Civil Service workers; there were several cooks, a preacher, a politician and an artist . . . .

The Golden Day itself, a tavern and whorehouse, attains a historical-mythical stature . . . . [Its clientele] suggests a collectivity of black experience. The intermittent allusions to a selective American history reinforce this idea as they contribute to a broader picture of Ellison's insight into a trauma of the Negro past, namely the redefinition of racial identity which followed the Negro's participation in the First World War. The taste for freedom acquired overseas in a Europe without Jim Crow, and the victory of "democracy" implicit in the War itself, helped to motivate the migration Northward in the post-War years, along with the aspirations of social improvement which accompanied it. (pp. 170-72)

Seen in this light, the irony of the lives of the imprisoned black veterans begins to take shape. The nature of their "madness," their relationship with the white world, and their responses to a degrading incarceration begin to reveal themselves. Beneath the "insanity" lies a ubiquitous proof of accomplishment. (p. 172)

Finally, and predictably, the "madness" of the vets is associated with political rebellion of a primitive form, mirrored both in the chiliasm of the prophet of "absolute armistice" and in another vet, a "student of history," who proclaims:

> The world moves in a circle like a roulette wheel. In the beginning, black is on top, in the middle epochs, white holds the odds, but soon Ethiopia shall stretch forth her noble wings.

Ellison is here developing a coherent argument for his theme of racism, first introduced in the concept of "invisibility." Despite the acidity of his irony and what may appear in this explication as the transparency of its form, the passage retains an elaborate rhetorical depth. Ellison is not content to leave the story on this level alone. To express the actual containment and suppression of black rebellion, Ellison allows the Golden Day to assume still another symbolic identity—that of the Negro mind. Supercargo, the veterans' guard and overseer from the asylum, becomes the "superego" of Ellison's symbolic architecture. He is described as a "stool-pigeon" and a "kind of censor," bellowing "I WANT ORDER" from the top of the stairs and kicking the vets back as they rush up to the whores' rooms, mimicking the act of mental suppression.

If Supercargo is the symbol of psychic order, he is also the representative of the white's mental manipulation of black aspirations. For he wears a "white suit" and "white shorts" and, when white folks are in the house, "[he] wan's *double* order." Talking to Mr. Norton after Supercargo has been beaten into submission by the increasingly unruly crowd, one vet doctor explains:

> The forces of destruction are rampant down below. They might realize you are what you are, and then your life wouldn't be worth a piece of bankrupt stock.

Supercargo's role is to keep the blacks from rebelling.

In Ellison's allegory, images of psychological suppression mingle confusingly with references to physical oppression. Is the entire Golden Day episode simply an allegorical recreation of the white's suppression of "the Negro Problem" and their subsequent forcing of it into the unconscious? Or is it a parody of the blacks' damnable gullibility before the talismans of white domination? On the broadest level, Ellison portrays the vets as a fearful swarm of undifferentiated sparks to the black unconscious. In this scheme, patterned after the psychical symbolism of the early sequence, Mr. Norton is merely a "trustee of consciousness"—a figure whom blacks deceive themselves into finding a "great white father . . . [or] the lyncher of souls," the alternate poles of security and fear delimiting choice. For Mr. Norton and the hero, in an upstairs room above the commotion, learn from the doctor vet that the others "know nothing of value" without Supercargo. In accordance with Ellison's revised terms of "invisibility," the trauma of post-War black America is volitional. (pp. 172-74)

One is constantly given the sense of a rending quality to the torturous path that Invisible Man travels in the course of the novel. Given the abruptness of the novel's change in the Epilogue, one feels that Ellison has been driven into a solution that abolishes contradiction by fiat, and into a literary strategy in which the products of American diversity can survive on a technical level, if not on an organic. Dream-symbolism, pastoral poetry, "hard-boiled" naturalism, and ghetto slang all meld into a unity whose boundaries are the ego. Unable to find a viable common ground for the white and black in his vision of American experience, driven by the logic of his own protagonist's descent into hell, Ellison reverts to a unity which no longer would exist in a common recognition of unity in diversity, but on the level of consciousness alone—the precise opposite of what he had set out to do. The work, in other words, tends toward a kind of solipsism.

The post-Invisible Man Ellison manifests the shift: "Good fiction is made of that which is real, and reality is difficult to come by. So much of it depends upon the individual's willingness to discover his true self." The notion that reality is somehow dependent upon one's knowledge of self, that the external world relies upon a subjective ordering becomes the fundamental principle:

> I whipped it all except the mind, the *mind*. And the mind that has conceived a plan of living must never lose sight of the chaos against which that pattern was conceived.

History is chaos, not only nature, but society, too, demands the discipline of the solitary will:

> I carried my sickness and though for a long time I tried to place it in the outside world, the attempt to write it down shows me that at least half of it lay within me . . . .

Looking closely, we watch a dialectic of will and determinism unfold. Freedom changes imperceptibly from the recognition of "possibility" to the recognition of necessity. We have travelled from an impassioned voluntarism to a nightmarish sense of inevitablity.

Imagination, discover, order—all these blossom from within, conferring enormous importance on the pre-existing order within. It is only natural, then, that a search for identity would become paramount. This is why the search for "freedom" (in the old protest sense) with which *Invisible Man* tentatively began, transmogrifies in the final pages to an equation with "identity gained." Translated to the specific world of the novel, this general idea (in retrospect) becomes the novel's moral core:

> It is what the hero refuses to do in each section which leads to further action. He must assert and achieve his own humanity; he cannot run with the pack and do this. This is the reason for all his reversals.

But, again, still taking the novel on its own terms, this can only be a half-truth. The evolution from throwing angry truth "into the guilty conscience of America" in 1945, the evolution away from "the will to confront the world" to the world of self-knowledge, describes a journey onto a terrain where the contradictions between American principles and racial inequality, between "high" and "low" culture, between social responsibility and spiritual fulfillment, can be collectively worked out.

By the terms Ellison originally laid out, we cannot help finding in this solution to the American synthesis and the inclusive novel a peculiar failure. . . . Unlike the earlier white writers who themselves were ill-equipped to portray the black man in the flesh, Ellison is unable, in practice, to see the black man any other way. The specific manipulations, injustices, and opportunism suffered upon the narrator are too concrete, too clearly a part of a common social understanding of a specific social oppression with localized perpetrators.

The novel's closing words raise in full force the problem of whom the work is addressed to: "Who knows but that, on the lower frequencies, I speak for *you*?" (emphasis added). Apparently, it is the "you" of humanity. However, it arises in an Epilogue which establishes in the immediately preceding pages a "we" of unmistakeable Afro-American identity. (pp. 177-79)

In the recognition of racial divisions, Ellison seems to reach out to whites in *Invisible Man*'s final words as if to say, "We have similar feelings and aspirations; we are human too." The concept is active; as he wrote in his review of *The American Dilemma,* it is to use "the Negro's strongest weapon in pressing his claims: his hold upon the moral consciousness of Northern whites." The very creation of a fully rounded black character would then itself be a kind of imaginative propaganda for the recognition of the harm of racism. This would be consistent with what he seemed to think in 1945 was the way to achieve the great synthesis.

As we saw at that time, he tried to portray a debilitating doublethink still identified with the whites' refusal to reconcile "the Negro Problem" with their own principles of freedom. In his acceptance speech for the National Book Award, Ellison locates the chief significance of *Invisible Man* in its contribution to the creation of a "personal moral responsibility for democracy."

But in the Epilogue in which blacks become as culpable as whites for their own alienation (in the old protest sense), it is no longer a question of recognition for a minority, of the great and noble unity in diversity, but of atomized individuals equally "invisible" to one another. Since the conscious suppression of the black problem (as Ellison had described it) changes in the era of *Invisible Man* to the "symbol [of the] underground aspect of human personality," the *primum mobile* of the novel has become centered in a dilemma specific to white consciousness. For this process of burying the facts of racism and inequality in the underground of the personality is a process peculiar to white consciousness; the black man lives, not only witnesses, his experience. Consequently, Ellison's transference of a social apprehension located in the unconscious to a symbol of that same unconscious, ostensibly forming the bridge between whites and blacks on the level of mental processes, seems in fact to abandon the journey to the black frontier.

In his acceptance speech mentioned above, Ellison explains his avoidance of understatement in *Invisible Man* because "understatement depends . . . on commonly held assumptions, and my minority status rendered all such assumptions questionable." In other words, the artist is responsible not only for the literal meanings of his text, but also its connotations, and these are shaped differently from subculture to subculture. When he admits the separation existing between the two halves of his audience, he shows the necessity of finding a metaphor which can communicate with both. The question is whether his symbol (both personal and American) for alienation—the agony of black experience—can accomplish this. (pp. 179-80)

For the Negro, the vividness of an actual racism along with Ellison's evocation of its terrible immediacy, burdens the transcendence of the symbol with the weights of a reasoned bitterness. For the whites, the "Negro Problem" (as Ellison himself had pointed out) is too uncomfortable a part of the national memory for them to decline Ellison's invitation to dissolve race in an exultation of the individual . . . . Under the centripetal pressures of solipsism, hope mutates into the stark and taunting picture of what cannot be. (pp. 180-81)

Timothy Brennan, "Ellison and Ellison: The Solipsism of 'Invisible Man,'" in CLA Journal, *Vol. XXV, No. 2, December, 1981, pp. 162-81.*

George Sim Johnston (essay date 1986)

[*In the following essay, Johnston reviews* Going to the Territory, *commenting on Ellison's development as a writer and thinker.*]

In 1965, the book-review supplement of the old New York *Herald Tribune* asked two hundred critics to pick the best American novels published since World War II. The resulting list of the "top twenty" was quite solid, as such lists go, and if it were to be revised today to take account of the novels published since then, it would, sad to say, require little revision. The first choice of the critics was Ralph Ellison's *Invisible Man,* which was published in 1952, and the book still stands as probably the best American novel to be published since—well, pick your favorite Faulkner.

Among Ellison's many accomplishments in that book was to demolish the Chinese Wall which critics like Philip Rahv had erected between the two main tendencies in American writing—between, as Rahv phrased it, the "palefaces" and the "redskins." Ellison's strategy was impeccably "literary"; he rejected the formulas of the social novelists of the 30's—given the story he wanted to tell, they must have suggested themselves as models—and took that he needed instead from the likes of Henry James and T.S. Eliot. The techniques of allegory and symbolism he learned from them gave his narrative both a depth and a surface texture which was beyond anything the writers in the naturalist camp were capable of. But at the same time, Ellison gave the impression that he was writing flat-out in good "redskin" fashion; he not only injected his dialogue with the rhythms of jazz and Harlem street talk, but also seemed to draw on an enormous fund of raw, primary experience. It was as though Henry James were improvising riffs with Charlie Parker on the corner of Lenox and 125th Street.

Among the lessons which Ellison's novel would seem to hold for younger American writers today is that it is possible to explore the subject of alienation without writing about an adolescent off in a corner doing lines of cocaine. It is a lesson that Ellison tells us he first learned from André Malraux. For implicit in his novel is the idea that the identity and fate of an individual are inextricably tied to the public life of the society in which he lives.

Ellison has also told us that as a young writer he deliberately set about making himself familiar with "the major motives of American literature" and in the process discovered books like *Moby-Dick* and *Huckleberry Finn.* (And these books *were* a discovery for a writer starting out in the 30's. Joyce and Eliot did not become acquainted with *Huckleberry Finn* until they were past middle age.) Even more, perhaps, than the modernists, Hawthorne, Melville, and Twain helped Ellison to write a novel that, while deeply political in its implications, went far beyond any "protest" novel in its exploration of the social realities of America.

National Book Awards presentation, 27 January 1953. From left to right: Ellison, Archibald MacLeish, Frederick Lewis Allen, and Bernard DeVoto.

Ellison is much taken with his own biography, and in his new collection of nonfiction pieces, *Going to the Territory,* we learn a great deal about how he turned himself into a novelist. *Invisible Man* is a work of such high order that we do not begrudge the information. But Ellison's one novel appeared thirty-four years ago, and only a few fragments of the big (or at least very long) novel which he has been writing since then have been allowed to leave the workshop. So far as his public is concerned, then, we may say that Ellison's main work since *Invisible Man* has been the crafting of himself as a man of letters.

It has been very careful and measured work, and has produced one of the more dignified, if somewhat mannered, presences on the literary landscape. I do not think Ellison would object to my implication that there is an element of calculation in his public persona, for in the strongest essay in this new book, **"An Extravagance of Laughter,"** he quotes Yeats on the necessity of fashioning a "second self" if one is to do any work in this world. According to Ellison, Yeats's demand for a "mask," for a self-elected identity, applies doubly for an

American, and triply for a black American like himself, because he lives in a fluid society in which the social identity of an individual is far more problematic than it is on the other side of the Atlantic.

Like *Shadow and Act,* which was published in 1964, *Going to the Territory* brings together some of the speeches, interviews, and articles which have come forth, at wide intervals, from the public Ellison. Like most artists who take it on themselves to instruct outside the medium of their art, Ellison turns out to have a few favorite hobby-horses which he mounts again and again. To begin with, he has a healthy obsession with the American writer's role as a continuator, as an improviser on the themes set down not only by past American writers, but also by the men who "conceived" America in documents like the Constitution and the Bill of Rights. Ellison understands American democracy much the way he understands literature—as a highly deliberate and self-conscious act. Like Emerson, he sees the writer as an energizer, teaching the possibilities of the individual in an open society. (Here, as elsewhere in these pieces, Ellison is playing the themes of *Invisible*

Man in a different key. Early on in that novel, the nameless hero is told to read Emerson, and the epilogue contains phrases which might have been spun during a walk in the woods around Concord.)

Ellison, of course, is not the only postwar writer to have taken the American classics to heart and set up shop as a public "witness" to the democratic experience. There has been Robert Lowell, for example. When Lowell read his poem, "For the Union Dead," to a cheering crowd of thousands in the Boston Public Garden, he went about as far as a writer can go along these lines. But Lowell's most famous public act was his refusal to accept Lyndon Johnson's invitation to the White House Festival of the Arts in 1965 because of his disagreement with Johnson's policies in Vietnam. Ellison accepted the invitation, and in a subsequent interview he took Lowell to task for mixing art and politics. And here we come to another major theme which connects many of the pieces in this new book with one another and with *Invisible Man.* Ellison does not care for partisan politics, and he thinks that an artist contributes far more to the commonwealth by sticking to his work than by going public with an agenda.

Ellison's distaste for political activism, which seems to date from his involvement with the Communist party as a young man, caused him to be subjected to a fair amount of abuse during the salad days of the New Left. In the same year that Lowell and Norman Mailer marched on the Pentagon, Ellison tweaked the nose of the New York literary establishment by quoting in *Harper's,* with approval, a speech of Lyndon Johnson to the effect that art is not a political weapon. Like Saul Bellow (who is far more prickly on the subject), Ellison is impatient with those who would force him into the reductive certainties of a "Position," and, again like Bellow, much of what he has put into print during the last few decades would seem to be an exasperated response to the sectarian clamor around him.

It would be a mistake, however, to say that Ellison rejects the use of political pressure to achieve ends like racial equality. But for him, that goal is promoted far more effectively by powerful *non-political* forces which are at work in this country. America's vernacular culture, he points out, is a potent leveler. It is the great solvent of social disparities, constantly eating away at traditional barriers of class and race. And in relation to the cultural whole, he writes, "we are all minorities," anyway. The implication of Ellison's argument—that Stevie Wonder and Bill Cosby are the cutting edge leading to a successful multiracial society—is not likely to sit well with those who are still intrigued by various forms of social engineering; but Ellison is supremely confident that our pluralistic culture will always manage to "outflank" politics.

Ellison's sheer relish of American vernacular culture expresses itself in just about every piece in this book. He is really most at home writing about jazz and folk humor. He points out that from the beginning our general culture has been strongly influenced by blacks—Ellison prefers the term "Negro American"—and that even in the South before the Civil War, blacks and whites shared in a cultural relationship which was nothing less than organic. Black artists, he says, should not subscribe to "the myth of the Negro American's total alienation from the larger American culture—a culture he helped create in the areas of music and literature . . . ." Cold comfort, perhaps, to a black musician who finds himself on the less remunerative side of the so-called "crossover" line, where records do not go triple platinum, but Ellison is making the valid point, which again will not sit well with those who have not yet graduated from the 60's, that a minority artist unnecessarily handicaps himself if he surrenders to "sociological notions of racial separatism."

The pieces in this book deal with a variety of subjects, but many of them, even when they have titles like **"Remembering Richard Wright"** and **"Homage to Duke Ellington on His Birthday,"** are heavily autobiographical. The writing varies in quality. Ellison is crisp and engaging when he addresses a concrete topic—his own past, for example, or jazz—but he tends to get windy when dealing with abstractions like culture and democracy. His generalities have a way of drowning in a sea of five-dollar words. ("So perhaps the complex actuality of our cultural pluralism is perplexing because the diverse interacting elements . . . ," and so on.) But one thing Ellison never loses is his humor. It is constantly brought forth by his contemplation of the American scene. James Joyce complained that not one of the critics of *Ulysses* saw that the book was "damn funny," and Ellison in effect makes the same point to critics of America. For all its problems and incongruities, the country is blessed with a vernacular culture which produces "an extravagance of laughter," and in that laughter, Ellison tells us, much that is painful can be transcended. (pp. 71-4)

George Sim Johnston, "Man of Letters," in Commentary, *Vol. 82, No. 6, December, 1986, pp. 71-4.*

Robert Butler (essay date 1988)

[*In the following excerpt, Butler explores the thematic role of urban environments in* Invisible Man.]

[Ellison's *Invisible Man* is a vivid example of a] pro-urban drive in Afro-American literature because it reduces to absurdity the hero's experiences in the rural South and extends to him the possibility of a kind of redemption in the Northern city. The small town in which the hero grows up, ironically given the pastoral name of "Greenwood," is revealed in the Battle Royal episode as a place intent on blinding him with illusions about American life and trapping him in the debilitating roles of a segregated society. The college he attends appears to be a kind of "Eden" but is in fact a "flower studded wasteland." The hero's experiences in both of these apparently bucolic settings arouse his hopes of finding a place for himself in the American dream but actually reduce him to the level of a robot controlled by people who use him for their own purposes.

His movement to New York City, however, suggests a way out of these traps. After he has been "expelled" from his false Eden and "cast into the darkness," he moves North to a larger and potentially more liberating world. As Ellison himself has observed to his hero in *Shadow and Act,* "He leaves the South and goes North; this, as you will notice in reading Negro folktales, is always the road to freedom—the movement upward. You have the same thing when he leaves his underground cave for the open." This is the Dreiserian "city of dreams," a "world of possibility" which the hero beholds in wonder as he steps off a Greyhound bus and contemplates Harlem for the very first time. As he observes late in the novel, New York is for him a fluid, open world with "all boundaries down," a new space where "you could actually make yourself anew."

What the hero must discover, however, is that the city which he beholds in such wonder is not a simple world containing one meaning but is in fact a tangle of painful contradictions. Like himself and American reality in general, the city is complexly double. He eventually discovers his own duality when he realizes that "there were two of me," a public self enslaved by society's expectation that he climb the ladder of outward "success" and a private self which is deformed by this "black rite of Horatio Alger." In the same way, he comes to see New York as two mutually opposed cities: First, the city classically portrayed in Horatio Alger novels, an urban world enticing him with external rewards such as money, power and status, and second, an existential city which offers an enriched consciousness leading to freedom and genuine selfhood.

His movements in these cities take two very different forms. The Algerian city invites him to move "upward" in American life toward various forms of outward success. But as the Battle Royal and his early experiences in New York clearly indicate, this upward movement exacts a terrible price, for it forces him to move away from the self toward various false roles eroding his identity. His movements in the existential city, however, are consistently *downward,* moving away from outward success and toward a greater degree of personal freedom, independence and self awareness. Rushing toward the center of Harlem late in the novel, he describes this movement as a race to the self: "I ran through the night, ran within myself."

But for much of the novel he is engaged in a fruitless "footrace against" himself as he moves blindly through an Algerian city mapped out by others intent on using him. He is sent to New York by Bledsoe ostensibly to redeem himself after the fiasco at the Golden Day. His letters of recommendation to various important people in the city apparently will put him in touch with the "sponsors" who in the Alger myth always open the doors of success for the hardworking young boy desirous

of "rising" in life. The hero temporarily takes up residence in Men's House, a place which has traditionally housed black men who have left the South to pursue the American Dream in the North. But when he finds out from Emerson's son that his letters will not lead him to sponsors interested in helping him to "rise" in life, but, on the contrary, will put him on a wild-goose chase toward a "horizon" which "recedes ever brightly and distantly from the hopeful traveler," he rejects everything which Men's House stands for and resolves to make his own way in the city.

Ironically, however, he uses another recommendation, the one provided by Emerson's son, and this brings him to Liberty Paint, which is described as a "small city". What he encounters there is another version of the Alger myth which now promises upward mobility by becoming part of a complex industrial society. Here again, the city seems to offer freedom from a restrictive Southern past but in fact provides him with another version of that past. Working for Kimbro, whom his fellow workers characterize as a "slave driver" and whom he sees as "a Northern redneck, a Yankee cracker," he becomes part of an urban plantation which reduces him to the level of a sharecropper at best and a slave at worst. The hero is exactly right when he thinks that "there were unseen lines which ran from North to South." Attaining one's freedom is not a simple matter of physically moving to a Northern city because the urban North has been contaminated by the same racism and brutality which characterizes the pastoral regions of the deep South.

Even in his acts of conscious rebellion against the Alger myth the hero ironically repeats the experience of slavery in the Northern city. Signing up with the Brotherhood because it promises him "the highest possible rewards" and a liberating role to play, he ultimately discovers that he is trapped in the same way that he was trapped in the Battle Royal. Here again he is carefully monitored by whites who want to make him "the new Booker T. Washington," a person who will channel black political energy into forms which are acceptable to whites. And just as his involvements in the Battle Royal result in self destructive violence for himself and others, his involvement in the Brotherhood culminates in the Harlem Riot which the Brotherhood engineers, a mad explosion which the hero ultimately describes as "not suicide but murder." Put another way, his Brotherhood experiences lead him to yet another dead-end, confinement in a Dantean "city of the dead," a Hell brought on by his own blindness and desires for power and status.

What he needs to enter the existential city of possibility is the kind of consciousness necessary to correctly *read* his urban experiences so that he can map his own way through the city and thus discover the city as a reflector and liberator of the self. In the Vet's words, he has "to learn to look beneath the surface." This ultimately brings him literally into an existential underworld which frees him by completely inverting the values of the

Horatio Alger myth, sending him *down* to the liberation regions of the self instead of up towards the material goals which have in fact enslaved him all his life.

Getting to the urban underworld, however, is no easy process, because he has always been trained to see success in Algerian terms as upward movement and freedom, or in Booker T. Washington's terms as rising from a condition of servitude. He begins the process of liberation leading to the "underground" of the self by spontaneously wandering through the hidden parts of the city, slowly becoming more aware of it as an emblem of the hidden parts of himself. Penetrating a city which he informally maps for himself, he gradually discovers the hidden recesses of his own nature.

This process begins shortly after the Hospital sequence where he takes the subway to Harlem and then passes out on the streets. Stunned by the explosions at Liberty Paint and the electro-shock therapy at the Hospital, the hero is freed from the Algerian "plan" for success imposed on him at the Battle Royal and reinforced in all subsequent episodes. Significantly, he moved to Harlem, which is a kind of underground, a "city within a city." His free movements in Harlem repeatedly result in increased self awareness as he discovers the falsity of an American Dream which promises freedom for all but creates an immense ghetto depriving enormous masses of their political, social and economic rights. Developing the habit, while living with Mary Rambo, of reading books from the library during the day and "wander[ing] the streets until late at night," the hero begins the slow process of reading the city and the self. Deciphering the codes contained in books and the urban landscape, he finally begins to interpret the secrets that have been deeply buried within himself for most of his life.

The first example of this occurs approximately half way through the novel when, hurrying through the streets one day, he comes upon a vendor selling yams. This key episode endows him with "an intense feeling of freedom" because it awakens in him a renewed respect for his folk traditions and their ability to "nourish" him more than the Alger myth, which has him rejecting soul food for a standard breakfast of toast, juice and coffee. This scene contrasts sharply with an earlier episode on the city streets when the hero meets the man calling himself Peter Wheatstraw. Whereas in the earlier episode, the hero was not able—and probably unwilling—to decipher the folk codes which are such a key part of his identity, here he understands what the street vendor is talking about and identifies strongly with the rich ethnic past which the sweet yams evoke. While the earlier street scene with Wheatstraw resulted in the hero rejecting his racial traditions, thinking "they're a hell of a people," this scene in Harlem culminates in his thinking with pride "What a group of people we were."

Shortly after this he moves into "a side street" where his perceptions are developed further as he witnesses an old black couple being evicted from their apartment. The vaguely-felt nostalgia induced by eating the yams be-

comes a much more disturbing feeling of anger and betrayal when he sees all of the couple's possessions thrown out on the street, reduced to what he will later describe as "junk whirled eighty-seven years in a cyclone." Again, the urban scene speaks to him in a vital way:

> I turned aside and looked at the clutter of household objects which the two men continued to pile on the walk. And as the crowd pushed me I looked down to see looking out of an oval frame a portrait of the old couple when young, seeing the sad, stiff dignity of the faces there; feeling strange memories awakening that began an echoing in my head like that of a hysterical voice stuttering in a dark street.

Here the outer cityscape becomes a compelling metaphor of the hero's self, which is tied to a cultural and racial past for which he finally takes responsibility. As he observes the dispossession of the old couple, he realizes that he too has been dispossessed of the same American Dream promised to them. The outward street thus becomes the "dark street" of his mind, filled with a critically important new sign of selfhood, the "hysterical voice" so long repressed since the Battle Royal but which now cries out for full articulation.

Throughout the remainder of the novel the hero continues to move into the self as he freely explores the existential city. He thus slowly becomes aware of the wisdom of Wheatstraw's statement that Harlem may be a "bear's den" but "it's the best place for you and me." Wandering the streets after he has witnessed Clifton's death, he thinks "It was as though in this short block I was forced to walk past everyone I had ever known." More importantly, he becomes increasingly sensitive to two voices which he had previously been trained to ignore—the voice of the city and the voice arising from the deepest levels of his consciousness. From his very first moments in Harlem he had been aware that these two voices are somehow related:

> I had always thought of my life as being confined in the South. And now as I struggled through the lives of people a new world of possibility suggested itself to me faintly, like a small voice that was barely audible in the roar of city sounds. I moved wide-eyed, trying to take the bombardment of impressions.

Just as the roar of the city awakens his sensations so that he sees and hears in an intensified way, it also releases in him a "small voice" of possibility which was muffled in the Battle Royal episode and completely silenced in his interview with Bledsoe. The vital roar of the city, so unlike the deadly silence of the campus, begins a true process of education for the hero because it draws from him the existential "voice" which is at the core of his self.

As the novel progresses, the hero's small voice amplifies as his consciousness of the city becomes more comprehensive and enriched. After delivering a Brotherhood speech, he thinks "I threw my voice hard down against the traffic sounds." While speaking at Clifton's funeral he imagines the crowd looking at "the pattern of my voice on the air." By the end of the novel, he has developed a voice which is as richly complex and sophisticated as the city itself. Moreover, he has switched from an oral to a written voice, moving from the status of orator to novelist. This is a crucial change for it makes him less dependent upon the needs of his immediate audience and better able to sound his own depths. The role of writer also grants his voice a greater degree of permanency and universality, enabling him to reach the "lower frequencies" which speak to all people.

Invisible Man, therefore, stops modeling himself on Norton, Bledsoe, the Founder and others who deceived him with the Horatio Alger myth, and he ultimately sees himself as a latter day Frederick Douglass, the man who liberated himself by moving from the rural South to the urban North and who transformed himself by becoming the master of his own voice. For he comes to regard Douglass as the man who "talked his way from slavery" and created his own name, thus signifying the fact that he was a truly self-made man, one who became humanly successful, not by accumulating wealth and status but by fully actualizing the self. In this way he rejects a superficial Algerian plan for success and celebrates a more essential American dream, an existential version of Emersonian self-reliance.

In her recent study of the American heroine [*Women Writing in America* (1984)], Blanche Gelfant argues that the city often becomes for women characters a modern equivalent of the West because it offers them the sort of free space necessary for achieving a "new life":

> In a city throbbing with dreams and desires, the heroine learns to identify her own needs, and living among strangers she has the privacy to cultivate personal desires usually condemned by family and friends as "selfishness".... Enjoying physical and social space in the city, the heroine moves about freely and experiences movement as freedom. For her, the territory ahead—the essence of freedom in male myths of the West—lies around the corner, a few streets away, in another neighborhood where nobody knows her and where she alone will say who she is.

Something very similar happens in **Invisible Man.** Rejecting pastoral settings such as the small town and the bucolic campus, the hero moves to the city where he is at first befuddled by the urban environment and is then controlled by others who possess greater awareness of how that environment functions. But he gradually experiences the city as a liberating frontier, a fresh version of the West offering the external and psychological space necessary for a new life characterized by radical forms of self-awareness, freedom and independence. The American frontier, which was described by Frederick Jackson Turner as "the meeting point between savagery and civilization," is reborn again in Ellison's underground, a "border area" which mediates between "the jungle of Harlem" and the decadent Manhattan of Emerson's Calamus Club and Jack's intricate political games. Although his underground, like the West, has been "shut off and forgotten during the

nineteenth century," he can reopen it through a prodigious act of will and imagination. A vital source of power and light, it converts him from an impotent robot into a fully conscious being able to direct his life in his own way. Ellison's positively imagined underground, therefore, is a revealing contrast to the ironic underworlds portrayed in Wright's "The Man Who Lived Underground" and Baraka's *Dutchman.* Whereas Wright's and Baraka's psychologically underdeveloped protagonists are murdered in tomb-like settings beneath the streets because they lack the experience and mental acuity to take full advantage of urban possibilities, Ellison's sophisticated, intellectually keen hero envisions his ingenious subterranean "home" as a place of "hibernation" providing him with the kind of new life which traditional American heroes have found in the West. Although a racist society forces him underground to kill him, he can, unlike Wright's Fred Daniels and Baraka's Clay, use his own inward resources to transform a cold, dead place into a warm, lifegiving space.

Paradoxically, the underground is for Ellison an urban equivalent of what the frontier was for Thoreau, a brilliant metaphor of the limitless possibilities of the self. Just as Thoreau exhorted his readers to become "the Lewis and Clark...of your own streams and oceans; explore your own higher latitudes," Ellison artfully interiorizes the Western myth by suggesting that selfhood may be attained by descending into our lower latitudes, the underground of the self which is "space, unbroken," a "dimensionless room" reflective of the self's "infinite possibilities." Converting the territories ahead into the territories *inside* his head, Ellison's hero becomes a true citizen of his own "city...of dreams."

He is careful to remind us, however, that this does not result in a neurotic escape, a puerile evasion of either his racial roots or his social responsibilities. As the Prologue makes clear, his descent into self is made possible only by encountering the full complexity of his racial past which contains both the pain of slavery and the transcendence afforded by black artists such as Louis Armstrong who have made "poetry" out of the racial experience, thus converting a condition of oppression into "a beam of lyrical sound." Moreover, his descent into the innermost reaches of the self paradoxically empowers him finally to return to the above-ground city where he is determined to play out a "socially responsible role." He lays great stress in the Epilogue on the fact that "the old fascination with playing a role returns and I'm drawn upward again." Several important new roles do indeed await him in the above ground world; for example, he does in fact become a writer who reveals the truth about his society, and he could become involved in political activity very different from that prescribed by either Jack or Ras. Now that he has effectively studied "the lesson of [his] own life" he could also become, like his grandfather, a teacher in the broadest sense of the word. These roles are liberating because they enrich the self while allowing the hero to connect himself to a larger social world in the city. In this way, each of these new roles is quite different from the old roles which nearly turned him into a robot because they arise from his own enriched, deepened, consciousness rather than the "plans" other people have devised for him. He therefore tells us that his "hibernation" in the underground is nearly over and that he goes above ground every night to seek out "the next phase" of his life.

Although he is not yet able (or willing) to define precisely the exact nature of the roles he will play for fear of being limited by them, the two anecdotes he relates about his above ground experiences offer ample proof that he is not "jiving" when he speaks of acting effectively in the city. Both of these stories, the fight which he describes in the Prologue and the conversation with Norton which he dramatizes in the Epilogue, establish the hero as fundamentally different from the victimized country bumpkin he was in his pre-underground days. Whereas he formerly lacked the consciousness necessary to direct his life and was therefore easily manipulated by others, he is not in full control of himself and his social environment.

Aware in the Prologue that his white attacker is a pathetic victim of a racist world which blinds his eyes and blunts his heart, Invisible Man can transform violence into awareness, laughing with "sincere compassion" at a man who was mugged by an invisible man. He thus saves himself from the self-defeating violence which has threatened him in nearly every major episode in the novel, from the Battle Royal to the Harlem Riot. He also extends the same kind of richly human "mixed feelings" toward Norton when he sees him pathetically lost on the subway and asking for directions to Centre Street, the locus of political power and government in New York City. Whereas he had earlier made Norton an Algerian sponsor and begged him for direction in life, he now gives subtly ironic directions to Norton who is too hurried and self-deluded to become aware of their meaning: "Take any train; they all go to the Golden D." No longer riding on the hard rails of other people's expectations which lead to madness, the hero can reject the Algerian city which still dominates Norton's life. Abandoning Norton's city of delusions once and for all, Invisible Man returns temporarily to his urban underground, laughing all the way at Norton's absurdity. He thus becomes more fully aware that his own life has ultimately found a truer "center"—the urbane consciousness which will allow him to transcend existentially the "fate" imagined for him by the Nortons of the world. (pp. 60-6)

> Robert Butler, "Down from Slavery," in
> American Studies, *Vol. 29, No. 2, Fall, 1988,*
> *pp. 57-67.*

FURTHER READING

Baker, Houston A., Jr. "A Forgotten Prototype." *Virginia Quarterly Review* 49, No. 3 (Summer 1973): 433-49.
> Compares *Invisible Man* with James Weldon Johnson's *Autobiography of an Ex-Colored Man,* noting: "The narrators of both works undergo many restless turnings within what appears to be a circular pattern (with the end in the beginning), each repeatedly colliding with the indisputable facts of the American situation—its denial of the black man and its avid willingness to co-opt and exploit his talents."

Bishop, Jack. *Ralph Ellison.* Black Americans of Achievement, edited by Nathan Irvin Huggins. New York: Chelsea House, 1988, 110 p.
> Heavily illustrated biographical and critical study of Ellison and *Invisible Man.* Intended chiefly for young readers.

Breit, Harvey. "Talk with Ralph Ellison." *The New York Times Book Review* (4 May 1952): 26.
> Brief biographical essay, offering comments by Ellison himself about the genesis of *Invisible Man.* Ellison states: "Several reviewers [of *Invisible Man*] pointed out parts of the book they considered surrealistic. I'll agree with that; however I didn't select the surrealism, the distortion, the intensity, as an experimental technique but because reality is surreal."

German, Norman. "Imagery in the 'Battle Royal' Chapter of Ralph Ellison's *Invisible Man.*" *CLA Journal* 31, No. 4 (June 1988): 394-99.
> Examines theme and imagery in the 'Battle Royal' chapter of *Invisible Man.*

Giza, Joan. "Ralph Ellison." In *Black American Writers: Bibliographical Essays,* edited by M. Thomas Inge, Maurice Duke, and Jackson R. Bryer, Vol. 2, pp. 47-71. New York: St. Martin's Press, 1978.
> Surveys criticism of Ellison's works, chiefly *Invisible Man* and *Shadow and Act,* through the year 1976.

Hersey, John., ed. *Ralph Ellison: A Collection of Critical Essays.* Englewood Cliffs, N. J.: Prentice-Hall, 1974, 180 p.
> Collects previously published criticism of Ellison's major works. Essays include: Saul Bellow, "Man Underground"; Irving Howe, "Black Boys and Native Sons"; James Alan McPherson, "Indivisible Man": and William J. Schafer, "Ralph Ellison and the Birth of the Anti-Hero."

Holland, Laurence B. "Ellison in Black and White: Confession, Violence and Rhetoric in *Invisible Man.*" In *Black Fiction: New Studies in the Afro-American Novel Since 1945,* edited by Robert Lee, pp. 54-73. London: Vision Press, 1980.
> Examines structural elements in *Invisible Man.*

McSweeney, Kerry. *"Invisible Man": Race and Identity.* Twayne's Masterwork Studies, No. 17. Boston: Twayne Publishers, 1988, 139 p.
> Book-length study of race awareness in *Invisible Man,* with commentary on psychological issues in the novel.

Nadel, Alan. *Invisible Criticism: Ralph Ellison and the American Canon.* Iowa City: University of Iowa Press, 1988, 181 p.

> Examines *Invisible Man* in light of contemporary notions of literary canon formation, maintaining that the work is "a perfect example of a novel which, through the use of allusions, can contain a literary-critical subtext."

O'Meally, Robert G. *The Craft of Ralph Ellison.* Cambridge, Mass.: Harvard University Press, 1980, 212 p.

> Comprehensive study of Ellison's life and works.

————, ed. *New Essays on "Invisible Man."* Cambridge: Cambridge University Press, 1988, 190 p.

> Essay collection. Contributors include: John F. Callahan, "Frequencies of Eloquence: The Performance and Composition of *Invisible Man*; Berndt Ostendorf, "Ralph Ellison: Anthropology, Modernism, and Jazz"; Thomas Schaub, "Ellison's Masks and the Novel of Reality"; and Valerie Smith, "The Meaning of Narration in *Invisible Man.*"

Parr, Susan Resneck, and Pancho, Savery, eds. *Approaches to Teaching Ellison's "Invisible Man."* Approaches to Teaching World Literature, No. 24. New York: Modern Language Association of America, 1989, 154 p.

> Collection of essays on *Invisible Man.* Essays include: Eleanor Lyons, "Ellison's Narrator as Emersonian Scholar"; R. Baxter Miller, "A Deeper Literacy: Teaching *Invisible Man* from Aboriginal Ground"; Neil Nakadate, "*Invisible Man* in an Ethnic Literature Course"; Mary Rohrberger, "Ball the Jack: Surreality, Sexuality, and the Role of Women in *Invisible Man*"; and Christopher Sten, "Losing It 'Even As He Finds It': The Invisible Man's Search for Identity."

Schultz, Elizabeth A. "The Illumination of Darkness: Affinities between *Moby-Dick* and *Invisible Man.*" *CLA Journal* 32, No. 2 (December 1988): 170-200.

> Compares *Invisible Man* with Herman Melville's *Moby-Dick,* focusing on thematic similarities.

Spillers, Hortense J. "'The Permanent Obliquity of an In(pha)llibly Straight': In the Time of the Daughters and the Fathers." In *Changing Our Words: Essays on Criticism, Theory, and Writing by Black Women,* edited by Cheryl A. Wall, pp. 127-49. New Brunswick, N. J.: Rutgers University Press, 1989.

> Examines family, racial, and sexual stereotyping in works by black American writers, noting of *Invisible Man*: "The entire tale of incest in *Invisible Man* is told by Trueblood.... For all intents and purposes, the wife/mother Kate and the daughter/surrogate lover Matty Lou are deprived of speech, of tongue, since what they said and did and when are reported/translated through the medium of Trueblood. These silent figures, like materialized vectors in a field of force, are curiously silent in the sense that incest fiction, even written by women, never, as far as I know, establishes the agency of the incestuous act inside the female character."

Stepto, Robert B., and Harper, Michael S. "Study & Experience: An Interview with Ralph Ellison." *The Massachusetts Review* XVIII, No. 3 (Autumn 1977): 417-35.

> Text of an interview conducted at Ellison's New York City home in 1976. The discussion focuses on the critical reception given to *Invisible Man* as well as on Ellison's growth as a writer.

Vogler, Thomas A. "*Invisible Man*: Somebody's Protest Novel." *The Iowa Review* 1, No. 2 (Spring 1970): 64-82.

> Close study of imagery in *Invisible Man,* focusing on two principal issues, protest and self-discovery.

Walsh, Mary Ellen Williams. "*Invisible Man*: Ralph Ellison's Wasteland." *CLA Journal* XXVIII, No. 2 (December 1984): 150-58.

> Explores apparent connections between *Invisible Man* and T. S. Eliot's *The Waste Land.*

Winther, Per. "Imagery of Imprisonment in Ralph Ellison's *Invisible Man.*" *Black American Literature Forum* 17, No. 3 (Fall 1983): 115-19.

> Explores images and symbols of imprisonment—for example, Brother Tarp's leg chain, Dr. Bledsoe's leg shackle from slavery times, and the electric shock machine—in *Invisible Man.*